Turkey

Footprint

The travel guide

Handbook

Dominic Whiting

It was three days to Lake Van, five to Tehran, and I was supremely comfortable. I went back to my compartment and propped myself at the window - a cool corner seat - and was lulled by the feel of Asia rumbling under the wheels.

Paul Theroux - The Great Railway Bazaar

Turkey Handbook
First edition
© Footprint Handbooks Ltd 2001

Published by Footprint Handbooks
6 Riverside Court
Lower Bristol Road
Bath BA2 3DZ. England
T +44 (0)1225 469141
F +44 (0)1225 469461
Email discover@footprintbooks.com
Web www.footprintbooks.com

ISBN 1 900949 85 7
CIP DATA: A catalogue record for this
book is available from the British Library

Distributed in the USA by
Publishers Group West

Credits

Series editors
Patrick Dawson and Rachel Fielding

Editorial
Editor: Stephanie Lambe
Maps: Sarah Sorensen

Production
Typesetting: Richard Ponsford, Leona
Bailey and Emma Bryers
Maps: Robert Lunn and Claire Benison
Colour maps: Kevin Feeney

Cover: Camilla Ford

Design
Mytton Williams

Photography
Front and back cover: gettyone Stone
Inside colour section: Elizabeth Whiting
Associates, Eye Ubiquitous, gettyone
Stone, Impact Photo Library, James
Davis Travel Library, Robert Harding
Picture Library.

Print
Manufactured in Italy by LEGOPRINT

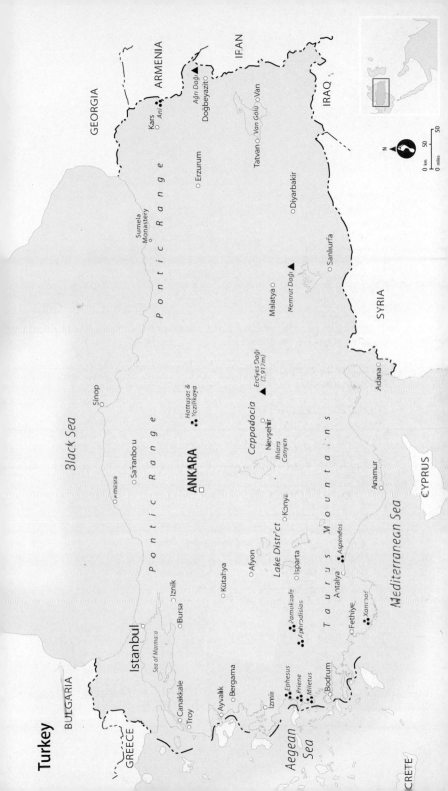

Contents

1

5	**A foot in the door**

2

17	**Essentials**
19	**Planning your trip**
19	Where to go
20	When to go
21	Tours and tour operators
23	Finding out more
23	**Before you travel**
23	Getting in
24	What to take
25	Language
25	**Money**
27	**Getting there**
27	Air
29	Road
30	Sea
32	Train
32	**Touching down**
32	Airport information
32	Tourist information
35	Rules, customs and etiquette
37	Safety
38	**Where to stay**
41	**Getting around**
41	Air
42	Road
47	Sea
47	Train
50	**Keeping in touch**
50	Communications
52	Media
53	**Food and drink**
59	**Shopping**
62	**Holidays and festivals**
64	**Sport and special interest travel**
66	**Health**
66	Before travelling
67	On the road
68	**Further reading**

3

71	**Istanbul**
74	Ins and outs
77	History
81	Modern İstanbul
81	The 'Old' City: Sultanahmet to the City Walls
82	Haghia Sophia
85	Topkapı Palace
95	Sultan Ahmet Camii (Blue Mosque)
96	The Hippodrome
103	Eminönü
110	The Theodosian Walls
113	North of the Golden Horn
115	Karaköy
117	Galata
118	Beyoğlu
120	Taksim Square
120	The Bosphorus
135	Museums
137	Excursions from the city
137	The Prince's Islands
141	The Black Sea Coast
143	Essentials

4

169	**The Marmara Region**
172	Termal
173	İznik
178	Bursa
190	Uludağ

5

193	**The Thrace Region**
196	Edirne
199	The Tunca Valley
204	The Thracian Coast
205	The Gallipoli Peninsula
206	Gelibolu
207	Eceabat
208	The Gallipoli National Historic Park
212	Gökçeada

6

213	**The Aegean Region**
216	Çanakkale
220	The Troad
220	Troy
226	Assos (Behramkale)
230	Ayvalık
236	Bergama (Pergamum)
241	Çandarlı
242	Foça
244	Manisa
247	Sardis (Sart)
249	İzmir
260	Çeşme
265	Selçuk
269	Ephesus (Efes)
274	Şirince
275	Kuşadası
279	The Büyük Menderes Valley
279	Priene
281	Miletus (Milet)
284	Didyma
287	Aphrodisias
289	Pamukkale
294	The southern Aegean coast
294	Heracleia under Latmos
296	Milas
298	Bodrum
305	Bodrum Peninsula
307	The Bay of Gökova

7

311	**Western Mediterranean**
314	Marmaris
318	The Reşadiye and Hisarönü Peninsulas

Left *Catching up on the news outside the Ulu Cami in Erzurum*

321	Köyceğiz
324	Dalyan
331	Dalaman
332	Fethiye
338	Ölüdeniz
341	Kaya Köyü
342	Tlos
346	Xanthos
347	Patara
350	Kalkan
351	Kaş
357	Kekova
361	Demre (Kale)
365	The Lycian Hinterland
368	Olympos and Çıralı
372	Tahtalı Dağı
373	Phaselis
374	Kemer
376	Antalya
387	The Pamphylian Plain
387	Perge
389	Aspendos
390	Köprülü Kanyon National Park and Selge
392	Side
397	Alanya

8

403	**Eastern Mediterranean**
406	Anamur
411	Silifke
417	Kızkalesi
420	Mersin
422	Adana
429	The Hatay
431	Antakya

9

437	**Western Anatolia**
440	Kütahya
445	Afyon
449	The Lake District
450	Isparta
453	Eğirdir
457	Beyşehir

10

463	**Central Anatolia**
466	Ankara
478	Gordion
480	Konya
488	Aksaray
489	The Ihlara Canyon
492	Cappadocia
511	Avanos
515	Kayseri
521	Niğde
523	The Aladağlar
528	Safranbolu
532	Hattuşaş
534	Yazılıkaya
535	Amasya
540	Tokat
542	Sivas

11

547	**The Black Sea Region**
550	Amasra
553	Sinop
556	Samsun
559	Ordu
559	Giresun
562	Trabzon
568	Sumela Monastry
571	Rize
573	Artvin
575	The Kaçkar Dağları

12

587	**Northeast Anatolia**
590	Erzurum
596	Kars
600	Ani
604	Doğubeyazıt

13

609	**Southeast Anatolia**
613	Karamanmaraş
615	Gaziantep
621	Nemrut Dağı
625	Malatya
627	Şanlıurfa
633	Harran
635	Diyarbakır
640	Mardin
643	Tatvan
647	Van

14

653	**Background**
655	**History**
685	**Economy**
688	Modern Turkey
689	**Culture**
689	People
690	Ethnic make-up
692	Religion
696	Art
698	Architecture
700	Language
700	Literature
703	Cinema
704	**Land and environment**
704	Geography
706	Climate
707	Flora
708	Fauna

15

711	**Footnotes**
713	Basic Turkish for travellers
718	Glossary
720	Food glossary
725	Index
728	Shorts
729	Map index
739	Colour maps

Inside front cover
Hotel and restaurant price guide
Dialling codes
Useful numbers

Inside back cover
Map symbols
Useful websites

Right The ruins of the Temple of Trajaneum, built in 125AD

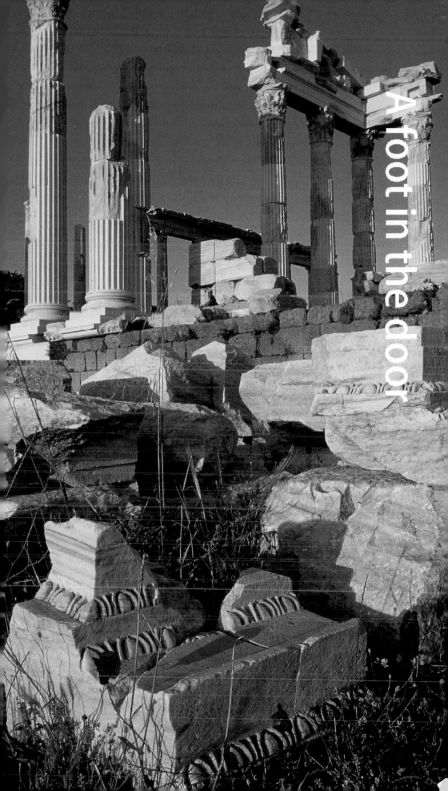

A foot in the door

6

Below The stone heads at Nemrut Daği stare out towards the dawn of civilization.
Right The beautiful Ishak Paşa Sarayı surrounded by lofty mountains.

Above The wonderfully preserved Roman theatre at Aspendos. **Right** Cruising along the rocky coastline of Kekova. **Next page** A winter wonderland, Cappadocia.

Highlights

Turkey, a land of mosques, minarets, kebaps, of exotic eastern bazaars, the mystery of the sultan's harem and shady-looking characters puffing on hubble-bubbles. Stepping off the plane in İstanbul such preconceptions are immediately strained as you're shepherded through a glittering new terminal, dazzled by acres of pale marble. Outside, a cab or the newly unveiled metro await to whisk you into the city. And still no-one wearing a fez, although the way the driver dodges incessantly between the lanes, leaning on his horn, feels pretty 'eastern'. But there, as envisaged, are the mosques and moustachioed men; the street-traders with trays balanced precariously on their head and the shoeshine boys. As you step onto the street the evening call to prayer reverberates across the city, an exotic cacophony loaded with eastern flavour. However, not far away you stumble across a trendy café, where the sound of the *ezan* is drowned out by pop music and carefully preened *İstanbullu* chat into mobile phones while sipping *latte*. In fact, modern Turkey falls beyond any conventional mould. Neither convincingly European nor wholly of the Middle East; tradition and modernity co-exist in a dynamic, eye-opening mosaic that justifies its clichéd title as the meeting place of east and west.

A road to ruin

The Hittites, the Phrygians, the Lydians, the Greeks, the Romans, the Byzantines; Anatolia, the land that makes up present-day Turkey, played host to a long line of distinguished guests before the Turks arrived. Like ancient calling cards, each civilization has left evidence of its passing in the form of ruins scattered liberally across the country. The scale and diversity of this legacy is hard to believe. There are the crowd-pullers such as Ephesus with its marble avenues and magnificent library of Celsius; the ancient theatre at Aspendos where performances are still held; or the mystical stone heads of Nemrut Dağı, toppled on a rocky mountaintop. There are also a wealth of lesser visited sites often found in exquisite settings. Take Arykanda with its most scenic of amphitheatres perched in the Lycian mountains; the bucolic peace at the ancient temple city of Olbia near Uzuncaburç or the ruins of an Armenian city at Ani in all its windswept isolation.

Coastal blues

Some 8,000 km long Turkey's coastline is lapped by four very distinctive seas. Off its northern coast the Black Sea is fickle, frequently forbidding and often lashed by rain. Squeezed between two continents the Marmara is an inland sea crossed by busy shipping lanes and harvested by rusting trawlers. Passing through the Dardanelles, the Aegean has secluded coves of aquamarine, fishing ports and the Greek islands floating on the western horizon. However, if its sand you're after and miles of it, then the real action is on the Med, where the likes of Iztuzu or Patara rate among the Mediterranean's finest beaches. A great way to experience the Turkish littoral, however, is on board a wooden *gület*, lazing on deck as you cruise along the pine-fringed coast.

Mountains & plateaus

Anatolia is a land of mountains and plateaus, buckled and folded by unimaginable forces in the geological past. Along the coast olive groves give way to slopes of fresh-smelling pine, gnarled cedar and juniper. Honey bees buzz lazily through the air and herds of black-haired goats chomp their way across scrubby mountainsides. Enclosed by the coastal ranges large parts of the rolling central plateau have a bleak austerity; an empty grain-planted sea dotted with isolated oases of civilization. From the Pontic Alps in the north vigorous torrents nourished by snow-melt spill down from the flower-studded meadows, crisscrossed by adventurous trekkers, to empty into the Black Sea. The rugged eastern mountains are blanketed in snow in the winter and ablaze with colour after the spring thaw. The people of Anatolia – townsfolk, farmers and herdsmen – add to the landscape, carving a living out of the often inhospitable terrain.

İstanbul

The queen of cities İstanbul, the enigmatic 'Queen of Cities', has many faces. Standing on the Galata bridge garrisoned by hopeful fishermen, a line of graceful imperial mosques punctuate the skyline and seagulls wheel noisily over-head diving for the scraps from a row of waterside fish stalls. Ferries shuttle busily to and fro across the choppy water, and tankers glide serenely up the straits, saluting the city in passing with their deep-throated horns. Having climbed the narrow twisting streets of Galata, a bell announces the passing of the rattling red tram car on Istiklal Caddesi, busy with shoppers. In Ortaköy the cobbled square is abuzz with chatter drifting from the rows of upbeat cafés while across the city in Fatih veiled housewives drape colourful lines of washing across the narrow streets.

Ottoman İstanbul The epicentre of the Ottoman world for over 400 years, not surprisingly İstanbul is a treasure trove of Ottoman architecture. Dotted with countless mosques, castles, seminaries, fountains and baths, the city's imperial foundations reached their peak of brilliance in the soaring domes of the Süleymaniye Camii. Nearby is the Selimiye Camii, which does justice to the prime spot overlooking the Golden Horn, and in Eminönü, the colourful tiles dance on the walls of the Rüstem Paşa Camii. Spread over a wooded hillside overlooking the straits, the Topkapı Palace, home to the sultans, now houses one of the world's richest museums, a labyrinth you could lose yourself in for days at a time. While along up the Bosphorus a string of ostentatious palaces and summer residences reflect the oppulent tastes of the later sultans.

Shop 'til you drop A veritable maze of covered arcades, passages and courtyards, the city's Grand Bazaar has been open for business since 1453. Whether you're after something in particular, a carpet or a piece of copper, or there simply to soak up the atmosphere, you'll be entertained. The aroma of spices tempt you inside the nearby Egyptian Bazaar, while outside itinerant traders crowd the narrow streets hawking everything from disposable razors to piles of fruit. More sensory feasts await in the numerous street bazaars where raucous stall-holders tout chunks of Anatolia cheese, buckets of olives and silvery fish. At the other end of the spectrum there are also bargains to be had in the rarified climes of the city's ultra-modern shopping complexes.

İstanbul nights As the sun sets the city's nightspots come alive. Evenings often begin with a leisurely dinner in a streetside restaurant or a convivial backstreet *meyhane* where you can eat and drink and perhaps be entertained by impromptu alcohol-fuelled serenades. Bar culture has exploded in the twisting streets of Beyoğlu, where you'll find trendy bars and hip jazz clubs alongside the sleazy drinking dens of old. Uptown you can get down with the glitterazi in a club where a round costs the equivalent of an average Turk's weekly wage. Finally stumbling out of a neon-lit soup kitchen, you head for bed as the call to prayer echoes across the hushed pre-dawn city.

Islands & suburbs Strung out along the Bosphorus are a series of villages which, despite having been absorbed by the city, maintain much of their individuality and charm. Beneath wooded slopes stand elegant waterside palaces, atmospheric tumbledown mansions and esteemed restaurants. Only a bracing ferry journey from the centre of town, they're light years away from the hustle and bustle. When an *İstanbullu* fancies a break from the traffic and noise they head out to the Prince's Islands – a glorious escape from the city since Ottoman times and a monastic retreat long before that. Graceful Art Nouveau mansions line the streets of Büyükada and Heybeliada, while horse-drawn carriages complete the feeling that you've been transported back in time.

Left As many goings on outside as inside, a traditional wooden house in the old city of İstanbul. **Below** Drinking tea and playing cards - the steady pace of life on Prince's Island.

Above After a catch of the day on a bridge across the Bosphorous. **Left** Brassed off, a shopkeeper awaits trade in the Grand Bazaar. **Next page** Smokin' - traditional waterpipe methods continue beneath Galata Bridge.

14

Right Crumbling and neglected, the Greek town of Ayvalık has an atmosphere of times gone by. *Below* Another legacy of the Greeks, the enchanting Sumela Monastery clinging to the craggy cliffside.

Above People of Van, earning a crust.
Right True Turkish blue - the tile work of Yeşil (Green) Cami in Bursa.
Next page Wash day.

Turkish delights

Towering minarets piercing the sky, arching domes floating ethereally above the prayer hall, exquisitely patterned İznik tiles: Edirne's Selimiye Camii is Ottoman architecture at its finest. Bursa, home of the döner kebap and first Ottoman capital, also has a celebrated collection of early mosques, like the elegant Yeşil Cami nestling beneath the green slopes of Mount Uludağ. Then there's Ayvalık, a work-a-day Aegean town with narrow cobbled lanes lined with crumbling Greek mansions. Sirince – or 'loveliness' – is on a smaller, more rustic scale, a quaint Hellenic village of timber-framed houses crouched picturesquely in the Aegean hills. Inland solid caravanserais like the Sultanhanı near Aksaray dot the empty steppe and the vivid blue tilework of Selçuk seminaries and tombs adds a splash of colour to Anatolian towns such as Konya and Erzurum. While crouched impossibly on a narrow ledge, the Sumela monastery clings to a soaring cliff-face in the Pontic Alps. **An architectural review**

The geological wonderland of Cappadocia is not to be missed, a place where wind and rain have sculpted the soft rock into a landscape of whimsical and unearthly beauty. Like a huge sci-fi filmset, you half expect the young Luke Skywalker to appear on his landspeeder, or sand people to jump out in ambush as you wander half-dazed through the rocky wilderness. Delving beneath the ground, cave churches harbour breathtaking frescoes and labyrinthine subterranean cities penetrate deep into the bowels of the earth. **Cave churches & underground cities**

In the baking, remorseless heat of a summer day in Şanlıurfa, Diyarbakır or Mardin, a fountain cools the shady courtyard of a solid stone house. Outside dusty alleyways lead down to the bazaar, a timeless warren bustling with mercantile activity despite the stifling air. The heady aroma of tanned leather and spices combine with the smoke from a streetside grill and the sound of Arabic, Kurdish and Turkish spoken in unison entertains your ears. Sitting down to eat your tastebuds are treated to tongue-tingling spices and cooled by sharp, creamy yogurt. This is the taste of Turkey's southeast, a distinctly Middle Eastern flavour. **Middle Eastern flavour**

Travelling in Turkey you'll have ample opportunity not just to marvel at, but also to live with the remnants of its long and colourful past. In İstanbul Ottoman mansions have been refurnished as pleasant 'boutique' hotels, while Bursa's Eski Kaplıca baths are still steam-filled after over 500 years. The old quarter of Antalya has more creaky Ottoman lodgings, or you could live out a period fantasy in the graceful timber-frame konaks of Amasya or Safranbolu. In many an Anatolian town you'll do your shopping next to a rock-tomb, eat in view of an amphitheatre or dance the night away beside a temple. Chunks of antique marble are built into modern walls; fortresses act as football fields; in Turkey present and past mingle like nowhere else. **Living with history**

Essentials

2

18

Essentials

19	**Planning your trip**	38	**Where to stay**
19	Where to go	41	**Getting around**
20	When to go	41	Air
21	Tours and tour operators	42	Road
23	Finding out more	47	Sea
23	**Before you travel**	47	Train
23	Getting in	50	**Keeping in touch**
24	What to take	50	Communications
25	Language	52	Media
25	**Money**	53	**Food and drink**
27	**Getting there**	53	Food
27	Air	57	Drink
29	Road	59	**Shopping**
30	Sea	62	**Holidays and festivals**
32	Train	64	**Sport and special interest travel**
32	**Touching down**		
32	Airport information	66	**Health**
32	Tourist information	66	Before travelling
35	Rules, customs and etiquette	67	On the road
37	Safety	68	**Further reading**

Planning your trip

Where to go

Turkey is a country which often surprises the first-timer with its geographical diversity. Indeed, it can offer something for all tastes and energy levels from visiting the many and varied historical sites to relaxing on sunny beaches, cruising along the coast on a chartered yacht or, for the more adventurous, skiing, trekking, rafting and climbing. There's such variety of options that your main consideration will be timing. Below are several suggested itineraries that give a broad picture of what there is to see and do, and the best times in which to see and do them.

A visit to İstanbul is not to be missed on any trip to Turkey, and with its wealth of **İstanbul** historical sights, museums, bazaars and nightlife the city deserves at least a couple of days out of anyone's programme. The city is a possible destination for a long weekend visit from Europe, although give yourself at least three days to look around the main sights and soak-up the atmosphere.

The Aegean and western Mediterranean coast are the focus for much of the country's **Western Turkey** tourism and contain the best beaches as well as a seemingly never-ending supply of archaeological sites, such as Troy, Bergama, Ephesus, Miletus, Xanthos and Phaselis, to name but a few.

A popular circular route from İstanbul, possible in seven to 12 days depending on your pace, goes south via Bursa to Selçuk and the fabulous ruins of Ephesus before returning along the north Aegean coast taking in Bergama, Ayvalık, Assos, Troy and the battlefields of Gallipoli. An excursion to visit the ruins and geological formations of Aphrodisias and Pamukkale could also be added into this.

A southern alternative if you only have a week would be to start in İzmir, visiting Ephesus and some of the other sights in the Büyük Menderes Valley, before continuing on to Bodrum or Dalyan for some relaxed beach time and nightlife. An extra few days would allow you to start or finish the programme with a couple of days in İstanbul.

Another option would be to catch a bus or fly from İstanbul to Antalya or Dalaman and explore the coast of the Lycian Peninsula, doing daily excursions from some of the southern resorts like Kaş, Fethiye or Dalyan. During the summer there are also package flights directly into Dalaman and Antalya as well as İzmir from European airports. Of course for those ruin-buffs who want to really immerse themselves in the history of the region it's possible to spend much longer exploring the many less-well-known, but equally fascinating, sites.

For those with more time on their hands a popular circuit is from İstanbul south to Antalya, taking in some of the towns and sights along the Aegean and Mediterranean coasts. From Antalya you can travel inland to explore the exceptional landscapes of Cappadocia, visiting en route the Lake District and Konya if time permits. The return leg to İstanbul could be broken by a day in Ankara to visit the Museum of Anatolia Civilisation and the Anıt Kabir. This route is just possible in two weeks using a combination of air, rail and bus travel, however, an extra week would give you time to do justice, at a less hurried pace, to the many fascinating places along the way. After all, it is quite easy to spend four or five days in Cappadocia alone, visiting the underground cities and Byzantine churches, walking in the Ihlara Valley and marvelling at the incredible geological formations around Göreme. A possible addition to this route could be to head northeast from Ankara to Amasya and the picturesque fishing towns of Sinop or Amasra on the Black Sea coast.

Essentials

Eastern Turkey

When making your travel plans it is important to remember that road conditions in the east & army check-points in the Kurdish region make for slower & less comfortable journeys by road. If time is short consider flying at least part of the way

A whistle-stop tour of the eastern part of the country departing from Ankara takes a minimum of two weeks, though it really warrants three. This would give you time to include visits to Cappadocia and the mountain top temple at Nemrut Dağı, followed by the eastern towns of Şanlıurfa, Diyarbakır, Van, Doğubeyazit and Erzurum. If time was short from Erzurum you could return to Ankara or İstanbul by plane, or catch buses and trains back via Amasya and the Hittite capital of Hattuşaş. Alternatively, with time to spare, from Erzurum you could travel to Kars and the ruined city of Ani on the Armenian border; even adding on an additional week for some trekking or rafting in the Kaçkar Mountains. This itinerary could be shortened by flying in to one of the eastern airports such as Erzurum, Van or Diyarbakır and then heading westwards by your chosen route, possibly ending on the Mediterranean coast for some beach time. Also don't forget about the *Turkish Maritime Lines* ferry departing from Trabzon as a very pleasurable way of returning to İstanbul after a tour of the east.

Black Sea coast

But for a few notable exceptions such as Trabzon with its interesting history and the Sumela Monastery or the Kaçkar Mountains, there are few places that will detain you on the Black Sea coast east of Samsun. Likewise, bar Amasra and Sinop the western part of the coast has few sights of specific interest, though it is pleasant to meander along, soaking up the beautiful scenery. Along the western half of the coast this is best done with your own transport, although it's also possible using buses and dolmuş. A journey along the Black Sea littoral could be coupled with a visit to picturesque Safranbolu and Amasya further inland, in about a week to 10 days, though this involves a lot of travelling. Don't forget the possibility of using the weekly *Turkish Maritime Lines* car ferry between İstanbul, Samsun, Ordu, Giresun and Trabzon.

Biblical sites

So-called 'faith tours' usually begin in İstanbul with its fabulous Haghia Sofia and other less well known Byzantine churches. The Aegean region also holds a significant place in early Christian history with the Seven Churches of the Revelation scattered across the area. Of the seven, Pergamum, Ephesus and Sardis are the most deserving of a visit and have an additional bonus in that their considerable historical legacy is not just limited to the Christian era. Pergamum and Ephesus are the most popular and are close to tourist centres with accommodation and other facilities. Visiting Sardis is also relatively easy as a day trip from İzmir, while the seventh church, Laodicea, is near the tourist attractions of Pamukkale.

Starting in İzmir, it is possible to take in five of the Seven Churches of the Revelation (excluding Philadelphia and Thyatira) within a week using public transport. This allows plenty of time for additional exploration of interesting places nearby and some time to relax. With your own transport you could visit all seven sites in the same amount of time, though this would involve a considerable amount of driving. There are several agencies offering tours of the Seven Churches from İzmir and İstanbul (see pages 164 and 258).

A longer itinerary could include the Seven Churches of the Revelation combined with visits to Tarsus near Adana, which is celebrated as the birth place of St Paul, and Antakya (Antioch) in the Hatay, which played a prominent role in the early development of Christianity. From there you could travel north to spend several days exploring the rock-cut churches and monastic communities of Cappadocia before returning to İstanbul via Ankara. This two to three week route could be shortened by taking internal flights, for example between İstanbul and İzmir, or Nevşehir and İstanbul.

When to go

High season in Turkey is from the end of June to the end of August, when Turkish schools, civil servants and many businesses have their holidays, and foreign arrivals are also at their peak. During this period prices rise considerably in tourist hotels and booking ahead is a good idea. The coastal resorts are at their busiest and it is scorchingly hot for much of the day, making sightseeing a somewhat exhausting experience. National and religious holidays (see page 62) can also put transport and accommodation under considerable pressure.

If you aren't tied to school holidays the best time to visit these regions is spring or early summer, before it gets busy, when prices are low and the weather is not yet too hot. The countryside is fresh and green after the winter rains and the meadows are carpeted with wild flowers. Autumn is also pleasantly quiet in the resorts and temperatures, particularly at night, are more comfortable. January and February are the wettest months; though extended periods of clear, sunny weather are not unusual in the winter. The Aegean Sea is warm from the end of May onwards, while in the south around Antalya it's possible to swim comfortably in April. The Mediterranean is like a warm bath during August and offers no relief from the heat and high humidity. In an average year it's warm enough to swim in the Aegean up to the end of October, later further south.

The Aegean & Mediterranean

İstanbul and the Marmara region enjoy a more temperate climate, but in August the heat and humidity can be debilitating.

İstanbul & the Marmara

Early summer is also a good time to visit Cappadocia and other parts of Central Anatolia, although the altitude and the dryness of the air mean that it never gets as hot as it does down on the coast, or in the southeast where temperatures soar to above 40°C. So, if you're planning to visit Diyarbakır or Şanlıurfa, make it in the spring or autumn. Winter is no time to be in northeast Anatolia, unless you enjoy sub-zero temperatures or you want to ski.

Central & Eastern Anatolia

Along the Black Sea coast winters are exceptionally mild and rainfall is high throughout the year. The coastal towns are crowded with domestic tourists during July and August, but things wind down quickly once the school term starts in September and some guesthouses may close for the winter. The swimming season in the Black Sea is shorter, roughly from the end of May to September unless you're brave.

Black Sea coast

Spring is the best time for walking along the **Aegean coast** and in the mountains of the **Lycian Peninsula**; autumn is also a pleasant time in terms of climate, but much of the vegetation has been burnt to a crisp by this stage in the year. In the high **Taurus Mountains** (the Aladağlar) the trekking and climbing season begins in June, although there is generally still snow on the higher passes. July is probably the best month, while the heat of August dries up many water sources and makes for tough going walking. In the **Kaçkar mountains** the season starts later with thick cloud and mists cloaking the coastal side of the range for much of the spring and summer. You have the greatest chance of dry weather from the middle of August, with the conditions in September often becoming more settled.

Trekking & climbing seasons

Tours and tour operators

UK and Ireland *Alternative Travel*, 146 Kingsland High Street, London, E8 2NS, T020-79233230. Turkish package operator, also specializing in golfing holidays. *British Museum Traveller*, 46 Bloomsbury Street, London, WC1B 3QQ, T020-73238895, www.britishmuseum.ac.uk Several themed archaeological tours led by eminently qualified specialists each year. *Dolunay Holidays*, Spread Eagle Court, Northgate Street, Gloucester, GL1 1SL, T01452-501978, F01452-501976. Good selection of cottages, villas and hotels along the Mediterranean coast. *Exodus*, T020-87723822, www.exodus.co.uk Well established worldwide operator. *Explore*

See also page 64 for special interest tour operators

Worldwide, 1 Frederick Street, Aldershot, Hants, GU11 1LQ, T01252-760000, F01252-760001, www.exploreworldwide.com Several group walking and minibus tours from this large operator. *Health and Fitness Holidays*, 133A Devonshire Road, London, SE23 3LZ, T020-82917981. Yoga, shiatsu and salsa courses in relaxed surroundings on the Bodrum Peninsula. *Huzur Vadisi*, 3 Crown Place, Aberath, Aberaeron, Dyfed, 8A46 OLL, T01970-626821. Selection of alternative courses, including yoga and cookery and accommodation-only stays in a *yurt* complex set in an unspoilt valley inland from Göcek. *President Holidays*, 92 Park Lane, Croydon, Surrey, CR0 1JF, T020-86887555. Large tour operator specializing in North Cyprus and İstanbul, also UK agent for *İstanbul Airlines*. *Savile*, 6 Blenheim Terrace, London, NW8, T020-76253001, F020-76258852, www.saviletours.com Upmarket villas, hotels and guesthouses in Cappadocia, İstanbul and along the Mediterranean coast. *Simply Turkey*, Chiswick Gate, 598 Chiswick High Road, Chiswick, London, W4 5RT, T020-87471011, www.simply-travel.com Specialize in self-catering villas along with a range of other quality package holidays. *Thomas Cook*, T0870-750750316, www.thomascook.com Good source of charter and discounted scheduled flights, as well as package holidays. *Travelbag Adventures*, T01420-541007, F01420-541022, www.travelbag-adventures.co.uk 15 Turk Street, Alton, Hants, GU34 1AG. Another large operator who offers walking and coach tours of the country. *Westminster Classic Tours*, Suite 120, 266 Banbury Road, Summertown, Oxford, OX2 7DL. T01865-728565, F01865-728575, info@wct99.com Upmarket historical tours, painting holidays and *gület* cruises.

North America *The Adventure Centre*, Toll free: 1-800-2288747, T510-6541879, F510-6544200. Several guided trips to Turkey. *Heritage Tours*, T800-3784555, www.heritagetoursONLINE.com 216 West 18th street, Suite 1001, New York City.

Tailor made tours throughout Turkey. *Mountain Trip Sobek*, 6420 Fairmont Ave, El Cerrito, CA, T510-5278105, F510-5257710, www.mtsobek.com *Gület* cruises, multi-activity and walking holidays. *Mythic Travel*, T831-4383031, F831-4388291, www.mythic-travel.com 1580 Tucker Road, Scotts valley, CA95066, USA. High class tours across Turkey, led by experts.*Tohum Anatolian Journeys*, T1413-7744140, F1413-7744634, www.tohum.com Alternative and "folkloric" tours, yoga workshops.

Finding out more

Current affairs www.bbc.co.uk/worldservice – the BBC World Service website has regional news bulletins, live web-casts and useful links; **www.turkishdaily news.com** – a selection of articles and features from the English language Turkish daily; **www.turkeynews.net/News** – an excellent resource for international press stories about Turkey; **www.turkey-news.com** – current news stories about Turkey; **www.turkeyupdate.com** – an excellent site with a news round-up, analysis and interesting articles.

Useful websites

Essentials

Currency converter www.oanda.com/converter/classic – converts between all major currencies instantly.

Cyber cafés www.netcafeguide.com – a list of over 2,000 internet cafés in 117 countries, plus language section and travellers' forum.

Hotels www.Istanbulhotels.com – this site has over 85 İstanbul hotels, mostly 3-4 star, discounts for on-line booking.

Maps www.nationalgeographic.com/resources/ngo/maps/atlas – on-line maps from the National Geographic atlas.

Travel advisories www.travel.state.gov/travel_warnings.html – US State Department travel advisories; **www.fco.gov.uk/travel/** – the UK Foreign and Commonwealth Office travel advisories.

Weather www.rainorshine.com/ – five-day forecasts for 800 cities worldwide.

Before you travel

Getting in

American, British, Irish, Israeli, Italy, Portuguese and Spanish citizens must obtain a visa when they arrive in the country. Tourist visas are valid for three months for multiple entries and take the form of a sticker stuck into your passport before you proceed through passport control. Visas currently cost £10 for British and Irish passport holders and US$45 for US citizens. These visa charges are subject to periodic change, so check with a Turkish Consulate (see page 24) before you leave (UK visa line: T0891-347348). Try and have the correct amount of hard currency with you as the visa officials, particularly at smaller entry points, may not always have change. A visa is not required for nationals of Australia, Belgium, Canada, Denmark, Finland, France, Germany, Greece, Holland, Iceland, Japan, New Zealand, Norway, Sweden and Switzerland.

Visas
Passports should have at least 6 months validity from your date of entry into the country

No special vaccinations are necessary for a visit to Turkey, however it's a good idea to be inoculated against typhoid and to have a tetanus booster if you need one. You may also consider being immunized against Hepatitis A and B. See page 67 for more details.

Vaccinations

Turkish customs regulations limit the importation of certain products. Some limits include 200 cigarettes (400 if bought from a Turkish duty free shop), 75 cl of spirits and 1.5 kg of instant coffee. Contact a Turkish Consulate before departure for a more complete list of import limits.

Customs

Essentials

 Turkish consulates and embassies

Australia *60 Mugga Way, Red Hill Canberra A.C.T. 2603, T6-2950227, F6-2396592.*

Austria *Prinz Eugen Str 40, 1040 Wien, T1-5041285, F222-5053660*

Belgium *4, Rue Montoyer 1000, Brussels, T2-5134095, F2-5140748.*

Canada *197 Wurtemburg St, Ottawa, Ontario KIN 8L9, T613-7894044, F613-7893442.*

Denmark *Rosbaeksvej 15, 2100 Copenhagen 0, T31202788, F31205166.*

Finland *Puistokatu 1B A3, 00140 Helsinki, T0-655755, F0-655011.*

France *16 Avenue de Lamballe, 75016 Paris, T1-45245224, T1-45204191.*

Germany *Ute Str 47/53179 Bonn 2, T228-953830, F228-348877.*

Ireland *11 Clyde Road, Ballsbridge, Dublin 4, T1-6685240, T1-6685014.*

Israel *202 Hayarkon Str, Tel Aviv 63405, T3-5241101, T3-5241390.*

Italy *Via Palestro, 28-00185 Rome,* *T6-4941547, F6-4941526.*

New Zealand *15-17 Murphy St, Level 8, Wellington, T4-4721290, F4-4721277.*

Norway *Halvdan Svartes Gate 5, N-0244 Oslo, T22449971, F22556263*

The Netherlands *Jan Everstraat 2514 Bs, The Hague, T70-3604912, F70-3617969.*

South Africa *1067 Church St, Hatfield 0181, Pretoria, T12-3426053, F12-3426052.*

Johannesburg *6 Sandown Valley Crescent, 2nd Fl Sandown-Sandt, T11-8849060, F11-8849064.*

Spain *Calle Rafael Calvo 18-2 Ay-B, Madrid 28010, T1-3198064, F1-3086602.*

UK *Rutland Lodge, Rutland Gardens, London, SW7 1BW, T020-75890949, F020-75846235.*

USA *1714 Massachusetts Avenue, N.W. Washington, D.C. 20036, T202-6598200, F202-6590744.*

When you enter the country details of your vehicle and personal items of value, such as hi-fi equipment, are entered in your passport to prevent you from selling them in the country.

The export of antiquities from Turkey is strictly forbidden and those caught doing so can expect to be dealt with severely. In an attempt to staunch the illegal flow of artefacts from the country, punishments handed down by the courts to would-be smugglers have included hefty fines and lengthy custodial sentences. Reputable shops will provide you with a certificate proving that your purchase is not an antique, however, if you are still unsure then contact a museum for advice.

What to take

Try and keep your luggage to a minimum particularly if you are planning to be on the move. The most convenient way to carry your things is in a rucksack, with a smaller bag for carrying valuables and for use as a daypack. Hybrid backpacks that can be converted into a more conventional suitcase are also good.

Clothing In the resort towns of western Turkey it's quite normal to walk the streets in **beachwear**, however, in other parts of the country you will attract a lot less attention and avoid causing offence if you are dressed more modestly. Loose cotton clothes are ideal during the summer with a pair of sandals on your feet. This will also give you protection from the sun and against the mosquitoes which plague parts of the country. Remember that summer nights in Cappadocia and other parts of central and eastern Anatolia can be chilly, so take a sweatshirt or a lightweight fleece. Women should avoid wearing revealing clothes and should keep a **headscarf** with them for covering their head and shoulders when visiting mosques. If you intend to do some walking **trekking boots** are recommended.

Medication Any medication you use regularly should be brought from home although it's probably available without prescription from one of the ubiquitous pharmacies. Pharmacists are generally very helpful and medication for the treatment of most common ailments, along with more severe conditions, can be bought across the counter in Turkey. However, this should not delay you from seeking proper medical attention if you are concerned about your health. Insect repellent, tampons and condoms (*prezervatif*) are also easily found but you may prefer to bring your own from home.

See page 66 for health information

Miscellaneous Today there's very little that you can't find in the shops of most Turkish towns and resorts. Print **film** is widely available, however, transparency or black and white film is harder to come by, so you should take your own supply. Carrying a spare camera battery will also give you piece of mind. If you have electrical appliances don't forget a travel **adapter** as well. During the summer a good **sun hat** and **sunscreen** are essential. Several well-known brands of sun cream are available at chemists in tourist areas, but don't expect to find it once you get off the beaten track. Insulated **bottle-carriers** are excellent for keeping your trusty bottle of mineral water cool. If you're staying in **budget accommodation** it's useful to carry a rubber **plug** for using in washbasins and bathtubs, as Turks generally wash only in running water. A cotton sheet sleeping bag is also a bonus when the sheets provided are not the cleanest.

Essentials

Language

Turkish is the official language and is spoken by the entire population either as their mother tongue or otherwise (see page 700). In the tourist areas of western Turkey most hotel and restaurant staff can speak English or sometimes German. However, amongst the general population only a minority of people have anything more than a very basic level of English, ie the few words they can remember from school. It's a good idea to try and master a few basics (see page 713) and any such effort will be very warmly received by Turks.

A pocket dictionary is an invaluable aid in many situations

Money

The Turkish currency is called the **Turkish Lira** which is abbreviated in signs and prices to 'TL'. In recent times Turkey has endured one of the highest inflation rates in the world with the value of the Turkish Lira depreciating steadily against other major currencies. Although things are starting to improve, the weakness of the Turkish Lira still causes great practical difficulties, not to mention amusement, for foreign visitors. Even a bus fare costs hundreds of thousands of Turkish Lira, while a hotel bill for the night runs into seven digits!

Currency *Small shops often don't have change for the larger bank notes, so try & keep some smaller change on you*

Try to get used to the colours of the various denominations, but until that happens take care when paying for things, particularly at night. At present the smallest bank note is 100,000 TL, while the largest is 10,000,000 TL. However, this may well have changed by the time you arrive unless the government decides to chop some noughts off. There are also a series of coins from 10,000 to 200,000 TL.

When travelling keep the majority of your money in hard currency and change up enough to last you for the immediate future. Travel agents, large shops and some other businesses are often happy to accept payment in hard currencies and you can sometimes negotiate a small discount for doing so.

Visa, **Mastercard**, **American Express** and **Diners Club** are widely accepted in shops, hotels and restaurants. A commission of up to 5% is charged on some purchases with a credit card, although this practice is slowly being phased out. Withdrawing money

Credit cards *See inside back cover for website details*

from an ATM is a very convenient way of getting cash. You can count on finding a choice of ATMs in provincial towns as well as in many smaller centres. The large domestic bank chains are affiliated to both the Visa/Plus and Mastercard/Cirrus systems, so money can be withdrawn using the vast majority of foreign cards, including most debit cards.

Though an extremely convenient way of getting local currency, the rate of exchange offered by credit card companies is slightly less competitive than at a **döviz** (bureau de change) or domestic banks. Such transactions are also subject to a small service charge levied by the credit card company.

Don't forget that credit cards aren't widely accepted in remote and rural areas, so make sure you always have some cash. Also remember to carry with you the international telephone numbers that are necessary to report your card lost or stolen. You will also need the card number to report if stolen.

Exchange
At the end of your trip, change your Turkish Lira back into foreign currency before you leave the country: you'll get a terrible rate back at home

There are no restrictions on foreign exchange and due to the steady depreciation of the Turkish Lira changing money to and from hard currencies such as US dollars or Deutsche Marks is a part of everyday life for many Turkish people. Exchange bureaus, or *döviz*, are not exclusive to tourist areas and can be found in most towns. If you can't find a *döviz* then shopkeepers, particularly gold merchants and jewellers, will normally change foreign notes. It is best to carry US dollars or Deutsche Marks, as these are the most widely used. Make sure you are familiar with the rate of exchange before beginning any transaction.

Travellers' cheques
Send a copy of the cheque numbers to your email address if you have one, along with your passport & credit card numbers in case you lose them too

Travellers' cheques are a safe and fairly convenient way of carrying your money in Turkey, although some banks may be reluctant to change them, particularly in small, out-of-the-way places. *İşbankası* branches are the most reliable at changing travellers' cheques but even they occasionally refuse. This is often simply due to laziness on the part of the staff, so in the event of a refusal try insisting politely. A commission of 3-5% is charged for changing cheques, but there may be a hefty minimum charge of up to US$8. Large hotels and also some tourism-related businesses may take travellers' cheques as payment. Generally only *döviz* in tourist areas change travellers' cheques. Remember to keep the cheque receipts in a different place to the cheques themselves and to have a copy of the telephone number to ring for replacement of lost or stolen cheques.

Money transfer
Western Union money transfers can be received at 28 branches of *Interbank* across the country. Below are likely to be the most useful branches or alternatively ring T0212-2126666 (İstanbul) for a complete list. **Ankara** Atatürk Bulvarı No 211/B, Kavaklıdere and Kazım Karabekir Caddesi, Nizam Oğlu İşhan No 72, Ulus; **Antalya** Ali Çetin Kaya Bulvarı No 12; **Bodrum** Kibris Şehitleri Caddesi, C3 Yuksel Çağlar İş Merkezi No 8; **Denizli** İkinci Ticaret Yol No 73, Saraylar Mahallesi; **Gaziantep** Atatürk Bulvarı No 6, Bey Mahallesi; **İstanbul** Millet Caddesi, Sorgut Caddesi No 1, Aksaray. Cumhuriyet Caddesi No 20, Elmadağ (near the *Divan Hotel*); **İzmir** Cumhuriyet Bulvarı No 109/A, Pasaport (near the main post office); **Kayseri** Millet Caddesi No 22; **Marmaris** Ulusal Egemen Caddesi No 19A.

Student cards
International student cards will get you discounted entrance fees for museums and archaeological sites as well as train fares and some, but not all, bus tickets.

Cost of living
The cost of living is considerably lower than in Europe, though not as low as other developing countries such as Thailand or India. Average monthly salaries have dropped precipitously in dollar terms due to the latest financial crisis. A junior school teacher now earns just US$150-200 per month and a low level civil servant US$150-300. Salaries in the private sector are considerably better.

A holiday in Turkey represents excellent value for money, particularly with the weakness of the Turkish Lira. If you are staying in the most comfortable hotels and dining at the best available restaurants you are likely to spend in excess of US$150 per day. On a more modest budget of US$45-75 per day, it is possible to stay in comfortable, midrange hotels, to dine at decent local restaurants and, if there were two or more of you, to rent a car. For the budget traveller staying in pensions and guesthouses, eating cheaply and using public transport, a daily allowance of US$20-30 is required. It's considerably more expensive to travel on your own as single room rates are normally 75% of the price of a double and of course staying put in one place greatly reduces your daily spend.

Cost of travelling

Getting there

Air

İstanbul's Atatürk airport is the country's largest and busiest, receiving scheduled flights from Europe, the Middle East, America and Asia throughout the year. There are some international scheduled flights into **İzmir**, though it's very busy with European package flights during the summer. **Antalya** and **Dalaman** airports also receive lots of package flights from Europe in the summer season.

Scheduled flights These fares vary according to the airline and the time of year, but expect to pay upwards of US$300 return from London, and often considerably more. *Turkish Airlines* fly daily services to İstanbul from most European cities, though sometimes these are via a third airport and in conjunction with another carrier. *British Airways* have two daily direct flights from London; *Air France* fly the same number from Paris; *Lufthansa* fly from Frankfurt; *KLM* fly from Amsterdam and *Olympic* fly twice daily from Athens. *Turkish Cypriot Airlines* have twice weekly flights from London to İzmir continuing on to Northern Cyprus. Turkey's second, much smaller airline, *İstanbul Airlines*, flies into İstanbul, Ankara, and Adana from a variety of European airports including Gatwick and Manchester, however, it's in financial difficulty at present and may be forced to close. The *İstanbul Airlines* agent in London is *President Holidays* (see page 22).

From Europe

Charter flights In summer these scheduled services are joined by a flood of charter flights from European airports. Several large UK tour operators such as *Thomas Cook* (see page 22) offer flight-only deals in season, or alternatively with prices as low as US$250

• •

Discount flight agents in the UK and Ireland

STA Travel *86 Brompton Road, London, SW7 3LH, T020 -774376262, www.statravel.co.uk Branches in Brighton, Bristol, Cambridge, Leeds, Newcastle and Oxford. Specialist is student fares, can also provide ISIC card and insurance.*

Trailfinders *215 Kensington High Street, London W8 6BD, T020-79375400. Also branches in Birmingham, Bristol, Cambridge, Glasgow, Manchester, Newcastle and Dublin.*

Usit Campus *52 Grosvenor Gardens, London, SW1 0AG, T0870-2401010, www.usitcampus.com Their main Irish branch is at 19 Aston Quay, Dublin 2, T01-6021777 but they also have branches in Belfast, Brighton, Bristol, Cambridge, Manchester and Oxford.* www.usitcampus.co.uk

Other recommended websites *www.fly4less.com; www.flynow.com; www.dialaflight.com*

• •

Discount flight agents in North America and Canada

Air Brokers International *323 Geary St, Suite 411, San Francisco, CA94102, T01-800-883 3273, www.airbrokers.com, consolidators.*

Council Travel *205 E 42nd St, New York, NY, 10017, T1-888-COUNCIL, www.counciltravel.com, specialists in student and budget travel, many other branches.*

Discount Airfares Worldwide On-Line *www.etn.nl/discount.htm, links to consolidators and discount agents.*

Flightfinders *www.flightfinders.ca, on-line Canadian discount agent.*

STA *5900 Wilshire Blvd, Suite 2110, Los Angeles, CA 90036, T1-800-777 0112, www.sta-travel.com, branches in New York, Boston, Miami, San Francisco and Washington DC.*

Travel CUTS *187 College Street, Toronto, ON, M5T 1P7, T1-800-667 2887, www.travelcuts.com Student and budget travel specials, also has branches in other Canadian cities.*

per week including accommodation, you can simply use the flight and head off on your own. Look out for good deals in the press or at local travel agents, especially at the end of the season when prices hit rock bottom. One drawback with charter flights, however, is that you're generally limited to a seven or 14 day return, though you can sometimes pay a supplement to extend this. It's also important to remember that there's an element of risk involved in buying heavily discounted charter fares, as the firms occasionally go out of business leaving passengers stranded.

Discount flights agents in Australia and New Zealand

Budget Travel 16 Fort St, Auckland, T09-3660061, also branches in other cities.

www.statravelaus.com.au and 10 High St, Auckland, T09-3666673.

Flight Centres 82 Elizabeth Street, Sydney, T13-1600 and 205 Queen Street, Auckland, T02 9-3096171, also branches in other towns.

Thomas Cook 257 Collins St, Melbourne, T(02)92486100, www.thomas cook.com.au

STA Travel 702 Harris St, Ultimo, Sydney; also 256 Flinders St, Melbourne,

Trailfinders Sydney: T02 9-247766, also branches in Brisbane, Cairns, Melbourne and Perth, www.travel.com.au

Essentials

Turkish Airlines fly daily direct from New York and three times a week from Chicago; while **Delta** have twice weekly flights from New York with prices ranging between US$438 and US$ 720 one-way depending on the time of year. There are no direct flights from Canadian airports, though **Turkish Airlines** along with several other European carriers operate services via Chicago or European cities such as London or Zurich.

From the USA & Canada

Turkish Airlines and the various national carriers have several flights per week from many Middle Eastern cities including Bahrain, Beirut, Dubai, and Kuwait. There are also three weekly flights from Amman for about US$300 one-way, US$390 return; twice weekly flights from Damascus for about US$260 one-way, US$310 return; also two flights a week from Tehran for about US$380 one-way, US$410 return and daily flights from Cairo for about US$370, US$415 return. **Turkish Airlines** and **Istanbul Airlines** operate flights between Northern Cyprus and Adana, Ankara and Antalya; while **Turkish Cypriot Airlines** operate a twice weekly service to İzmir. **El Al** and **Turkish Airlines** have two to three non-stop flights from Tel Aviv each day for US$330 one-way, US$360 return.

From the Middle East
Prices quoted are an average price for the year with considerable seasonal fluctuations

Turkish Airlines operate anything up to five weekly flights from Almaty, Askhabad, Baku, Bishkek, Tashkent and Tbilisi. Several of the national carriers such as **Azerbaycan Airlines** also have flights to İstanbul.

From Central Asia

Malaysian Airlines, **Singapore Airlines**, **Gulf Air** and **Egypt Air** are among the carriers offering flights from Sydney to İstanbul stopping at one or two other airports. Alternatively there's a much wider choice of connecting flight combinations if you're prepared to use two airlines. You could also consider flying to London and buying a cheap return from there to Turkey. Expect to pay between A$1,350 and A$1,900 return.

From Australia

Airlines generally only allow each economy passenger 20-25 kg of hold luggage; while those flying first or business class are allowed significantly more. Your baggage allowance is shown on your ticket. Baggage in excess of the limit may have to be paid for depending on how busy the plane is and how lenient the check-in staff are.

Baggage allowance

Road

From Britain you can drive to Turkey via France, Italy and Greece using the ferry service from Brindisi to Igoumenitsa. Alternatively, a more direct northerly route takes you through Belguim, Germany, Austria, Hungary, Serbia and Bulgaria.

You can also enter Turkey by road from Greece at the **Kipi-Ipsala** border crossing (see page 204) on the busy highway to the east of Alexandroupolis. It's about a 2½ to three hour drive from the border into İstanbul. The border crossing is open around the clock,

From Greece

though the on-site tourist office and *Turkish Touring and Automobile Association* (see page 44) branch are only open in office hours during the week. Alternatively, there is a much quieter border crossing to the north of Alexandroupolis at **Kastanies-Pazarkule** (see page 203), but this is really only useful if you're heading for Edirne. *Ulusoy*, T1-5240519 and *Varan*, T1-5135768 operate daily buses from Athens (US$70, 20 hours) and Thessaloniki (US$50, 12 hours). *Ulusoy* also operate bus services from Munich, Vienna, Belgrade and Moscow.

From Bulgaria The busy Turkish-Bulgarian frontier post at **Kapıkule** is open 24 hours a day. It's 18 km from the border to Edirne and there are regular buses and dolmuş in the daytime. There are several buses a week from Sofia to İstanbul, US$35, 12 hours.

From Iran Once well-used on the overland trail from India, the border crossing with Iran just to the southeast of **Doğubeyazıt** (see page 652) sees much less tourist traffic these days. Nevertheless, it's still open and dolmuş shuttle between Doğubeyazıt and the border every hour throughout the day. There's also another border crossing further south near **Yuksekova** in Hakkari province but its pretty remote and much more difficult to get to if you're relying on public transport. Several companies run daily buses from Tehran to İstanbul via Ankara, US$40, 40 hours. The prices are very low at present due to excessive competition so they could rise substantially.

From Syria The busiest border crossing from Syria is to the west of Aleppo at **Bab al Hawa**. On the Turkish side there's no public transport until **Reyhanlı**, 5 km inside the frontier and 40 km east of Antakya, though you can easily hitch or catch a taxi. There's also a quieter border crossing to the north of Latakia, which brings you into Turkey at the village of **Yayladağı**, from where there's an occasional dolmuş onwards to Antakya. There are also smaller crossing points to the east at Öncupınar to the south of Gaziantep, Akçakale and Ceylanpınar, though these are more likely to be closed due to border tension and public transport is less certain. There are daily buses from Damascus and Aleppo to İstanbul via Antakya and Ankara.

From Georgia The Georgian border crossing is at **Sarp**, 10 km east of Hopa. There are regular dolmuş from the border to Hopa. There are also several daily buses from Tiblisi and Batumi via Trabzon and Ankara to İstanbul. Daily buses from Azerbaijan also pass across the border here on their way to İstanbul.

From Armenia The Turkish-Armenian border is currently closed.

Sea

There are ferry sailings from Italy and mainland Greece to Turkey, as well as shorter hops from the Greek Islands and Northern Cyprus.

From Italy *Turkish Maritime Lines* (*TML*) operate car ferry services between Venice and İzmir and Brindisi and Çeşme. The **Venice-İzmir** service operates twice a month during December, January and February, increasing in frequency to once a week for the rest of the year. It takes a leisurely 63 hours. The **Brindisi-Çeşme** ferry takes only 31 hours and is more frequent with three weekly sailings from 8 June to 8 October, however, it doesn't operate the rest of the year. Below are some sample fares not including port tax of US$18 per person and US$28 per vehicle. All cabins have a bathroom with shower and a/c. 'A' class cabins have windows and are slightly more comfortable than 'B' and 'C' class cabins, both of which are without portholes. The cheapest option (slightly less than a Pullman seat) during the summer is to travel deck class, in which case you'll need a sleeping mat and bedding. Meals are available on board for US$11 per person.

Turkish Maritime Lines offices and agents in Turkey

These offices are open during normal office hours.
Ankara *TDI Denizyolları Acentesi, Adem Yavuz Sokak No 3/2, Kızılay, T0312-4171161/ 4256368, F4182374*
Antalya *TDI Denizyolları Acentesi, Konyaaltı Caddesi S, Gürsoy Apartments No 40/19, T0242-2411120, F2475095*
Çe[0254]me *TDI Denizyolları Acentesi, Yeni Liman, Çeşme, İzmir, T0232-7121091, F7120482*
Fethiye *Lama Tur AŞ, Hamam Sokak No 3/A, T0252 6144964, F6141404*
Giresun *Çakıroğlu Liman İşletmesi A[0222], Atatürk Bulvarı, Sultan Selim Mahallesi No 9, T0454-2161620, F2121734*
İstanbul *TDI Denizyolları Acentesi, Rıhtım Caddesi, Karaköy, T0212-2499222*

(reservations), T0212-2442502/0207 (info line, recorded message in English), F2519025
İzmir *TDI Denizyolları Acentesi, Yeni Liman 35220, T0232-4647847/ 4648889/64, F4647834*
Marmaris *TDI Denizyolları Acentesi, Yeni Liman, T0252-4130230, F4120449*
Mersin *Kuzeymanlar AŞ, Istiklal Caddesi, 31 Sokak, Verem Savaş Derneği Binası No 4/5, T0324-2312688, F2311069*
Samsun *Türer Alemdarzade Şti, Rıhtım, T0362-4451005, F4451604*
Rize *Ritur, Cumhuriyet Caddesi No 93, T0464-2171484/85, F2171486*
Trabzon *TDI Denizyolları Acentesi, Taksim Parkı Ustu, T0462-3217096, F3221004*

Private ferry companies Often a bit cheaper than TML, although they only run in summer. *Med Link Lines* operate ferries between Brindisi and Çeşme, calling in at Igoumenitsa and Patras, from June to September. Ferries depart Brindisi on Tuesday, Wednesday and Saturday arriving about 30 hours later. In Brindisi contact *Discovery Shipping Agency*, 49 Corso Garibaldi, 72100, T831-527667, F831-564070.

Super-ferries Operate a twice weekly service from Brindisi to Kuşadası, fares are US$200-480 and tickets can be bought through *Karavan Turizm* (see İzmir or Çeşme directories).

TML also operate a ferry between Gazimagosa in the Turkish Republic of Northern Cyprus and the port of Mersin. The overnight car ferry departs every Monday, Wednesday and Friday at 2200, arriving in the opposite port at 0800 the next morning. There are no cabins on this service and the fare is US$25 per person for a Pullman reclining seat, US$48 for a car. There are also daily car ferries run by private companies from Gazimagosa to Taşucu near Silifke (see page 410). **From North Cyprus**

A very popular way of entering the country is by ferry from the Greek islands just off the Turkish coast. Throughout the summer season small ferries and high-speed catamarans regularly make the short crossings from Lesbos to Ayvalık, Chios to **From Greece**

Turkish Maritime Lines sample fares

High*/low season	Luxury cabin	A Class	B Class	Pullman	Car
Venice-İzmir	US$387/530	US$315/415	US$290/320	US$165/210	US$175/205
Brindisi-Çeşme	US$275/350	US$205/250	US$190/230	US$90/115	US$181/140

*High season = Venice-İzmir (21 July-15 September); Brindisi Çeşme (20 July-17 September)

Essentials

Çeşme, Samos to Kuşadası, Kos to Bodrum and Marmaris to Rhodes. There are also less frequent, services to Kaş and Datça. During the winter months most of these ferries operate a skeleton service, while some cease entirely. For more information see the transport sections in the relevant town. The *Med Link Lines* service between Brindisi and Çeşme also calls in at Igoumenitsa and Patras (see above).

Train

Travelling from European cities to Turkey by train is now only for the dedicated rail enthusiast as its both expensive and slow when compared to flying or taking a bus. It's still possible to follow in the tracks of the **Orient Express**, though in considerably less opulent style and with the trip from London taking over 70 hours and involving changes in Cologne, Vienna and Budapest. The **Balkan Express** from Munich to İstanbul, also with changes at Budapest and Vienna, takes 40 hours and costs over US$200 one-way in second class. There are also daily trains from Belgrade, 20 hours, US$50, and Thessaloniki in Greece, 16 hours. There are no longer any rail services from Iran, but there's one weekly passenger train from **Aleppo** to İstanbul which takes 30 hours.

Touching down

Airport information

There is no departure tax when leaving the country Passengers arriving in Turkey have to progress through passport control having purchased the necessary visa (see page 23). Remember to have the right amount of money as they may not always have change.

Once you've collected your baggage and cleared customs at İstanbul's Atatürk airport, there are several 24-hour banks with ATM and change facilities in the arrivals hall. There's also a tourist office, car rental booths and several hotel booking agents who can make reservations for you at some of the city's hotels. A row of taxis wait outside to whisk passengers into the city. *Havaş* airport buses also wait outside, dropping people at the bus station, Aksaray or Taksim. See page 74 for further information.

There are also change facilities and ATMs at **Ankara**, **Antalya** and **İzmir** airports with *Havaş* airport buses and taxis waiting outside the arrivals halls to take you into the city. At **Dalaman** there are no airport buses so a taxi into the town's bus station or direct to one of the local resorts is the only option.

Tourist information

Tourist offices   Most provincial towns and all resorts have Tourist Information Offices, while large cities often have several including one at the airport. Their usefulness varies greatly although at the very least you'll receive a town plan and lots of glossy regional brochures. They generally keep normal office hours.

Disabled travellers   Unfortunately, as in many other developing countries, facilities for disabled travellers are woefully inadequate in Turkey. A few of the larger hotels, particularly the international chains, and restaurants in the main cities and resorts have wheel-chair access and adapted toilets. The vast majority, though, do not. The generally appalling, or even non-existent, condition of the pavements in Turkish towns and cities also presents a major challenge to those with walking difficulties or in a wheel chair. In fact, often the only practical solution is to use the street itself. Having said that, members of the public will usually go out of their way to help you and a few tour operators are beginning to feature special holidays catering for those with disabilities.

Touching down

Hours of business Banks, tourist
information and government offices:
0830-1200, 1330-1700, Mon-Fri. Shops
generally stay open until 1900 or even
later and are open on Saturday.
Official time 2 hours ahead of GMT.

Voltage 220 volts (50 cycles).
Weights and measures Metric system.
Useful numbers Ambulance: 112. Fire:
110. Police: 155. Directory enquiries: 118.
Traffic police: 154. International operator:
115. Jandarma (in rural areas): 156.

Essentials

Additional information can be found at the **Global Access-Disabled Travel Network Site**, www.geocities.com/Paris/1502 Also try the **Royal Association for Disability and Rehabilitation**, 250 City Road, London, EC1V 8AF, UK. Or the **Society for the Advancement of Travel for Handicapped**, 347 Fifth Avenue, New York, NY, T212-4477284. In İstanbul the **Turkish Association for the Disabled**, T0212-5214912, may be able to provide some information.

Ocakköy, near Fethiye, is one of the only hotels in the country with specially designed facilities such as a pool-lift.

Student travellers

Students in full time education should pick up an **International Student Identity Card** (ISIC), available from student travel offices and travel agencies worldwide. These entitle the holder to reduced entrance fees at most of the country's sights and museums, along with discounted fares on trains as well as some buses and airlines.

Women travellers

Many women travel to Turkey every year and leave having had a very positive experience, however, it's important to keep in mind a few things to help you get the most from your visit. Firstly, Turkey is a Muslim country and people's attitudes towards women are very different to those in the west. Outside of the major western towns and tourist areas you'll notice relatively few women on the streets and those you do see are often with a friend or family member. They'll also be dressed very modestly, with their arms and legs covered and often with a scarf tied around their head. In such areas women still marry young and attitudes towards them are very traditional. This means that as a foreign woman, particularly if you are travelling alone, you're likely to attract considerable attention.

Unfortunately, men are often encouraged by the negative stereotypes of foreign women, and particularly their moral values, that are portrayed in the Turkish tabloid press. To be fair, this situation also hasn't been helped by the behaviour of some women, for whom promiscuous sex with local men is an important part of a successful holiday.

The result is that women travellers may find themselves the subject of unwanted advances. If this is the case, be firm and don't worry about causing offence. Avoid making eye contact, which can be misconstrued as a come-on and reply to questions bluntly. Get up and leave if you feel uncomfortable. It may help to wear a wedding ring or to talk about your 'husband' and 'children'. Wearing modest clothes is also important so as not to give the wrong impression. It should be added that by no means all Turkish men behave disrespectfully towards foreign women. Such behaviour is seen as socially unacceptable, so you can expect the support of other people around you. Try learning a few simple phrases (see page 713) in order to get your message across.

Travelling with a male companion can drastically reduce these problems, while you can turn to a female friend for moral support in difficult situations. As in most countries there is a well trodden tourist route and it's easy to find western company if you want it. Travelling with others can help you feel more secure, particularly when arriving in a new place and finding accommodation.

In more conservative areas couples may be asked to prove their marital status before they can share a room, although this is generally not a problem in tourist areas. On buses single women are always seated next to other women, and a similar system operates on dolmuş, often with much awkward shuffling of passengers.

Travelling with children

Turkey must be one of the easiest countries in which to travel with children, as Turks exhibit an almost universal love of kids. Children often become the centre of attention in hotels and restaurants while misbehaviour is tolerated to a far greater degree than in the west. Travelling with children can also help bring you into contact with local families and the presence of a little face has been known to oil the wheels of officialdom.

Travelling on buses can be a stressful experience for both parent and child because of the confined space and lack of things to do. (Remember to take something like books or paper and colouring pencils to help keep children occupied during long journeys.) Travelling at night when children can sleep is a very good idea. Trains, although slower, tend to offer more opportunity for moving around, while motion sickness is also less of a problem. When travelling by air remember to take sweets for a child to suck during take-off and landing to help equalize the pressure in their ears. If you require a child seat for a hire car it's advisable to request it in advance.

On long distance buses you pay by the seat and there are no reductions for children. Most Turks don't buy their children a separate seat, even on long journeys, but have them on their lap. This can be extremely uncomfortable for all concerned on anything but a short hop and it's not to be recommended. On sightseeing tours a discount can generally be negotiated.

If hotel tariffs are on a per person basis then you will nearly always be able to negotiate a reduction for children. Particularly as two little ones can easily share a bed top-to-toe. Extra beds are often available for double rooms.

If you can't see anything suitable on the menu ask the restaurant staff, who will often be happy to prepare something specially for a child. It is also wise to carry some snacks with you particularly if you are travelling by public transport. Bananas and cartons of UHT milk, flavoured or otherwise, are two nutritious and widely available possibilities.

Gay & lesbian travellers

Despite a homosexual tradition running through Ottoman times and the existence of several widely adored transvestite singers, modern Turks, including many police officers, are generally pretty intolerant towards gay men and women. Gay sex is legal for consenting adults over the age of 18, though harassment, official and otherwise, is commonplace. Still there is a small but vibrant gay scene in western cities such as İstanbul, İzmir and, surprisingly, Bursa too. For more information, log-on to www.eshcinsel.net an extensive Turkish gay site or get in touch with LAMBDA İstanbul, PO Box ACL222, İstanbul 80800, T0212-2334966, lamba @lambistanbul.org a group which organises meetings and events for the gay community in İstanbul.

Working in Turkey

There are plenty of opportunities for casual work in the resort towns along the southern coast and despite low rates of pay many young holidaymakers choose to work in a bar or hotel as a means of extending their trip. If the thrill hasn't worn off by the time the three-month visa runs out, it's easy enough to make a day trip to one of the Greek islands off the coast, buying another visa on re-entry into the country.

Private, state and language schools, along with some universities, recruit native-English speakers to teach English. Most teaching jobs are found in the large cities in the west of the country, although some provincial towns also have private language schools. Rates of pay are generally low by western standards, but teachers in İstanbul are paid significantly more than elsewhere in the country, reflecting the higher cost of living in the city. Schools generally expect you to have a university degree and a TEFL-certificate when applying, though you may be able to find less formal employment with neither. It is best to apply for work and residency permits once you have found a job and in most cases your employer will take care of this for you. A good place to start looking for a teaching job is the **British Council** in Ankara, İstanbul or İzmir (see relevant sections).

Voluntary work The **British Trust for Conservation Volunteers** (BTCV), 36 St Mary's Street, Wallingford, Oxon, OX10 0EU, T01491-839766, F01491-839646, www.btcv.org, runs two-week turtle monitoring holidays in Çıralı and Akyatan on the Mediterranean coast. Volunteers patrol the beach each night collecting data on marine turtles visiting these important nesting beaches. No previous experience required. It costs £395, including flights and food. An İstanbul based company called *Genç Tur* (see page 164) organizes a wide variety of working holidays across the country.

Essentials

Rules, customs & etiquette

Hospitality is an art form in Anatolia, refined over centuries by the nomadic Turks. Contrary to western norms in Turkish culture the host is honoured by a visit, grateful of the opportunity to receive guests, be they old friends or strangers from afar. Although the traditions may be fading in the most urbanised and touristy areas, the old custom are very much alive elsewhere. Invitations are common place, endless cups of tea forthcoming, while the Turkish equivalent of welcome, "*Hoş geldiniz*" – literally "Your coming is pleasurable" – will ring frequently in your ears.

Hospitality

Cleanliness and neatness of dress are of the upmost importance to Turkish people. Although very tolerant of the way foreigners dress and behave, this should be remembered particularly if you're dealing with officials. A shirt and trousers or a long skirt kept for such occasions can be a great asset and can help ease red tape.

Clothing

It's also important to remember some regional differences in attitudes towards dress. Though it's perfectly acceptable to wear shorts and a t-shirt in the resorts and cities along the Aegean and Mediterranean coasts, such attire would raise eyebrows in more conservative areas of the country and may even cause offence. Women should take particular care to choose modest clothes, such as long skirts and baggy trousers, in order to avoid unwanted male attention.

Topless sun-bathing is only acceptable on the beaches of the main tourist resorts like Marmaris, Kemer and Alanya; though even there nude bathing is out of the question.

When entering mosques you should be respectfully dressed. This means no shorts or sleeveless tops for men or women and women should also tie a scarf over their heads. In a few of the touristy mosques, in İstanbul for instance, there are scarves hanging outside the door for you to borrow; but in the vast majority you'll need to have your own.

Turks are generally a courteous race and demonstrate a strong tradition of respect for elders and strangers. As in French, politeness is built into the grammar of the language with the use of the plural pronoun and it's relevant suffixes to denote respect. Despite this, Turks can sometimes seem abrupt to foreigners. Unlike European languages, 'thank you' is not used as often in everyday situations and doing so may well bring a smile to the face of the person you're dealing with. The easiest way to be courteous and earn yourself countless brownie points is to learn a few simple phrases of Turkish (see page 713). You'll be continually and shamelessly congratulated for uttering just a few badly pronounced words.

Courtesy

One of the areas where there's a distinct lack of courtesy is queuing and it's not unusual for people to barge right to the head of a line or to lean in front of you when you are buying a ticket. A loud 'tutt' will make the offender aware of your disapproval, and may even have some effect. In extreme situations you may have to use your body for strategic blocking manoeuvres.

Shaking hands is the normal way for men to greet each other, however, some women may not be comfortable shaking a strange man's hand. Men and women are greeting close friends, be they male or female, usually exchange kisses on either cheek.

It's particularly important to remain courteous when dealing with officials no matter how frustrated you are. Remember any official process takes much longer than expected, so be patient and avoid losing your temper at all costs, as it will do you no good.

Drugs The trafficking and use of illegal drugs carries stiff penalties in Turkey and although the penal systems has been considerably reformed since the days of *Midnight Express*, conditions in prison and on remand awaiting trial still fall far short of those in western countries. The government, due to pressure from the west, has vigorously suppressed the domestic production of illicit drugs and the only opium poppies you are likely to see nowadays are those grown under strict control for the pharmaceutical industry. Even so, Turkey is one of the world's main trans-shipment centres for narcotics, much of which passes across its eastern borders en-route for Europe.

Tipping In some more expensive restaurants a service charge of around 10-15% is added, although it's doubtful whether much of this ever reaches the staff. If the service was good you can add something on yourself – perhaps 5-10%. In cheap restaurants and cafés tipping is not expected, but rounding a sum up to leave a small amount will be greatly appreciated. Similarly, tipping is not necessary in budget hotels but porters who carry your luggage up to your room or carry out other tasks on your behalf should be rewarded with a tip of between US$0.50-1.50.

It's not customary to tip dolmuş, bus or taxi drivers but a fare displayed on a taxi meter will often be rounded up, or down, to avoid creating unnecessary change. If you are part of a tour group, it is normal practice to reward the driver and guide, if they deserve it, with a tip.

A 10% tip is given to the hairdresser cutting your hair or giving you a shave, along with a small additional sum to the person sweeping up. An official, compulsory, tip is payable to the porter on night trains and will be collected near the end of the journey, you may also wish to add on a small amount yourself.

Commissions Some hotels, shops and other businesses pay commissions to guides, taxi drivers or anyone else, for that matter, who brings them trade. This commission comes directly out of your pocket because it's added onto the price of whatever you buy. For example, if you visit a carpet shop with a tour group, typically 20-30%, but occasionally up to 40%, of what you pay for a carpet will go directly into the guide's pocket. The best way to avoid such hidden rip-offs is to avoid buying things while on an organized tour and instead seek out shops on your own. Also book hotels and tours directly rather than through a third party.

Responsible tourism The economic benefits of tourism for countries such as Turkey are undeniable, but tourist development has its share of negative impacts too. These environmental and social costs are most obvious at the mass, package, end of the market, though there is potential for independent travellers to cause considerable harm as well. Respecting local customs and acting in a responsible manner can reduce such problems. In the country's **national parks** and conservation areas follow guidelines and rules. This is particularly important on some **turtle nesting** beaches along the south coast where access is restricted to daylight hours to avoid disturbing nesting females.

In some fire-sensitive areas **lighting fires** is banned during summer months. Elsewhere, always take the upmost care. **Litter**, particularly plastic bags and bottles, is a great problem, and one that you can help to reduce by using bins provided or by carrying your rubbish to somewhere where it will be disposed of properly. Try re-using plastic bags and filling up drinking water bottles at places mentioned in this book. If you are staying somewhere for a while enquire locally about a potable spring or a water shop (*sucu*), because locals probably won't drink expensive bottled water. Much of the waste produced on boat trips is tipped straight over the side, so when booking a *gület* voyage enquire about arrangements for waste disposal. If you see a member of the crew dumping rubbish into the sea complain to the captain or the tour organizer.

Turkey is a signatory of the Convention on International Trade in Endangered Species of Wild Fauna and Flora (CITES), along with most European countries, the US and Canada. Importation of CITES protected species can result in heavy fines, confiscation of goods and imprisonment. Contact *Traffic International*, UK office T01223-277427, traffic@wcmc.org.uk, for details of legislative control and protective measures. Other useful addresses include: *Tourism Concern*, Southlands College, Wimbledon, Parkside, London, SW19 5NN, T020-89440464, www.gn.apc.org/tourismconcern A non-profit organization which aims to promote a greater understanding of the impacts of tourism. *Centre for the Advancement of Responsible Travel*, UK T01732-352757, has information on alternative and green holiday destinations and a range of publications.

Safety

Turkey is a relatively safe country: the incidence of petty street crime such as mugging is much lower than in most western countries. Still, it's important not to be complacent, particularly when in large cities and tourist areas. You should also be aware that in the southeast of the country the security situation is much less certain. British Foreign & Commonwealth Office's travel advisory website, and/or the US State Department's equivalent site can be useful sources of up to date information. However, you should bear in mind that these tend to be written by diplomats based in the capital or other major cities and they can be rather generic in their advice. FCO, T020 70080232, US State Department T202-6475225, website: www.travel.state.gov/travel_warnings.html

Although organized pick-pocket gangs and 'slashers' are not a common problem in Turkey, it's as well to keep all your documentation, credit cards and travellers' cheques in a secure place such as a money belt, leaving a small amount of cash in your pocket for day to day costs. In crowded areas such as market places shoulder bags can be vulnerable, carry them so that they are visible. Make photocopies of all your important documents and give them to your family and travelling partner. Always carry travellers' cheque numbers and credit card help-line numbers separately from your wallet. Valuables shouldn't be left in your hotel room but should be deposited with front desk staff or in a safe. Keep your passport with you at all times, as you'll be expected to produce it on demand by police and other authorities.

Protecting money & valuables
Send your passport, TC's & credit card numbers to an e-mail address so that you have them if everything gets stolen

Although still rare, there's been a worrying increase in the number of incidents involving the drugging and robbery of western travellers. Such scams sometimes involve nationals from other Middle Eastern countries, as well as Turks, who befriend tourists and slip a powerful drug into a drink or food. The victim falls into a deep sleep only to wake up hours, or sometimes days later, with a very sore head and relieved of all their valuables. To make matters worse the police can be less than sympathetic towards the victims themselves, suspecting them of using illegal drugs

Remember to stay alert and to avoid accepting gifts of food or drinks from strangers, even if they are staying in the same hotel as you. This presents some difficulties because Turkish people are by nature very generous and every offer shouldn't be regarded with suspicion. You will just have to judge each situation yourself and decline politely if your are even the slightest bit suspicious.

Con-tricks & drugging

A popular con-trick employed in İstanbul is for tourists, particularly lone males, to be invited into clubs or bars by people they meet in the street. After several drinks the unwary 'guest' will then be presented with an astronomic bill. Things inevitably get pretty nasty if they're unwilling to pay.

Southeast Anatolia Since the early 1980's the Kurdish Worker's Party (PKK) has been conducting a violent separatist campaign in the southeast of the country (see box, page 612). The military has responded by imposing marshal law and using massive force to try and wipe out its often-illusive foe. Since the capture of the PKK leader, Abdullah Ocalan, the conflict has entered a new, quieter, phase with Kurdish leaders calling on their fighters to lay down their arms. Foreign tourists travelling in the southeast have rarely been targeted by the PKK, however, there is always a remote possibility of this happening, particularly given the fact that small groups of separatists have ignored calls to disengage in fighting. Also remember that the border region abutting Iran, Iraq and Syria is a sensitive area. Foreigners are sometimes viewed with suspicion by security personnel, partly because very few tourists now travel in the region, but also because the Turkish State is extremely sensitive to foreign involvement in the Kurdish struggle.

Before visiting the region it is important to contact your embassy or consulate (see page 24) for details of the current situation and to advise them of your plans. You are also recommended to limit your itinerary to towns and tourist sites and to avoid straying off into rural areas. Restrict road journeys to daylight hours and keep your passport with you at all times for army checkpoints.

Police The responsibility of policing urban areas with a population of over 2000 falls on the shoulders of the blue-uniformed civil *Polis* force. *Trafik Polis*, who wear a similar uniform with a white cap, have the doubtful pleasure of bringing some semblance of order to the roads, which usually means directing traffic at intersections and giving out parking tickets. The *Jandarma* is a branch of the military, made up largely of conscripts, whose job it is to keep the peace in rural areas.

The only contact most visitors have with the Turkish law enforcement agencies is being asked to produce their identification. In less touristy areas a mixture of curiosity and boredom on the part of the police often motivates this intrusion. Don't be intimidated by the men in blue, or green, as they're usually only too happy to offer assistance, though their ability to help is generally limited by a lack of English. Tourist police in the main resorts and cities can normally speak English or German. As with all officials, be respectful and avoid losing your temper.

Despite widespread corruption it is not advisable for you to try and bribe your way out of trouble, as there is a good chance that you will make things worse. If you suspect that you are being asked for a bribe, the best course of action is to play the dumb tourist and pretend not to understand. When paying on-the-spot fines for traffic offences make sure you receive a receipt for the entire amount.

Where to stay

There is a large and varied range of accommodation available across the country, with something to suit all budgets and tastes, and many places which offer real value for money. Many hotels throughout the country are registered by the Ministry of Tourism as well as local authorities, who ensure that they meet certain standards. However, there are also lots of hotels and pensions which are not registered and which offer equally high, if not better, standards of service and facilities (possibly at a reduced price). So, just because a place has stars outside it, don't imagine that it will be better than the hotel next door without them.

Hotel price guide and facilities

LL (over US$201) to AL (US$101-150)
Most often found in the main cities and where there's a large concentration of tourists or business travellers. Comfortable and generally equipped with cable TV, a/c and an en suite bathroom. Amenities often include a pool, sauna, gym, business facilities, several restaurants and bars. A safe box is provided in your room or at reception. Credit cards are generally accepted and foreign currencies changed, though often at a poor rate.

A (US$71-100) *These hotels provide a high level of comfort; rooms with an ensuite bathroom , a/c, TV and telephone. Facilities such as a pool, fitness centre, restaurant and bar also may be on offer. A buffet breakfast and room service are usually provided, as are currency exchange facilities. Credit cards are widely accepted though discounts for cash, as well as longer stays can normally be negotiated.*

B (US$51-70) – C (US$41-50) *A bit simpler, though rooms usually have an en suite shower or bath, TV and telephone. Breakfast, buffet or otherwise, is provided*
and there may be a restaurant. Credit cards may not be accepted but prices are often open to negotiation.

D (US$31-40) – E (US$21-30) *There are some excellent bargains in these categories though rooms will vary from fairly comfortable to merely functional. An ensuite shower with hot water, as well as clean towels and bed linen, should be expected. A fan may be provided in hotter regions, while in the resorts there should be safe boxes at reception. A simple breakfast is generally included in the price.*

F (US$12-20) – G (under US$12)
Usually pretty simple and no direct-dial telephone. Bathrooms are often shared, though there may be a washbasin in your room. Hot water may only be available in the evenings and in the cheapest places there is an additional charge for using the showers. Standards of cleanliness may not be the highest. In touristy areas however there are some excellent value pensions and hostels in these price bands, offering spartan but clean rooms with lots of additional services such as lockers, kitchen facilities, cheap food and tours.

Essentials

   Top class hotels, including the well known international chains, can be found in the larger cities of İstanbul, İzmir and Ankara; in the main tourist areas; and in the occasional town such as Diyarbakır or Trabzon, which are visited by business travellers. In smaller centres and less touristy areas the choice of accommodation is not as good, though you will usually get considerably more for your money. İstanbul hotel prices are more expensive than the rest of the country but there are also some very good budget options. Generally, the pensions and hostels used by independent travellers are cheaper than those catering for package tourists, however, booking through an agent, in Turkey or before you arrive, can substantially reduce the difference. Despite claiming to offer 24-hour hot water, the definition of '24-hour' and 'hot' are sometimes rather elastic in the cheaper hotels. Check several rooms before making a choice and be aware of whether the hotel is close to a mosque, unless you don't mind being blasted by the *ezan* in the early hours.

   Generally hotels in the top price brackets do not include VAT (15%) in their rates, and most also do not include breakfast. This is the same with the really cheap pensions, although all the establishments in between generally provide a fairly standard breakfast country-wide, which consists of a hard-boiled egg, cheese, tomatoes, cucumber, jams and tea or coffee. It's great at first, though after several weeks of the same combination it can get a little boring. Most midrange places offer this as an open-buffet.

Essentials

The availability of rooms during the summer holiday period and national holidays (see page 62) is stretched and at these times it is advisable to book ahead if possible. You will very, very rarely not be able to find a bed at all, it's just that the nicer hotels and pensions may well be full. Checkout time is generally 1200, but ask when you arrive to make sure. Hotels usually have a luggage room in which you can put your stuff if you are not leaving until the evening.

Advice & suggestions

There is often a cluster of cheap accommodation around bus and railway stations. These can be very convenient if you are departing early or are just passing through, but generally there is little else to recommend them. Remember to consider road noise (generally worse in front rooms) and proximity to mosques if you want an undisturbed night's sleep. The prices posted on the wall of many hotel receptions are often far more than should be paid and are open to bargaining, especially if the place looks empty or it's low season. Some midrange places may also give you a discount for paying in hard currency. In the cheaper hotels and pensions there is usually far less room for discounting so consider whether the price is fair and represents value for money before trying to beat the price down just for the sake of it.

Bathrooms
'Sicak su yok' - there's no hot water

Turkish plumbing is at best adequate, but often downright terrible and after travelling for a few weeks you may well ask yourself if there is a competent plumber in the entire country. Strangely positioned toilets; taps that leak; dribbling showers and blocked drains are all things that you will almost certainly encounter, unless you stay in expensive hotels. To avoid making things worse, don't flush toilet paper and tampons down the toilet but use the bin provided. Also don't assume that hot water will come out of the 'hot' tap, and cold out of the 'cold'. Leave taps running for some time, check the temperature, and then get into the shower to avoid nasty surprises. If hot water isn't forthcoming after a couple of minutes, call the receptionist. The small pipe sticking into the toilet bowl is used by Turkish people to wash themselves. Once over their initial reservations some people find this method is a cleaner and more convenient alternative to using toilet paper. Squat-type toilets, where you crouch over a whole in the floor, are found in some cheap accommodation and when you get off the beaten track. A small plastic jug, standing beneath a tap, is provided for washing yourself and for flushing the toilet as well. Toilet paper should be carried with you when you travel in less touristy area as it may not be provided.

In many of the cheapest boarding houses there's an additional charge, usually about US$2, for using the showers. If you intend to have a shower it is often worth seeking out somewhere a bit nicer with an ensuite bathroom, as it will work out at about the same price in the end.

Treat electric sockets and shower units with great care: the combination of Turkish electrics and plumbing is potentially lethal. Try not to touch the appliance when it's on and step out of the shower before switching it off.

Youth hostels

The **Youth Hostel Association-Turkey** is an affiliation of close to 20 hostels located in many of the main tourist centres. The standard of accommodation available varies from hostel to hostel, although simple double and dormitory beds are usually available from US$5-10 per person in the high season. Most hostels are clean and friendly, with facilities such as a laundry, luggage room and lockers for your valuables. You don't need to be a member to stay at any of the member hostels, but discount cards are available for US$4 that entitle you to priority booking and some reductions. Pick up or send for a brochure from their head office: Caferiye Sokak No 6, 34400, Sultanahmet, İstanbul, T0212-5136150, www.hostelsturkey.org

Despite having come from nomadic stock, Turkish people aren't great campers. The average family camping trip is more like a major expedition involving loading a van or truck with everything bar the kitchen sink. Despite this, there are excellent opportunities for camping both on sites and in the 'wild'.

The services provided on campsites vary, though at the very least there should be clean toilets, hot showers and a place to cook. However, some of the more luxurious place may even have a swimming pool. Expect to pay from US$2-5 per person per night, US$4-7 for a caravan.

If you wish to camp 'wild', look around for someone to ask permission from. Near towns and villages it is best to remain discreet, erecting the tent as it gets dark and keeping out of sight of main roads. Nevertheless, some inquisitive person will probably spot you and, Turkish nature being what it is, come over to make sure you are all right and that you don't need anything.

Although theft is not generally a problem, don't risk leaving valuables in your tent when it is unattended, particularly in touristy areas. Remember to be extremely careful if lighting fires and to collect all your rubbish. If you are in a wilderness area faeces should be buried properly – a small trowel is useful for this – and toilet paper burnt or taken with you.

Camping
When camping take care to tap out your shoes in the morning to make sure nothing has crept in during the night

Essentials

Getting around

Travel within the country is a painless task when compared to many developing countries and using the excellent public bus system or the slower state railway network, not only gets you where you want to go, but also gives you a valuable insight into everyday life. Journey times tend to be long because of the large distances involved; the mountainous nature of the terrain and the frequently poor condition of the roads, particularly once you get away from the west of the country and large cities. This means that if time is short it is advisable to limit your itinerary geographically or to use the efficient domestic air network.

Air

Turkish Airlines (*Türk Hava Yolları*) have a virtual monopoly on internal routes and there are flights to all major cities and many provincial towns (see map). *İstanbul Airlines* also operate planes on a very limited number of routes, though these are essentially just continuations of foreign service. *Turkish Airlines* tickets are a bit cheaper when bought in Turkey, although once in the country there is no difference between buying from an travel agent or direct from *Turkish Airlines*. On the regular services like İstanbul-İzmir or İstanbul-Ankara you can usually turn up at the airport, buy your ticket and fly on the next flight. However, during the summer and on national holidays, and on routes with only a limited service, you should book well in advance.

All domestic flights are from İstanbul or Ankara, with no internal flights between the various smaller airports

It is worth flying stand-by if there are no seats available on a particular flight as many companies make block reservations that are never used. Passengers should check in at least 45 minutes before the departure time, or they risk losing their reservation. Before check in your luggage will be x-rayed and you will have to pass through a metal detector. Prior to boarding the plane you are required to identify your luggage on the tarmac. This is a way of preventing terrorists from checking an unaccompanied bomb on to the plane.

Road

Signs for toll roads have a green background, whilst those for normal highways are blue. Tourist sites are marked by signs with a yellow background

Turkey's road network is fairly good in the west of the country, though further east and away from the main cities its often a different story. Rough roads and mountainous terrain make for much slower and more uncomfortable journeys in the east. Even in the west once you leave the main intercity routes the quality of roads reduces dramatically with rutted and pot-holed surfaces as the norm. Lengthy sections of the main trunk routes have not yet been widened and the large number of slow-moving trucks on single-lane highways greatly lengthens journey times. Particularly slow sections include the Balıkesir-İzmir, İzmir-Ankara and Ankara-Samsun highways, along with unimproved sections of the Black Sea coastal highway.

Toll roads, similar to the French *péage,*have been constructed in the west of the country and these offer excellent driving conditions for a small charge – usually US$0.50-2. The national speed limits are 50 kmh in urban areas, 90 kmh on open highways and 130 kmh on motorways.

Bus

Buses are the most popular method of transport and Turkey has an extremely efficient and cheap bus system. A mind-boggling array of private companies as well as local *belediye* (councils) operate services to even the smallest of towns. Bus stations in the main centres are like small cities in themselves with dozens of ticket offices, hundreds of buses and thousands of passengers and staff

Most routes are covered by several different companies, so if you are travelling on a tight budget it can pay to shop around. Check the prices and departure times for all the various competing companies. Also bear in mind that you pay for what you get, with the cheaper companies undercutting their larger rivals by operating older, less comfortable buses and sometimes skimping on the costs of labour and maintenance. You don't need to be a genius to realize that this effects safety.

Where and when you are going may dictate what company you use, particularly on the less popular routes, however, below is a list of the best companies and the geographical regions they specialise in. *Varan* and *Ulusoy* are the best, but also the most expensive, companies. Their modern buses are fitted with comfortable reclining seats and they operate truly non-stop services between the major centres in the west of the country. Both companies also operate services to European destinations. *Ulusoy* also operate services to the Black Sea from İstanbul, İzmir and Ankara. With these top-tier companies it is always necessary to book in advance.

Kamil Koç and *Pamukkale* are most people's choice and they offer a huge number of routes concentrated mainly in the west of the country. Expect more stops, longer journey times and slightly less comfort than with the top companies, although both provide reclining seats and air-conditioning. *Has* are recommended if you are travelling to the south and east of the country, and they also have international routes particularly to Germany. Apart from the companies mentioned above there are a large number of smaller companies operating modern Mercedes 403 buses on specific routes.

Seats can be booked in advance at bus stations or company offices. On the busiest routes, for example between İstanbul, İzmir, Ankara and Antalya, it is generally possible to turn up at the *otogar*, buy your ticket and leave after just a short wait, however, it is safer to make a reservation. During holiday periods it feels like the whole country is on the move and booking is essential. When buying your ticket, look at the agent's seating chart and try to select a seat towards the front of the bus. The back rows are bumpy and uncomfortable, while the front passengers may be more at risk in the event of an accident. Women travelling unaccompanied are seated next to other women and sometimes you may be asked to swap seats to make this possible. Smoking has recently been banned on all buses

Longer journeys are usually made at night, although there may also be a slower day service. During a long journey you can expect to stop several times at service

No rules of the road

Narrow winding roads, poorly marked obstructions, rough surfaces and pot-holes all test a driver's skill. Then there are the other road users: overloaded trucks emblazoned with "Allah Korusun" (May God Protect), dolmuş stopping with little or no warning, suicidal motorbike riders and farm vehicles driving at night with no lights. Practices such as overtaking on blind corners and ignoring red lights also do little to improve road safety, and Turkey suffers from a soberingly high road accident rate. In order not to become one of the statistics, drive carefully, take your time and allow for plenty of stops en route. When driving at night pay particular attention for unmarked obstructions and domestic animals and do not be alarmed by the Turkish driver's habit of flashing their lights at on-coming vehicles – this is simply a way of letting you know that they're coming.

stations with toilets, cheap food and of course tea. Most importantly, though, stops give everyone the chance to have a cigarette or two. Don't leave your hand luggage unattended on the bus during such stops. The rest of your baggage is stowed in the hold and most companies give you a numbered plastic tag to present when collecting it. Soon after getting underway the steward will check everyone's tickets. He should also come through the cabin at regular intervals during the journey offering passengers drinking water and lemon cologne to refresh their hands and faces. When you arrive at your destination, enquire about minibus services into the centre of town (*servis araba var mı?*). These often leave quickly after the arrival of the bus, so don't hang around.

City buses operate in the country's larger towns and cities and are usually boarded having bought a ticket or pre-paid card from a kiosk or official vendor near main bus stops. At night, when such outlets are closed, hawkers often hang around bus stops selling tickets at a slight premium. In some large cities bus routes are operated by private companies and on many of these buses your fare is collected and a ticket issued by an employee on the bus itself.

Car

Driving allows you unrivalled freedom to explore the country. Once out of the cities and off the main routes, traffic is light so you can enjoy the scenery at your own pace. However, it is important to remember that the quality of the roads and the standard of driving generally fall far short of that of western countries.

Despite the general disregard for the rules shown by most Turkish drivers, traffic police do liberally hand out on-the-spot fines for minor offences. The issuing of fines has greatly increased in recent years in an attempt to bring some semblance of order to the roads. Make sure you are given a receipt when you pay for a fine or you will have unwittingly contributed to the police officer's salary. In urban areas take notice of all parking restrictions or you risk being towed away.

Documentation and border formalities Legal requirements for driving in Turkey include a full driving licence from your home country, or an International driving licence, along with the vehicle registration documents and insurance certificate. Carry all these documents with you in the vehicle at all times and if renting a vehicle, make sure that the rental company has provided them.

Cars must be equipped with a reflective triangle for emergency use & a spare tyre

Most insurers will extend Green Card insurance cover specifically for driving in Turkey – considered a high-risk country – for an additional sum. At the **border**, you will be asked to produce a driving licence, the registration papers for the vehicle, as well as an insurance document proving that you are covered to drive in the country. If you are continuing into another Middle Eastern country, you will also need a *Carnet de Passage* (Transit book). You will be issued with a temporary registration document

Essentials

Essentials

 Turkish Touring and Automobile Association Offices

Open 0830-1200, 1300, 1730 weekdays.

Ankara Maraşal Fevzi Çakmak Caddesi No 31/8 Beşevler, T0312-2228723, F2228557.

Antalya Milli Egemenlik Caddesi, Dallar Yıldız Çarşısı No 9, T0242-2470699, F2484574.

Gaziantep A Fuat Cebesoy Bulvar2, Orkide Apart No 24/A, T0342-3251610.

İstanbul (Head office) 1.Oto Sanayi Sitesi Yan2, 4. Levent, T0212-2828140, F2828042.

İzmir Atatürk Bulvar2 No 370, Alsancak, T0232-4213514, F4213542.

Mersin Mücahitler Caddesi, Karadağ İşhanı No 55, Kat 2/10, T0324-2320492, F2321247.

Trabzon Devlet Caddesi, Tünel Çıkışı No 2/2, T0462-3217156.

(*araba tezkeresi*) for the car, which is valid for six months and must be handed in when you leave the country. Your passport will also be stamped so that you cannot leave without the vehicle. If your car is written-off while your in Turkey you will need to take it to the nearest customs compound in order to have the stamp cancelled. Likewise, if it is stolen, you will need a report from the police and local administration (*Vilayet*) freeing you to leave the country.

In the event of a **Breakdown** cover and a recovery service are provided in Turkey by the **Turkish**
breakdown call the 24-hr **Touring and Automobile Association** (*Türkiye Turing ve Otomobile Kurumu*), who work
emergency line, in association with other international motoring organizations, such as the British AA.
T0212-2804449, They can also provide you with general motoring information and a list of recognized
although the operator repair shops. The association have offices in a number of cities (see box) as well as at
may not speak English the main border crossings.

Accidents It is against the law to move a vehicle that has been involved in an accident, so leave it where it is, even if it's obstructing the traffic, and wait for the traffic police to arrive. Moving your car before the police reach the scene is not only an offence, but it may also influence culpability for the smash.

For insurance purposes, you will need an accident report from the police (*kaza raporu*) and you may be required to give a breath-test for alcohol. If you are found to have been driving under the influence of alcohol you will be liable for prosecution and if it is a hire car your insurance will be void. Your insurance may also be cancelled if you don't report an accident to the firm within 48 hours.

Petrol and mechanics As with the rest of continental Europe, in Turkey you drive on the right. Finding a filling station is never much of a problem except in some regions of the east, where you should try and avoid running your tank too low. Petrol stations are generally open 24 hours a day and sell *normal benzin* (petrol), *süper benzin* (high-octane petrol), *kursunsuz* (lead-free) and *mazot* (diesel). Rental cars normally use *süper* or *kursunsuz* and it should say which on the petrol cap.

If you have mechanical problems or a flat tyre, head for a *sanayi*, the area of workshops on the edge of most towns, where you will have no problem finding a mechanic for the job. Spare parts for Renault, Fiat, Mercedes, Ford, along with the domestic brand Tofaş (essentially Fiats) are easily found, however, parts for other foreign models may be harder to come by. Turkish mechanics are highly ingenious and labour charges low, so even without the right part they can normally get you back on the road for a fraction of what it would cost in the west. Punctured tyres require an *oto lastikçi* which are a regular sight along the country's roads.

Hiring a car To rent a car you must be at least 21 and have a valid driving licence with you. Some companies may also require you to leave an imprint of your credit card or your passport as a deposit. All the large international rental companies such as *Avis*, *Hertz* and *Budget* have a presence in the main cities, airports and resorts of western Turkey and there are also smaller domestic firms. Rental rates are relatively expensive by international standards starting at about US$65 per day for an economy model (insurance is extra). Make sure you purchase insurance for every possible eventuality, including tyre and widescreen repairs. There are slight discounts on weekly rates and, with the large companies at least, it is possible to pick up and drop off the car in different cities. Local hire companies may offer cheaper rates, although the quality of the cars may not be as good. Inform the hire company in advance if you require child seats.

There are only a few rental outfits in the east of the country

Essentials

A growing number of foreign visitors are discovering the delights of cycling in Turkey. Cycle touring is an excellent way of exploring the country, particularly if you take to the backroads where traffic is light, and avoiding the main cities and highways when possible. The footpaths and forestry tracks found in areas such as Cappadocia or in the coastal mountains near the major resorts also offer some superb mountain biking, with lots of potential for more challenging routes in the higher ranges such as the Taurus.

Cycling

Airlines generally carry bicycles free of charge as part of your personal baggage allowance but you should contact them in advance to make sure. The tyres should be deflated and the peddles taken off before check-in. Bicycles are also carried without charge by most Turkish bus companies but, again, you should check before buying a ticket. Basic spares are available in most towns, although outside the main cities modern components are rare. It is best to bring a selection of spares including inner tubes and cables, along with a puncture repair kit, a pump and the necessary tools. A roll of gaffer tape and an elastic bungee may come in useful too. If you intend to travel any kind of distance you will need bottles holding at least 1.5 litres of water.

The best times for cycle touring are spring and autumn, and even then you should avoid cycling in the midday sun. Take great care on the roads and always use the hard shoulder where available. A mirror is a useful accessory to keep a wary eye on approaching traffic. Also remember to fill up your bottles at every opportunity. Roadside springs (*çeşme*) marked by a sign with a tap or which say '*İçme Suyu*' are safe to drink from. Don't drink from anything that says '*İçilmez*'.

Expect to attract lots of attention along the way: you will receive countless offers of tea and lots of waving. You may also attract less welcome attention from local dogs, who seem to harbour an in-bred hatred of bicycles. A couple of stones judiciously hurled at appropriate moments can help ward off such aggressive curs.

It is possible to rent reasonable bicycles relatively cheaply in most resort towns, but before setting off always check the condition of the brakes, tyres and gear mechanism.

Dolmuş are a ubiquitous feature on the Turkish roads and you will almost certainly use one during your stay. The *dolmuş* is a shared vehicle, anything from a four-door saloon to a large van, which plies a set route in towns and cities as well as the countryside. A simple hand signal brings them to a halt at the roadside, to the frustration of fellow road-users (except in some cities where *dolmuş* are only allowed to stop at designated places, often marked by a sign with a blue 'D'). Routes, particularly in urban areas, can be confusing for the uninitiated, although the ultimate destination, along with some major points on the way, is usually marked on the front. If you are unsure, ask the driver before getting on.

Dolmuş
The word dolmuş is derived from the Turkish word for 'full' or 'stuffed': no accident, they are frequently filled to overflowing

Once you get on, the fare, which is usually displayed somewhere at the front of the vehicle, can be handed directly to the driver or relayed to the front by your fellow passengers. Fares are very reasonable and generally on a par with local bus journeys. If

Essentials

TML agents abroad

Foreign agencies cannot make bookings for domestic services, see page 31 for TML offices and agents in Turkey.

UK *Alternative Travel, 146 Kingdom High Street, London, E8 2NS, T020-72412687, F020-79233118.*

Italy *Venice Bassani S.p.A, Vio XXII, Marzo 2414/30124, Venice, T0415208819,*

*F0415209211 and **96-98 Carso Garibaldi S.p.A.,**1972100 Zacmari,Brindisi, T831568633.*

TR Northern Cyprus *Kuzey Kıbrıs Türk Denizcilik Ltd, 3 Bülent Ecevit Bulvarı No 10, Gazimagosa, North Cyprus, T03923665786, F03923667840.*

you are not sure how much the fare is to a particular place, state your destination as you hand over the money and the correct change will be returned to you.

Passengers are expected to shuffle and swap their seats to make sure that unaccompanied women are seated next to another woman, or at the very worst only have a man on one side. The frequency of *dolmuş* varies greatly from round-the-clock services in some resort areas such as Bodrum, to the single daily *dolmuş* which leave many rural communities each morning for the local market town, returning sometime during the afternoon. The last thing to consider when travelling by *dolmuş* is how to stop the thing when you get to your destination. The phrase, '*inecek var*' (there is [someone] getting-off) is easy to remember and works admirably.

Hitch-hiking In rural areas where public transport is limited thumbing a lift – *otostop* in Turkish – is often the only way for local people to get about. This is good news for hitch-hikers: lifts are relatively plentiful, although longer waits should be expected in more developed areas of the country where a more cautious attitude towards hitch-hikers prevails. Also remember that traffic may be extremely light on some minor roads, so be prepared for long waits in summer by carrying some water and a hat.

Having a few words of Turkish (see page 713) is very helpful to explain where you are going and if you smoke, a cigarette will probably be gratefully received by the driver. As in any country hitching is potentially risky. Women should not hitch-hike alone and when a couple accept a lift, the man should always position himself next to the driver, who will almost certainly also be male.

Occasionally, you may be expected to pay a small sum by the driver, but usually not. As you are getting out, you could ask *Para vereyim mi?* – Shall I give some money? – though the request will generally be declined.

Taxis Yellow taxis are everywhere in the main cities, waiting at intersections and cruising the streets looking for fares. Many use natural gas, a cheaper and cleaner alternative to petrol. Taxi meter rates are set by the local administration and may vary from city to city. The rates are more expensive between midnight and 0600 (*gece*) than during the day (*gündüz*), so check that the driver has set the meter correctly. The driver is legally required to start the meter running when accepting a fare but some drivers in the large cities may try to demand a fixed, and often extortionate, fare. If this happens get out and look for another ride. Many of the taxi drivers in İstanbul and other large cities are recent arrivals from rural areas or the east who are simply driving the vehicle in return for a small portion, usually only 25%, of the fare. Consequently, they very rarely speak any English and also may have as little idea of where they are going as you do. It's a good idea to write down on a piece of paper where you want to go to avoid confusion.

For longer inter-city journeys it is possible to negotiate prices which can be quite reasonable if shared between several people. Taxis may also be the only way of getting to remote archaeological sites that aren't served by public transport.

Black Sea ferry timetable

Port	Arrival/Departure		
İstanbul	Monday: 1400	Rize	Wednesday: 1500/1900
Samsun	Tuesday: 2100/2200	Trabzon	Thursday: 2200/2300
Trabzon	Wednesday: 1100/1200	Samsun	Thursday: 1200/1300
		İstanbul	Friday: 1300/ –

Sea

Apart from the small passenger ferries operating along the Bosphorus and across the bay in İzmir, there are several longer domestic ferry services operated by the state-run *Turkish Maritime Lines* (TML). The first of these is the overnight car ferry sailing between **İstanbul and İzmir** every weekend, while the second is the excellent weekly service along the Black Sea coast from **İstanbul to Rize** and back. Both are an extremely pleasurable way to travel, offering the atmosphere of an, albeit old-fashioned, cruise liner at an extremely economical price. On board there are a range of cabin classes to choose from, along with a restaurant, tea saloon and bar to pass the time in. One of the highlights of these ferry journeys, however, must be the memorable view of the minaret-studded İstanbul skyline as you approach or slip away from the quayside on the Golden Horn. Tickets for both services can only be bought from domestic TML agents and offices (see below). Discounts of 20-30% are available on all services for children, students and over-60's.

This ferry leaves at 1500 on Friday, reaching İzmir at 1230 on Saturday. It returns 1400 on Sunday, docking in İstanbul at 0900 on Monday. There are four classes of cabin of varying comfort which sleep two, three and four people, each with a/c, shower and toilet. Cabin prices include breakfast and dinner. A one-way ticket costs US$100, US$70 or US$20 per person for a luxury cabin, an 'A' class cabin or a Pullman reclining seat respectively. 'B' and 'C' class cabins are on the lower decks and do not have windows. It is possible to stay on board on Saturday night once the ship has docked in İzmir for an additional fee. The one-way fare for a car is US$55.

İstanbul-İzmir

Again, there is a choice of cabin classes and seats with all two, three and four bed cabins having their own ensuite toilet and shower. Luxury and 'A' class cabins are more comfortable and have exterior windows. Sample fares from İstanbul to Trabzon one-way per person for a luxury cabin, an 'A' class cabin, a 'C' class cabin and a Pullman seat are US$86, US$60, US$47 and US$18 respectively. It costs US$85 for a car.

Black Sea
See box for arrival & departure times for this service

Train

The Turkish railway system was largely laid by German companies at the end of the 19th century with economic and strategic concerns factoring strongly in the routing. Despite a flurry of building activity in the early republican era, later investment has been concentrated on the country's road network and much of the rail system remains unmodernized. Trains are still operated by the loss-making *Turkish State Railways* (TCDD) with circuitous routes and ageing rolling stock making for long journeys and frequent delays. On the plus side, travelling by train is cheap and more comfortable than the bus, with the opportunity of getting a good sleep during overnight journeys. What's more, railway lines often pass through beautiful, unspoilt countryside away from the focus of development along the main roads. A leisurely pace and frequent stops at small backcountry stations give you lots of time to appreciate the scenery, while on board there is generally plenty going on.

Essentials

Train timetable

Ankara-İstanbul	Ankara	Eskişehir	Izmit	Haydarpaşa	Bostancı	
Boğaziçi Ekspresi	0800 / 2227	1140 / 1845	1512 / 1506	1645 / 1330	1629 / 1348	
Başkent Ekspresi	1020 / 1630	1256 / 1356	1540 / 1111	1650 / 1000	1637 / 1012	
Fatih Ekspresi	2330 / 0720	0230 / 0425	0540 / 0103	0730 / 2330	0708 / 2347	
Anadolu Ekspresi	2200 / 0712	0148 / 0335	0524 / 2335	0715 / 2200	0653 / 2220	
Ankara Ekspresi	2230 / 0804	0215 / 0417	0607 / 0005	0800 / 2230	0737 / 2248	
Eskişehir Ekspresi		0635 / 2326		1059 / 1855	1040 / 1915	
Ankara-İzmir	**Ankara**	**Eskişehir**	**Kütahya**	**Balıkesir**	**Manisa**	**Basmane**
İzmir Mavi Treni	1810 / 0820	2120 / 0515	2243 / 0344	0325 / 2250	0628 / 1939	0750 / 1820
Karesi Ekspresi	1910 / 1033	2256 / 0700	0022 / 0514	0525 / 2352	0836 / 2032	1003 / 1900
Ankara- İzmir	**Ankara**	**Eskişehir**	**Afyon**	**Uşak**	**Manisa**	**Alsancak**
Dumlupınar Mavi Treni	1835 / 1000	2215 / 0633	0125 / 0333	0358 / 0040	0759 / 2011	0925 / 1835
Eskişehir-İzmir		**Eskişehir**	**Kütahya**	**Balıkesir**	**Manisa**	**Basmane**
Ege Ekspresi		0730 / 1825	0855 / 1705	1350 / 1208	1712 / 0829	1844 / 0655
Ankara-Isparta	**Ankara**	**Eskişehir**	**Alayunt**	**Afyon**	**Karakuyu**	**Isparta**
Gülistan Mavi Treni	1835 / 1000	2215 / 0633	2331 / 0510	0145 / 0333	0420 / 0020	0605 / 2210
Ankara-Zonguldak	**Ankara**	**Çankırı**	**Karabük**	**Gökçebey**	**Çatalağzı**	**Zonguldak**
Karaelmas Ekspresi	0810 / 2023	1155 / 1625	1618 / 1215	1750 / 1036	1853 / 0934	1905 / 0920
Ankara-Adana	**Ankara**	**Kayseri**	**Niğde**	**Ulukışla**	**Yenice**	**Adana**
Çukurova Mavi Treni	2010 / 0805	0241 / 0124	0432 / 2332	0550 / 2220	0743 / 1954	0805 / 1930
Ankara-Elazığ, Diyarbakır-Ankara	**Ankara**	**Kayseri**	**Sivas**	**Malatya**	**Elazığ**	**Diyarbakır**
Eylül Mavi Treni	1940 / 0658	0247 / 0009	0700 / 2005	1150 / 1455	1429 / 1205	1720 / 0905

Services

Sleeping cabins as well as seats on many trains must be reserved in advance: reserve at least a day before you want to travel & considerably more on national holidays or weekends

The best services are the *Mavi trenler* (Blue Train), *Ekspres* (Express) and *Mototren* (Motor Train), which are relatively fast and comfortable when compared to the torturously slow *Yolcu* (passenger) and *Posta* (post) services. İstanbul and Ankara are well connected with various services, including express sleeper trains. These have modern and very comfortable air-conditioned cabins, as well as seating coaches and a restaurant. At the other end of the spectrum are the old trains that rattle eastwards towards Kars and Tatvan. Although they have a restaurant car serving a limited menu and alcohol, it is best to take your own supplies of food and water. If you enjoy long train journeys, then the *Doğu Ekspresi*, which traverses the length of the country from İstanbul to Kars in a leisurely 38-40 hours (if it's on time), is definitely for you.

Fares & discounts

Inter-rail passes are valid in Turkey but Eurail passes are not

Fares are incredibly cheap – a small part of the reason why the TCDD makes a huge financial loss each year. **Ankara-İzmir** in first class costs about US$12, **Ankara-Kars** slightly less! On sleeper trains (*yataklı trenler*) there is usually a choice of cabins. *Örtülü yataklı* cabins have four to six fold-out beds and are shared with fellow passengers unless there is a group of four or six of you. These cost US$8 on top of the first-class fare.

One, two and three person cabins are also available on most overnight routes, with

tanbul-Kars	Haydarpaşa	Ankara	Kayseri	Sivas	Erzurum	Kars
Doğu Ekspresi	0835 / 2145	1808 / 1215	0130 / 0400	0545 / 2345	1720 / 1200	2200 / 0710
İstanbul-Elazığ	**Haydarpaşa**	**Ankara**	**Kayseri**	**Sivas**	**Malatya**	**Elazığ**
Van Gölü Ekspresi	2005 / 2300	0650 / 1330	1448 / 0440	1915 / 0015	0135 / 1810	0434 / 1450
İstanbul-Ereğli	**Haydarpaşa**	**Kütahya**	**Afyon**	**Konya**	**Karaman**	**Ereğli**
İç Anadolu Mavi Treni	2350 / 0909	0634 / 0255	0825 / 0108	1230 / 2115	1357 / 1935	1509 / 1810
İstanbul-Kurtalan	**Haydarpaşa**	**Ankara**	**Sivas**	**Malatya**	**Diyarbakır**	**Kurtalan**
Güney Ekspresi	2005 / 2300	0650 / 1330	1915 / 0015	0135 / 1810	0740 / 1136	1052 / 0815
stanbul-Gazi antep	**Haydarpaşa**	**Afyon**	**Konya**	**Karaman**	**Adana**	**Gaziantep**
Toros Ekspresi	0855 / 1755	1805 / 0824	2225 / 0415	2352 / 0225	0505 / 2114	1135 / 1430
İstanbul-Konya, Uşak-İstanbul	**Haydarpaşa**	**Enveriye**	**Kütahya**	**Afyon**	**Uşak**	**Konya**
Meram Ekspresi	1920 / 0630	0045 / 0130	0224 / 2350	0430 / 2158	0703 / 1900	0821 / 1750
İstanbul-Eğirdir - Burdur - Denizli	**Haydarpaşa**	**Afyon**	**Dinar**	**Eğirdir**	**Burdur**	**Denizli**
Pamukkale Ekspresi	1735 / 0834	0245 / 2325	0529 / 2016	0850 / 1700	0705 / 1900	0820 / 1705
zmir- Isparta - Burdur	**Basmane**	**Selçuk**	**Aydın**	**Nazilli**	**Isparta**	**Burdur**
Göller Ekspresi	2130 / 0840	2302 / 0712	0013 / 0604	0103 / 0516	0624 / 2350	0624 / 2355
İzmir-Bandırma	**Basmane**	**Manisa**	**Akhisar**	**Balıkesir**	**Susurluk**	**Bandırma**
Marmara Ekspresi	0830 / 2238	0949 / 2110	1038 / 2010	1253 / 1803	1353 / 1702	1455 / 1600
Adana-Kayseri	**Adana**	**Yenice**	**Ulukışla**	**Niğde**	**Boğazköprü**	**Kayseri**
Erciyes Ekspresi	1730 / 1035	1802 / 1007	2040 / 0805	2153 / 0643	2342 / 0450	2400 / 0430
Elazığ-Adana	**Elazığ**	**Malatya**	**Gölbaşı**	**Fevzipaa**	**Osmaniye**	**Adana**
Fırat Ekspresi	0730 / 2015	1020 / 1740	1254 / 1445	1550 / 1200	1709 / 1008	1835 / 0840

the **Ankara-İstanbul** fare on the flashy *Başkent Ekspresi*, for example, costing US$37 for a two person cabin and US$30 for a single. More representative is the *Meram Ekspresi*, a nightly service between **İstanbul and Konya**, with seats costing US$8 first class, US$5 second class and US$20/38/56 for a single/double/triple cabin.

A compulsory tip is also collected by the attendant of each carriage at the end of your journey. There are student (*öğrenci*) discounts of 20%-30% on most routes (you'll need an ISIC card). Return (*gidiş-dönüş*) tickets are also discounted by 20% and there are reductions of 20%-30% for married couples with children. If you plan to do a lot of travelling by train and you are under 26 or over 55, enquire about the *Tren-tur* pass, which allows a month's unlimited travel on the Turkish rail network.

The timetable includes all the main train services, however these may be subject to periodic change, so check at the station before buying a ticket. Reservations should be made during holiday periods and for sleeper services at local stations or from the main reservation centres in İstanbul and Ankara. Bookings are also taken on the following numbers, but you will need a Turkish speaker to ring for you: Ankara T0312-3114994, Haydarpaşa T0216-3378724, İzmir T0232-4848638

Timetables

Frequency of trains

Van Gölü Ekspresi:	
Haydarpaşa-Elazığ	Monday, Wednesday, Saturday.
Elazığ-Haydarpaşa	Tuesday, Thursday, Saturday.
Güney Ekspresi:	
Haydarpaşa-Kurtalan	Tuesday, Friday, Sunday.
Kurtalan-Haydarpaşa	Monday, Wednesday, Friday.
Haydarpaşa-Diyarbakır	Thursday.
Diyarbakır-Haydarpaşa	Sunday.
Toros Ekspresi:	
Haydarpaşa-Gaziantep	Tuesday, Thursday, Sunday.
Gaziantep-Haydarpaşa	Tuesday, Thursday, Saturday.
Eskişehir Ekspresi:	Monday, Wednesday, Friday.
Gülistan Mavi Treni:	
Ankara-Isparta	Monday, Wednesday, Friday.
Isparta-Ankara	Tuesday, Thursday, Sunday.
4 Eylül Mavi Treni:	
Ankara-Elazığ	Monday, Wednesday, Friday, Saturday.
Elazığ-Ankara	Monday, Wednesday, Friday, Sunday.
Ankara-Diyarbakır	Tuesday, Thursday, Sunday.
Diyarbakır-Ankara	Tuesday, Thursday, Saturday.

Keeping in touch

Communications

Internet

There are several international directories listing internet cafés worldwide, try www.netcafeguide.com

The cyber revolution is gradually taking root in Turkey and although the number of users is still far behind that in western countries, travellers can gain access to the internet in most provincial towns and tourist centres. Internet cafés have sprung up across the country and some guesthouses and hotels also provide an internet service to non-residents as well as guests.

Internet cafés etc are listed in the directory sections of this book, however, with the rapid pace of change, towns without a listing may well now have a newly opened cyber café. Try asking young people or the local tourist office if there is no internet café listed in this book.

Prices for access vary considerably. Establishments in tourist areas cash in on the popularity of web-based email services, such as hotmail, for keeping in touch. In less popular areas, internet cafés are the preserve of local teenagers and prices reflect their small disposable incomes. Expect to pay US$1-5 per hour, with a minimum charge of 15 minutes. This works out substantially cheaper than telephoning or sending a fax, and is of course much faster than sending a postcard, so if you don't already have an email address, sign up for a free one at one of the sites below: **yahoo.com**, **hotmail.com**, **email.com** or **backpackers.com**

One of the main frustrations with accessing the internet in Turkey is its slowness, particularly at peak times such as during office hours. If possible, check your mail early in the morning or late at night, and to reduce loading times, empty your in-box regularly. You may also want to ask friends and family not to send you junk email or correspondence containing large files such as images. Remember that to keep your address viable you need to use it quite regularly.

Dialling out

All international codes are preceded by the prefix '00' and the initial '0' of the country area code is usually not dialled.

Australia: 61
Canada: 1
Ireland: 353

Netherlands: 31
New Zealand: 64
South Africa: 27
Turkey: 90
UK: 44
USA: 1

Essentials

The state-run postal system is cheap and reliable with *PTT* (*Posta, Telefon ve Telegraf*) offices easily identified by their black and yellow signs. Stamps can generally be bought and letters posted between 0800 and 2000, although some small post offices may only open between 0900 and 1700. Main post offices in large towns and cities stay open until 2300 or even 24-hours for buying telephone cards or using counter telephones (see below). Airmail letters and postcards (*uçak ile*) generally take seven to 10 days to reach European and North American addresses and should be posted in the *yurt dışı* (overseas) box, as opposed to the *yurt içi* (domestic) mail box. If it is urgent, sending a letter or parcel by express mail – *Acele Posta Servis or APS* - for an additional charge, usually gets it there in half the time.

Post

Poste restante Mail can be posted to any main post office. When picking up your mail, you will need some form of photo-ID. Envelopes should be addressed as follows: Your name, Poste Restante, Merkez Postane (*Central Post Office*), District, City, Province, Turkey.

The recently privatized telephone network is now operated by *Türk Telekom*, however, your best bet for finding a public telephone is to ask for the nearest PTT office. Banks of orange or blue public telephones are found outside post offices, as well as scattered around urban areas. In some places you may still come across the old *jeton* phones which take tokens, although these are rapidly being replaced by the modern phone or credit card telephones. Phone cards and *jeton* can be bought in post offices, some shops and from street vendors who often hang around near public telephones making a small profit on reselling the cards. Phone cards come in 30, 60 and 100-unit denominations with a 100 unit card necessary for all but the briefest international call. The cheapest time to ring is from 1800 to 0800, at weekends or on national holidays.

Telephone
Numbers are 7 digits long & must be preceded by a 4 digit area code if you are dialling from outside the province. These codes are listed at the beginning of each town & the inside front cover

Metered telephones Calls can also be made inside post offices and at some shops and kiosks on metered telephones (*kontürlü telefon*). The rate per unit should be displayed and when you have finished, the price of your call is calculated. Although useful in an emergency or when you can't find a public phone, *kontürlü telephonler* can be expensive in some shops and should only be used for local calls. When making a counter phone call, particularly an international one, in a post office ask for a receipt (*fiş*) as the meter is usually out of sight and over-charging is not uncommon.

Such counter telephones are particularly common in areas of the east where infrastructural development is lagging behind demand for telephones. This strain on the telephone system also means that in the east and in rural areas it may take several attempts to get through to a number, or to place international calls at peak times (eg during the evening).

Hotel telephones Hotels typically put a significant surcharge on all calls made from rooms, so you may pay dearly for the convenience. It is wise to check the rates with reception before dialling to avoid a nasty surprise when you come to pay your bill.

Toll free numbers

For credit card and reverse charge calls
Australia: *00 800 611177*
Canada: *00800 16677*
Ireland: *00800 3531177*
Netherlands: *00800 311177*

UK: *00 800 441177*
UK (Mercury): *0800 442277*
USA (AT&T): *00 800 12277*
USA (MCI): *00800 11177*
USA (SPRINT): *00800 14477*

International calls International calls are relatively expensive in comparison with other western countries: up to US$2 per minute to the UK or US$3 per minute to the US. Make use of reduced rates between midnight and 0700 and on Sundays. It is usually possible to dial an operator in your home country free of charge in order to place a reverse charge or credit card call but getting through can be difficult. See box for these toll-free numbers.

Fax Sending and receiving faxes is possible from most large post offices for about US$2 per A4 sheet. Some private businesses and shops, particularly in tourist areas, also offer fax services for more competitive prices.

Media

Newspapers A wide selection of international newspapers and publications, such as *Newsweek* and *The Economist*, are available in resort areas and at some bookshops and large hotels in the major cities. Such outlets are listed in this book in each town or city's shopping section. Unfortunately, all international publications are at least a day out-of-date, with the European edition of *The Guardian* or *The International Herald Tribune* generally finding their way to the news stands the fastest. An English language publication printed in Ankara, *The Turkish Daily News*, is also on sale at selected outlets. It's a fairly solid publication but does give an insight into contemporary issues along with some world news. *The Turkish Daily News* also has an on-line edition at www.turkishdailynews.com

Magazines *Atlas* is a glossy monthly travel magazine filled with beautifully illustrated photo-stories about Turkey and the wider world. It used to include English summaries of its articles, which made it a useful resource for travellers, however, this seems to have stopped. It's still worth a buy though, just to enjoy the photographs. An upmarket English language coffee-table magazine called *Cornocopia* comes out on a bi-monthly basis and has some interesting features on travel, culture and cookery.

Television Until comparatively recently, broadcasting in Turkey was controlled predominantly by the state through *Turkish Radio Television* (TRT). This began to change in the late 1980's with the dissemination of affordable satellite technology, however, it was the relaxation of state controls in the mid-1990's which really opened the floodgates, allowing a huge proliferation of commercial channels. Today, the words 'quantity' rather than 'quality' best describe Turkish television. Airtime on most channels is filled with cheap gameshows (Geri Halliwell fans will be astounded to hear that she appeared in one of them before she made it big), tabloid-style news programmes, soap-operas – including many old western favourites dubbed into Turkish – and films. Most larger hotels, along with some bars and restaurants in resort areas, have cable TV, which includes channels such as *CNN*, *BBC Prime* and *Eurosport*.

Radio The explosion in commercial television has been matched by a huge increase in the number of privately run radio stations. In remote areas the play-list of low budget local stations may not be to your taste, but around the large cities and resorts there is a varied choice of stations playing both Turkish and western music.

BBC World Service can be received in some parts of the country on the following short-wave frequencies: 3955, 6195, 9410, 12095, 15565, 17640 kHz. You could also try AM/medium-wave 1323 kHz. **Voice of America** broadcasts between 1900 and 2000 GMT; 9750, 6160, 11875 kHz.

Food and drink

Food

Heir to one of the world's richest cuisines, the food on offer in most restaurants today is considerably more simple than the court banquets of old, but still delicious nevertheless. Not surprisingly, for a people who descended from nomadic stock, meat (particularly lamb), cheese and yoghurt feature strongly in the national diet.

See also the food glossary on page 720

For most of us the *kebap*, popularized as a fast food across Europe, is synonymous with Turkish food. Having said that, before setting foot in the country, few people realize just how many variations on the theme there are, with the word *kebap* in fact used as a generic term for meat prepared and cooked in a huge variety of ways. So in addition to the humble *şiş kebap* – lumps of chicken or lamb grilled on a skewer – or *döner*, there is a host of less familiar *kebap* for you to try.

Meat

Turks also have an almost fanatical love of fish, ranging from trout, now largely of the farmed variety, to sea species such as tuna, grey mullet or bream. Fish are generally sold by weight, with the relatively high price of some species reflecting their growing scarcity. Still, expect to pay considerably less in all but the most exclusive (or tourist) restaurants than in Europe. Other types of fish, such as sardines, anchovies or trout, are an excellent bargain, particularly when in season or farmed locally.

When you arrive in a restaurant, you will be expected to select your fish from the glass-fronted refrigerator. Compare the price of various species and make sure you ask whether the price quoted is for the whole fish (*Bütün balık mı?*) or a portion (*Bir porsiyonu mu?*).

Fish is nearly always grilled (*izgara*) or fried (*tava*), the exception being the occasional fish soup and the weird and wonderful recipes prepared on the Black Sea coast using *hamsi* (Black Sea anchovies) such *hamsi tatlısı* (a fishy pudding) and *hamsi pilavı* (anchovy rice).

Fish

Before you get to your fish or *kebap*, restaurants typically have a large, and often rather daunting, array of starters, called *meze* (see box, page 55) displayed in a glass-fronted refrigerator. It is quite acceptable to choose a selection of these dishes by pointing at them, or a number of small plates may be brought to your table on a tray by the waiter, from which you can pick the ones you want. When the bill arrives remember to check that you haven't been charged for the dishes returned to the kitchen untouched.

Meze

As in other Mediterranean countries, the variety, freshness and flavour of locally produced fruit and vegetables is a tonic after the tasteless, pre-packaged goods we are presented with in most western supermarkets. Despite extensive glasshouse cultivation of vegetables such as tomatoes and peppers, other fruit and vegetables such as oranges, melons and grapes are much more seasonal.

Fruit & vegetables

Essentials

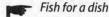

Fish for a dish

Alabalık - trout
Barbunya - red mullet
Çıpura - gilt-headed bream
Kalkan - turbot
Kefal - grey mullet
Kılıç - sword-fish
İstavrit - horse mackerel

Levrek - bass
Lüfer - bluefish
Mercan - common bream
Uskumru - mackerel
Hamsi - Black Sea anchovy
Palamut - bonito

Shopping

If you are after bargains, visit a market in the evening when the traders are packing up & virtually giving things away

The best place to buy fruit and vegetables, as well as fresh produce such as cheese and eggs, is in a *pazar* (market). Every town or area in the big cities has its own particular market day, when traders descend in their vans and lorries and set up stalls, stacked high with all manner of goods. Not only are goods fresh but prices are extremely low. Shopping in a bustling *pazar* with all its noise, smells and colour is also an enjoyable experience which makes pushing a trolley around a supermarket seem very dull and bland. Turkish housewives typically make a day of it, comparing prices, testing produce and haggling. It is quite acceptable for you to do the same. Try a variety of different olives or cheeses, for example, before making a decision on which to buy. Just point to one and say *Tadabilir miyim?* (Can I taste it?).

Most large towns and resorts have modern supermarkets such as the domestic chains *Migros* or *Tansaş*, where you will find a wide selection of Turkish and imported foods. In smaller places you will need to shop in a *bakal* – or grocer's – which usually stock most necessities such as mineral water, cartons of milk, cigarettes and canned food. Inevitably, prices are not as low as in the supermarkets and in tourist resorts they can be a real rip-off.

Vegetarians

'Et yemiyorum' – I don't eat meat

With the abundance of fresh fruit and vegetables you may expect Turkey to be the ideal place for the visiting vegetarian, however, maintaining a diet free of meat can be a bit tricky. This is because there is no tradition of vegetarianism in the country and in fact the eating of meat is an important part of Turkish cultural life. To complicate things further many dishes that should be suitable for vegetarians, such as bean casseroles, rice or bulgar wheat, are sometimes cooked using meat stock. To check if this is the case ask: *İçinde et veya et suyu var mı?* (Is there meat or meat stock in it?).

Don't despair though, there are some dishes, particularly *meze*, that are suitable for non-meat eaters. *Pide* (a type of bread) topped with *peynirli* (cheese) is a good, widely available, standby. In the food glossary dishes that are normally prepared without meat are followed by a (v), but in some cases it may still be wise to check. Cheese, nuts and fresh fruit and vegetables are also widely available and relatively cheap.

Restaurants

Generally, there is a broad spectrum of places to eat in Turkey, so you will almost always be able to find something to fit the bill. However, in small out-of-the-way towns and villages the choice will be much more restricted. At the top end are the up-market restaurants found in large hotels and the major cities and resort areas of the country. These generally have a varied menu consisting of both international and Turkish dishes, with some specializing exclusively in fish. Such restaurants usually have a good wine list that may include some imported wines.

Restaurants that typically serve *meze* and grilled meat dishes (*ızgara*), possibly fish in coastal areas, can be found in most large towns and are notch down in price and exclusivity. Alcohol is generally served, although the selection will probably be limited to *rakı*, beer and one or two types of wine. In the coastal resorts, menus often include a wide variety of non-Turkish dishes, reflecting the national tastes of foreign tourists. Don't be surprised to see roast beef and Yorkshire pudding or *shnitzel* on offer in restaurants in Marmaris or Kemer. Predictably, prices in these tourist restaurants are considerably

An A-Z of meze

*A meal in Turkey usually begins with
starters known as meze. These are divided
into* soğuk meze *(cold starters) usually
displayed in a glass-fronted fridge and* ara
sicak *(hot appetizers) such as calamari,
potato croquettes or deep-fried savoury
pastries. If you are only in the mood for a
light meal, then a choice of meze eaten
with bread often hits the spot. Many are
also suitable for vegetarians (marked here
with a 'v'). Meze are traditionally
accompanied by a glass or two of* rakı, *the
cloudy aniseed- flavoured spirit, and
savoured at a very relaxed pace.*

ahtapot salatası - octopus salad
antep ezmesi (v) - an often fiery mix of
finely chopped tomatoes, onions,
cucumber, peppers and garlic. Originates
from Gaziantep in southeast Turkey
arnavut ciğeri - spicy fried liver
barbunya (v) - red beans
beyaz peynir (v) - white cheese, popular
accompaniment for rakı
beyin salatası - lamb's brain salad
börülce (v) - black-eye pea salad
cacık (v) - watery yoghurt, flavoured with
garlic, mint and cucumber
çerkez tavuğu - shredded chicken with a
walnut sauce
dolma - peppers stuffed with delicately
spiced rice and pinenuts
enginar (v) - artichoke hearts
fava (v) - broad beans mashed with olive oil
haydari (v) - yoghurt with garlic

kalamar - fried calamari
kısır (v) - coucous salad
kızartma (v) - fried vegetables covered
with garlicky yoghurt
içli köfte - bulgur wheat parcels filled with
mince, onions, parsley and spices; a
speciality of the southeast
imam bayıldı (v) - "the imam (priest)
fainted" when he tasted this dish of
aubergines cooked with tomatoes, garlic
and onion
midye dolması - mussels stuffed with
spiced rice
midye tava - fried mussels
mücver (v) - fried courgette cakes
flavoured with dill
pancar (v) - pickled beetroot
patates kroket (v) - fried potato
croquettes
patlıcan ezmesi (v) - grilled aubergines
mashed with olive oil, garlic and salt
piyaz/pilaki (v) - white bean salad Sarma
- stuffed vine leaves
rus salatası (v) - diced potatoes, carrots
and peas in mayonnaise
sarma - vine leaves stuffed with rice and
sometimes meat
semizotu (v) - purslane, green vegetable
with garlic yoghurt
sigara böreği (v) - deep-fried filo rolls
filled with cheese
taze fasulye (v) - green beans
terator (v) - peppers and aubergine,
marinated in garlic sauce
zeytin ezmesi (v) - black olive paste

higher; you will probably pay US$10-20 per head for a meal including alcohol.

Hotel restaurants often aren't the best in terms of value for money or the quality of
the food, so apart from breakfast, which is usually included in the price of the room,
you would do well to go elsewhere.

Kebapçı, ocakbaşı and köfteci Given the Turks carnivorous tastes two popular
types of restaurant are the *kebapçı* – serving all manner of *kebaps* – and the o*cakbaşı*
which serve a selection of steak, chops and kebaps cooked in the dining room on a
charcoal grill typically hooded with shiny copper cowl. Décor and price vary greatly in
both types of restaurant, the more fancy ones serve alcohol (*içkili* - with alcohol) while
in others (*içkisiz* - dry) you will have to make do with *ayran* (see below) or soft drinks.
A salad and some plain yoghurt usually accompany main dishes, and there is often a
choice of desert. *Köfteci* specialize in meatballs which are generally eaten with a white
bean salad (*piyaz*) or in a sandwich. They are normally very economical places to eat, a
portion of *köfte* costing from US$1.50-3.

Essentials

Essentials

Dining out

In this book restaurants are divided into three price categories.

Expensive: Over US$25 per head These restaurants are very pricey by local standards and are only found in the largest cities or tourist resorts. In this class of restaurant you should expect a very high standard of food and service, with an extensive wine list and pleasant surroundings.

Midrange: US$5-25 There are a wide variety of restaurants in this category, from fish restaurants to decent kebapçı and tourist places in the coastal resorts.

Cheap: Under US$5 Most Turks would only spend more than US$5 on a meal for a special occasion, so there are plenty of tasty and nourishing options in this category.

Lokantalar For the average Turk, lunch is often eaten in a *lokanta*, where you can choose from a selection of ready-prepared dishes and soup, kept warm in shiny stainless steel steam trays. *Kebaps* and other types of food may also be on offer but don't expect a menu: you will have to make do with pointing and gesticulating. Bear in mind that because the food has been sitting around it is best to seek out a busy place where the dishes have probably not been on display since the day before, over even longer! *Lokanta* are usually pretty spartan affairs, with plastic chairs and tables and a separate dining area, or *aile salonu* (family dining room) for women and families. As a couple or a woman travelling alone you may feel more comfortable dining in the *aile salonu*.

Pideci and çorbacı A common feature of all Turkish towns, *pideci* are simple places serving a variety of different *pide* – thin dough bases, similar to pizzas, that are topped with cheese, mince or even chicken – and baked in a wood-fired oven. *Pideci* also serve *lahmacun*, a very thin dough base spread with spiced lamb. Leaves of *roka* (rocket) and a glass of ayran (yoghurt drink) usually accompany *pide*.

A *çorbacı* or *işkembe salonu* serves a range of soups, some of which may not appeal to western tastes. Concoctions such as tripe, brain or lentil are traditionally eaten for breakfast, but have also been a favourite snack with late-night revellers since Ottoman times. After a nocturnal outing in Galata, the old European quarter of İstanbul, Evliya Çelebi, the 17th-century chronicler, reported that, "At night many people assemble in their shops who in order to get rid of their wine eat tripe soup because, it is said, if tripe is eaten towards morning it produces that effect." *İşkembeci* in the main cities still do a brisk trade in the early hours serving up bowls of steaming soup which usually cost about US$1.50-2.50. Perhaps a bit bland at first, you will find that, having added some garlic lemon, vinegar, cumin, ground chilli, black pepper and salt – you have a tasty and very economical meal. No guarantees that it will prevent your hang-over though. Again, alcohol is rarely served and credit cards are not accepted.

Tatlıcı and pastane The brightly lit neon *tatlıcı* are another Turkish culinary institution, their windows crammed with trays of mouth-watering *baklava* (sweet pastries) and milk or chocolate puddings such as *sütlaç* (rice pudding). Usually fairly spartan inside, your choice of pudding or sweet is brought to your table along with a bottle of mineral water. Tea, coffee and soft drinks are usually available too.

Pastane are a little more like a cafés, serving cakes, biscuits, along with *baklava* and puddings. They are a favourite place for young people and families to meet for a chat. They also usually serve breakfast in the form of pastries or bread, butter and honey with tea or coffee.

Drink

Served in small tulip-shaped glasses, tea is drunk black, sweet and with incredible **Tea** regularity from first thing in the morning to last thing at night. It is made from leaves grown around the town of Rize on the Black Sea coast and is brewed into a strong liquour that is then diluted to taste with boiling water. *Çay*, as it's called, is normally taken strong, so if you prefer it weaker, ask for *açık çay*. Contrary to what you might think, drinking tea in hot weather actually has a cooling effect on the body by causing you to sweat. If this is not for you try one of the herbal brews, many of which are said to have therapeutic properties. *Kuşburnu* (rose hip) and *ada çayı* (sage) are both popular. *Elma çayı* (apple tea) has caught on in the tourist resorts, but nowhere else.

Coffee comes in two sorts, the instant-type, which is commonly referred to as *neskafe*, **Coffee** and traditional Turkish coffee which was first introduced from Arabia in the 16th century. Turkish coffee is boiled up in a small metal jug before being served in tiny cups without milk. Sugar is added during the brewing process, so when ordering a *türk kahvesi* you must decide whether you want it *şekerli* (sweet), *orta şekerli* (quite sweet) or *şekersiz/sade* (without sugar). Turkish coffee is not filtered so only if it's properly made do the grounds sink to the bottom of the cup. Leave them there and somebody may offer to tell your fortune by interpreting the shapes left on the inside of the upturned cup.

Despite the fact that the tap water in many areas is chlorinated and supposedly safe to **Water** drink, tourists and some locals stick to bottled mineral water, widely available at shops, petrol stations and supermarkets. In urban areas residents generally visit the local *sucu* (watershop) found in every neighbourhood or fill up large containers from a tanker which drives around the streets. In both cases the water will be from a potable local spring or filtration plant and will be regularly tested to ensure purity. People living in small towns and villages often rely on a local spring for drinking water, and in every area there will be a favourite from which the water is reputed to be particularly sweet. To help reduce waste, find out if there is a local spring or watershop nearby from which you can refill plastic bottles (*Çeşme veya sucu yakında var mı?* – Is there a spring or a water shop near here?). When you are on the road, springs are a common sight marked by a sign showing a tap or a sign saying '*İçme suyu*' (drinking water), not to be confused with '*İçilmez*' – not potable.

Salep is a hot milky drink made with an extract from the root of a particular orchid. **Other drinks** *Sıcak süt*, hot milk sweetened with sugar, is often drunk with pastries or *börek* at breakfast time. A wide range of carbonated and uncarbonated **soft drinks** and **fruit juices**, similar to those on the market in western countries, are widely available. *Ayran* is a refreshing mixture of yoghurt and water which is typically drunk with food. *Boza* is a lightly fermented beverage made from wheat or millet, prized for its healthiness.

Considering that the overwhelming majority of Turks are Muslim, you may find it **Alcohol** surprising to learn that many people enjoy a tipple. Alcohol is available throughout the country, although in the more conservative areas it is much harder to come by, or rather, you have to know where to look. A lively drinking culture exists in the major cities and resort towns of western Turkey, with plenty of western-style bars and pubs. The indigenous incarnation of the pub is known as the *meyhane;* typically a smoky all-male preserve, where glasses of *rakı* or beer are accompanied by often-excellent *meze*. Needless to say, such places are not recommended for women travellers unaccompanied by a man. Try not to be put off by appearances, as even in the dodgiest looking *meyhane* you will generally find a warm welcome and will emerge having experienced a true slice of local life.

Essentials

Essentials

 ### Tips on haggling

It is customary for a purchase to be preceded by an often-protracted haggling process. It is also essential if you do not want to be ripped off. Here are some unwritten rules as well a few techniques to help you achieve success.

Rule no 1: *Don't rush into the first shop you see, fall in love with a carpet and get out your credit card. Compare the goods in several shops, get a feel for what's on offer and for how much. When engaged in reconnaissance it's best to maintain an air of nonchalance and not to display too much interest in any one particular item.*

Rule no 2: *Having done the leg-work and spotted something you like at a not unreasonable first asking price, it's time to gauge what the thing is worth to you. Set yourself a maximum price, taking into account how desperately you want the thing and, of course, your current cash situation (ie don't cut short your holiday because you've invested in a leather jacket*

never to be worn once you get home).

Rule no 3: *Now it's time to get down to business but bear in mind that things are done at a more leisurely pace than in the west, so accept the inevitable offer of tea and engage in some small talk. When that is over, pitch your offer. There is no set rule but try about half of the first asking price. You'll probably be greeted with a sarcastic remark or even hysterics, particularly in İstanbul's Covered Bazaar where there is plenty of potential business. You can either raise the stakes slightly or turn the tables by asking the shopkeeper for a 'serious price'. Remember though, don't be pressurized into making an offer that you'll regret, because once a price is agreed it's considered binding. If the proceedings seem to be deadlocked, you can usually gain some leverage by offering to pay in hard currency. Don't forget that you are dealing with professionals who make their livelihood by bargaining.*

Spirits By far the most popular alcoholic beverage in Turkey is *rakı*, a strong aniseed-flavoured spirit which is diluted with water to form a potent milky concoction, respectfully referred to as *aslan sütu* (lion's milk). Broadly similar to other aniseed-flavoured liqueurs drunk in the Mediterranean region, *rakı* is sipped slowly with *meze*, particularly cheese and fruit, and is a favourite accompaniment to fish. State-owned *Tekel* is the only company producing *rakı*, most commonly sold as the *Yeni Rakı* brand. For the connoisseur, there are also two higher quality varieties containing more aniseed: *Kulüp Rakı* and *Altınbaş*. Other spirits produced by *Tekel*, including gin, vodka and cognac, have little to recommend them except their price: they are considerably cheaper than imported liquours. Such *yabancı likörü* (foreign spirits) are available in some bars and clubs in tourist areas or large cities.

Beer Rapidly gaining in popularity though rates of consumption are still far behind those in western countries. The best selling brand is *Efes Pilser*, a clean tasting lager, with its closest competitor the Danish beer *Tuborg*, which is brewed under licence in the country. Both brands have a low-alcohol 'light' variety and *Efes* have also tried to create a stout-type beer called *Efes Dark*. There are several other cheaper lagers, including one produced by a popular football team and emblazoned with the team's colours.

Wine There is now a reasonable selection of domestically produced red and white wines on the market. They range from the real cheapies, known colloquially as *köpek öldüren* (dog killer), to some very drinkable offerings at the higher end of the price range from Turkish vintners such as *Doluca* and *Kavaklıdere*. Smaller scale wineries are also to be found in Cappadocia, although their wine is hard to obtain in the rest of the country. Foreign wine is available at specialist shops and in high-class restaurants and hotels.

Carpet talk

There is a bewildering choice. There are carpets from the weaving areas of Thrace, Balıkesir, Bergama, Konya, Kayseri, Van and Hakkarı. Decent shops will also have carpets from Iran, Azerbaijan and the Central Asian republics. Pieces are made using various techniques and with a variety of materials, or combinations of materials, such as silk, wool or even mercerized cotton. It is useful to remember a few basic principles with regard to choosing the right carpet for the right price.

The size, of course, will affect the price tag as will the **material** it is made from. Pure silk-on-silk rugs are the most expensive, though silk can also be combined with wool very successfully, producing a cheaper finished product. Hand-woven all-wool carpets are cheaper still, while the synthetic mass-produced carpets, covering the floors of many Turkish homes, are the most economical though hardly worth the bother of carrying home. Wool can be identified by the tiny fibres sticking out of the yarn, or if you are really suspicious, pluck a strand and hold it to a lighter. Synthetic fibres will flame and leave a sticky residue, while silk and wool tend to smoulder and turn to ash.

How the carpet is made is also important. Look at the back of the carpet to check the **density of knots**, because as a general rule the tighter the weave the higher the quality and the more hard wearing it will be. Have a look at both the warp and the weft, to make sure they are definitely what they are meant to be. A **handmade** kilim will show the pattern clearly on their underside, unlike most machine woven rugs.

A rug's price will also be affected by its **age**: older, hand-woven pieces are prized for their rarity and individuality. However, you should check an old carpet carefully: excessive wear or areas where it has been mended or patched should be reflected in the price. Old carpets can also be repainted; while newer ones can be faded to look 'antique' by being left in the sun.

Ask whether a carpet has been coloured using natural or synthetic **dyes**. The former are more sought after and fetch a higher price. Synthetic dyes are generally brighter and there may be less tonal variation in each colour. Give the carpet a good rub, ideally with a damp cloth, to make sure the dye has been fixed properly.

Finally, don't forget to ask yourself whether it will work in your IKEA-based 'living space'?!

Getting it home... one option is to wait until the end of your trip. If things don't work out that way, shops normally offer to post your carpet back for a small extra charge or alternatively you can take it down to the post office yourself armed with wrapping paper, string and some scissors.

Shopping

The best shopping in the country is undoubtedly within the labyrinthine confines of the covered bazaar in İstanbul, where competition is at its fiercest and the range of goods at its best. The bazaars in large cities such as Bursa, Konya or Kayseri are also good spots to pick up souvenirs, although you won't find the same selection as in İstanbul. On the plus side, these provincial markets are more geared up for the local population, so you won't be continually pestered by over-enthusiastic salesmen. The shops and boutiques in the coastal resorts tend to be on the expensive side, although at the end of a quiet season and with plenty of haggling you can still pick up a bargain. You will find western-style shopping centres in all the major cities, with familiar brand names at not unfamiliar prices. Some of the domestic clothing chains do have some excellent bargains though, especially when the sales kick-off in June or July and after New Year.

Shops generally open 0900-2000, Mon-Sat, although in resort towns they often open mid-morning, when most people surface, & stay open well into the night

Essentials

Anatolian carpets

Carpet weaving is an age-old tradition imported into Anatolia with the Turks from Central Asia. The earliest fragments of carpet discovered have been dated to the fourth century BC, although it was under the Selçuks that a carpet weaving industry first developed in present-day Turkey. Conceived by nomadic people, carpets were a practical means of covering the floor of their yürt – black wool tent – though their bright colours and striking designs also attest to their decorative significance.

The process of carpet-making begins with the shearing of sheep (in late spring). Washed and dried in the sun, the raw wool was originally spun into yarn using simple drop spindles. Today you still occasionally see shepherds spinning like this while they tend their flocks, though most yarn is mass-produced in factories.

Dyeing is the next stage and the pigments were traditionally sourced purely from natural materials such as leaves, roots and minerals. Many are found locally, such as the yellow pigment made from the leaves of spurge – a type of euphorbia – while others like indigo have always been imported (in this case from India). The tone of the dye can also be adjusted by adding yoghurt, lemons, salt or urine. From the mid-19th century, natural pigments were increasingly replaced by a new generation of synthetic dyes, which were cheaper to produce and became hard to distinguish from the original colours. Now, synthetic pigments are predominantly used in mass-produced carpets, but thanks to growing demand in the last 30 years, there has been a renaissance in the use of naturally dyed yarns in the hand-weaving industry.

Carpets are made up of vertical yarns (warps) through which coloured horizontal yarns (wefts) are woven. These flat-weave carpets, or kilim, are usually woven into blocks of bold colour, while sumak or cicim have more delicate patterns brocaded on to them. Many contemporary designs date

Carpets & kilims
Try to find out the significance of the various motifs that adorn your rug! See also the boxes on pages 58 & 59

A carpet or kilim is high on most people's shopping list when they come to Turkey. In fact it's hard to avoid buying one as shops and persuasive salesmen seem to be everywhere you go in the tourist traps of the country. The combination of colours, patterns and materials available is huge, and the choice on offer in the average shop is quite simply mind-boggling. Carpet salesmen have also earned an unenviable reputation for their hard-sell tactics. Considering all this it is important to do your homework thoroughly. Visit several shops, preferably in different places, so you can build up a picture of what is on offer and for how much. It is also a good idea to have a look in a shop back home, because unless you buy carefully, there may not be the huge price difference you would expect.

Although different kinds of carpet traditionally come from distinct regions, today you can get almost anything anywhere. In fact, you will probably find the best selection of carpets, as well as the most competitive prices, in İstanbul, whose dealers secure contracts directly with regional producers. This means that even if you did find your way to a carpet-making village you might well be disappointed if all the rugs were being woven to fill orders from specific shops or dealers.

Leatherwear
Expect to pay US$150 at least for a decent jacket

Leather goods are another popular buy and you will have no trouble finding jackets, handbags, holdalls and wallets in all the bazaars and resorts. For the best value, you will need to find one of the large factory outlets (particularly around İzmir and İstanbul – the traditional centres of leather production) although even prices in the resort towns are probably substantially lower than back home. Generally prices are very reasonable, although as with anything they reflect the quality of the materials used and the workmanship. Finding the right style can be a problem along the Mediterranean coast, where the merchandise is predominantly aimed at German and back to the original motifs brought by nomadic Turkomen from the east. Researchers have traced this migration by comparing Anatolian designs with those used in Persian and Central Asian rugs. Motifs often reflected the pre-Islamic traditions and animist beliefs of a particular tribe but were also an expression of the weaver's feelings at the time. Geometric patterns predominate but there are also certain commonly used designs such as the scorpion, a symbol to ward-off evil, and the tree of life which signifies the axis of the world.

Weaving continued as nomadic tribes settled into sedentary life and village women produced rugs both for personal use and for their dowry. Though intermarriage and migration reduced the regional distinctiveness of rug design, each carpet remained a wholly unique creation, a very personal form of artistic expression. Some of this individuality was lost in the 19th century as demand for Turkish rugs in Europe caused the

commercialization of the weaving industry. Whereas previously women had produced carpets according to their own feelings and tastes, now dealers dictated designs and motifs as well as supplying the raw materials. In many respects this continues today, with carpet weavers contracted to produce rugs of a certain size, colour and design. However, despite a greater uniformity, close up each rug displays the subtle idiosyncrasies of its weaver: an originality that is part of the charm of a hand-woven carpet.

Russian package tourists, who seem to go for hideous colours and fluffy collars. İstanbul has a much better selection of shops selling modern, stylish designs.

Antiques

Shops selling antiques can be found wherever there are tourists, however be aware that much of what you see is in fact newly manufactured, something a reputable salesperson should bring to your attention before the bargaining begins. This is a good thing too, because Turkish law actually forbids the buying, selling and exporting of antiques, although the issue is clouded by the fact that there is no official definition of what constitutes an "antique". If you are worried, ask the shop for a certificate proving that the item is a replica or contact a local museum or KÜSAV (the Foundation for the Conservation and Promotion of Culture and Arts), see page 164. Copperware, coins, jewellery, miniatures and furniture are some of the items typically on sale.

Other souvenirs

Small items carved from **onyx** such as ash-trays and statuettes are a popular souvenir, and although you will find them almost everywhere, Cappadocia and particularly the town of Hacıbektaş are good places to pick them up. Popular with smokers are **meerschaum pipes**, hand-carved from the soft, white stone quarried near Eskişehir. Again, meerschaum crops up in gift shops all over the country, but the best choice and prices are in Eslişehir.

The centre of the country's **ceramics** industry, Kütahya, is a good place to stop if you are looking for decorated plates or tiles at bargain prices. Then there are the classic momentos such as the **hookah** (most of the ones you see in tourist shops are not actually designed to be smoked), and of course the **fez**.

There is a booming trade in **fake designer clothes**, with shops and stalls in İstanbul and the resort towns selling everything from Nike sweatshirts to Louis Vuitton handbags at suspiciously low prices. Although such gear may be emblazoned with an authentic-looking label, a close inspection will reveal that it has been cheaply made in a local sweat-shop, something that becomes obvious after a couple of washes.

Turkey is the world's fifth largest manufacturer of **gold jewellery**. Much of this is exported, though glittering gold merchants' shops are a common sight in all Turkish bazaars and main streets. Not only is gold jewellery widely worn by Turkish women, but it is also seen as a popular hedge against rampant inflation. The best place to buy gold is in the Covered Bazaar in İstanbul, where competition keeps prices low. Individual pieces are sold by weight, though the designs are frequently not to western tastes. Not domestically as popular as gold, **silver jewellery** is normally sold in distinct shops or from stalls in the main cities and resorts. Many of the rings and earrings are imported from the Far East, though you will also find some more traditional pieces made to old Anatolian designs.

VAT Value Added Tax, known as **KDV**, is payable on most purchases at a rate of up to 15%, although this is generally hidden in the price. As a foreign tourist you are entitled to claim back this KDV on items bought in shops authorized to make tax-free sales, easily identified by a sticker in the window. However, because it is a fairly long-winded procedure, it is only worth doing for large purchases. The retailer issues you with an *özel fatura* (special invoice) which is handed in to customs when you leave the country. Once this paperwork has been processed, a refund from the shop eventually drops through your letter box at home.

When making a large purchase such as a carpet, many shops offer to sell the item without adding the KDV. Although this sounds attractive, it is a bit risky because you will not be given an official receipt, and therefore won't be able to prove the value of the purchase if quizzed by customs when returning to your country.

Holidays and festivals

National holidays In addition to New Year's Day there are four public holidays observed in Turkey, with one extra for the lucky residents of İzmir. These four commemorate important landmarks in the history of the Turkish Republic, and all banks, schools, universities, museums and government offices, as well as some shops and many private businesses are closed. Public transport generally runs as normal but seats on buses, trains and planes will be in greater demand, so you should make reservations well in advance. National holidays are an opportunity for Turks to display their patriotism and Turkish flags are draped everywhere days in advance. Parades by local school children, officials and the military typically take place in towns and cities, and the ubiquitous Atatürk statues become the focus for wreath-laying and speech-making by local dignitaries. There is even the occasional folk-dance or musical recital. Such holidays also give people the chance for a change of scene and resorts are filled with domestic tourists.

23rd April – *National Sovereignty and Children's Day* Celebrates the inaugural meeting of the Republican Parliament in Ankara in 1920.
19th May – *Youth and Sports Day* Commemorates the start of the War of Independence.
30th August – *Victory Day* Anniversary of the victory over Greek forces by the nationalists at Dumlupınar in 1922.
9th September – *Liberation Day* A holiday in İzmir only celebrating the liberation of the city from Greek forces at the end of the War of Independence.
29th October – *Republic Day* Date of the birth of the Republic of Turkey in 1923.

In addition to these national holidays, there are a number of other important dates on the official calendar which are marked by pomp and ceremony, although banks and offices remain open: *Navy Day* (**1st July**), *Armed Forces Day* (**26th August**), *Anniversary of Atatürk's death* in 1938 (**10th November** – the country falls eerily silent at 9:05 am, the time of his death, as people everywhere stop what they are doing to observe a minute's silence).

Ramadan *Ramazan* in Turkish, the month of fasting when faithful Muslims abstain from eating, drinking and smoking during daylight hours. The level of observance varies across the country, with the fast almost universally adhered to in more conservative areas. Even in the cities and resorts of the west, where *Ramazan* is less strictly observed, you should be sensitive and avoid eating and drinking in front of people who are fasting. As far as shops, museums, offices and so on life generally goes on as normal. Restaurants and cafés are, of course, empty during the day but they quickly fill up with ravenous diners at sundown and it can be difficult to find a table. The only other time you may be aware that it is *Ramazan* is in the early hours of the morning when *davutlar*, traditional drummers, walk the streets making lots of noise in order to wake people in time for their pre-dawn meal.

Religious holidays *Despite Turkey being a secular state there are several religious holidays which are widely observed*

Essentials

Şeker Bayramı The end of *Ramazan* is marked by the three-day long *Şeker Bayramı* (Sugar Holiday) when family, friends and neighbours get together to celebrate. Children show respect to their elders by kissing their hands and are rewarded with gifts and sweets. Government offices, museums and some shops are closed, however, restaurants and hotels are generally open. Unless *Şeker Bayramı* falls over a weekend, the country more or less packs up work for an entire week.

Kurban Bayramı (Sacrifice Holiday) An important holiday universally observed by Muslims which involves the ritual sacrifice of a sheep, or less commonly these days, a cow or camel. Several million sheep are dispatched each year across Turkey by having their throats cut. This is a re-enactment of the Old Testament and Koranic story of Abraham who was ordered by God to sacrifice his son, Isaac, on Mount Moriah. However, at the last moment, convinced of his faith, God allows Abraham to spare his son, instead directing him to kill a ram caught in a nearby thicket. Traditionally only the most wealthy households could afford to make a sacrifice and this meat was eaten by the family and also distributed to the poor. As with şeker Bayramı it seems like half the country is on the move in the run-up to, and the days following, the holiday, so it is important to make reservations for transportation and hotels well in advance.

The dates of *Ramazan* and the two religious holidays are set according to the Islamic lunar calender, meaning they fall 11 days earlier each year in relation to the Gregorian Calender. Below are the dates of the beginning of *Ramazan* and *Kurban Bayramı* for the next few years.

Year	Ramazan	Kurban Bayramı
2001	17 November	16 December
2002	7 November	6 December
2003	29 October	27 November
2004	19 October	17 November

There are well over a hundred festivals organized in towns and cities across the country each year. Most of them are small, parochial affairs which are not worth a special trip, but can be interesting to visit if you are in the area anyway. There are also a handful of better known events listed here.

Festivals

Essentials

Manisa Festival, Manisa, end of **March**: A week of cultural events culminating in a well attended ceremony in which tonnes of *mesir macunu*, a sticky sweet made from a mixture of 40 different ingredients, is thrown from the roof of the city's most famous mosque.

İstanbul International Film Festival, İstanbul, **April**: A chance to see some of the best Turkish films, often with English subtitles, along with a selection of foreign productions.

Anzac Day, Gallipoli National Park, **25th April**: Ceremony commemorating the ill-fated Anzac landings on the Gallipoli Peninsula at the beginning of the First World War.

Conquest of İstanbul, shores of the Bosphorus, **29th May**: A festival including mock battles to celebrate the conquest of İstanbul by Sultan Fatih Mehmet in 1453.

İstanbul Festival of Arts and Culture, İstanbul, **mid-June to mid-July**: The most prestigious arts festival in the country, attracting well known artists and musicians from across Turkey and abroad.

International İzmir Festival, İzmir region including Ephesus and Çeşme, **mid-June to mid-July**. A selection of foreign and Turkish musical performances. The concerts in the spectacular surroundings of the Roman amphitheatre at Ephesus are particularly worth seeing.

Grease Wrestling, Kırkpınar, near Edirne, **mid-June**. The National Grease Wrestling championships are accompanied by folk dancing, music and craft exhibitions.

Kafkasör Festival, Artvin, last weekend of **June**. A truly folky affair. Thousands of people gather in the high pastures above Artvin for a weekend of merriment, including dancing, wrestling and bull fighting.

İstanbul Jazz Festival, various venues, **July**. Big name international acts from world of jazz, rock and blues.

Hacı Bektaş Veli Pilgrimage, Hacıbektaş, third week of **August**. Tens of thousands of people descend on the Hacı Bektaş Museum to pay their respects to the inspirational founder of the *Bektaşi* order of dervishes.

Mevlâna Festival, Konya, 10th–17th **December**. A chance to see the official 'Whirling Dervishes', a troop of folk dancers rather than practising Mevlevi dervishes, who re-enact a *sema* or spinning ceremony.

Sport and special interest travel

Walking, trekking & cycling

Turkey has a huge and barely realized potential for adventure tourism. The mountains and unspoilt rural scenery that cover much of the country lend themselves to walking and trekking, while in many places the quiet back roads, paths and tracks are ideally suited for mountain biking or longer distance cycle-touring. Some of the country's foremost areas for walking and trekking include the **Lycian Peninsula**, which is now girded by Turkey's first long-distance path (see page 339); the **Lake District** (see page 449); the high **Taurus Mountains** (see page 523); **Cappadocia** and the **Kaçkar Mountains**. In most of these areas there are possibilities for both interesting day walks or more challenging multi-day expeditions. Added to these are several areas in the east of the country, such as the **Cilo-Sat mountains** and the **Munzur range**, which are currently off-limits due to the still-smoldering Kurdish troubles.

Tour operators *Anatolian Adventures*, 21 Albert Street, London, NW1 7LU, T020-78741107, psunshine@hotmail.com A range of walking and trekking trips in the Kaçkar Mountains, Cappadocia and the Aegean region, bespoke adventures also organized. *Bougainville Travel*, Çukurbağlı Caddesi No 10, Kaş, Turkey, T0242-8363737, F0242-8361605, www.bougainville-turkey.com Local agents for several of the large international adventure travel firms, they also organize their own programme of trekking, mountain biking, canyoning and sea-kayaking trips in the area around Kaş. *Exodus*, T020-8772-3822, www.exodus.co.uk Well established worldwide operator with several trips in Turkey. *Inner Asia*, T415-9220448, T1-800-7778183, www.innerasia.com A US-based company offering upmarket walking and sailing tours. *Mountain Trip Sobek*, www.mtsobek.com An American firm which organises walking and trekking through a local subsidiary, also easy güllet cruises. *Sobek Travel*, Istasyon Caddesi No 42, 51100, Niğde, Turkey, T0388-2132117, outdoor activity holidays including trekking and rafting, the local agents for *Exodus* in Cappadocia and the Aladağlar. *Upcountry*, 24 St John's Road, Buxton, Derbyshire, lycianway.da.ru, T020-76818595. Guided walking trips along the Lycian Way and in the Turkish lake district.

Essentials

Rock-climbing

Rock-climbing is still in its infancy in Turkey, despite the activities of a small number of highly dedicated Turkish climbers and a few intrepid visitors. Particular areas of interest are the limestone faces of the **Beydağları**, near Antalya, and the **Aladağlar**. The Aladağlar not only offers some excellent single and multi-pitch rock routes, but also alpine and big-wall climbing on the larger peaks of the range.

Hang gliding & paragliding

Two sports that have also only recently caught on in Turkey. Most activity is concentrated on the Mediterranean coast near **Fethiye**. As with climbing, there is enormous room for development with ideal climatic conditions during much of the year and forestry tracks giving motor access high into many of the country's coastal ranges.

Skiing

Many people are surprised to learn that there are numerous possibilities for skiing across the country. Probably the best known resort is **Uludağ**, near Bursa, (see page 191) which is a favourite weekend get-away for the wealthy İstanbul set. The runs, which vary from easy to moderately difficult, are mostly below the treeline and are ideally suited for beginners or lower-intermediates. **Palandoken**, just outside Erzurum (see page 595) has longer and more challenging pistes, however, the treeless slopes can get very cold and windswept in the depths of the frigid eastern winter. The choice of accommodation is also limited at the moment, though this will certainly change in the future. There are also smaller ski-centres on the slopes of **Mount Erciyes** (see page 520), near Kayseri, and on **Boz Dağı** (see page 248) to the east of İzmir. Although probably not warranting a trip in themselves, these centres make for an interesting excursion if you are staying nearby. Facilities for renting equipment are available at all these places and you will find the whole experience very economical by European standards. There are no foreign tour operators offering skiing packages to Turkey at the moment. See individual sections for details including accommodation and the length of the season.

Rafting & kayaking

The **Çoruh River** in northeast Turkey is considered to be one of the foremost rafting rivers in the world (see page 581), and several companies offer multi-day trips down rapids which in early summer reach an adrenaline-pumping grade five. Other rafting rivers include the **Dalaman** and the **Köprülü Çayı** which, although not as wild as the Çoruh, are more accessible, being within easy reach of many of the Mediterranean resorts. The convoluted coastline and protected waters off the southern coast, particularly in the **Kekova area** (see page 354), are ideal for sea kayaking. There are only two commercial outfits offering group trips from **Marmaris** and **Kaş** at present, though this will undoubtedly change.

Tour operators *Adrift* (Head Office), PO Box 310, Queenstown, New Zealand, T034425458, F034425950, www.adrift.co.nz Organize rafting expeditions on the Çoruh. UK office: T01488-684509, F01488-685055. *AlternatifTurizm*, T0252-4135994, F0252-4133208, alternatifraft.com, Kenan Evren Bulvarı, Çamlık Sokak 10/1, Marmaris, Muğla, Turkey. Well-established and professional outfit offering multi-day rafting trips on the Çoruh and Dalaman, plus sea-kayaking around Marmaris. *Bougainville Travel*,

Çukurbağlı Cadessi No10, Kaş, Antalya, Turkey, T0242-8363737, T0242-8361605, www.bougainville-turkey.com

Diving   Diving is a popular activity along the Aegean and Mediterranean coasts and there are dive schools and equipment rental outfits in most of the larger resorts. Once beneath the waves, although the marine life is not immediately as spectacular as in certain other parts of the world, excellent water clarity and varied underwater terrain make for some interesting diving. The best diving in Turkey is said to be around **Kaş**, although there are some interesting spots along the **northern Aegean coast**. Those in search of **wreck dives** could consider the waters off the west coast of the Galipolli Peninsula where many First World War ships lie on the sea bed

Health

Hospitals & other medical facilities are listed in the relevant town's directory   In common with most other Mediterranean countries, a trip to Turkey involves no major health concerns. Generally, environmental conditions and high standards of hygiene mean that it is easy to stay healthy. Most visitors suffer nothing more than a mild stomach upset. Having said that, travelling to areas of eastern Turkey does involve slightly greater health risks, given the less developed nature of the region. This is particularly the case in the southeast where there is a risk of serious infectious diseases, such as malaria and typhoid.

Before travelling

The cost of private medical care is relatively high, so make sure you take out a suitable travel insurance policy that will cover the cost of treatment and repatriation by air-ambulance in the event of serious illness. If you take regular medication, make sure you are stocked up with enough to last you for the whole trip. The contraceptive pill is available from chemists without prescription, but it is more convenient to bring your own supply. Also pack a spare pair of glasses. Consider having a dental check-up and if you suffer from a chronic illness, such as diabetes or high blood pressure, arrange for a thorough medical examination prior to your departure. In such cases it may also be useful for your physician to write a letter explaining fully your medical condition.

Medical facilities
Your embassy representative or the local tourist information bureau can normally recommend the best hospital or a reputable doctor in the area. Most large hotels have a doctor on call   A three-tier health system operates in Turkey, with state, social security and private medical facilities. State hospitals (*devlet hastanesi*) or medical centres (*poliklinik*) can be found in cities, towns and some large villages. In the west of the country, these offer a reasonable standard of care particularly for minor complaints, although they are generally over-crowded and slow. Further east and in rural areas facilities are more rudimentary and should only be used in an emergency. Such hospitals accept non-Turkish citizens, although you will have to pay for all your treatment. Social security hospitals (*SSK hastanesi*) are for those contributing to the social security system, mostly public sector employees, and they do not accept foreign patients. Private medical facilities, where you can expect western standards of care and up-to-date equipment, are found in most cities and tourist centres, however, the best are located in İstanbul and Ankara. The doctors in private hospitals (*özel hastanesi*) often speak some English. For minor ailments you should visit a pharmacy, where the staff are generally well trained and helpful. Outside opening hours one pharmacy in a particular area or town remains open. This is known as the *nöbetçi eczane* and can be found by asking taxi drivers or the police. Other pharmacies will also have a note in their window informing you where the *nöbetçi eczane* is that particular night.

Most medicines are available in pharmacies over the counter without a prescription. The brand names of some may be different, so if you need something specific it is useful to know its active ingredients. Check the expiry dates on all medication before buying it and make sure the pharmacist explains the dosage instructions. If you are unclear about the dosage, it is usually not too difficult to find someone who can translate them for you. Try the staff at the local tourist information office or in your hotel. Although nearly all medical supplies are available at pharmacies, it is a sensible idea to carry at least a few basic things with you. If you are planning to visit more remote areas, however, it is essential to have a more extensive first aid kit.

Medicines
Chemists (Eczane) are ubiquitous in Turkish towns and cities

Checklist Antiseptic cream; plasters and sterile pads; pain killers; water sterilizing tablets; antacid tablets for indigestion; antibiotics for diarrhoea and other minor infections; an elastic bandage for twists and sprains; a larger bandage for supporting broken limbs; plenty of rehydration salts and travel sickness tablets. You may also want to take with you a supply of condoms (*preservatif*), though they are available in all pharmacies, and some fungicidal foot powder.

Some extra preparations are necessary if you are travelling with babies or children. As with adults, the most likely thing they will be afflicted with is mild diarrhoea and vomiting. These should be treated in the same way as with adults, although the risk of dehydration is much greater so it is particularly important to carry plenty of rehydration salts with you. Any treatment should be started earlier and carried on with more persistence. Breast-feeding your baby is best, however powdered milk is widely available. Bananas and other peeled fruit are nutritious and easy to prepare, possibly eaten with yoghurt for example. A course of antibiotics in case of upper respiratory infections and antibiotic ear drops for treating outer ear infections, which are quite common after swimming, should also be carried. A selection of plasters and some antiseptic cream is a good idea for the inevitable bumps and scraps. Nappies are easily found, as are wet wipes.

Children

Take special care to protect your children from the sun by applying high-factor sun cream regularly. A hat is good for keeping the sun off their face and a T-shirt can even be worn in the sea during the hottest part of the day.

No special vaccinations are necessary for a visit to Turkey, however it is a good idea to be inoculated against **typhoid** and to have a **tetanus** booster if you need one. You may also consider being immunized against **Hepatitis A,** along with the **B-strain** of the disease.

Vaccinations & immunization

On the road

Most of the time, intestinal upsets are due to the insanitary preparation of **food.** Undercooked fish, vegetables or meat, fruit with the skin on or food that is exposed to flies are all highly risky. Water can also be the culprit. Although the water in some Turkish cities is supposedly safe you should stick to bottled water or water from water shops (see page 57) or recommended springs. **Diarrhoea** is usually the result of food poisoning. The lynch pins of treatment for diarrhoea are rest, fluid and salt replacement, antibiotics for the bacterial types and special diagnostic tests and medical treatment for amoeba and giardia infections. All kinds of diarrhoea, whether or not accompanied by vomiting respond favourably to the replacement of water and salts taken as frequent small sips of some kind of rehydration solution. Any diarrhoea continuing for more than three days should be treated by a doctor.

Stomach upsets

Essentials

Heat & cold Full acclimatisation to high temperatures takes about two weeks. Drink plenty of water (up to 15 litres a day can be needed if taking vigorous exercise), use salt on food and avoid extreme exertion. Tepid showers are more cooling than hot or cold ones. The burning power of the sun is phenomenal. Wear a wide brimmed hat and use some form of sun cream or lotion on untanned skin. Always use high protection factor suntan lotions, designed specifically for high temperatures or for mountaineers or skiers. It is a good idea to protect your eyes too by wearing sunglasses. There are several varieties of 'heat stroke'. The most common cause is severe dehydration. Avoid this by drinking lots of non-alcoholic fluid and put extra salt on your food.

Malaria Malaria is only a risk in the southeast of the country where large scale irrigation projects have produced conditions suitable for the mosquito that carries the disease. If you intend to spend time in the rural areas of the Çukurova plain or around Şanlıurfa it's best to take precautions. To ward off mosquitoes sleep off the ground with a mosquito net and burn mosquito coils. Sprays and insecticidal tablets, heated on a mat plugged into the wall socket, are effective, as are personal insect repellents. The best contain a high concentration of Diethyltoluamide generally known as DEET. Liquid is best for arms and face (take care around eyes and make sure you do not dissolve the plastic of your spectacles).

Rabies Rabies is present in Turkey though it doesn't pose a serious threat. Pre-exposure vaccination gives anyone bitten by a suspect animal time to get treatment and also prepares the body to produce antibodies quickly. If you are bitten by a domestic or wild animal, don't leave things to chance. Scrub the wound with soap and water/or disinfectant, try to have the animal captured (within limits) or at least determine its ownership where possible and seek medical assistance at once.

Further reading

Architecture **Godfrey Goodwin**, *A History of Ottoman Architecture*, the best guide to the architecture of the era. **Spiro Kostoff**, *Caves of the Gods - Cappadocia and its Churches*, exhaustive though fairly uninspiring academic study. **Richard Krautheimur**, *Early Christian and Byzantine Architecture*, an interesting and informative study. **Cyril Mango**, *Byzantine Architecture*, examines the main buildings of the period.

History **Roderic Davison**, *Turkey: A Short History*, concise academic examination of Turkish history from the steppes of Central Asia to the modern republic. **John Freely**, *Inside the Seraglio*, thoroughly researched account of the trials and tribulations of the House of Osman. **OR Gurney**, *The Hittites*, readable history of Anatolia's first great civilisation. **Herodotus**, *The Histories*, the first historical and social commentary of the ancient world, written in the fifth century BC. **Lord Kinross**, *The Ottoman Centuries*, fairly thorough and accesible summary of Ottoman history. *Atatürk: the Rebirth of a Nation*, weighty and balanced description of the man and his times. **Seton Lloyd**, *Ancient Turkey - A Traveller's History of Anatolia*, thorough and readable early history of Anatolia. **Alan Moorhead**, *Gallipoli*, interesting and detailed account of the tragic battles and their wider context in the First World War. **Sir Steven Runciman**, *Byzantine Style and Civilisation*, a detailed look at the Byzantines. Also a definitive examination of: The Fall of Constantinople. **Richard Stoneman**, *A Traveller's History of Turkey*, a pretty good introduction to Anatolian history though it lacks detail. **Erik Zürcher**, *Turkey, A Modern History*, excellent for the history of the region from the beginning of the 19th century.

Neal Ascherson, *The Black Sea*, authoritative examination of the history, culture and ecology of the Black Sea basin, including an interesting section about the Laz and the Pontic Greeks. **Tim Kelsey**, *Dervish*, fairly dark but informative inquiry into modern Turkish life. **Lord Kinross**, *Europa Minor, Within the Taurus*, the accounts of a series of journeys made by the author during the 1940s and 1950s, filled with rich description and lots of interesting background information. **Irfan Orga**, *Portrait of a Turkish Family*, highly acclaimed autobiographical account of life for an upper class İstanbul family at the end of the Ottoman era, poignant and engaging. **Joan and David Peterson**, *Eat Smart in Turkey*, excellent examination of the history and custom of eating in Turkey, also lots of practical tips. **Freya Stark**, Ionian - *A Quest, Alexander's Path, Lycian Shore, Riding to the Tigris*, the journeys of one of the greatest female adventures. **Jeremy Seal**, *A Fez of the Heart*, an entertaining and sometimes illuminating look at modern Turkish society. Verges towards the banal at times (witness the title) but still worth a look. **John Tumpone**, *Scotch and Holy Water*, a warm and humourous account of the adventures of a debauched American defence contractor working in Turkey during the 1950s and 1960s. **Andrew Wheatcroft**, *The Ottomans*, lively and informative look at many aspects of the Ottoman Empire.

Useful city maps for İstanbul, İzmir and cities can be obtained free of charge from tourist offices and some large hotels.

Access to large scale topographical maps is restricted by the government. A few maps of greatly varying usefulness and accuracy have been produced for mountainous parts of the country popular with trekkers and climbers.

Non-fiction & travel

Essentials

Aileen Crawley, *The Bride of Suleiman*, an engrossing and historically accurate novel about the relationship between Roxelana and Sultan Süleyman. **Yaşar Kemal**, *Memed, My Hawk*, one of several epic novels set mostly in rural Turkey in the middle of the 20th century. The author's later works, mostly based in İstanbul, make for lighter reading, try the *The Sea Crossed Fishermen*. **Pierre Loti**, *Aziyade*, semi-autobiographical tale of romance and intrigue in Ottoman İstanbul penned by a French naval officer who lived briefly in the city. **Rose Macauley**, *The Towers of Trebizond*, witty tale of the adventures of three missionaries in eastern Turkey.

Novels

Feroz Ahmad, *The Making of Modern Turkey*, a study of the evolution and form of contemporary Turkish politics with chapters dedicated to the Atatürk years and the various military coups. **Nicole and Hugh Pope**, *Turkey Unveiled*, an illuminating look at the country's political landscape, as well as focusing in on particular issues such as Cyprus.

Politics

Asuman and David Pollard, *Teach Yourself Turkish*, relevant and useful dialogue, interesting excercises, and all the necessary grammar make this the best book on the market. Cassette also available. Langenscheidt's do a handy pocket-size *English-Turkish dictionary* (*sözluk*) which is widely available in Turkey. **Arın Bayraktaroğlu**, *Culture Shock: Turkey*, an illuminating and entertaining dissection of Turkish customs and habits from this excellent series. Particularly useful for those staying for a while.

Language & culture

George Bean, *Turkey's Southern Shore, Turkey Beyond the Meander, Lycian Turkey, Aegean Turkey*, excellent series of archaeological guides written by a lecturer from İstanbul University. Although they are over thirty years old now, they are still the most informative studies. **Blake and Edmonds**, *Biblical Sites in Turkey*, information on the biblical significance and associations of various places in modern Turkey. **Boyd and Freely**, *Strolling Through İstanbul*, a series of walks through the city with lots of interesting historic information. John Freely has also written a series of regional historical guides published by Red House Press. **Karl Smith**, *The Mountains of Turkey*, a

Specialist guides

Cicerone guide with climbing and trekking routes. **Welch, Moore, et al**, *Where to Watch birds in Turkey*, Greece and Cyprus.

Maps There are several general maps of Turkey which can be purchased in the country or before you arrive. *GeoCentre* do a reasonable pair of 1:800,000 sheets as part of their EuroMap series which are adequate for general use, though they aren't entirely accurate. The 1:500,000 maps produced by *Kartographischer Verlag Reinhard Ryborsch* in conjunction with the Turkish Ministry of Defence are much more detailed and cover the country in seven sheets. They can be ordered from *Stanfords*, 12-14 Long Acre, London, WC2, UK, T020-78361321, though they're quite hard to find in Turkey itself.

Essentials

istanbul

3

İstanbul

74 Ins and outs

77 History

81 Modern İstanbul

**81 The 'Old' City:
Sultanahmet to the
City Walls**

82 Haghia Sophia

85 Topkapı Palace

93 Around the Topkapı

95 Around Sultanahmet Medanı

95 Sultan Ahmet Camii
(Blue Mosque)

96 The Hippodrome

98 Sultanahmet to Beyazıt

103 Eminönü

106 From the Mısır Çarşısı to
the Covered Bazaar

107 Beyazıt to the City Walls

110 The Theodosian Walls

113 North of the Golden Horn

115 Karaköy

117 Galata

118 Beyoğlu

120 Taksim Square

120 The Bosphorus

122 The European Shore

130 The Asian side

135 Museums

137 Excursions from the city

137 The Prince's Islands

141 The Black Sea Coast

143 Essentials

143 Sleeping

151 Eating

İstanbul has one of the most stunning natural settings of any major city in the world, divided by the Golden Horn, then cleaved again by the bluey-green waters of the Bosphorus. Within this is a chaotic and inexorably expanding mass of humanity, streets choked with traffic and air filled with pollution.

It was the capital of two world empires, one Christian, the other Islamic. Over 25 centuries of uninterrupted history have left the city with a dazzling cultural and architectural heritage including dozens of castles, palaces, churches and mosques. Where else could you follow a visit to one of the world's greatest churches with an afternoon discovering the glories of Ottoman religious architecture? Shop in the world's largest covered bazaar? Stretch out on warm marble in a 300 year-old Turkish bath? Steam up the Bosphorus on a vintage ferry?

İstanbul is also a dynamic melting pot of tradition and modernity, wealth and poverty, east and west. A fashionably dressed career woman rubs shoulders with her tightly veiled compatriot; a horse and cart holds up a sleek modern tram; a bearded imam chats into a mobile phone in the hushed silence of a mosque courtyard. This is the fascination of İstanbul. A city at the epicentre of the Turkish nation that evokes enormous pride amongst its inhabitants and that makes a habit of seducing foreigners with its chaotic, enigmatic charm.

Ins and outs

Getting there

Atatürk airport
See page 27 for
flight information

Atatürk airport Opened for the new millennium, the international terminal (*dış hatlar*) at İstanbul's Atatürk airport is a vast structure built to relieve the chaos and congestion. Facilities include a duty-free shop, post office, chemist, restaurants, banks open 24-hours, a left-luggage facility, a tourist information desk and a hotel booking office. The domestic terminal (*iç hatlar*) is several hundred metres away from the international terminal, turn right as you come out of the arrivals hall. It's a short walk or the *Havaş* airport bus (see below) calls in at the domestic terminal on its way into the city.

Transport into the city

If you're on your way back to the airport at an odd time several private companies run shuttle buses which pick-up from the city's hotels. Enquire at your hotel

From the airport Atatürk airport, 25 km west of the city centre, is served by *Havaş* airport buses which depart from in front of the international and domestic terminals at 0500 and then every 30 minutes, 0600-2300, US$3 for Taksim. Unfortunately the closest it gets to Sultanahmet is Aksaray from where you'll need to get on a tram or hail a taxi (US$3-4). Airport taxis wait directly outside the front doors of both terminals with a typical fare into Sultanahmet and Taksim about US$10-12 respectively. *Havaş* also operate an erratic bus service to Esenler intercity bus station which is supposed to leave day or night when full US$3.25.

From the bus stations Most bus companies provide a free shuttle buses into Taksim and Sultanahmet from the main *otogar* at **Esenler**, 10 km from the centre. A taxi into Taksim or Sultanahmet costs US$5 and US$6 respectively. You could also use the metro to Aksaray although from there you'll need to get a taxi, tram or bus, depending on where you're going. It's sometimes possible to get buses to İstanbul's smaller **Harem** terminal on the Asian side of the Bosphorous. This is advantageous if you're coming down from Asiatic Turkey as you won't have to sit in the cross-town traffic to Esenler. From Harem it's a short ferry ride across to Eminönü – a good introduction to the city.

From the railway stations İstanbul has 2 mainline stations located on either side of the Bosphorus. **Haydarpaşa**, on the Asian side, is the terminus for services from Asiatic Turkey. Arriving at here the quickest way to cross to the European side is on one of the regular ferries to Karaköy which leave from in front of the station (US$0.80). A walk across Galata Bridge brings you to Eminönü where trams run up the hill to Sultanahmet. If you have alot of luggage, a taxi via the Bosphorus bridge is around US$8 to Taksim. There are also some hotels a walk or short taxi ride south in Kadiköy. **Sirkeci**, the smaller station south of the Golden Horn, handles trains from European Turkey and mainland Europe. Getting to accommodation in Sultanahmet from Sirkeci is simply a matter of boarding a tram which stops in front of the station (far platform). A taxi up to Sultanahmet is under US$2; about US$5 to Taksim.

Getting around

See also page 164 for
tour agencies

İstanbul is a vast and sprawling city which can be rather daunting to negotiate at first. Luckily many of the main tourist sights are within a relatively small area of the old city, which also boasts a good choice of accommodation. This means that your legs are all you need to explore much of what's on offer, with a taxi, bus, tram or ferryboat ride unlocking the city's other attractions. Needless to say, it is best to avoid travelling during the rush hours when all forms of public transport are packed to overflowing and the city's roads grind to a halt. If you have to make a trip during these times allow a lot of extra time.

İstanbul's huge fleet of buses (*otobüs*), made-up largely of ageing Hungarian-built vehicles, is operated by the government-owned IETT. On such buses you post a ticket (US$0.50), purchased from a kiosk or shop near major bus stops, into a box as you get on. It is worth buying a stock of bus tickets if you plan to use buses frequently. These tickets can also be bought from traders hanging around bus stops who add a small margin onto the price. On private buses, identified by a sign on the front saying '*Özel Halk Otobüsü*', passengers pay a conductor seated at the front. The bus number and final destination are shown on the front, with other important stops often listed in a side window. The Belediye is slowly bringing more modern buses into operation and some of these have wheel-chair access or are powered by natural gas.

Bus
Generally operate between 0600-2200, although some services continue until midnight. There are no night bus services

The petrol guzzling 1950s Cadillacs and Chevrolets which used to cruise the streets as dolmuş have been replaced with modern minibuses. Fares vary depending on the

Dolmuş

İstanbul

Istanbul orientation

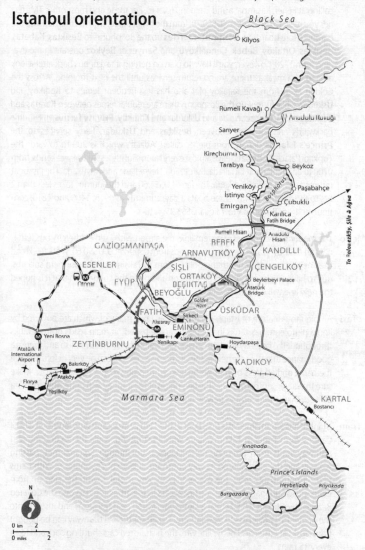

İstanbul

distance travelled (US$0.30-1). The new minibus dolmuş are brown or blue and operate on set routes including: *Eminönü-Taksim, Eminönü-Topkapı, Kadıköy-Üsküdar, Üsküdar-Beykoz, Taksim-Beşiktaş-Sarıyer, Taksim-Kadıköy, Taksim-Topkapı.*

Ferries
For details of other Bosphorus ferry services see page 122

Divided by the Golden Horn and the Bosphorus, there is a wealth of waterborne public transport. Not only do ferries often provide the fastest means of reaching a destination in the traffic choked city, but they are also a thoroughly civilized way to travel. They run well into the evening so catching one is a lovely way of starting the night off if, for example, you're having dinner in one of the Bosphorus suburbs, returning later by bus or cab. *Turkish Maritime Lines* operates a fleet of old ferries sailing regularly between **Eminönü** and Üsküdar (pier 1), **Kadıköy** (pier 2) and **Harem** (pier 4) on the Asian side of the Bosphorus. They leave every 15-30 mins, 0630 to 2200, later at weekends. There is also an hourly boat between **Balat** on the Golden Horn and **Üsküdar** calling at Fener, Kasımpaşa and Eminönü (pier 6). For these and most other TML ferries you need to buy a token (US$0.70) from the ticket office, which is then fed into the barrier before boarding. **Commuter ferries** up the Bosphorus to Beşiktaş, Kabataş, Beşiktas, Ortaköy, Bebek, Çengelköyü, and Sarıyer or Beykoz operate in the evening from 1720, however, you'll have to plan on getting a taxi or bus back after a look around or a meal as there are no return services until the next morning. Across the Golden Horn from the Karaköy pier also has less-frequent ferries to **Kadıköy** and **Üsküdar**, while further up the Bosphorus there are regular ferries between **Karataş** and **Beşiktaş** on the European side and **Üsküdar** and **Kadıköy**. **Private ferries** also shuttle backwards and forwards between Beşiktaş and Üsküdar. Ferry services to the **Prince's Islands** depart from pier 5, called 'Adalar', which is 200 m towards the Topkapı Palace. The boats leave almost every hour, slightly less at the weekends, from 0700 to 2230 calling at Kınalıada, Burgazada, Heybeliada and Büyükada. The last boat returns at 2130 from Büyükada. The fare is US$1.60 and the journey takes less than 2 hrs to the furthest island. Three boats a day, currently at 0915, 1400 and 1815, continue on from Büyükada to Yalova, US$3.25.

Metro

The modern, efficient metro system links the airport with Esenler intercity bus terminal and Aksaray. Trains run every 5-15 mins from 0500-2400, US$0.60. Work to extend the line northwards beneath the Golden Horn to Taksim and the northern suburbs, due to have finished in 2000, is grinding on adding to the congestion that it is hoped the new line will eventually relieve.

Taxi
The passenger is responsible for all toll-charges, ie crossing the Bosphorus bridge

A ubiquitous feature of İstanbul traffic, yellow taxis, many of which are powered by liquid petroleum gas tanks in the boot, can be hailed on main roads or from ranks throughout the city, day or night. Drivers generally do not speak English and there's a good chance that they are new to the city themselves, so it can be very helpful to have the name and address of your destination written down on a piece of paper. Make sure the driver sets his meter at the beginning of the journey and remember there's a 50% surcharge for journeys between 2400 and 0600.

Tram

İstanbul has 2 tram lines: the first, built in the 19th century, runs the length of Istiklal Caddesi from Tünel to Taksim Square without stopping; while the second modern tramway starts from Eminönü before looping up through Sultanahmet, passing Aksaray and the city walls on its way out to the suburb of Zeytinburnu. With trams every 5 mins, 0500-2400, the modern line is very useful, saving the slog up from Eminönü to Sultanahmet or giving fast access to the attractions beyond the Covered Bazaar. Buy a token (US$0.60) at a kiosk (*gişe*) found near the stops and insert it into the barrier to gain access to the platform. Tickets for the old tramway can be bought from kiosks at either end of the line with the historic red cars shuttling back and forth every 15 mins.

Known as *banliyö trenler*, the trains running from Sirkeci station around the peninsula **Train** and along the Marmara coast to Halkalı are a useful means of getting to Kumkapı, the Yenikapı ferry terminal or the city walls at Yedikule. However, beyond these destinations, or unless you have a particular interest in slow train journeys, İstanbul's suburban network will be of little concern to you. Tickets (US$0.50) are purchased before you get on the train, with services running every 15-20 mins, 0600-2330.

The Tünel Another relic of the 19th century, this funicular railway climbs steeply up *See page 116* inside a tunnel from near the Karaköy end of Galata bridge to Tünel Meydanı. Built by a French company in 1875 to save European merchants and bankers from having to climb the steep streets of Galata, it is equally useful today for footsore shoppers and tourists. Tokens (US$0.50) can be bought from the ticket booths in the two stations.

İstanbul

History

Legend attributes the founding of Byzantium, as the city was initially known, **Ancient** to a Greek expedition which set-out from the mainland under the command of **Byzantium** one Byzas the Megarian. Guided by the words of the oracle at Delphi who had *The history of what we* advised them to establish a city "opposite the land of the blind," the colonists *today call İstanbul is a* came ashore at Saray Burnu. They were so impressed by the site, surrounded *long & eventful one which* as it was by water on three sides and strategically placed to control the narrow *spans at least 3 millennia* straits, that they deemed the residents of Chalcedonia, a colony established earlier on the southern shores of the Bosphorus, must have been blind to have missed it. The oracular prophesy fulfilled, Byzas began in 676 BC to build a new *polis* which developed as an important trade and commercial centre. In co-operation with the Chalcedonians, tolls were extracted from ships loaded with olive oil, wine and luxuries bound for the Greek colonies of the Black Sea, and on their return south heavy with grain, salted fish, timber and skins.

Incorporated into the Roman Empire in 64 BC Byzantium enjoyed an unprecedented period of peace which was eventually brought to a tumultuous end by civil war in 196 AD and again in 305 AD. The second was a bitter and protracted struggle which culminated in Constantine's final victory near Chrysopolis on the Asian shores of the Bosphorus, an event which ushered in a new era for the Roman Empire and the city of Byzantium.

Constantine rapidly embarked on his plan to reinvigorate the Roman Empire **Byzantine** around a new capital. Having initially favoured Troy as the site of this 'New Rome', **Constantinople** Constantine was swayed by the superior position of Byzantium, which from then on was known as Constantinople in his honour. He began an ambitious building programme which transformed the city: constructing grand public buildings, churches and market places, all enclosed within a strong defensive wall stretching from the Sea of Marmara to the Golden Horn. In just four short years the work was completed and in 330 AD Constantine presided over an inauguration ceremony in the Hippodrome. As the focus of the Eastern Roman Empire, Constantinople's rapid growth over the next 50 years necessitated the building of a new defensive perimeter several kilometres to the west of the original wall. The Theodosian wall, named after the emperor who commissioned its construction, remains to this day one of the most enduring features of the Byzantine city.

The reign of Justinian the Great (527-565 AD) witnessed an even greater transformation of the capital as he rebuilt in grander style many of the public buildings destroyed during the 'Nika Revolt'. This uprising, sparked by discontent at high taxation, raged through the city in 532 AD before finally being brutally suppressed by mercenaries in the Hippodrome at the expense of

İstanbul

30,000 lives. Among the architectural achievements of this period, the church of Haghia Sophia stands as a glorious testament to what became a golden era for the Byzantine empire.

These heady days proved to be ephemeral as the Byzantines came under pressure from invading Lombards, Slavs, Avars and Persians. Emperor Heraclius briefly checked the decline in the seventh century, but shortly after his death Arab invaders ravaged Anatolia, penetrating right up to the walls of the city. The Theodosian defences were tested again in the following centuries as Bulgar armies repeatedly attacked Constantinople, however, subsequently the city's gravest threat came from the Latin armies of western Europe.

Old Istanbul

■ Sleeping		● Eating
1 Eyfel	5 Pisa	1 Darüzziyafe
2 Grand Gülsoy	6 Prestige	2 Hamam
3 Klas	7 Reşitpasa	3 Safran
4 Merit Antique	8 The President	4 Vefa Bozacısı

N
Not to scale

With little or no effective support from its Christian allies in Europe, it was only a matter of time before the beleaguered city of Constantinople was overwhelmed by the Ottomans. After several unsuccessful assaults, the young and determined Sultan Mehmet II prepared to mount a decisive attack on the city. In preparation he constructed the fortress of Rumeli Hisarı on the Bosphorus opposite the fort of Anadolu Hisarı, which effectively cut existing Byzantine lines of supply. He also enlisted the help of foreign experts to construct huge cannons which could hurl projectiles into the solid masonry of the Theodosian Wall. The siege began on 6th April 1453 with Mehmet II massing 100,000 troops who "surrounded the walls like bees". Over the next seven weeks the

The Ottoman conquest

İstanbul

Related map
A Sultanahmet, page 94
B Covered Bazaar, page 100
C Sirkeci & Eminönü, page 104

Byzantine defenders and their Genoese allies, outnumbered more than ten to one, gallantly fought off repeated attacks, frantically rebuilding the walls as they crumbled in the face of an awesome artillery barrage. In a cunning plan to outflank the mighty chain stretched across the Golden Horn, Mehmet II ordered a slipway built over the heights of Galata from the Bosphorus. On 23rd April 80 ships were dragged on sledges up the hill, and then sliding down from the heights of Galata, they were launched on the Golden Horn. Now the city was completely encircled and the siege became a battle of attrition. By the end of May sensing the defenders weakness, Mehmet II launched a decisive attack, concentrating his forces at a point of relative weakness in the northern section of the walls. The jannissaries' relentless attack eventually overwhelmed the defences at the Gate of Romanos (now called the Edirne Kapısı) and the last Byzantine emperor Constantine XI Palaeologus was killed fighting-to-the death on the battlements.

İstanbul   Having secured the city, Sultan Mehmet, from then on known as Fatih (the Conqueror), allowed the Ottoman horde to ransack the imperial city for three days before marching in to restore order. He proceeded directly to the church of Haghia Sophia, where having prayed he ordered the buildings conversion to a mosque.

The city's population, greatly diminished by out-migration during the twilight years of the Byzantine Empire, was swelled as people from across the empire were resettled, often forcibly, into new neighbourhoods. To its new Turkish residents the city became known as İstanbul, a corruption of the Greek words '*stin poli*' meaning 'to the city' or 'in the city'. Large Greek, Armenian and Genoese communities were joined during the 16th century by Sephardic Jews fleeing persecution in Spain, and later by Arabs, Moors and Europeans. Some measure of the city's former diversity can be gauged by the fact that it had more resident Greeks than Athens, more Armenians than any other city. This colourful ethnic diversity was to last until the beginning of the modern era, when violence and discrimination encouraged the minorities to flee.

During Sultan Mehmet's lifetime the new Ottoman capital was graced with many fine public buildings including the Topkapı Sarayı and the Fatih Camii. As the Ottoman Empire expanded under Beyazıt and Süleyman, much of the new found wealth was used to adorn the city with mosques, palaces, seminaries and fountains, most of which survive to the present-day. Over the following centuries the building continued apace despite the empires declining fortunes, with the European-style palaces built along the Bosphorus during the 19th century marking a final extravagant flourish which the Ottoman treasury could ill-afford. The tensions and conflicts within Ottoman society would frequently manifest themselves at the centre, with everyday life in the capital punctuated by violent intrigue, successional conflict and revolt.

The changing balance of world power during the 19th century also saw İstanbul exposed on several occasions to the threat of enemy occupation. This was avoided up until the Ottoman capitulation of 1918, when British troops marched in to secure the Straits and administer a *coup de grace* to the dying imperial administration. In response Atatürk and his fellow nationalists fled to Ankara from where they organized the struggle against foreign occupation and, subsequently, set-up the new Republic's administration. This left İstanbul politically marginalized, isolated from the centre of government for only the second time in over 1,500 years. However, despite losing its political pre-eminence to an upstart provincial town, it remains the industrial, financial, cultural, intellectual and emotional heart of the country.

Modern İstanbul

As with other major cities, particularly in the developing world, your first impressions of the "Queen of Cities", may not be all that regal. Banking low on your final approach into Atatürk airport, the ranks of high-rise apartments and shabby concrete ghettos stretch monotonously towards the horizon. This is one face of modern İstanbul, the result of explosive urbanization which has seen the city's population rocket from 700,000 in 1920 to an official figure of 9,000,000 today; although less conservative estimates put the population of Greater İstanbul at a staggering 15,000,000. Such unprecedented urban growth is largely the result of migration from rural areas, and particularly from the underdeveloped east. As the industrial and commercial powerhouse of the country, migrants flock to İstanbul in search of work and a better life, with anything up to 400,000 new arrivals each year. Many end up living in the illegal squatter settlements, or *gecekondu,* which ring the city. Although life is undoubtedly extremely hard for these families, recent research has shown that the *gecekondu* aren't necessarily places of destitution and despair. 90% of respondents to one survey viewed their situation in a positive way and believed that their children would have a better future in the city.

With their hopes and belongings, these migrants also bring with them the traditional values and conservatism of the Anatolia villages and towns. Buoyed in part by their support, and to the horror of western thinking İstanbullu, the Islamic Refah party took control of the city's administration in the 1994 elections. Despite dire predictions in the press about a prohibition on alcohol and women being forced to wear headscarves in the street, the new municipal government won over many of its opponents with its responsible governance. Not only were the streets cleaner and more of the city's buses running on time, but the administration remains largely untainted by accusations of corruption and sleaze.

The 'Old' City: Sultanahmet to the City Walls

Situated on the crown of a hill overlooking the Bosphorus and the Sea of Marmara, Sultanahmet was where Byzas the Megarian first stepped ashore to established his colony. The benefits of the site weren't lost on its later inhabitants either with the district becoming the administrative and spiritual centre of two great empires. It's hardly surprising therefore that the area is littered with such a rich historical legacy of churches, mosques, palaces, baths, cisterns and caravanserais. There's no mistaking the Old City for a museum, however, as all this history is set within the context of the contemporary city with its busy streets, lively bazaars and crowded residential neighbourhoods.

The imperial centre of Sultanahmet is where most independent travellers choose to stay and the advantages of having attractions like the Topkapı Palace, Haghia Sophia and Sultan Ahmet Camii (the Blue Mosque) right on your doorstep in a traffic-choked city like İstanbul, hardly need pointing out. You could spend days exploring Sultanahmet and the Bazaar area alone, without even venturing more than a 20-minute stroll from the comfort of your hotel room.

Beyond Beyazıt Square and the Covered Bazaar the tourist crowds thin and some of the Old City's lesser known historical sights lurk in densely populated working class neighbourhoods. Districts like Fatih and Topkapı are strongholds of religious conservatism an outward sign of which are women going about their business enveloped in the all-encompassing black *chador*. A row of imperial mosques marches down the city's backbone towards the Theodosian city walls, in whose shadow stands the Church of St Saviour of Chora, a repository for some of the city's most beautiful Byzantine frescoes and mosaics. In fact, with so much to do many visitors hardly leave the old imperial city at all; except perhaps to sample the nightlife around Taksim or for a ferry ride up the Bosphorus.

Haghia Sophia (Aya Sofya)

Haghia Sophia is like no other building in Turkey. Stepping inside the magnificent central hall you're struck by its scale and the immense passage of time since its foundations were layed by Byzantine builders a staggering 14 centuries ago. Church, mosque and for the last 70-odd years secularized as a museum, such changes are merely superficial with the colossal structure standing immovable and unchanging.

History

The walls were covered in 4 acres of decorative mosaics, designed to glitter in the light of thousands of oil lamps

Having brutally put down the Nika Revolt in 532 AD Emperor Justinian commissioned the architect **Anthemius of Tralles** and his assistant **Isidore of Miletus** to create a huge new church of unprecedented scale and grandeur. It was a massive project with 10,000 workmen toiling under a system of bonuses and rewards to increase their efficiency. Building material was sourced across the empire with new stone shipped from as far away as Algeria and antique marble looted from Ephesus, Delphi and Athens. Five years and 11 months after work began, and no doubt much to the relief of the architects who had no idea whether their radical design would actually work in practice, the incredible structure was completed. On stepping inside the church during the inauguration ceremony Justinian gasped in amazement, uttering the words: "*Glory to God that I've been judged worthy to complete such a monument. Oh Solomon! I have outdone you!*".

Indeed, for its time Haghia Sofia was truly revolutionary, a graceful dome hovering 54 m above the marble floor with the soaring interior completely uncluttered by supporting columns or piers. It became a major influence on architects in the proceeding centuries, although it was about 1,000 years before the Ottoman architect Sinan began to rival its achievements. Apart from a few structural problems, the dome collapsing 20 years after it was built and again in 1342 due to earthquakes, Haghia Sophia has survived the ravages of time remarkably well. It was a human catastrophe, the crusader occupation of Constantinople in 1204, which wrought the worst damage. During the sacking of the city the church was desecrated by the Latins with virtually everything of any value carted off.

The church was treated considerably better in 1452 after the Ottoman capture of the city, as Mehmet II proceeded directly to the church, falling to his knees in front of it and pouring

Haghia Sophia

1 Outer Narthex
2 Inner Narthex
3 Imperial Door
4 Coronation Square
5 Müezzin Mahfili

6 Mihrab
7 Hünkar Mahfili
(Sultan's Loge)
8 Library of Mahmut I
9 Pillar of St Gregory
the Miracle-Worker
10 Ramp to Gallery
11 Vestibule of Warriors
12 Mehmet the
Conqueror's Minaret

Not to scale

Istanbul

a handful of soil over his head in an act of humility. He promptly ordered its conversion into a mosque with a wooden minaret, later to be replaced with a more permanent brick one, added to the outside. Thankfully he also ordered the church's beautiful frescoes to be plastered over rather than destroyed and ironically this has helped preserve many of them to the present day. Successive Ottoman rulers added to it: a library constructed on behalf of Mahmut I and various mausoleums added outside. Haghia Sofia's 500-year interlude as a mosque was brought to an end by the republican government in 1932 when it was closed for renovations, opening two years later as the Aya Sofya Museum.

Recent concerns, particularly the deterioration of the mosaics of the main dome, led experts to begin a major conservation effort in 1993. They found that the metal pins driven into the ceiling in the 19th century to secure it had rusted, causing it to crack dangerously. They've also began the laborious task of removing hundreds of years of dirt and grime from the tiny pieces of coloured glass, or tesserae, which make up the church's mosaics.

The church From the gate at the southwest end of the church you proceed past an area littered with fragments of stone and marble to the entrance. Some of these pieces date from the fifth-century Theodosian church and were uncovered by German archaeologists in the 1930s. Passing through the Outer Narthex it takes a while for your eyes to adjust to the gloom but when they do you'll notice the walls of the Inner Narthex are revetted with beautifully patterned sheets of green, red and grey marble. Apart from the subdued light, you'll also notice the coolness of the air, a relief on a hot summer day. Three doorways lead from the Inner Narthex into the church's interior, the largest central one is known as the **Imperial Door** and was reserved in Byzantine times for the emperor and his entourage. In the lunette above the Imperial Door is a mosaic, uncovered during work in 1933, depicting Christ the Pantocrator seated on a throne, blessing an emperor prostrated at his feet. Stepping through this portal in imperial fashion, your eyes are pulled upwards to the apex of the vast interior, the fabled dome flanked by two semi-domes to its east and west. There's an amazing feeling of space inside the immense nave even with the restorers' scaffolding tower, a permanent feature since 1993, obscuring part of the view and it's easy to appreciate the wonder it must have evoked in Byzantine visitors.

Bringing your eyes back down to ground level have a look at the depressions worn into the marble floor on either side of the Imperial Door. These were made over the years by the chamberlains who would stand flanking the entrance during ceremonies. Walking into the centre of the nave the area of marble inlaid into the floor is known as the **coronation square** as it was here that the Byzantine emperors were crowned. Nearby is the *müezzin mahfili*, a raised platform from where mosque officials would read extracts of the Kuran, added in the 16th century. Obviously the Christian architects built their church with little concern for the direction of Mecca, so the *mihrab* marking the direction of the Holy city is out of line with the rest of the building. Another Ottoman addition to the left of the *mihrab* is the sultan's loge, designed to shield the ruler from the public's gaze while he was praying.

This is a good vantagepoint from which to look at the surviving **figurative mosaics**, which decorate the nave. These mosaics, along with more in the galleries upstairs, show biblical scenes and Byzantine royalty. High above on the ceiling of the apse is a large mosaic of the **Virgin Mary with the infant Jesus** on her lap. Lower down is a depiction of the Archangel Gabriel, part of his wing sadly missing, while opposite only a few fragments remain of the Archangel Michael. The four pendentives around the main dome were originally decorated with

It's staggering to think this structure is 1,400 years old, raised 1,000 years before the Blue mosque across the square

six-winged **seraphim**, angels which were believed to guard over the church and warn of impending danger. Added during the 19th century was an inscription in the apex of the dome, produced by the master calligrapher Mustafa Izzet Efendi. Mustafa Izzet was also responsible for the large hanging **medallions**, produced from camel leather and emblazed in gold Arabic letters with the names of Allah, the Prophet Mohammed and the first Caliphs.

In the south aisle (the far right-hand side of the building when looking from the door) behind a decorative metal grill is the **library of Sultan Mahmut I** which was constructed in 1739 to hold a collection of over 7,000 books and manuscripts, later moved to the library at the Süleymaniye.

On the opposite side of the church in the north aisle you'll notice two bulbous marble urns which are thought to date from Hellenistic or early Byzantine times. Used for ceremonial washing, judging from the grooves eroded into their marble bases by water dripping from their taps they've been around a while. Behind one of the urns is a column faced with copper known as the **pillar of St Gregory the Miracle-Worker**, or alternatively the 'weeping column'. Various legends are attributed to this column, one being that those inflicted with eye infections or blindness could expect a miraculous cure if they inserted their finger into a hole in the pillar and then wiped their eyes. A more popular story holds that if you insert your finger into the hole and make a wish, if it emerges moist then your wish will come true.

Also in the north aisle is the entrance to a ramp which leads up to the galleries in a tight series of switchbacks. Initially reserved solely for women, the galleries were later used by the royal family and church notables. They now harbour many of the church's best surviving figurative mosaics. The earliest of these depictions is high on the east side of the northwest pier. Dated to the 10th century it shows **Emperor Alexander** standing in ceremonial attire. On the opposite, western aspect of this pier is a bit of graffiti showing a sailing ship, which was probably carved by a bored Byzantine woman during an interminable religious ceremony.

The western gallery is where the empress would have sat, her throne positioned on the green marble circle in the floor. The south gallery contains more well preserved mosaics. Having entered it through the opening beside a pair of false marble doors, known as the **Gates of Heaven and Hell**, to the right on the west face of the pier is the **Deesis**. Although partly damaged, this beautiful 14th-century mosaic depicts a very serious looking Christ flanked by the Virgin Mary and St John the Baptist, who are both pleading with him for the salvation of mankind.

Continuing to the end of the south gallery there is a mosaic of **Christ with Emperor Constantine IX Monomachus and the Empress Zoe**. The Emperor is depicted offering Christ a bag, presumably filled with coins, while the Empress clutches a scroll reading: "Constantine, in Christ the Lord Autocrat, faithful Emperor of the Romans, Monomachus." Intriguingly, the Emperor's head and the scroll were altered sometime after the mosaic was finished and historians now believe this was made necessary by the convoluted love-life of the formidable Empress Zoe. Daughter of Constantine VIII, she was married belatedly at the age of 50 to Romanus III, who was probably originally shown in the mosaic with Zoe. However, Romanus III was found dead in the bath shortly after the wedding to be replaced shortly after by Michael IV, whom the empress also outlived, marrying her last husband Constantine. So in actual fact the mosaic we see today may have been changed twice.

One final mosaic of particular beauty is in the **Vestibule of Warriors**, now used as the museum's exit. In Byzantine times the emperor would have entered the church through this passageway leading onto the narthex, donning his crown and leaving his royal bodyguards, hence the name. Dating from the 10th century, the mosaic was buried beneath layers of plaster and paint and only re-discovered in 1933. It depicts the Virgin Mary sitting on a throne with the infant Christ on her lap and the Emperors Constantine and Justinian offering her models of Constantinople and Haghia Sofia respectively. This was a popular device for representing pious benefaction and can be seen in one of the mosaics adorning the Church of St Saviour in Chora.

Having emerged, blinking from the church's interior, the structure to your left was part of the sixth-century church that stood on the site, although it was used in Ottoman times as a mausoleum. There are several other Ottoman tombs in the garden including those of Murat III, Mehmet III and Selim II. The gorgeous Rococo şadırvan in the courtyard, with its overhanging roof, the underside of which is richly decorated with floral reliefs and gilding, is an addition from the mid-18th century.

■ *0900-1630, Jul-Aug 1700, daily except Mon. US$4. The entrance, garrisoned by salesmen and touts, is at the north end of Sultanahmet Meydanı opposite the Blue Mosque.*

Topkapı Palace

The palace is one of the most popular sights in the entire country attracting tens of thousands of visitors each year to wander through its many halls, apartments and pavilions. Topkapı doesn't immediately dazzle the visitor with its scale or grandeur, although its had its fair share of admirers including the 17th-century Ottoman chronicler Evliya Çelebi, who enthused: "Never hath a more delightful residence been erected by the art of man." Instead of one monumental structure, what you find is a collection of low buildings, notable for their lack of ostentation, grouped around a series of large, open courtyards. Even the most cursory of visits takes a couple of hours, though possibly much longer. The best strategy is to arrive early to get a head-start on the inevitable crowds and to secure yourself one of the limited number of tickets for the ever-popular harem tours. If you feel the need to be bombarded with facts and anecdotes, officially sanctioned guides waiting near the ticket office are available for private tours of the palace for US$20 per hour. ■ *Everyday except Tue, 0930-1630, 1530 for the harem. US$5.*

As well as its intrinsic historical & architectural interest, the palace is a huge repository housing a diverse collection of Ottoman & Islamic artefacts

History

Six years after his victorious entry into the city, Mehmet II ordered the construction of a new palace on the high ground overlooking the Bosphorus and Golden Horn. Originally car-marked for the rapidly growing Ottoman administration, the sultan later decided to take up residence himself in the palace, transfering his household in 1465 from the Eski Saray which stood on the site of İstanbul University. Occupied by successive sultans up until 1853, the Topkapı Palace was initially both the spiritual and administrative centre of the vast empire. The palace evolved gradually over the centuries, with its irregular and seemingly haphazard plan in fact a carefully considered expression of Islamic and Turkic traditions, and the practical necessities and ceremonies of the Ottoman State.

Orientation

The first courtyard of the palace, part of the public domain, was dedicated to services such as the palace bakery. Access to the second court which housed the Imperial Council was restricted to those on official business. Beyond, the third court was the preserve of government officials and members of the royal household, and was mostly taken-up by the buildings of the palace school which educated and trained the Ottoman bureaucratic elite. At the heart of the

İstanbul

Topkapı Palace

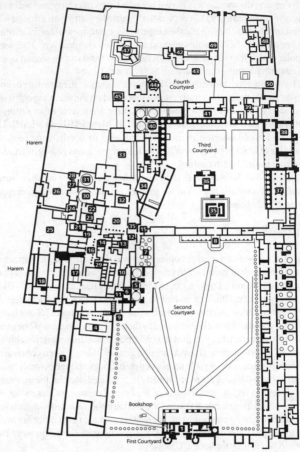

N

0 metres 20

0 yards 20

1 Orta Kapı
2 Cook's Quarters
  & palace kitchens
3 Privy Stables
4 Barracks of the
  Halberdiers
5 Divan
6 Divan Tower
7 Inner Treasury (collection
  of arms & armour)
8 Gate of Felicity
9 Carriage Gate & Harem
  ticket office

10 Court of the Black Eunuchs
11 Guard room
12 Harem entrance &
   gilded mirrors
13 Chief Black Eunuch's Quarters
14 Harem kitchen
15 Birdcage Gate (Kuşhane Kapısı)
16 Concubines Courtyard
17 Dormitories
18 Harem hospital
19 Sultan Ahmet Köşkü
20 Valide Sultan's Courtyard
21 Valide Sultan's Quarters
22 Sultan's Hamam
23 Valide's Hamam
24 Chamber of Abdül Hamit I
25 Harem garden
26 Terrace of Osma III
27 Ahmet III's dining room
28 Library of Ahmet I
29 Women's Hamam
30 Sultan's Quarters
31 Privy Chamber of Murat III

32 Kadın's Quarters
33 Selamlık & favourites
   apartments
34 Harem mosque & library
35 Throne room
36 Library of Ahmet III
37 Hall of Campaign Pages &
   exhibition of imperial costumes
38 Imperial Treasury
39 Museum Directorate
40 Pavilion of the Holy Mantle
41 Hall of the Treasury & exhibition
   of paintings & minatures
42 Kara Mustafa Köşkü
43 Tulip Garden
44 Rivan Köşkü
45 Circumcision Room (Sünnet Odası)
46 Iftariye Köşkü
47 Baghdad Köşkü
48 Mecidiye Köşkü & Konyalı
   Restaurant
49 Physician's Tower
50 Sofa Mosque

palace are the sultan's private quarters and the harem, an inviolate network of buildings where the ruler lived in relative isolation with his wives and concubines. The fourth court is essentially a walled garden with numerous pavilions dotting its terraces, its function dedicated to the pleasurable pursuits of the sultan. These various interconnecting courtyards were encompassed by a high defensive wall, breached along its length by several gates, one of which, Topkapı or "Cannon Gate", eventually lent its name to the whole palace.

The most commonly used entrance to the first court and the Topkapı museum itself is the Imperial Gate, or Bab-ı Hümayün, a monumental defensive portal just to the northeast of Haghia Sofia which has survived more or less intact, despite some major modifications, since the times of Mehmet the Conqueror. Above the portal notice the gilded inscriptions and imperial monograms, or *tuğra*, in flowing Arabic script that record work carried out on the gateway and palace at various times including during the reign of Mahmut II, the last sultan to live out his life in the palace. An inscription bearing the *tuğra* of Mehmet the Conqueror, also records the palace's completion in typically verbose prose: *"This is a blessed castle that has been put up with the consent of God and is secure and strong. May God the Most High make eternal the sultanate of the sultan of the two seas, the shadow of God in the two worlds, God's servant between the two horizons, the hero of the water and the land, the conqueror of the stronghold of Constantinople, Sultan Mehmet, son of Sultan Murat, son of Sultan Mehmet Khan, and may He place his position above the north star."*

The Imperial Gate
Presently guarded by a handful of army conscripts, in Ottoman times this busy gateway was permanently garrisoned by a contingent of 50 men. The alcoves on either side of the gateway were used to display the severed heads of those who fell from royal favour

İstanbul

Once through the gateway, the first courtyard is now an open area shaded by large plain trees and typically thronged by camera toting tour groups. In Ottoman days this would have been a bustling place dedicated to servicing the Palace and filled with workshops, storerooms, living quarters, the palace bakery and an infirmary for students of the Palace School. Today, there is nothing to be seen of these mostly wooden buildings, with the church of Haghia Eirene and the imperial mint beside it, left as the only survivors. At present neither the church nor the adjacent building which housed the **Imperial Mint and Treasury** are open to the public, although the former has in the past hosted concerts as part of the İstanbul International Festival. Next to the treasury a cobbled street leads down to the Archaeological Museum and Gülhane Parkı.

The first courtyard

Following the main pathway from the Imperial Gate across the first courtyard brings you to the **Gate of Salutations**, or Bab-üs Selam, more frequently referred to as the Orta Kapı (Middle Gate). Topped with crenallations and flanked by a pair of conical towers, the pale stone gateway resembles a fairy tale castle. This was the entrance to the inner palace as today it is for the Topkapı Museum, so before passing through the metal detector and having your bag x rayed, you'll need to buy a ticket from the office to its right.

Reserved predominantly for affairs of state, this courtyard has changed little since the times of Mehmet II, with paths fanning out across lawned gardens planted with upright cypress, plain trees and roses, and once roamed by exotic gazelle and strutting peacocks. Four times every week petitioners were given access to the courtyard to present themselves to the Imperial Council which occupied the building in the far left-hand corner when looking from inside the gateway. At such times the area was filled with ranks of Ottoman officials and a guard of honour numbering up to 10,000 strong, who stood in absolute silence, something commented on by several impressed foreign visitors. The courtyard was also the scene for more light-hearted festivities and displays held in the presence of the sultan on special occasions.

The second courtyard

The right side of the courtyard is bordered by a long portico through which several doors lead into the **palace kitchens** where food was prepared for the sultan, his retinue and members of the court and palace staff. This amounted to as many as 4,000 mouths to feed twice each day, a task shouldered by 1,500 chefs, 600 of whom were concerned with producing confectionery alone. Each of the 10 kitchens is a large, domed room surmounted by a tall chimney to vent the smoke from the ovens. Separate kitchens were reserved for the preparation of certain types of food or for particular members of the royal household, and when ready the dishes were relayed across the second courtyard to the harem and sultan's apartments by a line of over 200 waiters. Two of the kitchens formerly used to make sweets have been reconstructed with rows of brass pots and cooking utensils. Several other rooms now hold the palace's extensive collection of ceramics, mostly from China and the far east, which rates among the largest in the world. Opposite the kitchens several storerooms house an **exhibition of European glass and silverware** made in the imperial workshops or presented as gifts to various Ottoman sultans.

Across the courtyard from the kitchens, at the southern end of the portico, is the entrance to the **Privy Stables** which housed the Sultan's personal steeds. At the opposite end of the portico the Carriage Gate was one of the main entrances to the harem and is now mobbed by a long line of people waiting for their tour of the inner sanctum. Jutting out into the courtyard next to the Carriage Gate are the chambers of the **Divan**, the administrative centre of the Ottoman empire where the council of ministers would meet to discuss matters of state and receive petitions. Initially these sessions were attended by Sultan Mehmet II, however, he increasingly distanced himself from the day-to-day running of the empire, instead preferring to keep an eye on events in the Divan through a grill in the wall, known as "the Eye of the Sultan". Above the Divan rises a square tower, topped with a conical spire that projects skyward like a church steeple. Built in 1826 to replace a less elegant tower, the **Divan tower** (*1100-1400, US$3.50. Tickets from booth next to carriage gate in second courtyard*) gives a wonderful vantage point from which to survey the palace.

Another of the functions carried out in the second courtyard was the payment of Ottoman officials and Janissaries, which took place three times each year. The **Inner Treasury**, found next to the Divan, was used to collect the imperial income which flowed in from the provinces and dispense it in payments and salaries. The long room now contains the **collection of arms and armour**, with a varied assortment of exquisitely crafted Ottoman weaponry, some pieces made by the sultans themselves. At the eastern end of the second courtyard a portal known as the **Gate of Felicity**, or Bab-üs Saadet, leads through to the third courtyard. It was at this gate that the sultan, seated on a lavishly decorated throne, would receive the homage of his subjects on special occasions. In more turbulent times the Janissaries would march to the gate during their numerous revolts to present their demands to the sultan. Guarded by a troop of white eunuchs, no one was permitted through except for members of the royal household and a handful of high officials. Indeed the sanctity of the inner palace beyond was only violated once in nearly four centuries during a rebellion against Mustafa IV in 1808, when forces loyal to the crown prince, formerly Selim III, burst in to try and protect the heir to the throne.

The word harem derives from the Arabic for "forbidden". The harems inviolate status was carefully guarded by a troop of black eunuchs, whose leader, the *Kizlar Ağası,* was a powerful member of the Ottoman court. Essentially a palace within a palace, the labyrinthine network of over 250 rooms was home to the wives and concubines of the ruling sultan along with their female servants. These women and girls, generally of Christian origin, were captured in battle; procured from the slave markets of the empire or presented as gifts to the sultan. Having arrived in the palace they would be taught to read write, dance and sing, as well as practical skills which would be of use to them in their new life. Contemporary sources report there were 150 women in the harem of Selim the Sot, although this number grew substantially over the following centuries to reach nearly 700 by the 18th century. By no means all would have had intimate relations with the sultan. Only those lucky enough to catch his eye were set-up in private apartments to became imperial odalisques servicing his carnal desires, as well as entertaining him with song and dance. From amongst these concubines there would emerge a favourite, or *haseki,* who having born the sultan's eldest son would become the *birinci kadın,* or first woman. After the death of the sultan the *birinci kadın* as the mother of the new ruler would assume the position of *valide sultan* at the top of the harem's hierarchy.

Perhaps the best remembered favourite was Polish born Haseki Hürrem, known to the west as Roxelana, who stole the heart of Süleyman the Magnificent, becoming his *birinci kadın,* but more unusually as it was care for a sultan to marry at all, also his wife. Ambitious and manipulative, the indomitable Roxelana exerted considerable influence from behind the scenes, encouraging her husband to murder the grand vizier, Ibrahim Paşa, and the crown prince Mustafa, thereby clearing the way for her own son's accession to the throne. The precedent of strong, influential harem women set by Roxelana was continued by Nurbanu, the favourite of Selim the Sot, who encouraged her husband's debauched practices and effectively assumed control of the Ottoman administration, beginning a period known as the "Sultanate of Women".

The Harem Tour The harem is only open to visitors who join one of the official guided tours which depart every half an hour from the carriage gate in the second courtyard. It takes about 45 minutes to complete the tour. As one of the most popular sections of the palace long queues build up by mid-morning. The best idea is to proceed directly to the harem ticket office when you arrive and once you've bought your ticket you can head off for a look around. The groups are normally fairly large so as you're shepherded through the maze of apartments, courtyards and passages it's often hard to make out what the guide is saying. Don't be afraid of asking questions as the guides enjoy anything that breaks the tedium of spouting their well-rehearsed monologues.

Having entered through the **Carriage Gate**, so called because the women of the harem would only venture beyond it in a horse drawn carriage, you come into the guard room, its walls revetted with a stunning display of İznik tiles and the patterned floor made from coloured pebbles. Passing through this room you come out into the **Court of the Black Eunuchs**, where a contingent of up to 70 black guards charged with maintaining the harem's security lived. Generally bought by agents of the palace in the slave markets of Nubia, the black eunuchs were castrated before their arrival in İstanbul. Those that survived the operation and the journey were given ridiculous sounding names which reflected their virginity, "sweet and undefiled", such as Rose, Hyacinth or Narcissus. Enrolled in the palace school they would grow up alongside the royal princes and pages, before beginning their service in the harem. Their leader, the *kızlar ağası,* enjoyed unrivalled access to all the women of the harem

The Harem

A sequestered complex of apartments & halls reserved for the sultan & his female entourage the harem has long excited the western imagination

İstanbul

including the valide sultan, and from the time of Murat III became the most powerful official of the palace staff, frequently embroiled in the intrigues and power struggles of the court.

The entrance to the harem proper is at the far end of this courtyard, and is followed by a antechamber furnished with two flamboyant gold-framed mirrors. The tour then proceeds through a claustrophobic series of dormitories and apartments where the imperial concubines were quartered in less than salubrious conditions, leading to high rates of mortality amongst the women and their children.

A step up in comfort were the living quarters of the sultan's four favourite women which open off a long, narrow courtyard. Strategically placed beyond this, the apartments of the valide sultan were the centre of power within the harem. Next the tour passes into the sultans grand bath chamber where a pair of golden taps empty into a deep marble basin. It was here that Selim the Sot met a rather undignified end, slipping over and dying in a drunken stupor.

It comes as quite a relief to emerge into the spacious *selamlık*, the private quarters of the sultan much of which was built by Mimar Sinan in the 16th century. Without a doubt the grandest room in the entire harem, the **Imperial Chamber** was used by the sultan for entertaining female guests who would lounge on a low divan while the court musicians played on the balcony above. Another of Sinan's contributions to the harem is the **salon of Murat III**, which is decorated with İznik tiles and has a handsome bronze chimney. An elaborate fountain with water trickling musically into a series of marble troughs adds to the rooms appeal, however, this also had a practical purpose, masking any private conversation within the room from prying ears. Several adjoining rooms were added to this chamber by Murat III's successors, one of which is the **Yemiş Odası**, or "**Fruit Room**", which gets its name from the bowls of fruit painted onto the walls during the 18th century.

Next the tour passes the apartments of the Crowned Prince, known as **the Cage** or *kafes* in Turkish. After fratricide was abolished, it was common practice for the sultans to intern their male relatives within a secure apartment in the palace to remove any potential competition for the throne. Although this may seem like a step forward, initially conditions were far from humane, with the Cage's occupants imprisoned behind a high wall for years at a time. After such extended periods of confinement, often in fear of their lives, when the Cage's occupants were released on the death of the sultan, they were mentally and physically ill-prepared to rule. This led to a series of incompetent and short lived sultans such as Süleyman II, captive for 39 years, and his successor Ahmet II, a resident of the cage for 43 years, who between them ruled for less than a decade. Ahmet II's deficiencies are concisely summed up by a contemporary commentator: "*He affected to appear a lover of justice, though by reason of his stupidity, he could not perfectly discharge the function of a judge, and believed everything that his friends, bribed by the contending parties, represented to him.*"

Depending on the route you are taken through the harem you may also pass a large marble pool built during the reign of Murat III, where the more fun-loving sultans would frolic with their dwarves and concubines. A long paved corridor known as the **Golden Road** because sultans on ascending the throne would throw gold coins to their concubines assembled in the passageway, leads back to the exit of the harem, the **Kuşhane Kapısı**, or Bird-house Gate.

The Third Courtyard This was essentially a private area reserved for the sultan and his closest servants including pages enrolled in the palace school. In front of the portal stands the **Throne Room**, also referred to as the Chamber of Petitions, where the sultan gave audiences, received foreign ambassadors and approved decisions made by the Divan. Originally entered through one of two doors, a third being reserved for the sultan, you'll now have to satisfy yourself with peering in from outside at the richly decorated throne itself. Behind the throne room in the centre of the courtyard stands the elegant **Library of Ahmet III** constructed in 1719 of Proconnesian marble and adorned with a pretty ornamental fountain.

The **Palace school**, where young Christian boys collected in the annual tribute known as the *devşirme* were converted to Islam and trained to fill posts in the Ottoman bureaucracy and military, occupies many of the buildings around the third courtyard. The school was divided into six halls, with the preparatory halls where students received their initial education situated to the right and left of the Gate of Felicity. Having received a basic education promising students graduated to one of four vocational halls where they would receive further instruction. The first of these was situated in the building on the right-hand side of the courtyard, known as the **Hall of the Campaign Pages**, or Seferli Koğuşu, behind which were the school's main baths, the hamam of Selim II, where the debauched monarch slipped and fell, later dying of his injuries. Today, the hall houses the engaging **Exhibition of imperial costumes** which thanks to the practice of carefully preserving the garments of deceased rulers, has a wonderful selection of royal clothes worn down through the years since Mehmet the Conqueror. Among the most noteworthy are Selim I's pink and yellow spotted cape which seems incredibly gay for a ruler with such a grim reputation; the blood-flecked kaftan worn by the unfortunate Osman II, who met his end in the torture chamber of Yedikule, and a deep purple silk robe of Murat IV's.

Next to the Hall of the Campaign Pages, the two-storey **Pavilion of Mehmet II** was originally constructed as a suite of airy reception rooms opening off a wide colonnaded terrace, however, gradually the rooms were taken over by the Imperial Treasury. Today, the rooms are filled by the **Topkapı Treasury** and some of the densest crowds in the entire palace, attracted by the abundance of glittering jewels and precious metals. Among the highlights of the first room is a ceremonial chainmail suit encrusted with diamonds made for Mustafa III, while next door you'll find the Topkapı dagger, featured in the classic Peter Ustinov film *Topkapı*, its handle emblazoned with three huge emeralds, one of which lifts to reveal a hidden clock. Commissioned by Murat I as a gift for the Shah of Persia, the magnificent dagger never reached its destination due to Nadir Shah's untimely death. In the third room the Spoonmaker's diamond, which at 86-carats is the fifth largest of its kind in the world, is an inevitable crowd drawer. Nearby is a golden throne given to Sultan Murat III by the governor of Egypt and used by his successors up until the beginning of the 20th century. Many of the rest of the exhibits in this room, such as a pair of 1½-m high gold, diamond studded candlestick holders commissioned by Sultan Abdülmecid, cross the boundaries of good taste into the realms of the grotesque. Also on display in a glass cabinet are several bones said to be from the hand of St John the Baptist.

Across the courtyard the **Pavilion of the Holy Mantle** houses more holy relics, this time Islamic ones, which were acquired by Selim I during his conquest of Egypt in 1517. Above the entrance to the pavilion an inscription reads: "*The king of the world, the illustrious ruler. Sultan Ahmet, who follows the Holy Law.*" Decorated with beautiful İznik faïence, the domed halls of this building, only opened to the public in 1962, contain some of the most sacred relics of the Islamic faith and are the focus for pilgrimage from across the Muslim world. An object of particular reverence is the mantle worn by the Prophet Mohammed, hidden within a gold chest in a glass-fronted chamber next to which an *imam* continually recites passages from the Koran. Other relics include an imprint of Mohammed's foot in a piece of polished stone and hairs from his beard.

Next to the Pavilion of the Holy Mantle, the Hall of the Treasury contains the **Exhibition of Paintings and Miniatures**, a selection from the Topkapı's huge collection of over 13,000 miniatures. Following on from a tradition of miniature painting in Moghul India and Persia this became a popular artform in Ottoman times. Many of the exquisitely painted scenes were commissioned by Murat III, such as the *Surname* which depict events during the marathon 52-day festival held to celebrate the circumcision of Prince Mehmet.

The Fourth Courtyard From either side of the Hall of the Treasury passageways lead through to the Fourth Courtyard which is in fact a terraced garden dotted with numerous pavilions where the sultans idled away their time. The gardens were planted with tulips during the reign of Ahmet III and were the site of an annual festival held in April to celebrate the flowers blooming. It was an elaborate three-day affair with the gardens lit by hundreds of coloured lamps and filled with the sound of songbirds suspended from the trees in cages. Palace musicians and dancers entertained the sultan and his guests as they admired floral displays made especially for the occasion. It was extravagant events such as this, held regularly by the court and financed by the Ottoman treasury, that eventually lead to a violent uprising in 1790 which forced Ahmet III to abdicate in favour of his nephew Mahmut. There aren't any tulips left in the garden today, although the rococo **Kara Mustafa Köşkü** from where Ahmet would have surveyed his blooms is still standing.

To the south of the Kara Mustafa Köşkü stands a square, white building known as the **Physician's tower** because it was where the sultan's doctor would concoct potions and cures for the monarch and his household. To the north, standing at one end of a long portico, is the **Rivan Köşkü**. This portico was the site chosen for a musical organ presented to Mehmet III by Queen Elizabeth of England in 1599. The gift was delivered in the company of its maker, Thomas Dallam, who, while assembling the organ was given a rare tour of the sultan's apartments. The organ was a source of considerable wonder but was later destroyed by Mehmet's pious successor Ahmet I, who was offended by the figures which decorated it.

At the other end of the portico is the **Circumcision Room** (Sünnet Odası) constructed during the reign of Ibrahim I, known to his subjects as Deli (Mad) Ibrahim on account of his mental instability, no doubt the result of his 22 years of confinement in the Cage. The exterior is revetted with panels of beautiful İznik tiles which date from various periods including the golden epoch of Ottoman tilemaking during the second half of the 16th century. Flanking the Circumcision Room are a pool and fountain which were the scene for some of Deli Ibrahim's legendary sexual escapades. Conceived by Ibrahim during one of his more restrained moments and named after the evening meal taken during the holy month of Ramazan, the **Iftariye Köşkü** is a small balcony covered by a resplendent bronze roof which offers wonderful views over the tree-tops of Gülhane Park to the Golden Horn and Galata beyond. At the end of the terrace stands the most memorable pavilion, the **Baghdad Köşkü**, which was commissioned by Murat IV in 1638 to commemorate another of his military successes, the capture of Baghdad after a bloody five-week siege that cost the lives of 100,000 men. Decorated with İznik tiles, its wooden cupboards and shutters inlaid with exquisite mother-of-pearl, the building was a favourite retreat for Sultan Murat who in his latter years terrorized the palace with his psychotic behaviour, a trait that lived on in his son Ibrahim.

The **Mecidiye Köşkü**, built in 1840 by Abdül Mecit shortly before he abandoned the Topkapı in favour of the Dolmabahçe Palace, stands in a scenic position on a marble terrace overlooking the Bosphorus at the southern end of the gardens. On its lower terrace, reached down a flight of stairs, is a **café** and **restaurant**, where you can take the weight off your feet and enjoy a drink or some food while watching the ferries and ships plying the straits below. Not surprisingly this is a popular spot with tour groups so it gets very crowded around lunchtime.

Around the Topkapı

Before the Imperial Gateway leading into the First Courtyard of the Topkapı stands the Fountain of Ahmet III, a large square structure which is without doubt the city's finest Rococo street fountain. Commissioned by the fun-loving sultan in 1728, each of its four facets, shaded by a widely overhanging roof topped with five small domes, bears a tap surrounded by a richly carved facade. Penned by the Ottoman poet Seyit Vehbi, inscriptions on each of the faces compare the fountain's water to that of the sacred spring Zemzem, also praising its founder.

Fountain of Ahmet III

Spring water was not the only liquid dispensed, on special occasions silver goblets of fruit sherbet would have been offered to passers-by from the sebil, at each of its corners

From next to the Imperial Gateway a quiet cobbled street runs west between the outer defences of the Topkapı and Haghia Sofia. Soğukçeşme Sokak (Cold-spring street) is lined on its palace side with a row of *ahşap evleri*, the picturesque wooden houses, frequently ravaged by devastating fires, which once stood shoulder-to-shoulder along the streets of old Istanbul. Preserved by the Turkish Touring and Automobile Club in the 1980s, the pastel coloured houses, their windows covered with wooden screens known as *kafes* to frustrate prying eyes, are now run as the *Aya Sofya Pansiyonları* (see page 145). At the end of the row is a handsome Ottoman mansion, the Konut Evi, whose peaceful garden café makes an excellent place to relax during your explorations.

Soğukçeşme Sokak

A steep cobbled street leads down from the western end of Soğukçeşme Sokağı to Alemdar Caddesi, up which the modern tramway climbs from Eminönü. A gate in the walls here leads through to the Archaeological Museum and Gülhane Parkı which originally formed part of the outer gardens of the palace. It's now a popular place for *İstanbullu* to stroll, particularly on Sundays and public holidays when its paths are thronged by gaggles of sunflower seed nibbling youths. Within the park a pitiful collection of animals passes as a zoo, with an aquarium near-by interesting less for its finned captives swimming around in garishly lit tanks, than for the venue itself, which is a subterranean cistern of Roman vintage. Further north near the exit to waterside Kennedy Caddesi is a 15-m high granite monument known as **Goth's Column** due to the Latin inscription on it which reads: "*Fortune is restored to us by reason of the defeat of the Goths.*" Historians have speculated that this victory monument dates from the third century during the reigns of either Claudius II Gothicus or Constantine the Great. Crossing the coastal thoroughfare, Kennedy Caddesi, brings you out onto Saray Burnu jutting out into the busy waters where the Bosphorus and Golden Horn meet.

Gülhane Parkı

Descending down a flight of steps from the modern ticket office on Yerebatan Caddesi, there is little to prepare you for the serenity and grandeur of the city's largest subterranean cistern. Known in Byzantine times as the Basilica Cistern, the huge underground reservoir was constructed in 532 AD during the reign of Justinian to meet the growing water requirements of the imperial palace. Used throughout the Byzantine era, the cistern slipped into obscurity following the Ottoman conquest only to be rediscovered again in 1545 by Petrus Gyllius, a Frenchman investigating İstanbul's Byzantine legacy. His curiosity piqued by

Yerebatan Sarayı

İstanbul

the discovery that local people drew water, and occasionally fish, from shallow wells in their basements, the Frenchman succeeded in gaining access to the cistern through one of the houses above. The Yerebatan Sarayı was then brought back into use, providing the Topkapı Palace with water up until the end of the 19th century. Restoration work, including the removal of thousands of tons of

Sultanahmet

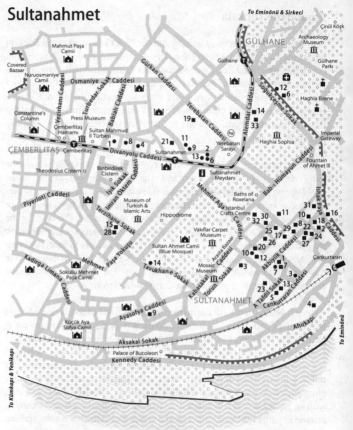

12 Hippodrome	31 Valide Sultan Konağı
13 Historia	32 Yeşil Ev
14 Hostel Merih	33 Yücelt Interyouth Hostel
15 İbrahim Paşa Oteli	
16 İshakpaşa	● **Eating**
17 İstanbul Hostel	1 Akdeniz Lokantası
18 Karasu Green & Restaurant	2 Amedros
19 Kybele	3 Balıkçı Sabahattin
20 Mavi Ev	4 Divan Pizza Shop
21 Nomade	5 Dubb
22 Orient Guesthouse	6 Lale
23 Sarı Konak Oteli	7 Magnura
24 Şebnem & Hanedan	8 Medrese Kafeterya
Guesthouse	9 Mosaik
25 Side & Pension	10 Rami
26 Spina	11 Rumeli Café
27 Sultan Tourist Hostel	12 Sarnıç
28 Turkoman	13 Sultanahmet Köftecisi
29 Universal Pension	14 Turkistan Aşevi
30 Uyan	

■ **Sleeping**
1 Acropol
2 Alp Guesthoue
3 Ararat
4 Armada
5 Avicenna
6 Aya Sofya Pansiyonlar
7 Bauhaus Guesthouse
8 Berk Guesthouse
9 Dersaadet Oteli
10 Empress Zoe
11 Four Seasons

mud which had accumulated over the centuries, was the prelude to the cistern being opened as a tourist attraction in 1987.

Despite the inevitable crowds, the huge cistern retains a magical quality enhanced by sensitive lighting and, at times, unintrusive background music. Walkways guide you past the majestic columns, 336 in total, which have been cannibalized from earlier buildings. An obligatory photo opportunity for most visitors are the **Medusa heads** exposed in the bases of two columns when the cistern was drained. Thought by some to be a shrine, their original position below the water line makes it more probable that they were simply re-cycled material from a previous structure.

■ *0930-1700 daily. US$2.50. The entrance is at the Haghia Sophia-end of Yerebatan Caddesi on the left-hand side when your back is to the Great Church.*

Around Sultanahmet Meydanı

The area between Haghia Sophia and the Sultan Ahmet Camii, known as Sultanahmet Meydanı, used to be the heart of Byzantine Constantinople. Today it is planted with formal gardens, criss-crossed by tourists walking between the sights around its perimeter and patrolled by persistent salesmen and would-be guides eager to offer their services. Its benches make an excellent place to sit and gaze at the staggering architectural monuments, the Byzantine church and the Ottoman mosque, left to commemorate the two empires.

On the opposite side of Sultanahmet Meydanı, standing between the Sultan Ahmet Camii and Haghia Sophia on Kabasakal Caddesi, are the Baths of Roxelana. Unfortunately for *hamam aficionados,* what would certainly be the grandest baths in the city is no longer in operation, with the building now housing a government-run carpet emporium. Built by Mimar Sinan at the request of Süleyman the Magnificent in 1556 and named after his wife Roxelana, the attractive twin-domed hamam was intended for the use of those praying in Haghia Sophia.

Baths of Roxelana

Also on Kabasakal Caddesi is the **Yeşil Ev**, a graceful Ottoman house carefully restored by the Turkish Touring and Automobile and now functioning as a hotel (see page 144). It has a lovely garden café/restaurant at the rear.

Ottoman house & seminary

Beyond the Yeşil Ev is the **Cedid Mehmet Efendi Medresesi**, a small Ottoman seminary restored in 1985. Dubbed the **İstanbul Crafts Centre**, the rooms opening off its pretty garden courtyard are used by artisans as workshops and showrooms. Traditional skills such as calligraphy, cloth printing and glass painting are all represented, giving visitors the opportunity to watch the craftsmen and women at work and to buy the finished products. ■ *0930-1830 daily.*

Sultan Ahmet Camii

The Sultan Ahmet Camii, known to western tourists as the Blue Mosque on account of the glorious İznik tiles covering much of its interior, stands magnificently across the formal gardens of Sultanahmet Meydanı from Haghia Sophia. For many the mosque, built for Sultan Ahmet I by the imperial architect Mehmet Ağa, stands at the pinnacle of Ottoman architectural achievement, however, paradoxically it was built at a time when imperial fortunes had already begun to decline. There was considerable opposition to the mosque's construction from those who viewed it as an extravagance the Ottoman treasury could ill-afford, while Mehmet Ağa's plans to adorn the building with six towering

İstanbul

Istanbul

minarets scandalized conservative elements of society, who viewed it as a sacrilegious attempt to rival the religious architecture of Mecca. Despite the objections, work began in 1609 with the sultan himself often taking an active role, working alongside the craftsmen and labours. The mosque was finished in seven years but sadly its enthusiastic patron died just a year later aged only 27.

The mosque

For dramatic effect the best way to enter the courtyard is through the gate facing the Hippodrome, from where you can fully appreciate the mosques wonderful symmetry & proportions framed by the tall, narrow portal

The mosque is approached via a large courtyard surrounded by a wide, domed portico and with a small hexagonal fountain at its centre. Ahead, the main entrance to the mosque is reserved for the congregation, with signs directing you around to the north entrance where plastic bags are provided for carrying your shoes and there are shawls for covering exposed legs and shoulders.

Inside, the mosque is almost square in layout with the soaring central dome, 43 m above the carpet, supported on four smaller half-domes, which are in turn flanked by a cluster of more semi-domes. The upper structure rests on four massive rubble-filled tiers, their size and squatness deliberately emphasized by the detail carved into their marble facing. Casting your gaze upwards the feelings of serenity and space evoked in mosques such as the Süleymaniye is lacking, although the intense decoration is nonetheless very impressive. Flowing arabesques, rather insipid copies of the designs original stencilled onto the inside of the domes, are flooded with light from scores of windows, originally glazed with Venetian stained-glass. Lower down the walls are enlivened with over 20,000 tiles produced by the artisans of İznik, a glorious display unrivalled in its extent. Closer inspection of the beautifully carved white marble *mimber* and *mihrab* is restricted by a fence which designates the area of the mosque dedicated to prayer, with the rich decoration beneath the sultan's loge, found on the balcony to the left of the *mihrab,* unfortunately also out-of-bounds to the lay visitor. Having surveyed the interior leave via the opposite doorway from which you entered. A mosque official collects voluntary donations while you put your shoes back on.

To the right as you exit, a stone ramp leads up to the **Imperial Pavilion**, used by the sultans and their entourage when they attended Friday prayer services and now housing the **Vakıflar Carpet Museum** (see page 135). A gateway beneath the pavilion leads down to the stables and an arcade of shops built in the 17th century to raise money for the pious foundations of the mosque. This arcade continues to fill its retail function as the **Arasta bazaar**, a parade of carpet, craft and souvenir shops staffed by silver-tongued salesmen.

The Hippodrome

Almost no trace remains of this huge Byzantine stadium which once filled the long square in front of the Sultan Ahmet Camii

An important focus of civic life in Constantinople, the Hippodrome was constructed as part of a city-wide building programme ordered by Emperor Septimus Severus after his sacking of the city in the second century. Later enlarged during the reign of Constantine the Great, a staggering 100,000 spectators are thought to have crammed into the arena to watch official ceremonies, games and chariot racing. These fiercely contested events became the expression for competition between rival political factions in the city, with "the Blues" associated with the wealthier, conservative citizens and "the Greens" supported by a more radical, lower class crowd. Temporarily united in opposition to Emperor Justinian, members of the two factions rioted in 532 AD. Much of the city was destroyed in the ensuing anarchy before an army of mercenaries commanded by General Belisarius restored order, massacring 30,000 rebels trapped in the arena in the process.

The Hippodrome was a huge structure 480 m long by 117 m wide with banks of seating rising up in tiers around the outside of an elongated track. The

Byzantine royalty watched events held in the arena from an imperial box called the *kathisma* which was connected directly to the Great Palace. Along the central axis of the stadium, known as the *spina,* stood a row of obelisks and columns brought back from across the empire. Three of these are left as the only conspicuous reminder of the hippodrome's existence. The northern-most is the **Egyptian Obelisk** dating from about 1500 BC and from Luxor some time in the fourth century AD. Thought originally to have been three times its present 20-m height, transporting even this fragment from Egypt must have presented enormous difficulties. The obelisk is set on a marble base into which are carved reliefs depicting Theodosius I and his entourage in the *kathisma* watching a chariot race; the emperor presenting the victors with a laurel wreath; prisoners paying homage to the emperor and the erection of the monument.

Nearby is the **Serpentine Column**, imported from the Temple of Apollo at Delphi by Constantine the Great. The column, consisting of three intertwined serpents, was dedicated to Apollo by 31 Greek cities in gratitude for their victory over the Persians in the battle of Plataea in 479 BC. Unfortunately, the monument lost its heads due to the actions of a drunken Polish official during the 18th century with one of the bronze pieces now on display in the Archaeological Museum.

The last of the extant ancient monuments to have decorated the *spina* is called the **Column of Constantine Porphyrogenitus** as it was the Emperor Constantine VII who restored it in the 10th century, encasing the dull masonry shaft in bronze. This embellishment was removed by the Crusaders along with anything else of value following their capture of the city in 1204. During the Ottoman era the area where the Hippodrome had stood was the centre of the Jannissary quarter and young soldiers would regularly climb the needle to demonstrate their bravery. A considerably less ancient structure is the fountain built to commemorate the state visit made by Kaiser Wilhelm II in 1898 found at the northern end of At Meydanı

Ibrahim Paşa Sarayı

A palatial residence given by Suleyman the Magnificent to his grand vizier Ibrahim Paşa in 1542, the Ibrahim Paşa Sarayı now houses the excellent **Museum of Turkish and Islamic Arts** (see page 135). The son of a Greek fisherman collected in the periodic levy of Christian youths, Ibrahim Paşa became close friends with the sultan while serving as a page in the royal household. Enjoying the sultan's approval the ambitious young man rapidly gained rank in the Ottoman administration serving as chief falconer and chief of the royal bedchamber before being awarded the grand vizirate. As grand vizier he displayed his considerable talents, not only leading the Ottoman horde on numerous campaigns but also amassing a huge personal fortune. In time his power grew to rival that of the sultan himself; a state of affairs that was unacceptable to both Süleyman and his scheming wife, Roxelana, and which ultimately brought about his strangulation at the hands of the royal mutes. The building later served as a dormitory, barracks and school with its balcony used by sultans as a vantage point from which to watch festivities held in the Hippodrome below.

Sokullu Mehmet Paşa Camii

The building was commissioned in 1571 by Sokullu Mehmet Paşa, who served as grand vizier under Süleyman the Magnificent, then enjoying unrivalled power and influence under his successors Selim II and Murat III. The courtyard, entered by climbing a steep set of steps from the street, also functioned as a *medrese* with the students lodged in cells beneath the surrounding portico and theology classes given in the hall above the staircase or the mosque itself. The most striking feature of the interior is the colourful Iznik faïence, predominantly turquoise in colour, which has been used to great decorative effect on

One of Mimar Sinan's most beautiful small mosques, Sokullu Mehmet Paşa Camii deserves more than the scant attention it receives from visitors to the city

İstanbul

İstanbul

the east wall surrounding the *mihrab* and the pendentives of the central dome. The spire of the *mimber* is also sheathed in tiles with fragments of black rock, said to be from the sacred Kaaba in Mecca, set into its marblework. Another fragment can be seen above the entrance, encompassed by beautifully painted arabesques. ■ *Getting there: Walk down Mehmet Paşa Yokuşu from the southwest corner of the Hippodrome, continue for about 200 m and the mosque is on your left.*

Küçük Aya Sofya Camii
Built in 527 AD, some five years before the Haghia Sophia, the building was later referred to as 'Little Haghia Sophia' because of its resemblance to the Great Church. In fact, although the two buildings are similar in overall form, each church demonstrates great individuality. The church has an irregular plan which allowed it to fit into the space available. The vaulted central dome is supported on an octagon of pillars around the top of which runs a beautifully carved inscription honouring Justinian, his wife Theodora and St Sergius, with mention of St Bacchus strangely missing. The gallery above provides an excellent view of the interior, which was lavishly decorated with golden mosaics and coloured marble facing. The building was converted to a mosque shortly after the conquest of İstanbul. ■ *Getting there: Walk down Ayasofya Caddesi which starts beyond the south end of the Arasta Bazaar. Alternatively, walk along the sea-front road past the ruins of the Palace of Bucoleon from Çankurtaran, in which case the church is reached by turning left after going under the railway tracks on Aksakal Sokak.*

The Palace of Bucoleon
It now requires a huge feat of imagination to conjure up the magnificence of a complex which dazzled medieval visitors to the city

A crumbling stone facade partially cloaked in vines and pierced by several large marble window frames is all that remains of the once magnificent Palace of Bucoleon. The palace was occupied for nine centuries by the royal court, only to be badly damaged during the sacking of the city by the Crusaders in 1261. Following the Latin interlude the palace was never restored for want of funds and the last Byzantine emperors ruled from the Palace of Blachernae built against the city wall in the northwest of the city. By the time of the Ottoman conquest the palace was in an advanced state of decay, prompting Mehmet II to quote a melancholy verse by the Persian poet Saadi as he surveyed the ruins following his triumphant entry into the city: "*The spider is the curtain-holder in the Palace of the Caesars, The owl hoots its night call on the Tower of Aphrasiab.*" The last five centuries have scarcely been any kinder with most of the Great Palace buried under new buildings, its constituent materials often reincorporated into other structures. The last remnants of the Bucoleon Palace are now sandwiched between traffic tearing along the coastal highway and the suburban train line behind, although the benches set in a small public garden at its base make a good place to contemplate its former grandeur. ■ *Getting there: On the seafront road, Kennedy Caddesi, 200 m east of Aksakal Sokak. Not warranting a trip in its own right it could be visited as part of an excursion to Küçük Aya Sofya Camii and Sokullu Mehmet Paşa Camii, possibly continuing along the seaside promenade to Kumkapı (see page 152).*

Sultanahmet to Beyazıt

Along Divanyolu
Walking west from Sultanahmet Meydanı takes you along Divanyolu, an important thoroughfare since Byzantine times and today the route of the tramline. A short distance along a left turn down Işık Sokak leads you to the **Binbirdirek Cistern** (Cistern of a Thousand and One Columns) which is reached via a staircase descending from a brick shack on the south side of a small municipal garden. At present the entrance is locked, so it's not possible to see what, at over 3,600 sq m, is the city's second largest cistern.

Opposite the *Piyerloti Hotel*, the imposing **Sultan Mahmud II Türbesi** contains the tombs of Mahmut II, the energetic sultan who succeeded in ridding the empire of the unruly Jannisaries, but whose efforts to revitalize the Ottoman Empire were ultimately frustrated. The baroque structure wasn't finished until a year after the monarch's death, which contemporary sources attribute to his addiction to fortified wines. ■ *0930-1630, daily except Mon*. On the other side of the street, a left turn down Piyerloti Caddesi, named after the 19th-century French novelist and Turkophile Pierre Loti, brings you down to the generally overlooked **Theodosius Cistern**. Situated beneath Eminönü Town Hall and reached via a doorway to the right of the main entrance, one of the employees hanging around during office hours will let you in and turn the light on. Constructed 408-450 AD during the reign of Theodosius II, the cistern is still in good condition with rows of marble columns supporting a vaulted masonry ceiling.

Continuing up Divanyolu brings you to **Constantine's Column**, raised in 330 AD to celebrate Constantinople becoming the capital of the Roman Empire. Originally standing at the centre of the magnificent oval-shaped Forum of Constantine, the decrepit extant remains are showing their considerable age. The statue of Constantine which once surmounted the column was brought down during a violent storm in 1106. Legend has it that a fantastic collection of Holy relics was buried at the base of the column during its inauguration ceremony including the axe used by Noah to build the Ark, the remains of the bread used by Christ to feed the multitude and pieces of the True Cross discovered in Jerusalem. The **Çemberlitaş Hamamı**, a 16th-century bathhouse constructed to plans by Mimar Sinan for Nur Banu, wife of Selim II, is still open for business on the corner (very touristy).

A right turn at the Column of Constantine takes you down Vezirhanı Caddesi, to the **Nuruosmaniye Camii**. Completed during the reign of Osman III in 1755, the mosque is one of the earliest examples of Baroque architecture in the city and although it demonstrates none of the refined aesthetics achieved during the classical period, the mosque was to set the trend for future buildings. A short distance beyond, **Mahmut Paşa Camii** (1462) is one of the oldest mosques in İstanbul exemplifying the early 'Bursa Style'. Beside the mosque is the octagonal tomb of its benefactor, Mahmut Paşa, a Byzantine noble who having converted to Islam served as the sultans chief minister for 20 years before finally losing favour and meeting a violent end at the hands of the imperial strangler. The large octagonal tomb, which is covered in blue and turquoise İznik tiles, is currently undergoing restoration work but should be open again in the near future.

Ottoman grave stones

High on the list of compulsory sights to be seen on any visit to İstanbul is the Covered Bazaar. Entered through one of 22 gates, the bazaar is a huge maze of covered streets, arcades and hans containing over 4,000 shops selling everything from cheap souvenirs to carpets, leatherwear to jewellery. Thought to be the largest retail area of its type in the world, the bazaar contains a school, a police station, banks, mosques, restaurants and cafés serving shoppers and an estimated 25,000 people employed

Covered Bazaar (Kapalı Çarşı)
Heaven on earth for the 'shopaholic', an exploratory wander can also be a fascinating experience for those who aren't in a buying mood

within its labyrinthine confines. Competition is stiff and the salesmen at their most persistent so be prepared to fend off a constant stream of leading questions and insistent invitations.

Built on its present site during the reign of Mehmet II, the character and function of the Covered Bazaar have changed surprisingly little over the years despite several catastrophic fires, the last of which swept through in 1954. Shops selling a particular type of goods continue to congregate in the traditional manner, although these groupings have become less rigid with time. Age-old trades have disappeared leaving street names such as Terlikçiler Sokat (Street of the Slipper-makers) and Fesçiler Caddesi (Street of the Fez-makers) as their epitaph, while the survivors have been joined by new shops selling modern manufactured goods and souvenirs.

Although much quieter now, the carpet auctions held in the hall every Mon & Thu at 1300 are worth a look

At the heart of the bazaar is the **İç Bedesten**, one of the few original buildings to have survived to the present-day. Originally used for storing valuable merchandise, its solid gates were kept locked and guarded at night. Today the İç Bedesten contains shops selling silver and antiques, while **Halıcılar Çarşısı** to the north is a good place to look for a carpet. At the junction of Halıcılar Çarşısı and Kuyumcular Caddesi, lined as far as the eye can see with gold merchants, is a quaint white kiosk built in the 17th century as a coffee house and now occupied, surprisingly enough, by a jewellery shop. A short distance to the north, **Zincirli Han** is one of the prettiest of the bazaar's 17 hans, some of which are still occupied by workshops producing goods for sale in the nearby shops.

Covered Bazaar

To Valide Hanı & Eminönü
N
Not to scale

If hunger strikes during your shopping expedition, you won't have to look far to find a snack bar serving-up sandwiches or döner kebap, or for a sit-down meal try the *Havuzlu Restaurant* (see page 153). If it's just a brief pit stop that you're looking for, seek out the traditional Şark Kahvesi on Yağlıkçılar Caddesi, or the trendy *Fes Cafe* on Halıcılar Çarşısı.

Tucked between the Covered Bazaar and Beyazıt Camii, the market has a long history stretching back to when the site was home to the Byzantine book and paper market, with the guild of booksellers counting itself among the oldest in the city. After the conquest, however, the markets original function changed as books, viewed by the Ottoman establishment as a corrupting influence, were outlawed. Turban makers and metal engravers replaced the booksellers and it was only the legalization of printing in the early 18th century that breathed new life into the Sahaflar Çarşısı. Despite losing some of their custom to modern bookshops and public libraries, the traders of the bazaar still ply their wares, selling everything from dog-eared novels to foreign dictionaries, watched over by a bust of Ibrahim Müteferrika, the Hungarian immigrant who set-up the first Ottoman printing press in 1732.■ *0800-2000, daily except Sun.*

Sahaflar Çarşısı
A small shady courtyard lined with second-hand bookstalls & shops

Standing aloof, set back from the chaotic traffic of Beyazıt Meydanı, the Beyazıt Camii was the second great mosque complex to be built in İstanbul. However, with the destruction of the original Fatih Camii during an earth quake in 1766, the Beyazıt Camii stands as the oldest imperial mosque. Completed in 1506, the building's carefully proportioned design was greatly influenced by Haghia Sophia, with a lofty central dome supported by two semi-domes. Unusual in its placing, the sultan's loge is found to the right of the *mimber*, supported on beautiful marble columns. Outside, the busy courtyard is paved with richly coloured marble with a pretty domed *şadırvan* surrounded by antique verd columns, at its centre. The tomb of Beyazıt II, who died suspiciously in 1512 having abdicated in favour of his son, Selim, lies nearby, along with the tombs of his daughter and the reforming grand vezir and leader of the 19th-century Tanzimat movement, Reşit Paşa. The *imaret*, which is thought to have served as a rest-house as well as a public kitchen, now houses the State Library, while the medrese at the western end of Beyazıt Meydanı is home to the **Museum of Calligraphy** (see page 136).

Beyazıt Camii

Standing on the site of the Eski Saray (Old Palace) constructed by Mehmet II as his imperial residence, the campus is entered through an imposing gateway overlooking Beyazıt Square. Nothing remains of the original building which was abandoned in favour of the Topkapı Palace in 1541 after a devastating fire. Rebuilt some years later, the Eski Saray served as the living quarters for the mothers, wives and concubines of deceased sultans, and so was commonly referred to as the 'Palace of Tears'. Today, there is no trace of this building either, with the university housed in a structure built by the French architect Bourgeois in 1866 to accommodate the Ministry of War. A hot-bed of leftist and, more recently, Islamic radicalism, the university has been the focus for often violent confrontation with the authorities, most recently involving students protesting against the ban on head-scarf in educational institutions.

İstanbul University

Situated on the campus grounds, the 50-m high **Beyazıt Tower** was constructed in 1828 as a fire watchtower. One hundred and eighty steps lead up inside the marble-faced structure to a gallery from where you used to be able to enjoy the best panoramic view south of the Golden Horn. Unfortunately, the tower is not open at present.

İstanbul

İstanbul

The Imperial Architect

*It's hard to go anywhere in İstanbul without bumping into something built by **Mimar Sinan**. This is hardly surprising as during his career he constructed at least 120 buildings in the capital alone, with another 200 scattered widely across the Ottoman empire. Not only the most prolific Ottoman architect he was also the most gifted, taking Ottoman architecture to new heights of style and grace.*

This remarkably gifted man came from humble origins: born to Greek or Armenian parents in the province of Kayseri, he was caught up in the annual levy of Christian boys, the devşirme, drafted into the service of the sultan. Having been converted to Islam, he received an education in the palace school before being selected in 1512 for service in the Jannissary Corps. He served as a military engineer on campaign with the army of Süleyman the Magnificent, gaining valuable practical experience, as well as inspiration from the various buildings he encountered in Anatolia and the Balkans.

Sinan must have impressed his superiors during his time in the Janisarries because in 1536 he was awarded the position of Court Architect, a prestigious posting which involved taking charge of

imperial commissions at a time when the empire was expanding rapidly. There certainly was no shortage of work, however, Sinan produced few exceptional buildings during his early years in the job, concentrating instead on civil projects such as caravanserais and bathhouses, bridges and aqueducts. The death of the Crown Prince in 1548 changed all that as Sinan was commissioned by a grief stricken Sultan Süleyman to produce the Şehzade Camii in his memory. Fifty years old at the time, he went from strength to strength, drawing on influences including Haghia Sofia to produce the finest work of Ottoman religious architecture to date, the Süleymaniye complex. Far from resting on his laurels, he went on to grace the capital and provinces with many other great buildings, including the Selimiye Camii in Edirne (1569-75), widely recognized as his crowning glory. Mimar Sinan continued working into old age dying in 1588, well into his 90s. Modest until the end, he was buried in a small tomb he'd prepared for himself on the grounds of the Süleymaniye Camii, a fitting place for a man credited as the father of the golden age of Ottoman architecture.

Süleymaniye Camii

Crowning the crest of a ridge above the Golden Horn, its massive dome and sharp minarets dominating the surrounding skyline, from afar the Süleymaniye is without doubt the most impressive of the city's imperial mosques. Set amid the well-kept gardens, it is a veritable town of buildings housing its various charitable foundations.

Commissioned by Sultan Süleyman, Sinan began work on what was to be his largest project in 1550. Built on part of the grounds of the Eski Saray, the huge construction project continued for over seven years with Mimar Sinan proudly proclaiming at the inauguration ceremony: "*I have built thee, O emperor, a mosque which will remain on the face of the earth until judgement day.*" Maybe a little on the optimistic side, the structure certainly hasn't weathered badly so far.

To enter the mosque you must first pass through a large rectangular courtyard which is surrounded by a wide portico supported on columns of porphyry, marble and pink Egyptian granite. Two pairs of minarets, said to represent Süleyman's position as the fourth sultan to rule from İstanbul, project skyward from each corner of the courtyard. Either side of the main entrance are the apartments of the mosque astronomer, one of whose duties was to calculate the daily times for prayer. In the centre of the courtyard is a small fountain, almost lost in the vastness of the enclosure, the main structure rising above it in a series of carefully balanced domes and semi-domes. The symmetry and understated grandeur of the exterior continue as you step through the narrow entranceway. The overwhelming feeling is one of space as your eye is drawn upwards to the lofty roof of the 53-m high central dome, part of which collapsed in the 1766 earthquake. The decor is suitably restrained except for the colourful stained glass windows, produced by the famous glazier Ibrahim the Drunkard, around the simple marble *mimber* and the baroque-style decoration added in the 19th century by the Fossati brothers.

Back outside, the small **tomb of Mimar Sinan**, who lived at the site for many years, is set in a triangular garden just outside the northwest corner of the outer courtyard. Around the corner from the tomb is a caravansarai, the first of the pious foundations which surround the mosque on its western and southern sides. Next along is the *imaret*, a large public kitchen which had the huge task of feeding not only the ranks of clergy, students and employees living within the complex, but also poor people from the surrounding area. The kitchens of the *imaret*, set around a peaceful courtyard shaded by an aged plain tree planted in 1550 at the time of its construction, house a restaurant. Turning the corner into Tiryaki Çarşısı, the "Market of the Addicts", so called because its cafés were once frequented by dealers peddling opium and hashish, the medical centre and sanatorium of the Süleymaniye *külliye* line one side of the quiet street. To the south behind a line of small shops and restaurants stand two identical *medrese*, the Sâni and Evvel seminaries, which contain the Süleymaniye library, an important collection of over 100,000 manuscripts and books. Within a walled garden to the east of the mosque, the tombs of Sultan Süleyman and his beloved wife Roxelana stand surrounded by Ottoman gravestones. Süleyman's *türbe*, which is also the last resting place of his daughter Princess Mihrimah and two later sultans, Süleyman II and Ahmet II, is a large octagonal building with a richly decorated inner dome supported on antique columns and walls enlived with colourful İznik tileswork. The triangular area beyond the graveyard to the east which presently serves as a car park was formerly the site of regular wrestling matches. ■ *0930-1630 daily except Mon.*

Eminönü

Beside the shores of the Golden Horn, Eminönü is a vibrant commercial district whose streets are permanently choked by day with traders, pedestrians and vehicular traffic, only to fall eerily silent when everyone has shut-up shop and gone home for the night. Historically the site of the city's docks, during Byzantine times the area was peopled largely by Genoese and Venetian merchants who enjoyed a privileged position within the empire due to generous concessions extracted from their Byzantine hosts. A large community of Karaite Jews, members of a sect which separated from Orthodox Jewry in the eighth century, also lived in the district, however, they were moved across the Golden Horn to Hasköy in order to make way for the Yeni Camii.

The streets that stretch up the hill towards Beyazıt and the Covered Bazaar is an area known as Tahtakale which still act as one huge and sprawling bazaar. Traders noisily hawk their wares, everything from plastic toys to metal tools, cloth caps to contraceptives from makeshift stalls or briefcases, and progress is often reduced to a shuffle by the sheer weight of pedestrian traffic. Being far too narrow and congested for motorized transport, goods are humped around the streets by *hammal*, porters who dart back and forth with boxes piled onto a wooden saddle on their backs. The **Mısır Çarşısı**, known to westerners as the **Spice Bazaar**, is the most distinguished of the markets, as well as being the areas biggest tourist draw. However, its historic partners, the fish and

İstanbul

vegetable bazaars, were moved to new sites in the 1980s in an effort to relieve the district's endemic congestion.

As a visitor to İstanbul it's practically impossible not to pass through Eminönü on your way somewhere else because of its pivotal position in the city's public transport network. A flashy new tram deposits passengers at platforms reached by darting beneath the traffic through underpasses lined with shops and fast-food joints. Crowded city buses leave from ranks on either side of the road to the west of the Yeni Camii, and ferries set sail from a line of quays on the waterfront.

Then there's **Sirkeci**, where the illustrious Orient Express pulled into town, and from where today, the rather less distinguished suburban trains depart. At rush hour the pavements are choked with commuters, serenaded on their way home by street musicians and tempted by vendors selling roast chestnuts or corn-on-the-cob. The smell of grilled fish hangs in the air, wafting from the boats moored up against the railings. At around a dollar, a sardine sandwich from one of these waterborne snack-bars, eaten leaning against the railings watching the show, is one of the most pleasurable, not to mention economical, snacks in the whole city.

Sirkeci & Eminönü

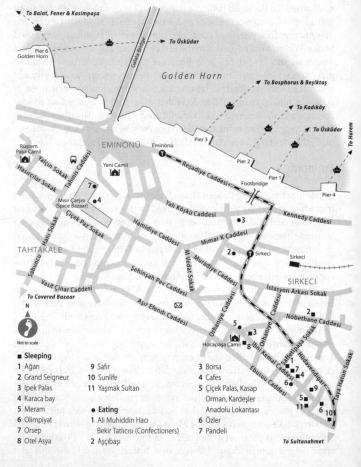

Sleeping

1 Ağan	9 Safir
2 Grand Seigneur	10 Sunlife
3 Ipek Palas	11 Yaşmak Sultan
4 Karaca bay	
5 Meram	**● Eating**
6 Olimpiyat	1 Ali Muhiddin Hacı
7 Orsep	Bekir Tatlıcısı (Confectioners)
8 Otel Asya	2 Aşçıbaşı

3 Borsa
4 Cafes
5 Çiçek Palas, Kasap
Orman, Kardeşler
Anadolu Lokantası
6 Özler
7 Pandeli

The Golden Horn

In typically pragmatic form the Turks have always called the gently tapering body of water which curves westwards from the Bosphorus the Haliç, the 'Estuary'. The origins of its more romantic Greek name Chrysokeras, translated into English as the Golden Horn, are however about as clear as the turbid waters themselves. It has been suggested that the name dates from the Ottoman conquest when terrified Byzantines hurled their valuables into the water rather than give them up to the rampaging Turks. It doesn't take a great leap of the imagination to come to a more plausible conclusion though, particularly if you've stood on the Galata bridge watching the evening sun set the water on fire as it dips towards the horizon.

Wherever the name came from, the Golden Horn is a wonderful natural harbour which has been used as such since the time of Byzas. As Constantinople's main port ships lined up along the wharfside to unload goods and slaves from across the vast empire. During the 16th and 17th centuries the dockyards at Kasımpaşa were a source of wonder to foreign visitors and as seaborn trade increased the Golden Horn became steadily more crowded. By the 1800s it was packed with caiques, dhows, coastal steamers and the warships of the Ottoman navy which anchored during the winter in its calm waters.

With a huge chain stretched across its mouth it was also a valuable defence, protecting the city's northern walls from attack until wily Mehmet the Conqueror came upon the plan of dragging boats over the heights of Pera from Beşiktaş. The Golden Horn's defensive function continued through Ottoman times, for although the city wasn't threatened by a marauding enemy until the 19th century, the water protected the good Muslims of the Old City from the temptations and sin of the Christian colonies to the north. The feelings of distrust and contempt were mutual and Europeans ventured across the Bosphorus by caique only to conduct business or to sightsee, returning to the comforts of Pera by nightfall.

As industry developed along its shores and the city's population expanded, the waters of the Golden Horn became anything but golden. Poisoned with sewage and effluent, the old Galata bridge, floating on pontoons, hardly helped matters by restricting the natural flow of water in and out of the Horn. The building of a new bridge and efforts by the municipality to reduce the flow of pollutants into the water have had some effect, however, it's still the unspoken nightmare of passengers jumping on and off the city's ferries to fall into its murky, smelly depths. Not that it's obviously polluted state dissuades the anglers who line the Galata Bridge from dawn until dusk pulling silvery fish from the foul water. And yes, they do eat their catch, although thankfully most of these are migratory species which live most of their lives in the more salubrious waters of the Black Sea or the Marmara.

Standing sentinel at the southern end of the Galata bridge, the Yeni Camii (New Mosque), or to give it its full title, the 'New Mosque of the Valide Sultan', was first commissioned in 1597 for the Valide Sultan Safiye, mother of Sultan Mehmet III. Safiye was a redoubtable woman who exerted considerable power in the Ottoman court in the face of her son's indifference to affairs of state. Progress was further slowed by the practical difficulties of building on a site so close to the water's edge and when Mehmet III died in 1603 the mosque was only partially completed. With Safiye banished to the Eski Saray, this was how it remained for 60 years until Valide Sultan Turhan, mother of Sultan Mehmet IV, decided to sponsor the buildings reconstruction. The court architect Mustafa Ağa was entrusted with the task and within a year it was completed.

Yeni Camii
Perhaps the most fascinating feature about the mosque is its human setting, permanently surrounded by a crowd of itinerant salesmen, worshippers & pedestrians; its front-steps thronged by sightseers & clouds of pigeons

İstanbul

Built towards the end of the classical epoch of Ottoman architecture, the Yeni Camii lacks the inspiration and grace of earlier imperial mosques. The ascetics of the building aren't helped by the grime from passing cars and ferries which collects on its pale exterior. Interesting features, however, are the three balconies on each of its minarets, from where a grand total of six *müezzin* used to call the faithful to prayer.

Mısır Çarşısı The Mısır Çarşısı, or Egyptian Bazaar, is a large L-shaped building just to the west of the Yeni Camii. Its Turkish name dates from when it was endowed with the customs duties from Cairo, although nowadays foreign visitors commonly refer to it as the **Spice Bazaar** on account of the large number of spice outlets occupying its vaulted arcades. There's also lots on offer besides, with shops selling everything from cheap watches and souvenirs, to Anatolian cheese and honey dripping from the comb. The eponymous spice merchants display their aromatic wares in colourful piles, everything from cinnamon to saffron; ready-mixed köfte spice to mysterious potions said to enhance the libido.

Rüstem Paşa Camii When it seems like there's no escape from the tightly packed crowds slip out the middle door of the Mısır Çarşısı and head west along Hasırcılar Sokak, you come across the peaceful courtyard of the Rüstem Paşa Camii, reached through an anonymous archway on the right and up some stone stairs.

Set on a terrace above the hustle and bustle at street-level, the mosque is the work of the masterly Mimar Sinan who was commissioned to build it in 1561 by Rüstem Paşa, grand vezir to Süleyman the Magnificent. Rüstem Paşa was known by the amusing nickname *Kehle-i Ikbal*, the Louse of Fortune, because his enemies had tried to stop him marrying Princess Mihrimah by spreading rumours that he was suffering from leprosy. When examined by the royal physicians it was discovered that he had nothing more serious than a nasty infestation of lice. He was given the green light to marry the princess and over the years used his privileged position to amass unrivalled power and riches, giving rise to the nickname *Kehle-i Ikbal*.

Some measure of the "Louse's" fortune can be gauged by the amazing display of İznik tilework which covers much of the inside of his endowment. Well-lit by daylight flooding in through the mosque's many windows, the faïence dates from a period when the tile-makers of İznik were producing their very best works. The panels include vividly coloured floral designs and a dizzying array of geometric patterns, using among other colours a rich red called "Armenian bole".

From the Mısır Çarşısı to the Covered Bazaar

This route takes you through the warren of narrow streets, dotted with historic hans, which is **Tahtakale**, eventually bringing you out near the Covered Bazaar. It's quite a steep climb, so you may prefer to explore this area after browsing around the Covered Bazaar. After leaving the Mısır Çarşısı progress is slow up Sabuncu Hanı Sokak (Street of the Soap-makers Han) which is usually choked with stalls and shoppers. Continue up this street past a row of toy shops, taking a right turn at the end on Çakmakçılar Yokuşu. This steep street leads up into an area of shops specializing in head-scarves and *yazma*, fine cotton cloths hand-printed with traditional designs. There's a row of particularly good shops on the left along Çarkçılar Sokağı which is aptly named the **Yazmacılar Çarşısı** (Market of the Cloth-printers). Just uphill on the left is a large gateway leading into the Büyük Yeni Han, a 18th-century han which is now used by fabric wholesalers. Continuing up on the opposite side of the street is the entrance to the **Valide Hanı**, the city's largest han which was commissioned in 1651 by Sultan Valide Kösem, the powerful mother of Murat IV and Ibrahim the Mad. In a state of atmospheric dilapidation, the han's central courtyard is occupied by fabric shops and dealers, many of whom are of Persian origin as the area was formerly an important focus for the city's Shiite community. About a 100 m further up Çakmakçılar Yokuşu, a left turn on Örücüler Caddesi brings you into the Covered Bazaar.

Beyazıt to the City Walls

Continuing west from Beyazıt Meydanı brings you into **Lâleli** and **Aksaray** beyond. Important areas for the rag and leather trade, the shops, hotels and wholesalers of this district cater predominantly for travelling entrepreneurs who flock to İstanbul from the countries of the ex-Soviet Union and Eastern Europe. Russian is the *lingua franca* in this part of town, with Cyrillic script sprinkled liberally across the shop fronts and travel agents advertising nightly departures for destinations like Sofia, Moscow or Baku. On the seedier side, this mercantile activity is accompanied by a service industry staffed by women from the aforementioned countries who work out of the cheaper hotels, bars and clubs.

Approaching the thick knot of roads which collide in a chaotic junction at Aksaray, the Lâleli Camii stands on the right-hand side of Ordu Caddesi. Designed by the accomplished baroque architect Mehmet Tahir Ağa, the Laleli Camii was commissioned by Sultan Mustafa III in 1759 shortly after he emerged from 27 years of captivity in the Cage. An attractive structure of brick and light-brown stone, the mosque conspicuously exhibits the growing European influences affecting the empire during this period, while inside the richly coloured marble decorating every surface strains the boundaries of good taste. Within the mosque's precinct are the tombs of Mustafa III and his luckless successor, Selim III, who having forced the pace of reform in the empire was deposed and killed for his efforts. Beneath the mosque a bustling bazaar fills a series of subterranean galleries, with the largest, central hall divided by thick pillars supporting the structure above.

Lâleli Camii

The 'Prince's mosque' and its attending civic buildings were commissioned by Sultan Süleyman in 1543 following the tragic death of his eldest son, Mehmet, from smallpox. As a fitting tribute to a young man who was set to inherit the Ottoman throne, the grieving sultan employed the services of the royal architect to build a mosque complex in his memory. The resulting structure, which Sinan described himself as his "apprentice work", is a lively one starkly at odds with the austerity of his later buildings. Red stonework and carving decorate the exterior, while inside the architect surrounded the central dome, supported on irregular shaped piers, with four semi-domes in an effort to increase the interior space. This symmetrical configuration was something of an experiment and, despite achieving its purpose, was never used again.

Şehzade Camii
Behind the mosque but not currently open to the public, are a series of tombs decorated with beautiful İznik tilework, the largest contains the remains of Şehzade Mehmet

Walking down Dede Efendi Caddesi beside the Şehzade Camii brings you into the working class area of Vefa which takes its name from Şeyh Muslihiddin Vefa, a 15th-century popular saint who devoted his life to the poor and is buried in a small *türbe* on Kâtip Vefa Caddesi. Also on Kâtip Vefa Caddesi is the **Vefa Bozacısı**, an İstanbul institution which has been serving *boza*, a thick drink made from fermented millet and topped with a sprinkle of cinnamon, since 1876. On the wall in a small cabinet is the glass from which Atatürk slurped during a visit earlier this century.

Vefa

İstanbul

Fatih Camii Commissioned by Mehmet II in 1463, the huge mosque and socio-religious complex which included eight *medreses*, an *imaret,* baths, a caravansarai, a hospital, and a primary school, was the largest of its time in the entire Ottoman Empire. Built on the site of the partially ruined Church of the Holy Apostle, burial place of many of the Byzantine rulers, the mosque's design was greatly influenced by Haghia Sophia. However, evidently its builders were under considerable pressure to out-do their Christian predecessors and Evliya Çelebi, the Ottoman chronicler, recounts how upon the mosques completion the sultan ordered the architects hands to be cut off for having failed to better the dimensions of the Great Church's dome. Inferior in scale, the original Fatih Camii also failed to match the longevity of Haghia Sophia, as it was destroyed by a violent earthquake which struck the city in 1766. Sultan Mustafa ordered that the mosque be rebuilt immediately, but this reincarnation was very different in character. Rebuilt in typically baroque style, the imperial architect, Mehmet Tahir Ağa, incorporated several parts of the original building that survived the earthquake, notably the porticoes surrounding the courtyard and the central *şadırvan* flanked by four tall cypresses. The colourful calligraphic inscriptions in İznik faïence adorning the walls at either end of the porch are one of the most outstanding features of the entire mosque. Inside there is less to get excited about with plain white tiles covering the lower walls and the upper reaches decorated with busy arabesque stencilwork.

The tombs of Mehmet the Conqueror and his favourite wife, Gülbahar, were also reconstructed after the earthquake in the graveyard to the east of the mosque. It was customary for new sultans to visit Mehmet II's *türbe* in the hope that such a pilgrimage would help them recapture their forefathers strength and courage, and indeed Fatih's resting-place continues to be a shrine popular with the citizens of İstanbul. Beyond the graveyard the Çorba Kapısı (Soup Gate), another beautifully decorated feature from the first mosque, leads onto the well-restored *tabhane,* a hospice for travelling dervishes. Flanking the great mosque stand some of the seminaries of the *külleyi* which at one time were occupied by as many as 1,000 students, however, no trace remains of the complex's huge caravansarai or hospital.

Today, the Fatih Camii is surrounded by a working class suburb of concrete apartment buildings to which it gives its name. A stronghold of religious conservatism, the feeling on the streets is a world away from that in the more progressive parts of town, with women universally clad in head-scarves and the black *chador* much in evidence. If possible time your visit to the mosque to coincide with the colourful Wednesday market which fills the surrounding streets with activity.

■ *0930-1630, closed Wed and Sun. Getting there: The Fatih Camii can be reached on buses 28, 90 and 91 from Eminönü; 90B from Beyazıt Meydanı or 87 from Taksim. Alternatively it is a 15-20 min walk from the Aksaray tram stop.*

The Greek Orthodox Patriarchate The Patriarchate has been situated at this site in the backstreets of Fener since 1601, however, despite remaining the spiritual centre of the Greek Orthodox faith, its ecclesiastical role has been marginalized by political events of the 20th century, with the mass exodus of Greeks after the War of Independence, anti-Greek riots and expulsions later in the century robbing the church of its flock. Today, inspite of the rapprochement in Greek-Turkish relations, the walled compound is accessed through a side entrance equipped with a metal detector. The main gate was welded shut in 1821 following the hanging of the Patriarch George V, found guilty of treason for inciting revolt against the Ottoman authorities. Within the enclosure the patriarchal church of St. George, a simple looking basilica built in 1720, contains a lavishly decorated pulpit, ostentatiously covered with gilding and adorned with Orthodox icons, while the Patriarchal throne is said to date from Byzantine times. ■ *0900-1630 daily. Getting there: On Sadrazam Ali Paşa Caddesi which starts across the road from the ferry landing in Fener. Catch bus no 99A from Eminönü or the 55T from Taksim, or use the hourly ferry departing from the Haliç quay to the west of Galata bridge.*

The mosque of Selim I is an attractive building whose shaded garden is popular with local people for its peaceful atmosphere and the sweeping views from its terrace, although tourist visitors are a rare species. Ironically, the building was commissioned by a sultan whose ruthlessness and barbarity earned him the epithet 'the Grim'. The inner courtyard is surrounded by a portico supported on an assortment of fine columns and enlivened by İznik faience in the lunettes above the grate-covered openings. The spacious interior, capped by a shallow dome pierced with stain-glass windows, is simply decorated with areas of beautiful İznik tilework. It seems the building was quite a sensation in Ottoman times for Evliya Çelebi reports: *"On examination, all mathematicians are astonished, for its dome is found to be one span wider than Aya Sofya."* Either side of the central prayer hall the smaller domed rooms are also notable as they are typically found in mosques of the earlier 'Bursa' period, when they were used to accommodate travelling dervishes. Particularly worthy of inspection is the fine paintwork and gilding beneath the sultan's loge.

In the garden behind the mosque are several tombs including that of Selim the Grim who died at the age of 50 having ruled for only eight bloody years. Among his more infamous achievements was the massacre of 40,000 Anatolian Shiites shortly before defeating the Shah of Persia in battle.

■ *Getting there: A 10-15-min walk from the Fatih Camii. Head-off north down Darüşşafaka Caddesi and then turn right on Yavuz Selim Caddesi. Alternatively you could take the hourly ferries from the Haliç quay to the west of the Galata bridge and get off at Fener, from where it is a 15-min walk up to the mosque.*

Selimiye

Hidden away in the backstreets next to a primary school, this multi-domed church built in typical Byzantine fashion from alternating courses of stone and red brick, was made the seat of the Greek Orthodox Patriachate after the Ottoman conquest. Late in the 16th century Murat III converted the church into a mosque to commemorate his annexation of Georgia and Azerbaijan, calling it the Mosque of Victory (Fethiye Camii). Despite some ruthless remodelling in the main hall of the building, a small side chapel adorned with beautiful mosaics survived relatively untouched. Created during the early 14th-century Byzantine renaissance, the mosaics on the walls depict saints and angels against a background of glittering gold, with Christ surrounded by 12 prophets staring down from the central dome. ■ *Getting there: Buses 90 from Eminönü and 90B from Beyazıt Meydanı pass near the church. Alternatively it is a 10-min walk from the Selimiye: leave the mosque by the northwest gate and walk up Sultan Selim Caddesi with the Cistern on your left, turn right at the end and continue down Manyasizade Caddesi for about 250 m to where it turns abruptly to the left and changes into Fethiye Caddesi. The church is reached down a narrow street on the right. To gain entrance to the side chapel requires written permission from the Directorate of Aya Sofya, located on the grounds of the Great Church in Sultanahmet.*

Fethiye Camii (Church of the Theotokos Pammakaristos) *It was to this church that Mehmet II came to discuss matters of theology with the patriach, Gennadius. The visits gave rise to rumours that the sultan was considering converting to Christianity*

Situated in a quiet residential area just inside the Theodosian city walls, the Church of St Saviour in Chora, known to the local Turkish population as the Kariye Camii, contains a priceless record of Byzantine art in the form of a whole series of beautiful frescoes and mosaics. Although the origins of the church go back much further, as suggested by the name "in Chora" which

Kariye Camii (Church of St Saviour in Chora)

means "in the country", the present structure dates from the late 11th century. Two centuries later the church underwent extensive reconstruction directed by the accomplished Byzantine intellectual and statesman, Theodore Metochites, with the mosaics and frescoes added between 1315 and 1321. However, with its conversion into a mosque in the 16th century, the church's exquisite pictorial decoration was lost beneath layers of paint, plaster and grime, only to be revealed 500 years later during a restoration programme conducted by the Byzantine Institute of America. The colourful depictions which have survived are largely concerned with the life of Christ, the series beginning with the dedicatory and devotional panels in the narthexes.

Yedikule   Mehmet II followed his victorious entry into the city with orders to repair the Theodosian Walls and raise a fortress inside them at their Marmara end. Garrisoned by about 50 troops, this stronghold became known as Yedikule (Castle of the Seven Towers) after the turrets which top its strong walls. Part of the Ottoman Treasury was secured in the keep with several of the towers functioning as prisons for luckless foreign emissaries and those who had fallen foul of the Ottoman authorities. Having entered through the small gateway, the Tower of Ambassadors on your left was one such place of confinement. Testaments of despair have been left carved into the stone around the outside by captives, giving the tower its other name 'Tower of Inscriptions'. Although the wooden floors have long since disappeared, you can climb up a dark staircase within its thick walls. A torch is very useful for exploring these passageways. Once at the top a walk around the battlements gives good views over the rooftops of the surrounding district and across railway lines to the **Marble Tower**, the southwestern conclusion of the land wall.

Across the courtyard, now overgrown with vegetation, the outline of a Roman triumphal arch, known as the **Golden Gate**, can still be recognized between two marble turrets. This monumental gateway was built by Theodosius I in 390 AD astride the *Via Egnatia*, an ancient thoroughfare leading into the city. Plated with gold and adorned with sculptures, it was through this resplendent archway that imperial processions passed following triumphs on the field of war. The tower to the left of the Golden Gate was used as a torture chamber during Ottoman times and among the grisly relics inside is the "well of blood" into which severed heads would roll.

■ *Getting there: The easiest way to reach Yedikule is by Banliyö train from Sirkeci or Çankurtaran. Having turned left after leaving the station, the narrow street brings you out near the entrance. If you have arrived by road you'll need to pass round to the city-side of the keep using the gate in the walls to the north (left) of the castle. Everyday except Mon, 0900-1700. US$1.25.*

The Theodosian Walls

Despite their semi-ruinous state the walls, stretching over 6 km from the Golden Horn to the Sea of Marmara, count among the most impressive legacies of İstanbul's past

Built to replace the earlier Byzantine defences, which by the fourth century had begun to restrict the city's growth, the ramparts were completed in 413 AD during the reign of Theodosius II. However, 34 years later much of this hard work was undone by a major earthquake which toppled 57 of the walls defensive towers. This disaster left the city completely exposed, and with the news that Atilla the Hun was baring down on the city with his Golden Horde, the entire population, even the mutually antagonistic Hippodrome factions, co-operated in the efforts to rebuilding the tattered ramparts. Within an incredible 60 days the landward approaches to Constantinople were secured not just by the single pre-quake wall, but also by a second outer wall and a 20-m wide moat. This formidable double curtain, guarded by 96 towers set at

50-m intervals along each wall and pierced by 11 gates, succeeded in repelling numerous armies over the next 1,000 years, finally succumbing in 1453 to the persistent attacks of Mehmet II. The conqueror promptly ordered the walls to be repaired and they continued to be well maintained up until the end of the 17th century. The modern era has been less kind to the slowly crumbling fortifications, with several wide gaps blasted in their length to allow the passage of railway lines and roads. Equally controversial has been the programme to restore, or rather rebuild, the walls, with many academics unhappy about the insensitive use of modern materials. On the positive side, seeing stretches of the battlements in something approaching their original condition gives us an idea of the huge effort needed to raise the wall, not to mention the manpower required subsequently to garrison it.

Today, the walls are flanked by intensively cultivated market gardens, tracts of wasteland and poor residential areas. For the enthusiast it's possible to follow the walls for most of their 6½ km length by taxi, dolmuş or on foot, using a path which weaves along parts of the battlements or walking in the streets running parallel. The best place to start such an expedition is at Yedikule (see above), from where the less-fanatical can walk as far as Belgrat Kapı or Silivri Kapı before catching a dolmuş on the main road outside the walls, onwards to Topkapı.

Exploring the walls alone is not recommended due to the relative isolation of certain sections

İstanbul

Just to the north of Yedikule Castle a Byzantine eagle carved from marble stands guard over the **Yedikule Kapısı**, through which competing lines of traffic are directed by a raucous official. From there you can follow a path along the main wall or the terrace below as far as **Belgrat Kapısı**, which gets its name from the prisoners forcibly settled in the district after Süleyman the Magnificent took Belgrade in 1521.

A tour

Onward to the next gate, **Silivri Kapısı**, the walls are also in relatively good condition. It was through here that a group of Byzantine soldiers forced their way into the city in 1261, beginning the recapture of the city from the Latins. The Byzantines called this portal the Gate of Zoodochus Pege after the sacred spring that survives to the present day surrounded by graveyards outside the wall. Called the **Balıklı Kilisesi** (Church of Fish) in Turkish, the waters of this shrine are held to have curative powers and were visited by successive Byzantine emperors on Ascension day. The spring maintained its significance through Ottoman times and its courtyard is filled with the tombs of Greek Orthodox clergy including several patriarchs. A small pool, reached down a set of stairs, contains fish which are said to have arrived miraculously shortly before the conquest of Constantinople. Legend has it that on hearing a monk profess that the chances of Constantinople falling to the Turks were as likely as fish coming back to life, the fish jumped from a frying pan into the pool. ■ *0830-1600 daily. Getting there: To reach the Balıklı Kilisesi head west down Seyit Nizam Caddesi which starts opposite Silivri Kapısı, bearing right after a short distance onto Silivri-Balıklı Caddesi.*

Unless you are particularly determined, the next leg north to the Mevlana Kapısı does not warrant continuing along because of the walls deteriorated condition. A dolmuş to Topkapı can be flagged-down on the main road outside the defences.

Under a kilometre beyond Mevlana Kapısı is **Topkapı** (the Cannon Gate), known in pre-conquest times as the Gate of St Romanus. It was against this part of the city's defences that Mehmet II concentrated fire from his specially made artillery piece known as Orban, with some of its huge stone projectiles preserved inside the gate. To the south of the historic gateway a gap has been torn in the walls to allow traffic to pass in and out of the city on the busy artery, Millet Caddesi. On the city side of Topkapı there are numerous cheap eateries and the **Kara Ahmet Paşa Camii**, a little known work by Sinan, is on the right as you walk down the street leading from the gate. Built in 1554 for the grand vezir of Süleyman the Magnificent, the well-proportioned mosque complex exhibits some lively İznik faïence decoration and a rare painted wooden ceiling. Topkapı is served by the modern tram giving access to Aksaray, Sultanahmet or Sirkeci.

Continuing to **Edirnekapı**, inside the city walls here, beside the ranks of buses in the belediye bus garage, the **Mihrimah Camii** sits atop a platform crowning the highest of the six hills in the old city. Another masterly work by the chief imperial architect Sinan, the *külliye*, which includes a hamam, a medrese, shops and a tomb, was commissioned in 1562 by the favourite daughter of Süleyman the Magnificent, Princess Mihrimah. Since its completion fate has not smiled on the complex with its various buildings sustaining major damage in two earthquakes, the last of which sent the mosque's single slender minaret toppling through the 37-m high central dome. Looking beyond the uninspired stencilling added during repairs carried-out after the last earthquake, the airy interior is well-lit by dozens of windows with some beautiful examples of Ottoman stained-glass. ■ *Buses to Edirnekapı include: 28 from Eminönü, 87 from Taksim, 39 from Eyüp.*

From Edirnekapı the Theodosian walls continue for over half a kilometre before being replaced by battlements added from the seventh century for the last stretch down to the Golden Horn. A short distance beyond the gate are the scant remains of the **Palace of Porphyrogenitus**, an imperial residence occupied during the final two centuries of the Byzantine Empire. The extant structure consists of little more than a grand three-storey facade built of limestone blocks alternated with courses of red brick, the rest of the building having disappeared in the intervening years. There is even less to see of the **Blachernae Palace**, another Byzantine palace situated where the fortifications near the Golden Horn.

Eyüp   Standing near the head of the Golden Horn, the suburb of Eyüp is home to the most sacred Islamic shrine in Turkey, the tomb of Eba Eyüp Ensari, companion and standard-bearer of the Prophet Mohammed. Legend has it that Eyüp was killed during the Arab siege of Constantinople in 674 AD and buried at an unknown location outside the city walls. Over 1,000 years later when the city was once again surrounded by a Muslim army, this time the Ottoman horde of Mehmet II, the sultan is said to have ordered a search for Eyüp's grave. Led by the *Şeyhülislam*, the most senior Ottoman cleric, this search miraculously uncovered a sarcophagus containing the man's remains. Although a pleasant story, other sources suggest that the tomb was never lost, and in fact enjoyed considerable respect during the Byzantine era. Whatever the truth, Mehmet II constructed a grand new tomb as part of a mosque complex raised at the site shortly after the conquest.

The **Eyüp Camii** enjoyed considerable importance during Ottoman times as the place where new sultans were girded with the sword of Osman, a ceremony that affirmed their ascendance to the throne. The mosque and tomb were joined by other elaborate mausoleums built as the final resting place for distinguished Ottoman citizens. By the end of the 18th century, however, the Eyüp Camii had fallen into disrepair, possibly as a result of the 1766 earthquake, and in 1798 it was torn down and replaced by the present baroque structure at the behest of Selim III. Today, the mosque complex has a well-kept air, with meticulously swept approaches, a wide cobblestone piazza and an ornamental fountain hinting at the generous patronage received from devotees. The mosque foundation, along with traders in the surrounding area, also profit from Eyüp's status as a site of pilgrimage for religious tourists from across Turkey and the Islamic world. Approaching the Eyüp Mosque complex on foot from the Golden Horn you pass several **mausoleums** set on either side of Cami-i Kebir Sokak. From the plaza just beyond you pass through an outer enclosure into an inner courtyard, partially covered by a colonnade. Two ancient plane trees are rooted in the centre beside the platform where the Ottoman sultans received the sword of their ancestors. An attractive structure of milky coloured stone and white marble, the mosque is nonetheless of secondary interest to the **türbe of Eyüp** which it faces across the courtyard. Many pilgrims direct their initial devotions towards the facade of the shrine, completely covered with İznik faïence panels. Having removed your footwear and donned suitably respectful attire, you may proceed into the vestibule of the tomb, also lavishly decorated with fine tiles, from where you can peer through a window at the sarcophagus itself. Once you have inspected the tomb and the footprint of Mohammed also on display in a glass case, leave via the exit at the far end of the vestibule.

■ *Getting there: The most pleasant way is on the hourly ferry which departs from the Haliç quay to the west of Galata bridge, US$0.70. Also bus no 99 from Eminönü, 55T from Taksim; 39 from Edirnekapı.*

North of the Golden Horn

Across the Golden Horn from Eminönü is the district of **Galata**. It rises steeply away from the waterline, a chaotic jumble of office buildings, warehouses and tenements topped by the conical, and rather incongruous looking, Galata Tower. The site of a Byzantine fortress guarding the Golden Horn since the earliest times, the area traces its origins back to 1261 when the land was granted to the Genoese as a reward for their help in reclaiming the city from the Latin Crusaders. They established a trading colony on the slopes beside the Golden Horn, which prospered and grew.

The Genoese were joined by Greeks, Armenians and Moors, along with a large influx of Sephardic Jews, welcomed into the empire by Beyazıt II to escape the Spanish Inquisition. Added to this colourful mixture were merchants, adventurers and seamen from across the Mediterranean, who arrived in town and decided to stay. Galata became the European quarter of the city, scathingly referred to by Turks as the Giaour City, the word 'Giaour' being a derogatory term for Christian!. However, many of these supposedly disapproving Muslims would cross the Golden Horn to escape the Islamic prohibition on alcohol strictly enforced in the old city. Indeed even in the earliest times Galata gained a reputation for its rowdiness and the 17th-century chronicler Evliya Çelebi wrote this description after a visit to the area:

When I passed through this district I saw many bareheaded and barefooted lying drunk on the street; some confessed aloud the state they were in by singing such couplets as these:
"I drank the ruby wine, how drunk, how drunk am I.
A prisoner of the locks, how mad, how mad am I"

The European powers established missions in the area and foreign merchants set-up trading houses. As the 19th century progressed, trade with Europe developed rapidly and many a fortune was made by the merchants. Fine European-style mansions, town houses and churches were built on the crest of the hill above Galata, an area which became known as Pera, after the Greek word

İstanbul

North of the Golden Horn

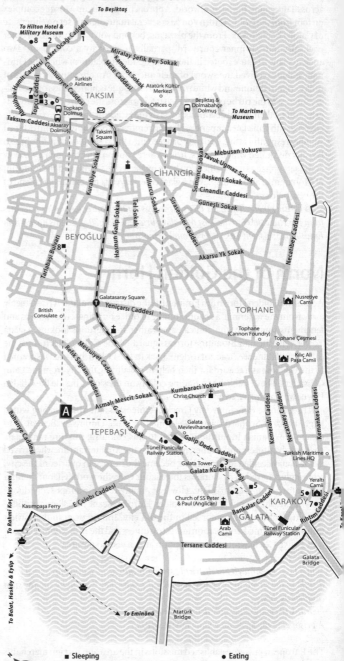

Istanbul

To Beşiktaş

To Hilton Hotel &
Military Museum

8   2   1

Miralay Şefik Bey Sokak

Asker Ocağı Caddesi

Camanrı Sokak

Mete Caddesi

Turkish
Airlines

TAKSIM

Atatürk Kültür
Merkezi

Beşiktaş &
Dolmabahçe
Dolmuş

**To Maritime
Museum**

7 6
3 6

Topkapı
Dolmuş

Taksim Caddesi

Aksaray
Dolmuş

Bus Offices

Taksim
Square

4

İmaml Hamit Caddesi

Cumhuriyet Caddesi

Topçu Caddesi

Mebusan Yokuşu

Tavuk Uçmaz Sokak

Somuncu Sokak

CİHANGİR

Başkent Sokak

Cinandir Caddesi

Güneşli Sokak

Kurabiye Sokak

Hasnun Galip Sokak

Tel Sokak

Billurcu Sokak

Sıraselviler Caddesi

BEYOĞLU

Tarlabaşı Bulvarı

Akarsu Yk Sokak

Nusretiye
Camii

Galatasaray Square

Yeniçarşı Caddesi

TOPHANE

Necatibey Caddesi

British
Consulate

Tophane
(Cannon Foundry)

Tophane Çeşmesi

Mesrutiyet Caddesi

Refik Saydam Caddesi

Kılıç Ali
Paşa Camii

Kumbaracı Yokuşu
Christ Church

Asmalı Mescit Sokak

G. Sofyalı Sokak

A

TEPEBAŞI

1

Galata
Mevlevihanesi

Galip Dede Caddesi

Bahariye Caddesi

4
Tünel Funicular
Railway Station

Galata Tower
Galata Külesi Sokağı

3

Kemankeş Caddesi

Necatibey Caddesi

Kemankeş Caddesi

Turkish Maritime
Lines HQ

Church of SS Peter
& Paul (Anglican)

2   5

5
7

Yeraltı
Camii

KARAKÖY

Bankalar Caddesi

GALATA

Rıhtım Caddesi

E Çelebi Caddesi

Kasımpaşa Ferry

Arab
Camii

Tünel Funicular
Railway Station

Tersane Caddesi

Galata
Bridge

To Rahmi Koç Museum

To Balat, Hasköy & Eyüp

To Eminönü

Atatürk
Bridge

Related map
A *Galata & Taksim
square, page 118*

0 metres   100
0 yards   100

■ Sleeping

1 Ceylan Inter-Continental
2 Divan
3 Dorint Park Plaza
4 Family House

5 Galata Residence
6 Lamartine
7 Otel Avrupa
8 Yonga

● Eating

1 Four Seasons
2 Galata Evi
3 Galata Tower
4 KV Café

5 Mevlana Et Lokanta
6 Ninja
7 Olimpiyat 1 & 3
8 Ristorante Italiano

for "beyond". In effect Galata and Pera became a separate Christian city, their residents rarely visiting Stamboul across the Golden Horn. The main street, the Grand Rue de Pera, now Istiklal Caddesi, was lined with shops selling western goods, while its inhabitants followed the latest European fashions. The contrast with the area across the water, where women only ventured onto the streets hidden behind thick veils and life continued much as it had done since the Middle Ages, could not have been more complete.

The 20th century saw great change sweep over Galata and Pera as the Armenian pogroms; the Treaty of Lausanne and the discriminatory taxes of the 1940s encouraged the areas ethnic minorities to leave. The final blow came in 1964 when the Turkish government retaliated against Greek involvement in Cyprus by expelling the Greeks of İstanbul. Losing its multi-ethnic population sapped the area of its vitality and what had once been a centre of Bohemian society reached a seedy nadir. Many of the grand 19th-century buildings were abandoned and fell into disrepair, while unplanned development continued unchecked.

Thankfully, however, in recent years Galata and Pera, known today as Beyoğlu, have pulled out of what looked like a terminal nose-dive and are undergoing something of a renaissance. New life has been injected into the area's main thoroughfare, Istiklal Caddesi, by its pedestrianization and it's now lined with clothing outlets, record shops, cinemas and a growing number of galleries. In 1989 the historic tramline from Tünel to Taksim was brought back into service adding both a useful means of transport and a feature of historical interest. A new generation of trendy cafés, bars and restaurants have sprung-up in the area, while many of the city's most happening nightspots are buried away in the narrow backstreets. Despite this superficial 'gentrification' once you're off the main drag Beyoğlu retains much of its dilapidated charm with its colourful street-life continuing remarkably unchanged.

Karaköy

At the opposite end of the Galata Bridge to Eminönü is the area of Karaköy which since Byzantine times has been an important commercial area. Known as Galata in Ottoman times, its streets were lined with trading houses and banks. Many of these buildings are still occupied by financial institutions today, although most are merely local branches as the regional headquarters of the country's main banks have relocated to more spacious and modern premise in the new city.

One of the larger buildings on Bankalar Caddesi, now housing a branch of the Central Bank, was the scene of a hostage crisis in 1896 when Armenian nationalists took over what was then the Ottoman Bank and threatened to blow it up if their demands for an autonomous homeland were not met. They later surrendered, however, the incident inflamed anti-Armenian feeling and resulted in massacres across Anatolia which left over 15,000 dead.

Karakoy still contains many shipping agents as well as the headquarters of *Turkish Maritime Lines* (Türkiye Denizcilik İşletmeleri), the state-run ferry company, which is a short walk east along waterside Rıhtım Caddesi from the Galata Bridge. On the way you'll pass a row of stalls where raucous traders peddle glistening fish from large trays and the air is filled with sea-gulls waiting to snatch any tip-bits thrown into the water.

Nearby in a maze of narrow streets is the **Yeraltı Camii**, or "Underground Mosque", which is reached down a set of stairs from street-level and was originally the cellar of a Byzantine castle built to defend the Golden Horn. Nothing remains of the keep except for the claustrophobic arched dungeons which

fill-up with men from the surrounding shops and businesses at prayer time.
■ *Getting there: Turn right off Karaköy Caddesi next to Akbank, and then take the second alleyway on the right.*

On the opposite side of Karaköy Caddesi, on Yüzbaşı Sabahattin Evren Caddesi, is the entrance to the **Tünel**, an underground railway built in 1875 to save the businessmen of Galata the steep climb up to Pera at the end of the day. Still operational, its old fashioned carriages shuttle the 500 m up to Tünel square at the end of Istiklal Caddesi every five to 10 minutes.

To the north of Yüzbaşı Evren Caddesi in an area crowded with tool shops and dotted with crumbling 18th-century Ottoman *hans*, formerly used to accommodate visiting merchants, is the **Arap Camii**. A solid rectangular building off Perşembe Pazarı Sokağı, its tall spire gives away its origins as a church, and in fact it was built in 1337 by the Dominican Order as the Church of SS Paul and Dominic. In the 16th century it was taken over by a group of Moors, hence its present name, who settled in İstanbul following their expulsion from Spain. Despite having been restored several times, it retains much of its original character as a Gothic church.

Returning to Perşembe Pazarı Sokağı, turning up the hill and crossing Bankalar Caddesi brings you to a flight of steps at the bottom of Galata Kulesi Sokağı. As its name suggests, this narrow street climbs steeply up to the Galata tower, however, you may prefer to catch the Tünel to the top of the hill and visit the tower on the way back down.

Tophane North of Karaköy the district of Tophane has several interesting monuments which most people only see from the inside of a bus or taxi heading up or down Necatibey Caddesi. Next to the busy road is the **Kılıç Ali Paşa Camii** which was commissioned by an Italian who, having converted to Islam, distinguished himself in the Ottoman navy, rising to the rank of High Admiral. Designed by Mimar Sinan in the year 1580 when he was 90 years old, the mosque is a scaled-down version of Haghia Sofia, however, it entirely lacks the majesty and grandeur of its predecessor.

Next to the mosque the **Tophane Çeşmesi** is one of the city's most beautiful baroque fountains. Dating from 1732, it's well worth getting up close as beneath the widely overhanging roof its marble walls are richly decorated with floral reliefs and fruit trees.

Having safely made it across the road walk up to the **Tophane**, or cannon foundry, which gives the surrounding area its name. Although a foundry has existed at the site since the times of Beyazıt II, the present building was constructed in the 17th century. Recently restored, the spacious interior has been opened to the public as an excellent venue used for exhibitions and cultural events by the Mimar Sinan University.

Further up Necatibey Caddesi on the right is the **Nusretiye Camii**, a strange looking mosque which departs from all Ottoman architectural tradition, instead blending various European styles. Designed by Kirkor Balyan, the first of a series of architects from this Armenian family to serve the sultans, it was called Nusretiye (Victory) by Mahmut II in celebration of his annihilation of the Jannissaries in 1826. Behind the mosque are several cafés which are crowded with local students and workers at lunchtime.

Hasköy Although it's hard to believe now, Hasköy, on the northern shore of the Golden Horn, was once an idyllic Royal Park favoured for its tranquillity by members of the Ottoman court. Today, the orchards and meadows have been buried beneath a sea of concrete with the only reminder of the past being an Ottoman Pavilion, the **Aynalı Kavak Kasrı**, which miraculously survives amongst the factories and warehouses. Restored in 1984, the royal summer

While you're in Hasköy you should also visit the Rahmi Koç Museum (see page 136) which is one of the city's more unusual museums

residence is thought to date from the reign of Ahmet III, although renovations were carried out later in the 18th and 19th centuries. Built into a slope, the palace's interior is lavishly decorated with an unusual double set of windows, decorated with colourful stained glass, along its seaward facade. The audience chamber is particularly beautiful, with a large brass brassier beneath a crystal chandelier in the centre of the room. As well as the period furnishings the pavilion is home to a collection of Ottoman instruments, the likes of which Selim III, an accomplished musician, may have played during his lengthy stays. ■ *0930-1600, daily except Mon and Thu. US$1.50. Hasköy can be reached on the Golden Horn ferry between Eminönü and Eyüp. The pavilion is just to the north of the ferry station. Bus no 47 from Eminönü and 54 from Taksim pass the approach road to the pavilion which is off Kasımpaşa- Hasköy Caddesi. Look out for the signs on your left.*

Galata

The Tünel disgorges its passengers where Istiklal Caddesi culminates in a small pedestrianized square: the turning place for the picturesque 1920s red tram which rattles its way down to Taksim square. It's an atmospheric area, with the dilapidated 19th-century apartment buildings giving the narrow streets and alleyways a distinctly continental feel. Antique book and map shops are gradually being joined by trendy cafés and bars, although the streets are still eerily quiet at night. From Tünel Meydanı Galip Dede Caddesi, named after a great Mevlevi poet and lined with shops selling musical instruments, heads steeply down the hill towards Karaköy.

At the top of Galip Dede Caddesi on the left-hand side, a gateway leads into the peaceful courtyard of the Galata Mevlevihanesi. The first Whirling Dervish *tekke* or lodge to be built in the city, it celebrated its 500th anniversary in 1991, functioning as a centre of education and worship for the followers of the teachings of Mevlana (see page 482) up until 1924, when all Sufi brotherhoods were proscribed by Atatürk. The *tekke* was reopened after extensive renovation work in 1972 as the Divan Edebiyat Müzesi (Museum of Divan Literature), with a collection of Ottoman poetry (Divan) on display at the site. The main 19th-century hall stands across the courtyard from the entrance and inside the polished hardwood floor where the *sema* (whirling ceremonies) were held is surrounded by a partly screened balcony for spectators. Beneath the balcony Mevlevi instruments and clothing are on display in cases. The *sema* is still periodically performed by a group of contemporary dervishes in the hall, however, this is officially a 'cultural event' rather than a religious one. Enquire at the ticket office about the next ceremony. Continuing down Galip Dede Caddesi from the Mevlevihanesi after a couple of minutes you'll spot the Galata tower between the buildings on your right. **Galata Mevlevihanesi**

The conical form of the 62-m high **Galata Kulesi** is a distinctive landmark on the Galata sky-line. It's also an excellent spot to head for a bird's-eye view over the rooftops of this part of town with access to the viewing gallery and restaurant (see page 154) by way of a lift or long spiral staircase. Originally called the Tower of Christ, the structure was built in 1348 as the highest point in the Genoese defences surrounding the colony of Galata. Rebuilt several times since, it functioned as a fire look-out post during Ottoman times. ■ *0900-2000, US$1.50.* **Galata tower**

In the shadow of the tower are several small antique and carpet shops, while narrow Galata Kulesi Sokağı dives down the hill between tall, ramshackled apartment buildings towards the Golden Horn. A short distance down on the left is a small café, the *Galata Evi*, which is housed in a renovated building that served as a police station during the British occupation of the city after the First World War. It's a quiet little place specializing in Georgian food which is a good spot to break your sightseeing, especially if you're slogging up the hill from Karaköy.

Beyoğlu

The city's principle shopping street, **Istiklal Caddesi**, cuts like a long canyon through the heart of Beyoğlu emerging at Taksim Square. For much of its length it is lined with shops blaring music, busy cafés and fast-food restaurants, however, there are also foreign consulates, churches and art nouveau buildings to remind you of its cosmopolitan past. Walking along its 1.2 km length from Tünel, the street becomes progressively more frenetic and crowded, although at first the atmosphere is sedate and calm. A number of free galleries dotting Istiklal Caddesi, many sponsored by the country's main banks, make a very pleasurable diversion (see page160).

Asmalı Mescit Sokak is a narrow street of *meyhane,* cheap hotels and frame shops which was once the haunt of a Bohemian crowd of artists and intellectuals including Salvador Dali and the celebrated Turkish photographer Ara Güler. Several of the local eateries, try *Refik* on Sofyalı Sokak or *Yakup 2* on Asmalı Mescit Sokak, are excellent spots to experience authentic meze and rakı culture.

Asmalı Mescit Sokak brings you out onto **Meşrutiyet Caddesi** near the fortress-like US Consulate and, to the right, the *Pera Palas Hotel.* Built in 1890 by the Belgian entrepreneur Georges Nagelmackers to accommodate passengers from the Orient Express, the *Pera Palas* was the finest, most luxurious hotel in the entire city. Its guestbook is littered with the name's of heads of state, politicians, poets and stars from the world of theatre and film. Agatha Christie was

Galata & Taksim Square

0 metres 100
0 yards 100

■ **Sleeping**
1 As
2 Büyük Londra Oteli
3 Devran Oteli
4 Dilson
5 Entes Apart Otel
6 Grace
7 Grand Star
8 Inka
9 Marmara
10 Mercure
11 Monopol
12 Pelikan
13 Pera Palas
14 Residence
15 Richmond
16 Saydam
17 Savoy
18 Silviya
19 Sultan
20 Taksim Square
21 Vardar Palace

● **Eating**
1 Afacan
2 Bursa Kebapcısı
3 Chan-ga
4 Çatı
5 Degustasyon Lokantası
6 Diknik
7 Ficcin
8 Galata
9 Hacı Abdullah
10 Hacıbaba
11 Huseyin Zihni
12 Indian
13 Lale Işkembecisi
14 Marko Paşa Şark Sofrası
15 Meşhur Selçuk
16 Nature & Peace
17 Pars
18 Refik
19 Rejans
20 Sanat
21 Saray Muhallebicisi
22 Şarabi
23 Tadım
24 T-Square
25 Yakup 2
26 Zindan

A night north of the Golden Horn

An atmospheric aperetif at the Pera Palas bar is a relaxed way to start the evening.

When hunger strikes head up Meşrutiyet Caddesi and take a right turn on to Balykoz Sokak which brings you to the Galata Restaurant where an excellent value set-meal is accompanied by fasil music and much cheer.

Stumbling up Istiklak Caddesi from the Galata, a left turn down Hamalbaşi Caddesi at Galata Square takes you to the Tarihi Pano Şaraphanesi (opposite the British Consulate) which has decent house wine by the bottle or glass and something of the atmosphere of an old Beyoğlu taverna. For another after-dinner drink the cool and very French-feeling Kaktüs Bar is a 10-minute walk further up Istiklal Caddesi on Imam Adnan Sokak (across Vakko).

Once digestion is well-advanced wander along Istiklal Caddesi to Zambak Sokak where you'll find Godet - a club/bar with the latest sounds from the world of techno and trance. If you prefer a more relaxed bassline get to the Riddim on Büyükparmakkapı Sokak (also off Istiklal Caddesi) and listen to some reggae. When it's time to get your dancing shoes on, a short walk down Sıraselviler Caddesi from Taksim brings you to Akarsu Sokak and the strobes and pulsating techno/trance of Milk. If this isn't your cup of tea stumble back down Istiklal Caddesi to Babylon where they have club nights until 0300, Wed-Sun (also an excellent venue to catch occasional live acts early evening). For a late bite there's plenty on offer around Taksim with a taxi back to Sultanahmet in the region of US$7.

a regular guest and it was during one of her stays that she was inspired to pen 'Murder on the Orient Express'. Other celebrated visitors included Atatürk, whose suite, no 101, is maintained in its original state as a museum, Zsa Zsa Gabor and Mata Hari, the infamous spy. The staff are happy to take you up in the creaky vintage lift and show you around; while the faded grandeur of the hotel bar or patisserie, where you can enjoy a pot of English tea, are excellent places to soak-up the nostalgic atmosphere. Continuing up Meşrutiyet Caddesi the ugly concrete exhibition centre on the left stands on the site of a 19th-century opera house. If you can't stretch to tea in the *Pera Palas*, the café on the far side of the terrace has good views down to the Golden Horn.

Further up Meşrutiyet Caddesi on the right, the *Büyük Londra Oteli* is another old survivor which was built around the same time as the *Pera Palas*. Despite the grand neo-classical facade it hasn't aged as gracefully as its neighbour, although the atmospheric bar complete with antique gramophone makes another nostalgic spot for a beer. Turning up the alleyway next to the Büyük Londra we leave the district of Tepebaşı and cut back to Istiklal Caddesi.

Across Istiklal Caddesi, hidden around a corner in Tütüncü Çıkmaz, is the **Fotografevi**, a gallery which exhibits the work of domestic and foreign photographers, and which has a café on the second floor.

Continuing a short distance along Istiklal Caddesi from Galatasaray Square, on the left, Sahne Sokağı is known as the Balık Pazarı or Beyoğlu's fish market. It's a busy covered street which, despite the name, is lined with all sorts of stalls selling spices and herbs, fruit and vegetables and fresh fish. It's an excellent place for a cheap snack as there is a row of chaotic places serving *midye tava* (fried mussels on sticks), *midye dolma* (stuffed mussels) and *kokoreç* (grilled intestines). A short distance into the bazaar on the left-hand side is the **Avrupa Pasajı**, a recently restored gallery of shops and upmarket delicatessen where Beyoğlu's expat residents come in search of hard-to-find delicacies such as pork sausages. While on the right, concealed between the shop fronts, is the entrance to the **Üç Horan Ermeni Kilisesi**, an Armenian church.

Balık Pazarı

Çiçek Pasajı   Next to the Balık Pazarı is the so-called "Passage of the Flowers", Çicek Pasajı, a narrow covered courtyard within the rococo-style Cité de Pera building. Originally lined with rough-and-ready drinking halls where the boisterous clientele would sit on barrels drinking rakı and snacking on offerings brought past by wandering street traders, since the buildings renovation in the 1980s things have been a bit more refined. The *meyhane* now have benches and tables outside, and diners, a large proportion of who are tourists, are serenaded by street musicians and hassled by hawkers. Unfortunately, its discovery by foreign visitors has been accompanied by a drop in standards and rise in prices, so locals-in-the-know now opt for *meyhane* further into the market area, such as those on Nevizade Sokak.

Taksim Square   Huge and rectangular, most people's first and most lasting impression of Taksim Square is the traffic, swirling around in the shadow of the *Marmara Hotel*, or for much of the day snarled-up on the approaches. Despite being the centre of modern İstanbul, unless you're waiting for a bus at one of the permanently crowded stops or eating in a fast-food restaurant there are remarkably few reasons to linger at all. One of these is the *Atatürk Kültür Merkezi*, situated on the east side of the square, which is the city's premier venue for concerts and the performing arts. You could also pop into the small **Taksim Sanat Galerisi**, a gallery next to the *Turkish Airlines* office on Cumhuriyet Caddesi which exhibits Turkish contemporary art. A coffee and a slice of cake at the *Marmara's* upmarket street side café could also occupy a bit of time.

Uptown: North of Taksim   Beyond Taksim, Cumhuriyet Caddesi heads north past many of the city's luxury hotels and the regional headquarters of TRT, the state broadcasting service, to the Military Museum (see page 136). At this point the traffic divides, with the right fork heading into the very upmarket residential and shopping area of Nişantaşı where alongside posh cafés and jewellery shops you'll find the likes of western chain stores such as BHS, Marks & Spencer, Mango, Top Shop and Espirit. The left-hand fork continues north through the shopping and commercial district of Şişli towards the affluent suburbs of Levent and Etiler.

The Bosphorus

A 36-km long channel varying in width from 660 m to 4,500 m the Bosphorus, Boğaziçi in Turkish, has always held an almost magical fascination for foreign visitors. Not only does it link the Sea of Marmara to the Black Sea, but it also divides the continents of Europe and Asia. So paradoxically throughout history it has been both an important route of passage and also a barrier to human movement. Legend has it that Jason and the Argonauts passed up the straits on their quest for the Golden fleece; while in 512 BC Darius, King of Persia, crossed its waters on a pontoon bridge heading to make war on the Athenians. The earliest myth concerning the straits recounts how Zeus transformed his mistress Io into a cow to conceal her from his jealous wife Hera. Unfooled by the deception, Hera set a gadfly on the heifer, forcing her to escape across the straits, an event which gave the Bosphorus its rather undignified name, "Ford of the Cow".

Porpoises are sometimes spotted swimming through the straits   Today, as in the past, the Bosphorus is a busy international waterway with a constant stream of ships and tankers plying the narrow straits. About 50,000 ships pass through the straits each year, 10% of which are tankers over 200 m in length which have limited manoeuverablility and require several kilometres to stop. Add to this pleasure craft, fishing boats and the dozens of ferries shuttling backwards and forwards between the two shores and it seems amazing that more collisions don't occur. According to the Turkish Maritime Pilots Association, in 1999 there were only 14 accidents in the Bosphorus, four of which were collisions. This is small comfort for campaigners, who rightly point out that accidents are happening with increasing regularity; a trend that will continue, they say, unless the government requires large vessels to take a local pilot on board to guide them through the tricky straits.

As well as its role as shipping lane the Bosphorus has a lighter side; providing İstanbul's residents with a release from their urban existence. On summer evenings the banks are lined with anglers casting-out into the deep blue waters to pull in their hooks loaded with wriggling fish. In the bright early morning flotillas of fishing boats bob off-shore; while later in the day families picnic along its banks or dine at tables overlooking the water.

Despite having been absorbed into the wider fabric of the city the suburbs strung-out along either side of the Bosphorus manage to retain a distinct character of their own. North of Ortaköy and Üsküdar the settlements have a village-like feel with stretches of woodland separating them and some of the city's finest surviving examples of vernacular Ottoman architecture: the beautiful wooden *yalı* built as summer retreats for the well-to-do. Today, these suburbs are still favoured by the wealthy with real estate prices among the highest in the city.

Ins and outs

The regular TML ferries working the Bosphorus route (*Boğaz hatı*) from Eminönü are designed for commuters not tourists; so in the morning ferries are heading into town, and only turn around again to head back up the Bosphorus in the evening. Of course these evening boats are perfect if you fancy a night out in one of the suburbs, but then you'll have to return by bus or taxi. Private commuter ferries, US$0.30, also operate between Beşiktaş and Bebek every 30 mins, 0745-0915 and 1730-2000, calling at Ortaköy and Arnavutköy along the way (timetables are posted near the jetties). There are several ferry services crossing the Bosphorus throughout the day further north. A useful one for visiting Anadolu Hisarı and Küçüksu Kasrı is the route between **Bebek**, on the European shore, and **Kandili, Anadolu Hisarı** and **Kanlıca** on the opposite side, 20 mins, US$0.50. From Bebek: 0900, 1000, 1200, 1330, 1445, 1635, 1730, 1830, 1845 and 1920. From Kanlıca: 0700, 0715, 0730, 0830, 0930, 1030, 1230, 1400, 1545 1700 and 1800. Another loop operates between **Çubuklu, İstinye, Paşabahçe, Beykoz** and **Yeniköy** every 30 mins 0715-1015; and then hourly 1445-1945. There are also private ferries between Yeniköy and Beykoz which leave when full.

Ferries
All services are restricted on Sun. An infrequent ferry service runs between Sarıyer, Rumeli Kavağı & Anadolu Kavağı

There are bus services operating up both sides of the Bosphorus as far as Rumeli and Anadolu Kavağı. It's a good idea to buy a supply of tickets before you set off and also to remember to check what time the last bus is, so you don't get stranded. Listed are some useful buses: **European side** 25E Eminönü-Sarıyer, 25A Eminönü-Rumeli Kavağı. **Asia side** 15 Üsküdar-Beykoz, 15A Üsküdar-Anadolu Kavağı, 101 Beşiktaş-Beykoz, 221 Taksim-Beykoz (double decker).

Bus

Useful dolmuş routes include: Taksim-Beşiktaş-Sarıyer, Üsküdar-Beykoz.

Dolmuş

A particularly nice stretch of the Bosphorus to walk along is between Arnavutköy and Bebek, which takes about 20 mins, and then on to Rumeli Hisarı about another 30 mins.

Walking

İstanbul

İstanbul

☞ *Up the Bosphorus*

*An excellent way of getting a taste of the picturesque suburbs and villages along the Bosphorus is the daily **TML sightseeing trip** (Boğaziçi Özel Gezi) up the straits. The atmospheric vintage ferries leave Eminönü (pier 3) three times daily Mondays-Saturdays in summer, usually at 1030, 1230 and 1400 (times may be subject to change, so check the day before). On Sundays there are more departures, however, during the winter the service is cut back to two daily boats at 1030 and 1330.*

After leaving Eminönü the ferries call briefly at Beşiktaş, Kanlıca, Yeniköy, Sariyer, Rumeli Kavağı and finally Anadolu Kavağı, about 1½ hours later, where there is enough time for a look around and

some lunch in one of the numerous fish restaurants. Keep your ticket to show to the inspector when getting back on. The ferries then return back down the Bosphorus, arriving at Eminönü during the afternoon. The trip costs US$6 per person and refreshments are available on-board. Make sure that you arrive early at weekends during the summer to secure yourself a good seat. In the winter don't forget to wrap-up warm as it can get very chilly out on deck. The whole journey, there and back, takes five hours.

There are also numerous private operators offering shorter cruises up the Bosphorus and you will undoubtedly be approached by touts trying to get you on-board.

The European shore

Strung out along the shore are a series of laid-back and progressively leafy suburbs. Ortaköy, for example, is a lively 'village' whose cobbled streets are dotted with bars, cafés and restaurants. To the north, Arnavutköy hangs on to many of its old Ottoman houses while a short walk away is the Rumeli Hisar, a castle constructed by Mehmet the Conqueror in preparation for his assault on Constantinople.

Dolmabahçe

Despite its indisputable scale & grandeur, the palace is overwhelming to modern sensibilities

Considering the Topkapı Palace to be out-dated and impractical in 1842 Sultan Abdülmecit commissioned Armenian architect Karabet Balyan and his son Nikogos to construct a new European-style imperial palace. The site chosen for the building was originally a small harbour, the one in fact that was used by Mehmet II to launch is amphibious attack on Constantinople. Over the centuries the inlet was gradually filled-in to extend the adjacent royal gardens, giving it its name, Dolmabahçe, literally "Filled garden".

By far the largest and most opulent of the Ottoman palaces constructed along the Bosphorus, the Dolmabahçe was finally completed in 1853 and the sultan moved in with the women of his harem and an army of attendants. The architects fusion of Oriental and European styles produces a tawdry, over-ornamented, result which strains the boundaries of good taste and leaves your head spinning. It seems that even 19th-century visitors, such as the French writer Theophile Gautier, didn't know quite what to make of it: *"It is not Greek, nor Roman, not Gothic, nor Saracen, nor Arab, nor yet Turkish."* The ostentatious display is harder to stomach as it belies the fact that the palace was constructed at a time when the Ottoman Empire, riven by internal revolt and besieged by aggressive foreign powers, was in terminal decline. The cost of construction was far beyond the means of the Ottoman treasury and the sultan borrowed heavily to finance it, helping to build up debts that would eventually bankrupt the state.

Opened to the public as a museum in 1960 having been restored, access is by guided tour only. The palace has a total of 285 rooms which according to Ottoman tradition were divided into the *selamlık*, where matters of state were conducted, and the *harem*, the private living-quarters of the sultan and his retinue. There are separate tours lasting 45-60 minutes of each section; or if you really want to overdose you can combine the two.

■ *0900-1600 (1500 Oct-Feb) daily except Mon and Thu. Tour of the Selamlık or Harem US$6, combined ticket US$10, camera fee US$6 (it's actually not worth paying this as photography is difficult in the low-light conditions inside the palace with tripods and flashes banned). Getting there: From Eminönü the palace can be reached on any Beşiktaş-bound bus (including 25, 28, 56). Taksim-Beşiktaş dolmuş pass the palace gates, as does the no. 40 bus. You could also catch a ferry to Beşiktaş from where it's a 15-min walk.*

Ihlamur Kasrı

If you have a passion for Baroque architecture, the evocatively named Ihlamur Kasrı, which translates as the 'Palace of the Linden Tree', is certainly worth a visit

Tucked away in a vale above Beşiktaş, this palace is in fact two separate pavilions which were once set in a huge area of parkland favoured for hunting and relaxing by the Ottoman sultans. The present buildings were constructed by Nikoğos Balyan in 1857. The Mabeyn Köşkü, or Ceremonial Pavilion, was used by the sultan and his guests, while the Maiyet Köşkü nearby was reserved for the harem. Built from sandstone and marble, the exteriors of both are embellished with ornate carving and the rooms inside, reached via a grand double staircase, are lavishly decorated in the style of the time. Set in a garden dotted with magnolias and camillias, the pavilions are now besieged by the city, however, sitting in the café it's still possible to appreciate what an enchanting spot this must once have been. ■ *0930-1700, daily except Mon and Thu. US$1.75, camera US$6. It's a 15-20 min walk up hill from Beşiktaş, or you may prefer to take a cab. Bus no 26 from Eminönü passes by.*

Beşiktaş

Centred on a bustling ferry terminal and an equally busy road junction where traffic clogged Barbaros Bulvarı climbs away from the Bosphorus, Beşiktaş is an affluent middle-class district which is home to one of the city's other two football teams. In Ottoman days it was an important port where the imperial fleet anchored and to remind us of this nautical past is the **Maritime Museum** (see page 137), to the west of the jetty beyond some public gardens. Also nearby is the octagonal **tomb of Hayretti Paşa**, better known as Barbarossa to the Christian sailors that he harried. A pirate of Greek descent, Barbarossa became a celebrated admiral in Süleyman the Magnificent's fleet, breaking Venetian naval supremacy in the Aegean and conquering large parts of North Africa. He is commemorated by a statue standing near the tomb, commissioned in 1946 on the 400th anniversary of his death, and on which is found a fitting verse penned by the poet and *Istanbullu* Yahya Kemal Beyatlı:

Whence on the sea's horizon comes that roar?
Is it Barbarossa now returning,
From Tunis or Algiers or from the Isles?
Two hundred vessels ride upon the waves,
Coming from lands the rising Crescent lights:
O blessed ships, from what seas are ye come?

The small stone and brick mosque on the corner of Barbarossa Caddesi is another one attributed to the prolific Mimar Sinan while across the busy road there's a lively **fruit and vegetable market** beneath a modern canopy.

Yıldız Parkı
& Sarayı

In a city with relatively
few areas of open space,
Yıldız Parkı provides a rare
opportunity to escape
from the noise & concrete

Early in his reign Sultan Abdül Hamit made the decision to move the imperial residence from Dolmabahçe. The motivations behind this move have never been fully explained, although the sultan seems to have felt uncomfortable and exposed in the huge waterside palace built for his uncle. Instead he decided to construct a palace for himself in the gardens of the Çırağan Palace which covered the hillside to the northeast of Beşiktaş. This extensive area of formal gardens and parkland had been a popular place for sultans to stroll and hunt since the 17th century, while in the 18th century it was the scene of some of the elaborate Tulip festivals attended by the court of Ahmet III.

The new sultan, shunning the excesses of his predecessors, lived in much simpler style in his new palace. Trained as a cabinet-maker during his youth, Abdül Hamit established a large workshop in the palace grounds which manufactured high-quality furniture to grace the imperial palaces; while in 1895 the Imperial Porcelain Factory, also on-site, began producing the European-style ceramics which were heavily in demand by the upper classes. During his increasingly autocratic reign the sultan effectively ran the Ottoman administration and government from the palace, building up a huge staff of 12,000 who were answerable only to him; evidence many say of his growing paranoia.

Yıldız Sarayı was built not as one building but rather as a collection of villas and mansions added to the pavilions, many constructed during the reign of Sultan Abdül Aziz, already dotting the park. Today, the main group of palace buildings and its former gardens, now a public park, form two distinct units.

Criss-crossed with meandering paths, its pleasant woodland and gently landscaped gardens are a favourite place for families to picnic and couples to court free from unwanted attention. Several pretty 19th-century pavilions scattered across the hillside received the attention of the Turkish Touring and Automobile Association in 1979 and are presently functioning as a café and restaurant. Entered by a gate to the north of the *Çırağan Hotel* you can walk up through the park to visit the various pavilions, or alternatively if you don't fancy the climb you could catch a taxi up to the gate on Palanga Caddesi which is near the Malta Köşkü, and then walk back down.

Beside a small lake to the northwest of the bottom entrance is the **Çadır Köşkü**, the "Tent-Pavilion", a neatly proportioned building with bright pink paintwork and shuttered windows. Despite its innocuous appearance, it served as a prison where the reformist politician and constitutionalist Midhat Paşa was confined after his conviction on trumped-up charges of murdering Sultan Abdülaziz. Now a café, its shady terrace is a perfect spot for a quiet drink.

Further up the hill, the **Şale Köşkü** is the most significant of the park's pavilions. Built in three stages during the reign of Sultan Abdülaziz, the first, resembling a Swiss chalet, was used by Winston Churchill and Charles de Gaulle during official visits. The adjacent sections were constructed to house Kaiser Wilhelm II when he visited İstanbul in 1889 and 1898. Entry to the pavillion is by official tour only with the guide drawing your attention to things of interest such as a huge Hereke carpet, the work of over 60 weavers, in the ceremonial hall. ■ *0930-1700, Oct-Feb 1600, daily except Mon and Thu, US$1.50.*

The **Malta Köşkü**, where Murat V was incarcerated for 27 years after being deposed in 1876, is now dedicated to lighter pursuits. Recently opened as a café and restaurant, you can sample 'Ottoman' fare in splendid period surroundings. Near the park gate the **Imperial Porcelain Factory** is still in operation, churning out mass-produced china; vastly inferior to the early pieces from the factory which grace museums and collections across the city. Tours of the factory can be arranged on weekdays for groups of more than five, however, your guide probably won't speak much English.

The **palace** itself is a 10 minute walk up Barbarossa Caddesi from Beşiktaş (not accessible from the park). Turn right on Ihlamur-Yıldız Caddesi and walk up past the Yıldız Camii to the end. Approaching the main gate the green **State Apartments** on the left date from the reign of Selim III. Once inside the courtyard, opposite you is the **Yıldız Palace Museum**, housed in a long building which was formerly the palace's carpentry workshop. On display inside is a collection of furniture produced by the 60 palace craftsmen, along with several pieces made by the sultan himself. Among them is a exuberantly decorated arabesque throne, covered with delicate carving and inlaid with mother-of-pearl. There are also some interesting old photographs including one of the sultan's entertainers – a motley looking crew of musicians, poets and dwarfs. Also on show is Sultan Abdül Hamit's smart European-style military uniform.

Next door in the **City Museum** you can examine a collection of fine porcelain and glassware well displayed in a grand marble-floored hall. Among the more curious pieces is a 19th-century glass walking stick, which judging from its chipped end was actually used. As you come out of the museum, the single storey neo-classical building in front of you was the palace armoury, or *Silahane*. More charming is the Adjutant's Department, a long building with wooden shutters and pretty carving work on its facade, which now houses the *Research Centre for Islamic History, Art and Culture*. Beyond it is a monumental gateway leading through to the palace harem; out-of-bounds to the general public today, as it was then.

■ *Yıldız Sarayı: 0900-1630, daily except Mon. US$2.25. City Museum: Open same times as palace. Free.*

İstanbul

On the waterfront between Beşiktaş and Ortaköy, the Çırağan Sarayı has had a very checkered history. Work began on the palace in 1855 during the reign of Abdül Mecit, however, it progressed at a snail's pace, only reaching completion 19 years later. By that time Abdülaziz had acceded to the throne, with the new sultan insisting the architect, Nikoğos Balian, add Arabic elements to the building's design, most conspicuous of which are the ornately carved stalagtite niches above the windows.

Despite all the effort and expense the sultan hardly used the palace, declaring it to be damp and uncomfortable. Ironically, two years after the Çırağan Sarayı's completion, Abdülaziz was overthrow and imprisoned in the palace, where on 4 June, 1876 he slit his wrists with a pair of scissors. His successor, Murat V, fared little better, as having shown signs of mental instability he too was replaced only months later by his brother Abdül Hamit.

The ill-fated palace lay abandoned and derelict for the next 30 years, enjoying a brief upturn in its fortunes in 1908 when it was chosen as the site of the new Turkish Parliament. However, two years later disaster struck and the palace was gutted by fire. And so it remained, a smoke-blackened shell, for nearly 75 years until in 1986 the German Kempinski group redeveloped it as a luxury hotel.

Today, the palace is rather eclipsed by the modern buildings of the hotel, however, the exterior has been lovingly returned to its original state. The building now contains 12 luxurious suites, but the hideously over-the-top decor is far from authentic. The Çırağan's Bosphorus-side swimming pool is certainly the city's most spectacular and is open to non-residents for a fee; with the well-recommended Sunday buffet brunch on the terrace nearby as another good excuse to pop-in for a look around.

■ *The Çırağan Palace is a 10-min walk along Çırağan Caddesi from Beşiktaş. Alternatively, jump on any bus from Beşiktaş which passes through Ortaköy (25E, 40).*

Çırağan Sarayı
No expense was spared during the construction: the final bill reached 5,000,000 gold lira, a staggering sum at the time, particularly in view of the parlous state of Ottoman finances

☞ *Bosphorus nights*

There's no better way to spend a summer night than to cruise up the Bosphorus on one of the evening commuter ferries which depart regularly from Eminönü pier no 3. The journey to Bebek takes about 30 minutes.

Once back on dry land buy a couple of cans of Efes in Bebek and walk towards Arnavutköy swigging your beer while watching the fishermen from one of the benches along the way.

In Arnavutköy check the times of the private ferries down to Ortaköy displayed on a board south of the picturesque old jetty, before having a nose around the charming backstreets. If you're after an appetizer try a plate of highly rated köfte

at Ali Baba, one block back from the front. Then on to Ortaköy.

Here, a row of stalls on Isele Sokak provides ample choice for snackers on a budget, although the Bodrum on the square is an excellent spot for a relaxed dinner of meze and fish in view of the lovely Mecidiye Camil and Atatürk bridge.

If you're going strong and you're wallet can take the strain, hop in a cab up to where the swanky Instanbullu dance at Scene or Laila. A cab home after midnight is about US$10 to Sultanahmet, US$5 to Taksim, though up until midnight there are occasional buses (40 to Taksim; 25E to Eminönü).

Ortaköy

Most evenings it's packed with a young, affluent crowd who flock to a row of fish restaurants & cafés overlooking the Bosphorus

Once a small fishing village with a large Jewish and Christian community, Ortaköy has metamorphosed in recent years into a fashionable area crowded with trendy cafés, shops and bars. Narrow cobbled streets, which on Sunday are lined with stalls selling jewellery and handicrafts, lead down to a waterside square and ferry station. On a promontory to the north, strikingly juxtaposed against the Atatürk bridge and beautifully illuminated at night, stands the **Mecidiye Camii**. Built in 1855 by Nikogos Balyan, the Armenian architect responsible for the Dolmabahçe, the mosque avoids the gross ostentation of the palace and is instead one of the city's most graceful Baroque buildings. The café behind the mosque makes an excellent place to enjoy the cooling sea breeze, while the local boatmen's association arrange lightning **tours of the middle Bosphorus suburbs** leaving from nearby every 20 minutes on summer afternoons, US$2.

Also to the north of the mosque and partially hidden behind a high wall are the skeletal remains of the **Küçük Esma Sultan Sarayı**, a 17th-century palace named after its most infamous resident, Küçük Esma Sultan, the daughter of Sultan Abdülhamit. Married to an important court official at the age of 14, Küçük Esma Sultan was widowed a decade later. However, instead of remarrying as was customary for Ottoman princesses, she embarked on a scandalous life of debauchery and excess more commonly associated with the sultan and his harem. Gutted by fire in 1975, the palace is now a venue for weddings, receptions and circumcision parties, a use its former owner would surely have approved of.

Back up on the main road and surrounded by a perennial traffic jam is a handsome double-domed **hamam** built in the 16th century by the masterly Mimar Sinan. Similar to the Baths of Roxelana in Sultanahmet it had separate sections for men and women, although the layout within is quite unique. Owned by the nearby *Princess Hotel*, restoration work on the building has recently been completed with plans to use the interior as some kind of cultural or exhibition centre.

■ *Getting there: Reached on bus no 25E from Eminönü, or no 40 from Taksim. The commuter ferries between Beşiktaş and Bebek, which pull in beside the ferry station every 30 mins during the morning and evening are a much more pleasurable way to arrive.*

Having escaped the confines of Ortaköy the traffic thunders beneath the 1,074-m long, 64-m high, Atatürk Köprüsü which was completed in 1973 for the 50th anniversary of the Turkish Republic. Beyond the bridge the journey north to **Kuruçeşme**, the next Bosphorus suburb, is fairly unremarkable except for a series of lavish nightclubs where the cream of İstanbul society come to prance, pose and pay-out extortionate sums of cash for the privilege. Apart from some very attractive wooden houses on the hill above the road, the main points of interest in Kuruçeşme are historical as it was the site of an important church dedicated to the Archangel Michael, built by Constantine the Great early in the fourth century. A century later Simeon the Stylite, a column sitting Christian ascetic, squatted on top of a pillar here for 27 years, attracting large crowds to share in his enlightenment. Nothing now remains of the pillar or the church which was demolished by Mehmet II to provide building materials for his fortress of Rumeli Hisarı.

North to Arnavutköy

Arnavutköy, the "Village of the Albanians", is a bit of a misnomer as for much of its history the area was inhabited predominantly by Greeks and Jews. Although the Jewish community has long since moved on there still remain about 25 families of Greek descent, many of them attending the local Orthodox church of Taxiarchs. Sweeping around the headland, the first impression of the suburb, a row of well-preserved 19th-century wooden *yalı*, unfortunately now on rather intimate terms with the busy shoreline road, is a positive one. The passing traffic also detracts somewhat from a series of still-popular restaurants and cafés along the front, although penetrating inland from the picturesque blue and white ferry station. Small shops, lively taverns and workshops dot the backstreets, along with a rich heritage of late-Ottoman wooden houses, a growing number of which are being restored. Unfortunately as the proposed site of a third Bosphorus crossing many of these historic buildings, which ironically should benefit from state protection, are currently threatened with destruction. Thankfully in the face of vociferous opposition to the bridge project from local residents and conservationists, the government is also considering other options including a tunnel, however, Arnavutköy's fate still hangs very much in the balance.

Arnavutköy
Retains a village-like feel far removed from the brash gentrification of nearby Ortaköy

Apart from wandering the streets soaking up the atmosphere, you may want to seek out the Church of Taxiarchs which is reached by walking up Gül Sokağı from the ferry station and taking the third turning on the right. The cream coloured building is approached through a courtyard filled with fragrant blooms in summer and the guardian, Yani, lets visitors in to inspect the interior on weekdays at 0800 or 1700. Housed in a chapel beside the church is a holy spring, or *ayazma*, reached down a highly polished marble staircase.

North of Arnavutköy the road rounds a promontory marked by a small green and white lighthouse. Known as **Akıntı Burnu**, or "Point of the Current", on account of the swiftly flowing waters which wash against the shore. It's a popular spot with local anglers who pull *tekir, barbunyu* (red mullet) and *Iskorpit* from the turquoise depths. Indeed the current is so swift at this point that in the past sailing vessels would sometimes have to be dragged up the strait by porters on the bank.

Scattered around a wide arching bay backed by verdant hills dotted with some very expensive real estate, Bebek is a genteel, well-to-do little place. Despite this evocative setting and a pleasant atmosphere, Bebek lacks the colourful street life of Arnavutköy attracting instead a very polished crowd, including more than a few students from nearby Boğaziçi University, to its numerous upmarket cafés and bars. To the south of a small park and ferry landing stands

Bebek & onwards to Rumeli Hisarı

İstanbul

the **Hıdıv Sarayı**, a waterside Art Nouveau mansion built for the Ottoman Governor of Egypt at the turn of the last century by the Italian architect Raimondo D'Aronco, and now occupied by the Egyptian Consulate. A few other vintage mansions survive in the backstreets with one particularly fine example reached up Hamam Sokağı from opposite the brownstone mosque. After several hundred metres you'll notice an Orthodox church on the left opposite an infants school, with a huge, dilapidated konak awaiting some benevolent soul with bottomless pockets on the hillside above. Continuing onwards the *Cafe de Pera*, housed in a pretty wooden house, is a good place to take the weight off your feet.

Continuing north from Bebek the waterside promenade is lined with pleasure craft used by wealthy local residents to make good their escape from the city on summer weekends. On the heights above the road the buildings of **Boğaziçi University** are scattered across a leafy campus. One of the country's most prestigious state-run universities which counts among its distinguished alumni the present prime minister Bülent Ecevit.

Rumeli Hisarı

Along the shore road there are several popular cafés including the down-to-earth Cafe Kale, while the village's old ferry station has been turned into a pricey but well-recommended fish restaurant

Overlooking a bend in the Bosphorus beyond Aşiyan point is the **castle** of Rumeli Hisarı which was built in 1452 as part of Mehmet II's hurried preparations for the siege of Constantinople. Planned personally by the sultan himself, the fort consists of three massive towers linked by long crenellated curtain walls up to 15-m thick. Incredibly, in spite of its scale the structure took only four months to complete, a testament as much to the strength and skill of the Ottoman workforce as to the healthy spirit of competition which developed between the sultan's three chief ministers, each entrusted with the task of building one of the main towers. Once garrisoned by a force of Janissaries and bristling with cannon, the fortress and its smaller predecessor on the opposite shore, achieved their purpose admirably, closing the straits to Byzantine shipping and effectively cutting the city's last remaining supply route. However, the fortress proved to be a victim of its own success as the fall of Constantinople left it largely redundant and over the following centuries it functioned primarily as a prison. Restored to something approaching its original state in 1953, you can now climb up on the battlements to enjoy the vista over the straits and the bracing seabreeze. A small open-air theatre within the fort's perimeter is a modern addition which hosts concerts in the summer months (see page 159). ■ *0900-1630, daily except Mon. US$2. Getting there: 1 km north of Bebek, buses no 25E from Eminönü and no 40 from Taksim pass beneath the walls.*

Rumeli Hisarı

The Belgrade Forest

Located to the west of Sarıyer, the Belgrade Forest has been a popular escape from the city since the 17th century when rich Ottoman and European residents would picnic there. An extensive stretch of forest and heathland, it's still popular today with city-dwellers who converge en-mass at weekends to spread out their rugs in it's shady glades and barbeque. It's quieter during the week, an ideal spot to stretch your legs and fill your lungs with fresh air.

Originally reserved as a royal hunting range, the forest also provided the city with its water supply transported via a system of aqueducts some of which were constructed by Mimar Sinan in the 16th century. Without your own transport you'll need to get a dolmuş from Çayırbaşı, between Büyükdere and Sarıyer, to Bahçeköy in the east margins of the forest. From there follow a road sign-posted to 'Bentler' which leads to **Büyük Bend** one of several reservoirs within the forest. It's under an hour walk in total, much of it through beautiful woodland. The best idea is to bring provisions for a picnic although there are several simple cafes along the way.

İstanbul

Continuing northwards the suburb of Emirgan is famous for its park which since the reign of Ahmet III, a time commonly referred to as the Tulip Period due to the flowermania which swept Ottoman society, has been the scene of a spring flower festival. Signposted off the coast road, these formal gardens make a lovely place to stroll, breaking you're wanderings at one of the three architecturally contrasting pavilions which have recently been converted into cafés. The Khedive's Palace nearby, which dates from the end of the 19th century, is now the home of Sakıp Sabancı, one of the country's leading industrialists.

At **Istinye** the road takes a sharp diversion around a long, narrow bay which has long been valued as a protected anchorage and is now densely packed with yachts and motor launches. Along with some nice cafés, there's a lively waterside fish market beside the road. A good place to break your journey is *Süreyya*, Istinye Caddesi No 26, T2775886, a Bosphorus institution established by White Russians which still serves Slavic treats such as chicken kiev, beef stroganoff and borsch as well as Turkish dishes. Expect your bill to top US$35 per head with advance reservations recommended.

Passing by road through **Yeniköy**, the next suburb to the north, you may notice the church of Ayios Yiorgios (Church of St George) which is still used by the remnants of the area's Greek community, although more difficult to miss, particularly if you're on a boat, are the brightly painted *yalı* fronting the Bosphorus.

The next suburb north, **Tarabya**, was formerly a Greek village favoured during the 19th century as a summer retreat by the European residents of İstanbul. It's pretty bay is now badly overshadowed by a monstrous concrete hotel. Beyond the eyesore of a hotel, **Kireçburunu** has a number of expensive fish restaurants overlooking the water such as the large, modern *Pescatore*. At **Büyükdere** the Bosphorus is at its widest, and the Black Sea finally comes into view to the north.

Emirgan to Sarıyer

Sarıyer is an active town far enough away from İstanbul to shake off the tag of "suburb". Down by the harbour which has recently been brutally pedestrinized, a raucous market is stocked by a large fleet of Black Sea trawlers. ■ *Getting there: The high-speed Deniz Otobusleri departs on its twice daily return journey to Kadıköy (currently at 0735 and 1730), although bus no 25 heads into Eminönü via Beşiktaş half-hourly until about 2230.*

Sarıyer & Rumeli Kavağı

It's a 10-minute drive along the coast north of Sarıyer to the fishing community of **Rumeli Kavağı**, the most northerly village on the European side of the Bosphorus and the last stop on this side of the straits for the TML sightseeing ferry. Its a scrappy place with an over-abundance of fish restaurants that earn their keep from the day-trippers you arrive from İstanbul. Slap bang in the middle of the village are the grass covered remains of an Ottoman fort, off-limits to the public due to their continued use by the military. At the far end of the wharf the reasonably priced *Ayder Balık Lokantası* serves-up the catch of the day complemented by views across the straits to Anadolu Kavağı on the opposite shore. ■ *Getting there: Ferries make the short hop across the water every 2-3 hrs, check the timetable on the jetty. If you're returning to the city in the evening the last bus to Eminönü departs from the square at 2005, although dolmuş to Sarıyer, from where there are later running buses and dolmuş, leave until about 2230. Double check these times when you arrive as you wouldn't want to get stranded here.*

The Asian side

Separated from the main sights and centres of accommodation on the European side of the Bosphorus, the Asian suburbs of the city receive only a trickle of foreign visitors. There are, however, quite a few things to see, with a journey across to the "other side" warranted if only for the ferry crossing itself, which gives you a chance to escape the confines of the city and enjoy an unrivalled glimpse of the İstanbul skyline. Üsküdar or Kadıköy make good places to head for first with regular ferries crossing from Eminönü (piers 1 or 2), Karaköy, Kabataş and Beşiktaş throughout the day. Once back on dry land bus and dolmuş services string together the waterside villages further north.

Kadıköy Fronting the Sea of Marmara, there has been a settlement at the site of modern-day Kadıköy since 670 BC, meaning that it predates even Byzantium itself. During Ottoman times it was the seat of a *kadı* or judge who administered justice over the Anatolian provinces, and from whom the area gets its name, "Village of the Judge". Today Kadıköy is slowly shaking-off its gritty, down-market image with the grid of pedestrianized streets leading up the hill from the waterside square peppered with clothes shops, trendy cafés and some excellent music outlets. During your wanderings you're also bound to come across a church or synagogue left by the sizeable non-Muslim communities who once made the area their home, though there's precious little else of any greater antiquity.

One of the largest & most colourful street markets in the entire city

Perhaps the best reason for making the trip to Kadıköy is to explore the massive **Salıpazarı**. As its name suggests the market is at its best on Tuesdays (Salı), with stalls of food and clothing sprawling over a huge area around Kuşdili Caddesi. On Sunday there are stalls selling jewellery, antiques and furniture. ■ *Getting there: Walk up Söğütlüçeşme Caddesi away from the water until you come to a roundabout with a golden bull, from where the narrow street opposite leads down to the market.*

Overlooking the northern side of Kadıköy harbour the terminus for trains from the Asian part of the country, **Haydarpaşa Station**, stands grandly on the waterfront. The building was completed in 1908 as part of the project to develop a railway network across the Ottoman Empire using German finance and expertise, one of a number of symbols demonstrating the cozy relationship that developed between Sultan Abdül Hamit II and Kaiser Wilhelm II.

Continuing north up Rıhtım Caddesi, which turns into Tibbiye Caddesi, the wide tree-lined avenue passes a large military hospital and a strange building with towers topped by onion-shaped domes that forms part of the campus of Marmara University. Turning right down Burhan Felek Caddesi past the military hospital's entrance brings you to the **British War Cemetery**, the last resting place for some of the soldiers who died in the Crimean War, First and Second World Wars.

On the left soon after, Çeşme-i Kebir Sokak leads down the hill from Tibbiye Caddesi towards the **Selimiye Barracks**. If you don't fancy the walk "Üsküdar" dolmuş departing from the waterfront in Kadıköy pass the turning, just ask for "Selimiye Kışlası". The barracks, one of the most recognizable landmarks on the Asian shore of the Bosphorus, were originally constructed in 1799 by Selim III to house the second regiment of a Western-style army known as *Nizam-i Jedid,* or New Order. Trained in western military tactics by foreign instructors, this army was intended as a replacement for the corrupt and ineffective Jannissaries, but instead their existence became the catalyst for a rebellion which cost the Sultan not only his throne but also his life. Burnt to the ground in 1808, the barracks were rebuilt in stone 20 years later after Mahmut II had finally succeeded in liquidating the troublesome Jannissary Corps. The huge building, which stretches around a massive parade ground and has over 1,000 windows, served as a military hospital during the Crimean War (1854-56) and it was in the north-west wing that an English nurse **Florence Nightingale**, lived and worked along with 38 colleagues This section of the building is now preserved in something approaching its original state as a museum dedicated to the remarkable lady, with exhibits including a copy of the lamp which earnt her the epithet "the Lady of the Lamp". Unfortunately, access to the museum has been made rather difficult by the military administration, who now require you to telephone or fax (T02163437310) ahead of a proposed visit to request permission- enough to put off all but the most devoted fans.

According to tradition Üsküdar, a corruption of the name Scutari by which the town was formerly known, was established at about the same time in the seventh century BC as Kadıköy. But enjoying a superior position at the head of the Bosphorus the town rapidly eclipsed its southerly neighbour, also benefiting from its status as the western terminus of the Roman road network which spread out across Asia Minor. In later times the Ottoman sultans would muster their legions in the town before heading off eastwards on campaign, while Evliya Çelebi, the distinguished Ottoman traveller, describes it thus: "Scutari is a great place of passage, because all foreigners from Anatolia, Persia and India, coming to Constantinople, pass through it."

The days of the Ottoman empire not only left Üsküdar with a rich legacy of Islamic architecture, but also as a centre of the syncretic dervish sects whose influence persists to the present-day despite their proscription by Atatürk in 1925. The area is home to one of the city's Mevlevi *tekke,* where followers of the Sufi mystic Mevlana gather periodically to perform their whirling ceremonial dances. In a major break from tradition this *tekke* has recently begun admitting women, a move which has shocked more conservative members of an order for whom tolerance and open-mindedness is supposed to be a central tenet.

On the ground Üsküdar is a bustling shopping area with the streets radiating inland from the ferry terminal choked by day with pedestrian and vehicular traffic. The traffic situation isn't helped by its other role as a transport node with buses and dolmuş clogging up the waterside square. Luckily most of the areas interesting buildings are within easy walking distance of the pier, with the Çinli Camii and Atik Valide Camii, on the hill above the centre, requiring a bit more effort to reach.

İstanbul

Üsküdar

Overlooking the bus station on the side of the main square, the **Iskele Camii** was constructed by Mimar Sinan in 1547-48 for the favourite daughter of Süleyman the Magnificent, Mihrimah Sultan, after whom the building is also sometimes known. Due to the constraints of the terrain the ever-resourceful Sinan abandoned convention, mounting the structure on a large terrace sheltered by a huge overhanging porch. The plan of the main building is also asymmetrical with a large central dome supported by three, instead of the more usual two or four, much smaller semi-domes. The end result isn't a resounding success, unlike his second major commission for Mihrimah Sultan which stands on the opposite side of town near the Edirne Kapı, although the architect seems to have made the best of a rather difficult spot. The terrace with its Baroque fountain added later by Ahmet II makes an excellent spot from which to survey the milling crowds below.

To the west of the ferry landing the **Şemsi Paşa Camii** is one of the smallest and most picturesque of the city's mosques. Built by Mimar Sinan in 1580 for the grand vizier of Süleyman the Magnificent, Şemsi Ahmet Paşa, the simple square building incorporates into its plan the tomb of its sponsor, which is separated from the prayer hall by a metal grill.

Walking along the coast road as it rounds Salacak point you are rewarded by some excellent views across the straits, with about 2 km of water standing between you and the point of Saray Burnu beneath the Topkapı Palace. Just off-shore stands a small white tower known as **Leander's Tower** in English due to its false association with the Greek myth of Leander, a young man who is said to have swam the straits, the Hellespont, nightly to visit his lover. Locals refer to the tower as Kız Kalesi, the Maiden's Tower, after a story about a beautiful Princess who was confined on the island by her father to frustrate a prophesy that she would die from a snake bite. Despite the best efforts of her father a snake found its way on to the island in a basket of fruit and duly fulfilled the prediction by biting the girl. Re-entering the realms of historical fact, the tower served as an anchor point for a chain stretched across the Bosphorus in Byzantine times to prevent ships evading their duties, while over the subsequent years it has filled the role of lighthouse, semaphore post, customs station, quarantine centre and film set (used in the James Bond extravaganza "Tomorrow Never Dies"). Now open as a café during the day (0900-1830) and restaurant by night (after 2030), it's an interesting and unusual venue, well worth visiting. Reservations are required, T0216 3424747.

Inland from Üsküdar

Built on a hilltop above Üsküdar, the **Atik Valide Camii** rates among the finest works by the prolific Ottoman architect Mimar Sinan, although it is also one of the least visited. The extensive complex which includes a medrese, an infirmary, a Koran school, a hamam and a caravanserai was commissioned in 1583 by Sultan Murat III, distraught after the death of his beloved mother Valide Sultan Nur Banu. An indomitable woman, as the favourite wife of Selim the Sot, the Venetian-born Nur Banu exerted huge influence over court affairs while her husband was distracted by the pleasures of the harem. After Selim's death she ensured the accession of her son Murat to the throne by having the other young princes strangled, thereby continuing a period of Ottoman history known as the Sultanate of Women. Once through the main gateway a well-proportioned courtyard shaded by cypress and plane trees leads via a double portico into the mosque. Under a wide central dome, wooden galleries stretch around three sides of the main hall with the floral patterns stencilled on their undersides particularly worthy of inspection. The İznik tilework around the *mihrab* is also a beautiful original feature although the decorative painting on the royal loge and the side aisles was added much later. Reached through a doorway in the west wall of the courtyard, the mosque's *medrese* is built on a lower level, while the hospital, or *şifahane*, is found on the opposite side of the building. ■ *Getting there: A 25-min walk from the jetty in Üsküdar or a US$2 taxi ride. On foot head south on the main thoroughfare Hakimiyet-i Milliye Caddesi from the square. Turn left up Çavuşdere Caddesi and continue climbing until you get to Çinili Camii Sokağı on your right (if you get to the Çinili Camii itself you've gone too far). The mosque complex is a short distance up on the left-hand side.*

For fans of İznik tilework **Çinli Camii**, whose name literally translates as the "Mosque with tiles", is definitely worth seeking out as its interior walls are revetted with a stunning display of beautifully patterned faïence. The *külliye* was founded in 1640 by Mahpeyker Kösem Sultan, the favourite wife of Sultan Ahmet I, who following in the footsteps of Nur Banu enjoyed enormous power and influence in the Ottoman court under her husband and subsequently during the reigns of her sons, Murat IV and Ibrahim the Mad. The bright, airy interior is well-used by locals at prayer times and also as a venue for religious instruction, with an excellent hamam, recently renovated and kept spotlessly clean, found around the corner on Çinili Hamam Sokağı. ■ *Getting there: Follow the instructions above for reaching the Atik Valide Camii, but continue climbing Çavuşdere Caddesi for a short way beyond Çinili Camii Sokağı.*

The peak of **Büyük Çamlıca**, which at 261 m above sea-level is the highest point in the city, has long been a favourite place for İstanbul residents, including numerous sultans, to take a stroll. On a clear day the view is exceptional with an urban panorama encompassing the great monuments of Sultanahmet, ridge top Beyoğlu and a great sweep of the modern town to the north, all laid out beyond the blue twisting ribbon of the Bosphorus. In the opposite direction the Prince's Islands hover off the coast and very occasionally, weather and air quality permitting, Mount Uludağ appears as a distant smudge floating on the horizon to the southeast. However, encroached on by illegal building, these impressive views would not have been available for the public to enjoy today had it not been for the timely action of the Turkish Touring and Automobile Club who leased the area from the Municipal government, creating a landscaped park complete with two period cafés. Since then administration of the gardens has reverted back to the city government with locals complaining about a resulting drop in the standards of maintenance and care. Still Büyük Çamlıca makes an excellent place to come for a wander although rather inevitably it gets mobbed at the weekends when it is a favourite destination for newly weds and their horn honking cavalcades. An adjacent, lower, peak known as Küçük Çamlıca is also topped by public park and café, and cloaked in thicker vegetation than its loftier brother. ■ *Getting there: By public transport from Üsküdar you'll need to catch an "Ümraniye" dolmuş from in front of the Iskele Camii. Tell the driver you want to go to Büyük Çamlıca and you'll be let-off after passing the entrance to Küçük Çamlıca in Kısıklı from where it is about a 20-30 min walk up the hill to the summit. Alternatively it's about a US$3 taxi ride from Üsküdar to the summit.*

North to Beylerbeyi

Heading north from Üsküdar you leave behind the hustle and bustle for a string of quiet "villages" the first of which, **Kuzguncuk**, had a large Armenian and Jewish population up until the beginning of the last century. Wandering the streets you'll come across a few handsome wooden houses with carefully carved balconies along with several Orthodox churches and synagogues all dating from the 19th century. Above the settlement and reached on foot up Icadiye Sokak is an extensive Jewish cemetery with marble graves scattered across the hillside. As good a reason as any to visit Kuzguncuk is to try the catch-of-the-day in the unassuming waterside institution, *Ismet Baba*. Under a kilometre north of Kuzguncuk just beyond the Atatürk Bridge the road passes the Beylerbeyi Palace.

Commissioned in 1861 by Sultan Abdül Aziz, the **Beylerbeyi Palace** was built as a summer residence and a place to lodge distinguished foreign visitors, who over the years included the Duke and Duchess of Windsor, Empress Eugénie of France and the Persian Shah. Designed by the architect Sarkis Balyan, brother of Nikoğos who was responsible for the Dolmabahçe, the 30-room Beylerbeyi Palace is an attractive three-story building surrounded by immaculately kept gardens and overlooking a marble quay from which royal bathers could slip into the water without risking their modesty from one of two pavilions. Built on the site of an earlier wooden palace constructed for Mahmut II and later ravaged by fire, the result of over four years work by a force of 5,000 men is certainly one of the most attractive palaces of its time. After donning plastic slippers visitors are taken on a compulsory whistle-stop tour around the two sections of the building, the *selamlık* and *haremlik*, reached from a magnificent central hall lit by glittering Bohemian chandeliers and cooled in summer by a marble pool and fountain. The floors are covered with Egyptian reed matting along with acres of Hereke carpet, and the rooms themselves are sumptuously furnished with pieces selected personally by Sultan Abdül Aziz. Up a grand twisting staircase, the tour takes you through the valide sultan's private apartment and on to the sultan's bedroom, where the imperial bed, lent to Empress Eugénie during her visit, looks rather small and uncomfortable. Back downstairs a set of wooden dining chairs bares the monogram of the Sultan Abdülhamid II, who evidently kept himself busy during his five years under house arrest in the palace before his death in 1918.
■ *0930-1630 daily except Mon and Thu. US$2.50. Camera US$6.50. Beykoz dolmuş leave from in front of Iskele Camii in Üsküdar or any bus going to Beykoz, Anadolu Hisarı or Anadolu Kavağı also passes by.*

Beylerbeyi to the Göksu River

Continuing north from Beylerbeyi brings you to the suburb of **Çengelköy** which has a number of fish restaurants around its pleasant square and a handsome 18th-century *yalı*, the reddy-brown painted Sadullah Paşa Yalı, on the shoreline to the south of the centre. North of the village the Kuleli Naval Officer's Training College occupies a long building on the waterline which is easily identified by its two conical towers. After passing through Kandilli you cross a small river, the Küçüksu, which together with the Göksu river just to the north were referred to evocatively as the "**Sweet Waters of Asia**" by European residents of Ottoman İstanbul. An area of grassy meadows shaded by poplars and willows, the land between the rivers was a favourite spot for elaborate picnics held by the Ottoman court and aristocracy.

Gracing "the Sweet Waters of Asia" is a neat rococo mansion built in 1856 by the court architect Nikoğos Balyan as a pavilion and base-camp for Sultan Abdülmecit's pleasure outings up the Bosphorus. Known as the **Küçüksu Kasrı**, it is one of the prettiest Baroque buildings in the city, particularly when viewed from the waterside with an elegantly curving double staircase up which the sultan would have padded having disembarked from his royal barge. The highly ornamented marble facade was originally more restrained, however, extra work was added to it after the sultan complained about it being too plain. As you'd expect, the mansion's interior is sumptuously decorated with Italian marble, Hereke carpets, crystal chandeliers and plenty of gold-leaf, although unlike the Dolmabahçe Palace the overall impression is not overpowering because of the buildings smaller scale. Originally intended simply as a pavillion, several rooms upstairs were later converted into bedrooms to be used by foreign dignitaries. Nearby, the Baroque Valide Sultan Mihrişah fountain was built by Selim III in memory of his mother in the year 1796. ■ *0930-1600, summer 1700, daily except Mon and Thu. US$2, camera fee US$4. 10-mins walk south of Anadolu Hısarı, get off buses or dolmuş from Üsküdar at the castle. Walk back across the bridge and turn right down the road parallel to the river, the palace is visible up ahead by the waterline.*

Along the shore between Anadolu Hisarı and the Fatih Bridge stands the **Köprülü Ancazade Hüseyin Paşa Yalı**, one of the oldest wooden residences on the Bosphorus which has survived moreorless intact since 1698. Built by Mustafa II's grand vizier, Hüseyin Paşa, the *yalı* was the scene for the signing of the Treaty of Carlowitz (1699), a humiliating document which confirmed the end of Ottoman territorial expansion westward into Europe. The building, which is currently under restoration, isn't visible from the road so you'll have to pick it out from a passing boat.

North of the Fatih Bridge stands the village of **Kanlıca** which is known locally for the creaminess of its yoghurt. Try some at one of the cafés near the ferry landing, although in this age of mass production it tastes much like any other. Also on the main square stands a nondescript mosque dating back to 1560 which is attributed to Mimar Sinan. An excellent venue for a special meal is *Körfez*, Körfez Caddesi No 78, T4134314, a refined waterside restaurant with excellent *meze* and fish including house-speciality, *tuzda levrek* (sea bass baked in salt). If there's a group of you the management will ferry you across the Bosphorus from Rumeli Hısarı in a private launch. Expect to pay at least US$30 per head.

Despite being one of the largest settlements on the Asian shore of the Bosphorus there isn't much to detain you in **Beykoz**, whose name, "Prince's Walnut", presumably dates from when the area was famous for its nuts. Walnut trees aren't much in evidence these days though, and modern development has swept away much of the original architecture. One of the towns only notable features, but hardly worth a journey in itself, is a celebrated 18th-century fountain on the main square which gushes water from 10 spouts.

Anadolu Kavağı has been identified as the site of the Temple of Zeus Ourious, or Zeus of the Favouring Wind, a compulsory stop for ancient mariners heading out onto the Black Sea. Today the village is the last port of call on the Bosphorus sightseeing ferries and nourished by boatloads of sightseers on summer weekends, fish restaurants and food stands have taken over most of the centre of town. *Yosun* has the best position right at the quayside. If you don't fancy sitting down to a seafood lunch, a 25-minute climb will see you up on the summit of Yoros Tepesi above the settlement, the site of an ancient fortress used in conjunction with the fort at Rumeli Kavağı to control access to the Bosphorus. Originally dating back to Byzantine times, the castle was rebuilt by the Genoese during the 14th century only to be garrisoned by the Ottomans soon after.

Museums

Housed in what's left of the **Ibrahim Paşa Sarayı**, the museum has a fascinating collection of over 40,000 artefacts, with the displays concentrating primarily on the Mamluk, Selçuk and Ottoman periods, but also featuring items from other Islamic cultures of the Middle-east. Downstairs in the ethnography section are a series of informative exhibits on the art and traditions of various nomadic groups, including the 'Karaevli', now settled near Adana. There is also an exhibition about traditional techniques used for producing natural dyes from plant and animal materials which is based largely on research by the Marmara University. The hall on the ground floor hosts visiting exhibitions and the café on the museum terrace is a good place to take the weight off your feet with excellent views across the Hippodrome to the Sultan Ahmet Camii.

Museum of Turkish & Islamic Arts (Türk ve Islam Eserleri Müzesi)

If you only plan to visit 1 museum while you're in town this should be it

Istanbul

■ *0900-1630 daily except Mon. US$2.50. Situated on the Hippodrome opposite Sultan Ahmet Camii.*

Vakıflar Carpet Museum (Vakıflar Halı Müzesi) A varied and interesting collection of Turkish carpets which charts their history from early Ottoman times to the 19th century, and includes rare pieces from most of the principle areas of production in the country. Fascinating for the rug enthusiast. ■ *0900-1200, 1300-1600. Closed Sun and Mon. US$1.25. Imperial Pavilion of Sultan Ahmet Camii, northeast corner.*

Mosaic Museum (Mozaik Müzesi) The museum contains some of the exquisite mosaics that once decorated the halls of the Byzantine Great Palace, built on the slopes leading down to the sea of Marmara. Preserved in-situ after their discovery earlier this century, the mosaics were later carefully removed to Haghia Eirene by a Turco-Austrian team to allow a new protective structure to be built. The extensive mosaic pavement which formed part of a peristyle, an open courtyard surrounded by a collonade, can now be viewed back where it was found from a series of walkways. The lively scenes laboriously created from thousands of coloured fragments include a donkey kicking an unlucky Byzantine and a monkey-like creature plucking dates from a palm tree. ■ *0900-1600 daily except Mon. US$1.25. Entrance on Torun Sokağı. Can be reached on foot by leaving the Arasta bazaar by the passage half-way along.*

Press Museum (Basın Müzesi) This small museum has a collection of antiquated cameras and other equipment formerly used by the press in Turkey. Bakerlite telex machines the size of washing machines make you realize how far technology has progressed. There is also an exhibit commemorating the assasination of Abdi Ipekçi, a well-respected journalist gunned down in 1978 by right-wing extremists, along with a replica of the first printing press used in the Ottoman empire. ■ *0930-1730, weekdays. Free. 2nd floor of building on Divanyolu near Cennet Restaurant.*

Museum of Calligraphy (Türk Vakıf Hat Sanatları Müzesi) Housed in the beautifully restored medrese of the Beyazıt mosque complex, the museum has a varied collection of manuscripts, treaties and religious texts drawn from the huge archives of the Turkish Calligraphy Foundation. The exhibits include calligraphic tools along with embroidery inscriptions and calligraphy carved into wood and stone. ■ *0900-1600, closed Mon and Sun. US$1.50. Overlooking Ordu Caddesi to the west of Beyazıt Camii.*

Rahmi Koç Museum (Rahmi Koç Müzesi)
This museum is 1 of the city's more unusual & interesting, particularly for the mechanically minded Founded by Rahmi M Koç, a Turkish industrialist and household name, in a disused 18th-century factory that once produced chains and anchors. On display inside the spacious halls of the sensitively converted building are Rahmi Koç's varied personal collection of mechanical toys, machines, steam engines and vehicles, such as an old Kadıköy-Moda tram. Visitors can play captain at the bridge of a ship, reconstructed accurately with explanations of all its instruments; make coins in a mechanical press or examine the inner workings of an engine from the Kalender, a steam ship built in the dockyards of Newcastle-upon-Tyne in 1911. ■ *1000-1700 daily except Mon. US$1.50. In Sütlüce at Hasköy Caddesi No 27, the museum can be reached on bus no 47 from Eminönü, 54HM from Taksim. Decent french restaurant on-site.*

Military Museum (Askeri Müze) The museum can trace its origins back to 1846. The collection of antique weaponry and equipment grew steadily over the proceeding years, necessitating several moves. As well as an impressive, clearly annotated collection of Mameluke, Persian, Ottoman and European weaponry, armour, medals and uniforms dating back to the 13th century, the museum has on display a beautiful series of richly decorated pavilions, used by the sultans and their ministers while on campaign. Perhaps the biggest draw, however, is the **Mehter Band** which performs in the museum courtyard every day between 1500 and 1600. Drawn from the ranks of the Janissary Corps, the musicians of the band would accompany the Ottoman horde into battle, motivating the troops with songs of bravery and heroism. Abolished by Sultan Mahmut II along with the Jannisaries in 1826, the band was revived in 1914 and in recent years has been touring the world to play at cultural events and concerts. ■ *0900-1700 daily except Mon and Tue. US$0.75, camera US$1.75, video US$3.50. Getting there: On the right hand side of Cumhuriyet Caddesi about a 10-15 min walk north of Taksim. Practically all buses north from Taksim pass by it (including: 46H, 59A, 559C), alternatively a cab won't be more than US$1.50.*

Uniformed conscripts, counting their blessings for such a cushy posting, stand guard at the entrance to this interesting collection of naval memorabilia. On display is a reconstruction of Atatürk's yacht, *The Savarona*, along with a collection of imperial caiques which transported various sultans up and down the Bosphorus. The garden is home to a collection of cannons, shells and the twisted remains of a German U-boat. Of more contemporary interest is an exhibition charting a Turkish couple's, Zuhal and Osman Atasoy's, circumnavigation of the globe in 1992; a four-year 10 month odyssey aboard their 8-m yacht, Uzaklar, during which Zuhal gave birth to a baby girl. ■ *0900-1230, 1330-1700. US$1.50. In a dull concrete building on Cezayir Caddesi, 150 m west of Beşiktaş ferry landing.*

Maritime Museum (Deniz Müzesi)

Excursions from the city

When the hustle and bustle of the city gets too much it's time to think about exploring what's beyond the sprawling city limits. If it's fresh air and peace you crave then jump on a boat to the Prince's Islands, by far the easiest escape from the city, although precisely because of that fact things can get a bit hectic on summer holiday weekends. The same is true of the Black Sea resorts, Kilyos, Şile and to a lesser degree Ağva, which boast some of the best beaches on the entire north Anatolian coast.

The Prince's Islands

An archipelago of nine islands strung out along the Anatolian coast 15 km to the southeast of the city, the laid back atmosphere and fresh air of the Prince's Islands make them feel a lot more distant. Indeed, at less than an hours boat journey away from the city, 20 minutes on the new hydrofoil, they make the perfect escape when things in the city get too much, a sentiment shared by many local families who keep summer houses on the islands.

Phone code: 0216

Getting there Ferries leave from 0700 to 2230, less often at weekends and during the winter. Boats generally call at **Heybeliada**, and sometimes **Kınalıada** and **Burgazada**, before continuing on to **Büyükada**. The last boat returns at 2130 from Büyükada. The fare is US$1.60 and it takes less than 2 hrs to the furthest island. Three boats a day at 0915, 1400 and 1815, continue on from **Büyükada** to **Yalova**, US$3.25. The **catamaran** (*Deniz otobüs*) leaves from **Kabataş** on the Bosphorus south of the Dolmabahçe Palace (buses 25E, 56 and 28 from Eminönü and 40 from Taksim stop near the Kabataş quay) and from Bostancı, on the Asian shores, several times a day in summer, 25 mins, US$3.75 (Bostancı is easily accessible by dolmuş leaving from the

Ins & outs
Getting to the islands is simply a matter of deciding whether you want to cruise leisurely on 1 of the old ferries or speed there on the new, less frequent catamaran service

large bus station to the southeast of the ferry terminal in Kadıköy). **Getting around** There are regular ferries between the islands themselves in summer, but you should check a timetable when you arrive as schedules change without notice. Outside the summer season boats between the islands are far less regular and you need to pay careful attention to timetables to avoid getting stranded.

Background   Known as the Kızıl Adalar or 'Red Islands', on account of the reddish cliffs which grace several of the chain, the islands have a long history of human occupation dating back to Classical times when copper ore was extracted from mines on Heybeliada. The Byzantines, favouring their seclusion, dotted the islands with monasteries and convents, several of which were used as places of internal exile. A three hour crossing from the mainland by oar-powered caique, the islands were generally ignored by the Ottomans, becoming a backwater favoured by the empires non-Muslim minorities. However in 1849 all this was to change as a regular steam ferry service brought the islands closer to city enabling wealthy Armenian, Greek and Jewish merchants to construct summer houses on the islands, many of which survive to the present-day. Nor were the pleasures of the archipelago lost on İstanbul's expatriate community and in 1857 the British Ambassador to the Sublime Porte Sir Henry Bulwer bought Yassıada and had a castle built on the small island. The same island was later to gain infamy as the site of the prison where Adnan Menderes and two members of his government were executed following the military take-over of 1960.

Only at the beginning of the Republican era did the islands begin to receive attention from the Turks of İstanbul, who flocked in ever increasing numbers no doubt encouraged by the example of figures such as Ismet Inönü, Atatürk's deputy and confidant, who bought a residence on Heybeliada. Among the distinguished foreign residents of the islands was Leon Trotsky, who having fled into exile from Communist Russia lived on Büyükada from 1929 to1933.

Modern times have seen the islands' popularity as a summer get-away threaten to swamp their unique character. New buildings have steadily joined the historic wooden mansions and conservation legislation, where in existence, is consistently ignored. Thankfully though the islands remain a car-free zone, so it is still possible to enjoy a respite from the noise and pollution associated with the internal combustion engine.

Büyükada
Largest of the islands, it is also probably the most interesting. The dreamy atmosphere is added to by the absence of cars

Having landed at one of the islands' piers you'll immediately become aware of the rich architectural heritage left by the islands' 19th-century residents. Wandering up past the clocktower the streets are lined with grand wooden villas, mostly shut-up behind louver shutters until the end of May when the island slowly wakes from its winter slumber. Immaculately kept gardens fill the air with sweet fragrances while luxuriant palms and pine trees cast dappled shadows over dazzling white Art Nouveau or Levantine Palladian facades. It comes as quite a revelation to wander streets so gloriously unclogged with traffic and quiet except for the chatter of sparrows and the wind in the trees. In the grid of backstreets beyond the clocktower the Roman Catholic church of **San Pacifico** (1886) hides behind a row of tall cypresses, while high on a forested ridge above town stands the largest surviving all-wooden building in the world, built by one Count Moris Bostari as a palatial hotel in 1898. Unfortunately for the Count permission to open the hotel was never granted, so it subsequently passed into the hands of a benevolent Greek businessman who pressed it into service as an orphanage. Known locally as the Greek Orphanage, it now stands forlorn and empty, attracting persistent rumours about its imminent redevelopment as a swanky holiday resort.

Sooner or later you'll come across one of the horse-drawn **phaeton** which are the main means of transport on the island. Drivers and their four legged beasts congregate in a square near the clock tower, waiting to set-off on tours around the island. To circumnavigate the entire island on a 'long tour' takes about 1½ hours and costs US$12; alternatively you may be happy with a 45-minute 'short tour', US$9. If you prefer to do things at your own pace, it's perfectly possible to explore the island on foot or using one of the bicycles for hire at **Yılmaz Bisiklet**, US$2.50 per hour, just up from the ferry station on Iskele Caddesi.

Heading west out of town on Çankaya Caddesi you pass some of the grandest residences, including the island's administrative headquarters, or *Kaymakamlık*, and the Izzet Paşa Köşkü at No 55 where Trotsky resided behind the ornately carved facade. Also on Çankaya Caddesi the **Büyükada Kültür Evi** (*1 May-15 Nov daily*) is a café, bookshop and art gallery housed in an attractive cream-coloured mansion. Continuing along Çankaya Caddesi you soon leave the town for the quiet pine woodland which cloaks much of the southern part of the island. Beyond a shady picnic area at Dilburnu, the road brings you down to **Yörük Ali Plajı**, a small holiday complex with restaurant, accommodation and swimming off a concrete jetty.

From the saddle in the middle of the island, dubbed Lunapark, a cobbled track leads up to the 202-m high summit of Yücel Tepe and the **Monastery of St George**. A series of buildings, one of which contains a sacred spring, the monastery is the scene of an annual pilgrimage on 23 April when Turkish mothers pant up the hill to pray for the saints intercession in the search for a good husband for their daughters. Things are quieter the rest of the year with a little café serving welcome refreshments.

From Lunapark a road loops around the sparsely inhabited and rockier southern half of the island, affording good views on a clear day across the sea to Yalova. There are several possibilities for a swim on the way round such as a short strip of pebbly beach at the extreme southern tip of the island, known as Kurşun Burnu.

Sleeping A *Princess Büyükada*, Iskele Meydanı No 2, T3821628, F3821949. Central, 100 m up from ferry terminal, modern reasonably well-equipped hotel with small pool, oddly shaped rooms have ensuite, a/c, TV and telephone as standard, US$120 for seaview. A *Saydam Planet Hotel*, Iskele Meydanı, 13822670, F3023848, next to the ferry terminal. Behind the shutters of renovated old building are attractive pine-fitted rooms, equipped with TV, telephone and nice bathroom, open all year, large suites with balcony US$200. Recommended. A *Splendid Otel*, 23 Nisan Caddesi No 71, T3826950, F3826775. Huge rambling hotel built in 1906 by Kazim Paşa, whose descendents still own it today. Recently gutted but by the time you arrive renovation work should be complete, worth a look for its nostalgia value alone, or if you can't stump the room rates dinner is an option, US$15. D *Ideal Pansiyon*, Kadiyora Caddesi No 14, T3826857, 5-mins walk from the ferry station past clock tower and then take left off 23 Nisan Caddesi. Unpainted and unpolished wooden konak, lots of atmosphere, large rooms with high-ceilings, very simple furnishings include a vintage refrigerator in each room, some have balconies, shared bathroom. Recommended.

With the limited availability of beds booking ahead is advisable during the summer months & essential on summer weekends

Eating There is a row of restaurants along waterfront Gülistan Caddesi to the east of the ferry terminal of which *Birtat* and *Milano*, offering a wide variety of meat and seafood dishes, come locally recommended. Expect to pay US$13-20 per head depending on what you order. One block inland on the main street *Taş Fırın* is a cheap and cheerful pide and lahmacun place. *Dolci Pasticceria*, next to the clock tower, is a favourite breakfast spot with pastries, cakes as well as ice-cream and drinks.

Directory Post office On main street. **Bank** On the main street, but don't expect to change TCs.

Istanbul

Heybeliada Second of the archipelago in terms of size is Heybeliada, "Saddle Bag Island", so called because of its shape. Blissfully devoid of traffic, outside the main holiday months a sleepy calm pervades the main settlement which climbs up the hillside behind a waterfront promenade dotted with a handful of small cafés and restaurants. On summer weekends things are a bit more intense, though, as boatloads of city-folk descend on the island.

The most conspicuous building in town, clearly visible as you approach, is the **Naval Academy** where young men receive an education before serving their country on the high seas. In comparison to Büyükada, however, the island's civil architecture is far less grand, although strolling around the streets you'll discover a few little 19th century and early Republic-style gems. As with its larger neighbour the horse-drawn carriage is the main means of transport on Heybeliada, although the island's gently contoured landscape and fragrant pine forests also lend themselves to exploration on foot or by **bicycle**, which can be rented at Imralı Sokak No 3. Phaetons queue up on Ayyıldız Caddesi, one block back from the water-front, waiting to whisk compliants off on a tour of the island. Sights along the way include the **Greek Orthodox School of Theology** built in the 19th century on the hill to the north of town as a repository for an important collection of Byzantine texts, but now only open with special permission from the Patriarchate in Fener. Your best bet for a **swim** are a series of small pebbly beaches along the island's northern coast which can be reached by climbing out of town on Refah Şehitleri Caddesi. In summer boats chug across to the small neighbouring island of **Kaşıkada**.

Sleeping **L** *Merit Halkı Palas*, Refah Şehitler Caddesi No 88, T3510025. There's been a hotel on the site since 1850, however, the present building was constructed in traditional style in 1991 after a fire destroyed the old building, decor is verging on the tasteless, comfortable rooms with lots of mod-cons: a/c, TV, minibar, some rooms have jacuzzi, a short phaeton ride from the village. **C-B** *Prenset Pansiyon*, Ayyıldız Caddesi No 74, T3519388, centrally located in Heybeli town. Good value, comfortable rooms, small swimming pool open in summer, the hotel is currently on the market so present, very amiable, management may have changed by the time you arrive.

All of the action is along the front or the main street, Ayyıldız Caddesi (Moon-star street), running parallel to it **Eating** *Başak Et-Balık Lokantası*, at Ayyıldız No 38, is a simple place serving a wide selection of meat dishes, döner and fish. Further on *Ada Kebap* has a similar choice with the addition of lahmacun and pide. *El Faro* on the front aspires to something slightly more sophisticated with a range of international dishes like beef stroganoff.

Directory Post office The PTT is on Gemici Kaynağı Sokak, behind the Naval Academy.

Burgazada Similar in size, these two smaller members of the archipelago attract far fewer **& Kınalıada** visitors and have retained a backwater feel despite in recent years being the target of extensive summer house development. The greener, more fertile of the pair, Burgazada is scattered with ruined monasteries and cemeteries, while in town you can check-out the home of the novelist Sait Faik, preserved as a museum. ■ *1000-1200, 1400-1700 daily except Mon and Sat afternoons.*

Kınalıada, "Henna Island", named after its red coloured cliffs, is a rockier more barren affair still favoured as a home or summer retreat by İstanbul's Armenian community. Facilities on both islands are limited to a couple of simple restaurants which shut-up shop for the winter at the end of the school holidays in September.

The Black Sea Coast

When things get hot in the summer many İstanbullu head for the Black Sea coast where a trio of seaside villages have accommodation, fish restaurants and very good beaches.

A 15-km road climbs its way over wooded hills scarred by villa developments from Sarıyer to the small Black Sea resort of Kilyos. A fairly forgettable tangle of mostly-modern houses, the main reason to visit is for the excellent beach which stretches away to the west of the village, however, care should be taken when swimming here because of potentially dangerous currents. A possible source of interest, the extensive ruins of a Genoese castle crowning a promontory above the settlement, are unfortunately closed to the public due to its use by the military.

Kilyos
Phone code: 0216
Accessible by dolmuş leaving from outside the PTT on the main street in Sarıyer, Kilyos could easily be visited on a daytrip from the city

Sleeping and eating There are quite a few options should you want to stay: book ahead at the weekend. **C** *Yalı Otel*, Plaj Yolu No 55, T2012210, F2011339. Modern place overlooking the beach, large, pleasant rooms, TV, telephone and balcony, fish restaurant on the top floor. **D** *Erzurumlu Otel*, Kilyos Kale Caddesi No 77, T2011003, F2011108. Concrete block above beach, reasonable rooms but the main draw is the swimming pool. **E** *Yonca Hotel*, Kilyos Kale Caddesi. Fairly decent rooms in 1 of older hotels, quite atmospheric restaurant serving fish and meze.

With your own transport Polonezköy, which translates as "the village of the Poles", makes a good destination for a day trip, possibly combined with a visit to the Black Sea coast. A strange aberration on the human map of Anatolia, as you might have guessed from the name, Polonezköy is a village peopled by Polish descendants. The approach to the village is through thick deciduous forests, a verdant feast for the eyes after the urban jungle of Istanbul and now protected as part of a nature park. A 4½ km walking track loops through the forests to the north of the village, although most visitors engage in more sedentary pursuits at one of the restaurant cum self-styled country clubs.

Polonezköy
Phone code: 0216

To explain how the Poles settled in this corner of the land you need to look back at the convoluted world of 19th-century international politics. Prince Adam Czartoryski, a Polish nationalist who sought exile in the Ottoman empire following a failed revolution against Russian rule in 1830, was given a tract of land by Sultan Abdülmecit in reward for bravely commanding a detachment of Polish soldiers who fought in the Crimean War. Also exempted from taxation, the Prince and his followers established a small farming community which retained its distinctive language and customs remarkably intact up until the modern era. Polish is now only spoken by a handful of the older villagers, while the original community has been diluted by cityfolk buying up weekend properties in the area. Despite this the 'Polish connection' has lured several important personages to the village over the years including Pope John Paul II and Lech Walesa.

Sleeping Relatively free from the moral constraints of the city, the village is a popular place for lovers to come for a quiet weekend with a number of guesthouses springing up in the village to accommodate them. Courting the higher end of the market, the **A** *Polka Country Hotel*, Cumhuriyet Yolu No 36, T4323220, polkahotel.com Has very comfortable 'rustic' rooms with use of a large swimming pool, however, you'll have to book well in advance for the weekend. You could also try the modern but much less refined **E** *Gülayım Hotel*, Cumhuriyet Caddesi No 64, T64323005.

Eating Pork sausages, a Polish culinary tradition which has long attracted less pious *İstanbullu* to the village, remains on the menu at the rather polished *Polka* and *Leonardo* restaurants. Expect to pay about US$8 per head for a plate of swine, which incidentally is no longer raised in the village but actually comes all the way from İzmir.

Transport Reached in less than an hr by **car** from İstanbul in reasonable traffic by crossing the Fatih Bridge and following signs off the motorway to Şile and then Polonezköy. Without your own transport you're in for a long and expensive **taxi** ride from Beykoz.

Şile Built near the site of ancient Kalpe, a port of call for Xenophon and the 10,000 on their long trek back from Babylon in 399 BC, Şile's proximity to İstanbul has ensured its rapid transformation from a poor Black Sea fishing and farming village into a holiday town catering to the summer crowds from the nearby metropolis. All this attention is not really surprising as the town occupies an attractive position on a hilltop overlooking a crowded harbour, sheltered by a rocky, wave-lashed promontory on top of which stand the remains of a Genoese castle. The big attraction, however, is a glorious dune-backed beach that arches away to the west of the harbour – well populated at first, it becomes progressively less crowded, but also more exposed, as you move away from town. As on other beaches along this stretch of coast care should be taken when bathing due to strong currents. A possible nocturnal activity is an inspection of the town's 19th-century lighthouse, the largest in the country, which is open to visitors after sunset. Something to look out for in town is the *şile bezi*, a loose weave cotton cloth produced locally and made into shirts and blouses decorated with hand embroidery.

Many local families rent rooms to visitors at economical prices. Try enquiring in the shops on the main street

Sleeping Room rates in Şile's ordinary collection of hotels are inflated due to the brevity of the season and the fact that most of their business during the summer is squeezed into just 2 days of the week. Mid-week occupancy is generally low, so try and bargain for a discount if you visit during the week. **A** *Grand Şile Hotel*, Plaj Yolu No 19, T7114676, F7114680. Modern building down near the harbour, most comfortable rooms in town with a/c, swimming pool, half-board weekend special US$165. **B** *Kumbaba Hotel and Camping*, Kumbaba, T7115038, F7114851, well-established German-run hotel, wonderfully secluded location on the dunes several kilometres west of the harbour, turn left at BP station just before Şile and ask anybody for directions, reached by catching a small ferry across a river and then following a path over the dunes, simple rooms are set in garden scattered with archaeological ephemera, rooms showing their age a bit, full-board only with meals eaten on terrace overlooking sand. The perfect antidote for the urban blues. **D** *Ruya Motel*, Plaj Yolu No 7, T7115070, F7115807, behind the beach at the harbour end. Simple rooms with balcony and ensuite, prices have rocketted this year, now well-overpriced for standard of accommodation. Cheaper accommodation can be found in a row of places backing the beach which offer basic bungalows with shared bathroom facilities for US$16. Try *Bacanaklar Camping*, T7120641.

Eating The best place to eat in Şile is in 1 of the fish restaurants near the harbour. The *Panorama* has tables on a terrace with excellent views, the *Iyot Restaurant* has a lovely location beside the water which unfortunately isn't matched by the very mediocre food and service.

Transport Buses leave regularly on the 2-hr, 75 km, journey from the main square in Üsküdar, US$1.50.

A twisty, stomach churning 30-km drive east of Şile, the pleasant little harbour **Ağva**
village of Ağva receives far less attention from the 'madding crowds' than its
neighbour. Set between two rivers, the Yeşilçay and the Göksü, it was essentially a small fishing community until residents and escapees from the city
began buying-up land in recent years. Even so, things are still pretty low-key
and the fine white sand beach, accessible by rowboat from many of the local
pensions, is excellent. The sea is subject to dangerous undercurrents so take
care when swimming.

Sleeping and eating Although if you set-out early it's possible to visit for the day,
the accommodation options have diversified considerably in the last couple of years,
so you may just decide to stay. **B** *Paradise*, Göksu Deresi Kenarı, T7218577. Idyllic spot
on the banks of the Göksu River, simple waterside bungalows, access by boat only so
ring ahead. **C-D** *Acqua Verde*, Kurfallı Köyü, T/F7217143. Comfortable rooms in modern but tasteful hotel, breakfast in large riverside garden, bike and boat rental.
D *Kurfal Tatil Evi*, Plaj Caddesi No 35, T7218493, F7218963, kurfal.com Across the
street from the beach, homely and comfortable small hotel, excellent wholesome
dinners. **D** *Riverside Club*, Yakuplu Mahallesi No 2, T7218293, F7218751, river-
side.com.tr Very relaxed place beside Göksu river, used as base for walking groups
from İstanbul so ring ahead at weekends, simple bungalows and rooms, camping
spaces, breakfast and dinner served on waterside terrace, canoes available.

In the summer & at weekends it's a good idea to ring ahead

Transport Some Şile buses from Üsküdar continue on to Ağva, however, when you
arrive enquire about the last return bus, usually 1800 in summer, 1700 in winter.

Essentials

Sleeping

İstanbul's accommodation scene is hugely diverse with something for everybody
from the footloose backpacker to the international business executive. As you'd
expect in a city so large there are several distinct areas where you can stay, each with
its own advantages and disadvantages.

There are 2 dialling codes for İstanbul: 0212 for the European side; 0216 for the Asian side

Within easy walking distance of many of the town's main sights, **Sultanahmet** is **Areas**
where you'll find most of the city's smaller and more interesting hotels. Budget hos
tels and pensions are concentrated on or near Akbıyık Caddesi, while there are also a
few more luxurious options dotted around, notably the lavish *Four Seasons Hotel* situated in what used to be a prison. Since the 1980s the area has witnessed the proliferation of 'Special Licence' or 'Ottoman' hotels, a trend started by the Turkish Touring and
Automobile Association when they converted several old Ottoman residences to take
paying guests. Exemplified by the *Ayasofya Pansionları* or the *Yeşil Ev* (see below),
these small atmospheric hotels give visitors the chance to live-out their own nostalgic
fantasy in splendid period surroundings, although due to the nature of the buildings
you may have to forgo the odd luxury. Most of these hotels, for instance, don't have a
lift. In recent years these 'Special License' hotels have been joined by a whole host of
other comfortable hotels housed in restored 19th-century buildings.

About 10-mins walk from the sights of Sultanahmet and Eminönü, the hotels in
Sirkeci tend to be slightly better value than those up the hill, although you won't
have the pleasure of looking out at Haghia Sofia from your roof terrace at breakfast.
Along with a selection of midrange package hotels, there's a cluster of cheap boarding houses on Ibni Kemal Caddesi, although as they're frequented mainly by visiting
workers some may not be suitable for women travelling alone.

İstanbul

A short tram ride from the Covered Bazaar and Sultanahmet, the backstreets of **Aksaray** and **Laleli** have a generous scattering of cheap and midrange hotels catering mainly for tourists and traders from the states of the ex-Soviet Union. Most are fairly standard package offerings, although they are well-equipped and represent much better value than a similar bed in Sultanahmet. The area also supports a thriving sex industry, so women walking alone at night may attract unwanted attention.

Across the Golden Horn the back streets of **Beyoğlu** hold numerous seedy boarding houses, along with a few little gems. Prices are generally very reasonable, although conditions may be a bit on the basic side. Also don't expect the company of other tourists as the cheaper places are generally frequented by visiting Turks. A good place to start for budget accommodation is Mescit Asmalı Sokakin Tepebaşı.

Around **Taksim** you'll find a large proportion of the city's modern package hotels, a well-equipped though fairly bland bunch; while just to the north are the big name luxury places like the *Hilton* and the *Swissôtel*. Staying in this part of town you have all the shopping and nightlife of Beyoğlu on your doorstep, although the majority of the big sights are a bus or taxi ride away.

Costs Although reasonable by European standards, hotel rates in İstanbul are considerably more expensive than the rest of the country. This is particularly the case in Sultanahmet where, except for the cheapest hostels, you pay a premium for being in the heart of the imperial district. As elsewhere, room prices in all but the lowliest boarding houses and hostels include a fairly standard breakfast. The prices quoted are high season rates, but in many places you'll be able to negotiate a discount of as much as 30% from September through until May. You may also be able to get a reduction if you're paying in cash, particularly hard currency, or if you're staying for more than a few days. Many places will also offer a free airport pick-up if you book ahead for more than 3 nights.

Booking Despite the abundance of hotels in the city it's a good idea to book ahead during the summer; on national holidays and when local events such as the İstanbul Festival are taking place. Booking in advance is particularly important for the small hotels in Sultanahmet, the best of which are very popular and only have a limited number of rooms. Bookings can be made by telephone, fax and, at a growing number of places, by e-mail too. Some places have started offering a small discount for on-line booking. In fact the internet revolution is at a much more advanced stage in İstanbul with a large number of the city's hotels having a presence on the world wide web. There are several sites offering information and in some cases an on-line booking facility for some of the hotels mentioned in this guide. Try: *istanbulhotels.com*; *istanbul.hotelguide.net* If you arrive at the airport without a hotel reservation there are 2 booking agents open 24-hrs a day at the far left-hand end (as you face the exit) of the arrivals hall. They have a database of mostly 3 and 4 star hotels and will deliver you free of charge.

Sultanahmet **LL** *Four Seasons Hotel*, Tevfikhane Sokak No 1, T6388200, F6388210,
See page 94 for map fourseasons.com Formerly the Sultanahmet prison, transformed into stunning luxury hotel in 1986, neo-classical architectural elements, set around courtyard with restaurant, sumptuous rooms, expansive marble bathrooms, conservatory restaurant, range of suites. Highly recommended. **L** *Hotel Armada*, Ahırkapı, T6381370, F5185060. Large well-designed, next to railway tracks and main coastal road, comfortable rooms, good restaurant. **L** *Yeşil Ev*, Kabasakal Caddesi No 5, T5176785, F5176780, yesilevhotel@superonline.com Became first Special License hotel after conversion in 1980s, unrivalled position on square between Haghia Sofia and Sultan Ahmet mosque, atmospheric 19th-century mansion, period furnishings throughout, comfortable but not overly luxurious rooms, bathrooms are slight disappointment, except for Paşa's Suite which has its own turkish bath, lovely garden café and restaurant serving traditional Turkish and international dishes. Recommended.

AL *Mavi Ev*, Dalbastı Sokak No 14, T6389010, F6389017, bluehouse.com.tr Conspicuous blue exterior, well-fitted and equipped, can't compete with atmosphere of nearby *Yeşil Ev* but comfortable, modern rooms, TV, minibar, a/c, excellent views of Sultan Ahmet from roof terrace restaurant. **AL** *Valide Sultan Konağı*, Ishakpaşa Caddesi, T5176558, F6380705, hotelvalidesultan.com, just down from Topkapı entrance. Wooden exterior, over-the-top decor, fake cornices and frilly curtains, over-priced, excellent views from top floor restaurant. **A** *Aya Sofya Pansiyonları*, Soğukçeşme Sokağı, T5133660, F5133669, between Haghia Sofia and the Topkapı palace. An entire row of Ottoman town houses lovingly restored by Turkish Touring and Automobile Club, atmospheric rooms and small 2-bedroom apartments which are perfect for couples with child, extra bed US$40, period decor and furnishings, like stepping back in time, peaceful setting, restaurant. Well recommended. **A** *Dersaadet Oteli*, Küçük Ayasofya Caddesi, Kapıağası Sokak No 5, T4580760, F5184918, just down the hill from Sultan Ahmet mosque and the Arasta Bazaar in residential neighbourhood. Corner building reconstructed in traditional Ottoman style, pleasant and very comfortable rooms, wooden floorboards and fittings, a/c, TV, refrigerator, telephone, 3 suites, roof terrace and leafy conservatory, discounts available for those in possession of this handbook. Highly recommended. **A** *Hotel Avicenna*, Amiral Tafdil Sokak No 31/33, T5170550, F5166555, avicenna.com.tr Special license hotel created from 2 Ottoman-era residences, not the most successful of conversions, lacking in atmosphere, comfortable rooms though with en suite, TV, telephone, a/c. **A** *Hotel Empress Zoe*, Akbıyık Caddesi No 10, T5182504, F5184360, emzoe.com Idiosyncratic 19-room hotel with lots of style and originality, walls decorated with Byzantine-style frescoes by Greek architect Nikos Papadakis, ancient masonry left exposed in reception, compact rooms stylishly furnished, residents include friendly cat, lovely little garden at rear, roof-top bar and terrace. Recommended. **A** *Hotel Spina*, Utangaç Sokak No 19, T6381727, F6381742, istanbulhotels.net/spina Restored Ottoman mansion, wooden facade, none of original features left unfortunately, comfortable rooms with large bathroom, facilities include TV, minibar, a/c, suites US$120, breakfast and BBQ's on roof terrace in summer. **A** *Hotel Turkoman*, Asmalı Çeşme Sokak No 2, T5162956, F5162957, turkomanhotel.com Splendid location overlooking the Hippodrome and the Blue Mosque, converted Ottoman residence which retains a homely feel, compact but comfortable rooms, metal bedsteads, wooden floorboards, ask for a front room, breakfast terrace and bar on the roof. Recommended. **A** *Ibrahim Paşa Oteli*, Terzihane Sokak No 5, T5180394, F5184457, pasha@ibm.net In sidestreet next to Museum of Turkish and Islamic Arts. 150-year old stone residence cleverly converted, stylish details, well-equipped rooms with all mod-cons, a/c, safe, TV, telephone, lift, pleasant ground floor café where breakfast is served, tiny roof terrace overlooking palace across the road. Recommended. **A** *Kybele Hotel*, Yerebatan Caddesi No 35, T5117766, F5134393, kybelehotel.com Small welcoming hotel, 10 out of 10 for novelty value and homeliness, filled with antiques and proprietor, Alparslan Akbayrak's, collection of over 2,000 glass lamps, rooms are nicely furnished and have decent marble bathrooms, singles are bit on small side though, triples on top floor have large balcony. Recommended home from home. **A-B** *Sarı Konak Oteli*, Mimar Mehmet Ağa Caddesi No 42, T6386258, F5178635, sarikonak@superonline.com Well-equipped rooms in pleasantly converted Ottoman building, architectural features such as wooden window screens retained, ensuite, TV, telephone, restaurant, front rooms have screened bay windows US$90, lovely roof terrace with conservatory. Recommended. **A-C** *Berk Guesthouse*, Kutlugün Sokak No 27, T5176561, F5177715. Small family-run guesthouse, plain rooms with toilet are a little over-priced, as are deluxe rooms available with a/c, TV, refrigerator, US$95, roof terrace and seating area, breakfast served in tiny garden at the rear.

B *Acropol Hotel*, Akbıyık Caddesi No 25, T6389021, F5183031, acropolhotel.com Well-appointed modern midrange hotel, comfortable rooms with TV, minibar, some have seaviews or small balcony, free airport pick-up for stays of over 3 days. **B** *Hotel Antea*, Piyerloti Caddesi No 21. Modern midrange hotel with reasonable, well-equipped, rooms, TV, radio, telephone, a/c. **B** *Hotel Ararat*, Torun Sokak No 3, Sultanahmet, T5160411, F5185241, ararat@turkport.com Newly opened near Arasta Bazaar, stylish interior by Greek architect/designer of Empress Zoe, artistic paint techniques, bare wooden beams, small rooms with ensuite, excellent views of Sultanahmet from front rooms and sitting area on top floor. Recommended. **B** *Hotel Pierre Loti*, Piyerloti Caddesi No 5, T5185700, F5161886, akturk.hotels.com Modern hotel fronting Divanyolu, has a lift, rooms equipped with TV, a/c, telephone, front rooms suffer from traffic noise. **B-C** *Alp Guest House*, Adliye Sokak No 4, T5179570, F5185728, alpguesthouse@turk.net Well-established place with decent rooms, prices increase as you move up the hotel, upper floors have seaview, breakfast on roof terrace in summer, cramped basement breakfast room in winter. **B-C** *Hotel Historia*, Amiral Tafdil Sokak No 23, T5177472, F5168169. Pretty wooden house, converted 9 years ago into hotel, small rooms are well-equipped but lacking in atmosphere, 3 have balconies, all are equipped with TV and telephone. **B-C** *Hotel Ishakpaşa*, Ishakpasa Caddesi No 15, T6386267, F6386027. Wooden-clad hotel built against Topkapı defences, modern, well-equipped rooms with TV, minibar, telephone, small garden, very convenient for palace and Haghia Sofia. **B-C** *Hotel Nomade*, Ticarethane Sokak No 15, T5111296, F5132404, just off Divanyolu Caddesi in busy sidestreet. Small welcoming reception, sofas make good place to people watch, rooms vary in size and lay-out, very pleasant decor, iron bedsteads, wooden floorboards, simple bathroom with shower, roof terrace, run by multi-lingual twin sisters Esra and Hamra. Recommended, particularly for women travellers.

C *Hotel Şebnem*, Adliye Sokak No 1, T5176623, F6381056, sebnemhotel.com Small pleasant guesthouse in quiet backstreet, efficient management, very pleasant rooms some with metal four-poster bed, fragrant pine floorboards, well plumbed bathroom with shower cabinet, large roof terrace with excellent views. Well recommended. **C** *Hotel Hippodrome*, Mimar Mehmetağa Caddesi No 17, T5176889, F5160268. Simply furnished but rooms come with TV, telephone, fan, showing its age a bit. **C** *Karasu Green Hotel*, Akbıyık Caddesi No 5, T6386600, F6386600, on corner. Plain rooms with ensuite, some have a/c, fan, popular restaurant downstairs. **C-D** *Hotel Uyan*, Utangaç Sokak No 25, T5164892, F5171582, uyanhotel.com Family house dating from 1930s, helpful staff, large rooms with plain decor, equipped with TV, some have balcony or a/c, excellent views from roof-terrace where breakfast is served, sunbathing deck. Recommended. **C-E** *Side Hotel and Pension*, Utangaç Sokak No 20, T5172282, F5176590, sidehotel.com Friendly proprietor, wide selection of different rooms, all clean and simply furnished, some with shared bathroom, US$25, single rooms US$5 less, also 12 deluxe rooms with wrought iron furniture and parquet flooring, equipped with TV and refrigerator, US$45, breakfast served on roof terrace with view. Recommended, good value.

D *Bahaus Guesthouse*, Bayram Fırın Sokak No 11, T5176697. Nondescript concrete building, rooms are pretty plain but they are clean, en suite, common room/eating area on the roof. **D** *Hanedan Guesthouse*, Adliye Sokak No 3, T5164869, F5174524, hanedan.com, just off Akbıyık Caddesi. Basic rooms with homely touch, all different shapes and sizes, roof terrace, restaurant, conscientious and friendly Malaysian manager. Recommended value for money. **D** *Universal Pension*, Akbıyık Caddesi No 18, T6382302, F5161827. Formerly the *Star Guesthouse*, plain and pretty uninspiring rooms with en-suite, some deluxe rooms and self-contained apartments. **D-F** *Orient Guesthouse*, Akbıyık Caddesi No 13, T5179493, F5183894, hostels.com/orienthostel

Backpacker favourite at the centre of Sultanahmet's budget accommodation district, simple rooms with plenty of clean shared toilets and showers on each floor, 4/8 person dorms US$6/7 each, more comfortable rooms at rear US$30, breakfast extra, rooftop café, basement bar, live entertainment evenings, travel agency on-site, cheap internet access. Recommended.

F *Hostel Merih*, Alemdar Caddesi No 24, T5139395, F5135271, short distance down from Haghia Sofia. Small hostel, quite cramped dorms but reasonable doubles. **F** *İstanbul Hostel*, Kutlugün Sokak No 35, T5169380, F5169384. Small, a relative newcomer to the budget accommodation scene, doubles with shared bathroom, dorm beds US$7, bar and restaurant in basement, breakfast extra. **F** *Sultan Tourist Hostel*, Terbiyik Caddesi No 3, Akbıyık Caddesi, T5169260, F5171626, feztravel.com Popular with backpackers, run by owner of *Fez Travel*, shared bathroom, single US$16, basic but clean rooms, newly renovated bathrooms, but there's only 1 on each floor, dorm beds US$7, café serving snacks, breakfast extra, games room. Recommended. **F** *Yücelt Interyouth Hostel*, Caferiye Sokak No 6/1, T5136150, F5127628, yücelthostel.com Large 300-bed hostel which has been around since the days of the overland trail to India, continues to provide excellent facilities although decor is a bit spartan, small basic doubles, singles US$16, all shared bathrooms, 6-bed dorms US$7, breakfast extra, safe, laundry, café, films daily, social events organized such as belly dancing evenings, IYHF discount. Recommended.

AL *Hotel Yaşmak Sultan*, Ebusuud Caddesi No 18-20, T5281343, F5281348, yasmaksultan@yasmak.com Modern well-appointed hotel, popular with continental package tours, comfortable rooms with TV, telephone, minibar, a/c, fitness centre, bar, restaurant, internet access. Recommended. **A** *Safir Hotel*, Ibni Kemal Caddesi No 14, T5205685, F5201009. Newly opened, plush reception and lounge furnished with comfy leather chairs, rich decor, modern rooms with all mod-cons, TV, telephone, a/c, good value at present but expect the prices to rise. Recommended. **B** *Grand Seigneur Hotel*, Nöbethane Caddesi No 30, T5121034, F5208910. Apocalyptic scene painted by the friendly proprietor on the wall of the breakfast room, rest of decor is more conventional: framed prints of city, homely and comfortable rooms with well-fitted bathrooms, views of the Golden Horn from some rooms on the upper floors, but no lift. Recommended. **B** *Hotel Olimpiyat*, Ebusuud Caddesi, Erdoğan Sokak No 5, T5119659, F5282160. Reasonable but certainly nothing special, small rooms with ensuite, TV and telephone. **C-D** *Sunlife Hotel*, Ebusuud Caddesi No 2, T5205111, F5205344, sunlife-hotels.com.tr, corner building. Very close to sights of Sultanahmet, modern, well-equipped rooms, telephone, TV, a/c, decent size bathroom, restaurant on roof, good value. Recommended. **C-D** *Hotel Orsep*, T5133586, F5133591. Place popular with visiting businessmen, TV, telephone. **E** *Hotel Ipek Palas*, Orhaniye Caddesi No 9, T5209724, F5261302, ipekotel@superonline.com Over 50 years old, rooms are bit disappointing after antique lift, equipped with ensuite, TV and telephone, 3-bed rooms available, not bad for the money. **E** *Hotel Karacu bay*, Ibni Kemal Caddesi No 28, T5133570, F5226133. Small simple rooms with TV and telephone, well-priced. **F** *Hotel Ağan*, Saffetipaşa Sokak No 6, T5278550, pretty basic but clean doubles. **F** *Hotel Güray*, Ibni Kemal Caddesi No 32, T5222868, 2-star hotel with tatty rooms, no breakfast. **G** *Hotel Meram*, Ibni Kemal Caddesi No 19, T5276295, basic but pretty clean rooms with simple toilet, also doubles with shared toilet for US$8.50, no breakfast, not recommended for women alone. **G** *Hotel Sultan*, Orhaniye Caddesi No 28, T5271986, plain but clean, artistic interior decoration, simple rooms with tiny bathroom, no breakfast, best of the areas rock-bottom boarding houses. **G** *Otel Asya*, Ibni Kemal Caddesi No 41, T5284442, F5227451, rock bottom place, basic, shared bathroom, popular with Central Asian workers and traders, not recommended for women.

Sirkeci
See page 104 for map

İstanbul

Beyazıt **A** *The President Hotel*, Tiyatro Caddesi No 25, T5166980, F5166998, presidenthotel.com, 100 m down hill from Beyazıt Convenient for Covered Bazaar, modern mid-range package hotel, comfortable rooms with TV, telephone, restaurant, 'English' Pub on premises.

Aksaray & Laleli **LL** *Merit Antique*, Ordu Caddesi No 226, T5139300, F5139340. Popular with business travellers, comfortable rooms with TV, a/c and minibar, there's a basement pool, jacuzzi and sauna, 4 restaurants including city's only kosher diner in atrium between buildings. **A** *Grand Hotel Gülsoy*, Şehzadebaşı Caddesi No 17, T5125842, F5266075, opposite Şehzade Camii. Modern hotel with mainly Russian clientele, comfy but rather cramped rooms with plenty of mod-cons. **C** *Hotel Klas*, Harikzedeler Sokak No 48. A solid midrange option, better equipped with restaurant, bar and sauna than *Hotel Pisa*. **C** *Hotel Pisa*, Kurultay Sokak No 3, T5261878, F5124220, up Fethi Bey Caddesi beside the Laleli Camii you'll find this one on a corner. A newish hotel, decent rooms with TV and telephone but tiny bathroom, ground floor bar and tables on the street, not bad value for money. **C** *Prestige Hotel*, Koska Caddesi No 8, T5188280, F5188290, in the street opposite the Laleli Mosque. Reception reached up escalator from street, pretty average package rooms which come with TV, refrigerator, telephone and a/c as standard. Good value. **D** *Hotel Eyfel*, Kurultay Sokak No 19, T5209788, up Fethi Bey Caddesi beside the Laleli Camii, first right, comfortable rooms with tiny bathroom, package hotel popular with Russian and German groups, restaurant, bar, good value. **F** *Fahri 2*, Nöbethane Caddesi No 32, Laleli, T5141597. Simple rooms in modern hotel, equipped with TV and telephone, good value. **F** *Hotel Reşitpaşa*, Büyük Reşitpaşa Caddesi No 34, Laleli. Plain unexceptional rooms with ensuite bathroom.

Edirne Kapı **A** *Kariye Oteli*, Kariye Camii Sokak No 18, Edirne Kapı, T5348414, F5216631, late 19th-century residence converted sensitively by Turkish Touring and Automobile Association, situated in backstreets next to the church of St Chora, peaceful location, homely rooms furnished in period style, excellent restaurant serving 'Ottoman' cuisine downstairs, terrace dining in summer, good value, however, quite a distance from the sights. Recommended.

Galata &
Tepebaşı
See page 118 for map
LL *Pera Palas*, Meşrutiyet Caddesi No 89-100, T2514560, F2514088. Built to accommodate passengers from the Orient Express in 1892, reputation attracted many famous people, refurbished in 1974 but retains something of its original atmosphere and splendor, faded gently by the years, 145 rooms are little changed, period-style furnishings, bathrooms a bit austere by today's standards, dine beneath chandeliers in restaurant, enjoy a drink at the atmospheric bar or a pot of English tea in the patisserie, attentive staff. Recommended for nostalgia. **LL** *Hotel Mercure*, Meşrutiyet Caddesi. Unappealling concrete tower, dated decor, comfortable rooms with excellent views, open-buffet breakfast, restaurant. **L** *Richmond Hotel*, Istiklal Caddesi No 445, T2525460, F2529707, on İstanbul's main shopping street near the Russian Consulate. Understated comfort and well-equipped rooms: hair-dryer, a/c, TV, telephone, back rooms look-out over Bosphorus and Golden Horn, scenic *Blue Cat* rooftop restaurant/bar lovely in summer, nightly entertainment, well-established and very upmarket café at street level. Recommended. **AL** *Grace Hotel*, Meşrutiyet Caddesi No 38, T2933955, F2524370, next to British Consulate. Modern hotel, rooms have a/c, minibar, telephone and TV, 4 split-level suites, bar with good views, restaurant. **C** *Büyük Londra Oteli*, Meşrutiyet Caddesi No 117, T2450670, F2450671. Opened in 1892 although it hasn't aged as gracefully as its neighbour the *Pera Palas*, atmosphere of decay pervades the place, eccentric decor, parrots in cages looking out of the windows from lounge, tatty rooms badly in need of renovation, recommended for a drink rather than the night. **C** *Hotel Inka*, Meşrutiyet Caddesi No 225, T2431728, F2492044. Modern, plain but well-equipped rooms, TV, telephone, some have a/c.

Recommended. **D** *Hotel Monopol*, Meşrutiyet Caddesi No 223, T2517326, F2517333. 3-star place near the US Consulate General, the clean rooms are a good size, comfortable but dated furnishings, equipped with TV, minibar and shower, represents good value, best of midrange places on Meşrutiyet Caddesi. Recommended. **E** *Hotel Saydam*, Asmalı Mescit Caddesi No 1, T2518116, F2440366. Small, cramped rooms in modern hotel, well-equipped: TV, telephone and refrigerator, breakfast extra. **E** *Hotel Silviya*, Asmalı Mescit Caddesi No 54, T2927749, F2436115. Newly-opened, well-fitted rooms with brand new furniture, telephone, TV, no breakfast, very good value but expect prices to rise. Recommended. **F** *Devran Oteli*, Tepebaşı Kallavi Sokak No 38, in alley next to *Büyük Londra Oteli*. Dated sitting area, simply furnished rooms with desk, basin and small bathroom, single US$10, triple US$16, no breakfast. **F** *Hotel Pelikan*, Asmalı Mescit Caddesi No 44, T2525803, F2518934. Plain rooms with TV and refrigerator, no breakfast.

LL *Ceylan Inter-Continental*, Asker Ocağı Caddesi No 1, T2312121. All the comforts and facilities you'd expect in this brash 390-room monster, also some you wouldn't (ie golf simulator), wonderful panoramic bar on top floor and several top notch restaurants, daily BBQ beside the pool. **LL** *Divan Hotel*, Cumhuriyet Caddesi No 2, T2314100, F2488527. Part of the Koç families huge business empire, unassuming luxury and excellent service distinguish this 180 room place, nicely furnished guestrooms, plenty of space except in bathroom, cable TV, a/c, bar, restaurant and famous patisserie. **LL** *Hilton İstanbul*, Cumhuriyet Caddesi, T2314650, F2404165, hilton.com Unattractive concrete block surrounded by 13 acres of lovely gardens, rooms with Bosphorus view US$355, comfortable rooms with large balconies, equipped with cable TV, a/c, minibar, safe, also has business centre, several restaurants, sports facilities including swimming pool, baby sitting service is useful if you want to go out on the town. **LL** *Marmara Hotel*, Taksim Square, Taksim, T2514696, F2440509, themarmara.com.tr Couldn't get more central than this well-established hotel on Taksim Square, comfortable rooms starting to feel a bit dated, rooms higher up have wonderful views, rooftop bar and restaurant, popular street-level café, excellent gym, sauna, Turkish bath, pool, various classes also on offer, recommended Sunday buffet. **LL** *Swissôtel*, Bayıldım Caddesi No 2, Maçka, T3261100, F3261122, swissotel.com One of city's foremost luxury hotels, excellent position surrounded by immaculate gardens, sweeping views of the Bosphorus, loads of services and facilities plus 6 restaurants to choose from, sumptuous tastefully furnished modern rooms. Recommended.

AL *Dorint Park Plaza*, Topcu Caddesi No 23, T2545100, F2547160, dorintparkplaza.com Part of German group, comfortable, well-furnished and equipped rooms, TV, telephone, safe, 24-hr room service, pleasant seating area on ground floor, basement pool, fitness centre, wood panelled bar and bistro with live music nightly, good value for money. Highly recommended. **AL** *Taksim Square Hotel*, Sıraserviler Caddesi No 15, T2926440, F2926449, taksimsquare hotel.com Smart, modern, catering mainly to businessmen, higher back rooms have Bosphorus view, front ones on lower floors are a bit noisy, restaurant. Recommended. **A** *Dilson Hotel*, T2529600, F2497077. Corny neo-classical decor in lobby, small rooms showing their age, front rooms give excellent vantage point for people watching, Bosphorus view at back reserved for suites, US$200, TV and telephone. **A** *Hotel Grand Star*, Sıraselviler Caddesi No 79, T2577070, F2517822. Modern, 4-star, reasonable rooms with all mod-cons, pool, fitness centre, some rooms at rear have Bosphorus views. Best of the bunch on Sıraselviler Caddesi. **A** *Hotel Lamartine*, Lamartine Caddesi No 25, T2546270, F2562776, 2-mins walk from Taksim. Good value midrange option, clean comfortable rooms with TV, telephone and refrigerator as standard. Recommended. **A** *Savoy Hotel*, Sıraselviler Caddesi No 29, T2529326, F2432010. No connection with London namesake, modern with business clientel, small but

Around Taksim & Maçka
See page 118 for map

İstanbul

well-equipped rooms, front ones suffer from traffic noise. **B** *Vardar Palace Hotel*, Siraselviler Caddesi No 54, T2522888, F2521527. Once-grand 19th-century building which has seen better days, good size rooms with high ceilings, unfortunately a bit dark and dingy, rooms have TV and telephone, noise is a problem in front rooms.

C *Hotel Residence,* Sadri Alışık Sokak No 19, T2527687, F2430084, in backstreet off Istiklal Caddesi. Small newly decorated rooms, very well-equipped for price: a/c, telephone, TV, some rooms have interconnecting door, noise from surrounding bars may be nuisance so ask for rooms on 5th or 6th floor, friendly staff, very good value. Recommended. **D** *Otel Avrupa*, Topçu Caddesi No 32, T2509420, F2507399. Recently had a facelift, simple rooms in corner building, homely breakfast room/sitting area on 1st floor, reasonable value for money but not as well-equipped as *Residence*. **E** *Hotel As*, Bekar Sokak No 26, T2526525, F2450099. High-ceiling rooms in old building, tiny bathrooms. **F** *Hotel Yonga*, Tarlabaşı Bulvarı, Toprak Lüle Sokak No 5, T2939391, F2512627, 5-mins walk from Taksim. Newly renovated reception, rooms haven't had the treatment yet, bit tatty but decent enough for the price, TV, telephone. Recommended. **G** *Hotel Sultan*, Nana Sokak No 22, basic, very small single rooms only.

Near the airport **L** *Polat Renaissance İstanbul Hotel*, Sahil Caddesi, Yeşilyurt, T6631700, F6631755, renaissance-hotels.com/renaiss, high-rise hotel within striking distance of the airport, decent rooms most with excellent panoramic views, a/c, telephone, cable TV, minibar, large outdoor pool, tennis courts, fitness centre, restaurant and piano bar. Recommended. **B-C** *Yeşilköy Aile Pansiyonu*, İstanbul Caddesi No 29, Yeşilköy, T6634812, F5738082. Charming 140 year old house in genteel suburb 5 mins by cab from the airport, owned by Mr Frenkel an Austria Jew whose family fled to Turkey from the Nazis, large high-ceiling rooms with bathroom, old fashioned furnishings, loads of atmosphere, breakfast on the terrace, single/triple/quad US$40/60/70. Recommended.

Apartments **AL** *Galata Residence*, Bankalar Caddesi, Hacı Ali Sokak, Galata, T2924841, F2442323. Colourful neighbourhood at bottom of Galata, 5-mins walk from Galata bridge, brick building constructed in 1881 by Jewish banking family, the Comandos, recently converted into comfortable, pleasantly furnished fully-equipped 2-bedroom apartments, sleep up to 4 people, kitchenette, restaurant on top floor and café, special discounted rates for extended stays. Recommended. **A** *Family House*, Gümüşsuyu, Kutlu Sokak No 53, Taksim, T2499670, F2499667, familyhouse@ihlas.net.tr Simply-furnished apartments in quiet backstreet, 2 mins from Taksim, sleep up to 4 people, perfect for families, baby-sitting service, equipped kitchenette, the manager, Atıl Erman, is very helpful, airport pick-ups organized, discounts in winter and for long-stay guests. **B** *Entes Apart Otel*, Ipek Caddesi No 19, Taksim, T2932208, F2931598, entesapart@ turk.net, in backstreet near Aya Triada. Compact, modern, open plan or with separate bedroom, sleep 2, 3rd on sofa bed, fully equipped kitchenette, impressive references, minimum stay 3 days, discounts for longer periods.

The Bosphorus **European shore** **L** *Hotel Princess Ortaköy*, Dereboyu Caddesi No 36, Ortaköy,
Suburbs T2276010, F2602148. Newish 5-star, mainly business clientel, rooms vary in size, all well-equipped with TV, telephone, a/c, minibar. Pool, fitness centre and meeting rooms. Renovation of the *Bebek Hotel* on the main street in Bebek is scheduled to be finished early in 2001; the smart waterside bar is still open though.

Asian shore Kadıköy Due to its proximity to Haydarpaşa station there is no problem finding a bed here, although with regular ferries and buses linking it to the European side there is also little reason to stay, unless of course you arrive late at night or just fancy something different. **A** *Hotel Eysan*, Rıhtım Caddesi No 26, T3462440,

F3472329. Yellow building on the busy waterfront road, plain but comfortable rooms, many have a Bosphorus view, on lower floors traffic noise could be a problem, a/c, TV, minibar as standard, restaurant with views across to Sarayburnu and Sultanahmet. Recommended. **D** *Hotel Zirve*, Reşitefendi Sokak No 36, T4145142, near *Hotel Eysan*. 2-star, plain, modern rooms, small shower, TV, telephone. **D** *Kent Otel*, Serasker Caddesi No 8, T3362453. Newly opened in shopping district 5 mins from ferry terminals, signposted up Muvakkithane Caddesi from square, left at Serb church and then first right, clean, modern rooms, marble floors, simple furnishings, at the moment bathrooms are shared, however, work is in progress to make facilities ensuite, free mineral water dispenser. Recommended. **F** *Hotel Okur*, Reşitefendi Sokak No 3, T3360629. Basic but clean rooms, best of several budget places inland from *Hotel Eysan*. **G** *Girne Oteli*, Kırmızı Koşak Sokak, T3369077, basic crash pad, cheaper rooms with shared bedroom. **Beylerbeyi LL** *Bosphorus Pasha*, Yalıboyu Caddesi No 64, T4220003, F4220012. Exclusive small hotel in restored 19th-century mansion house, fantastic Bosphorus-side position near Beylerbeyi Palace, very romantic setting, distinguished guests include John le Carré and Asil Nadir, large high-ceiling rooms are lavishly furnished with antiques, excellent restaurant on-site. Recommended.

Eating

As you'd expect İstanbul has by far the widest choice of restaurants in the country – everything from basic *lokantas* serving simple Turkish dishes to top notch establishments with extensive International menus. Fish restaurants are particularly popular with locals and tourists alike and they can be found in most parts of the city, although some of the nicest, and the most pricey, are along the Bosphorus. Kumkapı (see page 152) is an area particularly famous for its fish restaurants and riotous nocturnal atmosphere. The *meyhanes* of Beyoğlu are a excellent places to try *meze* accompanied by the national drink *rakı* and you may well have the bonus of live music as well. A popular place to eat out is the Çiçek Pasajı, off Istiklal Caddesi (see page 156), although tourists generally outnumber locals now (never a good sign) and standards of food and service have slipped considerably. Much better to seek out the quieter places in the backstreets off the Sahne Sokak, known as the Balık Pazarı (Fish market). If you've had enough of Turkish food there are decent Chinese, Japanese and European restaurants in Beyoğlu, Taksim and the city's 5-star hotels. Many of these luxury hotels also have themed food evenings and Sunday buffet brunches. Western fast-food places are ubiquitous too. For a fast inexpensive snack the fish sandwiches served-up from boats moored along the waterfront in Eminönü are hard to beat. Other snack food widely available on the streets are the sesame covered bread rings, *simit*, generally eaten for breakfast; roasted chesnuts and the tight coils of grilled tripe which are very much an aquired taste. Beef or chicken *döner* kebaps are also cheap and plentiful.

Expensive *Sarnıç*, Soğukçeşme Sokagı, T5124291, Turkish/French cuisine eaten in interesting surroundings of converted Byzantine cistern.

Sultanahmet & Divan Yolu
See page 94 for map

Midrange *Amedros*, Hoca Rüstem Sokak No 7, T5228356. Pleasant bistro owned by local architect, cozy wooden interior with open fire in winter, tables outside on street in summer, specialities such as *pither kebap*, delicately spiced lamb cooked in a clay pot with wine and vegetables, and *çoban kavurma*, lamb fried on a wok with tomatoes, peppers and spices, also pasta, crèpes and other international dishes, about US$15 per head before wine. *Balıkçı Sabahattin*, Çankurtaran, T4581824, dine in relaxed atmosphere on meze and excellent fish, there is no menu so surrender yourself to the daily choice of traditional Turkish starters and well-cooked seafood, in summer tables are put outside in the quiet street, expect to pay about US$15 per head with wine. *Dubb*, Incili Çavuş Sokak No 10, Sultanahmet, very reasonably priced little

☞ Lively streets

A meal in one of the dozens of restaurants which line the cobbled streets of **Kumkapı** ranks as one of the city's most memorable dining experiences. Formerly populated largely by Armenians, the district gets its name from a gate in the city walls known as the Kum Kapı, or Sand Gate, which used to lead out to the fishing harbour. Known as Kontoscalian in Byzantine times, the harbour is still used by a large and active fishing fleet which sets out daily to trawl the Sea of Marmara. Inland, the lanes radiating from the village fountain are today known for their lively fish restaurants. Tables are put out on the street and diners, well lubricated with rakı are serenaded by groups of musicians who wander from place to place. The atmosphere is riotous and fun, and it's quite usual for people to get up and have a dance.

Competition between the many restaurants is fierce with waiters thrusting menus into your face as you walk down the street. Don't let yourself be hurried. Have a good walk around and even check what a couple of restaurants have on display in their glass-fronted refrigerators before deciding on where to sit down. Expect to pay US$15-30 per head on a meal which includes meze, fish, desert and wine or rakı. If there is a group of you, negotiate a per person price before sitting down.

Some places to check-out are: **Çapari** or **Gölçek** on Çarpariz Sokak between the fountain and the bridge under the railway lines; **Yengeç** on Telli Odalar Sokak No 6, is a three storey restaurant with specialities including sword fish kebap and kiremitte balık, fish baked on an earthenware tile with cheese. A local speciality to try is lakerda (salted sea bass) a meze brought to your table from a local fish-mongers. If your budget won't stretch to, or you don't like, fish, then **Meşhur Tarihi Bursa Inegöl Köftesi** on Üstat Sokak No 10, inland from the fountain, is an unassuming little place serving soup, köfte or şiş for US$2.50.

Indian restaurant, tandoori oven, US$10 per head before wine, closed Mon. **Konyalı**, Topkapı Palace, T5139696, excellent position on terraces overlooking Bosphorus, monopoly on Topkapı lunchtime business, very average menu, also has self-service section with döner sandwiches and other snacks. **Magnura**, Akbıyık Caddesi No 26, Sultanahmet, old house stylishly converted, Turkish food with a distinctly Meditteranean influence, about US$12 per head. **Mosaik**, Ticarethane Sokak, Sultanahmet, homely little dining room warmed by old gas fire during colder months, in summer the windows are wide open to bustling street, food is a bit disappointing, dressed-up versions of traditional dishes, rather bland. **Rami**, Utangaç Sokak No 6, Sultanahmet, T5176593. Charming restaurant housed on 2 floors of quaint Ottoman house, very atmospheric antique-filled dining rooms warmed by wood burning stoves in winter, views of Blue Mosque from roof terrace, traditional Turkish cuisine, fish of the day also available. **Rumeli Cafe**, Ticarethane Sokak No 8, Sultanahmet, T5120008. Very ambient restaurant in what was old print works, unclad brickwork and bare boards, interesting menu, Greek influences, fried cheese, salads, try the Sultan Abdulazziz: sauteed lamb on an aubergine bechamel base, also have vegetarian dishes. **Saltanat**, Tahsinbey Sokak No 11, off Divanyolu, Sultanahmet, stone-clad exterior, touristy restaurant serving Turkish and international food including some Thai dishes. **Yeşil Ev**, Kabasakal Caddesi No 5, Sultanahmet, lovely location in garden of hotel, tables in shade near fountain, Turkish and European dishes, meat-orientated, traditional Turkish puddings, US$8-10 for a main dish.

Cheap *Akdeniz Lokantası*, Hoca Rüstem Sokak, Sultanahmet, basic, no-thrills lokanta serving decent stew-tray food, kebaps and puddings. *Cennet*, Divanyolu Caddesi No 90, Çemberlitaş, Anatolian food, *gözleme*, *ayran* and *mantı*, lounge at small tables on the floor and watch women in village outfits roll-out paper thin dough, favourite lunch spot for tourists. *Divan Pizza Shop*, Divanyolu Caddesi, Sultanahmet, just up from Et Meydanı on right, snack-bar serving pizza, lahmacun and grilled meat dishes. *Doy Doy*, Zıfa Hamamı Sok 13, south of the Hippodrome. Good quality standard fare with rooftop terrace overlooking the Blue Mosque. *Karasu Restaurant*, Akbıyık Caddesi No 5, Sultanahmet, convenient for those staying in pensions or hotels along Akbıyık Caddesi, pretty good kebaps, grilled meat, lahmacun and pide, sit at low tables or on cushions on the floor. *Lale Restaurant*, Divan Yolu No 18, Sultanahmet, favourite haunt for the hippy travellers of yesteryear, featured in scenes from Midnight Express, recently revamped and renamed for the new millenium, don't expect much of an atmosphere though, self-service style, good selection of stew tray stews, kebaps, grilled meats at slightly inflated prices. *Sultanahmet Köftecisi*, Divan Yolu No 12A, long-standing and much replicated meat ball and *piyaz* (white-bean salad) place, small, plain tiled interior, but it's for the *köfte* that people come, still good value despite recent inflation, leave full for less than US$3. *Turkistan Aşevi*, Tavukhane Sokağı No 36, Sultanahmet, behind the Blue Mosque, family-run Turkish folk restaurant serving traditional Anatolian fare, diners must take their shoes off at the door and sit on stools around low tables, staff are dressed in traditional costume, a bit corny but still very popular, also have nomadic *yurt* (tent) across the road which is open in summer.

Cafés *Basin Müze Cafe*, Basin Müze, Divanyolu Caddesi, Çemberlitaş, very pleasant café on ground floor of building housing the Press Museum, relaxed atmosphere, beer and snacks served. *Çiğdem Pastanesi*, Divanyolu Caddesi, near Sultanahmet tram stop, mouth-watering array of cakes and biscuits, good for pastries at breakfast too. *Derviş Çay Bahçesi*, Kabasakal Sokak, Sultanahmet, simple café with shady terrace next to Baths of Roxelana. *Konut Evi*, Soğukçeşme Sokak, Sultanahmet, take a break from sight-seeing in the garden of this Ottoman mansion. *Medrese Kafeterya*, Hoca Rüstem Sokak, Sultanahmet, café in restored Mehmet Ağa Seminary, popular with students and local intellectuals, hosts lectures and recitals, internet access *Traditional Mystic Water Pipe and Erenler Tea Garden*, Çorlulu Ali Paşa Medresesi, Divanyolu Caddesi, Çemberlitaş, not as corny as it sounds, sip tea and try smoking a nargile in historic courtyard of 17th-century seminary

Midrange *Asıtane*, Kariye Hotel, Kariye Camii Sokak No 16, Edirnekapı, T5348414, excellent Ottoman cuisine in pleasant surroundings of restored Ottoman house, dining outside on large leafy terrace during the summer, another good reason to visit the Church of St Saviour in Chora nearby. *Durüzziyafe*, Şifahane Caddesi, Süleymaniye, T5118414, dine on well-prepared Turkish dishes in magnificent location: restored 16th-century kitchens of the Süleymaniye mosque, some tables outside in shady courtyard beside fountain, convenient place to break for lunch while visiting mosque. *Havuzlu Lokantası*, Gani Çelebi Sokak No 3, Kapalı Çarşı, (see map, page 100) just the place to have a bite to eat in the Covered Bazaar, nothing amazing but reasonable grills and steam tray food served at tables in large dining room, service is generally good but it can be slow when it's busy. *Hünkar*, Akdeniz Caddesi No 21, Fatih, off Vatan Caddesi, unassuming family run place serving traditional Turkish/Ottoman cuisine in pleasant surroundings, colourful jars of pickles and preserves decorate interior. *Safran*, Çemberlitaş, Ottoman-style building on the corner across from tram stop, varied menu aimed at tourists, specialities include *çöp şiş* (chunks of lamb cooked on bamboo skewers) and *testi kebabı* (lamb cooked in clay pot), also international dishes like spaghetti and steak. **Cafés** *Fez Cafe*, Halıcılar Caddesi, Covered Bazaar, good place to break for a cappacino during shopping expeditions. *Pierre Loti*, Gümüşsuyu Balmumcu Sokak No 5, Eyüp, nice place to break for a drink having looked at Eyüp Camii (see page 112). *Şark Kahvesi*, Yağlıkçılar Caddesi, Covered Bazaar, more traditional café, favourite of local shopkeepers, drink tea serenaded by the click of backgammon dice.

İstanbul

Covered Bazaar & beyond

Sirkeci &
Eminönü
See page 104 for map

Expensive *Hamam*, Sepetçiler Kasrı, Kennedy Caddesi, T5116386, as locations go you couldn't get much better than this on a summer evening, occupies part of restored Ottoman fort which used to guard royal docks, fantastic views across the Golden Horn to Galata and up Bosphorus as far as Dolmabahçe, Turkish Ottoman cuisine, also fish and some international dishes. **Midrange** *Pandeli*, Mısır Çarşısı No 54, 1 of the city's oldest restaurants, moved to hall above entrance of Spice Bazaar in 1955 after anti-Greek riots, Greek/Turkish management, excellent traditional dishes such as *Kağıtta levrek*, sea bass baked in waxed paper to keep it moist, open weekday lunch times only. **Cheap** A number of well-frequented budget eateries are clustered near the Hocapaşa Camii on İbni Kemal Caddesi, to the south of Sirkeci station. Places such as *Çiçek Kebap*, *Kasap Osman* or *Kardeşler Anadolu Lokantası* serve-up soup, stew-tray stews and şiş kebap. Or try *Namlı Rumeli Köftecisi* where a meatball sandwich and a drink weighs-in at under US$3. *Özler Restaurant*, also on İbni Kemal Caddesi is a very popular *meyhane*, particularly when there's an important football match on TV, predominantly male crowd, meze, fried fish and grilled meat, washed down with rakı or beer. *Aşçıbaşı Restaurant*, Ankara Caddesi, Emir Han Sokak No 7/9, easily overlooked in a narrow street opposite Sirkeci station, small friendly self-service place on 2 levels, choose from selection of well-prepared Turkish dishes, good lunch spot with very reasonable prices, closes 1700, no alcohol. *Borsa*, Yalı Köşkü Caddesi, Sirkeci, up side street near pedestrian bridge across Kennedy Caddesi, large self-service caféteria style restaurant, very busy at lunch time, excellent range of Turkish food, also grilled meat and fish, alcohol served.

Galata, Tünel
& Tepebaşı
See pages 114 & 118
for maps

Expensive *Pera*, *Pera Palace Hotel*, Tepebaşı, T2430505, Turkish/international menu in atmospheric dining room of this old institution.

Midrange *Four Seasons Restaurant*, İstiklal Caddesi No 509, T2933941, Tünel end of İstiklal, Turkish/Continental menu served in intimate setting, starters include grilled liver or stuffed peppers, main dishes like duck a l'orange. *Galata Evi*, Galata Kulesi Sokak No 61, T2451861, on left 75 m down Galata Kulesi Sokak from base of the Galata tower, housed in building which served as British police station during post-Great War occupation, café and restaurant serving Georgian specialities such as chicken with walnut sauce, goulash and tatar mantı, US$8 per head, no alcohol, closes early evening unless prior reservation made. *Galata Restaurant*, Orhan Apaydın Sokak No 11, T2931139, F2456705, just off İstiklal Caddesi on same street as *Çatı*, entered through discreet wooden door, friendly, convivial atmosphere, live *fasıl* music every evening, set-menu: excellent selection of delicious hot and cold meze brought to the table, main dish is generally meat or chicken, desert and 2 double rakı, 3 beers or a small bottle of wine, US$16 (US$20 weekends), very popular so book well ahead at the weekends. *Galata Tower*, Büyük Hendek Sokak, Galata, worth putting-up with the mediocre food for the exceptional panoramic view and very entertaining floor-show, like a well-rehearsed adult pantomime, set-menu US$11 at lunch, US$17 at dinner, dinner and show US$75. *Olimpiyat 1 and 3*, Rıhtım Caddesi No 17 and 31, Karaköy, busy fish restaurants on front near Karaköy ferry station, best in the row of places, reasonably priced meze and seafood, informal atmosphere, bar downstairs, from some tables upstairs you can sit and watch the colourful waterside fish market. *Pars*, Meşrutiyet Caddesi No 187, opposite *Pera Palace*, small Persian restaurant, pictures of the dishes on menu for those who aren't acquainted with Iraninan cuisine, features grilled meat and stews served with spiced pilav, alcohol served. *Refik*, Sofyalı Sokak No 10, T2432834, well-regarded back-street *meyhane*, patronized by regulars who appreciate good food and a relaxed atmosphere, excellent meze including delicious *kereviz* (artichoke heart), *karalahana dolması* (stuffed black cabbage) and *ciğer tava* (spicy fried liver), leave room for fish or grilled meat after, good value at US$15 per head with alcohol, booking recommended. *Rejans*, Olivio Geçidi, just off İstiklal Caddesi, T2441610, old-fashioned, a bit dingy, dining room, meat-orientated menu, Russian/Eastern European specialities served along with lemon vodka charged by the shot from a bottle on the table, open for lunch and dinner, live music at weekends, booking recommended. *Sanat*, Nevizade Sokak No 23, T2441309, sophisticated little fish restaurant which attracts an intellectual crowd, reasonable prices and much better quality than near-by Çiçek Pasajı. *Şarabi*, Istiklal Caddesi No 174, smart wine-bar and restaurant serving sophisticated snacks and meals, delicious grilled quail with pomegranate sauce, US$10 per head before alcohol. *Yakup 2*, Asmalı Mescit Caddesi No 35, T2492925, another local favourite, no-nonsense eating and drinking in traditional *meyhane* atmosphere, good meze selection, fish and meat dishes, excellent value. *Zindan*, Olivio Geçidi, T2527340, below Rejans in dungeon-like cellar, hence name which means dungeon, don't be put off descending to this pleasant *meyhane*.

Cheap *Fıccın*, Kallavi Sokak No 7, T2933786, small smart place divided between 3 premises, simple Turkish cuisine, menu changed daily, popular lunch spot, closes 1700. *Huseyin Zihni*, Asmalı Mescit Sokak No 29, tiny place which does cheap and tasty dishes such as mantı. *Lale İşkembecisi*, Istiklal Caddesi No 238, soups and kebaps in pleasantly decorated place on the main drag. *Lila*, Istiklal Caddesi No 425, selection of steam tray stews and soups, salads and desert, self-service. *Mevlana Et Lokantası*, next to the Yeraltı Camii, Karaköy, simple corner restaurant frequented by local shop-keepers and traders, cheap soups and kebaps. *Piknik*, Istiklal Caddesi No 268, self-service restaurant specializing in grilled köfte and piyaz, but with lots besides.

Cafés and pudding shops *Galata Evi*, Galatakulesi Sokak No 61, quiet café in old Galata neighbourhood below the tower, building was British police station during the post Great War occupation, hot and cold drinks, also specialize in Georgian dishes such as chicken with walnut sauce. *Is-tav-rit*, Istiklal Caddesi No 237, café above music and book store, popular with students and young intellectual crowd. *KV Cafe*, Tünel Geçidi, in arcade opposite the top station, homemade cakes, biscuits and börek, popular with latte sipping bourgeoisie, filled with interesting antiques, back-dated and current newspapers to read, candle-lit tables outside in summer, ambience doesn't come cheap though. *Patisserie de Pera*, Pera Palas Hotel, Meşrutiyet Caddesi, cakes and a pot of English tea accompanied by classical music in period surroundings. *Saray Muhallebicisi*, Istiklal Caddesi No 98, delicious milk puddings and traditional sweets.

Expensive *Chan-ga*, Sıraselviler Caddesi No 87, Taksim, stylish, modern basement restaurant, ecclectic menu "designed" by Peter Gordon of the *Sugar Club* in London, talk-of-the town so you'll need to reserve at least a week in advance, you may have more luck getting a seat at the bar. *Citronelle*, Inter-Continental Hotel, Taksim, a fusion of Far Eastern and European influences go to make-up the refined menu of this highly regarded restaurant. *La Corne d'Or*, Swissôtel, Maçka, T3268268, billed as the best French restaurant in town, dine on delicacies such as pan-fried duck with pear chutney or rack of lamb with white bean stew, open winter only, in summer the menu changes and the restaurant moves up to a roof terrace overlooking the Bosphorus, expect a bill of about US$40 per head with wine. *Mezzaluna*, Abdi İpekçi Caddesi No 38/1, Nişantaşı, T2313142, modern Italian restaurant, extensive menu filled with delicious pastas, pizzas and other dishes, attentive service and pleasant atmosphere, imported Italian wines available. *Ninja*, Şehitmuhtar Caddesi No 22, T2372328, Taksim, held to be the best Japanese in town. *Safran*, Inter-Continental Hotel, Taksim, exceptional Turkish/Ottoman cuisine and excellent service in dining room high above the city. *Taşlık*, Swissôtel, Maçka, T3268268, housed in a wooden pavillion, traditional Turkish cuisine, excellent selection of hot and cold meze, refined kebaps, fish and dishes with a wider Mediterranean influence, delicious puddings, chef's recommendation set-menus for US$25 and US$30, excellent service.

Beyoğlu, Taksim & beyond
See page 118 for map

Midrange *California Brasserie*, *Inter-Continental Hotel*, Taksim, Pacific-rim cuisine in stylish surroundings, American buffet breakfast, also buffet lunch and dinner. *C Fischer*, Inönü Caddesi, T2452576, meat-based menu, starters include Albanian-style fried liver, grilled kidneys, hearty main courses like Hungarian goulash, Chateaubriand, US$12 per head before alcohol. *Degustasyon Lokantası*, Şahne Sokak No 41, Beyoğlu, smart *meyhane* on the Balık Pazarı, choose from excellent selection of *meze*, followed by fish or meat dishes, about US$10 per head. *Hacı Abdullah*, Sakızağacı Sokak No 17, Beyoğlu, highly regarded kebap restaurant with 110-year history, colourful homemade pickles, jams and preserves displayed in front window and glass cabinets inside, selection of ready-prepared Turkish/Ottoman dishes, typical offerings include green lentil stew, stuffed auberines, liver casserole, also döner, lahmacun and delicious regional variations on the kebap theme such as Adana, Urfa, Manisa, eat in grand old dining room and depart well-fed for less than US$7, no alcohol. *Hacıbaba*, Istiklal Caddesi No 49, T2441886, Taksim, well-established place serving kebaps and other Turkish dishes, pleasant dining room, bustling with staff and customers at lunch time, conservatory at rear overlooking courtyard of Aya Triada. *Nature and Peace*, Büyükparmakkapı Sokak No 21, Beyoğlu, Kebap-free oasis for the vegetarian or non-red meat eater, pleasant atmosphere with candle-lit tables, friendly staff and regular clientel, dishes include green lentil cakes, pasta and falafels, all served with complimentary salad and corn bread, all dishes are prepared fresh so you may have to wait a while if it's busy. *Indian Restaurant*, Zambak Sokak No 8, 2nd floor, vegetarian and meat dishes prepared by chef from the subcontinent, relaxed simple dining room, closed Sunday. *Ristorante Italiano*, Cumhuriyet Caddesi No 6, small trattoria next to *Divan Hotel*. *T-Square*, Sıraserviler Caddesi No 67, smart new-age restaurant and café, stylish decor, surprisingly quiet terrace at the rear, varied western menu including large tasty salads, pasta, burgers, about US$7 per head before alcohol.

Çicek Pasajı **Cheap** Day or night you won't have to look far to find something cheap to eat along Istiklal Caddesi, however the emphasis is on fast food rather than haute cuisine. For a quick bite there's a whole row of small places serving meat or chicken döner with a glass of ayran on the corner of Istiklal and Sıraselviler Caddesi. *Taksim Durum* is one of the better ones, also cooking şiş over hot-coals. *Afacan*, Istiklal Caddesi No 86, canteen-style place, choose from mind boggling array of soups, stews, casseroles and other Turkish dishes. *Tadım*, Meşelik Caddesi, excellent place for lunch, bright, good service, choose from the dishes on display, typically a variety of meat stews, spinach with egg, bean casserole, stuffed peppers, a soup and chocolate pudding, expect to pay less than US$4 for a hearty 3 course meal. *Bursa Kebapcisi*, Istiklal Caddesi, opposite French Consulate, busy kebap place, soup for US$1, iskender, şis or a choice of other kebaps to follow. *Meşhur Selçuk*, Kuçukparmakkapı Sokak, 30 m off Istiklal, civilized little place off the main drag, specializing in çöp şiş, köfte and lamb chops. *Marko Paşa Şark Sofrası*, Sadri Alışık Sokak No 4, in street opposite Ağa Camii, 1 of several small "folky" places, decorated with brass kettles, stuffed animals, jars of pickle and other bits and bobs, the food is simple and cheap, *gözleme* with a huge variety of fillings are prepared by women in traditional dress (US$1.25), there's also *mantı* washed down with *ayran* served in little metal cups. *Hala Mantı ve Gözleme*, Istiklal Caddesi No 209, another variation on the Anatolian theme restaurant, tasty traditional fare like *mantı*, *gözleme*, *ayran* and of course costumed 'village' women sweating over a hot stove. *Sahne Sokağı* (see page 119) is a covered market street next to Çicek Pasajı which is also known as the Beyoğlu Balık Pazarı (Fish Market). You can find lots of cheap and tasty snacks such as *midye tava* (mussels fried on a stick), *midye dolma* (stuffed mussels) or *koköreç* (fried tripe).

Cafés and patisseries *Divan*, Cumhuriyet Caddesi No 2, high reputation for its biscuits, cakes and desserts, all displayed in glass cabinets for you to drool over. *Hacı*

Bekir, Istiklal Caddesi No 129, sweets and Turkish delight from this grandfather of shops which has been around since 1777.

Expensive *Ferides*, Sabancı Kültür Merkezi, Çırağan Caddesi, Ortaköy, waterfront restaurant housed in grand Ottoman building which used to be a police station, renovated as part of the Sabancı Cultural Centre, grand dining room, however, terrace with views up the Bosphorus to Ortaköy and the Atatürk bridge is the real draw, wicker chairs and white table cloths, interesting and tasty dishes such as grilled wild quails on a chickpea mousse or chicken marinated with ginger and pomegranite, attentive service, reckon on about US$20 per head before wine. *Rumeli Iskele*, Yahya Kemal Caddesi No 1, Rumeli Hisarı, T2632997, well-regarded fish place built on the old village ferry station, wonderful location for which you pay premium, hot and cold meze, good selection of seafood and fish, US$25-US$30 per head with alcohol. *Mustafa Paşa Konağı*, Palanga Caddesi No 3, Ortaköy, T2274900, large restaurant in conservatory and garden of old house, attentive service, Turkish meat and fish dishes, live music nightly.

Bosphorus Suburbs: European side

Midrange *Bodrum*, Sağlık Sokak No 4, Ortaköy, on the waterside square, smart fish place with relaxed convivial atmosphere, tables in conservatory area or outside on cobblestone square, wicker chairs, good selection of fish. *Malta Köşk*, Yildiz Parkı, Beşiktaş, T2589453, wonderful location in Malta Pavilion in Yildiz Parkı, reasonable Ottoman/Turkish cuisine to compliment surroundings, choice of traditional deserts, no alcohol, breakfast and afternoon tea also served. *A la Turka*, Hazine Sokak No 8, Ortaköy, small modern café/restaurnant in backstreets behind waterside square, traditional Turkish dished such as *mantı*, *köfte and börek*.

Cheap *Köfteci Ali Baba*, 1 Caddesi No 92, Arnavutköy, small place with a deservedly large reputation for its meatballs and *piyaz* (bean salad), always packed so you may have to queue with other meatball aficionados. *Yazarlurın Evi Restorant*, Değirmen Sokak No 12, T2607741, Ortaköy, tiny 2-floor place, woman in window preparing *gözleme*, walls plastered with sayings which make more sense after a bottle of rakı, upstairs live music on Thu, Fri, Sat nights, extremely intimate! Good value Turkish food such as çiğ böreği- pastry pancakes, meze (US$1.30) and grilled meat. *Cafe Kale*, Yahya Kemal Caddesi, Rumeli Hisarı, 200 m north of the castle, simple café which is a popular local brunch spot, excellent eggs with *kaşar* (cheese), *sucuk* (garlic sausage), *sosis* (salami), or peppers, onions, garlic and tomato (*menemen*), also serve pastries, salads, gözleme (pancakes) and midye tava (fried mussels). *Bebek Köftecisi*, Hamam Sokak, opposite mosque in Bebek, tiny basement place serving soup, meat-balls and şiş.

Otantik Anadolu Yemekleri, Muvahhahit Sokak No 62, Kadıköy, traditional Anatolian fare, gözleme, börek and ayran, in modern shop on pedestrian shopping street leading up from Kadıköy. *Hacioğlu*, Hakimiyeti Milliye Caddesi, Üsküdar, large 2-storey lahmacun place on main street. *Kanaat Lokantası*, Selmanıpak Caddesi No 25, Üsküdar, next to the *Migros Supermarket*, well-established family place serving simple Turkish food at reasonable prices. *Saray Et Lokantası*, Balaban Caddesi, Üsküdar, simple lokanta opposite the ferry quay serving steam-tray food, kebaps and grilled meat. *Ismet Baba*, Sahil Yolu, Kuzguncuk, well-recommended fish restaurant overlooking Bosphorus, unashamedly old fashioned but reasonably priced, well-cooked fish.

Bosphorus Suburbs: Asian side

Bars

For an up-to-date listing of the city's pubs, bars, nightclubs and restaurants pick-up a copy of 'The Guide' a bi-monthly English-language magazine on sale at large book shops and some hotel lobbies, US$3.

Sultanahmet
Many guesthouses & hotels have pleasant bars open to non-residents but most of the action is N of the Golden Horn

Cheers, Akbıyık Caddesi, loud western rock and pop, mainly tourist crowd, cheap beer. *Istanblues*, Topkapı Palace, atmospheric jazz and blues bar. *Teras Pub*, Divanyolu Caddesi No 66, opposite *Imar Bankası*, entrance in alley, on top floor of building scenic views from balcony, live pop and classical music, belly dancing, mixed local/tourist crowd.

Tünel & Tepebaşı
Büyük Londra Oteli, Meşrutiyet Caddesi No 117, Tepebaşı, step in to the bar of this dilapidated hotel to savour the wonderful atmosphere of yesteryear, sit at the bar next to the antique gramophone, lacking the pretensions and considerably cheaper than its venerable neighbour the *Pera Palas*. *Galatea*, Asmalı Mescit Sofyalı Sokak No 16, Tünel, smart basement place, masonry arches, classic western rock played. *Gramafon Bar*, Tünel, right at the tram turn-around, live jazz most evenings, cover charge US$11. *Pera Palas*, Meşrutiyet Caddesi No 89, Tepebaşı, if you can't muster the money to stay, enjoying a cocktail at the long marble bar is a must. *Pera Sanat Evi*, Balyoz Sokak No 25, Tepebaşı dimly-lit atmospheric bar/café, local artists display work on walls, wood burning stove in winter, food served. *Tarihi Pano Şaraphanesi*, Hamalbaşı Caddesi, Beyoğlu, on corner next to British Consulate, reincarnation of Greek taverna established in 1898, row of barrels over the bar, stand at tables to drink very palatable house wines, packed every night so arrive early, food served. *Varelli Şaraphanesi*, Oteller Sokak No 7, Tepebaşı, next to *Mercure Hotel*, popular winebar with atmospheric wooden interior, delicious domestic and imported cheese and cured meats, sit or stand at up-turned wine barrels, very reasonable house wine.

Taksim & beyond
Bar Bahçe, Soğancı Sokak No 7, Cihangir, hidden away on the ground floor in quiet residential street of Siraselviler Caddesi, lively gay crowd, loud house and pop. *City Lights*, Ceylan Intercontinental Hotel, smart bar on top floor, breathtaking view at night more than justifies a visit. *Çınaraltı*, Balo Sokak No 14, Beyoğlu, popular new bar packed with jazz and blues fans, mostly standing room. *Godet*, Zambak Sokak No 15, Beyoğlu, just off Istiklal Caddesi, behind nondescript facade is a hugely popular bar, always cram-packed with a lively crowd who enjoy their techno loud, open until 4 am at weekends, also sell imported clothes and music. *Hayal Kahvesi*, Büyükparmakkapı Sokak No 19, Beyoğlu, trendy venue for jazz and rock fans, live sets from 2300-0200 at weekends, gets very crowded. *The James Joyce*, İstanbul Sanat Merkezi, Tarlabaşı Bulvarı, 1 of more successful attempts to recreate an authentic pub atmosphere, favourite with expats, serves food and imported beers, tango and latin dance nights. *The Lane English Pub*, Çalıkuyu Sokak, 4 Aralık No 14, Levent, set back off main road, very popular with local ex-pat community, meeting place for the İstanbul Hash House Harriers, fairly pricey at US$3.50 for a beer. *Madrid*, Ipek Sokak No 16, Beyoğlu, very popular backstreet bar, 5 floors of old building, lively crowd, reasonably priced beer and ambience. *Murphy's Dance Bar*, Divan Hotel, Cumhuriyet Caddesi No 2, themed dancing nights. *North Shields Pub*, Istiklal Caddesi No 24, successful chain of "English" theme pubs, drinks on offer include Scotch whisky, other branches include the airport and Beşiktaş. *Riddim*, Büyükparmakkapı Sokak No 8, Beyoğlu, let your hair down to some pumping reggae and African music, popular with local African community. *Şal*, Büyükparmakkapı Sokak No 18/A, off Istiklal Caddesi intimate, not to say cramped at times, little bar serving up live Turkish folk music. *Sefahathane*, Atlas Bazaar, Istiklal Caddesi No 209, relaxed café with jazz, blues and rock play list by day, harder, techno, trance, by night. *Türkü Bar*, Imam Adnan Sokak No 9, off Istiklal Caddesi, bar with live Turkish folk music and dancing later when the raki has worked its magic.

Bosphorus Suburbs
Gület Bar, Yelkovan Sokak, Ortaköy, 1 of nicer bars in the backstreets of Ortaköy, tables outside. *On the Rocks*, Kaymakçı Sokak, Ortaköy, candle-lit bar with loud western pop and rock on the playlist. *Pupa's Reggae Bar*, Sahil Yolu, Arnavutköy, small relaxed bar on waterfront road, mostly reggae played, also some latin sounds.

Nightclubs

İstanbul has a lively and diverse club scene with places to suit most tastes. In common with other European cities going out on the town is a costly affair with clubs charging an entry fee on top of inflated bar prices. Avoid the seedier clubs around Taksim which typically have a Turkish band and live entertainment, as it is not uncommon for foreigners to be forced into paying a grossly inflated bill. *Babylon*, Şeyhbender Sokak No 3, Tünel, babylon.com, excellent venue with a varied programme of live musical acts, both local and international artists, bar and café on-site. *Çubuklu 29*, Paşabahçe Yolu No 24, Çubuklu, the place for İstanbul society to see and be seen, dance the night away to Turkish and western pop, stroll in the torch-lit garden, have a dip in the pool, ferries shuttle across from Istinye on the European side, open summer only, US$20. *Dip*, Nispetiye Caddesi No 32, Etiler, hip and expensive club popular with gilded youth. *Discotheque 1001*, Sıraselviler Caddesi, Turk Sanat Muziği (a classical genre), transvestite scene. *Gülhim*, Istiklal Caddesi No 373, Beyoğlu, riotous and fairly seedy basement club, gay mixed crowd, Turkish/Western pop. *High End*, Nispetiye Caddesi No 4, Etiler, another trendy place which attracts a young, wealthy crowd from the surrounding suburbs. *Milk*, Akarsu Sokak No 5, Galatasaray, very popular dance venue, gets going late after most bars have closed, techno, house, drum n bass until morning. *Laila*, Muallim Naci Caddesi No 141, Kuruçeşme, dance the night away to Turkish and European pop beside the Bosphorus, *the* place to play spot the celebrity, will make a predictably large hole in your wallet, strict door policy. *Regine Revue*, Cumhuriyet Caddesi No 16, belly dancers and saucy acts from 2200 to 0300, US$22 entry including free drink. *Roxy*, Arslan Yatağı Sokak, Sıraselviler, Taksim, well-regarded, eclectic sounds from rock to trip-hop, foreign and local acts for which you pay a hefty cover charge. *Scene*, Muallim Naci Caddesi No 109, Ortaköy, open Wed, Fri, Sat only, dance the night away at this Bosphorus-side club complex in the shadow of the Atatürk bridge, imaginative decor and up-beat garage/techno playlist, not for the financially challenged. *Switch*, Istiklal Caddesi, Muammer Karaca Çıkmaz No 3, hippro.com, cutting edge of city's club scene, Turkish and foreign guest DJ's play house, techno and trance.

Entertainment

Bab Bowling, Yeşilçam Sokak No 24, Beyoğlu, T2511591, off Istiklal Caddesi, special **Bowling** off-peak price weekdays, book ahead.

The International İstanbul Film Festival, www.istfest.org has been running now **Cinemas** for nearly 20 years. More than 150 films from around the world shown at various cinemas across the city over a two week period starting 15th April. Ask at a tourist information office for a program. Cinema-going is popular in İstanbul with the city's screens showing a good range of films mostly the latest Hollywood blockbuster subtitled in Turkish, but also international independent movies and local fare. *Akmerkez*, Akmerkez Shopping Centre, Etiler, T2820505. *As*, Cumhuriyet Caddesi, Cebeltopu Sokak No 7, Harbiye, T2476315. *Atlas*, Istiklal Caddesi No 209, Beyoğlu, T2528576. *Alkazar*, Istiklal Caddesi No 179, Beyoğlu, T2932466. *Beyoğlu*, Istiklal Caddesi No 140, T2513240. *Broadway*, Bahariye Caddesi, Kadıköy, T3461481. *Emek*, Istiklal Caddesi, Yeşilçam Sokak No 5, Beyoğlu, T2938439. Kafika Bolahenk Sokak No 8, Cihangir, three small auditoriums which seat upto 25, available for hire, 2,500 DUD collection, US$5.50 p/p, minimum 4 people. *Feriye*, Sabancı Kültürel Merkezi, Ortaköy, T2362864. *Moda*, Bahariye Caddesi, Halil Ethem Sokak No 53, Kadıköy, T3370128.

Atatürk Kültürel Merkezi, Taksim Meydanı, T2515600, concert hall which hosts Turkish **Concerts** State Opera, Ballet and Symphony Orchestra. *Babylon*, Şeybender Sokak, Asmalımescit,

Tünel, T2927368, hosts diverse musical acts from home and abroad, call in for a program. *Cemal Reşit Rey Konser Salonu*, Harbiye, T2405012, large venue with varied programme of concerts, including Turkish Classical music. *Rumeli Hisarı*, classical concerts are held in the amphitheatre within the medieval walls of the castle during the summer months. Enquire at a Tourist information office or check 'The Turkish Daily News' or 'The Guide' for information. *Yerebatan Sarnıç*, concerts are periodically held in the haunting setting of this Byzantine cistern, check the entrance for posters or enquire at a Tourist information office. *Tarìk Zafer Tunaya Salonu* Şahkulu Bostanì Sokak No 8, Tünel, T2931270/2273390, varied programme of musical performances.

Galleries A stroll along Istiklal Caddesi, Beyoğlu, can be punctuated with forays into the many galleries found along its length. These are often supported by the larger domestic banks with entrance fees not charged. *Aksanat Kültürel Merkezi*, Istiklal Caddesi No 16, T2523500, exhibitions of art and sculpture, music and drama. *Borusan Kültür ve Sanat Merkezi*, Istiklal Caddesi No 421, T2920655, exhibits art along with hosting concerts and lectures, call in for a programme. *Fotografevi*, Tütüncü Çıkmaz No 4, Galatasaray, tucked around corner in small alley across from Galatasaray Lise, exhibits the work of domestic and foreign photographers, café on 2nd floor. *Mimar Sinan Universite Kültür ve Sanat Merkezi*, Boğazkesen Caddesi Tophane, housed in well-restored early 19th-century cannon foundry, excellent surroundings for displaying work of young contemporary Turkish artists. *Pamukbank Kültürel Merkezi*, Istiklal Caddesi No 261/7, Galatasaray, displays of contemporary Turkish art from this Bank's collection. *Taksim Sanat Galerisi*, Cumhuriyet Caddesi No 24, T2452068, next to *Turkish Airlines* pick-up point, exhibits mostly Turkish contemporary art. *Yapı Kredi Sanat Galerisi*, Istiklal Caddesi No 285, Beyoğlu, retrospectives by Turkish artists, near Galatasaray Lycée.

Most of the cities upmarket commercial galleries are found in the well-to-do suburbs of Nişantaşi and Maçka. *Urart Art Gallery*, Abdi Ipekçi Caddesi No 18/1, Nişantaşì, Smart private gallery above jewllery outlet. *Teşvikiye Art Gallery* Abdi Ipekçi Caddesi No 48/3, Nişantaşì, shows mainly work of celebrated contemporary Turkish artists.

Opera A visit to the city's Opera House is a possible night-time activity, with concerts and recitals also held in the large pink building on Atatürk Bulvarı, T3242210.

Shopping

Whether you want to hunt for bargains in the bazaars of the old city, browse the stalls of a colourful street market or check-out what's on offer in an ultra-modern shopping mall, İstanbul has lots to offer the foreign shopper.

Antiques Visit the shops clustered in the narrow residential streets of Çukurcuma, a 10-min walk down Sıraselviler Caddesi from Taksim, which are veritable Alladin's caves, stuffed with interesting treasures. Some places to try are: *Antikhane*, Faikpaşa Yokuşu No 41. *Bagu Antika*, Çukurcuma Caddesi No 74. *Oda Koleksiyon*, Çukurcuma Caddesi No 52, *Tombak II*, Faikpaşa Yokuşu No 34/A. There are also antique shops in the Covered Bazaar including: *Dilek Export*, Cevahir Bedesten, Şerif Ağa Sokak No 74, specializes in Greek and Russian icons and Cappadocian brasswear. *Metin Gürgen*, Cevahir Bedesten No 42, vintage watches including antique Rolex worth up to US$5,000. Antique books, prints and maps are sold in shops around Tünel. One of the most renowned is *Librairie de Pera*, Galip Dede Sokak No 22. Also try *Ottomania*, Sofyalı Sokak No 30, Tünel, while on the other side of the Bosphorus, *Sahaf*, Dumlupınar Sokak No 12, Kadıköy, also has a large selection of old books. Before buying any antiques read the section on export restrictions (see page 24). A useful source of information about antiques is *KÜSAV* (the Foundation for the Conservation and Promotion of Culture and Art), 3rd floor,

Sinanpaşa İş Merkezi, Has Fırın Caddesi, Beşiktaş, T2273485. The office is open odd hours so telephone before visiting. They also run courses.

Dünya Aktüel Kitabevi, Istiklal Caddesi No 469, Tünel, stocks limited selection of guidebooks and maps, lots of foreign newspapers and periodicals. *Galeri Kayseri*, Divanyolu Caddesi No 58, Sultanahmet, excellent collection of books on Islamic, Byzantine, Ottoman and contemporary Turkish history, culture and architecture, also stocks guidebooks. *Homer*, Yeni Çarşı Caddesi No 28/A, Galatasaray, stocks English titles. *Metro*, Istiklal Caddesi No 513, Tünel, English teaching books and dictionaries.*Net Bookstore*, Istiklal Caddesi No 79, Beyoğlu, foreign titles and newspapers, also branches in the Galleria and Carousel shopping centres. *Pandora Bookshop*, Büyükparmakkapı Sokak No 3, Beyoğlu, academic, local interest and assorted other English titles. *Remzi Kitabevi*, Akmerkez shopping centre, Etiler, foreign newspapers, range of guidebooks, children's books and other English-language publications, has café where you can read with a coffee. Also branch at Rumeli Caddesi No 44, Nişantası. *Robinson Crusoe*, Istiklal Caddesi No 389, Beyoğlu, wide selection of English-language books including novels, guidebooks and titles about local culture and history. You could also visit the *Sahaflar Çarşısı*, Beyazıt (see page 101) which is dedicated entirely to selling new and second-hand books, some of them in English, or the *Beyoğlu Sahaflar Çarşısı*, off Sahne Sokağı opposite the back entrance to Çicek Pasajı, Galatasaray, which fills a similar function. You can find the *Turkish Daily News* and foreign newspapers in shops around Taksim and Sultanahmet.

Books & newspapers
'No Name Book Exchange' on Bayram Fırın Sokak in Sultanahmet has over 1,200 books to swap for your old, battered paperback

Clothing

Running behind the Nusretiye Camii in Karaköy is a row of boutiques, known collectively as the Amerikan Pazarı, which sell western clothes and footwear from names such as *Versace* and *Timberland* at very competitive prices. Trendy Western brands like *Diesel*, *Espirit* or *Mango* are also available along Istiklal Caddesi and on Cumhuriyet Caddesi, north of Taksim square, as well as in Nişantaşi. Prices are considerably lower than in Europe, particularly during the end of season sales. *Vakko*, Istiklal Caddesi No 123, Beyoğlu, one of oldest and most exclusive department stores in town. *Beymen*, *Vakkorama*, *Mudo City*, *Cotton Club*, *Abbate* and other quality homegrown outlets can be found in the Akmerkez, Carousel and Galleria shopping centres. Bağdat Caddesi, stretching east from Kadıköy, also has many upmarket western and domestic outlets along its length, get on a Bostancı dolmuş from Kadıköy.

Carpets & kilims

İstanbul is a good place to buy that classic souvenir with well-stocked carpet shops dotted liberally across the city. Although prices may be slightly higher than in the regions of production, you will generally find a greater selection on offer. A good place to start looking is in the Covered Bazaar with a particular concentration of shops along, surprisingly enough, **Halıcılar Caddesi** (the Market of the Carpetmen). Recommended shops include: *Şirinoğlu*, No 36, specializes in sumptuous Turkish silk carpets of all sizes, and *Şişko Osman*, No 49. Also in the Covered Bazaar, *Selection*, Kalpakçılar Caddesi No 29, excellent collection of rare antique carpets from Anatolia and the Caucasus, also more affordable pieces. The Arasta bazaar behind Sultan Ahmet Camii has a large number of carpet shops such as: *Aziz Nomadic Art Gallery*, No 85, specialists in tribal and Kurdish carpets. Also in Sultanahmet, *Heritage*, Caferiye Sokak 6/A, has good selection of handmade carpets and kilims. Shops in other parts of the city include: *Hazal Halı*, Meridiyeköy Köprüsü Sokak No 27, Ortaköy. *Punto*, Gazi Sinanpaşa Sokak No 17, Vezirhan, Çağaloğlu, new and antique carpets on display in shop located in 17th-century han. *Sümerbank*, Istiklal Caddesi No 302, Beyoğlu, wide choice of reasonably priced carpets and kilims. *Şengör Halı*, Cumhuriyet Caddesi No 47/2, Taksim.

Crafts

The İstanbul Crafts Centre, housed in a restored Ottoman seminary on Kabasakal Caddesi, Sultanahmet, has small shops run by local artisans practicing traditional

İstanbul

crafts such as calligraphy, cloth printing, glass painting, pipe carving and embroidery. *Caferağa Medresesi*, Caferiye Sokak, a similar crafts centre and café situated in another restored theology school next to Haghia Sophia.

For **scarves** and **fabric** printed with traditional designs find your way to *Yazmacılar Çarşısı*, quite literally 'market of the fabric printers' which is on Çarkçılar Sokak near the Büyük Yeni Hanı (see page 106). Also try *Sivaslı İstanbul Yazmacısı*, Yağlıkçılar Caddesi No 57, Covered Bazaar, which specializes in hand-embroidered and woven fabrics. *Muhlis Günbattı*, Perdahçılar Sokak No 48, Covered Bazaar, stocks brightly coloured, hand-embroidered *suzanis* cloths from Central Asia, along with other interesting textiles and carpets.

Artisan, Iskele Sokak, Ortaköy, stocks Kütahya ceramics. *Deli Kızın Yeri*, Francalacı Sokak No 2, Arnavutköy, T2871294. "the Mad Girl's place", owned by long-term İstanbul resident Linda Caldwell, interesting gifts and clothing much of it hand-made on the premises, wraps decorated with *yazma* (traditional blockprinting) by local artist. *Le Fer Forgé*, Cevdetpaşa Caddesi No 125/1, Bebek, interesting wrought iron and metal pieces, showroom doubles as trendy café, unfortunately most pieces are on the heavy side for hand luguage! *Meddah*, Kaymakçı Sokak No 10, Ortaköy, beautifully hand-painted ceramics. *Negül Atelye*, Değirmenci Sokak No 10, Ortaköy, 1 of several shops in area selling avant-gard and more traditional glassware. *Sofa*, Nuruosmaniye Caddesi No 42, Cağaloğlu, east of the Covered Bazaar, calligraphy, marbling, and Ottoman minatures. *Paşabahçe*, Istiklal Caddesi No 314, Beyoğlu, takes its name from famous glass factory on Asian side of Bosphorus, delicate blue and gilded glassware.

Jewellery The Covered Bazaar is where you'll find the widest selection of jewellery with shops specializing in gold lining Kalpakçılar Başı and Terzi Başı Caddesi. Silver pieces are sold by the gram from dozens of tiny outlets in the Iç Bedesten. Also: *Antıkart*, Istiklal Caddesi No 209, Atlas Pasajı, Beyoğlu, interesting selection of Turkish silver, antique silver from Kurdish regions, also have good range of kilims. *Mudo Pera*, Istiklal Caddesi No 401, upmarket jewellery and gift shop, unusual designs and ideas, still not too expensive. *Urart*, Abdi Ipekçi Caddesi No 18/1, Nişantası, also have a concession in the Swissotel, contemporary gold and silver jewellery, many of the designs are inspired by ancient Anatolian art.

Leather For cheap leatherware your best bet is the Covered Bazaar, although the style and quality on offer in many of the shops is not the highest. There is a particularly large concentration of outlets around the Çarşıkapı entrance to the bazaar. For better quality try: *BB*, Gani Çelebi Sokak No 46, Covered Bazaar. *Derishow*, a more fashion-orientated, and expensive, leather shop, has outlets in the Akmerkez, Capitol and Galeria shopping centres, also found at Istiklal Caddesi No 140, Beyoğlu. *Desa*, Istiklal Caddesi No 140, Beyoğlu, high-quality jackets and bags.

Markets Every district has its weekly *pazar*, a colourful street market at which fresh fruit and vegetables, clothes and household goods are sold from stalls. Such street markets are an excellent place to stock up on picnic food and snacks. The *pazar* in Sultanahmet, conveniently close for the hotels and guesthouses in the area, is every Tue on Akbıyık Caddesi. Particularly extensive is the **Salı Pazarı** (Tue market) held at Altıyol in Kadıköy every Tue. Head up Söğütlüçeşme Caddesi from the ferry terminal to roundabout with statue of charging bull. Narrow road ahead leads down to the market. Every Wed the streets around the **Fatih Camii**, in Fatih are filled with a huge chaotic market. **Ortaköy**, every Sun the cobbled streets of this trendy Bosphorus suburb are lined with stalls selling jewellery and handicrafts. Bargain hunters and junk collectors shouldn't miss a visit to one of the city's flea markets, called *Bit Pazarı* (Louse Market). **Kadıköy**

Bit Pazarı, Özellik Sokak, off Soğutluçeşme Caddesi. **Horhor Bit Pazarı,** Kırık Tulumbe Sokak No 13, Aksaray, west off Atatürk Bulvarı on Baba Hasan Sokak, several floors packed with junk and furniture.

Shops selling and developing film are found in most areas, however there is a particu- **Photography** lar concentration around Sirkeci Station. Many of these sell transparency film.

Akmerkez, Nispetiye Caddesi, Etiler, large, modern shopping mall with cinema and **Shopping** extensive food hall. *Galeria*, Bakırköy, can be reached on the Banliyö train from Sirkeci, **centres** equally as large, also has fast-food restaurants plus an ice-rink. *Carousel*, Bakırköy, another modern mall with foreign names such as *British Home Stores* and *Mothercare*. *Stadium Florya*, Çatal Sokak No 2, Florya, suburb beyond the airport, can be reached on Banliyö train from Sirkeci, centre specializing entirely in sporting equipment and clothing.

Adrenalin, Büyük Beşiktaş Çarşı, PTT karşı, Beşiktaş, T2606002, on same floor of shop- **Outdoor** ping centre as PTT, camping and climbing equipment. *Atölye*, Muallim Naci Caddesi **equipment** No 65, Ortaköy, T2360595, on main road near the hamam.

Armador Denizcilik, Denizcilik Bankası Sitesi No 27/A, Tophane, T2452051, sailing **Watersports** equipment, marine maps. *Ogan Sub*, Kemeraltı Caddesi 81/A, Karaköy, T2490445, **equipment** diving equipment, wet suits.

Sports

There are lots of bicycle shops selling components and tools at the top of *Galip Dede* **Cycling** *Caddesi*, Tünel. *Atölye*, Palanga Caddesi No 8, Ortaköy, T2275680, bikes made-to-order or off the rack. *Yeşil Bisiklet*, Lalezar Caddesi No 8/1, Kardelen Apart, Selamiçeşme, Kadıköy, bike shop, maintenance, also organize biking weekends and holidays.

Turkish football is dominated by a trio of İstanbul teams – Galatasaray, Beşiktaş and **Football** Fenerbahçe – with the former team gaining an international reputation after its victory *See also page 699* over Arsenal in th UEFA Cup final in 2000, and some very ugly pitched battles between the opposing fans. The Turkish league runs from August to May with matches held Friday evening, Saturday and Sunday. Most weekends there is a fixture at one of the city's stadiums, often at all three. Tickets (US$6-110) go on sale two days before a match and are available at the stadiums (see below) or for Beşiktaş and Fenerbahçe matches from *Biletix* T0216-4541555, biletix.com credit card bookings by phone, on-line or at one of the branches in some Vakkorama clothes stores or *Migros* supermarkets. *Beşiktaş*, İnönü Stadium, Dolmabahçe Caddesi, Beşiktaş opposite the Dolmabahçe Palace. T0212-2367202. *Fenerbahçe*, Rüştü Saraçoğlu Stadium, Kadıköy, reservations T0216-3690784, on the Asian shore reached by bus or taxi from Kadıköy.

İstanbul Riding Club, Binicilik Sitesi, Uçyol, Maslak, T2761404, riding and instruction. **Horse riding** *Kemer Country*, Kemerburgaz, T2391913, golf, riding and country club near Belgrad Forest.

There is an ice-rink at the Galeria shopping centre, Bakırköy. T0212-5608550, US$6 for **Ice-skating** 45 mins, open 1000-2300, daily.

Most of the city's luxury hotels have swimming pools that can be used by **Swimming** non-residents for a fee. *The Hilton*, for example, has a nice outdoor pool set in its **pools** lovely gardens, although the most spectacular is without a doubt the Çırağan Palace's Bosphorus side pool.

İstanbul

Tour agencies

Abelya Tourism, Zambak Sokak No 21/4, Beyoğlu, T2923986, F2932962. Unusual daily tours of city, walks and excursions with an educational slant. *Genç Tur*, Yerebatan Caddesi No 15/3, Sultanahmet, T5205274, F5190864. Specialists in student travel, issue student cards, city tours, also arrange voluntary working holidays across country. *Karavan Tur*, Halaskargazi Caddesi, Gun Apartmentlar, No 245/251, Osmanbey, T2475044, F2415278, karavanist@superonline.com Greek and Italian ferry agents. *Marco Polo*, Divanyolu Caddesi No 54/11, T5192804, F5131781, marcopolo@unimedya.net.tr Flights and package holidays. *Meptur*, Büyükdere Caddesi No 26/17. City and nationwide tour organizer, hotel reservations, car hire. *Orient*, Yeni Akbıyık Caddesi No 13, Sultanahmet, T5168907. Agent attached to popular hostel, cheap international flights. *Hat-Sail Tourism*, Maçka, T2589983, organize Bosphorus cruises and private boat rentals. *Plan Tours*, Cumhuriyet Caddesi No 131/1, T2302272, F2318965, plantours.com Popular sightseeing tours, open-top bus tour, Bosphorus dinner cruises, Prince's Island and further afield, cultural tours. *Seven Student*, Divanyolu Caddesi No 52, T5121227, F5123641, info@seventur.com.tr Specialize in student travel, cheap flights. *She Tours*, Cumhuriyet Caddesi No 309/3, Harbiye, T2333670, F2333673, shetours@bitek.net.tr Range of city tours, also Bursa, Troy, Gallipoli, Cappadocia, Ephesus. *Sultan*, Cumhuriyet Caddesi No 87, Elmadağ, T2336098, F2300419. Flight agents. *Toyça Tours*, Yeni Akbıyık Caddesi No 16, T5184773, F5188561, in *Orient Youth Hostel*. City tours, car rental, cheap international flights. *Trek Turizm*, Aydede Caddesi No 24, Taksim, T2565556, F2531509. Large flight agent, destinations include Central Asia and Russia. *Yücelt Interyouth Hostel*, Caferiye Sokak No 6, Sultanahmet, T5136150, F5127628. Budget domestic tours, including Gallipoli, Pamukkale and Cappadocia.

Transport

Air

Atatürk Airport information line: T6630793

İstanbul is the main hub for **Turkish Airlines** domestic and international flights (see pages 27 for details). Their main office is in Taksim square, at Cumhuriyet Caddesi, T2511106, but there are also agents who can make reservations and issue tickets across the city. *Havaş* airport buses leave from the Taksim *Turkish 0* office and now from the Akmerkez shopping centre regularly during the day. For other airline offices see the directory.

Bus

Buses leave the huge Esenler bus station throughout the day and night to destinations across the country and to cities in Europe, Central Asia and the Middle East. The easiest way to get there by public transport is on the metro from Aksaray. Most bus companies have several offices in the city where you can buy tickets. There is also normally a complimentary transfer service to Esenler for ticket holders, so enquire when you buy your ticket (*servis var mı?*). Offices are clustered on Ordu Caddesi in Laleli and Inönü Caddesi and Mete Caddesi in Taksim. There are also some offices scattered along Divanyolu Caddesi. Outside of public holidays and the summer months it's generally possible just to turn up at Esenler without a reservation; find a bus going to your particular destination and depart within the hr. If the destination that you want is not listed below, trawl along the row of offices asking at a few. Remember that several companies often have services to the same destination, so check around before buying your ticket as there may be a difference in price or a bus leaving sooner. The larger, more-reputable companies with services to most major destinations are found at the following booths: **Kamil Koç 12-18, Metro 41, Pamukkale 58, Ulusoy 12, Varan 13.**

Within Turkey Adana, (102), every hr evening and night, US$20, 13 hrs. **Ankara** (40, 36), at least every hr, US$12, 6 hrs. **Amasya**, (68, 84, 87), regular buses, US$15, 12 hrs. **Antalya**, (40, 145), every hr, US$19, 12 hrs. **Artvin** (127), 1 evening bus, US$25, 22 hrs. **Bursa**, (145), every 30 mins, US$6, 4 hrs. **Çanakkale** (103), hourly buses, 0500-2400, US$11, 6½ hrs. **Doğubeyazıt**, (166) 1 bus daily, US$28, 22 hrs. **Erzurum**, 7 daily, mainly evening and night departures, US$22, 19 hrs. **Gaziantep** (96, 166), several evening buses, US$25, 14 hrs. **Göreme**, **Nevşehir** and **Ürgup** (18,28), several evening buses, US$16, 11 hrs. **İzmir** (40, 53), every hr, US$16, 8 hrs. **Kayseri** (60), 7 daily, US$16, 11 hrs. **Karabük (Safranbolu)**, *Ulusoy* have 4 buses daily, US$13, 6 hrs. **Konya** (78), 8 buses daily, US$17, 10 hrs. **Samsun** (127), *Ulusoy* have morning and evening buses, US$21, 12 hrs. **Trabzon** (40, 127), *Ulusoy* have several daily, US$25, 18 hrs. **Van** (48, 147), several evening buses, US$28, 23 hrs.

Buses arriving from Asiatic Turkey call-in at Harem on the way to Esenler, so you can save yourself the frustrating journey across the city (up to 2 hrs during the day) by getting off here and crossing the Bosphorus on a car ferry to Eminönü. Many people also prefer to start their journey in Harem, although the choice of destinations is not as wide as at Esenler.

Outside Turkey Austria *Varan* have weekly buses to Vienna, US$75, 38 hrs. **Bulgaria** *Öz Varol* (160), several a week to Sofia, US$35, 12 hrs. **Greece** *Ulusoy* (127) and *Varan* (15) operate daily buses to Athens (US$70, 20 hrs) and Thessaloniki (US$50, 12 hrs). Both companies also have offices on İnönü Caddesi, Taksim. **Iran** Tehran buses leave everyday (166), US$40, 40 hrs, prices are very low at present due to competition, expect them to rise. **Middle East** *Has* (102), T6583111, hasturizm.com, is a large, reputable company running services to Syria, Saudi Arabia, the Central Asian republics and Russia, some services are summer only, call-in for a schedule. Syria: Aleppo (via Antakya), daily, 22 hrs; Damascus (Şam), daily, 30 hrs, expect to change buses at least once.

Avis, Hilton Arcade No 4, Cumhuriyet Caddesi, Elmadağ, T2412917, Airport: T6620852. *Budget*, Cumhuriyet Caddesi 19/A Gezi Apart, Elmadağ, T2539200. *Tempo*, Şair Nedim Caddesi No 150, Levent Apartments, Beşiktaş, T2590685, F2608687. *Europcar*, Cumhuriyet Caddesi No 47/2, Taksim, T2547788. *Hertz*, Cumhuriyet Caddesi No 295, T2331020, F2331018, Airport: T6630807, F6636797. **Car rental** *All the companies below have an office at the airport in the arrivals lounge*

The *TML* Black Sea and *İzmir* ferry services (see page 47) depart from docks at Sarayburnu, about 600 m east of Sirkeci station along Kennedy Caddesi. Tickets for this and other TML services, including Mediterranean and Black Sea cruise holidays, can be obtained from the TML head office on Rıhtım Caddesi, Karaköy, T2499222, 150 m east of the Galata bridge. This is where cruise lines dock also. The high speed catamaran which take passengers and vehicles to **Bandırma** and **Yalova** departs from Yeni Kapı on the Marmara coast to the south of Aksaray. The *banliyö* train connects Yenikapı and Sirkeci, from where it's a tram up the hill. Bus stops are outside the terminal building. Bus no T4 is 1 of several buses to Taksim from Yenikapı. **Sea**

Trains to destinations in Asiatic Turkey depart from Haydarpaşa Garı on the Asian side of the Bosphorous north of Kadıköy. Information line: T0216-336 0475 (Turkish spoken), Reservations: T0216-3378724, Regular ferries cross from Karaköy to Haydarpaşa in 20 mins. Taxis take much longer. Trains bound for Edirne and destinations in Europe leave from the smaller Sirkeci station near Eminönü and Sultanahmet. **Train** *For details of train services see page 47*

Directory

Airline offices *Aeroflot*, Mete Caddesi No 30, Taksim, T2434725. *Air France*, Cumhuriyet Caddesi No 1, Taksim, T2373000, F2547614. *Azerbaycan Airlines*, Cumhuriyet Caddesi No 43/1, Taksim, T2374201, F2374200. *Bulgarian Airlines*, Cumhuriyet Caddesi No 8, Elmadağ, T2932239, F2939402. *British Airways*, Cumhuriyet Caddesi No 10/1, Elmadağ, T2341300, F2341308, 2 daily flights to UK. *Delta* Hilton Hotel entrance, T2333820. *Egyptair*, Cumhuriyet Caddesi, Harbiye, T6633301. *Iran Air*, Vali Konağı Caddesi No 17, Harbiye, T2250255/56, 2 weekly flights to Tehran. *Istanbul Airlines*, Atatürk Bulvarı 61/1, Kızılay. *KLM*, Nişantaşı, T2300311. *Syrian Air*, Hilton Hotel entrance, T2461781, F2326293. *Swissair*, Cumhuriyet Caddesi No 6, Elmadağ, T2196419. *Turkish-Cypriot Airlines*, Mecidiyeköy, T2670973.

Banks There are banks with ATM machines and change facilities throughout the city, however, branches around the main tourist areas of Sultanahmet and Taksim are more used to dealing with foreigners and so are more efficient. There are private change places along Divanyolu Caddesi which change TCs, and which generally give a preferable rate of exchange to the banks. Ask about commissions charged. Many of the large hotels also change cash and TCs, however, rates are not very competitive.

Baths *Çağaloğlu Hamamı*, Profesör Kazım Gürkan Caddesi No 34, Cağaloğlu, 18th-century bath complex, 1 of the best in the city but pretty touristy, US$15 for bath and scrub. *Çemberlitaş Hamamı*, Vezirhan Caddesi No 8, Beyazıt, bath US$8, massage US$15, historic baths, very touristy, 0600-2400. *Çukurcuma Hamamı*, Çukurcuma Caddesi No 57, Çukurcuma, bath and kese US$9. *Galatasaray Hamamı*, Turnacıbaşı Sokak No 24, modern baths built around historic core, US$16, kese massage US$18, expensive. *Tarihi Park Hamamı*, Doktor Emin Paşa Sokak No 10, Sultanahmet, off Dirvanyolu, small local baths, untouristy, US$4, Kese.

Communications **Internet** You'll come across internet cafés almost everywhere you go in town with a particular concentration off Istiklal Caddesi at the Taksim square end. *Antique cafe*, Kutlugün Sokak No 51, Sultanahmet, US$1.50 per hr. *Net Net Cafe*, Yerebatan Caddesi, 100 m on left from Haghia Sophia, US$1.50 per hr. *Solaris Cafe*, Mis Sokak No 14/1, off Istiklal Caddesi, Beyoğlu, US$1.25 per hour. *Taksim Intenet Cafe*, Tarlabaşı Caddesi No 20, Taksim, US$1.75 per hr. **Post office** The central post office is on Yeni Posthane Caddesi, Sirkeci. Open 0900-1730, letters 0800-2000, telegrams/phonecards 0800-2400. There are smaller post offices across the city with useful branches found in Taksim Meydanı, next to the bus terminal; in Beşiktaş in the shopping centre behind the mosque and in Kadıköy on Iskele Meydanı. There is a kiosk where you can buy stamps and post letters opposite Haghia Sophia. **Post restante** Mail should be clearly marked 'poste restante' and should be addressed to the central post office (see above). To pick letters up you'll need proof of identification. **Telephones** seem to be everywhere except when you need one. Useful clusters are found around Sultanahmet Meydanı, Çemberlitaş, Sirkeci station, Taksim Square.

Consulates *Australia*, Tepecik Yokuşu No 58, Etiler, T2577050. *Canada*, Büyükdere Caddesi No 107/3, Gayrettepe, T2725174. *Egypt*, Bebek Sarayı, Cevdetpaşa Caddesi No 173, Bebek, T263638. *France*, Istiklal Caddesi No 8, Beyoğlu, T2932460. *German*, Inönü Caddesi No 6, Taksim, T2515404. *Greece*, Turnacıbaşı Sokak No 32, Galatasaray, T2450596. *Iran*, Ankara Caddesi, Cağaloğlu, T5138230. *Ireland*, Cumhuriyet Caddesi No 26/A, Harbiye, T2466025. *Netherlands*, Istiklal Caddesi No 393, Tünel, T2515030. *Pakistan*, Abide-i Hürriyet Caddesi No 11, Hacıonbaşı Işhanı, 6th floor, Şişli, T2335801. Russian Federation, Istiklal Caddesi No 443, Beyoğlu, T2442610. *Sweden*, Istiklal Caddesi No 497, Tünel, T2435770. *Switzerland*, Hüsrev Gerede Caddesi No 75/3, Teşvikiye, T2591115. *Syria*, Ikıncı Bayırı Sokak No 8, Mecidiyeköy, T2327110. *UK*, Meşrutiyet Caddesi No 34, Tepebaşı, T2513602. *USA*, Meşrutiyet Caddesi No 104/108, Tepebaşı, T2513602.

Cultural centres *American Cultural Centre*, American Consulate, 104-108 Meşrutiyet Caddesi, Tepebaşı, T2512675. *British Council*, Istiklal Caddesi No 251-253, Örs Turistik Iş Merkezi, Beyoğlu, T2490574, library and teachers resource centre, programme of events. *Istanbul Kültur ve Sanat Vakıf*, Istiklal Caddesi No 146, T2933133, the organization behind the city's music, film, theatre and jazz festivals, pop-in to collect a programme of up and coming events.

İstanbul

Active Laundry, Dr Emin Paşa Sokak, just off Divanyolu, wash and dry US$2.50 per kg. *Hobby* **Laundry**
Laundry, Caferiya Sokak No 6/1, next to *Yücel Hostel*, café to while-away time. Most large hotels
have a dry cleaning service for their guests. *Modern Kuru Temizleme*, Rumeli Caddesi, Şafak Sokak
No 32, Nişantası, dry-cleaning. *Şık Çamaşır Yıkama*, Akarsu Yokuşu, Cihangir, US$1.50 per kg,
ironing service.

American Cultural Centre, (see cultural centres). *British Council Library*, (see cultural centres). **Libraries**
Istanbul Kitapçılığı, Soğukçeşme Sokak, Sultanahmet, reference collection belonging to the
Turkish Touring and Automobile Association, mainly books concerning history and culture. Open
weekdays 0900-1200, 1300-1700. *State Library* (*Devlet Kütüphanesi*), housed in *imaret* of Beyazıt
mosque, entrance next to Beyazıt Camii courtyard, important collection of Ottoman manuscripts
and books. Open 0830-1600.

Ambulance services *Ambulance 2000*, T2226161. *General Ambulance Ltd.*, T5412917/19, **Medical services**
Mobile 05323125129. *International Hospital Ambulance*, T6633000. **Dentists** *German Hospital
Dental Clinic*, Sıraselviler Caddesi No 119, Taksim. **Hospitals** *American Hospital*, Güzelbahçe
Sokak, Nişantaşı, T3112000. *Florence Nightingale*, Abide-i Hürriyet Caddesi No 290, Çağalayan,
Şişli, T2244950. *German Hospital*, Sıraselviler Caddesi No 119, Taksim, T2932150 has a dental
clinic open 24 hours daily. *Taksim Ilk Yardim* (emergency), Sıraselviler Caddesi, Taksim, T2524300.

Armenian Patriarchate, Şarapnel Sokak No 20, Kumkapı. *Chief Rabbinate of Turkey*, Yemenici **Places of**
Sokak No 23, Tünel, T2435166. *Christ Church*, Serdarı Ekrem Sokak No 82, Beyoğlu, T2515616, **Worship**
Anglican ministry, Sun service held regularly. *Greek Orthodox Patriarchate*, Sadrazam Ali Paşa
Caddesi No 35, Fener, T5252117. *St Anthony of Padua*, Istiklal Caddesi, Galatasaray, T2440935, 1 of
city's best attended Roman Catholic churches. *Union Church of Istanbul*, Postacılar Sokak,
Beyoğlu, T2445212, Anglican church. T5170970.

Atatürk International Airport, arrivals lounge, T6630793, supposed to be open 24-hrs, but don't **Tourist**
rely on it. *Istanbul Regional Directorate*, Meşrutiyet Caddesi No 57/5, Tepebaşı, T2433731, **information**
F2524346, open weekdays 0830-1730, in building across from the British Consulate. *Elmadağ*,
Hilton Hotel entrance, T2330592, open weekdays 0830-1730. *Karaköy*, Karaköy ferry terminal,
T2495776, open weekdays 0830-1700. *Sirkeci*, Sirkeci Station, T5115888, open weekdays
0830-1730. *Sultanahmet*, Sultanahmet square, T5188754, open weekdays 0830-1730.

Tourist police Alemdar Caddesi, T5274503, have some officers who can speak English, with a **Useful**
translator on call during the day. *Turkish Touring and Automobile Association*, (Known as **addresses**
'Turing') Birinci Oto Sanayı Sitesi Yanı, 4. Levent, T2804449/2827874, the people to see if you are
importing a vehicle into the country, also organize insurance and break-down cover.

The Marmara Region

4

The Marmara Region

172 Termal

173 İznik

178 Bursa

190 Uludağ

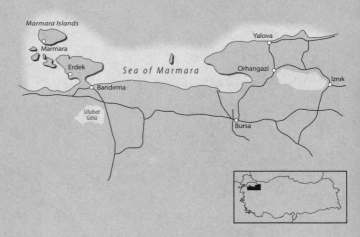

Along its southern shores the Sea of Marmara laps the land of ancient Bithynia, originally settled according to the New Testament by tribes from the Thracian plains. Wetter and greener than further south and east, and originally thickly forested, it's now an important agricultural region with groves of olives – which produce the choicest black fruit – carpeting the mountainsides. Its proximity to İstanbul has promoted rapid industrial development in a string of manufacturing centres such as Bursa and Izmit. Yet despite its indisputable historic and economic significance, the area lags well behind in the tourist stakes.

The region's main draw is the first Ottoman capital Bursa, now a progressive modern city with a fabulous architectural heritage of mosques, medreses and hans. A famous spa centre, there are also lavish marble baths to steam yourself in; while the winter sports and walking trails of Mount Uludağ are just a short cable-car ride away. Despite its illustrious past as a Byzantine Christian town and centre for ceramic art, lakeside İznik is a much more modest affair with a scattering of historic buildings encompassed by crumbling city walls. In the hills above Yalova, Termal is another, much smaller, thermal centre with a long distinguished past.

Most people pass straight through the unappealing port of Bandırma, though the nearby Kuş Cenneti (Bird Heaven) National Park is paradise for bird-watchers too. During the summer domestic holidaymakers descend on the rocky Marmara islands off the coast, but the resulting development sadly detracts from their attractiveness.

Yalova Situated at the mouth of the long, narrow Bay of Izmit, Yalova is a busy town which was badly hit by the 1999 earthquake. Evidence of the disaster remains in the form of uninhabited apartment blocks, ominous looking cracks running up their walls, and the empty lots, bulldozed flat, where buildings previously stood. There's nothing of interest in Yalova itself, though it's an important transportation centre where the high-speed catamarans arrive from İstanbul and buses cross the mountains to Bursa and İznik. You may also pass through on your way to the nearby spa complex at Termal.

Transport Bus The bus station is 100 m west of the ferry landing, although buses to Bursa, İznik and more distant destinations also meet passengers outside the ferry terminal gates on the left-hand side. **Bursa**, every 30 mins, 0630-2100, 2 hrs, US$3. **İznik**, hourly during the day, 90 mins, US$2. **Ferry** The high-speed car ferry (hızlı feribot) to Yenikapı is a fast and convenient way of getting into İstanbul. Ferries depart from a terminal 1 km east of the town centre at 0730, 0900, then every 2 hrs until 1900, 2130. The 1st service on Sun is at 0900. It takes 45 mins to cross the Sea of Marmara, saving a road journey of about 2 hrs. There is also a conventional ferry service across the Bay of Izmit from Topçular, east of Yalova, to Danca near Gebze, which is used by long distance buses and cars heading for İstanbul. The roll-on roll-off ferries run every 30 mins around the clock, saving a long and testing drive around the bay. The crossing takes 25 mins and costs US$10 for a car.

Termal

In a beautiful wooded valley in the hills 12 km from Yalova, the hot springs at Termal have been popular since Roman times. The buildings of today's complex, where you can still wallow in the therapeutic mineral-laden waters which issue from the ground at 37°C, date mostly from the end of the 19th century. In the republican era Atatürk was a frequent guest at the spa and he had an elegant house built on the valley side above the complex, surrounded by woods planted with exotic species of trees and shrubs.

Approaching the spa from the car park and dolmuş drop-off point, Atatürk's house is reached up a lane on the left (*0930-1600, 1700 daily except Mon and Thu in summer*). The Kurşunlu Banyo on the right is named after the *kurşun* (lead) dome of its roof. Here you can choose between an outdoor pool popular with families, US$3 per hour, or private baths which are US$5 for two people per hour. There are also the public steam baths where a 1½-hour session will set you back US$2.50. Better appointed and larger are the Valide and Sultan baths reached across a small footbridge which have private (US$4 for two people) and communal baths (US$1.50 per hour). You can also indulge yourself with a massage for a small addition fee.

Sleeping If you want to stay the night accommodation is available at the **C** *Çınar Hotel*, above
& eating the Sultan baths, T02266757400. Plain rooms with small bathroom, front rooms have balcony, evening meals are available in the restaurant in summer. When the *Çınar* is full guests are lodged in the nicer **Çınarcık** on the opposite side of the stream where rooms are set around a courtyard shaded by a plain tree. Cheaper lodgings can be found in the scrappy township of **Gökçedere** which has grown-up over the ridge less than 500 m from the spa complex. Popular with Middle Eastern holidaymakers. Try the **F** *Özen Motel*, T02666757647 or slightly more comfortable but equally unattractive from the outside **F** *Yeni Park Hotel*, T02666757100. Gökçedere also has a number of basic eateries serving kebabs, pide and lahmacun or in summer you could try the lahmacun and pide place near the Kurşunlu Baths.

The 1999 earthquake

At 3am on 17 August 1999 a massive earthquake registering 7.4 on the Richter scale shook northwest Turkey. Lasting just 45 seconds it wrought massive devastation over an area centred on the town of Izmit, collapsing hundreds of apartment buildings, severing roads and lines of communication and setting ablaze an oil refinery. Official estimates put the death toll at around 18,000, although the actual figure may have been twice that, with 200,000 people left homeless by the disaster. In economic terms the earthquake also cost the country dearly, hitting a heavily industrialized region which accounts for about 30% of Turkish GDP.

Sitting on a major fault zone, Turkey is no stranger to seismic activity. But in the aftermath of the August 1999 earthquake the question on everybody's lips was how could the country have been so ill prepared? The government drew heavy criticism for its ponderously slow reaction to the quake, as the desperate search for survivors trapped beneath the rubble was conducted mainly by local volunteers, joined later by specialist international teams (amazingly, Turkey had none of its own). Paralysed by the scale of the disaster the state took several critical days to begin the relief effort. Meanwhile, ordinary citizens from across the country stepped in, collecting essentials and transporting them to the devastated area.

The earthquake also exposed the sub-standard nature of many modern buildings as hundreds of concrete apartment blocks, thrown-up on unsuitable land by contractors using shoddy materials, buckled and collapsed. In the rush to build new homes regulations had been widely ignored, often with the connivance of local officials.

If you're interested in making a donation or offering assistance contact The Human Resource Development Foundation, T02122931605, ikgv@ikgv.org A non-profit organization in İstanbul called Genç Tur (see page 164) also organize working holidays helping children affected by the quake.

The easiest way to get to Termal is on one of the bright yellow dolmuş (US$0.50) that depart when full from near the Türk Petrol station between the high-speed ferry terminal and the bus station. After leaving town you pass rows of pre-fabricated houses occupied by people left homeless by the earthquake.

Transport

İznik

The approach to İznik is across an unspoilt rural landscape planted with olive and fruit orchards that sweep down from the Bithynian Mountains to the very edge of placid Lake İznik. The town could be one of countless others in the Marmaran hinterland, a sleepy place where most activity still revolves with the agricultural calendar and local farmers park their tractors on the dusty main street, passing endless hours in smoky teahouses. However, today's modest settlement is in fact the heir to a long and colourful history dating back over 2,000 years, although except for the crumbling defensive walls which still encompass the town and a scattering of pretty unimpressive monuments, you'd never know it. Apart from these rather scant remains, easily exhausted in a morning or afternoon on your way between İstanbul and Bursa, the town could provide a good base for bird-watchers species bagging in the reed beds and meadows surrounding the lake.

Phone code: 0224
Colour map 1, grid B4

Getting there İznik can be reach by turning off the busy Bursa-Yalova road after Gemlik or at the dismal town of Orhangazi depending on whether you're coming from the north or south. There are regular bus services from both Bursa and Yalova throughout the day. **Getting around** Possible to visit all the town's sights on foot.

Ins & outs
See page 178 for further details

History

The city probably owes its origins to Antigonus, the one-eyed general of Alexander the Great, who established it in 316 BC. Soon after, the city was wrestled from his control by another of Alexander's former generals, Lysimachus, who expanded the settlement, naming it Nicaea after his wife. For the next 200 years Nicaea or nearby Nicomedia (Izmit) functioned as the capital of the Bithynian Kingdom, until in 74 BC it shared the fate of Pergamon to the south and was bequeathed to the Roman Empire. As the centre of the Roman province, the city prospered until temporary decline was brought about by the marauding Goths. The city's fortunes improved under the Byzantines as it became the administrative and military headquarters of the surrounding region, graced with many grand public buildings and palaces.

İznik played an important role in the early history of Christianity as the site of two important church meetings. The main outcome of the first Ecumenical Council, convened by Constantine the Great in 325 AD, was the condemnation of the heretical teachings Bishop Arius, who held that Christ's nature was inferior to that of the Lord God's, and the issuing of the Nicene Creed, a statement affirming the divine nature of Christ. Another Ecumenical Council wasn't held in the city until 787 AD, when a meeting was called to solve the Iconoclastic Controversy which had been raging over the representation and worship of religious figures. Conservatives viewed idols as heretical, however, the synod issued a statement supporting "reverence" but not "adoration" of such depictions. Significantly, although this decree was endorsed by Pope Adrian I, it was misunderstood in the west due to a bad translation from Greek into Latin ultimately helping to bring about the final split between the Orthodox and Roman Catholic churches.

As an Ottoman city in the rapidly expanding empire, İznik flourished becoming a celebrated centre for the production of ceramics (see box). The good times didn't last, however, and with the decline of the local tilemaking industry İznik became just another backwater town which suffered terrible damage at the beginning of the 20th century during the struggle for independence.

Sights

Having passed through the city walls the first thing you'll probably notice about the town is its regular layout – a real boon for visiting tourists. This isn't the work of a zealous modern town planner, rather a legacy from the Hellenistic and Roman city's built previously on the spot. The grid of streets is dissected by Atatürk Caddesi and Kılıçaslan Caddesi which run north-south and east-west between the old city's main gates: İstanbul, Lefke, Yenişehir and Göl Kapıları.

Haghia Sophia (Aya Sofya) Situated right in the centre of town, the "Church of Divine Wisdom" hasn't stood the test of time very well and is little more than a roofless masonry shell. This is the third building to have graced the spot with excavations early last century revealing that the original church was destroyed by an earthquake in 1065. Rebuilt soon afterwards, the church was promptly converted into a mosque when Osman Gazi took the city in 1331, becoming the Ulu Cami. Damaged during the Mongol invasion and later by fire, the mosque's reconstruction was placed in the capable hands of the court architect Mimar Sinan. However, it again fell into disrepair at the end of the Ottoman era and was wrecked during vicious fighting between Greek and Turkish forces in 1922. After such a turbulent history it's hardly surprising that little remains but the

Miles of tiles

From the end of the 15th century a ceramics industry developed in İznik using local deposits of clay and quartz found in the nearby mountains. It was given a boost in 1514 when Selim the Grim captured Tabriz from the Persians, forcibly relocating the city's skilled artisans to the lakeside town. Inspired by the designs on imported Chinese porcelain and earlier Islamic art, these craftsmen and their descendants created beautiful ceramic plates, bowls and tiles. Initially decorated predominantly with cobalt blue geometric designs and floral motifs, later in the century other vivid colours such as 'Armenian bole', a bright red glaze produced using iron oxide, were introduced into the designs.

Tile production expanded greatly during the reign of Süleyman the Magnificent as İznik faïence was used to decorate the finest mosques in the empire. Some of the best examples can be seen in İstanbul, where the Rüstem Paşa Camii or the Blue Mosque are outstanding examples of İznik tiles used to wonderful decorative effect. The industry's heyday came during the 16th and early 17th centuries when over 300 kilns were operating in the area; but by 1620 the industry had gone into rapid decline. As demand contracted the special techniques for producing and decorating

ceramics were forgotten, leaving the early İznik-ware unrivalled by later, inferior pieces from Kütahya, which by the end of the 17th century had replaced İznik as the focus of production (see page 441).

Since 1995, however, a group called the İznik Foundation has attempted to revive the town's tilemaking tradition. Employing a group of local craftsmen and aided by ceramics experts and archaeologists, they've set about rediscovering the techniques used by the original masters. Decorated by hand using traditional designs, you can judge the results for yourself at the foundation's workshops on Vakıf Sokak, near the Saray Kapısı. There's also a show room in İstanbul at Öksüz Çocuk Sokak No 14, Kuruçeşme. Although at US$150 for a 23½ cm square tile you may decide they're a little pricey for redecorating your bathroom with.

Keep in mind that original İznik faïence is classed as an antique and exporting it from the country is an offence.

church's external walls. Inside, part of the mosaic pavement, which once covered the nave, is protected from the elements beneath a glass roof. A faded fresco of Jesus and Mary with John the Baptist also survives under an arch in the north wall. ■ *0900-1200, 1300-1630 daily except Mon. US$1.25. If the gate is locked enquire at the museum for the key.*

If you arrive at the bus station it makes sense to begin by walking several blocks further east on Çelebi Sokak to the **Yakup Çelebi Zaviyesi**, a dervish hospice established in the 14th century by the younger brother of Beyazıt I. Despite distinguishing himself in battle, Yakup was murdered by his older sibling after the death of their father at the Battle of Kosova. Beyazıt I justified this act by claiming that it was necessary to avoid a potentially damaging successional conflict, establishing a bloody fratricide tradition which lasted for over 200 years. In the courtyard of the hospice, later converted into a mosque, Yakup's tomb is covered by an open-sided, domed structure which has been rather insensitively rebuilt with concrete.

Ottoman buildings
Most of the town's Ottoman buildings, none of which are that spectacular, are east of Atatürk Caddesi

Nearby are the foundations of the eighth century **Church of Koimesis** levelled in the 1922 fighting. An imperial chapel, it was the last resting place of Theodore I Lascaris, the Byzantine emperor who fled from Constantinople after the Crusaders took the city, establishing the short-lived but successful Empire of Nicaea.

To the northwest of the church on Süleyman Paşa Sokak is the **Süleyman Paşa Medresesi**, a rough stone building with several chimneys protruding from its tiled roof. Still functioning as a Koran school nearly 700 years on, the religious seminary was founded by Orhan Gazi shortly after he took the city in 1313 and is the first of its kind established by an Ottoman ruler.

Mosques Continuing north to Kılınçaslan Caddesi, on the opposite side of the street stands the oldest mosque in town, the **Hacı Özbek Camii**, built in 1332 and rather brutal added-to since. A block north is the tomb of Eşrefzade Abdullah Rumi, a highly regarded sufic mystic, beside which rises a brick minaret, the only extant remains of a mosque destroyed in 1922.

Walking along Kılınçaslan Caddesi you'll come to a municipal park on the opposite side of which stands the **Yeşil Cami** (Green Mosque), a diminutive mosque with a squat minaret encased in red, turquoise and black tiles (the eponymous green tiles were replaced). The twin-domed building was commissioned in 1378 by Çandarlı Kara Halil Hayrettin Paşa, who apart from having a very long winded name, was commander of Orhan Gazi's army and later grand vizier under his successor Murat I. It isn't nearly as impressive as its

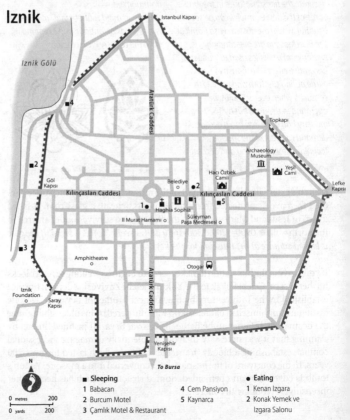

Iznik

Iznik Gölü

Istanbul Kapısı

Atatürk Caddesi

Topkapı

Archaeology Museum

Yeşil Cami

Göl Kapısı

Belediye

Hacı Özbek Camii

Kılınçaslan Caddesi

Lefke Kapısı

Kılınçaslan Caddesi

Haghia Sophia

Süleyman Paşa Medresesi

II Murat Hamamı

Amphitheatre

Otogar

Iznik Foundation

Saray Kapısı

Yenişehir Kapısı

To Bursa

N

0 metres 200
0 yards 200

■ **Sleeping**
1 Babacan
2 Burcum Motel
3 Çamlık Motel & Restaurant
4 Cem Pansiyon
5 Kaynarca

● **Eating**
1 Kenan Izgara
2 Konak Yemek ve Izgara Salonu

namesake in Bursa, although the minaret does provide a splash of colour in an otherwise pretty dour town.

Opposite the Yeşil Cami is the collapsed **Şeyh Kutbettin Camii**, its tottering minaret splinted by steel girders, and the town's archaeological museum (see below).

Nicaea was a well-defended city with a double ring of thick walls topped by 100 watchtowers constructed during Byzantine times. Even so, the ramparts were breached, and subsequently repaired, on numerous occasions and today they're a crumbling shadow of their former selves. At the eastern end of Kılınçaslan Caddesi is the **Lefke Kapısı**, one of the city's four principle gates which used to lead to the town of Lefke, now Osmaneli. It's in fact a treble gateway with a Roman triumphal arch, erected by Proconsul Plancius Varus in 123 AD to commemorate a visit by Hadrian, sandwiched between two portals. On the outside gate some ancient reliefs depicting a Roman centurion fighting against a barbarian are built into its outer face. About 400 m beyond this gateway is the tomb of Çandarlı Kara Halil Hayrettin Paşa the grand vizier who commissioned the Yeşil Cami.

The City Walls
The top of the ramparts is a good point from which to survey the surrounding area. Notice the aqueduct which used to supply the town with water

The town's south gateway, the **Yenişehir Kapısı**, is very much worse for wear having been the defensive chink used by the Selçuks, Byzantines and Ottomans to breach the city walls. As with the other gates traffic is now routed through a modern opening in the walls to help preserve what's left of the portal.

The **Saray Kapısı** (Palace Gate) to the west is reached along a lane which passes a much degraded ancient amphitheatre dating from Roman times. The setting is leafy and peaceful and having passed through the gate in winter you have to ford a small brook. Continuing straight ahead the track turns into Vakıf Sokak which brings you out at the lakeside. There's a concrete promenade and several cafés fronting the lake and in the height of summer you may even be tempted to have a swim.

Similar to the Lefke Kapısı, the **İstanbul Kapısı** has a triumphal arch dedicated to Hadrian between an inner and an outer gateway.

With your own transport or in a taxi you could visit an underground tomb known as the **Yeraltı Mezarı** which is about 7 km north of town. First, however, you'll need to enquire at the town museum for the key, and somebody will usually accompany you to the sight. Don't forget to give them a tip for the trouble. What you'll find is an early Byzantine burial chamber, the walls decorated with well-preserved frescoes.

Outside the city walls

İznik's archaeological museum is housed in the **Nilüfer Hatun Imareti**, a multi-domed soup-kitchen which was built in 1388 by Murat I in honour of his mother, Nilüfer Hatun, a Byzantine woman of noble birth. An intelligent and talented woman, she acted as regent managing state affairs while her husband was away pushing back the frontiers of the Ottoman realm. In actual fact the building began life as a *zaviye* (hospice) for the Ahi brotherhood, a fraternal society or guild made up of skilled artisans. The garden is littered with chunks of marble and stone: the fragmentary remains of sarcophagi and capitals left over from Roman and Byzantine times, along with early Ottoman gravestones including that of the 'head tile-maker'. Inside the cool halls of the *imaret* there is only a limited display of locally produced ceramics, with some damaged tiles recovered by archaeologists excavating the town's kilns and other later 16th-century pieces. Also on show are exhibits of Ottoman weaponry, handicrafts such as embroidery, and a handsome Roman sarcophagus. ■ *0830-1200, 1300-1700 daily except Mon. US$1.25.*

Archaeological Museum

Essentials

Sleeping
There are a few simple hotels which are perfectly adequate for a night, however, they can get busy on summer weekends when it's a good idea to book

E *Çamlık Motel*, Göl Kenarı, T7571362, F7571631. Certainly one of the nicer places in town, good position on lakeside road, simple rooms with en-suite, good restaurant with outside dining. Recommended. **E** *Burcum Motel*, Göl Kenarı, T7571011. 3 floors of simple rooms with en-suite, lake view from upper balconies is redeeming feature, not open in the winter. **F** *Cem Pansiyon*, Mustafa Kemal Paşa Mahallesi, Göl Sahili No 34, T7571687, cempansiyon@hotmail.com Formerly the *Murat Pansiyon*, plain but airy rooms, clean shared bathrooms, balconies overlooking lake, not a bad second choice, breakfast extra. **F** *Kaynarca Hotel*, Kılınçaslan Caddesi, M. Gündem Sokak No 1, T7571753, F7571723. Exuberant decor throughout, simple rooms are good value, equipped with TV and fan, kitchen area and terrace, internet access, centrally located but you may miss the lakeside breeze in the summer. Good budget option. **F** *Babacan Hotel*, Kılınçaslan Caddesi No 2, T7571211, F7574281, on main street opposite Belediye. Fairly characterless concrete building, large spartan rooms with and without bathrooms. **Camping** For a small fee you can pitch a tent in the gardens of the *Hotel Burcum* and *Çamlık Motel*.

Eating
The Çamlık Restaurant, Göl Kenarı, serves *meze*, locally caught fish including *yayın balığı* (catfish), grilled meat and kebabs in pleasant surroundings near the lake, expect to pay about US$8 per head with alcohol. Also on the lakefront road, the *Burcum* and the *Kırık Çatal* have similar menus and prices. On Kılınçaslan Caddesi there are several cheap eateries such as the *Konak Yemek ve Izgara Salonu*, where you can have grilled chicken and lamb chops (*pirzola),* döner during the day and some ready-prepared dishes. Across Atatürk Caddesi from Haghia Sophia, *Kenan Izgara* is a clean, modern place serving soup, *inegöl köftesi* and kebabs.

Transport
Bursa, every 30 mins, 0730-1830, 90 min, US$3. **Yalova**, hourly until 1800, 75 mins, US$3.50.

Directory
Banks There are several with ATMs near Haghia Sophia, they will not change TCs though. **Baths** *Il Murat Hamamı*, 15th-century baths constructed by Murat II, 1 block south of Haghia Sophia turn left off Atatürk Caddesi, wash and *kese* US$2.50. **Communications Internet**: Café below the *Kaynarca Hotel* on Gündem Sokak, US$1 per hr. **Tourist information** On the 1st floor at Kılınçaslan Caddesi No 130, opposite the Belediye building, T/F7571933. Open daily 0900-1200, 1300-1700, in winter closed at weekends.

Bursa

Phone code: 0224
Colour map 1, grid B4
250 km SE of İstanbul

The bulky forested mass of Mount Uludağ is an impressive backdrop to what is one of modern Turkey's pleasantest large cities. Affluent and self-assured, Bursa has industrialized rapidly, particularly in the last three decades, and is now an important centre for the textile, food processing and car manufacturing industries. Traditionally known as Yeşil (Green) Bursa, the unprecedented urban growth which has accompanied the city's industrialization has eaten-up much of the eponymous green space and sent the city sprawling outwards from its historic core. A huge influx of workers from rural and eastern areas has pushed the population to well over one million, however, the city lacks the disorderly, chaotic feel of İstanbul. As a celebrated spa centre since the days of Rome and the first Ottoman capital, Bursa attracts some attention from foreign tourists on account of its rich legacy of early Ottoman architecture and its steamy mineral baths fed by natural hot springs. For most though, it is little more than a cursory visit, bused in from İstanbul for a whistlestop tour around the main sights and a rushed session in one of the historic baths. Bursa deserves far more, a couple of days ideally to *appreciate the city's beautiful mosques; lose yourself in the bazaar district; ride the cable-car up Mount Uludağ and last, but by no means least, have a leisurely wallow in the therapeutic mineral baths.*

Ins and outs

Bursa is extremely well connected with regular buses to most Turkish towns and cities. The easiest way to travel between İstanbul and Bursa is using the high-speed ferry service from Yenikapı to Yalova, from where it's about an hours bus ride over the Bithynian mountains to Bursa.

Getting there
See page 189 for further details

Despite the sprawling suburbs, central Bursa is a compact, manageable size, particularly after İstanbul. You can see most of the sights on foot with a short dolmuş or bus ride only necessary to get to the more outlying areas like Muradiye or Çekirge. The centre of town is Cumhuriyet Meydanı, known as Heykel (Statue), where administrative buildings flank a statue of Atatürk which overlooks the busy traffic of Atatürk Caddesi, the principle avenue. The bus station is 10 km from the centre (moved to relieve congestion). Access to the city centre is on grey 'Terminal' buses, or buses no. 90A to Heykel, or alternatively no 92 to Çekirge, US$0.50.

Getting around

Bursa began life in 183 AD as the Bithynian capital of Prusias I, named Prusa after the tyrant himself. Gifted with copious hot springs, the city attracted the favour and patronage of the Romans, who adorned the city with splendid public buildings and bathhouses. The Byzantines, who like their predecessors appreciated bathing in hot water, continued the tradition also introducing silk production to the area.

History

The city's most illustrious period began, however, in 1326 when the Ottoman emir Orhan Gazi succeeded, after a decade long siege begun by his father Osman, in taking the city from the Byzantines. Renamed Bursa, the city became the first capital of the nascent Ottoman empire, a defining step in the Ottoman's metamorphosis from nomadic tribe to imperial dynasty. Though with the Ottoman pendulum of conquest swinging westwards into the Balkans, the capital was moved to Edirne less than 50 years later. Despite the move Bursa maintained its sentimental importance for successive Ottoman sultans who constructed fine public buildings and were laid to rest in the city.

The bazaar area

Bounded by the busy thoroughfare of Atatürk Caddesi to the south, the bazaar area contains a fascinating cluster of hans, mosques and market places which are still the focus of much of the modern city's retail and commercial activity. It's an interesting area to wander around soaking up the sights and sounds, stopping for a drink in one of several pleasant shady courtyard cafés.

Standing beside Atatürk Caddesi is the solid rectangular form of Bursa's Ulu Cami, or 'Great Mosque'. Commissioned by Beyazıt I in 1396 and completed three years later, the building is constructed out of stone quarried from the slopes of Mount Uludağ above the city. The mosque typifies the early style of Ottoman architecture with the interior space broken up by rows of thick columns supporting the multi-domed roof. An interesting feature is the three-tiered şadırvan found near the centre of the mosque beneath a glass dome. Originally open to the elements, this glass dome lights-up what would otherwise be a very dark interior, while the fountain fills the mosque with the relaxing sound of running water. Make sure you have a look at the richly

Ulu Cami
Well used by local residents & traders who pop in at prayer time or sit on the carpet near the shuttered windows reading the Koran

carved walnut *mimber*. Outside in the courtyard, shaded by plain trees, stall-holders sell colourful strings of worry beads and other religious paraphernalia.

From the courtyard of the Ulu Cami a flight of steps leads down into the **Emir Hanı**, its courtyard filled with the hum of conversation as people sit drinking tea around the pretty central fountain. In days gone by this was where overland caravans would pause to trade goods and rest.

The covered bazaar Beyond the Emir Hanı you enter Bursa's labyrinthine bazaar, one of the largest in Anatolia. Unlike the Kapalı Çarşı in İstanbul most of the shops cater for the needs of the local population and tourists are relatively thin on the ground. The 'hassle factor' is correspondingly low, so you can shop around in relative peace for bargains such as silk and cotton material, towels and clothing.

To the north of the Emir Hanı, across busy Kapalı Çarşı Caddesi, the **Bedesten** is the oldest part of the market. Built in the 14th century during the reign of Beyazıt I, the building has been rebuilt several times, most recently after a major fire in 1955. Today, it's known as the Kuyumcular Çarşısı (the Jeweller's Market) and its arching halls are filled with glittering gold and jewellery merchants. Leading off the opposite side of Kapalı Çarşı Caddesi, the **Eski Aynalı Çarşı** is an arcade of shops in what was formerly the Orhan Gazi Hamamı (1339), the first Turkish bath to be built by the Ottomans.

Koza Hanı Exiting the covered bazaar on to Uzun Çarşı, the entrance to Bursa's most beautiful caravanserai, the **Koza Hanı** is on your right-hand side. Built at the end of the 15th century by Beyazıt II, and handsomely restored in 1985 with funds donated by the Aga Khan Foundation, it's a two-storey stone building topped by peaked chimneys around a large central courtyard. In the centre of this open space, shaded by plain trees, is a diminutive octagonal *mescit* (prayer hall) ingeniously built directly over a fountain. Traditionally the centre of the city's silk industry, villagers would gather each year in the courtyard to sell sacks of white silk cocoons (*koza*) to dealers. Unfortunately, mechanisation and stiff competition from abroad have put paid to this colourful spectacle, and despite the efforts of Bursa's Silk Research Institute the local silk rearing industry has all but died out. There is some continuity with the past though, as many of the shops in the second floor arcade of the Koza Hanı are devoted to

Bursa

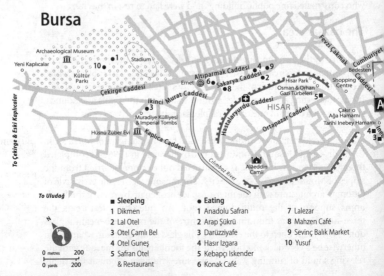

Sleeping
1 Dikmen
2 Lal Otel
3 Otel Çamlı Bel
4 Otel Guneş
5 Safran Otel & Restaurant

Eating
1 Anadolu Safran
2 Arap Şükrü
3 Darüzziyafe
4 Hasır Izgara
5 Kebapçı Iskender
6 Konak Café
7 Lalezar
8 Mahzen Café
9 Sevinç Balık Market
10 Yusuf

selling silk goods such as brightly dyed scarves, shirts, blouses and ties. Leaving the Koza Hanı by its front gate brings you out into a pedestrianized area called **Koza Parkı** with a fountain surrounded by benches, crowded by day with cloth-capped men and gaggles of sunflower seed nibbling students.

Other sights

To the east, the **Orhan Gazi Camii** was built in 1339, soon after the Ottoman conquest of the city. In fact it was originally constructed as a *zaviye*, a meeting place for dervishes, and has retained its T-shaped plan, with side chambers flanking the main hall, despite having been restored on several occasions. Next to the Orhan Gazi Camii, Bursa's town hall is a strange looking half-timber affair behind which is the cobbled **Çiçek Pazarı** (**Flower Market**) where flower sellers display their colourful wares on a row of stalls. Turning right, Tuz Pazarı and then Okçular Caddesi lead east to İnönü Caddesi, on the opposite side of which is a lively and interesting area known as the **Demirciler Çarşısı** (**Ironmongers' Market**). The narrow streets are lined with workshops where craftsmen beat, shape and weld all manner of metal goods.

Beyond the Gök Dere

Spilling down from the flanks of Mount Uludağ, the Gök Dere is one of several streams that score the city. It's crossed by several bridges, including the Setbaşı Köprüsü which is reached up the smart-shopping street of Namazgah Caddesi from Heykel. Once across take a left fork at the large plain tree and walk up Yeşil Cadde with the Yeşil Cami, Bursa's most celebrated imperial mosque, clearly visible crowning the hill ahead. The mosque's garden, shaded by huge plain trees, is a popular place for *Bursalı* to sit on summer evenings. As Bursa's biggest draw there's also a cluster of 'touristy' souvenir and antique shops catering for the groups bused in to admire the mosque and nearby tomb.

Yeşil Cami

The Yeşil Cami (Green Mosque) certainly has a prime spot overlooking the city, although the buildings of the residential area around it have encroached on what, in Ottoman times, must have been a wonderful view. Work on the mosque began in 1412 at the orders of the Mehmet I, who had just emerged victorious from a ten-year civil war with his two brothers, precipitated by the death of their father Beyazıt I. Construction dragged on for nearly a decade and the structure was still not completed in 1421 when he died. The project gradually lost steam and the building remains unfinished to this day, the most conspicuous omission being the portico on the mosque's facade. This hardly detracts, though, from what is Bursa's most graceful imperial mosque; a mosque which represents an emerging 'Ottoman' architectural style, with Selçuk and Persian influences no longer dominating. Notice the delicate carving picked out by a thin line of turquoise faïence around the grilled windows and the ornately

Related map
A Bursa centre,
page 183

To Yıldırım Beyazıt Camii

Phantom plays

Karagöz, also known as Hayal Oyunu (Phantom play), is a form of shadow puppetry which originated in Bursa in the 15th century. Legend has it that during the construction of the city's Ulu Cami work was delayed by the continual antics of a pair of workmen, Karagöz and Hacivat. Unamused by the comic duo and angry at the slow pace of construction, Sultan Orhan ordered their execution. Later regretting his actions the sultan had one of his officials make puppets of the unfortunate jokers, giving birth to the tradition of Karagöz.

Baring a striking resemblance to the shadow puppets of Java, Hayal Oyunu was probably the continuation of a much older tradition imported via Central Asia from the Far East; although other researchers suggest that it may in fact have originated in the Mediterranean. Made from thin sheets of camel leather treated with oil to make them translucent and then colourfully painted, the puppets are skilfully manipulated by several puppeteers – or hayalı – from behind a backlit white sheet. Karagöz was a popular form of entertainment in coffeehouses and cafés across the Ottoman Empire, with the hayalılar using their puppets to retell popular stories and satirised contemporary events. A bevy of well-known characters, such as Çelebi the dandy, Kayserili the sharp-witted merchant and Çift Tabancalı Matiz the roguish drunkard, join the two principal characters, Karagöz and his side-kick Hacivat, in their amusing and frequently bawdy adventures.

Sadly Karagöz has all but disappeared as a form of popular entertainment in the modern age of TV and radio, however, the determined efforts of a small group of puppeteers have managed to keep the tradition alive. Naturally enough Bursa is the focus of a modest revival in Hayal Oyunu with performances, seminars and exhibitions. See page 189 for these details.

worked stalactite niche above the entrance portal – a feature common in earlier Selçuk buildings. The interior's most impressive feature is the polychrome tiles covering almost every surface. This was the first time that coloured tiles had been used so profusely in an Ottoman mosque, a taste of what was to come a century later when İznik tiles became all the rage. Particularly dazzling are the tiles revetting the Sultan's Loge above the main entrance, although unfortunately this isn't usually open to the public.

Yeşil Türbe Overlooking the Yeşil Cami and reached up a flight of steps is the Yeşil Türbe. Built to contain the remains of Mehmet I, it's a striking octagonal building covered in turquoise faïence. Originally revetted with green tiles similar to those in the Yeşil Cami, these were replaced by the present tiles from Kütahya after the tomb was badly damaged by an earthquake in 1855. Stepping through the beautifully carved wooden doors, the interior is richly decorated with tiles, this time

Bursa centre

Kamil
Koç Office

Heykel
(Cumhuriyet
Meydanı)

Bookshop/Newspapers

Dolmuş to
Teleferik
(Uludağ)

■ Sleeping
1 Artıç
2 Bilgiç
3 Çeşmeli
4 Kent

● Eating
1 Beyler
2 Çiçek Izgara
3 Hacıbey Iskender
4 Küçük Saray
Pideli Köfte

0 metres 100
0 yards 100

the originals. Both the large *mihrab* and the sultan's tomb, as you'd expect the largest of the group, are covered with yet more panels of colourful decorative tiling, and there are also Koranic inscriptions above each of the windows.

Back a short distance towards the centre, the **Museum of Turkish and Islamic Art** (see page 186) is contained in the Yeşil Cami's *medrese*.

Although less visited by tourists because of its outlying position, the Emir Sultan Camii is extremely popular with pious *Bursalı* who come to pray at the tombs of several dervishes buried in the compound. Built during the 14th century the mosque endured major renovation work in 1805 and in 1985, so the architectural authenticity of the present structure is questionable. What isn't in doubt is the mosque's excellent position beside a rambling graveyard, commanding a view across the city. ■ *Getting there: The mosque is 300 m east of the Yeşil Cami on Emir Sultan Caddesi. It's an uphill walk, so you may prefer to catch a dolmuş from Heykel marked 'Emirsultan', and then walk back via the Yeşil Cami.*

Emir Sultan Camii

Known as Yıldırım, or 'Lightning bolt', because of the speed with which he switched his attention between campaigns in the Balkans and Anatolia, also managing to find time to lay siege to Constantinople on several occasions, Beyazıt I met a rather ignoble end. Defeated by the Mongol horde at Tamerlane at the Battle of Ankara in 1402, the sultan was dragged around in a cage until his death a year later. His death precipitated a decade long battle for supremacy between his sons, during which the future of the Ottoman empire hung in the balance.

Yıldırım Beyazıt Camii
If you're after a comprehensive tour of the city's mosques then you shouldn't miss this one

The mosque was constructed between 1390 and 1395 at the beginning of the sultan's ill-fated reign. Perched on a small hill to the east of the Gök Dere, the twin-domed marble structure is of a similar design to the Yeşil Cami with a modified T-shaped plan with several *eyvan* flanking the main prayer hall. Nearby is the tomb of the unfortunate Sultan and one of the *medrese* of the complex, now functioning as a health centre.

■ *Getting there: The Yıldırım Beyazıt Camii can be reached on foot in about 15 mins from the Yeşil Cami or the Emir Sultan Camii. Alternatively, catch a 'Beyazıt Yıldırım' dolmuş from Heykel.*

The Hisar & Muradiye

At the opposite end of Atatürk Caddesi to Heykel rises the Hisar (Fortress), also known as Tophane, the oldest part of the city dating back to Roman times. Originally enclosed within strong defensive walls, after the Ottoman conquest the city was encouraged to develop outwards to the east and west of the acropolis. Today, along with short sections of the ramparts, the area still contains a few surviving examples of Ottoman vernacular architecture, although many more beautiful wooden konaks have disappeared beneath a tide of concrete.

Osman & Orhan Gazi Türbeleri
Remember to take your shoes off at the door & give a small donation

At the eastern end of the Hisar is a small park which contains the Osman and Orhan Gazi Türbeleri, the last resting place of the founder of the Ottoman dynasty, and his son, who took Bursa from the Byzantines. The tombs are found in two rather uninspiring baroque buildings constructed after the 1855 earthquake flattened the original structures; but still they attract a fairly constant stream of reverential visitors. Inside, crystal chandeliers hang over them and the ceilings are covered with stencil work typical of the period. ■ *0900-1200, 1300-1700, daily except Mon and Thu.*

Beyond the tombs, in the shadow of a large 19th-century clock tower, are a series of pleasant cafés where *Bursalı* come to enjoy a glass of tea and a chat. The view from the cliff-top terraces is superb with ranks of offices and apartments disappearing into the haze that often hangs over the city. In good weather entrepreneurial locals hire out binoculars for US$0.05 per five minutes to scan the city below. A long staircase descends the front of the escarpment, passing several more cafés and sections of the old battlements, bringing you out on Cemal Nadir Caddesi at the bottom.

The backstreets

Before continuing on your way you could seek out some of the old Ottoman houses lurking in the quiet backstreets of the Tophane neighbourhood. During your wanderings you'll catch fleeting glimpses of Bursa how it was before the proliferation of drab concrete; a Bursa described by Lord Kinross in his travelogue 'Europa Minor':

The Turks of Bursa wash their houses in many colours – ochre or pink or tomato or chocolate – but mainly in this cerulean blue, creating the illusion that the sky has been poured into the town, making rivers and pools of it beneath the russet tiled roofs and their attendant spreading trees.

A good place to start is **Kaleiçi Sokağı**, reached by walking down Karadut Sokağı from Hastayurdu Caddesi. Another sight of marginal interest to aim for is the **Alâeddin Camii**, Bursa's oldest mosque which was built in the year the Ottomans conquered the city. It's a small, single domed structure that's recently been restored, however, it may take you a while to find in the maze of alleyways and it's only open at prayer time.

From the top of Orhan Gazi Caddesi and the entrance to the park, Hastalaryurdu Caddesi heads west across the Hisar, passing the town's hospital before winding its way down to the area of Muradiye beyond. It's about a 15-minute walk. Today, it's a residential quarter which, like the Hisar, has a few remaining Ottoman buildings. The streets around the Muradiye mosque complex are filled with a busy street market every Tuesday.

Muradiye Külliyesi

The Muradiye Külliyesi marks the end of Bursa's golden age of construction as it was the last imperial mosque complex to grace the city. Built over two years from 1424 for Murat II, father of Mehmet the Conqueror, the mosque is very similar in plan to the Orhan Gazi Camii and inside the walls are richly decorated with colourful tiles. Other buildings of the complex built at the same time include the *medrese*, functioning today as a health centre, and the *imaret*, which has been converted into an excellent Ottoman restaurant, the *Darüzziyafe* (see page 188).

Behind the mosque in a large, well-kept garden dotted with roses and cypress trees is the simple tomb of the mosque's founder Murat II. Surrounded by a delicately carved wooden porch, the roof of the building was left open at the Sultan's command so that the rain could fall on his grave. The Ottoman practice of fratricide, whereby a new sultan having seized the throne would eliminate all his male relatives, ensured that the garden is well stocked with other tombs built over the centuries. Nearby, the **Şehzade Ahmet Türbesi** contains the remains of Şehzade Ahmet, oldest son of Beyazıt II, who was murdered by his younger brother Selim. To consolidate his position Selim I went on to kill another brother, six nephews and three of his own sons, aptly displaying the cruelty which would earn him the epithet 'the Grim'. The tomb itself contains a beautiful display of İznik tilework, lit by sunlight filtering in through a stained glass window.

The **Şehzade Mustafa Türbesi** was built for the oldest son of Süleyman the Magnificent, strangled by the imperial mutes after the grand vizier, Rüstem Paşa, persuaded the sultan that he was being plotted against. Perhaps it was out of regret for his actions that the sultan had his son's tomb decorated so beautifully with lively panels of İznik faïence.

Another tragic occupant of the garden is Prince Cem, son of Mehmet the Conqueror. Despite an auspicious start as the first Ottoman prince born in the new capital of İstanbul, Cem lost a successional war with his brother, Beyazıt II, and fled into exile. Over the next fourteen years he tried in vain to solicit the support of various Christian powers, finally dying as a lonely and broken prisoner of the Pope in 1495. Despite their antagonistic relationship, the sultan welcomed his brother back into the empire after his death, burying him with honour in a richly decorated tomb.

■ *The tombs are generally open daily, 0830-1200, 1300-1700, however, you may have to seek out the warden to gain entry to some of them. Buses marked 'Muradiye' climb up Orhan Gazi Caddesi, passing the park and hospital. Get off when you see the Tarihi Murat Hamamı on the left-hand side.*

In a quiet backstreet near the Muradiye Camii, the Hüsnü Züber Evi, or 'Living **Hüsnü Züber Evi** Museum', is found in a rambling Ottoman konak authentically restored by local artist Hüsnü Züber. Originally built in 1836 as a guesthouse, the graceful timber frame building served as the Russian Consulate and a home to several families before being renovated in 1988. Recently turned over to the municipality, the rooms downstairs contain Hüsnü's collection of traditional wooden spoons collected from villages across Anatolia. Also on show are wooden implements decorated with traditional motifs using a technique known as 'pyrogravure', which involves burning the surface of the wood using heated metal tools. You'll be showed around by Hüsnü himself, who actually lives upstairs. ■ *1000-1700 daily except Mon. US$1.50. Follow the signs up the street beside the Tahiri Murat Hamamı.*

A short walk north of Muradiye is an area of semi-green space where *Bursalı* **Kültür Parkı** enjoy strolling on summer evenings and Sundays. Called the Kültür (Culture) Park, soon after arriving you'll notice that the Turkish idea of a park is quite different to the concept held generally in the west. There is very little grass or open space at all, the area is taken up instead by a matrix of paths, cafés, restaurants and assorted other buildings, including the **Archaeological Museum** (see page 187). It is relatively peaceful and car-free after the city though, and much of it is shaded beneath a canopy of trees. ■ *It's about a 15-20 min walk from Koza Parkı or Heykel get on a bus or dolmuş bound for Sigorta or Çekirge which pass along Çekirge Caddesi to the south of the park. US$0.10.*

To the west of the Kültür Parkı are the city's Yeni Kaplıcalar, or New Baths. **Yeni Kaplıcalar** Despite the name, they are nearly 500 years old, endowed by Süleyman the Magnificent's grand vizier, Rüstem Paşa, after the therapeutic waters cured a dose of imperial gout. The baths are still popular with those seeking a cure for ailments such as rheumatism or residents after a relaxing soak. In the men's section, beyond the fairly ordinary changing area and *soğukluk* is a grand marble pool filled to the brim with steaming water piped from hot springs which emerge at temperatures of up to 50°C. The women's section of the baths is unfortunately not as impressive. Next door is the **Karamustafa Çamur Banyosu** where you can subject yourself to a mud bath or wallow in small private cubicles. Couples may be asked for proof that they are married. If you're after a serious cure then the baths have basic rooms for US$20 per night, with a morning and evening bath included in the price. There's a small tea garden and simple restaurant on-site. ■ *Getting there: Çekirge and Sigorta-bound buses and dolmuş from Heykel pass within 200 m of the baths, which are reached down a road off Çekirge Caddesi. 0600-2300 daily. US$5, kese US$1.50. Mud-bath US$4.*

Çekirge

Several kilometres to the west of the city centre the suburb of Çekirge tumbles down the wooded flanks of Mount Uludağ. Famous since Roman times for its mineral springs and hot baths, today it's a well-to-do residential area scattered with hotels, many of which boast their own thermal pools.

Eski Kaplıcalar
If you're after a more refined bathing experience than the Yeni Kaplıcalar look no further

Known as the 'Old Baths', the multi-domed thermal complex next to the central roundabout in Çekirge can trace its origins back to the Byzantine Emperor Justinian and his wife Theodora, who is said to have arrived to take the waters with a retinue of 4,000 attendants. The stone building you see today was raised on Byzantine foundations during the reign of Murat I. It's been renovated several times since, most recently by the adjacent *Kervansaray Termal Hotel*, to which it's connected by an ugly modern walkway. Divided into men's and women's sections, the *hararet* of each has a large marble pool flanked by ancient columns. Don't forget to have a wash at the individual marble basins before taking the plunge. Having scrubbed and cooked yourself, relax in the domed *soğukluk* which is filled with the sound of a marble fountain. ■ *From Bursa get on a dolmuş or bus marked Çekirge or Sigorta (SSK). Daily, men 0700-2230, women 0730-2230. US$6, kese US$3, massage US$4. There's a bar for replacing those lost fluids.*

Hüdavendigâr (Birinci) Murat Camii

On the hill above the Eski Kaplıcalar is a mosque complex commissioned by Murat I, who liked to be known by the epithet Hüdavendigâr, which translates literally as the 'Creator of the Universe'. The mosque took over 20 years to build because the sultan was constantly on campaign, waging war against infidels in the Balkans. Finally completed in 1385, it was built to a unique design with a *medrese* on the first floor and two barrel-vaulted *zaviye* (side halls) for the use of travelling dervishes on either side of the main hall. The mosque's contemporary decor is spartan except for an ornate niched *mihrab*. Across the street is the tomb of Murat I, who was murdered by a Serbian defector in his royal pavilion after the Ottoman victory over a Serbian-led coalition at the Battle of Kosova in 1389.

Museum of Turkish & Islamic Art

The stone *medrese* of the Yeşil Camii provides an excellent venue for a collection displayed in halls around the seminary's lovely courtyard. On show are examples of pre-Ottoman, İznik and Kütahya ceramics; various items associated with dervish sects; some beautifully decorated Korans and metalwork including an interesting Mameluk chandelier. There's also a reconstruction of an Ottoman bath chamber complete with scantily clad dummies and some interesting paraphernalia. ■ *0830-1200, 1300-1700 daily except Mon. US$1.25. On Yeşil Caddesi, 50 m west of the mosque.*

Found in the middle of the Kültür Parkı, Bursa's provincial museum has a pre- **Archaeological**
dictable collection of Roman and Byzantine stonework, statuary and sarcoph- **Museum**
agi, along with some more unusual artefacts such as a Byzantine funerary cask
with parts of a skeleton inside. Also on display are pieces of ancient glassware
and metal jewellery and objects from sites across Anatolia. ■ *0830-1200,
1300-1730 daily except Mon. US$1.25.*

Essentials

The city centre, especially the roads off Atatürk Caddesi near the Ulu Cami, is the best **Sleeping**
place to look for budget accommodation. Most of the classier hotels, along with a few
more humble offerings, are out in the spa suburb of Çekirge. The hotels in Çekirge
generally have mineral baths for the use of their guests, with the Eski Kaplıcalar at
most only a short walk down the road.

City centre A *Kent Hotel*, Atatürk Caddesi No 69, T2235420, F2244015, right in the
centre of things opposite Koza Parkı. Front rooms are noisy, well-equipped with small
bathroom, a/c, refrigerator, telephone, TV, discounts available. **B** *Safran Otel*, Kale
Sokak, Tophane, T2247216, F2247219. Excellent location in Hisar neighbourhood,
across from the tombs of Osman and Orhan Gazi in picturesque Ottoman-style building. Well-appointed rooms with a/c, telephone and TV. Recommended. **D** *Hotel
Çeşmeli*, Gumuşçeken Caddesi No 6, Heykel, T2241511, F2241511. Centrally located,
efficient management, good bet for female travellers, spotlessly clean but rooms are
bit simple for the money, larger doubles with TV, fan and refrigerator US$40. Recom-
mended despite being a little over-priced. **D-E** *Hotel Dikmen*, Maksem Caddesi No
78, T2241840, F2204085, singles US$25. Dated 2-star place up street next to PTT. Rea-
sonably spacious rooms with refrigerator, telephone, TV, small terrace at the rear,
some rooms are a little noisy. Recommended. **E** *Hotel Bilgiç*, Başak Caddesi No 30,
Heykel, T2201289, F2227633. Tall, narrow hotel off Atatürk Caddesi. Oddly shaped
rooms with small bathroom, telephone and TV as standard. **E** *Hotel Artıç*, Atatürk
Caddesi No 95, T2245505, F2245509, just off Atatürk Caddesi across from Ulu Cami.
Large hotel with plainly furnished, rather dated rooms, telephone, TV, avoid rooms
facing street due to traffic noise. **E-F** *Otel Çamlı Bel*, Inebey Caddesi No 71, T2212565,
F2234405. Conveniently located for the sights, good choice of 1/2/3 bed rooms with
or without bathrooms, all simply furnished but some have TV. Recommended budget
option. **F** *Otel Güneş*, Inebey Caddesi No 75, T2221404. Traditional style house, rooms
are small and disappointing though, basic, shared bathroom, no breakfast. **F** *Lal Otel*,
Maksem Caddesi No 79, T2211710. Old-fashioned boarding house with clean but
waterless rooms. Recommended rock-bottom place.

Çekirge L *Kervansaray Termal Hotel*, Çekirge Meydanı, T2339300, F2339324. Very
comfortable well-equipped rooms, excellent facilities including health centre with
sauna and pool, good restaurant on roof terrace, internal access to Eski Kaplıcalar (see
page 186) next door. Recommended. **L** *Hotel Çelik Palas*, Çekirge Caddesi, 12333800,
F2361910, overlooking the Kültür Parkı between Çekirge and the centre of town.
Huge spa hotel established in 1935, spacious rooms with a/c, minibar, telephone and
cable TV, unlimited use of large domed mineral pool and sauna. **AL** *Hotel Anatolia*,
Çekirge Meydanı, T2339400, F2339408, overlooking the Eski Kaplıcalar. Modern hotel
with thermal baths and small outdoor pool, rooms are equipped with a/c, minibar,
telephone, TV, some have view of city, substantial off-season discount. **A** *Hotel
Dilmen*, Birinci Murat Caddesi No 20, T2339500, F2352568. 100 bright rooms with
minibar, telephone and TV as standard, mineral baths, gym and sauna. **C** *Hotel
Akdoğan*, Çekirge Birinci Murat Caddesi No 1, T2338200, F2363129. Fairly plain modern place behind the *Hotel Anatolia*, decent enough rooms with small bathroom.

D *Medine Tuğra Termal Otel*, Birinci Murat Camii Yanı No 2, T2343740, F2330324, in side street next to Hüdavendigâr Camii. Clean and simple rooms with shower, telephone and TV, marble baths in the basement. Recommended. **D** *Atlas Termal Hotel*, Hamamlar Caddesi No 35, T2344100, F2364605, 250 m up the hill from the Eski Kaplıcalar. Nice rooms in smart, wood panelled hotel, helpful staff, thermal baths on the premises. Recommended. **E** *Hotel Eren*, Birinci Murat Caddesi, Aralığı Sokak No 2, T2367105, F2368099. Next to the Hüdavendigâr Camii. Clean, simple rooms in family run pension. Good budget option.

Eating Bursa is the home of that Turkish institution, the döner kebap, which was invented in 1867 by a local chef named Iskender Usta. Although Turks had been spit roasting meat for thousands of years, Iskender was the bright spark who turned everything on its head, grilling the lamb or mutton in an upright position. This ensures that the 'elephant's foot' remains moist and doesn't char, with the meat sliced off using a long, thin blade. Served as a tasty fastfood across the country, the döner tradition has also been carried around the globe by immigrant Turks. In Bursa it's generally served as an *Iskender kebabı* or *Bursa kebabı*, consisting of slices of döner meat on a raft of pide bread soaked in a rich tomato, yoghurt and butter sauce. Another meaty speciality is *Inegöl köftesi*, grilled meat balls, which are often served with melted cheese as *Kaşarlı köfte*. If you're in the mood for seafood head down to Sakarya Caddesi, north of the Hisar, where there are a number of convivial fish restaurants with outside dining and plenty of alcohol. Alternatively, if it's relatively peaceful outside dining you're after, there are several restaurants in the Kültür Park which have terraces.

Expensive *Mercan*, *Kervansaray Termal Hotel*, Çekirge, T2339300, about as sophisticated as dining in Bursa gets, the Mercan has a diverse Turkish/international menu and tables outside on the hotel's roof terrace. **Midrange** *Anatolian Pizza*, Çekirge Meydanı, Çekirge, run by *Anatolia Hotel*, convenient stop-off after a bath at the Eski Kaplıcalar, pizza and pasta place with extensive menu, closed Mon. *Arap Şükrü*, Sakarya Caddesi, brightly lit fish restaurant in small half-timber houses on either side of this lively street, good range of seafood on display. *Darüzziyafe*, Ikinci Murat Caddesi No 36, Muradiye, T2246439, another good reason to visit this part of town, atmospheric dining in renovated public kitchens of Muradiye Camii, meat-based menu offering tasty and unusual Ottoman dishes, in keeping with surroundings no alcohol served, instead diners encouraged to try range of sweet *şerbet* drinks, outside terrace, very reasonably priced at under US$10 per head. *Hasır Izgara*, Sakarya Caddesi, Kuruçeşme Mahallesi, popular *meze* and fish place with friendly and informal atmosphere. *Safran Restaurant*, Kale Sokak, Tophane, T2247216, pleasant restaurant in Ottoman-style hotel in the Hisar, good selection of hot and cold *meze*, stews and grilled meat, salads and traditional deserts. Also under the same management is *Anadolu Safran*, T2208901, inside the stadium gate of the Kültür Parkı, offers equally tasteful surroundings and a similar menu, but with the added advantage of a peaceful location and outside dining. *Yusuf*, Kültür Parkı, near the stadium entrance, popular *meze* and kebap restaurant with some tables outside, alcohol served, about US$6-$10 per head. **Cheap** *Çiçek Izgara*, Belediye Caddesi No 15, behind the Belediye building, pleasant upstairs dining with extensive menu of grilled meats including fillet steak (*bonfile*) and lamb chops (*pirzola*). *Beyler*, Gümüşçeken Caddesi No 3, excellent new addition, brightly-lit modern place, extensive menu including soup, lahmacun, pide, *iskender* and *köfte*, efficient service. *Hacıbey Iskender*, Taşkapı Sokak No 4, in street opposite the town hall, said to be the home of the *iskender kebabı*, small bustling restaurant on 2 floors, Kütahya tiles on the walls and wooden furniture. *Kebapçı Iskender*, Ünlü Caddesi No 7, Heykel, well-established place that's been serving local speciality, along with other variations on the kebap theme, since 1950. *Küçük Saray Pideli Köfte*, Maskan Caddesi, popular diner which serves soup, pide, *köfte*, but no alcohol, convenient if you staying in one of cheap hotels nearby.

Lalezar, Ünlü Caddesi, Heykel, excellent little place serving soup and ready-prepared dishes, try the traditional puddings like *kabak tatlısı* (pumpkin pudding) after. *Sevinç Balık Market*, Sakarya Caddesi, Kuruçeşme Mahallesi, on corner with Altıparmak Caddesi, no-nonsense venue for cheap seafood, deep-fried fish or *midye* (mussels) served with salad, also huge fish sandwiches US$2.50, popular with local students because it's such excellent value.

Konak Cafe, Sakarya Caddesi, Kuruçeşme Mahallesi, convivial café in rambling old Ottoman house, popular with students from Uludağ University. *Geye*, Namazgah Caddesi, near Setbaşı bridge, indulge your sweet-tooth at this fairly upmarket cake and pudding shop. Next door is *Baba Yadigarı* which has similar range of sweet delicacies. *Mahzen Cafe*, Sakarya Caddesi, Kuruçeşme Mahallesi, popular with young studenty crowd, live folk and Turkish pop music in the evenings, snacks and food served. *Mahfel Çay Bahçesi*, tea garden on the east side of the Gök Dere near the Setbaşı bridge, benefits from cooling breeze funnelled down gorge from Uludağ.

Cafés & cake shops

For action after dark your best off heading down to Sakarya Caddesi, a lively street of bars, cafés and restaurants, many of them housed in old renovated buildings. Try *Barantico* or *Cevriye* both of which play mostly western rock and pop music to an affluent young crowd. There's a knot of fairly insalubrious bars at the top of İnönü Caddesi, such as *Uludağ* and *Bacanak*.

Bars

Theatre and festivals Traditional Karagöz shadow puppet shows and an annual festival are held at the Karagöz Art House (*Karagöz Sanat Evi*) daily except Sun, T2321871 on Çekirge Caddesi opposite a statue of Karagöz and Hacivat). Call for details of events and evening courses, which are usually, but not always, in Turkish. The annual *Karagöz Festival* is held in mid-Nov, during which Turkish *hayalılar* and foreign puppeteers gather for 5 days of performances and workshops.

Entertainment

For information on skiing see Uludağ, page 191. The facilities at the *Kervansaray Termal Hotel* are open to non-residents: swimming pool US$5, sauna US$6.

Sports

There's a new, ultra modern shopping centre with a Louvre-esque pyramid on Cemal Nadir Caddesi in the shadow of the Hisar. More traditional outlets for **fabric** and **towels** can be found in the covered bazaar. The Koza Hanı is the place to look for **silk**. To buy a Karagöz **puppet** seek out *Karagöz*, T2218727, Eski Aynalı Çarşı No 12, covered bazaar, to the west of the Koza Hanı, which is run by Şinasi Çelikkol, a *hayalı* who's been instrumental in re-invigorating the tradition locally. Puppets vary from US$10-35 depending on their size and whether they're painted with natural or artificial dyes; you may even get an impromptu performance thrown into the bargain. An edible local speciality are the candied **chestnuts** – *kestane şekeri* – found in shops across the city and even at the bus station. For English language **books** and **newspapers** try *TAŞ Kitapçılık*, Adliye Karşısı, Kültür Sokak No 8/A, in street behind Heykel.

Shopping

Karagöz Turizm, Eski Aynalı Çarşı No 4, T/F2218727, karagoz_tr@hotmail.com *Ottomantur*, Cemal Nadir Caddesi, Kızılay Pasajı, Çakırhamam, T2218878, F2218948, car rental, tours, ticketing.

Tour agencies

Local Bus Fares are US$0.50 with a major set of stops on Atatürk Caddesi opposite Koza Parkı. Some useful stops are no 1 for Yeşil, Emir Sultan and Teleferik; no 2 for Muradiye; no 3 for Kültür Parkı and the BOI Ekspres stop for the Hisar and Muradiye. **Dolmuş** US$0.40-0.75 depending on the journey. They are generally cars into which 5 passengers are squeezed. For Yeşil, the Emir Sultan Camii and Teleferik they leave from a 2-storey garage behind the government buildings at Heykel. Dolmuş for

Transport

The Marmara Region

Çekirge, which pass the Kültür Parkı and Yeni Kaplıcalar, depart from the east side of the Setbaşı bridge and from the top of İnönü Caddesi in Heykel.

Long distance Bus The huge out-of-town bus station (Şehirlerarası Otobüs Terminali) has regular departures to towns and cities across the country. To get there hop on a grey 'Terminal' bus at Koza Parkı. Allow 15-20 mins for the 10 km journey. A taxi will set you back about US$5. **Afyon**, 4½ hrs, 9 daily, US$9. **Ankara**, 5½ hrs, at least every hr, US$11. **Bandırma**, 2 hrs, every hr during the day, US$3.50. **Çanakkale**, 5 hrs, 12 daily, US$6. **Erdek**, 2½ hrs, 3 daily, US$4 (there is a regular bus service between Bandırma and Erdek, so don't wait around for a bus direct to Erdek), **İzmir**, 6 hrs, at least every hr, US$6. **Yalova**, 1 hr, every 30 mins, US$2.50. Minibuses for **İznik** depart every 15 mins from the **Kuzey Garaj**, reached on bus no 38 from the stops opposite Koza Parkı. **Car rental** Avis, Çekirge Caddesi No 139, T2365133, F2366918. **Ferry** The best way to get to **İstanbul** is on the high-speed ferryboat from Yalova to Yenikapı, however, if you've missed the last ferry buses leave hourly for İstanbul's Esenler and Harem bus stations. If you're heading for Sultanahmet consider getting a bus to Harem and then hopping on a ferry across the Bosphorus. Whichever make sure you get on a bus marked '*feribot ile*' (by ferry) as these use the roll-on, roll-off ferries across the Gulf of Izmit to save a long and tedious diversion via Izmit (Kocaeli).

Directory **Airline offices** *Turkish Airlines*, Haşim İşcan Caddesi, Tuğtaş İş Merkezi No 12/e, T2211167, F2221866. **Banks** With ATMs along Atatürk Caddesi and Namazgah Caddesi. **Baths** *Çakır Ağa Hamamı*, corner of Kazım Baykal Caddesi and Atatürk Caddesi, Tahtakale, open 0700-2300, US$3 entry, US$1.50 *kese*. *Tarihi Murat Hamamı*, Kaplıca Caddesi, Muradiye, part of Muradiye complex, open 1000-2300, men: Fri, Sun and evenings; women: 1000-1800 everyday except Fri and Sun. Prices as above. *Tarihi Yeşil Hamam*, Yeşil Cadde, Yeşil, unassuming baths near Yeşil Cami, 0700-2300, women: daytime and Mon all day, men: evenings. Prices as above. **Communications** Post office: The PTT is on Atatürk Caddesi opposite the Ulu Cami. **Internet:** *Ernet*, Bozkurt Caddesi No 3/C, Altıparmak Mahallesi, west end of Altıparmak Caddesi, US$0.50 per hr. **Hospitals** *Devlet Hastanesi*, Hastayurdu Caddesi, Tophane, west of Osman and Orhan Gazi tombs. **Tourist information** Orhan Gazi Altgeçidi, Koza Parkı, T2201848, facing the Orhan Gazi Camii in arcade beneath Atatürk Caddesi. Weekdays, summer 0830-1730, winter 0800-1700.

Uludağ

Directly to the south of Bursa rise the forested slopes of 2543-m Uludağ, which in antiquity was known as Mount Olympus, or Bithynian Olympus to distinguish it from the 20 or so other peaks of the same name in the region. Winding upwards on a torturously twisting road from Çekirge, the city's suburbs give way to stands of birch, chestnut and beech interspersed with settlements surrounded by meadows. Above, the massif's haunches are cloaked in thick coniferous forests, tracts of which make up the Uludağ National Park. In all but the coldest weather, weekends and public holidays are marked by a procession of overloaded cars wheezing up to a series of picnic spots on the mountain. Further up near the tree-line, and in view of the rocky peak itself, a cluster of hotels cater for alpine skiers and in summer conferences.

Ins & outs
The initial stretch is lined with restaurants with signs advertizing 'kendin pişir, kendin ye' or 'et mangal' where you can cook your own kebabs or chops on a charcoal braziers brought to the table

Getting there With your own transport follow a winding 32 km road which climbs up the mountain from Çekirge. About 4 km above Çekirge you could pause to have a look at the so-called '*Tarihi Ağaç*' (Historic Tree), a gnarled and hollow plain tree which is said to be over 700 years old. After 20 km you reach the entrance to the national park where officials collect a fee of US$2.50 per car. In winter it's compulsory to have snow chains and in recent years driver without have been forced into making the decision between returning to Bursa or buying them from entrepreneurial roadside salesmen at predictably inflated prices. The final stretch to the hotel zone is on a rough cobbled road so allow about 1 hr for the whole trip, longer in bad weather.

Without your own transport the most pleasant way up to Uludağ is by the red *teleferik,* reminiscent of cablecars in countless Alpine resorts. The terminal is several kilometres to the west of Heykel, and can be reached by dolmuş marked 'Teleferik'. Weather permitting the 40 person gondola swings its way up the mountain about every 30 mins, 0800-2200, US$5 1-way. The 30-min ascent is broken at a mid-station, Kadıyayla, where you change lifts for the final climb to Sarıalan. At Sarıalan passengers are met by a dolmuş which ferries them 6 km to the resort – the fare is usually about US$1, however, if there are only a few passengers you'll have to negotiate a price or wait for the next lift. Alternatively, you can take a dolmuş all the way from Bursa, although these only leave when full from their stop on Orhan Gazi Caddesi, so you may have to wait awhile for other passengers. Costs US$4 1-way, or about US$25 in a private taxi. You can often negotiate a discount on the way down as drivers are reluctant to return empty.

With a vertical range of approximately 750 m and 13 lifts, Uludağ is Turkey's **Skiing** most extensive ski area. Although by European standards the resort may be small, it does have some pleasant tree-lined runs ideal for beginners and lower intermediate skiers. There's also good potential for cross country and ski mountaineering on the flanks of Uludağ itself. The official season lasts from the beginning of December to the end of March, with the best conditions generally found in January and February. There are several rental places hiring reasonable boots, poles and skis for US$8-10 per day, or snowboards for US$10-12 per day. The lift situation is rather tedious as each hotel operates its own lifts for which you need a separate ticket. A popular winter hang-out for the İstanbul gliterazzi, a lot of immaculately dressed 'skiers' never even go near a pair of skis, instead spending their time posing in the resort's cafés and bars.

When the snow melts in Spring and the crowds return back to sea-level there **Walking** is some pleasant walking in the alpine meadows and forests around the resort, although as elsewhere in Turkey there is no system of marked trails. Due to its proximity to the Sea of Marmara, the weather on Uludağ is notoriously changeable with cloud, mist and violent storms possible throughout the year. Therefore it's imperative to set-out properly equipped for even the shortest of excursions. The best time to visit is early summer when there's the least chance of bad weather and the spring flowers are in bloom. Early autumn can also be a lovely time.

A path leads from the cablecar's mid station at Sarıalan through forest to the hotel zone in two to three hours. From the resort itself you can bushwhack your way up to the wide south ridge of the mountain which leads up to the large summit cairn in about 90 minutes. Alternatively, an obvious track climbs up to the tungsten mines in approximately 90 minutes, above which you can explore a series of beautiful tarns beneath the summit.

During the ski season, and particularly at weekends, it is advisable to book well in **Sleeping** advance. Room rates are generally full-board and special weekday discounts are offered *Only a few hotels remain* by most of the hotels. You can also pick up good value packages which include trans- *open during the summer* portation to Uludağ, accommodation, food and a lift pass from domestic travel compa- *& they cater mainly for* nies such as *ETS Tur* and *Asyatur.* **AL** *Kervansaray Uludağ,* T2852187, F2852193, US$85 *conferences* per night during the week, good location at the bottom of the nursery slopes. Decent rooms many of which overlook pistes, excellent facilities including pool and sauna for relaxing those battered muscles, massive open-buffet breakfast and dinner included, bar and entertainment during season, excellent for families. Recommended. **AL** *Hotel Grand Yazıcı,* T2852050, F2852048. Huge yellow building which is reminiscent of the hotel in 'The Shining', popular conference venue. **AL** *Otel Beceren,* T2852111, F2852119, opposite the Kervansaray. Alpine-style building, nice annex at the bottom of the nursery slopes, well-equipped rooms with cable TV, weekend rate US$260 for 2 people/2 nights full board, open buffet breakfast, lunch and dinner, closed in summer. For cheaper accommodation try the *Ulukardeşler*, T2852136, F2852139.

Eating With expansive open-buffets as the norm most people return to the hotel where they are staying to eat all their meals. There are fairly pricey places to get a snack or drink on the mountain, but if you're only coming up for the day you may prefer to bring a picnic.

Cumalıkızık An enjoyable outing from Bursa is to the village of Cumalıkızık, set on the verdant lower slopes of Mount Uludağ amidst the orchards and meadows. Said to have been established by Osman Gazi, the founder of the Ottoman dynasty, as one of seven villages presented to his seven sons, recent research has revealed the remains of a Byzantine church. Now under official protection, the village's tumble down Ottoman houses, built from stone and timber, survive remarkably undisturbed and wandering around the cobbled streets is a like going back in time. There are, as yet, no facilities in the village except a small shop so you may want to bring a picnic with you. Mr Şinasi Çelikkol at Karagöz Turizm (see tour agencies) organizes ethnographic tours to Cumalıkızık and several other interesting villages around Bursa. ■ *The village is 4 km south of the main Bursa-Ankara highway, 12 km east of the city. Infrequent dolmuş leave from Bursa's Eski Garaj on the 20 min journey, US$0.50.*

Bandırma
Phone code: 0266
Colour map 1, grid B3

A wholly uninteresting, and in winter dismal, concrete port town on the south coast of the Sea of Marmara, there really is no reason to extend your stay in Bandırma any longer than absolutely necessary. Most people arrive on the high-speed ferryboat (*hızlı feribot*) from İstanbul's Yenikapı, only to depart again as soon as possible on a train or bus heading for destinations on the Aegean coast or for Erdek and the Marmara Islands. It's a 250 m walk east from the ferry dock and train station to the main square, in fact a traffic roundabout with an interesting metal sculpture at its centre. The bus station is about 2 km southeast of the city centre and can be reached on dolmuş marked 'Garaj, 600 Evleri, Sanayi', US$0.40, which leave regularly from the rank in front of the docks, trawling up the main street, İnönü Caddesi.

Sleeping and eating AL *Eken Prestige*, Mehmet Akif Ersoy Caddesi No 7, T7147600, F7147804, ekenprestij@superonline.com Pink and grey building to the west of the docks, modern place with decent comforts such as a/c, telephone, TV as standard, also restaurant, fitness centre and pool in the summer. **D** *Türe Otel*, General Halit Caddesi No 15, T7145550, F7134594. 1 block inland from the main roundabout. Simple but perfectly adequate rooms with en suite. On your way through try a *Bandırma börek*, a deep-fried half-circle of pastry filled with cheese or meat, at the *Bandırma Börekçi* on the main square. If you want something more substantial there are several kebap places such as *Kebabsaray* on İnönü Caddesi.

Transport Bus Bursa, every hr, 2 hrs, US$4. **Çanakkale**, every hr, 3 hrs, US$5. **Erdek**, every 30 mins, 30 mins, US$0.80. **İzmir**, every 2 hrs during day, 4 hrs, US$7.50. For **Ayvalık** take a bus to Balıkesir, 2 hrs, US$4. **Ferry** High-speed car ferries to Yenikapı depart at 0700, 1230 and 1830 on the 2-hr crossing. **Train** *Marmara Ekspresi*, departs daily 1600 arriving İzmir 2240, US$3.

Kuşcenneti
Milli Parkı

One reason to over-night in Bandırma is if you're heading for Kuşcenneti Milli Parkı (Bird Paradise National Park), a 64 ha wetland reserve set up on the shores of Manyas Gölü in 1938. It's an important habitat for over 255 species of bird, many of which are only stopping off on their annual migration, so the best times to visit are April to June and September to November. ■ *0700-1730. US$1. Sign-posted 3 km off the Bandırma-Balıkesir highway, 15 km south of Bandırma.*

The Thrace Region

The Thrace Region

196 Edirne

199 The Tunca Valley

203 South of Edirne

204 The Thracian Coast

205 The Gallipoli Peninsula

206 Gelibolu

207 Eceabat

208 The Gallipoli National Historic Park

208 History

209 The Northern Battlefields

211 The Southern Battlefields

212 Gökçeada

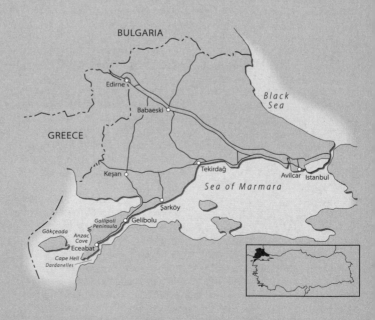

*A toehold on the continent of Europe, Thrace, or more correctly
Eastern Thrace because the rest of the region lies beyond
international boundaries in Greece and Bulgaria, makes up
only 3% of Turkey's area. Formerly the home of war-like tribes
credited by Herodotus as being "the greatest of Mankind", it
was later scored by the Via Egnatia, a Roman and then
Byzantine artery which marched westwards to Rome.*

*Modern Thrace is a predominantly agricultural region with
large expanses of rolling rather monotonous terrain. Tobacco
and wheat fields stretch to what seems like a very distant
horizon, with summer crops of sunflowers adding a welcome
splash of colour. In winter herds of goats range over the
stubbly fields watched by shepherds protected from the biting
Balkan wind by outsized sheepskin capes. South towards
Gallipoli the landscape softens and the peninsular itself,
protected within a national park, possesses a bucolic beauty
made more poignant by its association with bloodshed and
war. In a region largely devoid of touristic interest, the
battlefields and memorials of Gallipoli are by far the largest
draw. Coming a distant second is the graceful Ottoman
architecture of Edirne, including what is widely considered to
be the apogee of the empire's architecture achievement, the
magnificent Selimiye Camii. Then there's the well-kept secret
of Gökçeada, a rarely visited island off the Aegean coast
which has a long Greek history and some pretty fine beaches.*

Edirne

Phone code: 0284
Colour map 1, grid A2

Occupying a hill above the confluence of the Meriç and Tunca rivers, Edirne rose to prominence as a staging post on the Roman road to Asia Minor. It maintained its importance through Byzantine and Ottoman times, when for nearly a century it was the imperial capital. During the golden years of Ottoman conquest and expansion, the town was graced with some of the finest mosques in the empire. Most visitors come for a look at these buildings, with those that stay long enough discovering a pleasant, down-to-earth provisional town with a busy bazaar and some interesting vernacular architecture lurking in the backstreets. Tucked up against the Greek and Bulgarian frontiers, it's also within easy day-trip range of İstanbul, so there's no need to stay, though you may just decide you want to.

Ins and outs

Getting there
See page 202 for further details

Since the construction of the E-80 expressway Edirne is an easy 2 hr drive or 2½ hr bus journey away from İstanbul. Grandly dubbed the 'Trans-European Motorway', the E-80 is a toll rd and for around US$3 you'll have the privilege of driving along 235 km of the newest and smoothest road in the country. Buses depart every 30 mins throughout the day from Esenler bus station *peron* 103. If you've a train enthusiast with plenty of time there's 1 daily train at 1525 from İstanbul's Sirkeci station which takes 6 hrs – faster than a sultan on horseback who used to do it in 3 days.

Getting around

Many of Edirne's sights are clustered in a relatively small area around Hürriyet Meydanı (the centre of town) and can be visited easily on foot. There are also some outlying historic bridges and mosques along the course of the Tunca River which loops around the outskirts of town. You can walk between these along the Tunca valley, though the sights can also be reached by car or taxi from the centre. The *otogar* is a couple of kilometres southeast of town along Talatpaşa Bulvarı. Dolmuş pass the terminal regularly (opposite side of the road) on their way in to the main garage behind the Rüstempaşa Caravanserai. The same dolmuş can drop you near the train station which is about 3 km out along Talat Paşa Asfaltı.

Background

Edirne has a long history dating back to at least the seventh century BC when it was the 'capital' of one of the war-like Thracian tribes. This settlement was joined later by a Hellenic town and in 125 AD Roman Emperor Hadrian merged the two, calling the new city Hadrianopolis, corrupted later to Adrianopolis and then Adrianopole. Adrianopolis became an important garrison town with a thriving weapon making industry. In 323 AD the plains beyond the city walls were the scene of an important battle when Constantine the Great defeated his co-emperor Licinius, a victory which opened the way for the establishment of Byzantium as the new capital of the Roman Empire.

Over nearly a millennia Byzantine Adrianopolis' prosperity was only interrupted by a succession of enemies including the Bulgars, the Avars and the Crusaders, and the city finally fell to the Ottomans in 1361 during the reign of Murat I. With Ottoman Empire building concentrated initially in the Balkans, the capital was moved from Bursa to Adrianopolis later in the 14th century. Despite losing this status to İstanbul less than 100 years later, Edirne, as the city had become known, remained popular with the Ottoman court which relocated there on several occasions to avoid outbreaks of disease or unrest in the capital. Several sultans actually preferred living in Edirne free from much of the tedious ceremony and pomp which dominated life at the Topkapı in İstanbul.

A major earthquake shook the area in 1751 destroying many of the city's buildings and signalling a general downturn in its fortunes. Ottoman decline left Edirne exposed to attack by the Russians, who occupied the city in 1829 and 1879 as they pushed towards İstanbul, and new neighbours Greece and Bulgaria. The first disastrous Balkan War resulted in a brief Bulgarian occupation of the city in 1913, with Greek forces holding. In 1923 the Treaty of Lausanne acknowledged Turkish sovereignty over the city, however, the surrounding area has remained heavily militarised, and occasionally pretty tense, up to the present. Nowadays cross-border contact is more positive with Greek and Bulgarian families popping across the frontier at weekends to shop and sightsee. Students from the University of Thrace, whose main campus is on the outskirts of town, are also much in evidence in the town's cafés and tea gardens.

Sights

Right in the centre of town is Edirne's oldest surviving structure, the appropriately named Eski Camii (Old Mosque). Despite its longevity it's not wildly interesting, a square multi-domed building the inside of which is dominated by rows of pillars and arches. It is, however, a good example of the mosques built during early Ottoman times and if you're heading to Bursa you'll notice striking similarities with the Ulu Cami there. As with many of the other mosques in town it has recently undergone extensive renovation, so step inside for a look at the massive inscriptions on either side of the prayer hall; the grand *mihrab* and the colourful stencilling which enlivens the arches.

Next to the Eski Camii the **Bedesten** was built by Mehmet I to raise money for the upkeep of the mosque. It was the commercial heart of the city where valuable goods such as gold, jewellery and carpets could be stored and traded. Nowadays its spacious vaulted interior contains small shops selling far more mundane goods such as stationary and army surplus gear.

Across a small square from the Eski Camii, an interesting caravanserai constructed by Mimar Sinan in 1560. Since its award winning restoration 20 years ago it has reverted to its original function: providing travellers with a roof over their head. The building has two sections with the rooms around the first, small courtyard used to accommodate travellers and merchants; while the much larger courtyard reached through a passageway was a *han* occupied by local traders. This part of the building is Sinan at his best, with a shady courtyard surrounded by a two-storey arcade, the arches of which are stripped with red masonry and yellow stone. In summer the courtyard café is a peaceful place to relax after beating the streets.

A couple of minutes walk to the west, the town's covered bazaar the Semiz Paşa Çarşısı is entered via gates at its north and south end, or half-way along its length from Saraçlar Caddesi or Maarif Caddesi. Built by the prolific Mimar Sinan in 1568-69 for the highly capable grand vizier Semiz Ali and recently restored after a major fire, the bazaar is a long tunnel-like arcade lined with small shops selling all kinds of things. Across Talat Paşa Caddesi from the north entrance stands the only remaining defensive tower from the city walls built by Hadrian and then reconstructed in 1123 by the Byzantine emperor John II Comnenus.

To the southwest of the Semiz Paşa Çarşısı, Kaleiçi, "Inside the Castle", harbours a few grand old 19th-century houses. One of these rambling mansions at Maarif Caddesi No 18 was formerly the home of a Greek doctor and is now occupied by the regional offices of the state conservation department. Foreign

Eski Camii

Rustem Paşa Caravanserai

Semiz Paşa Çarşısı

Kaleiçi
A grid of quiet residential streets which was the heart of the medieval city

The Thrace Region

visitors provide a welcome distraction for the civil servants shuffling paper inside, so if you'd like a look around at the spacious rooms, one of which has an enchanting picture of Aphrodite painted on the ceiling and a collection of yellowed family photographs, then knock on the door during office hours.

Üç Şerefeli Camii

Just to the north of Hürriyet Meydanı, the Üç Şerefeli Camii gets its name, the "Three Balconied Mosque", from the trio of balconies on its tallest minaret. Built between 1437 and 1447 for Murat II, it's an odd but nonetheless appealing structure which represents a step in the evolution from early Bursa-style Ottoman architecture to the soaring structures of the Classical period, exemplified by the Selimiye Camii nearby. Restoration work has been dragging on for years, so unfortunately the courtyard may still not be open when you arrive.

The first thing you'll notice on approaching the building is that each of it's four minarets is totally different, with the eponymous "three-balconied" one, at nearly 70-m tall, ranking as the loftiest in the empire when it was constructed. Although it may not look like it, the courtyard with its central *şadırvan* was a radical departure from tradition which set a precedent for later mosque design. The main building itself was also pretty revolutionary for its time with a large central dome – which at 24-m wide was the largest in the empire for a while – resting on a hexagonal drum supported by just two squat piers. This was a definite advance from the rows of columns and pillars which crowd earlier mosques, though it still lacks the feeling of space attained in later works such as the Süleymaniye in İstanbul.

Across Hükümet Caddesi from the mosque is the **Sokullu Paşa Hamamı** which was built by Mimar Sinan in 1568-69. It's still in operation, though sadly it has lost much of its sparkle, along with the İznik tiles which once covered the walls, in the intervening years.

Selimiye Camii

Before leaving don't forget to have a look at the mihrab & mimber, both beautifully carved from marble & enlivened by colourful panels of İznik tilework

Dominating the high ground to the northeast of the town centre, the Selimiye Camii is held to be one of the finest works of Ottoman religious architecture and the culmination of the masterly Court Architect Mimar Sinan's long and brilliant career (see page 102). Designed and built by Sinan between 1566 and 1574 for Sultan Selim II, the mosque's four slender minarets tower up into the sky, a striking landmark visible for miles across the gently rolling Thracian countryside.

Approaching the mosque up Mimar Sinan Caddesi, you're struck by the building's harmonious form and symmetry with all of its features – domes, minarets, windows – carefully balanced in pairs. If you've just had a look around the Üç Şerefeli Camii the contrast with that building couldn't be more complete, a graphic lesson of how rapidly Ottoman architect progressed during the 16th century under Sinan's stewardship. The grand **courtyard**, centred on a beautifully worked *şadırvan,* is surrounded by a portico supported on antique columns pilfered from earlier buildings and arches of red and white stone.

The interior is no less impressive with the massive 31½-m wide dome resting 44 m above the floor on eight thick trunk-like piers. Cleverly incorporated into the structure these supports do little to impinge on the marvellous feeling of space inside the building, which is accentuated by light flooding in through the many windows. Directly below the dome, the müezzin's platform has a small marble fountain, an appealing feature unique to the Selimiye Camii, beneath it and some lovely decorative painting on its underside. This platform makes a good vantage point from which to absorb the scene, lulled by the sound of trickling water from the fountain, as does the balcony above the front entrance which is reached via a pair of red carpeted stairways.

Attached to the mosque were several pious foundations including the **Kavaflar Arasta** (the Cobbler's Bazaar) built by an apprentice of Sinan's, Davut Ağa. Reached down a staircase from the courtyard, the covered bazaar is still lined with shops, although there isn't a tailor in sight anymore. On the opposite side of the mosque a *medrese* now houses the **Museum of Turkish and Islamic Arts**. Arranged around a central courtyard, the rooms contain exhibits of locally made handicrafts, pottery and furniture. More unusual are a collection of colourful hand-knitted woollen socks from across the country and a display about *yağlı güreş*, the traditional wrestling event held annually at Kırkpınar (see page 200). ■ *0830-1730, 0830-1700 winter, daily except Mon, US$1.25.* The **Archaeological and Ethnographic Museum**, situated in a modern building across the road from the Museum of Turkish and Islamic Art, contains a small but interesting collection of artefacts dating from prehistoric times to the Ottoman era. The ethnographic section has a collection of local carpets and embroidery on show along with a display of traditional wedding dresses. ■ *0830-1730, 0830-1700 winter, daily except Mon, US$1.25.*

Market & museums

Topping a hill to the northeast of town and beyond a working class district of narrow streets and little houses, the Muradiye Camii isn't nearly as well visited as its illustrious neighbour the Selimiye, though it's worth a look if you have some time on your hands or you're a particular fan of Ottoman faïence.

Commissioned by Murat II in 1435 after, legend has it, Mevlana, spiritual leader of the Mevlevi dervish sect, appeared to the sultan in a dream and asked him to establish a resthouse for his followers. The resulting *zaviye*, or dervish convent, is a simple T-shaped building with two side chambers (*eyvan*) on either side of the main hall where the dervishes used to gather to read or pray. A single lonely minaret was added when Murat turned the *zaviye* into a mosque, relocating the dervish *tekke* to an adjacent building. Inside the *mihrab* is reverted with a truly stunning display of polychrome tiles often wrongly ascribed to the artisans of İznik. In fact, these tiles, decorated in blue, green, turquoise and vivid yellow geometric patterns were made before the kilns of İznik were producing their famous decorative works. Interestingly enough the tiles demonstrate the influence of earlier Islamic, but also Chinese designs, from imported Yuan and Ming dynasty porcelain. Similar displays of tiling can also be seen in the Yeşil Cami and the Yeşil Türbe in Bursa.

■ *Getting there: Continue down the hill on Mimar Sinan Caddesi from the Selimiye Camii and you'll be able to see it on the hilltop ahead. It's about a 10-15 min walk or US$2.50 in a cab.*

Muradiye Camii
Try to time your visit to coincide with prayer time & slip in when the men file out of the building as at other times the mosque is generally locked

The Tunca Valley

Arching around Edirne, the river Tunca lazily meanders along a wide valley past seasonally flooded meadows and coppices of upright poplar to its confluence with the Meriç southeast of the city. It's spanned by a number of historic bridges, the northern-most of which, the **Süleyman** and **Fatih Bridges**, connect either bank to a large low-lying island embraced by two arms of the river.

Known as Sarayiçi, this was formerly an imperial hunting reserve graced with a summer palace built in 1450 by Murat II. Nothing now remains of the palace as it was destroyed by fire during the Russian occupation of 1878. It's a peaceful spot except for the occasional passing car and the distant shouts of children playing football, that is unless you visit during the annual Kırkpınar oiled wrestling championships (see box, page 200) held in an ugly concrete stadium beside the road. Also beside the road is an incongruous looking stone tower with a

Sarayiçi

The Thrace Region

The Thrace Region

☛ *Oiled wrestling*

Once a year in the first week of July the quiet fields of Sarayiçi are transformed into a hive of activity as thousands of spectators and contestants descend on a purpose built arena to take part in the Kırkpınar Oiled Wrestling Competition. Popular throughout the country, oiled wrestling, or Yağlı Güreş, is a sport Turkic nomads are thought to have brought with them from Central Asia. The origins of this particular competition, the largest and most prestigious of hundreds held in towns and villages across the country, date back to early Ottoman times when Süleyman Paşa, son of Orhan Gazi, was crossing Thrace with a war party of forty soldiers. Legend has it that they camped in a meadow beside the Tunca River near Edirne and began wrestling with one another to pass time. Long after the other warriors had thrown in the towel, two of their number wrestled on, neither one willing to admit defeat. Eventually, long after midnight the pair collapsed from exhaustion and died. The next morning when the other soldiers awoke they found forty springs emerging from the meadow where they'd buried their companions the night before. To commemorate this miraculous event Süleyman Paşa established a wrestling lodge which every year since has held a three-day competition. Now in well over its 630th year, the event is touted locally as the oldest

sports contest in the world.

Strictly governed by tradition, matches take place between amateur wrestlers dressed in calf leather knickerbockers and smeared from head to toe in olive oil. The competitors are divided into 11 classes according to their height and having performed a series of ritualized warm-up exercises, the fun begins. There's no time limit on the bouts which last until one of the wrestlers pins his opponents shoulders to the ground – no easy matter when both are covered in slippery oil. Matches in each of the categories take place simultaneously with the winners from each class battling it out on the final day for the title of başpehlivan (champion wrestler). Along with the coveted gold belt, champions take home a small cash prize and the esteem of their countrymen, something which translates these days into lucrative advertising contracts and appearance fees.

The event itself remains pleasantly uncommercialized, more like a country fair than a national sporting event. The meadows surrounding the arena are turned into a huge fairground cum picnic site with a carnival atmosphere prevailing. Gypsies arrive from across the region and the festivities are accompanied by the ever-present sound of the zurna (reed pipe) and the davul (bass drum).

peaked roof called the **Kasr-i Adalet** (The Hall of Justice). Built during the reign of Süleyman the Magnificent it has two stones in front of it. Ottoman subjects would leave petitions to the sultan on top of one, while the other was used to display the decapitated heads of those who'd fallen from favour.

The walk gives you the opportunity to leave the noise of the city behind though the minarets of the mosques in the centre are always visible

Walk to Sarayiçi From the centre of town it is about a 15-minute walk along Mimar Sinan Caddesi and then, at the bottom of the hill, fork left following a small signpost for 'Kırkpınar'. Before crossing the Süleyman Bridge, another 16th-century structure by Mimar Sinan, you'll notice a track crossing the road and following the crest of an embankment. There's a similar track on the other side of the river protecting the farmland beyond from flooding and following either on foot you can visit the other sights along the Tunca Valley. Reckon on at least a couple of hours for a leisurely walk from the centre of town via Sarayiçi, the Saraçhane Bridge and the Ikinci Beyazıt Külliyesi, returning over the Gazi Mihal Bridge to the centre. Alternatively, you could head back into town on Horozlu Bayır Caddesi or Saraçlar Caddesi depending on how far you want to walk. Take some water and maybe even a snack as there isn't much along the way, though an excellent way to finish off your excursion could be a meal at one of the restaurants near the Tunca or Meriç Bridges (see eating).

After passing the **Saraçhane Köprüsü**, a narrow stone bridge over which modern traffic squeezes in single file, the Beyazıt II Külliyesi is visible on the far side of the river. The mosque was deliberately built beyond the city's boundaries to try and encourage suburban development, however Edirne's decline left the *külliye* stranded forlornly amongst the meadows. It is the largest mosque complex in the city with a religious seminary, hostel, bakery, soup kitchen, hospital and insane asylum contained within its perimeter wall. Built by the architect Hayrettin between 1484 and 1488, the mosque itself is pretty unexciting, particularly after a visit to the Selimiye Camii. To make matters worse many of the surrounding buildings are kept firmly locked.

(margin note) **Beyazıt II Külliyesi**

On the east side of the complex stands the *imaret*, or soup kitchens, where the mosque's workers, dependants and visitors were fed. Also on this side of the complex are the külliye's extensive storehouses. Behind the mosque in the western part of the outer courtyard stands the medical school, beside which is the *tımarhane* where insane patients were confined. They were treated in the domed *darüşşifa* next door, where a fountain filled the central courtyard with the soothing sound of water, accompanied several times a week by musicians playing calming melodies.

South of the Beyazıt II Külliyesi this small mosque sits beside the river, separated from its ruinous hamam on the opposite shore. Commissioned by Mihal Gazi, a Greek nobleman who converted to Islam, later earning himself the epithet "Warrior of the Faith", or *Gazi*, for his zealousness. The old stone bridge parts of which date back to the 13th century as bares his name.

(margin note) **Gazi Mihal Camii**

(vertical margin text) The Thrace Region

Essentials

C *Hotel Rüstempaşa Kervansaray*, İki Kapılı Han Caddesi No 57, T2252195, F2120462. Situated in the historic Rüstempaşa Caravanserai this hotel received the Ağa Khan Prize for Architecture in 1980 for its sensitive conversion, although you wouldn't guess it in winter when the hotel is only semi-operational and the small rooms available are a bit on the claustrophobic side. Things improve considerably in summer, larger rooms around pleasant courtyard, TV, telephone and heater as standard, hotel facilities include Internet café, billiards hall which are a favourite haunt for local students. **C** *Sultan Hotel*, Talatpaşa Asfaltı, T2251372, F2252156. Average rooms with en suite, TV and telephone in modern hotel, kebap restaurant, outside dining at rear in summer. **D** *Efe Hotel*, Maarif Caddesi No 13, T2136166, F2129446, on quiet street 2 mins from the centre. Clean rooms with homely touch, shower, TV, telephone and some with refrigerator, pleasant sitting/breakfast room. Recommended. **D** *Park Otel*, Maarif Caddesi No 7, T2254610, F2254635. 1980s-style place with large lounge on 1st floor, rooms are plain but comfortable, equipped with satellite TV and telephone. **E** *Otel Şaban Açıkgöz*, Tahmis Meydanı, Çilingirler Caddesi No 9, T2131404, F2134516, near the Eski Camii. Good value rooms with a/c, TV and telephone, triple room US$26, decor a bit worse for wear but nonetheless recommended. **F-G** *Hotel Aksaray*, Alipaşa Ortakapı Caddesi, T2126035, near the middle entrance to the covered bazaar. Old wooden house converted into a pension, 15 simple high ceiling rooms with shower, cheaper waterless rooms, no breakfast. Recommended. **F-G** *Otel Anıl*, Hürriyet Meydanı, Maarif Caddesi No 8, T2121782. Another creaky old house converted into a pension, similar rooms to the Aksaray but none have en suite bathroom, large 3/4/5 bed rooms. Recommended. **G** *Hotel Taşhan*, Üç Şerefeli Camii Karşısı, T2126088. Spartan affair behind the Sokullu Hamamı. Basic rooms are a bit noisy, only 1 bathroom for entire place.

(margin note) **Sleeping**
There's a reasonable selection of good value midrange places. On some summer nights tour groups occupy most of the better beds and during the Kırkpınar Wrestling Competition everything fills up. Book well in advance

Camping *Fifi Mocamp*, Demirkapı Mevkii, 9 km from town on the old İstanbul road (D100), inconveniently situated if you don't have your own transport, continue out on Talat Paşa Asfaltı past the bus station, campsite open from Apr-Oct, hook-ups for caravans, toilets and cooking facilities.

Eating In common with most other Turkish provincial towns Edirne's food scene isn't particularly sophisticated, though there are plenty of good value eateries, many of which sell the local speciality *ciğer tava* (deep-fried liver). There's a concentration of spartan *ciğerci* serving liver for about US$0.50 per portion around the square between the Eski Camii and the Rüstempaşa Caravanserai. Among them are: **Çiçek Ciğer and Yudum. Ciğerci Nedim**, Ali Paşa Caddesi, next to the middle entrance of the bazaar is recommended locally for liver. **Midrange** For a sophisticated lunchtime meal or evening out try the *Lalezar*, on the far side of the graceful Meriç bridge several kilometres from town along the road to Karaağaç, *meze*, fish, kebabs and grilled meat, tables outside in the riverside garden, live music some evenings, alcohol served. *Villa* nearby or the *Gazi Baba II*, between the bridges, are similar set-ups. If you don't fancy the walk jump on a Karaağaç dolmuş which stop in front of the PTT on Saraçlar Caddesi. *Park Restaurant*, Maarif Caddesi, below the *Park Hotel*, slightly less upmarket place serving kebabs, grilled meat and deserts. *Sultan*, Talatpaşa Asfaltı, below the *Sultan Hotel*, similar menu to *Park Restaurant*, also serve fish, decorated with a hideous fake stone waterfall and lots of mirrors, better in summer to sit at rear on the terrace. **Cheap** *Edirne Kebap Sarayı*, on the corner of Çilingir Caddesi, serves good kebabs, pide and lahmacun with baklava to follow, and there's a *aile salonu* upstairs. Opposite the Edirne Kebap Sarayı is a row of cheap lokantas with *Tahmiş Börekçi*, specializing in cheese and meat filled pastry, *Meşhur Serhat Köftecisi* serving meat balls and *Polat* offering a good selection of steam-tray food and soup. *Gaziantep Baklavacısı*, Çilingir Caddesi, across from the Edirne Kebap Sarayı, mouth watering sweets including *künefe*, a desert containing cheese from the southeast of the country. Also serve *boza* and, in the winter, *salep* to drink.

Cafés *Cafe E*, tables in Erdoğan Parkı in shadow of Üç Şerefeli Camii, popular with students from the University of Thrace. *Zogo Pastanesi*, Saraçlar Caddesi, opposite PTT, large well-established café serving hot and cold drinks, cakes, biscuits and puddings. *Cafe London*, Saraçlar Caddesi, small wooden building near Zogo Pastanesi, friendly place for a snack and drink. *Emirgan Aile Çay Bahçesi*, between the Tunca and the Meriç Rivers, pleasant tea garden with hot and cold drinks and snacks.

Bars *Efe English Pub*, Maarif Caddesi No 13, catering for groups staying at the *Efe Hotel* next door this place is rarely open. The bar in the *Hotel Rüstempaşa Kervansaray* is a better bet for a drink.

Festivals *Kirkpınar Oiled Wrestling Competition* usually held at the beginning of **Jul**. Exhibitions and performances are held in the week proceeding. The wrestling starts on Fri reaching its climax with the championship bout on Sun. Tickets must be reserved well in advance. Contact the local tourist office for details: T2251518

Transport **Bus** **Çanakkale**, 3 daily, 5 hrs, US$8. There are also more regular buses to **Keşan**, 2 hrs, US$4, from where there are regular buses to Çanakkale. **İstanbul**, at least every 30 mins, 0700-1830, 2½ hrs, US$6. **Train** Edirne-İstanbul, 0800, 5½ hrs, US$3. Returns from Sirkeci at 1525.

For transport to & from the Greek & Bulgarian borders see below

Directory **Banks** Found in the centre of town on Saraçlar Caddesi and Hürriyet Meydanı. There is a private change office, *Araz Döviz*, next to the Tourist Information Office on Hürriyet Meydanı. Only place in town you can buy drachma. **Baths** *Sokullu Paşa Hamamı*, Hükümet Caddesi, opposite the Üç şerefeli Camii, separate male and female baths, open 0700-2300, US$1.75 for wash and *kese*.

The Thrace Region

Communications Post office: The PTT is on Saraçlar Caddesi. **Internet**: *Hotel Rüstempaşa Kervansaray*, in 1st courtyard, US$1 per hr. **Tourist information** *Tourist Information Office*, Hürriyet Meydanı No 17, T2139208. Open 0800-1700. **Useful addresses** *Greek Consulate* (Yunan Konsolosluğu), İkinci Cadde, Kocasinan, several kilometres out of town along Atatürk Bulvarı. Open Mon-Fri, 0900-1200. *Bulgarian Consulate* (Bulgar Konsolosluğu), Talatpaşa Caddesi, 10-min walk from the centre on the way to the bus station. Open Mon-Fri, 0900-1200.

The border crossing at **Kapıkule**, 18 km northwest of town, is reached along the E-80 highway or from town by heading west along Talat Paşa Asfaltı. Getting there by public transport from Edirne presents no problem with regular buses and dolmuş throughout the day. **Dolmuş** marked 'Yıldırım/Kapıkule', US$0.50, leave from next to Rüstempaşa Caravanserai every 20 mins, 0700-2100. These dolmuş, as well as buses operated by the Belediye, can also be flagged down opposite the tourist office on Hürriyet Meydanı. The massive frontier complex is open around the clock, however, once you've crossed the River Tunca don't expect to find any transport on to the Bulgarian town of Svilengrad at night. Another option is the **Balkan Express** to Sofia and Budapest which leaves Edirne at about 0245, but check with tourist information about the current schedule. You'll probably be required to buy your ticket at Kapıkule as the office at Edirne is closed at that time of the morning.

Crossing into Bulgaria

Transit visas are available from the Bulgarian Consulate (see useful addresses above) for US$12–16 if you buy it at the frontier

The Turkish-Greek border crossing is 7 km west of Edirne, 2 km beyond the village of Karaağaç. It's less well-used than the major frontier post further south at Ipsala. The post is generally open daylight hours but it's wise to check at the tourist office in Edirne before making the trip out there. Getting to the border without your own transport is also slightly problematic as buses and dolmuş, US$0.30, which leave from behind the Belediye building every 20 mins, only run as far as Karaağaç. The final 2 km to the Turkish border post of Pazarkule you'll have to walk or take a taxi. Alternatively a cab all the way from Edirne to Pazarkule will set you back about US$5. You'll also need to hitch or catch a Greek taxi across no-man's land to the Greek border post of Kastaniés, from where there are infrequent buses and trains to Alexandroúpolis 3 hrs away.

Crossing into Greece

Try & cross as early in the day as possible so as not to be stranded in Kastaniés

Over 200 km of rolling countryside separate Edirne from İstanbul, but there really isn't much reason to break the journey. The only possible distraction is the town of **Lüleburgaz**, 75 km east of Edirne, or rather the **Sokullu Paşa Külliyesi** which stands in it. Commissioned by Sokullu Mehmet Paşa in 1549, surrounding the mosque courtyard are the classrooms of the complex's religious seminary which still fulfill their original function today, hosting the local Koran school. Also part of the complex are a bazaar of shops, the revenue from which paid for the mosque's upkeep, a caravanserai, which has all but disappeared, and a partially ruined hamam.

East towards İstanbul

Sleeping and eating in Lüleburgaz There are several hotels on İstanbul Caddesi, the best of which is opposite a small park **F** *Hotel Şentürk*, No 12, T02884172112, F0288412554, simple 1/2/3 bed rooms with shower, TV and telephone.

There are also several cheap eateries on İstanbul Caddesi near the mosque

South of Edirne

If you're heading for Gallipoli or Keşan by road you'll turn southwards off the İstanbul highway at the small market town of **Havsa**, unremarkable except for its **Sokullu Kasım Paşa Külliyesi**, a large mosque complex built by Mimar Sinan in 1576 for the grand vizier of Süleyman the Magnificent, Sokullu Mehmet Paşa.

There's very little of interest along this stretch of road, just miles of fertile steppe-like countryside. Some 36 km south of Havsa the road crosses a 1.2 km long Ottoman bridge with 173 arches before entering the town of **Uzunköprü** (Long Bridge). Constructed between 1427 and 1443 it has stood the test of time incredibly well. The İstanbul-Athens train line passes 4 km to the north of Uzunköprü and you could theoretically board trains in either direction from here, although they pass at rather inconvenient times of the night. Buses stop at the *otogar* on the Keşan road, 2 km southeast of town. If for some reason you are benighted in Uzunköprü the *Hotel Ergene* has decent enough rooms and there are a couple of simple restaurants nearby too.

Keşan is an another rather inconsequential little place which sits just south of the busy E84/D110 highway, the main road artery between Turkey and Greece. The only reason you might pass through is on your way somewhere else as the town's bus station is well connected to other destinations in the region such as Çanakkale, Edirne, Tekirdağ, İstanbul and Bursa. Once again, if needs be there are a couple of simple hotels and restaurants on the main square, a 2½ km walk or dolmuş ride from the *otogar*.

Heading west from Keşan along the E84/D110 bring you to the **Ipsala border crossing** into Greece, which is open 24 hours and boasts a tourist booth, banking facilities and an office of the TTOK (Turkish Touring and Automobile Association) where you can purchase vehicle insurance. However, these facilities are open normal office hours only, so you may want to have some Greek or Turkish currency with you. If you don't Turkish officials will generally be happy to change hard currency.

From Keşan public transport will only get you as far as the town of Ipsala, 5 km east of the border, from where you'll need to take a taxi (about US$7). Once at the frontier you'll have to hitch a lift across the 500 m of no man's land as it's forbidden to walk. From the Greek village of Kipi on the other side there are several daily buses onwards to Alexandroúpolis and beyond. Coming in the other direction by dolmuş or taxi it is best to continue on to Keşan which has much better bus connections than Ipsala.

The Thracian coast

The northern coast of the Sea of Marmara is fairly unremarkable and most people travelling along the E84/D110 highway are simply heading for İstanbul, Gallipoli or the Greek border.

Tekirdağ A predominantly modern port town whose population is swelled in summer by holidaymakers from İstanbul. The surrounding hills were once an important wine-producing region, though today not a trace of this viticulture remains. The main relic from Ottoman times is the 16th-century **Rüstem Paşa Camii**, designed by Mimar Sinan and standing on Hükümet Caddesi near the centre of town.

Essentials If you should need to stay the night there are several cheap pensions near the ferry quay or just to the east of town backing the town's beach, Akyaka Plajı.

Kumbağ & Heading along the coast, **Kumbağ**, 8 km west of Tekirdağ and accessible by
Şarköy dolmuş from the *otogar*, has a good stretch of beach, although inland the fields and orchards have been gobbled up by summer house developments. A short distance beyond Kumbağ what looks like a decent road on many maps degenerates into little more than a rocky track. Clinging to the mountains, this route is just passable in a car in good weather, however, care should be taken due to the loose surface and dizzying drops. Most people, including bus drivers, take

the main E84/D110 west towards Keşan. After about 50 km a road cuts south across rolling hills to the seaside town of **Şarköy**, a well-established little resort with a fairly good choice of accommodation along its tree-lined promenade.

The Gallipoli Peninsula

A narrow tongue of land lapped by the Aegean on the west and separated from the coast of Anatolia by the Dardanelles, Gallipoli – *Gelibolu* in Turkish after the peninsula's principal tourist town – has gained grim notoriety due to the bloody battles fought there during the First World War. Although most visitors arrive with the sole purpose of touring the various cemeteries and memorials, the peninsula's unspoilt pastoral scenery and beaches suggest extending your visit beyond the normal rushed day-trip – if you have the time that is. The peninsula's gentle contours and compact size lend themselves to exploring by bicycle either with camping gear or relying on guesthouses for accommodation. The most common base for visiting the area is across the Dardanelles in **Çanakkale** (see page 216), however, the pretty village of **Kilitbahir** or its far less endearing neighbour, **Eceabat**, also have some places to stay. Further north you'll also find a bed for the night or something to eat in **Gelibolu**, although it's distance from the battlefield sites make it inconvenient unless you have your own transport.

Gallipoli Peninsula

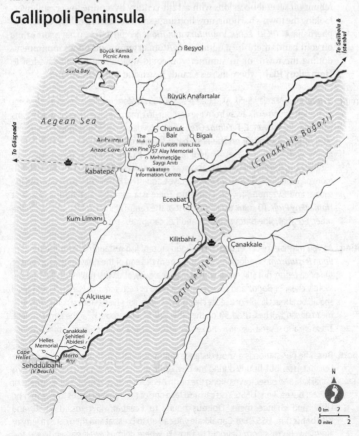

The Thrace Region

Approaching from the north along the E-87 you cross the narrow neck of the peninsular at **Bolayır**. Here is the tomb of Süleyman Paşa, eldest son of Orhan Gazi, who established the first Ottoman toehold in Europe when he conquered the fortresses at Gelibolu and Tzympe in 1354. Buried nearby is Namık Kemal, a playwright and influential member of the New Ottomans, a late-19th century nationalist group which believed in the reinvigoration of the Ottoman empire through democratization and reform.

Gelibolu

At the entrance to the Dardenelles, Gelibolu is an unassuming town with a crowded harbour and a busy fishing fleet. Rusty freighters are loaded and unloaded at the docks and the salt-laced sea breeze carries the smell of fish from the waterside canneries. Fish restaurants overlook the water and locally tinned sardines, anchovies and various vegetables – ideal picnic fare – are on sale in numerous shops along Liman Caddesi, the main street which climbs away to the east of the harbour.

An important crossing point and stronghold guarding the maritime approaches to İstanbul since medieval times, ferries still chug across the straits to Lapseki and there are several large military installations in the town. Originally constructed by Emperor Justinian, the town's fortifications were rebuilt on several occasions with a 12th-century Byzantine tower, still overlooking the town's harbour, now housing a small **collection** of historical paraphernalia. ■ *0830-1800. Voluntary donations accepted*. If you have some time on your hands there are a number of Ottoman tombs and minor monuments dotting the town, or in summer you could walk along Liman Caddesi to **Hamzakoy Plajı,** where there's a sandy beach and some restaurants.

Sleeping **E** *Hotel Oya*, Miralay Şefik Aker Caddesi, T5660392. Modern place down a sidestreet on the left as you walk away from the harbour up Liman Caddesi. Decent sized rooms with en suite shower. **E-F** *Yılmaz Otel*, Liman Meydanı No 8, T5661256, at the beginning of Liman Caddesi on the right-hand side. Brightly painted but a bit shabby, rooms with shower have TV and telephone. **F** *Otel Yelkenci*, Liman Meydanı, T5661022, at the end of the quay above a café. Rudimentary rooms with shared bathroom on each floor. **G** *Otel Hakan*, Belediye Caddesi No 8, basic place overlooking the square and Byzantine tower. **Camping** There is a campsite behind the beach at *Hamzakoy Plajı*, 10-mins walk northeast of the centre along Liman Caddesi. On the other, Eceabat, side of town there's another campsite.

Eating As you might expect Gelibolu has a good crop of fish restaurants with the modern *Ilhan Restaurant*, overlooking the straits from the end of the quay, at the top end of the price range, but still reasonable. Along the quay, also with tables outside, are the slightly cheaper *Boğaz* and *Liman* where a plate of fresh *sardalya* (sardines) and salad should be about US$6. For a really cheap snack there are several stalls serving sardine or meatball sandwiches, US$1.50, on the other side of the harbour near the ferry terminal. There are also several *lokantas* and kebap places on Liman Caddesi, east of the harbour.

Transport **Bus** The bus station is a short distance southwest of the harbour along the road to Eceabat. **İstanbul**, hourly during the day, some night buses, 4½ hrs, US$7. **İzmir** (via Çanakkale and other towns along the north Aegean coast), 6½ hrs, US$8. **Edirne**, 2 or 3 direct buses, 3 hrs, US$6. You can also take one of the frequent buses to **Keşan**, 1 hr, US$2, and change there. **Dolmuş** hourly to **Eceabat**, 45 mins, US$1.50, and **Kilitbahir**, 1 hr, US$2. For **Çanakkale** you can go to Eceabat and then catch a ferry or alternatively cross from Gelibolu to Lapseki, where dolmuş await passengers at the dockside during the day. **Ferry** Lapseki, 20 mins, foot passengers US$0.50, cars US$4. Ferries leave from next to the harbour on the 20-min crossing, nearly every 1-1½ hrs, 0630-1100, then on the hour 1300-midnight. From Lapseki ferries return every 1-2 hrs, 0630-1200, then on the hour 1400-midnight. There's a round-the-clock ferry service between Eceabat and Çanakkale.

The *Yılmaz Otel* (see above) organizes daily tours of the Gallipoli battlefield for US$13 **Tours** per person, though at present instead of a guide you'll be given a pre-recorded commentary to play on your walkman, if you have one.

Banks There are several banks with ATM on the main square and the PTT (see below) will **Directory** normally change foreign currency. **Post office**: There's a PTT kiosk beside the harbour. **Tourist information** The head of the town's Tourism Association, Mehmet Irdesel, mans a small kiosk next to the harbour. The author of a book on local history he gives away town plans, but unfortunately speaks no English.

Eceabat

A scrappy, unappealing collection of concrete blocks, the small town of Eceabat, 36 km south of Gelibolu, is an important transit point for traffic heading across the Dardanelles on the 24-hour ferry service to Çanakkale. The town's very ordinary hotels have only their proximity to the battlefield sites to recommend them, however, don't imagine that you'll find a free room leading up to Anzac Day when everything in the area is block booked by travel agents.

About 5 km south of Eceabat, the village of **Kilitbahir** is dominated by the imposing ramparts of a massive Ottoman castle built by Mehmet the Conqueror in the run-up to the siege of Constantinople. A sleepy little community a world away from the bustle of Çanakkale across the straits, cobbled streets lined with old wooden houses, the beneficiaries of a preservation order slapped on the village, climb up from a tiny harbour. Far more alluring than Eceabat it makes a charming place to stay which is especially convenient for touring the southern battlefields. The only hotel is the F *Otel Dardanel*, T8245001, a conspicuously newer cream and white building near the top of the village, run by amiable local artist, simple rooms with dated 1970s decor, splendid roof terrace with commanding view of the straits. Recommended. ■ *Getting there: A small private car ferry shuttles back and forth on an hourly basis from Çanakkale, and is met by a dolmuş heading north to Eceabat and, in season, south to the memorials at Cape Helles and Morto Bay.*

F *Hotel Eceabat*, Iskele Meydanı, T8142458. Reasonable rooms for the price with en **Sleeping** suite bathroom in characterless building opposite the ferry terminal. **F** *Hotel Boss*, **& eating** Cumhuriyet Bulvarı No 12, T8142311. Similarly unexciting place a few doors to the *Camping on the* east. **G** *Down Under*, Cumhuriyet Caddesi, T8142431, F8142430. Backpacker favourite *edges of town* east of the ferry terminal. Clean but utilitarian rooms with en suite shower, services include snacks and internet access, breakfast not included. **G** *Başak Pansiyon*, Cumhuriyet Caddesi No 9, 18142464, towards the eastern edge of town. Basic but very cheap rooms with shared toilet in newly-built block. A couple of simple local **eateries** on the front to the west of the jetty are joined in the tourist season by several ephemeral bar-restaurants.

Dolmuş depart from opposite the jetty every hour for Gelibolu, 45 mins, US$1.50, and **Transport** Kilitbahir, US$0.50, 10 mins. In summer dolmuş also depart when full for the jetty at Kabatepe, passing along the way the Kabatepe information centre and the turn-off up to the memorials on Çonkbayırı Hill. **Car ferries** depart for Çanakkale every ½ hr up until midnight, when the service is reduced to 1 every 2 hrs, passengers US$0.50, cars US$8.

The Gallipoli National Historic Park

Established in 1973, the Gallipoli National Historic Park (Gelibolu Yarımadası Milli, Parkı) covers the southern third of the Gallipoli Peninsula and encompasses all the area's First World War battle sites and memorials. Inspite of its tragic past it's a beautiful stretch of countryside, particularly in spring time when an abundance of wildflowers dot the fields and hedgerows. Having visited the various battle sites there are some good beaches for a refreshing swim.

Ins and outs

Getting there
Tours cost US$10-20, depending on their length & whether they include lunch

Many visitors to the national park enrol on an organized tour from Çanakkale, Eceabat or Gelibolu. The most popular itineraries tour the northern battlefields and usually include a visit to the Kabatepe Information Centre and some time for a swim in summer. Excursions to the Cape Helles sites are also available. *Hassle Free Tourism* and *Troyanzac* (see page 219) are 2 reputable firms in Çanakkale who can also organize private guides.

Getting around
The area can be divided in 2 with the **northern sector**, northwest of Eceabat, corresponding to the main Anzac field of operations and containing the Visitors' Centre at Kabatepe along with a major concentration of cemeteries and commemorative monuments on the highground to the north. Except for the irregular dolmuş service from Eceabat to Kabatepe, there is no public transport in this sector. If you don't have your own transport this narrows your options to enrolling on a tour (see above) or, if you're reasonably fit and have plenty of time, setting out on foot from the Visitor's Centre. You may also be lucky enough to get the odd lift but traffic is very light so don't count on it. Remember to take adequate water and supplies as there's nothing en route. There's another cluster of memorials and cemeteries around **Cape Helles**, the southern tip of the peninsular where the British and French landed. Under your own steam these sites can be reached from Eceabat or Kilitbahir via the village of Alçıtepe. There's also a dolmuş service from Kilitbahir to Alçıtepe, Sehddülbahir and the Turkish memorial which meets the ferry from Çanakkale in Kilitbahir during the season, taking passengers on a 2½ hr tour with stops at the main sites.

When to go
Quiet for most of the year, the area becomes the focus for commemorative ceremonies on 25 April – the anniversary of the Gallipoli landings declared a national holiday, known as Anzac (Australian and New Zealand Army Corps) Day, in Australia and New Zealand. Formerly a solemn occasion of remembrance attended by just a handful of veterans, in recent years Anzac Day has attracted thousands of mainly Antipodean visitors. The associated crowds, traffic jams, solidly booked hotels and inflated prices suggest steering well clear during this period.

History

When the Ottoman government allied itself with Germany at the beginning of the First World War, British commanders decided that Turkey must be taken out of the conflict as soon as possible, with a knock-out blow to İstanbul deemed the most effective way of achieving this end. A joint Anglo-French naval force was organised by Winston Churchill, then the First Lord of the Admiralty, to force the Dardenelles and attack the Ottoman capital. Having subjected the coastal batteries guarding the straits to intermittent bombardment for three months, on 18 March 1915 an armada of warships under the command of Admiral de Robeck attempted to run the blockade. An intense seven hour battle ensued with the allied ships penetrating 10 km up the straits before being forced to retreat. The allies lost over 2,000 sailors and only later did they discover that the Turkish defenders had been on the brink of abandoning their guns having almost run-out of ammunition. However, chastened by these losses the Anglo-French fleet retreated to the Greek island of Limnos where over the following months a force was prepared to secure the Dardanelles by occupying the Gallipoli Peninsula and the opposite Asian shore.

To achieve this end British and French troops were landed at the tip of the peninsular near Cape Helles before dawn on 14 April 1915, while a second force comprised mainly of Anzac units simultaneously went ashore on the peninsula's western coast. The plan was for these two forces to link-up, but things went seriously awry.

In the face of dogged opposition by the Turkish ninth infantry division, the British and French struggled to secure a beach-head, making only very limited headway over the following months at the expense of thousands of lives. Far worse was in store for the Anzacs, however, as they missed their intended landing zone on the beach at Kabatepe, instead ending up crammed beneath the cliffs beside Arıburnu several kilometres to the north. Not only was progress inland hampered by the steep terrain, but a determined counter-offensive led by one Lieutenant Colonel Mustafa Kemal, later to be known as Atatürk (see page 470), succeeded in driving the Anzacs back down the slope, giving the Turks time to reinforce their lines. Despite bitter fighting the Anzacs failed to break through and both sides dug-in for a war of attrition in which the allied commanders, having clearly underestimated the courage and strength of the defenders, sacrificed thousands of lives. Additional British landings at Suvla Bay in August failed to provide the desired breakthrough and the horrifically bloody campaign dragged on until December 1915, when the order was finally given to begin evacuating the allied troops.

They left behind an estimated 160,000 dead, with 86,000 Turkish defenders also killed in the nine month campaign. The scale, but also the futility, of the bloodshed has singled Gallipoli out as one of the most appalling episodes of the First World War, with much of the blame for the tragic misadventure laid at the door of the allied top brass. Of course this gives little credit to the Turkish soldiers and officers who mounted such a courageous defence of the peninsula.

As one of the terms of the 1918 Armistice, the British and French returned to formally bury their dead. Today there are over 31 cemeteries on the peninsular with the graves of the British and Commonwealth soldiers maintained by the **Commonwealth Graves Commission** (see page 220).

The Northern Battlefields

The logical first stop on a tour of this area is the **Kabatepe Information Centre** (Kabatepe Tanıtma Merkezi) where there is a collection of memorabilia, including lots of rusty metal items recovered from the battlefields, uniforms and letters, all exhibited in a modern bunker-like building, 7 km northwest of Eceabat. There's also an exhibition of photographs of the campaign and more recent commemorative ceremonies. The melted watch strap and blackened glasses of Talat Göktepe, a forestry official who died fighting a large forest fire which swept across the peninsular in 1994, also make a macabre spectacle. ■ *0830-1800, daily. US$1.*

A short distance beyond the information centre the road divides, the right fork leading to the northern memorials and the other road leading 2 km west to the tiny village of **Kabatepe**, where there's a campsite and ferries leave for Gökçeada (see page 212).

The road divides again with the left-hand option continuing along the coast passing the **Beach**, **Shell Green** and **Shrapnel Alley** cemeteries to **Anzac Bay**. This was the site of the first ill-fated landings and looking up at the scrubby mountainside it's easy to appreciate the difficulties faced by the young soldiers as they tried to scramble up the steep escarpment exposed to the Turkish guns along the ridge above. These slopes were turned into a barren wasteland by the fighting and as the front-line advanced upwards supplies landed on the beaches at night had to be laboriously ferried up through a maze of trenches by men and donkeys. Along with rows of graves, there's a Turkish monument at Anzac Cove which bares Atatürk's moving words:

"Those heroes that shed their blood and lost their lives... you are now lying in the soil of a friendly country. Therefore rest in peace... you the mothers who sent their sons from far away countries, wipe away your tears; your sons are now lying in our bosom and are in peace. After having lost their lives on this land they have become our sons too."

Beyond Anzac Bay and Arıburnu, are a series of widely spaced Allied cemeteries, including **Canterbury**, **No 2 Outpost** and the **Embarkation Pier**. Continuing north (left) at a fork brings you to Suvla Bay where British troops were landed in August 1915 to try and out-flank the Turkish positions on Chunuk Bair. Unfortunately, the British were unable to take advantage of these surprise landings and subsequently failed to make any headway in the face of determined Turkish opposition. Today, there's a beach and picnic area to the north of a large inlet at **Büyük Kemikli**.

Baring right at the earlier junction and following signs to Büyük Anafartalar and then Chunuk Bair (Çonkbayırı) you'll ascend to the largest concentration of sites on the heights above the coast. Chunuk Bair can also be reached by turning right at both forks from the Kabatepe Information Centre: a much shorter route if you're on foot.

Approaching from this direction you pass the **Mehmetçiğe Saygı Anıtı**, a monument dedicated to all the Turkish soldiers, known colloquially as "Mehmetçik", who've died in defence of their homeland. Over a kilometre further on is a large graveyard at **Lone Pine** which witnessed a brave assault by Australian troops on 6 August 1915 to divert attention and reserves from the British landings at Suvla Bay. This single attack claimed 2,200 Australian and 4,000 Turkish lives, though it achieved little in terms of territorial gain with the front-line remaining more-or-less static until the Anzac's eventual withdrawal.

Continuing onwards, the present road corresponds approximately to the front-line with the opposing trenches often only 8 m apart and extensive tunnel systems descending either side of the ridge. Bloody battles were fought all along this crest and the dead are buried in a row of cemeteries (Johnson's Jolly, Courtney's Post, Steele's Post and Quinn's Post). Further on is a memorial dedicated to the **Turkish 57 regiment** (57. Alay), virtually annihilated in a brave counter-attack 10 days into the campaign which was launched by Atatürk's now-famous words:

"I am not asking you to attack, I am ordering you to die. For in the time it takes us to die other soldiers and commanders will arrive to take our place".

Climbing further up the winding road takes you past more graveyards, memorials and key positions which saw some of the fiercest fighting, such as **the Nek**. On a lighter note, as you ascend towards the summit of Chunuk Bair, the main objective of the Anzac offensive, sweeping views open up across the surrounding countryside.

On the top is an **obelisk** commemorating the New Zealand dead beside which a section of the timber-lined **Turkish trench system** has been reconstructed. Signposts indicate the spot where Atatürk launched a crucial attack on 8 August 1915; the observation post from where he monitored the bloody proceedings and the place where he was saved from certain death when a piece of shrapnel lodged itself in his pocket-watch (now on display in Çanakkale's Naval Museum). Nearby are a group of five huge tablets inscribed with a commentary concerned primarily with the deeds of Atatürk and the course of the battles which raged in the early part of the campaign.

About 5 km south of Kabatepe village and information centre is a good beach at **Kum Limanı**. If you wish to stay the **D** *Kum Hotel and Camping*, T8141466, F8141917, has decent rooms with en suite shower or you can pitch your tent for US$6. There are several other secluded sandy beaches perfect for a swim as you progress down the peninsular towards Alçıtepe and Seddülbahir.

The Southern Battlefields

Heading south towards Cape Helles, where the British and French contingents came ashore, you'll pass through the village of **Alçıtepe**, with its interesting **private museum**. The aged owner, Mutlu Salim, has collected a large and diverse array of memorabilia connected with the war, including shell fragments, bullets, medals, pieces of uniform and poignant letters written by soldiers. He opens up the collection, displayed in several rooms of his house, when people arrive in the village in return for a voluntary donation.

Beyond Alçıtepe, the road continues across fertile cropland dotted with cemeteries towards the culmination of the peninsula. At a junction the right-hand road leads to **Seddülbahir**, a tiny community of farmhouses and holiday cottages overlooking a crescent of sand and flanked by the remains of some Ottoman-era defences. It's a tranquil spot today with the peace broken only by birdsong and the low hum of passing ships carried on the breeze. On 25 April 1915, however, this is where British forces landed in a terrifying hail of bullets. Known as **"V" beach**, two cemeteries on the bluff above the bay are the last resting place for some of the thousands of Turkish and British soldiers killed in the action. There are also some mock-ups of the trenches from which the out-numbered Turkish troops, commanded by one Yahya Çavuş (Sergeant Yahya), mounted their valiant defence of the beach. Despite its bloody past Seddülbahir is a lovely place to stay with a choice of several simple pensions such as **F** *Helles* or **F** *Kale*, as well as a couple of campsites.

About a kilometre west of the village down a signposted side-road is the **Helles Memorial**, a tall stone obelisk dedicated to British soldiers and sailors killed in the nine month campaign. Inscribed with the names and regiments of over 20,000 servicemen, it's a stark reminder of the terrible human sacrifice made in the battles for Gallipoli.

A short distance to the north of Seddülbahir a road heads east around Morto Bay passing the memorial and cemetery for French soldiers killed attacking Cape Helles. At the end of the lane the **Çanakkale Şehitleri Abidesi** is a monolithic four-legged structure, over 45-m high, built to commemorate all the Turkish dead. Occupying a commanding position overlooking the straits, there's a museum beneath the monument with an assorted collection of weaponry, medals, buttons and bullets unearthed in the area, as well as an exhibition of vintage photographs.■ *0900-1300, 1400-1800, US$0.50.*

Gökçeada

Phone code: 0286
Colour map 1, grid B1

One of the two Aegean islands – the other being Bozcaada (see page 224) – awarded to Turkey instead of Greece by the Treaty of Lausanne in 1923, the distant silhouette of Gökçeada is visible floating on the horizon 18 km off the western coast of Gallipoli. Some 30 km from end to end, the mountainous island was inhabited by a sizeable Greek population for at least 2,500 years. Except for the arrival of a few Turkish bureaucrats little changed on the island post-treaty. That is until 1964, when rising tensions over Cyprus caused the authorities to begin oppressing the Greek islanders: closing schools, confiscating land and resettling families from the Black Sea region on the island. Large numbers of troops were stationed on Gökçeada and in the tense climate which prevailed many Greeks chose to depart, with the islands Hellenic population dwindling from 8,000 to about 250, mostly old people. Today, the island's predominantly Turkish inhabitants are augmented by students studying at a branch of Thrace University and, during the summer months, a small but growing number of domestic holidaymakers, who come to relax on its quiet beaches.

Arriving ferries dock at the newly constructed harbour at **Kuzu Limanı** on the east coast, which has a strip of coarse sand backed by a few pensions. It seems to be popular in summer mainly because of its proximity to the harbour, so you may decide to get straight on the waiting dolmuş and proceed 6 km inland to **Gökçeada** (formerly called Panayia), the island's main town. Here you'll find the island's only bank, as well as a post office, chemist and some shops although once again there's little to hold your interest apart from several old Greek churches scattered around the dusty streets.

Kaleköy, a small fishing village watched over by the ruins of an Ottoman fortress, 4 km to the north, has more in the way of places to sleep (see below) and eat. Along the waterfront are several eateries serving excellent value seafood on roof-top terraces with views across to the Greek island of Samothraki. There's a beach in the village or for more secluded bathing spots, and good snorkelling, you could explore along the coast towards the beach at Mavi Koy.

From Gökçeada town a roads climbs through olive groves and scrubland, scattered in late spring with bright explosion of pink oleander, into the island's mountainous, partially forested, interior. There's no public transport so you'll need to have a bicycle or car, or hire a taxi. Heading westwards you pass the former Greek village of **Zeytinlik**; a large reservoir which supplies much of Gökçeada's drinking water and **Şahinkaya**, one of several villages settled by former residents of the Black Sea region. Soon after the abandoned community of **Dereköy** a road descends a pine forested valley for 7 km to a beach at Marmaros. More stretches of sparsely populated beach, such as the pristine and lengthy **Gizli Liman**, await discovery on the southwest coast around the tiny village of **Uğurlu**. Enquire in the village about renting a room or even a whole house.

Sleeping & eating On the main square in Gökçeada the **G** *Belediye Oteli*, T8873375 can provide simple food and lodgings. In Kaleköy the **F** *Gökçe Motel*, T8872726, set in a large garden, is 1 of a number of down-to-earth places offering decent rooms. Southeast of Gökçeada town the large protected bay at **Aydıncık Koyu** has several pensions and a campsite.

Transport
There is no unleaded petrol available on the island

Daily ferries leave from **Kabatepe** (reached by dolmuş from Eceabat) at 1100 and 1600, returning 1400 and 1800, 1½ hrs, US$1.50 passengers, US$8 car. There are also daily boats from **Çanakkale** in season at 1700 returning next day at 0800, US$2.50 passengers, US$12 car.

The Aegean Region

6

The Aegean Region

216 Çanakkale

220 The Troad
220 Troy
224 Bozcaada
226 Assos (Behramkale)

230 Ayvalık

236 Bergama (Pergamum)
241 Çandarlı
242 Foça
244 Manisa

247 Sardis (Sart)

249 İzmir
260 Çeşme
264 To Kuşadası

265 Selçuk

269 Ephesus (Efes)
271 The site
274 Şirince
275 Kuşadası

279 The Büyük Menderes Valley
279 Priene
281 Miletus (Milet)
284 Didyma
287 Aphrodisias

289 Pamukkale

294 The southern Aegean coast
294 Heracleia under Latmos (Kapıkırı)
296 Milas

298 Bodrum

305 Bodrum Peninsula

307 The Bay of Gökova
308 Akyaka (Gökova)

Stretching from Çanakkale in the north to the Bodrum Peninsula, the deeply indented Aegean coast has a climate as ideal for the visitor as it is for the region's many farmers. The rural economy is dominated by cotton, tobacco and fruit, though it is the ubiquitous olive grove, carpeted with fragrant blooms in the spring, that characterizes much of the landscape.

An extended history of human occupation spanning over 5000 years has left the region with a string of important archaeological sites, amongst them Troy, Pergamum, and Sardis, all heavyweights of ancient history, and a must for anyone remotely interested in the past. To the south of the important port and industrial city of İzmir is ancient Ionia, the centre of Greek civilization for a time, and an area peppered with yet more famous cities of antiquity: Ephesus, standing in all its marble splendour, as the greatest and now most visited. More recent memories of the Ottoman Greeks who lived in the region up until 1923 linger in the cobbled streets of many coastal towns, with contemporary life in Ayvalık played-out in a museum of 19th-century Greek architecture. In the mountainous hinterland are the extraordinary white mineral formations of Pamukkale which have been attracting the curious since Roman times.

Back down at the coast, the Aegean resorts, which although not naturally as well-endowed with golden sand as those along the Mediterranean, and generally suffering from similar problems of localized over-development, offer plenty of scope for enjoying some beach time. Then there is Bodrum, best known for its riotous nightlife, but also a starting point for leisurely cruises along the coast to the south.

The Aegean Region

Çanakkale

Phone code: 0286
Colour map 1, grid B1

Çanakkale's position beside the narrow straits, known as the Hellespont or the Dardenelles, separating the continental land masses of Europe and Asia, has ensured its strategic importance since antiquity. Despite its enduring geopolitical significance, the modern town, with its large student population and concentration of food processing and manufacturing industry, has little to detain the visitor and is generally used as a jumping-off point for tours to the Gallipoli battlefields to the north and Troy, 30 km to the south. If you have time, it is worth looking around the Naval and the Archaeological museums and spending a little time in the waterside cafés, gazing across at the little village of Kilitbahir, about a kilometre away on the European side, watching the fishermen pulling silvery sardines from the water and the massive ships passing-by.

Ins and outs

Getting there
See page 220 for further details

Çanakkale is regularly served by buses travelling between İstanbul and destinations along the northern Aegean coast and also to and from other cities across the country. Ferries carrying vehicular and pedestrian traffic depart every 30 mins for Eceabat, on the European side, from the dock in the centre of town. There is also a smaller private car-ferry chugging across to Kilitbahir, visible directly across from the town.

Getting around
The main focus of town is the docks, with most of the accommodation clustered in the narrow streets to the south (left as you face the water), around the Ottoman clock tower. The *otogar* is 1 km inland from the waterfront, on Atatürk Caddesi, however, many buses drop you at the dockside. The town's attractions are all within 5 mins walk of the clocktower, except for the Archaeology museum, which is several kilometres south on the road to Troy. The tourist office, T/F2171187, is on Cumhuriyet Bulvarı, next to the dock. The helpful staff can give you advice on accommodation and visiting local sights.

History

Depending on who you talk to, the name Çanakkale (pottery castle) is said to derive either from the brightly coloured ceramics for which the area was famous, or from the bowl-like shape of the city's fortress

The town's site at the Dardenelles' narrowest point, with just over a kilometre of water between the European and Asian shores, has made it both a natural crossing point and a valuable defensive position since antiquity. Herodotus recounts how two lines of vessels were lashed together and planks of wood laid between, to enable the passage of his troops. Alexander the Great crossed the Hellespont in 334 BC, at the beginning of his far reaching campaign into Persian territory and beyond. During his passage a bull was sacrificed in honour of Poseidon and wine was poured into the waters from a golden cup to placate the Gods.

The strategic importance of the Dardenelles was not lost on the Ottomans, with the massive ramparts of Kale-i Sultaniye, now known as Çimenlik Kalesi, and Kilitbahir Hisar, on the opposite European shore, being raised by Mehmet the Conqueror in 1453 to halt the passage of Christian ships and to tighten his grip on Constantinople.

The battlements, strengthened in the 19th century, once again demonstrated their importance by helping thwart allied naval attempts to force the Dardenelles in 1915, as a prelude to another occupation of İstanbul. Three British and French battleships were sunk by mines and artillery fire and 2750 sailors lost their lives. This action showed the impossibility of a naval force passing up the well-defended channel and precipitated the ill-fated landings on the Gallipoli Peninsula.

The mythology of the strait

The narrow strait of water that divides Europe and Asia has numerous myths associated with it. The first concerns **Phrixus and Helle**, the children of Nephele, goddess of the clouds. During a time of drought in Boeotia, their father King Athamas was persuaded by his evil wife Ino, the stepmother of the children, that offering them in sacrifice might assuage the displeasure of the Gods and relieve his parched kingdom. The children were rescued just in time by their mother, who flew down from the clouds and sent them off to safety on a golden-fleeced ram, given to her by Hermes. Unfortunately, the rescue went tragically wrong for Helle, who lost her grip as they flew eastwards and fell into the waters of the strait, where she drowned. The strait was named the Hellespont by the Greeks in her memory.

In Western Europe the Hellespont is known as the Dardenelles, after the less fantastical tale of **Dardanus**, a son of Zeus who founded a city named after himself on the Asian shore of the channel. Homer recounted the fable in his epics, read widely in Renaissance Europe, and from then on the strait gained the name that is still used today.

The narrowest point of the Dardenelles, between present-day Çanakkale and Kilitbahir, was the site of another tragic myth. This is the story of **Leander**, a young resident of Abydus, the ancient settlement on the Asian shore of the narrows, who would brave the treacherous waters each night, swimming across to visit his beloved Hero, a priestess at the Temple of Aphrodite. One stormy night the lamp which Hero would light to guide her brave lover across the water was blown-out and Leander was lost and drowned. When the body was discovered, Hero threw herself from her window in despair. The poet and romantic **Lord Byron**, inspired by the myth, swam the narrows in 1810 and a few days later penned the poem, 'Written After Swimming from Sestus to Abydus'.

Sights

There are a few interesting old buildings here, including a well-preserved **The bazaar area** Ottoman Han on Fetvane Sokak. There is a self-service café and restaurant in the cobbled courtyard and the rooms are used by local artists and craftsmen. A relaxed place, it makes a good place to have a glass of tea or a cold beer.

There is a small park surrounding the massive ramparts of the Çimenlik **Çimenlik Kalesi** Kalesi (Grassy Castle), the top of whose walls are still used by the military. In the gardens is a replica of the plucky minesweeper **Nusrat**, which played an important role in repulsing allied attempts to steam up the Dardenelles on 18th March 1915 by making night-time sorties to re-lay mines in areas previously cleared by the British and French navies. Clamber around on deck and have a look at the exhibition of newspaper cuttings below. The dock, with a string of mock-up mines, is a favourite fishing-spot and has good views across the water to the castle of Kilitbahir. Also in the park is the **Naval Museum**, which houses an interesting collection of photographs and military paraphernalia, including the infamous dented pocket watch which, by deflecting a piece of shrapnel, undoubtedly saved the life of its owner, Atatürk. ■ *The Naval Museum is open 0900-1200, 1330-1700. Entrance US$0.75, camera US$0.75, video US$1.25. The Nusrat is open the same hours as the museum. Getting there: From the docks walk past the clock tower and through the bazaar area. The park is open daily 0900-2200.*

The Aegean Region

Archaeology Museum The museum has well-displayed artefacts from sights around the Troad, including statuettes and other items found by Calvert at Troy. There is a good collection of coinage and other brass implements, wooden objects, terracotta and gold pieces, found during the 1974 excavations at Dardanos tumulus, 11 km south of Çanakkale. Some of the finest pieces, unearthed in the necropolis on the island of Bozcaada (Tenedos), are also on display. ■ *0830-1200, 1300-1730. US$1.25. Getting there: Several kilometres south of the town centre, walk up Demircioğlu Caddesi and turn right onto Atatürk Caddesi, from where you can get on dolmuş heading for 'Kepez' or 'Güzelyalı'.*

Essentials

Sleeping Most of the hotels and pensions are found in the area around the Ottoman clock tower, near to the docks, with the cheaper rooms found in the bazaar area. Around the 24th Apr most places in town are booked solid with tourists arriving for the anniversary of the Gallipoli landings. Accommodation is also harder to find during mid-Aug when the Çannakale/Troy festival takes place. At these times book in advance or, if you are desperate, try some of the places inland up Demircioğlu Caddesi.

B *Hotel Akol*, Kordonboyu, north of the docks on waterfront, T2179456, F2171069. Swimming pool, satellite TV, restaurant, bar, popular with tour groups. **C** *Otel Anafartalar*, on the waterfront next to the docks, T2174454, F2174457. 2-star,

Çanakkale

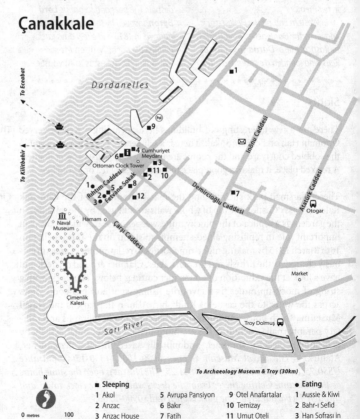

■ Sleeping		● Eating
1 Akol	5 Avrupa Pansiyon	9 Otel Anafartalar	1 Aussie & Kiwi
2 Anzac	6 Bakır	10 Temizay	2 Bahr-ı Sefid
3 Anzac House	7 Fatih	11 Umut Oteli	3 Han Sofrası in
4 Aras Oteli	8 Kervansaray	12 Yellow Rose	Ottoman Han

N

0 metres 100
0 yards 100

overpriced, sea views, open-buffet dinner. **C** *Otel Bakır*, on the clocktower square, T2172908, F2174090. Slightly overpriced although discounts available, some rooms with view of Dardenelles, all en suite **D** *Anzac Hotel*, on the clock tower square, T2177777, F2172018, good value, comfortable rooms with telephone, TV and minibar, meals available for US$4. Recommended. **D** *Hotel Temizay*, Cumhuriyet Meydanı, 50 m inland from docks, T2128760, F2175885. TV, telephone. Better value and closer to the waterfront. Recommended. **E** *Fatih Otel*, near the PTT, on the other side of the road, basic rooms, no breakfast, a good bet if everything else is full. **E** *Umut Oteli*, T2134246. Cheap and centrally located on the clock tower square, little else to recommend it, breakfast extra. **F** *Avrupa Pansiyon*, Matbaa Sokak No.8, T2174084. Run-down rooms with or without bathroom, single US$10, breakfast extra. **F** *Aras Oteli*, next to the docks on the clock tower square, T2171018. Clean, basic rooms, can be noisy, overpriced. **F** *Hotel Kervansaray*, Fetvane Sokak No.13, T2178192. Rooms in old mansion house which has seen better days, mostly shared bathrooms, triple room US$15, garden with fountain, washing machine, no breakfast. Recommended. **F** *Konak Oteli*, Fetvane Sokak No.14, T2171150. 1970's style, single rooms US$10, en-suite bathroom, heating. **F** *Anzac House*, Cumhuriyet Meydanı No.61, T2135969, F2172906, hasselfree@anzachouse.com Run by efficient English-speaking and foreign staff, youth-hostel environment, clean rooms, shared toilet, dormitory beds US$5, breakfast extra, very popular with backpackers. Good value for money. Recommended. **F** *Yellow Rose*, Yeni Sokak No 5, T2173343, yellowrose1@mailexcite.com Deservedly popular with Antipodean backpackers, dormitory beds US$5, breakfast extra, laundry service, table tennis, internet, tours. Recommended. **Camping** *Mocamp Trova*, Güzel Yalı, 14 km south of Çanakkale, off the Troy Rd, showers, kitchen facilities.

Midrange *Otel Anafartalar* restaurant has a good waterside location and reason- **Eating** able selection of meze. There are several other places specializing in seafood along the waterfront, however, be sure to ask prices before you order and to check your bill. **Cheap** *Bahr-ı Sefid*, Fetvane Sokak No.22, T2138288, self-service restaurant, for US$2 choose main dish and starter or dessert from range of Turkish specialities, extremely good value and pleasant surroundings. Recommended. *Han Sofrası*, further down Fetvane Sokak in a restored Ottoman Han, selection of traditional special-ities including local wild vegetables and plants, from US$0.75-3.50 per plate. *Boğaz Lokantası*, on the clock tower square, large choice of ready-prepared dishes. The soup place on the opposite side of the clock tower has chickens revolving in the win-dow, US$2 a portion. *Aussies and Kiwi Restaurant*, Yalı Sokak, T2121722, backpacker hangout, cheap seafood and meat dishes, alternative breakfasts, vegemite. There are numerous busy kebap and pide places on Demircioğlu Caddesi as you walk away from the docks, good value, local clientele. Head for the waterfront, to sit and enjoy the view and the sea breeze in one of the many **cafés**. The café in the Han Sofrası, on Fetvane Sokak, is also recommended for a quiet tea in relaxing surroundings.

TNT Bar, on the clock tower square, tastefully restored building, popular with travel- **Bars** lers and trendy locals, very roudy around Anzac day, run by the same people as *Anzac House*. The *Han Sofrası*, Fetvane Sokak is frequented by a more local, student crowd.

The *Çanakkale/Troy Festival* is held for a week in **mid-Aug**, and hosts a variety of tra- **Festivals** ditional and contemporary acts, exhibitions and contests.

Hassle Free Tourism, part of Anzac House, T2135969, F2172906, recommended daily **Tour operators** tours of the Anzac sites on the Gallipoli Peninsula and Troy. Anzac tour includes a packed-lunch and all transportation costs for US$17. A documentary and the film 'Gallipoli', starring Mel Gibson, set the scene the night before. Private tours, transfers and accommodation in affiliated hostels around Turkey also arranged. *Troyanzac*, on the clock tower square, T2175847, F2170196, interesting display of Gallipoli memorabilia, 25 years experience, private and group tours of the Anzac sites, Cape Helles and Troy.

Transport **Bus** All the bus companies have offices near the docks as well as at the bus station. When buying your ticket, enquire whether you can get on at the docks or if you have to go to the bus station. Remember that the departure time on your ticket may be from the bus station with the bus leaving the docks 10-15 mins earlier. Buses to: **Ankara**, every 2 hrs, 10 hrs, US$10.50; **Antalya**, departs midnight, 12 hrs, US$13.50; **Ayvalık**, 200 km, many buses, 3½ hrs, US$5; **Bursa**, every hr, 4½ hrs, US$6; **Edirne**, get on İstanbul bus and change at Keşan; **İstanbul**, 340 km, every 2 hrs from 0700 to 1900, plus one at 0100, 6 hrs, US$8½; **İzmir**, depart every hr, 5 hrs, US$6. For towns south along the coastal highway, such as **Ezine**, **Ayvacık**, **Edremit**, **Ayvalık** and **Bergama**, you can use buses bound for İzmir. **Dolmuş** Regularly depart for Troy in summer from the dolmuş garage on Atatürk Caddesi. For **Lapseki**, from where there is a ferry-boat to Gelibolu, dolmuş leave from the bus station. **Radar** has services to **Selçuk**, every hr, 6 hrs, US$8. Also has buses to destinations along the **Black Sea coast**. **Ferry** *Eceabat* car and passenger ferries depart from the docks every 30 mins up until midnight, when the service is reduced to 1 every 2 hrs, passengers US$0.50, cars US$8. The small ferry service to **Kilitbahir**, directly across from Çanakkale, departs approximately every hr, although the timetable is rather erratic.

Directory **Banks** There are numerous ATM kiosks around the docks, and several banks nearby on Demircioğlu Caddesi. **Baths** *Tarihi Yalı Hamamı*, Çarşı Caddesi No.46, T2172367, friendly staff, used to tourists, reasonable rates, US$6.50 including massage. **Post office** A short walk from the docks on İnönü caddesi. **Internet** *Yellow Rose pension* has facilities and charges US$1 per 15 mins. *Anzac House*, Cumhuriyet Meydanı No.61, also has several computer terminals with internet access. **Useful addresses** *Commonwealth War Graves Commission*, Çimenlik Sokak, next to the Naval Museum, Başkur İşhanı 10.

The Troad

The area between the main Çanakkale-İzmir road and the coast, historically referred to as the Troad, has several interesting places worth seeing, foremost of which is the ancient city of Troy. Gently rolling wheat fields and olive groves cover much of the land with the area at its most beautiful in spring when the scent of almond blossom carries on the air and the meadows are filled with wildflowers. Rarely visited by tourists, foreign or domestic, the Troad also has relatively undeveloped stretches of coastline with some good beaches for camping. However as you might expect, facilities are extremely limited and accommodation is available in only a couple of spots. One possible base is the pretty seaside village of Assos, where a handful of hotels clusters beside a picturesque fishing harbour, with classical ruins and a beach nearby. It is best to visit the area with your own transport, the quiet lanes and gentle topography make it ideal cycling country.

Troy (Truva)

The site of the ancient city, given-up as legend and only rediscovered in the 19th century, is 30 km south of Çanakkale, in the undulating landscape of the northern Troad. Troy is a name that conjures up great romance and mystery, a name immortalized by Homer's epic tales of Helen, Paris and the infamous wooden horse. But, the uniqueness of the site goes far beyond its Homeric association as it gives archaeologists and historians the opportunity to chart urban and cultural development at a single site over a great sweep of history.

This continuity can leave the untrained visitor in a state of confusion as they try to make sense of the stratified ruins left by over 3000 years of near-continuous settlement. Thankfully a system of explanatory signs help make the ruins somewhat more accessible, but even so, Troy is far less impressive than other sites in the region and in spite of its extent – covering several thousand square metres – the meagre remains can be a bit disappointing.

The site is 5 km west of the Çanakkale-İzmir highway, near the village of Teyfikiye. Dolmuş leave regularly from the Çanakkale dolmuş garage on the 35 min journey (US$1.50). Çanakkale or southbound buses can be stopped at the Teyfikiye turn-off. Visiting the site on a guided tour arranged through one of the agencies in Çanakkale can be very worthwhile.

The first settlement at Troy was built in the Late Bronze Age, about three millennia before the birth of Christ, on a small hill called Hisarlık. Over time, this mound rose by about 16 m as successive civilisations built on top of the remains of the preceding settlement, and archaeologists have now identified nine distinct layers of habitation, with over 46 sub-levels. **History**

Troy I (3000-2400 BC) seems to have been little more than a walled village of clay-brick houses with a layer of carbonized material suggesting that it met a disastrous end. Excavations show that **Troy II** (2400-2200 BC) was a larger settlement laid-out on terraces and that the city enjoyed its first period of prosperity, possibly due to its position on developing east-west trade routes. Metalwork of a distinctly Mesopotamian character has been found in these layers, showing that there was significant contact between the two civilisations. Other finds of pottery, made using a potter's wheel for the first time, have allowed archaeologists to date the arrival of this technology in the area. It was in this level, which he mistook to be 'Homeric' Troy, that the 19th-century archaeologist Schliemann discovered a horde of gold and precious stones, which became known as Priam's treasure.

For about 400 years (**Troy III-V**) there was only a succession of villages at the site, however, **Troy VI** (1800-1275 BC), peopled by Mycenaean immigrants, regained its splendour and the city was enclosed by a 10 m-high sloping wall, large parts of which can be seen today. Some archaeologists have suggested that this was the city of Priam, although general opinion now holds **Troy VIIa** to be the city which held-out against the Greeks for 10 years during the Trojan War.

After being destroyed by the victorious Achaean forces, Troy became a modest market town, although thanks to Homer its reputation attracted some important visitors.

Alexander the Great, believing himself to be a descendent of Achilles, made a pilgrimage to **Troy IX** after crossing the Hellespont in 334 BC. He gave the city special privileges and vowed to build a magnificent temple for Athena, a promise that was only honoured after his death by his successor Lysimachus.

Under the Romans, the city, now called **Ilium Novum**, continued to do well. Reviled as the place from where Aeneas, the sole Trojan leader to survive the war, had fled to establish Rome, the city enjoyed generous imperial patronage and was totally rebuilt at the behest of Augustus.

In Byzantine times the city narrowly missed being chosen as capital by Emperor Constantine. He decided on Constantinople instead, and thereafter Troy suffered a terminal decline due in part, as at Ephesus, to the natural advancement of the coastline, which had left it stranded miles from the sea. It was finally abandoned during Ottoman times, although its memory lived on. A steady stream of curious visitors was attracted over the years by the epic stories and romantic associations, but most of them departed disappointed that there was not a trace of the city to be seen.

The Aegean Region

The site The first sight that greets you is a model of the **wooden horse**. Carefully constructed to scale after consulting images on coins and pottery found at the site, it is now an obligatory photo-stop for arriving coach parties. The **visitors centre** has some very informative displays explaining the history of Troy and the archaeological excavations.

From the remains of the Roman perimeter wall you get a good view of the site, with the sloping wall of Troy VI, built of blocks hewn from local limestone, in front. Some blocks are cracked, evidence some say of an earthquake that destroyed the city

There is a path looping around the site beginning from next to the visitor's centre. Walking towards the site there are some examples of terracotta piping on the right, which brought water from Mount Ida to the palaces of Ilium Novum, the Roman city. There are also some simple stone mortars used for grinding grain in the Bronze Age and huge terracotta *pithoi* used for keeping foodstuffs.

The path passes through the **east gate**, built between two parallel walls for defensive reasons, and up some steps. What little remains of the **Temple of Athena**, the most important building of the Hellenistic-Roman city, is scattered around the next area you come to. Unfortunately, the huge north-south trench dug by Schliemann undercut the great monument and most of it was destroyed. The archaeologist had little interest in Ilium and his workers were told to discard any pieces of the later city that they found. The highest terrace, with polished paving stones, was the forecourt of the temple, where Xerxes, Alexander and later Roman emperors came to pay their respects. There is a good view across the cultivated plain of the Scamander, which used to be the sea, to the present coastline of the Dardanelles and beyond to the war monuments of Cape Helles. The archaic era well, covered by a grill, was built using a mortar containing egg white. Continuing down the path at the bottom is a jumble

Troy

1 City wall
2 City wall
3 East Gate
4 Temple of Athena
5 Ramp
6 Palace of Priam's
7 City wall
8 Sanctuary
9 Odeion
10 Baths
11 South Gate

Troy I
Troy II
Troy VI & VII
Troy VIII (Hellenistic)
Troy IX (Roman)

0 metres 30
0 yards 30

Well
House Foundations

▼ To Car Park & Visitors' Centre

The Aegean Region

Trojan Horse

of pieces from the temple, with one part of a ceiling plate decorated with a flower motif. This small symbol carved onto the surface is the architect's signature.

Leaving the temple, to the right are **house foundations** from Troy I. The walls were built to a megaron plan using a fishbone technique still used in the area nearly 5000 years later. From the wooden platform ahead you can see the vertical layers, from the Roman city, at the top, to the first settlement built onto the bedrock at the bottom. The bones of infants, buried in the kitchens of the first houses of Troy I, were an interesting discovery. Presumably they were placed here so that even in death they would be close to their mothers. The well-preserved **ramp**, used for ceremonial events, leading up to the gates of Troy II is still impressive. It was just inside the walls, to the left of the ramp, that Schliemann unearthed the treasure of Priam. Pass the foundations of a palace, thought to be Homer's **Palace of Priam** and the southern walls of Troy VI, you reach a Hellenistic **sanctuary** with two wells, the round one into which blood was channelled after sacrifices. Turning the corner you come into an area littered with fragments from the Roman city, with the **odeion**, unusually, built up against the walls of Troy VI for support. The **South Gate** of Troy VI and VII, past the odeion on the left, is reckoned to be the Skaian Gate of the Iliad. Notice the early sewage system, channels covered with paving slabs. ■ *0800-1700 (winter), 0800-1900 (summer). US$2.50. Getting there: The site is 500 m up a tree-lined road from the drop-off point in Tevfikiye.*

Sleeping & eating

Çanakkale provides a good base for visiting Troy, but there are several places to stay in the village of **Teyfikiye**, just east of the archaeological site. **E** *Hisarlık Hotel*, on the approach to the site entrance, T2831026, popular with tour groups, nothing exciting but reasonable rooms with ensuite, bit over-priced. **F** *Varol Pensiyon*, next to village mosque, above café, basic budget alternative. There are several tourist **restaurants** catering for the tour groups visiting the site.

The Aegean Region

Troy: Fact or Fable

The story of the Trojan Wars as recounted by Homer in the Iliad begins with the kidnap of beautiful Helen by the Trojan prince Paris. In the company of the heroes Ajax, Achilles, Agamemnon and Odysseus, King Menelaus of Sparta sails with a large armada to capture the city of Troy and recover his wife. The ensuing conflict lasts for 10 years with the besieging Greek forces camped-out for that time on the coastal plain before the city. The protracted struggle is finally concluded when the Greeks secretly enter the city in the belly of the infamous wooden horse.

Although there is little doubt about the epic nature of this tale, how much of it actually happened has always been a matter for considerable debate. The site of Troy has long been associated with the story, with illustrious visitors such as Xerxes, Alexander the Great and Julius Caesar making pilgrimages to the city. Homers inclusion of local geographical features, such as the river Scamander, Mount Ida and the island of Tenedos, gives substance to the story, but perhaps the writer simply used the familiar countryside as a backdrop for his imaginary characters and events.

Schliemann's discovery of a fantastic horde of treasure during excavations at Troy in the 19th century, seemed to prove that the Iliad was not merely fiction, and

that its characters could indeed have drawn breath. But having kindled the public's imagination, later, more scientific, work showed that the archaeologist's assumptions had been flawed and that the Priam's treasure in fact dated from a thousand years before Homeric Troy.

More recent archaeological research has proved that some version of events portrayed in the epic did actually take place. Evidence shows that the walls of Troy VI were quickly rebuilt after an earthquake, possibly as the Greeks advanced, and that a large number of people sheltered within the city walls, as they would do during a siege. A layer of carbonized material also shows that the city was destroyed by fire, maybe the work of a victorious army. Unfortunately, there is no trace of any definite evidence, such as the wooden horse.

Despite on-going academic debate, the consensus of opinion now is that Homer based his epic on stories of the siege of a Bronze Age city over 500 years before his time. These tales were part of an oral history, passed from generation to generation, and which Homer drew on, possibly adding from his own imagination for dramatic effect. Some people have also suggested that in fact the wooden horse was an offering to Poseidon by a conquering army in thanks for an earthquake which damaged the defensive walls.

Bozcaada (Tenedos)
For Gökçeada see page 212
If you are looking for somewhere to get away from it all the island Bozcaada, the more southerly of Turkey's two Aegean islands, the other being Gökçeada, may be for you. Mentioned in *The Iliad*, according to Homer there was a deep underwater cave nearby where Poseidon kept his horses. Today, much of the small island, which is about 6 km from end to end, is covered in vineyards, the fruit from which is used to make wine. The small port and arrival point for ferries is overlooked by a medieval fortress and some Greek domestic architecture survives along the quiet streets. Bar a few old survivors most of the Hellenic population have departed. Like Gökçeada the island has been discovered by domestic tourists, mostly from İstanbul, and during the summer the handful of simple pensions and campsites get quite busy. Even so it's a good place to relax and do very little either walking across the rolling countryside or seeking out local beaches.

Transport Leave the main highway, 5 km south of Troy, and follow the signs for Bozcaada. After 24 km the road passes through the small market town of Geyikli,

The discovery of Troy

Held as the discoverer of Troy, German-born **Heinrich Schliemann** advanced himself from humble origins using a flair for languages, of which he spoke 11 fluently. Having earned his first fortune as the St Petersburg agent of a German trading company, his sense of adventure then lead him across the Atlantic, where he participated in the California Gold Rush, amassing yet more money. It was only at the age of 40 that he decided to find Homer's Troy and with characteristic single-mindedness, he abandoned his family, learnt ancient Greek and set-out for Çanakkale in 1868. There he met Frank Calvert, a local American consular official, who was also convinced of the ancient city's existence in the local area.

Calvert showed Schliemann around the mound at Hisarlık, which lay on his farmland, and where he had started some initial excavations. The site's correspondence to physical references given by Homer in the Iliad was striking, and despite falling out with Calvert, Schliemann began excavations in 1871. Employing nearly 100 local workmen, Schliemann started digging a huge north-south trench into the mound. His methods were far from scientific and his total disregard for the upper, later, settlement layers caused irreparable damage.

After two fruitless years of work his determination finally paid off when he spotted something glimmering in the wall of the trench. Acting quickly, in order to, 'secure the treasure from my workmen and save it for archaeology', he called an early lunch break, using the time to cut a magnificent collection of gold and jewels, wrongly assumed to be Priam's treasure, from the earth. Disregarding his promises to the Ottoman government, the horde was smuggled to Athens, from where it was revealed to a stunned public.

Despite the importance of the find, there was considerable scepticism in academic circles about its authenticity. Schliemann's motives were also questioned, sparking a debate which continues to the present-day. Whether he was a self-aggrandizing treasure hunter or an obsessive amateur archaeologist, the significance of his work is undeniable. However, later excavations proved Schliemann's claims wrong, showing that the treasure was from 1000 years before the time of Priam.

What of the treasure? Donated to the people of Germany by Schliemann, it was exhibited in the Berlin museum. During the last chaotic days of the Second World War it was spirited away by occupying Russian forces and disappeared for nearly 50 years. It only resurfaced after the collapse of the Soviet Union, hidden away in the vaults of the Pushkin museum in Moscow. Its rediscovery has sparked a row between the Russian and the German governments, with the Turkish authorities claiming that it belongs to neither because it was stolen in the first place.

The Aegean Region

where there are no reindeer, despite the name meaning 'with reindeer' in Turkish. Continue 5 km along the newly built access road to the equally new ferry terminal from where there are sailings at 1000, 1400 and 1700. The price is US$8 for a van, US$3 for a car and US$0.50 for foot passengers.

Alexandria Troas

Little remains of this once important city except ruins which are estimated to cover a thousand acres. The city was established in 301 BC by Antigonus who became King of Macedonia after the death of Alexander. Initially called Antigonia, the city's name was changed to Alexandria after the defeat of its founder by Lysimachus, another of Alexander's former generals. Alexandria Troas quickly became the largest and wealthiest city in the Troad, benefiting from its position on the trade routes crossing the Hellespont. The main structure that can be seen today is that of the Roman baths and gymnasium built in 135 AD. The city maintained its importance during the early Byzantine period and was even considered, like Troy, by Constantine the Great in 324 AD as a possible site for the construction of his new capital. He later changed his mind in favour of Constantinople, condemning Alexandria Troas to decline as the focus of imperial trade and commerce shifted northwards. To add insult to injury, the city's ruins were later pillaged by the Ottomans for building material to be used in construction projects such as the Sultanahmet Camii in İstanbul. ■ *Getting there: Taxi dolmuş run between Ezine and Oduniskelesi, 5 km north, when full (US$0.90), there are also occasional dolmuş from Ezine to the hamlet of Dalyan on the coast near the site.*

Kestanbolu Kaplıca On the road to Gülpınar, 3 km south of Alexandria Troas, are the whitewashed buildings of this small hot-spring complex. You can bathe in the murky brown waters that emerge from the ground at a pleasant 72ºC in the communal baths for US$4. For a real 'kaplıca experience' rent your own room with an en-suite tub for US$14 per person per night full board.

Gülpınar Gülpınar is an unremarkable village except for the **Apollo Smintheos**. The remains of this temple are in a pleasant setting, shaded by pomegranate trees, on the western outskirts of the village. It was built in honour of Apollo Lord of the Mice in the second century BC by the legendary hero Teucer and his followers, who had arrived in the Troad after fleeing famine on the island of Crete. Before departing they had been told by an oracle, in typically cryptic fashion, that they should settle where 'the sons of the earth' attacked them. Waking-up one morning to discover that their equipment had been nibbled by mice, they decided that this must be the spot referred to and promptly built a settlement and temple. ■ *Getting there: Dolmuş leave 3 times daily on the 50 km journey to Ayvacık.*

Babakale Babakale is a windswept fishing village situated at the southwesternmost point of the Biga Peninsula, known as Cape Lekton to the Greeks. It's a sleepy place whose economy is based on the 60-vessel fishing fleet which sails from its new harbour and also the yachts from İstanbul that pass through on their way south into the Aegean. There is a ruined **fort** built in 1726 by the Ottoman Admiral Mustafa Paşa, which now serves as a football pitch for the local boys.

Sleeping and eating 1 of the reasons to venture as far as Babakale is to sample the fresh catch cooked in 1 of the restaurants overlooking the harbour. The modern **F** *Uran Motel*, T7470218, is 1 of several hotels in town offering clean, characterless rooms with breakfast.

Assos (Behramkale)

Phone code: 0286
Colour map1, grid B1

From some way off the village of Behramkale is visible across the stone walled fields and oak-dotted hills of the southern Troad, clustered on a hillside beneath the impressive remains of a Byzantine fortification. The village is in fact surrounded by the ruins of ancient Assos, many of the stones from which have been recycled over the years for building its houses. The protected status the area now enjoys due to its archaeological significance, has largely spared it from unsightly development, satellite dishes apart, and the holiday homes and pensions in the village itself, built in traditional style, do little to spoil its charm. The focus of hotel development is beside the picturesque harbour, which is tucked away at the base of cliffs, on the far side of the hill from the village.

Getting there The village is 19 km southwest of Ayvacık, which is on the main
Çanakkale-İzmir highway. Dolmuş depart from Ayvacık bus station every hr in summer (US$1.25), but less frequently at other times of the year. **Getting around** There
is a dolmuş service between the iskele (harbour) and the village at least once an hour
in the summer, or when full the rest of the time. It is about a 15-20-min walk down the
road, but a hot climb up.

Ins & outs

The city of Assos was established in the seventh century BC by colonists from
the island of Lesbos. However, research by American archaeologists suggests
that there was a settlement at the site as early as the Bronze Age. The city rose to
prominence in the fourth century BC under the rule of a wealthy banker
named Eubulus. He was succeeded by Hermeias, a eunuch, who had previously been the student of Plato and Aristotle in Athens. A school of philosophy
was set-up in Assos under the patronage of the ruler and Aristotle was invited
to lead it. The famous philosopher lived in the city between 347 and 344 BC,
during which time he married the ruler's niece. This brief golden age came to
an end with the Persian invasion and Hermeias was dragged off to the Persian
capital to be tortured to death by his captors. Soon after Aristotle fled with his
retinue to Lesbos, where he conducted some of his most important work.
Assos never regained its former importance. During the Byzantine era the
importance of the city steadily decreased, and it was little more than a village by
the time the Ottomans arrived.

History

Approaching from Ayvacık, the road crosses the River Tuzla beside a
well-preserved **Ottoman bridge** with a peaked arch. At the village crossroads
notice the **large sarcophagus** on the left, cracked open by raiders in search of
booty. After crossing the junction a cobbled lane on the left leads up to a small
mosque, shaded by a pine tree, and the village teahouse flanked by several

Sights

The Aecean Region

Assos

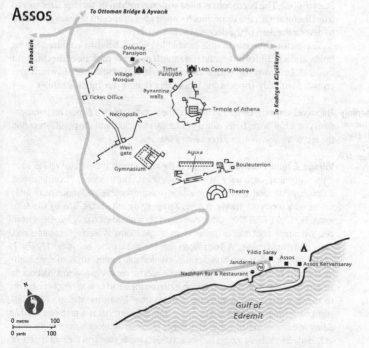

picturesque little shops. Continue climbing towards the top of the hill, past solidly built stone houses with flat roofs and courtyards, many of which contain traditional outdoor ovens. At the top of the cobbled lane, in the shadow of part of the **Byzantine keep** is the ticket booth (*US$1.50*) and a water tap, a good place to refresh yourself before making the final climb.

The **14th-century mosque** on the left is a simple domed structure built of the local stone and lacking the architectural refinements of later Ottoman buildings. Greek inscriptions in the marble above its entranceway show that it was built on the site of an earlier church, partly from cannabalized stone.

The **Temple of Athena**, built in the sixth century BC, crowns the hill and commands a spectacular view along the northern coast of the Gulf of Edremit and across to the Greek island of Lesbos. Excavated during the early 1880's by the American archaeologists Clarke and Bacon, significant parts of the temple were taken back to Boston by the pair, leaving little more than the platform itself and some column parts remaining. Portions of the colonnade have recently been re-erected as part of restoration work sponsored by the Turkish Ministry of Culture and Efes Pilsen Beer. The magnificent position with its panoramic view more than makes-up for the lack of tangible remains and it is easy to see why such a site was chosen both as a place of worship and a defensive position, commanding the southern coast of the Troad.

Looking down the seaward side of the acropolis a cobbled road winds steeply down to the iskele (village harbour) and hotels, with the **gymnasium**, **agora** and **amphitheatre** of the Hellenistic city found on terraces between. These can be reached by continuing on the harbour road, past the village turn-off, to a ticket booth on the left. From there, follow the path past the **necropolis** and through the **West Gate** of the city. This section of the city wall, remarkably well preserved, is one of the most impressive examples of its kind in the country. Unfortunately for Hermeias the walls were unable to keep the Persians out. The necropolis is filled with sarcophagi of varying sizes carved from the local andesite stone, much sought after in ancient times as it was said to devour the flesh of the deceased in just 40 days.

The picturesque **iskele** with its cobbled wharf, brightly coloured fishing boats, and handful of hotels and restaurants nestles at the base of the cliffs, just under 3 km from the village crossroads. It is a popular spot, which gets crowded with day-trippers and longer stay visitors during the summer.

Sleeping
All of the hotels are down by the iskele, but there are several less-expensive pensions in the village itself

Things get very busy by the iskele during the summer months & most accommodation is on a half-board basis, with a substantial reduction, and the possibility of B&B the rest of the year. Ask for a room with a sea view.

Village E *Timur Pansiyon*, 20 m right of the ticket booth at the top of village, small rooms opening onto nice terrace, bathrooms, great views. Recommended. **E** *Dolunay Pansiyon*, opposite the village mosque, double and much nicer triple rooms off a courtyard. **Iskele A** *Assos Kervansaray*, left up the lane by the *Assos Hotel*, T7217093, F7217200. Offers half-board accommodation only, excellent facilities, swimming pool, sauna, games room, single rooms available. Recommended, particularly for families. **A** *Assos Hotel*, on the left at the quayside, T7217017, F7217249. Also offers half-board option, comfortable rooms, small en-suite bathrooms, telephone, TV, minibar, a/c in some rooms, great views across harbour to Lesbos, good selection of meze and fish, eaten on the wharf or in atmospheric dining room. Recommended. **A** *Nazlıhan*, next to the Jandarma station, T7217385. Half-board, live music with dinner, noise from adjacent bar is a problem. **D** *Yıldız Saray*, at entrance to harbour, T7217025, F7217169. Small, friendly, larger sister hotel at Kadırga Beach, basic rooms, half-board US$60, meals eaten on the roof terrace or

Tobacco in Turkey

The country stands as one of the top five world tobacco producers. About half of this is grown in the Aegean region, stretching from Bergama in the north, south as far as Fethiye. It is also produced in the east of the country, around Adıyaman, and in the Black sea region, famous for the samsun variety, which gives its name to the lung-wrenching black-tobacco cigarettes favoured by hardened Turkish smokers.

First introduced to the Ottoman empire in the 16th century by European merchants, tobacco consumption grew slowly in the face of strong opposition from the conservative élite. Sultan Murad IV prohibited its use in 1621, imposing strict penalties on anyone caught having a smoke. After his death the laws were gradually relaxed and once tobacco was legalized, and taxed, by Ottoman authorities, smoking quickly spread. The hookah, a free standing waterpipe, became a common sight in cafés and houses of the time.

Some farmers also found that tobacco grew well under local conditions and it was planted as a profitable alternative to traditional crops. Cultivating tobacco is a labour intensive business which starts in early spring when seeds are sown into tightly packed beds. Transplanted into the fields several months later, they are left to grow for two to three months before the mature leaves are picked by hand, threaded onto long strings, and left out to dry. Racks of brown leaves drying in the sun are a common sight in the Aegean countryside at the end of summer. At this stage the leaves undergo an initial grading before being bailed-up and sold, the majority to the huge state-owned monopoly, Tekel.

In common with other developing countries, the number of smokers in Turkey is high with demand increasing rapidly. The majority of the adult population, along with more than a few children, smoke, and indeed meeting a non-smoking Turk is quite a rarity. This worrying trend is put down to the lack of anti-smoking education, in addition to the fact that cigarettes are both cheap and widely available. Smoking has however been banned on long-distance bus journeys; a small victory for the non-smoking lobby but hell for their nicotine-hooked fellow passengers.

floating pontoon. Cheaper accommodation and **camping** is found up the lane by the Assos Hotel. **E** *Antik Pansiyon*, 15 m from quayside, T7217452. Several small rooms above little restaurant, prices includes breakfast and dinner. *Dost camping*, T7217096, and *Şen camping*, T7217048, are up the track by the *Assos Hotel*, on the edge of the harbour village.

All the hotels mentioned have their own restaurants that serve the standard selection of mezes and seafood, often on the quayside. Cheapish vegetable and fish dishes are on offer at the *Antik Restaurant*, left up the lane by the *Assos Hotel*. The *Assos Kervansaray* has an open-buffet dinner available for non-residents. If you are hungry in the village, the *Timur Pension* has snacks and a bar to go with the view.

Eating
Many of the local women make gözleme, pancakes filled with cheese & greens

The Fenerlihan, at the western end of the quay, is Assos' night-spot, with live music during the summer. The interior's bare wooden beams and stonework are very atmospheric, with people drinking on the terrace or spilling out onto the adjacent rocks where a fire is lit.

Bars

Banks None in the village, but some of the hotels change foreign currency. **Post office** There is a tiny post office in the village square.

Directory

Assos
to Edremit

After leaving Assos, the rough road winds along the coast passing a long beach at **Kadırga** where there are numerous possibilities for accommodation including **D** *Yeni Yıldız Saray*, T7217204, a newly-built hotel with fully equipped rooms. Overlooking the beach 10 km east of Assos is the **A** *Assos Eden Gardens Hotel*, modern, 98-room, lots of facilities, restaurant, café, two swimming pools, sauna, fitness centre, table tennis and watersports.

Beyond Kadırga the coast is pretty unspoilt with olive groves marching up to the pebbly coast and a scattering of summerhouses and campsites some of them offering bungalows for rent. Once the busy coastal highway is reached at **Küçükkuyu**, the ratio of olive trees to concrete rapidly deteriorates with a discontinuous band of summer house developments, uninspiring hotels and motels stretching as far as Akçay 29 km away.

Akçay, at the head of the Gulf of Edremit, is a small seaside resort particularly popular with families from Ankara who come to enjoy the 5 km-long beach. It has plenty of hotels and pensions, packed with domestic tourists in summer.

Edremit, a short dolmuş ride east of Akçay, is the ancient city of Adramyttium mentioned in the Iliad. Nothing remains of its historic legacy, although the centre of this busy market town is pleasant enough, also providing man.

Ören, a former Greek village 4 km before reaching Burhaniye, has a lovely stretch of beach, less marred by development than those along the northern coast of the gulf. Famous for its wine and olives, there is an olive festival from 16 to 18 August. Served regularly by dolmuş from Burhaniye and a boat service from Akçay in summer.

Ayvalık

Phone code: 0266
Colour map 1, grid C2

Approaching from the coastal road the charming seaside town of Ayvalık appears as a chaotic jumble of ochre tiled roofs punctuated by brick chimneys that during the winter belch smoke, heavy with the pungent smell of the olive presses below. It is a down-to-earth place with a well-diversified economy based on the processing of local agricultural produce, primarily olives, and fishing. Inland from the sea-front, the old quarter is criss-crossed by narrow cobbled streets lined with Ottoman Greek houses. This picturesque architectural legacy, now mostly crumbling and neglected, attracts a steady stream of visitors, who come to stroll around and soak-up the delightful atmosphere of yesteryear. Another favourite activity for locals and tourists alike is to cross the bay to the island of Alibey, where the waterside fish restaurants serve up the catch of the day at waterside tables.

Ins and outs

Getting there
See page 234 for further details

The coastal highway passes several kilometres inland of the town. Buses travelling along the coastal highway can drop you at the junction to the town from where you can hitch or catch a dolmuş. Ayvalık-bound buses arrive at the inter-city bus terminal, 1.5 km north of the centre on Atatürk Caddesi. Those from the south, for example İzmir, pass through the square before reaching the terminal and you can ask to get off in the centre. Ferries from Lesbos arrive at the docks on Gümrük Meydanı.

Getting around
City buses (red and white) marked 'Çamlık' travel from the Inter-city bus terminal south into town. Buy a ticket from a nearby shop or kiosk (US$0.25) before getting on. The only way to explore the labyrinth of streets in the old town is on foot. City buses or a boat (much nicer) cross to Alibey island, joined to the mainland by a causeway, every 30 mins from the square. There is also a regular dolmuş to Sarımsaklı beach, departing from Atatürk Caddesi, 100 m south of the main square. The main **tourist**

information office is south of the town on the Sarımsaklı road, just past the new marina. There is an information kiosk on the seafront just south of the square.

The name Ayvalık (quince orchard) was inherited from the ancient Greek name for the town, when perhaps the area was renowned for its quinces. Today, olives are the mainstay of the local economy, with about 7,000 tons of what any local will assure you is the finest olive oil available anywhere in the Aegean region, being produced every year. The shops on the main street display a mind-boggling range of products derived from the humble olive, including soaps, purées, pickles, jams and of course oil. **Background**

The modern town developed from the 18th century with the mainly Orthodox Greek population enjoying significant autonomy within the Ottoman Empire due to a *ferman*, or Sultan's order. Migrants were attracted by the town's prosperity and freedom and by the early 19th century an academy and printing press had been established. There were also several European consular missions in the town, attesting to its relative international importance.

The administrative freedom enjoyed by Ayvalık, was abruptly withdrawn in 1821, when the town's inhabitants became embroiled in the Greek struggle for independence. In an infamous episode of local history, two passing Turkish warships were captured and burnt by some of the townsfolk. The result was six years of internal exile for the population on the Anatolian plateau, far from their beloved Aegean.

When the Greeks returned, Ayvalık continued its role as an entrepot, processing and exporting the produce from the surrounding orchards, fields, vineyards, and saltpans. Smuggling was also the basis of many a local fortune, with the narrow alleyways providing perfect conduits for contraband.

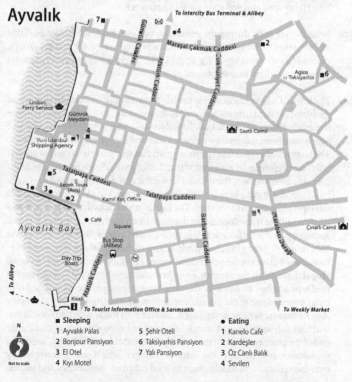

Ayvalık

To Intercity Bus Terminal & Alibey

Gümrük Caddesi
Atatürk Caddesi
Maraşal Çakmak Caddesi
Cumhuriyet Caddesi

Agios Taksiyarhis

Lesbos Ferry Service
Gümruk Meydanı
Yeni İstanbul Shipping Agency
Saatli Camii

Talatpaşa Caddesi
Sezek Tours (Avis)
Kamil Koç Office
Talatpaşa Caddesi

Barbaros Caddesi
Tarabası Deragi

Ayvalık Bay

Café
Square
Bus Stop (Alibey)

Çınarlı Camii

Day Trip Boats

To Alibey

Kiosk
To Tourist Information Office & Sarımsaklı
To Weekly Market

N
Not to scale

■ **Sleeping**
1 Ayvalık Palas
2 Bonjour Pansiyon
3 El Otel
4 Kıyı Motel
5 Şehir Oteli
6 Taksiyarhis Pansiyon
7 Yalı Pansiyon

● **Eating**
1 Kanelo Café
2 Kardeşler
3 Öz Canlı Balık
4 Sevilen

The Aegean Region

Ayvalık was occupied by the Greek army at the end of the First World War and although the occupation was brief, lasting until 1922, it was a major turning point for the town. The following 'liberation' by Turkish nationalist troops, the establishment of the Turkish Republic and the Treaty of Lausanne signed a year later, ensured the end of Ayvalık as a Greek town. Under the terms of the treaty the residents were uprooted to begin a new life on mainland Greece, while Turks from Crete, Macedonia and the nearby island of Lesbos were resettled, often unwillingly, in the town. With time, the new Turkish population began to prosper again, but the former days of wealth and opulence were never regained.

Sights

The old town There are few sights of specific interest in the maze of back streets, so it is best just to wander around appreciating the fine Greek architecture and the pervading atmosphere of dereliction. A good place to begin your explorations is the main square. Walk up the alleyway beside the police station, and heading inland away from the sea, make your way towards **Atarabası Durağı** (horse-cart stop), where horsemen, who negotiate the narrow streets with their brightly painted carts, wait for business. **Çınarlı Camii** (Plain tree mosque), formerly orthodox Agios Yorgis, is up the street to the east. As with the town's other churches, it was not destroyed by the new Turkish residents in 1923, but converted for use as a mosque. Nearby is the **Saatli Camii** (Clock mosque), which used to be the church of Agios Yannis (St John) and which gets its Turkish name from the clock that still keeps time on its façade. **Agios Taksiyarhis,** at the bottom of the hill in Ismetpaşa Mahallesi, is currently being renovated and will soon open as a museum.

Boat trips Boats depart daily during the summer on cruises from the quayside. Trips include visits to some of the 33 islands scattered across the coastal waters, swimming stops and lunch for about US$7. There are even some operators offering moonlight dinner cruises.

Alibey The town of Alibey is just across the bay from Ayvalık on what was known as the island of Cunda, now connected to the mainland by a causeway. There are some fine Ottoman Greek buildings along its wider cobbled lanes, many of which have been restored by wealthy Turks and foreigners as holiday homes. The large number of estate agents suggests that this process of regeneration is only just beginning. It also means that the ugly villa developments are set to continue creeping over the island. Despite the grandeur of some of the Greek buildings, the atmosphere is village-like, with a patchwork of artichoke fields interspersed between the houses. The **Taksiyarhis Cathedral** stands forlornly in the middle of the village. Badly damaged by an earthquake in 1944, a Greek speaking guardian, whose family migrated from Crete in 1923, will let you in to see a couple of fading frescoes which survive on the graffiti-covered walls. Further up the hill is a roofless church, now used as a stable, and the shell of a small chapel that crowns the summit. From here is an uninterrupted view across the roof tops and bay to Ayvalık. The main reason most people visit Alibey is to enjoy a meal in one of the quayside restaurants specializing in seafood. Try the *Ada Restaurant* for *Lor Böreği*, light pancake rolls made with cottage-cheese, and tasty fish soup. *Pizza Veranda*, if you've had enough fish, is also at the far end of the promenade from the bus stop. There are also stalls selling souvenirs (remember not to buy the natural sponges which are threatened by over-harvesting) and snacks, such as fried calamari, sandwiches and lokma.

■ *Getting there: The most enjoyable way is on one of the boats which depart Ayvalık from the waterfront near the tourist information kiosk every 30 mins. Buses also leave every 30 mins from the square, crossing via the causeway.*

Sleeping The guesthouses are generally over-subscribed during the summer and on national holidays, so booking ahead is essential. **AL** *Florium Resort Hotel*, after the causeway, T3310787, F3310790. Large modern place, great location fronting bay, gardens and pool, restaurant, bar, telephone, minibar. Recommended. **AL** *Ayvalık Beach*, on road towards Şeytan Sofrası, T3245301, F3245304. Half-board, bright, comfortable rooms, a/c, fitness centre, sports facilities, large swimming pool, restaurants, bar. **B** *Cunda Oteli*, on left 500 m before Alibey Village, T3271598, F3272464. Row of comfortable, modern rooms at water's edge, private beach, open-buffet dinner US$6.50. **E** *Artur Motel*, on front, above restaurant of same name, T3271014. Simple rooms with shower.

There are several guesthouses & good quality hotels in Alibey which offer an alternative to staying in Ayvalık

On a hilltop south of the town, near the resort of Sarımsaklı, there are several cafés and a small water-worn indentation in a nearby rock that is supposed to be a footprint left by the devil himself. The unobstructed panorama over the convoluted local coastline of bays, headlands and islands is impressive, particularly at sunset, and is popular with locals and tourists alike, who come to enjoy the view but the lack of public transport to the site, however, means that it isn't worth the bother, unless you have your own transport. ■ *Getting there: There is 1 crowded local bus in summer, leaving from opposite the post office at 1900 and returning after sunset.*

Şeytan Sofrası (Devil's dinner table)

Ayvalık's beach resort, about 8 km to the south, is a scrappy affair with nothing to recommend it except for several kilometres of good, white sand beach. Unfortunately, even this may not be enough to justify a visit to what is a perennially unfinished collection of tatty apartments, restaurants, cafés and package hotels. The unplanned development along the coastal strip is not only unsightly, but it has also blocked natural drainage lines, leaving a swampy, smelly mess just inland. If you do need some beach time, then the beach becomes progressively less developed towards the east. ■ *Getting there: Dolmuş depart from Atatürk Caddesi, 75 m south of the square. Also buses every 30 mins from the stops on the bayside of Atatürk Caddesi.*

Sarımsaklı

Essentials

There are some interesting pensions in old Greek houses in the town. With the sound of horses hooves in the streets outside and the period decoration it often feels like you have been transported back in time. They are very popular, so book ahead at weekends or in the season. **D** *Kaptan Otel*, Balıkhane Sokak No.7, T3128834. New hotel, nice rooms, 3 with sea view, terrace overlooking bay, interesting old photos of Ayvalık in the lobby. Recommended. **E** *Hotel Ayvalık Palas*, Gümrük Meydanı, T3121064, F3121046, modern, characterless, en-suite bathrooms, balcony, telephone, minibar, 6 year-old piranhas in tank in lobby, diving school. **E** *Aziz Arslan Otel*, Belediye Sokak, T3125331, F3126888. Small, centrally located, modern rooms, telephone, TV, bar. **E** *Yalı Pansiyon*, behind the PTT. Lovely restored Greek waterfront residence, Baroque-style painted ceilings, atmospheric, shared bathrooms, leafy garden beside the bay. Recommended. **F** *Bonjour Pansiyon*, Maraşal Çakmak Caddesi, T3128085. Former French consulate, small high ceiling rooms, sitting area furnished with antiques, tunnel said to run down to waterfront, shared bathrooms not in keeping with grandeur of building, good breakfast extra. Recommended. **F** *Taksiyarhis Pansiyon*, İsmetpaşa Mahallesi, behind the Taksiyarhis church, T3121494. Greek house lovingly converted, friendly staff, relaxed

Sleeping
The more luxurious hotels are found outside town, in Alibey & Sarımsaklı

The Aegean Region

atmosphere, 2/3/4 bed rooms, shared bathrooms, breakfast extra US$4, guests encouraged to use fully equipped kitchen, terrace with lovely views of town, bike rental, very popular so book ahead at weekends. Recommended. **F** *Kıyı Motel*, Gümrük Meydanı, T3126677. Small hotel, telephone, no breakfast. **G** *El Otel*, entrance just off Talatpaşa, T3122217, Basic rooms with or without bathroom, no breakfast. Recommended. **G** *Şehir Oteli*, Gazinolar Caddesi No.4, T3121569. Newly renovated boarding house, small rooms, shared bathroom, noisy.

Eating **Midrange** For fish, most people head to the waterside restaurants of Alibey, mentioned above. There are also the popular *Kardeşler Balık Restaurant* and *Öz Canlı Balık* on the cobbled wharf in Ayvalık. A meal with a selection of meze, fish and a bottle of wine costs about US$15 per head at either, with the second having better service. *Dayım Restaurant*, also in the centre, has a waterside terrace with meze, fish and meat dishes served.

Some of the large hotels in Sarımsaklı & Alibey have open-buffet dinners for non-residents

Cheap There are several soup places on Talatpaşa Caddesi, as well as *Gaziantepli*, serving lahmacun, pide and ready-prepared stews. *İstanbul Börekçi*, also on Talatpaşa Caddesi, has pastries which are good for a snack. *Kardeşler Pide and Kebap*, on the main street, serves kebaps and pide. *Sevilen Restaurant*, further down near the PTT, excellent lahmacun with wholemeal dough for US$0.75 each, also has mantı, ravioli-like dish served with yoghurt.

Cafés The quayside cafés opposite the main square are always busy. At the end of the quay is the trendy *Kanelo Café and Bar*.

Bars In the narrow streets of the market area are many *meyhanes*, local drinking clubs with cheap food, alcohol and plenty of atmosphere though not recommended for unaccompanied women. The town's nightlife, fairly low-key compared to the resorts further south, is clustered between Gümrük Caddesi and Talatpaşa Caddesi, near the water. Places include: *Sokak Bar* and *X-dancing Bar*.

Shopping Have a look in the shops along Atatürk Caddesi at the produce from the local olive industry, everything from jam to soap. The jars of olives stuffed with almonds or peppers are delicious. The weekly market, held on Thu, is a particularly colourful Aegean affair with villagers descending on the town from the surrounding area.

Tour operators *Sezek Tours*, Talatpaşa Caddesi No 67, T3128875, F3123734, Avis agents. *Yeni İstanbul Shipping Agency*, Gümrük Meydanı, T3126123, F3126123, Lesbos ferry tickets.

Transport **Bus** All the major bus companies have offices along Talatpaşa Caddesi. From the inter-city bus station buses leave for: **Ankara**, 2000, 2130, 11 hrs, US$13; **Balıkesir**, every hr, 2 hrs, US$3.5; **Bergama**, every hr, 45 mins, US$2; **Çanakkale**, regularly, 3½ hrs, US$4; **Edremit**, every 30 mins, 1 hr, US$1; **İstanbul**, 0845, 1200, 2100, 2230, 6 hrs, US$10; **İzmir**, every hr, 3½ hrs, US$4. You can usually board southbound buses in the square. Enquire when you buy your ticket. **Ferry** **Lesbos**: ferries depart Tue, Thu and Sat at 0900, returning at 1800. The crossing takes 2 hrs, US$50 one-way, US$65 return, US$120 car. There is also a port tax for those buying one-way tickets in Lesbos. Contact agent for details. You may have to give your passport to the agent a day before you travel.

Directory **Banks** Most banks, with ATMs, are situated along Atatürk Caddesi. **Post office** The post office is on Atatürk Caddesi, 500 m north of the square. **Medical facilities** *Doktor Özel Sağlık Hizmetleri*, Talatpaşa Caddesi No 17, T3127457. **Useful addresses** *Ayvalık Diving Centre*, T3121064, F3121046, in lobby of *Hotel Ayvalık Palas*. SSI-certificate courses, over 25 local dive sites.

Heading towards Edremit, 7 km north of Ayvalık along the main E87 coastal road, is a right-hand turn next to an olive oil factory, signposted for **Kozak** and Bergama (58 km). The road traverses a veritable sea of olive trees, before climbing into the mountains, where quiet villages are lost amongst the pinenut trees, orchards and vineyards. There are infrequent dolmuş from Ayvalık to Kozak, where there is a small restaurant, however, it is best to explore the area under your own steam, by car or bicycle.

Ayvalık to Bergama
Away from the focus of development on the coast, the countryside inland from Ayvalık is blissfully unspoilt

Formerly a quiet village, Dikili has grown enormously as a result of its active fishing fleet, domestic tourism and the deepwater quay where cruise-liners periodically dock and passengers disembark to visit the nearby ruins of Pergamum. The promenade is lined with cafés, crowded on summer evenings with Turkish families spending their holidays in the suburban summer house developments that surround the town. Apart from a good stretch of sandy beach, the town has little to offer, something reflected in the poor choice of accommodation available.

Dikili
Phone code: 0232

A possible excursion is to follow the narrow coastal road which heads through the dusty village of **Bademli**, where there are two campsites and several simple restaurants, and south along a stretch of unspoilt coastline eventually reaching **Çandarlı**. ■ *Getting there: Dolmuş run as far as Bademli from opposite the Ziraat Bankası in Dikili, but after that you'll need your own transport*

Sleeping **B** *Dikelya Hotel*, on beach 1 km from the bus station, right-hand turn at roundabout before town, T6718856, F6718871. Half-board, swimming-pool, bar, restaurant. Recommended. **B** *Dikili Ümmetoğlu Hotel*, near bus station. Modern, TV, minibar, restaurant. **E** *Perla Otel*, far side of town from bus station, 150 m beyond the square, T6714145, in row of apartment buildings overlooking harbour, simple rooms with bathroom, restaurant, bar. **E** *Sinka Otel*, in the centre of town, inland of Atatürk Parkı. 2/3/4 bed rooms with bathroom, bar on top floor, live music, restaurant below. Recommended. **G** *Özdemir Pansiyon*, Şehit Sami Akbulut Caddesi No 32, half-way between the bus station and square. Converted apartment, no breakfast, basic rooms, shared toilets, kitchen.

Eating *Liman Restaurant*, on the harbour-side, fresh seafood, reasonably priced. Next to *Since Hotel* there is a small square of cheap restaurants including *Blue and White*, every conceivable type of kebab; *Özgaziantep*, lahmacun and other southeastern specialities. Try a fish sandwich (US$1.50) from the stalls near the fishing co-operative gates.

Transport Long distance buses travelling along the coastal road let passengers off at the junction, 4 km from town, a distance regularly travelled by dolmuş. There are direct buses from the terminal to İzmir, Çanakkale, Bergama and Ayvalık.

Directory **Banks** Around Atatürk Parkı in the centre of town. **Post office** On Şehit Sami Akbulut Caddesi just before Atatürk Parkı.

Bergama

Phone code: 0232
Colour map 1, grid C2

The magnificent city of Pergamum was the capital of an empire which at its height stretched along most of the Aegean coast and inland as far as Konya. The site is breathtaking, with the remains of the Attalid acropolis and later Roman public buildings perched on top of a steep-sided mountain above the present-day town of Bergama. Less spectacular than the acropolis, the Asclepion at Pergamum grew to rival Epidaurus as a centre of ancient medicine and can be visited next to an army base in the southwest of the town. Besides these ancient sites, which are seen by most visitors as a day trip from Ayvalık or even further afield, the bustling Turkish town of Bergama has some lovely old buildings and a pleasant atmosphere, making it worth extending your stay, although few people do. Tobacco is an important crop in the countryside around the town and some of the surrounding villages produce carpets which are on sale in a handful of shops.

Ins and outs

Getting there
See page 241 for further details

Bergama is 107 km north of İzmir and 8 km inland from the main coastal highway. The town is within easy reach of the seaside towns of Çandarlı, Dikili and Ayvalık, which are 32 km, 30 km and 60 km away respectively, and is regularly connected by bus and dolmuş with all these places. Other long distance bus services running along the coastal road can drop you at the Bergama junction, from where you can catch a taxi (approx US$8) or wait for the regular dolmuş services (US$0.50) into the centre.

Getting around
The town is relatively spread out with the main sights of the acropolis & the Asclepion found, unfortunately, at opposite ends

The acropolis is 5 km from town via a road that encircles the steep mountain, and although you can shorten this on foot by making several short-cuts it is still a long, hot climb. The Asklepion is on the western edge of town, signposted off the main road as you enter from the coastal highway, about 3 km before the centre. If you don't want to walk to these outlying sights from the centre, then taking a taxi is the only option. **Tourist information** is next to the Hükümet Konağı (Government building) on Atatürk Meydanı, T6331862. Open 0830-1730, later in the summer.

History

Pergamum's rise was based on the spoils of war collected by Alexander the Great during his extensive campaigns and secured in the city after his death by the general Lysimachus. While Lysimachus was fighting for control of Asia Minor with Seleucus, another of Alexander's former generals, he appointed a eunuch named Philetarus to act as governor and guard the treasure. Lysimachus died in battle in 281 BC and Philetarus, with considerable guile, managed to remain in control of the fortune. He used the money wisely to consolidate his position and to establish a dynasty that ruled for 150 years.

Under the Attalid king's generous patronage Pergamum blossomed, becoming one of the foremost cultural centres in the Hellenistic world. A policy of alignment with the Roman Empire started by Eumenes II (197 BC - 159 BC) also greatly benefited the city. This relationship with Rome grew increasingly close, culminated with Attalus III bequeathing his kingdom to Rome in 133 BC. As part of the Roman Province of Asia, trade helped maintain the fortunes of the city and population increases caused the city to spread out onto the plain to the south of the acropolis. Many monuments and public buildings were added during this period, beautifully decorated by the local sculptures. In Byzantine times the city was an important Christian centre being the site of one of the Seven Churches of the Revelation and a bishopric.

Sights

The city of the Attalid kings, located on terraces carved from the top section of a steep-sided peak over 400 m above the valley floor, dominates the modern town of Bergama. From the car park, the remains of the **palaces** of the Kings of Pergamum, six groups in all, can be seen on the right (northeast) side of the site. To the left (south) is the **upper agora**, through which an ancient road passed before descending to the Middle city located on terraces below. Important structures of the **Middle city** include the **gymnasium**, the **Temple of Demetre** and the **lower agora**. Follow a faint path down, but remember it's a hot climb back up.

The acropolis

Above the upper agora is the **Altar of Zeus**, built during the reign of Eumenes II to honour both Zeus and Athena. A 120 m long relief carved into its outer wall was one of the finest pieces of Hellenistic craftsmanship. Carved after the victory over Antiochus III at Magnesia, it depicted a battle between the gods of Greek mythology and the Giants, meant to represent the Attalids defence of Hellenistic civilisation against the Persian and earlier Gaul barbarians. Pieces of this epic frieze were discovered in the 19th century by archaeologist Carl Humann and taken back to Germany to form the basis of a reconstruction in the Pergamum Museum in Berlin, something the contemporary inhabitants of Bergama are not very happy about. Today there's only the criss-cross foundations of the podium to give you an idea of the size of the temple and how much work it must have been to carve the 2.3 m-high relief stretching around it.

Next to the Altar of Zeus part of a temple dedicated to **Athena** stands right on the edge on the mountain, adjoining the famous **library**, which grew to rival the greatest ancient collection at Alexandria (see box). Look over the edge at the **amphitheatre**, one of the steepest of its kind in the Hellenistic world, with 80 rows of seats stacked in a vertical elevation of 36 m, and a capacity of 10,000 spectators. A short flight of steps and a tunnel leads down to the auditorium, however, originally the audience would have entered from the bottom. The stage building was made of wood with large beams inserted into extant square holes and removed again after performances in order not to obstruct the view.

The exposure is considerable from the top rows of the amphitheatre, with a wonderful view over the modern town & down the valley to the sea on a clear day. Definitely not for the citizen with vertigo!

After climbing back to the top, progress round to the **Trajaneum**, built to honour the deified Emperor Trajan by his successor Hadrian in 125 AD. The magnificent Corinthian temple has been partly reconstructed, using modern marble to replace pieces that have disappeared in the intervening millennia. The result captures the grandeur of the original structure and the view from the edge of the sacred enclosure is spectacular.

The mountaintop position of Pergamum presented contemporary engineers with the problem of how to supply the city with water. This was overcome by piping water from a source over 45 km away on Madra Dağı, which was sufficiently high to give the water enough pressure to reach the city. A modern irrigation canal, seen from the **arsenal**, beyond the Trajaneum, follows much the same course as the original pipeline, while a section of the Roman aqueduct, built in the second century BC to satisfy increasing demand, is also obvious below.

■ *0830-1700 daily. US$2.50. It is about 5 km by road from the centre of town, US$6 for a taxi. If you want to climb on foot to the acropolis the distance can be cut short by weaving your way up through the old district above the Red Basilica. It is impossible to give directions in the labyrinth of alleyways, however, it is relatively easy to keep on a direct course upwards. Keep veering right as you climb because there is a fence along the road further to the left.*

The Aegean Region

Kızıl Avlu (Red Basilica) This massive redbrick building on the road leading up to the acropolis is built over the River Bergama, which passes diagonally beneath it in two parallel tunnels. Constructed during the reign of the Roman emperor Hadrian, it was a temple devoted to the worship of the Egyptian gods Serapis, Isis and Harpocrates. It was later converted into a church, while today part of it functions as a mosque. ■ *0830-1200, 1300-1700 (later in summer) daily. US$2.50. Getting there: About 200 m beyond the main square on the Acropolis Rd.*

The Asclepion Of the gods of the Greek pantheon it was Asclepius who was the deity of medicine, and it was around him that the famous cult at Epidaurus on the Greek mainland developed into the world's foremost medical centre. In the fourth century BC the cult was introduced to Pergamum where it flourished. The Asclepion was unlike any modern hospital, with patients sleeping in small chambers within the sanctuary. Some awoke to find themselves miraculously cured, but for the rest, a course of treatment would be prescribed, based on an interpretation of their dreams. Such treatments typically involved drinking from the sacred spring, mud baths and special diets and often lasted for many months. Whether the success of the Asclepion was due to the medical treatments prescribed, auto-suggestion on the part of the patients, or divine intervention, the sanctuary was a very popular place, always crowded with priests, physicians, patients and spectators.

The place reached its peak during the second century AD, when Pergamum was the home of the greatest Roman physician, Galen, and it is from this time that most of the present ruins date.

From the car park you pass up the Via Tecta (Sacred way), a paved road which stretched from the Roman city and which was flanked with shops. As you enter the sanctuary the structure on the right was a library, with the theatre in the far corner also for the entertainment of the patients. The sacred well is where patients drank from, hoping to be cured, with the tunnel leading to the Temple of Telesphorus built to protect them from the elements. ■ *0830-1700 daily. US$2.50. Getting there: From Atatürk Meydanı follow signs up the road beside the mosque. A longer route leaves the main road shortly after you reach the edge of town and crosses an army base.*

Bergama

Archaeology Museum Houses an extensive collection of interesting artefacts recovered from Pergamum and other local archaeological sites. ■ *0830-1200, 1300-1730 every day except Mon. US$2. On the main street next to the small park.*

Other sights The **Çarşı Hamamı**, on the main street 50 m from the main square as you head towards the acropolis, dates from the Selçuk period. You can have

The library of Pergamum

The Attalid rulers not only used their great wealth to embellish their capital with beautiful temples, palaces and sculpture; but under their patronage Pergamum also developed as an important centre of knowledge and for education. A particular passion of Eumenes II, which developed into an obsession, was the collecting of books. The empire was scoured for manuscripts, while the learned men of the city were also kept busy producing works to stock his newly-built library.

In those days, manuscripts were written on long pieces of papyrus, about 30 cm wide, and wound around two thin sticks. The reader would slowly unwind the scroll as he or she read, simultaneously winding the text up with the other hand. Such manuscripts were very impractical for scholars and it was in Pergamum that the book with individual pages, called codex, was invented.

With time, the Pergamene library developed into a huge collection of 200,000 volumes, second only in the ancient world to the great library at Alexandria. An intense rivalry developed between the two institutions, and the Egyptians, worried that scholars would be lured away to Pergamum, halted the export of papyrus from the reed beds of the Nile. Starved of the material from which to make manuscripts, the Pergamene scientists were put to work to find an alternative. They refined an earlier Ionian method of using animal hide to make parchment. This caught on and within a few hundred years parchment had totally replaced papyrus as the material for making books. The word 'parchment' actually comes from the Latin for the material, 'pergamen'.

The library at Pergamum outlived the Attalid dynasty and remained in the city until it was taken to Alexandria by Mark Anthony, as a gift for his beloved Cleopatra. There it survived until the 6th century when its 'heretical' contents were burned by Caliph Omar.

a hot bath in historic surroundings for US$5, open 0600-2300. Across the street in the old market area is the **Incirli Camii**, whose diminutive brick minaret, dating from the 14th century, protrudes above the surrounding rooftops.

If you have some time on your hands it is worth taking a stroll across one of the stone bridges spanning the Bergama Çayı and exploring the quiet, narrow streets of the **old town** set on the lower slopes of the acropolis, where many houses of Ottoman vintage survive in various states of disrepair. To the southeast of town are two large tumuli, one close to the main road, near the Asclepion turn-off. Known as **Maltepe**, this circular grass-covered burial mound, was initially thought to be that of a Pergemene ruler, but has since been dated to the Roman era. A passageway leads into the centre of the mound where there were several burial chambers, although any remains have long since disappeared.

There is a controversial **gold mine**, west of the town at Ovacık (see box). In the interests of PR, staff at their office in town at Osman Bayatlı Caddesi No 11B, T6321946, can organize special group tours of the extensive site.

Essentials

B *Berksoy Hotel*, T6332595, F6335346, on your way into town from the coastal highway. 3-star hotel popular with tour groups, satellite TV, small bathrooms, shower, mini-bar, restaurant, bar, swimming pool, tennis, laundry service. Most comfortable place in town. **B** *Iskender Oteli*, on the edge of town, T6329711, F6329710. Modern, single US$55, larger bathrooms, a/c, restaurant, bar. **D** *Ersane Otel*, on the main road about 1 km before the bus station, T6326350, F6326333. Single US$25, comfortable rooms with en-suite bathroom, bar, roof terrace, small swimming pool open only in summer. **D** *Serapion Hotel*, opposite *Ersane Otel*, T6333434, F6332663. Single US$20, will give

Sleeping
The hotels are found along the main road as you enter the town, with the nicer pensions in the older parts of town past the main square

●●

Controversial mining

In 1989 a group of foreign companies revealed their plans to exploit a deposit of gold and silver to the west of Bergama, near the village of Ovacık. Despite Eurogold, having received government permission to begin operations, environmentalists and local people, strongly opposed to the plans, mobilized themselves to battle against the mine operations. A campaign of marches and blockades was organized and some militant eco-warriors even planted a bomb outside the company offices in İzmir.

The protestors' central concern was the use of cyanide in the production process and the potentially disastrous consequences should it escape into the environment. Eurogold countered these fears by pointing to the findings of an independent environmental impact study carried out on their behalf and to the stringent safety measures built into the extraction process. However, environmentalists were unimpressed,

pointing to the involvement of the parent companies in other mine operations in Papua New Guinea and Cyprus, which had resulted in pollution and environmental damage.

Advocates of the mine cited its economic benefits, with Eurogold estimating that over 1,000 people would be employed both directly and indirectly by the operations, which would produce 6 tonnes of gold and silver each year. Charges of putting economic interests before the well being of local people were levelled at the government and the fight to close the mine was taken to the courts.

Finally, after almost a decade of work, a court ruling banning production at the mine was both a rare victory and a defining moment for Turkey's nascent environmental movement. The mine is still in operating though, pending an appeal by Eurogold, so if you want to have a look what all the fuss is about contact Eurogold offices in Bergama.

●●

discounts. **F** *Gobi Pension*, on the main road near the bus station, T6332518. New building, triple rooms available, en suite bathrooms, 24-hr hot water. **F** *Acroteria*, entrance in alley next to Çarşı Hamamı, T6332469, F6331720. Rooms off quiet shady courtyard, triple rooms available at same price, small shower closet, breakfast not included, meals prepared on demand, terrace overlooking rooftops, 24-hr hot water. Recommended. **F** *Pension Athena*, Barbaros Mahallesi, İmam Çıkmazı 5, from the old centre walk up small street towards the river, take a sharp left before the bridge, T6333420. Original building 150 years old with several later additions, cheaper rooms available with shared bathroom, use of kitchen, friendly owner whose motto, 'we are not the best but trying to get there', sums up the place, basic rooms, ask to see room with safe built into the wall. Recommended. **G** *Nike Pension*, Tabak Köprü Çıkmazı No.2, cross bridge into old quarter, pension is ahead of you with entrance to the left, T6333901. 2/3/4 bed rooms, family house with simple facilities, shared bathroom, quiet leafy garden, excellent breakfast including home-made jams. Currently being refurbished, so expect prices to rise. **Camping** *Bergama Caravan*, on the left as you approach town from the coastal road, T6333902, F6331792. Tent US$4, caravan US$10, restaurant, bar, swimming pool.

Eating

The cheapest food is around the bus station. There are also some ice-cream places on the main road near the bus station

The food situation in Bergama is not very inspiring with a predictable choice of basic kebap, pide and soup places and a few restaurants offering a bland menu aimed at passing tour groups. The best of the bunch by far is *Bergama Caravan Restaurant*, just outside town on the way to the main road, serves a range of meze, grilled meat and fish, eaten outside on a terrace next to the swimming pool. More central is the *Saşlam 3*, İstiklal Meydanı, near the tourist office, has a range of ready-prepared *sulu yemek* and some specialities from the southeast of Turkey, such as *içli köfte* and *spicy güveç*. The row of restaurants on the main road in the old centre of town, *Arzu*, *Meydan* and *Gizem*, are relatively cheap and good.

There are several café/bars opposite the museum serving beer on tap. Across the road in the small park is another café. **Bars & cafés**

Carpets are produced using hand-weaving techniques and natural dyes in some of the villages surrounding Bergama and are sold in the shops opposite the Kızıl Avlu. Beware that there are also some carpets which have been produced in less traditional, more automated, ways. Prices start from about US$100 for a small piece. **Shopping**

Buses and dolmuş depart from the bus terminal on İzmir Caddesi. **Bus** Ankara, departs 2030, 9 hrs, US$12; **Ayvalık**, US$1.75, 6 buses daily; **İstanbul**, departs 2100, 8-9 hrs, US$13; **İzmir**, every 30 mins, 2½ hrs, US$2.5. Buses for **Çanakkale** and other destination to the north can be stopped on the main coastal road, 8 km from town. **Dolmuş** Regularly depart for **Ayvalık**, **Çandarlı** and **Dikili**, but the last direct dolmuş to Ayvalık leaves at 1700, after which you'll have to go via Dikili. **Transport**

Banks There are banks with ATM's along Bankalar Caddesi, near the Çarşı Hamamı. **Communications Post office**: The PTT is on Atatürk Meydanı, open 24-hrs. **Internet** The *Büyük Bergama Dersane* offers internet access for US$1.75 per hr. Follow the signs for the Asclepeium from Atatürk Meydanı and take the first left. **Directory**

Çandarlı

A sleepy seaside place 11 km off the coastal road, Çandarlı has become a popular weekend retreat for middle-class *İzmirli*, with the outskirts of town in danger of developing into an all-too-familiar tale of whitewashed concrete and steel girders. At present though the town, built on a sea-girt peninsular jutting into the calm waters of a protected bay, hangs on to just enough of its original character as a fishing and farming community to maintain its charm, with the local men-folk still driving into town on their tractors and the conversation in the cafés revolving around the size of the day's catch. *Phone code: 0232 Colour map1, grid C2*

Not surprisingly, given its naturally defensible position, the site was first settled over 2,000 years ago as the Greek town of Pitane, the northernmost city of the Aeolian league. Although nothing remains of the Greek *polis*, a 14th-century Genoese castle, restored by the government in 1950, stands guard over the community. Unfortunately, the gates of are kept firmly locked except on special occasions. This limits activities in the town to relaxing on the clean, coarse sand beach and eating in one of several fish restaurants: making Çandarlı the perfect place to get through that book you've been trying to finish. Contemporary life is focused to the east of the main square, where the bus stop, post office, a collection of shops and the aforementioned cafés are to be found.

E *Samyeli Hotel*, T6733428, F6733451. Modern, clean rooms with small bathroom, some with sea view, above restaurant. **F** *Bağış Pansiyon*, 1 road back from beach-front, T6732459. 20 small rooms around courtyard, breakfast extra. **F** *Kaya Pansiyon*, near bus station, T6733058. Friendly, good value, but noisy. **F** *Senger Pansiyon*, on beachfront, T6733117. Family-run, clean rooms with bathroom. **Sleeping** *The town's simple hotels & pensions are found on the western side of the peninsular near the beach*

On the sea-front the restaurant below the *Samyeli Hotel* and the *Kalender Restaurant* serve a good selection of grilled or fried fish. The *Senger Pansiyon* restaurant also serves fish. There are cheap soup and pide places, frequented by the locals, near the bus stop. **Eating**

Buses and **dolmuş** leave from the bus stand in the east of town for: **İzmir**, depart every hr, US$2; **Dikili**, at 10 mins past the hr, US$0.70; **Bergama**, 5 times a day, US$0.70. Services are drastically reduced out-of-season. **Transport**

Foça

Stretching around a pair of protected bays at the mouth of the Gulf of İzmir, this seaside town is a popular excursion from İzmir and at weekends during the summer its restaurants, bars and souvenir shops are crowded with day-trippers. The weekend throng is augmented by uniformed young conscripts from the town's large military base, enjoying a brief reprieve from the rigours, and boredom, of their national service. However, once the weekend is over the town settles back into its mellow repose with most activity centred around the busy fleet of trawlers which set off daily from its quayside. It is this relaxed atmosphere which attracts a small number of foreign tourists, who return to the town's family-run pensions, year after year. The rocky coastline to the north of town, apart from offering some rather chilly bathing, is also one of the last haunts of the highly endangered Mediterranean monk seal, the focus of a local WWF-sponsored conservation project.

Ins & outs

See page 244 for further details

Getting there Foça is 26 km off the E87 coastal road, 70 km north of İzmir. Regular buses link the town with Dikili, Çandarlı and İzmir, there are also dolmuş to Bergama. The bus terminal is near the centre of town. **Getting around** The bus station is just a short stroll from the seafront, restaurants and hotels, although you'll need to catch a dolmuş to the best bathing spots to the north of town. The **tourist information** office is in the square next to the bus station, T8121222. Open 0830-1900 weekdays; 1000-1300 and 1500-1900 weekends.

Sights

The fragmentary and wholly unsatisfying remains of Phocaea, as it used to be called, are limited to the recently rebuilt **Genoese fortress** on the headland between the town's two bays, Küçük Deniz (Small Sea) to the north and Büyük Deniz (Large Sea) to the south. Portions of the original **perimeter wall** are also still visible as you walk around the peninsula, which was initially identified as the centre of the ancient city by French archaeologists in the 1920's. Their excavations also uncovered the remains of a temple, probably dedicated to Athena, near the tip of the promontory; but this structure along with any other ancient buildings have long since been buried beneath the modern town. More recent research did, however, turn up a **sanctuary** dedicated to the Anatolian fertility goddess Cybele at the entrance to Küçük Deniz. Discovered in 1993, this temple consists of several small niches, some of which are now underwater, carved into the living rock and probably used to hold statuettes or oil lamps. There is also an unusual 6-m high rock-cut tomb, known as the **Taş Kule**, beside the road 8 km before the town. Without the help of any inscriptions, experts believe the burial chamber, reminiscent of early Phrygian monuments found further to the east, may date back as far as the eighth century BC.

Tour boats are moored along the wharf of Küçük Deniz. A typical tour around the coast and offshore islands, stopping for swimming and fishing, costs US$17 including a meal.

There are some small stretches of beach at the northern end of Küçük Deniz. The **Halk Plajı**, which can get crowded in summer, is just 3 km north of town and served by regular dolmuş leaving from the bus station. Heading along the rocky coast towards Yeni Foça (25 km), there are several good sand and pebble beaches, but these can also get crowded with day-trippers during the summer and are litter-prone. If you don't have your own transport jump on a dolmuş which depart roughly every 30 minutes during the season from the bus station. About 14 km from town is a stretch of shingle beach with camping facilities. Beyond this, the military have reserved one of the best beaches for their own use. Don't be tempted to ignore the signs and scramble down from the road. Sazlıca Plaj is another reasonable beach 19 km north from Foça.

On the brink: the Mediterranean monk seal

The Mediterranean monk seal (Monachus monachus) is a shy mammal which lives along isolated sections of the rocky coastline near Foça. Formerly found throughout the Mediterranean basin, its numbers have dropped dramatically in recent years and it is now classed as one of the 10 most threatened animal species in the world. Less than 400 seals are thought to remain in communities on some Adriatic islands, Madeira and the Atlantic seaboard of Morocco and Mauritania, with an estimated 20-50 adults living in the Turkish Aegean.

The monk seal's precipitous decline, with numbers down 80% since 1970, has been attributed to various causes including pollution of the coastal waters by sewage, plastics and heavy metals. Fishermen, many of whom regard the animals as competition for increasingly depleted fish stocks, have also been known to kill the mammals, while their nets accidentally entangle and drown hapless individuals. The reclusive seals are also sensitive to disturbance by leisure craft and scuba divers, particularly during the critical pupping season.

Since 1993, a project supported by the WWF and the Turkish Ministry for the Environment has been trying to conserve the last remaining monk seals, with the coast around Foça designated as a Specially Protected Area. Local and foreign volunteers are collecting data on the dwindling population and have also successfully raised public awareness (the seal has been adopted as the town's symbol, appearing on souvenir mugs and tea-towels). They also help enforce a ban on boating, diving and fishing around the Siren Rocks, an important breeding area, which some say got its name from the ghostly barking of the seals.

If you would like more information about the WWF Foça Pilot Project, visit their office on the second floor of the modern commercial centre fronted with restaurants, just past the fishing co-operative on Küçük Deniz (Fevzipaşa Mahallesi, 212 Sokak No6/B). Their mailing address is PK12, Foça, İzmir. Alternatively, there is information on volunteering at: www.ecovolunteer.org

The Aegean Region

Sleeping
Prices drop considerably outside of the summer holiday period

Small pensions, all charging about the same rate, are in abundant supply around town, although with the nicer places booking ahead is necessary. **D Villa Dedem**, on the waterfront, 25 m from beginning of Küçük Deniz, T8122838, F8121700. Reasonable rooms, en-suite bathroom, ask for room with sea view. **E Ensar Aile Pansiyonu**, 161 Sokak, next to Siren Pansiyon, T0121777, F8126159. Popular with Turkish families, smaller rooms than next-door with en suite bathrooms. **E Fokai Pansiyon**, 139 Sokak, north end of Küçük Deniz, T8121765. Clean rooms, roof terrace, use of kitchen. Recommended. **E Huzur Pansiyon**, 139 Sokak, T8121203. Small place on waterfront, next to Fokai, clean rooms, some with sea view, shaded terrace beside sea, use of kitchen. Recommended. **E Melaike Otel**, Ismet Paşa Mahallesi, 200 Sokak No.20, Küçük Deniz, in back streets behind İyigün, T0122414, F8123117. Reasonable prices, friendly guest-house aspiring to be a hotel. Recommended. **E Siren Pansiyon**, 161 Sokak, 150 m along Küçük Deniz, 50 m from seafront, T8122660, F8126220. Friendly family run pension, slightly cheaper than the others, roof terrace, use of kitchen, airport transfers US$35. Recommended. **F Aydın Pansiyon**, Fevzipaşa Mahallesi No.2, turn right off the main street, in back streets 100 m away, T8122941. Basic rooms, with colour TV, refrigerator, hot water, no breakfast.

Eating
Try the local speciality lokma, deep-fried balls of dough, sold on the main street

There are many fish restaurants around Küçük Deniz, also serving a selection of meze and meat dishes, including **Celep** and **Kordon**. **İkizler Restaurant** is always popular, with the **Sahil I**, next to the fishing co-operative, offering to cook fish that you buy or catch yourself. Delicious calamari is available in most of these restaurants for about US$2.50 a portion. Walking around to Büyük Deniz, there are several slightly cheaper seafood places on the promenade, beside where the fishing boats tie-up. Döner and kebap places are found back from the waterfront at the bottom of the main street. For a cheap and delicious fish sandwich look for the old man cooking on a trolley in the back streets, north of the Belediye building. Several other portable stalls serve fish sandwiches (*balık ekmek*) for about US$1.25. *Keyif Café*, Küçük Deniz, café beside the water, serves drinks and snacks. There is a café in the restored odeion, Büyük Deniz.

Bars *Balıkçı Bar*, Küçük Deniz, trendy wharf-side bar, serves snacks. *Anatolia Café and Bar*, back streets, inland from *Balıkçı Bar*, music cranked up in the evenings for lively sessions.

Transport **Buses** for İzmir leave every 30 mins, US$2. For other destinations further north get off an İzmir-bound bus at the highway, or continue on to Menemen, and flag down a passing bus. **Dolmuş** to İzmir from Menemen

Directory **Banks** Found on the main street between the bus-station and Küçük Deniz. **Communications** **Post office**: On the main street, 50 m from the bus station.

Manisa

Phone code: 0236
Colour map 1, grid C2

Manisa is located on the southern fringe of the fertile Gediz Valley, overshadowed by the towering, craggy form of Spil Dağı, known to the Greeks as Mount Sipylos. Decimated by the Greeks on their chaotic retreat towards the coast in 1922, this former Ottoman provincial capital is a predominantly modern city with an important concentration of manufacturing industries and a large military base, where newly-shorn conscripts undergo their initial training before being posted across the country. A few historic buildings of Selçuk and Ottoman vintage have survived to the present, making the city a worthwhile destination for the ardent admirer of Islamic architecture. There is little else to detain you though, instead it is much better to continue on your way, or even to visit on a day trip from İzmir, taking in the ruins of Sardis in the afternoon.

Ins & outs
See page 246 for further details

Getting there Manisa is on the main İzmir-Balıkesir highway and is well served by buses from the north and south. Dolmuş depart regularly from the *otogar* for Sardis, 50 km away. **Getting around** The town is relatively compact and all the sights are clustered in the southern part around Murat Caddesi, making it possible to see them all on foot in a morning or afternoon. To reduce the amount of walking, take a dolmuş labelled 'Muradiye' from the bus station and get off at the Muradiye Camii complex.

History
It is from this story that we get the word 'tantalize'

Manisa is associated with the legend of Tantalus, the King of Phrygia, and his son Pelops. The myth recounts how Tantalus invited the Gods to a banquet at which he fed them with the cooked remains of his son. All the gods but Demeter, who at the time was grieving for her daughter, passed this crude test of their perception and noticed the nature of the food set before them. Tantulus was duly punished for his insolence by being condemned to eternal thirst beside a lake in Hades that would recede each time he bent to drink from its waters.

Most of the historic quarter of the city was destroyed during the disorderly Greek evacuation, leaving room for a modern and obviously prosperous city to develop. Lord Kinross, who visited the city during the 1950's, described it as a miniature Bursa, and looking up its streets, past the minarets and plane trees to the green slopes of Spil Dağı, you are often reminded of the old Ottoman capital.

Sights The **Sultan Camii complex**, was raised at the behest of Süleyman the Magnificent (1522) to honour his mother Ayşe Hafize, who lived in the city while he was serving out his imperial apprenticeship as governor. The mosque was the centre of a *külliye* which included a *medrese*, a hospital, which now houses part of Celal Bayar University, and a hamam. Today, the mosque is the focus of the **Mesir Festival**, a week-long event including concerts and folk dancing held at the end of March, and culminating in a grand finale in which thousands of sweets are thrown from the mosque's minaret to an eager crowd awaiting below. Now in nearly its 460th successive year, the event celebrates a cure concocted for Ayşe Hafize, by a local chemist. She was so grateful for her full recovery that she ordered the *mesir macunu* (power gum), a mixture of 40 different spices and other ingredients, to be distributed annually to the citizens of Manisa.

Across Murat Caddesi, the **Saruhan Bey Türbesi** is the oldest building in the city and was built to hold the body of the Selçuk Emir Saruhan Bey who conquered the city at the beginning of the 14th century. A wily commander, he is said to have fooled the Byzantine soldiers garrisoning the fortress into fleeing by attaching torches to the horns of a herd of goats, giving the impression that a much larger force was about to overwhelm the defences.

Next door to the tomb is the **Muradiye Camii**, built in 1586 for Murat III who also served as imperial governor in the city before being girded with the sword of Osman. As you would expect from a mosque designed by the master architect Mimar Sinan, its slender twin minarets and large central dome, supported by four half-domes, are aesthetically very pleasing. The interior is no disappointment either, with colourful stained-glass windows and beautiful İznik tilework covering the *mihrab*.

Climb the steep steps behind the Muradiye Camii to reach the **Ulu Cami**, built in 1363 by the grandson of the emir Saruhan Bey. The oldest mosque in the city, it commands an excellent view across the city and the café next door is a fine place to have a drink. Entered through an elaborately decorated portal, the inner courtyard is surrounded by a colonnade of irregular pillars, some quite obviously pillaged from earlier structures. Inside, a large central dome is held aloft by yet more columns. Facing the building, notice the crumbling domes of the old hamam 30 m to the left, while to the right the *medrese* still functions as a Koran school. ■ *Getting there: If walking, head towards the mountain from the bus station for about 300 m until you reach Doşu Caddesi, turn left and then right, towards the mountain again, after the small park. Sultan Camii is visible at the top of the boulevard ahead. See also 'Getting around' above.*

Niobe Ağlayan Kaya (Weeping rock of Niobe) Legend has it that Niobe, daughter of the ill-fated Tantulus, boasted to the nymph Leto of her superior fertility having had 14 children compared with the latter's two. Unfortunately, for Niobe, Leto's two offspring were the gods Apollo and Artemis, who punished Niobe for this slight against their mother by killing all her children and then turning her to stone. The weathered outcrop of rock which is supposed to resemble Niobe, her head bowed in grief, is found at the base of Spil Dağı next to the open-air theatre. ■ *Getting there: Follow the narrow street between Ulu Cami and the café up to a main road, which you descend to the right.*

Taş Suret Along the road to Turgutlu, about 7 km from Manisa, is the weathered relief of a seated woman carved into a 5-m high niche in a rock face at the base of Spil Dağı. Initially mistaken for Niobe, it was later identified as a Hittite representation of Cybele, goddess of fertility. ■ *Getting there: Catch the Salıhlı or Turgutlu dolmuş as far as the Akpınar pool from where there is a roadside sign to the 'Cybele'. It is a short scramble up some scree from the road.*

An affair of the eyes

King Candaules, who ruled over Lydia in the fifth century BC, was so infatuated with his wife that he would never stop praising her beauty to all those around him. His favourite minister Gyges was a cautious man who deemed it wise not to be over-enthusiastic in his support of the monarch's praises. This angered the King and Herodotus recounts how he told his minister: 'Gyges, it is clear that you doubt what I tell you of my wife's beauty; seeing is believing so we must contrive that you see her naked.'

To Gyges' horror, Candaules devised a plan whereby the minister would sneak into the royal apartment and hide behind the door, from where he would be able to witness the queen getting undressed without being noticed. Gyges reluctantly agreed to carry out the king's wish and that night he concealed himself behind the door and watched as the queen disrobed. As he was slipping

out of the room he was spotted by the queen who, guessing her husband's complicity in the affair, stifled her scream. The next day she summoned Gyges to her and delivered this ultimatum: 'Gyges, you have seen me naked; you must therefore choose one of two courses: either you must kill Candaules, marry me and be king of Lydia, or you must perish here and now.'

Self-preservation led him to accept the first option and that night the minister hid behind the same door waiting until the king was asleep, before sneaking over and stabbing him to death. The next day Gyges claimed the throne of Lydia and this was the beginning of a new dynasty, which lasted 150 years. However, this betrayal eventually returned to haunt his descendants, with the Gods engineering the defeat of King Croesus by Cyrus of Persia in punishment for the sin of Gyges, his fifth ancestor.

Spil Dağı (Mount Siphylus) A road winds 20 km up the forested mountain (1517m) to a plateau where there are cabins for rent and a restaurant set in the pine forest. Book the cabins in advance from the Spil National Park office in Manisa, T2371065. It is possible to follow a dirt track to the summit and enjoy the superb view over Manisa and the Gediz valley. A well-marked trail descends a gorge from the plateau rejoining the road above Manisa. ■ *Getting there: No public transport on the mountain. Hitching a lift is possible at weekends when families drive up to picnic.*

Sleeping
The choice of hotels in Manisa is very limited: it is better to continue on to İzmir once you have seen the sights

A *Büyük Saruhan Otel*, on the İzmir-Balıkesir highway before town, T2332380. Moderno, over-priced, comfortable rooms, en suite bathrooms, a/c, bar, restaurant. **E** *Hotel Arma*, Doğu Caddesi, T2311980. Left over from 1970's, plain rooms, ones on the front suffer from traffic noise, bar, restaurant. **E** *Otel Niobe*, Sinema Park Caddesi, No 8, opposite PTT, T2312745. Once a modern hotel it is now very tatty, rooms have TV, breakfast not included. **F** *Atlas Otel*, Dumlupınar Caddesi, No 22, T2311997. Cheap, basic rooms, some have washbasin. **G** *Günaydın Pansiyon*, just off İzmir Caddesi, the bottom of the barrel in terms of comfort, very cheap and basic.

Eating The restaurant situation is as dire as the choice of accommodation with none of the kebap and pide places that are scattered around the centre being particularly noteworthy. The *Kent Lokantası*, serving the usual selection of soups, ready-prepared dishes, kebaps and pide is conveniently sited across from the bus station.

Shopping Every Thu there is a colourful weekly market selling food, clothes and household goods along Murat Caddesi.

Transport **Bus** To İzmir, every 30 mins, 45 mins, US$1.25; İstanbul, every hr, 8 hrs, US$10. **Dolmuş** To Salihli, which pass **Sardis**, leave from the bus station every 30 mins and cost about US$2. There are also regular dolmuş to **Menemen**. **Train** It is also possible, but much slower, to get to **Manisa** by 5 daily trains from İzmir's Basmane station.

Banks Most of the major banks, many with ATMs, can be found around the junction of Doğu Caddesi and İzmir Caddesi. **Baths** *Yeni Alaca Hamamı* on Murat Caddesi is 1 of oldest in the city. The *Sultan Hamam* is part of the Sultan mosque complex.

Directory

Sardis (Sart)

Sardis is an important archaeological site spread out near the simple farming community of Sartmustafa. Capital of the mighty Lydian empire, most of the extant ruins, including the impressive multi-story façade of the Marble court, are in fact from Roman and Byzantine times. Today, this is vine country with the surrounding land producing grapes and sultanas for the domestic market and export. Once you've had a look around the ruins there is little else to do in Sartmustafa. A way to extend a visit outside of the hottest months would be to bring supplies for a picnic at the temple of Artemis which is set in an idyllic pastoral setting.

Colour map1, grid C2
90 km E of İzmir

Getting there Just over 1 hr from İzmir by bus (US$1.25), it is best to visit Sardis as a day trip, although you can continue on the 9 km to Salihli, where there are a few hotels. There are also several daily trains from Basmane (İzmir) passing Sart, although these tend to progress at a very leisurely pace. The train station is a 1 km walk north of the highway. Dolmuş regularly travel between Manisa and Sartmustafa (US$1.75). **Getting around** Most of the ruins are conveniently situated next to the E96 highway though it's a pleasant 10-min walk to the Temple of Artemis.

Ins & outs
If you are leaving from İzmir make sure you do so early so you're not walking round the site in the midday sun

The origins of Sardis are lost in the mists of time, however, the city came to prominence as the capital of the Lydian Empire during the sixth century BC. The city's fantastic wealth was partly founded on the gold dust washed down from Mount Tmolos (Boz Dağı) by the river Pactolus and collected on sheepskins by the Lydians. The precious metal, at first mixed with silver, was minted into simple coins, stamped with the lion's head emblem of Sardis and guaranteed by the government, forming the earliest example of metal coinage being used as currency. This invention allowed the Lydians to make full use of their strategic position on an important route between the coast and central Anatolia and their widespread trading activities amassed even more wealth.

History

Sardis continued to prosper under Persian rule until the city was occupied by Alexander the Great in 334 BC. Sardis was then controlled by the Seleucids and Pergamum before becoming part of the Roman Province of Asia in 129 BC. It continued to thrive as the site of a highly revered temple dedicated to the worship of Artemis, later becoming an important centre for emerging Christianity, held as one of the Seven Churches of Asia in the Revelation. Fortune finally turned against the city with its sacking by the Sassanids in the seventh century AD and Tamerlane in 1401. By the time Richard Chadler visited Sardis in 1765, most of the city was buried under up to 9 m of sediment washed down by the river Pactolus and he scathingly referred to it as a 'miserable village'.

The site

From the car park walk towards the nearest corner of the ruins where there are the remains of some **Byzantine latrines** with several seats and the drainage channels clearly visible. A shopping arcade, lined with the crumbling foundations of Byzantine shops and restaurants, runs down the right-hand side of the

The gymnasium & bath complex

site. Off to the right near the perimeter fence, part of a 18.5 m wide **Roman avenue**, which flanked the complex, has been uncovered. This was one of the main thoroughfares of the city and was probably lined on either side by a colonnade. At the far end of the area the excavations started in 1958 by an American archaeological expedition continue.

The entrance to the **synagogue**, the largest of its time so far discovered, is on the left through some gates. It was given to the sizeable Jewish community in Sardis during the late Roman period and in addition to being a place of worship was probably used as a meeting place, school and dining hall. From the entrance hall three doorways (notice the marks made in the marble floor by the original doors) lead into the main hall, which was decorated with intricate geometric designs made from small pieces of coloured marble. At the far end is a solid table where the Torah, Old Testament scrolls, were brought from their shrines against the entrance wall, to be read aloud.

Leaving the synagogue the multi-story façade of the **Marble court** is visible across the open **Paleastra**, a colonnaded area used for sporting events. The Marble court is very impressive and gives a good impression of the size and grandeur of the whole complex. The reconstruction includes about 60% of the original ornamentation; however, the rubble and brick walls that support the columns were formerly hidden by marble facing. Behind the Marble court were the hot and cold baths where citizens washed after exercising, chatted and enjoyed a massage. ■ *0830-1730 daily, later in summer. US$1.75. Next to highway.*

The Temple of Artemis The temple is up the lane on the opposite side of the road to the gymnasium and bath complex. This track passes an area where Lycian workshops and houses have been uncovered and a Forestry Department depot before reaching the temple. There is a path leading off the road to the **Pyramid Tomb**, believed to be the final resting place of a Persian nobleman killed in battle in 546 BC.

A sandstone altar dedicated to Artemis was originally constructed at the site in the fifth century BC but the temple went through several subsequent building phases during Hellenistic times. The original design was radically changed to accommodate a temple for Zeus and an outer colonnade was also added. In 139 AD it was once more converted by the Emperor Antoninus, with the western part still dedicated to Artemis, while the other section became a temple of the Imperial Cult.

Several of the huge columns have been reconstructed and it is easy to appreciate the huge scale of what was one of the largest Greek temples in the ancient world. The site is particularly beautiful in spring, with the meadows surrounding the scattered fragments of stone carpeted in flowers and the sound of the river, which helped enrich ancient Sardis, adding to the peacefulness of the scene. Behind the temple rises a jagged eroded peak on top of which stood the **acropolis** of Sardis. There are still some sections of the Byzantine fortifications visible, perched precariously on the ridge.

Boz Dağı Between Sart and Salihli a side road, sign-posted for Boz Dağı and Ödemiş, winds up into the mountains of the Boz Dağları range. After 18 km is the quiet village of Boz Dağı, clustered beneath the peak of the same name. Renowned for its chestnuts, the village has an almost alpine feel to it during the winter, overlooked as it is by the snowy haunches of the mountain; while in summer the villagers are joined by a growing number of temporary residents, escaping the oppressive heat below.

There is a small ski-centre on the flanks of the mountain nearby with ski-rental facilities, several lifts and a few short beginners runs. There is some more exciting off-piste skiing from the summit chair-lift for the more accomplished skier. Snow is unreliable but the best conditions are generally in January and February.

Sleeping   Half-board accommodation is available at the **D** *Boz Daş Kayak Merkez Hoteli*, T5458333, which has simple rooms, price per person, **E** during the week. Huts (*kulübeler*), sleeping up to 5, are also available for US$166 weekend, US$133 weeknights. Make reservation in advance.

İzmir

İzmir is a modern industrial and commercial city blessed with a dramatic location sprawling around a long and narrow bay enclosed by barren mountains. Wide tree-lined boulevards and street cafés give parts of the centre a distinctly European flavour although the rapidly growing suburbs and shantytowns that ring the city are a very Turkish phenomenon. The combination of a catastrophic fire, which swept through the city in 1922, and rampant urban development, have left İzmir surprisingly devoid of historical and architectural interest, and few specific sights to lure the foreign visitor. Don't dismiss the place however as a day spent exploring the massive bazaar area, visiting the archaeological museum and having a cold beer in one of the relaxed waterside bars can be an enjoyable one.

Phone code: 0232
Colour map 1, grid C2
Population: over 3 mn

Ins and outs

İzmir's Adnan Menderes airport is 25 km from the city centre on the main road south. It is served by regular *Turkish Airlines* domestic flights and is busy with package flights during the summer. The airport is connected to the city by *Havaş* airport buses, which leave from the *Turkish Airlines* office, next to the *Efes Hotel*, 90 mins before *Turkish Airlines* departures. There are also hourly trains between the airport and Alsancak Garı, near the docks. A taxi to or from the airport takes about 20 mins and costs around US$20. The bus station has been moved to a new huge terminal at Pınarbaşı, about 15 km north of the city. Board one of the service buses to get to the centre of town.

Getting there
See page 258 for further details

In common with any large city, İzmir can be a little confusing to negotiate at first, particularly when you start venturing into the maze of streets in the bazaar area. Luckily, though, most of the main attractions are conveniently located in a small area around Konak, the centre of the city, and it is quite possible to walk between them. The bay is flanked along its entire length by Atatürk Caddesi, more commonly referred to as the Birinci Kordon (First Kordon) or simply the Kordon. Running parallel to the Kordon just inland is Cumhuriyet Bulvarı, often called the İkinci, or second, Kordon. These 2 thoroughfares run north to Cumhuriyet Meydanı, a square centred on an equestrian statue of Atatürk, with many of the plusher hotels found nearby, and beyond into the upmarket area of Alsancak. **Tourist information** Main office: *Akdeniz Mahallesi*, 1344 Sokak No 2, Pasaport, T4838086, pink building on waterfront near naval base, open 0830-1700, daily except Sun. Also *Çınkaya*, Gazi Osman Paşa Bulvarı No 1/1, between *Büyük Efes* and *Hilton Hotels*, T4457390. Also at the airport, T2742210.

Getting around
The İ Hilton, by far the tallest building & visible from most places, can be used as a useful landmark during your sorties

History

The suitability of İzmir's site for human habitation, with its protected harbour and rich agricultural hinterland has ensured a long and colourful history. The first settlement was situated at the northern end of the bay and dates back to 3000 BC. An Aeolian and then an Ionian city, it was in the ninth century BC that the city's most famous resident, the poet Homer, is reputed to have penned his epics in a cave nearby.

The town was re-established 300 years later across the bay at the behest of Alexander the Great, who, during a hunting trip from Sardis, stopped to sleep beneath a plane tree on the slopes of Mount Pagus, known today as Kadifekale. The Goddess Nemesis appeared to him in a dream and bid him establish a city at the site. The new city flourished becoming what Strabo, the ancient geographer and historian, described as, 'the most beautiful of all cities.'

Izmir

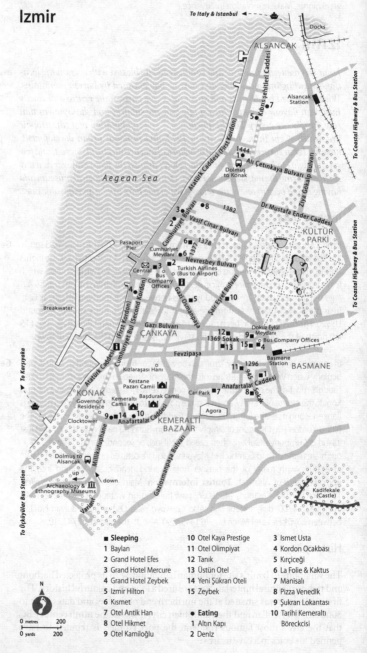

■ Sleeping	10 Otel Kaya Prestige	3 Ismet Usta
1 Baylan	11 Otel Olimpiyat	4 Kordon Ocakbaşı
2 Grand Hotel Efes	12 Tanık	5 Kırçiçeği
3 Grand Hotel Mercure	13 Üstün Otel	6 La Folie & Kaktus
4 Grand Hotel Zeybek	14 Yeni Şükran Oteli	7 Manisalı
5 Izmir Hilton	15 Zeybek	8 Pizza Venedlk
6 Kısmet		9 Şukran Lokantası
7 Otel Antik Han	● Eating	10 Tarihi Kemeraltı
8 Otel Hikmet	1 Altın Kapı	Böreckcisi
9 Otel Kamiloğlu	2 Denlz	

During Ottoman times it was scathingly referred to as Gavur (Infidel) Smyrna due to the large number of Italian, French, Dutch, British and Jewish merchants who flocked to the city. Levantines – Europeans living in the Ottoman Empire – began to outnumber Turks. A French traveller visiting in 1700 remarked, 'one seems to be in Christendom; the speech is nothing but Italian, French, English or Dutch there and the Taverns are open all Hours, Day and Night.'

Smyrna continued to prosper due to its position at the culmination of the Silk Route and at the centre of a rich agricultural hinterland producing valuable export crops such as cotton and tobacco.

The city was occupied by Greek forces in 1919, but they were driven from the mainland by nationalist troops under Atatürk just three years later. This victory marked the climax of the war to free Anatolia from foreign occupation and is celebrated throughout the country as a national holiday.

Sights

Many of the sites are clustered in and around the main business and retail district of Konak, named after the Ottoman Governor's mansion which stands on the landward side of a large pedestrianized area crowded with office workers, shoppers, hawkers and shoe-shine boys. Konak has an important administrative function with the mayor's office, police and city council headquarters housed in grim concrete buildings around the plaza. The monotonous urban landscape is partly relieved by an ornate **clock tower**, a gift to the city from Sultan Abdülhamit in 1901 which has become the city's official symbol and the pretty **Konak Camii**, its exterior decorated with brightly-coloured tiles.

From next to the Governors mansion, Anafartalar Caddesi leads into the main **bazaar** called Kemeraltı ('Under the arches'), after the arched arcade that used to be the centre of the market. Retail activity has spread out into a huge area on either side of the main thoroughfare and it is easy to become lost in a maze of alleyways and streets. There are few buildings of historic interest in Kemeraltı with the exception of **Kızlarağası Han**, but the atmosphere is relaxed and, unlike the Kapalı Çarşı in İstanbul, it's not geared up for tourism, rather the needs of the city.

Around Konak

From Konak progress up Anafartalar Caddesi and on the right you can stop for a refreshing glass of freshly squeezed juice at the **Konak Şerbetçisi**. At **Kemeraltı Camii**, the busy road veers right. Continue walking along it until you reach the **Başdurak Camii**, which has recently been restored. Turn left and facing the front of the mosque a row of small restaurants serve *kokoreç* (tripe) and delicious *midye dolması* (mussels stuffed with rice), for about US$0.20 each.

Passing the restaurants you will see an old fountain surrounded by butchers' shops, their shop-fronts festooned with red carcasses, tripe and tongue. Take the alleyway in the right-hand corner, past the shop selling hundreds of pickles colourfully displayed in jars and the pet shops alive with the sounds of a veritable Noah's Ark of small creatures. Continue straight down past several spice shops, their aromatic wares displayed in heaped buckets, and the **Kestane Pazarı Camii** (the Chestnut Market mosque) on your left to the pretty **Sadırvanaltı Camii** (1636), with its fountain and corner café, where men sit chatting and puffing away on their hookahs. Walk through the neon-lit arcade beneath the mosque and past another fountain. Take the first left after about 50 m and head straight towards the **Hisar Camii** (1598), visible ahead. Turn right at the doorway and enter the square, where there is a lively plant market, cafés and stalls selling worry beads and religious paraphernalia. Shaded by trees, two fountains take the edge off the summer heat, making this the most pleasant place

A walking tour
This circular route through the main bazaar can be done in just over an hour, but you could easily spend a lot longer soaking up the sights & buying a few bargains along the way

The Aegean Region

The Kordon

The recent history of the waterfront Kordon, eulogized throughout Turkey, has been a checkered one. Originally it was lined with graceful Leventine houses owned mostly by İzmir's well-to-do Christian minorities. Pontoons and boathouses jutted out into the crystaline waters, with the districts older residents able to remember the days when it was safe to swim off the seawall. Sadly, industrial effluent and raw sewage have gradually turned the waters into a noxious smelling, turbid soup.

Then in the late 1990s, the local government, keen to solve the city's rapidly worsening traffic problem, decided on a grandiose scheme to build a multi-lane highway along the front. With little local consultation thousands of tonnes of rubble were dumped into the bay and the Kordon was turned into an infernal, dusty building site. The project became a hot bed of political debate in the run-up to the 1998 elections and, in the face of mounting public opposition, construction ground to a

halt. And so things remained for months, with the view across the bay to the twinkling lights of Karşıyaka obscured by a mountain of rocky debris. The official word was that the rubble needed time to settle, however, in reality the mayor, Mr Özfatura, had realized his bludder: spending millions of dollars of tax payers money on a highly visible and very unpopular project. Touted as an example of government incompetence and mismanagement, the scheme contributed to Özfatura's defeat at the ballot box. Under his successor, one Mr Priştina, the plans were revised, thankfully taking greater account of the Kordon's aesthetic and social importance as a place to escape the confines of the city for a wander or an evening beer. What would have been six-lanes of traffic has thankfully been reduced to two, with the bars and restaurants now spilling out onto a wide cobbled esplanade. So the Kordon lives on and this story has a happy ending, well at least if the wind is blowing in the right direction.

to break your sightseeing for a pit stop. In winter the cafés serve hot *salep* sprinkled with cinnamon. In the corner of the square is the **Kızlarağası Hanı**, built in 1745 by the Chief Black Eunuch of Mahmut I. Handsomely restored in 1993, this is as touristy as the bazaar gets, with its arcaded passageways lined with carpet, leather and antique shops. Once you've finished browsing, walking straight down 861 Sokak after emerging from the opposite end of the *han* brings you out behind the office buildings at Konak.

To continue on to the Agora, retrace your steps to the Kestane Pazarı Camii, where a left turn takes you across the main drag and up through the food market, a lane lined with stalls and alive with the raucous cries of competing traders', to emerge from the bazaar on Eşrefpaşa Caddesi. On the opposite side of the road is a signpost for the Agora, pointing you down the side of a multi-storey car park and up some steps to the site entrance.

The Agora One of the only remaining parts of Hellenistic Smyrna left today is the Agora. Found at the base of Kadifekale, it's a conspicuously open area besieged by the modern city. It's a good place to relax and enjoy a bit of peace, particularly if you've just spent time in the frenetic confines of Kemeraltı, but paradoxically in Roman times this market place was a major focus of activity. First built in the middle of the second century AD, it was levelled some years later by a huge earthquake only to be reconstructed at the behest of Faustina II, the wife of Marcus Aurelius in AD 178. Parts of the Corinthian colonnade surrounding the courtyard have been restored and it is possible to walk beneath the well-preserved arches of the vaulted promenade, which was lined with tiny shops. There is little else to see except a jumble of assorted Ottoman tombstones, the best examples of which now adorn the archaeology museum. ■ *0830-1200, 1300-1700. US$1.50. Just off Eşrefpaşa Caddesi, behind a multi-storey car park.*

From the Agora it is a steep climb up through a labyrinth of streets to the **Kadifekale** (Velvet Castle), the ramparts of which are set on the flat-topped summit of ancient Mount Pagus. These hillside neighbourhoods are home to a large Kurdish community with many of the small homes, a few of which survived the 1922 fire, painted vividly in turquoise, yellow or red. Gangs of little children play in the streets, interrupting their games to shout their few words of English as you pass. Once at the top you can inspect the castle walls which date from medieval times, with nothing remaining of the original Hellenic construction, and join the young kite-flyers on top of the ramparts for an unrivalled view across the city, particularly impressive at around sunset. Access to the castle is unrestricted, however, nocturnal visits are not recommended. If you're not feeling very energetic you can save yourself the climb by boarding a bus, marked 'K.Kale', from near the archaeology museum in Konak.

Kadifekale
The atmosphere is a world away from the city below, as if you've been miraculously transported eastwards to a small Anatolian town

If you need a break from the hustle and bustle of the city catch one of the ferries which regularly cross the bay from the Konak or Pasaport piers to Karşıyaka, the suburb on the opposite (karşı) side of the bay. The trip takes about 20 minutes during which time you can enjoy a drink and the fresh air as you watch the city skyline recede. Once you've landed, the wide promenade, flanked on its landward side by gardens, is a good place to stroll, particularly in the cool of the evening when you'll be joined by young couples and families relaxing after work. Allow at least an hour for the roundtrip which costs US$1.

Karşıyaka

The archaeology museum houses a varied collection of finds from ancient Smyrna and other sites around the region. Many fine Roman statues are exhibited, including those of Poseidon and Demeter, unearthed at the Agora. There are also displays of metalwork, jewellery and terracotta from various periods along with artefacts discovered at the Tepekule site in Bayraklı. Exhibits are labelled in Turkish and English and there is a guidebook available. ■ *0830-1700, daily except Mon. US$2.75 (half-price with student card). Getting there: 5-mins walk from Konak up the winding road called the Variant. The entrance to the museum is on the downhill carriageway.*

Archaeology Museum

Alsancak is an upmarket residential and business area to the north of Cumhuriyet Meydanı. It has a European flavour with wide avenues and tree-lined boulevards radiating at odd angles from several large roundabouts. Café culture is well-developed and the area's affluent residents gather, designer labels and mobile phones much in evidence, in trendy establishments to see and be seen. The main street, Kıbrıs Şehitleri Caddesi, is pedestrianized and runs the length of Alsancak parallel to the bay front. In the back streets off it survive some terraces of 19th-century houses, constructed originally by European merchants who lived in the area. Some have been beautifully restored to begin life anew as family homes, while other are occupied by bars and clubs. The area is in fact the centre of Izmir's nightlife, with the waterfront Kordon and the back streets leading to it from Kıbrıs Şehitleri Caddesi, dotted with places, many playing live music of greatly varying quality. Thankfully, despite the best efforts of the city's previous mayor (see box), the Kordon is still a lovely place for an evening stroll, stopping at one of the bars which spill out onto the wide esplanade to enjoy a drink and the view across to the blinking lights of Karşıyaka.

Alsancak

The Aegean Region

Kültür Parkı An area of relatively green space east of Cumhuriyet Meydanı, the Kültür Parkı is where the İzmir International Fair is held from the 20 August to 9 September. The fair is a pretty uninspiring event consisting mainly of commercial exhibitors. The rest of the year the park, which covers an area of about 75 acres, is a pleasant enough place to stroll, although with a large number of exhibition halls, a pitiful zoo, cafés, sports facilities and a registry office, the ratio of concrete to open space is only marginally better that in the city itself. ■ *0700-2400. US$0.20.*

Essentials

Sleeping The expensive international hotels are clustered around Cumhuriyet Meydanı. Cheap
Prices in the midrange hotels are found in the area around Basmane, with the cheapest along 1296 Sokak.
establishments, These are mostly used by seasonal workers and are generally pretty grim – not recom-
particularly near mended for women travelling alone. Good value rooms with better facilities can be
Basmane, are often open found on 945 Sokak and around 1369 Sokak which heads east from 9 Eylül Meydanı.
to negotiation depending
on the time of year & how
busy they are **LL** *Grand Hotel Mercure*, Cumhuriyet Bulvarı No 138, across street from main post office, T4894090, F4894089. Modern luxury hotel with all the comforts, including indoor pool, popular with NATO personnel. **LL** *The İzmir Hilton*, Gazi Ozmanpaşa Bulvarı No 7, T4416060, F4412277. The most luxurious bed in town with 2 restaurants, bars, swimming pool, 2 roof-top tennis courts, 2 squash courts and all the other facilities you'd expect. The 40-storey giant is visible from throughout town. Special weekend rates available. **L** *Grand Hotel Efes*, Gazi Osmanpaşa Bulvarı 1, T4844300, F4415695. An İzmir institution overlooking Cumhuiyet Meydanı, now a little dated, bar, restaurant, tennis court, swimming pool. **AL** *Otel Kaya Prestige*, corner of Şair Eşref Bulvar and 1371 Sokak, T4891940, F4831498. Modern 4-star hotel, comfortable rooms with TV, telephone, a/c, minibar, also has fitness centre, bar, restaurant. Recommended for the price. **AL** *Otel Marla*, Kazim Dirik Caddesi No. 7, Pasaport, T4414000, F4411150. 4-star, new 68-room hotel, cable TV, rooftop restaurant, parking, over-priced. **A** *Hotel Hisar*, Fevzipaşa Bulvarı No.153, T4845400, F4258830. Modern, restaurant, TV, a/c, minibar, car park. Discounts available. Recommended.

B *Hotel Baylan*, 1299 Sokak No 8, Basmane, T4831426, F4833844. In quiet alley off 1296 Sokak, comfortable 1,2,3 and 4 person rooms, minibar, TV, telephone, bar, represents pretty good value, beautiful iron balcony on house opposite. Recommended. **B** *Otel Kilim*, Atatürk Bulvarı, Pasaport, between 1st and 2nd Kordons, T4845340, F4895070. Rooms with TV, minibar, telephone, bath, ask for larger corner room. Good selection of seafood in restaurant. Recommended. **B** *Otel Kısmet*, 1377 Sokak No 9, Alsancak, T4633850, F4214856. Well-equipped rooms, bar and good restaurant, situated in quiet back street. Recommended. **C** *Üstün Otel (Alsancak)*, 1420 Sokak No 79, Alsancak, T4630346, F4634764. Modern hotel on same street as Özel Sağlık hospital, clean well-equipped rooms with a/c, TV, minibar, telephone, safe, triple rooms available for US$60. Recommended. **D** *Otel Antik Han*, Anafartalar Caddesi No.600, Çankaya, T4892750, F4835925. Round the corner from the Agora. Nicely furnished rooms in newly renovated 19th-century building which was owned by Atatürk's father-in-law, excellent value, en suite bathrooms, telephone, single and triple rooms available, suites opening onto courtyard US$40, English-speaking staff. Recommended. **D** *Hotel Tanık*, 1294 Sokak No 4, Çankaya, T4414503. 2-star, with old piano in reception, reasonable rooms with TV, telephone, no breakfast. **D** *Üstün Otel (Çankaya)*, 1361 Sokak No.14, Çankaya, T4842595, F4848814. Good value rooms with a/c, TV, minibar, telephone, safe, friendly English-speaking manager. Recommended. **D** *Hotel Zeybek*, 1368 Sokak No 5-6, Basmane, T4896694, F4835020. Brightly lit and decorated, small formica-panelled rooms with bathroom, TV, telephone, open-buffet breakfast included, owned by local entrepreneur Ömer Zeybek who also runs *Grand Hotel Zeybek* across the road and cheaper *Hotel Lalesi* next door, US$21 not including breakfast.

E *Otel Kamiloğlu*, 1369 Sokak No 63, Basmane, T4837159. Old-fashioned place, plain rooms with shower, no breakfast. **F** *Otel Akpınar*, 1294 Sokak No 13, Basmane, T4463896. Basic rooms with shower cubicle in corner, breakfast extra. **F** *Otel Gönen*, 1294 Sokak No 19, Basmane, T4840569. Basic rooms, no breakfast, hot water in mornings and evenings. **F** *Otel Hikmet*, 945 Sokak No 29, Basmane, off Anafartalar just uphill from Dönertaş (small stone kiosk covered with Arabic carvings), T4842672. Homely place (in contrast to most of the other budget hotels), reception full of kitsch, clean, simple rooms, cheaper ones without bathroom, breakfast extra. Recommended. **F** *Otel Isık*, 1364 Sokak No 11, Basmane, T4831029. Basic rooms, cheaper rooms without bathroom, no breakfast. **F** *Otel Olimpiyat*, 945 Sokak No 2, Basmane, T4251269. Old Czechoslovakian switchboard in reception, cosy attic rooms on top floor, simple but clean, cheaper rooms without bathroom, breakfast available for US$1.50. Recommended. **G** *Otel Güneydoğu Palas*, 1296 Sokak No 15, Basmane, T4849201. A palace it isn't, typical of places on 1296 Sokak, basic rooms with shared bathroom, intermittent hot water. **G** *Haci Büro*, 945 Sokak No 29, Basmane, T4895967. You can't miss the paintings of the clocktower and a scene which looks like Monet's lily pond by the front door, original cornices and carving preserved under new layer of bright paint, enthusiastic owner, very basic, shared bathroom, no breakfast. **G** *Yeni Şükran Oteli*, Anafartalar Caddesi No.61, Kemeraltı, 100 m into bazaar on left, T4255068. High-ceilinged rooms around bustling courtyard, formerly used by camel-drivers, basic facilities but loads of atmosphere, for a real cheapy look no further, check out balcony overlooking main drag, use safe provided at reception for valuables. Recommended.

Expensive *Collonade Restaurant*, 8th floor of the Hilton, T4416060, specially themed buffets for US$37 per person with unlimited alcohol. Recommended. *Deniz Restaurant*, Kordon, Atatürk Caddesi No 188-B, T4220601. The town's best seafood restaurant, well-cooked fish and attentive service, popular for business dinners. **Eating**

Midrange *Çato*, Varyant (ascending carriageway). Turkish cuisine with an excellent view. *Ismet Usta*, Cumhuriyet Bulvarı, one block north of İzmir sineması, T4840132. Up-market soup restaurant, *mercimek* (lentil) *işkembe* (tripe) and lots more. *Otel Kısmet Restaurant*, 1377 Sokak No 9, Alsancak, T4633850. Varied menu with tasty continental and Turkish cuisine. *Pizza Venedik*, 1382 Gül Sokak 10-B, Alsancak, T4222735. Large and popular pizza restaurant, tables outside. *Altın Kapı*, 1444 Sokak, Alsancak, just off Kıbrıs şehitleri Caddesi, T4222709. Institution which is slowly taking over whole street, kebaps of all shapes and sizes including chicken şiş, also newly opened fish restaurant. *La Folie*, Nevresbey Bulvarı, behind Grand Efes Hotel. Pasta, sandwiches, salads, along with more substantial Mediterranean cuisine. *Le Trio*, 1386 Sokak, Alsancak. The closest thing to a bistro that you'll find in town, meat-orientated menu, tasty dishes such as chicken with a cream and almond sauce, very popular with locals, tables outside.

Cheap **Konak and the bazaar** There are several good *iskender* and *köfte* places around the Kemeraltı Camii in Konak: *Uludağ Iskender Salonu*, opposite the mosque on 853 Sokak, delicious *iskender* drenched in yoghurt and butter; also the *Bursalılar* next door, serves köfte (meat-balls) at very economical prices; *Şaşlik Ocakbaşı*, 30 m up 866 Sokak from mosque, slightly smarter meat restaurant, tables outside, still very reasonable prices, special of meatballs, *piyaz* (white bean salad) and a drink for US$2.50. *Park Café Konak*, Şehit Fethibey Caddesi No 4/1, smart, modern self-service restaurant, very economical Turkish dishes and western fast food, köfte US$2. *Şükran Lokantası*, in courtyard of *Yeni Şükran Oteli*, Konak, popular with local traders, simple steam-tray food and kebaps. *Tarihi Kemeraltı Börekcisi*, on Anafatalar Caddesi just past Kemeraltı Mosque, Konak, good selection of börek, served with warm milk for breakfast. In the bazaar the small square beside the Kızlarağası Hanı is an excellent place to have a pit-stop. Around the shady courtyard are stalls selling baked potatoes and *söğuş* (mutton, sheep's brain, slices of tomato and parsley wrapped in a pancake) along with several kebap places such as *Çevirme Döner ve Kebap*, which serves *iskender* and a drink for about US$2.50.

Basmane Opposite Basmane station and on 1369 Sokak there are lots of cheap restaurants serving kebaps, pide and ready-prepared dishes, including *Ödemiş, Azım* and *Tokat*. A good place to head for a cheap meal is 1379 Sokak, off Şehit Nevresbey Bulvarı, where a line of snack-bars serve **baked potatoes** (*kumpir*) with a choice of fillings for about US$2. *Pide Fabrika 2*, Fevzipaşa Bulvarı, 100 m down from station on left, 'the pide factory', modern place serving all types of pide, the more unusual varieties include potato and chicken.

Alsancak and Çankaya *Kırçiçeği*, Kıbrıs Şehitleri Caddesi No 83, Alsancak, T4220691. Good soup, pide and kebap restaurant serving 24-hrs, try their *manisalı kebabı* – köfte on a raft of bread, drenched with butter, yoghurt and tomato sauce, crowded with clubbers in the early hours, also serve beer. *Kordon Ocakbası*, opposite *Topcu'nun Yeri*, Cumhuriyet Bulvarı. Excellent *pirzola* (lamb chops) and other grilled meats. *Manisalı*, Kıbrıs Şehitleri, Alsancak. One of several other places serving Manisa kebaps, delicious variation on a theme. *Pizza, Pizza*, Kıbrıs şehitleri Caddesi, Alsancak. One of several places which are permanently crowded, slices of pizza and fries. *Terrasse Et Lokantası*, 1379 Sokak No 59, Çankaya, next to Karaca Cinema, road between *Hilton* and *Büyük Efes Oteli*. Ready prepared meat and vegetable dishes, kebaps, grills, fish. *Topçu'nun Yeri*, Kazim Dirik Caddesi No 3, Çankaya. Large place which has built its reputation on soup and *çöp şiş* – tender pieces of lamb grilled on small bamboo skewers, also have a bar, open late with tables on the street.

Street snacks Mussels stuffed with delicately spiced rice and pine-nuts (US$0.20 each), hawked from silver trays by street vendors throughout the city, are a delicious snack. There are also several places serving mussels in Kemeraltı (see walking tour). Avoid eating them during the hot summer months, though. Another good snack are the toasted rolls filled with cheese, egg, and salami (US$1.50) prepared at street stalls across the city. Ask for a 'karışık sandviç' with meat or 'peynirli' with just cheese. One particularly popular kiosk is at the Lozan Meydanı, to the west of the Kültür Parkı. The *İzmirli* are particularly fond of sweet milky puddings and there are several chains of brightly lit tatlıcı (sweet-makers), such as *Hasan Usta* or *Özsut*. Specialities include *kazan dibi* (bottom of the pan), a creamy desert with a burnt, caramelized top, and *tavuk göğsü*, a glutinous pudding which contains finely shredded chicken.

Vegetarian *Vejetaryan Restaurant*, 1375 Sokak No 11, Çankaya, near the American-Turkish Cultural Centre. The city's only vegetarian restaurant, good selection of dishes including some with chicken. Set menus for under US$5.

Cafés *Café Biyer*, Mustafabay Caddesi No 3/B, Alsancak. Up-market café which has extensive menu: pastas, salads, meat and chicken dishes served all day. *Bonjour*, corner of Plevne Caddesi and Dr Mustafa Ender Caddesi, Alsancak. Very popular café, serve huge sandwiches which come with fries and salad, tasty crepes, ice-creams and cakes. *Café Cine*, 1379 Sokak, Çankaya, next to Karaca cinema. Excellent cakes and cookies. *Café Plaza*, Mustafabay Caddesi No 4, Alsancak. Trendy café popular with wealthy young things. *Reyhan*, corner of Plevne Caddesi and Dr Mustafa Ender Caddesi, Alsancak. A selection of the best cream cakes in town for a very upmarket clientele. There are several more down-to-earth cafés on Kıbrıs Şehitleri Caddesi, where local workers and students sit on plastic stools and watch the world go by.

Bars The waterfront Kordon, where you can sit outside and watch the promenade, is by far the nicest place to drink and there is certainly no shortage of places to choose from. A small selection includes: *Deniz Atı*, south of German Consulate, small rock bar popular with İzmir's middle-class biker crowd; *Baryum*, upmarket bar/restaurant, with live Turkish classical music, tables outside; *Mexican bar*, semi-latin feel, snacks and light-meals served; *La Sera*, large bar and restaurant, live Turkish and Latin music nightly, tables outside. Elsewhere in Alsancak: *Eko*, tables on the street in square where Cumhuriyet Bulvarı and Ali Çetinkaya Caddesi meet in Alsancak; *Doy-doy*, corner of Cumhuriyet Bulvarı and 1407 Sokak, shady tables on the street, darts, popular with ex-pats, particularly NATO personnel; *Kybele Rock Bar*, just off Kıbrıs Şehitleri Caddesi, near Italian Consulate, small intimate place with lively, regular crowd, live rock and dancing. **Clubs** *Always*, First Kordon, by Pasaport, techno, hip-hop and Turkish. *Club 33*, same street as Punta, away from the bay, techno. *Mavi*, converted Leventine house on Cumhuriyet Bulvarı, behind German consulate, live band playing classic rock, good atmosphere. *Outside*, opposite the Kapalı Spor Salonu, techno, lasers, lights. *Punta*, far end of Kıbrıs Şehitler Caddesi, 2 floors, roof terrace, live bands. *Tatoo*, in side street off Kıbrıs Şehitleri Caddesi, opposite Italian Consulate, heavy metal, rock, studenty crowd.

Bars & clubs
Quite a variety of night spots with the distinction between bars, clubs & restaurant often blurred. Some bars charge an admission fee, which normally includes a free drink, while many of the bars along the Kordon serve food & have live music

There are cinemas throughout the city showing the latest western releases with Turkish subtitles. For programs check the Turkish Daily News. Tickets cost US$3.50, half-price for students. *Sema Sineması*, top floor of Kemer Plaza shopping centre, Anafartalar Caddesi. *Çınar Sineması*, Konak SSK, E blok, the big concrete buildings lining Millikütüphane Caddesi, T2771100. *İzmir Sineması*, Atatürk Caddesi No 188, T4214261. *Karaca*, 1379 Sokak, between *Grand Efes Hotel* and *Hilton Hotel*, T4839354.

Cinemas

The International İzmir Festival runs from **mid-Jun** to the **end of Jul** and includes some top international acts. The events are held in İzmir, Çeşme and Ephesus. For a list of ticket agents and the programme of events contact the İzmir Culture Foundation, Şair Eşref Bulvarı, Park Apartment 58/4, T4630077 or the tourist office. *The İzmir International Film Festival* in **Apr** is a chance to see foreign and Turkish films at a number of venues around the city. Contact the tourist office for a programme.

Festivals

İzmir does not have much to offer in the way of shopping, although the boutiques of Alsancak have fashionable clothes at reasonable prices, while the best place to hunt for souvenirs is in the Kızlarağası Hanı in the bazaar area. Carpet shops in the restored 17th-century *han* include *Ahtamara*, No 21/P36. There are also stalls selling silver jewellery and a couple of antique shops: *Pazar Antik*, No 19/P35 and *Anatolian Collection*, inner courtyard, antique copper and metalware. *Toprak Çocukları*, inner courtyard, sells interesting locally produced ceramics. Strolling down *Sevgi Yolu* (Lover's Lane), a pedestrianized street between Gaziosmanpaşa and Şehit Nevresbey Bulvarı in Çankaya, you're bound to come across a few trystic couples, but the street is also home to street artists, second-hand book sellers and silver stalls. **Bookshops** *Net Bookshop*, Cumhuriyet Bulvarı 142/B, Alsancak, 1 block north of Cumhuriyet Meydanı on right, good selection of newspapers and magazines, small selection of English books. *Dünya*, Cumhuriyet Bulvarı 143/B, Alsancak, next to cinema, English newspapers and magazines. *Yavuz Kitabevi*, Tibaşhan, Konak, take first right off Anafartalar Caddesi, 50 m on the left, foreign newspapers and magazines. **Photography** *Foto Reşat*, 857 Sokak No17 P/15, Konak, T4836311, first right heading north from the clocktower, cameras, tripods, good selection of film. For **camera repairs**: *Hüseyin Sayar*, Kemeraltı, Havuzlu Çarçısı No 12, T4843771, is recommended. *Havuzlu Çarşısı* is on the left after the Kemeraltı Camii, his shop is at the far end. *Chroma Copy*, Şehit Nevres Bulvarı No 9, Alsancak, T4632998, develop transparency and print film. *Mehmetler*, Kıbrıs Şehitler Caddesi No 4, Alsancak, T4226287, 1 of many places around town offering fast print processing.

Shopping
There are no bookshops with anything more than a very limited selection of foreign books. Newspapers are on sale at some large hotels

The Aegean Region

Sport **Football** You can buy tickets to watch the local team Altay at the *İzmir Stadium*, Şehitler Caddesi, follow the traffic past the Alsancak harbour. **Basketball** Matches are held in the *Kapalı Sports Salonu*, Ali Çetinkaya Bulvarı. Alsancak stops when there is a home victory as boisterous fans celebrate in the streets. **Cycling shops** There are lots of small shops along Fevzipaşa Bulvarı between 1361 and 1366 Sokak. *Sundu Bisiklet*, 1361 Sokak No9, T4412463, is the best, good selection of parts and accessories. *Granite*, Plevne Caddesi, Alsancak, T4222125, owner will put together bikes from the components of your choice. Regular outings organized at the weekends. Highly recommended. **Scuba diving** *Ege Barakuda*, Mithatpaşa Caddesi, 334/1, Karataş, T4450379, sells good selection of equipment, PADI courses, regular weekend trips.

Tour operators *Ihlas Turizm*, Gaziosmanpaşa Bulvarı No1/1-F, Alsancak, T4892881, F4890539, next to
There are lots of travel tourist office, range of tours, flight bookings. *Opal Travel*, Gaziosmanpaşa Bulvarı
agents in the area No1/1-B, Alsancak, T4456767, F4898865, daily and longer tours, yacht trips, flights.
inland of Cumhuriyet *Karavan*, 1378 Sokak 4/1-C, Alsancak, T4223725 F4224168, karavan@superonline.
Bulvarı, around the com, round the corner from *Net bookshop*, Chios and Italian ferry boat agent, domes-
international hotels tic and international flights, tours. *FAI*, Akdeniz Caddesi No8, Alsancak, T4467110,
F4894031. *Esin Turizm*, Şehit Fethi Bey Bulvarı No.122/F, T4461050, F4830031. *Rainbow Tour Turkey*, Halit Ziya Bulvarı No72/602, www.rainbow.turkeylink.com, near
Grand Hotel Efes, T4461637, specialize in tours of the Seven Churches of the Revelation and other faith tours.

Transport **Local** **Yellow taxis**, many of which are powered by natural gas, are a fast and relatively cheap way of getting around central İzmir. Make sure the driver turns on the meter when you get in. The cities **buses** are generally slow and crowded. You must first purchase a ticket (US$0.30) from 1 of the kiosks or shops located near main bus stops and this is posted into the box as you get on. There are also a growing number of modern buses run by Izulaş, a private company, on which you purchase a ticket once you get on. The **taxi-dolmuş** operating between Alsancak Garı and Konak (US$0.40) are particularly useful for traversing the centre and can be flagged down anywhere on their route: south along the waterfront on the Kordon and Cumhuriyet north along Bulvarı, before turning inland on Talatpaşa Bulvarı. Regular passenger **ferries** cross the bay from Konak and Pasaport to Karşıyaka and Bayraklı on the opposite side of the bay. After years of work the eagerly awaited **metro** opened for the new millenium. It crosses the city from the northern suburb of Bornova to Üçyol, south of Konak. Unfortunately, it is of little use for visitors except for travelling between Konak and Basmane railway station. The modern trains run every 5-10 mins, 0600-2400, US$0.30.

Long distance Air Adnan Menderes airport information line, T2742626. 13 flights daily to **İstanbul** and 7 to **Ankara**. Flights to other cities and international destinations are via İstanbul or Ankara. *Turk Kıbrıs Havayolları* have direct flights to London Heathrow on Sat and Mon.

Bus Depart regularly from the monolithic bus terminal in Pınarbaşı for destinations all over the country. Buy your ticket in advance particularly at weekends and during the holiday season as things get very booked up. Public transport to the bus terminal is inadequate with only the infrequent bus no 601 running from Montro and Alsancak. It is better to buy your ticket from the bus company offices clustered on Gaziosmanpaşa Bulvarı opposite the *Grand Hotel Efes* or the Dokuz Eylül Meydanı, near Basmane, and use the free shuttle services. **Ankara**, every hr, 8 hrs, US$16; **Antalya**, every 2-3 hrs, 9 hrs, US$16; **Bergama**, every hr, US$4, **Bodrum**, every hr, 4 hrs, US$8; **Denizli**, every hr, 4 hrs, US$9; **İstanbul**, every hr, 8 hrs, from US$16.50; **Konya**, every 2 hrs, US$16; **Kuşadası**, every hr, US$3; **Manisa**, every 30 mins, US$2;

Marmaris, every 2 hrs, 6 hrs, US$12; **Sardis**, bus every 30 mins to Salihli, US$3; **Selçuk**, every 30 mins, 0600-1900, 1½ hrs, US$2.75. Luxury services to İstanbul, Ankara and Antalya are operated by *Varan* and *Ulusoy*, whose offices are on Gaziosmanpaşa Bulvarı, opposite the *Grand Hotel Efes*. Buses to **Çeşme** (1½ hrs) and **Karaburun** (2 hrs)depart from the Üçkuyular terminal, 6 km west of Konak. City buses run from next to the waterfront in Konak to Balçova, passing the terminal.

Car hire In town, car rental offices are clustered around Cumhuriyet Meydanı. *Avis*, Şair Eşref Bulvarı No 18, Çankaya, T4414417, F4414420. *Bil di Tur*, 1377 Sokak No.8/D, Alsancak, T4644332, F4631308, opposite *Otel Kısmet*. *Budget*, Şair Eşref Bulvarı No 22/1, Çankaya T4419224. *Europcar*, Şehit Fethi Bey Caddesi No 122, Çankaya T4415521, F4830031.

Most car hire companies have an office at the arrivals terminal of the airport

Ferries Turkish Maritime Lines, T4211484, F4211481, operates car ferries to: **İstanbul**, Sun 1400, 18 hrs, cabin half-board is US$56-$43 per person depending on cabin, seat US$20; **Venice**, Wed 1600, 62 hrs, double cabin full-board, class A: US$328, B: US$311, C: US$250, single US$185. Ferries depart from the docks at the end of Atatürk Caddesi (Kordon) in Alsancak.

Train Train services leave from Basmane station, T4848638. From Konak catch a dolmuş from Millikütüpane Caddesi to the station. **Ankara**, *Durnlupınar Mavi Treni* via Manisa and Afyon at 1835 daily, 16 hrs; *Ankara Mavi Treni* via Manisa and Kütahya at 1820 daily, 14 hrs; *Karesi Ekspresi* via Manisa and Kutahya at 1900 daily, 15 hrs. **Bandırma**, *Marmara Ekspresi* via Manisa at 0830 daily, 9 hrs; **Denizli**, *Denizli Ekspresi* via Adnan Menderes airport, Selçuk, Aydin and stations along the Büyük Menderes Valley at 0830, 1515 and 1805 daily, 5 hrs. **Isparta**, *Goller Ekspresi* via Selçuk and stations along the Büyük Menderes Valley at 2130 daily, 12 hrs. **Eskişehir**, *Ege Ekspresi* 0640. Bandırma and Ankara trains stop at **Manisa**, extra services at 0630 and 1800, US$0.75.

Airline offices *Turkish Airlines*, Gaziosmanpaşa Bulvarı No 1/F, Çankaya, next to *Grand Hotel Efes*, T4841220, T4258280 (reservations), open 0830-1930, 0830-1730 Sun, office at the airport is open longer hours; *İstanbul Airlines*, Gaziosmanpaşa Bulvarı, Çankaya, opposite *Grand Hotel Efes*, T4213666, open office-hours, Tue flight to İstanbul; *Turk Kıbrıs Havayolları*, Şehit Nevres Bulvarı, Çankaya, behind *Grand Hotel Efes*, T4649095, open 0830-1700 weekdays; *Swissair*, Atatürk Meydanı No 11, Çankaya, T4634960. **Banks** There are banks with ATM throughout the city. There are also private change places to the north of the clock tower in Konak and at the southern end of Kıbrıs Şehitler Caddesi in Alsancak. **Baths** *Hamam*, Anafartalar Caddesi No 501, tiled building facing a multi-storey car-park, despite the highly inflated 'tourist price' set by the local government, you should be able to negotiate a wash and *kese* for about US$8. **Communications** Post office: the main post office is on Cumhuriyet Meydanı is open 24-hrs. You can make International calls using counter-phones and also send faxes, open 0800-1900. There are local post offices throughout the city. Internet: the Tourist Police booth at the Konak end of Anafartalar Caddesi offers free internet access to foreign travellers. *Artek Internet centre*, Meriç Apartmanlar, 1st floor, 1408 Sokak, Alsancak, across Şair Eşref Bulvarı from the Alsancak Camii, US$1.50 per hr. *seçkin Internet Café*, Mimar Kemalettin Caddesi No 16, above restaurant of same name, US$1.50 per hr. **Consulates** *UK*, 1442 Sokak, No 49, Alsancak, T4635151, F4212914. *Germany*, Atatürk Caddesi No 260, Alsancak, T4216995. *Netherlands*, 1881 Sokak No 30, Balçova, T4210542, F4636458. *Norway*, 1378 Sokak No 4/1, Kordon Işhanı Kat 2/201. *Sweden*, 1378 Sokak No 4/1, Kordon Işhanı Kat 2/202, Alsancak, T4222322, F4220690. **Cultural centres** *The British Council*, 1374 Sokak, Selvili Iş Merkezi No 18, floor 3, D:301, Çankaya, T4460132. *French Cultural Centre*, Cumhuriyet Bulvarı No 152, Alsancak, 14636142. *Turkish American Association*, Şehit Nevres Bulvarı No 23, Çankaya, T4218873. **Medical facilities** Hospitals: *Özel Saşlık Hastanesi*, 1399 Sokak, Alsancak, good private hospital. *Alsancak Devlet Hastanesi*, Aliçetinkaya Bulvarı, Alsancak, state hospital, recommended for emergencies only. **Language schools** *Tömer*, Kıbrıs Şehitleri Caddesi No 55, Alsancak, T4640544, tomer@bi.net.tr, branch of Ankara University which runs Turkish and other foreign language

Directory

T-e Aegean Region

courses. **Laundry** *Büyük Otel Efes Kuru Temizleme*, Gaziosmanpaşa Bulvarı, next to tourist information office, rather expensive dry cleaning. **Places of Worship** *St. John's*, 1442 Sokak No 49, Alsancak, Anglican church, Sunday services held. *St Mary's*, Gaziosmanpaşa Bulvarı, Çankaya, opposite tourist information office, Catholic church, mass held 1100 Sun. *International Protestant Fellowship*, Cumhuriyet Bulvarı No 88, Kat 6, T4259458, lighthouseic.org, along with weekly prayer meetings, the church's members are involved in a variety of other activities including voluntary work with local street children. **Useful addresses Tourist Police**: *Konak*, small booth near beginning of Anafartalar Caddesi, free internet access, T4890500. *Basmane*, 9 Eylül Meydanı, beside entrance to Kültür Parkı.

Çeşme

Phone code: 0232
Colour map 1, grid C1

Çeşme is at the western end of a peninsular that reaches out into the Aegean almost touching the Greek island of Chios. An impressive Genoese fort dominates the town, which in season gears-up for the arrival of domestic holidaymakers and a few foreign package tourists. There are some reasonable beaches in the surrounding area, particularly favoured by windsurfers due to the strength and constancy of the wind. The town is the arrival point for ferry services from Chios and ports in Italy, which in summer disgorge a procession of ex-patriot Turks returning for their summer holidays.

Ins & outs
See page 263 for further details

Getting there Çeşme is at the end of a 6-lane strip of blissfully smooth toll-road stretching the 85 km from İzmir (US$1.50). Avoid the motorway on Sun evenings in the summer when half of İzmir pack-up their picnics and head for home. Buses link the town with İzmir every 20 mins, passing through the outlying resorts of Alaçatı and Ilıca on the way. **Getting around** The *otogar* is 1 km south of the main square. If you arrive aboard a ferry from Italy then the town is across the harbour, a 10-min walk or 2-min taxi ride away. The tourist office is in front of the castle, next to the police station. T/F7126653. Open weekdays 0830-1900, weekends 0900-1700.

Sights

Dominating the harbour the **castle** was built by the Genoese in the 14th century and strengthened after its capture by the Ottoman Sultan Beyazıt. It is possible to climb up to the battlements to enjoy the view over the marina and across to Chios while in the north tower there's a small exhibition from Erythrae. ■ *0830-1200, 1300-1700 daily. US$1.*

Situated next to the castle is a **caravanserai** constructed in 1528, by order of Süleyman the Magnificent. It was restored in 1980 and now houses a hotel. On the other side of the castle stands the **statue of Cezayirli Gazi Hasan**, who was a famous Ottoman admiral and politician. It is nice to walk around some of the back streets of the town where a few **old Greek buildings** have survived. The **Orthodox church** halfway-up Inkilap Caddesi has recently been restored and will host cultural events in the near future.

Beaches
Boats leave on day-trips calling at points around the peninsular from near the Ertan Oteli. Prices are US$13.50 per person including lunch

Dolmuş depart regularly from behind the tourist information office for all the outlying villages and beaches. One of the best beaches is 6 km east at **Ilıca**, where a long stretch of fine white sand is backed by holiday homes, strangely reminiscent of suburban Florida and hotels. There are hot springs at the end of the beach (which gets very crowded at the weekends). İzmir buses call in at the bus station near the main road. There is very little in the way of accommodation, an interesting exception being **F** *Karabina Sahil Oteli*, on the front near the marina, T7231010, a long Greek building with shuttered windows, plenty of character though the waterless rooms are pretty simple, downstairs tiled tubs are filled with hot water from thermal springs, said to have been used by Atatürk.

Several kilometres beyond **Alaçatı**, having passed beneath the İzmir-Çeşme highway, there are some exposed beaches popular with windsurfers. **Surf**

paradise is on the large, shallow bay just beyond the marina. There is a snack bar, camping facilities and board rental open from mid-April to November. A board and wetsuit cost from US$38 per day and you can also take lessons. The strength and constancy of the wind, the very thing that attracts windsurf aficionados, makes it less than ideal for beginners and bathers. Nearby is **D** *Herman Surf Paradise Pansiyon*, T7166295, newly-built, clean rooms with bathroom and balcony, rooftop bar and restaurant, very convenient for windsurfing.

Altınkum is a series of small white-sand coves, 10 km south of Çeşme, just beyond the village of **Çiftliköy**. There are several campsites and places offering bungalow accommodation including *Altınkum Turistic Motel and Camping*, T7221221, bungalows overlooking sea, gets very hot in summer.

The one-time village of **Dalyan Köy**, just to the north, is now little more than a suburb of Çeşme where Turks come to indulge their love for seafood in the expensive harbour-side restaurants. There is a small beach protected from the omnipresent wind, but it gets very crowded.

The Karaburun (black nose) Peninsula juts out northwards from the Çeşme Peninsula almost enclosing the Gulf of İzmir. The turn-off to Karaburun is signposted on the İzmir-Çeşme highway after the town of **Urla**. The two-lane road then winds along the coast past scattered summerhouse developments and litter-prone beaches popular with picnickers from İzmir. After 20 km you reach the village of **Balıklova**, where there are several small fish restaurants, shops and a couple of bakeries selling delicious crusty bread. A sharp left turn on the far side of town, takes you across the neck of the peninsular past the melancholy ruins of a Greek village and through olive groves carpeted with flowers in spring.

Karaburun Peninsula

Spared from major development due to its craggy coastline & sinuous roads & so manages to retain a wild, windswept feel. The cold clear waters off the coast are favoured by divers

The Aegean Region

Çeşme

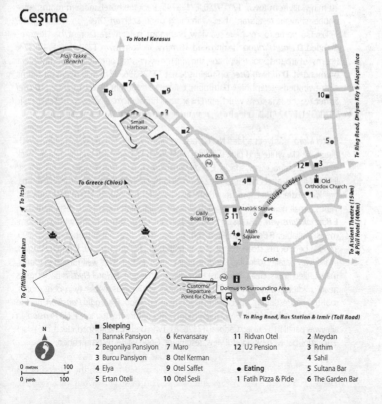

N

| 0 metres | 100 |
| 0 yards | 100 |

■ Sleeping			
1 Bannak Pansiyon	6 Kervansaray	11 Rıdvan Otel	2 Meydan
2 Begonilya Pansiyon	7 Maro	12 U2 Pension	3 Rıthım
3 Burcu Pansiyon	8 Otel Kerman		4 Sahil
4 Elya	9 Otel Saffet	● Eating	5 Sultana Bar
5 Ertan Oteli	10 Otel Sesli	1 Fatih Pizza & Pide	6 The Garden Bar

At a junction ahead the left-hand fork takes you south towards Erythrae and Çeşme, while the other road winds along the western coast of the peninsular past several pebble beaches, clean and deserted even in summer. Continuing from Balıklova towards Karaburun, the road passes *Karanoz Camping*, in a cove with a pebbly beach, which has toilets, showers and a restaurant serving simple food. From **Mordoğan**, which is an uninspiring place with possibilities for accommodation and restaurants, the coastline becomes more rocky with views across to Foça on a clear day. **Kaynarpınar** is a tiny fishing village, amidst the olive and citrus trees with a restaurant and the simple *Marina Pansiyon*, T7381042. The town of **Karaburun** itself is an anti-climax, however, there are several good fish restaurants by the harbour (*iskele*) and a beach to the north of town. From Karaburun the road continues its loop around the desolate treeless north of the peninsular to the old Greek village of **Kuçukbahçe**. ■ *Getting there: Regular dolmuş from İzmir's Üçkuyular bus terminal running along the coastal road to Mordoğan and Karaburun. No public transport on the west side of the island.*

Sleeping

Dominated by pensions & small hotel, 2 & 3-star hotels found in the main square & along the ring-road, just outside town. Luxury hotels are found outside the town in Boyalık & Ilıca

L *Hotel Boyalık Beach*, 2 km from centre on Ilıca road, white monolith backing beach, T7127081, F7127331. Facilities include restaurants, bars, swimming pools, tennis, watersports, disco. **AL** *Hotel Kerasus*, 1½ km from town past Tekke Plajı, T7120506, F7127938. Large 4-star hotel, 4 pools, sauna, fitness centre, private beach, suites, restaurant, bar. **C** *Otel Kerman*, next to Tekke Plajı, T7127112, F7127728. Good location, relatively expensive, small rooms with bathroom, sea views, small balconies, family suites, restaurant, roof bar, yacht tours organized. **C** *Kervansaray Hotel*, T7127177, F7126492. 30 double rooms with bathroom in historic Caravansarai, backrooms cheaper, telephone, bar, restaurant. **D** *Hotel Çalış*, on the ring road opposite Pırıl, 10-min walk from town, T7129750, F7129745. Package hotel, modern rooms, telephone, shower, restaurant, bar, swimming pool. **D** *Ertan Oteli*, on main square, T7126336. Some rooms have sea view, bathroom, balcony, restaurant, bar. Recommended. **D** *Hotel Pırıl*, on the ring road, 10 min walk from town, T7127538, F7127574. Rooms set around pool, telephone, shower, fitness centre, sauna, bar, restaurant. Recommended. **D** *Ridvan Otel*, on main square, T7126336, F7127627. Pleasant rooms with twin beds, telephone, bathroom, balcony, restaurant. Recommended. **D** *Otel Saffet*, reached via steps which start near small harbour, road access past Tekke Plajı, T7120331, F7127152. Telephone, restaurant, open buffet breakfast, safe box.

E *Otel Maro*, Hürriyet Caddesi No. 68, behind *Otel Kerman*, T7126252, F7127267. Wedding cake-like white and pink building, triple room **D**, clean and bright, cheaper back rooms, front terrace, bar, snacks. **E** *Seda Pansiyon*, coming from castle take first left off Inkilap Caddesi after church, T7126228. Small family pension, clean comfortable rooms, breakfast extra. **E** *Otel Sesli*, from castle take left after the church, 150 m past Seda and Venüs. Small neat hotel, rooms with shower, small swimming pool, restaurant, bar. **E** *Barınak Pansiyon*, upstairs on far side of harbour. Quiet, simple rooms with bathroom, meals available. **F** *Begonilya Pansiyon*, on the front near small harbour, T7120990. 1/2/3/4 bed rooms, clean, bright, shared bathroom. Recommended. **F** *Burcu Pension*, in alleyway parallel to Inkilap Caddesi, near church, T7120387. 9 well-furnished rooms, marble tiled floors, clean, breakfast extra. Recommended. **F** *Hotel Elya*, in back streets near children's playground, T7128327. Good value, reasonable twin-bed rooms, roof-top bar/restaurant, specializing in southeastern food. **F** *Köroğlu Pansiyon*, next to small harbour, T7126086. Basic triple rooms with bathroom, terrace. **F** *U2 Pension*, in alleyway parallel to Istiklap Caddesi, T7126381. Twin beds, pine finished, clean, breakfast extra, roof-bar with wonderful view, restaurant. Good value, recommended.

Midrange *Castle Restaurant*, entrance in seaward wall of castle, romantic setting, Turkish dishes and seafood. *Meydan* and *Sahil* Restaurants, both on the main square, have meze, fish and pizza, however, you are better off walking along the front, where there are lots of smart places including *Körfez*, *Bistro Penguen* and *Papillon*, which serves a good selection of pizza at lunch. For seafood look no further than *Rıhtım Restaurant*, beside the small harbour, with tables next to the water. Good selection of meze and the catch of the day. **Cheap** *Inkilap Caddesi* has a wide choice of cheap kebap restaurants. Clustered around the church are several snack bars and pide places, including *Fatih Pizza and Pide*. Try a 'kumru', a toasted sesame seed roll with cheese (peynir), meat (karışık) and tomatoes from the stands beside the castle.

There is a rapid turn-over of bars in the town with most lasting just a season. A survivor is *Sultana Bar*, Köste Caddesi, first left after church when coming from castle, small, friendly, Turkish music. *The Garden Bar*, 25 m up Inkilap Caddesi from the square on the right, has interesting interior with trees incorporated into bar, reasonably priced, eclectic music.

Çeşme is a venue for *International İzmir Festival* events, check at the tourist office for details. The *Çeşme Film Festival* is held every year at the end of **Aug**.

There are several shops on Inkilap Caddesi selling local-made **jams** and **preserves** (*reçel*). The white one is made from *sakız*, pinegum, which is the main product of the adjacent island of Chios and from where it gets its Turkish name, Sakız Adası.

Agencies dealing with ferry tickets are found beside the castle and along the main road approaching the harbour. *Ertürk*, Beyazıt Cad. No7/8, Çeşme, T7126768, F7126223, specialize in Chios and Italian ferry services, rent-a-car. *Karavan Tourism*, Belediye Dükkanlar No.3, Çeşme, T7127230, F7126987, flights and ferries to Italian ports, also have an office in İzmir.

Bus Services run from İzmir's Üçkuyular bus terminal at least every 30 mins via **Ilıca** and **Alaçatı** (US$2.50), taking 75 mins. There are also services to **İstanbul**, **Ankara**, **Marmaris**, **Bodrum** and **Fethiye** by various companies including *Ulusoy*, *Varan* and *Kamil Koç*. **Ferry To Chios**: ferries depart from the docks in front of the castle, from where there are services to **Samos**, **Lesbos**, **Pireaus** and **Thessaloniki**. It is possible to go for a day trip, returning in the evening. During the winter there is 1 boat per week leaving on Thu at 0900. In May and Oct boats leave on Tue and Thu at 0900. In Jun boats leave on Tue, Thu and Sat at 0900 and Sun at 1600. From 1st Jul to 10th Sep boats leave at 0900 on Tue, Thu and Sat and at 1600 on Fri and Sun. From 11th to 30th Sep services on Tue and Thu at 0900, Fri and Sun at 1600. All ferries return from Chios at 1800, except those from 1st Nov to 30th May, which return at 1600. **To Italy**: *Turkish Maritime Lines* have regular ferries to **Brindisi**, Mon 2300, Tue 1100, Fri 1100 and 2300, (32 hrs), prices are the same as İzmir-Venice, but this ferry is much faster. Ferries also depart for the Italian ports of **Trieste**, **Bari** and **Ancona** from the docks on the opposite side of the harbour from the town. These services are subject to frequent changes and are particularly unreliable in the winter. It is best to check with an agent in Çeşme (see above), İzmir or İstanbul on the current services.

Banks Many banks with ATM machines and bureau de change facilities can be found on the main square and Inkilap Caddesi. **Baths** *Tourist Baths*, past the *Kervansaray Hotel*, name leaves little to guess about the authenticity, expensive at US$15 for a complete wash and massage. **Communications Post office**: The PTT is on the waterfront 100 m from the main square. **Medical facilities Dentist**: *Zafer Gürbüz*, Inkilap Caddesi, No. 66, Çeşme, T7126969, T7126907 (home). **Doctor**: *Dr Sirus Afşaroğlu*, Inkilap Caddesi, No 2, Çeşme, T7127492, T7167792 (home).

Eating

Bars

Festivals

Shopping

Tour agencies

Transport

Directory

To Kuşadası

The coast south to Kuşadası is relatively undeveloped except around Gümüldür & Özdere where summerhouses crowd the coastal plain. On the other hand there is little to get excited about

Leaving the İzmir-Çeşme highway at the turn-off for Kuşadası and Seferhisar, the road crosses the base of the Çeşme Peninsula 21 km to the town of **Seferhisar**. Reached through the orange groves, 9 km west of Seferhisar, is the small fishing town of **Sığarcık** which, until recently, was enclosed entirely within the walls of a Genoese fortress. It's a sleepy place where fishermen mend their nets on the quayside and idle away their time in the cafés. This may be all set to change with the completion of a 400-yacht marina complex. Walking around its back streets you'll also discover some fine Ottoman houses. Its hotels and pensions are a favourite haunt of *İzmirli* men enjoying an afternoon of extra-marital activity. Past the marina a road winds over the peninsular to **Akkum**, a short stretch of white sand in a sheltered cove, backed by several restaurants, shops, changing facilities and the large *Atlantis Holiday Village*. Windsurfers (US$16 per hour) and wet-suits (US$20 per hour) can be hired from the place at the end. They also organize mountain bike excursions.

Continuing along the road you pass the Teos forestry picnic area amongst the pines before winding down a hill to the ruins of **Teos**. An important city of the Ionian league, Teans were great seafarers establishing a trading colony on the Nile delta. However, in 546 BC when threatened by the Persians courage deserted them and they took to the sea abandoning their city for a new settlement in Thrace. Except for portions of the great Temple of Dionysus, little remains of the city today, although it occupies an idyllic spot, particularly in spring when the surrounding meadows are carpeted in blooms.

Sleeping & eating

B *Otel Çakırağa*, just outside town on the road to Akkum, T7457575, F7457023. Rooms in nicely designed villas around swimming pool, pool-side bar, restaurant. Recommended. **F** *Teos Sunset Pension*, on the waterfront around the corner from square, T7457463, F7457616. Homely place run by Beer de Zoeten and his girlfriend Füsun Bilgin, comfortable rooms, restaurant, internet access, dive trips organized. Recommended. **G** *Sahil Pansiyon*, on waterfront promenade, T7457464. Basic rooms, 3 and 4 bed rooms, bathrooms en-suite, breakfast extra, fish restaurant next door. *The Liman Restaurant* and the *Burç Restaurant* are at the quayside and offer good meze, fish and meat. There is another slightly more expensive fish restaurant on the road to Akkum.

Transport

Buses leave İzmir's Üçkuyular bus station for **Seferhisar**, and from there dolmuş and belediye buses continue on to Akkum at least every 30 mins. Dolmuş also travel south along the coast to **Kuşadası** and **Selçuk** departing every hr (US$1.75).

Gümüldür, Özdere & beyond

Heading south from Seferhisar after 20 km you reach **Gümüldür** with its long but fairly scrappy beach backed by ranks of identical villas. There are a few hotels along the rather uninspiring strip with an ATM machine in the town centre. **Özdere** is much the same: a strip of estate agents, shops and restaurants with several large hotel complexes on the coast near-by. Beyond the town the mountainous topography has put a brake on development, with the road snaking along between small coves, some of which are good for camping.

At **Sahilevleri**, 11 km from Özdere, there is a short stretch of beach and several small pensions. At the junction turn left for the ancient site of **Claros**, found 2 km up the valley amongst the citrus orchards. Claros was not a city but the sight of a famous temple and oracle of Apollo. Delegations came from across the ancient world to consult the oracle, who would, having sipped from a secret fountain, answer them without hearing their questions. The oracle was one of the last to survive in the era of Christianity, but the temple was finally destroyed by an earthquake and slowly buried in silt by the stream which runs nearby.

Deniz Pınarı beach, 3 km along the coast road from Sahilevleri, has showers and some good snorkelling and fishing along the rocky coast. It gets crowded with picnickers during the summer. After a few more windy kilometres the road drops down onto the Kuçuk Menderes Plain, an area of marshland important for wildlife, which was a large bay in antiquity before sedimentation advanced the coastline. The amphitheatre at Ephesus is visible over 8 km inland.

Selçuk

Selçuk is in the agriculturally rich Kuçuk Menderes Valley surrounded by orchards and fields of tobacco and cotton. Approaches to the town are dominated by views of the Byzantine fortress and the basilica of Saint John crowning Ayasoluk hill. The town developed at the base of the hill after nearby Ephesus was abandoned when silt from the Kuçuk Menderes blocked its harbour. In more recent times its proximity to Ephesus has transformed it into an important tourist centre acting as a base for seeing the extensive ruins, along with the Virgin Mary's chapel and the Greek village of Şirince nearby. The tourist explosion of the 1980s left the town with the predictable array of hotels, restaurants, leather and carpet shops. However, the town has not sold its soul to the same degree as nearby Kuşadası and manages to retain some of its original character.

Phone code: 0232
Colour map 4, grid B2
70 km S of Izmir

Getting there Selçuk is linked regularly to Kuşadası and İzmir by the *Elbirlik* bus company, while there are also dolmuş departing from the bus station for the beaches of Pamucak, Kuşadası and smaller destinations in the surrounding area. **Getting around** It is possible to walk around the compact centre of town, much of which is pedestrianized. **Tourist information** is in a new building opposite the museum, T8926945. Helpful staff can provide information on Ephesus and travel in the country. Open every day, 0830-1730, later in summer.

Ins & outs
See page 269 for further details

Sights

The name Ayasoluk, which was also shared by the town until 1914, developed from the original name of Ayio Theologo given to the hill venerated as the resting place of Saint John the Theologian, who arrived in Ephesus with the Virgin Mary. The sight became a focus for early pilgrimage and in the sixth century AD the benevolent Emperor Justinian had a magnificent basilica built to honour the Apostle. The remains of the huge **Basilica of St John**, being excavated using funds from the Turkish Ministry of Culture and an American Christian foundation based in Ohio, are on the top of the hill reached through the **Gate of Persecution**. This gateway was made of recycled material and owes its name to a relief depicting Achilles in combat which was brought from the amphitheatre at Ephesus in Byzantine times and misinterpreted as a Christian being martyred in gladiatorial combat. There is a good model of the basilica at the site, showing the cross-shaped building with its six domes. The pillars that supported these domes can still be seen, along with some areas of marble flooring which look as if they were laid yesterday. However, the rest of what was a highly decorated interior must be left to the imagination. Nearby is a scale plan of the area which gives a good idea of how the process of sedimentation advanced the coastline and doomed the city of Ephesus. While at the site you may be approached by men claiming to be members of the archaeological staff and offering you artefacts for sale. These are probably fakes, but if not, they have been stolen from this and other sites and should under no circumstances by bought. ■ *0830-1730 daily. US$2. Getting there: Follow sign from the main road.*

Ayasoluk Hill
The picturesque Byzantine fortress occupying the other end of the hill is not pen at present

The Aegean Region

Isa Bey Camii Walking down the cobbled road on the opposite side of Ayasoluk Hill brings you to the Isa Bey Camii, a solid 14th-century stone mosque which represents a classic example of the *beylik* architectural style which formed a transition between Selçuk and Ottoman periods. If the building is locked, ask in the museum about gaining access.

The Temple of Artemis

One tall column has been re-erected & the foundations are just discernible, but in its present state it takes a very vivid imagination to picture the building in all its former splendour

Early in its history Ephesus was as an important place of pilgrimage for those worshipping the Anatolian goddess of fertility Cybele. Cybele was assimilated into the cult of Artemis by the Ionian Greeks after their arrival and the temple continued to attract an ever-increasing number of devotees. This was not only of spiritual significance to the Ephesians but like modern day tourism it also brought great economic benefits to the city.

The earliest temple, thought to date from the eighth century BC and destroyed by marauding Cimmerians, was still in the process of being replaced when Croesus took the city 200 years later. He generously donated some of his fantastic wealth to the building fund and it was finally finished. But in 356 BC the temple was burnt to the ground by a lunatic named Herostratus, whose self-confessed motive which he duly achieved was a desire to go down in history. The Ephesians immediately set about building an even more magnificent building, which was only partially completed when Alexander the Great passed through in 334 BC. He was sufficiently impressed by what he saw,

Selçuk

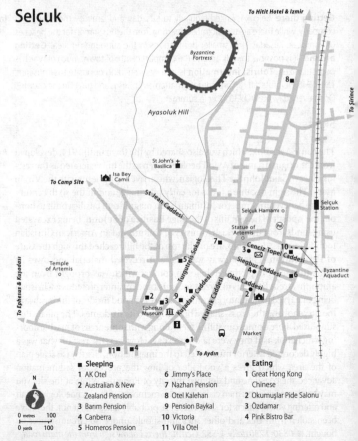

To Hitit Hotel & İzmir

Byzantine Fortress

Ayasoluk Hill

To Şirince

8■

St John's Basilica ■

Isa Bey Camii

To Camp Site

St Jean Caddesi

Selçuk Hamamı

Selçuk Station

Statue of Artemis

7■   ● 3 *Cenciz Topel Caddesi* 10■

Turgutreis Sokak ■5   Siegbur Caddesi

Temple of Artemis ○

■2 ●9 ■1 *Okul Caddesi* ●2

Ephesus Museum 🏛

Atatürk Caddesi *Kuşadası Caddesi*

●1

Byzantine Aquaduct

To Ephesus & Kuşadası

Market

11■ ■4

To Aydın

■ **Sleeping**
1 AK Otel
2 Australian & New Zealand Pension
3 Barım Pension
4 Canberra
5 Homeros Pension
6 Jimmy's Place
7 Nazhan Pension
8 Otel Kalehan
9 Pension Baykal
10 Victoria
11 Villa Otel

● **Eating**
1 Great Hong Kong Chinese
2 Okumuşlar Pide Salonu
3 Özdamar
4 Pink Bistro Bar

N

0 metres 100
0 yards 100

though, to offer to pay for the building costs himself. This time the benevolent offer was tactfully declined by the Ephesians, saying that it was not proper for a god to make a dedication to another god. The completed temple was magnificent, becoming known as one of the Seven Wonders of the World.

The Byzantine era saw the steady decline of the temple as Christianity developed at the expense of the old pagan beliefs and it was finally closed, along with all the other temples in the empire, in 392 AD. Over the years the site was buried in silt and forgotten, waiting until 1869 to be discovered by the clever detective work and determined effort of English engineer John Wood. Finding the temple became an obsession for Wood and he spent 11 years digging, finally achieving success by following a deeply buried ceremonial way from the Magnesia Gate of Ephesus.

It is well worth visiting the museum with its extensive collection of artefacts recovered mainly from Ephesus. One of the highlights is the large statues of Artemis Ephesia dating from the Roman period and portraying the goddess with a multitude of glands, now thought to be testicles, hanging from her chest. They were hidden by priests in order to save them when the temple was closed by edict of Theodosius I. There are informative displays about the history of Ephesus and life in its terraced houses, while outside in the garden are more artefacts and ethnographic exhibits including a traditional tent-like dwelling, called a *topuk ev*, used by Turkic nomads. ■ *0830-1200, 1300-1700 daily. US$3.50.* **Ephesus Museum**

Essentials

There is a good choice of budget accommodation in town along with a couple of more comfortable guesthouses and lower to mid-range hotels, however, for a more luxurious bed you will need to continue on towards Kuşadası. Competition between the hotels and pensions is intense, particularly around the bus station where touts wait to pounce on new arrivals. If you already have a place in mind be firm and don't be dissuaded by their offers or comments. **Sleeping**

B *Otel Kalehan*, on main İzmir road at the edge of town, T8926154, F8922169. Mock Ottoman architecture, decorated tastefully with old furnishings and local handicrafts, en-suite bathrooms with showers, a/c, deluxe rooms have minibar, small swimming pool, traffic noise problem in front rooms, good restaurant. Recommended. **C** *Hitit Hotel*, on İzmir road just outside town, T8926960, F8922490. Large modern 4 star, satellite TV, telephone, restaurants, bars, room service, a/c, safe box, swimming pool. **C** *Victoria Hotel*, Atatürk Mahallesi, Cenciz Topel Caddesi No.2, T8923203, F8923204. Central location near post office, a bit overpriced, restaurant on ground floor, excellent views into adjacent stork nests. **E** *Ak Otel*, Kuşadası Caddesi No.14. 60 rooms with small balconies and en-suite bathrooms, garden restaurant, bar, popular with tour groups. **E** *Nazhan Pension*, Saint Jean Caddesi, 1044 Sokak No.2, up the hill on the way to the basilica, quaint, homely rooms, breakfast served in leafy courtyard, equally verdant roof terrace bar is excellent place to unwind, meals cooked, friendly management. One of the nicest places in town.

F *Australian and New Zealand Pension*, 1064 Sokak, No.12, T8926050, F8919594, oznzpension@superonline.com Run by Turkish/Australian brothers, dorm rooms US$4, full board US$10 per person, roof terrace bar and lounge area, choice of breakfasts, laundry service, internet access, book exchange and a carpet shop on-site. Recommended. **F** *Barım Pension*, T8926923, behind the museum. Small pension in 18th-century house, colourfully decorated, breakfast included, lovely sitting room. Recommended. **F** *Pension Baykal*, Atatürk Mahallesi, Uğur Mumcu Sevgi Yolu No.2, T8926908, F8914623, run by ex-journalist and national squad football player Cengiz Baykal, helpful host can provide lots of info on the surrounding area, small rooms with showers, nice rooftop double US$27. Recommended. **F** *Canberra Hotel*, 1067 Sokak No.13, behind hospital, T/F8927668. Reasonable 2-star place, small en-suite bathrooms, singles available, bar, restaurant: dinner US$3. **F** *Homeros Pension*, Atatürk Mahallesi, Asmalı Sokak No.17, T8923995, F8928393. Family place run by bubbly hostess, enjoy some good home cooking in the evenings, breakfast extra US$2.50, use of kitchen and laundry, superb views from roof, boat trips organized. Recommended. **F** *Jimmy's Place*, Atatürk Mahallesi, 1012 Sokak, No.2, T8926191, jimmy@egenet.com.tr Formerly *Artemis guesthouse*, leased by enthusiastic Turk and his Australian girlfriend, eccentric décor, DVD video system, bar, internet facilities, use of kitchen, popular with Antipodean backpackers, breakfast extra US$2.50. **F** *Villa Otel*, 1 Spor Sokak No.11, T8926299, F8926331. 2-star, better option than *Canberra Hotel*, rooms with TV and en-suite bathrooms, breakfast included, US$12 half-board with meals eaten at *Leylek Restaurant* nearby, shuttle service to camping site near Dilek National Park. **F** *Turem Otel*, Otogar Yanı, T8922651, next to bus station, run by local government and staffed part of the year by students from the tourism department of the local college, uninspiring concrete building, reasonable rooms with ensuite and balcony represent fairly good value. **Camping** *Garden Camping*, behind Isabey Camii, T8926165.

Eating

Most of the hotels have restaurants & the smaller guesthouses generally prepare evening meals on request

Midrange The restaurant in the *Hotel Kalehan*, T8926154, serves a Turkish/European menu at reasonable prices in pleasant surroundings. *Özdamar Restaurant*, Cengiz Topel Caddesi No.65, near the main road end, T8914097. A good selection of meze, pizza, fish and meat dishes. There are several other similar establishments also with tables on the street further down Cengiz Topel Caddesi. *Karameşe Restaurant*, next to Isabey Camii, 'Anatolian village' open-air theme restaurant, Turkish dishes served at low tables with cushions on the floor. *Great Hong Kong Chinese Restaurant*, corner of Atatürk and Kuşadası Caddesi, near Tourist Information, surprisingly good place with Chinese chefs, 1 or 2 person set-menus are good value, US$6.50-20 per head. **Cheap** *Ak Restaurant*, Kuşadası Caddesi, opposite the small mosque, tables on the street, serving pide, pizza and soup. *Kodalak Restaurant* in the bus station serves standard ready prepared dishes and soup. Check the prices before ordering. *Tolga* and *Petek,* sandwiched between the *otogar* and the highway serve çöp şiş, kebaps and a range of other dishes for reasonable prices. The neon-lit roadside places just outside town heading towards İzmir specialize in çöp şiş, small pieces of lamb or beef, barbecued on bamboo skewers, which have been a local favourite since ancient times. *Okumuşlar Pide Salonu*, Nakım Kemal Caddesi, serves good pide and lahmacun.

Cafés There are tables in the small **Ahmet Ferahlı Parkı**, near the museum and tourist office, although the café at the train station is a much quieter, more pleasant place to have a tea in the shade of some pine trees, serenaded by chirping sparrows.

Bars *Pink Bistro Bar*, Saigburg Sokak No.24, T8914015. Music and tables on the street.

Festivals The amphitheatre at Ephesus hosts events for the *İzmir International Festival* held in the **Jul** and **Aug**. *Camel wrestling* also comes to town sometime during the winter. Enquire at the tourist office for information on both.

Shopping There are many carpet shops in the centre of town and although you can expect better prices than in nearby Kuşadası, you won't find any real bargains. Embroidery bought from the villagers in Şirince can make a nice souvenir, but the wine doesn't travel well. Visit the colourful Saturday market and stock-up on cheese, olives, tomatoes and other picnic food.

Most of the hotels and pensions can organize day trips around the ruins of Ephesus **Tour agencies** and to other sites in the area. *Ekol*, Uğur Mumcu Caddesi No.26, T8923157, ekol@okotravel.com   next to *Baykal Pension*, organize daily tours, car rental and bookings, have been recommended.

Bus Buses from Kuşadası and Bodrum bound for **İzmir** can be stopped on the main **Transport** road by the bus station, just hold out your hand. **Karadeveci** have buses between **İzmir** and **Bodrum** every hr. There are regular services to **İstanbul** (US$12.50, 9½ hrs), including expresses at 0945, 1200, 1700, 2200 and 2300. **Pamukkale**, several direct buses per day, or catch a **Denizli** service, depart every 30 mins, US$4, and get a dolmuş at the other end. **Dolmuş** Regular dolmuş depart from the *otogar* for **Ephesus, Şirince, Tire, Belevi, Pamucak, Söke** and **Seferhisar**. **Car rental** *Avis*, Atatürk Bulvarı No.5, T8922226, F8914230.

Banks There are several banks with ATM's in the streets around the post office. **Baths** *Selçuk* **Directory** *Hamamı*, T8926198, next to the police station, mixed sex bath and massage, US$12, predictably touristy. **Communications** **Post office**: PTT, Cengiz Topol Caddesi, open 24-hrs, also changes money, telephone boxes opposite. **Medical facilities Doctor**: *Özel Sağlık Hizmetleri*, T8927928, opposite the small mosque on Kuşadası Caddesi. **Laundry** *Pamukkale*, Koçak Sokak No.19, T8922980, efficient dry-cleaning service. **Useful numbers** Tourist Police, T8926910, on the main roundabout by the bus station.

Ephesus (Efes)

Known as the 'first and foremost Metropolis in Asia', Ephesus had a long and illustrious history, reaching its golden era as the capital of the Roman province of Asia. The city has also enjoyed a great deal of attention in modern times and the classical ruins uncovered are the most extensive and impressive anywhere in Turkey. Crouched between the scrubby slopes of Mount Pion and Bülbül Dağı, the grandest surviving buildings are the great theatre and the Library of Celsus, although ongoing excavations have revealed much more of interest besides. Still, despite the intensive efforts of archaeologists, it is estimated that only a fraction of the city has been unearthed. It is, however, a glorious white marble fraction, which gives an unrivalled glimpse of life in a Greco Roman city. The popularity of the site has brought with it the inevitable commercialization and the coach loads of camera-toting tourists can be a distraction. Though looking on the bright side, with a bit of imagination the crowds can help to give a more accurate impression of what it was like to be in a living, breathing Roman centre.

History

In fact, Ephesus was not one, but several cities, having been re-established during its long history as a result of conquest and because of the inexorable advance of the coast, which now lies 8 km to the west. Legend has it that the first Ionian settlement was established by Prince Androclus who arrived with his followers from Greece in 1000 AD. They chose a sight on the northern slope of Mount Pion, which in those days was beside the sea, having consulted an oracle. In typically cryptic terms the oracle had told them to build the new city where a fish and a wild boar showed them. One day while Androclus and some fishermen sat cooking, one of the fish jumped off the brazier with a hot-coal attached to its tail. The coal set fire to a nearby thicket in which a boar was sheltering. The boar fled, fulfilling the prophecy and the Ionians built their city on the site.

Ionian Ephesus grew and prospered because of its busy harbour and the sanctuary of Artemis, an important pilgrimage site for worshippers of the

Anatolian fertility goddess Cybele since Prehistoric times. The Ionians cleverly combined the cults of Artemis and Cybele and the indigenous goddess was assimilated into the Greek system of beliefs.

The city was forced to relocate for the first time from around the Temple of Artemis after its conquest by King Croesus. As the tyrant had approached the citizen's of Ephesus had tried to make up for their inadequate defences by stretching a rope from the Temple of Artemis to the city, in the vain hope of receiving divine protection against the Lydian minions.

The arrival of Lysimachus, about 300 years later, heralded another move for the city as the harbour was becoming blocked with silt washed down by the River Cayster. The city was rebuilt on the opposite side of Mount Pion. When the ungrateful citizens showed a reluctance to leave their homes, Lysimachus gently persuaded them by having the city drains blocked during a downpour, flooding the city.

After the death of Lysimachus, Ephesus gave its fickle allegiance to the Seleucids, the Ptolemies, Antiochus the Great and Pergamum, before coming under the control of Rome. It was as the capital of the Roman province of Asia that the city reached its zenith, becoming the most important trading centre on the Aegean coast with a population of over 250,000. Pilgrims, including several emperors, travelled from far and wide to visit the temple of Artemis Ephesia, one of the 'wonders of the world', stimulating business for local craftsmen and shopkeepers.

Despite the importance of the cult of Ephesia Artemis, Christianity took root quickly in the city and the success of St Paul's proselytizing after his arrival in 53 AD threatened established economic interests. The silversmiths, who made a living manufacturing silver likenesses of Artemis, were one group whose livelihood was jeopardized by the new religion. A meeting was called by a silversmith called Demetrius to discuss the situation and tempers quickly flared as he alleged that Christianity was affronting the Goddess's dignity. Rumours spread throughout the city and people took to the streets. The crowds converged on the theatre shouting, 'Great is Artemis of the Ephesians'.

Ephesus

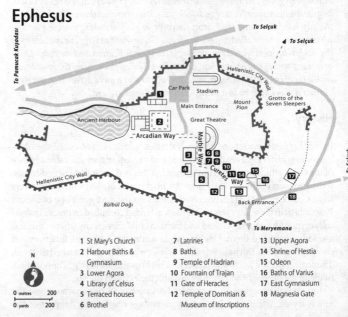

1 St Mary's Church	7 Latrines	13 Upper Agora
2 Harbour Baths &	8 Baths	14 Shrine of Hestia
Gymnasium	9 Temple of Hadrian	15 Odeon
3 Lower Agora	10 Fountain of Trajan	16 Baths of Varius
4 Library of Celsus	11 Gate of Heracles	17 East Gymnasium
5 Terraced houses	12 Temple of Domitian &	18 Magnesia Gate
6 Brothel	Museum of Inscriptions	

N

0 metres 200
0 yards 200

Anarchy prevailing until the secretary of the city council restored calm, also securing the release of several Christians who'd been swept-up in the crowd. St Paul wisely left soon after.

The rise of Christianity and the corresponding decline in the fortunes of the cult of Artemis continued, as did the silting up of the harbour. In spite of Roman attempts to alleviate the problem by dredging the advancing coast slowly strangled the city's commerce. By the time Byzantine Emperor Theodosius I issued an edict in 392 AD closing all pagan shrines in the empire the glory of Ephesus was fading fast. Battered by Persian, Arab and Selcuk invasions, medieval Ephesus became little more than a provincial town clustered at the base of Ayasuluk hill, the silted up harbour finally abandoned.

The site

The archaeological site is several kilometres to the southwest of Selçuk and accessible by dolmuş from the bus station. It is also possible to walk there along a tree-shaded path, named after Doktor Sabri Yayla, which runs from near the tourist information centre along the Kuşadası road, in about 30 minutes.

The majority of people visiting independently stay in Selçuk however Kuşadası or Şirince could make alternative, more distance, bases for a visit

A good walking tour, that fills the best part of a day, passes the Temple of Artemis on the way to the main entrance of Ephesus. Work your way through the city, which can take anything from a couple of hours to well over half a day depending on your level of interest, and out of the back entrance. Turn left and a short distance down on the left is a track leading around Mount Pion to the Grotto of the Seven Sleepers. From here continue along to a track on the right, which leads you through the fields and orchards for over a kilometre to a cemetery and the main road. This route can also be done in reverse taking the track through the cemetery. This has the advantage of descending down through the ruins of Ephesus to the main entrance, where you can take a dolmuş if you are tired.

Ephesus gets very hot in summer. Make an early start if possible, take water & a sun-hat

The impressive **Great Theatre** draws the eye as you enter the sight. Built into the western slopes of Mount Pion in the time of Lysimachus, it was the largest theatre in Asia Minor, seating 25,000 people. It was reconstructed by the Romans to improve the acoustics, which are still excellent today. This is where the mob angered by the Christian proselytizing gathered, shouting 'Great is Artemis of the Ephesians!'

Walking tour

The **Arcadian Way**, leading from the ancient harbour up to the theatre, was a main thoroughfare in Roman times. Built by Emperor Arcadius, it was a wide colonnaded avenue, paved with mosaics and lined with small shops and street lights.

From the theatre you walk along the **Marble Way** which would have been busy with Roman feet. Goods arriving in the harbour were carried along here to the main commercial area, the **agora**. Notice the ruts worn by cartwheels and the remnants of the city's water and sewage system running underneath the marble paving slabs. On the right-hand side of the Marble Way, chiseled into a paving stone, are some small engravings of a heart symbol, a left foot and a woman wearing a crown. These are a cryptic advertisement for the city's brothel, deciphered as, 'Go this way and turn to your left, to find a woman and love.' The 'house of love', on the left side of the street at the far end, was part of a complex including baths and public lavatories, and had a mosaic of the Four Seasons on the floor of the dining hall.

Ahead is the restored façade of the **library of Celsus**, which ranked as the third largest library in the ancient world after Alexandria and Pergamum containing well over 1,000 scrolls. It was built by Consul Tiberius Julius Aquila in honour of his father, Gaius Celsus Polemaenus, who died in 110 AD and was buried underneath. The building was constructed in a narrow gap between two other buildings, so the canny Roman architects usde some clever techniques to give it a monumental appearance. The dimensions of the central columns and capitals are larger than those on the outside, and the façade is slightly convex, thereby giving the illusion of greater size. The library was built with a double external wall to inculate the recious manuscripts from heat and cold, while the facade was embellished with statues representing the virtues of Sophia (Wisdom), Arete (Valour), Ennoia (Thought) and Episteme (Knowledge). Destroyed by the Goths in the third century AD the library was restored with help from Austrian Archaeological Institute, although the original statues remain in the Ephesus Museum in Vienna. Just to the right of the library is the **Gate of Mazeus and Mithridates** built by two slaves in gratitude at having been set free.

Curetes Way leads up the hill, its marble paving stones polished smooth by years of pedestrian traffic. This was a very busy street lined with shops and numerous temples, fountains and statues. On the left are the public toilets, for the use of men only, built as part of the brothel complex and now a favourite photo-stop. It was in the small well by the entrance that the well endowed figure of Priapus, the god of sex, was found and put on display in the Ephesus Museum.

Next on the left is the Corinthian style **Temple of Hadrian**. Built in the second century AD, the delicate friezes around the top of the porch depict the story of Androclus establishing the city were added later. The carving above the doorway which looks like Medusa, is in fact a female figure symbolizing fertility.

Opposite the temple is an area where on-going excavations have uncovered a residential area of the Roman city. The **terraced houses** built into the hillside around the first century AD were for the wealthiest inhabitants of the city and many of the fine mosaics, statues and frescoes that decorated them have survived and now grace the museum in Selçuk. Fronting onto Curetes Way is a row of small shops with mosaic covered floor.

Passing the **Fountain of Trajan** on the left, the marble flagstones climb up to the **Gate of Heracles**, what was a two-storey structure with carvings of Heracles on each pillar. The **Temple of Domitian**, on the right, was the first temple to be dedicated to a Roman emperor in the city. Its huge statue of the deified emperor was smashed by a mob in 96 AD after his assassination. One part of the temple is used to display the inscriptions found throughout the site.

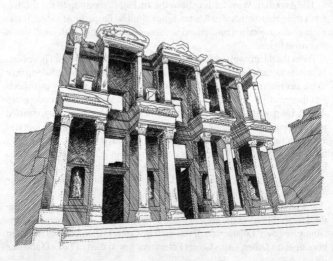

Library of Celsus

The Virgin Mary (Meryemana)

Remarkably little is known about the life of the Virgin Mary after Christ's ascension to heaven and her last days are shrouded in mystery. It has been suggested that this was deliberate in order to avoid her becoming a focus of reverence, or hatred, that could distract from the extraordinary story of Christ which had become central to the emerging Christian faith.

Orthodox schools of thought hold that Mary died on Mount Zion in Jerusalem after John was martyred there in 44 AD. However, conflicting stories tell how she accompanied John to Ephesus, where she lived out her days on a mountain south of the city. Although there is no evidence to support either story in the bible, local Christians from the village of Kirkince, now known as Şirince, traditionally made a pilgrimage into the mountains on Assumption Day.

In the 19th century, Lazarist priests from İzmir set out to discover the exact spot where Mary had lived. They interviewed local monks and used the descriptions given by Catherine Emmerich, a German nun, who had seen Mary's house in a dream. Miraculously, despite never having visited the area, Catherine Emmerich's recollections of the dream were detailed enough to help lead the searchers to the foundations of a small building.

Once news spread of the discovery, a steady stream of pilgrims began visiting to pay their respects and a small guesthouse and chapel were built. The site was officially recognized by the Vatican and Pope Paul VI celebrated mass there in 1967. Its potential for tourism was belatedly realized by the local government and today hundreds of thousands of people visit the site each year. A service is conducted on Assumption Day (15 August) each year to commemorate Mary's accession into heaven, and is attended by both Orthodox Christians and Muslims, who revere Meryemana as the mother of a great Prophet.

The Sacred Way then runs along the north side of the **state agora**, and was considered sacred because it leads to the **Shrine of Hestia**, the goddess of the hearth. The flame in the altar of this shrine, which is on the left at the beginning of the sacred way, was brought from Athens and kept continually burning by followers of her cult. Next to the temple is the **odeon**, used for meetings of the town council and musical performances. Beyond, there is little left of the **Baths of Varius**, **East Gymnasium** and **Magnesia Gate**. ■ *0830-1700 daily (1800 in summer). US$5, US$1.25 parking charge, free for students.*

On the opposite side of Mount Pion to the ruins of Ephesus is the place where seven young Christians and their dog are said to have been sealed in a cave by soldiers of the Roman Emperor, and notorious Christian-hater, Decius. They awoke over 200 years later when an earthquake unblocked the cave's entrance and walked back into town, which had become Christian in the intervening years. This was widely held as a miracle and when the seven died and were reburied in the cave, the site became the centre of a popular cult. A small chapel was built and the tombs of other, later, Christians can also be seen.

Grotto of the Seven Sleepers
It is a short walk from the back gate of Ephesus

After the magnificent marble of Ephesus it is a little disappointing, but the restaurants at the entrance make up for it by serving delicious *şac boreği* (thin pancakes filled with meat or cheese) and creamy *ayran*.

The site, high on the forested slopes of Bülbül Dağı 8 km from Selçuk, is reputed by some Christians to be the last home of the Virgin Mary (see box). Officially recognized by the Vatican in 1896 and more recently restored, the house/chapel has become an important place of pilgrimage for Muslims and Christians alike, who come to drink from the sacred spring and pay their respects. Meryemana is

Meryemana (House of the Virgin Mary)

The Aegean Region

also firmly on the coach tour circuit, so it gets crowded with less pious visitors as well. There is a basic restaurant, several shops selling trinkets and picnic tables in the surrounding municipal park. ■ *Open dawn till dusk. US$2. Getting there: There is no public transport. A taxi costs about US$10 from Selçuk.*

Şirince

Nestling in the fertile hills, 8 km above Selçuk, is the former Ottoman Greek village of Şirince, meaning 'loveliness'. The setting amongst the vineyards, orchards and meadows lives up to its name and strict controls have helped preserve the village's many old buildings. It was once a sizeable place with an industrious population of over 9,000 Greeks, several churches, a school and a hospital. However, the former residents reluctantly left their homes as part of the populations exchanges between Greece and Turkey in 1923, an event chronicled by Dido Sotiriou in her poignant novel 'Farewell to Anatolia'.

Home to just over 800 people today, many of the houses in the village have a ramshackled, melancholy air about them, and look in imminent danger of collapse. Others have had their cracked plasterwork and sagging beams lovingly restored, to begin life anew as a second home or guesthouse. The villages two churches have also enjoyed a thorough renovation thanks to a benevolent US-based foundation and are now open to visitors during the day.

At weekends, particularly during the summer, the village gets crowded with day-trippers who eat in the village's restaurants and browse the handicraft stalls lining the main street. Despite this attention, Şirince retains a rustic air and it is pleasurable to wander around the cobbled lanes. During your visit you may receive an invite to have a look inside one of the old houses where you'll be shown lace and other handicrafts for sale.

Sleeping
Şirince could make a pleasant alternative to staying in Selçuk as regular dolmuş connect the two

A few pensions have sprung up in recent years and the village is a lovely place to unwind – a sentiment shared by others, so book ahead on summer weekends. **A *Şirince Evleri*,** contact Ahmet Koçak in his shop 'Motif' in advance, right at mosque, opposite Özlem Gözleme, T8983099, F8983099. 2 lovingly renovated 19th-century properties packed with interesting antiques, 1 self-contained property, with 2 double bedrooms and sitting room, 2nd house has 3 rooms, wonderful breakfast served on terrace overlooking village, all rooms have telephone and a/c, unique experience, booked in advance. Recommended. **D *Erdem Pansiyon*,** T8983069, F8983226, turn right after passing the mosque and pension is on the right after 25 m. Handsomely restored Greek house, interesting rooms with many of original features retained, some have ensuite bathrooms, delicious breakfast served on patio, very popular so advanced booking essential. Recommended. **F *Esra Pansiyon*,** up alley opposite *Artemis Restaurant*, T8983140. 7 compact rooms in converted family house, rooms upstairs with shared shower are preferable, downstairs ones with ensuite are claustrophobic, shady terrace, the owner, Ercan, takes walking tours into the surrounding hills, bread is baked in traditional oven outside, English and German spoken. Recommended. **G *Huzur Pension*,** straight ahead past village mosque, T8983060. 3 rooms with shared toilet and small kitchen, 1 room sleeps up to 6, good value, breakfast extra. Recommended.

Eating
A visit is not complete without tasting the local plonk in 1 of the several winehouses

Artemis Şarapevi and Restoran, T8983201, in the restored school-house, has perfect location at the entrance to the village, an interesting menu, including spit-roast lamb and Şirince köfte, specially-produced wines, reasonable prices, thoroughly recommended. There are several places overlooking the square and higher up in the village.

Transport
During the day dolmuş shuttle up from the bus station in Selcuk every 20-40 mins, US$0.50.

Near the small dusty agricultural community of Belevi is the rarely visited **Belevi**
Belevi Mezar Anıtı, a large monumental sepulchre hewn from the living rock *10 km N of Selcuk, just*
of a mountainside. Originally decorated with statues and holding a tomb con- *off the road to Izmir*
taining the remains of a nobleman of Persian or Syrian origin, little else is
known about the mausoleum. Despite having been stripped of its marble panelling – the statues and tomb have also been removed for safe-keeping and are
now on display in the Ephesus Museum in Selçuk – it's easy to imagine how
impressive it would have looked. The tomb's setting, amongst the olive and fig
orchards, must have been peaceful until the İzmir-Aydin highway was constructed just 100 m away. ■ *Getting there: The tomb is 2 km beyond the village
on the road towards Tire. A signposted track passes under the highway. From
Selçuk catch 1 of the regular Tire or Belevi dolmuş.*

Kuşadası

Kuşadası was once a quiet coastal town whose economy was based on its fish   *Phone code: 0256*
ing fleet, the surrounding farms and trade conducted from its harbour. In the   *Colour map 4, grid B2*
last 20 years it has undergone a metamorphosis. The town has been catapulted
into the world of mass tourism and a bewildering number of hotels now cater
for package tourists arriving from northern Europe for a week of sun. The
apartment buildings and summerhouse developments ringing the town are
also proof of the popularity of the town as a destination for domestic tourists.
Cruise-ships regularly call at the harbour, disgorging their passengers for tours
of Ephesus and Pamukkale, and there are also regular ferry services to and
from the Greek island of Samos.

Getting there Kuşadası's *otogar* is on the ring-road about 10-15-mins walk from town.   **Ins & outs**
There are direct connections with İzmir, Bodrum and other more distant destinations. The   *See page 278 for*
Elbirlik bus service to İzmir passes through Selçuk and the entrance to the airport. Dolmuş   *further details*
leave from the *otogar* for Söke, Selçuk, Dilek National Park and other places in the surrounding area. **Getting around** Şehiriçi dolmuş operate in the local area, connecting
the town centre with the *otogar* and beaches. **Tourist information** at İskele Meydanı, on
corner opposite the docks, open 0830-1200, 1300-1800, later in high season.

The town owes its name, Bird Island, to the small island called Güvercin Adası   **History**
(Pigeon Island) which is just off the coast to the west of the marina and is now
connected to the mainland by a causeway. Venetian and Genoese traders settled during the Middle Ages and built the fort on Güvercin Adası was one of
the town's defences against attack by pirates. Kuşadası was incorporated into
the Ottoman empire in 1413 and it was at the command of Grand Vizier Öküz
Mehmet Paşa that the caravanserai and the Kaleiçi mosque complex, which
survive to the present day, were constructed in 1618. Apart from these exceptions, the town is devoid of historical interest and the tourist population seem
to divide their time, rather predictably, between sunning themselves on the
crowded beaches nearby, buying leather, jewellery and carpets and getting ine-
briated in the hundreds of bars.

The **Kaleiçi Mosque** is in the centre of town on the main parade, Barbaros   **Sights**
Hayrettin Caddesi, while the restored **caravanserai** nearby is now a hotel, where
they hold regular evenings of folk and belly dancing. If you have had enough of
the touts and tourists take a stroll up the hill on **Yıldırım** or **Arslanlar Sokak**,
where Turkish life continues in the narrow streets, between crumbling Ottoman
houses. Notice the wooden screens, or *kafes*, over many of the windows that
stopped prying eyes from violating the privacy of the households.

The Aegean Region

Beaches The beaches within the immediate area are really nothing to get excited about, **Pamucak** (see previous section) and **Dilek National Park** to the south are better bets. **Yılancı Burnu** is a short beach past the Güvercın Ada. **Kadınlar Denizi** (Ladies' Beach), 2 km south of the centre, is the town's best known beach. It is, however, hardly deserving of such a distinction, being a miserly piece of crowded sand backed by hotels and restaurants. The water is often none-too-clean either. Şehiriçi dolmuş constantly trawl for business along the coast road and from the bus station to the beach. **Kuştur** beach, about 5 km to the north of town, is a bit better, although it is also very crowded during the summer. Catch a dolmuş from the waterfront, towards the new marina.

Sleeping

Luxury is found to the N along the old Selçuk rd & beyond Kadınlar Denizi to the S. For budget rooms head up Yıldırım or Arslanlar Caddesi into what is left of the old town

If arriving by bus expect to be harassed by touts as you get off

A *Club Caravanserail*, T6144115, F6142423. Converted 17th-century Öküz Mehmet Paşa caravanserai, all the comforts, café/restaurant in central courtyard, venue for belly and folk dancing evenings, loud if you want to sleep, open-buffet dinners. **C** *Atınç Otel*, Atatürk Bulvarı No.42, T6147608, F6144967. 4-star, a/c, minibar, TV, swimming pool, restaurant, bar. Recommended. **D** *Hotel Derici*, Atatürk Bulvarı No 40, T6148222, F6148226. Not as good value as the *Atınç Otel*, most of the same facilities except no swimming pool, good fish restaurant. **E** *Bahar Pansiyon*, Cephane Sokak No12, T6141191, F6149359, walking from the harbour take the first left off Barbaros Haryrettin Bulvarı, reasonable rooms, telephone, a/c, safe box in reception. **E** *Hotel Sungarden Flash*, Arslanlar Caddesi No 68, T6143806. 'Backpacker comfort zone' (!), modern pension, restaurant, bar, small swimming pool. **F** *Park Garden Village Pension*, Arslanlar Caddesi No 17, T6143917. Old Greek building with some very atmospheric high ceiling rooms, run by a Welsh lady and her Turkish husband, garden at the rear with plunge pool to cool-off in and bar, laundry service. Recommended. **G** *şeçkin Pansiyon*, Yıldırım Caddesi No 35, up the road past the Hamam, T6142263. Small rooms with bathroom, use of kitchen, friendly owner, breakfast extra. **G** *Cennet Pension*, Yayla Sokak No 1, entrance is in fact near the top of Yıldırım Caddesi, T6144893. Nice rooms in family run place, triple rooms, shared bathrooms, use of kitchen, friendly owner, fantastic view of town from roof terrace, breakfast extra. Recommended. **G** *Golden Bed Pansiyon*, in small cul-de-sac off Arslanlar Caddesi, T6148708. Small rooms with bathroom, breakfast extra, terrace with a great view.

North of town **L** *Pine Bay*, 6 km north on the old road, T6149370, F6149379. Huge 5-star resort complex, rates are half-board, substantial off-season discounts, bungalows available, indoor and outdoor pools, tennis courts, private beach, watersports, conference centre, an endless list of other facilities. **AL** *Hotel Kısmet*, on headland above the new marina, T6142005, F6144914. Unobtrusive luxury, have a look at the photographs of some of the distinguished guests including Queen Elizabeth on her visit in 1971, several former heads of state, actors and industrialists, views over Kuşadası from the garden and terraces, buffet dinner open to non-residents US$20, 3 bars, swimming pool, tennis courts, lounge with uninterrupted sea views. Recommended. **A** *Turtel*, just off the new Selçuk road to the north of town, T6149270, strange architectural fusion, like something from 'Thunderbirds', lots of facilities including pool, restaurants, bars, nightclub at the top of the turret.

Kadınlar Denizi **L** *Imbat Hotel*, at the far end of beach, T6127750, F6124225. 5-star resort with all the facilities you'd expect including a private beach. **D** *Hotel Asena*, tall modern hotel right on the front, T6148923, F6148916. Half-board, modern rooms, TV, minibar, restaurant, bar, swimming pool on top floor. **F** *Balcı Pansiyon*, *Kadınlar Denizi*, on the road behind the front, T6147546, F6125851. Pension housed in several buildings, also home to diving club which has been operating for 15 years.

Camping *Tur-Yat*, Kuştur, T6141087, right on beach front road, camping complex with space for caravans, 100-bed hotel, restaurant.

Midrange *Kısmet Hotel*, Akyar Mevkii, T6142005. Open-buffet (US$20) or à la carte menu, enjoy a civilized evening on the terrace overlooking the town. *Club Cappello*, on the old road past the *Kısmet Hotel*, T6144043. Turkish cuisine, grilled meats, fish and meze, go there for an afternoon to enjoy the swimming pool overlooking the sea. *1-A Grand*, parallel to Barlar Sokağı one street up, T6148409. Leafy terrace restaurant, understandably popular with local ex-pat community, Turkish-European cuisine, speciality steaks, bar. There are several places serving meze and fish in the Municipal plaza overlooking the old harbour including *Ali Baba*, T6141551. *Hotel Derici Restaurant*, Atatürk Caddesi, T6148222. European and Turkish dishes. *Chinese Restaurant*, Atatürk Bulvarı opposite the new yacht harbour, eclectic range of international dishes. There are many other restaurants in the back streets of the Kaleiçi area.

Cheap Expect to pay considerably more than other less-touristy towns even in the cheapest looking places. Many of the budget pensions will prepare food if notified in advance and this represents the best value food in town. *Konya Restaurant*, Karamanlar Caddesi, next to *E-Café*. Kebaps and pide. There are some other reasonably priced places further up Karamanlar Caddesi towards the bus station. *Adana Kebap*, in the alley behind the Kaleiçi Camii specializes in spicy Adana kebaps.

Eating
The café next to the caravanserai is a good place to watch the world go buy, there are also numerous buffets along the sea front

Kuşadası

Sleeping
1 Atınç Otel
2 Cennet Pension
3 Club Caravanserail
4 Derici
5 Kısmet
6 Park Garden
   Village Pension
7 Sungarden Flash

Eating
1 1-A Grand
2 Ali Baba
3 Konya

The Aegean Region

Bars Kuşadası is certainly well-endowed with watering holes and 1 entire street, imaginatively renamed *Barlar Sokağı* (Bar street), is crammed with establishments such as *Lobly Jubly*, *The Yorkshire Arms*, *Molly Malone's* and *Jimmy's Irish Bar*, all competing for the patronage of the flocks of pink package tourists. Once your anthropological curiosity has been satisfied, head for the maze of narrow streets behind the Kaleiçi Camii, where you'll find a diverse collection of bars and clubs playing every type of music from techno (*Ecstacy*) to traditional Turkish (*Kervan Bar*).

Nightclubs There is a nightclub on the Güvercin Adası where you can dance the night away to Euro-pop and techno. *The Temple*, playing slightly more sophisticated music, is on Atatürk Bulvarı opposite the new marina. There are other clubs, many with a life expectancy of just one season, in the Kaleiçi area. *Sandals*, Kadınlar Denizi, at the far end of the strip behind the *Blue Sky Hotel*, upbeat and Latin rhythms played for an affluent, mainly local crowd.

Shopping Kuşadası is commission city, the retail activities of the town a tangled web of reciprocity between hotels, restaurants, taxi drivers, street traders, guides and the hundreds of gold, leather and carpet shops. Prices are generally high and the hassle from the countless salesmen can be a minor annoyance as you walk around town. With the state of things as they are it is almost impossible to recommend buying anything from anywhere. One exception, *Turcam*, Ataturk Bulvari stocks UNICEF goods, kilims etc, helpful owner.

Tour operators *Diana Travel Agency*, on 1st floor of building opposite docks, T6144900, F6127295, Samos tickets and boat excursions. There are many other agents around the harbour selling ferry tickets. *Sisan Tours*, Yıldırım Caddesi No 17, around the corner from Barlar Sokağı, daily tours, custom itineraries, car rental and plane flights.

Transport **Bus** Buses and **dolmuş** leave for: **Bodrum**, frequently in season, 2½ hrs, US$7; **İzmir**, passes Adnan Menderes airport, every 30 mins, 90 mins, US$3; **Pamukkale**, frequent buses to Denizli, then catch dolmuş, 3 hrs, US$7; **Selçuk**, every 15 mins in summer to 2100, 30 mins, US$1.25; **Söke**, regular dolmuş, 30 mins, US$1.25. For **Priene**, **Miletus** and **Didyma** catch dolmuş from Söke *otogar*. **Car hire** *Avis*, Atatürk Bulvarı near junction with İnönü Cadddesi. *HK Rent a car*, Adnan Menderes Bulvarı, opposite bus station, T6148210. **Ferries to Samos** Tickets are available from most travel agents in the town. Ships depart at 0830 from Apr to the end of Oct, returning at 1700, with an additional ferry leaving at 1700 from May to the middle of Oct. A single fare costs US$30, US$35 round-trip. A car costs US$70 one-way. There is also a twice weekly ferry to Brindisi, Italy between Jun and Sep (see page30).

The bus station is quite a walk from the centre of town, so visit the bus company offices on İnönü Caddesi to buy a ticket

Directory **Banks** Banks with ATM's can be found throughout the centre of town. **Baths** Of the tourist type, mixed sex groups. *Kaleiçi Hamamı*, T6141292, behind the Kale mosque. *Belediye Hamamı*, T6141219, just up Yıldırım Caddesi on the right. **Communications** **Post office**: The PTT is on Barbaros Hayrettin Bulvarı opposite the caravansarai. **Internet**: *Café Net*, Karamanlar Caddesi No.57/6, near the small mosque, T6125500. **Medical services** The state hospital is on Atatürk Bulvarı, near where it joins İnönü Caddesi.

Dilek National Park The relatively undisturbed forests and abundant wildlife of Dilek National Park, 30 km south of Kuşadası, are an antedote to the coastal experience. Set up in 1966, the park largely owes its existence to the Greek island of Samos only a few kilometres off-shore at the end of the peninsula, and a large portion is a military zone off-limits to the public. Whatever its *raison d'être*, the concrete miraculously stops just short of the park boundary and the mountain slopes, cloaked thickly in vegetation, are a haven for rarely seen wildlife including wildcats and jackals. However, you're much more likely to see the not so wild boar that clean up around the picnic areas once the humans have departed in the evening.

A road winds along the coast from the park entrance past several good beaches. **İçmeler Koyu**, a small cove with protected beach ideal for children, is under 2 km from the park entrance and has a snack bar, showers and picnic area. **Aydınlık Koyu**, 3 km further on, is a long pebble beach with an approach at either end, picnic tables, showers and changing facilities.

A kilometre beyond the first track down to Aydınlık Koyu is a sign-posted track on the left heading up a **canyon**. The track climbs up the gorge, through verdant mixed forest until you reach the summit of **Dilek Tepe** (1237 m) in four to five hours. This track is also good, but strenuous, on a mountain bike. A day-trip popular with local walkers follows this route up, descending on the opposite side of the mountains to the village of **Yukarı Doğanbey**, from where there are dolmuş to Söke. Remember to leave early, as the last dolmuş from Yukarı Doğanbey leaves at around 1600.

Kavaklı Burunu, 8 km from the park entrance, has another good stretch of pebble beach and similar facilities, with Karasu at the end, beyond which the military area begins.

The park gets busy at the weekends during school holidays. Lighting fires and camping are strictly prohibited throughout the park and if you are driving make sure not to leave any valuables in the car. ■ *0800-1800 daily. US$0.50 per person, car US$2.50. To get there, follow the Söke road out of Kuşadası, taking a turn to Davutlar, Güzelçamlı and Dilek Milli Parkı. Dolmuş depart from Söke and Kuşadası bus stations for Güzelçamlı and the national park.*

The Büyük Menderes Valley

Penetrating deep into the Aegean hinterland from its estuary south of the Dilek National Park, the Büyük Menderes Valley is a rich agricultural area with extensive fields of cotton and wheat, orchards of fruit and groves of olive trees. Called 'the worker' by the ancient commentator Herodotus on account of the speed with which it changed the coastline, the silt it washes down is still extending the land by up to 6 m a year. Manufacturing and processing industries have sprung up around the larger centres such as Aydın and Denizli, and there has been an influx of people from the surrounding countryside and from further east to find work. There are a series of interesting archaeological sites as you progress up the valley, such as Nyssa and Aphrodisias, with the white travertines and mineral waters of Pamukkale as most people's ultimate goal. South of Söke, on the flat cotton plains, are the varied Ionian ruins of Priene, Miletus and Didim and the package resort of Altınkum.

Söke A market town on the edge of the deltaic lower Menderes valley, Söke is also an important centre for the production of marble, which is carved from huge scars in the mountain. The bus terminal is an important transport hub with services to places in the surrounding area.

Priene

Remarkable neither for its importance as a member of the Ionian League, nor for the scale of the ruins uncovered, Priene, 20 km southwest of Söke, is still a special place. This is partly because of its position perched on a terrace cut into the side of Mount Mycale and looking out across miles of cotton fields and irrigation channels to the mountains, on the opposite side of the Menderes valley. Archaeologically speaking, Priene is also notable as a predominately Greek city, having missed out on the Roman building phase which dominates most of the ancient ruins of the region.

Phone code: 0256
Colour map 4, grid B2

Less-visited than other sites in the area, the peacefulness of the spot means that the ever-present wind may often be your only companion

Ins & outs	**Getting there** Priene, Didim and Miletus are sign-posted 5 km south of Söke on the Milas/Bodrum road. The site is 14 km ahead at the far (western) end of the strung out village of Güllübahçe. **Getting around** From the carpark, reached up a steep track from the village, it is a short walk to the site.
The site & some history	The city was founded some time around 1000 BC by Greek settlers. Moved in the fourth century BC from its first unknown site close by, probably because of the advancing coastline, the city was laid out in a rectangular grid plan with the streets intersecting each other at right-angles. Known as the Hippodamian model, after a citizen of nearby Miletus who first developed the linear city plan, all the main avenues run east to west and are joined by stairs climbing south to north. Each rectangular unit contained four houses or a public building, which sometimes occupied adjacent blocks also.

After entering through the **northeast gate**, walk along what was one of the city's main east-west thoroughfares to the **theatre**, which seated 5,000, and which is one of the best surviving examples of its type in Turkey. Notice the altar in the middle of the first row where offerings to Dionysus preceded each performance and the marble thrones used by local officials.

Activity in the city would have been focused to the south where the **agora**, **Temple of Zeus** and **council chamber** are found. Twenty-five metres further west along the main avenue is the **Temple of Athena Polias**, designed by the architect Pythius, who helped build the Mausoleum in Halicarnassus, one of the Seven Wonders of the World. Its construction was financed by Alexander the Great, a fact we know because of an inscription found at the site which is now in the British museum. The temple dominated the city and was used as a model for later buildings of its type. Some of the Ionic columns that surrounded the sanctuary have been reconstructed, while a jumble of other pieces lie scattered about. This is a good place to enjoy the view and to imagine looking out across what was a large bay in ancient times.

In the western (far) section of the city, near the west gate, are several blocks of well preserved houses, one of which was used as a shrine to Alexander the Great. There is also a **Temple of Demeter** on the hillside above the Temple of Athena reached via a small path. Little remains of the temple except for the bases of some Doric columns and a pit for offering sacrificial blood to the gods of the underworld. At the bottom of the site, inside the southern ramparts are the **gymnasium** and **stadium**.

Priene

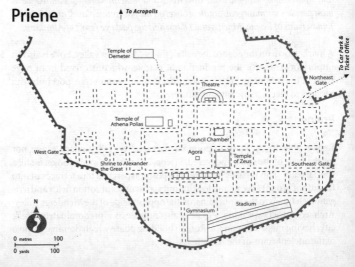

Temple of Apollo

The Aegean Region

F *Priene Pansiyon*, behind the village mosque, 50 m east (right when looking at the **Sleeping**
Şelale Restaurant) of the bus station, T5471725. 11 rooms shaded by citrus trees, nicely **& eating**
finished, with bathroom. Recommended. Camping also possible. There are several
touristy restaurants like the *Şelale Restaurant* next to the dolmuş stop. *Shadow Café*,
near the track up to ruins, tables set in nice garden.

Dolmuş run to and from **Söke** every 30 mins, 0800-1900, less frequently in winter, **Transport**
US$1.25. To continue to **Miletus** flag down a dolmuş bound for **Altınkum, Akköy** or
Balat on the main road.

Miletus (Milet)

Thought to be oldest of the Ionian cities, the great maritime port of Miletus was
built on a peninsular of land jutting into the Latmian Gulf. An important centre of
ancient trade and commerce, the citizens of Miletus founded colonies across the
Mediterranean and Black Sea, with the city also producing some of the most gifted
ancient minds (see box). Today the site is stranded 8 km from the sea and
approached across the tobacco and cotton fields of the Menderes Plain. Scattered
across bramble-choked, seasonally flooded fields, it requires a major feat of imagination to reconstruct the city's former splendour from the scattered extant ruins.

Getting there Miletus is 10 km off the Söke-Milas highway near the village of Balat. **Ins & outs**
Without your own transport you need to get a dolmuş and hitch-hike or walk.
Getting around From the carpark the ruins must be toured on foot.

A natural choice for a trading city, pottery finds have shown that the peninsu- **History**
lar site was first occupied by Minoans from Crete in about 1600 BC.
Mycenaeans then inherited the colony which was probably peopled predominantly by indigenous Carians. The Ionians, intent on making a more lasting
presence, put to death all the male inhabitants of the city upon their arrival and
married their women. Herodotus tells how in response the Carian women
made a pact not to eat with their husbands nor call them by their names.
    Despite this inauspicious start the city flourished becoming the most
important city of the Ionian League, a great commercial and cultural centre

(see box) and a colonial power with 90 trading settlements dotted around the Black Sea, the Sea of Marmara and the Dardanelles.

The Milesians were a major player in the Ionian Revolt against Persian rule from 499 BC, paying a heavy price for their rebelliousness when the Persian navy scored a decisive victory off the coast. The city was burnt to the ground and the inhabitants enslaved. Miletus took another knock when it was razed again by the Persians two decades later, however, from the ashes the ground-breaking city planner, Hippodamus, redesign the city on a regular grid system, the first time this much-replicated lay-out had been used.

In Hellenistic times the city came under the control of various powers finally being incorporated into the Roman Province of Asia. As a 'free city' of the empire Miletus maintained its importance, although its fortunes were gradual eclipsed by the ascendency of its neighbour, Ephesus. Its latter history is a familiar story of decline as silt brought down by the Meander (Büyük Menderes) river left it stranded from its life-blood: the sea.

The site The buildings seen today date from after the rebuilding of the city in the fifth century BC, with most from the Roman era. The most impressive feature visible from some way off is the large theatre which was enlarged during the Roman period to seat a crowd of about 15,000. You can still walk through the huge vaulted passageways much as the spectators would have done over 2,000 years ago. Inscriptions in the fifth row reserve seats for 'the Jews also called the God fearing', while one further up records a labour dispute resolved after arbitration by the oracle at Didyma. The hill above is crowned by a **Byzantine castle**, from where you can get a bird's eye view of the rest of the site.

To the northeast (opposite side of the hill to the theatre) was one of the city's busy harbours, known as Lion Bay because of the two **stone lions**, now partially uncovered, that stood guard at its entrance. The remains of a **naval monument** commemorating the victory of Augustus over Cleopatra in 31 BC is at the head of the harbour.

Miletus

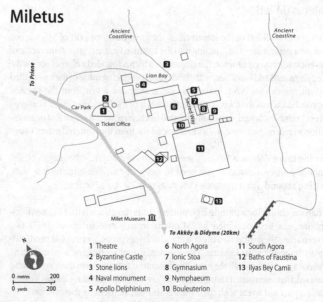

1 Theatre
2 Byzantine Castle
3 Stone lions
4 Naval monument
5 Apollo Delphinium
6 North Agora
7 Ionic Stoa
8 Gymnasium
9 Nymphaeum
10 Bouleuterion
11 South Agora
12 Baths of Faustina
13 Ilyas Bey Camii

Ancient Coastline

Ancient Coastline

To Priene

Car Park
Ticket Office

Lion Bay

Sacred Way

Milet Museum

To Akköy & Didyma (20km)

N

0 metres 200
0 yards 200

The thinkers of Miletus

While the seafarers of Miletus travelled far and wide founding colonies and enriching the city, back home there were some great thinkers at work. Although Miletus was not alone among the Ionian cities in being home to intellectual heavyweights, it does seem to have had more than its fair share of brilliant individuals, who pushed forward the boundaries of knowledge in fields such as astrology, mathematics, philosophy and geography.

First there was **Thales**, an early scientist whose remarkable hypothesis that all things were 'made of water' was way ahead of its time. His theory formed the basis for future speculation on the make up of the universe. Among his other notable achievements was the prediction of a solar eclipse in 585 BC, which he made using the help of observations by Babylonian astronomers. By using simple logic he also worked out the height of the Pyramids in Egypt by measuring their shadow at the time of day when a man's shadow was equal in length to his height.

Fellow Milesians, **Anaximenes** and **Anaximander** were also busy theorizing about the universe, the first believing that air was its fundamental building block, while the second attributed it to something he called the 'Infinite'. Anaximander has also been dubbed the father of geography for drawing the first map of the world. This was quite a feat for someone who had never travelled, something that can at least partly explain its wild inaccuracies. The wandering was left up to another citizen of Miletus, **Hecataeus**, who journey widely, recording his observations in his ancient travel book, 'Geography'.

Finally there was **Hippodamus**, the ancestor of modern city planners, who arranged Miletus in a regular grid pattern, the first of its kind and an early

The Aegean Region

The main civic buildings were to the south of the harbour, with a colon-naded avenue leading to the most important sanctuary of Miletus, a shrine to **Apollo Delphinium**. In the form of a dolphin Apollo was the patron saint of this seafaring city and was believed to guide Milesian ships across the waves. The bases of four semi-circular altars are still visible and nearby is the beginning of a **sacred way** which originally stretched all the way to Didyma. There's also a restored Ionic stoa, the remains of a **gymnasium** and an ornate **nymphaeum** on one side of the sacred way. Facing these are the **north agora** and the **bouleuterion** where the city council met.

Nearby, the **Baths of Faustina** was built at the behest of the wife of Emperor Marcus Aurelis. Though better preserved than other buildings at the site they're unremarkable except for the fountains carved into the shape of a lion and the local river god Meander, now sadly missing its head.

To the south the **Ilyas Bey Camii**, constructed in 1404 when Miletus was part of the *beylik* (principality) of Menteşoğlu, is near the site entrance. The structure is a testament to the robust building practices of the time having survived an earthquake in 1954 which levelled the nearby village of Balat, depriving it of its practitioners.

The **Milet Museum**, with its interesting collection of artefacts from Miletus and other sites, is beside the road a short distance before the entrance. ■ *0800-1900 daily, US$1.25. Museum open 0830-1230, 1330-1730, US$2.*

Dolmuş from Güllübahçe and Söke pass nearby on their way to **Altınkum**, **Balat** or Akköy. From Akköy you may have to hitch the last 5 km or ask in the village café for a lift. **Transport**

Didyma

In the very south of Ionia, 20 km beyond Miletus, Didyma was not an ancient city, but the site of a temple of Apollo, home to the most renowned oracle of the Hellenistic world. Even today it is an extremely impressive structure thanks to its huge scale and the extensive efforts of French and German excavators.

History
Excavation has been a very multi-national affair; begun in the 18th century by English archaeologists subsequent work by French & German experts continues to the present day

Originally a Carian sanctuary, Didyma sat on Milesian territory and was administered by hereditary priests or priestesses from the noble Branchidae family. When consulted by petitioners, who would travel from across the ancient world, the oracle of Apollo Branchidae would slip into a trance-like state and utter prophecies believed to be the words of Apollo. For such services the temple was lavished with rewards.

The sanctuary was destroyed along with Miletus in 479 BC by Xerxes, and the Branchidae, having given up the temple treasure to the enemy, packed their bags and left with the Persians. When Alexander the Great came upon their descendants in Persia 50 years later, he had them executed in revenge for this treachery. Destroyed again by the Persians, the construction of the present structure started in Hellenistic times, but was never fully completed even after 500 years of work due to the huge costs and engineering problems involved. Although incomplete it ranked as the third largest monument in the ancient world and continued functioning up until Theodosius I banned pagan worship in 392 AD. Since then it has suffered from damage by earthquake and at the hands of villagers, carting off chunks of marble to use as building material.

The site
The size of the structure, towering above the contemporary houses that surround it, is still very impressive. Of the original forest of over 100 columns supporting the roof, only three are left standing to their original height. Even so the column bases are still huge and walking up the front steps, you can well imagine the awe felt by suppliants arriving to consult the oracle.

In front of the building is a **well** where pilgrims performed their ritual ablutions before making a sacrifice at the raised **circular altar** in the porch area. The much-reproduced **Medusa head** was part of a relief adorning the architrave, high up above the outer columns. It was in the front porch area that petitioners would pose there questions to temple priests who would relay them to the prophetess in the **oracle room**. Broad steps lead down to the **central courtyard**, which was open to the sky. Around the back of the temple parts of one of the huge pillars lie where it toppled to the ground. Also notice the inscriptions- ancient graffitti- carved into the blocks of the perimeter wall.

Sleeping & eating
There are 2 options close by, or else head down the hill into the beach resort of Altınkum

F *Medusa House*, just past temple towards Altınkum, T8110063. Slightly better rooms than Oracle (see below), but no views of temple, shady terrace, chunks of ancient marble used in building, boat tours arranged. Recommended. **F** *Oracle Pansiyon*, next to the temple, T8110270. Simple 2/3 bed rooms, comfortable seating area overlooking the temple, wonderful at night. Recommended. There are several touristy restaurants catering for coach parties visiting the temple.

Transport
There are regular **dolmuş** to and from **Söke** and **Milas** passing by on their way to **Altınkum**.

Altınkum
Suffering from its popularity with Turkish and British holidaymakers, the beach resort of Altınkum at least lives up to its name – 'Golden Sand' – with an excellent stretch of fine white sand, gently sloping off into the turquoise water. Unfortunately, the beach is backed by a jumble of restaurants and hotels aimed solely at the short-stay package market. Prices are advertised in pounds, with

Deve Güreşi-Camel wrestling

Camel wrestling is popular throughout the Aegean and western Mediterranean regions, but its heartland is the Büyük Menderes Valley. During the winter mating season, between November and March, up to 30 competitions are held at the weekends in small towns and villages. The events attract large crowds and a carnival-like atmosphere prevails with much eating, drinking and merriment.

Male camels begin their wrestling career at the age of four and may compete for anything up to 15 years. Named after their home town or a contemporary film star, they carry large brightly coloured felt saddles with a bell attached. For the owners –or savranlar– camel wrestling rates as a very serious hobby with a winning beast worth anything up to US$25,000.

A match begins with two males, roused into a state of aggression by their proximity to one another, being paraded around the arena, spilling trails of saliva from their mouths. They are then charged together to start the bout which lasts anything up to four minutes. Once locked together, the belligerents use their long necks to lever their opponent's legs out from underneath them. The intensity of the resulting tussle varies considerably

with some pairs remaining locked motionlessly together, much to the crowds dissatisfaction, while others spin and jostle in a blur of long brown necks and legs. An outright win is achieved if one of the camels falls to the ground or makes a break for it, with two teams of urgancı on hand with long ropes to pull the camels apart at the end of a bout.

Matches are supervised by a committee of judges and a referee on the look-out for any illegal biting or kicking; while the cazgır provides a running commentary on the proceedings in language peppered with traditional rhyming quatrains and sarcastic humour. Surprisingly, no gambling takes place and the only money changing hands is the final prize – usually about US$250– awarded to the overall winner at the end of the day. But the runners-up don't go home empty handed as all the participants receive a carpet for their trouble.

The İzmir tourist information office has a list of events in the region, however, this is sometimes wrong. Double check with local tourist information offices. Competitions take place in towns from Çanakkale to Antalya, including some of the resorts such as Bodrum and Kuşadası.

The Aegean Region

doubtful treats such as the 'English Breakfast' and 'Sunday Roast' on offer; while the beer is cheap and plentiful.

Sleeping The accommodation scene along the front is dominated by 2- and 3-star package hotels such as **B** *Golden Sand Hotel*, T8131380. Double rooms overlooking sea, pool, restaurant, bar. **F** *Damla Otel*, T8131632. One of several more basic places near the police station.

Transport A useful **ferry** service connects Altınkum with Bodrum in 2 hrs, leaving every day 0900 and returning at 1900, US$8. There are **buses** from the bus station to destinations across the country.

The administrative centre of a province of the same name, Aydın is surrounded by fertile agricultural land irrigated by water from the Büyük Menderes River. Formerly the important Roman city of Tralles and later the capital of a 14th-century Turcomen principality that controlled the area, there is little left to see of either today, thanks to several earthquakes, the retreating Greek army in 1922 and the Turkish military, who now occupy the hilltop site of Tralles. The only reason most people visit, briefly, is to get on a dolmuş or bus to one of the

Aydın
Phone code: 0256
Colour map 4, grid B2

sites nearby. Tourist information is beside the roundabout on the main highway, to the east of the bus station, T2254145, F2126226, open 0900-1700.

Sleeping and eating If you want to spend the night, there are a couple of good hotels north of the main square on the continuation of Adnan Menderes Bulvarı, Hükümet Bulvarı (see below). There is also **C** *Turtay Hotel*, outside town on road south towards Muğla, T2133003, F2130351, large 4-star hotel, comfortable rooms have ensuite and TV, swimming pool, restaurant, bar. **F** *Hotel Kabaçam*, Hükümet Bulvarı, 11 Sokak 2/B, T2122794. Double rooms with bathroom. Recommended. The cheaper *Hotel Vardar* across the street is not recommended. As far as food is concerned Aydın offers the standard selection of reasonably priced kebap and pide places.

Transport Buses depart from the bus station on the main road, 1 km south from the town centre, for **İzmir**, very frequently, 2 hrs, US$5; **Denizli**, also very frequently, 2 hrs, US$4. There is a free bus service from the bus station to the centre of town. **Dolmuş** leave for **Sultanhisar, Nazilli** and other points in the area from the dolmuş station on Gazi Bulvarı. **Train** services between **İzmir** and **Denizli** pass through 3 times daily, also stopping at **Nazilli, Selçuk** and **Menderes** airport. However, the bus is faster and more reliable. Check locally for departure times.

Directory Post office: In the centre of town just west of the main square, open 24 hrs.

Nysa Just to the north of the village of Sultanhisar, 28 km east of Aydın, are the ruins of Nysa, an important city during the Imperial Roman era. Seldom visited today, the remains of the city are scattered amongst the olive trees, surrounded by peaceful rural scenery.

The famous geographer Strabo (63 BC-25 AD) was one of a large number of pupils who studied in the city, which was a celebrated centre of learning. He described it as a: 'double city, so to speak, for it is divided by a torrential stream, which at one place has a bridge over it, joining the two cities, and at another it is adorned with an amphitheatre, with a hidden underground passage for the torrential waters.'

It's possible to walk through the 150 m long **Roman drainage tunnel** Stabo describes in summer and to explore the scattered remains of the city's **theatre**, the important **library**, the **gymnasium**, the **bouleuterion** and scattered **Byzantine buildings**. Nothing remains of the ancient bridge though. The warden, present during daylight hours, can give you a brief tour in return for a tip. Above all Nysa makes a good place to take a break from the road and have a picnic. ■ *Open during daylight hours. US$1.50. Getting there: From the highway the ruins are 2 km beyond town on a hill.*

Transport Dolmuş travel regularly east and west along the E87 highway and can be stopped at Sultanhisar, as does the plodding İzmir-Denizli**train**.

Nazilli A substantial market town 14 km east of Sultanhisar, there is no reason to stop in Nazilli unless you're using public transport to get to Aphrodisias. The bus station has frequent buses to İzmir, Denizli and Selçuk, passing through Ortaklar, and there are dolmuş south to Geyre, the Turkish village near Aphrodisias, or Karacasu about 10 km away from the ruins. Buses depart several times a day for more distant destinations, such as İstanbul, 12 hours, US$21; Antalya, six hours, US$10 and Konya, eight hours, US$8. The İzmir-Denizli train also passes through in each direction.

If you have to stay the night, try **E** *Hotal Metya*, opposite the petrol station near the bus station, T3128888, which has decent rooms with ensuite.

Aphrodisias

Excavations have revealed that Aphrodisias, 40 km south of the Aydın-Denizli highway near the village of Geyre, has been inhabited for 5000 years. However, it's the Graeco-Roman ruins including the Temple of Aphrodite, the goddess of love, which attract most visitors. Despite the scale and interest of the discoveries unearthed since the 1960s, Aphrodisias remains refreshingly uncommercialized. Situated in a wide valley flanked by rounded mountains, streaked with snow well into spring, the site has a wild isolation which is a relief after the crowds and touts of Ephesus. The on-site museum, crammed with statuary carved from the creamy local marble by some of the most gifted ancient hands, is excellent.

Phone code: 0256
Colour map 4, grid B3

Originally called Ninoe after the Akkadian fertility goddess who had a shrine here, the town developed quickly after its association with the Greek goddess of love, Aphrodite. This assimilation of an existing cult into the Greek pantheon turned out to be very fortuitous for the town. Aphrodite was the mother of Aeneas, the mythical founder of Rome, and her temple attracted a large number of pilgrims as well as the patronage of Roman emperors, like Julius Caesar, who claimed direct descendence from her. The city was awarded free status by Octavian in 39 BC and was embellished with magnificent public buildings. These were decorated beautifully using pale marble quarried from the slopes of nearby Baba Dağı. The work of the prolific local sculptors was esteemed across the ancient world and exported throughout the Roman Empire.

History

During medieval times Stavropolis (City of the Cross), as it was renamed, in an effort to shake-off its pagan past, was beset by various calamities and its population was finally dispersed by the Selçuks at the end of the 13th century. And so the ruins lay, half-buried beneath farmland and visited by various romantically inspired travellers, until the first excavations by a French engineer named Paul Gaudin in 1904. The most important discoveries though, which stunned the archaeological community, were found by a team led by the late Professor Kenan Erim who dedicated himself to the excavations before his untimely death in 1990.

Aphrodisias

1 Tetrapylon
2 Professor Erim's Grave
3 Stadium
4 Temple of Aphrodisias
5 Bishop's Palace
6 Odeion
7 Baths of Hadrian
8 Portico of Tiberius
9 Double Agora
10 Acropolis Mound
11 Theatre
12 Tetrastoön
13 Theatre Baths
14 Sebasteion

0 metres 200
0 yards 200

A pathway loops around the extensive site passing all of the main buildings. However, due to on-going work and an accompanying paranoia of theft, access to some is restricted. The Turkish village of Geyre originally covered much of the archaeological zone, but was moved to its present position, 1.5 km to the north, after being damaged by an earthquake in 1950. The paved area between the museum and the archaeologist's living quarters was once the village square.

The site

Taking the right-hand path after the museum, you pass the foundations of some wealthy residences before the magnificent **Tetrapylon**, a monumental gateway that led into the sanctuary of Aphrodisias, comes into view. The recently re-erected

T-e Aegean Region

structure, with half its columns baring striking spiral fluting, was built in the second century AD and originally had a rich frieze carved into its pediment. The grave of the archaeologist Kenan Erim is nearby, a fitting resting-place for a man who invested so much energy uncovering the ruins.

Follow a path across an open meadow to the **stadium** which is so remarkably complete you can easily imagine a baying crowd of up to 30,000 Aphrodisians watching gladiatory battles or the sporting, musical, theatrical and religious events which it also hosted

Continuing south the **Temple of Aphrodisias** is rather disappointing, although some of the columns have been erected to give you an idea of its former grandeur. The paucity of the remains is largely due to sweeping alterations made by the Byzantines, who transformed it into a basilica. Adjoining the temple are the foundations of the **Bishop's palace**, and a well-restored second century **odeion**, originally enclosed by a roof.

The **Baths of Hadrian** are next along the path with the chequer-board tiling around the square pool and a Corinthian column base at each corner are well preserved. Built in honour of a visit by the emperor, the baths had separate male and female sections and an under-floor heating system. Past the **Portico of Tiberius**, the large **double agora** is on the left, surrounded by Ionic and Corinthian colonnades. A hot climb in summer leads up to the **theatre**, built into the side of the **Acropolis mound** where excavations have revealed stratified settlement layers dating back to the Bronze Age. Inscriptions reveal that the theatre was built in the first century AD by a freed slave, with some later remodelling work carried out to protect the crowd from the wild animals and gladiators who did battle on the stage.

In front of the theatre is the **Tetrastoön**, used as a market place after the city's agora was subject to flooding following a rise in the water-table and the **Theatre Baths** to the south. Back near the modern buildings is the recently excavated **Sebasteion**, two parallel porticoes over 80 m in length, built in honour of Roman Emperor Augustus.

A visit to the **museum**, packed with sculptuary produced by the prolific ancient craftsmen from the creamy local stone, rounds off a visit to Aphrodisias perfectly. Opened in 1979, under joint sponsorship of the Turkish government and the National Geographic Society, it holds most of the artefacts unearthed by Professor Erim and his team. ■ *Site: 0830-1900. US$2.50. Museum: 0830-1800. Additional fee: US$2.50.*

Sleeping & eating
Near the village of Geyre and 13 km east of the small town of Karacasu, local options are limited to the *Anatolian Restaurant*, on the main road about 1 kms before the site, which also offers **camping**, and the reasonable **F** *Aphrodisias Hotel and Restaurant*, T4488132, clean doubles with ensuite, pleasant garden and roof-top restaurant. Before it, is the simpler **G** *Chez Mestan*, T4488046, with basic rooms with sink and shower, shared toilet. Above the bus-station in Karacasu, the *Otogar Moteli* is a last resort if you get stranded. The approach to Karacasu is also punctuated by restaurants used by Aphrodisias-bound tour buses.

Transport
There are several direct buses every day from İzmir (3½ hrs, US$9) and Selçuk (2½ hrs, US$8) to Karacasu, from where you can get a dolmuş to Geyre. Dolmuş also leave regularly from the well-connected Nazilli bus station for Karacasu, often continuing on to Geyre. If you are dumped in Karacasu, get a local dolmuş, taxi (US$8 return) or hitch the final 13 km. Remember to leave early to avoid being stranded, particularly out-of-season. Without your own transport the easiest way to visit Aphrodisias in summer is by enrolling on a tour from Pamukkale or even Selçuk. These are arranged by several companies and usually depart at 1000, returning early afternoon, costing US$10.

At the eastern end of the Büyük Menderes Valley, 110 km from Aydın, is the large provincial town of Denizli. The moderating influence of the distant Aegean is weaker here and the climate has a definate continental feel with snow lingering late on the surrounding mountains and the summers hot and dusty. At the centre of a rich agricultural hinterland, manufacturing industries, particularly textile mills and garment factories, have sprung up on the outskirts of town attracting workers from far afield. Several earthquakes and the recent building boom have left little reason to prolong your stay though; indeed most tourists are just passing through en-route to nearby Pamukkale.

Denizli
Phone code: 0258
Colour map 4, grid B3

Sleeping and eating If, for some reason, you want to stay there are lots of hotels within easy reach of the bus station, including the following. **C** *Bellona*, Cumhuriyet Caddesi, T2419828, F2650338. tastefully designed to cater for visiting businessmen, comfortable rooms. Recommended. **E** *Napa Otel*, Cumhuriyet Caddesi, T2420428. Reasonable rooms with ensuite, restaurant. Recommended. **E** *Yıldırım Otel*, next to bus station, T2633590. Average rooms, a/c, ensuite, convenient for *otogar*.

Transport Pamukkale Ekspresi, departs for İstanbul via Eğirdir and Afyon every day at 1705, 15 hrs. There are also 3 daily trains to **İzmir**, taking a leisurely 6 hrs, US$3.50. More regular **buses** do the journey to İzmir in 4 hrs, US$10. Buses also leave frequently for destinations including **Antalya**, **Ankara**, **Eğirdir**, **Göreme** and **Konya** (see page 293). Regular **dolmuş** and **city buses** for **Pamukkale** leave from the bus station throughout the day.

The train & bus station face one another across the busy highway

Pamukkale

The travertines of Pamukkale are one of the classic images of Turkey, used in countless tourist brochures, pamphlets and posters to entice people to visit the country. Having seen the pictures of scantily clad tourists lounging in turquoise pools amongst the startling-white mineral formations, it's easy to be very disappointed with the reality marred, as it is, by some thoughtless development and blatant commercialization. However, attempts are being made to redress some of the problems and if you set your expectations at a more realistic level, a visit can still be enjoyable and interesting.

Phone code: 0258
Colour map 4, grid B4

Getting there The turn off for Pamukkale is on the highway to Afyon and Isparta near the edge of Denizli. Dolmuş shuttle between Denizli bus station and Pamukkale, a distance of 19 km, until 2300 during the summer. There are some long-distance buses which call en route at the much busier Denizli bus station. In the highly competitive accommodation market, most guesthouses and hotels will pick you up for free from Denizli if you telephone them. **Getting around** From Pamukkale village it is a short climb up through the travertines to the plateau and ruins of Hierapolis, called Örenyeri. In a car you can drive to the north entrance, on the road to Karahayıt and 2.5 km from the centre of the ruins, or to the south entrance, reached from Pamukkale village, which is much closer. Dolmuş from Denizli stop in the village before continuing up to the centre of Örenyeri, every 30 mins, US$0.50. There is a **tourist information** office at the top of the travertines, T2722077, open 0800-1200, 1330-1700, and an information kiosk near the south entrance.

Ins & outs
See page 293 for further details

The mineral waters and unique formations they created have been attracting people for thousands of years. A city was first established by one of the kings of Pergamum in the second century BC, but it is from the later Roman city of Hierapolis that most of today's ruins date. Just like now, Romans came to bathe in the warm waters which were attributed with healing qualities.

History

The Aegean Region

Inscriptions reveal that several emperors were among those that came for a soak and the city benefited handsomely from imperial patronage. This was a good thing because it sat in a geologically unstable zone prone to earthquakes, one of which flattened it completely in 60 AD.

The Travertines   The mineral formations, visible from far away as a white smudge on the valleyside, owe their existence to the calcite-laden waters that issue from a spring in the slopes of Çal Dağı. Emerging at about 35°C, the water flows off the edge of the plateau, cooling and depositing some of its mineral load as calcium carbonate, chalk, in great petrified waterfalls and curtains of stalactites. Over thousands of years this process has built up the tiers of pools and cascades that we see today. Known to the Turks as Pamukkale or 'Cotton castle', walking across the terraces is a strange sensory experience, visually like being on a frigid glacier surrounded by icicles and snow, but pleasantly warm and without the fear of slipping over.

Unfortunately, Pamukkale's popularity has come at a considerable cost with the passage of thousands of tourist feet wearing away the delicate chalky layers. The mineral-rich waters, valued since Roman times, were also used to fill hotel pools along the plateau rim, depleting the amount cascading over the travertines. The combined effect was a gradual discolouration with brown patches appearing through the whiteness.

Despite the existence of a management plan and the site being added to the UNESCO World Heritage list, only recently has action been taken to halt this deterioration. Access is now restricted to a limited area of the travertines and only with bare feet. Relaxing in the pools is also now a thing of the past. Amazingly the hotels along the top which spoilt the view and monopolized the precious water have all been knocked down by order of the local government, belatedly reacting to the possibility of losing an important tourist attraction and source of revenue. A re-whitening programme is also now in progress with water switched between different areas of the formation in strict rotation. Only time will tell whether this action is enough to reverse years of decline.

The site   The best way to approach the site on foot is via the ramp leading directly up to the base of the travertines. A guard will prompt you to take off your shoes before commencing your ascent for real. If some of the shallow pools look suspiciously angular, that's because they are man-made attempts to replicate the natural ones damaged during earlier construction. The pathway up through the travertine terraces gets crowded and you may prefer exploring the area further to the southeast (right as you look from the bottom) where access is so far unrestricted, although the formations are not as spectacular.

With the razing of the hotels in Örenyeri, what was the Pamukkale Moteli is now the **Turaş Pamukkale Thermal**. It's a fairly modern complex encompassing a large pool littered with chunks of ancient marble and is the only place for a swim above the travertines, entry US$3. However, subject to the outcome of a pending court case even this may be gone by the time you arrive. A row of souvenir stalls selling drinks has survived, along with the **museum** and **tourist information** centre.

Hierapolis: east section   A road leads past the museum and Turaş Pamukkale Thermal up to the **Nymphaeum**, **Temple of Apollo** and **Plutonium**. Built on Hellenistic foundations, what remains of the sanctuary dedicated to Apollo is from the third century AD. The Plutonium, within Apollo's temple, was formerly thought to be the entrance to Hades and was the focus of worship of the god of the underworld. A grotto filled with poisonous gases bubbling up from a fissure, the ancient Geographer Strabo described how, '... any living creature that enters will find death upon the instant.' He also reported mysteriously that eunuchs from the temple could enter the grotto without holding their breath. The gas is still just as deadly and a metal grate prevents any tragic repetition of earlier accidents caused by foolhardy tourists trying to emulate the eunuchs. The well-preserved **Roman theatre** and the fifth-century **Martyrion of St Philip** are further up the track. The second, along a pathway on the left, was a centre of pilgrimage and worship dedicated to the saint.

Hierapolis: west section From the souvenir shops walk about 500 m north along the road to the **colonnaded street** just outside the **city walls**. Alternatively, if you are at the Martyrion of St Philip you can cut down directly westwards on a path. This was the commercial heart of the Hellenistic city, a wide marble way bisecting it from wall to wall and ending in a monumental gateway at each end. The **triple arch** dedicated to Domitian in 83 AD is the only survivor of the pair. Nearby the restored **tomb of Flavius Zeuxis**, a local merchant and traveller, marks the beginning of the **necropolis**, one of the most extensive and interesting of its kind in Anatolia. Hundreds of sarcophagi, burial mounds and elaborate tombs dating from the Hellenistic to the early Byzantine period are scattered along either side of the road. Many of the tombs were surrounded by well kept gardens and carried inscriptions over 300 of which have been translated.

Sleeping

Most visitors stay in 1 of the many hotels or guesthouses in Pamukkale Village, conveniently situated at the bottom of the travertines. These typically have a pool filled with mineral water channelled down from the spring on the plateau above, which because of the distance has lost its heat. The more luxurious accommodation, used by visiting tour groups, is in Karahayıt, with a range of 4 and 5-star resort hotels to choose from. The competition between places in Pamukkale village, particularly in light of dwindling tourist numbers, is fierce. This does keep prices low but on the downside it also means you are pounced on by touts as soon as you arrive in Denizli or Pamukkale and subjected to an often aggressive sales pitch. To avoid this have a place in mind (perhaps arrange to be picked up) and take no notice of claims that the place you have chosen is shut, full or has burnt down'.

The Aegean Region

Hierapolis

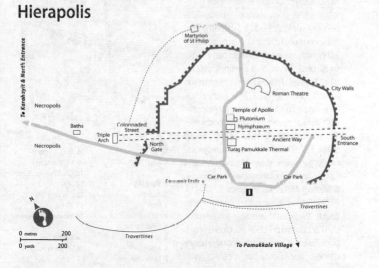

Karahayıt A *Club Hierapolis*, T2714100, F2714143. Mock classical buildings, comfortable rooms, immaculate gardens, pools, health spa, mud treatments, restaurant. Recommended. **B** *Hotel Villa Lycus*, past larger *Lycus River Hotel*, T2714351, F2714508. Double rooms with a/c, TV and telephone, 2 pools, thermal centre, fitness centre, restaurant. Recommended. **D** *Pam Thermal Hotel*, right up lane from road, T2714140, F2714097. Modern blocks, double rooms with bathroom, TV, telephone, balcony, thermal centre, pool, bar, restaurant. **E** *Kur-Tur Otel*, at the end of lane on right in trees, T2714071, F2630818. Small rooms with bathroom, a/c, set around pool, shaded by greenery. Recommended. **G** *Selçuklu Kaplıcaları*, up lane on right beside brightly colour hotel, T2714189. Small local-run place, Turkish customers, each room has kitchenette, fridge, mineral bath, bath in garden. Outstanding value if you're looking for something cheap. Recommended.

Pamukkale Village C *Hotel Hal-Tur*, on the main road heading out of town, T/F2722723. Modern, flashy, looks out on travertines, rooms with satellite TV, minibar, a/c, pool, sauna, bar. Recommended if you like your creature comforts. **D** *Best Hotel*, T2722916, Cumhuriyet Meydanı, bit tatty, small courtyard and pool squeezed in. **D** *Koçak Otel*, 50 m down Menderes Caddesi from centre, T2722492, F2722112. Comfortable rooms around swimming pool, sauna, restaurant. **E** *Konak Sade Hotel*, at the top of Atatürk Caddesi, car park access from main road, T2722002, F2722175. Good position for which you pay a slight premium, sound of mineral water filling pool from rooms, terrace restaurant with views, wood-panelled attic rooms are particularly nice. Recommended. **E** *Koray Otel*, Fevzi Çakmak Caddesi, T2722222, F2722095. Rooms around swimming pool and gardens, half-board, buffet breakfast, heating, friendly, good value. Recommended. **E** *Melodi Motel*, on the main road opposite the base of the travertines, T2722274, F2722275. Pool, bar, restaurant, open buffet in season. Recommended for its position, not the rooms. **F** *Alida Otel*, T2722602, F2722823. 2/3/4 person rooms, courtyard with pool and views of travertines, restaurant, set menu for US$7 including soft-drink. Recommended. **F** *Kervansaray Hotel*, down Turgut Özal Caddesi, left after bridge, T2722209, reasonable rooms with bathroom, small pool, rooftop terrace, 10% discount with this book. **F** *Sympathy Paradise Pension*, T2722047. 7 simple rooms, 2/3 person, some with shared bathrooms, small pool, views of travertines, restaurant. **F** *Hotel Türkü*, back entrance on Atatürk Caddesi, T2722181. Family run, nice wood-panelled rooms, rooftop bar with view of travertines, pool, good value. Recommended. **G** *Alida Otel*, Kuzey Sokak, T2722180. Basic rooms, run by local family, panoramic views of travertines and town from rooftop bar, restaurant. **G** *Meltem Motel*, Kuzey Sokak, T2722413, F2722157, meltemmotel@superonline.com.tr Breakfast extra, single-room US$7.50, dormitory US$4.50, clean rooms, pool, internet, use of telephone, money change, restaurant, bar, popular with

Pamukkale village

To North Entrance & Karahayıt

To the Travertines

Menderes Caddesi
Health Clinic

Kuzey Sokak

Cumhuriyet Meydanı

Turgut Özal Caddesi

Atatürk Caddesi

Oğuz Kağan Caddesi

Mehmet Akif Ersoy Bulvarı

To Denizli

N

Not to scale

■ **Sleeping**
1 Alida Otel
2 Best
3 Hal Tur
4 Kervansaray
5 Koçak Otel
6 Konak Sade
7 Koray Otel
8 Melodi Motel
9 Meltem Motel
10 OASE Pension/Camping
11 Rose
12 Star Otel
13 Türkü
14 Weisse Burg Pension

● **Eating**
1 Bergoma Aparatif
2 Han

backpackers, best cheap bed in town. Recommended. **G** *OASE Pension and Camping*, as you approach village on left, T2722030. Bit ramshackle but good value, rooms facing large pool, garden, restaurant serves tandır kebaps. Recommended. **G** *Hotel Rose*, on the right after south entrance, T2722205. A-frame bungalows with bathroom, pool, camping, nice location. Noise nearby club can be problem. **G** *Hotel Şahin*, left before Melodi, T2722180. Simple doubles, pool, panoramic view from roof terrace. **G** *Star Otel*, at base of travertines, T2722639. Motel-style, basic rooms around pool and garden, breakfast extra, restaurant, camping. **G** *Weisse Burg Pension*, down Turgut Özal Caddesi, across bridge on left, T2722064. Nice rooms beside pool, good value. Recommended.

Camping *OASE Camping*, see above, offers free camping and use of bathrooms. There are several other campsites suitable for caravans along the main road before the village. *Star Pension* and *Sympathy Paradise* also have camping spots.

Midrange The *Konak Sade Hotel* has a terrace restaurant looking out onto the travertines, live music and a reasonable selection of Turkish and European food. *Han Restaurant*, one of many touristy places in the centre of the village. **Cheap** *Bergoma Aparatif*, Cumhuriyet Meydanı at bottom of Atatürk Caddesi, good soups, vegetable and meat dishes.

Eating
The restaurant situation is not very inspiring: most places are mediocre at best & expensive

The bars are an ephemeral species, here one season gone the next, so it is pointless trying to make any recommendations.

Bars

There are several on Atatürk Caddesi who can arrange transportation, car hire and tours. *Magic Valley Cappadocia Tours*, have an agent at Atatürk Caddesi No 7.

Tour operators

Bus There are several agents for the major bus companies along Atatürk Caddesi. Most buses depart from Denizli bus station except during high-season, so ask about a service bus before buying your ticket. **Antalya**, 8 buses daily, 5 hrs, US$5; **Çanakkale**, 1800, 9 hrs, US$11.50; **Eğirdir**, every 2 hrs, 3.5 hrs, US$5; **İzmir**, 0930, 1630, 1700, US$4; **Ürgüp/Göreme**, 1330, 1900, 2000, 10 hrs, US$9.

Transport

Medical facilities The health clinic is on the corner of Menderes and Bahçe Sokak. **Communications Post office**: There is a PTT at the top of the travertines, near the museum and information centre.

Directory

Around Pamukkale

Karahayıt is the site of an iron-rich spring and is also where most of the area's top-notch hotels are to be found. The spring is nothing to get excited about, the hot Kırmızı Su (Red water) welling up into a pool and trickling down a small set of discoloured deposits. This hasn't stopped the attraction being ruthlessly commercialized with a row of souvenir shops, a murky bathing pool and a large café detracting from the already tame spectacle. ■ *Getting there: Dolmuş arrive from Pamukkale village at least every 30 minutes.*

Karahayıt

Coming from Denizli, about 13 km before Pamukkale, you may notice a large yellow signpost for the remains of the **ancient city** of Laodiceia. What little remains of the city is scattered over a desolate flat-topped hill between two small river valleys. Built by the Seleucid King Antiochus II in the third century BC and named after his wife, it became part of the Roman Empire after the Seleucid defeat. It was an important Christian centre and site of one of the Churches of the Revelation. It was decimated by a catastrophic earthquake in

Laodiceia

494 AD from which it never fully recovered. What's left is mainly from the Roman city and includes a nymphaeum, stadium, baths complex, gymnasium, theatre, and Ionic temple. All in all it's a fairly forgettable place, particularly if you've already seen several of the better known archaeological sites, and is mostly visited because of its biblical association. ■ *Getting there: Denizli-Pamukkale dolmuş will drop you on the main road, 500 m from the site.*

The southern Aegean coast

The ancient kingdom of Caria begins in the hills south of the Büyük Menderes valley, and its capital at Halicarnassas, the modern-day resort of Bodrum, is a Mecca for holidaymakers. But there are also some quieter spots nearby, generally overlooked by people dashing for the bright lights.

Lake Bafa After traversing the flat Büyük Menderes valley on a monotonously straight ribbon of tarmac, the mountainous relief of ancient Caria comes as quite a relief. The highway at this point winds along the shore of Lake Bafa with the serrated ridge of Beşparmak Dağı, ancient Mount Latmos, reflected in its brackish waters.

The area has been designated as a nature park in recognition of its importance as an over-wintering site for numerous species of bird In ancient times this was the Latmian Gulf, a tongue of water stretching inland from the Aegean and dividing the cities of Priene and Miletus, on its northern and southern shores. With the passage of time the silt-laden waters of the River Meander (Menderes) advanced the coastline, cutting the ancient cities off from the sea and trapping a body of water inland forming Lake Bafa.

The *Turkish Society for the Protection of Nature* has a hide at the western end of the lake near the village of **Dalyan**. Dalmatian pelicans, white-tailed eagles and pygmy cormorants are just a few of the visitors that can be spotted, while beneath the waves swim grey mullet (*kefal*), sea bass (*levrek*) and eels (*ihlan baliği*). All these species are threatened by water diversion for agricultural use on the adjacent Büyük Menderes plain; pollution and illegal hunting. The southern shore is largely undeveloped with a few basic restaurants and camp sites catering mainly for passing trade. G*Ceri'nin Yeri* is best with a restaurant, camping and basic rooms.

Heracleia under Latmos (Kapıkırı)

Phone code: 0252
Colour map 4, grid B2 Despite the huge volume of tourist traffic passing along the busy highway to the south of Lake Bafa, the village of Kapıkırı nestling beneath the rocky haunches of Beşparmak Dağı, ancient Mount Latmos, remains a tranquil backwater. Surrounded by the ruins of ancient Heracleia under Latmos, life continues much as it has done for generations. That is except for a small but growing collection of guesthouses and simple restaurants catering for those that do make it the 11 km from the main road.

Lake Bafa

Getting there Buses plying the highway north or south can be stopped in the vil- | **Ins & outs**
lage of Çamiçi, about 11 km from Kapıkırı. The Söke-Milas dolmuş, every 30 mins during the day, is another alternative. From Kapıkırı itself an unreliable dolmuş leaves in
the morning for Çamiçi, returning in the evening to Kapıkırı. On Fri, market-day in
Çamiçi, there are 3 services. Hitching is possible, although traffic on the road is light.
Getting around From 1 of the village's guesthouses the ruins can be visited on foot
in a morning or afternoon. More time is require to visit the outlying monasteries.

In antiquity Heracleia was a port city at the eastern end of the Latmian Gulf. | **Background**
Blessed neither with ample territory nor an ideal position from which to conduct sea-trade – Miletus was much better placed for that – the city never rose
to any kind of prominence. Of Carian origin, the city, then known as Latmos,
was moved for some unknown reason in the late Hellenistic period. Any
prospect of the city's fortunes picking up were dashed by the advancing
coastline of the Meander River, which cut off the Latmian Gulf from the open
sea, forming Lake Bafa.

Indeed, Heracleia would have sunk deeper into obscurity had it not been
for the legend of a local shepherd boy associated with the area. Endymion,
who tended his flock on the slopes of Mount Latmos, was visited each night
by the moon goddess Selenes as he slept. When Zeus found out about the liai-
son he granted the handsome shepherd a wish. Endymion asked for eternal
sleep and as he lay in slumber he was visited each night by the lustful Selenes
who bore him 50 children. Later, Christian clerics held that Endymion was in
fact a Carian mystic who wished to learn the name of God from the moon.
When he achieved this he promptly died and later his coffin became a focus
for pilgrimage once a year, when the bones were said to hum, apparently in
an attempt to pass on the name of God. During the Middle Ages, a thriving
monastic society developed in the area, with anchorite hermits living in
monasteries dotted throughout the mountains.

The houses of the present village are scattered amongst huge boulders and
the remains of ancient Heracleia. About 300 villagers traditionally make a living from the spindly olive trees covering the mountainside and the fields to the
west of the village. Also along the lakeshore to the west are small houses where
the villagers traditionally moved in the summer to take advantage of the cooling
wind blowing off the lake. This *yayla* – summer community – is now abandoned
and partially drowned by the rising lake. Tourism is of increasing importance to
the local economy and there is talk in the village of creating a society to help promote the area and control the negative impacts of such development.

The **Temple of Athena**, with its solid masonry largely intact, grabs your eye as | **Sights**
you approach the village. Notice the small inscription on the left as you enter. It
is reached via the village schoolyard which was the ancient agora. The
bouleuterion is further up on the right, with the **theatre** and **nymphaeum**
beyond the centre of the village. Follow the path up past the unsightly relay station to get a closer look at the magnificent city walls as they climb up the rocky
ridge. Some sections are well preserved with the blocks bedded directly into
grooves cut into the rock. It is hard to imagine the time and workmanship
needed to complete such a task.

Back down beside the lake, a **Byzantine fortress** sits on a promontory and
past this is a **Carian necropolis** with scores of coffins carved directly into the
rock, some with their lids nearby. The foundations of what is believed to be the
Sanctuary of Edymion are further to the west, near the *Zeybek* restaurant.
You can swim or wade, depending on the water level, out to the ruins of a fortified **Byzantine monastery** on an island just offshore.

The Aegean Region

For a good walk follow a track through the idyllic fields to the west of the village to the beginning of an ancient path which hugs the coastline for several kilometres, reaching a Byzantine fortress known as **Ikizada**. The fortifications crown an island connected to the coast by an isthmus of coarse sand. This is one of several possible stops on boat trips organized through pensions or restaurants in the village.

There are other monasteries worth visiting in the rocky hinterland of Mount Latmos, several with the remains of colourful frescoes depicting biblical scenes, though walking is not advisable in the heat of summer. Guides can be arranged locally, as with the boat trips, through the village restaurants or pensions. A London-based company, *Anatolian Adventures*, T0207 8741107, psunshine@hotmail.com, also arranges walking and trekking trips in the surrounding mountains.

Sleeping & eating

E *Agora Pension*, in the village, T5435445, F5435567, has fourteen simple but nicely finished rooms, also 3 cosy wooden bungalows, restaurant and bar, buffet breakfast, airport transfers. Recommended. **F** *Kaya Pansiyon and Restaurant*, lower (left) fork, past Zeybek and Selenes, T5435579, several simple rooms with bathroom on the hillside, also has lovely free camping spot across the road by the lakeshore. Recommended. **F** *Pelikan Pension*, on the edge of village, T5435880. Basic rooms, some with view of lake, restaurant. **F** *Yasemin Pension*, past *Agora Pension*, in the village proper. Simple rooms, terrace, friendly family-run place, plenty of rustic noises. Recommended. **F** *Zeybek Pansiyon*, left at fork, on headland beside lake, great position, T5435441. Small wooden cabins, also camping, US$1.50 per person with no breakfast.

Milas

Phone code: 0252
Colour map 4, grid B2

Milas is little more than a blur of apartment blocks and a junction in the road for most travellers intent on making their way south to Bodrum as quickly as possible. But such fleeting visits do little justice to a town with a considerable history. It could be worth sparing an hour or two to visit the town's mosques and Roman relics, after which you'll almost certainly be ready to move on. The tourist information bureau is in the Sudi Özkan Iş Merkezi on Muştak Bey Caddesi.

Sights

Probably the most interesting thing to see is the **Gümüşkesen**, meaning 'cuts-silver', a monumental Roman tomb built during the first century AD. The similarity of its Corinthian colonnade and pyramidal roof to the great Mausoleum at Halicarnassus is no accident and it was obviously built as a miniature version of the nearby 'Wonder of the World'. A curious feature is the hole in the floor of the platform through which mourners poured libations to the departed soul. ■ *No admission fee or opening hours. From the town centre walk west up Kadiağa Caddesi which turns into Gümüşkesen Caddesi.*

The **Baltalı Kapı** 'Gate with an Axe' in the north of the city, was one of the portals in the perimeter wall of Roman Mylasa. The double-headed axe, a symbol of Zeus and from which it gets its name, is carved faintly into the north-facing keystone. It's 100 m north of Orhan Bey Camii.

Scattered around town are some interesting mosques, the legacy of pre-Ottoman days when the town was under the control of the Turcoman Menteşe. **Ulu Cami** (1378) and **Orhan Bey Camii** (1330) are both on Şair Ülvi Akgün Caddesi, and **Firuz Bey Camii** (1394), built using much recycled material from earlier Hellenistic and Roman buildings, is near the Belediye. The **Çollühanı** is a caravanserai, a rarity because it is still serving its mercantile function and has not been turned into a hotel like so many others of its kind.

A look around the sights shouldn't take more than a couple of hours, so there's little **Sleeping**
need to stay in Milas. However if you do want to stay overnight, there are various simple options along Kadıağa Caddesi. **F** *Otel Arıcan*, beside the Hacı Ilyas Camii, T5121215, good value rooms with shared bathroom. **F** *Hotel Çınar*, T5125525. reasonably comfortable rooms with bathroom and balcony. **F** *Otel Sürücü*, Atatürk Bulvarı near the statue, T5124001, the best of a fairly mediocre bunch, decent rooms with bathroom and TV.

The town's restaurants offer pretty standard fare running to pide, soups, ready-prepared **Eating**
stews and of course kebaps. *Pamukkale Pide*, on Menteşe Caddesi is popular with locals, while the *Sürücü* and *Arican Hotels* both have their own restaurants.

The **market** is at its liveliest on Tue when tour groups are bussed in from Bodrum to **Shopping**
haggle for locally produced carpets, olive oil and honey.

Bus Buses leave the bus station, situated at the edge of town on the main road north, **Transport**
regularly throughout the day for **Muğla**, **Söke** and **Bodrum**, while there are also longer distance services passing through. There are regular shuttle buses into town from the *otogar*.

Banks In the centre of town. **Baths** *Yeni Hamamı*, near *Otel Arıcan* on Hacı Ilyas Sokak. **Directory**

From Milas the highway south climbs up into the mountains through pine **South of Milas**
woods dotted with beehives. Roadside stalls sell the golden honey produced by local bee-keepers as well as royal jelly. The honey generally comes in two varieties: *çam balı*, a darker, stronger tasting honey made by bees feeding in pine (*çam*) forests, and *çiçek balı*, a fragrant wildflower honey.

Shortly before reaching Yatağan the highway skirts a large open-caste mine where lignite, a low-grade coal responsible for the poor air quality in many Turkish cities during the winter, is extracted. On the eastern edge of the mine, in the shadow of huge piles of slag which threaten to engulf it, is the ancient city of **Stratonikea**. Established in the third century, the centre grew to prominence under the Romans with scattered ruins remaining from this time. Of additional interest are the more recent remains of Eskihisar, a deserted village whose population was relocated due to the mining operations.

The signpost for Iasos, about 10 km northwest of Milas, is generally ignored by **Iasos**
travellers heading south and on first impressions the strung out, dusty little fish- **(Kıyıkışlacık)**
ing village doesn't really justify the detour. However, some interesting ruins on a sea-girt peninsula; a couple of down-to-earth fish restaurants and a string of nice pensions on the hill above the village deserve a bit more attention. On-going excavations by an Italian team at the site of ancient Iasos have identified objects dating back over 5000 years, while the ruins of a Hellenistic city have been uncovered on the neck of the promontory. Iasos is also associated with the story of a local boy who was befriended by a dolphin. When the story was told to Alexander the Great as he passed through on his way to besiege Halicarnassus in 334 BC, he was so enchanted by the tale that he took the boy with him, later installing him as the head of the priesthood of Poseidon in Babylon.

Sleeping E *Kaya Pension*, T5377439. Nicely furnished rooms with bathroom, large *All 3 of the village's*
scenic terrace and swimming pool, evening meal provided as extra, perfect get-away, *pensions are up on the hill*
good value. Recommended. **E** *Pension Zeytin*, T5377008, F5377327. Pension and art *& are reached by*
school run by a friendly Danish couple, courses in drawing, painting, sculpture and *following the rough track*
mosaic design, rooms with bathroom may be available, courses should be booked in *up through the village*

The Aegean Region

advanced, summer: number above, winter: Denmark T49221905. Recommended. **F** *Cengiz Pansiyon*, T5377181. 7 pleasant rooms with shower, homely atmosphere, owner Cengiz speaks English, evening meal can be provided. Recommended.

Güllük On the road to Bodrum, 16 km from Milas, is a turn-off signposted for the small town of Güllük. Although there are some major villa developments on the hillside above it, life continues much as it always has done. Dozens of freighters wait off-shore to be loaded with locally-mined bauxite ore at the dock in town and the local fishing fleet sets out regularly on its Aegean forays. There are two bays either side of the centre, the southern one dominated by a petroleum company's private resort. There is a narrow strip of sand on the northern bay but this is very windswept at times. Tourism is low-key and mainly domestic in nature with lots of villas, a couple of guesthouses and a single large four-star hotel. All this adds-up to an unassuming kind of place, refreshingly free of the commercialisation of the main resorts.

From the limited range of accommodation there is still something to fit most budgets

Sleeping B *Corinthian Güllük Hotel*, on hilltop overlooking town, T5222911, F5222009. 36 a/c rooms with bathroom, TV, minibar, private beach and watersports, pool with great view over Mandalya Bay. Recommended. **D** *Knot Hotel*, T5222427, F5222426. 3-star, just to the south of town, rooms with balcony, bathroom, sea-views, swimming pool. Recommended. **F** *Pascal Motel*, signposted on right as you come down into town, T5222822, F5222026. Double rooms with bathroom, balcony looking on to citrus trees, open all year, single US$11, 2 apartments. Recommended. **F** *Kemer Pansiyon*, on road in, overlooking town, T5222143. Small rooms with bathroom, some have no external window, breakfast extra, excellent views from roof terrace. Ask at the *Barbaros Café*, on the bay to the north of the centre, about free camping.

Eating There are plenty of fish restaurants along the waterfront, which offer good value for money and a excellent place to watch the sunset.

Tours Boat excursions across the bay to Iasos and to nearby beaches can be arranged by some of these places or through the guesthouses.

Bodrum

Phone code: 0252
Colour map 4, grid B2

Originally the Carian capital of King Mausolus and later an outpost of the Knights of St John, Bodrum is now a resort town whose reputation has spread far beyond the turquoise Aegean shores. It is well known to both Turks and European visitors for its relaxed atmosphere and nocturnal activities, namely drinking and dancing in the town's innumerable bars, clubs and discos. The fishing town of yesteryear has been besieged by ranks of condominiums and holiday developments but in spite of this Bodrum has maintained a charm lost by other Turkish resorts; a certain sophistication that gives it appeal beyond the British package tourists for whom it's so popular. Joining the evening promenade or sitting in one of the marina-side cafés looking across a forest of masts to the solid ramparts of the Castle of St John are thoroughly pleasant experiences. And once you've had enough of the hustle there are also some quieter spots on the peninsular nearby.

Ins and outs

Getting there
See page 304 for further details
The town is 250 km south of İzmir on a toe of land protruding from the southwestern coast. Roughly equidistant, the airports of Dalaman to the south and İzmir to the north are typical arrival points for package tourist from Europe. The town also has a

The Aegean Region

small airport of its own, served by domestic and charter flights. Regular buses from destinations across the country arrive via the town of Milas, where a good highway leaves the coastal road, winding 52 km to the resort. Regular ferries link Bodrum with the Greek island of Kos on the horizon to the south.

In an attempt to regulate traffic in the town centre large areas have been pedestrianized. There is also a one-way system in operation which can be of some frustration to the first-time visitor arriving by car. This sends you down Cevat Şakır Caddesi towards the harbour, along waterfront Neyzen Tevfik Caddesi, up Cafer Paşa Caddesi before returning along Turgut Reis Caddesi. The best thing to do is abandon the car as soon as possible and, after orientating yourself, park closer to your accommodation if need be. Dolmuş run from the bus station around this one-way system and on to Gümbet. **Tourist information** is on Iskele Meydanı, on the left as you walk out towards the castle, open 0830-1730, later in summer.

Getting around

Blessed with a very pleasant Mediterranean climate the area around Bodrum is important for citrus production during the winter months with tourism, the mainstay of the local economy, picking up in spring. Despite some unsightly development, the recurring image as you walk around the back streets is the violent pink of bougainvillaca against a backdrop of whitewashed walls.

The area

There are no good **beaches** in the town itself, so to get wet, unless you have a hotel pool, means travelling a short distance to the bays of Gümbet or Bitez just to the west, or further afield to the other beaches on the peninsula. Bodrum has an important marina with ranks of wooden hulled gülets waiting to be chartered for the day or for longer Blue Water voyages. Ferry services also depart for the Greek island of Kos and points north and south along the coast, saving long bus journeys. The interesting castle of St John and the Mausoleum of Halicarnassus, neglected by many visitors, are worth a look, as is the Underwater Archaeological Museum.

Halicarnassus rose to prominence as the capital of the Carian king Mausolus in the fourth century BC. Beautified with grand monuments and enclosed in a strong city wall during his reign, it was the magnificent mausoleum, unfinished in his lifetime, that brought particular renown, becoming one of the Seven Wonders of the World.

History
Birthplace of the ancient chronicler Herodotus

Hellenistic Halicarnassus passed from the Ptolemies of Egypt to the Seleucids of Syria, before being absorbed into the Roman Empire in 129 AD. The Roman city survived until the arrival of the Arabs who promptly razed it. Christians and Turks played tug-of-war with the city during Byzantine times with the Knights Hospitallers of St John capturing Bodrum from the Ottomans in 1402. They built the castle that you see today using marble from the mausoleum to make lime. Chunks of ancient masonry were also used to embellish the fort. As an outpost of Christianity its thick walls survived against the Ottoman tide until Rhodes fell to Süleyman the Magnificent, and it was finally abandoned.

Ottoman Bodrum was a backwater, the mountains of Caria effectively isolating it from the activities of the empire. Writer Cevat Şakir Kabaağaçlı was internally exiled to the town for his political views in the last paranoid years of Ottoman rule. Charged with murdering his father, he was returned by the new republican authorities under a commuted death sentence in 1923. Far from languishing away, Cevat worked energetically to preserve Bodrum's historical legacy, while also penning works based in the local area. His sailing trips along the Aegean and Mediterranean coasts, described in his story 'Mavi Yolculuk' (Blue Voyage) were the precedent for today's yacht chartering industry (see box, page 315).

The Aegean Region

Sights

The town At the bottom of Cevat Şakır Caddesi, behind the Adilye Camii, are the streets of the **bazaar** area, now pedestrianized and the old shops replaced with boutiques, banks, restaurants and travel agents. From near the castle begins pedestrian Dr Alim Bey Caddesi, which continues parallel to the outer harbour, turning into Cumhuriyet Caddesi. This is the main thoroughfare, lined with shops, restaurants, bars and clubs, crowded with two-legged traffic and called Uzunyol (Long street) by the locals. To get a feel for normal life in the town, walk inland from Neyzen Tevfik Caddesi, up one of the narrow roads towards Turgut Reis Caddesi. Things are quieter and there are some lovely gardens tucked away.

The Mausoleum
Held as one of the Seven Wonders of the World the structure was built to last, only succumbing to an earthquake over 1600 years after it was raised

Designed by the architect Pytheos, the monument was huge, with the burial vault surrounded by 36 pillars and surmounted by a stepped pyramid at the top of which stood a statue of Mausolus himself, riding in a chariot with his wife and sister Artemisia. The whole structure towered 60 m high and was richly decorated with friezes and statuary, carved by the best contemporary sculptors.

Today, despite the efforts of a Danish team of archaeologists there is little to be seen and it takes a major feat of imagination to picture the mausoleum in all its former glory. The lack of remains is largely the fault of the Knights of St John who scavenged the rubble left after the earthquake for building material and

Bodrum

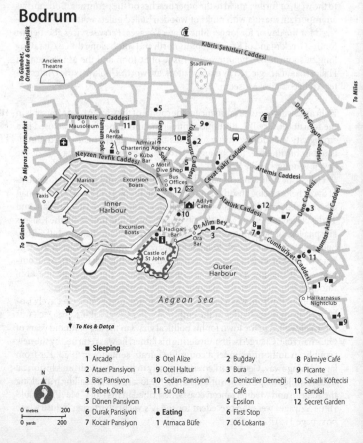

■ **Sleeping**
1 Arcade
2 Ataer Pansiyon
3 Baç Pansiyon
4 Bebek Otel
5 Dönen Pansiyon
6 Durak Pansiyon
7 Kocair Pansiyon
8 Otel Alize
9 Otel Haltur
10 Sedan Pansiyon
11 Su Otel

● **Eating**
1 Atmaca Büfe
2 Buğday
3 Bura
4 Denizciler Derneği Café
5 Epsilon
6 First Stop
7 06 Lokanta
8 Palmiye Café
9 Picante
10 Sakallı Köftecisi
11 Sandal
12 Secret Garden

N

0 metres 200
0 yards 200

burnt many of the exquisite reliefs for lime. Luckily, parts of the marblework were carted-off to decorate the castle and in 1846 these were spotted by the British Ambassador, Lord Stratford, who obtained permission to ship them to England. Later exploration by Charles Newton uncovered the site of the mausoleum itself and more fragments from the building found their way to the British Museum, including the figures of the tyrant and his wife/sister. ■ *0830-1200, 0100-1730 daily except Mon. US$1.50. On Turgut Reis Caddesi in the midst of a residential area.*

The Knights of St John built the initial fortifications over an existing Selçuk castle in 1402. A Christian outpost on the edge of Ottoman territory, the castle was manned by knights from across Europe, motivated by a mixture of religious fervour, a sense of adventure and greed. Over the course of a hundred years the rest of the fortress was constructed, much of it from the characteristic green marble of the mausoleum, with the German, Italian, French and English towers reflecting the international composition, and funding, of the order. When Süleyman the Magnificent finally succeeded in capturing Rhodes in 1523, Bodrum was abandoned and the Knights returned to Malta. ■ *0830-1200, 1300-1700 daily except Mon. US$3.50.* **The Castle of St John**

The entrance to the castle is through the west gate, facing the Inner harbour. On the right is the chapel which served as a mosque after the Ottomans captured the city and which was badly damaged by the French navy bombardment of Bodrum during the First World War. It now houses the **Museum of Underwater Archaeology**, unique in Turkey, with finds from along the coast, spanning history from the late Bronze Age. ■ *Opening hours are the same as the castle, US$3.50.*

The **Glass Shipwreck Hall** is well worth a look as it contains a reconstruction of a trading ship, discovered by sponge divers in 1973 and later recovered from its resting place by an international team of marine archaeologists. Painstaking research has revealed that the flat-bottomed vessel was carrying a mixed consignment of glass to a port along the Black Sea coast, when it sank in 1025 near present day Marmaris. To protect the original timbers used in the mock-up, the room is climatically controlled and only 20 visitors at a time are allowed in ■ *Mon-Fri, 1000-1100, 1400-1600. Additional entrance US$1.50.*

The **Carian Princess Hall** houses artefacts recovered from a tomb discovered nearby in 1989 during building activity. The find is particularly exciting because the sarcophagus was unlooted and contained the skeletal remains of a female, who died between 360 and 325 BC. Using the latest pathological techniques, experts at Britain's Manchester University reconstructed the woman's face from a cast of the skull. The result, at the far end of the hall, is a likeness of the Carian Queen Ada that greatly resembles her bust displayed in the British Museum. ■ *Opening hours are the same as the castle. Additional fee US$1.50.*

The **English Tower**, built during the reign of King Henry IV of England, contains standards from the opposing Ottoman and Christian forces along with a collection of armour and weaponry. Notice the Latin graffiti chiselled into the window niches by bored knights.

Within the upper courtyard are the **Snake tower**, so-called because of the plaque of a serpent above the entrance, the **German tower** and the **dungeons**. Used as a place of incarceration and torture by the Knights of St John, a plaque in Latin above the doorway to the dungeons reads 'Where God does not exist'. Inside are macabre reconstructions of torture methods complete with red lighting and pre-recorded screams.

The Aegean Region

Boat trips   Many of the *gülets* lining the inner harbour are available for charter for periods from a single day to several weeks (see box, page 315). A small boat for six people costs about US$120 for the day, but in slack times or with good bargaining skills you may find something a bit cheaper. Larger boat owners charge US$12-15 per person, which usually includes a basic lunch. Chartering your own boat gives you choice to decide where to go and how long to stay.

Another option is to sign up for one of the boat excursions touted along the quayside and throughout town. These generally last from 1000 to 1700, and follow a fairly standard route, calling at Karaada, with its hot springs, the beach at Ortakent Yalısı and Akvaryum, a cove known for its good visibility and fish.

Essentials

Sleeping   As you would expect, Bodrum has a wide variety of accommodation from simple pen-
There are no campsites in   sions to 5-star hotels. The pensions are spread fairly evenly across the town centre
the vicinity of the town   with some good ones along Türkkuyusu Caddesi. Higher standard hotels are mostly found a bit further out, particularly in the resorts of Gümbet and Bitez. Prices are generally high in Bodrum, particularly when compared to less-touristy areas.

A *Hotel Karia Princess*, Canlıdere Sokak No 15, T3168971, F3168979. Luxury hotel on the way to Gümbet, comfortable rooms with A/C and lots more besides, pool, sports facilities including tennis court. **B** *Su Otel*, Turgutreis Caddesi, 1201 Sokak, T3166906, F3167391, suotel@superonline.com in middle of residential area. Colourful place, relaxed atmosphere, 12 rooms with bathroom, telephone and a/c, swimming pool, slightly on the expensive side but still recommended. **C** *Baç Pansiyon*, on busy Cumhuriyet Caddesi, T3161602, F3167917. Unostentatious comfort and style, rooms with TV, a/c, balcony, minibar, some have sea-view, bar, terrace. Recommended. **C** *Napa Otel*, Atatürk Caddesi, far end heading out of town, T3164940, F3164943. 3-star, double rooms, some with sea-view, in villa complex, access from the seafront, swimming pontoon, bars, restaurant. **D** *Otel Alize*, Uçkuyular Caddesi, T3161401, F3168611. Centrally located place with twin-bed rooms and ensuite, swimming-pool, safe box. Recommended. **D** *Hotel Arcade*, Halicarnassus end of waterfront, T3133185, F3134876, well-finished rooms with a/c, roof terrace, pool, nice bar, noise from Halicarnassus could be problem in front rooms. Recommended. **D** *Bebek Otel*, Kumbahçe Mahallesi, right off Atatürk Caddesi, waterfront location, T3162441, F3133155, bebekotel@turk.net Popular with Scandinavian tour groups, austere reception area but decent rooms wuth kitchenette and minibar, TV room, pool, bar, restaurant, car-park. Recommended. **D** *Otel Haltur*, Paşatarlası Caddesi, Kumbahçe Mahallesi, waterfront location, next to *Bebek Otel*, T3162597, pleasant terraced garden, shaded seating area, mostly Turkish clientele, small 2 and 4 bed rooms with bathroom, bar, a bit out of the way but still recommended.

E *Ataer Pansiyon*, on harbour-side of Tevfik Caddesi, 50 m before Tepecik mosque, T3167552, great location, 1/2/3 bed rooms but singles are very small, the best room is at the front with a balcony. Recommended. **E** *Dönen Pansiyon*, Türkkuyusu Caddesi, near Melis Pansiyon on the left, T3164017. 2/3 bed rooms with bathroom, peaceful sitting area, plans for swimming pool, car-park (access from next lane on the left). Recommended. **E** *Melis Pansiyon*, Türkkuyusu Caddesi, on right, T3160560, clean, plain rooms, some with balcony, 3-bed room with kitchenette, no breakfast, bar, snacks served in small courtyard at rear. **E** *Sedan Pansiyon*, Türkkuyusu Caddesi No 121, at end of alley on right, past *Şenlik Pansiyon*, T3160355. 2 buildings around a garden, fairly basic rooms, use of kitchen, good view from the roof terrace, counter phone, car-park. Recommended. **E** *Şengül Pansiyon*, just off Atatürk Caddesi on Hamamı Sokak, T3165530, decent rooms with pine fittings, bathroom, roof terrace, bar.

F *Durak Pansiyon*, Kumbahçe Mahallesi, 30 m below Gümbet on Atatürk Caddesi, T3161564. family-run, rooms with refrigerator, roof terrace, guest-kitchen, breakfast extra, also run the Villa Durak Pansiyon nearby which has slightly better rooms. Recommended. **F** *Esen Pansiyon*, left off Türkkuyusu Caddesi, T3163539. One of the cheapest beds in town, nothing to write home about, discounts if empty, small, basic, 3/4 bed rooms, US$7 for dirty mattress on roof, no breakfast. **F** *Kocair Pansiyon*, Atatürk Caddesi, 2426 Sokak, T3161321. Run by 4 sisters, 2/3 bed rooms with bathroom, leafy courtyard, good value, breakfast extra. Recommended. **F** *Uslu Pansiyon*, on pedestrianised Cumhuriyet Caddesi, T3130665. 30 years old, 1/2/3 bed rooms, very clean, stark white, small roof terrace, top rooms are very hot, back facing rooms not noisy, no breakfast.

Expensive *Bura Restaurant*, Dere Caddesi, T3132042. Meat and seafood, high quality interesting food, nice surroundings. *Epsilon Restaurant*, left off Turgut Reis Caddesi, up small alleyway, T3132964. Ottoman and European cuisine, menu changed daily, art exhibited, jazz and classical music. *Picante*, T3160270. Mexican, cool hangout, ambient and Latin tunes, limited but good menu, beware of extortionate imported beer. **Midrange** *Secret Garden*, garden of old house off Atatürk Caddesi, T3134479. Mediterranean cuisine, recommended. *Sandal*, T3169117. Chinese and Thai food, including green and red curry for US$6, authentic, best of its kind in town. *Poncho's*, near Halikarnas, disco, Argentinian steak house. *First Stop Restaurant*, on the front, Outer harbour, tourist favourite, 210 different dishes. *Körfez Restaurant*, Inner harbour, Turkish and seafood. *06 Lokanta*, junction of Üçkuyular Caddesi and Cumhuriyet Caddesi. Try the Çökertme kebaps, spiced lamb on a layer of fried potatoes with cream. There are many fish restaurants along the main thoroughfare, Cumhuriyet Caddesi. Check prices before sitting down, as some fall into 'expensive' category. **Cheap** *Sakallı Köftecisi*, first right after Adliye Camii, favourite with office workers, cheap soups, kebaps and köfte. For cheap food look along Cevat şakır Caddesi between the petrol station and the post office. *Kebabistan*, past fruit and vegetable stalls just off Cevat Şakır Caddesi. *Guneş Pide/Pizza*, next to the former, serving mostly locals. *Atmaca Büfe*, next to petrol station, döner in half-loaf of bread for US$1.40, garden to eat it in. There are many other döner and snack places as you walk along Cumhuriyet Caddesi, but prices are a bit higher. *Via Boyle*, just a couple of tables on side street at beginning of beach, soup, fish and a couple of other choices. *Duğday*, Türkuyusu Caddesi, good selection of vegetarian dishes, including tofu, at reasonable prices.

A favourite place to sit and watch the promenade is the **Denizciler Derneği Café** (Boatmen's Association Café) on the quayside next to the tourist office. *Mado*, Cumhuriyet Caddesi, ice-cream and coffee on seaside terrace. *Palmiye Café*, first of the row of snack-bars, with stripy umbrellas, on Neyzen Tevfik Caddesi, has ice-cream, pastries and biscuits.

Lowery's, Inner harbour, loud, pseudo-Irish bar, cans of Guinness are saving grace. *Küba*, cool Latin music, terrace, not the cheapest. *Westside*, relaxed terrace bar *Hadigari*, next to mosque and the castle, drink on terrace with wonderful views along Outer harbour. *Ora Bar*, Dr Alim Bey Caddesi nicely decorated, open-fronted, mix of music. *Capanella*, at beginning of Cumhuriyet Caddesi, first floor, Turkish music, sometimes live. *Körfez Bar*, past Arby's just-off Cumhuriyet Caddesi on left, cheaper beer, rock music. *Seagull*, same street as Körfez bar, low-key place amidst the hype, small terrace overlooking sea. Once you reach the beach there are a string of bars, competing for customers, and trying to drown-out each others music. *White House*, bottle-juggling bar staff and pumping music. *Red Lion*, similar deal, screens showing sport instead of juggling bar staff. *Alem*, far end of Outer harbour near Halikarnas, Turkish Sanat (Art) music. *Oasis*, also near Halikarnas, mellower scene, rock and pop.

Eating
Bodrum's restaurant scene is predictably diverse with everything from the usual kepap & pide places to Mexican & Thai cuisine

Cafés

Bars
Generally speaking the bars along the Inner harbour are more relaxed with the decibel level rising as you head down Dr Alim Bey & Cumhuriyet Caddesi

The Aegean Region

Nightclubs As with other places, the distinction between bars and clubs becomes very blurred in Bodrum, with many of the bars above playing loud music and having dance floors. *The Temple*, Cumhuriyet Caddesi, several bars, dance floor on ground floor, chairs on the beach. *Robin Hood*, Inner harbour, open-fronted building, statues, flooded with UV light and saturated with electronic sounds. *Halikarnasus*, best known and largest venue in town, on point at the end of Cumhuriyet Caddesi, follow the lasers, entry US$12, open-air, lights, lasers, mock-Classical terrace, Euro-house and techno.

Festivals The town's *International Film Festival* is held at the beginning of **Jun**.

Shopping There is no shortage of souvenir shops along Cumhuriyet Caddesi, where you will also find leatherwear at predictably touristy prices. The weekly market held near the bus station is a colourful affair and more orientated towards the local population. Enquire locally about which days it is happening. *Migros* supermarket is on Turgut Reis Caddesi, near the junction with Kıbrıs Şehitleri Caddesi. There is also a *Tansaş* supermarket near the bus station.

Sports **Diving** is another activity popular in the surrounding waters with over 15 sites used regularly by local operators. For qualified divers a 2-dive day plus lunch is around US$50, with a full programmeof certificate courses and tuition also offered. *Motif Diving Centre*, Neyzen Tevfik Caddesi No 48, T3166252, F3166198, dive trips daily in glass-bottom boat. *Poseidon*, Neyzen Tevfik Caddesi No 80, T3138727, shop selling equipment, boat near Kos ferries, free hotel pick-up.

Tour operators *Borda*, Neyzen Tevfik Caddesi, *İstanbul Airlines* agent. *Director Tour*, Cevat Şakır Caddesi No 26, down from bus station, T3160563, ferry and airline tickets, transfers, rent-a-car, accommodation, jeep safari. *Margaret Tour*, Cevat Şakir Caddesi, opposite side to petrol station, T3160403, F3161440, rent-a-car, large selection of tours. *Hi Tour*, office next to *Denizciler Derneşi Café*, T3164615, boat trips and other excursions.

Transport **Air** *Turkish Airlines* have flights between **İstanbul** and **Bodrum** every day, and to and from **Ankara** on Fri and Sun. *İstanbul Airlines* also fly in from İstanbul 3 times a week. Contact a travel agent to buy tickets. During the season there are also various charter flights arriving from Europe. The newly built airport is on the Milas-Bodrum road, 35 km away.

Several of the large bus companies have offices at the eastern end of Neyzen Tevfik Caddesi, so you don't have to walk out to the bus station to buy a ticket

Road Bus Buses leave the terminal for **Ankara**, 1000, 1900, 2100, 11 hrs, US$14; **Antalya**, morning and evening, 8 hrs, US$10; **Denizli** and **Pamukkale**, several a day, 5 hrs, US$5; **İstanbul**, several during the day and every night, 12 hrs, US$16.50; **İzmir**, every hr, 3½ hrs, 0600-1800, US$5; **Kaş**, via **Fethiye** and coast road, 1215, 7 hrs, US$10; **Marmaris**, every hr, 0830-1730, 3 hrs, US$5. **Milas** and **Muşla**, frequent buses and dolmuş, 45 mins and 2 hrs. *Has* run services to **Konya**, continuing on to **Adana**, at 1600 and 1830, 12/16 hrs, US$13/$15. **Ulusoy** and **Varan** have several luxury services daily to **İstanbul**, US$25, and **Ankara,** US$21. **Car hire** International and local firms have offices along Neyzen Tevfik Caddesi.

Ferry Boats for the Greek island of **Kos** leave from the end of the Inner harbour, past the castle, at 0900, return 1600, 1 hr, one-way US$6, return US$8, car US$20. Services for **Datça** also depart in the morning, 2 hrs, 1-way US$4, return US$7, car US$12. **Altınkum**, leaves every day 0900 and returns at 1900, US$8.

Directory **Banks** There are lots of banks with ATM's in the pedestrianised area at the bottom of Cevat şakır Caddesi. Several private exchange offices on Cevat Şakır Caddesi are open until 2300. **Communications** Internet: *Palmiye Café* at the far end of Neyzen Tevfik Caddesi, near marina.

Post office: PTT office is at the bottom of Cevat Şakır Caddesi. International Calls can be made from inside (counter) or the booths outside. Faxes sent. **Laundry** *Can Çamaşırhane*, Türkkuyusu Sokak, US$3 per load. **Medical services** *Bodrum Private Hospital*, Mars Mabedi Caddesi, off Kıbrıs şehitleri Caddesi, T3136566. Open 24 hrs. **Useful addresses** Yachting agencies: *Admiral Tours*, Neyzen Tevfik Caddesi No 78, T3161781, F3162627, admiral@superonline.com, long-established agency, custom packages on range of crewed güllets. *Borda*, Neyzen Tevfik Caddesi No 48, T3165632, F3166198, bare-board and crewed charters.

Bodrum Peninsula

Despite only covering about 700 sq km, the landscape on the Bodrum Peninsula varies considerably, from the bare rocky contours of the southwest to the greener forested mountainsides along the northern coast. The villages and resorts also differ both in character and in their levels of development. At one extreme is Gümbet, a spill-over from Bodrum with wall-to-wall package hotels, while at the other end is Gümüşlük, an altogether sleepier affair popular with those seeking a bit of quiet beach time.

Named after the domed cisterns that dot the countryside, Gümbet is now a white concrete jungle housing many of the thousands of British package tourists who flock to Bodrum each year in search of sun, sea and cheap beer. Only 2 km from Bodrum, there is little reason for the independent traveller to visit, outside of an anthropological interest in the holiday habits of the young package holidaymaker. **Gümbet**

The next bay to the west, known as Bitez or Ağaçlı ("with trees"), is a definite improvement with a gently sloping coarse sand beach backed by hotels and guesthouses. The sheltered cove and shallow water are perfect for learning to windsurf and there are several shacks offering equipment and lessons. A board costs US$10 for an hour, US$38 for a day. **Bitez (Ağaçlı)**

Sleeping and eating B *Otel Okaliput*, T3637780, F3637957, middle of beach, half-board as standard, cool rooms in nicely designed units, surrounded by well tended gardens, pool, beachside restaurant, shaded beach loungers. Recommended. **D** *Yalıhan Hotel*, T3637772, F3638184, near western end of beach. Small hotel with rooms around pool, a/c room **B**, pool table. Recommended. **F** *Sultan Motel*, T3637791, near the middle of the beach. Step down in luxury from the other 2, but good basic rooms above restaurant. Recommended. *The Sultan* is the closest thing to a Turkish restaurant, meze on display, with various other touristy alternatives along the beach. *Balıkçının Restaurant* has seafood at reasonable prices.

Transport Dolmuş shuttle between Bitez and the Bodrum bus garage every 15 mins from 0730 to 2400, US$0.75.

The southwest

Despite its length of over 2 km, there's little to recommend the beach between Ortakent and Yahşi. It is better to continue, turning off the main road at Gürece to **Kargı** and **Bağla** beaches, though they're also visited by most boat tours from Bodrum. **Akyarlar** is a proper village 30 km from Bodrum, showing evidence of its former Ottoman Greek population. There are some decent eateries, a few pensions along with the omnipresent villa developments. ■ *Getting there: Regular dolmuş in high season pass through Kargı, Bağla and Akyarlar.*

Turgutreis   Approaching Turgutreis, 20 km from Bodrum on the west coast of the peninsula, the countryside becomes more mountainous with rocky volcanic peaks
rearing up. The seascape is no less dramatic with several angular islands seem-
ing to float offshore. Unfortunately, the town itself, named after an Ottoman
admiral, doesn't live-up to its surroundings. Package hotels, a weedy uninvit-
ing coastline and a thoroughly over-pedestrianized centre devoid of anything
close to an atmosphere, sum the place up. ■ *Getting there: Dolmuş from
Bodrum, every 10 mins, 24 hrs in season, US$0.90.*

   Kadikalesi, 4 km to the north, is an improvement in the beach department,
however, unless you are booked into one of the package places, accommodation is sadly lacking.

Gümüşlük   Turning off the main road just after Gürece, a narrow lane winds through some
refreshingly unspoilt scenery, passing a row of crumbling windmills on an
exposed ridge. Gümüşlük is little more than a few houses, post office and a
couple of shops, but 2 km further on is the real draw in the form of a collection
of fish restaurants, a long sand and gravel beach and several simple pensions.
You may have to blink and rub your eyes: no hotels and no villa complexes,
although there is some suspicious activity on a mountainside to the south. The
reason for the miraculous lack of development is ancient **Myndos**, which lies
scattered across the area, and for the protection of which the government
strictly controls all building. The sheltered anchorage, between a large headland topped with an army watch-tower and Tavşan Adası (Rabbit Island) is
favoured by passing yachts, and it is possible to snorkel around exploring
some of the submarine ruins.

Sleeping Along the beach are a few alternatives for accommodation. All seem to
cash in on Gümüşlük's appeal, charging a bit over the odds for what are simple rooms.
C *Sysyphos*, right on beach, far end, T3343016. Shady courtyard with cushioned seating area, basic rooms with bathroom and balcony. Nicest place but overpriced.
D *Özak Pansiyon*, T3943388, simple bungalow-type rooms. **E** *Gümüşlük Motel*,
T3943007. Row of 10 reasonably simple rooms above restaurant, lovely view of wharf
and harbour. Recommended. **Self catering** *Arriba Apart*, T3943654, middle of the

Bodrum Peninsula

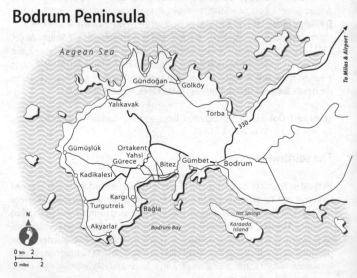

beach, fully-equipped apartments, sleep 4 people, US$300 per week, camping for US$5 per person, use of kitchen, toilets. *Hera Apart*, T3943065, apartments with kitchen, sleeps 4, just back from beach, US$360 per week.

Eating For food there are two good beach restaurants and the well known fish establishments for which people drive from Bodrum. A speciality of the *Gümüşlük Restaurant* is *tuzla*, fish baked in a casing of salt, which is cracked off at the table.

Boat trips Veteran diver, Feridun Boruk, organizes diving trips from the *Gümüşlük Hotel* and he'll be glad to show you his medals and interesting photograph collection, T3943045. Snorkelling equipment also available.

Transport Dolmuş to Bodrum leave every 45 mins from 0800 to 2200, US$1.20.

Yalıkavak is accessible along the narrow coastal road from Gümüşlük or via a main road from near Ortakent. It's a resort popular with Turkish families but British tour companies *First Choice* and *Sunquest* also have a presence. The village has suffered extensive remodelling with roads closed off from traffic, landscaping and lots of sand imported to make up for the deficient local supply. The end result is still not worth the bother.

The northern coast
Dolmuş depart frequently from Bodrum for these places though out-of-season frequency reduces

    Gündoğan, to the east, is something of an improvement, well – at least the beach is better, protected at the head of a narrow bay. There is a small marina at mid-point where the ferry from Didim docks and passengers are transferred to minibuses. Further east still, **Gölköy** is reached through lovely pine forests. It is a well kept secret from the foreign masses with a gravel beach punctuated by small jetties and numerous guesthouses and small hotels catering for the aforementioned crowd.

    Next stop on the circumnavigation, **Torba**, is easy to miss, hidden amongst the holiday homes and hotel developments. Beachless, there is really nothing else to justify seeking it out.

The Bay of Gökova

From Bodrum, the coast stretching east along the Bay of Gökova is mountainous and relatively unspoilt. The poor quality of the coastal road, little more than a track in places and often impassable in winter, has put a brake on building, with just a few embryonic developments serving passing yacht traffic. Between Ören and Akyaka there is no public transport and so the scenic track suggests itself as a perfect stretch to mountain bike.

*Phone code: 0252
Colour map 4, grid B2*

Ören is the only sizeable place sitting along this stretch of coast. With a reasonable stretch of sand and pebble beach it hasn't escaped attention by domestic tourists though development is very low-key and it retains a village-like atmosphere. It's 49 km south of Milas on a good tarmac road. Two large lignite burning power-stations, the focus of considerable environmental controversy, do not bode well as you approach, but the village of whitewashed houses, with a PTT and shops on its narrow cobbled main street, is a sufficient distance away to be unaffected. The government has banned building because the village sits on the ruins of ancient **Keramos**, which can be explored on foot.

Ören

    A clutch of small hotels, popular with Turkish families, is to the south on the beach. All get very booked in the summer, so it's wise to telephone ahead and reserve a room. **E** *Dolunay Motel*, west end of beach, T5322194. Comfortable bungalow rooms, garden, jetty. Recommended. **F** *Kerme Hotel*, next to *Dolunay Motel*, T5322065. Wooden bungalows. **F** *Keramos Motel*, T5322065.

The Aegean Region

More basic doubles with bathroom. There are a collection of **restaurants** on the beach and a couple of bars that constitute the nightlife.

To Akbük & Akyaka For a glimpse of what much of the Turkish coastline used to look like before the hotels, marinas and summer houses, continue east from Ören on the rough track which climbs into the mountains, passing several farming villages before returning to sea-level at **Akbük**, a protected crescent of pebbles which is a favourite anchorage for yachts. There are a couple of restaurants for the yachties and tour boats that occasionally turn up from Akyaka, but precious little else.

From Akbük, the track winds through coastal pine forests for over 20 km to Akyaka (see page 308) at the head of Gökova Bay. The forested scenery scattered with lines of brightly coloured beehives and the views across the sparkling bay to the Datça Peninsula are fine distractions from the rutted, back-jarring track.

Akyaka (Gökova)

Phone code: 0252
Colour map 4, grid B3

Nestled at the head of the deeply indented Gulf of Gökova the village of Akyaka – often called Gökova – has become a modest resort favoured particularly by Turkish and British families. Approaching from the north the coastal highway sweeps down a steep limestone escarpment in a series of long switchbacks from the **Sakar Geçidi** (670 m), a favourite spot for paragliders to launch themselves from a platform signposted off the road. If you're under your own steam consider stopping at the large restaurant complex perched by the roadside, if nothing else then to appreciate the stunning view.

Akyaka is a couple of kilometres off the highway at the bottom of this long descent, and consists of a fairly well-planned grid of streets on a pine forested hillside below the village square. In a heartening departure from the usual non-architecture of Turkish resorts, most of Akyaka's villas, pensions and small hotels replicate the vernacular Muğla-style Ottoman houses with large wooden balconies and wide overhanging roofs. At the base of the hill a hard-packed sandy beach flanks the clear-running Gökova Çayı, spanned by a wooden footbridge with brightly painted boats tied-up along its banks. More secluded bathing spots can be found over the bridge to the south, though the water is very shallow and sometimes not that clear. There's a second, pebble beach about 2.5 km west of town beyond a cluster of restaurants and houses known as Iskele.

There are daily **boat tours** from Akyaka's jetty in summer which cross the bay to Cleopatra Adası and Incekum beach, 1000-1800, US$10 including lunch.

Sleeping
Many places close for the winter

Most of Akyaka's accommodation is in family pensions, of which there's a selection below. All charge a fairly standard rate **E** for simple rooms often with a kitchenette and balcony. Rates plummet outside the main holiday season when a lot of business comes from Muğla University students. **B** *Hotel Yücelen*, T2435108, F2435434, a *Sunquest* affiliate inland at the west end of the beach. Pleasantly laid out a/c equipped villa-rooms in lush gardens complete with swimming pool, pond and resident ducks, half-board option US$70 per double. **E** *Gülen Apart Pansiyon*, Çimen Sokak No 52, T2435526. Small self-contained apartments above family house, accommodates 4 at a squeeze using pull-out sofa-bed. **E** *Gökovalı Apart Pansiyon*, T2435096. Zambak Sokak No 99, simple rooms with ensuite near the sea. **E** *Erdem Otel*, Akyaka Beldesi, T2435849, F2434326. Another *Sunquest* hotel with small neat rooms overlooking pool, 100 m inland from the beach. **E** *Gülemce Apart Pansiyon*, T2434245. Clean 2-bedroom apartments up a lane from the square, 5-10-min walk down to the sea. **F** *Setenciler Hotel Nil*, T2435441, F2435440. Off the main street below the square, 5-min walk to the beach, nice rooms, pine furniture, small ensuite and balcony, open year-round.

The restaurant at the *Hotel Yucelen* has an extensive and reasonably priced **Eating** open-buffet dinner, US$7; also fish and meat dishes. Down by the beach the *Kardelen* is good for snacks, pizza and more substantial Turkish dishes. The *Gülşalı Restaurant* has a variety of food including steak. There are more simple eateries near the beach at the Iskele, 2 km west. There's a small fruit and vegetable **market** on the right side of the road near the PTT, while the taps opposite the post office are suitable for filling your water bottles as it's pure **spring water** from beneath the limestone mountains.

There are regular dolmuş to and from Muğla, 40 mins, US$1.75, as well as 2 direct **Transport** buses to **Marmaris,** 30 mins, US$1.50, every day. Many more buses and dolmuş pass along the highway, so catch a Muşla dolmuş to the highway and wait by the roadside.

Banks The nearest banks are in Muşla. **Post office** The small PTT is on the main street 150 ms **Directory** below the square.

Muğla's attractions don't add up to enough to justify a special detour, though **Muğla** if you're waiting at the busy *otogar* you may decide to have a look around.

The administrative centre of a province which contains a string of coastal resorts, Muğla is a prosperous, well-heeled town clustered on the edge of a wide cultivated basin. Populated by a predictably large number of civil servants, as well as students studying at the local university, it's an orderly place by Turkish standards with rows of well-built apartment buildings flanking the tree-lined streets. However, reminders of the town's Ottoman past linger in the bustling **bazaar district** at the base of the hill and reached up Ismet İnönü Caddesi from the main roundabout, centred on a statue of Atatürk. While a stroll up the streets beyond the market reveals a neighbourhood of remarkably well-preserved Ottoman houses.

Sleeping and eating Conveniently placed across from the bus station is the **E** *Hotel* *Should the need* *Yalçın,* T2141599, F2141050. Clean rooms with large ensuite. Heading out towards *arise there are plenty* the highway on the western outskirts of town is the more comfortable **B** *Hotel Grand* *of hotels in town* *Brothers,* T2122700, F2122610. Sauna and swimming pool. There are several cheaper places, such as *Doşan Pansiyon,* in the bazaar area, where you'll also find plenty of budget eateries. Nearer the *otogar* on Cumhuriyet Caddesi there are several restaurants around the Mustafa Muşlalı Işhanı, a modern office block to the southeast of the main roundabout.

Directory Banks There are several banks in the vicinity of the roundabout. **Post office** Some 500 m west of the roundabout on Necat Güreli Bulvarı. **Tourist information** The tourist office, T/F2143127, is on the roundabout. Open weekdays, 0830-1200, 1330-1730.

The Aegean Region

Western Mediterranean

7

312

Western Mediterranean

314 Marmaris

318 **The Reşadiye and Hisarönü
Peninsulas**
319 Datça
321 Köyceğiz

324 **Dalyan**
331 Dalaman

332 **Fethiye**
338 Ölüdeniz
341 Kaya Köyü

342 **The Xanthos Valley**
342 Tlos
346 Xanthos
347 Patara
350 Kalkan

351 **Kaş**
356 Cyaneae (Kyaneai)

357 **Kekova**
358 Üçağız
361 Demre (Kale)

365 **The Lycian Hinterland**

368 **Olympos and Çıralı**

369 **Olympos**
369 Chimaera (Yanartaş)

372 **Towards Antalya**
372 Tahtalı Dağı
373 Phaselis
374 Kemer

376 **Antalya**

385 **Around Antalya**

387 **The Pamphylian Plain**
387 Perge
389 Aspendos
390 Köprülü Kanyon National Park
and Selge

392 **Side**
397 Alanya

*Fragrant pine forests, towering mountains and arching
turquoise bays, the western Mediterranean coast, from
Marmaris to Alanya, encompasses some of the most stunning
of Turkey's coastal scenery. Not surprisingly it's also become
one of the most touristy parts of the country with the summer
months witnessing an invasion of domestic and European
visitors. A string of burgeoning resorts such as Marmaris,
Kemer, Side and Alanya cater for the package crowds
funnelled in through the international airports at Dalaman
and Antalya. Antalya is the largest city in the region, modern
and rapidly growing, but with an appealing historic core and
good transport links to other sites in the vicinity. Between
these chaotic, overdeveloped holiday centres are other more
laid-back resorts far better suited to the independent traveller,
such as easy-going Dalyan on the banks of the slow flowing
Dalyan Çayı; Patara with its fantastic beach or the one-time
fishing town of Kaş. An energetic programme of road building
in the last two decades has also opened-up remoter spots
previously accessible only by rough shepherds tracks or from
the sea, with Kekova and Olympos suggesting themselves as
places to get away from it all and really unwind.*

*But this part of the country isn't just about relaxing by the
pool or sitting on the beach. Formerly the ancient lands of
Lycia, Pamphylia, as well as southern Caria, the area is
peppered with archaeological sites, many of which – like
Pinara, Tlos, Arykanda and Selge – occupy the most
evocative contemporary settings. Partly crossed by Turkey's
first long-distance path, the Lycian Way, there's also ample
scope for other outdoor pursuits such as trekking, canyoning
and mountain biking in the majestic Taurus (Toros)
Mountains or rafting on the Dalaman and Köprülü Rivers.*

Marmaris

One of the only good reasons for dropping in today is to set-off again onboard a yacht or gület, as the marina – the country's largest – is also Turkey's main centre for yacht-based holidays

Sitting on a deep bay ringed by pine-clad mountains, Marmaris earns full marks for its position. Unfortunately though, the quaint fishing port of yesterday has been catapulted into the age of mass tourism, achieving the status of mega-resort – brash and down-market. Waterside Barbaros Caddesi is thronged on summer evenings by a slow moving tide of pink-skinned tourists – mainly British – trawling past silver-tongued cockney-accented touts eager to entice customers in to one of a hundred bland eateries. In the modern bazaar district traders brazenly hawk fake Gucci handbags and dodgy Nike T-shirts, while your ears are subjected to the omnipresent thump of Euro-pop. What's left of the old town – in fact little more than an over-restored castle and caravanserai founded by Süleyman the Magnificent – is now besieged by new development which sprawls for miles in a chaotic mess along the coast. As the package hotels and apartment blocks have multiplied, so the reasons for an independent traveller to visit have dwindled.

Ins & outs
See page 317 for further details

Getting there Buses arrive regularly at Marmaris' *otogar* from destinations across the country. There are also frequent sailings from the Greek island of Rhodes during the summer, while the nearest airport is Dalaman. **Getting around** Arriving at the new *otogar* on the edge of town most companies have a free minibus service into the centre, which drops you on Ulusal Egemenlik Bulvarı, inland of the waterside square, Atatürk Meydanı. There are also regular dolmuş into the centre, US$0.40, from the bus station. From Atatürk Meydanı, it's easy to orientate yourself with the labyrinthine bazaar, the main concentration of waterfront restaurants and bars; the castle and the marina all to your left (east) as you look at the sea.

Sights

There's very little to see in the town itself, with the small **castle**, home to an assortment of historical curiosities with a strong nautical flavour, *0800-1200, 1300-1730, US$1.50* and the nearby **bedesten**, easily missed amongst the carpet shops of the bazaar, surviving as the only relics of old Marmaris. Both buildings were endowed by Süleyman the Magnificent in 1522 after he successfully captured Rhodes from the Knights of St John, a feat that demanded an army of 200,000 men who were loaded onto ships in Marmaris' protected bay.

To the east of the centre and reached across a footbridge from the end of *Barbaros Caddesi* is the **Netsel Marina**, where quays lined with sleek yachts and glittering gin-palaces are backed by a rarefied waterside complex of yachting agency offices, posh shops and upmarket restaurants. Every year in May the marina is the focus of the *Marmaris Yacht Festival* – mainly an event for boat owners and the trade; while in October the *Marmaris International Yacht Club*, T4123835, PO Box 132, 48700, holds its annual regatta.

For a major holiday resort, the local stretches of **sand** are very disappointing. Those fronting the hotels and apartments to the west of town are crowded in summer and the water is not particularly clean. **Içmeler**, a 10-minute dolmuş ride to the west, is a bit more enticing, though it's congested with parasols and sunbeds and backed by the same large hotel complexes. On the plus side the water is cleaner than in Marmaris and there are plenty of water-sports on offer. For an altogether better beach experience head across the mountains to **Turunç** (see page 317) where you'll probably end up staying.

A popular pass-time in Marmaris is taking an outing on one of the hundreds of excursion **boats** which line the waterfront. Competition is cut-throat and itineraries vary little with boats calling-in at several places in the vicinity for swimming stops and lunch, for an all inclusive price of US$10-15 depending on demand. Some companies also offer trips down the coast to Kaunos and the

Blue Water Voyage

One of the most memorable ways to experience the Mediterranean coast is aboard a yacht or gület – the graceful wooden motor-sailing vessels. Popularized by an autobiographical account of the maritime exploits of the novelist-dissident Cevat şakir Kabaağaç in the 1950s and 1960s, the term 'Mavi Yolculuk' or 'Blue Water Voyage' has come to describe any such leisurely foray. These days yacht chartering has grown into big business on the Turkish littoral, particularly along the deeply indented coastline between Bodrum and Antalya where the sheltered coastal waters offer innumerable secluded anchorages.

There are several ways of experiencing your own 'Blue Water Voyage', the first being to charter a vessel yourself, complete with a skipper and cook. This is possible through travel agents and yacht brokers in your home country or on the spot in one of the coastal resorts. The cost depends on the type of yacht and the time of year with typical prices for an eight berth yacht varying from US$400-900 per day in May or October, to US$600-1,500 in July or August, the most expensive months. Charter prices generally exclude food which works out at US$15-25 per person.

If you can't assemble a group of people all is not lost, as many companies offer the chance to simply charter a berth on a shared yacht. Called a cabin charter such trips generally follow a set itinerary, for example an eight day cruise from Marmaris to Fethiye or Datça and back. The cost of cabin charters varies from US$300-600 per person per week depending again on the time of year, but if you're on your own there's often a surcharge of 50% if you want your own cabin. Eser Yachting, 35. Sokak No 21/3, Yatlimanı, T4123527, F4126994, eser-yachting.com, is a reputable Marmaris-based company offering cabin charters.

If you fancy learning to skipper a yacht yourself Yüksel Yachting, Netsel Marina E-12, Marmaris, T4121016, F4125420, yukselyachting.com, offer a range of courses in sailing and seamanship. When you're a qualified captain and are comfortable handling your own vessel then you can hire a yacht yourself. Known as a bareboard charter, a six berth boat costs upwards of US$1,350 in low season, US$1,900 in high. A large well-established firm dealing in bareboard charters is Setur, Barbaros Caddesi No 223, Marmaris, T4126530, F4124608.

The Marmaris International Yacht Club, PO Box 132, 48700, Marmaris, T4123835, can provide details of other yachting agencies offering standard, bareboard and cabin charters.

mud-baths at Dalyan. Alternatively, for a more flexible programme you can charter your own boat for about US$100 for four people, or US$25 per person, including lunch.

The accommodation scene in Marmaris is dominated by package hotels and holiday complexes of which there are dozens spread along Kemal Seyfettin Elgin Bulvarı and its continuation Kenan Evren Bulvarı. Some of the places in the bazaar area, although central, are affected by noise from adjacent restaurants and bars. **B** *Otel Lidya*, Kenan Evren Bulvarı, T4122940. Near the edge of town, well-established place which is ageing gracefully, pleasant rooms with ensuite and a/c, good service. Recommended. **D** *Sariana Apart and Hotel*, 24 Sokak No 4, T4136835, F4122656. Immaculate apartments beside the canal inland from the marina, fully equipped kitchens, small sitting room, a/c, TV, balcony and swimming pool, weekly rate US$210, also 3 bed available. Recommended. **D** *Otel 47*, Atatürk Caddesi No 10, T4121700, F4124151, just west of Atatürk Meydanı. Old favourite with nicely furnished rooms, ensuite, a/c, some also have sea-view. **E** *Hotel Mavi*, Atatürk Caddesi No 72, T4123618, F4121822. Fairly standard package hotel, reasonable rooms with TV, telephone and balcony, street noise may be a

Sleeping
For something quieter consider the family-run pensions in Armutalan, a 10-min dolmuş ride to the W of town & within easy reach of Içmeler

Western Mediterranean

problem. **F** *Otel Karadeniz*, Atatürk Caddesi No 68, T4123614, F4121064, far end of Atatürk Caddesi. Reasonable value rooms with shower, telephone and balcony, ask for 1 at the back room as they're quieter, roadside restaurant not the nicest place to have breakfast. **F** *Hotel Aylin*, 1 Sokak, Kemeraltı Mahallesi, T4128283. Tacky looking place on a quiet backstreet, rooms above the restaurant and bar are good value though, single US$7. Recommended budget hotel. **F** *Interyouth Hostel 1*, 42 Sokak No 45, T4124095, interyouth@turk.net A popular backpacker place in the heart of the modern bazaar near the PTT, follow the signs off the waterfront just east of Atatürk Meydanı, simple double rooms with shared bathroom, also dorm beds US$6, no single rooms. Or *Interyouth Hostel 2*, T4122940, on the Datça road, 10-min walk from the centre, similar set-up but much quieter than its sister. **F** *Hülya Pansiyon*, Burdurlular Sokak No 9, Armutalan, T4123345, on edge of town going towards Içmeler. Simple rooms in family-run place with use of kitchen. Recommended. Next door is *Yılmaz Pansiyon* which has a similar set-up but the rooms are not as nice. **G** *Yaprak Pansiyon*, Kemeraltı Mahallesi, T4123001, around the corner from *Otel 47*, basic rooms, very good value singles at US$6. There are 2 **campsites** at **Aktaş**, 2 km east around the bay. Dolmuş leave from opposite *Tansaş Supermarket* on Ulusal Egemenlik Caddesi every 30 min.

Eating

The best place to sit & have a drink, & watch the promenade, are the cafés on Barbaros Caddesi east of the castle: Pegasus or Nil, for example

Predictably the vast majority of restaurants in town, particularly those lining waterfront Barbaros Caddesi, cater for the package masses and offer standard tourist fare, with smaller portions at a substantially higher price. There are a few exceptions, particularly in the marina, which are frequented by discerning locals and the yacht-set. **Midrange** *Mr Zek*, Barbaros Caddesi, visible above the waterside places, excellent Italian orientated menu, interesting seafood, baby calamari stuffed with mozarella, pizza, pasta, accompanied by the view across the harbour, about US$20 per head. *Drunken Crab*, Haci Mustafa Sokağı, good selection of fish, including scorpion fish, sea bass and sea bream, eaten at tables on this narrow street. *Türkay*, Haci Mustafa Sokağı, a well-cooked Turkish/French menu, locally recommended. *Sam Dodds*, Netsel marina, bar/restaurant, another smart Italian place with pizza, pasta and seafood. Classier are *Sea Club or Antique*, Netsel marina, varied menus and attentive service, popular with yachties and well-to-do locals. **Cheap** There are several cheap restaurants opposite the huge *Tansaş supermarket* on Ulusal Egemenlik Bulvarı. The best, all neon and white tiles is Kırçiçeği, just down a sidestreet, tasty and good value soups, kebaps, pide, pizza and lahmacun. Also serves alcohol. *Ney Birgül*, occupies a small converted house in a backstreet parallel to Barbaros Caddesi, refreshing place serving authentic Turkish cuisine, meze, grilled meat and köfte, convivial atmosphere. *Idil*, Haci Mustafa Sokağı, marina end of the bar-street, gözleme, ayran and döner kebaps at tables on street. *Captain's Pub*, amidst exclusive boutiques and yachting agents this is a down-to-earth place serving excellent soups, ready-prepared dishes. There are several stalls in the vicinity of Atatürk Meydanı which serve döner kebaps and *kumpir* (baked potatoes), with a large choice of fillings.

Bars & nightclubs

Marmaris' nightlife is concentrated along narrow Haci Mustafa Sokağı, running parallel to Barbaros Caddesi east of the castle. Imaginatively dubbed 'Bar Street', with the various establishments, set shoulder to shoulder, coming quickly in and out of vogue. Fronting the marina are a few decent watering holes amidst the rubbish: *Sila Cafe Bar*, Barbaros Caddesi, east of the castle, traditional Turkish folk music, the sound of a *saz* to remind you that you're still in Turkey! *Ivy Reggae Bar*, Barbaros Caddesi, at the marina end, small and friendly place the playlist is not strictly reggae. Situated in the Netsel marina are the slightly the more upmarket bars *Pineapple* and *My Marina*, fraternised predictably by the yachting set.

Shopping

Acres of shops and boutiques in the covered bazaar hold precious little of interest, unless you want to pick-up some fake designer T-shirts, perfume or a pair of Levis.

Diving *European Diving Centre*, AYC Marina, Kayabal Caddesi, İçmeler, T4554733,
F4554734, europeandiving.com.tr Local office of highly regarded Fethiye-based
company. *Octopus*, Rıhtım Sokak, Ayyıldız Pasajı No 3, T4120989, boat is moored on
the front near the Tourist Office. **Sea-kayaking and whitewater rafting** *Alternatif
Rafting*, Kenan Evren Bulvarı, Çamlık Sokak No 10/1, T4135994, F4133208,
alternatifraft.com Experienced outfit who organise sea-kayaking excursions and
white water trips on the Dalaman River and further afield.

Air *Turkish Airlines* provide a bus service from their office on Atatürk Caddesi to
Dalaman airport during the summer. **Bus** The bus companies all have offices on
Ulusal Egemenlik Bulvarı, around the *Tansaş* supermarket, with free minibus transfers
to the *otogar*. Ankara, 1 morning and 3 night buses, 12 hrs, US$18. **Antalya**, 5 daily, 7
hrs, US$11. Bodrum, hourly buses in season, 3 hrs, US$7. **Denizli/Pamukkale**, several
daily, 4½ hrs, US$8. **Muğla**, every hr, 1¼ hrs, US$2. **Fethiye**, hourly buses, 3 hrs, US$5.
İstanbul, regular buses, 14 hrs, US$20. **İzmir**, buses every hr, 4½ hrs, US$9. **Ortaca** and
Dalaman, every hr, 1½/2 hrs US$3.50/US$4. **Car and motorbike hire** *Avis*, Atatürk
Caddesi No 30, T4122771, F4126413. *Budget*, Ulusal Egemenlik Caddesi, Girginç Apart
No 12, T4124144, F4125774. There are also literally dozens of local agencies on nearly
every second corner. *Ares*, Kemal Elgin Bulvarı No 2/1, T4133999, F4133999. *Yoshi
Moto*, Kemal Elgin Bulvarı No 16/5-6, T/F4121825, is a reputable motorbike hire firm.
They also organise weekly off-road and touring trips. **Hydrofoils to Rhodes** During
the summer there are daily hydrofoils departing at 0915 on the 1 hr crossing to
Rhodes Town, returning 1630, US$26 single, US$30 day return, US$50 open return,
plus US$10 port tax. In winter the service is reduced to three sailing a week. Book your
ticket at least a day in advance at one of the many travel agencies in town and you'll
need to turn-up 90 mins before departure at the terminal to the east of the Netsel
marina. If you book through *Yeşil Marmaris Tourism* (see Tour agencies) they'll pick
you up at your hotel free of charge, otherwise a taxi shouldn't be more than US$4.

Airline offices *İstanbul Airlines*, Kenan Evren Bulvarı No 88, T4126627. Open weekdays
0830-1700.*Turkish Airlines*, Atatürk Caddesi No 50, T4123751. Open weekdays, everyday in
summer, 0830-1730. **Banks** There are banks with ATM and change facilities on Ulusal Egemenlik
Caddesi and along Barbaros Caddesi. There are also private change offices in the centre offering
better exchange rates. **Baths** *Sultan Baths*, in modern centre on Cumhuriyet Meydanı. Mixed.
Open 1000-2400. Entrance wash and massage US$8. **Communications Internet** *Marmaris
Internet Cafe*, Yat Liman Girişi, near Netsel Marina, beside canal. US$3.75 per hr, Open 0900-0100.
MŞ Internet, In narrow street next to the *Tansaş Supermarket* on Ulusal Egemenlik Caddesi, US$4
per hr. **Post office** The PTT is in the bazaar on 51 Sokak, look-out for the signpost on Kordon
Caddesi. **Consulates UK**, Barbaros Caddesi No 249, T4126486, F4125077, emergencies:
T262/661/5023, above *Yeşil Marmaris Travel Agent*, Open weekdays 0930-1200, also in summer
Mon-Thu 1430-1700. **Hospital** The State Hospital is off Datça Caddesi, 10-min walk from the
centre. **Medical services** *Marmaris Assistance*, Kemal Seyfettin Elgin Bulvarı, T4125824, private
doctors on-call 24 hrs-a-day. **Laundry** Marin Laundry, Netsel marina, 1 load US$4.50. **Tour
agencies** Yeşil Marmaris Tourism, Barbaros Caddesi No 11, flight bookings, ferry tickets, yacht
charters and car rental, near the Tourist Office. **Tourist information** The tourist information
office is on Kordon Caddesi west of the castle. Open everyday, 0830-1730, 1900 In summer.

Turunç, with its sweep of sandy coastline framed by craggy limestone mountains, has so far been spared the hyper-development of near-by Marmaris and
İçmeler and remains a quiet haven, favoured by those who want to relax on the
beach and do little else. Accommodation, mostly in villa developments scattered across the hillside, is dominated by several British tour operators, however there are also plenty of friendly hotels and pensions.

Western Mediterranean

Expect substantial discounts on room rates out-of-season

Sleeping and eating **C** *Hotel Diplomat*, T4767145, F4767147, on the main street overlooking the beach. Family-run place with pine-fitted rooms, ensuite, telephone, a/c as standard, suites also available. **E** *Balçı Apart*. Airy apartments with bathroom, kitchenette and balcony in a modern block overlooking the Jandarma post at far end of town. **F** *Alpin Otel*, T4767372, at the far end of the main street. Small nicely furnished rooms with balcony, telephone, breakfast served on the roof terrace. Recommended. **F** *Çardak Pansiyon*, T4767047, above restaurant at far end of village. Small plain rooms, open onto terrace, kitchen, no breakfast. Another good budget option.

Transport Dolmuş climb over the steep mountain barrier from Marmaris every 30 mins, US$2, and the local co-operative also run a regular boat service.

The Reşadiye and Hisarönü Peninsulas

Phone code: 0252
Colour map 4, grid B2 & 3

Like a thin sinewy finger pointing out into the Aegean, the Reşasiye Peninsula extends westwards for over 100 km, separated from Bodrum and Greek Kos by the long Gulf of Gökova and with the bulky form of Rhodes, floating on the horizon to the south. In this part of the world yachts are the preferred means of transport, but you can also visit by road. Leaving the forests around Marmaris, a narrow, twisting – though recently much improved – blacktop hugs the peninsula's rocky spine passing into a land of maquis – covered mountainsides and sweeping seascapes. The main port of call is the upstart resort of Datça, 75 km east of Marmaris, with the ancient Dorian city of Knidos, 35 km beyond, a goal only for the dedicated aficionado or the terminally curious due to its dead-end status.

From the peninsula's southern shore a second projection, known as the Hisarönü or Loryma Peninsula, after the ancient city which crouched on its rocky toe, juts into the sea. To the ancients this area was known as Rhodian Peraea, an isolated backwater ruled by the city-states of Rhodes for 800 years from the sixth century BC. Today, despite its physical proximity to Marmaris and an on-going road building campaign it hangs-on to an air of remoteness, with the sleepy little anchorages of Orhaniye and Selimiye and the harbour village of Bozburun attracting a trickle of land-based visitors too.

Orhaniye
Over 15 km west of Marmaris a paved road turns south towards Orhaniye, Selimiye and Bozburun. After just 8 km the road skirts a narrow bay bounded by fields, olive groves and a scattered collection of houses which collectively form Orhaniye. The main reason for the village so far being ignored by the developers is its deficiency in the beach department, with the bay bordered instead by a muddy shore. What Orhaniye does boast, however, is a long spit of sand dubbed **Kızkumu** – the Maiden's sand – which has become a minor attraction giving tourists who paddle their way along it the appearance of walking on water.

Sleeping As yet there are only a couple of purpose-built places to stay of which the roadside **E** *Kızkumu Otel*, T4871023, F4871024, with its shady restaurant beside the water, is the best. Simpler, but still clean and pleasant, is the **F** *Erol Pansiyon*, T4871018, or for a really rustic experience the family-run **F** *Aktaş Pansiyon*, T4871034, offers basic rooms with an equipped kitchenette opening onto a farmyard.

Bayırköy & Selimiye
Continuing south towards Selimiye, a lane on the left is sign-posted for the village of Bayırköy tucked-away in the mountainous interior of the peninsula, and from where tracks lead down to several isolated bays on the east coast. A short distance along the Bayırköy road is the **Kanlı Eğren Şelalesi**, a pretty waterfall cascading into a pool deep enough for a refreshing swim. Some 9 km

Western Mediterranean

south of Orhaniye, Selimiye is another small community on the shores of an enclosed bay. Overlooked by the remains of an Ottoman fortification, the village has a collection of tiny pensions and restaurants which do most of their trade with passing yachts.

Bozburun, 12 km further on, is a more substantial place with a small yacht-filled **Bozburun** harbour at the head of an inlet bounded by an amphitheatre of dry, craggy mountains. A scarcity of water has kept a lid on the village's growth, but the short waterfront promenade boasts of few restaurants and shops, while the village's stone houses have been joined by a growing number of holiday homes and villas. There's no beach in town, another explanation for Bozburun's slow development, but you can swim off the rocky coastline to the south of the centre.

Sleeping and eating The best accommodation in town is actually across the bay at **B** *Sabrina's House*, T4562045, F4562470, which boasts various amply proportioned rooms set in a verdant garden beside the sea, waterside restaurant, call to be picked-up at the dock or alternatively walk past the *Hotel Mete* for 20 mins around the bay. Along the waterfront to the south of the harbour are a number of pleasant pensions such as the **G** *Uslu*, T4562006, with a nice shady terrace, clean waterless rooms, use of the kitchen and a swimming dock just opposite. **G** *Suna Pansiyon*, T4562119, is slightly simpler and cheaper, or you could try **G** *Yılmaz Pansiyon*, T4562167. Next to the harbour you could try the *Akvaryum* or *Bozburun Restaurant* for meze followed by seafood or meat dishes, while the reasonably priced *Kandil Restaurant*, on the tiny square, also has soup and ready-prepared dishes.

Transport The village's dolmuş departs for Marmaris (via Selimiye and Orhaniye) from next to the post office at 0630, 0930, 1130 and 1630; returning at 1200, 1430, 1700 and 1900, US$1.50.

Datça

Twenty years ago Datça was a Shangri-La for foreign travellers, a quintessential Mediterranean fishing community of white-washed stone houses and narrow cobbled streets relatively unchanged by modernity. In the intervening years a rash of development – mostly villas and pensions rather than large hotels – have modified things somewhat, pushing the communities boundaries inexorably outwards and gentrifying the harbour area which in summer receives a large volume of yacht traffic. Still far quieter than other neighbouring resorts, the new, not necessarily improved, Datça remains a pleasant enough place to laze around and do, well, not much at all.

Phone code: 0252
Colour map 4, grid B2

Iskele Caddesi, the main street, leads right through town past the square to Iskele Mahallesi, squeezed on a rise between the harbour and east bay, and down across a short causeway to what was formerly the island of Esenada, now graced with a newly constructed amphitheatre surrounded by a small park. Across the harbour, the quayside is lined with a short strip of restaurants, cafés and bars.

There's a **beach** of compacted sand, known as Kumluk Plajı, just to the south of the main street, though more secluded bathing spots can be found to the west of the harbour, along a sand and pebble beach called Taşlık Plajı. If there's sufficient demand **boat trips** are organised along the coast to Knidos, also stopping briefly at several other place for swimming, 0930-1700, US$12. Shorter options are also available. On summer weekends you can cross over on a daytrip to the Greek islet of **Simi**, though currently there is no ferry to Rhodes.

Sleeping

Datça's accommodation is characterised by simple pensions in functional concrete buildings which multiply by the year

There are a few reasonable choices in Iskele Mahallesi between the harbour and the bay, such as **F** *Huzur Pansiyon*, T7123052, just off Iskele Caddesi or the nearby **F** *Kaya Pension*, T7123489, which also has plain rooms with ensuite shower. Off the main drag **F** *Yılmaz Pension*, T4562167 is possibly a bit quieter and it also has good sea-views. Crossing the isthmus, on Esenada you'll find the **D** *Hotel Dorya*, T7123593, F7123303, unsympathetic white blocks but set in lovely gardens running down to the sea, accessed from a swimming platform, large but rather austere rooms with balcony and seaview, fairly rudimentary bathrooms, swimming pool. **F** *Esenada Oteli*, T7123014, row of basic rooms in white-washed building, shared bathroom, pleasant location particularly in summer when there's usually a cooling breeze. Recommended. **C** *Villa Carla*, T7122029, F7122890, quiet hillside position beyond the Taşlık Plajı about 2 km from the centre, small and homely hotel set in well-kept garden with pool, private access to the sea.

Eating

Midrange There are a number of fish restaurants at the bottom end of Iskele Caddesi with terraces overlooking the harbour. *Emek* and *Taraça* have a wide selection of reasonably priced *meze*, meat and seafood served at outside table with a view, US$10-15 per head with wine or beer. Further up Iskele Caddesi a narrow alley leads to *Hüsnünün Yeri* which has a similar menu and shady waterside table. *Yasu Restaurant*, also has a nice position on the hillside above the harbour and serves barbeque meat and tasty garlic chicken, also some vegetarian dishes. **Cheap** For a cheaper meal try 1 of the places along the main street such as *Kemal Restaurant* where you can eat döner or köfte and a drink for about US$3, or the *Korsan Restaurant*.

Transport

Bus The *otogar* is 1 km east of the centre, but buses generally continue right into the bus company offices on Iskele Caddesi. **Marmaris**, 10 daily, 2 hrs, US$3.50. **Muğla**, 2 early morning buses, 3½ hrs, US$5. There are also daily services to **İzmir**, **İstanbul** and **Ankara** in summer, though at other times of year you'll need to change in Marmaris. **Ferry** *The Bodrum Ferryboat Association*, T7122143, local agent is *Deniz Hotel*, next to the main square, operates car ferries from Bodrum to Körmen, 9 km north of Datça, 3 times a week in summer, free service bus departs 0900 from town, US$10 1-way, US$16 return.

Directory

Banks There are several banks with ATM and change facilities on Iskele Caddesi. **Tourist information** The Tourist Office, T7123163, is beside the main square. 0830-1730 daily in summer, closed weekends Oct-May.

Datça to Knidos

It's 35 km from Datça to Knidos, passing along the way turn-offs down to several secluded bays frequented mainly by yachts but also offering possibilities for staying in quiet pensions or camping. After about 12 km, a road on the left leads 5 km down to the hamlet of **Mesudiye**, where you'll find a couple of campsites and basic pensions inland of a sand and shingle beach. Reached down a sign-posted track from the Mesudiye road, **Hayıt Bükü** also has a number of simple guesthouses and eateries including the **G** *Gabaklar Pansiyon*, T7280158, near another protected crescent of sand and pebble beach. About 28 km west of Datça and reached down a similar side road **Palamut Bükü** has more of the same.

Knidos

In a lonely, windswept spot at the very tip of the Reşadiye Peninsula are the scant remains of Knidos, at one time one of the wealthiest cities in the ancient world. Founded in 400 BC by Dorian traders, the settlement benefited from its position astride maritime trade routes, with the Knidians also establishing colonies on the coast of Sicily and Egypt. The city was best known, however, for its statue of Aphrodite which stood proudly over the sanctuary of Aphrodite

Euploia, Knido's patron deity. Crafted by the master sculptor Praxiteles, and said to have been modelled on his mistress, this statue achieved widespread notoriety as the first nude representation of the goddess of love, attracting besotted admirers from across the Mediterranean. In 1967 an American team unearthed the foundations the temple of Aphrodite, although the infamous statue had disappeared, leading some to believe it may have been taken along with other artefacts by the 19th-century archaeologist Charles Newton.

Occupying a large partially terraced area of scrubland beside two arching bays, despite continuing excavations there's really not very much to see. Unless you're a committed ruin buff the sign-posted remains uncovered to date, which include a Hellenistic theatre, several Byzantine basilicas, one with an extensive mosaic, a bouleterion and an agora, are not enough to justify the long journey in themselves. The spot has a certain rugged attraction though, and if you feel like stretching your legs the mountains overlooking the site provide a stunning 360°C panorama which on a clear day includes Kos and the Bodrum Peninsula to the north as well as the Greek islands of Nisiros, Tilos and Rhodes dotting a great expanse of sea to the west and south.

■ *Getting there: With taxi firms in Datça charging US$40-50 for the journey to and from Knidos a boat excursion offers by far the most pleasant and cost effective way of visiting the site. If you decide to take a taxi make sure the driver understands you want at least 90 minutes at the site.*

Köyceğiz

On the north shore of Köyceğiz Gölü, a large but shallow lake bordered by dense reed beds and marshland teeming with bird and animal life, Köyceğiz is a run-of-the-mill market town far more involved with the day-to-day concerns of agricultural production than tourism. Herein lies the place's appeal and apart from a stroll along the brutally landscaped promenade, or a browse around the Monday market which turns the centre into a raucous hubbub of activity, there's very little else to do. However, Köyceğiz does suggests itself as an alternative, far quieter, base for visiting the ruins of Kaunos or the hot-springs at Sultaniye (see below), with several of the local pensions arranging trips across the lake if there's sufficient interest.

Phone code: 0252
Colour map 4, grid B3

The town itself is of the one-horse variety – although admittedly things are changing fast – with a pot-holed main street leading down to the lakeside promenade. There are several pleasant cafés where it's nice to sit and enjoy the

Western Mediterranean

Köyceğiz

To Otogar (2 km) & Highway

To Sultaniye Hot Springs & İkincik

Hürriyet Caddesi

Atatürk Caddesi

Anatolia Camping

Cengiz Topel Caddesi

Köyceğiz Gölü

N

0 metres 200
0 yards 200

■ Sleeping	4 Flora Motel	8 Panorama Plaza	● Eating
1 Alila	5 Fulya Pension	9 Pansiyon Beyaz Konak	1 Çiçek Lokanta
2 Çiçek Pension	6 Kaunos	10 Tango Pension	2 Gülenoğlu Baklavanı
3 Evcegiz Otel	7 Özay		3 Meşhur Ali Baba

view across the lake's placid waters. For a swim walk to the western edge of town where there's a small beach near *Anatolia Camping*.

With your own transport or on a rented motorbike or bicycle you can explore the beautiful countryside around town, much of it devoted to orchards of squat citrus trees which produce abundant crops of oranges and tangerines in the winter. The area is also renowned for its liquidambar trees, the petrified sap of which forms amber after millions of years, and a government reforestation scheme occupies land along the highway to the west of the town. Mountain-biking, canyoning and jeep safaris in the rarely visited Gölgeli mountains to the northeast of town can be arranged through the *Flora Motel* (see sleeping).

Western Mediterranean

Sleeping

In recent years Köyceğiz has gathered quite a collection of hotels & pensions, which represent good value for money. The best places tend to be W of the centre: turn right along Cengiz Topel Caddesi as you face the water

B *Panorama Plaza*, Cenghiz Topel Caddesi, No 69, T2623773, F2623633. A 10-min walk west from the square, modern place with comfortable rooms, ensuite, TV telephone, a/c. **D** *Hotel Kaunos*, Cengiz Topel Caddesi No 37, T2624288, F2624836. Aged tour hotel overlooking the water, you can find better elsewhere. **E** *Hotel Alila*, Emeksiz Caddesi, T/F2621150. A short distance west of the mosque, newly-built hotel with small bright rooms many of which overlook the lake, all have ensuite shower, pool and lakeside terrace. Recommended. **E** *Hotel Özay*, Kordon Boyu No 11, T2624300, F2622000. Older 2-star place on the front near the Alila, slightly cheaper rooms which are still comfortable, equipped with TV, telephone, a/c, pool too. **F** *Flora Motel*, Cengiz Topel Caddesi No 110, T2623809, F2624076. Very recently opened place on the waterfront beyond the *Kaunos Hotel*, nicely fitted rooms with balcony, though no lake view, simple set menu dinner US$3.75, the owner, Alp Giray, can organise adventurous excursions into the nearby mountains. Recommended. **F** *Evceğiz Otel*, Ali Ihsan Kalmaz Caddesi, T2622343, F2622342, in the midst of a residential area inland from the *Flora Motel*. Homely rooms with ensuite in ugly concrete block, pool squeezed in, restaurant in season, friendly host. **F** *Fulya Pension*, Ali Ihsan Kalmaz Caddesi, Ulucami Mahallesi, T2622301, 1 road back from the lake-front. Plain and simple rooms with ensuite, breakfast served on the roof, boat trips arranged. Recommended. **F-G** *Tango Pension*, T2622501, F2624345, tangopension@superonline.com Popular backpacker haunt, relatively new and smart place with well-furnished rooms, dorm beds US$4, daily tours and activities, windsurfer rental. Recommended. **G** *Çiçek Pension*, Çarşı Meydanı, T2623038. Located squarely in the centre of town which means it may be noisy, has the distinction of offering the cheapest and most historic – it occupies a 120-year old han – beds in town, basic rooms with creaky floorboards and high ceilings, shared bathroom. **Camping** *Anatolia Camping*, T2624750, shady wooded site among the liquidambar trees on the western edge of town, near the beach.

Eating

Dining options in Köyceğiz are rather limited, but in addition to the places here food can often be organised by the hotels & pensions

Çiçek Lokanta, just off the main street on Alihsan Kalmaz Caddesi, is a cheap restaurant with ready-prepared dishes and grilled meatballs. For something sweet afterwards simply cross the street to the *Gülenoğlu Baklavaları. Meşhur Alibaba*, on the main square, is a friendly little place serving pide, lahmacun, ready-prepared dishes and kebaps. For something slightly more sophisticated try one of the lakeside fish restaurants such as the *Şamdan* or the *Çınaraltı*.

Transport

The otogar is situated 2 km from the town itself. Half-hourly dolmuş service between 0800 & 2000 into the centre. A taxi's about US$3

Bike rental *Şah Market*, opposite the *Çiçek Pasiyon* has scooter for US$16 per day. **Bus** Conveniently there's a Kamil Koç office beside the old bus station, so you don't have to trek out to the *otogar* to buy your tickets. Dolmuş for the *otogar* leave from here every 30 mins. Being on the main coastal highway Köyceğiz's tiny bus station is pretty busy. **Fethiye** (via Ortaca and Dalaman), 15 daily, 1½ hrs, US$2. **İzmir**, 9 daily, 5 hrs, US$10. **Marmaris**, 14 daily, 1½ hrs, US$2. **Muğla** (for Bodrum), regularly, 1¼ hrs, US$1.75. There are also a couple of direct buses to **Bodrum** each day, 3½ hrs, US$7 and night buses to **İstanbul** (14 hrs, US$20) and **Ankara** (16 hrs, US$22).

Banks There is an *Işbankası* with ATM on the main street. **Post office** The PTT is just west of the town square on Cengiz Topel Caddesi. **Tourist information** The Tourist Office, T2624703, is on the east side of the square, opposite the mosque.

Directory

Across the lake from Köyceğiz and reached by an 18 km road, or boat trip from either Köyceğiz or Dalyan, are the hot mineral baths at Sultaniye. In use since Roman times, hot mineral-charged water emerges from the ground at about 40°C and is channelled into a large murky pool enclosed in a tatty domed structure. Although this doesn't sound particularly enticing, the setting on the pine-fringed lakeshore is enchanting and thanks to their relative isolation the baths receive fewer visitors than the mudholes at Ilıca, so off-season there's a chance you may have the place to yourself. Having soaked in the soporific waters, said to be beneficial for sufferers of rheumatism, skin complaints and gynaecological problems, there's nothing more exhilarating than plunging headlong into the lake.

Sultaniye Kaplıcaları

If you want to prolong your visit there's a row of basic huts beside the baths which may or may not be in a fit state to occupy when you arrive. Alternatively, the guardian usually doesn't mind people pitching tents nearby. A more comfortable option is to stay in Karaağaç at the **C-D** *Sultan Palas Hotel*, T2842103, F2842106, sultanpalas.co.uk, open May to October, airy rooms with a/c or fan, telephone and balcony overlooking large pool, restaurant, free shuttle boat to Dalyan.

■ *Getting there: To get to the baths turn off the main coastal highway to the west of Köyceğiz at a sign for the Sultaniye Kaplıcaları and Ekincik; or drive out of Köyceğiz west along Cengiz Topal Caddesi. It's a decent road for most of the way until you turn left at the hamlet of Karaağaç, for the final kilometre approach along a gravel track. The only public transport is an elusive dolmuş said to depart the Köyceğiz otogar for Ekincik (see below) every afternoon in summer, returning the following morning.*

Continuing southwards past Karaağaç and the turning for Sultaniye brings you after a 10 to 15 minute drive to the isolated village of Ekincik, clustered inland of an arching coarse sand beach enclosed within steep forested mountains. It's a quiet spot which until very recently was only visited by passing yachts, however, now its also enjoyed by the guests of the pleasant beachside **D** *Hotel Ekincik*, T2660203/4, F2660205 or the simpler **F** *Ekincik Pansiyon*, T2660179, on the hillside behind. Far more threatening for Ekincik's status as a tranquil backwater is a group of concrete shells which look suspiciously like the start of a summer house development. There's an excellent walk east along the coast to Dalyan (see page 328) which initially follows a track to the yachting restaurant in the adjacent bay, subsequently climbing up the mountain beside its barbed wire perimeter fence.

Ekincik

As the administrative centre of the district containing Dalyan, Ortaca has benefited enormously from the tourist trade, as demonstrated by the furious pace of building around town. However, the only conceivable reason to call-in is enroute for the aforementioned resort. Apart from the restaurants in the bus station, you could get a bite to eat in the 24-hour soup place next to the roundabout.

Ortaca

Transport Dolmuş to Dalyan leave the *otogar*, off the main highway, every 15 mins until 1900, earlier in the slack months. A taxi costs US$13. There are also minibus services to **Dalaman** and **Sarıgerme** every 15 and 30 mins respectively, US$0.75. All buses plying the coastal route stop-off at **Ortaca**, including services to: **Antalya**, 5½ hrs, US$10. Make sure you get a *"Yayladan"* bus which goes the shortest route via **Korkuteli**. **Bodrum**, only a few direct buses so change at **Muğla**, 1½ hrs, US$3. **Fethiye**, every 30 mins, 1 hr, US$2. **Gökova**, every 45 mins, 75 mins, US$2. **İstanbul**, several evening buses, 15 hrs, US$22. **İzmir**, almost hourly, 6 hrs, US$10. **Köyceğiz**, about every 30 mins, 20 mins, US$1.50. For **Kalkan** (3 hrs) and **Kaş** (3½ hrs) get on a *sahildan* (coastal) **Antalya** bus, or changing at **Fethiye** may be quicker.

Dalyan

Phone code: 0252
Colour map 4, grid C3

Spread along the east bank of the lazy Dalyan Çayı river and overlooked by the dramatic Lycian rock tombs, Dalyan was formerly an agricultural community concerned with raising oranges, cotton and wheat from the rich alluvial soil. Fishing was also an important local pursuit with the town earning its name from the wooden traps, known as dalyan, built across the river to ensnare fish swimming upstream to spawn in Lake Koyceğiz. Now a popular package destination, Dalyan has so far managed to retain something of its original laid-back charm with a grid of small hotels and guesthouses and a long riverside boardwalk. The arrival of the large hotels – often the death knell of a place for the independent traveller – has been indefinitely postponed by the dogged opposition of local people and environmental campaigners, keen to conserve the wildlife-rich Dalyan Çayı delta and the pristine turtle beach at Iztuzu. However, a more immediate threat now comes from the veritable armada of tour boats which ply up and down the river to the beach; the ruined city of Kaunos and the mudbaths, attractions which make Dalyan both an interesting and enjoyable place to stay.

Ins and outs

Getting there
See page 330 for further details

Dalyan is 13 km south of Ortaca, which is a halting point for buses plying the coastal highway. From Ortaca's *otogar* dolmuş depart every 15 mins until 1900 – earlier in winter – for **Dalyan** or it's about US$12 in a taxi. A taxi from **Dalaman** airport will set you back about US$20.

Getting around

The centre of Dalyan is compact enough to walk around easily, and even the more outlying hotels are no more than a 10-min stroll away. For Iztuzu beach you'll need to get on one of the regular dolmuş-boats, while a visit to the ruins of Kaunos or a closer look at the Lycian rock tombs is simply a matter of being rowed across the river (see below) by one of the boat-women, followed by a short walk.

Sights

Kaunos & the rock-tombs
To see most of Dalyan's sights involves getting on a boat of some description

Under excavation since the 1960s, the archaeological site is scattered across a scrubby hillside dotted with bushes and trees above a reedbed which was once the city's harbour. It's a pleasant spot shared by wildlife such as lizards, frogs, tortoises and the odd heron or crane. In summer it's blistering hot by mid-morning, so visit as early as possible and take some water.

A Carian foundation of around the ninth century BC, Kaunos by nature of its geography interacted closely with Lycia, adopting many aspects of its southerly neighbours culture – a prime example being the rock-tombs carved into the cliff nearby. Renowned for their sallow complexions and ill-health – something remarked upon by the ancient historian Herodotus and passed off as a symptom of their over-indulgence in figs – historical hindsight suggests that in fact malaria was endemic amongst the city's population. However, a more terminal threat to the city's livelihood came from the Dalyan Çayı itself,

A turtle change

Turkey's long Mediterranean littoral provides some of the most important nesting sites for two types of marine turtle: the endangered loggerhead turtle, Caretta caretta, and the even rarer green turtle, Chelonia mydas. Thirteen principal nesting beaches have been identified by conservationists with the loggerheads concentrated along the western part of the coast from Dalyan to Anamur and the Göksu Delta; and green turtles nesting mainly on the beaches of the Çukurova Delta between Mersin and Yumurtalık, as well as at Samandağı in the Hatay. Every year between May and October female turtles pull themselves up on to these beaches to lay a clutch of up to 120 soft-shelled eggs in a nest laboriously excavated from the sand using their back flippers. Having reburied the nest, the mother heads back to the sea leaving the eggs to incubate in the sun-warmed sand. After about two months the baby turtles hatch, digging their way to the surface and making a dash for the sea under cover of darkness when they stand the best chance of escaping detection by predators and also not being fried by the

intense summer sun. Very few of these hatchlings survive to adulthood and those that do are threatened by human activity. Although few turtles are now killed in Turkey for their meat or shells, a grave danger to both species comes from sand extraction; fishing nets; industrial and agricultural pollution and litter, particularly floating plastic bags which they're thought to mistake for jellyfish, a common prey.

However, large-scale tourist development is considered to be the most pernicious threat and by an unhappy coincidence the wide, sandy beaches favoured by nesting turtles are also those most in demand by tourists and developers. Huge swathes of coast have been built-on with the noise, but more critically, the light from beachside hotels deterring females from nesting and also confusing newly-emerged hatchlings. For more information on turtle conservation contact the Turkish Society for the Protection of Nature (DHKD), Büyük Postane Caddesi No 43-45, Kat 5-6, Bahçekapı, İstanbul, T02125282030, F02125282040, dhkd.org.or

which silted-up the harbour and advanced the coastline to its present position 5 km south, cutting the city off from seaborne trade.

From the ticket booth a path passes the skeletal remains of the so-called Palaestra **church**, an early fifth-century structure which is among the oldest in Anatolia. Further to the east, the Hellenistic **theatre** is largely intact, making a it good place to rest your feet before sweating up the **fortified acropolis** for an impressive bird's eye view of the river's snaking path towards the sea and the ruins scattered below you. Further down the hill is a **temple complex** dedicated to Apollo and the city's **agora** where goods were brought for sale from the dockside wharves.

■ US$2. 0800-1700. *Getting there: Situated on the opposite side of the Dalyan Çayı, about 1½ km south. Included in most boat tours, it's also possible to visit independently. A couple of women wait to ferry people across the river in rowboats (US$0.50) from the southern end of the boardwalk opposite the tombs. From the other side, where there are several rustic places serving* gözleme, ayran *and soft drinks, it's a 10-min walk. Along the way you pass close to the finest group of monumental rock-tombs, although a fence prevents you from climbing up for a closer look at the fourth century BC sepulchres. If you don't fancy the walk to Kaunos, the boatman's co-operative have services at 1000, 1400 and 1600, returning an hr later, US$5.*

Ilıca Mud Baths Another popular sight included in the much-touted boat trips are the thermal baths 10 minutes upstream at Ilıca, where you can wallow in a series of open-air pools of thick, glutinous mud. Valued for its therapeutic properties – the warm mud is said to cure a whole range of ailments from rheumatism and gout to male impotence and gynaecological problems – it's now mostly just a bit fun for the boatloads of tourists ferried here from as far afield as Köyceğiz and Marmaris. Needless to say, in summer avoid arriving in the midday rush when things are hopelessly crowded, and instead try and organise an early morning or evening

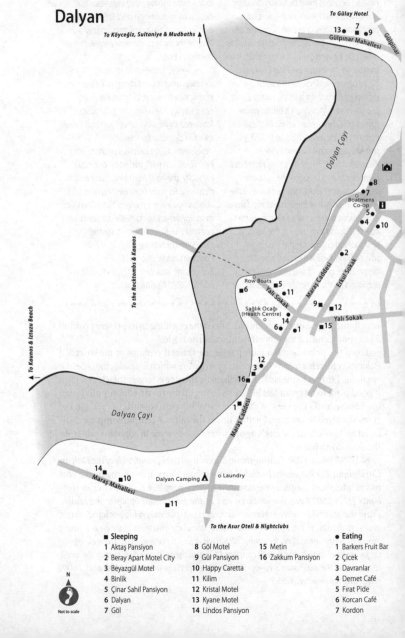

Dalyan

■ **Sleeping**

1 Aktaş Pansiyon	8 Göl Motel	15 Metin
2 Beray Apart Motel City	9 Gül Pansiyon	16 Zakkum Pansiyon
3 Beyazgül Motel	10 Happy Caretta	
4 Binlik	11 Kilim	
5 Çinar Sahil Pansiyon	12 Kristal Motel	
6 Dalyan	13 Kyane Motel	
7 Göl	14 Lindos Pansiyon	

● **Eating**

1 Barkers Fruit Bar
2 Çicek
3 Davranlar
4 Demet Café
5 Firat Pide
6 Korcan Café
7 Kordon

Western Mediterranean

visit. ■ *US$3. Getting there: The boatman's co-operative run boats at 1030, 1400 and 1700, giving you two hours at the bath before returning.*

There's another, slightly quieter, set of hot-springs 1 km or so along the lake shore from the mud baths at Sultaniye. Not on the standard boat tour itineraries you'll need to charter a boat for the trip.

Iztuzu Beach

A magnificent swath of golden sand stretching from the mouth of the Dalyan Çayı southeast for over 5 km, Iztuzu is an important nesting site for the endangered loggerhead turtle. As a result of a highly publicised campaign by environmentalists to halt a luxury hotel development in the mid-1980s, the beach remains pristine and undisturbed along most of its length. The gently sloping beach naturally attracts some human interest, although most activity – two snack bars, plus ranks of sunbeds and parasols – is confined to relatively short, but at times densely populated, stretches at either end. This means it's easy enough to turn your back on the crowds and find yourself a more secluded spot, though there's a universal lack of natural shade so don't forget a hat. During the turtle nesting season – May to October – access is forbidden between 2000 and 0800 and the use of parasols, which can damage buried nests, is also restricted. The most popular way down to the beach is on one of the boats (US$2 return) which depart every 30 minutes during the morning from the quayside near the mosque. It's an enjoyable 40-minute cruise down the river, flanked by reedbeds and girded by wooden fish traps (*dalyan*), to the beach. Return times are noted on a sign next to the quay, as are the restrictions aimed at protecting the turtles and their nests. ■ *Getting there: You can get to the other (south) end of the beach – by car, on a rented bicycle or, in high summer, by dolmuş – via a 13 km road from Dalyan.*

Boat trips

Lined up side by side along Dalyan's quay are dozens of brightly painted wooden boats waiting to whisk passengers off on excursions up and down the river. Most are operated by boatmen belonging to the local co-operative whose office is south of the mosque near *Köşem Restaurant*.

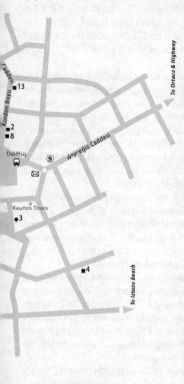

Kordon Boyu
13
2
8
Dolmuş
(Gülpınar) Maraş Caddesi
İnayegiz Caddesi
Kaunos Tours
3
4
To Iztuzu Beach
To Ortaca & Highway

8 Köşem
9 Melodi
10 Narin
11 Pembe
12 Riverside
13 Sürmen
14 The Oldest House in Dalyan

Western Mediterranean

The standard tour on offer runs 1030-1800 and includes visits to the mud baths, Kaunos, Iztuzu beach and some caves along the coast towards Ekincik. It's excellent value at US$6 per person, though you may feel the pace is a little rushed. The co-operative also offer early morning trips to feed the fresh water terrapins which live in the river, but you'll need to sign-up for this one the day before, US$5. On Mondays there's another outing across the lake to visit the large weekly market in Köyceğiz, also US$5.

The alternative to enrolling on a tour, particularly if there's a group of you, is to charter a boat and make your own itinerary. The rate is currently about US$60 per day for a boat capable of carrying up to 12 people, although you can also hire them for less time. The *Otel Caria* on Yalı Sokak has several decent 2-man sea-kayaks available for US$7 per hr, or US$35 per day.

Walking to Ekincik A wonderful walk from Dalyan is west along an unspoilt stretch of coastline to Ekincik, a quiet backwater village on a crescent-shaped bay enclosed by mountains. It's about a three hour walk along a reasonably well-marked path through pine forests for most of the way. However, unless you want to overnight in Ekincik or pay the extortionate US$120 demanded by the local boatman's co-operative for a ride back to Dalyan, you'll need to return on foot, making it somewhat more of a challenging day. It's advisable to get an early start, taking the row-boat ferry (US$0.50) across from the southern end of the quay. If there's no one around a few whistles or shouts may be required.

From the other side of the river follow the track past Kaunos towards the small, community of Çandır, which seems a world away from the hustle and development of Dalyan. Cross over the bridge in the village and follow the road around the mountainside towards the village's harbour, avoiding two tracks that climb away on the right. About 100 m before the dock near a small house, a path, marked with yellow spots, starts in a small gully on the right.

Ascending the forested slope in a series of switchbacks, this trail is easily lost beneath the thick carpet of pine needles, so keep a sharp eye out for the tell-tale yellow spots. It bares broadly right, crossing a dry stream bed and emerges after a 20-minute climb on to a stony slope. Continue up until you meet a track which traverses right, climbing to the crest of a ridge from where you can see along the coast towards Ekincik. Don't be tempted down a track on the left, but instead continue for about five minutes to a graveyard.

Cross the graveyard diagonally picking up a trail marked with red flashes which passes through a gate in a barbed wire fence. This path descends past a water trough and some antique marble blocks to a cluster of tiny bee-keepers huts in an olive grove. Dropping into a deep gulley it climbs the other side, joining a well-trodden ancient trail which snakes its way along the coast, offering some excellent views along the way, to Ekincik.

Essentials

Sleeping
The best places get very full in summer, so booking may be a good idea
Most of Dalyan's accommodation is in small hotels and guesthouses which, more often than not, are family-run. Many of the nicest places are in Maraş Mahallesi, a quiet neighbourhood 5-mins walk from the centre. These often front the river and have views of the rock-tombs. Gülpınar Mahallesi, a 5-min walk north is similarly quiet, although there's no access to the river. Prices are set by the municipality and as a result of several mediocre years in terms of occupancy rates prices are low. This could change, with the cheaper places jumping up a bracket.

A *Asur Oteli*, T2843232, F2843244, at the southern end of Maraş Caddesi about 10-min walk from town. Comfortable, airy rooms in single-storey octagonal kiosks designed by the award-winning architect Nail Çakırhan, intricate woodwork, all mod-cons, set in gardens with lovely pool, the Iztuzu boats will even stop at the hotel's private pier. Recommended. **A** *Dalyan Hotel*, Yalı Sokak, T2842239, F2842240, dalyanotel.com Superb location surrounded on 3 sides by the river and just a 2-min walk from the town, well-equipped but austere rooms facing circular pool. **D** *Hotel Metin*, Erkul Sokak No 14, Maraş Mahallesi T2842040, F2842066. Well-appointed tour hotel, rooms around a circular pool, lots of mod-cons, fridge, ceiling fan, a/c. **D** *Hotel Binlik*, Sulungur Sokak No 16, T2842148, F2842149, binlik@superonline.com 3-star tour hotel, comfortable rooms off an atrium, 2 pools, bar, restaurant, booked-up in season. **E** *Göl Motel*, Kordon Boyu, T2844647, F2844648, centrally located on waterfront north of the mosque. Plain rooms, a curtain separating shower, roof terrace. **E** *Hotel Göl*, Gülpınar Mahallesi, T2842096, F2842555. Simple place just north of the centre, roof terrace and pool. **E** *Gülay Hotel*, Gülpınar Mahallesi, 48 Sokak No 23/1, T2843397, F2843677. 300 m up Gülpınar Caddesi and turn left, small package hotel in quiet location, clean, homely rooms, with balcony, garden bar and pool. **E** *Beyazgül Motel*, Balıkhane Sokak 26-28, Maraş Caddesi, T2842304. 4 atmospheric rooms in a restored old house which is short stroll south of the action, very popular so booking required. **E** *Aktaş Pansiyon*, Maraş Caddesi, T2842042, F2844380, near the Beyazgül. Nice little rooms with view of rock-tombs, attic ones are hot in the summer, use of kitchen and barbeque, riverside garden, canoe for guest-use. Recommended. **E** *Kilim Hotel*, Maraş Mahallesi, T2842253, F2843464, kilimhotel@superonline.com Friendly hotel just off Maraş Caddesi, relaxed atmosphere, large rooms with mosquito net, some have balcony, pool in the garden, communal evening meals. **E** *Happy Caretta Hotel*, Maraş Mahallesi, T/F2842109. Fairly simple rooms but lovely riverside garden, swimming off jetty, friendly owners. Recommended. **F** *Beray Apart Motel City*, Kordonboyu, T2843139, F2843483. Despite the name this is a good budget option if you want to be in the middle of things, simple rooms with ensuite, roof terrace. **F** *Gül Pansiyon*, Erkul Sokak, T2842467, F2844803. Pleasant family-run guesthouse just behind Maraş Caddesi, attic rooms equipped with kitchenette, roof-top breakfast room and sitting area, evening meals prepared, proximity to the main drag makes some rooms a bit noisy in the evening. **F** *Kristal Motel*, T2842263, F2842743. Opposite the *Gül Pansiyon*, another family affair, a bit quieter though, small pool and roof terrace. Recommended. **F** *Kyane Motel*, Gülpınar Sokak No 30, T2842222. Another decent cheapy, this 1 has the advantage of a quieter position and garden, plain 2/3 bed rooms with tiled floors and balcony, use of kitchen. Recommended. **F** *Lindos Pansiyon*, Maraş Mahallesi No 24, T2842005, F2844460. In quiet cul-de-sac off Maraş Caddesi, 10 immaculate rooms and 1 apartment, lovely setting with breakfast and evening meals on terrace overlooking the river and tombs, informal tours arranged. Recommended. **F** *Zakkum Pansiyon*, Maraş Mahallesi, T2842111. Family-run waterside place, row of compact rooms with small ensuite, outside kitchen for guest use, tables next to the river.

Dalyan Camping, Maraş Caddesi, T2844157, well-kept site within easy strolling distance of centre, clean toilets and small waterside restaurant, use of boat, only possible problem could be noise from adjacent bar if you're an early sleeper, US$5 per tent, US$16 for a wooden cabin that sleeps 2.

Camping

Midrange Overlooking the river to the north of the centre, the *Sürmen* and *Melodi* have extensive Turkish menus including *meze*, kebaps, grilled meat and fresh seafood to go with the peaceful setting. For a similar ambience and choice of food you could try the pleasant *Riverside Restaurant* south of the centre. Also on the waterfront near the mosque the popular *Köşem* and *Kordon* offer a similar choice of food at slightly lower prices. On Maraş Caddesi *Onur Restaurant* has a vegetarian menu including curries, vegetable provençal and spinach and mushroom casserole. *Çiçek Restaurant* is an old-favourite serving a good selection of *meze* and Turkish dishes at outside

Eating

In common with all the tourist resorts Dalyan has a fast turn-over of very average dining spots, however, from among the mediocre crop a few good places stand out

Western Mediterranean

tables. *Pembe*, Yalı Sokak, is an atmospheric garden restaurant and bar serving traditional Turkish cuisine, such as *dolma* (stuffed peppers), *köfte* (meat balls), as well as trout. **Cheap** Although the surroundings aren't immediately the most appealing the modern retail development at the top end of Maraş Caddesi, across from the mosque, are popular and represent good value. Of these places *Narin* has good *meze*, ready-prepared soups and stews, grilled meat and specials such as *saç kavurma*. At *Fırat Pide* opposite you can eat soup, pide or lahmacun and a drink for about US$5. Nearby, *Davranlar* also has tasty ready-prepared dishes, grilled meats, kebabs and *mantı*. All these places serve alcohol too.

Cafés Demet Cafe and Patisserie, Maraş Caddesi, well-established café serving pide and burgers, as well as cakes, biscuits, garden at the rear. *Barkers Fruit Bar*, on Maraş Caddesi just south of Yalı Sokak, indulge yourself with a pancake, milkshake, fresh juice or fruit salad while you surf the net. Across the road the *Korcan Cafe* has a comfortable cushioned seating area and serves *gözleme* and pancakes with all manner of sweet and savoury fillings. Nearby on Maraş Caddesi *The Oldest House in Dalyan*, serves traditional pastries, tea and coffee, in atmospheric surroundings of restored house.

Bars The *Jazz Bar* on Kordon Boyu is a relax outside venue with melodious tunes. *Efe's Bar*, at the top end of Maraş Caddesi, is a good place to sit and watch the promenade. Further down Maraş Caddesi, *Albatros Bar* is a livelier street-side place. Across from the school *Crazy Dancing Bar* has a tacky modelled facade and high-decibel music. *The Blues Bar*, Maraş Caddesi, popular venue which has recently relocated from the centre of town, run by friendly couple Murat and Robyn Yücel, open jam-sessions led by Murat nightly.

Clubs Sound restrictions after midnight in the centre have encouraged a couple of nightspots to open at the far end of Maraş Caddesi beside the river. *Gel Gör* is 1 of the longest running.

Shopping A local speciality are hand-made leather sandals available at *Özen Kurdura* next to the mosque.

Tour agencies *Kaunos Tours*, Maraş Caddesi, T2842816. F2843157, good selection of outdoor activities and tours, bicycle rental US$5 per day, rent-a-car.

Transport **Bus** There are very few direct bus services from **Dalyan** itself, so you'll usually have to get a dolmuş to **Ortaca**, every 15 mins, US$0.50. Last dolmuş leaves 1900, earlier in winter. Buses leave for **Göcek** and **Fethiye**, **Köyceğiz** and **Marmaris** at 1000 and 1100 everyday during the season from the dolmuş stand near the PTT. In summer there is also a minibus service on Mon to the **Köyceğiz market**. **Taxi** To Dalaman airport costs US$24, with the prices to other places in the surrounding area clearly displayed outside the town's cab ranks.

Directory **Banks** There are several banks with ATM and change facilities near the post office. **Communications** Internet: *Barkers Fruit Bar* (see Cafés), Maraş Caddesi just south of Yalı Sokak, US$3.50 per hr. **Post office**: The PTT is just to the east of the mosque and main square. **Hospitals** The local health centre (*Sağlık Ocağı*) is off Maraş Caddesi near the *Dalyan Hotel*. **Laundry** *Çamaşırhane*, Maraş Caddesi, across from Dalyan Camping. **Tourist information** The Tourist Office, T2844235, is just off Maraş Caddesi in a small alley. Open 0930-1200, 1430-1800.

Dalaman

A well-known name because of its busy regional airport, where thousands of *Phone code 0252*
package tourists touch-down each year, unless you're arriving or leaving by air *Colour map 4, grid B3*
it's hard to think of another reason to spend any time in Dalaman. A uniformly
modern and fairly drab market town layed out on a characterless grid of dusty
streets, you approach the centre from the main highway along an interminable
5 km boulevard. Called Kenan Evren Bulvarı, it meets the town's main street,
Atatürk Caddesi, at a roundabout with the small bus station just to the east of
the junction in a sidestreet. Most of the town's functional accommodation and
restaurants are also in this direction. Continuing straight-on at the roundabout brings you after 6 km to the airport, which isn't served by public transport. An expensive US$8 taxi ride is the only option for getting there.

A *Hotel Dalaman Park*, Kenan Evren Bulvarı, T6923158/9, F6923332. Heading out **Sleeping**
towards the airport this modern hotel, frequented by tour groups, is the best on offer in *Dalaman's hotels*
town, has a pool and tennis court. B *Airport Hotel Sevilen*, Kenarı Evren Bulvarı, *are mainly of the*
T6922451, F6922452. Across from the Dalaman Park this is a marginally simpler alterna- *functional, rather than*
tive, guest-rooms with shower have TV, telephone and a/c, also a pool. D *Hafizoğlu* *inspirational, variety*
Hotel, Meltem Sokak, T6925078. Uninspiring concrete building on the opposite side of
Atatürk Caddesi to the *otogar*, rooms with ensuite have telephone and TV. E *Çaktuğ*
Hotel, Atatürk Caddesi, T6925265. A short walk down the main street, the serviceable
rooms aren't much different to the *Hafizoğlu Hotel*, making it better value, rates also
seem to be open to adjustment when it's quiet. F *Yılmaz Pansiyon*, Cenghiz Topal
Caddesi, Sokak 2, T6925511. The sign is just visible in street to the northeast of the bus
station, rudimentary but passable rooms in detached house, shared bathroom.

On Atatürk Caddesi the *Alakart Restaurant* is a pide place aspiring to greater things **Eating**
with a tacky upstairs dining room complete with a pair of neo-classical columns; the
reasonably priced pide, lahmacun and kebaps can't be faulted though. For something
more sophisticated you could try the *Hotel Dalaman* restaurant.

Dalaman's *otogar* is well-served as all buses plying the coastal highway to and from **Transport**
Fethiye call-in. **Antalya**, 7 daily, 5 hrs, US$10. Make sure you get a "*Yayladan*" bus
which goes the shortest route via *Korkuteli*. **Bodrum**, only a few direct – change at
Muğla, 1½ hrs, US$3. **Fethiye**, every 30 mins, 1 hr, US$2. **Gökova**, every 45 mins, 75
mins, US$2. **İstanbul**, several evening buses, 15 hrs, US$22. **İzmir**, almost hourly, 6½
hrs, US$10. **Köyceğiz**, about every 30 mins, 45 mins, US$1.50. **Ortaca** (for Dalyan),
every 15 mins, last leaves at 1900, 15 mins, US$0.50. **Pamukkale/Denizli**, regular
buses, 4 hrs, US$8. For **Kalkan** (2½ hrs) and **Kaş** (3 hrs) get on a *sahildan* (coastal)
Antalya bus, or changing at Fethiye may be quicker.

Banks *İşbunkası* is opposite the bus station. There's a Yapı Kredi with ATM next to the junction of **Directory**
Kenan Evren Bulvarı and Atatürk Caddesi. There are also 24 hr change facilities at the airport.
Tourist information There's a tourist information desk at the airport.

Some 15 km south of Dalaman, but most easily accessible by regular dolmuş **Sarıgerme**
from Ortaca, is the long sweeping beach of Sarıgerme. The road stops abruptly at
a group of large luxury hotels discreetly set-back from the sand amongst the pine
trees. There are sun-beds and a snackbar, while the aforementioned establishments make sure the gently sloping beach is kept immaculately clean, with an
island just off-shore giving a degree of protection. A possible day-trip from
Dalyan if you fancy an alternative venue for your beach lounging, it's doubtful
you'd want to overnight in the soulless township of Osmaniye, 2 km inland,

which consists mainly of leather shops and a restaurant or two. If the mood does take you there are several guesthouses such as **F** *Myra Pension*, T2868382.

Göcek On its winding passage through the lovely forested mountains between Dalaman and Fethiye, the D-400 highway skirts the edge of Göcek, a small seaside town at the head of a narrow bay leading onto the Gulf of Fethiye. It's a well-to-do, polished little place with a wide landscaped promenade and a large marina packed with ranks of sailing boats and pleasure craft. A favoured port of call for the affluent British and Turkish yacht-set, Göcek's attractions for the land-based visitor only stretch as far as a scrappy stretch of beach to the west of the marina and some predictably pricey restaurants and cafés along the waterfront esplanade. The town holds its annual regatta at the end of June.

Sleeping and eating If you decide to stay there are a number of hotels along, or just behind, the front: **B** *Deniz Hotel*, T6451902, F6451903. Very well-appointed small hotel with comfortable rooms and lots of trimmings, can be booked through *Simple Turkey* in the UK. **F** *Pansiyon Tufan's*, Iskele Caddesi, T6451334. Modest B&B place, some of the rooms overlook the marina. **F** *Ünlü Pansiyon*, T6451170, F6451380. Another unassuming pension fronting the street inland from the marina. **F** *Zelga Hostel*, Iskele Caddesi, T6451875. On the outskirts of town as you come in from the highway, simple rooms and **camping** too. For a cheaper bite than the water-front restaurants try the street one back from the promenade where you'll find *Deniz Kızı* with soup, ready-prepared dishes and *şiş kebabı;* or there's a pide place *Bizim City* on the pedestrianised square.

Transport There are several dolmuş to and from Fethiye each day, or else you can walk the 1 km out to the highway, north-west along Iskele Caddesi, and wait near the petrol station to flag down one of the many passing buses.

Directory Banks There are several banks with ATMs around the central square. **Post office** The PTT is on the square.

Huzur Vadisi High above Göcek in a peaceful valley is one of Turkey's more unusual places to stay, accommodation is in a group of *yurt* – Turkic nomadic tents – with a few less traditional mod-cons such as beds, mosquito nets and electricity added for comfort, vegetarian menu, pool, trips organised, also hosts programme of alternative holidays. Recommended. Contact T6452419, UK, 01970626821.

Göcek to It's a 32 km drive between Göcek and Fethiye with the highway twisting past
Fethiye the turn-offs for **Küçük Kargı** and **Katrancı**, two forestry department campsites set on lovely pine-fringed bays. Accessible in summer by dolmuş from Fethiye's minibus garage, alternatively you could simply get-off a passing bus, they can get quite crowded during the main holiday months, though the rest of the time things are much quieter.

Fethiye

Phone code: 0252
Colour map 4, grid C3

Blessed with a well-protected bay and an extensive hinterland of flat, agriculturally productive land – both rare commodities along this stretch of coast – it's no wonder Fethiye has had a long history. Originally known as Telmessos, it's been around for at least 2,500 years, although two cataclysmic earthquakes, the last of which struck in 1957, have left only fragmentary traces of this historic city. Instead, a vibrant modern town has risen rapidly from the rubble, nourished increasingly in the last

20 years by the tourist industry. A breed apart from many other Turkish resorts, though, tourism remains just another string in Fethiye's bow, a very profitable addition to its existing roles as a market town, administrative centre and exporter of chromium ore sourced in local mines. This breadth of character is refreshing in comparison to the saturation of mega-resorts such as Marmaris or Kuşadası, and although it may not be the most scenic of coastal towns, or have its own white sand beaches, it could make an excellent base for exploring the surrounding area. Peppered with ancient sites, the Xanthos Valley is within easy reach, while closer at hand are the ghost village of Kayaköy and the beaches of Ölüdeniz, Çalış, or for something altogether quieter, Gemiler or Katrancı. Then there are the boat trips around the turquoise waters of Fethiye bay.

Ins and outs

The nearest airport, served by international and domestic flights, is just over an hour north by road at Dalaman. The town's *otogar* is very well-connected to destinations far and wide.

Getting there
See page 337 for further details

The core of the town, between Iskele Meydanı and Çarşı Caddesi, is a grid of narrow streets known as the Paspatur district. Fethiye's bus station, 2 km east of the Paspatur, is served by regular dolmuş which pass by on Süleyman Demirel Caddesi. Turn left out of the entrance, walk up to the roundabout and wait across from the petrol station. Süleyman Demirel Caddesi turns into 1-way Atatürk Caddesi which heads straight into the centre. Traffic is then directed back out along Çarşı Caddesi to the south. City dolmuş (US$0.40) trawl around this 1-way system and out to the *otogar* regularly. Some dolmuş, labelled "jandarma", also continue west past the marina to Karagözler. A taxi from the bus station to Karagözler is about US$5. The dolmuş garage for Ölüdeniz, Çalış and other nearby places is about 1 km east of the centre, though people also wait next to the small mosque on Kaya Sokak, off Atatürk Caddesi.

Getting around
Hotel touts usually stake-out the bus station waiting to pounce on new arrivals, so it's good to have an idea of where you want to go

Sights

The remains of ancient Telmessos are fairly scanty, the most conspicuous being the monumental rock-cut tombs in the cliff above the town. Attractively illuminated at night, the most famous is known as the Tomb of Amyntas on account of a Greek inscription identifying its occcupant as one "Amyntas son of Hermagios". Built in the fourth century BC to imitate an Ionic order temple, the builders paid amazing attention to detail even carving metal studs in the panelled doorway. Reached by walking south, up the hill from Atatürk Caddesi, the tomb can get crowded at sunset during the summer when people climb up for the view across the town and bay. Further to the west, reached off Çarşı Caddesi, a badly ruined castle tops the acropolis above the centre. Originally the site of a Lycian settlement, later moved to the coastal plain below, the fortress was rebuilt in the 15th century by the Knights of St John. Apart from some Lycian sarcophagi dotting the streets, the only other sizeable reminder of ancient Telmessos is the 6,000 seat Hellenistic theatre, sitting inland from the harbour. Adapted later by the Romans, it became a useful source of pre-cut stone after the 1957 earthquake, although since 1994 this damage has largely been reversed by a locally funded restoration team. ■ *0830-1900, 1730 in winter. US$1.*

Telmessos

If you're looking for something to do, Fethiye's archaeological collection has some interesting artefacts from sites in the nearby Xanthos valley. Among the most intriguing is a fourth century BC stela recovered from Letoön, which

Fethiye Museum

bares a trilingual dedication in Lycian, Greek and Aramaic to the eponymous founder of the city of Kaunos, near present-day Dalyan. The museum also has a series of stone statuettes and some jewellery found at other nearby sites. ■ *0830-1700 daily except Mon. US$1. Getting there: Turn north off Atatürk Caddesi about is about a km east of the centre.*

Beaches The easiest beach to reach from town is 5 km north of the centre at Çalış. Several kilometres long, it's backed by a continuous strip of package hotels and touristy restaurants. Despite the views across the island-studded bay, the beach itself is pretty mediocre: coarse gravely sand and over-crowded with sun-loungers. ■ *Getting there: Dolmuş (US$0.40) leave every 10 mins from Kaya Caddesi, or by taxi-boat departing from the quayside in Fethiye every 20-30 mins until 2300.*

Far nicer are the beaches at Küçük Kargı, Katrancı (see page 337) or Ölüdeniz (see page 338) which are all within easy striking distance of the town.

Boat trips There are dozens of excursion boats moored along the waterfront which set-out daily on whistle-stop tours of Fethiye bay, stopping at a number of the 12 islands dotting the off-shore waters. Good value for money and fun these cruises typically depart at 1030, returning by 1830, and cost about US$10 per person. If you want to explore less-frequented parts of the coast at a more leisurely pace then you can charter your own boat and crew for US$100- 200 per day.

Scuba diving Scuba diving is a popular activity in the coastal waters around Fethiye and although the marine environment has been adversely affected in recent years by overfishing, pollution and disturbance from pleasure craft, there's still a lot to see. The coast around Fethiye is noted for its spectacular underwater

Fethiye

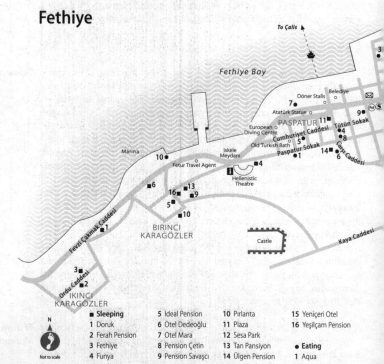

■ Sleeping	5 Ideal Pension	10 Pırlanta	15 Yeniçeri Otel
1 Doruk	6 Otel Dedeoğlu	11 Plaza	16 Yeşilçam Pension
2 Ferah Pension	7 Otel Mara	12 Sesa Park	
3 Fethiye	8 Pension Çetin	13 Tan Pansiyon	● Eating
4 Funya	9 Pension Savaşçı	14 Ülgen Pension	1 Aqua

Not to scale

scenery rather than abundant fish life, though there's always the chance of running into barracuda, octopus and even the odd turtle.

Of the dozens of outfits in town the British-owned **European Diving Centre**, Atatürk Caddesi No 12/1, T6149771, F6149772, europeandiving.com.tr is particularly well regarded. They run a weekly 21 site programme for qualified divers, as well as offering the full range of PADI courses and excellent value diving cruises.

Essentials

There's certainly no shortage in Fethiye, though in season the best places get fairly booked-up. Staying east of the centre and in the bazaar district you're conveniently close to the restaurants and bars as well as the *otogar* and dolmuş station. On the down-side some of these places can be pretty noisy. To the west of the centre in the hillside suburbs of Birinci (1st) and Ikinci (2nd) Karagözler things are much quieter, with the slog up to your hotel rewarded by fantastic views across the bay. The disadvantage, especially in Ikinci Karagözler, is that it's a fair old hike, or a short dolmuş ride, to the centre. You could also think about staying at Çalış, the town's seaside suburb 5 km north of the centre; although frankly you can find far better beaches elsewhere. Of the dozens of package hotels along the coastal strip, many are block booked by tour groups in season, so if you plan to stay more than a few days it makes sense to book through a travel agent before arriving.

Sleeping
Prices can fluctuate wildly depending on the time of year & how good a season everybody is having

The bazaar and east of the centre B *Otel Mara*, Yalı Sokak No 2, off Kral Caddesi, T6146722, F6148039. Comfortable hotel in the backstreets north of the PTT, rates seem to fluctuate widely depending on how busy they are so try bargaining, comfortable rooms with telephone, TV and ensuite, a little bit worn. **D** *Sesa Park Hotel*,

Akdeniz Caddesi No 17, T6144656, F6144326. Well-established tour hotel on corner near the sea, neat rooms with a/c, telephone, TV and balcony. **D** *Yeniçeri Otel*, Akdeniz Caddesi No 15, T6148583, F6141324. Similar style of rooms to the *Sesa Park* next-door, also have a/c, cable-TV and telephone. **E** *Hotel Plaza*, Atatürk Caddesi No 2, T6149030/1, F6141070. Centrally located on corner with Çarşı Caddesi, front rooms may be noisy, perfectly adequate but uninspiring rooms equipped with a/c and ensuite as standard. **F** *Ülgen Pension*, Cumhuriyet Mahallesi, T6143491, F6142911. Family-run pension on the hill above Çarşı Caddesi, reached up staircase opposite the *Rıhtım Pastanesi*, comparatively quiet despite central location, pretty basic rooms with showers but front ones have excellent view. Recommended. **F** *Pension Çetin*, Yüzüncü Cadde, T6146156, F6147794, just off seafront Akdeniz Caddesi. Simple rooms with ensuite in friendly pension, regular clientel.

Map labels:
To Çalış
Akdeniz Caddesi
Sedir Caddesi
Atatürk Caddesi
Dolmuş to Ölüdeniz & Çalış
Çarşı Caddesi
Dolmuş Station
To Otogar, Petrol Station, Letôon Hospital, Ölüdeniz & Kmalye (ID 400)
Lycian Monumental Tombs
Tomb of Amyntas

2 Güneş Lokanta
3 Indian Paradise
4 Meğri Lokanta
5 Ordukan
6 Pizza Pepino
7 Rafet
8 Rıhtım Pastanesi
9 Saray
10 Yacht

Western Mediterranean

The Marina and Karagözler B *Hotel Doruk*, Yat Limanı Karşısı, T6149860, F6123001. Pleasant, well-equipped hotel overlooking the marina. **C** *Hotel Pırlanta*, Birinci Karagözler, T6144959, F6141686. Steep climb up to the top of the district, modern hotel with large pool, sauna, restaurant, disco and billiards room, airy, a/c equipped rooms with excellent view from balcony. **D** *Fethiye Hotel*, Ikinci Karagözler, Ordu Caddesi No 16, T6146813, F6143663. *Thompson Holidays* affilliate so it may be booked in season, decent rooms equipped with fridge, a/c and TV, friendly bar and locally recommended terrace restaurant. **E** *Funya Hotel*, Fethibey Parkı Yanı, T6141602. Next to the amphitheatre, plain simple rooms which are overpriced, suffers from traffic noise. **E** *Otel Dedeoğlu*, Iskele Meydanı No 1/1, T6144010, F6141707. Fairly forgetable package place overlooking the marina. **F** *Pension Savaşcı*, Birinci Karagözler, T6146681, F6131528. Friendly family-run pension which is worth the climb, wonderful unobstructed views across the bay from terrace and balconies, simple rooms with tiled floor and ensuite, large breakfast. Recommended. **F** *Yeşilçam Pension*, Birinci Karagözler Yokuşu No 91, T6123518, F6124289. Simple white-washed rooms in tall building with rooftop terrace. **F** *Tan Pansiyon*, Birinci Karagözler, Eski Karagözler Caddesi No 89, T6141584. Clean but fairly plain rooms in guesthouse run by friendly old lady, breakfast on the scenic terrace. **F** *Ideal Pension*, Zafer Caddesi No 1, Birinci Karagözler, T6141981. Long-running favourite with the backpacking fraternity, 1/2/3 bed rooms with ensuite, some also have a balcony, panaramic terrace bar, laundry service and food available, free pick-up from the *otogar*. Recommended. **F-G** *Ferah Pension*, Ordu Caddesi No 21, Ikinci Karagözler, T6142816, F6127398, backpackingeurope.com Another good budget guesthouse on the backpacker circuit, basic rooms with shared toilet, dorm US$5, free pick-up from the bus station. Recommended.

Çalış D *Hotel Idee*, T6221164, F6221172. Towards the nicer, southern, end of the strip, comfortable rooms with a/c as standard, price includes open buffet dinner. **E** *Hotel Mutlu*, T6221180, F6221181, near the Fethiye-end of the beach. *Thomson Holidays* hotel in pleasant garden with pool, restaurant overlooking the beach, fairly standard rooms with ensuite. **E** *Kumsal Pension*, T6221207. Overlooking the beach near the dolmuş drop-off point, more simple rooms above restaurant, noise may be a problem.

Eating Fethiye has a wide choice of places to eat from touristy fish and *meze* restaurants in the Paspatur district to cheap-and-cheerful local diners near the market. It's common practice at a few of the town's restaurants to bring unordered dishes to the table, which then have a habit of creeping onto your bill. Return such unwanted dishes and check your bill to avoid being overcharged. **Midrange** On the seafront there are several fish restaurants where you can enjoy pleasant outdoor dining. Try *Rafet* near the Atatürk statue, which has a formidable selection of *meze* to begin, and possibly end, your meal, as well as seafood and meat dishes. The fish soup is also tasty. The *Ordukan Restaurant* in the Paspatur near the hamam also has an excellent range of *meze* followed by your choice of seafood, kebaps or other meat dishes. For a civilised meal at outside tables overlooking the marina you could try the *Yacht Restaurant*. If you fancy a pizza, *Pizza Pepino* on Çarşı Caddesi near the *Ottoman Han Bar* serves good ones served on wooden boards at tables beneath a leafy vine. Alternatively if it's curry you're craving the *Indian Paradise* beside *Uğur Mumcu Parkı* is well recommended locally. *Aqua Restaurant*, Hamam Sokak No 33, Paspatur, modern Mediterranean and ecclectic international dishes such as Thai-style fish, vegetarian pasta, lamb shank in barley and red wine sauce, finished off with rich chocolate mudcake, tables on terrace beside cooling water-feature. **Cheap** There are several excellent value lokantas west of the market, for example the *Güneş Lokanta*, serving soup, fish, meat dishes and ready-prepared stews, reached down the alleyway beside the *Işbankası* on Atatürk Caddesi. The *Saray Restaurant*, opposite the PTT, has a good menu including soup, *meze*, pide, pizza and kebaps, served inside or on a terrace to a healthy mix of locals and tourists. There's a row of döner stalls on Atatürk Caddesi near the statue where you can have a *dürüm* and soft drink for US$2.50. The *Meğri Lokanta*, at the west end of Çarşı Caddesi, is a popular local diner serving a mind-boggling array of soups, stews and ready-prepared dishes.

The *Rıhtım Pastanesi*, at the western end of Çarşı Caddesi has good biscuits, cakes and rice pudding that can be savoured at a couple of street-side tables. Alternatively, the waterfront promenade is lined with cafés and ice-cream parlours where you can indulge your sweet touch and recline in comfy chairs.

Cafés

Car Cemetery, on Hamam Sokağı is a cool place for a drink surrounded by bits and pieces of old automobiles, they sometimes have live acts, wide choice of liqueur coffees. On the same street is the loud and brash *Music Factory* where you can dance until the wee hours alongside tourists and locals, mostly men. Further towards Çarşı Caddesi, the *Otantik Bar* is located in one of the town's few surviving Ottoman houses. Nearby, the *Yes! Bar* on Cumhuriyet Caddesi is another place for a dance. For a really wild night out locals and tourists alike head up to the clubs and discos of Hisarönü (see page 340).

Bars & nightclubs
Fethiye's bars & nightclubs are concentrated in the narrow streets of the Paspatur

The streets of the Paspatur district, especially Hamam Sokağı, are amply supplied with leather, carpet and jewellery shops, but you'll need to bargain hard to get a bargain. For picnic stuff the town's lively and colourful produce **market**, open everyday, is between Atatürk and Çarşı Caddesis near the centre of town. But for an altogether overwhelming shopping experience head to the huge weekly market, held every Tue to the north of the stadium, where you'll find an abundance of fresh produce brought from the surrounding countryside, as well as cheap clothing and household goods.

Shopping

There's a concentration of agencies near the marina: *Alesta Yachting and Travel*, Telegraf Apartments, Fevzi Çakmak Caddesi, T6141861, F6142571, alestayachting.com, car rental, yacht charters, transfer. *Scirocco Tourism*, Körfez Apartments, Fevzi Çakmak Caddesi, T6125921, F6125926, fethiye.net/compass, flight ticketing, tours and excursions, yacht charter, car hire.

Tour agencies

Air To reach Dalaman international airport, an hour north of town, there are regular service buses departing from outside **Fetur**, the local sales agent for *Turkish Airlines* (see Directory). **Bus** Long distance services depart from the *otogar*, however, buses and dolmuş to destinations in the **Xanthos Valley** (Kınık, Kumluova and Saklıkent), as well as **Ölüdeniz**, **Çalış**, **Katrancı** and **Kargı**, leave from the minibus station, south of Atatürk Caddesi 1 km east of the centre. Some long-distance services include: **Ankara**, several night buses, 9 hrs, US$15. **Antalya**, *yayla* route via Korkuteli, 4½ hrs, US$6; *sahil* route via Kaş, 7½ hrs, US$8. Departures every 30-60 mins. **Denizli/Pamukkale**, 8 daily, 5 hrs, US$6. **İstanbul**, 3 daily, 13 hrs, US$18. **İzmir**, 10 daily, 7 hrs, US$12. **Kalkan**, hourly, coastal route Antalya bus (*sahildan*), 2 hrs, US$3. **Kaş**, hourly, 2½ hrs, US$3.50. **Marmaris**, hourly, 3 hrs, US$5. Buses to Marmaris and İzmir pass through Göcek (20 mins), Dalaman (1 hr), Ortaca (1¼ hrs) and Köyceğiz (2 hrs). For **Bodrum** get on a bus to Muğla (3½ hrs, US$5) and change. **Car and motorbike rental** *Avis*, Fevzi Çakmak Caddesi No 1/B, T6146339, F6146339, near the amphitheatre. *Budget*, Karagözler Yokuşu, Karagözler Mahallesi, T6146166, F6122401. *Tiger Rent-a-Car*, 1st floor, Kadioğlu Işhanı, Doktorlar Sitesi, T6125267, rent scooters, motorbikes and cars. **Hydrofoils to Rhodes** During the summer they operate on Thu, Fri and Sat mornings (subject to periodic change). 1½ hr trip costing US$45 1-way, or US$80 open return. Available from tour agents along Fevzi Çakmak Caddesi near the marina.

Transport

Western Mediterranean

Directory **Airline offices** *Fetur*, Fevzi Çakmak Caddesi, 9 Körfez Apartments, T6142034, F6143845, near the marina, agents for *Turkish Airlines* and departure point for Dalaman shuttle bus. **Banks** *İşbankası* and several other banks with ATMs are located on Atatürk Caddesi near the PTT. **Baths** *Old Turkish Bath*, T6149318. *Hamam Sokak*, Paspatur district. **Communications Internet:** *Line Internet Café*, Yalı Sokak No 5/B, T6127155, US$2 per hr, just inland of the seafront near Akdeniz Caddesi. There's also an internet café on Atatürk Caddesi near the European Diving Centre. **Post office**: The PTT is on Atatürk Caddesi east of the centre. You can send (US$3 per page) and receive (US$0.50) faxes at Çelik Ticaret, a small shop on Atatürk Caddesi near the statue. **Hospitals** *Letoön Hospital* Özel Fethiye Hastanesi is a large private hospital 2 km to the east of the *otogar* along Süleyman Demirel Bulvarı, T6125480. Devlet Hastanesi, state hospital, 1½ km north of the centre on Akdeniz Caddesi. **Laundry** *Guneş Laundry*, Fevzi Çakmak Caddesi, between *Prenses Hotel* and the Marina. **Tourist information** The Tourist Office, T6141527, with helpful English-speaking staff, is on Iskele Meydanı near the amphitheatre. Open daily 0830-1200, 1300-1730, closed at weekends in winter. Fethiye Turizm Derneği, the local tourism association, whose staff can help with hotel reservations and provide information on yachting, is conveniently located next-door.

Ölüdeniz

Phone code: 0252
Colour map 4, grid C3

An alluring turquoise lagoon, fringed by pine-forested slopes and protected from the sea by an arching spit of golden sand, Ölüdeniz is the most widely touted image of Turkey, plastered across innumerable promotional posters and brochures. Not surprisingly it's become a magnet for tourists, foreign and domestic alike, and in the last twenty odd years a fully fledged resort has grown-up inland of the Belceğiz public beach, just to the southeast. Lined with restaurants and lively bars, Belceğiz's newly-built beach-front promenade backs onto a jumble of hotels, guesthouses and campsites which creeps irresistibly further inland each year. Certainly no place to come in search of peace during the hectic summer season, the view as you descend the vertiginous road to the resort is still – concrete aside – achingly beautiful: a narrow valley hemmed-in by forested mountains and opening onto the blue Mediterranean. So, if you're disinclined to share such a spectacular setting with thousands of others, it's best to visit between October and May.

Ins & outs Ölüdeniz is a windy 10 km drive over the mountains to the southeast of Fethiye, passing along the way the tacky new resorts of Ovacık and Hisarönü (see below). Dolmuş leave on the 30-min journey from Fethiye's minibus garage every 15-30 mins until 0030 (earlier in the winter), US$1. Conveniently, these dolmuş also pass the *otogar*, so wait outside the entrance. Having wound down the steep hill into Belceğiz, dolmuş terminate at the northern end of the public beach where the road turns sharply right and continues past the Jandarma post and PTT to skirt the lagoon, 500 m west.

The lagoon & beaches Called "Dead Sea" in Turkish because of the serene calmness of its waters, Ölüdeniz is enclosed by a spit of sand, partially colonised by scrub and pines. Designated the Ölüdeniz Tabiat Parkı (Nature Park), the long curving beach within this fenced area is accessible during daylight hours. *US$0.50 per person, US$2.50 for a car. Toilets, showers and a drinks stand.*

Continuing along the road brings you to a series of campsites and bungalow outfits before reaching the *Hotel Meri*. Several places rent kayaks and the warm, still water is perfect for young children. Once a favourite anchorage the lagoon is now off-limits to yachts in order to prevent pollution.

About 2 km to the south of Ölüdeniz, the Kıdrak Orman Parkı is a pleasant pine-shaded campground and beach, though its now completely overshadowed by the sprawling *Club Likya World* complex next-door.

The Lycian Way

Turkey's first and, so far, only long-distance trail, the Lycian Way threads its way 500 km from Ovacik near Fethiye to Hısar Çandır, 25 km short of Antalya. Weaving a meandering course along ancient paths, mountain tracks and forestry trails the path cuts across some of the region's most beautiful and unspoilt countryside; skirting isolated stretches of coastline but also climbing into the mountainous Lycian hinterland, where it attains a 1,800 m high-point near the summit of Tahtalı Dağı.

Clearly marked using the Grande Randonnée system of signposts and painted flashes it can be undertaken as a fairly epic six week expedition; divided up into smaller sections or even just followed as a short excursion from one of the resorts or towns along the way. A companion guide written by Kate Clow, who conceived the idea for the path and was sponsored to waymark the route by a private Turkish bank, is available through the UK distributors Cordee Ltd, 39 De Montford Street, Leicester, LE1 7HD, T(0)1162471176, or from Bougainville Travel in Kaş (see page 356). Information also on-line at: www.lycianway.com

Butterfly Valley

A verdant canyon enclosed by towering limestone cliffs, Butterfly Valley owes its name to the profusion of flying insects, including the endemic Jersey Tiger, which flitter to and fro particularly in the spring. Such a lovely spot couldn't stay secret for long and in season the small beach is visited by a procession of tour boats from Ölüdeniz and Fethiye. Served by a rudimentary beach restaurant, there's also free camping and simple accommodation in treehouses, US$4 per person. Three daily boats leave from near the dolmuş station in season. A treacherous and exposed path climbs out of the valley to the hamlet of Faralya, also reached on a motorable track along the dizzying clifftops from Ölüdeniz. The **C** Değirmen, Faralya Köyü, T6421179/ 6146864, F6146992, is a rustic stone retreat with large pine-scented rooms and a pool in the garden. Recommended.

Walk to Kaya Köyü

A pleasant way to escape the crowds & catch a glimpse of the unspoilt coastline to the W of Ölüdeniz is to walk to the abandoned Greek village of Kaya Köyü

The fairly well-trodden path to Kaya Köyü (see page 341), marked by red dots, begins at the head of the bay beyond the *Hotel Meri*, climbing through the pine forests to emerge at some meadows, where a family of shepherds sometime spend the summer. Following parts of an old road, the path climbs steeply across the mountainside, with views west along the pristine coast towards Gemiler, eventually emerging after 2-2½ hours on a saddle above Kaya Köyü. Stout shoes are advisable for this excursion and don't forget to take some water.

Paragliding

In the shadow of Baba Dağı, the 1976 m-high slopes of which are climbed by a rough four-wheel drive track, Ölüdeniz is the undisputed paragliding capital of Turkey. At certain times of the day the sky is literally filled with minute dots which gradually materialise as they descend towards several landing zones on the beach. If you're not a qualified flyer you can sample the action with one of the many outfits offering tadem flights for about US$100. *Easy Riders Paragliding*, Han Camp No 5, T6170114, F6170148, has over seven years experience. Watersports such as kayaking, water-skiing and parasailing are also available on Belceğiz beach.

Sleeping

Most of the hotel accommodation, largely monopolised by package operators during the summer season, is located inland of the Belceğiz beach. It can sometimes be hard to find a bed during high season, so you may have to take whatever's available and continue your search early the next day. Remember to consider the noise factor when choosing a room as the bars along the beach-front strip are open for most of the

Western Mediterranean

night. A short walk west of Belceğiz there are a few quieter campsites with wooden bungalows and cabins fronting the lagoon. The *Öludeniz Tourism Development Co-operative* has an information kiosk on the right side of the road as you approach the dolmuş stand and beach. It provides details about many of the local hotels, though not, unfortunately, room rates or whether they currently have any vacancies.

Belceğiz A *Club Belcekız Beach*, Belceğiz, T6170077, F6170372, belcekiz.com Sprawling holiday village with huge pool and loads of amenities such as a Turkish bath, gym and 3 restaurants. **B** *Hotel Asena Beach*, Belceğiz, T6170154, F6170487. Large modern complex set-back from the middle of the beach also has a shopping centre, gym, numerous restaurants and bars. **C** *Hotel Karbel Beach*, Belceğiz, T6170411, F6170096. Less polished version of the *Asena*, well-fitted rooms with tiled floors around kidney-shaped pool, quite good value. **E** *Ilkiz Hotel*, Belceğiz, T6170251, F6170016, turn left 150 m before dolmuş stand and continue past *Oba*. Small package hotel with a/c equipped rooms around pool, also have several simpler rooms. **E** *Hotel Bronze*, Belceğiz, T6170107, F6170182, inland from *Deniz Camping*. Small hotel with pleasant rooms around small pool, cheaper rooms without a/c. **E** *Ünsal Hotel*, Belceğiz, T6170031, 200 m inland from the road (west) end of the beach. Plain rooms which aren't as nice as the *Oba* opposite. **F** *Oba Öludeniz*, Belceğiz, T6170470, F6170522, fethiye-net.com, turn left 150 m inland of the dolmuş stand. Set back enough from the beach to be reasonably quiet, pine bungalows with or without ensuite shower, also beds in bamboo dorm US$5 per person, safe box, good on-site restaurant. Recommended. **F** *Deniz Kamp*, Belceğiz, T6170045, F6170054. Popular campsite behind the beach-front *Buzz Bar*, expect a good deal of noise until the early hours, simple cabins with communal showers.

The Lagoon A *Hotel Meri*, T6170001, F6170010, 1 km west of the dolmuş stand at the end of the Lagoon road. Recently revamped and considerably more upmarket than before, nicely furnished rooms with TV, a/c and scenic balconies on the mountainside, reached by a funicular lift, pool and restaurant fronting the lagoon, protected beach, full-board only at present. Recommended. **F-G** *Öludeniz Camping*, T6170048, F6170181. Popular backpacker place fronting the lagoon 600 m west of the dolmuş stand, tent pitches as well as basic wooden bungalows, also more deluxe cabins with ensuite, excellent value open-buffet dinners. Recommended. Next door, the **F** *Asmalı Pansiyon and Camping*, T6170137, also has some bungalows, but mostly shady tent and caravan pitches. Continuing along the road Suara Camping, T6170123, is a pleasant campsite. Approaching *Hotel Meri* **Osman Çavuş Camping** and **Çağlar Camping** also have space for tents and rudimentary bungalows.

Eating

The staff in restaurants along the beachfront change on a seasonal basis, so the best thing to do is ask someone who's been around for a few days for a recommendation

Prices are generally high, by Turkish standards anyway, and the quality of the food can be pretty variable. Heading inland you generally get better value for money. Try the popular *Oba Restaurant*, attached to a pension of the same name (see sleeping), which has a reasonably priced and interesting menu. For a cheap snack there is a döner stand which does *dürüm* for about US$3 just inland of the dolmuş stand. There's also a refreshingly unpretentious soup restaurant, called *Soup Salad*, next to the *Asena Hotel* that serves various varieties for US$2 and is open until 0500 – perfect for a late night snack.

Directory **Banks** The nearest ATM machines and change facilities are in Hisarönü. **Post office** The PTT is 150 m along the lagoon road from the dolmuş stand.

Ovacık & Hisarönü

Bound for Ölüdeniz the mountain road from Fethiye climbs steeply up to a dry plateau which is the unlikely site for the rapidly developing, and increasingly overlapping, resorts of Ovacık and Hisarönü. Conceived as an overflow for housing the package hordes descending on Ölüdeniz – just 10 minutes down the other side of the mountain – they are one-street tourist ghettos consisting of burgeoning ranks of tour hotels, pensions, tacky restaurants, obnoxiously loud bars and travel agents. The best idea is to pass-on through, turning left at the roundabout for Ölüdeniz or right for Kaya Köyü, although you might need to use an ATM machine or car rental outfit in Hisarönü (also right at the roundabout).

Kaya Köyü

A interesting excursion from Fethiye or Ölüdeniz – or indeed a peaceful alternative place to stay – Kaya Köyü is a quiet farming community sitting in a cultivated basin sown with crops of tobacco and wheat. Its real claim to fame, however, is the "ghost" town of Levissi which spills down a mountainside overlooking the village. Originally an Ottoman Greek settlement populated by migrants from the Dodecanese islands, Levissi, like other Greek towns along the Aegean and Mediterranean coast, thrived on a mixture of farming and trade.

In the 1980s the idea of developing Levissi as a holiday village was floated by a tourist firm. Plans were dropped by the government in the face of a vocal opposition from Greek & Turkish groups

Swept-up in the geopolitical maelstrom following the First World War, Levissi's population were forced to abandon their homes under the conditions of the 1923 Treaty of Lausanne and join the exodus of Orthodox Greeks leaving the newly proclaimed Turkish Republic for Greece. They settled near Athens, establishing a suburb which still bares the name Nea (New) Levissi in memory of their historic home.

A sizeable settlement of about 2,000 houses, the ruins of Levissi have a melancholy, brooding atmosphere which is particularly evocative late in the day when the sun casts long shadows from the weathered buildings. Open to the elements, the rows of cottages seem to stare across the valley with their empty windows and it's easy to appreciate why the Muslim arrivals in 1923 refused to reoccupy the town, believing that it had been cursed. A network of paths weave around the weed-choked site, although apart from several churches there is little of specific interest. Sign-posted from the car park are two of the villages principle churches which, despite the elements and local vandals, retain some very faded frescoes and sections of pebble mosaic floor.

The path to Ölüdeniz (see page 339) climbs over an obvious saddle above the eastern (left as you're looking at it) side of Levissi; follow the red dots. At the western end of the site a second trail passes over a saddle to the left of a small chapel to Cold Water Bay, a popular anchorage with a small restaurant in season.

A tranquil haven after Ölüdeniz or Fethiye, Kaya Köyü now has some good places to stay, although there's a very limited number of beds in the village so you'd be wise to telephone ahead in summer. **D-E** *Les Jardins de Levissi*, T/F6167422, on the road out of the village to Gemiler. Newly-built but very sympathetic stone and wood building, 4 well-designed studio rooms, French/Turkish cuisine prepared by friendly hosts Figen and Michel Tesson, who can provide information on the local area. Recommended. **E** *Villa Rhapsody Pension*, 16166551, F6166987, also on the Gemiler road. 16 carpeted rooms with ensuite, balcony and telephone in villa, small pool and bar in immaculately kept garden. Recommended. **F** *Çavuşoğlu Motel*, T6166749, F6166751. Prime site at the foot of the ruins, popular pension, simpler balconied rooms overlooking pool. **F** *Selçuk Pansiyon*, T6166757. Cheaper and plainer rooms with shower. **F** *Kaya Apart Pansiyon*, T6167295. Rudimentary but serviceable rooms with ensuite, also have an apartment with kitchenette.

Sleeping

Apart from the first 3 pensions mentioned above which can all furnish a decent meal, at the *İstanbul Restaurant*, signposted off the road, you can barbecue your own

Eating

Western Mediterranean

meat. **Bulent's Place** on the road into the village has tasty *gözleme* and refreshing *ayran* or soft drinks, and makes an ideal spot to wait for the dolmuş.

Transport   In season there are hourly dolmuş to Kaya Köyü from Fethiye via Hisarönü, though this service drops off to 1 or 2 a day in winter. It's only 1 hr on foot through the pine woods from Hisarönü. With your own transport, another alternative is to take the steep 7 km road directly from Fethiye which starts as Çarşı Caddesi. Follow signs off Çarşı Caddesi. If you're feeling energetic you can also walk this route in about 2 hrs, abandoning the black-top at several points to follow the old cobbled road through the trees.

Gemiler   West from Kaya Köyü the tarmac quickly disappears, replaced instead by a bumpy track which snakes its way over the mountains for 7 km to an isolated bay known as Gemiler. It's a pleasantly out-of-the-way little spot, though there's little to get excited about except the spectacular views of Baba Dağı and the pristine coastline to the south of Ölüdeniz. A couple of scruffy beach restaurants stand on the tiny shingle beach and there are camping spot just inland. Offshore the fragmentary ruins of a Byzantine monastery top Gemile Adası, a rocky island which provides a popular anchorage for yachts, as well as a destination for boat tours from Ölüdeniz. ■ *Getting there: In summer 3 Kaya Köyü dolmuş a day, 1 morning, 1 midday and 1 late afternoon, are said to continue down to the bay, but don't count on it. To walk in from Kaya Köyü takes about 2 hrs.*

The Xanthos Valley

From Fethiye the coastal highway is forced inland by mountains, only to turn southwards again upon reaching the Xanthos Valley. Covered with a patchwork of cultivated fields, orchards and pinewoods and flanked to the east by the towering Ak Dağı range, this wide valley was a centre of Lycian civilisation, and today harbours a string of interesting sites. Tlos, Pinara, Xanthos and Letöon – not forgetting the impressive gorge at Saklıkent – can all be visited on day-trips from Fethiye; though Patara, with its pristine beach and yet more ruins, or Kalkan could be used as alternative bases.

Tlos

Largely unexcavated & frequently overgrown, the ruins of Tlos don't add up to much in themselves, although, as at Pinara, their setting, dotted across a patchwork of rough meadows, cultivated fields & hedgerows is very appealing

Clustered around a rocky promontory on the eastern side of the Xanthos Valley, Tlos is one of the most beautifully situated ancient cities in Lycia. It is also likely to be one of the oldest, as the settlement is mentioned in a Hittite inscription of the second millennium BC as "Dalawa in the land of the Lukkas". As a powerful member of the Lycian Federation it enjoyed the maximum three votes in the assembly, while later under direct Roman rule it was referred to in glowing terms as "the brilliant metropolis of the Lycian nation."

The most conspicuous building, visible from some way off as you approach, is a **fortress** crowning the acropolis. Overlaying earlier Lycian and Roman fortifications, this structure is comparatively recent, having been built in the nineteenth century by Kanlı Ali Ağa, a petty local potentate. Little more than an empty shell, it affords excellent views down the Xanthos valley.

The precipitous eastern face of the acropolis is riddled with numerous **Lycian tombs**, the most notable of which is the so-called tomb of Bellerophon, a splendid mock-temple cut from the cliff. The elaborate sepulchre, reached via a rough track around the acropolis and a short rusty ladder, takes its name from a carving on the porch of the mythical hero who flew to slay the Chimaera on the winged horse Pegasus. It's generally accepted that the tomb must have belonged to a local leader for the ruling elite of Tlos claimed descendency from Bellerophon himself.

At the base of the acropolis on the east (car park) side are the remnants of a **stadium** with some of the marble seats and granite column drums from a portico remaining. Following the track beyond the car park a path on the right leads 100 m to a **bath complex**, consisting of three chambers. An apse with seven arches, known locally a Yedi Kapı (Seven Gates), sticks out from the buildings southern aspect providing a lovely view over the countryside. On the other side of the main track stands a Roman **theatre**, largely intact but slowly being reclaimed, atmospherically, by bushes and weeds. Continuing up this track brings you after 2½ km to the *Yaka Park Restaurant*, where fresh trout and other dishes are served at shady tables beside a cooling stream: and idyllic spot in summer.

■ *Getting there: The turn-off to Tlos is clearly signposted off the Fethiye-Patara highway. Getting to the site without your own transport, however, requires some determination. Catch a Saklıkent dolmuş (see below) and ask to be let-off at the turning for Tlos, from where it's a 4 km walk.*

The Saklıkent Gorge is a 18-km long fissure incised deeply into the Akdağ **Saklıkent** Mountains by a swift-flowing, icy torrent. The 12-km drive from the main highway is through a bucolic landscape of tiny hamlets dotted between the cotton and wheat fields, olive groves and meadows which are filled with a profusion of wildflowers in spring. The road is garrisoned by stalls selling *saç böreği* and *ayran* and at its end a knot of touristy restaurants sit on either side of the river where it emerges from a narrow canyon. Having paid your entrance fee (US$2), and a parking charge if you're in a car, a disconcertingly bouncy boardwalk secured to the rock wall leads 100 m up the canyon to a restaurant nestled beside the river. A vigorous spring issues forth from the ground and even in the height of summer the air is refreshingly cool. It's an enchanting spot where you can savour the atmosphere at one of several restaurants serving fresh trout at charming wooden platforms; though the magic of the whole experience is somewhat lessen in summer by the inevitable crowds. Further exploration of the river demands getting your feet wet in the toe-numbingly cold water with rubber shoes (US$0.50) conveniently on hand for those who lack suitable footwear. The walls soar spectacularly upwards for hundreds of metres and depending on your ability at scrambling over greasy rocks you can continue onwards for another 10-15 minutes without special equipment.

An expedition first descended the full length of the gorge in 1993, however, *Bougainville Travel* in Kaş (see page 356) offer an adventurous daytrip down part of the canyon for groups of at least six people, accompanied by two qualified guides.

Crossing the bridge at the canyon mouth an unmetalled track makes its way south across beautifully unspoilt countryside, through the village of Palamut to the main highway near Kınık and the ruins of Xanthos.

Sleeping and eating At the *Saklıkent River Bar Restaurant*, across from the car park, you can roll-out your sleeping bag on the riverside platforms for free if you have an evening meal or breakfast.

Transport The road to Saklıkent is signposted off the D-400 highway about 36 km from Fethiye. It's a further 12 km to the canyon mouth. In season there are several morning dolmuş to Saklıkent from next to the minibus garage in Fethiye, as well as one from Kalkan. Alternatively you could hire a taxi or enrol on a tour from one of the nearby resorts.

☞ *The Lycians*

The Lycian people occupied the mountainous peninsular between modern-day Fethiye and Antalya from the most ancient times. Thought to have been an indigenous Anatolian race or settlers from Crete, they are reckoned to be the mysterious "Lukka" mentioned in some Hittite texts. The first solid reference to the Lycians comes in The Iliad, *with Homer mentioning the presence of a Lycian force led by the heroes Sarpedon and Glaucus in the armies that attacked Troy. Renowned for their martial skills, the ancient historian Herodotus left us this description of Lycian warriors:*
"They wore grease and corslets; they carried bow of cornel wood, cane arrows without feathers, and javelins. They had goatskins slung round their shoulders, and hats stuck around with feathers. They also carried daggers and rip-hooks."
The Lycian heartland was the wide and fertile Xanthos valley where three of the six principal cities – Xanthus, Pinara and Tlos – were situated, along with the main religious centre of Letoön. Originally a matrilineal people speaking their own language and worshipping a pantheon of Anatolian gods, the Lycians enjoyed a highly developed system of government with 23 city-states organised into a Federation whose assembly of democratically elected officials were charged with handling affairs of state.

Despite this organisation and a fiercely independent streak, the Lycians were nominally subjugated by a series of foreign powers, though the area generally maintained a high degree of autonomy because of its isolation and the difficult terrain. In 540 BC it was conquered by the Persian general Harpagus, subsequently enjoying a brief interlude as a member of the Delian League, before the Persians returned once more. In 333 BC the Lycian cities wisely surrendered to Alexander the Great, with control of the area passing after his death to the Ptolemies. A subsequent period of Rhodian rule was replaced by semi-independence under the aegis of Rome, though by this time the Lycians had become thoroughly Hellenised having abandoned their native tongue in favour of Greek. During the Roman civil war the Lycian League refused to support Brutus, a miscalculation which precipitated the destruction of Xanthos and, a year later, the region's formal incorporation into the empire.

Today, Lycia is littered with interesting and beautifully located archaeological sites, though the most conspicuous mark left by the ancients are the numerous rock-cut tombs, often elaborately designed to resemble temples or houses, carved into cliffs across the region.

Pınara
The name Pinara comes from the Lycian word for "something round": probably in reference to the acropolis mount which towers dramatically over the city

Nestled on the mountainous western slopes of the Xanthos Valley, Pınara was one of the largest and most important cities in ancient Lycia. Initially settled sometime in the fifth-century BC with people from the overcrowded city of Xanthos, little else is known about Pınara, except that it minted its own coins and fell to Alexander the Great in 333 BC. Approaching the site, the cliff-girt table-top mountain is visible from someway off, its precipitous east face honeycombed with hundreds of **rock-cut tombs**. Cutting these rectangular tombs into the vertical cliff-face clearly demanded some kind of hanging scaffold along with considerable acrobatics skill on the part of the builders.

Scattered amongst the fragrant pine woods and stony fields below the acropolis is the city itself. It's a beautiful spot: wild and isolated with uninterrupted views across to the Akdağı Range on the opposite side of the wide Xanthos Valley. This idyllic setting more than compensates for the sparcity of the actual remains and as it receives only a handful of visitors each day during the summer, you may well have the site to yourself.

From the ticket booth (*US$1 when the warden is present*) an marked path crosses a rocky streambed shaded by oriental plains to a series of Roman tombs carved into a cliff. The most impressive of these is the so-called **Royal tomb** whose porch is decorated with an amazingly detailed relief depicting views of a walled city – possibly Pinara itself – complete with houses, tombs and a few people. A second frieze above shows a procession of animals and people.

A steep ramp leads from the tombs up to a small saddle between the upper and lower **acropolis** which is scattered with an unidentifiable jumble of column drums and blocks. Picking your way north across the meadow, thought to have been the city's **agora**, an **odeon** on your right is just discernible amongst the pine trees. Following a path to the right, you have a good view across the stony fields below to Pinara's modest 3,200 seat **theatre** which was built into a rocky outcrop outside the city walls. On the steep hillside below are several more "**house tombs**", one of which is decorated with a pair of ox horns carved into its roof as some form of ancient talisman.

■ *Getting there: Pinara is sign-posted off the main highway over 40 km by road from Fethiye. It's 3 km from this junction to the village of Minare, from where its a further 2 km up a rough track, passable in an ordinary car, to the site. Without your own transport getting to the site involves being dropped on the main road by a passing bus or dolmuş and then walking. Make sure you take plenty of water and a snack, though you may find a small shop open in Minare.*

Letoön was once the religious heart of Lycia and as the site of the famous temple of Leto hosted national festivals and religious ceremonies. Legend has it that Leto gained the admiration of Zeus whose jealous wife Hera mercilessly drove the poor nymph from place to place. Having given birth to her two sons, Apollo and Artemis, Leto was led to the river Xanthos by wolves, where she bathed her infants and drank. In gratitude to the animals she renamed the land on the banks of the river Lycia, "lykos" meaning wolf in ancient Greek. Leto, along with her local-born children, became the paramount Lycian deities worshipped in three magnificent temples at Letoön.

Letoön

Approached through the farmland and greenhouses of the lower Xanthos Valley, Letoön's surroundings don't have the same rugged, solitary appeal as Pinara's. Spread across a low lying sun-baked field, they're also far less extensive than those at Xanthos, appealing more to the dedicated enthusiast than the casual visitor.

In front of the site entrance (*0830-1700, US$1*) are ranks of column drums and blocks of marble lined-up by the excavators who've been working intermittently at the site since 1963. Ahead of you, beyond the agora, are the foundations of the **three temples** contained within the sanctuary, which were dedicated to Apollo, Artemis and Leto. The building on the right (west) was identified as the temple of Leto by an inscription on a marble sacrificial altar, while the discovery of coins within the fabric of the Ionic structure dates it to the second century BC. Lying on the far left (east) is a Doric order structure that archaeologists have dated to the second or first centuries BC from surviving fragments of a mosaic which once covered the floor. Protected beneath a corrugated iron roof, this **mosaic** depicts a rosette, a lyre, a quiver and a bow, which led experts to conclude that it was a temple dedicated to Apollo and Artemis – the lyre being a symbol associated with Apollo, the quiver and bow with Artemis. Between the Doric and Ionic temples is a smaller, earlier structure which has been identified by an inscription as a fourth century BC temple dedicated to Artemis.

Walking past the three temples brings you to a **nymphaeum** which is normally flooded because it sits below the shallow water-table. The foundations of a **church** are just visible adjoining the nymphaeum to the east. The best-preserved building is the **Hellenistic theatre** in the northeast corner of the site. Entered through an arched passageway, its most interesting feature is a row of comic and tragic masks carved above the south-western tunnel.

■ *Getting there: Letoön is sign-posted off the main highway shortly before Kınık. It's 4½ km off the highway, 300 m beyond the village of Kumluova which is served by occasional dolmuş from Fethiye. Approaching from the other direction get-off a Fethiye-bound dolmuş at the turn-off and hitch, walk or wait for a dolmuş.*

Xanthos

On a rocky spur above the Eşen Çayı (formerly the Xanthos River) stand the ruins of Xanthos, one of the principle cities of ancient Lycia. Legend has it that the city was ruled by King Iobates and Bellerophon after he succeeded in killing the Chimaera, with the hero's descendants leading the Lycians into the Trojan Wars on the side of Troy. Archaeological evidence suggests there was a settlement at the site as long ago as the eighth century BC, though Xanthos first crops-up in historical texts when Herodotus recounts the tale of a siege of the city in 545 BC. Encircled by the armies of the Persian general Harpagus, the Xanthians retreated into their city where, having sworn to fight to the death, they burnt their families and possessions on a huge pyre. The Xanthians fanaticism was in evidence again in 42 BC during the Roman civil war when they resisted an imperial expedition led by Brutus. The Romans eventually succeeded in overcoming the city's defences, but not before the inhabitants had set fire to everything within, killing themselves rather than be taken prisoner. Under the Romans Xanthos prospered as the capital of the Lycian Federation, later becoming the seat of a Byzantine bishopric.

Abandoned and forgotten following the Arab raids of the seventh and eight centuries, Xanthos was visited by the traveller Charles Fellows in 1842. He had the best marble statuary and inscriptions loaded aboard the HMS Beacon and shipped to England, where controversially they remain on display in the British Museum to this day. Extensive excavations by a French team in the 1950s uncovered many of the city's main buildings, and the contemporary site is an engaging one to visit, particularly in spring before the intense summer sun has withered the grass and wildflowers which carpet the area.

Approaching the site up the hill from Kınık you'll notice a **Triumphal Arch of Emperor Vespasian** and the remnants of an earlier Hellenistic portal in the city walls on the left. Far more impressive, though, are the remains of a **Roman theatre**, the cavea littered with blocks of stone from the backstage building and upper rows of seats. The auditorium overlooks a **Roman agora**, while to its west stands a fifth century BC funerary monument called the **Harpy Tomb** on account of the reliefs on its exterior showing Harpies – mythological winged women – carrying off the daughters of

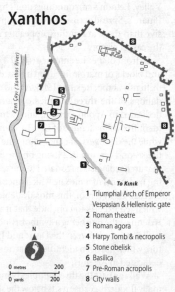

Xanthos

Eşen Çayı (Xanthos River)

To Kınık

1 Triumphal Arch of Emperor Vespasian & Hellenistic gate
2 Roman theatre
3 Roman agora
4 Harpy Tomb & necropolis
5 Stone obelisk
6 Basilica
7 Pre-Roman acropolis
8 City walls

N

0 metres   200
0 yards   200

Pandareos, a Lycian hero. Another, more plausible, interpretation is that the bird-women are in fact Sirens, flying off to deliver the souls of the dead, depicted as children, to the Isles of the Blessed. Whichever is correct, the present carvings are concrete casts of the originals which are on display in the British Museum. Beside the Harpy Tomb in what was the pre-Hellenistic era **necropolis**, is a Lycian-style sarcophagus perched unusually on the top of a tall pillar. Nearby, there's also a Roman tomb built in the first century AD to resemble a tower and a classic example of a Lycian house-tomb. Behind the theatre on what was the pre-Roman era acropolis, are the remains of a Byzantine structure with scattered fragments of mosaic pavement.

Walking past the agora brings you to an imposing fifth century BC **stone obelisk** whose weather-worn faces are completely covered with a lengthy inscription in a dialect of ancient Lycian. Partly translated using the help of proper names and short passages of ancient Greek within the text, linguists have ascertained that it recounts the story of a brave young noble, who was presumably buried inside what was in fact another tower tomb rather than an obelisk.

Reached along a path to the east of the car park is a Byzantine **basilica**, with a monastic complex from the same period found to the north near the city walls. Notable in its absence is the Monument of the Nereids, the most celebrated and beautiful of Xanthos' temples which was carted off to the British Museum by Charles Fellows.

■ *Officially open 0730-1900 in summer, 0800-1700 in winter, however, the site is unfenced. US$2, parking fee US$1. Getting there: Dolmuş between Fethiye and Kalkan or Patara pass through Kınık, which is about a 20-30 min walk from the hill top site. Let the driver know you want to go to Xanthos and he'll drop you at the appropriate spot.*

Patara

An important Lycian city and home of the venerable temple and oracle of Apollo, Patara was later the birth-place of St Nicholas, who spawned the celebrated legend of Santa Claus. Abandoned for nearly 500 years the ruins of this distinguished city, although by no means the most impressive you'll encounter in Lycia, enjoy an evocative coastal setting partly drowned by dunes beside a marshy lagoon teeming with wildlife. These day, however, it's Patara's marvellous 9 km beach that receives most attention. Kept gloriously free of development by the tireless efforts of environmentalists, it's a magnet for tourists and marine turtles alike. The latter arrive to bury their eggs during the summer nesting season, while a straggly township of hotels, guesthouses and restaurants 3 km inland at Gelemiş cater for the holiday-makers.

Phone code: 0242
Colour map 4, grid C4

Getting there During the summer there are plenty of dolmuş to Patara from Fethiye, Kalkan and Kaş, although out of season these services drop-off dramatically. Most dolmuş pass through Gelemiş (where the hotels and restaurants are) before continuing down to the ruins and the beach, however, buses generally drop passengers at the Patara turn-off on the highway, 3½ km from the village. From there you can take a taxi, or wait for a dolmuş or stroll. **Getting around** Gelemiş is a village naviqable on foot. To get to the beach and ruins it's about a 15-min stroll or there are beach dolmuş in summer or some of the hotels offer a free shuttle for their guests.

Ins & outs
See page 349 for further details

Blessed with a large natural harbour, now completely silted-up, Patara became a significant port city in Classical and Hellenistic times. Mentioned by the early historian Herodotus, coins and inscriptions discovered at the site show its original name as PTTRA. The city was celebrated for it's temple of Apollo and

History

the highly esteemed oracle, said to have rivalled the prophetess at Delphi in exactitude, who dwelt there. As yet, however, the location of this temple has eluded excavators.

An important port and commercial centre for the Xanthos valley, Patara also became a major naval base in the wars of succession following the death of Alexander the Great. As one of region's most important cities Patara wielded three votes in the Lycian assembly, while also being entrusted with the federation's archives. In 42 BC, after some hesitation, the Pataranscapitulated to Brutus, thereby avoiding the bloody fate of nearby Xanthos. Under the Romans Patara's good fortune continued, with the city subsequently becoming an important centre for early Christianity. Famous as the birth-place of Saint Nicholas, the city's bishop represented the whole of Lycia at the Council of Nicaea in 325 AD.

The site

Open 0730-1900 in summer, 0830-1700 in winter, US$3, with your ticket valid for a week

The largely unexcavated ruins of ancient Patara are scattered across marsh and agricultural land just inland from the sea. Despite continuing work by archaeologists from the Akdeniz University, it's hard to build-up an accurate picture of the city's lay-out from the fragmentary and widely spaced remains so far unearthed. These ruins are linked by a series of footpaths which cut across reed beds and fields from the road. It's best to visit early or late in the day to avoid the excessive daytime heat in summer, and also to carry some water.

Having past through the site entrance at the southern edge of the village, the road skirts a necropolis and enters what would have been the city beside a **monumental gateway**. One of Patara's more impressive extant structures, the triple-arched portal was built in the first century AD. Continuing along the road the remains of a **Roman baths complex** and a later basilica stand off to the right beside an exotic looking clump of palm trees.

A path leads southwest from the baths to an unidentified Corinthian order **temple** with a richly carved doorway giving on to a single chamber. Beside it survives one of the few remaining sections of the city's **defensive wall**, while a short distance further south, a Roman **theatre** is built up against the acropolis hill. Reached through dense bushes, it's an enchanting spot with the cavea partially buried in a drift of windblown sand.

Starting behind the theatre a path climbs to the summit of the hill from where there's an excellent view along the inviolate dune-backed beach to the west. Switching your gaze inland the city's **harbour** is still discernible despite having been silted-up and turned to marshland and reed beds, with the ruins of a **granary**, similar to the one at Andriake near Demre, on its west side.

A deep circular pit with a teetering **stone column** rising up from its centre also awaits inspection near the hill's top. Originally thought to be the remnants of an ancient lighthouse, archaeologists now believe that it was infact a cistern, part of Patara's water system prior to the construction of two Roman aqueducts. The remains of what is reckoned to be a lighthouse stands on the seaward side of the hill overlooking the beach.

The beach

A wide strip of fine, golden sand backed by extensive dunes, Patara's beach is certainly one of Turkey's finest. It's an important nesting site for marine turtles (see page 325) so access is restricted to daylight hours. Make sure you observe the rules posted on the signs next to the path. The beach is reached by following a road across the archaeological site to a small car park, separated from the sea by 300 m of dunes. A wooden boardwalk leads out onto the beach, emerging near the eastern end of its 9 km sweep. This part of the beach is fairly densely populated in summer, though the crowds melt quickly away as you walk west. There's a snack bar on the sand serving cold drinks and sustenance such as *döner kebaps* and *gözleme*, as well as a simple eatery, which often seems to be closed, next to the car park. With your own transport you can also access the beach at **Çayağızı** several kilometres west at the mouth of the Eşen Çayı river. It's 5 km down a track sign-posted off the approach road to Gelemiş to the beach and a collection of simple restaurants.

Patara has lots of good value accommodation with many of the cheaper hotels and pensions along the main street and beyond the PTT to the west of the village center. There are several more comfortable hotels on the hill to the east of the village which have nice views and often benefit from a cooling breeze in summer. These places also tend to be quieter. A multi-storey eye-sore built without permission on a hill to the west of the center, the Hotel Beyhan Patara is not recommended and will hopefully have been pulled down by the time you arrive. **D** *Hotel Merhaba*, T8435199, F8435133. Lovely position on a wooded hill above the beach road, simple but comfy rooms with mosquito net and balcony, convivial restaurant and bar. Recommended. **E** *Hotel Sisyphos*, T8435043. Centrally located on the main street, not too hectic though, reasonable rooms, swimming pool. **E** *Hotel Patara View Point*, T8435184, F8435022. Secluded location on east ridge above the village, British/Turkish management, pleasant rooms, with ceiling fan and mosquito nets, some also have a/c, and some balconies, relaxed seating area and open fire on terrace, pool and outdoor marble bar, free shuttle to the beach and tours organised. Recommended. **E** *Hotel Delfin*, T8435091, F8435169, on hillside above the road. 25 plain rooms with attached shower, terrace restaurant and pool. **F** *Likya Pansiyon*, T8435068, F8435211, pleasant pension with pool on the beach road. **F** *Zeybek 1*, T8435072, F8435132, at the end of the road past the PTT. Friendly family-run place with a pool, rooms are equipped with fan and mosquito nets. Recommended. **F** *Beyoğlu Pension*, T8435153. Simple family-run pension, plain rooms with en-suite and mosquito nets. **F** *Ali Baba Pansiyon*, Plaj Yolu Üzeri, T8435261. On the main street before the T-junction, utilitarian rooms above restaurant of the same name, a bit unkempt. **F** *Topaloğlu Pansiyon*, T8435030. Past the PTT, basic rooms. **F** *Leton Otel*, T8435218, F8435216. Basic but clean place in the centre.

Sleeping

Most of the hotels and pensions have a restaurant or can provide excellent value home-cooked meals for their guests. Of the hotel restaurants the *Patara Viewpoint* and the *Merhaba* are particularly worthy of note. Without a view but with a shady vine-covered terrace instead, you could try the *Sisyphos* on the main street. There are many other restaurants around the village with the *Tlos Terrace* recommended locally. For a simple snack there are a couple of stalls selling *gözleme*, US$1.50, on the road.

Eating

Gelemiş Turizm, Hotel Patara Viewpoint, T8435105, F8435008, run by Muzaffer Otlu, the co-manager of the hotel, selection of day-tours to local sights in the area such as Saklıkent, Kekova and Patara.

Tour agencies

Dolmuş depart regularly throughout the day for **Fethiye** (1½ hrs, US$3.50), **Kalkan** (25 mins, US$1.50) and **Kaş** (1 hr, US$2.50) during the season, but only a couple of times a day in the winter. It's a good idea to reserve a seat on your chosen dolmuş during the summer as they often fill-up with beach-goers from Fethiye and Kalkan. For most **long-distance services** you'll need to travel to Fethiye, however, some buses to Ankara, İstanbul and İzmir do pass along the main road from Kaş and Kalkan.

Transport

Banks There's no bank in Gelemiş, although there are several private money-changers. **Post office** The PTT is in the centre of the village.

Directory

Western Mediterranean

Kalkan

Phone code: 0242
Colour map 4, grid C4

Formerly the Ottoman Greek village of Kalamaki, Kalkan tumbles down a steep hillside to a small harbour at the head of a protected bay. Up until fairly recently the community survived by producing charcoal, fishing off the rocky coast and farming. Since the tourist boom of the 1980s, however, Kalkan has been reinvented as a small Mediterranean resort catering to a predominantly British, and fairly upmarket, crowd. The cobbled lanes leading down to the marina are thoroughly gentrified, lined with expensive jewellery and carpet shops where prices are displayed in pounds sterling. The whitewashed fishermen's cottages have been transformed into holiday homes or small pensions and hotels, joined on the edge of town by several unsightly resort hotels. All this development has left little room for ordinary Turkish life; creating in its place a agreeably genteel but rather sterile holiday village. There's not much to do in town itself except lie-out on the beach to the east of the harbour. It's large pebbles aren't particularly enticing though, so most people head for Kaputaş or Patara. Kalkan also suggests itself as an alternative base to Patara or Fethiye for visiting sights in the area, such as Saklıkent, Xanthos and Pınara.

Sleeping

Kalkan still has a reasonable choice of accomodation with some good pensions in the centre of town

C *Hotel Pirat*, T8443178, F8443183. Large modern hotel to west of harbour, comfortable rooms lookout over pool and the harbour. **D** *Samira Hotel*, T8443817, F8443396, samira.hotel@superonline.com Small package hotel overlooking the roundabout at the top of town, pleasant rooms, pool set in gardens. **D** *Hotel Tekinberk*, Kalamar Yolu No 31, T8443090, F8443398. Package hotel overlooking town, pool in gardens, roof-top terrace restaurant, comfortable rooms with a/c and small ensuite, excellent end-of-season deals. **D** *Zinbad Hotel*, Yalı Boyu Mahallesi No 18, T8443404, F8443943, kalkan.org.tr./kalkan/zinbad/, off Mustafa Koca Kaya Caddesi. Small, well-managed, comfy a/c equipped rooms, roof terrace, some rooms have sea-view. Recommended. **D-E** *Korsan Apartments*, T8443260, F8443274, kalkan.org.tr/kalkan/korsan/ On the front, small nicely furnished rooms with bathroom in bourvillaea-hung white-washed house, available through *Simply Turkey* in the UK. Recommended. **E-F** *Ay Pansiyon*, Yalı Mahallesi, T8443058. 1 block back from the front, a range of differently sized guestrooms in old family house with a pleasant rustic feel. **F** *Pasha's Inn*, Onuncu Sokak No 8, T8443666, F8443077. Simple rooms in old house several blocks back from the harbour, comfortable kilim-drapped seating area, roof-top terrace, helpful English management. Recommended. **F** *Kalamaki Pension*, Yalı Boyu Mahallesi, T8445649, F8445654. Inland from the *Kaptan Restaurant* at the beach end of the front, plain rooms in traditional-style building, British management, popular roof-top restaurant. **F** *St. Nicholas Pension*, Yalı Boyu Mahallesi, T8443855, F8442134. A good budget option in the quiet backstreets just to west of the Kalamaki Pension, cramped but clean rooms with tiny balcony and bathroom, use of nearby pool. *Kalkan Bay Customs House*, Kalkan Customs House, T2870672, F8442736, cemttt@yahoo.com 19th-century building overlooking the beach and harbour, recently converted into airy, white-washed apartments, sleeping 2-5 people, simple furnishings and fully equipped kitchenette, US$400-800 per week in high season.

Eating

There's certainly no shortage of good restaurants in Kalkan, though by local standards many are quite pricey

Midrange Down beside the harbour are a number of fairly pricey restaurants such as the *Patara*, with tables on the quayside, wide selection of dishes including fish and seafood, try the stuffed seabass. Nearby the *Korsan* has traditional *meze* such as *arnavut ciğer* (spicy Albanian liver) and *yaprak dolma* (stuffed vine-leaves), while the *Patlıcan* has unusual specials like wild boar and salmon encroute. Just inland *Doy-doy* and *Akın* are 2 popular restaurants where you can eat as much as you like *meze* for just US$4, followed by seafood or a meat dish if you still have room. *Zeki's*, on Mustafa Koca Kaya Caddesi, has an Anglophile menu with traditional dishes such as rack of lamb, you can even finish off with a glass of port. **Cheap** *Alibaba*, 20 m down from the roundabout, good value local restaurant serving soup and ready-prepared dishes such as white beans and beef stew. *Kaptan Restaurant*, small place with parasol-shaded tables overlooking the beach, limited menu including breakfasts, Şiş *kebabı* and casseroles. *Nostalji İstanbul Restaurant*, at the top of Mustafa Koca Kaya Caddesi, by local standards this is an expensive pide restaurant but you can still get a couple of lahmacun or a pide and a drink for about US$5, also other Turkish dishes like *hünkar Beğendi*, friendly owner. Across the road, *Foto's* is a rustic cabin where you can enjoy Turkish food such as *mantı*, *gözleme* and *menemen* at low tables.

Moonlight Bar, 100 m down from the roundabout, old-converted house is the venue for a fairly loud rock bar. *Anatolia*, on Hasan Altan Caddesi, is a more sophisticated roof-top bar playing jazz. **Bars**

Kalamus Specialty Tours, Yalı Boyu Mahallesi, T/F8442456, kalkanturkey.com, offers a range of tours to local sights such as Bezirgan, Letoon, Pinara and Saklıkent, also yachting and canoeing excursions. *Armes Tours*, Yat Limanı, T8443169, F8443468, down by the harbour, day tours, yacht trips and car hire. **Tour agencies**

There are dolmuş every hr during the day to **Antalya** and **Fethiye** from the roundabout at the top of Mustafa Koca Kaya Caddesi where all the bus companies have their offices. **Kaputaş**, get on a Kaş-bound dolmuş, 10 mins, US$0.50. **Kaş**, every 20-30 mins, US$1.25, 45 mins. **Patara**, every hr 1000-1500, book your return when you depart, 20 mins, US$1.75. **Saklıkent**, 1 dolmuş per day in season departs 1030, returning 1700, US$7.50. During the season there are daily buses to **Ankara**, **İstanbul** and **İzmir**. **Transport**

Banks There are several banks with ATMs below the roundabout. **Communications Internet**: *Cimbirlik Internet Cafe*, at the top of town, 75 m above the roundabout, in side road next to *Tespa Shopping Centre*, US$1.25 per hr. **Post office**: The PTT, which changes foreign exchange and TCs, is also just down from the roundabout. **Tourist information** There's no Tourist Office in Kalkan, but information is posted on the town's web-site: kalkan.org.tr **Directory**

The 27 km journey between Kalkan and Kaş is along a rocky, inhospitable coastline with the road hugging the steep mountainside above cliffs which tumble directly into the sea. About 7 kms east of Kalkan the road crosses a narrow canyon, known as **Kaputaş**. There's a small strip of beach reached down a long flight of steps from the highway which is often densely packed with bathers from Kaş and Kalkan in the summer. The plaques on either side of the bridge record the human cost of the coastal highways construction, commemorating four workers who lost their lives while building this stretch of the road in 1962-63. **Kalkan to Kaş**

Kaş

With its back to the craggy Lycian mountains, Kaş looks out across a calm bay to the Greek island of Meis floating offshore. Like Kalkan, not so long ago it was a simple fishing community of whitewashed houses clustered around a harbour. Things have changed dramatically since then with tourism now weighing-in as by far the most important economic activity. However, despite becoming a major Mediterranean resort and administrative centre, Kaş retains something of its original character and easy-going charm. Ignored by the major package operators, accommodation is predominantly in small hotels and pensions and after sunset in summer the narrow cobbled streets are thronged with European and Turkish holiday-makers, strolling between the numerous convivial restaurants *Phone code: 0242 Colour map 4, grid C4*

Western Mediterranean

and bars. Lacking a good beach of its own – the nearest stretch of sand is a 20 minute dolmuş ride away at Kaputaş – such maritime outings, along with diving and sea-kayaking, are a popular activity, while the town's proximity to the unspoilt mountains of the Lycian hinterland is also promoting it as a base for adventure sports such as mountain biking, trekking and canyoning.

Ins & outs
See page 356 for further details

Getting there Kaş is on the main coastal highway and buses between Fethiye and Antalya call-in at the small *otogar* regularly throughout the day. The town is roughly equidistant between the airports of Dalaman and Antalya, each about 3½ hrs away by road. **Getting around** It's only a couple of minutes walk down Atatürk Caddesi from the *otogar* to the harbour and the centre of town. Unless you are staying in one of the more luxurious hotels out on the Çukurbağ Peninsular, in which case a taxi ride into the centre is your only option, you won't need anything but your legs to get around.

Sights

As ancient Antiphellus, Kaş developed as an important port town, also sitting, as it does today, on the road between Phaselis and the cities of western Lycian. With its dry, rocky hinterland ill-suited for agriculture, the town relied on exporting timber from the highlands, also extracting fish and soft sponges from the sea for its livelihood. Later the town, peopled until 1923 largely by Greeks, became known as Andifli.

Ancient Antiphellus
There are a few conspicuous reminders of Antiphellus as you wander about the modern town. At the top of Uzun Çarşı a tall, handsome **tomb with a Gothic lid** and bosses carved in the shape of lions sits on a solid base inscribed with an indecipherable Lycian text. Nearby, steps lead up to a group of **Lycian tombs** cut into the cliff above Yeni Yol Caddesi and now partially hidden behind new apartment buildings.

On the other side of town, Recep Bilgin Caddesi leads via a flight of steps to a small white-washed **basilica**, now functioning as a mosque. Further to the north a path leads to an interesting **Doric tomb** consisting of a single chamber carved from the living rock and containing a bench, decorated with carved figures, on which the body would have rested.

Walking down Yeni Camii Caddesi the town suddenly gives way to olive groves and a short distance beyond a **Hellenistic theatre** is the most substantial ancient building left standing. Also reached along Hastane Caddesi, the well-preserved auditorium is splendidly located, facing across the bay to Meis.

Beaches & boat trips
Kaş is severely deficient in the beach department with **Kuçuk Çakıl** (Small Pebble), a five minute walk southeast of the harbour, adding up to little more than a stony ramp, squeezed between rocky outcrops. In the absence of sand many of the sea-front hotels have constructed terraces descending the rocky foreshore, with a small fee charged in season for the use of their sun-loungers and access to the water via metal ladders.

Büyük Çakıl (Large Pebble), a kilometre walk further along the coast, is also a pebbly cove, but this time just large enough to squeeze in a couple of rows of sunbeds and several restaurants which compete to provide refreshments.

The trip across the bay to **Liman Ağızı**, accessible by dolmuş-boat from the harbour for about US$2, is where you'll find crystal clear water and several simple eateries. It's makes a good outing but again you won't find any sand.

The nearest beach is at **Kaputaş**, 20 minutes west by dolmuş, though it can be crowded in summer so you may prefer to continue on to the expansive beach at Patara.

Due to the scarcity of sand many people opt for a boat trip during their stay. The boatmen's co-operative (*Kaş Deniz Taşıyıcıları Kooperatifi*) organise daily excursions in glass-bottomed boats around the coast to Kekova. A typical tour, lasting from 1000 to 1730, includes a visit to Simena, the Batık Şehir and the Tersane and costs about US$15. Alternatively, you can hire a boat and make your own programme from US$125 for up to 10 people, and an additional US$3.50 per person for a picnic lunch.

An aberration on the political map of the eastern Mediterranean, Meis is a Greek island stranded just three nautical miles off the Lycian coast. Formerly a close trading partner with Kalkan and Kaş, the island was occupied by Italy in 1918, with its subsequent hand over to Greece demoting it to the status of an isolated backwater, cut off from the Turkish mainland by a tense international boundary. In more recent times the island's economy was buoyed by visiting yachtsmen and day-trippers from Kaş, more than a few of whom were foreign workers and expats nipping across to secure themselves a new three-month tourist visa. However, lately such trips have been severely curtailed by the introduction of exorbitant harbour duties by the Greek authorities. So, until sense prevails and these inflated tie-up charges are reduced, boats cross the bay on a demand only basis with the short trip costing at least US$40 per person

Meis (Kastellorizo)

Western Mediterranean

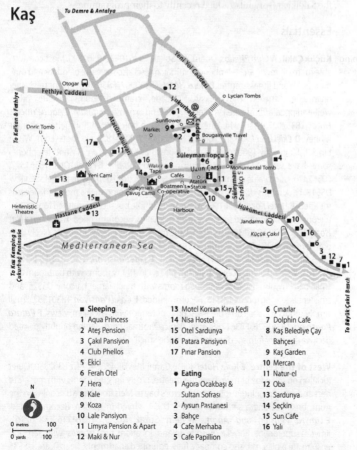

Kaş

To Demre & Antalya

To Kekova & Fethiye
Fethiye Caddesi
Otogar
Yeni Yol Caddesi
Çukurbağ Caddesi
o Lycian Tombs
Sunflower
Market
Bougainville Travel
Doric Tomb
Atatürk Bulvarı
To Kaş Kamping & Çukurbağ Peninsula
Hellenistic Theatre
Yeni Cami
Water Taps
Süleyman Topçu S
Uzun Çarşı
Monumental Tomb
Cafés
Atatürk Statue
Süleyman Çavuş Camii
Boatmen's Co-operative
Süleyman Sandıkçı
Hastane Caddesi
Harbour
Hükümet Caddesi
Jandarma
Küçük Çakıl
Mediterranean Sea
To Büyük Çakıl Beach

N

0 metres 100
0 yards 100

■ Sleeping	13 Motel Korsan Kara Kedi	6 Çınarlar
1 Aqua Princess	14 Nisa Hostel	7 Dolphin Cafe
2 Ateş Pension	15 Otel Sardunya	8 Kaş Belediye Çay
3 Çakıl Pansiyon	16 Patara Pansiyon	Bahçesi
4 Club Phellos	17 Pınar Pansion	9 Kaş Garden
5 Ekici		10 Mercan
6 Ferah Otel	● Eating	11 Natur-el
7 Hera	1 Agora Ocakbaşı &	12 Oba
8 Kale	Sultan Sofrası	13 Sardunya
9 Koza	2 Aysun Pastanesi	14 Seçkin
10 Lale Pansiyon	3 Bahçe	15 Sun Cafe
11 Limyra Pension & Apart	4 Cafe Merhaba	16 Yalı
12 Maki & Nur	5 Cafe Papillion	

with a minimum of six people necessary to make the trip financially viable for the boat-owner.

Diving Interesting submarine topography, excellent water clarity and, for the Mediterranean, varied sea-life make Kaş one of the most popular diving spots on the Turkish coast. A veritable army of outfits offer everything from brief introductory sessions to advance certificate courses. For qualified divers and beginners alike the area offers a good selection of easily accessible sites between eight and 40 m which include underwater caves, canyons, the wrecks of several unfortunate sea-vessels and the hulk of a downed Second World War bomber. Two reputable local companies are: *Kaş Diving*, Ferah Hotel, Küçük Çakıl, T8364045, F8364150, kas-diving.com and *Bougainville Travel* (see below).

Sea-kayaking & other adventure activities An ideal, low-impact way to explore the coastline and sunken ruins of Kekova, *Bougainville Travel* (see below) organise daily sea-kayaking trips to the area east of Kaş. The cost of the daytrip, including equipment, transport, a guide and lunch, is US$33 per person, with a minimum of four people required. Sea-kayak rental is only US$22 per day.

The same company also have a programme of guided walking and mountain biking excursions in the nearby mountains, with a canyoning trip down the Saklıkent Gorge also added recently to their programme.

Essentials

Sleeping
Kaş has a good choice of accommodation scattered around the town centre or out along the seafront in Küçük Çakıl Mahallesi.

Many hotels in this area have a small pool & sea views from the front rooms

Küçük Çakıl **A** *Club Phellos*, Doğru Yol Sokak, T8361953, F8361890. Most comfortable rooms in town, a/c, telephone, minibar, guests also have use of indoor and outdoor pools and fitness centre. **B** *Hera Hotel*, T8363062, F8363063, herahotel@super online.com Tasteless mock-Classical facade, cramped rooms despite price, well-equipped: a/c, satellite TV, minibar, pool and expensive *hamam*. **C** *Aqua Princess Hotel*, T8362027, F8361044. Unexciting package hotel, you'll find better value for money. **D** *Ekici Hotel*, Arısar Sokak No 1, T8361824, F8361823, ekicihotel.com White block built in early 1980s, very dated, rooms have minibar, a/c, TV and telephone, some have seaview, large swimming pool and *hamam*. **E** *Ferah Otel*, T8361377, F8362476. Good value rooms with a/c and balcony, side rooms with partial sea-view US$18, back rooms US$15, small swimming pool, evening meals prepared. Recommended. **E** *Hotel Koza*, T8361066, F8362331. Simple but nicely furnished rooms, a/c, telephone, uninterrupted seaviews from balconies. Recommended. **E** *Maki and Nur Hotel*, T8363479, F8361388. Small package hotel, mostly European guests, nicely decorated rooms with a/c, telephone and ensuite, shower cabinet in bathroom is a rarity, breakfast on seaside terrace, BBQ once a week. **F** *Lale Pansiyon*, T8361074, F8361575. At the town-end of the front, family-run place, clean, airy rooms with bathroom and small balcony, also have a/c equipped rooms with much larger balcony, US$25, and smaller backfacing rooms, US$15. Recommended. **F** *Çakıl Pansiyon*, T8361532. Small simple rooms with balcony, breakfast on roof terrace with excellent views. **F** *Patara Pansiyon*, T8361328, F8361788, ersu_yapici@hotmail.com Behind brightly painted doorways simply furnished rooms are on the small side.

West of the centre **E** *Kale Hotel*, Kilise Camii Mevkii, T8364074, F8362850. Quiet location on the edge of town near the theatre, nicely finished rooms with mosquito nets and ensuite, uninterrupted views across bay to Meis from large balconies on the front, breakfast and a set menu dinner, US$4, served in garden. Recommended. **E** *Limyra Pension and Apart*, Meltem Sokak No 5, T8361716, F8362161, limyra@superonline Popular despite inland location, neat rooms with fan and ensuite are a bit small, also compact, fully-equipped apartments, sleep 2, a/c, US$35 per night, advance booking required in summer. **E** *Otel Sardunya*, Hastane Caddesi, T8363080, F8363082. Plain rooms, no view, leaves a/c the only reason to stay. **F** *Nisa Hostel*, Hastane Caddesi No 48, T/F8363581. Plain rooms, en-suite, popular with backpackers, roof-top bar, use of kitchen, laundry service, internet access, triple room US$20. **F** *Motel Korsan Kara Kedi*, Yeni Camii Sokak No 7, T8361887, F8363086. The name of this place, which translates as "Motel Pirate Black Cat", gets top marks for originality, good value, use of a small pool and kitchen, unfortunately recent construction on an adjacent site has robbed most rooms of their seaview. **F** *Pınar Pansion*, Meltem Sokak No 1, T8361104. 1 of several simple, family-run places on this street which you could try if all else fails. **G** *Ateş Pension*, Yeni Cami Caddesi No 3, T8361393, ates_pension@hotmail.com On the hill behind the Yeni Camii, basic rooms, ensuite, excellent value, also dorm beds for US$6.50, or for those on a really tight budget US$5 will secure you a place on the terrace, satellite TV and laundry service.

Camping *Kaş Kamping*, Çukurbağ Peninsula, 300 m beyond the amphitheatre. Deservably popular spot since the days of the overland hippy-trail, quiet pitches amongst the olive trees, swimming off a private platform, tents are US$2.50 per person, caravans US$7.50, also small, tiled-roof cabins which sleep 2 for US$12, breakfast and evening meals are available. There are 2 more campsites, *Can Mocamp* and *Olympos Mocamp*, 3 km to the west of town on the road to Kalkan.

Midrange Of the fish restaurants on the main square the *Mercan* at the quayside is a well-established institution serving *meze* followed by a wide variety of fish and seafood on its terrace, try the fish soup to start. *Bahçe Restaurant*, Uzun Çarşı, a locally recommended garden restaurant above the tomb, excellent selection of over 18 different *meze*, followed by seafood and meat dishes. *Dolphin Cafe*, Hükümet Caddesi, informal eatery in converted house with terrace overlooking the harbour, menu includes *meze* and seafood. *Natur-el*, Uzun Çarşı, worth seeking out in back alley running off Uzun Çarşı, small selection of traditional Turkish dishes such as *mantı, çiğ böreği* and *aşure*, about US$6-8 per head with a soft drink. *Oba*, Çukurbağlı Caddesi, congenial place serving simple but tasty Turkish cuisine in a pleasant garden setting, alcohol served, good value too. *Sardunya*, Hastane Caddesi, under the same management as the mediocre *Otel Sardunya* this place is worth seeking out for its peaceful terrace overlooking the sea, good selection of *meze* followed by fish or grilled meat. *Sun Cafe*, Hükümet Caddesi, varied menu featuring seafood, salads and *meze* followed by fish and a selection of tasty meat and vegetarian dishes, convivial surroundings, candle-lit tables on the terrace. **Cheap** *Çınarlar*, Çukurbağlı Caddesi, a popular pide and lahmacun place with tables on the street, at breakfast time they bake delicious flat bread in their oven for US$0.30 a time. *Seçkin*, Atatürk Bulvarı, small spartan *lokanta* on the corner across from the mosque, *şiş kebabı, piyaz* and a soft drink for US$3.50. A bit further up Atatürk Bulvarı the *Yalı Restaurant* is another place serving cheap food. *Kaş Garden*, east side of the market area, wide choice of good value dishes from steam-tray range, also pide, lahmacun, kebaps and güveç (stew). Nearby, on a street between Çukurbağlı Caddesi and the north-east corner of the market area, *Agora Ocakbaşı* and *Sultan Sofrası* are two very reasonably priced restaurants with tables outside which are fraternised mainly by locals. For something sweet head for *Aysun Pastanesi*, a defiantly normal cake-shop in the south-east corner of the market area which has the best baklava in town. Also toasted sandwiches and biscuits.

Beside the harbour are several popular cafés such as the *Palmiye Tea Garden*, where you can sit outside with a cup of tea, a glass of freshly squeezed orange juice or an ice-cream. Just inland and shaded by eucalyptus trees, the Kaş Belediye Çay Bahçesi is a favourite local meeting spot. *Cafe Merhaba*, Çukurbağlı Sokak, near the PTT, enjoy a slice of cake, home-baked using organic ingredients by the friendly owner, Tülin Diren,

Eating

Cafés

Western Mediterranean

foreign newspapers also on sale. *Cafe Papillion*, Orta Sokağı, trendy coffee-shop near the PTT serving cappuccino, milkshakes and ice-creams at streetside tables or bar.

Bars & nighclubs There's a clutch of perenially popular bars in the corner of the main square, including *Deniz Altı Bar* and the *Mavi Bar* in an old fisherman's cottage. The *Sun Cafe* (see eating) is a more sophisticated place to have a drink with soothing world music and a relaxed seating area. *Habessos*, Hükümet Caddesi, leafy garden bar perched on a terrace above the road, live Turkish and western music. *Reggae Bar*, Hükümet Caddesi, informal venue where you can unwind to reggae and latin beats. *Hi Jazz Bar*, Zumrut Sokak, intimate backstreet jazz bar in small renovated building. *Full Moon Disco*, high decibel nightclub located a sensible distance outside the town on the Kalkan road, entry US$5, free shuttle service from the harbour. Also, the *Oasis* nightclub near the harbour.

Shopping Nautica, Uzunçarşı No 21, upmarket bric-a-brac and antiques with a maritime theme. *The old houses along cobbled Uzun Çarşı are now mostly occupied by expensive antique, jewellery & carpet shops* *Topika*, Uzunçarşı Sokak No 11, excellent selection of jewellery. *Galeria Seramik,* Orta Sokak, across from the PTT, nice selection of jewellery and pottery. *Kaş and Carry*, Orta Sokak, long-standing carper outlet near the PTT, recently diversified into ceramics also. *Gallery Anatolia*, Hükümet Caddesi, gallery/workshop selling handmade ceramics designed and painted by local artist Sibel Düzel, also hand-printed fabrics. *Tufan,* Çukurbağlı Caddesi, clothes hand-tailored from locally spun cotton, a bit pricey by local standards.

Tour agencies *Bougainville Travel*, Çukurbağlı Caddesi No 10, T8363142, F8361605, bougainville-turkey.com Rent-a-car, airline ticketing, airport transfers, guides, as well as diving and a range of adventure tours. *Sunflower*, Orta Sokak, T8363991, F8363992, near the PTT, programme of more conventional tours including day-trips to Kekova, Xanthos, Saklıkent and Gömbe.

Transport **Bus** Antalya, every 30 mins, 4 hrs, US$5. **Fethiye**, every 30 mins, 2½ hrs, US$3. **Demre**, every 30 mins, 1 hr, US$2. *Özkaş* dolmuş leave for **Kalkan** (30 mins, US$1.75) and **Patara** (1 hr, US$2.50) when full. Daily buses to **İstanbul** and **Ankara** in the summer, although **Fethiye** and **Antalya** are far better served by long-distance services. **Car rental** *Alibaba*, Hastane Caddesi No 42, T8362501, F8363254. *Tüzgölü Tourism*, next to the Süleyman Çavuş Camii, rents scooters for US$16 per day.

Directory **Banks** There are banks with ATMs on Atatürk Bulvarı. **Communications** **Internet**: *Magic com* and *Net-house* are on Çukurbağlı Caddesi across from the PTT, US$1.75 per hr. **Post office**: The PTT is on Çukurbağlı Caddesi, 150 m north of the main square. **Hospitals** The State hospital is on Hastane Caddesi near the antique theatre. **Laundry** *Rose Laundry*, Askerlik Şubesi Yanı, off Çukurbağlı Caddesi near the main square, US$5 per load for wash and dry. **Tourist information** The Tourist Office, T/F8361238, is on the east side of the main square. Open weekdays 0800-1900 in summer, 1700 in winter, at weekends 0800-1900 summer-only.

Cyaneae (Kyaneai)

The remains of Cyaneae are rarely visited; you'll almost certainly have the place to yourself Topping an escarpment above the roadside village of Yavu, 24 km east of Kaş, are the ruins of the ancient town of Cyaneae. A community of considerable local standing and influence, inscriptions at the site suggest the town existed as long ago as the fourth century BC, though little else is known about its history. Cyaneae prospered during Roman times, and it's from this period that most of the remains date, later becoming a Byzantine bishopric seat. Dubbed locally "the city of sarcophagi" because of its crowded necropolis, the name Cyaneae in fact comes from the ancient Greek word for "dark blue", though no explanation has yet been uncovered for this appellation.

Pick up the path at the base of a rocky gully above the village from where it traverses left across the mountainside towards a conspicuous tree. After zigzagging upwards for 15 minutes or so you'll pass half a dozen tombs, some inscribed with Lycian epithets, cracked open by treasure-hunters and scattered amongst the bushes. Shortly after these tombs the path levels out and the acropolis, protected on its three exposed sides by a defensive wall, comes into view across some stony fields. Its another five or 10 minute scramble to the top passing several more tombs and the remains of some unidentifiable buildings. The view from the ramparts of the overgrown citadel takes in a great sweep of empty mountains including the distant snow-streaked peak of Akdağı to the northwest. A path threads its way across the **acropolis** past the ruins of a library, a bath-house and two Byzantine churches to the more satisfying remains of a well-preserved **theatre**. The slope nearby is littered with dozens of free-standing **Roman tombs** with peaked lids, some of which are decorated with handles in the shape of a roaring lion. There are also several more tombs on the steep south face of the acropolis which must be approached with great care.

■ *Getting there: Easily accessible by bus from Kaş or Demre, the final 30-45 min approach from Yavu up a steep, but well-defined, path requires some perseverance. Even in spring and autumn it's best to arrive at Yavu as early in the morning as possible to avoid climbing in the hot sun. The first Antalya bound bus from Kaş leaves at about 0700, giving you enough time to explore the site and be back in Kaş for a late morning swim. Back down on the highway the Çeşme Restaurant, 750 m east of the village, serves simple food as well as hot and cold drinks. The German and English-speaking owner, Gülay Akkuş, can act as a guide to the local sights.*

Following part of an ancient roadway linking Cyaneae with Teimiussa, this walk is an enjoyable way of getting to Üçağız (see below), in Kekova, if you don't have your own transport. The walk starts down a track on the Kaş (west) side of the Çeşme Restaurant, looping around a group of houses on a small hill, turning sharply to the left and descending a slope towards a tall fence with concrete posts. Cut across the field next to this fence, turning right on a track that runs around the bottom of some scrubby hills. Once past the fenced area the track passes beneath some power lines and around a hill to a small shepherd's encampment, where you may encounter some aggressive dogs. If there's no one around to control them give the camp a very wide berth and keep a handful of rocks ready to throw at them should they get too close. Beyond the encampment an ancient trail, in places still paved with slabs of stone, descends the right-hand side of a scrubby valley which opens out after about 30 minutes above the small community of Çevreli. It's a 20-minute descent to the village and the Üçağız road down a rocky mountainside and then through orchards of widely spaced carob trees. The black-top is reached near the village mosque from where it's a hot 3-km walk over the hill to Üçağız.

Walking from Yavu to Üçağız
Allow 2½-3 hrs for the entire walk & make sure you take sufficient water as there are no springs along the way

Kekova

Kekova is an area of dry scrubby mountains dotted with ancient Lycian sites, some evocatively submerged off-shore beneath the crystal-clear turquoise water. The convoluted coastline of rocky bays, inlets and islands provides a wealth of secluded anchorages for yachts, while on dry land official protection has so far managed to put a brake on development, making it one of the most unspoilt parts of the Lycian coast.

Phone code: 0242
Colour map 4, grid C4

Western Mediterranean

Ins and outs

Getting there The majority of people visit Kekova on a boat tour from Kaş or Çayağazı (Demre), or drop anchor in one of its protected coves as they sail along the coast in a chartered *güllet* or yacht. Approaching by land the roadhead and main village of the area is Üçağız which suggests itself as a base, at least initially, for your explorations; with excursions on foot or by boat to places of interest in the surrounding area. Üçağız is 21 km off the coastal highway, 15 km east of Kaş. A new road has recently been completed east to Demre, however, it will probably be a while before this shows up on any road map. There's no public transport to Üçağızı at present, although locals are hoping that the completion of the new road will mean some coastal buses are re-routed via the village. Hitching down to Üçağız from the highway can be frustrating because there's very little traffic, but on foot you can follow a pleasant and much shorter path from the village of Yavu (see Kyaneai, page). When it's time to depart a lift up to the main road or Kaş can sometimes be arranged on the truck that delivers the morning bread. Enquire locally the day before you want to leave.

Üçağız

Look out for roadside stalls selling keçi boyunuzu pekmezi, a sweet syrup made locally from carob beans

Sitting on a placid inlet almost cut-off from the sea by a pair of narrow peninsulas, the name Üçağız, "Three Mouths", refers to the channel which slips between these two arms and the passages on either side of Kekova island beyond. Valued as an anchorage since antiquity, the village is built on the site of Teimiussa, an ancient Lycian settlement dating from the fourth century BC. After the First World War the area's remoteness made it a base for guerrilla operations against occupying Italian forces, while the villagers recount how during the war itself a German ship was secreted away from the British Navy in the bay. Later, this isolation attracted a growing number of yacht-borne tourists looking for a place to get-away and in the last twenty years the traditional activities of fishing and farming have increasingly been supplemented by tourism. Many of the village's bougainvillaea draped cottages are now guesthouses, while the peace is frequently shattered by the clatter of diesel-powered launches ferrying passenger across the bay. A row of restaurants lines the wooden docks where tour groups come ashore and inevitability the odd carpet shop has materialised in recent years. Government controls have, however,

Kekova area

managed to keep a lid on this development and although things get busy in the summer, the village's original laid-back atmosphere is still in evidence, particularly if you visit outside July and August.

The scant remains of ancient Teimiussa lie on the east side of the village, with several free-standing **Lycian tombs** and a relief showing a naked man, a cape in his hand, behind the ugly *Koç Pension*. Continuing east there are good views across the placid water to several islands at the mouth of the bay which were quarried down to near the waterline to provide building material for the ancients. On the slopes overlooking the sea more tombs are scattered liberally amongst the bushes and rocks. Typical Lycian sarcophagi, they're carefully sculpted from local stone with tight fitting lids and one is decorated with a wheel or sun-like motif.

Because of the enclosed nature of the bay swimming is not recommended in the village. However, many of the pensions provide their guests with a free ride across the bay to a small beach on the seaward side of the western peninsula.

E *Ekin Pansiyon*, T8742064. A row of small well-appointed rooms with balcony in a garden on the west side of the village, the owners, Ali and Yusuf Pehlivan, can organise visits to local sights such as Apollonia, use of the kitchen, 30% discount out of season. Recommended. **E** *Koç Pension*, T8742080. Concrete eyesore in the eastern part of the village, clearly built without permission. **F** *Onur Pension*, T8742071, F8742266, onurpension@yahoo.com On the front next to the mosque, reasonable rooms with ensuite opening onto large balcony overlooking the quayside, restaurant and internet access, free boat service to local beach. Recommended. **F** *Gönül Pansiyon*, T8742074. A variety of well-sized rooms in a converted family house, bathroom is shared, good value. **F** *Flower Pension*, T8742043. Another renovated family house next to the main car park and slipway, cheap fish available, could be noisy in summer.

Sleeping

On the front there are several restaurants frequented by "yachties" and tour groups. The long standing *Ibrahim Restaurant* is recommended for its open-buffet starters US$2.50, after which it's debatable whether you'll need any fish or kebaps. There's a shady tea garden serving *gözleme* (US$1) and drinks to the east of the centre.

Eating

The recent establishment of a local boatman's co-operative means that the prices and itineraries of the various excursions are more-or-less fixed. Members of the co-op wait near the entrance to the village for potential business. There are two choices, a "short tour" lasting about two hours which takes in Simena, the Batık Şehir – the Sunken City – and Tersane, or a longer four hour trip which goes right around the Kekova island visiting several places along the south shore in addition to those previously mentioned. The cost of these tours on a boat capable of carrying up to eight passengers is US$15-20 and US$25-35 respectively, with larger craft also available. A one way crossing to Kale costs US$10 for up to five people, so if you're on your own hang around at the dock for some other passengers.

Boat trips

Kale's picturesque medieval fortress, built by the Knights of St John beside the ancient settlement of Simena, crowns a peninsula to the south of Üçağız. Reached by a short boat ride (see above) or an enjoyable hour-long walk around the bay following a path that has become part of the Lycian Way (see page 339), the village's tumble-down stone cottages climb a rocky hillside from the water's edge. Despite being favoured as a secluded holiday retreat by a number of wealthy Turks, it has a charming rustic feel which, coupled with its superior location, make it more appealing than Üçağız. Chickens scratch around in the dirt and once the tour groups and yachting parties have departed

Kale & Simena
Don't confuse the village of Kale with the nearby town of Kale, also known as Demre

Western Mediterranean

for the day, there's only the sound of the water lapping gently against the rocks and a flag on the fortress flapping in the breeze.

The **castle** affords an impressive panorama across the surrounding coastline and is best visited early in the morning or later in the day when the sun dips below the mountains to the west. Within the well-preserved walls a **small theatre** has been carved from the rock. Capable of seating a mere 300 people the auditorium hints at the small size of ancient Simena, which together with the neighbouring towns of Aperlae, Appolonia and Isinda commanded just one vote in the Lycian assembly.

To the east of the village the ridge is littered with Roman sarcophagi standing atmospherically between wizened olive trees and thickets of carob and holly-oak. Another much-photographed tomb sits on the other side of the village surrounded by the sea.

Sleeping and eating Rooms in the village are very limited so it's probably advisable to ring ahead in the summer. You should also expect to pay considerably over-the-odds for what amounts to fairly rudimentary accommodation, however, recently luxuries such as a/c have made an appearance. **D** *Kale Pansiyon*, T8742111, F8742110. The first accommodation in the village, fairly simple rooms in several waterside fisherman's cottages, some are a/c equipped, restaurant, idyllic get-away but price is a little steep and there's little discount out of season. **E** *Mehtap Pansiyon*, T8742146, F8742261. On the hill in the western part of the village, pretty basic rooms in converted house, nice terrace area, also camping US$7.50 per person, free shuttle to Üçağız and guided walks organised by patron. Hasan's *Roma Restaurant* and *Deniz Restaurant* serve seafood and other dishes at the quayside.

Kekova Island Across the bay to the south of Kale lies the long, rocky island of Kekova which is fringed along its northern coast by the remnants of an ancient city drowned by the sea. Known as the **Batık Şehir** – or "Sunken City"- the remains of numerous buildings, streets and a harbour wall are visible beneath the translucent water. The sea around this mini-Atlantis is out-of-bounds for swimmers and divers to try and prevent the theft of antiquities, although in all honesty anything of value has probably long since disappeared. Instead you'll have to satisfy yourself with peering beneath the surface from a boat, with the flat bottomed variety giving a superior view. Another excellent way to see the ruins is to join a sea-kayaking tour organised by *Bougainville Travel* in Kaş (see page 356).

Boat tours generally call-in at a pebbly beach on the south-western tip of the island which is overlooked by the apse of a ruined Byzantine church. Locally called the **Tersane**, or the "Dockyard" there's no restriction on entering the sea here so it's a popular place to cool-off.

Aperlae Along the coast to the west of Üçağız is the isolated site of Aperlae, a ruined Lycian town which formed a coalition with four other local settlements, Simena, Appolonia and Isinda, to secure itself a single vote in the federal assembly. The citizens of this political unit were collectively referred to as Aperlites and they minted coins marked with the initials APR or PRL in the fifth century BC.

From Üçağız it's an hour's boat ride followed by a 20-30 minute walk over the neck of the Sıcak Burnu Peninsula to the site. Allow a total of five hours for the visit, which costs about US$30. On foot the site can be reached down a track from Appolonia (see below) in 2½ hours or by following a path along the coast from Üçağız in about the same time. Both these approaches are clearly marked as they're part of the Lycian Way. You'll need to set out with plenty of water and some food as the whole outing, including time to look around the site and swim, takes most of the day. This excursion is not recommended in July and August.

The ruins of various unidentified buildings are scattered across a hillside enclosed on three sides by the remains of a city wall. Usually deserted, you can snorkel around the submerged remnants of an ancient jetty and the foundations of some other buildings just off-shore.

Clearly visible on a rocky hilltop above Kılıçlı, a village about half way between Üçağız and the coastal highway, stand the ruins of Appolonia, a member of the Aperlite federation. Seldom visited except by goat-herders and local shepherds, the ruins are reached up a rough but motorable track which passes the village mosque and climbs to a saddle several hundred metres east of the site. Approaching the acropolis a path passes through an extensive **necropolis** with handsome Roman tombs, including a diminutive child-size one on a tall base, spread widely across the stony hillside. On the crest of the ridge stands a 3-m high **stella** with tombs cut from the bedrock beneath it, while on the south side of the hill there are several deep **cisterns** and an impressive **monumental tomb**. Unmistakably of Roman origin, this sepulchre is decorated with a lion relief and mock Corinthian order columns. The **Hellenistic fortress** crowning the peak is very overgrown and a ruined **Byzantine basilica** lurks in the bushes to the west of the walls.

Apollonia

Demre (Kale)

Swooping down a long grade from the west, the coastal highway affords a bird's eye view of the Demre, officially known as Kale. The community is essentially a market town which earns a living from supplying the nation with fruit and vegetables raised intensively under protective canopies of plastic and glass. Boasting the Church of St Nicholas and the ancient ruins of Myra on its northern outskirts, the town, not much in itself, is a stop-off point for coach groups, but few extend their visit much beyond a whistle-stop tour of the sights and a sit-down lunch at one of several purpose built restaurants. For those on a more leisurely schedule this standard itinerary could be complimented with a visit to nearby Andriake and some cold water springs or a swim at the unspoilt Sülüklü Beach.

Phone code: 0242
Colour map 4, grid C4

The main attraction in Demre is the Church of St Nicholas, who is known as Noel Baba in Turkish, and to whom we supposedly owe the celebrated legend of Father Christmas. A fourth century bishop of Myra, Nicholas anonymously aided the district's poor by providing dowries for local girls whose families could not otherwise afford to have them married. The bishop's largess was delivered covertly at night, spawning the custom of giving secret gifts to children on Christmas Eve. Whether fact or romantic fable, Nicholas was martyred during the reign of Emperor Diocletian, only to be beautified later in recognition of his charitable deeds. His grave became an important site of pilgrimage with miraculous events reported by visitors to the tomb. As well as children, Nicholas became the patron saint of virgins, sailors, pawn-brokers and Holy Russians, attracting a large number of pilgrims to his sepulchral tomb. In 1087 the saint's revered, but also extremely valuable, remains were stolen by the Crusaders who shipped the sarcophagus to Bari in Italy where it remains to this day.

Church of Saint Nicholas
All in all a visit to the church is a fairly forgettable experience, although the appealing, but much exaggerated, myths surrounding the building attract the tourists in droves

After this fantastic tale the church itself, protected by an unsightly plastic roof, is a bit disappointing. The present stone building bares little or no relation to the original third-century church having been rebuilt several times since, most recently in 1862 when extensive remodelling work was funded by

Western Mediterranean

Tsar Nicholas of Russia. Mostly unadorned, badly faded frescoes are just visible on some of the walls, while areas of colourful mosaic pavement survive in the nave and south aisle. Next door is a sarcophagus held to be that of Saint Nicholas, although doubt is cast on this assertion by reports that the bishop was in fact buried beneath a stone pavement. Decorated with rich carvings, the tomb more likely contained the remains of the man and woman shown on its lid. A special service is held annually on the 6 December which is supposed to be the true birthday of Saint Nicholas.

■ *0800-1730, 1900 in summer, daily. US$3. 200 m west of the main crossroad on Müze Caddesi.*

Myra The modern town of Demre is built to the south of the far more ancient settlement of Myra, one of the most accessible, and so most visited, of the Lycian cities. Firmly on the summer tour-bus circuit, it's best to arrive when the site opens or just before it closes in the evenings, thereby also avoiding the scorching sun in the middle of the day.

The city emerges from obscurity in the first century BC, although the Lycian inscriptions and coins found at the site hint at a far longer history. As a dominant member of the Lycian Confederacy Myra grew wealthy, enjoying continuing prosperity under the Romans. By the second century she became a metropolis, benefiting richly from the patronage and status which that conferred. Within the Byzantine Empire, as well as an important administrative and commercial centre, Myra's Church of St Nicholas became an important pilgrimage site, however, a combination of earthquakes and Arab raids caused the city's abandonment by the 11th century.

Approaching **the site** you must first run the gauntlet of a row of shopkeepers selling souvenirs and other nick-nacks, emerging from the citrus orchards in front of a large **theatre**. Partly propped against the rocky acropolis behind, either side of the large cavea is supported on two concentric galleries, with the outside one giving access to the auditorium via a set of stairs. Originally two stories high, the backstage building has collapsed, littering the orchestra with chunks of the decorative facade. Some of the fragments are exquisitely carved, with one showing two theatrical masks now lying upside down.

Even more compelling are the Lycian **rock tombs** cut into an outcrop to the left of the theatre. The most striking of these sepulchres are the so-called "house tombs" which were carefully crafted to resemble Lycian dwellings. Although universally damaged by treasure-hunters they have retained interesting features such as fake wooden beams, carved to resemble roof supports. Clamber up to individual tombs for a closer look and also try and spy the relief of a warrior, handing his helmet to a page, which is carved onto the rock above and to the left of the main group of mausolea. Nearby there is also a funerary scene carved onto the rockface.

For the enthusiast a second cluster of less impressive tombs, known as the **river necropolis**, are cut into a cliff face on the far side of the acropolis. These can be reached by retracing your steps to the road from Demre and turning left, instead of right towards town. Continue along this road for about 150 m to the first of two white buildings, where you should turn left down a track beside a glass house. Turn left after a house and follow the path across a rickety bridge towards the base of some crags. The tombs are on the mountainside several hundred metres further round.

■ *0730-1900 in summer, 0800-1730 in winter, daily. US$1.25. Getting there: Under your own steam walk 2 km north from Demre's main crossroads, turning left at a signposted road for the final 500 m. A taxi from Demre to the site and back, including 30 mins waiting time, is about US$6.*

The ancient geographer Strabo informs us that Myra was 20 stades, about 4 km, from the sea. This meant that a port, known as Andriake, grew up to the southeast at the mouth of the Androkos River to handle the city's maritime trade. Today, the spot, called Çayağız, is a scrappy collection of cafés, restaurants and shops which service the armada of yachts and excursion boats that set-off daily down the coast for Kekova. The local boatman's co-operative, the *Deniz Taşıcılar Koop*, T8713750, organises outings to Kekova costing US$25-35 for a small boat that can take up to eight people. In summer it's sometimes possible to join forces with other people or tag along with another group.

Approaching Çayağız, the ruins of Andriake are across the valley on the south side of the Androkos River and a wide marshy area. To reach them turn left on a road about 750 m before Çayağız, passing a small stream fed by a **cold mineral spring** to the east of this side road. Said by locals to be therapeutic for stomach problems if drunk early in the day, it's probably safer just to bathe in the sulphur-rich pools.

Continuing up the road a track on the right beside a small farm leads across the fields to Andriake's most significant surviving building, **Hadrian's Granary**. A well-preserved stone structure divided into eight separate chambers, it was built as part of the Roman's grain distribution system, essentially a warehouse used to store wheat before it was loaded onto ships for transportation across the empire. An inscription running along the front of the building dates its construction to 119-139 AD also identifying its founder as Hadrian. A relief above the central doorway depicts the Emperor and his wife, Sabina, while another frieze further to the right shows two unknown deities. A path continues west from the granary through pine woods to Çayağız.

■ *Getting there: Çayağız is about 3 km southwest of Demre and is signposted off the coastal highway. There's no public transport to Demre so you'll have to walk, hitch or catch a taxi. There's no accommodation at Çayağız, however, locals recommend a camping spot beneath a stand of trees at the far end of the 600 m long beach. It's certainly pretty secluded, but you'll have to carry-in your own drinking water.*

About 1½ km south of Demre and reached by crossing the coastal highway at the *Hotel Andriake*, is a long pebble beach backed by a few scrappy restaurants that cater mainly for locals at the weekend. Continuing along the road and crossing a headland brings you to a wonderfully pristine stretch of white sand beach with a couple of cafés. It's amazing that such a lovely beach has remained undeveloped, although there are plans afoot for a new holiday complex in the dunes behind. This road continues over the hills to the Çayağız road. ■ *Getting there: There's no public transport from Demre to the beaches, so once again you'll have to walk, hitch or get a taxi.*

E *Hotel Andriake*, Finike Caddesi, 18/14640, F8715440. On the coastal road, pretty soul-less modern place, most comfortable rooms in town though, front facing ones likely to be noisy, shower, a/c, TV, telephone. **E** *Grand Hotel Kekova*, PTT Caddesi, T8714515, F8715366. On eastern edge of town past the post office, a close second in the comfort stakes, rooms are also equipped with a/c and telephone, quieter. **F** *Noel Pension*, Myra Yolu No 29, T8712304. Situated on northern edge of town on way to Myra, basic rooms in little concrete building, over-priced. **G** *Şahin Otel*, Müze Caddesi, T8715686. Run by Yusuf Kamil who is the local *muhtar* (elected leader), fairly plain rooms with ensuite, included in the room price is a lift to the beach and Çayağızı, tours to Kekova can also be arranged on hotel's boat. Recommended. **G** *Hotel Simge*, PTT Caddesi, T8714511. Simple rooms which are comfortable for the price, telephone. Recommended budget option.

Sleeping
*The hotels in Demre
are certainly nothing to
get excited about, though
they're perfectly adequate
should you decide to
stay the night*

Eating *Ipek Restaurant*, on the right-hand side of Müze Caddesi as you walk towards St Nicholas, is the favourite local eatery and it's always pretty busy serving şiş, adana kebabı and other grilled meats, along with soup and some ready-prepared dishes at lunch time. There are several other simple lokantas around the main crossroads such as *Şehir Restaurant*, which also has kebabs and some stew-tray stew. At the *Inci Pastanesi* on Müze Caddesi, a tasty, light cheese börek sprinkled with sesame seeds and a glass of tea make a good snack.

Transport **Antalya**, about every 30 mins during the day, 3½ hrs, US$4. **Fethiye**, every 90 mins, 3½ hrs, US$4. **Kaş**, 0900-1630 every 30 mins, also 3 evening buses, 1 hr, US$1.75. For **Patara** get on a Fethiye-bound bus, 1½ hrs, US$2; while for **Olympos** you'll need an Antalya-bound bus, approximately the same journey time and price in the opposite direction.

Directory **Banks** There's an *Işbankası* with ATM on Müze Caddesi opposite the *Ipek restaurant*. **Communications Internet**: *Serra Net Cafe*, south of the *Şahin Hotel*, on the street parrallel to Müze Caddesi, US$1 per hr. **Post office**: The PTT is a couple of mins walk east along PTT Caddesi from the centre.

Finike Sitting at the western end of a long bay, Finike is a modern working town which, except for its large marina, has missed out on the Turkish tourist boom. Built on the site of ancient Phoenicus, any traces of this previous settlement have long since disappeared beneath the uninspiring concrete boxes. East of the centre there's a very mediocre beach backed by some scrappy holiday developments and forlorn hotels, but most visitors are simply in transit, stopping off for a nights sleep or a meal. Beyond breaking your journey, you may decide to make Finike a base for an excursion north to the antique cities of Limyra and Arykanda, possibly continuing for a look at the upland town of Elmalı. Tour groups also call-in to use the shiny new Turkish baths (see directory).

Several hotels are conveniently situated on the highway which is called Şerbetçi Bulvarı as it cuts through town

Sleeping **E** *Bahar Otel*, Cumhuriyet Caddesi No 14, T8552020, F8552093. Situated in the street behind the *Engin Otel*, marginally more comfortable rooms than its competitor and certainly less affected by traffic noise, equipped with a/c, TV and telephone. **F** *Simena Guesthouse*, Elmalı Caddesi No 2, T8551629, white building visible on hillside to the north of the bus station, reached by daunting staircase, 26 fairly basic rooms some with ensuite, several built against rock face, large terraces where meals are served, US$11 per person half-board option, enthusiastic owner Sabri Uysal organizes minibus and boat tours which amazingly are included in the room price.

Eating Popular locally, *Deniz 2* on the highway across from the marina has a wide choice of reasonably priced food including fish, alcohol served. Across the road the *Petek* has a similar choice of dishes but a superior location overlooking the marina. There are several cheap *lokantas* on Cumhuriyet Caddesi which runs parallel to the coast road behind the *Engin Hotel*. Try *Birlik Restaurant*, a spartan place with a good selection of steam-tray food and grilled meat, beer and *rakı* also available. Nearby is the *Mevlana Pide ve Lahmacun* where you can have soup followed by pide or lahmacun and a drink for about US$3.

Directory **Banks** There's an Işbankası on Şerbetçi Caddesi near the *Engin Hotel*. **Comunications Post office**: The PTT is just off the coastal highway on the road to the bus station and Elmalı. **Internet**: *Internet Cafe*, visible across the river from the PTT. **Baths** *Finike Hamamı*, Elmalı Caddesi, T8551467, on the road to Elmalı next to the bus station, modern baths with plunge pool, US$8 entry and *kese*, call to make a reservation as it's frequented primarily by tour groups, closed Tue.

The Lycian Hinterland

North of Finike the D-635 highway climbs its way into the mountainous hinterland of Lycia towards the traditional town Elmalı noted for its apples and a district of crumbling Ottoman houses. It's a two-hour journey by car, longer by bus, passing along the way the archaeological sites of Limyra and Arykanda, the latter of which, perched in a position that's second to none, is by far the more alluring. These sights aside, it's a pleasure to leave the heat on the coast for the invigorating freshness of the mountain air as you ascend through fragrant forests of pine and cedar, above which desolate rocky peaks are silhouetted boldly against the sky. With your own transport consider taking the quiet mountain road from Kaş via Kasaba to Arif (Arykanda).

Phone code: 0242
Colour map 4,
grid B4 & C4

Established sometime in the sixth century BC, Limyra grew to prominence 200 years later as the capital of an independent Lycian kingdom, whose freedom-loving dynast, King Pericles, successfully defended his territory against the Carian tyrant Mausolus. Little is heard about the city, until 4 AD when Gaius Caesar the adopted son of Emperor Augustus died in the city from a stab wound inflicted by a Parthian assassin. The seat of a Byzantine bishopric, the city was decimated by the Arab raids of the seventh and eighth centuries, eventually disappearing from the map entirely until 1839, when its ruins were rediscovered by the English traveller Charles Fellows.

Limyra

The fragmentary remains of Limyra are scattered between the greenhouses and dwellings of a small village, so it's very difficult to get an accurate impression of the scale or lay-out of the city. In good shape is a **Roman theatre** beside the road which also provides a vantage point from which to spot the other ruins. Further to the east, a free-standing **Lycian sarcophagus** is visible on the hillside below the obvious pylon line. Reached up a path from the road, it is decorated with carvings depicting scenes from its occupant's, a relative of Pericles named Xatabura, life. Walking back past the theatre, a path on the left leads beyond a large partially excavated **temple** building to a swift-flowing river fed by several powerful springs. A favourite place for local children to swim, these subterranean streams are mentioned in several ancient sources. An escarpment above the village is peppered with rock-cut tombs and an obvious track leads up the mountain from beside the mosque to a **monumental mausoleum** on the top of Tocak Dağı. Called the Heroon, it's an impressive relief decorated double tomb, presumed to be the last resting place of King Pericles. It's a hot 30-40 minute climb from the village.

■ *Getting there: The site is 3 km east of Turunçova, a small town on the road to Elmalı, 6 km north of Finike. Dolmuş to Turunçova leave every 15 mins from Finike otogar, but from there you'll have to walk or hitch a lift.*

Well off the usual coast hugging tourist itinerary, it's quite possible that you'll have the place to yourself, that is apart from the conscientious guardian, Ramazan Demir, who breaks the monotony of looking after the site by giving visitors an informative tour.

On-going excavations by Ankara University have uncovered remains dating back to the fifth century BC, but experts suggest there may have been a settlement on the site at least a thousand years before. What is certain is that Arykanda became a member of the Lycian Confederacy in the second century BC, also benefiting from its position straddling an artery of trade linking the Lycian highlands with the coast. The Arykandans took to Christianity early as demonstrated by a third-century petition to the emperor Maximinius requesting the

Arykanda

Superbly situated high in the Lycian mountains, a visit here is rewarded as much by the cool air & surroundings, as by the interesting ruins themselves

Western Mediterranean

suppression of pagan practices and idolatry. Known as Acalanda the settlement persisted, be it in a much diminished form, during Byzantine times, only to be abandoned in the 11th century for unknown reasons.

Sitting amongst the pine woods and rough fields on a mountainside above the small community of Arif, **the site** is reached up a kilometre long signposted track which passes several springs where you can enjoy a refreshing draught and refill your water bottle. The lower parking area is flanked by toilets and the **lower acropolis**, a crumbling structure with steps leading up beneath an arch to a series of chambers, formerly occupied by a blacksmiths and shops. You can also identify the brick columns that supported the floor of a small bath-house.

Continuing up the track, on the left is a **Byzantine basilica** with fragments of a mosaic pavement protected from the elements beneath a corrugated iron roof. On the other side of the track more **mosaic flooring** has been uncovered in the ruins of some houses.

To the southeast of the upper parking area, a Roman **baths** and **gymnasium** complex is the most substantial building still standing. Pierced by numerous windows, the bath's facade stands two stories high, with a mark along the walls showing clearly how much debris had to be removed to uncover the structure.

Back at the upper parking area stone steps climb up to the **agora**, on a large rectangular terrace cut from the slope. Formerly the commercial heart of the city, it's now covered with lush grass in spring and a small tree sprouts symmetrically from its centre. Overlooking the agora and reached through three arched doorways is a small **odeon** which has received generous attention from modern restorators. Above it, the city's 2,000 seat **Hellenistic theatre** is also in excellent condition. Nestled into the hillside, the rugged mountains of the Akdağ range across the valley form a stunning backdrop for its gracefully curving cavea and well-preserved backstage building. Up another level, several pine trees sprouting from the ancient **stadium** provide a shady spot to soak-up the beautiful surroundings or even for a picnic.

After your visit you can have a cold drink or sample some trout raised in a large pool at the simple **Kervan Lokantası**, just up the main road, which also provides a convenient place to wait for the dolmuş. High on the precipitous canyon wall behind are fragments of an ancient aqueduct which presumable supplied Arykanda with water.

■ *Getting there: Arykanda is above the village of Arif, 30 km north of Finike on the road to Elmalı. Without your own transport you'll need to get on a bus for Elmalı which depart Finike bus station about every hr, 0800-1700, 1½ hrs, US$1.50. Ask to be let off at Arif and having looked around return to the main road and wait for the next passing bus or hitch. A taxi from Finike to the site with an hr waiting time is about US$25.*

Elmalı From Arif the road continues climbing steadily topping the Avlanbeli Pass (1120 m) before cruising out onto a wide open plain, or *ova,* ringed by rugged mountains. This upland basin is agriculturally important, producing large crops of wheat, potatoes and sugar beet. The cooler climate at 1000 m is also ideal for growing apples and the area's extensive orchards lend the district capital its name: Elmalı, "With Apples".

Clustered at the base of a streaked, rocky peak, Elmalı is a conservative market town which has much more in common with urban centres in the Anatolian heartland than those along the westernised coastal strip. It receives only a trickle of foreign visitors attracted by the graceful timber-framed houses which crowd the old quarter of town. However, these are now under siege by the gritty modern town; and most are picturesque but in a terrible state of repair.

The main street, Hükümet Caddesi, leads up to the old town passing the 17th-century **Ömerpaşa Camii**, a classical Ottoman building with attractive lunettes of faïence on the outside, but a rather dark and disappointing interior. The courtyard is backed by a multi-domed *medrese*, now a library, and further up the street is the truncated base of a Selçuk minaret, though the accompanying mosque has disappeared. That's the sum total of Elmalı's sights; hardly enough to justify a special trip, although a short visit would give you the chance to experience another, more traditional, side of Turkey, light-years away from the coastal resorts. The colourful **weekly market** occupies the streets near the bus station on Mondays.

Sleeping and eating F *Belediye Otel*, Hükümet Caddesi, T6183137. Opposite the mosque, serviceable hotel run by the municipality. **G-F** *Toros Otel*, Hükümet Caddesi, T6185040. Across from the mosque, newly-opened, clean rooms with or without ensuite, no breakfast. There are several simple *lokantas*, such as *Gören*, on Hükümet Caddesi. The *Lezzet Lokantası*, on the corner up from the bus station has a better choice of food. A snack bar in the bus station does tasty cheese or *köfte* sandwiches for US$0.75.

Transport Antalya, every hr, 1½ hrs, US$1.50. **Finike**, every hr, 2 hrs, US$2. **Gömbe**, every 30 mins, 0900-1900, US$0.75. **Kaş**, 3 daily, 3 hrs, US$3.

Directory Banks Several with ATM on Hükümet Caddesi. **Communications Internet**: *Toros Internet*, on Hükümet Caddesi opposite Şen Lokantası. **Post office**: The PTT is also on Hükümet Caddesi.

Adrasan

Thanks to its relative isolation and position inside the Beydağları National Park, Adrasan has so far remained a backwater: a quiet resort-in-the-making consisting of an incontinuous strip of pensions and small hotels lining an arching shingle beach. Approached across a hinterland of citrus orchards, fields and greenhouses from the one-horse agricultural community of Çavuş Köyü, a cool tree-shaded river empties into the sea at the north end of the beach, while a procession of concrete lamp-posts marching along the coastal track provides a jarring note to the otherwise attractive scene. Boat trips along the pristine local coastline can be organised by several of the pensions (see below). ■ *Getting there: There's no public transport down to Adrasan from the coastal highway, so you'll have to rely on a taxi or hitch-hike.*

Sleeping and eating C *Ikizler Ev Pansiyon*, T8835227. Nice wooden bungalows beside the beach-front road, some with sleeping platforms which are perfect for children, prices are half-board, bar, restaurant, airport pick-ups and diving trips organised. Recommended. **E** *Golden River*, T8835220. Riverside pension reached across suspension bridge from the road, lovely location, plain rooms with ensuite, boat trips organised, pleasant trout restaurant with cool tables next to the water. **F** *Şimşek Pansiyon*, T8835419. Simple place beside the road to the beach. **F** *Riverside Garden Pension*, T8835212. Reached across a footbridge from the road, a row of fairly basic rooms overlooking the river, also has a decent fish restaurant. There are also several simple beachfront eateries which aren't attached to a pension or hotel.

Olympos and Çıralı

Phone code: 0242
Colour map 4, grid C5

Enjoying some degree of official protection within the Beydağları Coastal National Park, the area around the ruins of ancient Olympos and the nearby village of Çıralı have remained remarkably unspoilt. Blanketed in forests of pine, rocky ridges march towards the coast, where a wide 3-km strand of sand and pebble beach is overlooked by the towering pyramidal peak of Tahtalı Dağı. The countryside is at its most beautiful in spring when clear-running rivers rush seawards and the heady scent of orange blossom drifts on the breeze; though at any time of year it provides a peaceful spot to relax and unwind. In addition to lazing on the beach or exploring the atmospheric ruins of Lycian Olympos, the extraordinary natural spectacle of the Chimaera is just a short hike away. There are also several more excursions into the surrounding mountains taking in parts of the Lycian Way (see page 339).

Ins and outs

Getting there   Olympos and Çıralı are in adjacent valleys, 10-min walk along the beach from each other. Olympos is reached down a side road sign-posted for "Olympos and Adrasan" which leaves the coastal highway about 20 km northeast of Kumluca. After about 8 km a signposted track on the left leads 3 km to the ruins and accommodation. During the day an hourly dolmuş (US$1.25) descends from the highway making this the easiest place to head without your own transport. A short distance beyond the Olympos turn-off a second side road signposted for "Çıralı/ Yanartaş/ Chimaera" winds down to the village of Çıralı, 7 km. There's no dolmuş service to Çıralı, so you'll need to hitch or get a taxi (US$7) from the junction. Having crossed a little stone bridge a sign board has directions for the villages various pensions which are strung out along 2 parallel tracks inland from the beach. Antalya and Fethye bound buses can be flagged down on the highway during the day.

Getting around   The most usual form of transport is your feet, although a bicycle can be useful too.

Background   The area's archaeological and environmental significance as a nesting site for marine turtles have helped keep development to a minimum, with strict regulations governing land-use and building. Despite this a thriving local industry has sprung up to cater for the growing number of foreign backpackers and domestic tourists who descend on Olympos and Çıralı each year. Although development is still low-key in comparison to other Turkish resorts – accommodation is generally in single storey buildings or wooden huts – the summer crowds are inevitably accompanied by problems such as litter and nocturnal disturbance during the critical turtle nesting season. The financial rewards from tourism have also encouraged illegal building, as extra bungalows are surreptitiously added and makeshift restaurants sprout along the beach.

In the face of such pressures the Turkish Society for the Protection of Nature (DHKD), funded by a grant from the EU, is involved in creating a management plan for the area. Not without its critics in the local community, the organisation also conducts educational schemes and research on turtle nesting behaviour using volunteers from the British Trust for Conservation Volunteers (see page 325). The DHKD site office is signposted off the beachfront road near the school.

You can contribute to the area's conservation by avoiding the beach at night during the turtle nesting season and refilling your water bottles at the freshwater springs beside the path through Olympos or on the approach road to Çıralı.

Olympos

The ancient city's remains lie widely scattered across a verdant valley, hidden amongst tangled thickets of oleander and fragrant bay on the banks of a placid river. It's an idyllic spot which is alive with butterflies, lizards and birds, such as the Krüper's nuthatch and the green woodpecker; though in the summer there are a fair few tourists too.

Though its exact origins are uncertain, Olympos is thought to have taken its name from the nearby peak of Mount Olympos, known today as Tahtalı Dağı. According to the ancient geographer Strabo, the city was an important member of the Lycian League wielding the maximum number of three ballots in the federal caucus. A prosperous port-city, Olympos was a centre for the worship of Hephaistos, god of fire, with a temple built in his honour at the nearby Chimaera. In the first century BC Olympos, along with neighbouring Phaselis, came under the control of marauding Cilician corsairs. The pirate leader Zenicetes established his headquarters in the city, introducing the worship of Mithras, a god of Persian origin, to it's citizens. With the defeat of Zenicetes by Pompey in 67 BC, Olympos regained its fortunes, assuming its position in the Lycian Confederacy under the *pax Romana*. Later in Byzantine times the city suffered once more at the hands of marauding pirates. During the 11th and 12th centuries Olympos enjoyed a brief revival as a base for Genoese and Venetian trading activity, however, it was finally abandoned in the 15th century.

Starting from the sea you'll notice what's left of **Byzantine fortifications** on the crest of the low cliffs overlooking the beach. A steep path leads up from the landward side of the ridge, where a sweeping view along the beach makes up for the fragmentary state of the defences. At the base of the cliffs, beside the creek, are two recently unearthed **Lycian tombs**, one inscribed with a poignant poem that's translated on the adjacent sign. Inland the main path passes a **potable spring** beyond which a medieval irrigation channel provides a passage through the undergrowth to a **Byzantine villa**, complete with a small section of **mosaic floor**. Nearby are several free standing **tombs**, while a magnificent **marble door frame**, topped by a carved lintel, looms out of the vegetation to the south-west. The imposing portal of a second century AD temple that's long since disappeared, a statue base at its foot is dedicated to the Emperor Marcus Aurelis, and dated 172-175.

Along the river banks sections of the Hellenistic **harbour wall** are still visible, and to the south a path leads from the beach passed the ruins of the **harbour baths** to a badly degraded **Roman theatre**. Also on the south side of the river, further upstream, the city's extensive **necropolis** covers a wooded hillside. Along with an ornate Roman sarcophagus and the more usual free-standing Lycian tombs, are a large number of vaulted funerary chambers. Inside the walls were plastered and the crossbeam above the small entranceways are inscribed with an epithet or a variation of the "dice-oracle" seen at other Classical sites, such as Termessos (see page 386), which in this case were used to consult the ancestral spirits. (*Officially open only during daylight hrs, US$1 when wardens are present*).

Chimaera (Yanartaş)

On a rocky mountain about an hour's walk north of Çıralı is an extraordinary natural phenomena known as the Chimaera. Gas seeping out of the ground spontaneously ignites as it escapes, creating a series of flaming crevices clustered on a bare hillside. Known in Turkish as the Yanartaş, of "Burning Rocks", the flames can be extinguished by blowing on them or covering them with earth, only to reignite spontaneously within seconds.

Western Mediterranean

Ancient sources reveal that the fires burned considerably higher in the past and were even used by ancient mariners to navigate off the coast. Not surprisingly the site developed as a focus for the worship of Hephaistos, the god of fire, known to the Romans as Vulcan; though the ruins on a terrace below the flames are of a Byzantine chapel which superseded the earlier temple.

The site was also held to be the lair of the mythical Chimaera, a hideous fire-breathing monster which was part lion, part snake and part goat. Legend has it that the virtuous Bellerophon, grandson of Sisyphos and King of Corinth, was ordered to kill the monster by King Iobates of Lycia as punishment for the alleged rape of Stheneboea. Enjoying the favour of the gods, Bellerophon saddled the winged horse Pegasus and flew-off to overcome the Chimaera by pouring molten lead into its mouth.

Even today, the flames of Chimaera are a strange and magical sight which attract a procession of curious visitors each night, when they're at their most impressive. Most people make an evening of it, and in the summer there's usually a drinks stand run by an enterprising local.

■ *Getting there: From the car park at the foot of the mountain it's a 20 minute walk up to the flames; with a second, smaller set of fires about 15 to 20 minutes higher. Remember to take a torch for the way up and down. The car park can be reached along the track from Çıralı in about 30-45 mins.*

Walking to Ulupınar A pleasant excursion from Çıralı or Olympos is to the village of Ulupınar, just below the coastal highway, where there are several shady trout restaurants that make an excellent venue for lunch. From the stone bridge in Çıralı, walk inland for 3 km to where the road bends right and begins climbing in earnest towards the highway. Leave the tarmac before this bend, crossing the stream on the right and picking up a well-worn path that skirts a meadow and an old mill. Follow the path up the Ulupınar Çayı valley for about 90 minutes to where it emerges at a track on the edge of Ulupınar village. Turn right and the restaurant is several hundred metres further on. It's a lovely spot to escape the heat with shady seating platforms surrounded by running water, and the food is reasonably priced too. It can be reached in a car by leaving the highway at a sign for Ulupınar, several kilometres towards Antalya from the Çıralı turn-off.

After a meal you can return the way you came or take an alternative route via the Chimaera. This path starts about half-way down the Ulupınar Çayı valley, breaking left down a steep embankment and crossing the river, before ascending the right-hand side of an obvious side valley. It's a steep climb through pine forest, but the path is well marked with red and white flashes, being part of the Lycian Way. After about 90 minutes you emerge on a saddle that affords excellent views of Tahtalı Dağı and the higher set of flames are a short way down the opposite side. If you time it right you can arrive here at dusk, but remember to carry a torch for the way down.

Sleeping

If on a shoe-string budget try Gipsy's, beyond the river crossing, where there's space to roll-out your sleeping bag above the restaurant/bar but don't expect much privacy or sleep!

Olympos Accommodation in the Olympos valley is dominated by small, informal pensions. Most offer rustic "treehouses" – in fact mostly wooden bungalows on stilts – but the quality and comfort of these structures varies considerably with all of them having one thing in common: they're chilly in the winter. Hot water can also be a problem in the colder months (or when it's overcast) when the solar water-heaters don't get enough direct sunlight to provide everyone with a hot shower. Despite these drawbacks the "treehouses" are immensely popular with foreign and Turkish travellers alike, so in Jul and Aug you're advised to call-ahead. All the places in the valley offer a bed, breakfast and dinner package as standard making them exceptionally good value. However, don't expect an à la carte menu as the emphasis is on filling, mostly vegetarian, fare for which you generally queue-up to help yourself from a row of plastic bowls. **F** *Kadir's Place*, T8921250. 1 of the original treehouse encampments and still very popular despite being about 15-mins walk from the beach, some *bono fide* tree dwellings and a lot more bungalows clustered around a volleyball pitch, restaurant and café, very much on the backpacker circuit, partly staffed by western travellers, a few recent complaints about standards of hygiene in the kitchen don't seem to put people off, direct minibuses to Cappadocia, Antalya and other popular destinations, internet access, lively bar. **F** *Olympos Sheriff's*, T8921301. 500 m beyond Kadir's, well-established place before the river crossing, reasonably comfortable bungalows with or without bathrooms set amongst the orange trees, also more basic stilt-cabins which sleep up to 3 people, US$8 per person, shady seating area. Recommended. **F** *Caretta Caretta*, T8921292. Much smaller, more intimate place beyond Sheriff's and Turkmen, relaxed seating area overlooking river, cramped conventional rooms with toilet but much nicer wooden bungalows. Recommended. **F** *Olympos Orange Pansiyon*, T8921242/1317. 30 m beyond the river crossing, wood-panelled rooms with small ensuite bathrooms, also rows of wooden bungalows squeezed into the citrus grove behind, transfers and tours arranged, laundry service US$2.50 per load, internet access. **F** *Lemon Pension*, T8921255. Quiet location where the valley widens beyond Kadir's Place, basic rooms and simple cabins. **F** *Çavuşoğlu Pansiyon*, T8921322. Another new addition at the head of the valley, ugly double-storey row of concrete rooms, a 25 min hike to the beach makes this a last resort option, although the family running it seem very friendly.

Çıralı There are lots of pensions and small hotels dotted along the plain just inland from the beach. These places generally offer more comfortable lodgings than their counterparts in the Olympos valley and attract more Turkish holiday-makers and families. Room rates are slightly higher, though they still represent good value for money, with comforts such as ensuite bathrooms and air-conditioning more widely available. **A** *Olympos Lodge*, PO Box 38, Kemer, Antalya, T8257171, F8257173. First hotel in the area, still a cut above the rest, comfortable bungalows set in gardens roamed by peacocks, superb position on the beach, prices are half-board, 20% discount for children under 12, airport transfer arranged, car rental. **E** *Blue and White Hotel*, on the beach front road, T8257006, F8257263. 2 regimented rows of modern concrete bungalows, en suite bathrooms, twin beds available, hot water, restaurant. **E** *Guneş Pansiyon*, Çıralı village, T8257161. Simple rooms with en-suite bathrooms, hotwater, restaurant. **E** *Barış Pansiyon*, Çıralı village, T8257080. Small rooms with bathrooms, solar-heated water, restaurant, convenient for beach and restaurants, slightly overpriced. **E** *Fehim Pansiyon*, T8257250. 500 m along beachfront road, popular with Turkish families, plain rooms with en-suite bathroom, hotwater, restaurant. **E** *Martin Ranch*, T8257044. A km along the beach-front road, ranch theme doesn't go beyond the wagon wheels out front, well-appointed bungalows with ensuite bathrooms set in lush garden, freshwater pool in summer, expect to pay a bit extra here. **E-F** *Yıldız Pansiyon*, T8257160. On the beach front road next to Martin Ranch, pleasant family-run pension with choice of a/c equipped or normal rooms, also several cheaper cabins, tasty food including freshly caught fish, table tennis table, boat trips organised by owner, Ali. Recommended. **F** *Aygün Pansiyon*, Çıralı village, T8257146. Friendly place with en-suite bathrooms, hotwater, a/c doubles US$27, half-board option. Recommended. **F** *Rüya Pansiyon*, T8257055. Small rooms in set in a garden behind the village school, all have en-suite bathrooms, restaurant, table-tennis table. Recommended.

Camping *Green Point Camping*, well-kept site opposite *Star Pansiyon*, washing facilities and clean toilets, beach restaurant, on-site caravans for hire, sleep 2-3 at a squeeze, US$10 per person, a bit hot in the summer unless you have one of the few shady pitches.

Eating Eating in the Olympos valley is limited to the pensions although there are a couple of places along the road selling snacks such as gözleme and *ayran*. In Çıralı there is more choice with most of the action in a row of makeshift beach-front restaurants to the north of the river. Serving a similar menu, concentrating on *meze* and seafood, they go in and out of vogue so it's best to choose the one which is crowded on the day. You may want to bare in mind that these places are built illegally close to the sand and may disturb nesting turtles. The *Inka Cafe* is a shady retreat beneath a grove of towering plane trees near the stone bridge in Çıralı, food, refreshments and eclectic music.

Bars Should you be looking for some action after dark, the area's nightlife is restricted to *Gypsy's* and the *Ökuz Bar* at Kadır's Place. Both are in the Olympos valley so it's a long walk if you're staying in Çıralı.

Towards Antalya

The southern approach to Antalya is particularly impressive with the coastal highway following a meandering path beneath the jagged limestone peaks of the Beydağları which dip their forested feet directly into blue Mediterranean. Unfortunately despite the rugged beauty of this stretch of coast, much of which falls within the Beydağları National park, there isn't much to detain the independent traveller with the tourist scene along the way dominated by package hotels and holiday villages. An exception is the ancient city of Phaselis, occupying an evocative site between Tekirova and Kemer, which is well-deserving of a visit, or, if you fancy a spot of trekking, the towering peak of Tahtalı Dağı.

Tahtalı Dağı

It's possible if you're fit to climb to the summit & back in a fairly gruelling 8-9 hrs, although it's far nicer to takes things at a more leisurely pace & camp enroute

Rising abruptly to 2366 m, Tahtali Dagi is an impressive pyramidal peak looming to the west of the coastal road between the turn-offs for Çirali and Phaselis. Partially cloaked in thick forests of pine and cedar- hence the mountains contemporary name meaning "wooded", though in ancient times it was known as Mount Olympos - it's a challenging hike to the summit from where in the words of the Roman geographer Strabo: 'one may look down on the whole of Lycia and Pamphylia and Pisidia and Milyas.'

Although a little exaggerated, the view on a clear day is indeed magnificent, stretching from the Akdag range in the west past the greenhouses of Kumluca to the Cape of Gelidonia, then right around the arching Gulf of Antalya as far east as Side.

When to go The best time to ascend Tahtali Dagi is in late spring/early summer when the snow has melted off the upper mountain, but it's not too hot. Whenever you choose to climb you should be adequately equipped with sturdy boots, a large water bottle and a jacket incase the weather turns. If you're planning to camp on the mountain remember that even in summer the temperature drops significantly at night.

The trek The route begins in the village of Beycik on the haunches of the mountain and reached up a twisting road from the coastal highway. There's no public transport to the village which means a taxi from Kemer, Tekirova or Çirali. Another alternative is to follow the Lycian Way (see page 339) from where it crosses the highway north of Ulupinar, a walk of about three hours, or even from Çirali which would add about half-a-day.

Above Beycik the path starts beside a huge plain tree, passing the village's *yayla* – or summer pastures – before ascending through ancient cedar forests to an obvious forested col southeast of the summit pyramid. This age-old path has become part of the Lycian Way, so it's now clearly marked with distinctive red and white flashes. There are camping spots at the *yayla*, which has a spring where you should refill your bottles, or on the broad saddle amongst the cedars. From here it's a 3½ to four hour roundtrip to the summit, initially following a cairned path up a steep, energy-sapping scree slope. From the top of this slope follow the cairns across an undulating plateau to the final summit ridge. Join this at its lowest point and follow it southeast (right) up to the top. Take care of the steep drops down the north side of the mountain and don't forget to sign the summit book tucked away in a lead box in the summit cairn.

Having descended back to the saddle you can return to Beycik the way you came or follow the Lycian Way down the other side to a vigorous spring and possible camping spot at Çukuryayla, 30-40 minutes away. From here its a three to four hour descent to the village of Gedelme, where there are several simple eateries. In summer a dolmus leaves Kemer bus station at 0800 for Gedelme, returning back down the mountain at 1700. Alternatively, you can normally find a lift in the village.

Phaselis

"As we cruised southwards, lazing in the sunshine, the pine-forests thickened, the landscape grew wilder and emptier. Presently there came into view, beneath the wooded slopes, a city of some evident size. We glided into a small but well-built harbour, with substantial quays and breakwaters. But there was not a soul to be seen."

So Lord Kinross describes his arrival at Phaselis in his travelog *Europa Minor*, and although you'd be lucky to have the place to yourself these days, the ancient city's location scattered amongst the fragrant pine woods around three sparkling bays is still enchanting.

Phaselis began its days as a colony of Rhodes, established about 690 BC. The city rapidly became an important trading centre, exporting goods such as cedar wood and rose oil as far afield as Egypt. The Persian occupation of Asia Minor in the sixth century interfered little with the commercial life of the city and Phaselitan coins of the period are emblazoned with the prow of a merchant ship. However, Phaselis' pragmatic citizens were less happy about their "liberation" by the Athenians in 469 BC, though considerable arm-twisting eventually persuaded them to join their fellow Greeks in the Athenian maritime league.

The city next crops up in the fourth century when it concluded a treaty with Mausolus, aiding the Persian satrap (governor) of Caria in his subjugation of the Lycian Kingdom based at Limyra. The same self-serving instincts motivated the Phaselitans to send envoys to greet Alexander the Great as he approached the city in 333 BC; not only offering the surrender of their city, but also presenting Alexander with a golden crown. Their obsequiousness seems to have paid off as the Macedonian commander stayed around long enough to rid the city of some troublesome Pisidian neighbours.

After the death of Alexander Phaselis came under Persian control once more, only regaining it's independence as part of the Lycian League in 167 BC. Over the next century the city suffered greatly due to harassment by Cilician pirates, although things improved with its incorporated into the Roman empire. Under the Byzantines Phaselis remained a busy port-city.

History
Legend has it that the city was founded on land bought with salted fish, giving rise to the popular ancient saying "a Phaselitan offering", meaning a cheap gift

Western Mediterranean

The site

Open 0800-1900,
1730 in winter. US$2

Today, the site is reached down a 1 km access road from the highway. As you reach the car park you're greeted by several fragments of a **Roman aqueduct** and the blue Mediterranean sparkling between the pine trees. This aqueduct channelled water from a spring in the woods to the north of the site to the centre of the ancient city, located on a peninsula bounded by two large bays. The **northern bay** was generally too exposed to use as a harbour and as an obvious landing-point for attackers it was defended by a strong 3-m high defensive wall, segments of which are still visible.

On the east coast of the peninsula is a small enclosed bay which was formerly known as the **city harbour**. Protected by a strong wall and two defensive towers flanking its narrow mouth, small ships would tie-up at a stone quay on the south-west side of the harbour with the goods ferried up and down to warehouses behind. Largely silted-up in the intervening years it's now a lovely spot for a swim.

Scattered across the peninsula to the south-west of the city harbour are the ruins of the inner city, divided by a wide avenue lined with principal buildings such as the 1,500 seat **theatre**. Built into a low hill during the Roman era, the theatre was a focal point for civic life as well as being a central feature of the city's lay-out. The cavea remains largely intact, though the backstage building, which became part of the city's defensive wall in Byzantine times, is in a worse state. Also bordering the main thoroughfare is a **baths complex** with several roof arches intact. The piles of round stones formed part of the baths' under-floor heating system. Across the street and less well-preserved are the remains of the **tetragonos agora**, thought to have been the city's administrative centre in Roman times, and a Byzantine **basilica** beyond. There's little to see of the large warehouses and market places where city's merchants and middlemen used to conduct their business.

At the far end of the main avenue are the remnants of a **monumental gateway** built in honour of a visit by the Roman Emperor Hadrian in 129 BC. Previously, this end of the street was secured by a large gate giving access to the **south harbour**. The largest of the city's harbours, it was protected by a 180 m breakwater and was lined with a long quay where ships of up to 100 tons could be safely loaded and unloaded. The breakwater is now submerged and the docks have disappeared, but the fleet of tour boats anchored offshore in the summer gives you some idea of what things must have been like.

Kemer

Phone code: 0242
Colour map 4, grid C5

Despite the spectacular backdrop provided by the forested mountains of the Beydağları Range, Kemer is a modern, state-planned resort which has very little to offer the independent traveller. Catering for crowds of sun-seeking German and Russian

Phaselis

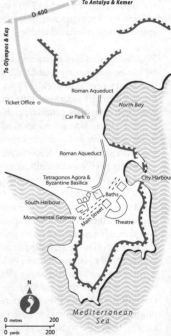

To Antalya & Kemer

D 400

To Olympos & Kaş

Roman Aqueduct

Ticket Office

North Bay

Car Park

Roman Aqueduct

Tetragonos Agora &
Byzantine Basilica

City Harbour

Baths

South Harbour

Monumental Gateway

Main Street

Theatre

Mediterranean Sea

N

0 metres 200
0 yards 200

package tourists, its streets are lined with dazzling white condos, hotels and apartment complexes. Carpet shops, gold merchants and designer clothing outlets crowd the central shopping area; and between the town's two crescents of crowded sand, there's a large marina packed with yachts and pleasure craft. Baking in the sun seems to be the most popular activity in town, although down at the beach camel rides, water skiing and windsurfing provide alternative distractions. Daily boat trips along the coast to Phaselis and Olympos are also organised by dozens of agencies, with a typical seven hour excursion costing US$15-US$20 per person including lunch.

Thoroughly westernised, the only concession to local culture to be found in Kemer is the Yörük Parkı, a predictably awful recreation of a nomadic encampment, complete with plastic dummies engaged in traditional pursuits such as spinning wool and weaving. In all truth the only plausible reason to seek-out the open-air museum on the wooded peninsula beyond the marina is to enjoy a *gözleme* and a glass of *ayran* in an open-sided black wool tent, lavishly decked out with carpets.

Sleeping

There are numerous pensions in Yenimahalle, between Atatürk Bulvarı & the beach

If you should decide to stay there's a reasonable selection of accommodation, although in summer much of it is block-booked by tour operators. Several cheap pensions are to be found on Atatürk Caddesi beyond the PTT, while the larger hotels are along the beach front and near the marina, at the southern end of the main street, Liman Caddesi. Expect large off-season discounts. **B** *Otel Hotel*, near the harbour, T8143181, F8143190. Comfortable 4-star offering with pool and restaurant, price is half-board. **B** *Nona Hotel*, Deniz Caddesi No 17, T8143170, F8141389. 1 of a row of package hotels backing the north beach, en-suite rooms with a/c, facilities include pool, fitness centre and restaurant. **F** *Doğan Pansiyon*, Atatürk Caddesi, T8142801. 150 m north of the bus station, past PTT, basic rooms with sink and shower, 1 of several cheap places frequented mainly by Turkish families, may not be open in winter.

Eating

Though expensive by local standards there are several reasonable restaurants overlooking the marina which serve an international menu including steak and seafood. There are several places near the PTT on Atatürk Bulvarı. Try *Mudurnu Restaurant*, for spit-roast chicken, döner and other kebaps, or *Aspaura Restaurant*, 100 m north, for tasty lahmacun and pide

Transport

The otogar is 3 km off the main highway, just north of the town centre and south of the PTT. **Dolmuş** shuttle between Antalya and Kemer every 15 mins, US$1.75, 1 hr; but make sure you get on an " Ust Yoldan Ekspres" service which use the main highway instead of the slow old road. There are also dolmuş every 15 mins to **Tekirova** and **Kemer. Buses** to Olympos, Finike and Kaş don't enter the town, so you'll have to get a taxi (US$3) or walk out along Atatürk Bulvarı and wait by the main highway. Arriving on a bus from this direction you'll be let-off at one of the Kemer exits from where you'll need to do the reverse. There are daily buses to more distant destinations such as Ankara, Istanbul and İzmir. The deluxe companies *Varan* and *Ulusoy* have evening services to these cities departing from their offices on Atatürk Bulvarı, north of the PTT.

Directory

Banks The PTT change TCs and foreign exchange. There are also ATMs nearby. **Post office** The PTT is on Atatürk Bulvarı, north of the otogar. **Hospitals** *Kemer Yaşam Hastanesi*, Akdeniz Caddesi No 26, T8145500, T8146070 (emergencies), private hospital and health clinic. **Tourist information** The Tourist Office, T8141537, F8141536, is in the Belediye (Municipal) building, near the harbour. Open weekdays, 0830-1230, 1330-1730.

Western Mediterranean

Antalya

Phone code: 0242
Colour map 4, grid B5

Stunningly situated on an arching bay, flanked to the west by the towering peaks of the Beydağları Mountains, Antalya is a rapidly expanding and predominantly modern city. With a population of about a million people, it's a centre for light industry as well as the administrative and commercial hub of a province which contains many of Turkey's main tourist resorts. Hundreds of thousands of package tourists are funnelled through the city's modern airport each summer, en-route for the sun-loungers and swimming pools of Alanya, Side, Kemer and Kaş. Some of this influx choose to stay in the city itself, though Antalya's beaches, pebbly Konyaaltı and well-developed Lara, are nothing to write home about. Far more alluring is the city's old quarter, Kaleiçi, clustered about the old harbour. Though thoroughly gentrified its charming streets are lined with Ottoman houses, many of which have been converted into hotels, restaurants and boutiques. This is the centre of things for the independent traveller; a pleasant place to spend a couple of nights and an excellent base for visiting the archaeological sites in the surrounding region.

Antalya

Related map
A Kaleiçi, page 378

0 metres 200
0 yards 200

Ins and outs

Antalya has excellent bus connections with towns and cities across the country. There are daily domestic flights from Ankara and İstanbul, as well as international charter flights during the holiday season.

Getting there
See page 384 for further details

The new modern otogar is 4 km north of the centre on the D-650 highway. Grey 'Terminal' buses (US$0.30) head into Kalekapısı from the bus station or a taxi into the centre costs about US$4. The airport is 10 km north-east of the city, off the D-400 coastal highway. Regular service buses bring passengers into the Turkish Airlines office on Cumhuriyet Caddesi. A taxi should be in the region of US$10. Around Kaleiçi all you need is your legs to see the sights, however, you may want to make use of the new tram (US$0.40), operating every 10 mins between Cumhuriyet Meydanı and the western end of Kenan Evren Caddesi, to get to the museum.

Getting around

Antalya was formerly known as Attaleia, a name received in honour of its second century BC founder, King Attalus II of Pergamum. Despite being a comparative late-comer in this region of very ancient cities, Attaleia became the

History

main Pamphylian port under Pergamene and later Roman rule. The city continued to prosper during Byzantine times with it's harbour acting as a staging post from where the Christian Crusaders embarked on ships for the voyage east to the Holy Land. Antalya was captured by the Selçuk Turks in 1207, briefly falling into the hands of King Peter of Cyprus and then the Turkomen Hamidoğlu clan, before Murat I took the city in 1387 for the Ottomans. Antalya became a provincial backwater under the Ottomans, renowned primarily for the fruit produced in its carefully tended walled gardens. In 1918 Italian forces took over the city along with a large chunk of south-west Anatolia, only to be dislodged in 1922 by Atatürk's nationalist forces. A year later the city's substantial Turkish-speaking Greek population was obliged to leave for Greece as part of the post-Treaty of Lausanne population exchanges.

Sights

The historic, and touristic, heart of Antalya is the Kaleiçi area around the harbour. Kaleiçi is just south of the modern city centre, pedestrianised Cumhuriyet Meydanı, centred on an equestrian statue of Atatürk, and Kalekapısı, which is flanked by a 19th-century clock-tower.

Kaleiçi   Overlooking the horse-shoe shaped harbour, Antalya's historic core, known as Kaleiçi (Inside the castle), is bordered by Cumhuriyet Caddesi and Atatürk Caddesi. After the soulless urban sprawl and busy traffic of the modern city,

Kaleiçi

■ **Sleeping**	7 Erkal Pansiyon	14 Villa Perla	4 Cumba
1 Alp Paşa	8 Kleopatra Pansiyon	15 Yeni Kont Pansiyon	5 Han
2 Antique Pansiyon	9 Marina Residence		6 Karavan Café
3 Begonvil	10 Mond Pension	● **Eating**	7 Mermerli
4 Çinar Pansiyon	11 Ninova Pension	1 Ayda Pastanesi/Internet	8 Yeşil Antalya 'Balık Evi'
5 Dedehan Pansiyon	12 Tunay Aile Pansiyon	2 Café Rolan	9 Yörükoğlu
6 Doğan	13 Urcu	3 Club 29	

it's a haven of relative tranquility with a network of twisting little streets overhung by the upper stories of Ottoman houses. Kaleiçi has enjoyed a renaissance in the last two decades as many of these old crumbling houses have been renovated and converted into hotels, guesthouses, restaurants and art galleries. The main street down from Kalekapısı, Uzun Çarşı Sokak, is lined with touristy shops and stalls.

Soaring land-values and spiralling rents have inevitably squeezed out many of the area's ordinary residents, though some semblance of the quarter's original flavour still persists in the backstreets. Down by the waterside the Roman harbour has been redeveloped with restaurants and cafés now overlooking wharves where fishing vessels are outnumbered by tour boats and pleasure craft. Although lacking in authenticity and thoroughly commercialised it's a very pleasant place to join the evening promenade or to relax with a cold beer.

Kaleiçi harbours a few specific sights the best known of which -because of its appearance on endless tourist brochures and promotional posters- is the **Yivli Minare**, which translates as the "Fluted Minaret". Visible to the south of Kalekapısı, the eponymous minaret, built of red brick set with turquoise tiles, was part of a mosque complex commissioned by the Selçuk sultan Alaeddin Keykubat I in the 13th century. That mosque was replace later with the rather plain multi-domed building we see today. Nearby, the medrese has been jarringly converted into a modern exhibition hall. Just to the west and accessible by stairs from Cumhuriyet Caddesi, is a dervish *tekke*, or meeting hall, also built in the 13th century and now occupied by Antalya's **Guzel Sanat Galerisi (Fine Art Gallery)**.

Resist descending to the harbour from here and instead walk along Cumhuriyet and Atatürk Caddesis to **Hadrian's Gate**, a triple-arched monumental gateway in the city walls, built to commemorate the emperor's visit in 130 AD. Beyond the portal quiet Hesapçı Sokak leads down to Akar Çeşme Sokak and the **Mediterranean Civilisations Research Institute** (see directory), which has a museum housed in the immaculately restored church of St George opposite. Entering beneath a relief of George slaying the dragon, inside there's a collection of rare Çanakkale ceramics and some delightful old photographs documenting Ottoman subjects engaged in various trades, though these may have changed by the time you visit.

Continuing down Hesapçı Sokak you'll pass the **Kesik Minare Camii** (the Mosque with the Cut-off Minaret) which in fact began life in the second century as a Roman temple. Converted subsequently to the Church of the Virgin Mary, the Selçuks turned it into a mosque when they took the city. After a brief interlude as a church when Peter I of Cyprus took the city, the building was converted yet again by the Ottoman Prince Dede Korkut in the 15th century. Despite this convoluted history the mosque was used up until 1896 when it was reduced to its present ruinous state by fire.

At the bottom of Hesapçı Sokak the **Mermerli and Karaalioğlu Park** stretches along the clifftop to the south; while in the other direction sits the **Hıdırlık Kulesi**, a squat Roman tower thought either to have been a tomb or part of the city's defences. Far more compelling is the breathtaking view across Antalya bay to the hulking peaks of the Beydağları Range.

Past the tower a flight of steps and a steep street descends to Mermerli Banyo Sokak (Street of the Marble Bath). Turning left brings you to the Mermerli Restaurant (see eating), which has a small strip of beach for its customers, and another flight of stairs that descends to the harbour. Alternatively you could wander up Mermerli Banyo Sokak for a look at one of Kaleiçi's most splendid Ottoman mansions, standing defiantly unrestored on the right. Further up is the **Kale Burcu**, a tower left from the Roman defences which is now used as a shop, and the foundations of a bath complex.

Bazaar District

The place to look for souvenirs or buy picnic stuff is the city's central market, east of the junction of Ali Çetinkaya Caddesi & Ali Fuat Cebesoy Caddesi

To the north of Cumhuriyet Caddesi Antalya's bazaar is a bit disappointing. Though the grid of narrow lanes is bustling with people, the area lacks the character or atmosphere of İstanbul's Covered Bazaar. One interesting exception is the **Iki Kapılı Han**, a 500-year old caravanserai which has recently been renovated. The L-shaped courtyard now hosts an excellent restaurant (see eating) and a row of fabric shops, but in days gone by villagers from the surrounding countryside would converge on the han to sell their produce. To find it turn left next to the Pazar Hamamı, an Ottoman bath complex also now being renovated, and take the second right.

Antalya Museum

One of the best provincial museums in the country, Antalya's diverse collection of archaeological & ethnographic artefacts is definitely worth a visit

Well-displayed in a series of galleries and annotated in English as well as Turkish, the exhibits date back as far as the Stone Age. Of particular interest are the silver and ivory pieces recovered from a Phrygian funerary mound near Elmalı. Also on show are various bits of pottery including some delicate clay figures recovered from a burial chamber in Patara. As you might expect in a region so richly endowed with ancient sites the collection of Roman statuary is very impressive, with all of the 15 classical deities represented in the Gallery of the Gods. One of the rooms is devoted to icons brought from various churches in the province; accompanied by several pieces of bone alleged to be from Saint Nicholas. While next door a horde of 187 gold coins found near Finike form part of the museums' glittering collection of historic money. Save some time for the ethnographic section which includes a display of regional costumes and an interesting assortment of coffee-making paraphernalia, as well as the usual selection of antique weaponry and carpets. ■ *0900-1800 daily except Mon. US$3.50. Getting there: The museum is at the west end of Cumhuriyet Bulvarı about 2½ km from the centre. Get on a tram near Cumhuriyet Meydanı and ride it to the end.*

Beaches

Antalya really isn't a beach resort though there are several places where you could have a swim. Some 3 km west along Cumhuriyet Bulvarı from the centre is **Konyaaltı Plajı**, a long arching swath of pebbly beach overlooked by some of the city's top notch hotels. Convenient for an evening dip, you probably wouldn't want to spend a whole afternoon here, particularly at weekends when it's predictably crowded. About 10 km to the east of the city **Lara** is more promising with a long sandy beach, accessible for a small fee, backed by hotels and condominiums. Lara is accessible by dolmuş (US$0.50) which start across the road to the west of the market or you could opt to stay out near the beach (see sleeping), although most people prefer to stay in town.

There are lots of tour boats moored in the harbour offering a variety of pro- **Boat tours** grammes from multi-day 'Blue Water' cruises to day trips around Antalya bay. A popular excursion is to the **Lower Düden Falls** which cascade into the sea to the east of the city. The tour lasts two to three hours and costs about US$10, with substantial discounts for group bookings. A longer four to six hour trip including visits to the falls, some off-shore islands or Çaltıcak beach, with lunch provided, costs US$15-25. Enquire about the exact itinerary and what you'll be getting to eat for comparison with other operators.

Essentials

Most independent travellers stay in the Kaleiçi area where many of the old tim- **Sleeping:** ber-framed houses have been converted, with varying degrees of success, into pen- **Kaleiçi area** sions and hotels. There is a huge selection to choose from with many places boasting quiet gardens or panoramic roof terraces where you can enjoy your breakfast. Outside the main seasons of Jul and Aug prices are generally open to negotiation, with discounts also given if you decide to forgo breakfast. The city's package and luxury establishments are found along the coast to the east and west of the centre within spitting distance of the beaches.

LL *Sheraton Voyager*, 100 Yıl Bulvarı, Konyaaltı, T2432432, F2432462. To the west of the city centre near the museum, large luxury hotel set in gardens overlooking Konyaaltı beach. **L** *Marina Residence*, Mermerli Sokak No 15, Kaleiçi, T2475490, F2411765. Exclusive 42-room hotel housed in 3 luxuriously renovated old residences set around a pool and restaurant, some of comfortable rooms are a bit on the small side but come very well-equipped with a/c and safe as some of the standard features, attentive service, sauna and Turkish bath. **L** *Dedeman Antalya*, Lara Caddesi, T3213930, F3213873, dedemanhotels.com, on the way to Lara beach, 3 km west of the centre, part of domestic luxury chain, modern rooms have lots of facilities, several restaurants and bars, lively night club, swimming pool, fitness centre, beach access and free entry to adjacent *Aqua Park* water-slides.

A-B *Hotel Alp Paşa*, Hesapçı Sokak No 30, Kaleiçi, T2475676, F2485074, alppasa.com Old mansion converted into smart hotel, many of original features retained, lovely old wooden doors open onto large, individually decorated rooms, some have jacuzzi baths, swimming pool squeezed into coutyard, restaurant. Recommended. **B** *Doğan Hotel*, Mermerli Barıyo Sokak No 5, Kaleiçi, T2474654, F2474006, doganhotel.com 3 buildings around pleasant courtyard with cooling water-feature and swimming pool, comfortable, nicely furnished rooms with a/c, TV, telephone, some of upper rooms have sea-view, very good value. Recommended. **C-D** *Villa Perla*, Hesapçı Sokak No 26, T2489793, F2412917. 12 pleasant rooms in rambling old house, large glazed veranda overlooking quiet courtyard garden with mini-pool, well-regarded restaurant.

E *Mond Pension*, Paşa Camii Sokak No 25, T2471212, F2410763, Kaleiçi. Nice, pine-fitted rooms in elegantly restored old house, small bathrooms, a/c, telephone, top-floor room has private balcony, US$27. Recommended. **E** *Ninova Pension*, Hamit Efendi Sokak No 9, Kaleiçi, T2486114, F2489684. Old stone and wood building with authentically restored exterior, 19 simply furnished but very nice rooms, wooden ceilings and floors throughout, small bathrooms, plenty of room to relax in the shady walled garden, on the balcony or in a comfortable sitting area, evening meals available on request. Recommended. **E** *Hotel Urcu*, Hamit Efendi Sokak No 6, Kaleiçi, T2436700, F2470931. Simply furnished but very spacious rooms in converted old residence surrounded by quiet garden, sofa-bed in each room can be used by third person, a/c, telephone. Recommended. **E** *Antique Pansiyon*, Paşa Camii Sokak No 28, Kaleiçi, T2424615, fatih.sertel@garanti.net.tr Old rambling house, large high-ceiling rooms, breakfast served in small garden at rear. **E** *Begonvil Hotel*, Mescit Sokak No 23, Kaleiçi, T/F2429486. Small rooms with a/c and ensuite in modern building, breakfast served in courtyard.

F *Senem Family Pansion*, Zeytingeçidi Sokak No 9, Kaleiçi, T2471752, F2470615, just behind the Hıdırlık Kulesi. Run by friendly Seval Unsal and her husband, simple but scrupulously clean rooms with tiny ensuite, most rooms open onto balconies, cheaper, smaller rooms at rear of building, one of the best views in Kaleiçi from the roof terrace. Recommended budget choice. **F** *Erkal Pansiyon*, Kandiller Geçidi No 5, T2440159, F2410757. Small bright rooms, with a/c, telephone and the use of a refrigerator they're well-equipped for the price, some have balconies, also larger rooms with sitting area which could accommodate 3 people, US$20. Good budget option. **F** *Sabah Pansiyon*, Hesapçı Sokak No 60, T2475345, F2475347. Family-run place which is popular with backpacking fraternity, helpful English-speaking staff, small, clean rooms with ensuite, available with a/c for US$18, travel agency on-site, bus-tickets, rent-a-car and rafting trips organized, also has a laundry. Recommended. **F** *Dedehan Pansiyon*, Mescid Sokak No 29, T2483787, Kaleiçi. Spacious rooms in old family house, cozy attic rooms are hot in the summer, friendly owners. Recommended. **F** *Yeni Kont Pansiyon*, Kandiller Geçit No 12, T2414990. 8 small rooms in little old house, tiny ensuite. **F** *Kleopatra Pansiyon*, Çikmaz Sokak, T2434721, Kaleiçi. Plain rooms in large, modern building, some more spacious than others and equipped with ceiling fan, superb view from breakfast terrace on the roof and upper balconies. **G** *Tunay Aile Pansiyon*, Mermerli Sokak No 7, Kaleiçi, T2428143. Basic rooms in ramshackled family house, some have ensuite, small sitting area on top floor overlooks castle wall, noise from bar opposite may be a problem. **G** *Çınar Pansiyon*, Paşa Camii Sokak No 33, Kaleiçi, T2481197. Basic rooms with tiny bathroom in badly converted and very rickety old house, single rooms are expensive, small courtyard garden.

Sleeping: Lara
Lara dolmuş which leave from the Doğu Garaj in the city centre pass all the places listed here.

AL *Hotel Sera*, Lara beach, T3493434, F3493454, clubsera.com Large, modern hotel with extensive facilities including casino, pool, tennis courts, night-club. **E** *Motel Ekici*, Lara beach, T3231247, F3232320. about 1 km beyond the Hotel Sera, wooden bungalows with ensuite set in gardens just back from the beach, café and restaurant. Excellent alternative to staying in the city. There are also lots of pretty average hotels catering mainly for Turks and a few German package tourists. These include: **F** *Grand Bistro*, Lara Caddesi No 3888, T3492428, on right before the Sera Hotel, **F** *Şimşek Hotel*, Lara Caddesi, T3493705, on hill down to Sera Hotel, plain rooms but pretty good value with a/c, telephone, swimming pool.

Camping The *Motel Ekici*, (see above) has a camping area and is easily accessible from the city centre. To the west of the city near the harbour is *Denizer Kamping*, T2591765.

Eating   **Expensive** *Marina Residence*, Mermerli Sokak No 15, garden restaurant of Marina Residence Hotel, relaxed ambience, choice of well-cooked dishes including fish from an oversized menu, attentive service.

Midrange *Club 29*, Yatlimanı, a cavernous, candle-lit 200 year-old building overlooking the harbour supplies an unrivalled setting for the evening, wonderful terrace bar for an aperitif, varied, tasty menu and after dinner move next door to the night-club which gets going in the small hours. **Cumba Restaurant**, Kocatepe Sokak No 3, Kaleiçi, down-to-earth place with plastic tables and chairs scattered around a leafy garden, live *fasıl* music nightly which doesn't seem to impress the resident duck, menu is meat orientated: meze, grilled chicken and kebaps, good value at about US$6 per head with a beer. **Mermerli Restaurant**, Mermerli Banyo Sokak, Kaleiçi, varied menu including fresh fish and meat dishes, specials such as 'Balkan Kebabı' – a beef casserole with mushrooms, topped with cheese – superb views along coast, relax after lunch on their small private beach. **Han Restaurant**, Paşa Camii Sokak, Kaleiçi, 1 of a large number of garden restaurants in the Kaleiçi, tables set-out in a large leafy courtyard, choose from a selection of meze, fish, grilled meat dishes and kebaps, in the evening you'll be serenaded by live fasıl, a genre of Turkish classical music, reckon on about US$10 per head before wine. **Villa Perla,** Hesapçı Sokak No 26, recommended restaurant in leafy courtyard of small pension, Turkish/ Mediterranean menu includes some unusual dishes, about US$12-15 per head. **Yeşil Antalya 'Balık Evi',** Yatlimanı, run by the a local fishing co-operative, you can rely on this place for fresh seafood, very reasonable prices and good service, pizza and pasta dishes aren't bad either, on the downside despite its waterfront location it's not the most atmospheric of places.

Cheap The Ottoman sherbet-makers who gave this street its name are long-gone and instead **Eski Şerbetçiler Sokak** is often jokingly referred to as "Dönerciler Çarşısı", "Market of the Döner-makers". It certainly lives up to its new name with a long, modern arcade of cheap eateries serving döner, as well as other kebaps, *kokoreç* (fried tripe) and *midye dolması* (stuffed mussels). Many of these place also serve *kuzu tandır*, large pieces of fatty roast mutton sold by weight, with a 200 gram portion costing about US$3.50. Competition is stiff and you'll be collared by insistent waiters eager to guide you up to their respective dining areas on the 1st floor.

Demirciler İçi Less frenetic are the row of restaurants on 419 Sokak, known as Demirciler İçi, which starts next to the PTT office on İsmet Paşa Caddesi. **Islama Köftecisi,** serves meat-balls and piyaz (white-bean salad), along with *Şiş kebabı* and other grills. **Mustafa'nın Yeri,** has a similar menu with sweet *kabak tatlısı* (pumpkin pudding) to finish-off. **Değirmen,** sells börek, baked pastry, for US$2.50 a portion, with a choice of meat (*kıymalı*), cheese (*peynirli*) or spinach filling (*ıspanaklı*). **Arnavut Çigeri,** specializes in fried spicy liver.

Bazaar and Kaleiçi At **Gaziantep Dürüm Restaurant** in the bazaar area you can enjoy a meal of meze, fish, grilled meat and kebaps in slightly more refined surroundings. To find it turn left from next to the Pazar hamamı and then take the first right. The best restaurant in the bazaar area, however, is the **Hancı** which for lunch serves an excellent selection of really tasty ready prepared stews at shaded tables in the courtyard of the recently restored İki Kapılı Han. There's *fasıl* music at lunch and during the evening, when meze and grilled meat dishes, such as *çerkez pirzola*, marinated lamb-chops baked with a covering of sauteed potatoes, are on offer. For a quick bite to eat in Kaleiçi try the **Karavan Cafe,** at the top of the steps leading down behind the İskele Camii, which does *gözleme* with traditional fillings like cheese, potatoes, spinach or meat, US$1.75, washed down with a glass of freshly squeezed orange juice, US$1.50. **Yörükoğlu** on Paşa Camii Sokak near to the mosque fills the street with the enticing aroma of grilled meatballs, US$3.50, during the evening.

Vegetarian **Vejetaryen,** Haşim İşcan Mahallesi, 1295 Sokak No 5, simple but interesting veggie menu changed daily, dine in 1 of several rooms of old house or the garden, also a health-food shop selling a limited range of organic foods, venue for talks and classes (generally in Turkish).

Cafés *Cafe Rolan,* Cumhuriyet Caddesi, tables overlooking Kaleiçi and harbour, lovely place at breakfast time for a coffee with a pastry bought from the *Ayda Pastanesi* opposite the Tourist Office. In the evening join the promenading families in Mermerli and Karaalioğlu Parks where there are numerous tea gardens to relax. *Yeni Kahramanmaraş Pastanesi,* Ali Çetinkaya Caddesi, rather inconveniently situated 250 m east of the market, this family-run place has a major reputation for its glutinous ice-cream, walls are hung with kilims and signed photographs of admiring politicians and prime ministers.

Entertainment **Art galleries** *Güzel Sanatlar Galerisi,* housed in Mevlevi tekke which is part of Yivli Camii complex, Kaleiçi. Entrance free. Open 0900-1800. **Festivals** A series of concerts, ballet and operatic performances are held in the antique theatre at *Aspendos* during Jun. Programs and tickets are available from an office near the Tourist information, with a complimentary coach service to and from the venue for ticket holders. During the **Altın Portakal Film Festivalı,** held every year from the last week of Sep to the first week of Oct, cinemas across the city show foreign and Turkish films.

Shopping For souvenirs you could try the stalls at the top of Uzun Çarşı Sokak, Kaleiçi, which are leased to local craftsmen by ANSAN, the city's association of artisans. Another place to look for gifts or to buy picnic stuff is the city's main food and clothing market east of the junction of Ali Çetinkaya Caddesi and Ali Fuat Cebesoy Caddesi. **Books** *Ardıç Kitabevi,* Selekler Çarşısı No 67, in the modern shopping plaza to the west of the Tourist information office, small selection of English books and maps. *Owl Bookshop,* Akar Çeşme Sokak No 21, Kaleiçi, new and second-hand bookshop with lots of English titles.

Sports **Motorcross** *AS Adventure,* Mescit Sokak No 9, Kaleiçi, T2432009, F2445692, adventuretour.netfirms.com, cross-country guided motorbike holidays, flexible programs, also BMW bike rental from US$75 per day.

Tour agencies There are dozens of tour agents in Kaleiçi and along Cumhuriyet Caddesi offering daily tours to the local sights, as well as multi-day trips to Cappadocia and Pamukkale. *Yanartaş Turizm,* Özel Idaire Çarşısı, Cumhuriyet Caddesi, next to the *Turkish Airlines* office.

Transport **Air** *Turkish Airlines,* Özel Idare Işhanı Altı, Cumhuriyet Caddesi, T2434383, F2484761, have 3 daily flight to **Ankara** and 4 to **İstanbul**. Service buses leave regularly for the airport from outside the office, US$2. **Bus** There are numerous bus company offices on Cumhuriyet and Atatürk Caddesi and they usually provide a free service bus to the otogar for their passengers. Grey 'terminal' buses pass Kalekapısı as do dolmuş labelled for 'Yeni Otogar'. **Adana**, (via Anamur and Silifke), 5-6 daily, 12 hrs, US$13. **Alanya**, every 20-30 mins, 2 hrs, US$4. **Ankara**, regular buses, 8 hrs, US$11, **Bodrum**, several direct buses or change at Muğla, 11 hrs, US$13. **Eğirdir**, regular buses to Isparta where you'll need to change onto a dolmuş, 3 hrs, US$5. **Fethiye**, very regular service but make sure you get a yayla bus which takes direct inland route, 4 hrs, instead of the sahil (coastal) bus, 8 hrs, US$6. **Göreme/Ürgüp**, several evening buses, 10 hrs, US$15. **İstanbul**, regular buses, 13 hrs, US$20. **Kaş**, every 30 mins, 4 hrs, US$4. **Olympos/Çıralı**, get on a Kaş bus, 90 mins, US$2.50. **Pamukkale**, regular Denizli buses some of which continue to Pamukkale, 4½ hrs, US$7. **Side/Manavgat**, every 20-30 mins, 1½ hrs, US$2. The deluxe company Varan have nightly services to **Ankara**, **İstanbul** and **İzmir**. They have an office on Cumhuriyet Caddesi, next to the Tourist Office. Aksu buses for **Perge** stop at the beginning of Aspendos Bulvarı, a 10-min walk down Ali Çetinkaya Caddesi from the centre. **Car rental** In Kaleiçi there are dozens of small, local firms offering very competitive rates: about US$25 per day for a Fiat Uno or Tofaş Şahin. *Say Rent-a-Car,* Mescit Caddesi No 22, T2430923,

F2430924, is recommended. The large international chains have offices in the city and at the airport: *Avis*, Fevzi Çakmak Caddesi, Talya Apartments, No 67/B, T2425642, F2419483. *Hertz,* Gençlik Mahallesi, Fevzi Çakmak Caddesi, 1312 Sokak No 5/2Gençlik Mahallesi, T2415711, F2473268.

Banks There are many banks with ATM and change facilities on Cumhuriyet Caddesi and Ismet Paşa Caddesi. Private döviz which keep longer hrs are also well-represented around Kalekapısı and the bazaar. **Baths** *Sefa Hamamı,* Kocatepe Sokak, Kaleiçi, vintage baths which are over 600 years old, still heated by wood-burning underfloor system, US$10 for a kese and massage. Open 0600-2400. *Nazır Hamamı,* Paşa Camii Sokak, Kaleiçi, another old bathhouse, US$8 kese and massage. Open 0700-2300, mixed sex. **Communications Internet**: *Ayda Internet,* Cumhuriyet Caddesi, above Ayda Pastanesi which is opposite *Turkish Airlines*, US$1 per hr. *Natural Internet*, next to fountain in shopping arcade to west of Cumhuriyet Meydanı, US$2 per hr. **Post office**: There is a post office with post, telephone and fax facilities on Ismet Paşa Caddesi. **Consulates** UK, Kızılsaray Mahallesi, Dolapdere Caddesl, Pırıllı Sitesi, Kat 1, T2477000. **Norway**, Cumhuriyet Caddesi, 59 Sokak, No 8, T2411622. **Russian**, *Ofo Otel*, Lara, T3494000. **Sweden**, Gün Oto Aş, Konyaaltı Bulvarı No 78, T2489061. **Hospitals** *Devlet Hastanesi* (State Hospital), Pınar Caddesi, inland from the museum. **Universite Hastanesi**, west of the city on Dumlupınar Caddesi, better equipped and staffed than state hospital. **Laundry** *Sabah Pansiyon* (see sleeping), Hesapçı Sokak No 60, US$5 per load for wash and dry. **Places of Worship** *International Church of Antalya*, St Paul's Cultural Centre, Yenikapı Sokak No 24, Kaleiçi, T2446894, services Sun 1100 and Wed 1900. **Tourist information** Cumhuriyet Caddesi, Özel Idaire Işhanı Altı, T/F2411747. Open 0830-1730, 1800 in summer. **Useful addresses** *Mediterranean Civilizations Research Institute* Kocatepe Sokak No 25, Kaleiçi, akmed.org.tr Sponsored by the Rehmi Koç Foundation, library and resources for historical and archaeological research, also has an exhibition centre. *Toros Doğa Sporları Klübü,* T2481391, club with programme of outdoor activities, frequent trips to surrounding mountains. *Tourism Police,* Kaleiçi Yat Limanı, T2431061, F3454113. By the harbour in the old city. *Turkish Touring and Automobile Association*, Milli Egemenlik Caddesi, Dallar Yıldız Çarşısı No 9, T2470699, F2484574. *Turkish Maritime Lines*, Akça Denizcilik, Konyaaltı Caddesi, S Gürsoy Apartments No 40/19, T2411170, F2475095.

Around Antalya

There are a number of places to visit beyond the city limits, however, some, such as Katrain and Kurşunlu Şelalesi, are a bit problematic to reach without your own transport. Consider hiring a car from one of the many reasonably priced rental agencies in Kaleiçi and including these attractions in a longer excursion to visit the ancient cities of Pamphylia or Köprülü Kanyon. Another alternative is to hire a taxi or join a tour organised by one of the many travel agents in Antalya.

Just clear of the city's northern suburbs is the waterfall of Yukarı (Upper) Düden enclosed within a wooded park managed by the state water authority. The falls themselves, with a concrete pathway running behind them, are a pleasant enough sight on a hot day, though they're certainly nothing to get excited about. The ruthless pedestrianisation of the surrounding area with its ranks of picnic tables, snack bars and souvenir stands hardly adds to the natural spectacle either, particularly at weekends when it's choked with day trippers. The Lower Düden falls which cascade into the sea to the east of town can be visited on a boat tour from Antalya's harbour (see Sights). ■ *0700-2000, 1800 in winter, daily. Getting there: Dolmuş (US$0.40) depart from Ali Çetinkaya Caddesi, across from the market, or catch a no 14 bus from near the Petrol Ofisi station beside the market.*

Düden Şelalesi

Marginally less commercialised than Düden is the Kurşunlu waterfall, 18 km east of Antalya near the town of Aksu. Reached through a pine wood dotted

Kurşunlu Şelalesi

with picnic tables, a path descends into a lush canyon where the falls cascade into an emerald pool teeming with well-fed fish. It's a beautiful spot, but the enticing water is off-limits so there is very little to detain you unless you've brought some picnic stuff. ■ *0800-1900, 1730 in winter, daily. US$0.50. Getting there: Kurşunlu Şelalesi is signposted off the coastal highway east of the airport. There are no dolmuş to the falls, so you'd have to get on an Aksu-bound bus and hitch from the highway.*

Termessos

One of the most rewarding excursions from Antalya is to the ancient city of Termessos, dramatically nestling high in the rugged limestone mountains to the west of the city

The ruins are enclosed within the **Güllük Dağı National Park**, created as much in recognition of the area's natural beauty and wildlife as its history. Termessos was inhabited from the earliest times by a war-like people mentioned by Homer in *The Iliad* as "the glorious Solymoi". They shared a language with the tribes who settled in the rugged mountains to the north of Pamphylia; hence the city's classification as a Pisidian, rather than a Lycian, city. Little is known about the Termessos until 333 BC, when it successfully held-out against the forces of Alexander the Great. The Termessians did their fair share of attacking too, however, going to war with neighbouring Lycia and Isinda on several occasions. In the Mithridates Wars they judiciously sided with the Romans, subsequently concluding a treaty of friendship with Rome that gave the fiercely independent Termessians significant autonomy within the empire.

From the park entrance the ruins are a 9 km climb up through beautiful forest cloaking the slopes of Güllük Dağı (1,066 m). The road ends at a car park beside the fragmentary remains of a **temple of Hadrian**, formerly entered through the ceremonial gateway – the only part of the structure left standing. A steep path strikes up the canyon following the approximate route of the **King's Road**, an ancient thoroughfare constructed in the second century using donations from the citizens of the city. After a short climb the path passes the **outer wall** which, like the rest of the city's defences, remains in good condition with a gate and watchtower still partially intact. Look out for an inscription on the inside of the wall to the left of the gate which has been identified as part of a "dice oracle". These consisted of a numbered list of prophesies carved into the wall of a temple or public place which would be selected at random by the role of several dice, known as astragali. Far more convenient than traipsing off to the nearest oracular shrine, which could be a considerable distance away, this form of fortune-telling enjoyed mass appeal during Roman times. Not surprisingly the pronouncements were very vague, typically offering only positive and negative responses that would fit any question posed.

After a stiff climb the path levels off and hidden amongst the bushes are a **gymnasium** and part of a **colonnaded street**. The best, however, is yet to come, because the **theatre**, overlooking the rocky slopes of Güllük Dağı and a steep sided canyon dropping down to the coastal plain, is certainly one of the most impressive in the country. A small theatre with a capacity of about 4,000, it's essentially a Greek style structure, though later it underwent extensive Roman modifications.

Nearby to the south are the remnants of a small **odeon** that was used for spectator sports such as wrestling, a second gymnasium and the well-preserved **temple of Zeus**, the divine patron of Termessos. A short walk further up the hill brings you to the city's extensive **necropolis** with tombs chaotically scattered amongst the trees and bushes. Most of the sarcophagi bare an inscription identifying the occupant, which is often accompanied by a warning of the financial penalties incurred by those caught desecrating the tomb. Walking back down the hill a path breaks left towards the grand, relief-decorated **tomb of Alcetas**, one of Alexander the Great's general who held the area briefly after the Macedonian commander's death.

■ *0800-1800, 1700 in winter, daily. US$2.50, car US$3.50. Getting there: The entrance to the Termessos Milli Parkı is clearly marked on the E-87/D350 highway, 28 km west of Antalya. Leaving the city follow signs for Burdur and Isparta, turning onto the E-87, signposted for Korkuteli, Denizli and Muğla, about 10 km beyond the city limits. With your own transport you could combine a visit to Termessos with a look at the Karain Cave (see below). To reach Termessos by public transport get on a Korkuteli-bound bus from Antalya otogar and get-off at the national park entrance. From there it's a 2 hr walk up to the site, though you may be able to hitch a lift.*

On-going excavations at the Karain Cave, hidden in a wooded valley in the **Karain Cave** mountains to the northwest of the city, have revealed a staggering history of human occupation spanning over 20,000 years during the Palaeolithic era (30,000 BC to 8,000 BC). Occupied by a tribe of primitive hunter-gatherers, archaeologists have discovered a range of stone tools and weapons, bone implements and skeletal fragments from humans and exotic species, such as elephants and rhinoceros, which formerly inhabited the area. The best of these discoveries are now on display in the Antalya Museum and the Museum of Anatolian Civilisation in Ankara, although a modest selection have been kept for the small on-site museum. From the museum it's a 15 minute walk up to the caverns themselves which are set into a cliff face high above the valley floor.
■ *Getting there: You need your own transport to visit Karain. Coming from Antalya take the Burdur/Isparta highway and turn-off at a road on the left which is signposted for Karain, Yeşilkoy and Yeşilbayır after the E-87 highway to Korkuteli. Alternatively, there is a signposted side road off the E-87 near the entrance to Termessos, from where it's 12 km to the site.*

The Pamphylian Plain

East of Antalya the Taurus Mountains retreat into the hazy distance and the busy coastal highway cuts across an agriculturally rich and well-watered plain planted with cotton fields and vegetables. To the ancients this fertile region was known as Pamphylia, a land settled in the second millennium by Greek tribes, often referred to as the "mixed multitude", who drifted south from the northern Aegean establishing a series of cities along the Mediterranean seaboard. Hemmed-in by mountains Pamphylia was a remote region, cut-off from the major routes of trade and communication to the north, and hence side-lined for much of history. Despite this the Pamphylian cities of Perge, Sillyon, Aspendos and Side developed into important centres of regional culture and trade, a position they maintained through Hellenistic and Roman times. For the modern visitor the ruins of these ancient cities are the area's main attraction. All can be reached as an excursion from Antalya, though outside the main summer months you could also base yourself in Side, which has metamorphosed into one of the Turkish Mediterranean's largest holiday resorts.

Perge

Within easy day trip range of Antalya, the ruins of Perge are the most extensive and impressive of any of the ancient Pamphylian cities. Legend has it that the settlement was founded by the "mixed multitudes", though the first solid reference to the city comes in the fourth century BC. A thriving riverine port city, Perge seems to have welcomed the arrival of Alexander the Great in 333 BC and he subsequently used the city as a base for his operations in Pamphylia.

Perge was renowned for its temple of Artemis Pergaea which enjoyed generous donations from devotees and was awarded the coveted right to offer asylum by Emperor Domitian in the first century AD. Sometime later St Paul visited the city and as a metropolitan bishopric it sent a representative to the influential Council of Nicaea in 325 AD. Perge maintained its importance into Byzantine times but the Persian and Arab invasions reduced it to a village.

The site Approaching the site you pass Perge's 14,000 seat **theatre**, originally constructed during the Hellenistic era but modified later by the Romans. On the other side of the road is a large **stadium**, open at the southern end to allow charioteers or competitors to enter the arena.

Having curved around the stadium you reach the car park and ticket office, to the north of which is the **walled city**, enclosed within its third century Seleucid defences. Outside the ramparts, to the right of a small Roman gateway, is the **tomb of Plancia Magna**, a woman who simultaneously held the posts of high priestess at the temple of Artemis and city governoress. Her name appears in dozens of inscription, identifying her as the benefactor of many of the town's monuments and public buildings.

Passing through the gateway there are the foundations of a **Byzantine basilica** on your right, opposite which are the remains of a **Roman baths complex**. However, the view ahead is dominated by something far more impressive: a **Hellenistic gateway** flanked by two solid stone towers. This magnificent portal is the only surviving part of the original city defences, although the inner court and the monumental archway are later additions. The niches around the inner courtyard were formerly occupied by statues of the city's legendary founders, including Calchas and Mopsus, supposed leaders of the great migration from Troy.

As you walk back along the avenue notice that some of the antique paving slabs have been rutted by the passage of cart & chariot wheels

From the inner courtyard you have a sweeping view north up what was the city's main thoroughfare. This wide **colonnaded avenue** was lined with marble statues and shops, and divided in the middle by a water channel running from an elaborate fountain at the far end. The reclining figure that decorates this **nymphaeum**, now sadly missing its head, is a deification of the river Cestrus, known today as the Aksu river.

Turning west at a crossroads in the main street brings you to the **palaestra**, a Roman gymnasium complex that would have included classrooms and baths around a central courtyard. A **necropolis** lies beyond the city walls to the west; while the **acropolis** provides a good vantage point from which to survey the site.

■ *Daily 0800-1900, 1730 in winter. US$3, parking US$0.75. Getting there: Perge is 2 km north of the town of Aksu which is 15 km east of Antalya on the coastal highway. Without your own transport get a bus to Aksu from the roundabout at the end of Ali Çetinkaya Caddesi in Antalya. From Aksu it's a 10-15 minute or you may be able to hitch. It's possible to combine an excursion to Perge with a visit to Aspendos or even Köprülü Kanyon and Selge.*

Sillyon Far less visited than either Perge or Aspendos, the ruins of ancient Sillyon may be worth a look if you have your own transport, especially if you enjoy savouring such sites without a crowd of other tourists around. The city occupied a flat-topped mesa which is still a prominent landmark visible for some distance across the Pamphylian Plain. Sillyon's naturally defensible position enabled it to repulse an attack by Alexander the Great in 333 BC. He continued on his way after this failure and the city sinks back into obscurity, never to appear again in the historical records.

A pair of stone ramps guarded by several towers gives access to the mountain-top, on which are scattered the remains of ancient houses; a well-preserved city gate and a theatre. Of particular interest to archaeologists was the discovery of a door jamb inscribed with a lengthy inscription in Pamphylian, a dialect of ancient Greek of which few examples have survived.

■ *Getting there: Without your own transport it's a fairly major walk, unless you're lucky enough to hitch a lift. Turn north off the coastal highway at a signposted side road opposite the entrance to the Belek Turizm Merkezi. The ruins are 1 km beyond the village of Asar Koyü which is about 8 km from the main road.*

Aspendos

A distinguished city of ancient Pamphylia, today Aspendos is synonymous with its wonderfully preserved Roman theatre which ranks among the finest in Asia Minor and still hosts productions to this day. The city, though, was founded considerably before the days of Rome, by Greek settlers from Argos in the Peloponnese, later coming under Persian rule. In 467 BC the Persian fleet was beaten in a famous engagement off the Pamphylian coast and Aspendos became a member of the Delian League paying tribute to Athens. The city again came under the Persian yoke in 411 BC, only to be liberated by Alexander the Great. The Aspendians welcomed the Macedonian commander with open arms surrendering their city and agreeing to his terms. But shortly after his departure they reneged on their agreement, fortifying the city's defences and refusing to part with the horses they'd promised to provide. On hearing of the Aspendians treachery Alexander promptly returned where his renewed presence was enough to force the city into another, far less favourable, treaty.

During the Roman era Aspendos prospered modestly exporting locally produced salt across the empire. The city issued coinage declaring itself the "proud and honoured... ally of Romans", and during the second century AD an architect named Zeno constructed the famous theatre. Although its good fortune initially continued under the Byzantines, Aspendos later shared the fate of the other Pamphylian cities, suffering at the hands of Persian and Arab invaders. Occupied by the Selçuks in 1078, by the time the Ottomans took over in 1392 Aspendos had been reduced to a small village which was subsequently abandoned.

The theatre Approaching Aspendos from the coastal highway you first pass through the village of Belkis whose houses are dwarfed by huge tax-free shopping centres and restaurants frequented by visiting coach parties. Arriving at the site (*open daily, 0800-1900, 1730 in winter, US$3*) the car park is overshadowed by the impressive multi-storey backstage building, later converted by the Selçuks into an imperial residence. The theatre entrance leads directly into the orchestra with the 20,000 seat auditorium rising up steeply in front of you. Partly built into the acropolis mound, the upper stories of the semi-circular cavea are supported on barrel vaults.

Climbing up past the front row, which was reserved for VIPs, you get an excellent view of the backstage building towering 25 m above the present wooden stage. The facade of this structure, a typical feature of Roman as opposed to Greek theatres, was richly adorned with marble columns and statuary and in the centre a relief showing Dionysus surrounded by floral patterns has survived on part of the pediment. Despite losing most of the rest of its decorative marble, it still makes a stunning backdrop for contemporary theatrical and musical performances.

It's well worth getting **tickets** if you're in the area when a production is on because crowded with people and filled with sound you get an unrivalled feeling for what things must have been like nearly 2,000 years ago. Look out for posters advertising upcoming events, usually held during July and August, or contact local Tourist Information Offices. In Antalya you can buy tickets from a booth next to the Turkish Airlines and Tourist Office. Seats are very reasonable at about US$5, including a bus service to and from the theatre. In fact, we largely have Atatürk to thank for the theatre's continued use as he proclaimed after a visit that it should be returned to its original function rather than converted into a museum.

Other ruins Not having benefited from the attention lavished on the theatre, ancient Aspendos' other remains are of only passing interest, although the walk itself can be enjoyable, also giving you the opportunity to view the theatre from another prospective. A path between the theatre and the toilets leads up to the top of the acropolis, passing a badly deteriorated **stadium** on the right and climbing an original section of road, complete with a central channel for drainage, to an **ornamental gateway**. Partly hidden by undergrowth, the remains of a **council chamber**, **agora** and **Byzantine basilica** are scattered across the hill top, with a well-preserved **Roman aqueduct** found 200 m to the north.

■ *Getting there: Aspendos is signposted off the coastal highway just over 40 km east of Antalya near a recently restored Selçuk bridge across the Köprülü Çayı. If you're coming by bus from Antalya, Serik or Manavgat-bound services will drop you at the turn-off, from where you'll need to hitch, walk or catch an overpriced taxi the last 4 km to the site passing through the village of Belkıs. From the east Antalya-bound buses can also drop you at the turn-off.*

Köprülü Kanyon National Park and Selge

High in the forested Taurus mountains the Köprülü Kanyon National Park has been created around a majestic Roman bridge which spans a deep canyon formed by the Köprülü Çayı, a river that's the focus for numerous local rafting operations. Even if you don't intend shooting the rapids, a visit to the Köprülü Kanyon gives you the chance to escape the oppressive summer heat on the coast and to see some beautiful mountain scenery. Another reason to make the journey is to visit the isolated village of Zerk, 12 km beyond Köprülü Kanyon, where a collection of stone houses cluster amongst the ruins of ancient Selge.

Ins & outs A sideroad signposted for Köprülü Kanyon (45 km) and Beşkonak (37 km) leaves the coastal highway 5 km east of the turning for Aspendos, 48 km east of Antalya. With your own transport it's possible to visit Selge and Köprülü Kanyon in a day trip from Antalya, possibly also stopping off at Aspendos or Perge along the way. The approach is on a windy but good quality black-top through cultivated valleys and forested mountains. About 30 km off the coastal highway you reach a road on the left which crosses the Köprülü river and progresses up the opposite side of the valley to the Roman bridge. Instead of taking this it makes sense to continue straight on and approach the bridge through the village of Beşkonak, returning via the other, rougher, road if you have your own transport. From Beşkonak it's just over 7 km to the bridge which it's still possible to drive across. On the opposite side a road climbs steeply for 12 km up to the village of Zerk, officially known as Altınkaya, and the ruins of Selge. The last section is very rough but passable in an ordinary car.

Without your own transport visiting Köprülü Kanyon and Selge generally means staying overnight in the mountains, unless you can afford US$90 to hire a taxi from Antalya for the day. One daily dolmuş leaves for Beşkonak and Zerk (2½ hrs, US$1.50) from behind the Belediye building in Serik at about 1430 each day, returning first thing the next morning. Serik is served by regular buses from Antalya, but if you're approaching from Alanya you'll have to get off on the coastal highway and walk 500 m north into town. If time is not a problem hitching up or down shouldn't be too much of a problem in summer.

Köprülü Kanyon

Approaching the canyon there's a large logging camp beside the road and a row of restaurants from where raft loads of tourists set-off down river. At the far end the *Köprülü Restaurant* serves fresh trout and salad (*US$3.50*) at tables set out on shady riverside platforms. About 150 m beyond the restaurant, the bridge itself is in remarkable shape considering it's been in use for about 2,000 years, although if anything a recent restoration job has made it look too new. On the far side of the span a narrow rocky path heads up the canyon passing above several large, river-sized springs issuing forth from the canyon walls. Several places demand some care to negotiate but after 250 m the canyon widens and there's a secluded spot to swim and picnic.

A much more popular, and on summer weekends crowded, picnic place is reached by descending the road on the other side of the bridge for 500 m to where it crosses a picturesque stone bridge. There's a very inviting pool for swimming, overlooked by a shady gazebo where you could surreptitiously roll-out your sleeping bag in summer. Continuing down this stabilised road takes you past several rafting centres as well as the F *Kanyon Pansiyon* and the F *Selge Restaurant and Pension*, eventually bringing you out at the road down to the coast.

Selge

Guides & mules can also be arranged in the village for the 2-3 day trip up Bozburun Dağı

From the Roman bridge the road climbs steeply, switchbacking upwards into a landscape of strangely eroded limestone formations scattered with cypress and pine trees. Magnificent vistas open up across the surrounding mountains and far below the Köprülü Çayı is visible snaking its way northwards. At 900 m above sea-level the village of **Zerk** is little more than a dozen or so houses scattered around a small cultivated basin where in summer crops of barley, wheat and vetch are grown. Walnut and chestnut trees shelter many of the stone buildings which are overlooked by an amphitheatre built into a rocky slope to the north. This theatre, dramatically silhouetted against the peaks of the Bozburun Dağları, is the most visible remnant of the ancient city of Selge.

The origins of the settlement are obscure, though it's clear from various sources that the Selgians were gifted in the arts of governance and war. They also became prosperous exporting storax, a fragrant resin sourced from liquidambar trees which was valued for its medicinal properties and as an ancient perfume. In 333 BC the Selgians judiciously surrender to Alexander the Great as he approached, however, up until its first century incorporation into the Roman empire the city remained wholly independent, protected from would-be aggressors by its remoteness and isolation. Considering the present communities problematic water supply it seems amazing that a city with a population that reached 20,000 at its peak could have been supported in these dry mountains, but Selge survived in one form or another well into the Byzantine period.

Arriving today you pay a nominal charge at the entrance to the village, before proceeding along a track past the school. Village children frantically try and persuade you to park outside their house, for which you'll be asked for a small fee. Most visitors also accept the services of one of these youngsters as a guide for which they'll deserve a small tip. A tour of the ruins usually begins at the **theatre** which survived remarkably intact until a bolt of lightning during a storm in 1948 reduced the stage building to the heap of rubble you see today. The cavea has faired better and from its top there's an uninterrupted view across to the rocky peak of Bozburun Dağı (2504 m). An even better vista awaits those who climb a hill to the southwest of the village, which is crowned by a jumble of stone that archaeologists have identified as a **temple of Zeus**, as well as a large **cistern**. Walking back east the remains of a **Byzantine church** and Selge's **agora** are on a lower hill overlooking the village. Apart from bits of a **stadium** that have been incorporated into several houses beside the theatre, there's very little else of ancient Selge to see, although the charming contemporary village and its rugged setting are worth the journey in themselves. If you want to prolong your stay overnight several of the families in the village will offer you a place to sleep for a small sum, although you should bring a sleeping bag or blanket with you.

Rafting on the Köprülü Çayı   Although experienced rafters and adrenaline junkies may scoff at the Köprülü Çayı, a rafting trip down the river can be fun, particularly in the spring when the water is at its highest. Rafting trips are now on offer in all the coastal resorts with a typical package including transport to and from the river, equipment, lunch and insurance. With over 50 operators now working on the river competition is fierce and prices are dropping fast. Expect to pay US$30-50 for the excursion.

Side

Phone code: 0242
Colour map 4, grid B5

Side, meaning "pomegranate" in some long-forgotten Anatolian tongue, enjoys a superb position on a promontory sticking out into the Mediterranean. Chosen by the ancients for its natural defensibility and harbour; the last 20 years have seen the peninsula colonised seasonally by foreign tourists, attracted primarily by those magic ingredients of a beach holiday: sun, sea and sand. The scale of this annual invasion, accompanied by the inevitable hotels, restaurants, carpet shops, leather outlets and change bureaux, has completely overwhelmed yesterday's sleepy fishing village, turning it instead into something which at times resembles an ill-planned historical theme park. Having said that, Side remains a very popular package resort, particularly suited for families with young children or those who are looking simply for some relaxed beach time. Far less brash and on a more human scale than Alanya, there are some pleasant small hotels tucked away in the quiet backstreets, while the ruins of the ancient city are never more than a stone's throw away. High season should certainly be avoided as things are hopelessly crowded, but things are far less hectic outside the summer months.

Ins & outs
See page 396 for further details

Getting there Side is well sign-posted off the coastal highway several km west of Manavgat. During the summer some bus companies run direct services to **Side**, although most will drop you in **Manavgat**, 4 km away, from where you'll need to catch a dolmuş (US$0.40). Dolmuş pass on the bus station side of the coastal highway every 10 mins, so just walk up to the dolmuş stop and wait. Alternatively, the bus may dropped you at the Side turnoff on the coastal highway, where again you can just wait for a dolmuş. **Getting around** The centre of Side is closed to all but essential vehicles from 1400-0100, so it's best to leave your car in the car park and then walk or take a tractor pulled train into the village. Buses and dolmuş also drop you at the car park, from where it's 500 m down Side Caddesi, past the museum and the ruined city, into the centre. Side village itself is very compact and there's no need for anything but your legs to get around.

History   Founded around 600 BC by Aeolian Greek settlers from the Aegean coast, Side gained an infamous reputation as an important centre for the regional slave trade. Hundreds of thousands of slaves passed through its markets each year with the city elders turning a blind eye to the illegal, but highly profitable, business. Despite its ill-gotten wealth the city played little part in the broader machinations of history, surrendering to Alexander the Great in 333 BC and later becoming part of the Seleucid realm. As a Roman free-city Side continued to be an entrepot for Cilician slavers and pirates until Pompey finally cleared the coast in 67 BC. In spite of losing its illicit revenues the city continued to flourish, surviving attacks by Scythian corsairs and Isaurian tribesmen to become a thriving Byzantine port-city and the seat of a bishopric. However, the Arab invasions of the seventh century sent the city into a rapid decline with the site eventually abandoned and its inhabitants moved to Antalya. And so it remained for 900 years, a desolate site buried in wind-blown sand, until it was occupied by Greek-speaking Turks who fled from Crete at the beginning of the 20th century.

Sights

Although 19th-century visitors commented on the paucity of Side's remains, **Ancient Side** over 50 years of diligent work by archaeologists have transformed the site and the modern resort is now surrounded by ancient ruins. Approaching from the car park the road passes through the **defensive wall** which once secured the landward side on the city against attack. Beside the road on-going excavations have revealed part of a **colonnaded street** that led south-west from the main gate to the city's **agora**, on the left, where unfortunate slaves were bought and sold. The area is currently closed due to work on the adjacent theatre, though there's not much to see anyway apart from rows of column bases and the structure's foundations.

On the opposite side of the road housed in a clumsily renovated fifth century bath house is the local **museum**. On display are a wealth of marble statues, sarcophagi and reliefs recovered from the site and watched over today by a bust of the late Dr Arif Müfid Mansel who led the excavations from 1947 to 1966. Unfortunately, most of the statues were defaced by religious zealots during the early Christian era. ■ *0800-1200, 1300-1700, daily except Mon, US$3.*

From the museum the road passes through a Roman **monumental gateway** which was partially closed-up during Byzantine times when a second city wall was constructed across the peninsula to secure it against attack. Next to the wall is a small **fountain** built in 74 AD to honour Emperors Vespasian and Titus. The largest and most impressive of Side's ancient ruins is the 20,000 seat Graeco-Roman **theatre**, one of the biggest of its kind in Anatolia and visible for miles across the surrounding countryside. Constructed on the site of an earlier Hellenistic structure, it has a three-storey free-standing auditorium which doesn't rely on a hill or mountainside for support. Originally built for hosting theatrical performances it was later also used for city meetings and gladiatorial contests. Restorators are currently shoring up the building, hence the crane, though it is usually still open to visitors.

On the tip of the peninsula commanding the entrance to the ancient harbour stood the city's main religious monuments, the **temples of Apollo** and **Athena**. Dated by archaeologists to the second century AD, little remains of the two identical Corinthian temples except for a jumble of marble fragments scattered across the ground. Five creamy-white columns have been re-erected to give some idea of the scale and grandeur of the original structure, while also providing a very evocative silhouette against the evening sky. To the east of the temples are the ruins of a large **Byzantine basilica**. Scattered in the backstreets are several antique **bath complexes**, while the path to the east beach passes through a gate in the city walls into an open area scattered with fragments of carved marble which are thought to have been part of a second **agora** or market place.

Western Mediterranean

Beaches Modern Side's reason d'etre are its excellent beaches which stretch away to the east and west of town. For much of their length they're backed by luxury hotels and beach restaurants, with sun-loungers and watersports on offer at regular intervals. Although hardly ideal if you're looking for a pristine beach experience, and crowded in places during high season, Side's beaches are perfect if you just want to soak-up the sun. There's also a small beach in town on the south side of the peninsula known as **Küçük Plajı**, which is ideal for families with small children, though inevitably it gets pretty packed in season.

Some 3 km to the east at **Sorgun** there's a stretch of public beach which it's quite possible to reach along the coast on foot from Side. Alternatively, it's served by dolmuş from Manavgat. In the other direction **Kumköy** has more large hotel developments, restaurants and beach clubs.

Side

■ Sleeping		● Eating	
1 Ani Motel	6 Kleopatra Otel	1 Gama Starlight	6 Uğur Lokantası
2 Belen	7 Lale Park	2 Gül	
3 Güven Motel	8 Pan Motel	3 Mercan Cafe	
4 Hanımeli Pansiyon	9 Sur Motel	4 Moonlight	
5 Kamer Motel	10 Yıldırım Pansiyon	5 Soundwaves	
	11 Yükser Pansiyon		

N
0 metres 50
0 yards 50

Essentials

Sleeping

D *Hotel Lale Park*, Lale Sokak, off Barbaros Sokak, T7531131, F7533567. Well-established package hotel 1 row back from town's small beach, small but well-equipped rooms, a/c, fridge, telephone, TV as standard, helpful staff. **D** *Kleopatra Otel*, Turgut Reis Sokak, T7531033. No prizes for the architecture of this angular concrete structure, rooms are reasonably comfy and have a/c and seaview on the sunset side. **E** *Hanimeli Pansiyon*, Liman Caddesi, T7531100. Despite promising Ottoman-style exterior rooms ordinary and overpriced. **E** *Belen Hotel*, Sümbül Sokak No 12, T7531043, F7532740. Nice wood panelled rooms with balconies, the 2 attic rooms have seaview, garden courtyard, friendly management. **E** *Kamer Motel*, Barbarosa Caddesi, west of the Kücük Plajı. Wooden clad building, functional, unexciting rooms, real bonus are balconies overlooking the sea. **E** *Yıldırım Pansiyon*, Lale Sokak, T7533209. Convenient for beach to east of town, small, homely pension with pleasant café and games room. **E** *Yükser Pansiyon*, Sümbül Sokak No 4, T7532010, F7534297. Quiet backstreet location, simple but pleasant rooms with ceiling fan and ensuite shower, *First Choice* affiliate so reservation advisable in season. **E** *Ani Motel*, Barbarosa Caddesi, T7533364. Convenient for east beach, small wooden bungalows set in gardens, equipped with fan and small ensuite, only drawback is that some may be hot in summer. **E** *Sur Motel*, Liman Caddesi, T7531087. Right in the middle of things so a bit hectic, plain rooms with balcony. **E** *Pan Motel*, Leylak Sokak No 129, T7531089, F7533874. Entered through ruins of what could be ancient temple, mediocre rooms off courtyard planted with banana trees, could be noisy at night. **F** *Güven Motel*, Barbaros Caddesi, T7531091. Very clean but lacking character, friendly British/Turkish management. **Camping** Several small campsites can be found on the road to the west beach, although they seem to change management and name annually. Enquire at the Tourist Office for this seasons recommended site.

Despite the huge number of hotels it's wise to book well ahead as many of the nicest places are block booked by British or European tour operators. Between Sep-May things are much quieter & cheaper but many places are closed

Eating

Midrange *Gül Restaurant*, Gül Sokak, informal locally recommended place with wide selection of Turkish and international dishes. *Soundwaves*, corner of Lale and Barbarosa Caddesis, more upmarket international menu with choices such as steak, fish or garlic mushrooms with a cream sauce, about US$10-12 per head before alcohol. *Moonlight*, Barbarosa Caddesi near Kamer Motel, garden restaurant with some tables overlooking the sea,

To Kumköy, Manavgat & Tourist Office

Otogar & Car Park

Side Caddesi

Agora

Ancient Theatre

Agora

Gate

To East Beach

Lale Sokak

Kücük Plajı

Western Mediterranean

wide choice of dishes including seafood such as grilled prawns, about US$15 per head with wine. *Gama Starlight*, Barbarosa Caddesi, just west of the Küçük Plajı, ambient restaurant with good selection of meze and Turkish dishes such as saç kavurma and Şiş kebabı. **Cheap** *Mercan Cafe*, Barbarosa Caddesi, good place for a snack on your way to the beach, gözleme or grilled meatballs. *Uğur Lokantası*, in side street off the top of Liman Caddesi, simple lokanta serving soup, ready-prepared dishes and kebaps, 1 of the more reasonbly priced places in town. For an economical lunch try 1 of the **fastfood stalls** on Liman Caddesi where a döner kebap and drink costs about US$2.50.

Bars *Mehmet's Bar*, Barbarosa Caddesi, Küçük Plajı, simply a row of stools beside the street, friendly atmosphere and good music. *Apollonik Bar*, garden bar with tables overlooking the harbour. If you want something more lively try *Baracuda, Stones* or *Temple Bar* which compete for trade on the seafront near the temples of Apollo and Athena.

Shopping Needless to say it's hard to find bargains in Side's overpriced leather and carpet outlets.

Tour agencies *Ora Tours*, Liman Caddesi 49/A, T7534250, daily tours to Manavgat, Köprülü Canyon, Aspendos and other local sights.

Transport **Bus** In the summer buses depart from Side's *otogar* for destinations across the country, however, at other times of the year you may have to get on a bus in **Manavgat**. Manavgat dolmuş leave every 8-10 mins from the otogar, US$1. There is no direct dolmuş to **Sorgum** so you'll have to go via Manavgat (see page 397). **Car rental** *Avis*, Fatih Caddesi No 25, T7531348, F7532813. *Budget*, Kumköy Yolu, opposite the *Kervan Otel*, T7531486, F7533767.

Directory **Banks** There are numerous banks and private change places along Liman Caddesi. **Post office** The PTT is at the bottom of Liman Caddesi on the main square. **Tourist information** The Tourist Information Office, T7531265, F7532657, is inconveniently situated on the main road into town beyond the bus station.

Manavgat A small market town whose inland position ensures that most tourists simply pass through on their way elsewhere, Manavgat is girded by the alluring jade-green waters of the Manavgat River. Rising deep in the Taurus Mountains, the Manavgat is at the centre of the government's ambitious plans to export water to the Middle East from a recently completed US$120 million terminal at its mouth. Presently, however, the town has a profitable sideline in shipping boatloads of tourists up to a scenic horseshoe-shaped waterfall known as the **Manavgat Şelalesi**, 4 km upstream. It's certainly a beautiful spot, although unfortunately in summer you'll have to share it with the crowds, and the cafés, restaurants and stalls that serve them. Boats leave from along the bank opposite the otogar on the 80 minute excursion, US$6 per person with minimum of four people required. You can also catch a dolmuş to the waterfalls, US$0.30. A second option is a three to four hour trip downstream to a long spit of sand at the mouth of the Manavgat River, where there's time for a swim and lunch. The cost of this is US$12 per person, but once again you need at least four people.

In the height of the summer season you could think about using Manavgat's hotels as a cheaper alternative to staying in nearby Side or if you're just passing through

Sleeping **E** *Hotel Gönnetlioğlu*, Çayboyu Caddesi No 51. New hotel beside the river, rooms have a/c, telephone and TV. **F** *Hotel Nil*, Çayboyu Caddesi, T7465289, F7465290. Comfy rooms with TV and balcony overlooking river. Recommended. **F** *Otel Kervan*, Fevzipaşa Caddesi, Arzu Sokak No 1, T7464400. Quiet position overlooking the river, 250 m downstream from the bridge, rooms with telephone, TV and small ensuite. **G** *Yılmaz Pansiyon*, Çayboyu Caddesi, T7463908. In the bowels of the Vergi Dairesi building on the riverside, entrance is in alleyway at rear, basic 2/3 bed rooms, shared toilet and no breakfast.

Eating There are several smart riverside restaurants, such as *Develiler* and *Çukurova*, serving *meze*, meat dishes and seafood upstream from the bridge on the east bank of the river. Nearby, the open-air *Belediye Çay Bahçesi*, run by the municipality, has excellent value meze, trout, Şiş kebabı and sandwiches if you don't mind sitting at plastic tables. The *Fatih Restaurant* in the otogar is good for a quick snack before getting on a bus.

Transport Bus The bus station is on the highway just west of the Manavgat River. **Antalya**, every 20-30 mins, 75 mins, US$3, **Alanya**, every 30 mins, 75 mins, US$3. **Konya**, regular buses, 6 hrs, US$8. There are also several daily buses to Adana, Ankara, Istanbul and İzmir. **Dolmuş** for **Side** and **Sorgun** drive along the main highway on the same side as the bus station about every 10/20 mins respectively.

Directory Banks There are several banks with ATMs on the main highway. **Communications Internet**: *Akdeniz Internet Centre*, on the main highway near the bus station. **Post office**: The PTT is on the main highway west of the bridge.

Alanya

Superbly situated on the landward side of a rocky, castle-topped peninsula with beaches sweeping away to the east and west, it's hardly surprising that the last 20 years have seen Alanya catapulted into the world of mass tourism. The quiet fishing town of yesteryear has been transformed beyond recognition, becoming one of the main resorts on the Mediterranean coast. The town's celebrated banana groves have given way to modern apartments and hotels catering mainly for European package tourists. This development leaves little room for the independent traveller, although outside the busy summer months you could stop-by to visit the Selçuk Castle, have a night out and then recover on the beach.

Getting there Over 140 km east of Antalya, which incidentally is the closest international airport, Alanya is well-served by buses from most major cities, as well as services along the coastal road east towards Silifke and Adana. **Getting around** The palm-lined incantation of the coastal highway, Atatürk Caddesi, cuts a swath through the centre of the modern town, becoming Keykubat Caddesi as it heads out around the bay to the east. Most of the action is south of this road, particularly along Damlataş Caddesi which leads east across the neck of the peninsula to the greatest concentration of bars, restaurants and shops, north of the harbour. The bus station is 1½ km west of the centre near the beach front. To get into town catch a Belediye bus (US$0.30) along Atatürk Caddesi from the stop across the road or alternatively it's a 15-20 min walk.

Ins & outs
Once established you can generally get around on foot, although you may want to hop on a bus to get to the beach or to save yourself a sweaty climb up to the Kale

Alanya rose to prominence following its surrender to the Selçuk Turks in 1221. Renamed Alaiye, Sultan Alâeddin Keykubat I built a large harbour and fortified the naturally defensible peninsula, handiwork which is still in evidence today. As the Selçuk's principal port the city thrived, counting among its exports the valuable cedar logs felled in the Taurus Mountains and floated down the nearby Dimçay River. However, the disintegration of the Selçuk Empire saw a gradually declined in Alaiye's fortunes, reducing it eventually to the unimportant little fishing town that Captain Beaufort visited in 1811. And this is how it remained until just a few decades ago, making its rapid transformation into a full blown tourist Mecca all the more remarkable.

History

Alanya's remorseless development has buried most traces of its former character beneath a tide of apartment buildings, restaurants and hotels. There are still a very few old buildings dotted incongruously around the centre of town with

Old Alanya

Western Mediterranean

most of these now pressed into service as bars or restaurants. Thankfully, the Selçuk fortifications on the towering promontory to the southwest of town, known locally as Iç Kale, have been more judiciously preserved; but before making the climb there are also a few sights in the harbour area.

Standing massively just beyond the harbour is the 35 m high **Kızılkule** (Red Tower) which formed part of the city's Selçuk defences. Built in 1226 by a Syrian architect in the employ of Sultan Alâeddin Keykubat I, and cleverly restored in the 1950s, antique column drums incorporated into the walls of the octagonal tower give an unusual visual effect. Another interesting feature are the protruding machicolations from which stones or hot oil could be dropped on an enemy below. Today the tower houses a small **ethnographic collection** (*0800-1200, 1330-1700, US$1*), though the view from the top is more enthralling. Following the **city walls**, which are beautifully illuminated at night, for 200 m along the coast brings you to the **Tersane**, a Selçuk dockyard guarded by another tower.

Kale Iç Sitting on a towering promontory jutting out into the Mediterranean, Alanya's citadel occupies a stunning naturally defensible position with precipitous cliffs dropping on three sides directly into the sea. The main road to the top, Kale Caddesi, begins near the Tourist Information Office, meandering its way up to the 6 km long outer walls which formerly enclosed the Selçuk town. Passing through one of several old gates you enter another world where official restrictions have helped preserve an area of orchards and fields, dotted with old houses outside which local women display hand-woven blankets and tablecloths.

Crowning the top is the Kale Iç (Inner Citadel), garrisoned today by more salesmen and women instead of guards. Once through the gate (■ *0800-1900, US$2.50*) there is surprisingly little to see, although the pathway does skirt the ruins of a Byzantine chapel and several red brick cisterns. These were among an estimated 400 cisterns built to collect rainwater as there was only one spring in the entire old town.

Along the west side of the keep the walls are built right up to the edge of the cliff and a metal platform affords amazing views along the coast towards Side. It was down this precipice that prisoner were hurled to their death, however, today tourists try in vain to thrown stones so that they land in the sea far below.

You can reach Kale Iç in about an hour on foot from the town, but it's a long and, in summer, hot climb. If you don't fancy the exertion take a city bus which pass the Tourist Office at five minutes past the hour and then walk down. A pleasant alternative to descending on the road is to take a narrow lane which leads past the *Bedesten Hotel* (see sleeping), and the Süleymaniye Camii into a peaceful hamlet known as Ehmedek. At the end of the path is the gate that lends this enchanting area its name, guarded by a watchtower from which you can gaze out across the rooftops of Alanya.

Below the double gate a narrow path zigzags down towards a pine wood which would make a lovely spot for a picnic. Continuing through the trees you emerge on a quiet street next to a graveyard. Turn right and this street leads down to Kale Caddesi at the *Yamaç Cafe*.

Damlataş Mağarası To the south of the Tourist Office, the Damlataş Mağarası is a cave that was discovered by chance in 1948. It's now firmly on the tour circuit and its entrance is besieged by restaurants, cafés and gift shops. Once through the turnstiles you descend a flight of stairs to a large cavern, its walls decorated by a profusion of stalactites and stalagmites. The air inside remains at a temperature of 24°C which, coupled with the high humidity, is supposed to be beneficial for asthma sufferers. If you aren't searching for a bronchial cure though, it's a fairly pedestrian experience.■ *1000-1900 daily. US$1.25.*

A popular daytime activity for the package hordes are the boat excursions which leave from the harbour. The itineraries are fairly standard with the boats calling-in at a series of cave around the base of the peninsula, giving you ample opportunity for swimming and sunning yourself. Remember to take a hat and suncream. Tours usual run from 1100 to 1600 and include lunch for about US$15, however, there are also shorter alternatives. If the idea of being crammed on a boat with a load of other tourists doesn't appeal then you could look into chartering a boat for yourself.

Boat trips

An enjoyable excursion from Alanya is to the Dimçay River which reaches the sea about 6 km east of the centre. A road off the main highway follows the river past numerous trout restaurants and places to cool-off in the refreshing water. After 8 km *Pınarbaşı Restaurant*, where you can eat trout at tables actually in the shallow river for about US$3 per portion, is locally recommended. Unfortunately there's no public transport up the valley, though during the summer it gets pretty busy so hitching shouldn't be a problem. You could also pay a visit to the recently discovered **Dim Mağarası**, a 60 m long cave about 7 km from the main road.

Dimçay Valley

Cleopatra's Beach Situated on the western side of town these hotels are convenient if you want to do the sun and sea routine, however, most are pretty bland and unexceptional. Half-board packages are standard, although prices below are B&B. **B** *Hotel Grand Zaman*, Atatürk Caddesi No 153. Large, impersonal, strange decor in reception, good facilities including pool and fitness centre, make sure you ask for a room with a sea view. **D** *Azak Otel*, Atatürk Caddesi No 161, T5139155, F5123966. 1 of better package hotels, on the beach, comfortable, well-equipped rooms, swimming pool, restaurant and bar. **D** *Kont Otel*, Atatürk Caddesi. On the beach where Atatürk Caddesi veers inland, standard package place, plain wood-panelled rooms with a/c, telephone, pool is hemmed in by other buildings. **E** *Şavk Otel*, Atatürk Caddesi No 159, 15134031, F5139103, savk.com.tr Nicest of a cluster of package places, pool bar, restaurant, easy beach access. **F** *Aysev Hotel*, Güzel Yalı Caddesi No 74, T5137358, F5120225. Modest family-run place catering to mostly Turkish clientel, 1 of cheapest sea-views you'll find, simple rooms have ceiling fan, a/c and balcony. Recommended.

Sleeping

Damlataş Caddesi and the harbour B *Hotel Kaptan*, İskele Caddesi No 70, T5134900, F5132000. Smart package place with nautical theme, small comfortable rooms with a/c, telephone, TV, minibar, cheaper rooms on back with no sea-view. **E** *Dolphin Apart Hotel*, İskele Caddesi, T5132996. Simple but spacious rooms with kitchenette and balcony overlooking harbour. Recommended. **E** *Bayırlı Otel*, İskele Caddesi, T5136487, F5134320. Small, comfortable rooms, basic bathroom, balcony overlooking harbour. **F** *Pension Best*, Alaaddinoğlu Sokak No 3/23, T5130446, F5110171, bestapart@hotmail.com Behind the museum, look for sign on 4th floor of apartment block, owned by extremely consciensious and friendly Ahmet Kan, spotlessly clean and homely rooms, also fully-equipped apartments which sleep up to 4, outings and airport pick-ups organised. Highly recommended. **F** *Yalı Pension*, Alaaddinoğlu Sokak. 2nd left after museum, clean and spacious rooms with kitchenette in apartment block, white tiles throughout, good value.

The Kale On the slopes of the castle-mount in a pleasant suburban setting with good views there are several places offering apartments and rooms to rent. Try Mrs Fusun on Melthem Sokak, T5123278 (she speaks no English), right turn at *Yamaç Café* on way up to the İç Kale, sign-posted in German. **C** *Bedesten Hotel*, Kale, T5121234, F5137934. Certainly the best located hotel in town, set in peaceful surroundings on the top of the castle-mount, however rooms around courtyard of unsympathetically renovated Selçuk bedesten are claustrophobic and dark, much nicer suites near swimming pool, has its own 13th-century cistern, under new management who have plans to do better justice to the site, definitely worth a look.

Eating

A wealth of restaurants though most cater firmly for the tastes of the package masses: a bland selection of European & corrupted Turkish dishes at relatively expensive prices

Expensive *Kaptan's Guverte Restaurant*, Iskele Caddesi, classy terrace restaurant and bar overlooking the harbour, Mediterranean/Turkish menu with well-presented dishes such as Şaşlık kebabı -grilled lamb marinated with bay leaves, about US$25 per head with wine. **Midrange** *Ottoman House*, Damlataş Caddesi, garishly lit 19th-century house, pleasant tables outside, large menu with touristy and more traditional fare including seafood. *Eski Ev*, Damlataş Caddesi, half-way along, another restaurant in a restored house, tables in garden, meze followed by Turkish dishes such as saç kavurma, also pasta, childrens menu available. Along the harbour front are a number of predictably touristy fish and steak restaurants, such as *Marina*, *La Luna* and *Mahperi*, where you can expect to have dinner with a bottle of wine for about US$12-15 per head. For a more romantic atmosphere try the waterside *Iskele Restaurant*, which serves Turkish, European and seafood dishes in the shadow of the Kızılkule. *Yakamoz Restaurant*, Iskele Caddesi, steak and seafood restaurant with good views over harbour, 14 types of steak, fish, calamari and grilled prawns. **Cheap** There is a knot of busy kebap and pide places frequented by locals and tourist alike between Hükümet Caddesi and Gazipaşa Caddesi near the park. Prices are only slightly inflated so you can still have a decent meal and a beer for US$4-5. *Esin*, Damlataş Caddesi, 200 m down from the museum, snack bar with delicious döner kebaps and freshly squeezed orange juice. *Yılmaz Restaurant*, in backstreet running parallel to Atatürk Caddesi near the post office, kebaps and ready-prepared dishes, local clientel and reasonable prices. *Has Konyalı Mevlana*, Atatürk Caddesi, bright neon-lit place serving pide and lahmacun, as well as soup, kebaps and ready-prepared stews.

Cafés
There is a simple teahouse on the harbour breakwater, as well as a number of tea-gardens on Kale Caddesi as you climb up to the castle.

Bars & nightclubs
Nightlife being a principal holiday ingredient for most of Alanya's visitors there are plenty of bars and clubs to choose from, although most are loud and brash, catering predominantly for a young, European crowd. On the harbour front the huge, partly-open air *James Dean* and *Bistro Bellman* compete with loud, pulsating Euro-house and huge TV screens. *Boomerang Bar*, Gazipaşa Caddesi, popular with tourists and locals, band nightly, Turkish and western pop music. For something more relaxed try the *Kaptan Büfe* on the harbour break-water, where a mainly local crowd sip beer and enjoy the view.

Shopping
The bazaar district north of Atatürk Caddesi is a good place to look for picnic things and souvenirs, particularly on Fri when there's a large food market.

Sports
Alanya Triathlon, held every year in May. Contact Tourist Information for details.

Tour agencies
There are literally dozens of tour agencies scattered across town offering daily tours, car rental and ticketing. *South Tours*, Eski PTT Caddesi, Uzay Apartments No 22, T5127959, F5132470.

Transport
Air The nearest airport is **Antalya**. **Bus** Dolmuş to the otogar leave from the dolmuş station in the bazaar area passing along Atatürk Caddesi. Buses call-in at Alanya's bus station en-route for destinations across the country, so it is important in summer to make reservations well in advance. **Adana**, every 3 hrs, 10 hrs, US$17. **Anamur**, every 2-3 hrs during the day, also several night buses, 3 hrs, US$6. **Antalya**, every hr, 2 hrs, US$4. **Konya** (via Beyşehir), regular buses, 6½ hrs, US$11. **Mersin**, every couple of hrs,

getaway tonight on

www.exodus.co.uk

exodus
The Different Holiday

exodus
9 Weir Road
LONDON
SW12 0BR

2

8½ hrs, US$15. **Silifke**, every 2-3 hrs, 7 hrs, US$12. There are also daily services to destinations further afield such as **Ankara, Istanbul** and **İzmir**. For Olympos, Kaş and Fethiye you'll have to change at Antalya. **Car rental** *Avis*, Atatürk Caddesi No 13, T5133513, F5119496. *Budget*, Atatürk Caddesi, Oral Apartments 192/B, T5137382, F5139088. *Race*, Atatürk Caddesi No 49/A, T5121501, F5125224.

Banks There are numerous banks with ATMs on Atatürk and Hükümet Caddesi. **Directory**
Baths *Kleopatra Baths*, Güzelyalı Sokak No 14/1, separate baths for men and women, evening families, US$8 entry and assisted wash. **Communications Internet**: *Ezgi Internet*, Damlataş Caddesi, near junction with Kultur Sokak, US$1 per hr. There are several cafés on Iskele Sokak. **Post office**: The main PTT is on Atatürk Caddesi. **Doctors** *Universal Medical Klinik*, Atatürk Caddesi, 100 m east of *Azak Otel*. **Laundry** *Sema Yikama*, Zamanoğlu Sokak, 100 m north of *Yalı Pension*, US$4 per 1 kg. **Tourist information** The office, T5131240, F5135436, is at the west end of Damlataş Caddesi. Open weekdays 0830-1730.

Eastern Mediterranean

8

Eastern Mediterranean

406 Anamur

411 Silifke

414 North of Silifke

417 Kızkalesi

420 Mersin

422 Adana

429 The Hatay

431 Antakya

East of Alanya the Taurus mountains bulge southwards in a bulbous knot, marching up to and then dropping precipitously into the sea. Known in ancient times as Cilicia Tracheia (Rough Cilicia), it's a remote and rugged coastline which has historically harboured pirates, as well as the reclusive monk seal. Today, the area's inaccessibility and the torturously twisted coastal road equate to low tourist densities, although aside from a few secluded coves backed by banana plantations, there is little to pause for. That is until you reach Anamur, which, in addition to an improbably picturesque castle and the ghostly ruins of Anemurium, boasts some decent stretches of beach. Striking east again, the road twists and turns endlessly to Taşucu, a little port with hydrofoils and ferries to Cyprus. Lost in the mountains beyond Silifke are a number of rarely visited archaeological sites, foremost of which is Uzuncaburç, where the ruins of a great Graeco-Roman city lie scattered amongst the houses of an upcountry village. Back down at the coast, the beach and offshore castle at Kızkalesi attract a mainly domestic crowd with the jumble of associated development rather detracting from the scene.

To the east the mountainous coastline gives way to the monotony of the fertile cotton-growing Çukurova Plain, with the modern industrial cities of Mersin and Adana offering few distractions. As the birthplace of St Paul, Tarsus has more luck at woeing visitors, although in fact there's disappointingly little to see. Instead it's probably best to press on to the Hatay where a handful of specific sights, such as the cave-church of St Pierre and the fabulous Mosaic Museum, are augmented by the local Arab culture and cuisine.

Anamur

Phone code: 0324
Colour map 5, grid C1

Nestled on a small plain enclosed by an amphitheatre of mountains, Anamur enjoys a balmy climate that allows the cultivation of sweet, finger-sized bananas, along with verdant citrus orchards and fields of vegetables. Set back from the sea, the town itself – modern and without interest – hardly does justice to its beautiful surroundings. On the coast nearby, Anamur's budding resort, Iskele, is also fairly uninspiring, although the winding coastal road and its distance from the nearest airport mean that it's far less developed than Alanya. Even so, the town's population of 50,000 trebles during the summer months, with domestic tourists accounting for most of this influx. On a more positive note Anamur makes a good spot to break your journey along the coast, with the haunting ruins of ancient Anemurium and the absurdly picturesque Mamure Kalesi providing some interest when you're bored with lying on the beach.

Ins & outs
See page 409 for further details

Getting there Sitting between Alanya (129 km) and Silifke (144 km), Anamur feels quite isolated due to the slow approach along the torturously twisted and narrow coastal road. Allow plenty of time for the journey if driving. Buses make the trip regularly in either direction. **Getting around** Most of the town's accommodation is on the coast 3 km south at Iskele. Dolmuş from behind the bus station shuttle to Iskele every 30 mins, 0630-2330, midnight in summer.

Sights

Anemurium
Clustered on a hillside 6 km SE of Anamur are the remains of Anemurium, a veritable ghost-town of Byzantine ruins

The origins of this settlement go back probably to the Phoenicians, with the town having enjoyed a period of prosperity under the Romans when it struck its own coinage. Having reached its apogee mid-way through the third century the Persian invasion of Cilicia and subsequent raiding by warlike Isaurian tribes from the Taurus Mountains brought about a gradual decline in Anemurium's fortunes. The Arab invasion of the eighth century seems to have been the final straw for the town's inhabitants and the site was abandoned soon after. And so it has remained, with the passage of time leaving us the well-preserved ruins that we see today.

As you approach the site the first thing you'll notice is an extensive **necropolis** spilling down the scrubby mountainside. From a distance the tombs look like stone houses with arched roofs, however, on closer inspection most consist of an antechamber leading onto the actual sepulchral tomb. Several of these mausolea contain fragments of mosaic pavement and faded frescos, although without the help of the warden you'll have to resort to trial and error to find them. It's altogether easier, particularly if it's hot, to locate the **necropolis church** which despite its ruinous state has the best preserved mosaic pavement, hidden beneath a layer of protective pebbles. Look out for a tower of stone – in fact part of the building's apse – on the right 30 m before the ticket office.

At the site entrance there's a car park and a café, beyond which on the left are the crumbling remains of a large third-century **bath complex**. A path leads through the ruins to a square pool, its bottom lined with tiny squares of marble and a drain hole clearly visible on the far side. Fragments of mosaic are also still visible around the edge of the pool, hinting at the bath's former splendour.

Back on the track you next come to the city's 1.7-km long **outer walls**. Before entering the town proper though, a path leads up to a **mausoleum** containing several very worn pieces of mosaic. This tomb was an unlikely beneficiary of the Cold War, having been restored with funds donated by the strategic alliance CENTO in 1965. However, today it's hard to see what they spent their money on, except of course for the concrete stairs mounting the side of the structure. On the way back down look into a smaller tomb on the left where a pair of peacocks adorn a wall of the inner chamber.

Inside the city walls there's a badly degraded **theatre** on the right which is hardly worth scrambling up to inspect. Further on the **odeon** is in better shape and the rows of seats where the city council would have sat are still visible. Continuing down the track you arrive at a lovely pebbly beach and having clabbered around the ruins in summer it's difficult to resist diving into the crystal clear water.

If you're still feeling energetic after looking around the ruins climb up to the city's **inner keep** crowning the top of Cape Anemurium. As you might expect the view is stunning with the mountains of Cyprus visible across the sea to the south on a clear day.

■ *US$1. Getting there: Reached down a signposted side road which leaves the coastal highway to the southwest of Anamur. Catch an Ören Belediye dolmuş (US$0.30) which pass along the main road by the Anamur bus station on the hour. This will drop you at the turn-off from where it's a 1½-km walk to the ruins. The Ören dolmuş returns at about 30 mins past the hour during the day, or you could try hitching.*

Several kilometres from the other side of Anamur next to the main road is an impressive medieval castle known as Mamure Kalesi. Built 900 years ago by the Armenian rulers of Cilicia on the site of an earlier Roman or Byzantine castle it was later occupied by the Crusaders, the Selçuk and the Karamanidsand has been rebuilt several times, most recently by the Ottomans who garrisoned it after the British took Cyprus in 1878. It was used again by the Turks during the First World War to guard this stretch of coast, though since then it's been abandoned,

Mamure Kalesi
Overlooking the Mediterranean, its long crenellated walls & tall watchtowers look like the film set for a medieval drama

Anamur area

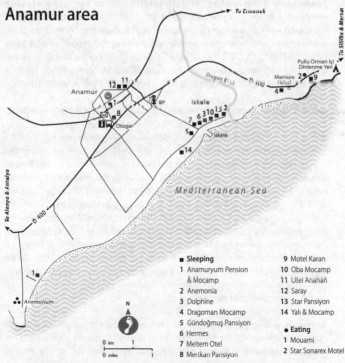

To Ermenek
To Silifke & Mersin
Pullu Orman İçi Dinlenme Yeri
Dragon R (L)
D 400
Mamure Halesi
Anamur
İskele
BP
Otogar
İskele
To Alenya & Antalya
D 400
Mediterranean Sea
Anemurium
N
0 km 1
0 miles 1

■ Sleeping
1 Anamuryum Pension & Mocamp
2 Anemonia
3 Dolphine
4 Dragoman Mocamp
5 Gündoğmuş Pansiyon
6 Hermes
7 Meltem Otel
8 Mertkan Pansiyon
9 Motel Karan
10 Oba Mocamp
11 Utel Anahan
12 Saray
13 Star Pansiyon
14 Yalı & Mocamp

● Eating
1 Mouami
2 Star Sonarex Motel

visited only by the occasional coach load of tourists . It's still in excellent condition and once across the narrow moat, water-filled and teeming with terrapins and other aquatic life, you can clamber up inside the towers and walk along the parapet. There's very little inside the walls except for a small mosque formerly used by the troops garrisoning the fort. If you fancy something to eat the *Kale Restaurant* across the road from the castle does trout, *köfte* and other meat dishes. ■ *0800-1700 daily. US$3.50. Dolmuş (US$0.30) passing the "Kale" wait near the BP station at the junction of the Iskele and the coastal road.*

Other sights   The whole coast from Anemurium to Mamure Kalesi is basically one long **beach** divided to the northeast of Iskele by the Dragon River. The least populated sections are found at either end away from Iskele. If you enjoy beach walking you could stroll along the coast from Anemurium to Iskele or visa versa, but remember to take some water as it's about 5 or 6 km and there's not much along the way. Also bear in mind that marine turtles nest along some parts of the coast, particularly northeast of the Dragon River, so avoid nocturnal visits or planting parasols into the sand.

Essentials

Sleeping   Most of Anamur's accommodation is found on the coast at Iskele which is quickly
The road from Anamur   gaining the trappings of a modest seaside resort. Unfortunately the hotels are gener-
reaches the coast at a   ally unimaginative concrete boxes. For an altogether quieter scene you could stay out
small square & a jetty   near Anemurium or in 1 of the pensions or campsites near Mamure Kalesi. There's lit-
with hotels strung out   tle reason to stay in town itself except perhaps if you arrive after the Iskele dolmuş
along the beachfront   have stopped running, when a taxi is the only solution.

Town centre **E** *Otel Anahan*, T8133511, F8141045, Tahsin Soylu Caddesi No 109, from the bus station go up the hill and after 800 m turn right at the statue of Atatürk. The hotel is at the other end of the street, about 600 m away. Reasonable 2-star place, rooms with TV, telephone and shower, breakfast served on top-floor, no lift. **F** *Saray Hotel*, T8141191, F8142933, Tahsin Soylu Caddesi, just west of the *Otel Anahan*, simpler rooms with ensuite. **G** *Mertkan Pansiyon*, T8165810, Atatürk Bulvarı No 99, a basic crash-pad across from the bus station, could be useful if you arrive late at night.

There are numerous **Iskele** **C** *Hermes Hotel*, T8143950, F8143995. Most comfortable place with swim-
other family-run pensions   ming pool and restaurant, the 70 guestrooms have recently been renovated, a/c, tele-
in the backstreets   phone, TV, central, may be a bit noisy, closed in winter. **D** *Hotel Anemonia*, T8144000, F8141443. Quieter, 750 m east of the *iskele* near Dragoman River, well-appointed 2-stars, reasonable rooms with shower and balcony, some have sea-view. **D** *Hotel Dolphine*, T8143435, just east of the *iskele,* popular garden restaurant but the a/c equipped rooms upstairs are a bit cramped. **E** *Yalı Hotel and Mocamp*, T8143474, F8141435, 1½ km west of the *iskele*, simple bungalows overlooking beach, restaurant and campsite, tents US$4, caravans US$6. **F** *Meltem Otel*, T8142316, across from the *iskele*, large modern block with utilitarian tiled rooms, could be noisy. **G** *Gündoğmuş Pansiyon*, T8142336, set back from road next to army base to west of *iskele*, family-run place, small rooms with shower, good value for money, breakfast extra. **G** *Oba Mocamp*, T8142346, east of the *iskele* at a bend in the road, row of little A-frame bungalows right next to the road so expect noise, shady camping spots right on the beach are more attractive, US$4 per tent.

Anemurium If you're arriving on a bus from the west the driver may be willing to drop you at the turn-off for Anemurium, from where it's just over 1 km walk to the pension **F** *Anamuryum Pension and Mocamp*, sign-posted left off the road to

Anemurium 500 m before ticket office. Quieter spot despite arrival of summer house developments, within easy walking distance of Anemurium, basic rooms and camping , tent US$7, on-site restaurant.

Mamure Kalesi If you're approaching on a bus from the east the driver may be willing to drop you somewhere near where you want to stay. If not, then get off the bus at the Iskele turn-off, recognisable by the statue of a woman carrying a bunch of bananas in the middle of the road, and catch a dolmuş back eastwards from next to the BP station. *Pullu Orman İçi Dinlenme Yeri*, 7 km from Anamur, run by Forestry Service, excellent campsite spread across 5 hectares of pine woodland, beach and restaurant, US$2 per person entrance, plus tent US$3, caravan US$5. *Dragoman Mocamp*, a new campsite just west of the castle and facing the beach, wooden bungalows US$18 per double, tents US$4, restaurant on-site, some of the pitches could be a little low on shade until the vegetation grows up.

In Anamur town there are a number of simple lokantas, such as the *Mouami*, on Bankalar Caddesi which runs east from the Atatürk Statue. In Iskele most hotels and pensions have a restaurant attached. The pide and lahmacun place beneath the *Star Pansiyon* is particularly popular locally. You could also try the *Avşaroğlu Restaurant* to the east of the *iskele*, serves kebaps and meat dishes. The *Hotel Dolphine* has a pleasant garden restaurant with a wide choice of dishes including seafood. Out near Mamure Kalesi there are several restaurants along the road including the *Kale Restaurant* (see sights). The *Star Sonarex Motel* has a decent rooftop restaurant.

Eating
Delicious local bananas hang in huge bunches outside greengrocers

Anamur's nightlife is confined to a few bars and clubs in Iskele, which are only open during the summer season. The *Hermes Hotel* has a popular bar and disco on the roof. *Yakamoz Bar*, east of the *iskele*, popular with local students, live music some nights.

Bars

Bus Alanya and Antalya, every 2-3 hrs, 4/6 hrs, US$5/8. **Silifke**, every 1-2 hrs during the day, also several night buses, 3½ hrs, US$5. **Konya**, 2 daily, 6 hrs, US$12. Several daily to **Ankara** and **Istanbul**. **Ferries** In summer Fergün *Denizcilik* operate several ferries a week to **Girne** in Cyprus. Contact the *Meltem Otel*, T8142316, for details.

Transport

Banks There are banks with ATMs on Bankalar Caddesi, in the town centre east of the Atatürk statue. **Communications** Internet: *Idea Internet Cafe*, Bankalar Caddesi, on left 150 m east of Atatürk statue. **Post office**: The PTT is on the hill leading up from the *otogar* to the centre of town. **Tourist information** On the 1st floor on the bus station, T8144058.

Directory

East from Anamur the highway winds along the rugged coast towards Silifke, 144 km away, often quitting the sea for long stretches to climb up and over pine covered mountains. Some 12 km east of Mamure Kalesi the small town of **Bozyazı** nestles on the narrow coastal plain amongst the banana groves. Overlooked by a ruined Armenian castle known as **Softa Kalesi**, which can be reached up a road starting in the village of Çubukkoyağı. Beyond Bozyazı the road progresses eastwards across forested mountainsides and through small communities which make a living from the crops raised in glasshouses as well as bananas.

The town of **Aydıncık**, 58 km east of Anamur, is strung out along the highway for several kilometres. Founded in the fifth century BC by colonists from Samos, it's one of the oldest settlements on the Cilician coast, however, the modern town, devoted to farming, fishing and forestry, is neither interesting nor attractive so you're unlikely to want to stay long. From Aydıncık the road continues its stomach churning meanderings and shortly before the banana growing community of **Sipahili** there's a large restaurant complex and a good stretch of sandy beach where you could stop for a swim.

Anamur to Taşucu

After climbing through some beautifully unspoilt forested scenery the road returns to the coast west of **Yeşilovacık**. Further east **Boğsak** was once a base for pirates, but now its protected sand-fringed bay has several campsites, a pension and a large motel. A possible trip could be to charter a boat from the harbour and cross to an offshore island to explore the ruins of several medieval churches and an extensive necropolis. On a headland east of Boğsak the 14th-century Armenian castle of **Liman Kalesi** comes into view, beyond which **Akçakıl** has a neat roadside campsite and some cabins next to a crescent of pebbly beach. From here its only a few kilometres to Taşucu, a port and departure point for ferries to Cyprus.

Taşucu Once a sleepy little harbour village, Taşucu has changed beyond recognition. About 10 km west of Silifke it's status as the main port for Cyprus-bound ferries and hydrofoils has fuelled its rapid transformation, with a mercilessly redeveloped dockside square lined with ferry company offices, a couple of restaurants and a small museum displaying amphoras discovered off the coast. There's no reason to prolong your stay in Taşucu unless you're waiting for a ferry. If you have some time to kill there's a small shingle beach 500 m to the east of the port, although its proximity to the town's paper factory and the port may make you think twice about swimming.

Sleeping **B** *Taşucu Best Resort Hotel*, Atatürk Caddesi No 97, T7416300, F7413005. West of the port on the highway, a rather mediocre modern 4-star which is the most comfortable option in the area, decent rooms with uninterrupted sea-views, large pool, rates fluctuate wildly depending on how busy they are so bargain. **D** *Lades Motel*, Atatürk Caddesi No 89, T7414008, F7414258, ladesmotel.bizland.com, a simpler option with pool and sweeping seaviews, plain but adequate guestrooms. On the main road north of the centre, you could try the **F** *Hotel Fatih*, T7414125, which has utilitarian doubles and singles with shower and balcony. There are also some family pensions to the east of the port backing the beach, such as **F** *Meltem Pansiyon*, T7414391, which has seaview rooms with a basin, fridge and balcony.

Eating *Dilek Lokantası*, on the front just east of the ferry terminal, popular, perfect for a snack before getting on your ferry, soup, ready-prepared dishes and grilled meat are all on the menu. *Gaziantepli Lahmacun ve Pide*, also on the square has a pretty self-explanatory menu and very reasonable prices. Nearby, the *100. Yıl Restaurant* is a little bit more refined, serving grilled meat and kebaps with wine or beer.

Transport Most **buses** passing through Silifke also call-in at Taşucu's *otogar* next to the main square. If it doesn't then simply get on a local bus to Silifke and ask to be let-off at the *otogar*. **Ferries and hydrofoils to Northern Cyprus**: There are several ferry companies with offices opposite the docks which compete fiercely for passengers. *Fergün Denizcilik*, T7412323, F7412802, operate daily car ferries (*feribot*) to Girne departing at midnight, 6 hrs, US$18 passenger, US$38 car. Returning from Girne at 1100. An additional ferry may leave at 1500 if there is sufficient demand. They also have hydrofoils (*denizotobüsü*) leaving daily at 1100, 2 hrs, US$23. Returning from Girne at 0930. *Mediterranean Sea Jets*, T7414874, F7414876, also operate hydrofoils leaving at 1100, 1200 and 1400. The prices and crossing times are the same as above. Make sure you arrive at least 90 mins before departure so you have time to complete the official formalities. There is a small reduction for buying a return ticket. 3-month tourist visas are multiple entry, so if you return while it's still valid there's no need to buy a new one.

Directory **Banks** There are several banks with ATMs on the main square. **Communications** Post office: The PTT is on the main square east of the ferry dock. **Internet**:

Internet Cafe, infront of the docks in 1st floor of building next to Jandarma HQ. **Laundry** *Gözde Çamaşır*, Atatürk Caddesi, next to *Lades Motel*, to wash and dry 5 kg is US$1.75.

Silifke

Spread out on either side of the Göksu River, where it emerges from the Taurus Mountains, Silifke is a friendly but fairly unexceptional market town which rarely finds itself on the itinerary of foreign visitors. Indeed, it's only because of its proximity to Taşucu, a departure point for ferries to Cyprus, and its status as a transit point for the ruins of Uzuncaburç that it receives a trickle of curious visitors at all, with most of them measuring their stay in hours rather than days. As such life goes on blissfully unaffected by the tourist industry with the town presenting itself as a good place to experience a slice of ordinary Turkish life, if nothing else.

Phone code: 0324
Colour map 5, grid C2

Silifke's *otogar* is 1 km east of the town centre near the junction of the D-715 to Konya and the D-400 coastal highway. Dolmuş for the centre (US$0.30) pass the *otogar* on the opposite side of İnönü Caddesi. The town is split in 2 by the Göksu River, although barring the helpful tourist information office and the dolmuş stand for Uzuncaburç, which are reached across an old stone bridge spanning the river, everything you'll need is on the south bank.

Ins & outs

Silifke began life as one of a dozen settlements founded by Seleucus I Nicator, general to Alexander the Great and founder of the Seleucid Empire. The town enjoyed a golden age following its incorporation into the Roman Empire in 72 AD and was endowed with beautiful public buildings, few of which survive today. As the capital of the Byzantine province of Isauria, Seleucia, as it was called, was a focal point for early Christianity as the last resting place of Saint Thecla, who had accompanied Saint Paul on his missionary journeys following her conversion in Iconium (Konya). The town next crops-up in history in the 12th century when Frederick Barbarossa, the Holy Roman Emperor, drowned while crossing the Göksu River at the head of his army, a rather ignominious end for a Christian warrior on his way to free the Holy Land.

Background

In the more recent past Silifke was an important market centre for the nomadic pastoralists of the Taurus, known as the *Yörük*, who would descend from the mountains to sell cheese and yoghurt to the lowlanders. Indeed, the town's yoghurt was so esteemed that it's entered popular folklore in the form of a song which can be recited by every Turkish child. These days you're unlikely to find any of the rich and creamy traditional goat's yoghurt around town, as it's been superseded by the relatively bland factory produced stuff.

The **stone bridge** that you'll no doubt cross sometime during your stay was originally constructed at the behest of the Roman Emperor Vespasianus in 78 AD, though it's been almost completely rebuilt on several occasions since.

Sights

On a strategic hill-top to the north of the centre sit the crumbling walls of the Silifke's **medieval citadel**. Raised by the Byzantines against marauding pirates and Arab invaders, early in the 13th century the castle was granted to the Knights of St John by its new Armenian owner, King Leon II. This arrangement lasted until 1224, when the knights sold the fortress back to the Armenians, who managed to hang on to it until the Mongol invasion of the 14th century. A succession of other Muslim rulers occupied the castle before it was taken by the Ottomans in 1471. It's a hot 10 to 15 minutes climb up to the castle from Menderes Caddesi, though you're rewarded with a good view over the town and the farmland of the Göksu delta. From the battlements you'll also be

Eastern Mediterranean

able to see a large cistern on the southeast slope of the hill which supplied the Byzantine city with water.

More easily accessible beside Inönü Caddesi half-way out to the bus station are the fragmentary remains of a second-century Roman **Temple of Jupiter**, although besides a single lonely Corinthian column, usually topped by a crane's nest, and some overgrown foundations there is little to get excited about. Several mosaic pavements and a statue were among the artefacts uncovered at the site. They're now on display at the museum.

In the backstreets between Inönü Caddesi and Fevzi Çakmak Caddesi is the **Atatürk Evi**, a beautifully restored traditional house where Mustafa Kemal stayed during his visit to the town in 1925. With its graceful wooden balcony and curious octagonal roof turret it's a poignant reminder of how things used to be before the proliferation of shoddy apartments and characterless concrete buildings.

Archaeological Museum

Stuck out on the coastal highway, five minutes walk to the east of the *otogar,* Silifke's museum has an interesting and varied collection of objects from sites across the region. You're greeted as you climb the front steps by a stone lion recovered from Uzuncaburç, while inside displays include a large collection of coins unearthed locally and some exquisite Roman statuary. ■ *0830-1230, 1330-1730 daily except Mon. US$1.25. Catch a dolmuş to the otogar which pass up Menderes Caddesi from the stone bridge and then along Inönü Caddesi. Get off at the roundabout and walk 350 m southeast along the Taşucu/Antalya road.*

Aya Tekla (The Church of St Thecla)

All that's left of Zeno the Isaurian's basilica is a piece of the apse; though even from this small fragment it's possible to imagine the former grandeur of the building which commands a magnificent view across the fields & orchards of the Göksu Delta

Beyond the edge of town to the southeast stand the ruins of the fifth-century Church of St Thecla which was built by the newly crowned Byzantine emperor Zeno the Isaurian and dedicated to Thecla, the patron saint of Isaurians, a warlike people who inhabited the rugged Taurus Mountains. Saint Thecla was an important figure in the early development of Christianity who followed Saint Paul on his missionary journeys, later fleeing from persecution to Seleucia ad Calycadnus (Silifke), where she continued to proselytise until her death. She was popularised in medieval times by the widely read *Acts of Paul and Thecla* and her burial place in a grotto to the north of the church became an important pilgrimage site.

Nearby a set of stone steps descends to an earlier cave church where Thecla is said to have lived and conducted clandestine church meetings. It was renovated in Byzantine times with the addition of mosaic pavements and marble panelling on the walls, however, except for a few fragments these adornments have been lost to looters. The cave church is kept locked but a warden will let you in and show you around. Every year on the 23rd and 24th September the Greek Orthodox Patriarch arrives from Istanbul to conduct a service in the cave-church.

■ *Getting there: The church is sign-posted off the Taşucu/Antalya road about 4 km southeast of town. Catch a Taşucu dolmuş from east of the PTT and ask to be let off at Aya Tekla. From the main road it's about a 10-min walk up the hill.*

Göksu Delta

Rather romantically called the Göksu, "Skywater", after the vivid blueness of its water, a visit during spring will reveal a far less appealing brown river, swollen with snow melt from the Taurus mountains and clouded with silt. Over the millennia this sediment has been deposited to form a flat alluvial plain projecting from the coast about 8 km into the Mediterranean. This 14,500-ha delta, which includes a large freshwater lake, known as Akgöl, salt water lagoons and extensive dune areas, is of great environmental significance, supporting a huge diversity of plant and animal life.

Over 334 of Turkey's 450 species of bird are found in the area, with many of these only temporary residents stopping-off on their trans-continental migrations. Feathered rarities such as the dalmatian pelican, white-tailed eagle and marbled duck make the Göksu delta a bird watcher's paradise. The sandy coastline is also an important nesting site for two types of marine turtle, the Green Turtle (*Chelonia mydas*) and the Loggerhead (*Caretta caretta*), both of which are endangered species. The delta's natural vegetation includes five endemic species found nowhere else, as well as rare plants such as the sand lily whose delicate white blooms dot the upper beach in late summer.

Needless to say the delta's flat, fertile land is of considerable agricultural significance too, producing abundant crops of strawberries, tomatoes, citrus fruit and rice. Large areas have been converted to farmland with the loss of important natural habitats compounded by the widespread use of chemical fertilizers and pesticides. Summer house developments have also begun sprouting along the coast, with the long-term impacts of the Kayraktepe Dam upstream of Silifke as yet uncertain. In the face of such threats the Göksu Delta was designated a Specially Protected Area by the government in 1990. Eight years later an area wide management plan, funded by the European Union and implemented with help from the Turkish Society for the Protection of Nature (DHKD) came in effect. However, despite enjoying nominal protection from Ankara and the involvement of domestic and international organisations, the area's future hangs very much in the balance.

■ *Getting there: Access to the delta is via the village of Kurtuluş, 8 km southeast of Silifke, or by a secondary road which leaves the coastal highway east of the SEKA paper factory on the outskirts of Taşucu. Disturbance should be kept to a minimum between Apr-Jun when many birds are nesting. Also avoid nocturnal visits to the beach during the turtle nesting season from May-Sep.*

Sleeping Accommodation in Silifke is limited to 3 fairly rudimentary hotels, so if you want something more elaborate then you'll have to stay in Taşucu or even Kızkalesi. What there is though, is pretty good value for money. F *Hotel Eren*, Sakarya Caddesi No 74, T7121160. Clean, neat rooms with telephone, also has waterless doubles for US$10. F *Arısan Otel*, İnönü Caddesi No 89, T7143331. 10-mins walk from centre but conveniently close to the *otogar*, simple, airy rooms, good value as they're equipped with telephone, a/c, large bathroom. Recommended. G *Hotel Akdeniz*, Menderes Caddesi No 76, T7141285. Basic boarding house, small but bright single and double rooms, with or without ensuite, no breakfast, tiny roof terrace on top floor.

Eating
The restaurant situation is rather restricted especially as most of the places seem to shut-up shop by 9 in the evening

Off Menderes Caddesi near the PTT, *Gözde Restaurant* has the best choice of food in town, serving tasty and good value ready-prepared dishes such as chickpeas (*nohut*), patlıcan güveç (aubergine stew) and yoğutlu ıspanak (spinach with yogurt), with iskender and adana kebabı also on offer and delicious baklava to round things off. A hearty meal shouldn't be more than US$4. *Pavurya*, in the alley opposite Gözde, is a rough and ready little *meyhane* which advertises yengeç (crab) and fish, with the former arriving fresh daily in the afternoon. There are several other smaller places on Menderes Caddesi, while out by the bus station *Babaoğlu*, on Fevzi Çakmak Caddesi, has tasty grilled meat and kebaps. An unassuming place 20 m towards town from Babaoğlu does an excellent and very cheap bowl of chicken soup, along with an assortment of stews.

Transport
Bus Adana, at least every hr, 3½ hrs, US$5. Alanya and Antalya, 3 day and 4 night buses, 7/9 hrs, US$8.50/10. Anamur, every 1-2 hrs during the day, also several night buses, 3½ hrs, US$5. Ankara, several daily, 8 hrs, US$12. Istanbul, several daily, 14 hrs, US$19. Kızkalesi, get on any Mersin bus, which leave every 15 mins throughout the

Easter Mediterranean

day, US$0.80. **Konya**, 12 daily, 4½ hrs, US$6. **Mersin**, direct buses leave every hr, 2½ hrs, US$2.50. **Taşucu** buses leave from the stop to the east of the riverside fairground every 15-20 mins, US$0.30.

Directory **Archaeological information** An experienced guide and local resident, Celâl Taşkıran, does a series of information sheets for archaeological sites in the area including Uzuncaburç. They're available at some of the sites or enquire at the Tourist Office where to get them in town. **Banks** *İşbankası* is on the corner of Menderes and Fevzi Çakmak Caddesi. **Communications** Post office: The PTT is 1 block east of the bridge. **Internet**: See Taşucu. **Hospitals** The State Hospital is off Atatürk Caddesi, north of the river. **Tourist information** The helpful office, T7141151, F7145328, is off Atatürk Caddesi on Veli Gürten Bozbey Caddesi, north of the river. **Useful addresses** Celâl Taşkıran, PK 56, 33941, Silifke, professional guide.

North of Silifke

Without your own transport patchy dolmuş services & empty roads makes hiring a taxi the only real option

The dry mountains to the north of Silifke are scattered with some seldom visited archaeological sites such as the ancient temple city of Olba, 28 km away at Uzuncaburç. Ruins aside an excursion into the foothills of the Taurus can also provide a pleasant break from the summer heat on the coast, while giving you the chance to catch a glimpse of traditional life in the villages along the way.

Demircili

Leaving Silifke the road climbs steeply up a gorge into a parched limestone landscape of scrubby pine forests interspersed with rocky fields. After 7 km you come to a small cluster of one-story buildings called Demircili which was known in antiquity as Imbriogon. Nothing remains of the old settlement except a group of six handsome Roman mausoleums. Looking rather incongruous on a hillside to the west (left) of the road are two double-story house tombs, their grand facades carefully sculpted to resemble miniature temples.

Uzuncaburç

The extensive site, with ruins strewn across a large area between the fields & houses, has a charming unkempt feel with some of the ancient buildings actually incorporated into the fabric of the modern village

Continuing for another 23 km through several more tiny villages and past herds of goats cropping the hillsides, you turn right at a sign-posted road for the final 5 km approach to Uzuncaburç, on the site of the **ancient city of Olba-Diocaesarea**. The contemporary village is a simple farming community whose inhabitants have traditionally made a living by cultivating grapes and cereal, herding goats and chopping lumber. These days though, most of the villagers seek employment down at sea-level, labouring on the farms of the Göksu Delta or working in Silifke. Apart from a basic shop and teahouse in the village centre, and a couple of makeshift stalls selling local handicrafts, there are no facilities for tourists, not that many make the journey anyway.

Undoubtedly of great antiquity, Olba-Diocaesarea's exact origins are uncertain. What is clear, however, is that Olba was taken by Seleucus I in 300 BC and that the Seleucid emperor established a temple of Zeus. This sanctuary grew in wealth and importance and within a century its head priests had established a dynasty which exerted political control over the surrounding area. Olba's line of priest-kings ruled over much of western Cilicia until the first century AD, when the city came under Roman control and was renamed Diocaesarea.

A good place to start your wanderings is the parking area overshadowed by five pillars of what was once a **monumental Roman gateway** on the city's main street. The statues of emperors and distinguished public figures would have rested on the shelves protruding from the columns. The colonnaded thoroughfare corresponds to a dusty, rutted track leading west, past a jumble of blocks on the right which was once a **nymphaeum**, or monumental public fountain.

On the left is the famous **temple of Zeus** established by Seleucid I, which has the distinction of being the earliest known Corinthian temple in Anatolia.

Converted later into a church, it has been degraded by the years into two rows of partially fluted columns, four of which are miraculously still crowned by their capitals. Originally these capitals supported a richly decorated entablature and pediment, with pieces of the frieze and architrave, covered in floral motifs and lively carvings of domestic animals, scattered on either side of the path. There is also a Roman sarcophagus decorated with several Medusa heads against the perimeter wall.

At the western end of the track the **temple of Tyche**, the Roman goddess of chance, is reached across the yard of an adjacent house. A row of five slender columns which supported the temple's porch survive, along with part of the architrave above. Looking back towards the ornamental gateway at the other end of the lane you can appreciated the regularity of the ancient city's plan, a lay-out which has to some degree been inherited by the modern village. Walking back towards the parking area you'll notice one of the **monumental gates** of the city down a track to the north (left).

Back at the parking area a left turn takes you up through the centre of the village, where men park their tractors and spend hours playing cards in the teahouse. A track on the right after the *Belediye* (local government) building leads to a Hellenistic **tower** that was originally part of the city walls, and which gives the village its name, Uzuncaburç meaning "High Tower". The rest of the defences have long since disappeared, but the 22 m high structure remains standing defiantly despite several ominous-looking cracks in its masonry. An inscription above the door reveals the tower has already undergone repairs in the third century AD, and it looks like it will shortly be in need of some more.

Back at the road a signpost near the Atatürk bust points 500 m north to an extensive **necropolis** containing Greek, Roman and Byzantine tombs. Before leaving cast your eye over a ruinous **Roman theatre** squeezed between two stone houses a short distance back along the approach road from the parking area. About 1 km south of the village and visible from the road is a striking stone **mausoleum** dating from the Hellenistic era and capped by a stone pyramid.

■ *Getting there: Public transport to Uzuncaburç amounts to a single dolmuş departing from the west end of Atatürk Caddesi in Silifke at 1330 (1130 in winter) everyday, however, it doesn't return until the following morning which is a problem as there's no accommodation in the village. This leaves hiring a taxi as the only alternative with the return trip from Silifke including an hour or so to walk around the ruins costing US$25-30. Returning via Karadedeli (see below) adds about an extra US$5 on to the price, although some drivers won't be happy about taking this diversion.*

With your own transport and plenty of petrol it's possible having regained the road 5 km from Uzuncaburç to turn right, instead of left, and head through the mountains to Mut (see page 416), over 80 km away. The road passes through a remote, rugged area with empty tableland stretching off towards the snow-flecked mountains of the High Taurus in the distance.

Uzuncaburç to Mut

An alternative route is to follow a stabilized road, rough at present but currently undergoing improvement, which descends past a series of minor archaeological site to the coastal plain at Karadedeli, 10 km east of Silifke. The road starts on the left after the village of Yenibahçe, then branches right at a fork ahead. After about 5 km you'll pass the scattered ruins of **Işıkkale** on the left which include a ruined Byzantine basilica converted from a Corinthian temple. Another couple of kilometres brings you to the more extensive remains of a Greco-Roman settlement at **Karakabaklı**. A number of buildings are scattered across some small wheat fields with others nearer the road converted into stables by the local shepherds. Take care of the shepherd's dogs which can be aggressive towards strangers. The final descent to Karadedeli, a large village inhabited by the descendants of Turkoman nomads who once roamed the mountains with their flocks, is through rocky scrubland. From Silifke the D-715 follows the Göksu Valley, flooded along much of its length by the Kayraktepe Dam, deep into the Taurus Mountains. After 9 km at a scenic look-out by the roadside there's a plaque erected in 1971 by the German Consulate in Ankara to commemorate the accidental death of the Holy Roman Emperor Barbarossa. The Emperor drowned in 1190 while crossing the Göksu River, an event which led many of the German knights to head for home. Nevertheless the remnants of the Christian army pushed-on to the Holy Land taking with them the pickled remains of Barbarossa who was finally laid to rest in Antioch (Antalya).

Mut & Alahan The small town of Mut, 82 km from Silifke, is guarded by a medieval fortress, rebuilt later by the Karamanids. Continuing north towards Karaman brings you after about 15 km to a signposted turn-off to **Alahan**, 2 km off the road. Excavations by a team from the British Institute of Archaeology during the 1960s revealed an extensive monastic complex at the site which occupies a spectacular spot high on the mountainside overlooking the Göksu Valley. Standing on a number of terraces are the remains of several basilicas including the amazingly well-preserved **East Church** whose stone walls stand almost completely intact. Nearby is a cave church and a necropolis of tombs cut into a rock face, one of which bares an inscription identifying its occupant as one Tarasis the Elder who died on the 13th February, 462 AD. Most of Alahan's buildings have been dated to the fourth century when Zeno the Isaurian, a native of this region, was the Byzantine Emperor and the area enjoyed generous royal patronage. Buses between Silifke and Konya or Karaman will let passengers off at the turn-off for Alahan. Having looked around the ruins return to the roadside and wait for the next bus. There are no facilities at the site so pack a bottle of water and some food.

East of Silifke

Narlıkuyu A 20 km drive east of Silifke is this tiny fishing village whose name translates as "the Well of the Pomegranate". These days, however, it's famed for its fish restaurants which cluster around a narrow rocky bay, their terraces overlooking the sparkling clear water. In the centre of the settlement are the ruins of the fourth-century **Baths of Poimenius**, referred to locally as the Kızlar Hamamı (Bath of the Maidens), after a mosaic of the "three fair-checked Graces", the daughters of Zeus, which decorated it. Protected by a rude modern structure you can still see the enchanting mosaic (*US$1*) and a Roman fountain reputed in ancient times to have been the Fountain of Knowledge, whose waters would confer wisdom unto those who drank from it. An underground river still empties into the sea at several points around the bay, with one icy underground stream exiting next to the *Yunus Restaurant*.

In addition to the half-dozen fish restaurants, where a meal of *meze* and fresh seafood will set you back US$7-15 per head depending on what you order, you can rent simple rooms for about US$4 per person in a house next to the *Lagos Kafeterya*. This could provide a pleasant alternative to staying in Kızkalesi if you don't mind fairly rudimentary lodgings.

Over a kilometre east from Narlıkuyu the village of **Akkum** has a good crescent of beach and several pensions including the simple but well-recommended **F** *Kökler Pansiyon*, Akkum Plajı Karşısı, T/F7233214, which is visible, a white building draped in vines, on the landward side of the highway. Unfortunately though, the busy coastal road does rather encroach on things.

Cennet ve Cehennem Mağaraları (The Caves of Heaven & Hell)

Opposite the turning for Narlıkuyu a side road leads 3 km into the dry limestone hills to the Corycian caverns, a group of evocatively named caves. On arrival there's a refreshment stand and car park where you'll need to pay an entrance fee (*US$1*) before descending 70 m via a rocky staircase into the **Cennet Mağarası** (Cave of Heaven), which is in fact a huge chasm 90 m wide by 250 m long, formed when the roof of a large subterranean chamber collapsed. The steps lead down to the bottom of the canyon and a well preserved Byzantine church known as the **Chapel of the Virgin Mary**, which guards the entrance to the **Cave of Typhon**. A slippery pathway continues down into this cavern, which was formerly thought to be the home of Typhon, a hideous fire-breathing monster with 100 heads. Above the eerie hum of the sodium lights you'll be able to hear rushing water below you in the darkness, the same underground river that flows into the sea at Narlıkuyu. When the ancient geographer Strabo visited the cave he noted that it became progressively harder to breathe as he descended, leading him to conclude that it must be one of the entrances to the underworld.

Having hauled yourself back up to the surface follow a path that skirts around the rim to another sink hole further north, the **Cehennem Mağarası** (Cave of Hell). There's no way down into this 120-m deep chasm which according to legend was where Zeus held the monster Typhon captive until he could entomb it beneath Mount Etna in Sicily. To add to its infamy, the hole was supposed to be another entrance to hell.

Some 300 m up the road from the car park is the **Asthma Mağarası** (*US$0.20*), a 17-m deep cave entered via an alarmingly wobbly spiral staircase. Once at the bottom you follow a path through several galleries festooned with stalactites and stalagmites, and garishly lit by coloured lamps. The warm, humid air in the cavern is supposedly beneficial for asthma sufferers.

Kızkalesi

Phone code: 0324
Colour map 5, grid C2
26 km E of Silifke

A particularly dense cluster of cheap hotels and pensions squeezed tightly one up against the other announces your arrival in Kızkalesi. The reason for this profusion of unplanned development, now hidden from the highway by all the concrete, is a wide arc of gently sloping sand, certainly one of the best beaches on the eastern Mediterranean coast. Adding to the spots appeal is the eponymous Kızkalesi, or "Maiden's Castle", a medieval fortress which seems to float above the waves 200 m offshore. Inevitably the intense building of the last 15 years detracts seriously from the spots intrinsic charm, although outside the summer holidays when things are hopelessly crowded, Kızkalesi still makes a good base from which to explore some local sights or have a day on the beach.

Ins & outs

Getting there Buses between Silifke and Mersin (60 km) pass regularly through town in either direction, just stand in a visible position and stick out your hand when one approaches. **Getting around** Compact enough to get around on foot.

Sights

In antiquity Kızkalesi was known as Corycus, an important port and commercial city protected by **two fortresses**, one built on a rocky headland, the other on an island connected to the coast by a long causeway. Occupied by the infamous corsair Zenicetes, who terrorized the coast of Cilicia and Pamphylia during the first century AD, the castles were taken for Rome in 78 AD, later becoming Byzantine and then Armenian strongholds.

Legend has it that the **offshore castle** was the spot where an Armenian monarch confined his beautiful daughter having received a prophecy that she would be killed by a poisonous snake. Unfortunately for the princess the prediction came true when a snake slipped on to the island in a basket of fruit and bit her. If this story sounds curiously familiar it's because it's associated with several other islets around the Turkish coast. Today, fishing boats ferry tourists out to the island from a pier at the western end of the beach for a look around, although apart from the ramparts themselves there's little to see.

On the headland to the east of the beach the **second castle** is more accessible and offers an excellent vantage point from which to admire the Kızkalesi. Inside its double walls, built making extensive use of recycled ancient stone, a path loops around the overgrown keep past a small chapel.

Across the road from the castle is an extensive **necropolis** which contains hundreds of free-standing sarcophagi and tombs cut into the sides of a shallow valley. Most of these date from the fourth century AD and some are beautifully decorated with carvings of flowers, animals and even some human figures. The epitaphs on the tombs reveal fascinating information including the former trade of their occupants with potters, weavers, wool makers, cobblers, goldsmiths, olive oil makers, ship owners and vintners among those laid to rest. The remains of the outer wall of Corycus, a Roman temple, several cisterns and two Byzantine churches also lie scattered across this area of orchards and scrubland north of the coastal road.

About 6 km inland from Kızkalesi is a set of 17 reliefs carved into a cliffside. Known as the **Adam Kayaları** – "People's Rocks" – they depict men, women and children dressed in typically Roman costume, with one stretched regally out on a divan holding a cup of wine in his hand. Each of the figures is accompanied by an inscription, however, they have been damaged by would-be treasure hunters and the elements to the point where they give us little help in understanding who each person was. ■ *Getting there: The road up to the reliefs begins next to the mosque on the main highway, continuing to where a signpost points 1 km down a track to a set of steps cut into the side of a rockface. Taxi drivers or pension owners in Kızkalesi are usually happy to drive up to the Adam Kayaları, which could be included with a visit to the Caves of Heaven and Hell on a ½-day tour, costing in the region of US$27.*

Sleeping

Prices drop dramatically outside the summer season & you should be able to negotiate yourself a handsome discount

With the explosive development of Kızkalesi there's no shortage of accommodation. Most are pretty uninspiring though, aimed squarely at the domestic tourists who flock here after the schools break-up at the end of Jun. There is also a cluster of better quality, midrange hotels, catering mainly to European holidaymakers, at the western end of the beach. **B** *Hotel Kilikya*, Kızkalesi, T5322116, F5232084. West end of the beach, reasonably comfortable package hotel, rooms have partial sea-view and are equipped with TV, minibar, a/c, large pool. **C** *Club Hotel Barbarossa*, Kızkalesi, T3281957, F5232090. West end of beach, medium-sized package hotel favoured by German clientel, set back from sand, small garden, swimming pool, represents good value for money particularly out-of-season when prices drop by nearly 50%, rooms have a/c and telephone, sauna and restaurant. **E** *Hotel Peyda*, Mavideniz Mahallesi Birinci Plaj Yolu, T5232607, F5232082. In the thick of things overlooking statue of Atatürk and beyond to the sea, clean airy rooms with tiled floors, some have sea-view, equipped with fridge, telephone and TV, restaurant on ground floor. **E** *Hotel Hantur*, Erdemli, T5232367, F5232006. Friendly family-run place in the middle of the beach, clean, decent size rooms with ensuite, front ones have full sea-view from their balconies, others make do with partial view of the beach and castle. Recommended. **E** *Öz Kızkalesi Motel*, Kızkalesi Plajı, T5232857. A row of simple bungalows with small ensuite right on the sand. **F** *Best Motel*, İkinci Plaj Yolu No 6, T5232074. Plain rooms with sink and bathroom, simply furnished, tasty home-cooked food on demand. **F** *Tolga Pansiyon*, Birinci Plaj Yolu, T5232037. Inland of Atatürk Statue above a café, utilitarian rooms which may not be available out of season.

There are also a few restaurants down by the beach. For fish you may prefer to make the trip to Narlıkuyu, a few kilometres west. *Tütüncü Restaurant*, off the main road overlooking east end of beach, scenic restaurant with *meze*, fish and meat menu, lovely place for dinner as sun goes down. *Düzen Restaurant*, beach front restaurant, limited selection of *meze*, reasonably priced fish and meat dishes served at tables outside.

Eating
Most of the hotels & pensions cook simple food for their guests which can be tasty & reasonably priced

Banks The nearest banks are in Erdemli or Silifke a short bus ride away, although you may find one of the hotel owners or taxi drivers is willing to change foreign currency.

Directory

The ruins of ancient Corycus dot the scrubby countryside east towards the village of Ayaş, 3 km away, which is nestled amongst the remains of another ancient city called Elaeusa-Sebaste. Among the ruins are a Roman aqueduct; a 15th-century Selçuk tomb; a theatre and several cisterns. On the peninsula you'll find a ruined Roman temple and a Byzantine church. Each of the village's three beaches is rather exposed to the road, although the middle one is probably the best for a swim.

Ayaş

Continuing eastwards after 7 km a well-signposted road winds up into the scrubby mountains for 3 km to what's left of the ancient city of Kanytelis, known today as Kanlıdivane. Occupied since Hellenistic times the site consists of extensive ruins scattered around a huge sink hole measuring 90 m by 70 m. On the rim of this huge hole, formed when the roof of an underground cavern collapsed, stands a partially ruined Hellenistic tower solidly built of polygonal stones. Halfway up the southwest corner of it two sets of inscriptions identify that the tower was dedicated to Olbian Zeus in 200 BC. Beyond the tower an ancient staircase descends 60 m into the chasm, the perpendicular limestone walls of which are decorated with several reliefs. The first, on the south wall beneath the tower, represents a group of six figures, possibly a family; while on the northwest wall a Roman soldier occupies a small niche. Local legend has it that convicted criminals would be hurled off the edge into the hole, where their remains would be devoured by wild animals. Walking around the west rim of the sinkhole you pass four ruined Byzantine basilicas, the earliest of which is thought to date from about the fifth century BC. You'll also notice a more recent Turkish graveyard used by local people and a large cistern with wide stone arches spanning it, partially hidden in the undergrowth. Scattered amongst the bushes to the northeast of the chasm are the tombs and sarcophagi of a necropolis. ■ *US$1.75 when the warden is present. Getting there: Without your own transport get-on a Silifke-Mersin bus and let the driver know you're going to Kanlıdivane. From the junction where you'll be dropped it's a 3-km walk uphill, so bring some water and try to avoid making the trip in the midday sun. To avoid the walk back you could catch a lift back to the highway with the warden who drives down at about 1700. There is a small shop selling soft drinks at the site.*

Kanlıdivane

Continuing eastwards the highway is shadowed by a Roman aqueduct visible crossing many of the valleys inland as you head towards the small town of **Erdemli**. Beyond Erdemli the coastal plain widens gradually as the Taurus Mountains step back from the sea. Covered largely with citrus orchards only a decade ago, the coast to Mersin is being remorselessly developed with hotels and apartment complexes stretching almost without interruption for 45 km.

Towards Mersin

Eastern Mediterranean

Mersin

Phone code: 0324
Colour map 5, grid C3
30 km W of Tarsus

Even by Turkish standards Mersin has undergone a rapid transformation, growing in less than 100 years from a humble fishing village into a major port and industrial centre with a population of over a million. Officially renamed Içel – though most people still prefer Mersin – the city is surrounded by a tapestry of warehouses, factories and wasteland; a chaotic industrial landscape set against the bluey silhouette of the distant Taurus Mountains. Once you've penetrated the outskirts, however, Mersin's centre is surprisingly orderly; a planned grid of streets lined with mostly-modern buildings. As a very youthful, working city there's predictably little to attract tourists, although as a departure point for TML ferries to Cyprus you may just need to pass through.

Ins & outs The city is pretty easy to negotiate with the main street, Istiklal Caddesi, running west from the train station into the centre. It's an easy walk unless you've got heavy baggage, however, from the *otogar* you'll need to get a cab or a city bus. To catch a bus leave via the front exit, turn right and walk up to the main road. Buses heading into the centre pass on the other side of the road.

Sights If you're looking for a way to pass some time you could visit the provincial **museum** which is a short walk west of the centre on Atatürk Caddesi. It contains a range of well-displayed artefacts found across the region, while upstairs there are various ethnographic curiosities. ■ *US$0.75, 0900-1200, 1300-1630 daily except Mon*. You could while-away a bit more time at the **Atatürk Evi**, also on Atatürk Caddesi, where you'll find a fairly predictable collection of paraphernalia connected to the esteemed man on display in an old stone house. Walk back along the shoreline promenade which is backed by gardens.

For some local colour stroll through the **fish market** which runs parallel to Soğuksu Caddesi. There are several excellent spice shops with sacks of brightly coloured spices lined-up out front and luffers hanging from the ceiling, as well as stalls selling the fresh catch-of-the-day.

Sleeping
If you should want or need to overnight in Mersin there are places to fit most budgets

Most of the city's restaurants and hotels are between Istiklal Caddesi and Ismet Inönü Bulvarı, the busy sea-front road. **A** *Merit Hotel*, Kuvay-ı Milliye Caddesi No 165, T3361010, F3360722. 46 floor luxury hotel which dominates the city's skyline, comfortable rooms with excellent views, facilities include a pool, 2 restaurants and a bar on the top floor. **AL** *Mersin Oteli*, Gümrük Meydanı, T2381040, F2312625. Ugly block overlooking Ismet Inönü Bulvarı, very 1970s decor, though rooms are comfortable and well-equipped, also sauna, bar and restaurant. **D** *Hotel Gökhan*, Soğuksu Caddesi No 20, T2316256, F2374462. Corner hotel which is the fanciest of the row, slightly better rooms than the *Hitit* and the *Savran* for which you pay US$10 premium, equipped with telephone, a/c, TV and a fridge. **E** *Hotel Hitit*, Soğuksu Caddesi No 12, T2316431, F2339394. 1 of several hotels on street parallel to fish market, central location, reasonable rooms although bathroom on the basic side, telephone, TV, a/c, breakfast extra but still represents good value. **E** *Hotel Savran*, Soğuksu Caddesi No 46, T2324472, F2385361. Not much to choose between this and the *Hotel Hitit*, similarly equipped, some large 3-bed rooms, breakfast also extra. **F** *Star Hotel*, Soğuksu Caddesi No 22, T2390141. Simple rooms with twin or double beds, a small step up the ladder in terms of comfort, and price, from the *Hotel Side* next-door, a/c, telephone, TV. **G** *Hotel Melida*, T2314084, 29 Sokak No 7, just off Istiklal Caddesi opposite the Jandarma HQ. Family-run, basic rooms but with an all-too-often neglected homely touch, also have TV and telephone, shared squat toilet and shower, sitting area downstairs hung with carpets, no breakfast. Recommended budget option.

There are several reasonably priced restaurants on Istiklal Caddesi including *Uysal* **Eating**
Ocakbaşı, which has a brick oven in the front and a pleasant *aile salonu* upstairs,
serves lahmacun, grilled meat dishes and kebaps. Next door, *Sabah* has a large vat of
işkember soup boiling 24-hrs a day, with ready-prepared stews, lahmacun, kebaps
and several types of desert also on offer. For an evening meal the best place to head is
the atmospheric fish market where *Balıkçı Yaşar* is one of a number of lively fish restaurants. Dine on fried fish or calamari, salad and wine or beer at tables outside on the
street. Prices are incredibly reasonable at about US$3-5 per head. There's always
plenty of action to entertain you while you eat and street vendors periodically come
past with trays of *içli köfte* -delicious parcels of bulgur wheat stuffed with spicey
minced lamb and parsley. For something more refined try 1 of the 2 restaurants at the
Merit Hotel which serve international/ Turkish cuisine.

Caner, Ismet İnönü Bulvarı, Güvenç İş Merkezi No 15, T2383134, F2312970, flight tick- **Tour agencies**
eting, car rental, hotel reservations.

Bus Dolmuş to the *otogar* pass along the seaward carriage-way of Ismet İnönü **Transport**
Bulvarı, stopping across from the PTT. Bus tickets can be bought from a small office on *On the D-400 coastal*
the entrance ramp to the underground car park beneath the central mosque. **Adana**, *highway Mersin is*
dolmuş leave every 10-15 mins from next to ticket offices, US$1.50, 45 mins. **Antalya**, *well-connected to the*
10 buses daily between 0800 and 0100, 11 hrs, US$12. Antalya buses stop en-route at *rest of the country by*
Anamur, 5 hrs, US$8 and **Alanya**, 9 hrs, US$10. **Konya**, every 2½ hrs, 0030 2030, 5½ *bus & local trains*
hrs, US$9. **Göreme/Nevşehir**, 1 evening bus, 6½ hrs, US$9. Other destinations *chuntling regularly to & from Adana (the closest*
include Erzurum, Diyarbakır, Istanbul, Ankara and İzmir. *Silifke Turizm* run buses to *provincial airport)*
Kızkalesi (50 mins), **Silifke** (75 hr) and **Taşucu** (90 mins) from Peron 22. Get on a direct
bus which leave every hr as the dolmuş can be very slow. **Car rental** *Avis*, Ismet
İnönü Bulvarı, Uysal Apt No 100, T2323450, F2323450. *Anıl Rent A Car*, Ismet İnönü
Bulvarı Uysal Apartmanı No 100/A, T2313411, F2373689. **Ferries to Cyprus**: Turkish
Maritime Lines operate ferries to Gazimagosa in the Turkish Republic of North Cyprus
at 2400 every Mon, Wed and Fri. The crossing takes 10 hrs and costs US$25 for a pull-
man seat or US$48 for a car and passengers. Ticket are sold on the 1st floor of the ferry
terminal which is reached off Ismet İnönü Bulvarı, near the Tourist Office. At the time
of writing no visa is required for citizens of the EU, United States, Canada, Australia or
New Zealand. You may prefer to catch the much faster **catamaran** services from
Taşucu, near Silifke, which do the crossing in about 3 hrs (see page410).

Airline offices *Turkish Airlines*, Istiklal Caddesi Caddesi No 27, T2315232, F2321277. **Directory**
Banks There are banks on Istiklal Caddesi and around Gümrük Meydanı, which is also a good
place for private *döviz* **Communications** Post office: The PTT is just off İnönü Caddesi to the
east of the Mersin Oteli. **Internet**: *Bilgi Internet Cafe*, 3rd floor, Soğuksu Caddesi No 30, across
from the *Side Hotel*, US$1.50 per hr. **Hospitals** The State hospital is at the north end of Kuvayi
Milliye Caddesi. **Places of worship** *Saint Anthony's Roman Catholic Church*, south of train
station, mass daily at 0800 and 1830, 1100 Sun. **Tourist information** The Tourist Office is in a
white building on Ismet İnönü Bulvarı, south of the station.

Once a famous port city whose merchants grew wealthy on trade passing **Tarsus**
through the Cilician Gates, still an important transport corridor between central Anatolia and the Mediterranean coast, present-day Tarsus is a mundane
manufacturing town 32 km east of Mersin and stranded far from the sea.
Despite an arch over the highway into town grandly proclaiming Tarsus as
"the centre of the ancient world", there are very few reminders of this illustrious past amidst the modern concrete sprawl. Most tourist traffic takes the
form of coach tours which stop briefly at a couple of historical sights that have
survived. For the independent traveller there's also no reason to extend your
visit beyond the couple of hours it takes to see these attractions.

First up, conveniently found right next to the small bus station, is the so-called **Cleopatra's Gate**, which despite its name has no connection with the Empress. Of undisputed Roman origin, the triumphal gateway, know rather ignominiously in Turkish as Kancık Kapısı ("the Gate of the Bitch), has been much restored and is now stranded on a traffic island at the south end of the town's main street. Walk north up this road for about 500 m to a fountain, where a signpost for the **Antik Şehir (Ancient City)** points you left down Atatürk Bulvarı to a large open area where excavations have uncovered a section of Roman road. Discovered by chance during the redevelopment of a bank, the road is made of irregular basalt slabs and has a steep camber with drainage channels on each side. A team from Selçuk University, sponsored by a local textile firm, are currently working on the site, so you'll have to satisfy yourself with examining it from behind the perimeter fence.

Following the road up the side of the excavations towards a small mosque brings you to **Saint Paul's Well** (Senpol Kuyusu), a rather unexciting hole in the ground which has no known association with the Apostle. Surrounded by a fenced-off grassy area, the water from the borehole is drawn with a metal bucket on a chain and offered to visitors for a small fee. More compelling is a row of dilapidated half-timber houses nearby, which serve as an incongruous reminder of how things used to be before the proliferation of characterless concrete.

Retracing your steps back to the fountain on Mersin Caddesi, cross over the junction and walk down the street opposite to the 19th-century **church of St Paul**. Once again the basilica has no known link to its namesake, though it has recently benefited from a thorough renovation and will soon be pressed into service as the town's museum. Inside the church is decorated with *trompe l'oeil* and curious landscape paintings above the galleries. Have a look at the long crack running up the exterior wall of the apse, the result of an earthquake.

Having returned to the fountain you'll need to walk back down Mersin Caddesi to get back to the bus station. Along the way there are several *lokantas* where you can get a bite to eat or if it's something sweet you're after try **Gaziantepli Develler Baklava** to the west of the fountain at the beginning of Atatürk Caddesi. As you walk down Mersin Caddesi from the fountain glance along the first road on the left where the exclusive **Tarsus College**, an American school established in 1888, is housed in a large cream building.

■ *Getting there: Buses leave every 10-15 mins for Adana and Mersin. The frequent local trains between Adana and Mersin stop in Tarsus, although the station is inconveniently situated for the sites.*

Adana

Phone code: 0322
Colour map 5, grid B3
Population: over 1.5 mn

A large modern town, Adana has grown explosively in recent years, spreading inexorably outwards across the Çukurova Plain. The interminable approach to the city is along a dye straight highway cutting through a suburban landscape of housing developments, factories and warehouses. Much of this expansion has been fuelled by the city's fertile agricultural hinterland, with the area's cotton crop supporting a huge textile industry that has sucked in workers from across the region. As you might expect the centre is traffic clogged; not the most endearing of places in the sticky heat of summer. With only a few attractions of very passing interest, it also has little to offer foreign tourists, except, that is, for its busy airport, railway station and otogar which are useful points of transit if you're heading to the Hatay or west along the Mediterranean coast.

Ins and outs

Adana has good transport connections with the rest of the country. Excellent new toll-highways snake eastwards to Gaziantep (206 km) and west to Mersin (75 km), dramatically cutting journey times. It also sits near the main Trans-Taurus E-90 highway used by buses travelling between cities in western Anatolia and the southeast. There are also daily express trains from Kayseri, Ankara and Istanbul via Konya, as well as daily non-stop flights from Istanbul and Ankara.

Getting there
See page 426 for
further details

The main coastal highway (D-400) cuts right through the middle of town making it easy to access the city centre by car. If you're driving east or west along the E-90 expressway, however, you'll need to exit the junction signposted for *Adana Küzey 1*, which will bring you south to the coastal highway. Local buses arriving from the east, for example from Ceyhan or Osmaniye, terminate at the Yüreği *otogar*, on the main road 500 m east of the Seyhan River. The main *otogar* is also on the highway, but it's inconveniently situated 5 km west of the centre. Bus companies provide minibuses into the centre. The city's airport is 2 km closer to the centre than the bus station and a taxi downtown is about US$4. The train station is at the far end of Ziyapaşa Caddesi, 1½ km north of the city between the highway and Beş (5) Ocak Meydanı. Most city buses and dolmuş (US$0.30-0.50), including those to the bus and train stations and the Seyhan Barajı, stop on Atatürk Caddesi next to Inönü Parkı.

Getting around

Sights

There are few relics of Adana's lengthy history, one of the most tenacious survivors being the **Taş Köprüsü**, a second-century stone bridge crossing the Seyhan river which was commissioned by the Emperor Hadrian. On your way to have a look at the bridge pass the city's **Ulu Cami**, a 16th-century mosque constructed by a local Turkoman emir shortly before the Ottoman take over. It's most striking feature is an imposing crenellated portal decorated with a fluid marble inscription in Arabic and a recessed stalactite niche above the doorway. Around the other side of the multi-domed building rises a solid looking minaret, beside which is a colourful portal made from bands of yellow, grey and black stone. This gateway formerly gave access to the courtyard, but the mosque is currently closed for restoration.

Crossing the small palm shaded gardens behind the Ulu Cami brings you out beside another of Adana's landmarks, a 19th-century **clock tower** dividing the traffic. If you have some spare time you may want to explore the city's **bazaar area** to the south and west of the clock tower which is a warren of covered alleyways, crumbling *hans* and grimy arcades.

If you're out at the Archaeology Museum (see below) it's hard not to notice the huge, sparkling new mosque which towers up on the banks of the Seyhan River. Built over 10 years from 1988 with funds donated by Sakıp Sabancı, one of Turkey's most successful industrialists, the **Sabancı Merkez Camii** can accommodate over 25,000 people at one time and has the highest dome in the country. Superlatives aside, it's a graceful building which is a lot more pleasing to the eye than most modern mosques.

On display in a modern building off Fuzuli Caddesi, the town's collection of historical artefacts majors strongly on the Hellenistic and Roman periods, although the Urartian and Hittite eras are also represented. Exhibits include a Roman mosaic recovered from Misis, to the east of the city, bronze statues and some beautifully carved tombs, such as the noteworthy **Achilles sarcophagus** which is decorated with reliefs depicting scenes from the Iliad. ■ *0830-1200,*

Archaeology Museum

Eastern Mediterranean

1330-1730, US$1 daily except Mon. About 10-mins walk northeast of the centre and could be reached by heading north along Seyhan Caddesi from the end of Abidin Paşa Caddesi, having had a look at the Ulu Cami.

Seyhan Barajı On hot and sticky summer days Adana's residents flock out to the restaurants and cafés ringing the Seyhan Barajı Gölü, a large reservoir impounded by the Seyhan Dam. Only 5 km north of the centre and accessible by dolmuş or city buses marked "Universite" or "Baraj" stopping next to Inönü Botanik Parkı on Atatürk Caddesi, there are also bathing areas and several sailing clubs so don't forget your swimming stuff.

Adana

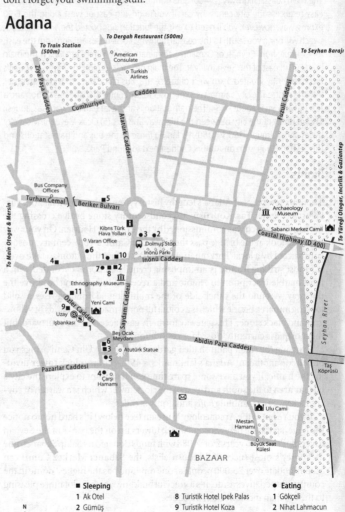

■ Sleeping		● Eating
1 Ak Otel	8 Turistik Hotel Ipek Palas	1 Gökçeli
2 Gümüş	9 Turistik Hotel Koza	2 Nihat Lahmacun
3 Otel Mercan	10 Turistik Otel Duygu	3 Onbaşılar
4 Otel Selibra	11 Zaimoğlu Oteli	4 Öz Asmaaltı
5 Otel Seyhan		5 Öz Baloğlu
6 Otel Yeni Park		6 Şahinoğlu Baklava
7 Sürmeli Çukurova		7 Zümrüt Et Lokantası

0 metres 100
0 yards 100

Eastern Mediterranean

A vast deltaic plain stretching south from Adana, the Çukurova was formed over **Çukurova**
millions of years by silt deposited by the Seyhan and Ceyhan rivers. With such
fertile alluvial soils and a very conducive climate the area has an extremely long
history of human settlement. In fact, the first people ploughed and planted on
the plains about 10,000 years ago in what has been dubbed the Neolithic Revolution, when man began to abandon hunting and gathering in favour of a more
sedentary existence. Later, Çukurova was part of the neo-Hittite kingdom of
Kizzuwadna which had its heyday in the ninth century BC.

Today, vast areas of the delta are given over to cotton, making it one of the
most important agricultural regions in the country. Hundreds of thousands of
tonnes of "white gold" are produced each year, providing the raw material for
local industry and jobs for migrant workers. Unfortunately, the down side has
been the loss of extensive areas of environmentally important wetland,
drained for farming or poisoned by fertilisers and pesticides. Large areas of
marsh and several freshwater lakes do still exist along the southern fringes of
the delta and its beaches are an important nesting area for two species of
marine turtle, the Loggerhead (*Caretta caretta*) and its more endangered
cousin the Green Turtle (*Chelonia mydas*).

There are a few points of minor touristic interest on the Çukurova plain, one
being the seaside village of **Karataş**, a monotonous 50-km drive south of
Adana, which has become a low-key resort frequented at weekends and public
holidays by city dwellers. Several rudimentary pensions, including the **Ünal
Pansiyon**, some fish restaurants and a good beach are the sum total of the place,
which could feasibly be a pleasant afternoon escape from the summer heat of
Adana. ■ *Getting there: Dolmuş for Karataş depart from the western end of the
Taşköprü in Adana, US$1.25, 40 mins.*

Essentials

L *Sürmeli Çukurova*, Özler Caddesi, T3523600, F3521945. Large, modern hotel fre- **Sleeping**
quented mainly by visiting businessmen, comfortable rooms with all the mod cons,
facilities include restaurant, bar and sauna, substantial discounts available on displayed rate. **AL** *Otel Seyhan*, Turhan Cemal Beriker Bulvarı No 18, T4575810,
F4542834, otelseyhan.com.tr. Situated on the north side of the highway this smart
hotel is a landmark on the Adana skyline, all the facilities and comforts you'd expect
for 5 stars. **A** *Zaimoğlu Oteli*, Özler Caddesi No 22, T3635353, F3635363. Large
well-equipped and furnished rooms with cable-TV, minibar and a hairdryer in the
bathroom, attentive staff and value for money suggest this hotel above the more
expensive places. **B** *Turistik Hotel Koza*, Özler Caddesi No 103, T3525857, F3598571.
60 decent, if a bit plain, rooms, a/c, TV, telephone, avoid rooms fronting noisy Özler
Caddesi.**C** *Turistik Otel Duygu*, İnönü Caddesi No 14, T3631510. Horrible pink decor
and very mediocre, a/c, TV and telephone. **D** *Otel Selibra*, İnönü Caddesi No 50,
T3633676, F3634283. 50 room hotel, good value for money, don't be put-off by the
pink reception, a/c, minibar, telephone, decent shower, ask for one at the back to
avoid traffic noise. Recommended. **E** *Turistik Hotel İpek Palace*, İnönü Caddesi No 89,
T3633512, F3633516. Opposite the *Turistik Otel Duygu*, fairly drab 1-star place, fan,
telephone and TV, breakfast extra. **F** *Ak Otel*, Özler Caddesi No 19, T3514208,
F3523878. Uninspiring place, simple rooms with or without shower, carpets in need
of a good clean, no breakfast. **G** *Otel Mercan*, Melek Girmez Çarşısı, T3512603. Visible
in a narrow street running off west from Beş Ocak Meydanı, clean doubles with fan
and ensuite are reached up smart marble staircase, best of the budget options by far,
no breakfast. **G** *Gümüş Hotel*, İnönü Caddesi No 87, T3630128. Next to the *Hotel İpek
Palas*, much more appealing despite the simplicity of the newly decorated rooms,
each has a basin, showers are shared, no breakfast.

Eating

In Adana you begin to feel the culinary influence of the SE as many dishes are laced with a liberal sprinkling of chilli & accompanied by a pile of fresh mint leaves

The town is famed for its *adana kebabı*, a skewer of spicy minced lamb wrapped in a *durum* (wheat pancake) and accompanied by fiery green chillies, red onion, mint and parsley. Wash it down with a glass of *şalgam* (turnip juice) or *ayran*. One of the best, not to mention cheapest, evenings meals in town can be had in the car park next to the Tourist Information office, where a busy stall serves delicious *adana kebabı*, with a pile of tomatoes, parsley and mint, at little tables. An added bonus in a town where things shut pretty early is that it's open well into the night. **Midrange** For something a bit more sophisticated than the run-of-the-mill kebap restaurants head north of the highway to where Atatürk Caddesi makes a 90 degree turn towards the train station. There you'll find *Dergah Restaurant*, T4532835, which has a more varied menu, evening entertainment and a swimming pool for day-time use. **Cheap** *Öz Asmaaltı*, Pazarlar Caddesi, in street to the west of Atatürk statue in Beş Ocak Meydanı, convenient if you're staying in the vicinity, spartan place but locally recommended for kebaps, grills and pide, also serves cold beer. *Öz Baloğlu*, Melek Girmez Çarşısı, opposite *Otel Mercan*, simple place serving soup, *döner kebap* and ready-prepared dishes like stew or *taze fasulye* (green beans). *Onbaşılar Restaurant*, Atatürk Caddesi, 1st-floor dining room to the north of the park, an Adana institution, with a fairly predictable but well-cooked selection of meat dishes and kebaps, fairly brusque service, alcohol served. *Nihat Lahmacun*, off Atatürk Caddesi past *Onbaşılar Restaurant*, as the name suggests serves lahmacun, pide, but also chicken döner and *çiğ köfte*. *Gökçeli*, *İnönü Caddesi*, opposite the *Hotel Ipek Palas*, fast-food place with *döner kebabı* US$1 or burger and fries US$2.75. *Zümrüt Et Lokantası*, İnönü Caddesi, near the *Hotel Ipek Palas*, kebaps and grilled meat. Visit 1 of the many juice bars around town which typically serve freshly squeezed *portakal suyu* (orange), *havuç suyu* (carrot), *muz sutu* (banana) and *şalgam* (turnip). There's 1 next to the *Salibra Otel* on İnönü Caddesi. *Şahinoğlu Baklava*, Ziya Paşa Caddesi, to northeast of junction with İnönü Caddesi, mouthwatering array of sweets including *kadayıf* sprinkled with pistachios.

Shopping

There are several shopping centres along Özler Caddesi, with the largest, *Çetinkaya*, overlooking Kuruköprü Meydanı.

Transport

Air *Turkish Airlines*, Prof Dr Nusret Fişek Caddesi No 22, T4570222, F4543088, has 6 daily return flights to Istanbul and 2 to Ankara. A service bus leaves their offices 90 mins before flight departures. *Kıbrıs Türk Hava Yolları (Turkish-Cypriot Airlines)*, Atatürk Caddesi, south of Tourist Information, direct flights to Cyprus everyday except Tue and Thu.

Road Bus: Most companies have offices where Ziya Paşa Caddesi crosses the main highway and will provide a service to the *otogar*. **Ankara**, every 2 hrs, 9 hrs, US$12. **Antakya**, hourly, 3 hrs, US$5. **Antalya** (via Silifke and Anamur), 4 or 5 daily, 12 hrs, US$13. **Konya**, regular, 6½ hrs, US$10, **Mersin**, every 15 mins, 1 hr, US$1.75. **Niğde**, 4 daily, 3 hrs, US$4. **Dolmuş** to **Ceyhan**, **Misis** and **Yumurtalık** depart from the Yüreğir Otogar, 500 m east of the Seyhan River. **Car rental**: *Avis*, Ziya Paşa Bulvarı, Hürriyet Apt No 5/B, T4533045, F4534824. *Budget*, Stadyum Caddesi, Serhat Apt. 37/C, Seyhan, T4590016, F4591109. *Can Oto Kiralama*, Baraj Yolu, 5½ Aurak, Sümer Mahallesi, 39 Sokak, Kulak Apt, Block 6/B, T2283573, F2250315, canoto@dostmail.com

The train station can be reached by jumping on a dolmuş going N up Atatürk Caddesi from İnönü Botanik Parkı

Train *Çukurova Mavi Tren*, departs for **Ankara** via Niğde at 1930, 12 hrs. *Toros Ekspresi*, passes through en-route for **Gaziantep** Tue, Thu, Sun at 0505, 6½ hrs; returning en-route for **Istanbul** via Konya and Afyon at 2114 on Tue, Thu and Sat, 21 hrs. *Erciyes Ekspresi*, departs Adana 1730 everyday arriving in **Kayseri** at 2400, 6½ hrs. *Fırat Ekspresi*, departs Adana everyday at 0840, arriving in **Elazığ** at 2015. There are also local trains to **Tarsus** and **Mersin**, every 30-40 mins, 1 hr.

Airline offices See above. **Banks** *Işbankası*, Özler Caddesi, opposite Yeni Cami. **Baths** *Çarşı Hamamı*, Büyük Saat Kulesi, next to the clock tower, 0730-2300, women-only. *Mestan Hamamı*, Pazarlar Caddesi, old baths on west side of Beş Ocak Meydanı. Open 0530-2330, men-only, US$4 for bath and *kese*. **Communications** Post office: There central PTT is on Kızılay Caddesi, parallel to Abdin Paşa Caddesi. **Internet**: *Uzay Internet Café*, 2nd floor, Arpacı İşhanı, Özler Caddesi No 210, T3511620. **Foreign consulates** *American Consulate*, Atatürk Caddesi, Vali Yolu, T4539106. **Hospitals** *Seyhan Hastanesi*, Barajı Yolu Caddesi, private hospital. **Tourist information** Office at Atatürk Caddesi No 13, T3591994, F3526790. Open weekdays 0800-1700.

Taking the highway, as opposed to the E-90 expressway, east from Adana brings you after 17 km to **Yakapınar** on the banks of the Ceyhan River. Formerly known as Misis, excavations have revealed that the small town, situated next to an important river crossing, has been inhabited more-or-less continuously since Hittite times. Archaeologists have unearthed artefacts spanning this huge period of time, however, Roman mosaic pavements have pride of place in the small museum.

Continuing east a dramatically sited 12th-century Armenian castle, the **Yılan Kalesi** (Snake Castle), comes into view on the crest of a ridge rising to the east of the Ceyhan River. Motor access to the ruins is via a long winding road, sign-posted on the right, with a predictably fine vista across the Çukurova Plains as reward for the climb.

On the banks of the languid Ceyhan River, 47 km east of Adana, is the thoroughly unexciting market town of **Ceyhan**. The only reason you might consider a fleeting visit is if you're heading for the coastal village of Yumurtalık, 34 km to the south.

A lonely road cuts south from Ceyhan across an open, empty landscape of sweeping cultivated fields and low hills to Yumurtalık. It's a scrappy, but endearing, little place with a busy fishing fleet that sets out daily to harvest the rich off-shore waters. The harbour is overlooked by a very moth-eaten medieval tower with the village mosque actually nestled inside the walls of the keep. These remains are from Ayas, an important port city which was visited twice by Marco Polo. Some more historic masonry survives on a small island to the east of the harbour, visible as you approach the centre along a short promenade lined by holiday apartments. The beach in front is gently sloping and pretty clean, setting the village up as a popular weekend get-away for residents of near-by Adana, as well as the odd party of off-duty servicemen and women from the US base at Incirlik. Everything comes alive after the schools break-up in June, but the rest of the year things are pretty quiet. Beyond town to the west, reached by following the road past the harbour and PTT, several kilometres of coastline offer more solitary bathing opportunities.

Sleeping and eating The only hotel at present is **F** *Öztur Otel*, T6712107/0, F6712163, on beach front Atatürk Caddesi. Simple rooms with ensuite facilities and a balcony, larger 'suites' with kitchenette are ideal for a small family, US$25. There are also several family-run pensions including: **G** *Küçük Aile Pansiyonu*, Kumrulu Caddesi No 19, T6712215. A 5-min walk past the harbour and the post office on the other side of town, uninspiring concrete building, but rooms are clean with ensuite bathroom, balcony, kitchen on each floor, owned by friendly local fisherman. Food-wise there's a row of cheap *lokantas* on the main street, such as *Deniz Lokantası*, serving ready-prepared dishes and kebaps, or you could try *Babanın Yeri*, down by the harbour, for fish. *Erzin Sahil Restaurant* at the village end of the beach has the most varied menu with very reasonably priced seafood, lahmacun and kebaps.

Transport Coming from Adana you'll need to get a dolmuş to Ceyhan, 1 hr, US$1.30, from the Yüreğin *otogar* on the main road to the east of the Seyhan River. Let the driver know where you're going and he'll drop you at the Yumurtalık dolmuş, 40 mins, US$0.75. These depart when full, which can be quite a wait out-of-season. Approaching from the east you'll probably have to be dropped at the Ceyhan turn-off on the main road, from where dolmuş crawl into Ceyhan every 15 mins.

Anazarbus

The ruins here are scattered across agricultural land & amongst the houses of the contemporary village of Anavarza, set at the base of a steep-sided limestone escarpment

A half-hour drive north of Ceyhan brings you to the hill-top remains of the fortress-city of Anazarbus. Benefiting from its advantageous position astride the caravan routes between Anatolia and Syria, Anazarbus grew to prominence in the Hellenistic era. Annexed by the Romans in 18 AD, it maintained its strategic and commercial significance through the subsequent Byzantine period. Lost to Arab raiders in the eighth century, the city was briefly regained by Constantinople before becoming part of the Cilician Kingdom of Lesser Armenia. Periods of Mongol, Turkish and Mameluk rule ensued with the city's decline accelerated by several earthquakes.

The first thing you'll see are the city walls, pierced by a gateway; while turning down a track on the right brings you after 250 m to an open-air museum (*daily, US$0.50*), which has various marble fragments and some solid stone sarcophagi on display. More compelling is a mosaic of the goddess Thetis which formed the bottom of a Roman pool. Beyond the museum is a Roman triumphal arch constructed in honour of Septimius Severus with the ruins of a stadium, a theatre, a Byzantine basilica and a baths complex nearby. It's a steep 15 to 20 minute climb up to the citadel on the mountaintop.

■ *Getting there: North of the Adana-Osmaniye highway, reached by turning off the highway towards Kandirli and Koza between the Yılan Kalesi and the Ceyhan Junction. It's 26 km to the village of Ayşehoca, where a road on the right leads 5 km to the village. Without your own transport catch a Kandirli dolmuş, which depart from the Yüreği bus station in Adana. Get off in Ayşehoca. From there you have to walk or hitch. The village has a small shop but don't expect more than a drink and snack. Pack plenty of drinking water.*

Karatepe-Arslan taş National Park

The setting for the archaeological site amongst the pine forested hills overlooking a turquoise blue reservoir formed by the Ceyhan Dam is enchanting

Another possible detour best made with your own transport is this national park that encompasses the remains of Karatepe, a city occupied between the 12th and eighth centuries BC by the rulers of the neo-Hittite Kizzuwadna kingdom. The ruins so far uncovered are far less extensive than those at the Hittite capital of Hattuşaş, although they do include several long inscriptions as well as some well preserved reliefs. The site guardian will conduct you on a tour of the archaeological zone. Parts of the city's 1,000-m perimeter wall are still visible, encompassing what was a hilltop summer palace built by the Kizzuwadna king, Azitawadda. The palace's southern gateway is guarded by stone lions and sphinxes, with carved panels flanking the entrance vividly depicting an elaborate royal feast. More stone figures and a relief showing various Hittite deities are found on the other side of the hill. Also unearthed at the site is a lengthy bilingual inscription recording the founding of the city. Written in both Hittite and Phoenician script, this text was of huge significance to archaeologists because it allowed them to decipher the previously impenetrable Hittite language. ■ *0800-1200, 1400-1730; 1300-1530 in winter, daily except Mon. Park fee US$1, ruins an extra US$1, cars US$3. Good picnic and camping possibilities near the park's entrance and a buffet selling cold drinks and snacks, and toilets. Getting there: About 35 km northeast of Osmaniye on a road sign-posted for Karatepe-Aslantaş Müzesi and Hierapolis (see below). No public transport to the site although you could hire a taxi in Osmaniye for the trip, also taking in the ruins of Hierapolis on the way, for about US$30. Osmaniye is well served by buses and dolmuş to Adana, Iskenderun and Gaziantep.*

Settled since Hellenistic times Hierapolis Castabala was, like Anazarbus to the west, an important garrison town of the Tarcondimotus Dynasty who ruled over the Cilician plain and paid tribute to Rome. Subsequently occupied in turn by Romans, Armenians, Byzantines, the Crusaders and Mameluks; today the city's impressive fortress, atop a rocky crag, towers over the surrounding meadows and cotton fields. From the site entrance walk along a Corinthian colonnaded avenue, flanked by a Roman bath complex and temple. There's also a ruined theatre beyond the citadel outcrop and the remains of several medieval Armenian churches. ■ *US$0.50, if somebody is present. Getting there: 15 km north of Osmaniye, you could combine a look around with a visit to Karatepe-Aslantaş National Park, above.*

Hierapolis Castabala

The Hatay

Looking at a map of Turkey the Hatay is a conspicuous feature: a small toe of territory jutting south into Syria. Culturally it's also an aberration: peopled mainly by Arabs, small Syrian and Greek Orthodox communities also co-exist with a Turkish minority, making it one of the most multi-cultural provinces in the country. Links with the Middle East are close geographically speaking and because many of the area's men reside as guest workers in the Gulf States. In return Arab holidaymakers cross the border to sightsee and enjoy the relative freedoms denied them back home. Not surprisingly a strong Syrian influence permeates many aspects of daily life, from the locally spoken Arabic dialect, peppered with Turkish words; to the tasty regional cuisine that combines the flavours of fresh mint, parsley and lemon with the spice of red chilly.

Conquered by Alexander the Great during his lightning campaign, the Hatay became part of the huge Seleucid realm after his death, with the imperial capital moved to Antioch, modern-day Antakya, at the beginning of the third century BC. The Seleucid collapse saw a brief period of Armenian rule, before Pompey marched in and annexed the area for Rome in 66 BC. Christianity made an early appearance in the region; established by those escaping persecution in Jerusalem. The new religion attracted a large following, eventually ranking Antioch alongside the Patriachates of Constantinople and Jerusalem in terms of importance. Indeed it was here that the term "Christian" was first used in reference to the church's followers.

History
The Hatay has been prized since antiquity for its strategic position astride important trade routes south into Syria & beyond

The Byzantine tenure was ended in the seventh century by the Arab invasions, with subsequent, comparatively brief, periods of Byzantine and Selçuk rule replaced in 1098 by a feudal principality founded by Count Bohemund, one of the leaders of the First Crusade. This peculiar Frankish state lasted for nearly 200 years, however, its demise at the hands of the Egyptian Mameluks was particularly bloody, with 16,000 soldiers massacred and the luckless population of Antioch sold into slavery.

Incorporated into the Ottoman empire the Hatay remained under Turkish control until its occupation by the French after the First World War. Despite Turkish opposition, the Treaty of Lausanne formalised this *status quo* and the province was ceded to the French Protectorate of Syria. This left a significant Turkish population the wrong side of the frontier, a situation that was unacceptable to Atatürk. But Turkey had little success in pressing its claims until the run-up to Syrian independence in 1936, when the area was awarded significant autonomy from Damascus. This still didn't satisfy the Turks and as the storm clouds of war gathered over Europe, France caved-in to continued pressure, agreeing to a plebiscite on the province's fate in an effort to curry favour with

Eastern Mediterranean

Ankara. Turkish vote rigging and intimidation ensured that the election went the right way and in 1938 the independent Republic of Hatay came into being. However, it was to be a short-lived state, as within a year its fledgling national assembly, dominated by Turkish deputies, voted for a union with Turkey. Since then tensions have periodically arisen between the Hatay's Arab population and the government, though the community's demands generally fall far short succession, instead concerned primarily with developing their cultural rights.

Iskenderun

The town centre is unexceptional rather than unpleasant, but there's no reason to stop despite an impressive history

The important port and industrial town of Iskenderun could hardly be a worse introduction to the Hatay. Approaching from the north along the narrow coastal plain hemmed in to the west by mountains, you're greeted by a grim industrial landscape of smokestacks, electricity pylons and warehouses which form one of the country's largest petro-chemical and steel complexes. The military are also much in evidence, guarding the strategic industrial plants and garrisoning the road and railway lines north.

Sleeping and eating If for some reason you want to stay there are several options in the centre of town near the waterfront promenade. From the bus station walk south to the highway. The main street, Şehit Pamir Caddesi, can be reached by crossing the highway and turning right. Walking to the end of Şehit Pamir Caddesi brings you to seafront Atatürk Bulvarı and the main square. **D** *Hotel Cabir*, Ulucami Caddesi No 16, T6123391. 1 block east of Şehit Pamir Caddesi, comfortable rooms with ensuite, telephone and TV. **E** *Hotel Altındişler*, Şehit Pamir Caddesi No 11, T6171011. Simple rooms with shower and fan.

Transport All buses heading to and from Antakya call in at the town's *otogar*.

Directory Banks There are banks with ATMs on Şehit Pamir Caddesi. **Tourist information** The Tourist Information Office, T6141620, F6132879, Atatürk Bulvarı No 49. Open weekday, 0830-1230, 1330-1700.

Iskenderun to Antakya

South of Iskenderun the highway leaves the coast, climbing its way across the Amanus Mountains by way of the 740-m Belen Pass. Known in Roman times as the *Porta Syriae* – Gate of Syria – it has always been a strategic point on the trade route between Anatolia and Syria, and today the modern descendants of the caravans of old, articulated trucks, still wheeze their way up the steep incline. Descending the southern side you get your first view of the fertile Amik plain, planted with a checkerboard of wheat fields and dotted with prehistoric tumuli. A few kilometres from the base of the pass a turning on the right leads 4 km to the village of Bakras, overlooked by the impressive remains of a **medieval castle**. Constructed in the eighth century by the Arab caliph Harun al-Rashid, the citadel had a turbulent history and was occupied in the following 400 hundred years by Armenians, Selçuks and the Knights Templar. The Ottomans took the castle in 1516, abandoning it to the ravages of time and frequent earthquakes.

Antakya

Sitting in a wide open valley at the southern edge of the Amik plain, Antakya began life as the glittering capital of the vast Seleucid empire. An important Roman city, it also played an influential role in the early history of Christianity. The cave church of St Luke still attracts modern-day pilgrims. However, earthquakes, conquest and rapid urban development have left few other reminders of the town's illustrious past. Instead, Antakya is a fairly modern provincial town with a large Arabic speaking population and a pleasantly laid-back feel. On summer evenings swifts wheel and dive above the rooftops as the sound of a church bell mingles with the müezzin's call to prayer. In the narrow backstreets of the old town men cluster around backgammon boards. Tourism is low-key, consisting of an occasional coach load of "faith tourists" bused in to see the cave church and to whip around the town's outstanding "Mosaic Museum". Few extend their itineraries much beyond this, which is a pity as a night or two in town gives you the chance to visit other minor sights in the area as well as time to soak-up Antakya's subtly different atmosphere.

Phone code 0326
Colour map 5, grid C4
Altitude 85 m

Ins and outs

The only way to reach Antakya without your own transport is by bus, of which the city is extremely well-served with services from across the country. If you can't stand long bus journeys, the closest you can get to the city by rail is Iskenderun, about an 1 hr north, or Adana if you're flying, 2-3 hrs away by road. As you might expect Antakya is also connected by regular buses to cities in Syria, Jordan and Saudi Arabia.

Getting there
See page 435 for further details

Antakya is a manageable size with most of its sights, services and accommodation found within spitting distance of Rana Köprüsü, the main bridge across the River Asi. From the bus station a 5-min stroll down Istiklal Caddesi brings you into the centre. The only significant sight which you'll need to muster some energy to visit is the Church of St Peter, situated on the edge of town 2 km to the northeast of the bridge.

Getting around

Antioch ad Orontes, to give the city it's full title, was established in 330 BC by Seleucus I, one of Alexander the Great's generals and the founder of the Seleucid Dynasty. It became the capital of the vast Seleucid Empire in the third century BC, growing into a large and prosperous city of 500,000 people by Roman times. Christianity found fertile ground in the city's large Jewish population with missionaries building a significant local community by 50 BC. Distinguished residents included St Peter, for seven years becoming the city's first bishop, while Paul and Barnabas also enjoyed an extended stay.

History

Devastated by numerous earthquakes, the first recorded tremor came in 148 BC. Some 200 years later the Roman Emperor Trajan was nearly killed in an earthquake during a visit to the city, with several subsequent quakes causing widespread destruction and killing thousands. Further damage came in the form of war. It's strategic position on an important route of movement also meant that Antioch was frequently ravaged. Sacked by the Persians several times during the Roman and Byzantine eras, the city was lost to the Arabs in the seventh century. Briefly recaptured for Byzantium by Emperor Nicephorus, it was lost again in 1084, this time to the Selçuks. The city fell to the Crusaders later in the 11th century becoming the capital of a feudal Christian Kingdom which lasted until its bloody termination by the Mameluks in 1268. By the time the Ottomans arrived in 1516 the city had lost its prominence, becoming a relatively insignificant backwater town.

Eastern Mediterranean

Sights

The city has expanded from its original site on the east bank of the River Asi, the ancient Orontes, to occupy a large area on the west side of the watercourse. This new part of the city is devoid of interest, consisting mainly of wide tree-planted boulevards lined with apartment blocks. In contrast the old core of the city on the opposite side has lots more atmosphere, as well as most of the town's surviving vernacular architecture.

Antakya

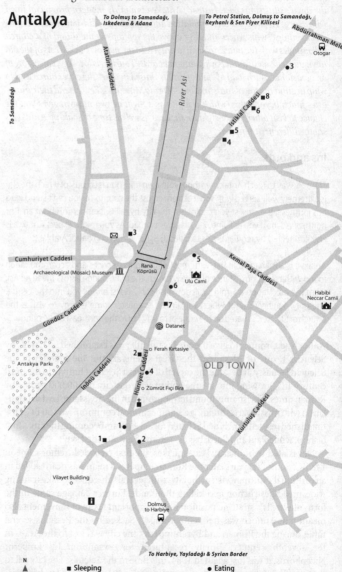

Sleeping
1 Antik Beyazıt
2 Atahan
3 Büyük Antakya Oteli
4 Jasmin
5 Onur
6 Orontes
7 Saray
8 Turistik Divan

Eating
1 Anadolu
2 Antakya Evi
3 Dörtler Lokantası
4 Han
5 Şamlıoğlu Künefe Salonu
6 Seyran Künefe

Opposite Rana Köprüsü is the Selçuk **Ulu Cami** whose irregular courtyard is partly shaded by ornamental orange trees. A rather unexceptional looking stone building, its most conspicuous feature is its well-proportioned minaret.

Walking south along Hürriyet Caddesi from the Ulu Cami, after a bend in the road an **Orthodox Church** is reached through a gateway and up some stone steps on the left. It's in immaculate condition, reflecting the vitality of the tightly knit local community, and there's usually somebody around to let you in for a look at the interior.

Beyond the church on Sihlalı Kuvvetler Caddesi are some old houses dating from the beginning of the 20th century, with elegant wrought iron balconies and wooden shutters. Turning left (northeast) down one of the narrow streets leads you into a traditional residential area, a maze-like district of narrow alleyways and passages, crowded with houses and the odd workshop. It's relatively cool and peaceful except for the sounds of family life continuing behind closed doors and shuttered windows. There's little hope of finding your way anywhere in particular, so it's best just to wander in a vaguely northeast direction which will probably bring you out somewhere along Kemal Paşa Caddesi.

At the far end of Kemal Paşa Caddesi is the **Habibi Neccar Camii**. Named after a locally revered Muslim saint who lived in a cave on the mountainside above town, it was converted from a church during the 13th-century Mameluk occupation. The courtyard is a popular spot for children to play in the shadow of a tall Arab-style minaret, topped by a wooden balcony and a conical roof. Obviously of ancient origins, a marble pillar standing in the courtyard suggests there may originally have been a temple on the site, before both mosque and church.

Old Antakya

On the west side of the river, beside the busy roundabout, is a small building constructed of beige stone which functioned briefly as the parliament of the short-lived Republic of Hatay. Today, it's devoted to less noble pursuits as an adults-only cinema. Also overlooking the traffic circle is the Belediye (town hall) and the post office.

Pop-in to the *Büyük Antakya Hotel* on Ataturk Caddesi for a look at an exhibition of old photographs in the mezzanine above the reception. Atmospheric black and white poses show a fly-blown, one-horse town; images which, except for the inclusion of local landmarks, are hard to reconcile with the realities of modern Antakya outside.

A short walk down Gündüz Caddesi from the roundabout brings you to the entrance for **Antakya Parkı** where you can join local families on their promenade on sultry summer evenings. A long avenue shaded by cypress trees runs the length of the park, lined on one side by cafés where Antakya's youth congregate to play cards and chat. Buy yourself a bag of *çekirdek* (sunflower seeds) or an ice-cream as you stroll or sit for a glass of tea.

New Antakya

Eastern Mediterranean

Sometimes called the 'Mosaic Museum', the main attraction is a stunning collection of Roman mosaics mainly recovered from excavations at nearby Harbiye, formerly the ancient resort of Daphne. Laboriously created from thousands of individually coloured pieces, the beautiful mosaics depict mythological scenes or recreations of contemporary life in a vivid, life-like way. Produced between the first and fifth centuries AD to decorate opulent Roman villas and palaces, the mosaics remain in excellent condition except for a few missing patches, and are well-displayed in several naturally lit, high ceiling rooms. Particularly memorable pieces include the huge Buffet Mosaic; one depicting Narcissus gazing adoringly at his reflection in a pond of water and a representation of Thetis and Oceanus, holding court with a bevy of sea-creatures. There's an interesting mosaic showing the Evil Eye being waylaid by wild animals, and a rather undignified portrait of Dionysus stumbling drunk.

Archaeological Museum
Excellent archaeological collection stands head & shoulders above the average provincial museum

A collection of other artefacts from various periods are displayed in the other rooms with Salon V dominated by an impressive pair of stone lions from the eighth century BC. Less satisfying are the fragmentary remains of a Hittite fresco discovered at the burial mound of Açana, one of many tumuli dotting the Amik plain to the north of town. Also on show are collections of delicate glassware, bronze figureens and well-preserved Hittite spearheads. ■ *0830-1200, 1330-1700 daily except Mon. US$3.*

Sen Piyer Kilisesi (Church of St Peter) The biggest draw in Antakya, attracting a steady stream of "faith tourists" and curious Turks, is the Church of St Peter located on a mountainside just beyond the outskirts of town. Held to have been a meeting place for the town's early Christian community, Luke the Evangelist is said to have preached regularly in the cave-chapel, with Barnabas and Paul setting-off from here on their first missionary journey.

The stone facade of the church, built into the cliff-face by the Crusaders in the 12th century, is pierced by three star-shaped windows and a door which leads into the cave behind. Refreshingly cool on a hot-day, the cavern is bare except for a simple marble altar and some fragments of mosaic flooring. The walls glisten with moisture and in one corner there's a bucket containing a cup with which to drink the "holy water" collected inside. In the other corner a blocked passageway, presumed to be an escape route for the congregation in times of peril, leads a short distance back into the rock. Mass is still celebrated in the church most Sunday mornings, while every year on the 29th June Christians congregate in the church to mark the anniversary of St Paul's death. The church also makes a haunting venue for periodic classical concerts and recitals. Look out around town for posters advertising such events, or you could enquire at the Tourist Information Office.

The mountainside above the church is honeycombed with small tunnels and tombs and a path to the left of the entrance leads 200 m across the slope to a curious relief carved into the rock. Although badly weathered, it's possible to make-out a veiled figure, thought to be Charon, the mythological ferryman who rowed spirits across the River Styx to Hades. There appears to be a small figure on his shoulder which could be the Seleucid monarch Antiochus IV, who may have commissioned the portrait in the second century BC during a period of great drought.

■ *0830-1200, 1330-1630 daily except Mon. US$0.75. Getting there: Reached by walking along Kurtuluş Caddesi until you reach a sign-post on the right, from where it's a further 300 m up a track. A taxi there and back should set you back about US$5 with 20 mins waiting time at the church.*

Essentials

Sleeping
Antakya's selection of hotels is pretty good with a reasonable option in most price brackets

A *Büyük Antakya Oteli*, Atatürk Caddesi No 8, T2135858, F2135869. Large hotel with well-equipped rooms, TV, telephone, a/c, minibar, restaurant, lovely old photographs of Antakya on mezzanine floor. **A** *Antik Beyazıt Hotel*, Hükümet Caddesi No 4, T2162900, F2143089. Near the the *Vilâyet* building, without doubt the most interesting hotel in town, turn of the century building recently renovated, well-furnished rooms, some have old iron bedsteads, a/c, modern shower, telephone, minibar, family rooms on ground floor sleep 3, good value at US$110. Recommended. **C** *Hotel Orontes*, Istiklal Caddesi No 58, T2145931, F2145933. Good midrange hotel, popular with package groups, rooms bit dark though, TV, telephone, a/c, shower, open-buffet breakfast. **D** *Atahan Hotel*, Hürriyet Caddesi No 28, T2142140, F2158006. Plain rooms lit by florescent tube, telephone, TV, a/c, attractive decorative tilework of floors, avoid front rooms although they have balcony due to noise from street. **D** *Onur Hotel*,

Istiklal Caddesi No 14, entrance in alley off Istiklal Caddesi. Despite dark reception rooms are actually pretty comfortable, as well-equipped as *Hotel Orontes* but better value, TV, telephone, a/c. Recommended. **F** *Turistik Divan Hotel*, Istiklal Caddesi No 62, T2151518, F2146356. Showing its age a bit, nonetheless represents excellent value particularly for single rooms, TV, telephone, rooms at front are noisy, no breakfast. Recommended. **F** *Hotel Saray*, Hürriyet Caddesi No 3, T2149001, F2149002. Above restaurant of same name, despite being right in the middle of things back rooms are peaceful, views of old town and mountains, good value, clean, telephone, TV. Recommended. **G** *Jasmin Hotel*, Istiklal Caddesi No 14, T2127171. No thrills place, basic but clean rooms, shared showers and toilets, avoid front rooms due to traffic noise, no breakfast, good budget option.

Midrange *Antakya Evi Restaurant*, Silahlı Kuvvetler Caddesi, excellent place to sample traditional local dishes in pleasant surroundings of old restored house, try the *Halebi kebabı*- a delicious patty of minced lamb with spices, garlic and pine nuts, attentive staff and relax atmosphere make this by far the nicest place in town, very reasonably priced US$6-10 per head depending on whether you have wine. **Cheap** *Saray Restaurant*, Hürriyet Caddesi at the bridge-end, bustling fast-food place with *döner* and ready-prepared dishes such as *kuru fasulye* (white beans). *Han Restaurant*, Hürriyet Caddesi, on the same side at the other end of the street to the Saray, squeeze through the fierce heat of the kitchen and upstairs to pleasant open-air tables on balcony overlooking street, enjoy *şiş* or *döner* with a cold beer for about US$4. *Anadolu Restaurant*, Hürriyet Caddesi, favourite local place for *meze* and meat dishes, occassionally some fish, tables in small garden, alcohol served. *Dörtler Lokantası*, Istiklal Caddesi, busy place near the *otogar* serving ready-prepared dishes, kebaps and pide, about US$3 per person. Call-in to one of the many places around the Ulu Cami and try the local sweet *künefe*, a predictably sweet concoction made from shredded wheat, white cheese and sugar syrup. Local favourite is *Şamlıoğlu Künefe Salonu*, with *Seyran Künefe* at the beginning of Hürriyet Caddesi also serving a breakfast of cheese, olives, honey and tea.

Eating
Antakya has a particularly rich local cuisine which, as you'd expect, exhibits a strong Arab influence. Dishes are a bit spicier than elsewhere & accompanied by a pile of mint leaves to nibble on

Zümrüt Fıçı Bira, Hürriyet Caddesi, at far end near the church, tiny place with draught *Efes* and sport permanently on the television.

Bars

Ferah Kırtasiye ve Kitabevi, Hürriyet Caddesi No 17, good selection of foreign language newspaper.

Shopping

Titus Tourism, Atatürk Caddesi, next to the *Büyük Antakya Hotel*, T2161025, F2139141, car rental, local tours, ticketing.

Tour agencies

Bus Adana, every 30 mins, 3 hrs, US$5. Ankara, about every 2 hrs, 10 hrs, US$14. Antalya, 5 daily, 10 hrs, US$15. Kayseri, 3 daily, 8 hrs, US$12. Gaziantep, regular buses, 4 hrs, US$8. Tarsus, every 45 mins, 3½ hrs, US$6.

Transport

Banks *Işbankası* and other banks with ATMs are on Istiklal Caddesi, northeast of the *Orontes Hotel*. You can change money in many of the jewellery shops around the bus station. **Communications** Internet: *Data Net Cafe*, Hürriyet Caddesi, on the left 25 m past the *Saray Hotel*, US$1.25 per hr. Post office: The PTT is across the roundabout from the Rana Köprüsü. **Places of Worship** *Catholic Church*, Kutlu Sokak No 6, off Kurtuluş Caddesi, Sunday mass. **Tourist information** The Tourist Information Office has recently moved to the top floor of the government building to the left of the *Vilayet* (Provincial government building) as you approach from Hürriyet Caddesi. Open 0800-1200, 1300-1730.

Directory

Into Syria Onward travel into Syria requires a visa issued by the Syrian Consulates in Ankara or Istanbul, or obtained before departure in your home country. With the necessary visa you can cross the border at Yayladağı, 57 km south of Antakya and on the mountain road to Lattakia, or Cilvegözü, 50 km to the east near Reyhanlı. Several **bus companies**, including reputable *Has*, operate services from Antakya's *otogar* to **Halab** (Aleppo), several daily, 4 hrs, US$12; **Şam** (Damascus), several daily, 8 hrs, US$20. There are also long-distance buses to **Amman** (Jordan), 4 days a week, 10 hrs, US$25. There's no longer a bus service to Lattakia, although you could get a dolmuş to Yayladağı from opposite the bus station. These leave when full and cost US$1.25, though they stop 5 km short of the border so you'll have to pay an extra US$3 to be dropped at the frontier, or you could hitch. Bare in mind that traffic is relatively light on this section of road and that you're only option on the Syrian side is to hitch or hire a taxi. It's also possible to get a Reyhanlı dolmuş (US$1.25) from next to the Petrol Ofisi station on Istiklal Caddesi beyond the *otogar*. The driver will drop you at the border for an extra couple of dollars, or you can hitch the last 10 km. On the Syrian side you'll need to catch a microbus or shared taxi 54 km to Aleppo.

Western Anatolia

9

Western Anatolia

440 Kütahya

444 Around Kütahya

445 Afyon

448 Around Afyon

449 The Lake District

450 Isparta

453 Eğirdir

456 Around Eğirdir

457 Beyşehir

458 Walking and trekking

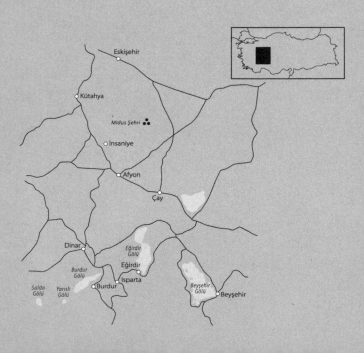

Western Anatolia is a region between the coastal lands of the Marmara, Aegean and Mediterranean and the Anatolian plateau to the east. Rippled by mountain ranges, it's drained by a series of long rivers, the Sakarya, the Gediz and the Menderes, which cut wide valleys sown with large fields of wheat and dotted with solitary oak trees. To the south a series of tectonic basins have flooded to form shallow lakes, scattered between the folds of the Taurus Mountains – an area known as the Turkish Lake District. The climate is distinctly Anatolian and even in summer you'll notice a refreshing chill in the nocturnal air. The inhabitants also share more in common, in terms of religiosity and conservatism, with their compatriots to the east.

Since the beginning of history Western Anatolia has been criss-crossed by armies as well as important trade routes. Today it's also traversed by travellers on their way elsewhere: Ankara to the Aegean, Bursa to the southern coast. Relatively few stop at all, though a string of towns with modest attractions suggest themselves as spots to linger for a while and experience a slice of authentic Turkish provincial life.

Starting in the north, Kütahya is the home of modern Turkish ceramics; a place to stock-up on eminently breakable souvenirs and pay a visit to the amazingly well preserved Temple of Zeus at Aizanoi nearby. Afyon has rather more to offer with a district of vernacular Ottoman residences in the shadow of a craggy fortress. Its Selçuk-era Ulu Cami is one of the finest mosques of its kind and the town makes an ideal base for visiting the neglected minor Phrygian sites to the north. South again, Eğirdir is the undoubted star of the Lake District, if not the whole region. It's a perfect place to unwind in one of the sedate island pensions or from which to explore the varied local sights – little-known ruins, unspoilt mountains and of course lakes.

Eskişehir Despite its name, which means 'Old City', modern Eskişehir is a drab industrial centre surrounded by large textile and food processing factories. Apart from a noisy military airbase and university, its only other claim to notoriety is as the centre of the meerschaum craft industry. Known as sepiolite to specialists and *lületaşı* to Turks, meerschaum is a white porous rock mined in an area to the east of the city. Chunks of the rock are carved while wet and soft into a variety of objects such as earrings, archtrays, walking sticks, but above all, pipes which are sold in shops across the country and also exported. Typically fashioned into a decorative head meerschaum pipes are prized by dedicated smokers for their cool draw. There are lots of shops around the centre selling meerschaum items, but the city's premier outlet is *Işık Pipo*, Konya Işhanı 12/17, Sakarya Caddesi, with craftsmen on-site doing their stuff.

There are lots of cheap kebap place dotted around the centre **Sleeping** At the junction with Yunus Emre Caddesi you'll find many of the city's hotels. Top of the bunch **A** *Atışhan Otel*, Yunus Emre Caddesi No 93, T2201666, F2324547. Comfortable rooms with en suite and a restaurant. Nearby the **C-F** *Otel Dural*, Yunus Emre No 97, T2331347. Reasonable rooms with or without en suite shower.

Transport Eskişehir is situated on the mainline between Ankara and Istanbul, with regular train services in both directions. The station is just northwest of the city centre. There are also hourly buses from the huge new *otogar* on the outskirts of town to **Ankara** (4 hrs, US$9), **Istanbul** (5½ hrs, US$10), **Bursa** (2½ hrs, US$6) and **Kütahya** (1 hr, US$3). When it's time to leave get on a dolmuş marked 'Yeni Garaj' or 'Terminal' from Yunus Emre Caddesi.

Directory Banks There are banks with ATMs in the centre. **Tourist information** The tourist office is in the Vilayet (Government) building at Iki Eylül Caddesi No 175.

Kütahya

Phone code: 0274
Colour map 1, grid C4
Altitude: 949 m

A small, pleasant town set against a backdrop of forested hills and overlooked by a ruinous fortress, the name Kütahya is synonymous above-all-else with ceramics. Whether produced in huge out-of-town factories, or carefully crafted and hand-painted by Kütahya's artisans, the industry is the modern heir to a tradition dating back over 500 years. Pottery aside, the town is also home to Dumlupınar University, whose students inject some extra life into the local cafés and restaurants. A well-stocked museum, some Ottoman buildings and several rarely visited sights in the surrounding area also suggest the town as a worthwhile stop-off.

Ins & outs
See page 444 for further details
Getting there There are regular bus services from Kütahya *otogar*, known locally as the *Çinigar* because of its covering of ceramic tiles, to destinations including Eskişehir, Ankara and İzmir. **Getting around** The town's central roundabout, flanked by the town hall and provincial government building, is a 500-m walk up Atatürk Bulvarı from Çinigar, with the main street, Cumhuriyet Bulvarı, beyond. Regular services also leave for Afyon and Çavdarhisar (Aizanoi), passing the town-centre bus-stop on Afyon Caddesi.

Sights

Most of the town's sights lie at the top of Cumhuriyet Caddesi, a five-minute walk from the roundabout at Belediye Meydanı, which is easily recognized by its fountain in the shape of a large ceramic vase. At the head of the street in the middle of the town's bazaar district stands the venerable **Ulu Cami** (Great Mosque), construction of which was commenced by Beyazıt I in 1410. Next to

Potty about pottery

Kütahya's modern ceramics industry is rooted far back in history when the nearby deposits of pale clay were first fashioned into pots and plates. By Ottoman times a well-established local industry existed, although it lacked the scale or refinement of nearby İznik (see box, page 175), the centre of pottery production in the empire at that time. Far from the centre of demand in the imperial capital Kütahya was sidelined up until the end of the 16th century. However, this situation was reversed with a slow decline in the İznik ceramic industry directly benefiting the town. Patronage also boosted local tile making with the grand vizier of Süleyman the Magnificent, among others, establishing a workshop – or atölye – in the town. By 1648 the Ottoman chronicler, Evliya Çelebi, reported there were 300 ceramic workshops in the town, although most were turning out simple household items and not decorative faïence.

Over the years Kütahya faïence developed a distinctive character with heavily stylized patterns and bold motifs, possibly influenced by the local carpet-making tradition. They were used to decorate many mosques, palaces and public buildings.

The 20th century brought hard-times for the industry with the forced departure of the town's Armenian potters and the subsequent War of Independence. By 1922 there was only one working atölye in the town and the future of ceramic production hung in the balance.

The determined efforts of a few local craftsmen brought the industry back from the brink as new apprentices were trained and workshops established. By 1950 there were 50 atölye and the years since have witnessed explosive growth with a large number of workshops, and more recently factories, opening-up to provide a diverse range of pottery, tiles and modern ceramic products. The emergence of a mass market for Kütahya faïence has inevitably resulted in a general drop in quality, with the master çinici (potters) still in business deploring the use of non-traditional patterns and industrially produced pigments. However, you'll be glad to know that most of the 50 workshops in town do still turn-out some high-quality pieces, known as özel iş (special work), using the old ways and these are on display in some of the shops around Belediye Meydanı.

the mosque stands next to the **Vecidiye Medresesi** which pre-dates the Ottoman period. The medrese was constructed by Umur bin Savcı in 1314 as an observatory and school of science and mathematics and the interior is centred on a marble pool beneath a glass dome in the roof. The building has recently been beautifully restored and is now home to the town's archaeological museum (see below).

The stone building next door was originally part of a religious complex built by Yakup Bey II and now hosts the newly opened **Çini Museum**, where a range of new and antique ceramic works are on display in the hall of the old medrese. Many of the exquisitely decorated pieces were donated by Rıfat Çini a prominent local artisan. ■ *0800-1200, 1330-1730. US$1.50.*

Built by the Byzantines and then subsequently much restored by the Selçuks, the Germiyanids and the Ottomans, to scale the heights to Kütahya's ruined **fortress** follow the signs for the Dönen Gazino from near the Ulu Cami. ■ *Getting there: Dolmuş no 1 will reduce the uphill slog by dropping you 600 m from the walls. Along with the* Dönen Gazino, *a restaurant serving grilled meat, kebabs and other fare, there's a scenic tea garden with excellent views over the town.*

Archaeological Museum Well worth a look, not least for a glimpse of the domed interior of the medrese, this collection includes artefacts uncovered from excavations across the province, spanning history from the Chalcolithic Age to the Roman and Byzantine eras. Pride of place goes to the Amazonlar Lahti, a magnificent marble tomb embellished with a lively frieze depicting soldiers in battle, found at the site of ancient Aizanoi in 1990. Also on display are some photographs of cave dwellings and churches in the nearby Valley of Frig. ■ *0830-1230, 1330-1730 daily except Mon. US$1.50.*

Kossuth Evi
Other Ottoman houses survive in the backstreets of town with a particularly high concentration to the north of the Kossuth Evi on Germiyan Sokak

Reached up a side street beside the Çini Museum, the Kossuth Evi is a 19th-century house typical of those which once lined the streets of Kütahya's wealthier districts. From 1850-1851 it was the home of the Hungarian nationalist leader Lajos Kossuth (1802-1894) who was forced to flee his native country after a failed uprising against the Habsburg Empire in 1848. As a result of its former occupant the house has been wonderfully preserved much as Kossuth would have left it, with the period decoration and furnishings giving you the chance to experience how an upper-class Ottoman household lived. ■ *0800-1200, 1330-1730 daily except Mon. US$1.*

Kütahya

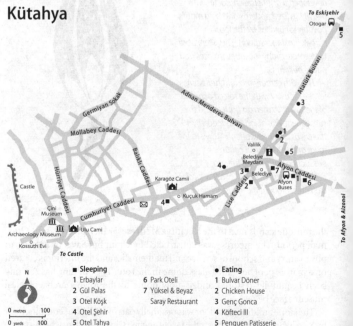

■ Sleeping		● Eating
1 Erbaylar	6 Park Oteli	1 Bulvar Döner
2 Gül Palas	7 Yüksel & Beyaz	2 Chicken House
3 Otel Köşk	Saray Restaurant	3 Genç Gonca
4 Otel Şehir		4 Köfteci III
5 Otel Tahya		5 Penguen Patisserie

Kütahya mosque

Essentials

D *Otel Tahya*, Atatürk Bulvarı, T2243070. A modern hotel convenient for the bus station, comfortable rooms, TV and telephone. Recommended. **C** *Gül Palas*, Belediye Meydanı, T2161759. Another decent place, recently refurbished, rooms have en suite, TV and telephone. Recommended. **C** *Hotel Erbaylar*, Afyon Caddesi No 14, T2236960. Spacious rooms in a very plain hotel, en suite bathroom, telephone and refrigerator come as standard. **F** *Otel Köşk*, Belediye Meydanı No 1, T2162024. Plain rooms with a shower cabinet in the corner and balcony, front rooms are probably noisy as they face the square. **F** *Hotel Yüksel*, Belediye Meydanı No 1. Clean, simple rooms with en suite, waterless rooms also available. Recommended. **F** *Güneş Oteli*, Atatürk Bulvarı No 65. Very basic, over-priced. **G** *Otel Şehir*, Cumhuriyet Caddesi No 65, T2161520. Basic but clean rooms with en suite, best bet for those on a really tight budget. Recommended. **G** *Park Oteli*, Afyon Caddesi No 20. Boarding house, cheap waterless rooms, for those only on determinedly tight budgets, not recommended for unaccompanied women.

Sleeping

Bulvar Döner, at the top of Atatürk Bulvarı, small brightly lit place serving tasty stew-tray food, including chick-pea stew for vegetarians, soups and kebabs. *Chicken House*, Atatürk Bulvarı, half a roast chicken accompanied by rice and salad is only about US$3.50, also soup to start. *Genç Gonca*, Atatürk Bulvarı, a smart little place which is popular with students, serves tasty mantı, kebabs and pasta, specials changed daily. *Beyaz Saray*, Belediye Meydanı, old Kütahya institution with white-table cloths below the *Hotel Yüksel*, serves a highly regarded Iskender as well as a selection of other kebabs. *Köfteci III*, Cumhuriyet Caddesi, a small busy place serving excellent value soups, köfte and kebabs, also a choice of dessert. For sweets such as baklava, *sütlaç* (rice pudding), biscuits or cakes try the *Penguen Patisserie* on Afyon Caddesi opposite the *Hotel Yüksel*.

Eating

There are lots of restaurants serving-up reasonable food at very economical prices on Atatürk Bulvarı, Belediye Meydanı & Cumhuriyet Caddesi

There are several open-air cafés mid-way along Cumhuriyet Caddesi which are popular with students and local families on warm evenings. If you're feeling energetic you could hike up to the cafés at the fortress, where a hot or cold drink is complemented by the view.

Cafés

Western Anatolia

Bars　*Biraderler Bira Salonu*, Cumhuriyet Caddesi, a popular student hangout with a convivial pub-like atmosphere.

Shopping　You can't walk ten paces in town without passing a shop selling Kütahya ceramics, everything from traditional patterned tiles to vases, jugs and plates. Be aware that the quality and price vary greatly from the mass-produced items churned-out for the souvenir market to the pieces laboriously crafted by one of town's master craftsmen. Drop into the showroom of Sıtkı Usta on the corner of Atatürk Bulvarı and Abdurrahman Kara Bulvarı, to see some of the work produced by this internationally exhibited craftsman. A controversial local figure, Sıtkı has broken away from traditional concepts of pattern and colour to create original designs using a variety of influences. He also has plenty of more traditional pieces on display.

Transport　**Bus** **Afyon**, every 90 mins from 0930, 1½ hr, US$5. Afyon buses conveniently pass the terminal on Afyon Caddesi. **Ankara**, 10 daily, 4 hrs, US$12. **Bursa**, 7 daily, 3 hrs, US$6. **İstanbul**, 6 daily, 6 hrs, US$14. **Eskişehir**, every hr, 1 hr, US$2.

Directory　**Banks** Banks with ATM machines are found on Cumhuriyet Caddesi. **Baths** *Tarihi Vakıf Küçük Hamamı*, on Cumhuriyet Caddesi about half-way along, 0730-2300. **Post office** The PTT is on Cumhuriyet Caddesi. **Tourist information** There is an information kiosk open in summer at Belediye Meydanı. At other times of year seek out the tourist information office in the *Özel İdare* building, Fuatpaşa Caddesi, Floor 4, T2231962, F2243189.

Around Kütahya

The Frig Valley　An area to the east of the Eskişehir highway, centred around the village of Inli, the Frig Valley was an important area of settlement in Phrygian, Roman and Byzantine times. Scattered across this agricultural district are houses, temples, churches and tombs carved into the soft volcanic rock. It would certainly be rewarding to explore this area, although you'll need your own transport as the villages of Söğüt, Inli, Sabuncupınar and Fındıkköy are only served by local dolmuş which come into Kütahya in the morning, returning in the evening. For more information contact the Kütahya museum director Metin Türtüzün, who has done extensive research in the area. There is also a publication based on research carried out in Phrygia, including the Frig Valley, by archaeologist *Emilie Haspel* titled 'The Highlands of Phrygia' (1971).

Aizanoi　Near the present-day town of Çavdarhisar, about 55 km southwest of Kütahya, stands one of the best preserved, though seldom visited, Roman temples in the whole of Anatolia. Built during the reign of emperor Hadrian (117-138 AD) the temple was dedicated to the worship of Zeus and the indigenous Anatolian fertility goddess, Cybele. Despite suffering some damage during an earthquake in 1970, the Temple of Zeus has endured the years remarkably well, and the two rows of columns making up its colonnaded porch are still largely standing.

Unfortunately, the huge statue of Zeus which once graced the temple and which is shown on coins found at the site, has long since disappeared. There are a few bits of statuary on show in a fenced area beside the temple but other finds have been shipped off to the Kütahya Museum for safe-keeping. Down a set of stairs at the rear of the temple and beyond, however, a gate kept locked by the amiable guardian is a representation of Cybele, thought to have been the focus of cult-worship at the site.

The other buildings of the city have not fared as well as the temple with the badly degraded ruins of an **amphitheatre** and **stadium** complex to the north. To the east are the remains of an **agora**, beyond which you'll find a **macellum** on the other side of a small stream spanned by an antique bridge. This circular meat market – is the only one of its kind in Anatolia and has weathered inscriptions on the walls setting prices. The guardian can also guide you to a **bath complex** where part of the original mosaic floor is kept safe in a locked shed.

■ *Getting there: Gediz, Emet and Simav-bound buses all pass through Çavdarhisar, which is sign-posted off the main Kütahya-Afyon road. These services depart from the Çinigar regularly from about 0930, calling-in at the bus stop on Afyon Caddesi. When you get to Çavdarhisar enquire about returning dolmuş before exploring, though buses pass fairly regularly throughout the day. There are shops and several simple restaurants at the junction near Çavdarhisar.*

Afyon

Afyon is an unassuming, down-to-earth provincial town dominated by several rocky volcanic protrusions and a crumbling fortress perched on the 226-m summit of the highest. It was this castle that earned the town its original long-winded and rather sinister title of Afyonkarahisar (Opium Black Castle) with the other half of the name derived from the colourful fields of opium poppies which are still widely cultivated in the surrounding province. Wandering the streets of the town's old quarter there are still plenty of Ottoman residences to appreciate, along with some interesting mosques. Afyon is also famous for its hot thermal waters which bubble-up from the depths at numerous hot-spring complexes in the vicinity. All this adds up to make the town a worthy overnight stop if you're heading through with time to spare.

Phone code: 0272
Colour map 1, grid C5
Altitude: 1021 m

Getting there Located at an important intersection in the national road network, the town is well served by buses from all directions. The *otogar* is to the northeast of the centre on the ring-road. Get-on a dolmuş marked 'Garaj, Sanayi, Çarşı', US$0.25, which wait inside the terminal for the 5-min ride into the centre. Trains stop at Afyon station, located at the end of Ordu Bulvarı, en route for İstanbul, İzmir, Konya, Denizli and Gaziantep. A taxi into the centre from the *otogar* or the station is under US$3. **Getting around** Once in the centre of town everything is within walking distance.

Ins & outs
See page 448 for further details

Afyon's prominent fortifications are thought to date back to Hittite times, with every power that occupied the strategic town over the following millennia modifying or rebuilding them. It also became an important Mevlevi centre, second only to Konya, a distinction it maintained after it was absorbed into the Ottoman empire in the 15th century.

Background

Afyon was occupied by the Greek Expeditionary Force which invaded much of western Anatolia at the end of the First World War, marching to within striking distance of Ankara and the fledgling nationalist government of Atatürk. The desperately fought Battle of Sakarya stopped this advance and marked the turning point of the War of Independence, with a bold counter-offensive the following year breaking the Greek army and sending the survivors into full-scale retreat towards İzmir. For three weeks during the campaign of 1922 the town hall in Afyon served as the nationalist headquarters, a period of local history commemorated by the Zafer (Victory) Museum.

Since this tumultuous time things have been considerably quieter. Afyon carpets, *sucuk* (garlic sausage), *pastırma* (pastrami), *kaymak* (clotted cream) and confectionery are all local specialities made with the produce from the town's rural hinterland. The town is also the centre of Turkey's opium producing region, where the exceptionally beautiful, benign looking poppies colour great swathes of the countryside in early summer. The industry, which accounts for over 25% of the world's legally produced opium used in the pharmaceutical trade, is carefully regulated with the young flowers collected and taken to local factories for the sap to be extracted.

Sights

The mosque has an adjacent public garden where Afyonlu come to sit & talk

Coming in from the *otogar* on Kurtuluş Caddesi you pass the **Imaret Camii** with its striking spiral-fluted minaret inlaid with blue tiles. This mosque, which shows elements of Selçuk and early Ottoman design, was completed in 1477 as part of the Gedik Ahmet Paşa complex which included a hamam (recently brought back into service, see directory) and medrese.

In the centre of town at Hükümet Meydanı is the imposing black **Zafer Anıtı**, a monument commemorating the nationalists victory over the Greek expeditionary force in 1922. Facing the monument from across Bankalar Caddesi, the old government building which served as Atatürk's headquarters, is now the **Zafer (Victory) Museum** (*0900-1700*) and contains old photographs, an assortment of weaponry used in the battles and a reconstruction of the office where the commander himself worked.

Walking up Uzunçarşı from Hükümet Meydanı takes you into the old town and towards the fortress. To the left before you reach the Ulu Cami is the **Mevlânaevi Camii**, which was the *tekke* (meeting hall) for Afyonkarahisar's large and important dervish community from the 13th century. The current twin-domed building was built in 1908 and is locked except at prayer time. The *imam* will usually let you in though to have a look at the collection of instruments and ceremonial costumes on display in the *semahane,* where the dervish used to conduct their *sema* (spinning ceremony).

Continuing up the road brings you to the venerable **Ulu Cami** (1277), a Selçuk mosque which is the oldest surviving building in town. The outside of the mosque has been modified during restoration, however, the superb

Afyon

■ **Sleeping**
1 Grand Özer Termal Otel
2 Otel Hocaoğlu
3 Otel Lale & Restaurant
4 Otel Oruçoğlu
5 Sinada

● **Eating**
1 Adem Usta
2 Cheap Lokantas
3 Ikbal Lokantas

interior with its low wooden ceiling supported by a veritable forest of forty pillars with carved capitals is unmistakably the real thing. Once again the mosque is usually kept locked except at prayer times, though the *bekçi* (guardian) isn't usually too far away. In the narrow, twisting alleys around the Ulu Cami stand lots of wood-beamed **Ottoman houses** their upper bay windows covered with *kafes* (wooden lattices) for privacy and overhanging the street. Most are in need of urgent and extensive repairs, but they still retain an air of grace despite the peeling paintwork and crumbling masonry.

Opposite the Ulu Cami a narrow street leads to the bottom of a very long flight of steps climbing up to the **fortress**. At the top you can scrabble around what remains of the battlements, mostly of Byzantine vintage, and enjoy the sweeping views and the sounds rising up from the town spread-out below.

The museum has a collection of artefacts dating back to the late Bronze Age. There is a particularly fine display of Roman era busts and statuettes, including a diminutive representation of Eros. In the ethnography section next door, curiosities include a felt tent used by the nomadic pastoralists who roamed the mountains of western Anatolia with their flocks until comparatively recently. ■ *0830-1200, 1330-1730 daily except Mon. US$1.50. The museum is on Kurtuluş Caddesi about 1 km from the centre of town. Dolmuş to the otogar pass-by.*

Afyon Museum

Essentials

C *Grand Özer Termal Hotel*, Süleyman Gönçer Caddesi No 2, T2143300, F2143309. Reasonably priced 4-star hotel with the most comfortable rooms in town, amenities include mineral baths and a restaurant. **D** *Otel Oruçoğlu*, Bankalar Caddesi, T2120122, F2131313. After 17 years of service the Oruçoğlu is still providing spacious, good value rooms with en suite, TV and telephone, though as you might expect it's looking a bit dated, breakfast is extra. Recommended. **E** *Hotel Soydan*, Turan Emeksiz Caddesi No 2. Horrible colour scheme but the rooms, with a tiny en suite, TV and telephone, are fairly reasonable for the price. **E** *Otel Hocaoğlu*, Ambaryolu No 12, T2138182. Clean, simple rooms with en suite, TV, telephone, breakfast extra. **F** *Sinada Hotel*, Ambaryolu No 25, 150 m down from Bankalar Caddesi on the left. Quiet place with plain rooms, TV and telephone, single/treble rooms US$12/$27. Recommended. **F-G** *Otel Lale*, Bankalar Caddesi No 23, T2151580, across from the Şeker Bank. Solid budget option, basic rooms have en suite shower, also cheaper waterless doubles but front-rooms noisy. The *Otel Mesut* on Dumlupınar Caddesi No 2 is closed indefinitely.

Sleeping
All of Afyon's accommodation is found on or near Bankalar Caddesi in the centre of town

Midrange *Ikbal Lokantası*, Uzunçarşı, just up from Hükümet Meydanı, a local institution since 1956, white table cloths but very reasonable prices, about US$8 per head for a two-course meal, grilled meats, kebabs and a few local surprises are on the menu. The restaurant on the top-floor of the *Hotel Oruçoğlu* is worth a try for a fairly standard, but well-cooked, menu of grills and kebabs, plus the view over the roof tops. **Cheap** *Lale Pide*, Bankalar Caddesi at the end closest to the Imaret Camii is a clean and busy pide and lahmacun place. *Adem Usta,* Ordu Caddesi, 50 m down from main junction, is locally recommended for its soup, lahmacun and kebabs. There is also a row of small lokantas opposite the *Oruçoğlu Hotel* including *Arzu Lokantası,* where a steam-tray stew and a drink will set you back about US$3.

Eating
Plenty of cheap eateries along Bankalar Caddesi, particularly near Hükümet Meydan

There are lots of shops in town where you can stock-up on locally made *sucuk, pastırma* or one of the many varieties of sweet *lokum*- Turkish delight. Don't worry if you forget because there are also rows of brightly lit shops at the bus station and lining the roads out of town which make a living by enticing passing motorists to stop.

Shopping

Western Anatolia

Transport **Bus** All the bus companies have offices on Bankalar Caddesi opposite the PTT and generally provide a free transfer service to the *otogar*. **Ankara**, hourly buses, 4 hrs, US$8. **Antalya**, regular buses, 5 hrs, US$12. **Isparta**, 5 buses daily, 3 hrs, US$7. **İstanbul**, every hr, 8 hrs, US$17. **İzmir**, almost every hr, 5 hrs, US$9. **Kütahya**, every hr, 1½ hrs, US$3. **Denizli/Pamukkale,** regular buses, 4 hrs, US$8. **Train** The train station is at the end of Ordu Caddesi and serviced by a regular dolmuş from the centre. The *Gülistan Mavi Tren, Toros Ekspresi, İç Anadolu Mavi Tren, Meram Ekspresi* and the *Pamukkale Ekspresi* all stop in Afyon (see page 48 for timetable).

Directory **Banks** The main banks with ATM machines are along Bankalar Caddesi. **Baths** *İmaret Hamamı*, part of Gedik Ahmet Pasa complex, entrance on Kurtuluş Caddesi, women 0900-1700, men 1800-2400, US$2.25. **Post office** On Bankalar Caddesi. **Internet** *Bürmak Internet cafe*, just around the corner from the PTT on Dumlupınar Caddesi, US$1.50 per hr. **Tourist information** The tourist information office, T2135447, F2132623, is just opposite the Anıt park, Hükümet Meydanı. Open 0830-1730.

Around Afyon

Hot springs The area around Afyon is well-known for its hot-springs which seep out of the ground at temperatures of up to 80°C, laden with minerals such as bromide, calcium and fluoride. Needless to say they're accredited with having various therapeutic powers for conditions ranging from rheumatism to gout and neuralgia. Hot-springs complexes include **Gazlıgöl**, 20 km north on the Ihsaniye road; **Heybelli**, 25 km east on the Konya road and reached by Sultandağı or Akşehir dolmuş, and **Ömer**, 15 km north on the Kütahya road, where you can stay in the huge, modern **C** *Oruçoğlu Termal Tesisleri*, T2515050, where the baths and treatments are also open to non-residents. If the name sounds familiar it's because its emblazoned across bottles of mineral water sold across the country. Several of these complexes are accessible using dolmuş that depart from the local bus-station adjacent to the *otogar* with the tourist office able to provide full details on the various springs and how to get to them. With your own transport you could also head for a wallow in the mud-baths at **Hudai**, reached off the Denizli-bound highway to the south of Sandıklı, where you'll also find the respectable **D-E** *Yeni Kaplıca Otel*, T5126947.

The Phrygian sites around Ihsaniye

With your own transport exploration in this area could be combined with a visit to Midas Şehri a more significant Phrygian site located between Afyon & Şehitgazi

The area around Ihsaniye, 36 km to the north of Afyon, is scattered with Phrygian sites that are well-worth seeking out if you're interested and have your own transport or don't mind the vagaries of village transport. The soft volcanic rock underlying the area has also been eroded in places into strange pinnacles and cones which are similar, if on a much smaller scale, to the formations found in Cappadocia.

One of the most interesting sites is near the village of **Ayazin**, where there is a cave settlement dating back to Phrygian times carved out of a large outcrop of rock. Some of the caves were apparently also used as burial chambers, complete with lion relieves carved into the walls. A striking rock-cut Byzantine church also survives nearby. Occasional dolmuş leave in the mornings for Ayazin or the village of Kunduzlu on the Afyon-Şehitgazi road from where you'll have to hitch or walk the last 5 km.

Beyond Kunduzlu on the road to Şehitgazi, there is a left turning marked for Göynüş Vadisi, which contains the **Arslantaş**, **Yılantaş** and **Maltaş**, monuments of Phrygian origin embellished with carvings of lions, a snake and sheep respectively.

An important Phrygian city founded 700 years before the birth of Christ, the **Midas Şehri**
ruins of Midas şehri lie scattered around a rocky plateau that rises 30 m above
the surrounding countryside. The city actually consisted of two parts with a
fortified acropolis on the outcrop and a lower section near the contemporary
village of Yazılıkaya to the north. The most striking feature of Midas Şehri is a
17-m high monumental facade, known as **Midas Tomb**, carved from the
escarpment on its northwest aspect. Topped by a decorative pediment and
covered with regular bands of relief, the face has a niche cut into it just above
ground-level which was originally thought to have been a tomb.

Visited by a group of European travellers in 1800, one of the party, Captain
Leake, misread some of the inscriptions on the monument and wrongly concluded that it was the tomb of King Midas. The passage that Leake interpreted
as 'to King Midas' was in fact another word for Cybele. More recent research
has confirmed that the monument is in fact a shrine to the fertility goddess, the
niche having contained a likeness of the deity.

There are more altars, tombs and lesser monuments around the periphery
including another unfinished relief called **Küçük Yazılıkaya**. Up on the plateau's top, accessed via a long flight of steps on the east side of the outcrop is a
well-preserved **step altar**, a throne hewn from the living rock on which a statue
was placed. Other exciting finds at the site include a sixth-century iron foundry.

■ *Getting there: Reaching Midaş Şehri without your own transport is a difficult task which involves relying on uncertain village dolmuş and hitch-hiking on
the quiet backcountry roads. Probably the easiest way is from Eskişehir south to
Şehitgazi by dolmuş from where you may be able to find a connection onwards to
Yazılıkaya. However, you may be forced to catch a minibus south in the direction
of Gazlıgöl or Afyon and then get-off at the village of Kümbet, from where you'll
have to hitch the remaining 17 km. By car the site is accessible from Afyon via
Gazlıgöl, Kunduzlu and Kümbet and a visit can be combined with stops at some
of the other Phrygian sites around Ihsaniye or the hot-springs at Gazlıgöl (see
above). From the north the approach is via Mahmudiye and Çifteler.*

The town of Akşehir on the road between Afyon and Konya is celebrated as the **Akşehir**
home of the 14th-century folk hero Nasrettin Hoca. Typically depicted wearing an outsized turban riding his bow-legged little donkey, his memory lives
on in the many satirical stories and anecdotes that are still told about him –
though these jokes seem to lose something in the translation, as they never
provoke the same howls of laughter from a foreign audience. If you are a particular fan of Nasrettin Hoca, you may want to make a pilgrimage to his simple
tomb which is set in a small garden near the town's *otogar*.

The Lake District

*Occupying a large chunk of land between Denizli, Afyon, Konya and Antalya,
Turkey's very own Lake District is dominated by the Taurus Mountains and, of
course, the scattering of disparate water bodies which lend it its name. An area of
wide cultivated basins – known for their apple orchards and rose gardens –
divided by mountain ranges, it's generally ignored by foreign tourists, with most
travellers simply passing through on their headlong dash for the beaches or
Cappadocia. However, those that stick around a bit longer discover an unspoilt
region only very superficially affected by tourism. Burdur and Isparta are relatively
dull provincial towns with few sights and little intrinsic interest. Lakeside Eğirdir,
on the other hand, has far more to offer both in terms of character and as a base for
further exploration. Beyond these centres the Lake District harbours rarely-visited*

ancient sites like Antiochus ad Pisidia and examples of early Islamic architecture such as Beyşehir's Eşrefoğlu Camii. There are also possibilities for cave exploration at Zindan as well as bird watching, trekking and cycle tours.

Isparta

Phone code: 0246
Colour map 4, grid B5

As the region's main town and transportation centre you may well pass through Isparta, however, few are the reasons for prolonging your visit beyond the time it takes to change buses. Spread across a wide basin overlooked by the lofty, and for most of the year, snow-clad Mount Davraz (2,635 m), it's a predominantly modern town which counts among its sons the ex-president Süleyman Demirel. The surrounding region is also well-known for the production of carpets and rose-oil (see box).

Ins & outs
See below for further details

Getting there On the main route south to Antalya, Isparta has excellent bus connections as well as several train services each week from Ankara and İzmir (motor train). There are also a couple of *Turkish Airlines* return flights from İstanbul each week. The *otogar* is inconveniently situated 5 km from the centre of Mimar Sinan Caddesi, with free service buses into town. Dolmuş for Eğirdir, Ağlasun and Barla depart from the Çarşı terminal, near the centre, which can be reached on a Belediye buses ($0.40) from the *otogar*. **Getting around** The centre of town is the Kaymakkapı Meydanı roundabout with the main street, Mimar Sinan Caddesi, leading off it.

Sights

Settled since Hittite times, Isparta's few buildings of historical merit date from after the local Hamidoğlu dynasty handed control of the town over to the Ottomans in 1381. The principal monument is the **Ulu Cami**, a sizeable early 15th-century mosque. Nearby on busy Mimar Sinan Caddesi, the **Firdevs Bey Camii** is a later work of the prolific palace architect Mimar Sinan.

Also on the same street behind the Belediye building is the Halı Sarayı, a large 'carpet palace' where dealers and joe public come to buy carpets and kilims, many of which are churned out on the town's machine looms.

Sleeping
Isparta has a reasonably good selection of hotels, including a couple of fairly luxurious offerings

A *Büyük Isparta Oteli*, T2324422, F2324422. Located in a prominent position on busy Kaymakkapı Meydanı, above brash reception are comfortable rooms with telephone, TV and en suite, substantial discount will probably be forthcoming. **C** *Otel Bolat*, Süleyman Demirel Bulvarı No 67, T2239001, F2185506. Within striking distance of Kaymakkapı, slightly cheaper but still has decent rooms with cable-TV and en suite, plus restaurant and bar. **E** *Hotel Akkoç*, Mimar Sinan Caddesi No 34, T2325811. Pretty good value rooms with shower, minibar and TV, room service available. **F** *Hotel Bayram*, Mimar Sinan Caddesi No 43, T2181480. Serviceable boarding house across from the Halı Saray, no breakfast. **F-G** *Lüx Hotel Yatbay*, Mimar Sinan Caddesi No 37, T2181288. Another boarding house, rooms with/without shower, judging by the photos of Mecca adorning the lobby unmarried couples may not be welcome here.

Eating

There are several popular local eateries on Kaymakkapı Meydanı near the Büyük Isparta Oteli with *Kebapçı Kadir* getting good marks for its kebabs and grilled meat selection. There are also lots of reasonably priced diners along Mimar Sinan Caddesi or the side street next to the Firdevs Bey Camii serving kebabs and steam tray food. For a more refined meal you could try the *Büyük Isparta Oteli*.

Lake District Peaks

Barla (2,799m)
Eğirdir Lake
Eğirdir
Isparta
Sav
Davraz (2,635m)
Kovada Lake
Aksu
Beyşehir Lake
Yenişarbademli
Dedegül (2,992m)
To Konya
To Antalya
N
Not to scale

Western Anatolia

A scent of roses

It may come as a surprise to learn that Turkey is the world's second largest producer of rose oil, an aromatic raw material used by the concocters of perfumes and scents. Commercial rose cultivation in fact has its origins in Bulgaria – still the world's number one grower – however, bushes were brought back to Turkey at the end of the 19th century when Bulgaria won its independence. These shrubs were planted around Isparta – an area thought to have similar climatic conditions to their native land – and sure enough the rose bushes thrived.

Today, over 13,000 tons of rose petals are produced each year with a particular concentration of growers around the village of Islamköyü to the north of the Isparta-Eğirdir road. From mid-May to the end of June fields of the pink Kazanlık roses come into bloom, with teams of dextrous pickers rising at first light to harvest the newly-opened flowers before the volatile oil is evaporated by the sun. It's a spiky business but a proficient picker can gather a staggering 12 kilograms per hour.

These flowers are then carted off to one of several local factories where the oil is extracted by steam distillation. After a lengthy process of boiling, evaporating and condensing 500 kilograms of rose petals produces just 125 grams of the fragrant attar, but at US$4,000 a kilo on the world market it's an important source of foreign exchange. Most of Isparta's rose oil goes to the perfume-makers of Grasse in the south of France, though there's also a profitable sideline in selling rose water, a scented by-product of the process esteemed by pious Muslims at home and abroad.

Tour agencies **Akita Turizm Seyahat Acentası**, Çağlar Apartments No 23/1, Istasyon Caddesi, Istiklal Mahallesi, 12322592, F2323279, local agents for *Turkish Airlines*, also rent-a-car organized.

Transport The following services leave from the main *otogar*. **Bus** Afyon, hourly buses, 2½ hrs, US$4. **Antalya**, hourly buses, 2½ hrs, US$3.50. **Burdur**, at least every hr during the day, 45 mins, US$1.75. **Denizli/Pamukkale**, regular buses, 2½ hrs, US$4. İzmir, frequent buses day and night, 7½ hrs, US$9. **Konya**, regular buses, 4 hrs, US$6.50. Dolmuş to **Eğirdir** (every 30 mins, ½ hr, US$1) and **Ağlasun** (every hr, ½ hr, US$1) depart from the Çarşı Terminal in the centre of town. **Train** The station is 500 m from the centre on Hükümet Caddesi. **Gülistan Mavi Tren**, departs for Ankara via Afyon and Eskişehir at 2210 on Tue, Thu and Sun, 12 hrs. **Göller Ekspresi** (motor train), leaves for İzmir via Denizli, Aydın and Selçuk at 2350, 9 hrs.

Directory **Banks** With ATMs and *döviz* on Mimar Sinan Caddesi. **Post office** The PTT is south of the centre on Hükümet Caddesi. **Tourist information** The Tourist Office, T2184438, F2121065, is on the 3rd floor of the Valilik Konağı (Town Hall) near Kaymakkapı Meydanı. Weekdays 0800-1200, 1330-1700.

Sagalassos

The sweeping views from this site down to the red roofs & minarets of Ağlasun partially hidden amidst the verdant orchards & southwards across the mountains are superb

Perched high above the town of **Ağlasun**, 40 km south of Isparta, on an exposed rocky slope backed by towering 2,000-m peaks, are the remains of the ancient city of Sagalassos. Certainly one of the oldest settlements in the region – its name appearing in inscriptions dated to 1224 BC. The city's inhabitants were known for their war-like tendencies and according to the historian Arrian were '... conspicuous even among a nation of fighters'.

Like Pisidian Termessos, the city refused to surrender to Alexander the Great in 333 BC, instead gallantly attacking the Macedonian army as it climbed towards the city. However, the lightly armoured Sagalassian warriors were no match for the battle-hardened Macedonians and the battle ended in a rout. The city suffered similar humiliations at the hands of the Pergemene and Roman armies, although sitting astride an important corridor of trade between Pisidia and the coast it enjoyed a golden era in the second and third centuries. Terminal decline was subsequently brought about by earthquakes and plague.

The site is currently under excavation by a Belgium-led team enjoying corporate sponsorship, but outside the summer work season the lofty spot is a lonely one which, apart from the warden, you'll probably have to yourself. From the car park three marked trails of varying length meander between the ruins scattered widely across the boulder strewn mountainside. By far the most impressive structure is the Hellenistic theatre, although several temples, a nyphaeum, and two agoras have also been unearthed.

■ *Getting there: Dolmuş to Ağlasun depart from Isparta every hr, 30 mins, US$1. There are also 4 dolmuş per day to and from Burdur, 1 hr, US$1.25. It's a 7 km climb up a winding tarmac road from Ağlasun to the site. There's no public transport so if you intend to ascend on foot make sure you start early and take water and supplies.* **G** Sagalassos Restaurant, *T0248-7313551, in the centre of town has large basic rooms with shared bathroom, should you need to stay.*

Burdur Sitting near the southern shore of saline Burdur Gölü, the provincial town of Burdur has a large army base and a minor concentration of light-industry, but nothing too enticing in the way of tourist attractions. That is unless you're an ornithologist as the nearby lake is a major over-wintering ground for the white-headed duck, with hundreds of thousands of birds living out the colder months around the shore.

Excursions Insuyu Mağarası, 9 km from Burdur beside the highway south to Antalya, is this 600-m long cave system containing several beautiful subterranean lakes. It's a popular outing with residents of Burdur and there are several cafés at the cave's entrance. You may want to take a jumper down with you in summer as it gets pretty chilly. ■ *Getting there: From Burdur get on an hourly dolmuş to Bucak, US$0.50, which passes the turn-off to the cave.*

About 5 km south of Insuyu a signposted sideroad leads over a craggy limestone range for 14 km to **Ağlasun** and **Sagalassos** (see page 451).

Heading west from Burdur on the quiet road to Denizli, 6 km beyond Yeşilova the highway skirts **Salda Gölü**, a small turquoise lake tucked amongst the mountains at the foot of the 1280-m Salda Pass. Surrounded by startlingly white mineral deposits it's an excellent place to break your journey for a swim in the mildly alkaline water with a conveniently placed picnic site on the shore. There's nothing to stop you camping to the west of the picnic site amongst the pine trees, or alternatively, at the eastern, less attractive, end of the lake you have the choice of several camp grounds or the fairly comfortable **E** Şahman Hotel, T02486180480. Leaving Salda Gölü the road winds over the **Salda Pass** to the *ova* of Serinhisar, a flat cultivated plain planted with fields of wheat and opium poppies, and dotted with almond trees. Eventually the road reaches the main Denizli-Antalya highway. There's no public transport along this road so hitching is the only option if you're without your own transport.

Sleeping If you need to stay there are several reasonable options on Gazi Caddesi such as the **F** *Burdur Oteli*, at No 37, T2332245, F2334106, dated decor but decent enough rooms with en suite, telephone and TV; or **F** *Hotel Özeren*, at No 51, T2339607, F2341600.

Transport The **bus station** is on the eastern edge of town, a 10-min walk down Gazi Caddesi from the centre. Belediye buses also run into the centre from outside the bus station.

Eğirdir

At the heart of the Lake District, Eğirdir nestles at the base of a rocky mountain on the shores of Eğirdir Gölü, Turkey's fourth largest lake. Encircled by high peaks that retain their snowy blanket well into spring, the lakeshore is ringed by apple orchards and meadows watered by rushing mountain streams. It's an enchanting spot which, despite the bland domestic architecture, a sadly typical story of unimaginative concrete blocks not helped by a sprawling army base on the edge of town, is very appealing.

Phone code: 0246
Colour map 4, grid B5

Getting there There are direct bus services to Eğirdir from many towns and cities in western and central Turkey, or alternatively you can get on a bus to Isparta, 54 km west, from where there are regular dolmuş. The *Pamukkale Ekspresi* passes through twice daily on its way between İstanbul and Denizli. **Getting around** The *otogar* is in the middle of town, 10-15 mins walk from the island of Yeşilada where you'll find most of the accommodation. City buses ($0.40) make the journey about every hr, less often out-of-season. The train station is on the road to Isparta, 3 km from the centre, with dolmuş and city buses passing on their way in to town.

Ins & outs
*See page 455 for
further details*

Sitting astride historic trade routes, today Eğirdir is a popular stopping point for coach parties travelling between Cappadocia and the Mediterranean, while in summer Turkish holidaymakers escape the heat and the mosquitoes at sea-level for the town's pleasant climes – at 914 m temperatures are moderated agreeably by the altitude, helped usually by a cooling breeze off the lake. In spite of this attention Eğirdir preserves its relaxed ambience, particularly on the island of Yeşilada, recently tethered to the mainland by a kilometre-long causeway, where most of the local guesthouses are fortuitously to be found. On Yeşilada the main pass-times are refreshing swims or fishing expeditions out on to the lake, though for most visitors these bursts of activity are interspersed by long periods of relaxation: sitting by the shore with a good book or sipping a cold beer as the evening sun slips behind the mountains.

The area
*The town is also the main
base for trekking &
walking trips into the
nearby mountains
(see page 458)*

There are a few noteworthy historical buildings in Eğirdir, the most obvious being the early 13th-century **Hızırbey Camii**, found right in the midst of things flanking the main street. A portal beneath the mosque's minaret gives access to the small courtyard with the roof inside supported on wooden pillars in the style of earlier Selçuk buildings.

Across the alleyway is the decorated entrance to the **Dündar Bey Medresesi**, originally constructed during the reign of the Selçuk Sultan Alâeddin Keykubat I as a caravanserai, and only later converted into a religious seminary. Today, its interior is occupied by small shops – a function more in keeping with its original purpose.

Strolling out towards Yeşilada the road is guarded by the town's semi-ruined **fortress** possibly dating from as long ago as the fifth century BC, though subsequently much rebuilt. What you see today is primarily the handiwork of the Selçuks, with a Turkish flag flapping in the breeze from the battlements.

Over on Yeşilada the Byzantine church of **Ayios Stefanos**, spiritual focus for the island's Greek community for over 700 years, is currently being rescued from destruction by restorators. Less fortunate are the few decrepit wooden houses which survived a rash of indiscriminate development only to be left to rot ignobly.

Sights
*On Thursday the town
centre is crowded with a
colourful weekly market*

Yeşilada's lack of beaches doesn't stop people from having a refreshing dip off the rocky shore, though more sandy spots aren't far away. Off the Isparta road

Beaches

Western Anatolia

less than a kilometre north of the centre, the **Belediye Plajı** is conveniently close but in the midst of a residential suburb it's hardly the most appealing place to relax. Down the hill from the train station, 3 km from the centre, **Altınkum** also suffers from its proximity to Eğirdir. A gently sloping fine sand beach ideally suited for kids, it's garrisoned by sun-loungers and parasols and overlooked by holiday villas. However, the best beach, reached in under an hour on a bicycle, is a long tree-lined stretch at **Bedres**, 12 km north along the road to Barla, where there's a campsite and restaurant open only in summer.

Day-trips Having strolled the perimeter road on Yeşilada you may decide you want to take to the water. Most of the pension owners in town can organize a **boat-trip** on the lake, usually incorporating a barbecue lunch and some swimming and fishing. The possibilities for non-nautical excursions from Eğirdir include the Kovada National Park, Adada and Çandır; the Zindan Caves and the ruins of Antioch ad Pisidiam (see below). Without your own transport you have the choice of hiring a taxi – not as expensive as it sounds if there's a group of you – or enrolling on a tour organized by one of the local hoteliers. These generally vary in price depending on the itinerary and the size of the group, though during the quieter months it can be difficult to muster enough people.

Sleeping The cheaper pensions are found in Kale Mahallesi, the tumbledown residential area beyond the castle, while Yeşilada island also has some excellent value guesthouses recommended for their tranquillity, fresh air and uninterrupted views. Several more expensive hotels with extra mod-cons are found on the mainland, though these are still reasonably priced.

Town centre B *Hotel Eğirdir*, Poyraz Sahil Yolu, T3114992, F3114219. Dated hotel popular with tour groups, comfortable rooms with bath, TV, telephone, some have lake view, restaurant and bar. **E** *Eğirtur Hotel*, Güney Sahil Yolu No 2, T3123700, F3115598. Modern place across from the bus station, reasonable rooms with shower and telephone, some also have balconies, may be noisy in the front rooms. **E** *Otel Apostel*, Ata Yolu No 7, T3115451, F3123533. Another modern one on the road to Yeşilada 50 m from the bus station, small rooms with TV, telephone and shower.

Kale Mahallesi F *Lale Pension*, Sokak 6 No 2, T3122406. A popular backpacker place run by friendly family, simple but pleasant rooms with en suite in new building, boat

Eğirdir

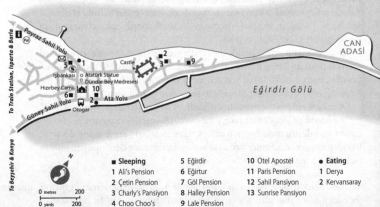

■ **Sleeping**	5 Eğirdir	10 Otel Apostel	● **Eating**
1 Ali's Pension	6 Eğirtur	11 Paris Pension	1 Derya
2 Çetin Pension	7 Göl Pension	12 Sahil Pansiyon	2 Kervansaray
3 Charly's Pansiyon	8 Halley Pension	13 Sunrise Pansiyon	
4 Choo Choo's	9 Lale Pension		

tours organized, bicycle rental, laundry service, traditional food. Recommended. **F** *Çetin Pension*, Sokak 4 No 12, T3122154. Fairly basic rooms in converted house, lovely lakeviews. **G** *Charly's Pansiyon*, Camii Sokak No 5. Basic waterless rooms in creaky 100-year old Ottoman house with loads of atmosphere and exposed woodwork, quirky features such as a shower in a converted cupboard, excellent views across lake from terrace, food prepared. Recommended.

Yeşilada E *Paris Pension*, T3115509. Simple but clean rooms above fish restaurant, en suite showers and large shared balcony. **E-F** *Göl Pension*, T3122370. Well-appointed pension on the south side of the island, rooms have balcony and shower, two top rooms open onto roof terrace with superb view, breakfast served beside the lake, no single rooms. **E** *Choo Choo's*, T3114926, next to the *Göl Pension*. Managed by eccentric American-Turkish team, tastefully furnished and very well-finished rooms with en suite and lakeviews. Recommended. **F** *Halley Pension*, T3123625. On the south side of the island, hospitable family-run place with bright rooms with balcony, roof terrace, good home-cooking. Recommended. **F** *Ali's Pension*, T3122547. Popular family-run place set back from the road on the far side of the island, spacious rooms with wooden floors and clean en suite, also roof terrace and tasty traditional food, fishing trips and tours organized. Recommended. **F** *Sunrise Pansiyon*, T3123234. Quiet position on the northeast corner of the island, plain rooms with cramped en suite, breakfast served on the terrace. **F** *Sahil Pansiyon*, T3122167. Newish place next to *Paris Pension*, bright clean rooms opening onto balcony overlooking the lake, en-suite shower, restaurant, excellent value. Recommended.

Eating

Kervansaray Restaurant, on the mainland opposite the *Otel Apostel*, white tablecloths and a pleasant waterside location add-up to the town's fanciest, but still reasonably priced, restaurant. The menu has a fairly predictable selection of *meze*, kebabs and meat dishes, but there's also a choice of fish. In a similar vein the *Derya Restaurant*, across from the *Hotel Eğirdir* on the opposite side of town, also has waterside tables in summer and serves alcohol. In town *Halil Ibrahim Sofrası* near the Atatürk statue on Posthane Caddesi is a keenly priced *lokanta* with soups, stews, ready-prepared dishes and puddings. There's a very cheap *lokanta* on the first floor of the bus station where a soup and *şiş kebabı* will set you back about US$2.50.

Many of the pensions on Yeşilada double as restaurants serving tasty home-cooked dishes including fish – usually perch or carp – caught fresh from the lake. A welcome variation to the usual battered and fried variety is *buğlama* – fish baked with tomatoes and herbs – which is a local speciality. Places to try include *Paris*, *Ali's* and, for something a little different, *Choo Choo's*, where the menu changes daily but may include delicacies such as *kuzu güveci* (lamb stew), cray-fish or oven-baked fish stuffed with bulgur wheat, mint and carp's roe.

Transport

Bus Instead of waiting for a bus in Eğirdir it's sometimes quicker to get a dolmuş to **Isparta** (every 30 mins, ½ hr, US$1) and catch a bus at the *otogar* there. **Ankara**, 3 buses daily, 6½ hrs, US$7.50. **Antalya**, regular buses, 3 hrs, US$3.50. **Göreme/Ürgüp**, 2 day and 2 night buses in the summer, 7½ hrs, US$10. **İstanbul**, 1 daily bus, 11 hrs,

US$13. İzmir, 6 buses daily, 8 hrs, US$9. **Konya**, hourly buses, 3½ hrs, US$6. **Train** Pamukkale Ekspresi, calls in on its way to Denizli at 0850, returning at 1700 en-route for İstanbul.

Directory **Banks** There are several banks with ATM in the centre of town. **Baths** Hızır Bey Hamamı, in the centre next to the Hızır Bey Camii, 12th-century baths still in use everyday 0800-2300, separate sections for men and women. **Post office** The PTT is past the Eğirdir Hotel on the road out of town to Isparta. **Tourist information** The Tourist Office, T3114388, F3122098, is also on the Isparta Rd 500 m from the centre. Open 0830-1200, 1330-1730.

Around Eğirdir

Barla
25 km NW of Eğirdir

The village of Barla is nestled in a steep valley, dominated by a dramatic limestone spur which plunges down from the Barla massif. Until 1923 the village used to be inhabited by a fifty-fifty mix of Turks and Greeks and many of the now sadly neglected brick and timber houses that line the streets were built prior to this date. Orchards of walnut, cherry and apricot trees compliment the melancholic charm of the houses, as do the numerous village springs, twisting cobbled lanes and minarets. Seldom visited by foreigners, and inhabited by religiously conservative but friendly locals, Barla is worth a look, though there's little to do but wander and savour the rustic atmosphere which permeates life there.

Perched above the village stand the substantial remains of the 19th-century church of **Ayios Georgios**, with a Greek inscription above the doorway. Higher still lay the Roman *colonia* of **Parlais**. A massive defensive wall can still be traced and a single rock cut tomb pierces the rocky ridge above the ruins.

Lower down in the village a spreading plane tree shades a house once occupied by **Sait Nursi**, an Islamic revivalist of Kurdish origin whose ideas brought him into collision with the staunchly secularist republican regime. Exiled here for some time in the 1920's, after his death the paranoiac authorities secretly reburied his body to avoid it becoming a focus for veneration. Though this didn't have the desired result as Nursi's former home is now a shrine for his numerous adherents (the Nurculuk or 'followers of light').

■ *Getting there: There are no buses or dolmuş to Barla, so without your own transport your options are limited to hiring a taxi from Eğirdir. Alternatively, it's a lovely, mildly strenuous bicycle ride, easily possible in a day if you start early. Remember to take water and a snack, plus your swimming stuff if you want to stop at Bedres beach along the way.*

Antioch ad Pisidiam

Set high on the rolling hills of the Anatolian plateau to the northeast of Lake Eğirdir, Antioch ad Pisidiam, excavated continuously over the last 20 years, would certainly be one of Turkey's major sites if it wasn't for its remote location and resource starved status. As it is the ruins attract a steady procession of Christian pilgrims because of their association with St Paul (it was here that the apostle first tried to convert non-Jews to Christianity), though there's actually very little to see today.

Founded in the late third century BC, Antioch became a *colonia* settled by legionary veterans from Gaul around 25 BC. Its growing importance was recognized towards the end of the third century AD when it became the capital of the newly formed province of Pisidia. At its height the city may have had a population as large as 100,000 people, making it a very sizeable place for its time.

Wandering around the rather exposed site, the obvious remains to look out for are the solidly built courses of the **aqueduct** to the north; the sizeable **bath house** and several sections of well **paved street**, lined in places with columns.

The focal point of the town was the **temple of Augustus**, with its most unusual semi circular stoa partially carved from the underlying rock. Christians will be disappointed by the scant remnants of the fourth century **Church of St Paul**, as the few courses of blocks that remain form little more than a ground plan of the building.

■ *Getting there: A bus taking 1½ hours each way departs daily from Eğirdir at 1030 to Yalvaş (2 km northeast of the site), returning at 1700.*

Zindan Mağarası

A popular outing from Eğirdir is to the Zindan Caves, 27 km southeast near the town of Aksu. Once in town head up the main street, Cumhuriyet Caddesi and cross a well-preserved Roman bridge to get to the caves. They've only been superficially developed as a tourist attraction so bring a torch and old clothes if you want to explore the 2.5 km long system of passages and caverns.

Kovada Gölü Milli Parkı

South from Eğirdir a quiet road follows a wide, flat-bottomed valley planted with apple orchards and carpeted with wildflowers in spring. To the west pine-forested slopes rise to the bare summit triangle of Davras Dağı (2635 m) and 35 km after leaving town the road reaches the Kovada Gölü Milli Parkı (Lake Kovada National Park). A small, rarely visited national park encompassing some beautiful stands of mature pine, oriental plain and oak, it's a haven for birds, insects (particularly butterflies) and some large mammals including wild boar and, supposedly, wolves and bears. There's a camp ground near the park entrance, though a lack of public transport and the quietness of the roads means reaching the park without your own transport is difficult.

Yazılı Canyon & Çandır
Road maps universally misrepresent the area, so be prepared to ask directions if you get lost

Lost in the mountains to the south of Lake Kovada and reached only by the most adventurous souls and the occasional tour group is Yazılı Canyon. It's a tranquil spot where a clear, swift flowing river emerges from a steep-sided canyon flanked by a well-preserved section of the ancient King's Road (Kral Yolu) which in the fifth century BC stretched from the Aegean coast to Babylon. There are camping spots beside the water and following the gorge upstream you pass several inscriptions, from whence the canyon gets its Turkish name – *Yazılı* meaning 'with writing', cut into the cliff-face. Continuing along the path brings you in about 15 minutes to a meadow where a river-sized spring gushes from the mountainside. Swimming in the freezing water is possible in numerous shady pools. There's a tiny shop in the village of Çandır, 1.5 km below the canyon, and you can usually buy trout from fish farms along the road.

■ *Getting there: Çandır is reached down a rough 14 km track, just passable with care in an ordinary car, though not after bad weather, which is signposted off the Aksu-Sütçüler road. It can also be approached from the Isparta-Antalya road initially following signs for Eğirdir/ Sütçüler, then Çandır/Şeyler.*

Beyşehir

Phone code: 0332
Colour map 4, grid B6

On the eastern margins of Beyşehir Gölü, the largest freshwater lake in the country, stands the small town of Beyşehir. An ancient settlement which has been in existence at least since Hittite times, possibly much longer, it enjoyed a golden era in Selçuk times as a staging post on the road between Konya and Alanya, the summer capital.

These days most people simply pass through on their way elsewhere, though a few are enticed to stop by the town's famous **Eşrefoğlu Camii**. Constructed in 1297 by a local emir, Şeyheddin Süleyman Bey, it is one of the most outstanding medieval mosques surviving in Anatolia. Outwardly a rather plain flat-roofed building, stepping through the ornately carved wooden

Western Anatolia

portal reveals an interior dominated by rows of thick wooden columns topped by niched capitals more usually seen in stone. A central skylight and windows high on the wall illuminate the richly coloured woodwork with exquisitely carved geometric patterns along the balustrades of the balcony and on the *mimber.* Exhibiting elements of Selçuk and Persian design, the Eşrefoğlu Camii is an excellent example of the *beylik* style which preceded the Ottoman domination of Anatolia.

The mosque, which may be locked outside prayer times, is accompanied by the founder's tomb and a *medrese,* also with an ornately carved entrance. Nearby is the **Dokumacılar Hanı,** a domed commercial bazaar dating from the same period as the mosque, but now generally kept locked. Conveniently close to the town's small *otogar,* having looked around the mosque you may decide to continue onwards to Konya or the Mediterranean coast. On the other hand there are a couple of sites in the vicinity, as well as some lovely unspoilt scenery that may justify extending your stay. See walking and trekking below.

Around
Beyşehir

Covering 650 square km and dotted with nearly two dozen small islands, on calm evenings **Beyşehir Gölü** presents a breathtaking scene reflecting the towering bulk of Dedegöl Dağı on its mirror-like surface. The lake attracts a wide variety of interesting birdlife to the reedbeds around its perimeter, while more promising beaches for bathing exist along the southern shore. On the west coast survive the remains of **Kubadabad,** a summer palace built for the Selçuk Sultan Alâeddin Keykubad I. Enquire in the nearby village of Gölyaka for a boat and boatman to ferry you there. There is no public transport to Gölyaka.

On the opposite side of the lake is another local curiosity, the Hittite shrine of **Eflatun Pınar** (Violet Spring) which is signposted off the Eğirdir highway 15 km north of Beyşehir. About 7 km after leaving the main road you come to a series of large spring-fed pools in a small valley frequented by flocks of geese and cows. Flanking the corner ponds are several stone blocks embellished with much-weathered figures their arms raised to heaven.

Sleeping

Overlooking the river is Beyşehir's nicest hotel the **F** *Beyaz Park,* Atatürk Caddesi No 1, T5124535. Rooms with showers in an old stone house and lovely garden restaurant, request a room facing the river. There are also several very basic boarding houses in the main square such as **G** *Park Oteli,* T5124745, though its worth paying a bit more to stay at the *Beyaz Park.*

Transport
Lots of regular bus connections

Bus The *otogar* is 2 km southwest of the centre of town on the banks of the Çarşamba River. There are regular dolmuş from there into town. **Antalya,** every 1-1½ hrs, 4 hrs, US$8. **Ankara,** 4 daily buses (or change in Konya), 5 hrs, US$9. **Eğirdir,** hourly buses, 2 hrs, US$4. **Konya,** hourly buses, 1½ hrs, US$3.

Walking and trekking

The limestone mountains circling the beautiful highland lakes of Eğirdir and Beyşehir are a western extension of the mighty Taurus range, which runs parallel to Turkey's southern Mediterranean coast. Of greatest interest to trekkers are the mountain massifs of Davraz, Barla and Dedegul, each with its own distinctive character and profile. The area lends itself to relatively short treks (two to three days) and peak-bagging for the more adventurous.

In spring the mountainsides bloom with wildflowers including iris, scilla, grape hyacinth and wild tulips. Although goats and woodcutters have accounted for much of the forest which once covered the area, pine and cedars still clad some of the lower slopes, and pollarded willows shade the springs on

Barla. Vultures, eagles and choughs soar over the peaks and cliffs, but walkers with a real interest in birds should come in May as the area is on a very important migration route. Fox tracks criss cross the snow, and ground squirrel burrows are everywhere.

From spring through to late autumn the black goat hair tents of Yoruk nomads can be seen all over the mountains, and the tinkling bells of their flocks of sheep and goats is an ever-present background noise. The Yoruk families are likely to be both surprised and delighted to see 'travellers' on their mountain, and may well invite you into their tents to share tea or even a meal.

The climate of the region is semi-arid, with most of the precipitation in winter and early spring, though be warned that sudden storms can occur at any time of the year, with cloud and rain obscuring summits and lightning a potential hazard. The first snows usually hit the highest slopes in November, and icy conditions can last well into May following a severe winter. Summer temperatures reach up to 30°C in the daytime, even on the peaks, but are never unmanageable.

Eğirdir is the best base for exploring the region's mountains, but unfortunately none of the massifs can be reached using public transport so you'll have to rely on local taxis or a hire car (it is possible to rent a car in Eğirdir but it's probably cheaper from a coastal resort).

Getting around
Most pension owners can help you arrange transport

Eğirdir's tourism manager, Gültekin Dabanci, T3114388, can organize guides and give route information, though you may need help translating. The owner of the *Donatim Ticaret* outdoor equipment shop, Belediye Cad 15, Sokak 7/A T/F02463116080, speaks some English and knows the mountains well. It may also be possible to join ETUDOSD, the local trekking club, on a weekend trip, T311 6195.

Guides & information

Upcountry Turkey, T/F02422431148, kateclow@ixir.com, an Antalya-based company can arrange treks and also provide information for independent trekkers.

Trekking agencies

These are high and remote mountains and you need to be adequately prepared with stout walking boots, a good quality tent, sleeping bag, stove and warm and waterproof clothing. A compass is also recommended. For winter and spring an ice axe is mandatory, crampons and helmet advisable.

Equipment

Rising up directly behind Eğirdir, Sivri Dağı is a useful warm-up and orientation point from which to get your bearings. Assuming you walk all the way, the whole expedition shouldn't take more than five hours.

Sivri Dağı (Needle Mountain)
Altitude: 1,749 m

1 Walk south out of Eğirdir and turn right just before the Orthopedic Hospital, up hairpins on the Akpınar village road until you reach a graveyard. If you want a head-start you can take a taxi to this point.

2 Turn right (north west) here and follow a tractor track to the left of the electricity pylons. Where the track swings left, aim at the saddle between Sivri Dağı and Gavurevleri Tepesi (Unbelievers Hill). The remains of a Roman period fortification and associated buildings can be seen here.

3 Head northwest for the summit, following a reasonable path over steep and rocky ground. A metal Turkish flag decorates the high point, and the views are superb. Return the way you came, as the north side of Sivri is a training camp for commandos and consequently out-of-bounds, while the east face is craggy and precipitous.

Western Anatolia

Davraz Dağı
Altitude: 2,635 m

Davraz has a craggy north face, split by numerous steep gullies, making it appear pretty forbidding. This northern aspect is fairly precipitous with crags of rotten rock and tiresome scree slopes. Despite this, there are several non-technical routes to the summit, though some care must be taken if visibility is bad not to stray off route.

Davraz Massif trek

The normal route conveniently starts at the Davraz Kayak Merkezi (Davraz Ski Lodge), a tiny ski centre set on the treeline at 1,700 m, half an hour by road southwest from Eğirdir. It has comfortable rooms and there's a newly constructed ski lift, though the grandiose plans to develop the area for golf and high altitude soccer training haven't materialized yet. The lodge can be used as a base for walks around Davraz, including a traverse below the north face to the village of Sav on the Antalya-Isparta road (around four to five hours). The real attraction, however, is the summit itself with the acsent and descent taking a minimum of two days.

1 Climb southwest up the hummocky hillside until you reach an undulating plateau, and then head for the base of a path which can be traced running southeast across the steep scree slopes above.
2 Follow this path with care until you reach a rocky ridge, pierced by a narrow gap.
3 Pass through the gap, negotiate a tricky section over a drop and swing southwest, reaching a grassy meadow with a spring at about 2350 m (about three hours). Unless you've started very early it's probably a good idea to camp here.
4 From the meadow walk south and then west, ascending the broad summit ridge, pocked with hollows and rocky steps, before climbing the rounded summit outcrop (around two hours). The views across the Isparta plain and Lake Eğirdir are excellent.
5 Retrace your steps or continue southwest down some steep scree to a viewpoint over Isparta (2550m).
6 From here turn northwest then north before the deep gully. Head down more scree to the moraines at the foot of the peak, ensuring that your line of descent does not take you over the smaller, but still dangerous, cliffs punctuating this end of the massif.
7 Turn and head east northeast across the plateau to the ski lodge.

The Barla Massif
Altitude: 2,799 m

Barla Dağı presents a more rounded profile than Davras or Dedegul and its prominent whale back summit ridge dominates the skyline to the north west of Eğirdir town. Barla village (see page 456) is the starting point for this two day walk.

1 Leave the village, heading uphill to a ruined Greek church. Continue northwest, with a ridge on the left to a spring marked by a plane tree (one hour). Here, amidst the ruins of Parlais, the path meets a dirt track.
2 Turn left to a spring and continue uphill for an hour towards a clump of willows below the end of the ridge.
3 Follow a tractor track over the pass in front, descending on a path across the stream bed ahead.
4 On the other side of the stream climb steeply upwards (west north west) to the pass above in about two hours. Here, you're rewarded with superb views back to the lake and Dedegul; while to your left is a cairned rock pinnacle.
5 Zigzag west down the slope to a stream bed in the valley below, and continue

south-west, following a path uphill until you reach shepherds' huts on a moderate rise which bisects the valley. About five hours out of Barla this makes a good spot to camp.

6 The best route to the main summit above is to head southwest to meet the summit ridge, then turn north and follow it to the top in two to three hours.

7 If you don't fancy retracing your steps along the ridge, you can drop down the steep gully scarring the east face of the mountain directly to the campsite.

Barla Massif trek

8 It's possible to take a different route down to Barla, initially following a shepherds' path southwest over the saddle; then descending gently towards the Kalkan Pass where stone huts enjoy a lovely view over the lake.

9 Descend northeast from here to Kocapınar spring distinguished by a cluster of willows and two more huts, then following a tractor trail which leads to a dam across the valley in about two hours.

10 Beyond the dam, take the left fork in the dirt road and continue until the minaret of Barla's main mosque is on your left shoulder. Here branch left to find a clear mule trail running down the gorge into Barla village itself.

Dedegul is the largest and most complex of the Lakeland massifs, with a series of rocky satellite peaks radiating out from its true summit at 2,992 m. The best approach is via Melekler Yaylasi, a summer pasture to the south of the Aksu – Yenişarbademli road about 1½ hours southeast from Eğirdir.

Dedegul

1 To reach the *yayla* turn right onto a dirt road by a forestry sign at the top of a pass. After 2 km the track curls right around the yayla and descends to meet a second dirt road from Yaka village below. Camping on the grassy meadows at 1,800 m, the summit ridge of Dedegul is due south, above magnificent rocky crags.

2 From the junction of the two dirt roads, follow a path towards the mountain, circling above two shepherds' huts and entering the pine forest. With a stream bed on your right, emerge from the forest and aim at the gully to the left of the crags ahead. After about 30 minutes you'll join a zigzag path which cuts up the left bank of the gully, on to Elmahosaf ridge (2,000 m).

3 From here the path bears southeast and climbs with Beyşehir lake coming into view below. After about 1½ hours bear right up a ridge and then swing further right (south), following the cairned path as it zigzags up a wide steep scree slope, aiming for the crags at the top.

Dedegul & Kartal Tepe trek

4 Passing these crags, the basin of Bostan Çukuru, a huge sink hole down which snow-melt drains into underground channels beneath the mountain, lies below and to the right. From here, the path ascends southwards to the summit ridge reached at Kartal Tepe (2887 m) after about 30 minutes.

5 Dedegul summit itself is 1.3 km (30 minutes) further south – southwest along the main ridge. If you don't mind a little scrambling, it's possible to return via the stream gully which runs northwest, then north, off Kartal Tepe; this emerges at the plateau of Elmahosaf, just below and to the left of the main path.

Central Anatolia

10

Central Anatolia

466 Ankara

478 Gordion

480 Konya

488 Aksaray

489 The Ihlara Canyon

492 Cappadocia

493 Nevşehir

495 Uçhisar

497 Göreme

505 Ürgüp

510 The underground cities

511 Avanos

515 Kayseri

519 Around Kayseri

521 Niğde

523 The Aladağlar

528 North Central Anatolia

528 Safranbolu

531 The Hittite sites around Boğazkale

532 Hattuşaş

534 Yazılıkaya

535 Amasya

540 Tokat

542 Sivas

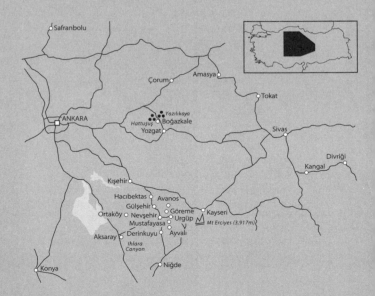

Central Anatolia is a high plateau region dominated by rolling steppe. Huge swathes of grass and arable land reach to the empty horizons and tiny villages are lost in the immensity of the landscape. In winter much of the region lies under snow, while the summer sun turns the ephemeral colours of spring to a monotony of brown. The region also boasts mountains, two exceptional examples being the volcanic cones of Erciyes and Hasan Dağı. It's them that we must thank for creating the geological wonderland of Cappadocia, undoubtedly the regions most popular tourist attraction.

Despite the seemingly inhospitable terrain, this region has witnessed over 8,000 years of human settlement dating back to the first Neolithic communities. Over the great span of history since, numerous great civilisations have waxed and waned, and countless armies have passed through leaving not just destruction in their wake, but also a rich archaeological record at sites like Kültepe, Hattuşaş and Gordion.

Central Anatolia is also the Turkish heartland where the first Turkic tribes settled during the 10th century. The towns are generally drab exceptions being the imperial capital and centre of the mystical Mevlevi dervish order, Konya, as well as Kayseri and Sivas, which were richly endowed with fine buildings during this period, many still on their feet to this day. Far more appealing in terms of setting and character is the riverside Amasya, city of the Pontic kings and now at the heart of the country's apple growing region. Anatolia was also the bastion into which Atatürk withdrew to muster the nationalist forces for the War of Independence, and where he chose to build the republics new capital, Ankara.

Ankara

A predominantly modern city lost in the rolling emptiness of the Anatolian steppe, Ankara is above all a creation of the Turkish republic. Prior to becoming the capital, it was a dusty provincial town, unexceptional except as a centre for the production of angora. Since then much has changed, with a mostly-planned, western-style capital developing with great rapidity. Representing the states progressive, western and secular aspirations, the city has a down-to-earth feel, peopled as it is by the administrators and civil servants of the country's huge bureaucratic machine.

Unable to compete with the history, culture or sheer energy of cosmopolitan Istanbul, a visit to Ankara is nonetheless essential for those who want to gain an understanding of contemporary Turkey. Despite the growth and change, bits of the old city persist around the castle with its quaint village-like districts and scattering of historical remains, such as the Roman era Temple of Augustus. The city also boasts some particularly fine museums, the Museum of Anatolian Civilisation, charting over 10,000 years of history in Asia Minor, standing head and shoulders above the rest. Then there are the shrines of the modern republic, including the early parliamentary buildings and Atatürk's imposing hilltop mausoleum, the Anıt Kabir. All in all there's enough to keep you busy for a day or two, although you probably won't want to stay much longer.

Ins and outs

Getting there
Ankara is extremely well connected by bus, rail & air to the rest of the country. See page 486 for further details

The city's Esenboğa airport is busy with international flights and *Turkish Airlines* also operate regular services to and from major cities in the country. From the huge bus terminal to the west of the city centre, known by the acronym AŞIT, buses fan-out across the country, leaving for most towns and cities at all hours of the day and night. Finally, trains arrive at the central station having lumbered across the country from destinations including Istanbul, Zonguldak, İzmir, Konya, Adana, Diyarbakır, Kars and Van.

Arriving at the **airport**, over 30 km to the north of the city centre, jump on one of the regular buses to the *Turkish Airlines* terminal next to the train station, operated by *Havaş* (US$3.50). A taxi into the centre will set you back between US$15-20. Conveniently, there are also *Havaş* buses between the airport and bus station.

From the **bus station** the easiest way into the centre is on the Ankaray metro, with the station found across a walkway in the centre of the mid-floor of the terminal. Buy a card (the minimum is 5 journeys for US$2.25) and get on any of the trains which all head into Kızılay in about 10 mins. If you are heading for accommodation in Ulus, change onto the other northbound line known as Metro at Kızılay. The metro runs 0630-0025, 2350 on Sun. Alternatively, get a dolmuş directly to Ulus from outside the front of the bus station, with city bus 623 heading into Kızılay.

The **train station** is within 5-mins walk of Maltepe metro station, follow signs for 'TCDD'.

Getting around
Ankara is relatively easy to get around using the modern metro system & plentiful city buses

Atatürk Caddesi forms the main axis running north to south from Ulus, where the cheaper accommodation is to be found and with the old city nearby, through the city centre, Kızılay, to the wealthy suburbs of Kavaklıdere and Çankaya in the south. There is never a shortage of buses running up and down this thoroughfare, the state-operated red ones requiring you to buy a ticket (5 rides for US$2.25) from the kiosks near the main stops before boarding. Taxis are also relatively cheap with a journey from Kızılay to Ulus or Kavaklıdere costing around US$3, more at night.

Climate
Situated at an altitude of 850 m and far from the moderating influences of the sea, Ankara has a continental climate with warm, dry summers and cold winters, the

temperature in Jan regularly dropping below freezing. Built in a natural basin surrounded by mountains, traffic, industry, but above all, the poor quality coal burnt for domestic heating during the winter months, have in the past caused a serious air pollution problem in the city. These winter smogs have been reduced by the introduction of natural gas, although in the burgeoning *gecekondu* – scanty towns – that ring the city coal is still used.

History

Despite much of the city rising from the steppe this century, Ankara has a long history of human occupation with Neolithic remains discovered by archaeologists at several burial sites in the city. Probably the site of a Hittite town, it was with the subsequent rise of the Phrygian empire from 1200 BC that it became an important centre on the Royal Road linking Sardis with Susa in Mesopotamia. Alexander the Great past through in 333 BC staying just long enough to accept the town's surrender; while in 278 BC it was overrun by marauding Celtic tribes. With their defeat by Attalus I of Pergamum, the war-like Gauls settled in Phrygia, setting-up a confederacy of tribes with Ancyra as capital of what became known as Galatia. Scholars believe this name comes from the Greek word for 'anchor', possibly derived from an indigenous Anatolia cult who were depicted with crooked anchor-like horns. Whatever its origin, the city's name first appears on coins minted during the reign of the King Deiotarus, shortly before Galatia was annexed by the Romans in 25 BC. As a provincial capital of the Roman empire, Ancyra grew into a thriving city of 200,000 people and was embellished with many fine buildings of which only the Temple of Augustus remains today.

Christianity appeared early in the city, although pagan worship, in response to which Paul wrote his reproachful 'Letter to the Galatians' after his 51 AD visit, stubbornly persisted until the fourth century AD. During Byzantine times the city continued to help it prosper, though the Persian and subsequent Arab invasions of the seventh and eighth centuries marked the prelude to an extended period of instability. In common with the other Anatolian cities, Ancyra endured conquest by the Selçuk Turks, Crusaders, Danishmendid, Eretnids, Ottomans and Mongols, before being incorporated into the Ottoman empire by Mehmet I in 1414.

As an Ottoman provincial capital the city was a relative backwater, far from the centre of power in Istanbul and cut off from maritime trading routes. And this is how it remained until 1919, when it took centre stage in the nationalist efforts to forge a Turkish state from the wreckage of the Ottoman empire. The town hosted the fledgling Grand National Assembly, set-up by Atatürk to serve as a *de facto* government, and it was from Ankara that the struggle to free Anatolia from foreign occupation and to establish an independent state was organized. With the nationalists victory in 1923 the city was proclaimed capital, a role for which it was hardly prepared.

Sights

A commercial district of grim concrete blocks and home to many of the city's budget hotels, Ulus is not a particularly pleasant introduction to the city, particularly at night when its streets are eerily devoid of life. Nevertheless, the area contains the few structural survivors of the Roman city, along with several museums and the vibrant fruit and vegetable market.

Any exploration of the area will inevitably take you past the busy crossroads of Ulus Meydanı, overlooked by an equestrian statue of Atatürk. Down the hill

Ulus & around

Central Anatolia

on Cumhuriyet Bulvarı are the buildings which housed the Turkish Grand National Assembly. The first, used up until 1925, now serves as the Liberation War Museum, while the second, to where the parliament was moved subsequently, is the Museum of the Republic (see museums).

Walking north along Çankırı Caddesi brings you to the **Roman Baths** situated on the west side of the road. Entering the gates before you is the *palaestra*, an open area originally surrounded by marble colonnades in which the athletes exercised before taking a bath. Of the baths themselves little remains except for parts of the lower walls and the brick pillars which supported the floors, allowing hot air to pass beneath them and heat the rooms. ■ *0830-1230, 1330-1730 daily except Mon. US$0.75.*

Slightly more impressive is the **Temple of Augustus** which lies to the north of Hisarparkı Caddesi stranded in a large pedestrianized area. Built at the behest of Emperor Augustus from 29-25 BC, the temple stands on the site of an

Ankara centre

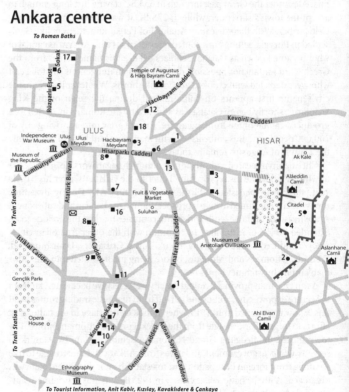

7 Otel Akmam	● Eating
8 Otel Buhara	1 Boğaziçi
9 Otel Bulduk	2 Erzurum Oltu Kebabı
10 Otel Fuar	3 Istanbul Börekçisi
11 Otel Güleryüz & Gaziantepli	4 Kale Washington, Hisar Kule
Fethi Bey Restaurant	& Zenger Paşa Konağı
12 Otel Gülpınar	5 Kınacılar Evi Restoran
13 Otel Pınar & Hisar Otel	6 Özgaziantepli Tabildot
14 Otel Sipahi	Lokantası
15 Otel Üçler	7 Urfalı Hacı Mehmet
16 Otel Zümrüt	8 Urfalı Kebap, Lahmacun
17 Turist	ve Tatlı Sarayı
18 Ulus	9 Uludağ

N

Not to scale

■ **Sleeping**
1 Barbaros Pansiyon
2 Devran
3 Hittit
4 Kale
5 Oğultürk & Yıldız
6 Olimpiyat

earlier shrine dedicated to the worship of the fertility goddess Cybele and Phrygian god Men. With the emperors death in 14 AD, his autobiographical work, *Res Gestae Divi Augusti*, 'The Achievement of the Deified Augustus', was engraved on to all the temples in the empire dedicated to his worship. One of the best preserved of these is the temple in Ankara and it forms an invaluable source of information for archaeologists and historians.

Crossing Hisarparkı Caddesi, Susam Caddesi brings you to the lively fruit and vegetable **market**, with stalls and shops selling all manner of produce. Heading through the market brings you out in front of the **Suluhan**, a 17th-century caravanserai only recognisable by the rows of pointed chimneys on its roof. Recently restored, the inner courtyard contains a *mescit*, a tiny mosque, supported on wooden stilts and several shops selling kitch plastic flowers. A small café also in the courtyard is an excellent place to relax with a glass of çay after the hustle and bustle of the market. From here, to continue onto the sites of the acropolis means crossing Anafartalar Caddesi and heading up to the Hotel Kale, where a left-hand turn brings you back out on Hisarparkı Caddesi below the outer walls of the citadel.

Old Ankara, crowded on to the top of the acropolis hill, is a world apart from the modern city which surrounds it. Walking its crooked streets lined with a jumble of small, white-washed houses is like turning the clock back to the days when the city was just a quiet provincial town. Today, the area is known as Hisar (Castle) after the Byzantine fortifications which crown the top of the hill.

Old Ankara (Hisar)

At the top of Hisarparkı Caddesi a flight of steps leads through the outer defences of the citadel, built in the ninth century by emperor Michael II but reconstructed later, to Inönü Parkı. Following the path right through these gardens brings you out across from the **Museum of Anatolian Civilisation** (see museums) housed in two beautifully restored Ottoman buildings. The street beside the museum leads up to a small gate in the **outer walls**, flanked by a white clock tower. Passing through this gateway, known as Saatlı Kapı, are quiet cobbled lanes lined with diminutive old dwellings. The atmosphere remains village-like with only the distant roar of city traffic to remind you of where you are.

Further on the thick wall of the **inner citadel**, incorporating several chunks of Roman marble, are pierced by a defensive double gateway. It is possible to scale the ruinous tower to the right of the gateway for an unrivalled view of the surrounding city, depending on the haze. The **Alâeddin Camii**, just inside the citadel walls, was built in 1178 and is a rather nondescript whitewashed building except for a row of classical columns used to support the porch area. Inside, however, the carved walnut *mimber* is an extremely fine example of Selçuk workmanship.

At the far end of the citadel, the fortifications culminate in the **Ak Kale**, a large tower which is no longer open to the public. From a vantage point nearby it's possible to look over the *gecekondu*, squatter settlements which are a very 20th-century urban phenomenon.

After looking around the kale, descend the narrow lane opposite the Saatlı Kapı into an interesting area of small shops and stalls. Easily missed on either side of this street at the top are two caravanserais, the **Çengel Hanı** (1522), now derelict, and the **Pilavoğlu Hanı**, built sometime in the 16th century and still used for commercial purposes.

Several hundred metres below the citadel stands the **Ahi Elvan Camii** built during Selçuk times and named after the Ahi sect, a guild of craftsmen who enjoyed considerable political influence and power in the medieval city. Outwardly rather plain, the structure is what's known as a 'forest mosque', with the wooden ceiling inside supported by a veritable forest of wooden columns.

Central Anatolia

'Father of the Turks'

*No matter how brief your stay in Turkey you'll be hard pressed to leave without become familiar with the piercing eyes, clipped moustache and arching hairline of **Mustafa Kemal Atatürk**. His statue graces every town square. His portrait is a mandatory feature of all government offices, also assuming pride of place in the homes and businesses of millions of secular Turks. Whether you're queuing up in the bank; waiting to buy a train ticket or tucking into a kebap, you'll probably be doing so under his ubiquitous stare. Widely admired, even adored, within the country, outside of Turkey the man is hardly known. Indeed for many visitors the reasons for and scale of this personality cult are quite unfathomable.*

Born in Salonika in present-day Greece in 1881, at school Mustafa was a diligent worker, earning the name Kemal, meaning 'perfection', from one of his teachers. After the death of his father, a secular-minded petty customs official, Mustafa Kemal enrolled at a military school where he excelled. In 1902 he won a place at the Staff College in Istanbul, which along with other military institutions had become a hotbed of anti-government feeling. He became an member of the revolutionary Committee of Union and Progress, playing an important role in the military take-over that swept the Young Turks to power in 1909.

As a low ranking officer in the infantry, Mustafa Kemal was posted to various far-flung corners of the embattled empire

before ending up as the military attaché in Sofia. With the outbreak of the First World War, he was recalled and sent to Gallipoli in expectation of the allied landings. It was there on the bloody battlefields that he distinguished himself as an able and courageous commander, rising to the rank of colonel and then general, but also earning himself widespread respect in both military and civilian circles. For the remainder of the war Mustafa Kemal commanded the increasingly demoralized Ottoman forces in the Middle east, returning to Istanbul after the armistice of 1918. As the Great Powers' intention to divide Anatolia between themselves became clear, he rallied supporters to the revolutionary cause, leaving the capital ostensibly in his new capacity as military inspector of eastern Anatolia. In fact his landing in Samsun on 19 May 1919 marked the beginning of his efforts to create a nationalist resistance movement, which were given new urgency by the Greek landings on the Aegean coast.

In Amasya a month later Mustafa Kemal made his first open call-to-arms in a rousing speech against the Sultan's discredited government and the occupying foreign armies. Over the summer he convened congresses in Erzurum and Sivas, establishing the political foundations and aims of the nationalist movement in a document known as the National Pact. His role as

The **Aslanhane Camii**, a bit higher-up the hill to the east, is another Selçuk 'forest mosque', its architectural form unaltered by later reconstruction. Built in the 13th century at the behest of Ahi Şerafettin, whose body is buried in the adjacent octagonal tomb, the mosque's ceiling and *mimber* display some particularly fine decorative carving.

Kızılay Kızılay is the undisputed heart of Ankara, a huge crossroads flanked by high-rise office buildings, shops and ranks of bus stops. Flights of stairs descend beneath the busy traffic to the cavernous subterranean metro station, reached via wide corridors lined with shopping arcades. To the southeast of the junction are several pedestrianized streets, the liveliest of which is **Karanfil Sokak**, its cafés and restaurants thronged by office workers and students studying in the many local colleges. On a prominent hilltop nearby stands the modern **Kocatepe Camii**, an expression of contemporary piety in this bastion the head of the resistance movement was confirmed by his election as president of the newly-founded Grand National Assembly in Ankara. However, the odds were stacked heavily against the nationalists as Mustafa Kemal threw himself into the task of forging a cohesive movement. This demanded all his considerable political skill and energy – cajoling, encouraging, threatening the various factions and groups – but over the next two years he succeeded in beating back the enemies threatening the country, taking a personal role in the decisive military victory over the Greeks at Sakarya, the turning point of the war for independence.

Military victory was followed by hard-won success at the negotiating table in Lausanne and the declaration of the republic in 1923. Though for Turkey's first president, Mustafa Kemal, this was only a first, important step. His agenda now was to create a modern, secular state in the western mould through a series of bold and often contentious reforms. An ardent secularist he viewed religion as a conservative force slowing his country's development. Essentially a populist, in private he expressed an arrogant superiority towards the people, illuminated by a quote from is diary: 'Let me not resemble them: they should resemble me'.

A keen advocate of democracy, he was not adverse to using authoritarian methods to get the desired result, also ruthlessly crushing opponents who threatened his reforms. However, the label dictator is ill fitting as he avoided the megalomania that infected other contemporary European leaders, using his power to achieve very specific, non-military, goals.

In his private life Mustafa Kemal had considerably less success with a short, troubled marriage ending in divorce. Though he never had a child of his own, he adopted several poor girls over the years providing for their education and well-being. He remained down-to-earth despite his privileged position, enjoying nothing better than a bottle of rakı and a game of poker with his friends. However, by 1937 years of heavy drinking and gruelling work had caused a steady deterioration in his health. He died of liver cirrhosis in the Dolmabahçe Sarayı in Istanbul on 10th November the following year. His untimely departure plunged the country into mourning and this dark moment is remembered in an annually observed minute of silence. For the majority of Turkish people Atatürk - a name meaning 'Father of the Turks' awarded him by the Grand National Assembly in 1934- was the creator of modern Turkey; a national saviour who had come to embody the achievements and aspirations of the new secular, westernising Turkish state.

of secularism. Built in Classical Ottoman style and only completed in 1987, the mosque sits on top of a shopping centre and car park.

The mausoleum of the Turkish Republic's founder, Mustafa Kemal Atatürk, **Anıt Kabir** stands on a hill-top surrounded by immaculately kept gardens to the west of Kızılay. A very imposing rectangular structure constructed between 1944 and 1953, the building serves as a shrine for secular Turks, illustrating the continued depth of feeling for the man widely seen as the father of the modern Turkish state (see box, page 470). It's a compulsory trip for all the region's school children, while secular Turks from across the country try and make what amounts to a pilgrimage sometime in their lives. Even as a foreign visitor it's difficult not to be moved by the solemnity and grandeur of the Anıt Kabir.

The approach is up a wide flight of steps and along a long colonnaded walkway guarded by Hittite-style stone lions and stern-faced ceremonial guards.

Central Anatolia

Beyond a pair of huge bronze doors leads into the mausoleum, the outside of which is inscribed with exerpts of a speech made by Atatürk on the tenth anniversary of the republic in 1933. The body itself is interned beneath a large but simple red marble cenotaph looking out over the city. Across a huge expanse of polished yellow marble bordered by more colonnades is the tomb of Ismet Inönü, loyal friend and colleague of Atatürk, who became the first prime-minister of the republic and president after Atatürk's death. Housed in one of the flanking colonnades is a collection of memorabilia from the great man's life.

The **Atatürk museum** contains some interesting vintage photographs of the man and his family, along with various gifts from fellow heads of state, including a beautiful portable vanity set presented by the King of Afghanistan. Also on display is a gun, stealthily disguised as a walking stick, the rowing machine on which Atatürk exercised and an assortment of his clothing. ■ *0900-1700, museum 0930-1230, 1330-1700. Free. Getting there: Can be reached using bus no 265 from Ulus and Kızılay, which drops you at the rear entrance to the mausoleum. Within easy walking distance of Tandoğan metro station.*

Uptown: Kavaklıdere & Çankaya

A short distance south of Kızılay, Atatürk Bulvarı passes the present parliamentary building, or *Meclis*, on the right and for the remaining several kilometres to the suburb of Kavaklıdere, is lined by foreign consulates and the smart head-offices of financial institutions and corporations. Kavaklıdere is the beginning of 'uptown' Ankara, a desirable suburb of leafy streets and expensive apartments where much of Ankara's best accommodation, dining and nightlife are to be found. The main street, **Tunalı Hilmi Caddesi** heading north from Kuğulu Park, has plenty of expensive boutiques and cafés, while for the real western shopping experience try the **Karum** shopping mall on Iran Caddesi.

From the roundabout in Kavaklıdere, Cinnah Caddesi and Atatürk Caddesi climb away from the city into wealthy **Çankaya**, another step-up the ladder in terms of wealth and exclusivity, and home to the **Presidential Palace** (Çankaya Köşkü) and Atatürk's former residence, a chalet-like building which has been immaculately preserved with its original 1930s decor and furnishings. ■ *Sun 1330-1730, no charge but you'll need your passport.*

Except for an anthropological interest in the lives of Ankara's elite, the only other reason to make the trip to Çankaya is to ride the lift to the top of the **Atakule** (US$1.50), a very 1970's looking space-age tower. Not a place for sufferers of vertigo, you can enjoy a drink or a meal with an excellent view in the revolving restaurant.

Kavaklıdere

To Kızılay & Ulus

Akay Caddesi

To Meclis (Parliament)

Atatürk Bulvarı

Esat Caddesi

Kennedy Caddesi

US Consulate

German Consulate

Tunus Caddesi

Besteka Sokak

Tunalı Hilmi Caddesi

To Australian Consulate

Abay Kunanbay Caddesi

Kuğulu Parkı

French Consulate

Iranian Consulate

Güvenlik Caddesi

Karum Shopping Mall

Tahran Caddesi

To Atakule, Indian & Syrian Consulates

To Çankaya, Presidential Palace & British Consulate

N

Not to scale

■ **Sleeping**
1 Best
2 Büyük Ankara Oteli
3 Dedeman Ankara
4 Hilton International
5 Otel Aldino
6 Otel Tunalı
7 Sheraton

● **Eating**
1 Cambo Iskender
2 Food Plaza
3 Kuğulu Park
4 Öz Annem
5 Tekne
6 Yakamoz

Museums

This museum charts the long history of civilisation in Anatolia with a stunning range of artefacts collected from sites across the country. The cream of the treasures discovered at Çatal Höyük, Kültepe, Boğazkale, Alaca Höyük, Gordion and many other archaeological sites besides are on display in chronological order starting from the dawn of mankind in the Stone Age and progressing right up to the Classical period. Particularly impressive are the Hittite mythological scenes from the Herald's Wall at Boğazkale. The exhibits are well annotated and the surroundings, the museum is housed in two beautifully restored Ottoman bedestens set in immaculate gardens, are wonderful. This is the one museum in town, and possibly the entire country, that you definitely shouldn't miss. ■ *0900-1730 daily except Mon. US$2.50. On the slopes of the Citadel, 100 m down from the Saatlı Kapı. On foot it can be reached up Hisarparkı Caddesi and through İnönü Parkı.*

Museum of Anatolian Civilisation (Anadolu Medeniyetleri Müzesi)

Housed in the building which functioned as the first Grand National Assembly, the exhibits chronicle the 1919-23 War of Independence with a collection of photographs, documents and other paraphernalia. The small parliamentary chamber is also preserved with a wax model of Atatürk standing on a raised podium. The likenesses of later presidents of the Republic are also on display. ■ *0830-1230, 1330-1730 daily except Mon. US$0.75. On Cumhuriyet Bulvarı just down from Ulus Meydanı on the right.*

Independence War Museum (Kurtuluş Savaşı Müzesi)

This collection is concerned with the achievements of the early Republican era, such as Atatürk's sweeping reforms. Unfortunately displays are labelled in Turkish only. The building was host to the Grand National Assembly after 1925, with the assembly hall open for inspection. ■ *0830-1230, 1330-1700 daily except Mon. Free. On the opposite side of Cumhuriyet Bulvarı to the Independence War Museum.*

Museum of the Republic (Cumhuriyet Müzesi)

Built as an administrative building in 1925, the mansion which houses the city's ethnographic collection was the resting-place of Atatürk's body up until the completion of the Anıt Kabir in 1953. His tomb held pride of place on the white marble slab inside the entrance. Exhibits include an interesting collection of costumes, furniture and other household items assembled into several recreations of Selçuk and Ottoman-era rooms. ■ *0830 1230, 1330 1730 daily except Mon. US$1.50. On Talat Paşa Bulvarı overlooking the Opera house.*

    In the same building as the ethnography collection are the **Korutürk Galerisi** and the **Arif Hikmet Koyunoğlu Galerisi** which exhibit art and sculpture by Turkish and foreign artists. ■ *0900-1200, 1300-1700 daily except Mon. Free.*

Ethnography Museum

Essentials

Ulus has most of the budget and lower midrange hotels fraternized by visiting traders and workmen. Many of the cheaper places are fairly dispiriting and because of the clientele women travelling alone may not feel comfortable. Such establishments also tend to charge an additional fee for using the bathroom.

Sleeping: Ulus

B *Hotel Oğultürk*, Rüzgarlı Eşdost Sokak No 6, T3092900, F3118321. Modern, reasonable option, rooms with TV, telephone and minibar, discounts available. Recommended. **B** *Hittit Hotel*, Hisarparkı Caddesi No 12, T3108617. Well-established tour hotel, large reasonably comfortable rooms, but nothing special particularly in view of price. **C** *Turist Hotel*, Çankırı Caddesi No 37, T3103980. Not up to its 3-star rating, reasonable ensuite rooms with TV, telephone, facilities include *hamam*, restaurant, bar, single US$31. **D** *Otel Güleryüz*, Sanayi Caddesi No 3, T3124122. Simple rooms with TV, telephone and ensuite, overpriced despite promise of discounts. **D** *Hotel Kale*, Anafartalar Caddesi, Alataş Sokak No 13, T3113393. A bit down-at-heel particularly in view of the price simple rooms, breakfast extra. **E** *Otel Bulduk*, Sanayi Caddesi No 26, T3104915, F3112617. Good-sized rooms with TV, telephone and ensuite. **E** *Hotel Yıldız*, Rüzgarlı Eşdost Sokak No 4, T3127581. Large, modern, small well-equipped rooms with TV, telephone, minibar, tiny ensuite. Recommended. **E** *Hotel As*, Rüzgarlı Sokak No 4, T3103998. Small, bright rooms with bathroom and telephone, breakfast extra, single US$15. **E** *Otel Buhara*, Sanayi Caddesi No 13, T3107999, F3243327. Good value place behind the post office, simple rooms with bath and balcony, single US$14. Recommended. **E** *Olimpiyat Hotel*, Rüzgarlı Eşdost Sokak No 18. Pretty ordinary rooms, some with TV, ensuite. **E** *Otel Akmam*, Kosova Sokak, T3244140. Old-fashioned, 2-star, unexceptional rooms have TV, telephone and ensuite.

F *Otel Zümrüt*, Şehit Teğmen Kalmaz Caddesi No 16, T3091554, off Sanayi. Deservedly popular with visiting businessmen, arriving late in the day you may find it full, large simple rooms, clean, good-sized ensuite, telephone, also waterless doubles for US$14, singles US$12. Recommended. **F** *Otel Pınar*, Hisarparkı Caddesi No 14, T3118951. Basic rooms with shower in the corner, overpriced, no breakfast. **F** *Hotel Devran*, Opera Meydanı, T3110485. Well-established place on the corner, 1 of the best in the row of cheapies, clean, simple but comfortable rooms with ensuite, rather small singles for US$13. Recommended. **F** *Hisar Otel*, Hisarparkı Caddesi No 6, T3119889. Singles US$10, clean basic rooms, shared bathroom, no breakfast. Reasonable option for those on a tight budget. **F** *Otel Sipahi*, Kosova Sokak No 1. Worn, peeling paintwork and depressing rooms. **G** *Hotel Ulus*, Hacıbayram Meydanı, T3105036. Atmospheric old boarding house with high-ceiling rooms, shared bathroom, single US$7, no breakfast. Recommended budget option. **G** *Otel Gülpınar*, Hacıbayram Caddesi No 6, T3115998. Very small basic rooms, use of shared bathroom extra US$3.50, no breakfast. **G** *Otel Fuar*, Kosova Sokak No 11. Used by visiting workers, adequate rooms with basin, shared toilet, bathroom charge US$2.50. Not a bad cheapy. **G** *Otel Üçler*, Kosova Sokak No 7, T3106664. Basic, a bit grimy but passable, shower charge US$2.50. **G** *Barbaros Pansiyon*, Kevgirli Sokak No 21, T3241246. Just down from junction with Hisarparkı Caddesi on left, very basic rooms, old residence that has seen better days, rock bottom prices, shared bathroom, no breakfast.

Sleeping: For more salubrious surroundings, Kızılay has a range of mid-priced and more luxuri-
Kızılay ous hotels, although inevitably with some of these places the price is more a reflection of the location than the facilities on offer. **LL** *Dedeman Ankara*, Büklüm Sokak No 1, T4176200, F4176214. Part of a national chain of luxury hotels, comfortable rooms and lots of facilities, discounts available. **LL** *Hotel Merit Altınel*, Gazi Mustafa Kemal Bulvarı, Tandoğan, T2317760, F2302330. Actually in Tandoğan near Anıt Kabir, luxury hotel with facilities including bar, restaurant, pool, sauna. **A** *Otel Melodi*, Karanfil Sokak No 10, T4176414, F4187858. Pleasant, large comfortable rooms with TV and telephone, car park, you're paying a hefty premium for the central location. **B** *Hotel Metropol*, Olgunlar Sokak No 5, T4173060, F4176990. Small well-appointed place, pleasant rooms with TV, telephone, single US$55. Recommended. **B** *Özilhan Otel*, Akay Caddesi No 9, T4175066, F4170243. Fairly ordinary rooms with minibar, TV and telephone, bar, restaurant, again you're primarily paying for the location with this one. **C** *Otel Elit*, Olgunlar Sokak No 10, T4174695, F4174697. Quiet but central place with reasonably priced rooms for location, ensuite, telephone, minibar and TV as standard, car-park. Recommended. **C** *Hotel Ergen*, Karanfil Sokak No 48, T4175906, F4257819. Standard rooms with TV and telephone. **D** *Otel Erşan*, Meşrutiyet Caddesi No 13,

T4189875, F4184092. Rooms on the small side but equipped with TV, minibar and telephone. About the cheapest in this part of town.

LL *Hilton International Hotel*, Tahran Caddesi No 12, T4682888, F4680909, www.hilton.com All the luxuries you'd expect. **LL** *Sheraton*, Noktalı Sokak, T4685454, F4671136, www.sheraton.com Another well-endowed favourite with visiting businessmen. **LL** *Büyük Ankara Oteli*, Atatürk Bulvarı No 183. Oldest of the luxury bunch, has had distinguished guests such as Queen Elizabeth. **L** *Otel Aldino*, Tunalı Hilmi Caddesi, Bülten Sokak No 22, T4686510, F4686517, just off Tunalı Hilmi on the right. Modern hotel with very comfortable but small rooms, TV, telephone, minibar as standard, sauna, restaurant. **AL** *Hotel Best*, Atatürk Caddesi No 195, T4670880, F4670885. Mid-size hotel with lots of comforts, has sister hotel *Apart Hotel Best*, Uğur Mumcu Sokağı 71, T4468080. Situated in much quieter suburb of Gaziosmanpaşa, a/c rooms, swimming pool, tennis courts, sauna, restaurant. **A** *Otel Tunalı*, Tunalı Hilmi Caddesi No 119, T4674440, F4274082, www.hoteltunali.com.tr Well designed modern place, well-equipped rooms with TV, refrigerator, telephone, also restaurant and bar, represents excellent value for this part of town. Recommended.

Sleeping: Kavaklıdere
Kavaklıdere is home to most of the city's luxury accommodation

Although not particularly renowned for its cuisine, Ankara does have a reasonable selection of places able to fit most budgets. Generally speaking the cheapest food is to be found in Ulus and Kızılay, with the more expensive restaurants predictably uptown in Kavaklıdere. The exceptions to the rule are several more upmarket and very atmospheric restaurants which have opened in the Hisar area which are often used by tour groups.

Eating

Midrange *Kınacılar Evi Restoran*, T3126500, Kale Sokak, Kaleiçi, near the gate to the inner citadel. Exquisitely restored late-Ottoman era konak, loads of atmosphere, tables inside or in courtyard, selection of Turkish dishes and meze, set-menus from US$15 per head. *Kale Washington*, T3114344, restored 300 year-old building. Pleasant terrace with views over city, a favourite with visiting tours, around US$20 per head. *Hisar Kule Restaurant*, T3097898, Kaleiçi. Renovated Ottoman building but not as atmospheric as the others, popular with tour groups, also has a terrace, Turkish dishes, grilled meat and fish, good value set-menus from US$15 including alcohol. *Zenger Paşa Konağı*, T3117070. Also located in several old houses, kitch 'museum' on 2nd floor, 1 dining room decorated with gaudy paintings of Atatürk, top floor has excellent views, traditional dishes including gözleme, mantı, m-long pide served at table, along with grilled meats and meze. A bit cheaper than the other restaurants in the castle area.

Eating: Ulus & the citadel

Cheap *Özurfa Kebap*, behind *Sipahi Hotel*, Kosova Caddesi, soups, kebabs and lahmacun, average place but convenient if you are staying in one of the nearby hotels. *Gaziantepli Fethi Bey*, Opera Meydanı, large place serving wide range of dishes including soups, stews, iskender kebap, döner, lahmacun. *Urfalı Hacı Mehmet*, Kızılbey Sokağı, in backstreet behind PTT, bright clean place serving south-eastern specialities, *lahmacun*, adana kebap, with *künefe* - a baked sweet made from shredded pastry, cheese and sugar syrup – for dessert. *Urfalı Kebap, Lahmacun ve Tatlı Sarayı*, Hisarparkı, up from Ulus Meydanı, grandly called a 'palace', popular eatery particularly at lunchtime, soups, kebabs, *lahmacun*, *baklava* and other tempting desserts. *Özgaziantepli Tabildot Lokantası*, Hisarparkı Caddesi, near junction with Kevgirli Caddesi, choice of 3 dishes from set-menu which are eaten off metal trays, unbeatable value at under US$2. *Erzurum Oltu Kebabı*, opposite Hisar Kapısı of Citadel, döner and Oltu kebabs, tiny place serving small skewers of lamb grilled over charcoal which is a speciality of eastern Anatolia. *Boğaziçi*, well-established place at top-end of Denizciler Caddesi, iskender, stews and sweets, all displayed on photographs. Desserts include *aşure*, a sweet stew of beans, pulses and wheat traditionally eaten after Ramazan. *Uludağ*, Denizciler Caddesi, No 54, huge and smart place built on Iskender

There is no shortage of good value kebap & lahmacun places in Ulus, many of which are run by people from the southeast region. Also cheap bites from the stalls along Hisarparkı Caddesi and Kosova Sokak at night. Choose one which is busy

kebabs. *Istanbul Börekçisi*, Hacıbayram Meydanı, sweet and savoury *börek*, pastries, biscuits. Good with hot milk or tea for breakfast. There are several more breakfast places across Hisarparkı Caddesi on Susam Sokak.

Eating: Kızılay **Midrange** *Göksu Restaurant*, Bayındır Sokak No 22/A, a notch up from the other kebap places, classy old-fashioned dining-room, tables on terrace, very reasonably priced menu including kebabs, grilled meat, fish, alcohol served. *Yeşil Bursa*, Karanfil Sokak near Olgunlar Sokak, specialising in Inegöl köfte and kebabs. *Anadolu Mutfağı*, Karanfil Sokak, bright modern place with reasonably priced kebabs and other Turkish dishes. *Pizzeria*, corner of Karanfil Sokak and Meşrutiyet Caddesi, pasta, pizza, salads and a pleasant atmosphere. **Cheap** Along Karanfil Sokak and the adjacent pedestrianized streets, snack bars serving *kumpir* (baked potatoes), burgers, sandwiches, gözleme and the like, abound. *Rumeli Işkembecisi*, Bayındır Sokak, popular institution serving soups, ready-prepared dishes and kebabs 24-hr a-day. *Iskender Evi*, Karanfil Sokak, unmistakable with its wooden facade, iskender and other kebabs, ready-prepare soups and stews, pasta and omelettes. *Özgaziantepli Tabildot*, Karanfil Sokak, sister restaurant to favourite in Ulus, similarly good value, set-menu with 3 choices of food for under US$2.50. *Kıraç Türk Mutfağı*, Konur Sokak, Turkish dishes in pleasant, modern surroundings. *Çömlek Güveç Evi*, Akay Caddesi opposite Konur Sokak, cheaply priced and delicious stews and soups, bean-stew contains meat, also serves *mantı* and various kebabs.

Eating: Kavaklıdere **Expensive** Several of the restaurants in the town's luxury hotels are worth a try with the 1 in the *Büyük Ankara Oteli* and the *Hilton* particularly well-regarded. **Midrange** *Neyzen*, Atatürk Bulvarı No 211/6, T4683968, next to the Interbank building, tastefully decorated and intimate place, live music evenings, fish, grilled meats and meze on the menu, US$22 set menu. *Kuğulu Park*, Atatürk Bulvarı 241, café/restaurant overlooking the park, a favourite meeting spot after shopping, mixed menu of snacks and heavier meals, terrace in summer, large open-fire warms atmosphere in winter. *Yakamoz*, Tunalı Hilmi Caddesi No 114, well-regarded fish and seafood restaurant around the back of Kuğulu Park. *Tekne Restaurant*, Tunalı Hilmi Caddesi No 73, where the young professional crowd comes to eat fish, convivial atmosphere, good meze, excellent value set-menu: meze, fish and unlimited alcohol US$14. *Food Plaza*, Tunalı Hilmi Caddesi No 85, fast-food centre, pizza, lahmacun, döner, burgers, all under one roof. *Cambo Iskender*, Tunalı Hilmi Caddesi No 105, up-market kebap place, crowded at lunchtime. *Cafe des Cafes*, Tunalı Hilmi Caddesi, bistro/café, diverse menu but mainly popular with locals for a coffee and a chat. *Öz Annem*, Tunalı Hilmi Caddesi No 66/2, Turkish cuisine, nice tables outside, reasonable prices.

Cafés There are lots of cafés in Karanfil Sokak and the adjacent streets of Kızılay. **Kuğulu Park**, Atatürk Bulvarı 241, café/restaurant overlooking the park. *Mado*, Tunalı Hilmi Caddesi, patisserie, ice-creams and breakfasts.

Bars & nightclubs
Ankara's nightlife, like the restaurant scene, is rather limited for a city of its size, however there are enough bars to keep you busy for a night or 2

In the SSK Işhanı on Ziya Gökalp Caddesi, 150 m from the Kızılay junction, are a whole gaggle of smoke-filled bars and drinking halls, some more enticing than others, most with live music and outdoor seating. Choices include *Tuana Cafe Bar*, *Naturel Bar*, *Ada Bar* and *Turkuaz Cafe Bar*. For something a bit more classy head uptown to Kavaklıdere and Çankaya. *Dolphin Cafe Bar*, Tunalı Hilmi Caddesi No 99, small stylish place, slow rock and blues played. *Marilyn Monroe's*, Tunalı Hilmi Caddesi, rub shoulders with the ex-pat community. *Papsi Bar*, Tunalı Hilmi Caddesi, small friendly place that gets very crowded. *Bira Parkı*, Kennedy Caddesi, near tall, white Işbankası building, lively rock bar, popular with student crowd. *Old School* and *Siyah*, louder than *Bira Parkı* next-door, heavy metal and hard rock. *A Soul Bar*, Cinnah Caddesi, stylish place, western pop and jazz. *Jade Bar*, Cinnah Caddesi No 56, frequented by the young and affluent of Çankaya, rock, blues and an occasional live act. *PM*, Cinnah Caddesi No 29, similar professional crowd, live Turkish music. Around the *Dedeman Ankara Hotel* are several large Turkish cabaret clubs, including *Altınkapı* and *Tropicana* on Esat Caddesi, Kavaklıdere. *Holiday Dance Café*, Tunalı Hilmi Caddesi, Kavaklıdere, basement place currently under restoration, pop play-list. For more clubs with a western-orientated play-list head out to Farabi Caddesi in Çankaya, where choices include *Paradise* and *Graffiti*.

Opera A visit to the city's **Opera House** is a possible night-time activity, with concerts and recitals also held in the large pink building on Atatürk Bulvarı, T3242210. **Bowling** Büklüm Sokak, beneath the *Dedeman Hotel*, US$2 per game. **Cinema** The cinemas below screen current international releases, generally with original soundtrack and Turkish subtitles. Tickets cost about US$3. *Kavaklıdere*, Tunalı Hilmi Caddesi No 105, Kavaklıdere. *Akun*, Atatürk Bulvarı No 227, Kavaklıdere. *Batı*, Atatürk Caddesi No 151, Bakanlıklar. *Derya*, Necatibey Caddesi No 57, Kızılay. *Kızılırmak*, Kızılırmak Sokak 21, Kızılay. *Megapol*, Konur Sokak No 33, Kızılay. *Metropol*, Selanik Caddesi No 76, Kızılay.

Entertainment

Although there is nothing to rival the experience of the Kapalı Çarşı in Istanbul, the streets on the eastern slope of the citadel harbour some colourful mercantile activity. There are also some carpet and antique shops on the main drag up to the castle, positioned to attract the passing tourist trade. Should you wish for an a/c shopping centre try *Beğendik*, underneath Kocatepe Camii in Kızılay or *Kavrum*, Iran Caddesi, Kavaklıdere. The area for book and music shops is around Karanfil Sokak. *Bilim ELT*, Konur Sokak, selection of Classics and novels in English. *Dost Kitabevi*, Karanfil Sokak 11/A, again novels, but also some coffee-table books.

Shopping

Parlemen-D, Ince Han, Atatürk Caddesi No 103, T4194545. *Ultra Turizm*, Inkilap Sokak No 18/b, Kızılay, T4193278. *Vista*, Cinnah Caddesi No 64/B, Çankaya, T4423020, ticket@vistatourism.com *Ecoadventure*, Cinnah Caddesi No 19, Çankaya, T4687131. *Bekset Turizm*, Cinnah Caddesi No 31/A, Çankaya. *Anki Travel*, Cinnah Caddesi No 22, Çankaya, T4276353. *Midas Tourism*, Bestekar Sokak No 74/2, Kavaklıdere, T4275943/44, arranges tours to the Hittite sites of Boğazkale.

Tour agencies
Scores around the main junction in Kızılay & along Cinnah Caddesi who deal with international flight bookings & arrange domestic tours

Air *Turkish Airlines* have direct internal flights to the following destinations: **Antalya**, 3 daily in summer. **Dalaman**, 3 weekly. **Erzurum**, 2 daily. **Gaziantep**, 2 daily. **Istanbul**, 17 flights daily. **İzmir**, 6 daily. **Trabzon**, 3 daily. **Sinop**, daily in summer. **Urfa**, daily. Flights to other destinations are via Istanbul.

Transport
For trains see the timetable on page 48

Bus The AŞIT bus-terminal is a mammoth horseshoe-shaped building on 2 levels with a bank, PTT, toilets, left-luggage office (*emanet*) and shops. Buses depart from gates on the 1st floor, behind an endless row of ticket booths. Arrivals are on the ground-floor. If the destination that you want is not listed below, trawl along the row of offices asking. The larger, more-reputable companies with services to most major cities are found at the following booths: *Kamil Koç 12-18*, *Metro 41*, *Pamukkale 58*, *Ulusoy 12*, *Varan 13*. Ulusoy also have their own terminal nearby on Ismet İnönü Bulvarı. **Adana**, regular buses, US$10, 8 hrs. **Afyon**, every 30 mins, US$4, 5 hrs. **Amasya**, (6, 60), every 90 mins, 4 hrs, US$9. **Antalya**, every hr, US$14, 9 hrs. **Bursa**, (58), at least every hr, 8½ hrs, US$10. **Çanakkale**, (70) every 2 hrs, US$15, 10 hrs. **Erzurum** (68, 80), US$19, 12 hrs. **Gaziantep**, every 90 mins, US$18, 12 hrs. **Göreme, Ürgüp and Avanos** (Nevtur, 50), every 1½ hrs during day, US$7.50, 5 hrs. **Istanbul**, every 30 mins, US$12, 6 hrs. **İzmir**, every hr, US$14, 8½ hrs. **Kayseri**, (Kent, 54) every hr, US$8, 5 hrs. **Konya** (Kontur, 39), every hr 0600-2200, US$8. 3½ hrs. **Kütahya**, (14, 18), every half-hr, US$3, 4 hrs. **Polatlı** (28), every hr, US$2.50, 1 hr. **Safranbolu**, (15, 4) regular buses, US$8, 5 hrs. **Samsun**, every hr, US$12, 6 hrs. **Sivas**, (27), regular, US$11, 6 hrs. **Trabzon**, several night buses, US$20, 10 hrs.

Several companies often have services to the same destination, so check around before buying your ticket as there may be a bus leaving sooner

Central Anatolia

Car rental Avis, Tunus Caddesi No 68/2, Kavaklıdere, T4672313, F4675703, **Best**, Büklüm Sokak No 89/9, Kavaklıdere, T4670008, F4670205. **Ekan**, Kavaklıdere Sokak No23, Kavaklıdere, T4269459, F4277161. **Europcar,**Akay Yokuşu No 25/C, Bakanlıklar, T4183430. **Hertz**, Atatürk Bulvarı No 138/B, Kavaklıdere, T4681029, F4681926.

Directory **Airline offices** *Aeroflot*, Cinnah Caddesi No 114/2, Çankaya, T4409874. *British Airways*, Atatürk Bulvarı No 237/1, Kavaklıdere. *Air France*, Atatürk Bulvarı No 231/7, Kavaklıdere, T4674400. *Istanbul Airlines*, Atatürk Bulvarı 61/1, Kızılay. *Lufthansa*, Iran Caddesi No 2, Kavaklıdere. *Turkish Airlines*, Atatürk Bulvarı No 154, Kavaklıdere. T4280200/2315572. At Esenboğa airport: T3980100. *Turkish-Cyprus Airlines*, Selanik Caddesi No 17, Kızılay. **Banks** There are banks with change facilities and ATM machines throughout the city. The central PTT in Ulus will also change foreign-currency outside working hours, although not TCs. **Baths** *Hisar Hamamı*, Hisarparkı Caddesi, Ulus, next to the *Hisar Hotel*, 0800-2300, men-only. *Küçükesat Hamamı*, Esat Caddesi No 81/A, men everyday except Tue 0700-2200, women Tue 0730-1800. **Communications Telephone** There is a row of telephone booths behind the central PTT on Sanayi Caddesi. They are also scattered around the city. **Post office** The central PTT office, open 24 hrs, is on Atatürk Bulvarı in Ulus. **Internet** There are lots of internet cafés in the vicinity of Karanfil Sokak. *Internet Café* Karanfil Sokak No 47, US$2.50 per hr. *Izci Internet Evi*, Konur Sokak No 53. Also in Maltepe near the Tourist Office is the *Atatürk Internet Evi*, Gazi Mustafa Kemal Bulvarı, US$1.50 per hr. **Cultural centres** *French Cultural centre*, Atatürk Bulvarı No 131, Bakanlıklar, T4311458. *Turkish-American Association*, Cinnah Caddesi No 20, Çankaya, T4262648. *Turco-British Association*, Bestekar Sokak No 32, Kavaklıdere T4191844. **Foreign consulates** *Australia*, Nenehatun Caddesi No 83, Gaziosmanpaşa, T4461180, F4461188. *Austria*, Atatürk Bulvarı No 189, Kavaklıdere, T4190431. *Canada*, Nenehatun Caddesi No 75, Gaziosmanpaşa, T4361275, F4464559. *France*, Paris Caddesi No 70, Çankaya, T4681154. *German*, Atatürk Caddesi No 114, Kavaklıdere, T4265465. *Great Britain*, Şehit Ersan Caddesi No 46/A, Çankaya, T4686230. *Italy*, Atatürk Caddesi No 118, Kavaklıdere, T4265460. *Japan*, Kırlangıç Sokak No 9, Gaziosmanpaşa, T4660414. *Netherlands*, Uğurmumcu Caddesi No 16, Gaziosmanpaşa, T4460470. *New Zealand*, Iran Caddesi No 13, Floor 4, Kavaklıdere, T4679056. *Pakistan*, Iran Caddesi No 37, Gaziosmanpaşa, T4271410. *Russian Federation*, Karyağdı Sokak No 5, Çankaya, T4392122. *South Africa*, Filistin Sokak No 27, Gaziosmanpaşa, T4464065. *Sweden*, Katip Çelebi Sokak No 7, Kavaklıdere, T4286735. *Switzerland*, Atatürk Bulvarı No 247, Kavaklıdere, T4675555. *Syria*, Abdullah Cevdet Sokak No 7, Çankaya, T4409657. *USA*, Atatürk Bulvarı No 110, Kavaklıdere, T4686110. *Uzbekistan*, Ahmet Rasim Sokak No 14, Çankaya, T4392740. **Hospitals** Ring your consulate to get advice on the best medical facilities, however, below are several options. *Hacettepe Hastanesi*, Hasırcılar Sokak, şıhhiye, state hospital with some English-speaking staff. *Acil Kavaklıdere Tıp Merkezi*, Şimşek Sokak No 6, centrally located private medical-centre. *Bayındır Medical Centre*, Eskişehir Yolu, modern health centre, some English speaking staff. **Tourist information** Gazi Mustafa Kemal Bulvarı No 121, Tandoğan, near Maltepe metro station, T2292631, F2293661. Mon-Fri 0900-1830, Sat 1000-1700. There is also an information kiosk at Esenboğa Airport.

Gordion

Phone code: 0312
Colour map 2, grid B1
Leaving early it's easily
possible to visit the sight
in a day-trip from Ankara

The mysterious tumuli sprouting up out of the monotony of the Anatolian steppe are the first, as well as the most lingering, impression of a visit to the ancient Phrygian capital of Gordion. Representing huge feats of ancient civil engineering, the stunning artefacts recovered by archaeologists from the University of Pennsylvania within several of these burial mounds have helped unlock many secrets about life in Asia Minor over 2500 years ago. However, burial mounds apart, there isn't a great deal else for the contemporary visitor to get excited about at Gordion.

History Excavations have revealed more or less continuous occupation from the late Bronze Age onwards, however, it is mainly with the capital of the Phrygian Empire that the site of Gordion is associated. Established some time in the ninth century BC, the city became the capital of the expanding Phrygian

Empire during the reign of King Gordios. Legend has it that the King, having sought the advice of an oracle concerning his lack of an heir, was told that he would be succeeded by a man who arrived in an oxcart. This prophesy was fulfilled when the young Midas entered the city by that very form of transport and was proclaimed heir to the throne. Needless to say King Midas, grateful at being plucked from obscurity by the hands of fate, had the wagon placed in the temple of Cybele, where it remained for over 500 years. During this time a myth developed that the person untying the knot in the rope linking the cart to its yoke would become the master of Asia. The task was finally achieved by Alexander the Great, who impetuously severed the rope with his sword, going on despite his unconventional tactics to fulfill the prophesy.

The Acropolis Begin your exploration of the site at the acropolis which was a **The site** relatively small defensible enclosure probably only inhabited by the Royal family and garrison. Ruins of the huge **gateway** leading into the Phrygian city from the southeast are the most impressive extant remains. This entrance, destroyed by the Cimmerians, was flanked by two defensive towers and courtyards used for storing goods and foodstuff, with large *pithoi* (storage vessels) unearthed by archaeologists during excavations. At a later date the Persians raised a second wall on the rubble of the Phrygian defences.

In the middle of the acropolis stood the **royal palace**, with four *megara*, solidly built flat-roofed halls, surrounded by a wall. One of these *megara*, the floor covered in a mosaic of geometric patterns, was probably where the royal family lived, while another of these halls is thought to be the temple of Cybele where Alexander severed the Gordion knot.

The Tumulus Tombs The tumuli raised above the tombs of the Phrygian kings are the most striking features of Gordion. Visible for miles across the open landscape, they are graphic testaments to the great, but ultimately transitory, importance of the city and its rulers.

To the southeast of the acropolis is **Küçük Höyük** (Small tumulus) a mound of clay beneath which a walled suburb of Gordion stood. Discoveries have shown that the settlement was destroyed by fire, probably after a siege, with carbon-dating techniques suggesting that this was at the hands of the Persian army in 546 BC. After this defeat the mound was raised on top of the garrison post and the tomb of the defeated king.

Büyük Höyük (large tumulus) to the east of the village is the largest of the burial mounds with an original height of over 70 m. Time has seen this height gradually reduced by the natural processes of erosion, so today it stands at a still-impressive height of 53 m, with a diameter of 300 m.

American-led excavations in the 1950s reached a chamber at the core of the mound. Built from cedar and juniper, the sepulchre contained the skeletal remains of a man, scientific analysis revealed had died in his sixties, surrounded by offerings including 178 bronze vessels and three large cauldrons now on display at the Museum of Anatolian Civilisation in Ankara. The artefacts discovered also dated the tomb to the mid-8th century, well after the deaths of both King Gordios and King Midas, one of who was thought to be buried inside.

Across the road from the Büyük Höyük the museum has a collection of artefacts **Museum** from the site, rather impoverished by the removal of the best pieces to Ankara. Outside the mosaic floors recovered from one of the *megara* of the royal palace are on display. ■ *US$1.50. Daily except Mon 0800-1230, 1330-1700.*

Central Anatolia

■ *Getting there: 15 km northwest of Polatlı, straddling the E90 highway about 100 km west of Ankara. There are regular buses to Polatlı from the Ankara otogar (booth 28). If coming from the other direction, any Ankara-bound bus will let you off in the town. From Polatlı the going is slightly less certain with dolmuş leaving occasionally from the town centre for the village of Yassıhöyük, a short walk from the site. A return taxi fare is in the region of US$20.*

Konya

Phone code: 0332
Colour map 5, grid B1
Altitude: 1061 m

The approach to Konya is across miles of featureless arable country, a wide open landscape covered with cereal fields known as the Turkish 'wheat basket'. Hot and dusty in the summer, winter brings a blanket of snow and icy temperatures. Once reached, the first impression is of a modern, prosperous city of apartment blocks and processing industries, but Konya also has a rich history dating back to prehistoric times when early farmers first began cultivating the fertile soils. For those interested in Selçuk architecture, Konya has an abundant supply of mosques, seminaries and tombs built when this was the capital of the Sultanate of Rum. As the adopted home of Mevlâna, the Sufi mystic and founder of the Mevlevi order of whirling dervishes, the city is now the destination for pilgrims who come from across Turkey and beyond to visit his tomb in the orders seminary.

Ins and outs

Getting there
See page 486
for further details

Konya is well-integrated into the national bus network with regular departures throughout the day to destinations both near and far. Several train services a week link the city with Istanbul, Adana and Gaziantep. There is also a small domestic airport handling hourly flights throughout the day to Istanbul. A modern tramway links the new *otogar* with Alâeddin Tepesi, or get on a dolmuş outside the tourist office when you want to return. Municipal buses link the centre with the train station (US$0.30).

Getting around
Many of the sights are clustered in and around the park on Alâeddin Tepesi, with the Mevlâna Museum and Tourist Information just over a kilometre's walk down Alâeddin Caddesi from the hill.

Climate
Konya's climate, like the religious views of many of its residents, tends towards the extreme, with the distance from the moderating influence of the Mediterranean subjecting it to hot, dusty summers and cold winters.

Background
The area around Konya was one of the earliest centres of civilisation in Anatolian with settlements dating back to 6800 BC. These Neolithic communities were among the first to practice sedentary farming and so represent an important landmark in the evolution of human civilisation.

Iconium, as Konya was called, grew up as just such a farming town, but later became an important way-station on the trade routes which developed across the Anatolian steppe. The Hittites, Phrygians, Lydians and Persians were some of those who built successive cities on the acropolis at Alâeddin Tepesi, while it was from Roman Iconium that St Paul and St Barnabus had to flee having enraged certain parts of the community with their sermons.

Soon after their victory over the Byzantines at Malazgirt, the Selçuk Turks overran the city. Laying aside their nomadic tendencies the Selçuk court chose Konya as the capital of their Anatolian empire, the Sultanate of Rum. They then set about beautifying it with many impressive public buildings, also establishing the city as an important cultural and religious centre. The empire reached its peak during the 12th century, about the time that Mevlâna Celaleddin Rumi, a mystic and religious philosopher, moved to the city (see box). Mevlâna gained great respect for his visionary teachings during his lifetime, and his philosophies lived on after his death, spread across Anatolia by the Mevlânaevi order of dervishes.

Today, the city is a conservative stronghold whose inhabitants uphold a stricter, more orthodox form of Islam. It is rare to see a woman in the street without a head scarf and female visitors will be given considerable attention if not dressed modestly. A visit during Ramazan, the holy month of fasting, can also be difficult as there are very few places to eat during the day, while you must also remember not to eat, drink or smoke in public out of respect for those fasting.

Sights

Alâeddin Camii Standing on Alâeddin Tepesi this large mosque was started during the reign of Sultan Ruknûddin Mesud I in the tenth century. Several subsequent phases of building over nearly a century resulted in the irregular structure which is seen today, a unique example of the development of Selçuk religious architecture. The main hall, the roof of which is supported by Byzantine columns, is built in Arab style, while the exquisitely carved *mimber* is one of the oldest works of Selçuk art, dated to 1155. In the courtyard are two tombs, the eastern ten-sided structure housing the graves of four Selçuk Sultans, with the other octagonal türbe containing the sarcophagus of Sultan Alâeddin Keykûbad I, after whom the mosque is named.

Büyük Karatay Medresesi To the north of Alâeddin Tepesi is this Islamic seminary established by Emir Celaleddin Karatay in 1251. Now called the Karatay Museum the building houses a beautiful collection of tiles and ceramics, with the interior of the domed main room covered with tiles of vivid turquoise, blue and gold which represent the heavens. The first verse of the Koran is written below in stylized, decorative calligraphy, with the names of first four prophets repeated below that. A square pool in the centre of the room was fed by a fountain, the water draining down a carefully sculpted curly drain, with the sound this created adding to the pervading atmosphere of calm and coolness. The tomb of Celaleddin Karatay who served as regent under several Sultans is also in the main room. Next door are interesting examples of tiles dating from the Selçuk and Ottoman periods. ■ *0900-1200, 1300-1700 daily except Mon. US$1.50. Cross Alâeddin Bulvarı near the remains of the Alâeddin Pavilion, now straddled by an ugly concrete structure to protect it from the elements.*

Ince Minare Medresesi This medrese, whose names translates as the Medrese with the Slender Minaret, was built in 1258 at the orders of Emir Sahip Ata Fahrettin Ali. A lightning strike on the aforementioned minaret in 1901 considerably shortened it. The imposing portal is typical of the grand entranceways found in Selçuk buildings, with the facade covered in elaborate carving. The students of theology who once studied in the medrese have been replaced by an interesting collection of Selçuk stonework and wood-carving. You will notice that the work of early Selçuk craftsmen was not confined by the Islamic prohibition on recreating likenesses of living things and many animals and humans are included in the carvings.■ *0900-1200, 1300-1700 daily except Mon. Entrance: US$1.50. On the opposite side of Alâeddin Tepesi to Alâeddin Bulvarı.*

Mevlâna and the Mevlevi

The Mevlevi are probably the best known of the heterodox Islamic sects which developed in Anatolia after the Selcuk invasion. Commonly referred to as the 'whirling dervishes' on account of their ritualized spinning ceremony, the Mevlevi followed the teachings of the great mystical philosopher and poet Mevlâna Celaleddin Rumi.

Mevlâna was born in Balkh, within the borders of present-day Afghanistan, in 1207. His father Bahâeddin Veled was a scholar of high regard, respected for his wise teachings and sermons. With the gathering Mongol threat to the east, Bahâeddin Veled set off westwards with his family, eventually settling in Konya upon the invitation of the Selçuk Sultan Alâeddin Keykûbad I.

In his new home Mevlâna studied diligently under his father, developing a keen sense of perception and intelligence. He became an expert in matters of Islamic law and theology, also mastering several foreign languages and studying Persian, Arabic and Greek literature. In 1244 when he was teaching at the Iplikçi seminary in Konya, Mevlâna was approached by a wandering dervish from Persia named Şems-i-Tabrizi. Mevlâna recognized the exceptional qualities of the mystic and a strong friendship developed between the two men. He abandoned his teaching, preferring instead to spend the days locked in philosophical debate with Şems. Mevlâna's withdrawal from society aroused the jealousy of his followers and they eventually murdered Şems, but not before the dervish had had a fundamental effect on Mevlâna.

For a long time Mevlâna was inconsolable at the loss of his friend and spiritual guide, but with the encouragement of those around him he embarked on writing his epic work of poetry, the Mathnawi. It was a huge undertaking, running to six volumes, in which he set out his mystical philosophies in the form of stories. On the 17 December, 1273, soon after completing the work, Mevlâna died.

His message of freedom of thought, love, tolerance and charity did not die with him though, becoming enshrined as the guiding principles of the Mevlevi order set up after his death by devoted followers.

Leadership of the Mevlevi sect was assumed by Mevlâna's son Sultan Veled, who established the tekke in Konya as the centre of a brotherhood whose influence spread over the next 650 years across Anatolia and into all levels of society. It was this influence and the resulting political power enjoyed by the Mevlevi, that Atatürk felt was a dangerous obstacle to his secular reforms, resulting in the ban on all dervish orders in 1925.

Life for the Mevlevi dervish was highly ritualized, with even the most mundane tasks taking on a spiritual significance. Novices wishing to join the order had to serve 1001 days of retreat during which they carried out the daily chores of the tekke, learning the discipline and devotion necessary to become a dervish. Having completed the noviciate the dervish were allowed to leave the monastery, marry and seek a career. Some, however, stayed on to be trained as musicians, poets, linguists or artists, with many of the most talented men in Ottoman society belonging to the Mevlevi order.

West of Alâeddin Tepesi
Aziziye Camii: a mosque with a difference

Walking down Alâeddin Caddesi is the **İplikçi Camii**, the oldest mosque still in use in the city which has been restored several times since it was built in 1230, with the large **Şerafettin Camii** on the opposite side. The **Aziziye Camii**, south of Alâeddin Caddesi at the Mevlâna Museum end, is a mosque built in the Ottoman Baroque style, incorporating eclectic elements such as classical capitals and Gothic-style spires reaching for the heavens, with the minarets capped by distinctive covered balconies. Constructed in 1671 it was rebuilt after a fire with the help of Sultan Abdülaziz in 1891.

Sema - the Universal movement

Today the Mevlevi are best know for the whirling ceremonial dance, the Sema, performed by its members. An act of worship, Mevlâna described the Sema as a way to reach spiritual unity with God through acts of controlled ecstasy. Traditionally conducted on Monday evenings, the proceedings are carried out according to a strict set of rules, carefully watched over by the şeyh or master. The Sema is made up of four periods of spinning, each representing a particular stage of man's journey to enlightenment and oneness with God. Every element of the proceeding is loaded with symbolism.

The dervish's dress in white robes, representing their ego's shroud, the tall felt hat their ego's tombstone. A black robe worn over the top is discarded as they shake-off their worldly existences to begin spinning as a slowly revolving formation. Arms out-stretched the dervish receive the blessings of God with each rotation through their upturned right palm, channelling them down to earth with their opposite, down-turned palm. This is in keeping with the belief that the dervish are nothing but vessels conferring love from God to man.

An inseparable part of the Sema is the music provided my the dervish orchestra, and particularly the poignant "voice" of the ney, reed flute. This instrument is held as a symbol of perfection, with a soul that cries out for its home, the reedbed.

It is possible to see the 'whirling dervishes' in Konya during the Mevlâna Festival starting on the 10th of December and culminating on the 17th, the day of Mevlâna's death, referred to by his followers as the 'Wedding Night'. Tickets must be bought well in advance for the performances, which are conducted in a local gymnasium by folk dancers who have no relation to the original Mevlevi dervishes. For a more authentic affair it is better to visit the semahane in Galatasaray, Istanbul, where Sema are regularly conducted by a group of modern dervish.

Each year multitudes of pilgrims from across the country come here, and more than a handful of curious tourists too. It is the *tekke* at the spiritual heart of the Mevlevi dervish order. This complex of buildings with its unmistakable fluted tower covered in turquoise tiles was built over the centuries after Mevlâna's death to serve as a centre for religious teaching, art, music and literature. Closed in 1925 as part of Atatürk's ban of the dervish orders it was reopened a year later as a museum. This attempt to 'secularise' what is an important religious shrine, was unsuccessful and to the present-day a stream of faithful Turks visit the tomb of Mevlâna to pay their respects, seek guidance and pray. In keeping with Mevlevi philosophy all visitors are welcome regardless of religion or creed, however, remember it is a sacred place and you should dress accordingly.

Upon entering there are fountains in the courtyard where people conduct their ablutions and drink the sacred water. After removing your shoes proceed with the crowd into the **mausoleum**, with the tombs of Mevlâna, his father and other important Mevlevi leaders draped in heavy cloth and topped by outsized symbolic turbans. The original tomb was built after Mevlâna's death, but it was reconstructed and other buildings added during the 15th and 16th centuries. It is here that the depth of feeling still held for Mevlâna is visible, with visitors praying, often bleary eyed with emotion, and caressing the pillars with great reverence. Beside the entrance is a bronze bowl called the **Nişan taşı** (April bowl), used to collect the April rainwater. This water was considered sacred

Mevlâna Museum
This is undoubtedly the most interesting sight in Konya

Central Anatolia

and was thought to have miraculous healing properties when administered to a patient by the end of Mevlâna's turban.

The **semahane** was where the dervishes performed their religious dances, spinning with outstretched arms on the polished wooden floor. Today, there is no more 'whirling' in the semahane, which is far too small for the crowds that turn out every December to witness the spectacle. Now the room contains various exhibits including a *ney* (reed flute), an important instrument in dervish music whose mournful 'voice' is thought to be a cry from the human soul at its separation from God. Also displayed is the original *Mathnawi*, the inspirational work of poetry composed by the Mevlâna and much studied since, along with many fine carpets and beautifully decorated Korans presented to the Mevlevi order by wealthy followers. At the centre of the room is a display case containing hairs from the beard of the Prophet Mohammed.

Back out in the courtyard flanking the entrance are the cells used by the Mevlevi for meditation, while in the corner is a mock-up of the living quarters complete with wax dummies dressed in authentic dervish garb. ■ *0900-1700 daily. US$2. Tucked behind the Selimiye Camii. Look out for the turquoise tiled tower.*

Koyunoğlu Museum Donated by a private collector, the museum contains a diverse selection of exhibits including stuffed birds, mineral samples, fossils, ancient coinage, jewellery, antique kilims, traditional costumes and an exhibition of old photographs of the city. It's worth a visit; as is the **Koyunoğlu Konya Evi** next door, a traditional Konya house complete with all the original trappings of a

Mevlâna Museum

19th-century home. ■ *0830-1730 daily except Mon. US$0.50. About 1 km walk down Topraklık Caddesi, flanking the graveyard, from the Selimiye Camii. Walking through the graveyard is not recommended, particularly if alone.*

Excursions

Discovered by the British archaeologist James Mellaart in 1958 this was the site of a Neolithic settlement inhabited from 6500 BC, making it the earliest community of its kind so far uncovered in Anatolia. Subsequent excavation of the stratified mound has revealed a town of mud-brick houses with each dwelling conforming to a similar plan. The houses were entered via a hole in the roof and contained several rooms including a family shrine, the walls of which were decorated with depictions of the mother-goddess of Anatolia and baked mud figurines. Most of what was discovered is on display at the Museum of Anatolian Civilisation in Ankara and but for the double mound there is little to see at the sight. Excavations by Cambridge University are continuing at the site with more information about progress available online at: www.catal.arch.cam.ac.uk/catal/catal ■ *Getting there: If you still want to have a look take a dolmuş to the village of Çumra, off highway 715 to Karaman, from where you must hire a taxi for the last 10 km.*

Çatal Höyük

An outing, possible only with your own transport, is to the medieval rock-cut churches of Glistra (marked Lystra on some maps) about 45 km to the southwest of Konya. The landscape and man-made alterations, in the form of churches and houses carved from the soft volcanic rock, are reminiscent of Cappadocia, all-be-it on a much smaller scale.

Gökyurt (Glistra)

Another interesting excursion by car is to Binbir Kilise, meaning 1001 Churches, found on the slopes of the volcanic Kara Dağ mountains, north of Karaman. A refuge for Christians during the Middle Ages, a thriving community existed here until the area came under Selçuk control in the 11th century. The ruins of basalt churches, monasteries, fortifications and houses are scattered across an extensive area, along with some Hellenistic, Roman and Hittite remains. From Karaman proceed 24 km north to the village of Dinek, where a rough road leads 9 km to the village of **Madenşehir**, around which there is much evidence of past ecclesiastical life. At **Degile**, a small village 8 km beyond, is another concentration of remains.

Binbir Kilise

Essentials

A *Hotel Balıkçılar*, Mevlâna Karşısı 1, T3509470, F3513259, opposite side of the roundabout to the Selimiye Camii and Mevlâna Museum. The best that Konya offers, some rooms have views of Mevlâna Museum but being on the street-side they may be noisy, equipped with TV, a/c, minibar, also restaurant, sauna, billiards and a bar. Recommended. **B** *Otel Hüma*, Alâeddin Sokak, No 8, T3506618, F3510244. Modern hotel across from Alâeddin Tepesi, good size rooms with TV, minibar and telephone, lovely wooden pictures on the walls, weekend discounts available. Recommended. **C** *Hotel Konya*, Mevlâna Meydanı No 8, T3519212, F3521003. Atmospheric wood-panelled reception and lounge, small rooms are a bit disappointing though, ensuite, TV and telephone, wooden furniture, roof terrace. **C** *Otel Şems*, Şems Caddesi No 10, T3505738, F3511771. Small comfortable rooms with balcony overlooking Şems Türbesi, equipped with telephone, minibar, TV, fan. Recommended. **D** *Hotel Şahin*, Hükümet Alanı No 39, T3526225, F3512376. Modern place on the main street so the front rooms are a bit noisy, good value rooms with ensuite and telephone, bar,

Sleeping

Central Anatolia

restaurant. Recommended. **D** *Köşk Esra Otel*, Yeni Aziziye Caddesi, Kadılar Sokak No 28, T3520671, F3520901. Small well-appointed modern hotel in quiet backstreet, singles are US$24. Recommended. **E** *Otel Sema*, Mevlâna Caddesi No 59, T3504623, F3523521. Good rooms for the price, well-finished bathrooms, TV, telephone, restaurant. Recommended. **E** *Bella Hotel*, Aziziye Caddesi No 19, T3514070. Reasonable rooms with bathroom, but traffic noise problem in front ones. **E** *Çatal Aile Pansiyonu*, Naci Fikret Sokak No 14, next to the *Hotel Konya*. Old-fashioned pension with plain guestrooms, cheaper rooms without toilet, roof terrace, use of washing machine, no breakfast. **F** *Hotel Fatih*, Kazanlı Sokak, T3528307, off Alâeddin Caddesi at Alâeddin Tepesi end. Clean, simple rooms with washbasin, TV and heater, shared bathroom, breakfast extra. Recommended. **F** *Otel Derviş*, Bostan Çelebi Sokak No15, next-door to the *Mavi Köşk*. Slightly better rooms than the *Mavi Köşk* with toilet and shower, no breakfast. **F** *Otel Yasin*, Yusufağa Sokak, No 25, T3511624. Old fashioned guesthouse with cheap but fairly passable 1/2/3/4 bed rooms, breakfast extra. Recommended budget option. **F** *Mavi Köşk Oteli*, Bostan Çelebi Sokak No13, T3501904. Grotty rooms with sink and shower, hot in summer, breakfast extra.

Eating

The food in Konya is far less refined than on the coast.

The cafés on Alâeddin Tepesi are a good place to rest those weary feet after sightseeing

The local speciality, *fırın kebabı*, consists of a lump of greasy roasted mutton or lamb served with plain pide. *Etli ekmek*, translated literally as bread with meat, is the local version of pide. Most places in Konya don't serve alcohol. One oasis you can find a cold beer is the *Alâeddin Restaurant*, or alternatively the other option is to search out a 'Tekel Bayii' (Off License) and take some well-disguised bottles or cans back to your hotel room. **Midrange** *Konya Mutfağı*, Topraklık Caddesi 66, 5-mins walk from *Hotel Balıkçılar* towards Koyunoğlu Museum, opposite Akçeşme Ilkokulu (school), traditional Turkish foods served in atmospheric restored building, full meal for under US$10 per head. *Alâeddin Restaurant*, Mimar Muzaffer Caddesi, another restaurant in a restored house which also has a pleasant ambience particularly at the weekend when diners are serenaded by cabaret acts and local musicians, alcohol served. **Cheap** There are many cheap places to eat along the main street including the modern and popular *Şifa Restaurant*, Mevlâna Caddesi, serving kebabs and pide. The *Sema Restaurant* opposite has a similar menu and prices. *Halil İbrahim Sofrası*, Mevlâna Karşısı, next to *Hotel Balıkçılar*, serves a similar range of kebabs, including *etli kebap*, and pide. There are also some cheap eateries in the bazaar area.

Festivals The *Mevlâna Festival* is held every year during the week leading up to the **17th Dec**. Buy tickets for performances of the Sema well in advance. For information and tickets contact the Tourist Information Office or the Konya Culture and Tourism Association, on the opposite corner facing the Selimiye Camii.

Shopping Over 500 villages in the Konya region produce woollen carpets many using natural dyes and featuring the distinctive triangular 'dervish' motif. There are plenty of shops on Mevlâna Caddesi. Also unique to Konya, though not to everybody's taste, are the chalky, delicately perfumed sweets, known as *Mevlana Şekeri* (Mevlana's sweets), sold in bags in all the city's souvenir shops.

Tour agencies *Mona*, Alâeddin Caddesi, Fevzi Çakmak Sokak No 2, on the 1st floor of corner building, car rental and plane tickets organized.

Transport **Air** *Turkish Airlines*, Mevlana Caddesi No 9, T3512000, F3502171, daily flights to **Istanbul**. A service bus shuttles passengers to and from the airport, dropping them at the *Turkish Airlines* office on Alâeddin Caddesi. **Bus** Aksaray, regular buses, US$6, 2½ hrs. **Ankara**, every hr during the day, US$7, 3 hrs. **Antalya**, every hr, US$9, 5 hrs. **Beyşehir**, every hr, US$3, 1¼ hrs. **İzmir**, 5 buses daily, US$11, 8 hrs. *Lider Aksaray* have service to **Nevşehir**, continuing to **Göreme** and **Avanos**, 0900, 1100, 1400, 1700,

Central Anatolia

The Selçuk caravanserai

The caravanserai or han is a common man-made feature of the rolling Central Anatolian landscape, although they were also built right up to the shores of the Aegean and eastwards along the continental trade routes. Typically constructed with thick walls and a richly ornamented portal leading into a courtyard surrounded by vaulted arcades, the caravanserai is an architectural form particularly associated with the Selçuks.

The construction of caravanserais by sultans, vezirs and other important Selçuk officials was part of an official policy to encourage trade as a source of revenue for the state. There was a flurry of building during the 12th and 13th centuries with 132 hans raised in just 80 years. Built along the main caravan routes, caravanserais were essentially fortified inns. However, they provided much more than just shelter from the elements, also offering food and security for the weary traveller and stabling for their animals. Generally there were also a mescit (small mosque) and a wash-house, while resident craftsmen could repair broken equipment and veterinarians would tend to sick animals.

Although the Selçuk system of caravanserais was not without precedent – the Romans also built barracks at regular intervals along their roads as did Genghiz Khan in Central Asia – it was unique in offering its services to everybody. Partly maintained by an annual tax levied on merchants, the system was egalitarian, making no distinction between the race or religion of those who used it.

The Selçuk court also provided state guarantees for traders, one of the earliest known insurance schemes, and robberies were reduced by holding local people responsible for the safe passage of caravans. In areas where banditry occurred punitive taxation was imposed, whereas those living in safer areas were rewarded with a lighter tax burden. All this helped to ensure an unprecedented level of security on the Anatolian road network with its being said that you could walk safely from the Aegean to Van with a pot of gold on your head.

To ensure such beneficial conditions for trade required a strong central government and with the defeat of the Selçuks by the Mongols in 1243 the glorious age of the caravanserai came to an end. Although they continued to be built and used during Ottoman times, they were never again to form part of such an integrated system. Today, you will see many caravanserai along Turkey's modern trade routes, most in ruin, although others have been restored to begin a new life as a hotel or shopping arcade. Ones to look out for are the Koza Hanı in Bursa, the Sarı Han near Avanos; the Sultan Hanı (see below) between Konya and Aksaray and the Karatay Hanı, east of Kayseri; though there are many more besides.

US$8, 3½ hrs. **Pamukkale**, 5 daily, US$8, 6 hrs. **Train** Surprisingly there is no line between Konya and Ankara, although the are 3 overnight services to and from Istanbul. *Meram Ekspresi*, departs for Istanbul via Afyon and Kütahya at 1750 everyday, 11 hrs. *İç Anadolu Mavi Tren* passes through en route for Karaman everyday at 1230, 3 hrs; returning en route for Istanbul via Afyon and Kütahya at 2115, 11 hrs. *Toros Ekspresi* passes through en route for Gaziantep via Adana, Tue, Thu and Sun, 2225, 13 hrs; returning en route for Istanbul via Afyon at 0415, 13 hrs.

Banks There are lots of banks with ATMs and change services around Hükümet Alanı. **Baths** The traditional *hamam*, with male and female sections, behind the Şerafettin Camii is excellent. **Communications Post office** On Hükümet Alanı, opposite Şerafettin Camii. **Tourist information** Mevlâna Caddesi No 21, near the Mevlâna Museum, T3511074, open weekday 0830-1230, 1330-1730.

Directory

Central Anatolia

Sultanhanı
Phone code: 0382

Turning its back on Konya, Highway 300 scores its way across miles of empty, rolling steppe country towards Aksaray. After 110 km of driving, featureless except for a couple of dusty villages of low, sod-roofed houses lost in an endless sea of wheat fields and grassland, is Sultanhanı. The village gets its name from the Selçuk caravanserai which in days gone by provided shelter for passing traders (see box). Built in 1229 at the behest of Sultan Alâeddin Kaykobad I, this particular caravanserai is the largest in Anatolia, and has been restored several times during its long history, most recently in the 1970's. It's an impressive structure built of blonde stone with the typically ornate marble entranceway giving onto a large courtyard with a small mosque at its centre. The accommodation, kitchens, workshops and *hamams* (baths) for men (erkek) and women (kadın) were along either side, with the large stables opposite the entranceway at the far end. ■ *0700-1900 daily. US$1.25. 100 m south of the main road*

Sleeping and eating For the modern traveller Sultanhanı offers several pensions with camping facilities and the *Sultan Restaurant*, opposite the caravanserai, has everything else you could need, including a place to leave your bags. **F** *Kervansaray Pansiyon and Camping*, T2422008, over a 100 m east of the *han*, simple doubles with ensuite bathroom. **F** *Sultan Pansiyon*, T2422393, also close-by and with similar facilities. **F** *Kervan Pansiyon*, T2422325, friendly. Family-run 750 m south past the centre of the village, doubles with ensuite, evening meals available, also camping. Recommended.

Aksaray

Phone code: 0382
Colour map 5, grid B2
Altitude: 980 m

Approaching Aksaray from the west the orchards and coppices of tall popular trees surrounding the town are a welcome change after miles of monotonous steppe-country. The conical form of Hasan Dağı looming to the south also provides interest, although the mostly modern agricultural town itself has very little to detain the contemporary traveller. Indeed most people simply pass through en route to the Ihlara valley, though there are a couple of historic buildings to see if you should have an hour to spare. If you have a passion for pre-Ottoman Islamic architecture then seek out the **Zinciriye Medresesi**. Built in 1336 at the behest of the Karamanid leader, it now houses the towns limited archaeological collection. Turning left passed the *Çakmak Pansiyon*, walk up to the main square where the police station and local government are housed in well-restored buildings. Also on the square is the **Ulu Cami** built during the Karamanid period.

Sleeping & eating **D** *Hotel Üçyıldız*, Bankalar Caddesi No 6, T382/2140404, at the far end of the main street. Modern 3-star hotel with decent rooms, singles for US$25. **F** *Otel Yuvam*, Eski Sanayi Caddesi, T2120024. Good value place next to the Ulu Cami, rooms with TV, telephone, bathroom and large beds. Recommended. **F** *Aksaray Pansiyon*, Eski Otel Ihlara karşısı, T2124133, from the bus station head towards the centre on Eski Sanayi Caddesi, take second right and the hotel is 50 m up on the right. Simple but comfortable rooms with bathroom, terrace, use of kitchen. Recommended. There are several restaurants along Bankalar Caddesi including the *Merkez Lokantası*, opposite the police station, which serves kebabs and ready-prepared stews.

Transport
The bus station is 10 mins walk from town

Ankara, several direct buses, 4½ hrs, US$6. **Güzelyurt**, about every 2 hrs, last at 1730, 1 hr, US$1. **Ihlara**, Belediye buses leave at 1100, 1400 and 1800, 1 hr, US$0.75. **Konya**, regular buses during the day, many are continuing-on somewhere else, 2½ hrs, US$4. **Nevşehir**, every 1½ hrs throughout day, last at 1745, 1½ hrs, US$2.50. **Niğde**, depart regularly during the day, 2 hrs, US$3.

Banks On the main street Bankalar Caddesi. **Tourist information** Ankara Caddesi, which starts next to the Ulu Cami, Dinçer Apt 2, 2nd floor. 0800-1200, 1330-1730 weekdays.

Directory

The Ihlara Canyon

A deep gash carved into the rolling basalt plains to the southeast of Aksaray, the Ihlara Canyon is a hidden shangri-la. Confined within its precipitous rock walls are 16 km of beautiful scenery with coppices of poplar and willow alive with birds and the rushing river. In medieval times the gorge harboured a thriving monastic society which left numerous rock-cut churches adorned with colourful frescoes. Mercifully overlooked by the majority of visitors to nearby Cappadocia, the canyon is far less touristy than the area around Göreme and has so far retained much of its wild beauty.

Phone code: 0382
Colour map 5, grid B2

Getting there Belediye buses leave Aksaray *otogar* 3 times a day for Ihlara village (US$0.50), passing Selime and the Belisırma turn-off en route. At present the times are as follows, although these may be subject to change. From Aksaray: 1100, 1400 and 1800. From Ihlara: 0700, 0730, 1300 and sometimes 1600. **Getting around** With a reasonable level of fitness you can comfortably walk the entire length of the canyon in a day, setting-off from either Selime at the bottom or Ihlara village at the head of the gorge. It is also possible to enter or exit from the gorge mid-way along at the village of Belisırma, however, walking down from here would mean missing the rock-cut churches situated in the upper section of the canyon. To see the entire canyon in a day independently would mean hiring a taxi to Ihlara village from Aksaray, at least US$15 one-way, or US$40 return with the taxi waiting in Belisırma to pick you up.

Ins & outs
Accommodation is available in Selime, Belisırma & Ihlara village which gives you plenty of flexibility when planning your visit

Ihlara Canyon

Mainly clustered on the steep sides of the narrow Melendiz valley, Ihlara village is a sizeable community of crumbling stone buildings. The town square, several cafés and the start of the path down the canyon are all at the bottom of the valley. Over the rim on the flat land above is the modern village built since the 1960s, where you will find the accommodation. Many of these buildings were built by locals who saved money working in Britain, mostly in the London restaurant trade. On the rim of the canyon about 1 km from the village is a tourist centre with a restaurant and a rather unappealing camping area. Access to the gorge is via a long flight of steps. ■ *Officially open 0800-1900 daily. US$2, the same charge is payable if you enter from the village.*

Ihlara village

Sleeping and eating F *Bişginler Ihlara Pansiyon*, T4537077, on the right as you enter the village. Simple 1/2/3 bed rooms with ensuite. **F** *Akar Pansiyon*,

Central Anatolia

T4537018, also on the main road. A row of clean, modern rooms with large spartan bathrooms, good restaurant at rear, owner also runs local shop where you can buy basic supplies, Recommended. **F** *Anatolia Pension*, T4537018, on the side road to the gorge tourist centre and entrance, surrounded by nice gardens, simple rooms with ensuite, recommended spot to camp, US$3 per person. **F** *Star Motel*, T4537429. Pleasant position in the old village near the river, plain rooms with shared bathroom, open all-year-round, restaurant. Recommended. **F** *Pansion Famille*, T4537098, on left as you come into the village. Top floor of a family house, a bit more basic than the rest but also cheaper, US$9 without breakfast, use of kitchen, small terrace.

The Upper Canyon

Situated in the far southeastern corner of the Roman province of Cappadocia, the Peristrema, as the gorge was then known, provided the seclusion and safety necessary for a major monastic society to develop within its walls. Cut-off from the rest of Byzantium it was largely unaffected by the turbulence that rocked the empire during the Iconoclastic period, with the churches of the valley showing a remarkable continuity of use right up until the 14th century and the arrival of the Selçuk Turks.

The most visited churches are grouped around the entrance from the tourist centre, with a map at the bottom of the stairs to help you locate them. There is also an excellent book 'The Rock Churches of the Ihlara Valley' on sale in the tourist centre, possibly in Ihlara as well, giving a detailed account of all the churches. One of the most interesting churches, the **Yılanlı Kilise**, is found across a small footbridge on the east side of the river. Its frescoes, in strong green, red and yellow pigment, include a line of figures standing shoulder to shoulder painted in memory of forty Christians martyred in Sivas.

At head height on the left is the scene which gives the church its name, 'The Snake Church', depicting four women being punished for their sins by serpents. The fresco also includes one of the rare depictions of the devil, now badly damaged, eagerly awaiting the sinners' souls. On the far left St Michael stands in judgement with a pair of scales in his hand.

From here it is a 90-minute walk downstream to Belisırma with the path threading its way through a patchwork of fields and shady stands of willow and poplar. Other churches with sections of intact fresco that you pass along the way include the Sümbüllü Kilise, Kokar Kilise and Eğritaş Kilisesi.

Belisırma

At the small village of Belisırma the valley widens and the angle of the canyon walls relent enough for a collection of stone, mud-roofed houses to perch on its rocky flank. The approach in either direction is through a mosaic of intensively cultivated fields, bordered by a grid of slender poplar trees which are cropped to make beams for building or fencing. Beside the river are two restaurants specialising in trout or saç kavurma, brought sizzling to your table in a meat pan. Both restaurants also have simple camping facilities and will even rent a tent to those without one. Up in the village several of the houses offer simple accommodation, including **G** *Belisırma Ev Pansiyon*, T4573037, where you'll find a cosy water-less room in a friendly household, meals available on request. ■ *Getting there: Motor access to the village is by a left-hand turn off the Aksaray-Ihlara village road about 1 km south of Yaprakhisar. Also on the main road, 2 km away from the village, is the **Ziga hamamı**, where you can have a soak in naturally-fed mineral baths (0800-2200, US$1).*

The Lower Canyon & Selime

Below Belisırma the canyon broadens and there is more agricultural activity in evidence. Although there are no churches in this section, the scenery is equally, if not more, entrancing. Eventually the valley splays out into a wide cultivated basin enclosed by rocky escarpments. The path reaches the main road between the villages of Yaprakhisar and Selime. The *Çatlak Restaurant* beside a bridge over the river serves trout, roast chicken, saç kavurma and delicious sheep's yoghurt at shady water-side tables and makes a good place to wait for the bus if you're leaving for Aksaray. If you're in no rush **Selime** could be a pleasant place to stay either before commencing your walk up the canyon or at the end.

A short distance beyond the bridge a Selçuk tomb stands incongruously in the village's roadside graveyard, with a large monastic settlement carved into the tufa pinnacles and cliffs above. Tunnels, which are thought originally to have led to the summit, give access to various interconnecting chambers the most impressive of which is a huge cathedral burrowed from the rock. The **F** *Piri Motel*, T4545114, F2131493, offers clean, simple rooms with large bathrooms, and the owner, Mustafa, can point you in the direction of several more churches in the area. The owner of the Çatlak restaurant also has a pension inconveniently stuck out on the other side of the village, but frankly it really isn't worth the bother even if he does offers you a lift. The Aksaray-Ihlara buses pass along the main road and there are also some additional services leaving in the morning from Selime village itself.

The 3268m volcanic cone of Hasandağı dominates the skyline to the south of **Hasandağı** Aksaray. It was eruptions from Hasandağı and Mount Erciyes near Kayseri which covered Cappadocia in the ash and lava flows that have produced the strange eroded landscape. Long since extinct the mountain presents a less serious proposition for trekkers than its higher cousin nearby, with the ascent of Hasandağı possible in two days. It makes an excellent continuation to the walk up the Ihlara canyon and there's also the added interest of some Byzantine ruins on the lower slopes to recommend it. For guides and/or transport to the two trailhead villages of Yenipınar or Helvadere, 15 km from Ihlara, enquire at the Akar Pansiyon in Ihlara village.

A large farming village nestled high on the flanks of Güllü Dağı, Güzelyurt had **Güzelyurt** a predominantly Greek population up until independence and was known as Kaballa. In the 1923 population exchanges Kaballa's Greek community was exchanged for Turkish families who emigrated from the town of Kavala in northern Greece. Today, the village is a quiet place where the male population seem to spend most of their time in the café on the main square. A short walk down a steep signposted lane from this square brings you into the so-called '*Manastır Vadisi*' (Monastery valley) where you can explore an area littered with rock-cut churches and monastic settlements. The village's very own 'underground city', although much less extensive than others in the region, is refreshingly undeveloped, with a switch at the entrance to turn on the lights illuminating the passageways and chambers. A short distance past the underground city is a six-level complex (*US$1.25 when warden is present*) carved into the cliff with several large dusty halls, living quarters, storage rooms, wineries and a canteen connected by narrow tunnels, ladders and stairs that you can scrabble through. The warden will show you around and provide you with a torch if you don't have one in return for a small tip.

Nearby the **Church of St Gregorius**, named after the founder of Güzelyurt, now functions as a mosque. Knock on the gate to gain entry into the courtyard where a long flight of stairs descends to a small subterranean chamber filled with water, reputed locally to have healing powers.

The valley beyond contains a number of rock-cut churches and cave dwellings. The most noteworthy church, the Kızıl Kilise, stands photogenically on a hill above a small reservoir to the southwest of the village and can be reached along a path starting on the Aksaray road.

Sleeping and eating E *Otel Karballa*, T4512103, F4512107, a 19th-century monastery restored by Yıldız Teknik Üniversitesi in Istanbul overlooking the main square, now a pension with simple rooms with ensuite bathroom, retains a dormitory-like feel, half-board option US$23 per person, bicycle rental and horse riding. Rooms are also available in several houses in the village. Try the house above the ceramics shop on the main street, although the US$18 they wanted for a plain double room is over the top. Mr. Veysel Dik also offers rooms in his family house on the opposite side of the mosque for US$12 including breakfast. *Güzelyurt Pide and Kebap*, on the main street, is simple eatery serving thick wholesome *mercimek* lentil soup as well as pide and kebabs.

Transport There are 6 dolmuş daily from Aksaray *otogar*, last 1745, 45 mins, US$1.

Cappadocia

When a trio of volcanoes erupted over 30 million years ago the area of Cappadocia was blanketed in a thick layer of ash. Partly overlaid by basalt lava flows, this ash was compressed into a soft, porous rock called tufa, which subsequent erosion by the wind and rain has sculpted into a weird and wonderful landscape of fantastically-shaped turrets, crags and pinnacles. To add to the geographical improbability of this scene, several thousand years of human occupation have left the countryside riddled with caverns, temples and troglodyte dwellings all hacked from the cream-coloured rock. Christianity then arrived and Cappadocia developed into an important monastic centre, the legacy of which are hundreds of rock-cut churches, many decorated with frescoes that form an unrivalled record of early Christian art.

Despite its barren appearance this rock produces fertile soils that support a variety of crops, including the grapes which form the raw material for a thriving local wine-making industry. However, it's not the traditional activities of agriculture, carpet-weaving or pot making which dominate the modern Cappadocian economy. Today tourism is king with the area attracting hundreds of thousands of visitors each year to its handful of principle sites. Places such as the Göreme Open Air museum, Zelve and the underground cities of Derinkuyu and Kaymaklı are on the itineraries of most large tour operators, along with the obligatory stop at a carpet factory. Though, for the independent traveller who wants to avoid the crowds the possibilities are enormous. Simply venture out of the core Nevşehir-Avanos-Ürgüp triangle or take to the footpaths which criss-cross the area to experience another, less crowded side to this extraordinary place.

History Evidence of human occupation as far back as the Neolithic Age has been uncovered by archaeologists at several sites. Later the area was settled by the Hatti, before becoming an integral part of the great Hittite Empire which had its capital at Hattuşa. With the decline of Hittite power, the region fell under the influence of various powers before being incorporated into the Persian empire by the tyrant Cyrus the Great.

Alexander the Great stormed through Cappadocia in 333 BC, liberating the region from its Persian masters and clearing the way for the establishment of an independent kingdom with its capital at Mazaca, present-day Kayseri. This kingdom lasted for over 300 years, until it was finally annexed by the Roman emperor Tiberius. Under the Romans, Cappadocia became a relative backwater far from centres of commerce and trade. This neglect helped to create the right conditions for the rapid development of early Christianity. In the remoteness of the Cappadocian hills, anchorite monks found the solitude they desired in caves and chambers hacked from the tufa. Loose religious communities grew-up and these became more organized, particularly after St Basil set-out his code for monastic life in the fourth century. During the Arab incursions of the sixth and seventh centuries, the Cappadocians did what they'd already been doing for thousands of years, headed underground into subterranean cities to wait until the storm had passed.

Despite the numerous Muslim invaders who crashed through the region on their way west, Cappadocia's Christian population remained largely intact until the beginning of the 19th century when it was finally extinguished by the population exchanges after the Treaty of Lausanne.

Nevşehir

Situated at the western edge of Cappadocia proper, it's around Nevşehir that one begins to catch glimpses of the highly eroded tufa landscape that you've travelled so far to see. Despite this, the town itself is a dreary provincial affair of concrete apartments which is geared up for its administrative role rather than tourism. An important transport hub for local bus companies, your visit will probably be limited to a brief glimpse of the modern *otogar*, though there's also a museum and celebrated mosque.

Getting there The *otogar* is 1 km from the centre on Gülşehir Caddesi. Dolmuş regularly pass up the hill to the centre. If you are exploring Cappadocia by public transport sooner or later you'll pass through Nevşehir, probably on your way south to the underground cities at Kaymaklı or Derinkuyu. Local bus and dolmuş services to towns across the region depart from the *otogar*, while buses coming from further afield call-in, although they usually continue-on to Göreme, Avanos or Ürgüp rather than dumping you here. There are twice weekly return flights to Istanbul. **Getting around** Once in the centre you can walk between the sights listed below.

Ins & outs
See page 499 for further details

Cappadocia region

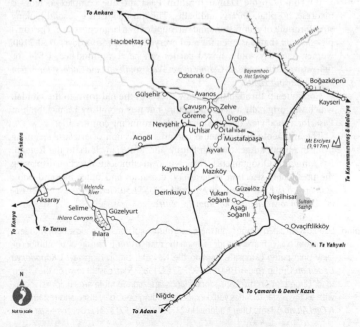

To Cap it all

With such a wealth of interesting spots you could easily spend a month exploring Cappadocia. Unfortunately, most visitors have considerably less time to appreciate the region so if you don't fancy taking an organised tour here are some suggested itineraries.

Day 1: Visit the Göreme Open Air Museum first thing before the crowds. Spend the afternoon wandering in the beautiful valleys near Çavuşin, climbing up to the Kızılçukur lookout for sunset.

Day 2: Walk up the Güvercinlik Vadisi (see page 499) to Uçhisar. Scale the castle to admire the panorama and descend for a

buffet feast at the Kaya Oteli, or a gözleme in the village. Explore one of the underground cities in the afternoon.

Day 3: Balloon flight (see page 499) at dawn; then on to the potteries of Avanos and lunch beside the lazy Kızılırmak River. Have a Turkish bath or soak in the hot-springs at Bayramhacı; or alternatively visit Zelve.

Day 4: Window shopping in Ürgüp; then stroll around Mustafapaşa, stopping-in for a tasting at the local winery. Drive south to Soğanlı or explore the countryside around Mustafapaşa on foot.

Sights Nevşehir is a pretty ugly town dominated by concrete apartments. Although not aesthetically pleasing to western tastes, these blocks with their electricity, modern kitchens and proper plumbing are what most cave-dwelling Cappadocians dream of. Few would think twice about exchanging their traditional troglodyte existence for such a 'dreary' urban life, as indeed most who can afford it are doing.

Apart from the citadel and Damat Ibrahim Paşa mosque complex there is also the interesting archaeological museum to look around and the picturesque village of Nar just to the north is also worth a visit.

Built in 1726 the **Damat Ibrahim Paşa** mosque complex includes a medrese, hospital, library, and baths. The mosque itself is a solid looking structure built of yellow stone and surrounded by a large courtyard. The complex *hamam* (bath) is open for men everyday except Saturdays, 0730-2100, women Saturdays only, mixed parties can be accommodated, US$4 for full-wash and massage. ■ *Getting there: Walk south up Lale Caddesi for 300 m and it's on your right.*

Continue up through the narrow streets of the old town to the **citadel**, which was originally a Selçuk structure but was rebuilt by Damat Ibrahim Paşa, for a good view over the town and surrounding countryside.

The **archaeological museum** contains a selection of artefacts spanning from the Bronze Age, through Hittite and Phrygian times to the Roman, Byzantine and Ottoman eras. There is also an ethnological section displaying the predictable selection of jewellery, costumes and other bits-and-bobs. ■ *0800-1200, 1300-1700 daily except Mon. US$1.50. Getting there: On the eastern edge of town, about 1 km from the centre.*

Sleeping Should want a bed for the night there are a number of hotels to choose from with several luxury places found outside town on the road to Ürgüp. The are also a number of fairly uninspiring campsites fronting the Nevşehir-Ürgüp highway. **L** *Kapadokya Dedeman*, Ürgüp Yolu, T0384/2139900, F2132158, 2.5 km east of town on the Ürgüp road. Large blot on the Cappadocian landscape, comfortable a/c equipped rooms with all the 5-star facilities you'd expect including pool, bar, disco and restaurants. **A** *Otel Altınöz*, Ragip Üner Caddesi No 23, T2135305, F2132817. Decent 4-star hotel with comfortable rooms, amenities include pool, sauna, restaurant and bar. **E** *Hotel Şekeryapan*, Gülşehir Caddesi No 8, T2128184, F2134051, between the bus station and the centre. The large rooms with en-suite bathroom are a bit worn, downstairs there's a disco and restaurant serving limited menu, also a hamam. **E** *Hotel Şems*, Atatürk Bulvarı No 29, T2133597. Centrally located, reasonable rooms with bathroom, telephone, TV. **G** *Ipek Palas*, Atatürk Bulvarı No 99, T2131478, at west end of the main street. Basic budget option, front rooms are a bit noisy, single US$6.

Midrange *Park Restaurant*, situated behind the tea gardens off Atatürk Caddesi near the PTT, favourite with local businessmen, meze and grilled meat, alcohol served, about US$10 per head. **Cheap** *Açlan Pide*, just off Atatürk Bulvarı at the Arçelik shop and this clean, bright pide place is around the corner on the right, best lahmacun this side of Gaziantep and *ayran* served in silver bowls, also excellent kebabs and pide. There are also several restaurants with ready-prepared dishes and kebabs, such as the *Şölen*, on Atatürk Caddesi.

Eating

Anahita Tourism, Esentepe Mahallesi, Ürgüp Caddesi, T2142202, F2142203, range of daily Cappadocian tours, rent-a-car.

Tour agencies

Bus Nevşehir is an important local transport centre with dolmuş and bus services departing for **Avanos, Derinkuyu, Gülşehir, Hacıbektaş, Niğde**, and **Ürgüp** every 30 mins during the day. **Göreme** co-operative minibuses depart from the centre of town by the tourist office and most others will also pass by there on their way from the bus station. The Göreme minibuses operate every 30 mins, 0700-1900. Although Avanos Belediye buses pass through Göreme, the drivers are reluctant to take away business from the co-op drivers, so if you can't see a minibus just get on the first bus that passes. Nevşehir *otogar* is also the departure point for longer journeys including: **Aksaray**, 7 departures daily, 0845-1745, 1½ hrs, US$2. **Ankara**, several morning and afternoon buses, 4½ hrs, US$7. **Antalya**, several evening buses, 10 hrs, US$11. **Istanbul**, several evening buses, 11 hrs, US$12. **İzmir**, 1 evening bus, 12 hrs, US$15. **Kayseri**, regularly throughout day, 2 hrs, US$2.25. **Konya**, several buses daily. **Trabzon**, 1 evening bus, 12 hrs, US$17. **Yozgat**, 1 afternoon bus, 3 hrs, US$7.

Transport

Banks On Atatürk Caddesi there are several banks with ATMs and exchange facilities. **Post office** On Atatürk Caddesi west of Lale Caddesi. **Tourist information** On Atatürk Caddesi, just east of Lale Caddesi. Very helpful staff who speak English, French and German. Open everyday during the summer, winter closed on Sun, 0830-1200, 1300-1730.

Directory

Uçhisar

Clustered around a huge tower of rock, riddled with cave dwellings and capped by a medieval fortress is the village of Uçhisar. Spared the intensive development of nearby Göreme, an atmosphere of tumble-down decay pervades much of the lower village, where you can still catch glimpses of traditional Cappadocian life. Boasting several good cave pensions – at the other end of the spectrum there's also a *Club Méditerranée* – the village is favoured by French travellers seeking a more peaceful base from which to explore the area.

Phone code: 0384
8 km E of Nevşehir
Even if you don't stay here make a visit to climb the Kale

The vista across the Cappadocian countryside from the top of the Kale is superb, particularly at sunset, when the eroded landscape takes on a myriad of pastel hues and the snow-covered cone of Mount Erciyes looms ethereally to the east. Aesthetics apart, it is also a very good point from which to get your bearings. ■ *0800-2000 daily. US$1.*

Central Anatolia

Walks from Uçhisar Uçhisar is the starting point for several walks, the first descending the picturesque **Güvercinlik Vadisi** (Pigeon Valley), which gets its name from the pigeon roosts carved into its rockwalls and towers, to Göreme. The path begins by the *Tandır Evi Restaurant* on the road to Ürgüp and after dropping into the valley you progress through beautiful scenery enclosed within walls of white tufa. There is a short steep section where care must be taken, however, this can be circumvented by a path which climbs up to the left a short distance before, leading over into a subsidiary canyon which descends back into the main valley. The walk takes less than two hours, although you will probably want longer to soak-up the scenery and do some exploring, before eventually emerging in Göreme below the *Ataman Hotel*.

A second walk follows **Ak Vadi**, also known locally as Aşk Vadisi (Love Valley), which begins to the northeast of the village on the Göreme road. A track leads down the side of an onyx factory, before forking right after 250 m. The path then drops into the valley, narrow and rocky at first, but then opening out, passing plenty of phallic looking pinnacles and strange tufa formations along the way. Walking for about 90 minutes brings you out onto a tarmac side-road leading right over a small rise to the main Göreme-Avanos road. Dolmuş pass in both directions, right to Göreme or left to Çavuşin and Avanos.

Sleeping **D** *Kaya Oteli*, east of the square on the rim of Pigeon valley, T2192007, F2192363. *Club Med* hotel with a superb position, terrace and swimming pool overlooking Cappadocian landscape, full and half-board options, comfortable rooms, good restaurant open to non-residents. Recommended. **C-F** *Les Jardin des 1001 nuit*, on the north side of the Kale above the Göreme road, T2192505. A range of rooms carved from several fairy chimneys, varying in price from US$15-US$50 per night, more expensive rooms have views and en suite bathrooms, lovely subterranean dining room where evening meals are served. Recommended. **E** *Kaya Pension*, on the north side of the Kale, above Göreme Rd, T2192441, F2192655. Pleasant hotel with non-cave rooms, US$30 rooms have view and large balcony, terrace with excellent view, restaurant. Recommended. **F** *Villa Pension*, next to the PTT on the road toward Ürgüp, T2192089, F2192680. Modern building with 2/3 bed rooms, shaded terrace and restaurant. **F** *Erciyes Pansiyon*, also to the east of the square on the road to Ürgüp, T21920990. Simple, conventional rooms in a family-run pension with lovely garden, good views from the front rooms. Recommended. *Les Maison de Cappadoce*, T2192813, F2192782, www.cappadoce.com A series of carefully renovated and tastefully decorated stone villas which sleep 2-8 people, prices vary from US$90-US$300 per night with advance booking necessary, the office is in the main square.

Eating *Uçhisar 96* and *Asena Restaurant* on the village square serve a similar choice of food, including *kiremit kebabı* (lamb baked on an earthenware tile) and *pirzola* (lamb chops). The village's best food is to be found at the Kaya Oteli's *Bindallı Restaurant* which does an extensive lunch-time buffet for US$10 and has an a la carte menu in the evenings.

Transport Nevşehir-Göreme dolmuş pass the junction to the west of town every 30 mins or alternatively Uçhisar Belediyesi also runs hourly buses to Nevşehir's *otogar*.

Directory **Banks** The nearest banks are in Nevşehir or Göreme. **Post office** The PTT is east of the square on the road towards Ürgüp.

Göreme

At the heart of Cappadocia the formerly sleepy village of Göreme sits in a basin surrounded by startling white tufa cliffs and dotted with fairy chimneys. This marvellous situation and its proximity to sites such as the Open Air Museum, Zelve and Çavuşin have made it the focus for much of the areas tourism, particularly at the budget end of the market. The village now boasts a bus station, restaurants, travel agents, carpet shops and scores of pensions and guesthouses many of which offer their guests the opportunity of sleeping in cave rooms carved from the soft rock. Indeed today, the local economy is almost entirely devoted to the tourist industry and the character of what 20 years ago was a simple farming community has been fundamentally changed. Despite this explosive growth Göreme retains a relaxed and pleasant feel with something approaching traditional life persisting in a few of the back lanes. Some subterranean dwellings remain unrenovated and inhabited by local families, though the number dwindles each year as the temptation to sell-up and move to more modern buildings becomes too great.

Phone code: 0384
Colour map 5, grid A3
3 km E of Uçhisar

Getting there The bus companies *Göreme* and *Nevtur* run long-distance services to Göreme from many cities across the country, however, generally these terminate in Nevşehir from where a minibus takes passengers the last part of the journey. Be warned that if you travel with other companies, particularly if the bus is continuing elsewhere, you may be left stranded at Nevşehir *otogar* at a very inconvenient hour, even if you've been sold a ticket to Göreme. A co-operative runs minibus services between Göreme and Nevşehir every 30 mins, and there are also minibuses between Ürgüp and Avanos which pass the roundabout at the beginning of the Open Air Museum road every 2 hrs. **Getting around** The place is easily navigable on foot.

Ins & outs
See page 502 for further details

There's been a farming community on the site of the present-day village at least since Byzantine times when the community was known as Matiana. The inhabitants formerly made a living farming the surrounding land, using the nutrient rich pigeon droppings collected from coops carved into the surrounding cliffs to fertilize their fields, orchards and vineyards. This pattern of life continued remarkably unchanged up until the 1980s when tourism in Turkey went ballistic and the village once more shed its name, choosing Göreme, '*unseen*', in reference to the valley of hidden churches nearby. Now known as the Göreme Open Air Museum this is the principal attraction in the area and is within easy walking distance of the village. Göreme is also a good base for exploring other parts of the surrounding countryside on foot, although it is not really advisable for women to wander these quiet footpaths alone.

The area

The village's rapid growth has inevitably threatened the very reason that people visit Göreme and despite the work of a local pressure group, problems such as illegal building have continued. The problem is not a lack of protective regulation just that the rules are not strictly enforced or are ignored in the search for short term profits.

There is relatively little to see in the village itself, although during a wander around the backstreets you can still experience a slice of traditional life. Women sit out in the alleyways gossiping and in the summer pumpkins are laid on sheets to dry in the sun, eventually yielding the prized white seeds which Turks love to nibble. Walk-up through the old village to the **Konak Türk Evi**, an Ottoman residence lovingly restored by Dutch architect Nico Leissen which now houses a restaurant. The terrace is a good place to have a drink, overlooking the village, while also giving you the chance to inspect the

Sights

Central Anatolia

frescoes in the atmospheric *selamlık* and *haremlik*, originally painted by a noteworthy local artist who also decorated scenes in the Ahmet III dining room of the Topkapı Palace. Back down in the centre you can't miss the **Roman tomb** carved into a large pinnacle of tufa, its lower portion eroded over the years.

Göreme Open Air Museum (Göreme Açık Hava Museum)

One of the most visited sights in Cappadocia included on virtually all tour programmes

Situated in a small rocky valley, a monastic community existed here between the ninth and 11th centuries, excavating cave churches to worship in, some of which are beautifully decorated, as well as refectories, kitchens and living quarters. Due to its popularity and the nature of the churches, most of which have a single small entrance that is also the only source of light, it is best to arrive early to avoid the inevitable congestion. Tour guides are meant to limit the time spent in each church, however, with a large coach party it can still be a long wait. Much better to continue to the next church and return later. A torch is useful to appreciate some of the frescoes that are poorly lit. There is a café selling drinks, several souvenir shops and a post office on site.

Near the entrance are the ruins of a **convent** with living quarters on the first two floors and a chapel above. Large circular doors, like those found in the underground cities, on the floors above could secure the convent in times of danger.

Çarıklı Kilise (the Church of the Sandals), reached by steel steps, is an 11th-century church which gets its name from the footprints below the Ascension scene. Restoration of its frescoes took over 10 years, giving an idea of the painstaking nature of the work.

There are several small unnamed churches between the Çarıklı Kilise and the superb **Karanlık Kilise** (the Dark Church) for which an additional entrance fee (*US$8*) is collected. The vivid frescoes, restored to something of their original

Göreme

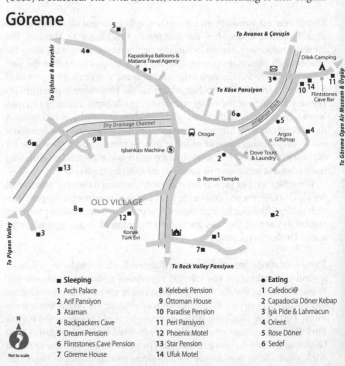

■ **Sleeping**		● **Eating**
1 Arch Palace	8 Kelebek Pension	1 Cafedoci@
2 Arif Pansiyon	9 Ottoman House	2 Capadocia Döner Kebap
3 Ataman	10 Paradise Pension	3 Işık Pide & Lahmacun
4 Backpackers Cave	11 Peri Pansiyon	4 Orient
5 Dream Pension	12 Phoenix Motel	5 Rose Döner
6 Flintstones Cave Pension	13 Star Pension	6 Sedef
7 Göreme House	14 Ufuk Motel	

Central Anatolia

splendour, depict scenes from the life of Christ in a very lifelike way. The zigzag patterning is thought to have been a temporary measure, filling the blank space on the pillars until a suitable artist could be found to complete the frescoes. The overall effect is mesmerizing as your eyes skip from the Nativity to the betrayal of Christ by Judas, from the Last Supper to the Crucifixion.

Below the Karanlık Kilise and built at about the same time is a **refectory complex** with a larder, kitchen and dining room, complete with benches and tables hewn from the living rock.

Next up is the **Yılanlı Kilise** (Church with the Snake), so called because of the fresco of Saints George and Theodore battling with the dragon. Beside this painting is a depiction of Constantine the Great and his mother Saint Helena, holding the True Cross, which she is said to have recovered from Jerusalem at the age of eighty after it appeared to her in a vision. She in fact unearthed three crosses, identifying the correct one by placing each on the grave of a dead young man. Legend has it that when touched by the True Cross he was miraculously brought back to life. Opposite them is a portrait of St Onophrius, a hermit who subsisted on nothing but dates in the Egyptian desert.

The cruder depictions of the **Barbara Kilise** (Church of St Barbara), predominantly painted in ochre-coloured paint, suggest that it was built at the end of the iconoclastic period, however, it too has been dated to the 11th century. St Barbara, the patron saint of architects, artillery men, stonemasons and grave diggers who was killed by her father for her Christian faith, is among the figures painted on the walls. There is also a picture of Christ making a three-figured hand gesture symbolizing the Holy Trinity. Recent research has identified the strange insect-like symbol nearby as a Byzantine military insignia. The **Elmalı Kilise** (Apple Church) on the other side of the outcrop has recently reopened after a long period of restoration which involved cleaning centuries of grime and soot off its superb frescoes.

On the way down the hill to the car park is the **Tokalı Kilise** (Church with the Buckle), one of the most interesting churches in Göreme. Named after a buckle-shaped decoration in one of its archways, parts of the Tokalı Kilise date from early in the 10th century, while the majority of it was constructed later. The church is unusual because it is of the transverse nave, Mesopotamian type. It is richly decorated with frescoes typical of the Archaic period, the dominant background colour being a deep blue pigment made from lapis lazuli.

Balloon flights
An unforgettable way to view the Cappadocian landscape is from the basket of a hot-air balloon. *Kapadokya Balloons Göreme*, T2712442, F2712586, fly@kapadokyaballoons.com, have daily flights at dawn throughout the season, with the US$230 price tag including transfer to and from your hotel and a champagne breakfast upon your return to *terra firma*. Their office is set back from the main road, heading out towards Uçhisar from the bus station.

Walks from Göreme
Several walks begin from points along the Open Air Museum road. Exploration of the **Zemi Vadisi** stretching southwards towards the Ürgüp-Nevşehir road can start either on the track next to the *Turistik Hotel*, or 100 m beyond via the **Saklı Kilise** and the **El-Nazar Kilise**, with the path beginning beside a small café.

A popular walk up Güvercinlik Vadisi starts near the Ataman Hotel & is detailed in reverse in the preceding Uçhisar section, see page 496

A signposted path to the **Kılınçlar Vadisi** (Valley of the Swords), named after some particularly sharp tufa pinnacles, starts 50 m past the Saklı Kilise on the left, before climbing over a low ridge. There are the remains of extensive subterranean settlements to explore on the ridge, while turning right the valley quickly narrows into a canyon. Further progress is up steep rock steps with handholds and footholds carved into the perpendicular rock, allowing access to pigeon houses carved into the canyon walls. Care must be taken following this route which is only for those who are comfortable scrambling up steep sections of rock. A torch would also be useful for passing through several sections of dark irrigation tunnel. The canyon eventually widens and a path climbing up the right-hand side leads to the Ürgüp road above the Open Air museum.

Following the path down Kılınçlar Vadisi brings you out onto a straight and rather boring track leading north-east to **Çavuşin**. Better to strike-off right before reaching this on one of several possibilities and then weave your way through the orchards and fields until you reach a group of substantial tufa cones and a particularly large outcrop of rock into which a multi-level monastic settlement is carved. If you have followed the straight track, turning right up a path opposite a football pitch will bring you to the same spot. Beyond this a path leads through vineyards and up a deeply eroded gully. A sharp left turn in the gully brings you over the ridge and down to the **Meskendir Vadisi** (see Çavuşin, page 503).

Sleeping The relaxed atmosphere in the village belies fierce competition between Göreme's 80 or so guesthouses and hotels, something you'll be immediately aware of if you arrive at the tout-guarded bus station. This may sound like good news but in fact it hurts many of the better establishments which are forced to drop their prices and standards in order to compete with the cheaper *pansiyons*. To try and break this vicious cycle, hotel and pension owners have attempted to set standard rates. A room at the bus station has also been set-up as an information centre displaying posters from all the pensions, setting out their prices and facilities. Unfortunately, this co-operation seems presently to have disintegrated.

AL *Ataman Hotel*, T2712310, F2712313, info@atamanhotel.com, follow the drainage channel up from the bus station. Superb position overlooking Pigeon Valley, a veritable maze of corridors and rooms cut into rock, carefully decorated and furnished rooms with a homely feel, well-equipped also with kettle and hairdryer among the standard luxuries, cavernous subterranean bar and terrace restaurant. A little on the pricey side but still recommended. **A** *Turist Hotel*, Müze Yolu, T2712430, F2712011, on the Open Air Museum road 300 m from the village. Uninspiring concrete exterior, rooms inside are not much better, popular with tour groups, large swimming pool, restaurant. **E** *Göreme House*, T2712668, F2712669, up the lane next to the village mosque. New hotel built in traditional style with comfortably furnished rooms off courtyard or balconies, suite available for US$100, scenic roof terrace. Recommended. **E** *Arch Palace Hotel*, T2712575, up-hill next to the mosque and near Göreme House. New, well-furnished rooms with arched stone ceilings and en suite. **E** *Ottoman House*, Orta Mahalle No 36, T2712616, F2712351, ottoman@indigo turizm.com.tr Comfortable, well-managed hotel, conventional non-cave rooms with en suite and telephone, breakfast extra US$5, suite US$75, roof terrace restaurant and pleasant basement bar. Recommended.

F *Dream Pension*, T2712082, as you come down hill from Uçhisar up a track on the left. Popular choice with a selection of cave rooms, some showerless for US$12, dorm US$4, foreign management and friendly atmosphere, barbecues and meals available. Recommended. **F** *Kelebek Pension*, T2712531, F2712763, at the top of village past the Phoenix Motel. Popular pension in an excellent position overlooking the village, 2/3/4 bed cave rooms varying in size and price, dorm beds US$4, honeymoon suite US$25, varied breakfasts are a relief if you're bored with the standard hotel fare, barbecues organized also bar, laundry service, Recommended. **F** *Ufuk Motel*, T2712157, just off the Museum road. Clean modern place, cave rooms with amusing carvings decorating the walls, also normal rooms, dorm beds US$5, restaurant and tours organized. **F** *Peri Pansiyon*, Müze Yolu, T2712136, on museum road at the edge of town. Built around several large fairy chimneys, various cave rooms US$14-US$20, also more conventional rooms with en suite off a pleasant garden courtyard, laundry service, free email, restaurant with a set-menu US$5. Recommended. **F** *Flintstones Cave*, T2712555, walk up drainage channel from bus station. Basic cave rooms for US$8 per person without toilet, camping US$4, quiet position but a bit shadeless, swimming pool in the summer. **F** *Phoenix Motel*, T2712602, in the middle of village. 2/3/4 person rooms off an open sitting area and bar.

F *Backpackers Cave*, T2712705, F2712736, from bus-station cross the footbridge bridge, turn left, second road on right. Part of Interyouth Hostel Group, well-managed and clean place with fairly small cave rooms with en suite, dorm US$5, garden area and bar, good value. Recommended. **F** *Köse Pansion*, north of the main road, T2712294, F2712577, follow signposts from opposite the bus station. Favourite with backpackers, simple but clean rooms in conventional building, 1/2/3 beds, rooftop dorm, large swimming pool, selection of breakfasts (extra) and other meals. Recommended. **F** *Arif Pansion*, T2712361, climb up road beside mosque to top. Small cave rooms some with en suite, superb views over the village from the terrace, breakfast extra. Recommended. **F** *Rock Valley Pansion*, T2712153, walk up the mainstreet to the end. Quiet position, basic but clean rooms in one of the village's cheaper places, also rooms without toilet, dorm beds US$4, friendly staff and meals cooked on request, plans for a swimming pool. Recommended budget option. **F** *Paradise Pension*, T2712248, at the Ürgüp-end of the village. Simple but pleasant rooms off small courtyard, subterranean and conventional rooms, also dorm beds, breakfast extra, laundry service. **G** *Star Pension*, follow drainage channel, 500 m from bus station. Quiet with basic cave rooms cut into the cliff-side, dorm beds US$4, friendly staff, breakfast extra, meals and barbecues prepared. Recommended.

Göreme Panorama Camping, T2712352. An excellent position on the Uçhisar Rd as you begin descent to the village, unfortunately the great views aren't complemented by the dusty pitches or the basic shower and kitchen facilities. US$1.25 per tent, caravan and electrical hook-up, plus US$2 per person. *Dilek Camping*, beginning of Museum Rd. Simple campsite with nice pitches amongst the trees, US$2.50 per person, clean bathrooms, swimming pool and restaurant. Recommended. *Kaya Camping*, T3433100, F3433984, on the road to Ortahisar beyond the Open Air Museum. Scenic spot 2 km from the village, well-managed site with clean kitchen facilities, bathrooms and a swimming pool, US$3.50 per person, plus US$2 per tent, US$2.50 per caravan.

Camping
Take care not to leave anything of value in your tent as there have been problems with theft from campsites in the area

Midrange *Ataman Hotel Restaurant*, T2712310. Turkish and European cuisine, pleasant surroundings on terrace or in intimate dining room, some brave attempts at more unusual dishes like soufflé are not altogether successful, about US$10 per head. *Konak Türk Evi Restaurant*, T2712463, in the old village, left at *Phoenix Hotel*, selection of traditional Turkish dishes eaten on terrace or in wonderfully restored dining rooms of old house. *Ottoman House Restaurant*, a la carte or 3-course set-menu for US$8 eaten on the roof terrace, often with musical entertainment. *Sedef Restaurant*, opposite bus station on the main road, a busy place with the widest choice of Turkish and European dishes in the village. *Orient Restaurant*, on the left-hand side as you walk out of the village towards Uçhisar, meze, grilled meat and specialities including *kiremit tava*, (lamb baked on an earthenware tile) are served at tables on a terrace or inside dining room, about US$6-US$8 per head with wine.

Eating

Cheap The options for really cheap food around Göreme are limited, however, most pensions can prepare evening meals for their guests and this represents the best value, and often the nicest, food in town. Many pensions also organize barbecues which are normally also open to non-residents. Those at the *Kelebek* and *Dream Pensions* have been recommended. *Rose Döner*, just down from the bus station, small place serving kebabs, pizza and döner kebabs. *Işık Pide and Lahmacun*, opposite the road to the Open Air Museum, more of a traditional place offering good value lahmacun and pide. *Capadocia Döner Kebap*, behind the *otogar* near the temple, as the name suggests cheap chicken döner kebabs and soft drinks.

Bars *Cafedoci@*, next to *Kapadokya Balloons*, beginning of the Uçhisar Rd, definitely the slickest bar in town with a properly stocked bar including foreign spirits, good food, mammoth burgers, sandwiches, DVD videos and films plus the internet for entertainment. *Flintstones Cave*, Open-air Museum Rd, convivial cave environment with live music sometimes.

Shopping Observing the rule that where there are tourists, there are carpet salesmen, Göreme has a predictably large number of shops selling carpets and kilims. If you do want to buy one use this to your advantage. Shop around extensively and get a feel for prices before taking the plunge. For other present ideas call in at *Alaturka*, next to *Sedef restaurant* which has a range of shoes and bags made from old kilims. *Argos*, to the east of the bus station, sells pottery and leatherwear, also amusing caricature posters by Orhan Coplu.

Tour agencies The proliferation of accommodation in Göreme has been accompanied by a huge growth in the number of travel agencies offering daily tours of the area as well as longer programs outside of Cappadocia. Tours are a good way of seeing the main sights particularly if you are limited for time, however, they can be a bit rushed with much of the day being spent getting on and off your tour bus. Also remember that you pay for what you get, and lowering the price by a few dollars means operators are forced to cut corners. This generally results in large groups, inexperienced guides and long stops at carpet shops along the way, where your guide will earn handsome commissions on anything you buy. Better then to go with a reputable agency whose prices may be a little higher. Agencies to consider include: *Dove tours*, in the centre of town has a range of daily tours for up to US$30 including lunch. *Matiana Travel*, T2712902, F2712903, next to Cafedoci@ on the main road, interesting selection of day and longer tours, also including walking trips. *Şovalye Tourism*, T/F2712622, across from the bus station, reputable organizers of local tours.

Transport **Bike hire** There are numerous outfits in the village renting bicycles, mopeds and motorbikes. Expect to pay about US$9/20/25 per day respectively. Make sure you check the bike, including brakes and bodywork, properly before signing anything. You'll need to leave your passport as a deposit. **Bus Local**: Dolmuş run to **Uçhisar** and **Nevşehir** every 30 mins, 0700-1900, 1800 in winter. **Ürgüp** dolmuş pass every 2 hrs, 0815-1715, 1615 in winter, wait at the beginning of the Open Air Museum road. **Avanos**, pass on the main road every 30 mins, 0815-1915, 1815 in winter. **Long distance**: *Nevtur* and *Göreme* have services to destinations across the country. Most of these actually depart from Nevşehir, where all the passengers from Göreme, Avanos and Ürgüp are ferried by minibus. **Ankara**, 2 buses in the morning and afternoon, 4 hrs, US$7. **Antalya**, 2 evening buses, 10 hrs, US$10. **Eğirdir**, 2 evening buses, 7 hrs, US$9. **Istanbul**, several evening buses, 11 hrs, US$12.50. **Kayseri**, every 2 hrs, 0715-1715, 1½ hrs, US$2.50. **Konya**, 3 buses daily, 3 hrs, US$6. **Trabzon**, 1715, 12 hrs, US$17.50.

Directory **Banks** There is an İş Bankası ATM machine in the centre of the village. The post office also changes TCs, as do some of the travel agents. **Communications Post office** In a side street roughly opposite the Open air museum Rd. Open 0830-1730. **Internet** *Göreme Internet Cafe* just down from the Sedef Restaurant, US$4 for 1 hr, US$1.50 for 15 mins. *Cafedoci@*, on the main road, US$4 per hr. **Laundry** *Wet and Dry laundry*, around the corner from the Roman temple.

Tourist information Despite all the signs there is no official tourist information office in Göreme. **Useful addresses** *Rainbow Ranch*, T2712413, see the valleys from horseback, novice to experienced, US$12 for 2 hrs. A company has also just started offering *camel tours* of Love, Rose and Zemi valleys, contact T2712491.

The village of Çavuşin is clustered beneath a strangely shaped outcrop of yellow tufa, just off the Avanos road 5 km south of Göreme. Farming is still the most important activity here, as you'll be able to tell by the number of tractors and bits of agricultural machinery parked in the square. The cave houses that riddle the outcrop above the village were abandoned comparatively recently because of the danger of rock-fall and they now make for some interesting exploration, if you're careful. Also nearby is the **Church of St John the Baptist**, a large basilica which was constructed in the fifth century, making it one of the oldest in Cappadocia. The façade carved into the cliff-face is particularly impressive, with the interior predominantly decorated with pre-iconoclastic frescoes.

Çavuşin
A haven of tranquillity when compared with Göreme

Walking from Çavuşin Çavuşin makes a particularly good base from which to explore the valleys descending from the southwest flank of Aktepe. Valleys such as Güllü Dere and Kızılçukur Vadisi contain some exquisite rock formations, with the former getting its name, the Rose Valley, from the pink hue of the local tufa. There are also well-tended gardens and vineyards irrigated by a complex system of underground cisterns and channels.

If you're staying in Göreme these walks can be linked in with exploring the Kılınç Vadisi. You could even make a large loop up the Meskendir Vadisi and back down the road to visit the Göreme Open Air museum. The possibilities, as with the number of paths and tracks, are endless.

From the main square walk up past the village mosque and turn right at the end. Continue on this track past the graveyard and signposted on the left is a footpath up the lovely **Güllü Dere** (Rose valley), which contains the **Üçhaçlı Kilise** (Three-cross Church) and the **Ayvalı Kilise** (Quince Church). There is a drinks stand at the second of these churches set-up by an enterprising local man. After a pit-stop he'll be happy to point you in the direction you want to go from there. From the Ayvalı Kilise climbing the steep path on the opposite side of the valley brings you out onto a flat bluff. Following this up to the left, you can descend into the next valley along via the **Haçlı Kilise** (Cross church) or traverse around to the Kızılçukur lookout.

The **Meskendir Vadisi** is also reached by the same track past the graveyard, but this valley is considerably longer stretching several kilometres southeast towards the Göreme-Ürgüp road, with the well-trodden path emerging beside Kaya Camping. Alternatively, you could turn left up the **Kızılçukur Vadisi** which contains several churches, and climb up to the Kızılçukur look-out.

There is also a path leading around the northern flank of Aktepe from Çavuşin to **Zelve**, see below.

Sleeping There is a good pension which should satisfy most peoples needs. **F** *Green Motel*, T5327050, F5327032. Large and pleasant place set in its own garden, variety of rooms at different prices, camping US$2 per person, toilet and kitchen facilities available, meals prepared. Recommended. There are several restaurants on the village square. Down on the main road are several reasonably priced onyx shops.

A trip to explore the troglodyte village of Zelve, located on the northeast flank of Aktepe, 3 km off the Avanos-Çavuşin road is an interesting experience. Originally a monastic settlement, Zelve was inhabited until 1952 by Turkish villagers, when it was abandoned, like the cave-homes of nearby Çavuşin,

Zelve

because of the danger of rockfall. A warren of rock-cut houses and even a small mosque – formerly a church – await exploration with plenty of scrambling and climbing for the adventurous. A torch is very useful to negotiate a section of tunnel and to see into some of the dark chambers.

There are also several churches in the valley, although these are decorated simply with crosses carved into the ceilings and walls. An exception is the Üzümlü Kilise (The Grape Church), which has simple pre-iconoclastic images of grapevines, palm leaves and fish painted on its walls. Zelve is a popular stop for tour groups, so it is best to arrive early or later-on in the evening. Flanking the entrance are stalls selling souvenirs, such as the all-too-familiar miniature fairy chimneys, a café and post office. ■ *0800-1900 daily, closes 1700 in winter. US$2.50. Avanos-Ürgüp dolmuş will drop you off on request, alternatively it is a pleasant walk from Çavuşin.*

Valley of the Hermits Some 2 km before Zelve on the Avanos road, you'll pass a valley known as Paşabağı, easily recognized by the line of souvenir stalls. From the vineyards sprouts a veritable forest of fairy chimneys many of them hollowed out by solitary monks, lending the area its other name 'Valley of the Hermits'. Out of one particularly handsome three-pronged pinnacle, St Symeon Stylite, a Byzantine saint famed for sitting on a pillar for 37 years, hacked his three-storey hermitage.

Ortahisar A visit to Ortahisar, just south of the junction of the Göreme and Nevşehir-Ürgüp roads, will give you a glimpse of what an ordinary Cappadocian village relatively unaffected by tourism is like. Farming is still an important activity for its residents and in the evening the menfolk gather in the çay houses around the main square to gossip and play cards. The only sight as such in Ortahisar is the 86-m high turret of rock, which used to accommodate most of the village in chambers and caverns burrowed from it. If you're feeling energetic you can climb the stairs to the top (*0730-2030 daily. US$1.50*), a great vantage point from which to look-out over the surrounding countryside. A 45-minute walk from the square down a sign-posted track is the Pancarlık Vadisi which contains the rarely visited **Pancarlık Kilise**.

Another interesting sight nearby which you'll probably have all to yourself is the **Hallaç Hospital Monastery**. Signposted off the Nevşehir-Ürgüp road to the east of town, it can also be reached by a track which leads off the side-road down to Ortahisar from the main road, passing the village graveyard (*mezarlık*). This monastic settlement cut into the side of a rocky escarpment included an inn for travellers passing on the road nearby. It's a very peaceful spot today, the carved and painted façade of one rock-cut chapel overlooking a field of tomatoes. You can clamber through an opening into a larger, square rock-cut chapel, the sky showing through a gap in the roof, which gives access to a hall beyond. A curiosity is the spiderman-like figure hanging in the corner of the chapel above the entrance, which looks like it was carved recently.

Sleeping and eating If you should want to stay in Ortahisar there are several options. **D** *Hotel Yeni Yükseller*, on the edge of town. Comfortable rooms with en suite, swimming pool and restaurant. **F** *Hotel Özyel*, T3432219, off the road into town near the belediye building. Plain rooms with en suite. **G** *Hotel Gümüş*, T3433127, near the PTT. Rooms are a bit more simple but still have en suite shower, terrace with excellent views. A reason in itself for visiting Ortahisar is to have the tasty and very reasonably priced pide or lahmacun at *Hisar Pide Salonu*, on the main square.

Transport There are regular belediye buses from Nevşehir. Avanos-Ürgüp buses pass the turn-off to Ortahisar, about 1 km from the square.

A popular spot to look out over the Cappadocian landscape at sunset is **Kızılçukur** Kızılçukur on the southeast side of Aktepe. The look-out is reached by a 2 km side-road off the Nevşehir-Ürgüp road, opposite the turning for Ortahisar. Any bus passing along this road will let you off at the junction from where it is an easy walk. There is usually no problem in finding a lift back to where you're staying when everybody departs after sundown. Paths also descend from the view-point into the Kızılçukur Vadisi, which has several rock-cut churches, and the Güllü Dere (see page 503).

Ürgüp

A market town and close to all the Cappadocian sights, Ürgüp has also developed into an important tourist centre, though the majority of its beds are found in larger hotels fraternized by tour groups. Initially not as appealing as its upstart neighbour, Göreme, the town's down-to-earth atmosphere is nonetheless quite endearing. Ordinary life, rather than being displaced by tourism, continues alongside it, with farming still a major contributor to the local economy. The town also has a thriving wine-making industry, a legacy of the Ottoman Greeks who left in 1923. With its varied choice of hotels Ürgüp suggests itself as an alternative base for exploring the region, particularly if you have your own transport.

Phone code: 0384
Colour map 5, grid A3
Altitude: 1060 m
23 km E of Nevşehir

Ürgüp is connected to the surrounding towns and villages by regular bus and **Ins & outs** dolmuş services. The *otogar* is near the middle of town. Within town everything is accessible on foot.

Some fine examples of Ottoman domestic architecture – solid houses built of **Sights** the pale local stone – survive in the backstreets of the old quarter, though the centre itself around Cumhuriyet Meydanı has been thoroughly, and rather blandly, redeveloped.

There isn't really much to do in town though you could climb up to the **Temenni** (Hill of wishes) on the rocky hilltop to the northeast of the centre by way of a long flight of steps starting opposite the 13th-century **Kebir Camii**. As you ascend, the steps pass cave dwellings formerly inhabited by townsfolk but now mostly abandoned and slowly disintegrating. On top the tomb of Kılınçarslan IV, murdered by his brother for the Selçuk throne in 1264, and a small stone *medrese* are surrounded by gardens and a café. ■ *0830-1800 daily. US$1.*

A visit in town on market day reveals that the countryside around Ürgüp still produces bountiful harvests of fruit including apples, apricots and grapes. The latter form the raw material for the local wineries, the produce of which can be tested at the **Tekel Bayii** on the corner of Cumhuriyet Meydanı and Posthane Caddesi. It is also possible to visit one of Ürgüp's half-dozen wine producers for a sampling, with the **Turasan winery**, situated on the Nevşehir road at the edge of town, producing what are considered to be some of the best Cappadocian wines. There is also a wine festival held at the beginning of June at which you can gargle and spit all of the local brews.

Another way of filling some time is to visit the town's small **museum** which has a limited collection of artefacts found in the surrounding area. ■ *0800-1730 daliy except Mon. US$0.75*

Central Anatolia

Sleeping

Most of the areas large hotels favoured by tour groups are found on the eastern outskirts of town beside the road to Kayseri

L *Otel Mustafa*, Kayseri Caddesi, T3413970, F3412288. Large modern 4-star hotel, facilities including pool, restaurants, bar, tennis court, sauna and Turkish bath. **A** *Büyük Almira Hotel*, Kayseri Caddesi No 43, T3418990, F3418999. Large hotel not too far from the centre, single US$70, the guestrooms have en suite, TV and telephone, also swimming pool, restaurants and bar. **B** *Ürgüp Evi*, Esbelli Mahallesi No 46, T3413173, F3416080, on the western edge of town near the Turasan winery. Luxurious cave rooms furnished with antiques, well-finished en suite bathrooms, terrace with wonderful views over countryside, suite with private jacuzzi and sauna US$250. Recommended. **B** *Esbelli Evi*, Esbelli Mahallesi No 8, T3413395, F3418848, suha@esbelli.com.tr, also near the winery. 6 traditional houses carefully restored and converted, lovingly furnished with antiques, family atmosphere with use of kitchen, pleasant rockcut rooms, family room with cot, breakfast terrace, washing machine, internet use. Recommended. **C** *Asia Minor Hotel*, Istiklal Caddesi, T3414645, F3412721, cappadocia50@hotmail.com Handsome Ottoman-Greek house with garden, newly restored and nicely furnished rooms with en suite, several more basic rooms for US$20, meals with family in evening, close to centre but peaceful. Recommended.

D *Hitit Hotel*, Istiklal Caddesi, T3414481. Simple family-run pension occupying converted church and house, subterranean bar, escape tunnel and caverns at the bottom of the garden, slightly over-priced. **E** *Hotel Elvan*, Istiklal Caddesi, Hayrettin Sokak No 2, T3414191, F3413455. Family-run place in newly restored stone building, 1/2/3/4 bed rooms all with en suite, meals available on request. Recommended. **E** *Otel Kral*, Kayseri Caddesi No14, T3412655, F3412656. Newly built from local stone, rooms with vaulted ceilings, telephone, restaurant, bar. **E** *Türkerler Otel*, Dereler Mahallesi, T3413354, just off Nevşehir road near the top of the hill. 250-year old mansion with simple rooms, bit run-down but set in lovely garden and with large pool. **E** *Hotel Surban*, Yunak Mahallesi No 55, T3414603, F3413223. Modern hotel with comfortable rooms with en suite, good value but lacks atmosphere. **F** *Yıldız Hotel*, Kayseri Caddesi, T3414610, F3414611. Large house converted into a pension, plain rooms with en suite. **F** *Bahçe Hostel*, Dutlu Camii Mahallesi, T3413314, F3414878, on the west side of Cumhuriyet Meydanı opposite the hamam. Centrally located hostel with simple 2/3/4 bed rooms in converted monastery, arched ceilings, relaxed atmosphere, garden courtyard and roof terrace, laundry. Recommended budget option. **G** *Born Hotel*,

Ürgüp

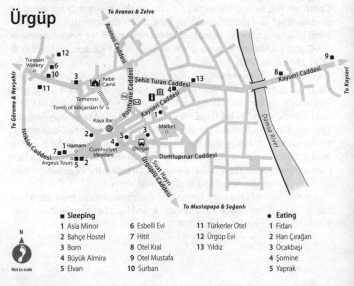

■ Sleeping
1 Asia Minor
2 Bahçe Hostel
3 Born
4 Büyük Almira
5 Elvan
6 Esbelli Evi
7 Hitit
8 Otel Kral
9 Otel Mustafa
10 Surban
11 Türkerler Otel
12 Ürgüp Evi
13 Yıldız

● Eating
1 Fidan
2 Han Çırağan
3 Ocakbaşı
4 Şomine
5 Yaprak

T3414756, on the way up the hill from Cumhuriyet Meydanı, near the Kebir Camii. Rambling old mansion with loads of atmosphere, the high ceiling rooms are fairly basic, some have toilet, breakfast extra. Recommended.

Midrange *Ocakbaşı Restaurant*, T3413277, don't be put off by the location in the bus terminal building on the first floor, excellent grilled meats and meze, US$9 for a full meal before alcohol. *Şömine*, on the main square, good menu including local specialities such as *kiremit kebabı*, lamb baked on a tile which absorbs the fat during cooking, again the location isn't very atmospheric but there are outside tables. *Han Çırağan*, T3412566, on Cumhuriyet Meydanı at the bottom of the hill, tables in the front courtyard or dining room of an old stone house, good local specialities and live music in season if there's enough demand. The *Karakuş Centre* T3415353, F3415356, outside town on the road towards Mustafapaşa, is a large restaurant which puts on a nightly programme of entertainment such as folk and belly dancing during the summer season. A three-course dinner with unlimited wine, beer or rakı is US$15, but it's very popular with tour groups so advance reservations is required.

Cheap The best bet for cheap food is around the bus station with *Yaprak Restaurant*, opposite the terminal, serving soup, ready-prepared dishes and kebaps at tables outside on the street. The nearby *Arkadaş Döner Salonu* has tasty döner and *ayran* for less than US$3.50. *Fidan Restaurant*, in the street opposite the El Sanatları Çarşısı does chicken doner wrapped in a durum (wheat pancake) for just US$1.50. There are more budget restaurants along Dumlupınar Caddesi south of the bus station. You could try the *Şölen Restaurant* for pide, kebabs and pizza served at street side tables in the summer; or the *Kardeşler Pizza Restaurant* opposite which has a similar choice of dishes.

Eating

Ürgüp doesn't have much of a bar scene though you could try the *Kaya Bar*, on Cumhuriyet Meydanı, 1st floor, which usually has a good convivial atmosphere.

Bars

Along Kayseri Caddesi are some interesting shops selling antiques, jewellery and other bits and pieces, there are also some very well stock carpet shops.

Shopping

Argeus Tourism, Istiklal Caddesi No13, T3414688, F3414888, inform@argeus.com.tr, reputable operator who are housed in a beautifully restored building which was formerly the local prison, agents for *Turkish Airlines*, also offer a range of tours including walking and mountain biking. *Cappadocia Tours*, Istiklal Caddesi No19/9, T3417485, F3417487, www.cappadociatours.com Newly established agency with experience and conscientous guides, range of local tours and private guide. *Magic Valley*, Terminal Yanı No 7, T3412145, in arcade next to bus station, various daily programmes, also ballooning and horse-riding.

Tour agencies

Road Bus: **Ankara**, very frequent buses during the day, 5 hrs, US$7.50. **Antalya**, evening buses, 11 hrs, US$14. **Istanbul**, several evening buses, 11 hrs, US$12.50. **Kayseri**, every 2 hrs, 0715-1715, 1½ hrs, US$2.50. **Konya**, 0800,1300, 1800, 1900, 2000, 4 hrs, US$6.25. **Dolmuş**: Leave for **Mustafapaşa**, **Göreme** and **Ortahisar**, every hr during the day, **Nevşehir**, every 30 mins. **Taxi tours**: The taxi co-operative on the corner next to the tourist information office do various tours including Soğanlı. A day long tour costs in the region of US$80.

Transport
Buses depart from the terminal just to the NE of Cumhuriyet Meydanı

Banks There are several banks along Kayseri Caddesi. **Baths** *Tarihi Şehir Hamamı*, west side of Cumhuriyet Meydanı, predictably touristy and expensive baths frequented by tour-groups, mixed groups accepted, US$10 for entry and *kese*. **Communications Post office** On Posthane Caddesi, around corner from Tourist Information Office. **Internet**: *Kaya Bar*, Cumhuriyet

Directory

Meydanı, several terminals, US$3 per hr. **Tourist information** Tourist Information Office is at Kayseri Caddesi No 37. Open everyday, 0800-1800, later in summer.

Mustafapaşa
South from Ürgüp the road weaves a sinuous path through verdant fields & orchards to Mustafapaşa, 5 km away There are buses every hr from Ürgüp, US$0.50

Formerly the Greek village of Sinasos the original inhabitants left in the population exchanges of 1923, although locals insist that a few old Greeks remained up until the 1950s. Whenever they finally departed the Greek legacy lives on in the grand stone buildings still on their feet in the village, though many are slowly crumbling under the weight of time.

Generally ignored by the camera toting crowds, the village remains a quiet backwater where you can experience a slice of Cappadocian life less altered by tourism. Several simple pensions provide a good base for exploring the surrounding countryside, as well as an excellent place to unwind. And where better to start than at the **Kapadokya Şarap Fabrikası**, a small family-run press producing about 600,000 litres of wine every year. Pay a visit to the factory which is up a narrow lane beside the *Old Greek House Otel* for an informal tour followed by a tasting.

There are also several churches around the village with the fresco decorated 10th-century church of **Ayos Vasilios**, a kilometre from town on the edge of a small canyon, reached down a signposted lane from the village roundabout. Before making the trip, though, enquire about the key in the village. Beside the main square at the bottom of the hill is **Ayios Konstantinos** (1729), one of the oldest free-standing churches in the area. There are also several more churches on the other side of the village including **St Nicholas** and **St Stephanos**, 2 and 3 km away respectively.

On foot there is some beautifully unspoilt countryside to explore to the southwest of Mustafapaşa, with paths leading across fields, meadows and orchards to the strangely eroded rockscapes of the **Gomeda Valley** or the farming community of **Ayvalı** (see below). Both walks begin by climbing up the cobbled lane from opposite the Belediye building in the village square. After a kilometre you reach the Ayvalı-Mustafapaşa road at a spring. Continue down the track opposite to a fork after 400 m. The track branching right leads into the Gomeda Valley, while the left option heads up to the village of Ayvalı.

Sleeping D *Otel Sinasos*, T3535009. A tour hotel in the upper part of the village, comfortable rooms with en suite in modern annex to old Greek house which hosts atmospheric restaurant. E *Old Greek House*, T3535306. A rambling 19th-century mansion with loads of atmosphere which was formerly the mayor's residence, cavernous rooms are simply furnished and equipped with en suite shower, also a small hamam and terrace, lunch and evening meal as available. Recommended. F *Hotel Pacha*, T3535004. Overlooking the roundabout as you enter the village, 22 reasonable rooms with shower opening onto a leafy courtyard or upstairs balconies, upper rooms have good views, restaurant serving home-cooked food. F *Lamia*, T3535413, in the upper village past the square. 5 very homely rooms, carefully furnished and opening onto flower-filled courtyard, modern en-suite bathrooms, perfect get-away. Recommended. F *Monastery Pansiyon*, T3535005. Conveniently situated on main square, basic rooms with shower, also an underground restaurant and bar open in the summer.

Ayvalı
There is no public transport to the village so hitching or walking are the only options if you don't have wheels

The small farming community of Ayvalı, 10 km south of Ürgüp, is even further off the beaten track then Mustafapaşa. Coming from Ürgüp, take a right turn several kilometres before Mustafapaşa. The lane climbs gently through the vineyards and orchards with some good views north across the heavily eroded countryside towards Ortahisar.

The villagers originally lived in houses cut from the walls of a narrow gorge, reached by following the road up through the square and turning left down a narrow lane. However, the extensive network of caverns and passages now lies abandoned, slowly crumbling. There is a small rock-cut church on the far side of the gorge which can be followed on foot for 7 km upstream. Above all a visit to the village gives you a true insight into authentic village life in the region.

Sleeping At present the only place to stay is the **B** *Gamirasu Hotel*, Ayvalı Köyü, T3545815, F3545815, www.gamirasu.com, which has been painstakingly converted from 5 old houses by Ibrahim Baştutan and his German wife, Sabrina, now lovely rooms which are carefully furnished, soft locally made woollen mattresses, set in immaculate garden, organic produce used in kitchen, plans to run alternative therapy and healing courses. Recommended.

South from Mustafapaşa the quiet road passes down a wide valley through **Soğanlı** beautifully unspoilt scenery. With no public transport and light traffic making hitching uncertain, it is best to have your own transport to continue southwards. After the village of Taşkınpaşa, overlooked by hillsides covered in fairy chimneys, the road climbs up onto the basalt plateau-land which dominates this part of the region, before dropping into another wide canyon incised into the ancient lava flows. Yukarı (upper) and Aşağı (lower) Soğanlı are lost in a side canyon off this valley. About 35 km south of Ürgüp their relative inaccessibility helps the villages retain a feeling of isolation lost by other parts of Cappadocia. The lower village, consisting of rows of ugly tin-roofed houses, was built as part of a well-intentioned but ill-conceived government plan to preserve the traditional dwellings of the upper settlement by relocating their inhabitants. Needless to say it didn't work as many locals still prefer to live illegally in their original houses, renting out the houses in the lower valley.

Home to a monastic community up until the 13th century, the area around Soğanlı originally contained an estimated 150 churches, although many of these have been lost to erosion or turned into pigeon houses by the local people. Pigeon coops, their entrances surrounded with bright paint to attract the birds, still honey-comb the cliff-faces. The churches that do remain are distinct from those further north, being cut from outcrops of rock rather than excavated from cliff-sides. Between Yukarı and Aşağı Soğanlı the road passes several churches clearly indicated by signs, however, the most interesting are located above the original village in the right-hand gorge. To reach these follow the road which forks right just before the upper village. You'll pass several churches as you progress up this road.

From the end of the road a path crosses a bubbling stream and climbs the other side of the valley to the **Kubbeli Kilise** (Church with the Dome) which is carved out of a pinnacle of rock and cleverly worked to resemble a more conventional stone-built structure. Back at the village a track leads to several more churches in the left-hand canyon.

Visited only by the occasional tour bus, facilities are limited to the small Cappadocia restaurant beside the village square. Simple meals are available here and you can also find a basic room for the night. Many of the village women supplement their meagre agricultural incomes by hawking colourful knitted dolls to arriving tourists. Far from being a local handicraft produced during long winter nights, these dolls are actually made in Kahramanmaraş, though don't let that stop you buying one.

Central Anatolia

The underground cities

The extraordinary wonders of the Cappadocian region are not confined to the surface but extend beneath the ground in the form of intriguing underground cities. These subterranean networks were burrowed out of the soft tufa by local people as a response to the marauding armies which swept through the region with monotonous regularity. At the first signs of trouble the whole population of towns and villages would disappear below ground, taking with them their livestock and enough supplies to remain there until the danger had passed.

Archaeologists believe that the first subterranean settlements date back to at least Hittite times and possibly a lot further. Xenophon, who past through Cappadocia with The Ten Thousand, mentions the existence of houses underground where the people lived along with their domestic animals. Such underground networks were also used as sanctuaries during the Christian period, as proved by the existence of underground churches.

Today, the underground cities of Derinkuyu and Kaymaklı, the largest so far discovered, are on the itineraries of most tours companies in Cappadocia. This means that they remain crowded for most of the day, with queues sometimes forming in the passageways and chambers. Looking on the bright-side, at least this gives you a better impression of what it was like when the city was filled with people sheltering for perhaps months at a time in such cramped conditions. All the passageways are well-lit and your path through the system is guided by arrows, a good thing because otherwise you'd almost certainly get lost. Some parts require you to bend almost double and the whole experience is definitely not one for those who suffer from claustrophobia. Something to consider before entering the underground cities is that the area now open to the public represents a tiny fraction of their original extent. Extensive areas remain uncleared and it has even been supposed that there may be a tunnel linking the underground networks of Derinkuyu and Kaymaklı, a distance of 9 km.

Derinkuyu
This underground labyrinthe reaches a maximum depth of 55 m

The underground city of Derinkuyu is found 29 km south of Nevşehir on the road to Niğde, in the midst of rolling farmland covered with fields of wheat and potatoes. The complex was discovered in 1963 below the scrappy village and extends eight levels into the earth. The upper levels were used predominantly as living quarters and stabling for domestic animal, although there are also armouries, churches and a wine press. The chambers below functioned as meeting halls, store rooms, churches and there is even a dungeon for holding captives or criminals. A complex system of ventilation shafts kept the chambers supplied with fresh air and deep wells were dug down to the water-table 85 m below the surface. An interesting feature that reminds you of the motivation behind the building of these extraordinary subterranean networks are the circular stone doors in many passageways. These were rolled closed with the aid of a pole inserted into a hole in the centre to seal off the chambers in times of insecurity. ■ *0800-1900 daily, closes earlier in winter. US$2. Getting there: Derinkuyu belediye or Niğde-bound buses leave Nevşehir every 30 mins, reaching Derinkuyu after 30 mins, US$1.50. Follow signs for the Yeraltı Şehri.*

Kaymaklı

Kaymaklı underground city is also on the road to Niğde, 20 km south of Nevşehir. Although less extensive than the underground city at Derinkuyu it also has an impressive network of chambers, living-quarters, and smoke-blackened communal kitchens, all linked by passageways and ventilation shafts. It can be less crowded than Derinkuyu. ■ *Opening hours and entrance fee same as Derinkuyu. Getting there: Buses from Nevşehir to Derinkuyu and Niğde pass through.*

Central Anatolia

Other underground cities in the area include those at **Mazıköy**, 10 km east of Kaymaklı, **Acıgöl**, 21 km west of Nevşehir on the road to Aksaray and **Özkonak** (see page 513).

Avanos

Sitting on the banks of the lazy Kızılırmak River, Avanos is paid scant attention by most visitors to Cappadocia despite being a very pleasant town with an interesting district of old houses – many of them built by its former Armenian residents – which stand in varying states of atmospheric dereliction on the hill above the modern town. It's also home to a thriving pottery industry which dates back over 4,000 years. Above all, though, the town is refreshingly normal after the commercialization of Göreme, and although not surrounded by weird and wonderful rock formations it suggests itself as an alternative base for exploring the area.

Phone code: 0384
Colour map 5, grid A3
Altitude: 910 m

The town is 18 km northeast of Nevşehir, connected to the rest of the country and other Cappadocian centres by regular bus and dolmuş services. The bus station is south of the river about 10-mins walk from the centre of town.

Ins & outs

As Venessa, Avanos enjoyed considerable wealth and influence within the Roman empire due to its role as a provincial capital and centre of a cult worshipping Zeus. It was also highly regarded as a source of pottery made from clay deposited by the Kızılırmak (Red River), the ancient River Halys. Today there are still over 50 workshops in the town producing earthenware plates, bowls, mugs, lampshades and a hundred other things besides, continuing a tradition that is thought to date back to Hittite times. While the men were engaged in the workshops and kilns, the women of Avanos made carpets, a tradition introduced by the Selçuk Turks that is unfortunately slowly dying-out in the modern era.

Background

Crossing the Kızılırmak you are greeted by the **Konak Evi**, a grand building built of the local blonde volcanic stone. Formerly the governor's residence it has recently been carefully restored and there are plans to open it as a carpet museum in the near future. Turning left at the roundabout takes you to the

Sights
See page 513 for excursions

Cental Anatolia

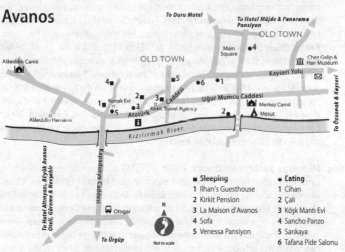

Avanos

To Duru Motel

To Hotel Müjde & Panorama Pansiyon

OLD TOWN

Main Square ● 4

Alâeddin Camii

OLD TOWN

Chez Galip & Hair Museum

Kayseri Yolu

4 ■

■ 5

● 6 ● 1

2 ■
Konak Evi ● 3 3 ■
1 ■   Kırkıt Travel Agency
● 5
Alâeddin Hamamı Atatürk

Uğur Mumcu Caddesi

Merkez Camii
2 ●   Mesut

To Özkonak & Kayseri

Kızılırmak River

To Hotel Altınyazı, Büyük Avanos Oteli, Göreme & Nevşehir

Kapadokya Caddesi

Otogar

N
Not to scale

To Ürgüp

■ **Sleeping**
1 Ilhan's Guesthouse
2 Kirkit Pension
3 La Maison d'Avanos
4 Sofa
5 Venessa Pansiyon

● **Eating**
1 Cihan
2 Çalı
3 Köşk Mantı Evi
4 Sancho Panzo
5 Sarıkaya
6 Tafana Pide Salonu

Alâeddin Camii, a small Selçuk mosque built in the 13th century. In the opposite direction the pleasant **main square** has a shady café and a large monument, far more interesting than yet another bust of Atatürk, celebrating the local pottery and carpet-weaving industries.

To the east of the main square are some of the local **pottery workshops**, many occupying sections of an underground network of tunnels and chambers which stretched beneath the old town on the hill above. It is possible to watch the craftsmen at work and even have a go at throwing yourself. One of the best-known potteries is Chez Galip, where a huge array of earthenware and porcelain pieces are on display in the subterranean showrooms. One chamber is home to the **'hair museum'**, a bizarre collection of locks, about 5,000 at last count, left by visitors from all over the world over the last decade. Several of the potteries also arrange courses in throwing and other local crafts, contact the Tourist Information Office for details.

Sleeping **A** *Hotel Altınyazı*, Kapadokya Caddesi, T5112010, F5114960. Modern 4-star hotel on the road to Göreme, rooms are equipped with TV and minibar, restaurant, bar and sauna. **C** *Büyük Avanos Oteli*, Kapadokya Caddesi No 46, T5113577, F5114863, hotel@buyukavanos.com.tr, on the Göreme road outside town. Owned by a French-Turkish couple, large modern hotel with decent rooms, paintings scattered around the walls add a pleasant personal touch, tennis court and pool in the garden. **D** *Sofa Hotel*, Orta Mahalle No13, T5114489, F5114489. Originally several small houses, now a family-run hotel, sweet rooms with low ceilings and kilims on the walls, single US$15, shady courtyard and restaurant. Recommended. **E** *Duru Motel*, Cumhuriyet Meydanı No15, T5114005, F5112402. View from the vine-covered terrace and the lovely garden make-up for what is a fairly unappealing concrete structure, inside the simple rooms have en suite, local specialities prepared in kitchen, informal tours organized by helpful management. Recommended. **E** *Ilhan's Guesthouse*, Orta Mahalle, Zafer Sokak No1, T5114828. Rooms in an old house near the bridge, run by a retired teacher and his wife, lots of atmosphere, simple have en suite, also small terrace. **F** *Kirkit Pension*, in alleyway parallel to Atatürk Caddesi, T5113148, F5112135, kirkit@service.raksnet.com.tr Originally 4 Ottoman houses, now combined to form atmospheric pension, cheaper rooms without toilet, cave bar and lots of comfortable sitting areas, walking, biking and horse-riding tours organized. Recommended. **F** *Venessa Pansiyon*, Hafızağa Sokak No 20, T5113840. Run-down old house in the process of being renovated, loads of atmosphere but the rooms are basic and the bathrooms shared. **F** *La Maison d'Avanos*, Atatürk Caddesi, T5113552, old house with basic rooms, shady terrace overlooking main street, rooms affected by traffic noise. **F** *Hotel Müjde*, Büyükdere Sokak No 34, T5115565, F5115470, at the top of the old town, follow signs from Chez Mumtaz pottery. Simple guesthouse with clean rooms, en suite bathrooms, rooms are hot in summer, breakfast extra. **F** *Panorama Pansiyon*, Yukarı Mahalle, T5114828. Good budget option away from the hustle and bustle at the top of old town, row of simple bungalows and cheaper rooms with shared toilet, excellent views across Cappadocian landscape. Recommended. **Camping** *Mesut Camping*, T5113545, behind the new mosque, centrally located riverside site, shower and toilet facilities, caravan US$7, tent US$5.

Eating **Midrange** *Sarıkaya Restaurant*, T5113560, F5113562, huge subterranean restaurant, hosts coach groups, dinner and entertainment by local folkdancers, US$28 all-inclusive, advance booking required. *Bizim Ev Restaurant*, near *Sofa Hotel* in Orta Mahalle, has been recommended for its setting in a restored Ottoman house and attentive service, a range of traditional Turkish dishes are on the menu. **Cheap** There are lots of simple eateries around the main square including the busy *Cihan Restaurant* which has kebabs, lahmacun, pide and ready-prepared stews on the menu.

Sancho Panzo, on the east side of the main square serves pide, pizza and güveç (stew) along with beer and wine. Nearby the *Tuvanna*, has a varied, slightly more expensive, menu including meze, pizza, kebabs and steak. *Tafana Pide Salonu*, Atatürk Caddesi, a smartish place serving tasty pide and lahmacun. *Köşk Mantı Evi*, off Atatürk Caddesi, traditional Turkish food brought to low tables in rock-cut dining room, soup, grilled meat or mantı with salad and sweet for US$5. *Çalı Restaurant*, T5114399, next to the footbridge across the river, waterside tables shaded by willows, trout and occasionally *yayın balığı*, a huge bottom-dwelling fish that lives in the Kızılırmak and can grow to weigh 125 kg. *Aytemur Pastanesi* on the main square is the place to head for pastries, biscuits and liquid refreshments. Or you can join the local menfolk in the main square for a glass of çay.

In a town of potters there's no shortage of earthenware souvenirs. The main problem **Shopping** is getting them home in one piece, however, there are plenty of smaller more porta- ble things too. To see some of the locally made carpets visit the Duru Carpet Shop, at the top of main square, run by the owner of the *Duru Hotel*.

Kirkit Voyage, T5113259, F5112135, visit their office on Atatürk Caddesi, organize **Tour agencies** standard sight-seeing trips as well as riding, walking, biking and snow-shoeing tours.

Ankara, 0700,0900,1200,1500,1700, 4 hrs, US$7.50, **Istanbul**, 3 evening buses, 11 hrs, **Transport** US$16 **Kayseri**, every 2 hrs, 0715-1715, 1½ hrs, US$2.50. **Konya**, 4 buses daily, 3 hrs, US$6. **Trabzon**, 1 afternoon bus, 12 hrs, US$17.50. **Hacıbektaş**, Ankara bus via Hacıbektaş, 0700, 1200, 1½ hrs, US$2.50. Belediye buses every 30 mins to **Nevşehir** via **Çavuşin** and **Göreme** throughout the day. **Özkonak** dolmuş depart every 30 mins from outside the new mosque just to the east of the main square.

Banks On Atatürk Caddesi and the main square. **Baths** *Alâeddin Turkish Bath*, traditional **Directory** bath complex now frequented by tour groups. Open 0800-0200, wash and massage US$6, near the Alâeddin Camii. **Post office** The PTT is east of the main square on Atatürk Caddesi. **Tourist information** The Tourist Information Office is on Atatürk Caddesi, local manager Kemal Uslu is very helpful, although unfortunately his second language is French. Open 0800-1200, 1300-1730, later in summer. **Useful addresses** *Avanos Riding Centre*, T5114240, hourly or daily rides, lessons also available.

Some 19 km north of Avanos is the village of Özkonak, below which a system **Özkonak** of underground caverns and passages was carved-out of the soft tufa to house *This complex is thought to* local people in times of conflict. Discovered by the village *müezzin* (mosque *have had a capacity of* crier) in 1972 and opened to the public twelve years later, this underground *60,000 people* city is less well-known than those at Kaymaklı and Derinkuyu and therefore less crowded. The subterranean network is 40 m deep with 10 levels, although at present only four of these are open to the public making it rather a limited experience. An interesting feature of the system are the microtunnels used to communicate between levels and in times of conflict, when hot oil could be poured through them onto attackers. There are also several circular stone doors which were rolled across the passageways in order to seal them off. ■ *0830-1700 daily, 1900 in summer. US$1.50. Getting there: Follow the Kayseri road for 12 km before taking the turn sign-posted for Özkonak, a further 7 km. Continue through the village until you see signs for the Yeraltı Şehir. Dolmuş leave for Özkonak from outside the new mosque in Avanos every 30 mins.*

A short distance beyond the turning for Özkonak is a road signposted on the **Bayramhacı** right for the hotsprings of Bayramhacı. The complex includes separate outside **Kaplıcaları** pools for men and women (*US$0.50*) and smaller private baths that can be

Central Anatolia

hired for up to two people (*US$3 per hour*). There is also a simple restaurant on-site serving trout and salad. ■ *Getting there: There is no public transport to Bayramhacı.*

Gülşehir   A quiet town situated in the Kızılırmak Valley, the only reason to visit Gülşehir is to explore the **Açık Saray**, a Byzantine monastic centre 7 km before town. Several churches and a three-storey palace are cut into a low tufa escarpment just off the Nevşehir road, with more rarely visited churches awaiting discovery further-up the Çat valley. Beyond a coppice of trees stands a strange mushroom-shaped rock, which has been adopted as the town's official symbol. During the day a warden is on duty and he will show you around for a small tip. ■ *Getting there: Buses between Nevşehir and Gülşehir (US$1) pass the Açık Saray at least every hour in each direction.*

Hacıbektaş   The small town of Hacıbektaş, 45 km northwest of Nevşehir, is unremarkable except as the site chosen by Hacı Bektaş Veli, the founder of the influential Bektaşi sect of dervishes, for his centre of scientific study. After his death the tiny hamlet of Suluca Karahöyük was renamed in his honour and a monastery complex was constructed around his tomb. Finished in the 14th century this became the headquarters of the Bektaşi order, and a centre of considerable religious and political importance within the Ottoman empire. Following the banning of the dervish orders in 1925, the monastery became the **Museum of Hacıbektaş** though despite this cosmetic secularization the complex has maintained its spiritual significance for followers of the teachings of Hacı Bektaş. ■ *0800-1200, 1300-1700 daily except Mon. US$1.50.*

The extent of contemporary feeling towards the man can be seen in mid-August each year, when hundreds of thousands of faithful descend on the town to pay their respects. Needless to say the rest of the time things are considerably quieter, although from the amount of new building going-on in town it would seem that Hacıbektaş is profiting handsomely from its legacy.

The museum is in fact a series of courtyards, the first being the former laundry and baths of the complex. The second courtyard contains the kitchens in which stands a large black cauldron known as the **Karakazan**. This was of spiritual significance to the Bektaşi as the source of their communal food, while such vessels were also used by the jannisaries to express their displeasure at the Sultan, with the upturning of the Karakazan the presage of many a violent revolt. On the left the **Meydan Evi**, with its well-restored wooden roof, was used for initiation ceremonies. Today it houses various objects of significance to the Bektaşi order, including a portrait of Hacı Bektaş sitting in a reflective pose, his hand stroking a lion sitting at his side. At the far end of the complex the third courtyard contains the tombs of important members of the Bektaşi order, with the burial place of its founder reached through a white marble portal known as the Akkapı.

Having looked around the museum there is no reason to extend your stay in Hacıbektaş, except possibly to have a browse through the souvenir shops outside. Many of these sell carved onyx pieces for which the town is famous.

Sleeping & eating

There are a row of simple eateries on Hacı Bektaş Veli Bulvarı, including Dostlar Sofrası

If you get stranded in Hacıbektaş there are a couple of serviceable hotels. Everything gets booked solid around the time of the August pilgrimage: you'll need to reserve well in advance to secure a room. **F** *Hotel Hünkar*, Karayalçın Parkı No 73, T4413344. In the commercial development across from the museum, plain rooms with en suite. **E** *Otel Cem*, Kırşehir Caddesi, T4412414, F4143562, follow Hacı Bektaş Veli Bulvarı down from the museum, the hotel is about 1 km away on the edge of town, though it's not really worth the journey unless the *Hotel Hünkar* is full, plain rooms with en suite.

Road Buses and dolmuş depart from the corner of Cumhuriyet Caddesi and Hacı   **Transport**
Bektaş Veli Bulvarı, near the white ceremonial arch. **Ankara**, several daily, 3 hrs, US$5.
Nevşehir, from Ankara, 5 daily, 45 mins, US$1.50. There are also regular dolmuş from
across the street. **Kırşehir**, 4 daily, 30 mins, US$1.50.

Tourist information The tourist information office is on Cumhuriyet Caddesi near the   **Directory**
ceremonial arch. Open weekdays 0830-1200, 1330-1730.

Kayseri

An important town on the trans-Anatolian caravan routes, Kayseri has   *Phone code: 0352*
enjoyed a tempestuous history marked by conquest and reconquest at the   *Colour map 5, grid A4*
hands of over a dozen armies. Originally known as Mazaca and then Caesarea   *Altitude: 1054 m*
after the Roman emperor Tiberius, it was subsequently held for varying
lengths of time by the Byzantines, Selçuks, Mongols, Eretnids, and
Karamanids before being taken by the Ottoman. The inevitable destruction of
war was often accompanied by building with the town boasting a rich architectural heritage, especially from its time as an important Selçuk town. Kayseri's
recent history has been considerably quieter with the town growing into a
modern, provincial centre of nearly 500,000 people. The *Kayserili* are a fairly
conservative bunch, content living in what by Turkish standards is an orderly
town, complete with such rarities as bicycle lanes and parking meters.

Getting there There are daily flights from Istanbul to Kayseri's Erciyes Airport with a   **Ins & outs**
minibus transfer (US$2) to the *Turkish Airlines* office in the centre of town. At an impor-   *See page 519 for*
tant junction in the national road and railway networks the town is well-served by   *further details*
buses and trains. **Getting around** Visiting the town's sights is easily done on foot,
but arriving at the *otogar*, 1 km west of the centre, you'll need to get on a dolmuş
marked 'DSI, Osmanlı Sitesi' or 'Terminal' which pass by the front of the bus station on
the opposite side of the road. From the train station, about the same distance north of
the centre, get on a 'Terminal' dolmuş passing outside.

Archaeological research has shown that the area around Kayseri has been   **Background**
inhabited for well over 4000 years. During Hellenistic times the town was the
capital of a Cappadocian Kingdom which in 17 AD became a province of the
Roman empire. Its citizens eagerly adopted Christianity with the last pagan
temple destroyed during the reign of Julian the Apostate (361-363 AD). The
town became an important centre for the emerging religion, counting among
it notable offspring St Basil, the great ecclesiastical writer and teacher.

Despite being surrounded by strong walls the town lived in constant fear of
attack, a state of insecurity that continued in the face of the Arab and later
Selçuk invasions. Under Selçuk rule the town became the second city of the
Sultanate of Rum and its streets were graced with many fine mosques and public buildings, many of which survive to this day. Fanatics of Selçuk architecture
will also find dozens of *kümbet*, free-standing tombs often decorated with
inscriptions and patterns carved into the stone, scattered across the town.

Modern Kayseri is an important manufacturing centre, well-known for its
textiles and metal goods. Also renowned for its sharp businessmen, several of
the country's leading industrialists are native *Kayserili*. The once-important
local tourist industry has never recovered from the twin blows of the Gulf War
and PKK insurgency far to the east, with the town eclipsed by the
newly-developed tourist centres of Cappadocia to the west. The city's promot-
ers are, however, hoping to attract visitors to the newly developed ski resort on
the flanks on Erciyes, 25 km to the south.

Central Anatolia

Sights The busy junction at **Cumhuriyet Meydanı** is the centre of modern Kayseri, with the well-preserved walls of the medieval castle standing just to the south. First constructed from black basalt blocks by the Byzantine emperor Justinian in the sixth century, it was later rebuilt by the Selçuks and Ottomans. Inside the walls – 3 m thick and topped by 19 towers – is a shopping precinct with several restaurants and lots of stalls selling clothes and consumer goods.

Across Seyyid Burhanettin Bulvarı is the **Hunat Hatun Camii** part of a complex built in the early 13th century for the Greek wife of the Selçuk sultan, Alâeddin Keykubat. With its low-ceiling and solid arches dividing up the interior, the overall feeling is one of confinement, very different to the spatial experience in later Ottoman mosques. Have a look at the intricate patterning around the *mihrab* which contrasts with the austerity of the rest of the interior. A hair from the prophet Mohammed's beard is kept in the wooden box to its left, while of the two columns flanking the *mihrab*, one can now be spun, showing that the building has sunk on one side since its construction over 700 years ago.

To the west of the citadel is what has always been the commercial heart of the city. A vibrant area of narrow streets and interconnecting buildings busy with shoppers and traders, it's still a lot of fun to explore. The solid stone

Kayseri

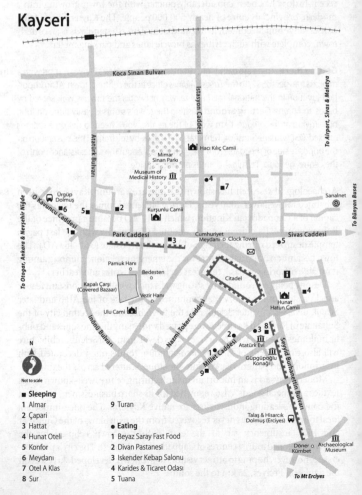

■ Sleeping
1 Almar
2 Çapari
3 Hattat
4 Hunat Oteli
5 Konfor
6 Meydanı
7 Otel A Klas
8 Sur
9 Turan

● Eating
1 Beyaz Saray Fast Food
2 Divan Pastanesi
3 Iskender Kebap Salonu
4 Karides & Ticaret Odası
5 Tuana

Hacı Bektaş Veli and the Bektaşi order

There is much speculation and very little fact known about the life of Hacı Bektaş Veli. What is certain is that he was born in Persia early in the 13th century and after receiving an education in Khorasan, he moved to Anatolia living briefly in Kayseri, Kırşehir and Sivas, before finally settling in the hamlet of Sulu Karahöyük. During these travels he developed a religious philosophy which incorporated orthodox İslam with elements of Christian and shamanistic beliefs.

Hacı Bektaş set-out his mystical philosophies in the Makalât, a great work which described the path to enlightenment through a series of stages. During this evolution the dervish would learn to differentiate between right and wrong, subsequently demonstrating his devotion to God through a process of prayer and self-effacement. Hacı Bektaş interpreted Islamic law in a flexible, pragmatic way, which included a disregard for traditional Muslim rituals such as regular prayer and the veiling of women. On the subject of women his unorthodox views,

which seem light years ahead of their time, are remembered in his oft quoted saying: 'a nation which does not educate its women cannot progress.'

The teachings of Hacı Bektaş became the tenets of the Bektaşi order of dervishes and proved to be extremely attractive to the common people of Anatolia, many of whom couldn't identify with the dogmatic religious ideologies of the Byzantine or Turkish states. After his death the Bektaşi order grew steadily becoming an important instrument of Islamization in Anatolia. Within the Ottoman empire the sect gained significant political power and was associated with the elite jannisaries corps, from whose ranks it drew many of its members. Paradoxically, it was the conservatism of the increasingly unruly jannisaries, an obstacle to reforms proposed by Sultan Mahmut II, that led to the violent destruction of the force in 1826 and the proscription of the Bektaşi order. Despite this, and Atatürk's subsequent banning of all dervish orders in 1925, the sect remains hugely popular for its liberal tenets.

Bedesten was originally built in 1497 to house a cloth market; while the nearby **Vezir Hanı**, recognizable by the pointed chimneys sprouting from its roof, was constructed at the orders of Damat Ibrahim Paşa in 1727. Today, the caravanserai houses wool and leather dealers as it always has done, with bundles of woollen fleeces and cured skins sitting in the courtyard and carpet dealers working from the gallery upstairs. Also nearby the **Kapalı Çarşı** (Covered Bazaar) is one of the largest of its kind in Anatolia. Over 500 shops lining the brightly-lit arcades are still very much open for business and unlike the Covered Bazaar in Istanbul the hassle-factor is low as tourists are a bit of a rarity these days. Just south of the Kapalı Çarşı is the town's oldest mosque, the **Ulu Cami** which looks in remarkable shape considering its age. Built in 1136 by a Danışmend emir its roof rests on rows of unmatched columns pilfered from earlier buildings and there's a nice carved wooden *mimber*.

The museum is housed in Kayseri's oldest seminary, the Çifte Medrese, which was founded as a medical school and hospital by the Selçuk Sultan Keyhüsrev in 1206. The two seminary buildings are occupied by various artefacts from the world of Selçuk medicine with reconstructions of the Ameliyathane (operating room), Akıl Hastanesi (Mental Hospital) and chief doctors' office. Unfortunately, all of the displays are currently only labelled in Turkish though the museum is certainly worth a look anyway. ■ *0800-1200, 1300-1700 daily except Mon. US$1.50. The Çifte Medrese is in Mimar Sinan Parkı, north of Park Caddesi.*

The Museum of Medical History

Central Anatolia

Güpgüpoğlu Konağı   The ancestral home of the influential Güpgüpoğlu clan is now occupied by Kayseri's ethnography museum. The interesting collection includes Selçuk and Ottoman ceramics, weaponry, coins and personal effects, however, it's the house itself which is the real draw. Built of roughly dressed volcanic stone, parts of the solid looking two storey building date back to the 15th century. According to tradition it's divided between a *haremlik* (women's quarters) on the left and the *selamlık* containing reception rooms next door. Authentically decorated and furnished the house gives an insight into life in a wealthy provincial household during Ottoman times. ■ *0830-1630 daily Mon. US$1.25. The entrance is on Tennuri Sokak just inside the city walls.*

Atatürk Museum (Atatürk Evi)   Across the road from the Güpgüpoğlu Konağı is another old house with historical significance. The building is a well-preserved Ottoman-era house where Atatürk stayed in December, 1919. On display are a collection of letters, photographs and other bits-and-bobs associated with Atatürk and the foundation of the Turkish Republic. A very life-like wax model of the man himself greets you in the bedroom upstairs. ■ *0800-1700 daily except Mon. US$1.25. The museum is on Tennuri Sokak, nearly opposite the Güpgüpoğlu Konağı.*

Archaeological Museum   Kayseri's excellent provincial museum contains many well-displayed artefacts discovered in Cappadocia and at the nearby site of Kültepe. Displays include Hittite stone carvings, artefacts from the Assyrian trading community at Kanesh, along with various Hellenistic and Roman curiosities. Walking out to the museum along Seyyit Burhanettin Bulvarı you pass the Alaca and Döner Kümbets, two of the cities many **Selçuk mausoleums**. ■ *0830-1730 daily except Mon. US$1.50. On Kışla Caddesi, just to the northeast of the Döner Kümbet.*

Sleeping   **A** *Hotel Almar*, Osman Kavuncu Caddesi, T3090435, F3115677. 3-star hotel which is the best in town, comfortable rooms with TV, minibar, television and air-con. Recommended. **C** *Hotel Çapari*, Donanma Caddesi No 12, T2225278, F2225282. 2-star hotel with small rooms, TV and telephone as standard, cleaner and better managed than other mid-range options. Recommended. **C** *Hotel Konfor*, Atatürk Bulvarı No 5, T3200184. Small comfortable rooms with wood panelled walls, en suite shower, TV and minibar, restaurant. Recommended. **D** *Hotel Hattat*, Park Caddesi No 21, T2226558, F2326503. Large hotel with small well-equipped rooms but tiny bathroom, decor is a bit worn. **D** *Otel A Klas*, Mete Caddesi No 6. Small reasonably well furnished rooms with cable TV and en suite. Recommended. **D** *Hotel Sur*, Talas Caddesi No 12, T2224367. Hotel inside the city walls with small rooms equipped with TV, telephone and shower, some don't have external window but at least you won't be bothered by any traffic noise. **E** *Hotel Çamlıca*, Gürcü Sokak No 14, T2314344. Reasonable rooms with TV, telephone and en suite shower, waterless doubles for US$16, singles for US$11. **E** *Hotel Turan*, Turan Caddesi No 8, T2225537. Well-established hotel which is now a little bit run-down, still conveniently place with spacious, comfortable TV and telephone-equipped rooms, breakfast on roof terrace. Recommended. **F** *Hotel Büyük*, İnönü Bulvarı No 55, T2325340. Opposite Hatıroğlu mosque, simple rooms with en suite in small hotel, cheaper waterless rooms available. **F** *Hotel Meydanı*, Osman Kavuncu Caddesi No 12, T3303548. Clean but pretty basic rooms with basic shower, also cheaper waterless rooms for US$13. Recommended although for a bit extra you can do a lot better. **G** *Hunat Oteli*, Zengin Sokak No 5, T2324319. Centrally located behind the Hunat Hatun Camii complex, old fashioned boarding house with friendly manager, Ömer Bey, plain simple waterless rooms. Recommended for those on a really tight budget.

Kayseri's specialities are of the pastoral type: *pastırma* (sun-dried spicy meat), *sucuk* (spicy sausage), *salam* (salami) and *tulum peyniri* (cheese matured in goatskin), all of which you will see in shops around town. **Midrange** *Karides*, Istasyon Caddesi No 16, 8th floor, T2223947, above the Ticaret Odası (Chamber of Commerce), favourite with the town's business community at lunchtime, also live music at weekends, menu includes meze, fish, grilled meats, accompanied by a great view over the city. *Tuana*, Sivas Caddesi, 1st floor, large modern restaurant reached via lift, local dishes such as beans with pastırma, mantı, kebabs, good desserts, very attentive service and good value at US$7 for 3 courses. **Cheap** *Ibrahim Sofrası*, snack bar inside the castle serving döner, *iskender kebap*, juices and ayran, good place to take the load of your feet while sightseeing. *Beyaz Saray Fast Food*, Millet Caddesi, very popular locally, serves soups, kebabs including eastern speciality *otlu kebap* (beef cooked on a spit over charcoal) and pizza. *Iskender Kebap Salonu*, Millet Caddesi No 5, perennially popular place on 1st floor serving döner and delicious iskender kebap. *Divan Pastanesi*, Millet Caddesi, very popular pastry shop and café with excellent baklava.

Eating

Being a fairly conservative place there isn't a huge selection of restaurants, as people don't really make a habit of eating out in the evening

Carpet weaving is an important economic activity in some areas of Kayseri province. To see some of the results try the shops in the Vezir Han.

Shopping

Bremer Tour, Ahmet Paşa Caddesi No 17/102, T/F2229946, programme of trekking holidays in the Aladağlar, also car rental and airline reservation.

Tour agencies

Air *Turkish Airlines*, Yıldırım Caddesi No 1, T2223858, F2224748, has 2 daily flights to Istanbul. Airport buses leave from the office 45 mins before check-in time. **Road Bus**: **Adana**, 6 buses daily, 5 hrs, US$8. **Ankara**, every hr, 5 hrs, US$8. **Antalya**, several evening buses, 10 hrs, US$14. **Diyarbakır**, 4 daily, 9 hrs, US$13. **Erzurum**, several night buses, 9 hrs, US$12. **Göreme**, 5 daily, 75 mins, US$2. **Istanbul**, 5 daily, 8 hrs, US$15. **Kahramanmaraş**, 5 daily, 4 hrs, US$6. **Van**, 4 daily, 16 hrs, US$18. **Car hire**: **Avis**, Mustafa Kemal Paşa Bulvarı No 7, T2226196, F2224965. **Dolmuş**: **Ürgüp** dolmuş leave from a separate terminal on Osman Kavuncu Caddesi, every 1½ hrs, 0800-1900, 1½ hrs, US$2. **Train** The train station is at the end of Istasyon Caddesi with regular dolmuş services from the centre. At a major rail junction Kayseri is well-served by trains to and from **Ankara** and **Istanbul**, as well as other parts of the south and east of the country. The *Çukurova Mavi Treni, 4 Eylül Mavi Treni, Doğu Ekspresi, Güney Ekspresi* and the *Van Gölü Ekspresi* all pass through Kayseri, often at uncivilized times of the night. See page 48 for complete timetable.

Transport

Airline offices Turkish Airlines, Yıldırım Caddesi No 1, T2223858. **Banks** There are banks with ATM machines and change facilities on Nazmi Toker Caddesi. **Baths** *Hanat Hatun Hamamı*, part of Hanat Hatun complex with separate sections for men and women. **Post office** The PTT is on Cumhuriyet Meydanı opposite the castle. **Internet** *Sanalnet*, Teoman Sokak No 13/A, walk up the road opposite the Tuana restaurant, take first right and walk down 100 m past Kristal Kuaför and its on your left, US$2 per hr. **Tourist information** The tourist information office, with helpful multi-lingual staff, is on Seyyid Burhanettin Caddesi next to the Hunat Hatun complex. Open weekdays 0800-1700.

Directory

Around Kayseri

Excavations at the site of Kültepe, 20 km northeast of Kayseri near the present-day village of Karahoyuk, have revealed evidence of human settlement since at least the middle of the third millennium BC. From around 1900 BC, what was then the city of Laneş contained an Assyrian trading community which flourished for over 200 years under the protection of the local Hatti rulers. One of nine such communities scattered across Anatolia, these *karum* had an important influence on the indigenous pre-Hittite cultures of the time, introducing

Kültepe

Central Anatolia

Mesopotamian technology and ways of life to the area. However, this cultural exchange and commerce came to an abrupt end after two centuries for unknown reasons and with the Assyrian's departure the *karum* was destroyed.

A record of the transactions carried-out, in which goods such as textiles and tin imported from Mesopotamia were exchanged for cattle, copper and silver, has survived in the form of over 15,000 **clay tablets** unearthed at the site. Inscribed in the commercial language of Mesopotamia, Akkadian, the tablets reveal much about contemporary life, including the intermarriage of Assyrians with their Anatolian hosts. Seals, alabaster idols, furniture and decorated earthenware vessels were also uncovered by archaeologists in the **Royal Palace**. These artefacts now grace the museums of Ankara and Kayseri, with the on-site remains consisting mainly of the stone foundations of the mud-brick community, including its palace. A visit is only recommended for those with an enduring fascination for early Anatolian history as there is actually very little to be seen.

■ *Getting there: To reach Kültepe by public transport take a Bünyan-bound bus which depart from along Sivas Caddesi. Get-off after 18 km at the turning sign-posted for 'Kültepe' and walk the remaining 2 km to the site.*

Erciyes Dağı The conical form of 3917 m Erciyes Dağı rears-up abruptly from the Anatolian plateau just to the south of Kayseri. An extinct volcano which last erupted about 30 million years ago, the peak, known as Mount Argaeus in Hellenistic times, has always held considerable mythological importance. More recently a ski resort has been developed on its slopes, though the upper mountain remains the preserve of trekkers and mountaineers intent on bagging what is one of the loftiest, if not the most interesting, peaks in the country.

The ski-season is officially from mid-Nov to mid-Apr, however, the best conditions are from Jan-Mar

Skiing The Tekir ski-centre is on the eastern side of the mountain, 25 km from Kayseri town centre. Several lifts presently carry skiers up to an altitude of 2700 m, with easy and moderately difficult runs descending 500 m to the resort. Plans are afoot for up to 5 new lifts which will considerably increase the 'skiable' area. Although the skiing is characterized by bare, treeless slopes which are rather bleak at times, the local climate generally produces decent, powdery snow.

Climbing Erciyes Dağı is a popular destination for mostly-domestic mountaineers, although this popularity is as much on account of its size and accessibility as the actual quality of the ascent. Snow remains on the upper mountain all-year-round, with much of the climb from Jun onwards being over barren, rocky slopes. Approaches to the mountain are via the ski-centre at Tekir or from the northwest via the village of Hacılar. The former is the easier of the two being possible in one long day. From Tekir continue up beyond the top of the ski-lifts to a wide basin, from where the easiest option is to follow the long ridge to the south as it swings round towards the summit (4-5 hrs). The last section involves some scrambling up steep, loose rock. Alternatively, a more direct line climbs the obvious couloir called Şeytan Deresi (Devil's Valley) starting directly to the west of the basin, but this route is steeper and remains choked with snow until late in the summer. Though relatively straightforward neither route should be tackled without adequate equipment, including plenty of water and an ice-axe, or by those without some previous mountaineering experience. Guides can generally be arranged through the Kayak Evi in Tekir or the Belediye in Hacılar. Also try enquiring at the helpful tourist information office in Kayseri. More detailed route descriptions can be found in '*The Mountains of Turkey*', Karl Smith, Cicerone Press.

Sleeping and eating Most accommodation takes the form of hostels reserved for state employees, but there are two other options: **A** *Dedeman Hotel*, T3422003, F3421117. 3-star hotel with comfortable rooms and restaurant, rates increases to

US$120 at weekends during the ski season. **B** *Erciyes Ski Lodge*, T3422031, F3422032. More simple rooms but still perfectly adequate, rates are fullboard, out-of-season prices are much reduced to US$13 per double, no food available. The ski-centre is on the road from Kayseri to Develi, with regular Develi dolmuş (US$1.25) leaving from the *Talaş durağı* on Seyyit Burhanettin Caddesi.

A large flat basin to the south of Erciyes, Sultansazlığı is recognized as one of the most important bird habitats in Turkey (see box) and as such has recently been designated a national park. The huge number of bird species that live-in or seasonally visit the lakes, marshland and reedbeds of the area, make this a must for avid ornithologists, however, those with a less fervent interest in feathered creatures may also enjoy a trip out into the reedbeds.

Sultansazlığı
See box, page 524

Access to the lakes is via the village of Ovaçiftlik, east of the Niğde-Kayseri highway on the road to Yahyalı. Any Yahyalı-bound bus from Kayseri (every hour, 0930-1700, US$1), will drop you in the village. A kilometre beyond the village is a watch-tower which provides good viewing at dawn during the spring and early summer when water-levels are high. Alternatively, a boat trip out onto Eğri Göl can be arranged for about US$20 for 4 people. There are several simple pensions in the village including **F** *Sultan Pansiyon and Camping*, T6585549. ■ *Getting there: With your own transport other parts of the park can be reached through the villages of Soysallı, Sindelhöyük and Çamısgözü, to the northeast of Ovaçiftlik.*

Niğde

Well to the south of the Cappadocian wonderland, Niğde is a fairly unexceptional provincial town set on a broad saddle between brown mountains. Although its origins may date back as far as Hittite times, the town first emerges from obscurity as a Selçuk settlement in the 11th century. Since then, however, nothing notable has occurred and Niğde continues to be a quiet place, its largely agrarian economy based on the crops of potatoes, cereal and fruit produced in its fertile hinterland. The only justification for a special visit is to see the well-preserved frescoes in the Eski Gümüşler monastery 10 km away, with a few other early-Islamic buildings in the town itself worth a look for the real aficionado.

Phone code 0388
Colour map 5, grid B3
Altitude: 1229 m

Niğde is a transit point for trekkers & climbers heading for the Aladağlar. Also worth a visit for the Eski Gümüşler monastery

Getting there Despite being relatively small, Niğde's *otogar* is well-served by buses to destinations close at hand, departing throughout the day, and further afield, mostly leaving at night. **Getting around** Coming out of the *otogar* turn right and walk up Faik Şahenik Caddesi to the large roundabout, where a left turn down Bankalar Caddesi brings you to Atatürk Caddesi (the centre of town) in just under 10 mins. Dolmuş marked 'SSK, Doğum ve Çocuk Hastanesi' (US$0.25) also ply this route.

Ins & outs
See page 522 for further details

The town's **fortress**, constructed on the foundations of an earlier Byzantine fort, can be found by walking along Istasyon Caddesi from Atatürk Meydanı. Nearby, on the southern slopes of the fortress mound is the **Alâeddin Camii** which was constructed by the Selçuk governor in 1223 and qualifies as the town's oldest mosque. It's also one of the most eye-catching with its horizontally stripped stonework and impressively carved entranceway. Further south again is the **Sungur Bey Camii** another Selçuk mosque which underwent extensive modification by the Mongols in the early 14th century.

Sights

The **Archaeology Museum** is situated south of the centre in the Ak Medrese, a seminary of Karamanid vintage. A variety of artefacts span the ages from the Bronze Age but the most intriguing, not to say macabre, exhibit is the

Central Anatolia

mummified body of a nun found in one of the cave churches of the Ihlara Canyon. ■ *0830-1200, 1330-1700, daily except Mon. US$1.25.*

Eski Gümüşler The Eski Gümüşler monastery, 10 km to the east of town, is an interesting Byzantine rock-cut monastery neglected by most visitors to the region, inspite of the well-preserved frescoes which adorn the walls of its chapel. Indeed, it's a mystery how these paintings remained in such good condition, avoiding damage by religious zealots and vandals, as well as the elements. Rediscovered in 1963 the monastery is near the village of Gümüşler which is surrounded by fertile orchards of apple and cherry trees.

At the centre of the monastic community was a large courtyard, now entered through a gated passageway. Around this courtyard are several sepulchres with skeletons still visible inside; a communal kitchen and a wine-press with large vessels carved from the rock for fermenting the grapes in. The big draw, however, is the main chapel reached through an arched doorway opposite the entranceway. Two rows of false pillars rise up to the high ceiling giving the feeling of being in a conventional church rather than a cave. On the walls are a series of beautifully painted and colourful frescoes dating from between the seventh and 11th centuries. They vividly depict biblical scenes such as the nativity, while the cross-hatch pattern also seen in other churches in the region probably dates from the Iconoclastic era when the representation of figures and living things in religious art was banned. Reached up a metal ladder from the chapel is a dormitory where the monks slept on beds hacked from the walls. There are more paintings on these walls showing a hunting scene and a soldier dressed in what looks like Roman garb. ■ *0800-1200, 1330-1730 daily. US$1.50. To reach the monastery get on a Gümüşler belediye bus which leave the otogar every 45 mins. Under you own steam Gümüşler is signposted off the main highway just to the east of town.*

Sleeping **C** *Hotel Evim*, Cumhuriyet Meydanı, T2323536. Comfortable rooms with TV and telephone in a smart newly refurbished hotel, you should be able to negotiate a discount on the rather steep posted rates. **F** *Otel Nahita*, Terminal Caddesi, T2325366, 100 m from the *otogar*. Bit worn but decent enough rooms for price, en suite, balcony, TV and telephone as standard. **F** *Otel Murat*, Eski Belediye Yanı No 5, T2133978. The rooms in this centrally located place are a bit spartan but relatively clean, cheaper waterless rooms also available. **G** *Otel Star*, Istasyon Caddesi No 47, T2131645. A boarding house with basic waterless rooms, no breakfast.

Eating Niğde doesn't have anything approaching *haute cuisine* with kebabs and pide about
There are several small all that's on offer. **Cheap** *Saruhan*, Istiklal Caddesi, 200 m south of Atatürk Meydanı,
cheap pide & kebap a decent pide and kebap place in a renovated stone han. *Sultan Restaurant*, Istiklal
places opposite the Caddesi, a local favourite with reasonable soup, burgers and kebabs. *Boğaziçi*, oppo-
otogar if hunger strikes site the *Sultan Restaurant*, crowded at lunch time, döner, iskender and pide on offer.
while waiting for a bus

Tour agencies Sobek Travel, Istasyon Caddesi, Çeşmeli Sokak No 1, T2329151, in side street opposite the clock tower, agent for *Turkish Airlines*, also organize trekking holidays in the Aladağlar.

Transport **Adana**, 6 daily, 3 hrs, US$5. **Ankara**, 2 daily, 6 hrs, US$10. **Kayseri**, nearly every hr, 0600-2200, 90 mins, US$3. **Mersin**, 5 daily, 3 hrs, US$5. **Nevşehir** (via Derinkuyu), every hr, 1 hr, US$2. **Istanbul**, several evening buses, 12 hrs, US$18.

Directory **Airline offices** See tour agencies. **Banks** Banks with ATM are found on Bankalar Caddesi. **Post office** The PTT is on Bankalar Caddesi. **Tourist information** There is a Tourist Information Office on Istiklal Caddesi near the roundabout. Open 0830-1200, 1330-1730.

The Aladağlar

The Aladağlar, or Crimson Mountains, are a lofty massif of the eastern Taurus Mountains, 50 km to the east of Niğde. Turning off the Kayseri-bound highway you approach the range across a pastoral landscape of rolling hills covered with fields of wheat, barley, but above all potatoes irrigated by long plastic pipelines. Stands of upright poplar and orchards of fruit trees hide the villages dotting the countryside, and until early summer wild flowers add bright splashes of colour to this idyllic scene. The first view of the mountains from this direction is stunning, a row of jagged peaks centred on the towering 3756 m pyramid of the aptly named Demirkazık (Iron Spike). Boldly rearing up out of a wide undulating valley the Aladağlar are a tightly packed range of snow-streaked, rocky mountains scored by deeply incised valleys. Indeed, after such a dramatic introduction it's easy to believe that the range is one of Turkey's premier spots for trekking and climbing.

Ins and outs

Getting there The compact nature of the Aladağlar makes access, particularly from the Niğde-side, relatively easy. The tiny village of Demirkazık, in the shadow of its namesake mountain, is a popular starting point, giving good access to the northern and central mountains. Above the village and its apple orchards is the Dağ Evi (refuge), an unsightly concrete structure which provides food and lodgings for mainly Turkish trekkers and mountaineers. Camping is also possible in the rocky meadow behind the refuge. Access to the southern parts of the range, such as the Emli valley, is easiest from the village of Çukurbağ several kilometres further down the valley.

Çamardı dolmuş leave the local bus garage next to the Niğde *otogar* every 90 mins during the day. Except for a direct service at 1400, these dolmuş do not enter Demirkazık, instead passing along the main road 3 km away from the village, to Çamardı. Ask to be let-off at the clearly sign-posted side-road and then walk or hitch a lift. All dolmuş pass through Çukurbağ where there is accommodation available at the **F Şafak Pansiyon**, the owner Ali Şafak can arrange guides and is very knowledgeable about the range. For the return to Niğde, dolmuş leave Çamardı at 0700, 0900, 1100, 1200, 1330, 1515, 1630, and 1730, passing the Demirkazık turn-off about 20 mins later. There are also several buses a day from Adana and Kayseri to Çamardı.

On the other side of the range dolmuş depart for Yahyalı from the isolated villages of Barazama and Karpuzbaşı early weekday mornings, US$3, returning in the evening. Secure yourself a seat the night before as these are often packed to overflowing. To hire a minibus for the journey costs US$35. It's a rough 70 km ride to Yahyalı, which is served by regular buses to Kayseri.

When to go The trekking season is considered to be from Jun until Sep, although in a normal year you are likely to encounter snow on the high passes until mid Jun. Early on in the season there is also a greater chance of unsettled weather, though conditions in Aug becoming unbearably hot and many sources of water also dry up. Having taken all this into account late Jun and Jul present themselves as the best times to venture into the high mountains.

Whenever you go you should be properly equipped with boots, waterproofs, tent, cooker, provisions & waterbottle

The Aladağlar are a karstic limestone range with a characteristically dry landscape devoid of surface water for much of the year. On their northwestern flank, facing the Anatolian plateau, the mountains are stark and dramatic, their abrupt contours largely naked of vegetation. Further south and on the opposite side of the range, however, a cloak of pine forests softens things.

Sultansazlığı: bird paradise

Sultansazlığı is home to a huge diversity of animals and plants, though it's best known as a paradise for birds. Some 301 winged species have been identified in numbers that top 700,000 at certain times of the year. Such an impressive concentration birds are attracted to the 40,000 ha area due to the variety of ecosystems within the basin. Ducks and geese, white pelicans, pigmy cormorants, spoonbills, herons, egrets and marsh harriers frequent the fresh-water marshlands, while the reedbeds of saline Yay Gölü are a nesting ground for species such as the great flamingo, black-winged stilt, spur-winged plover and slender-billed gull. For stone curlew, black-bellied sandgrouse, lark and wagtail the surrounding scrubland is home.

The position of Sultansazlığı on important migration routes also contributes to the high species diversity. Some birds are summer migrants arriving to take advantage of the ideal breeding habitats available. Others fly south from northern latitudes in the Autumn to over-winter in the area, while a third group of birds are merely in transit, stopping briefly to stock-up their energy reserves before flying onwards to destinations in Europe and the Middle East.

A sejour in Sultansazlığı is not, however, without its risks. Added to the danger from natural predators such as foxes, jackals and pine-martins, in the past up to 300,000 eggs a year were collected for sale by villagers. The area was also threatened by a government plan to drain the lakes and marshes to make way for arable land, an ill-conceived plan that was thankfully stopped by a public outcry. The harvesting of cane from reed beds and nearby pumice mines disturb breeding birds, while the water level and salinity of several lakes have been altered by the diversion of water for farming. Sultansazlığı has received some official protection since becoming a national park in 1988, although the enforcement of bans on egg-collection and hunting are crippled by a lack of resources and man-power.

Buried beneath deep snow during the winter, snowmelt and spring rains nurture a burst of life in the alpine meadows, carpeting them with a profusion of wild flowers. Also rich in bird life, the area is home to many interesting species including the elusive caspian snow-cock, a rare bird which lives high-up in the rocky wastes of the range. If you're lucky you may spot one of the ranges indigenous large mammals, although sadly the number of wolves, jackals and ibexes has been greatly reduced by hunting. Thankfully the Aladağlar have been designated a national park and as such enjoy some degree of official protection. Fees (*US$1.50 per person per day*) are only collected at Demirkazık village. Make sure you are given a ticket.

Trekking routes

Mules are available for load carrying from all the trail-head villages. Enquire at the Dağ Evi in Demirkazık or *Şafak Pansiyon* in Çukurbağ.

Cimbar Canyon & Çağal Yaylası This route passes through the dramatic Cimbar Canyon, circling around the base of Küçük Demirkazık to the Çağal Yaylası, set in a spectacular amphitheatre of high rocky mountains. It is possible as a long, exhausting day-trip, however, it's much better to camp at Çağal Yaylası and give yourself time to explore the upper Cimbar Valley and soak-up the scenery. From here your options are limited with an unpleasantly steep pass giving access to the top of the Narpuz Valley, making possible a circumnavigation of the highest peak in the Aladağlar range. However, you may decide to return the way you have come, with several deviations possible on the way back.

1 To reach the beginning of the Cimbar Canyon follow the road past the Dağ Evi for about a kilometre. The canyon, with its soaring limestone walls, is heaven for rock-climbers and a very pleasant spot to explore particularly when the stream is running early in the year.

2 Continue up the canyon taking the right-hand option when it forks. The left-hand canyon also ends up in the upper Cimbar Valley, although it is considerably longer. The path weaves its way up the narrow gorge, emerging at its head after about 90 minutes.

3 From the top of the canyon you pick-up a path leading up the Cimbar Vadisi from Arpalık Yaylası. This climbs consistently over scree and rocky meadows for an hour to a narrow defile, through which it passes before dropping down to Teke Pınarı, a perennial spring and possible campsite. Fill-up your water bottles here as the upper Cimbar Vadisi is dry particularly later in the season.

4 The path then continues up the valley as it swings right around the base of Küçük Demirkazık. The limestone scenery at this point is very rugged, the

Aladağlar treks

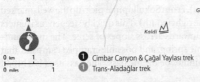

❶ Cimbar Canyon & Çağal Yaylası trek

① Trans-Aladağlar trek

precipitous mountainsides bristling with rocky spires like a gothic cathedral. After an hour the valley begins to open out rewarding your effort with views of the north face of Demirkazık and the other high peaks encircling the upper basin. There is an obvious campsite, 3½ to 4 hours above Demirkazık village, amongst the flower-filled meadows near the river and it makes an idyllic spot to spend the night.

5 A possible side-trip crosses the river and climbs-up towards the north face of Demirkazık. Near its base is a camp used by climbers attempting the huge perpendicular wall and a short way beyond is a broad scenic saddle between Demirkazık and Küçük Demirkazık to the north. The Apışkar valley descends steeply from the opposite side of this col, making a possible alternative, knee jolting, route down to the mid-section of the Cimbar Vadisi.

6 If you are intent on crossing the Demirkazık pass to the Narpuz Valley, a side valley heads southwest towards the col, which is at the bottom of the east ridge (left-hand skyline) of Demirkazık. Half-an-hour brings you to a small lake at the base of the col, with the east face of Demirkazık towering up on your right. From the lake, which dries-up later in the season, it is a 2½—hour slog up steep, unconsolidated scree to the pass.

7 The initial descent into the Narpuz is over huge slopes of scree, with a faint trail then leading down the valley bottom to the gorge, Narpuz Boğazı. Here the valley narrows to a rocky gorge which can be negotiated by scrambling down a series of rocky steps. Alternatively, a path of sorts stays high on the right, traversing above the gorge over steep slabs. About 20 minutes beyond these narrows (2½ hours from col) is a possible campsite at Kayacık Pınarı, although the campsite of Sokullupınar, beyond the last gorge, is less than an hour away.

Trans-Aladağlar (Sokullupınar to Karpuzbaşı)

The route is easy to follow being used regularly by muleteers & trekking parties, with several local trekking companies maintaining permanent camps along the route during the season

Crossing over the main ridge line of the central Aladağlar, this route passes through the rugged Yedi Göller basin, before descending the dramatic Hacer Valley to the forested eastern side of the range. The fascinating spectacle of huge waterfalls erupting from the strata of a steep mountainside at Karpuzbaşı, along with a couple of trout restaurants, makes for a fitting finale to the trek. Allow for a minimum of four days for the route, although there is plenty of scope for spending an extra day walking and scrambling around Yedi Göller.

The initial climb up to the Çelikbuyduran Pass is an arduous one involving over 1000 m of vertical gain. All but the most masochistic should consider hiring a mule to carry their bags at least to the top of the col (one day hire), or even beyond to Yedi Göller.

1 From beside the Dağ Evi in Demirkazık follow the jeep track up to the campsite of Sokullupınar (2½ hours), which is a series of meadows near the entrance to the Narpuz valley. There is also a slightly shorter path from Çukurbağ village leading up the Yalak Deresi past Yalak Köyü

2 The next day involves climbing up the Yalak Deresi, much of which is steep scree-slopes, to the Çelikbuyduran Pass (3450 m), before dropping down into the Yedi Göller basin (six hours). From Sokullupınar pick-up the well-marked trail heading over the rise to the right (south). This quickly steepens as it enters the Yalak Deresi, zigzagging upwards across slopes of scree. The main landmark of the ascent is a welcome spring, and possible cramped campsite, that emerges from the rocks, 45 minutes below the pass. The pass itself is a broad

col between the peaks of Kızılkaya (3725 m) and Emler (3723 m), the latter of which can be climbed easily in about 30 minutes for a spectacular view over the surrounding mountains. The cairned path then descends into the rocky wastes of the Yedi Göller basin, making its way in about an hour to a yayla and campsites near the rock tower of Direktaş. If you pass the summer encampment of Yörük herdsmen, there are several other pitches nearer the lake across from the base of Direktaş.

3 The trail passes the shell of an unfinished building, before dropping down in large steps into the Hacer Vadisi, its U-shaped profile the result of immensely powerful past glacial action. Once the valley bottom is reached the going becomes easier, with the view of distant forests to spur you onwards. Shortly after reaching the first stands of hardy pine (2½ hours), the path widens into a rough jeep track which continues through thickening forest towards Soğukpınar. Following a short ascent, where the valley turns abruptly to the right, the campsite is visible up a track on the right. Total time from Yedi Göller four to five hours.

4 Cut directly down from the campsite through rocky meadows to join the jeep track. After 30 minutes a path on the right is marked by cairns. Follow this path, faint at times, through lovely mixed forests down to where it meets the jeep track again and you have the first view of Barazama (1550 m) below. Cross the track and continue descending the path towards the village which is reached in about an hour. The villages facilities are limited to a tiny shop and café, but the inhabitants are friendly and you'll probably be offered a cup of tea.

5 If you camped at Soğukpınar then it will still be early enough to press-on to Karpuzbaşı and the waterfalls. Walk out of the village (south) and take the first track on the left, followed by a path on the right which leads you to the river. The path follows the river briefly before climbing away through stony fields, only to rejoin it again 45 minutes from the village at a wooden bridge and excellent swimming spot. Having crossed the bridge the path maintains its height on the forested mountainside and on reaching a fork take the left (upper) of the two choices. Two hours after leaving Barazama, the path drops down towards the river and there is a bridge on the right. Cross the bridge and follow the rough road for the last 30 minutes to the hamlet of Karpuzbaşı, with the waterfalls a short distance beyond. These make a fascinating spectacle, with a staggering volume of water pouring out from the cliff-face in a series of falls. There are several stands selling refreshments and camping is also possible, though it's not a particularly desirable spot. Much better to continue along the road, taking the first right which leads down to a small *mahalle* of houses. There beside the rushing torrent you'll find a basic pension and restaurant serving-up fresh trout. You could probably camp here too.

The Emli Valley

Located in the southern part of the Aladağlar, the scenery in the Emli Valley is some of the loveliest in the whole range. Vegetation softens the landscape lower down, while a chain of lofty snow-clad peaks popular with mountaineers rises-up above the high-alpine pastures. The easiest access to the valley is provided by a jeep track from the village of Çukurbağ, walkable in about two hours. From the end of this track, continuing up the valley for another three hours brings you to a campsite and good base for exploration of the upper valley at Akşam Pınarı (Evening Spring) Yaylası.

Trekking companies *Sobek Travel*, İstasyon Caddesi, Çeşmeli Sokak No1, Niğde, T2132117, F2324904, regular trekking programmes in the summer, *Bremer Tour*, Ahmet Paşa Caddesi, Örnek İş Merkezi, No 17/102, Kayseri, T(0352)2229946, F2328267, also have an office in Yahyalı, trekking and rafting trips in the Aladağlar.

Further reading **Books** *The Mountains of Turkey*, Karl Smith, Cicerone Press, descriptions of climbing and trekking routes. *The Aladağlar*, Ömer Tüzel, Cicerone Press, climbing and trekking routes, slightly more detailed. **Maps** There are no commercially available maps of the Aladağlar, though photocopied army charts and maps from the Turkish Mountaineering Federation do surface occasionally.

North Central Anatolia

The Selçuk architecture of Sivas; the pleasant riverside town of Amasya; the Hittite ruins of Hattuşaş or the picturesque Ottoman village of Safranbolu; the northern portion of central Anatolia has a very mixed bag of attractions. Though out-of-the-way and separated by miles of fairly empty and mountainous terrain they receive only a trickle of foreign tourists, with many of them on their way towards Samsun on the Black Sea coast or east to Erzurum.

Safranbolu

Phone code: 0372
Colour map 2, grid A1
Altitude: 350 m
Over 200 km N of Ankara

Picturesque Safranbolu is a tonic after the unattractive townscapes which dominate much of urban Turkey. A well-preserved snap-shot of the past, several hundred timber-framed Ottoman houses survive tucked away in the bottom of a valley. Forming what amounts to a living museum, many of these venerable timber and stucco residences have been restored over the last 25 years and pressed into service as atmospheric accommodation. The town has been attracting domestic tourists for some time, though apart from the expat community in Ankara, foreigners have been rather slow to cotton-on. Of course this is mainly because it's decidedly far from the main tourist centres. Though this is all the better for those that do make the effort, as Safranbolu has thus far managed to retain its charming atmosphere and wandering the narrow cobbled lanes between the old houses is still like slipping back in time.

Ins & outs
See page 531 for further details

Getting there With its growing popularity as a tourist destination, access to the town has much improved. Whereas buses approaching from Ankara used to terminate 10 km away in the grim industrial town of Karabük, from where you had to get a dolmuş, most services now make it all the way to Kıranköy, the modern part of Safranbolu. **Getting around** From the main street of Kıranköy dolmuş descend every 30 mins into Eski (Old) Safranbolu, a 5-min journey which is something akin to riding in a time machine, transported as you are from the concrete reality of contemporary urban Turkey into a period set of 19th-century provincial life.

History Although Safranbolu's origins are considerably more ancient, the town began to prosper during Ottoman times thanks to its position on an important corridor of trade north to the Black Sea. Wealthy landowners built solid wood and stucco mansions and graced the town with numerous public buildings. The workshops of the bazaar area were busy with craftsmen, and saffron, painstakingly gathered from autumnal crocuses which sprouted around the town, was an important local product. It is from this saffron, prized for its delicate flavour and colour, that the town derives its name.

These glorious days came to an end with the First World War and the establishment of the Turkish Republic, as Safranbolu lost the Greeks and Armenians who made-up almost a quarter of its population. Subsequently, many of the graceful mansions fell into disrepair, a state in which they remained for most of the century. Overlooked except by a few Turkish photographers and artists, it was not until the late 1970's that restoration work began on some of the buildings. Since then the towns potential for tourism has been realized, with many of the *konaks* returned to their original splendour and now serving as restaurants or hotels for visiting coach parties. Despite the changes brought by tourism, Safranbolu remains a living, breathing town where normal life manages to continue, as yet far from being overwhelmed by its new industry. Its designation as a World Heritage Site by UNESCO will hopefully aid its conservation.

Sights Although there are a handful of specific buildings worthy of attention, the most pleasurable thing to do is wander the cobbled streets soaking-up the ambience. Early evening is a particularly good time to explore the backstreets, when the setting sun bathes the cracked plasterwork and dark weathered beams of the houses in its warm, flattering light. For a good vantage point, climb up Hükümet Sokak from the main square to the former **Government building**. Sitting on the foundations of an earlier fortification, the once-grand building is now a sad burnt-out shell awaiting future development.

On your way up you will have passed the **Mumtazlar Konağı**, one of several show houses in town where for a small fee you can examine the carefully recreated interior and get an idea of the style and layout of a well-to-do 19th-century Ottoman household. ■ *0800-1730 daily, US$0.50*.

Back down at the main square stands the 18th-century **Kazdağlı Camii** and the **Cinci Hamamı**, topped unmistakably by domes covered with nipple-like glass protrusions which allow light to penetrate into the steamy baths below. Built in 1645 and recently restored, the baths have separate sections for men and women. ■ *0800-2300 daily, entry US$2.25, kese US$1*.

The narrow street beside the Cinci Hamamı leads down to the newly restored **Köprülü Mehmet Paşa Camii** (1662), with a right turn through its courtyard bringing you to the **arasta**, formerly the cobblers bazaar, but now lined with

Central Anatolia

Safranbolu

To Havuzlu Konağı, Kıranköy & Ankara

Meşçit Sokak

Former Government Building

Hükümet Sokak

Kazdağlı Camii

Dolmuş to Kıranköy

Cinci Hamamı

Mumtazlar Konağı

Arasta Sokak

Köprülü Mehmet Paşa Camii

İşbankası

Cinci Hanı

To Çiftlik Ev Pansiyen

To Kaymakamlar Evi & Hıdır'lık Parkı

To Kastamonu

N

0 metres 200
0 yards 200

To İzzet Mehmet Paşa Camii

■ **Sleeping**
1 Arasna Otel
2 Çarşı Pansiyon
3 Dedebağ Ahmetbey Konağı
4 Hatice Hanım Konağı
5 Otel Tahsin Bey & Paşa Konağı
6 Selvili Köşk
7 Teras

● **Eating**
1 Asiyan Köy Sofrası

2 İmren
3 Kadioğlu Şehzade Sofrası
4 Köşk Ocakbaşı
5 Nimet Lokantası

souvenir shops. The original tradesmen who occupied the arasta continue their trade in little workshops in the surrounding streets. Continuing down past the Köprülü Mehmet Paşa Camii you can't miss the imposing **Cinci Hanı**, sprouting numerous pointed chimneys from its roof. Built at the same time as the baths, the building is empty at present with plans afoot to turn it into a hotel.

Further down Manifaturacılar Sokağı is the **İzzet Mehmet Paşa Camii** and a picturesque area of largely unrestored houses, mostly occupied by local families who fill the cobbled alleys with the sounds of domesticity. Having explored this district, the street behind the Cinci Hanı climbs up past the **Kaymakamlar Evi**, a period show-house (*0800-1230, 1330-1730 daily except Mon, US$0.50*), to the **Hıdırlık Parkı**. Another scenic spot from which to overlook the town, there is a café and the tombs of several local notables on a wide terrace.

As you came down the hill from Kıranköy, you may have noticed the **Havuzlu Konak** about 500 m before the main square. This is a fine example of one of the summer residences scattered across the countryside which were occupied seasonally by Safranbolu's wealthy residents. It is now a comfortable hotel, though it retains characteristic features of these mansions such as the large courtyard pools which cooled the interior during the balmy days of summer.

Sleeping   **C** *Otel Tahsin Bey & Paşa Konağı*, Hükümet Sokak No 50, T7126062, F7125596. Cosy and comfortable rooms in 150-year old house, lots of modern trappings such as telephone, hairdryer and TV, for which you pay a premium, single room US$40. **C** *Havuzlu Asmalar Konağı*, Mescit Sokak, T7212883, F7123824. One of first konaks to open as a hotel, situated 500 m up the hill from the main square, summer mansion built around a traditional pool (*havuz*) though it's not for swimming, well-furnished and comfortable rooms with tiny bathrooms, good restaurant. Recommended, though you may prefer something closer to the centre. **C** *Selvili Köşk Hotel*, Mescit Sokak No 23, T7128646. Beautifully restored konak built in 1883 with many original features such as the magnificent carved wood ceilings, comfortable rooms with en suite. Recommended. **D** *Dedebağ Ahmetbey Konağı*, Karaüzüm Sokak No 3, T7123319. Quiet rooms in rambling old family house, shared bathrooms, again beautiful carvings on the ceilings and lovely cushioned sitting areas, authentic feel. Recommended. **D** *Hatice Hanım Konağı*, Naip Tarla Sokak No 4, T7128745, behind the Cinci Hanı. Assorted rooms in a renovated traditional house, all vary in size and shape, some have en suite others waterless. **E** *Arasna Otel*, Arasta Sokak, T7124170. Small rooms in centrally located restored house, noise from the bar downstairs may be a problem at the weekends. **E** *Hotel Teras*, Mescit Sokak No 4, T7251748. Simple well-priced rooms in a renovated house on the corner of the square, may be noisy, interesting features retained such as closet bathrooms. **F** *Çarşı Pansiyon*, Bozkurt Sokak No 1, T7251079. Small plain rooms, some simply with a mattress on the floor, singles are particularly diminutive. **F** *Çiftlik Ev Pansiyon*, Akçasu Mahallesi No 12, T7121970, 5 mins walk east from the square. Modern house but a warm family welcome, simple rooms with clean, shared bathroom, delicious *gözleme* made for breakfast. Recommended budget option.

Eating   **Midrange** *Köşk Ocakbaşı*, on main square, small place specializing in grilled meat
There are several good, reasonably priced restaurants in town, with many of the hotels & pensions also cooking simple evening meals if you wish   and kebabs, US$6 for 3 courses with a beer. *Kadıoğlu Şehzade Sofrası*, just past the Kazdağı Camii, popular with tour-groups, plenty of space inside or at tables in courtyard, specialities include kuyu kebabı (roasted lamb), şiş, saç kavurma, also choice of desserts, reasonable prices. **Cheap** *Nimet Lokantası*, tiny place opposite the Köprülü Mehmet Paşa Camii, tasty köfte (meatball) sandwiches, ready-prepared stews and soup, excellent value. *Asiyan Köy Sofrası*, Arasta Sokak, *köfte*, şiş kebap, *mantı* (ravioli-like dish served with yoghurt), *gözleme*, served at little tables. *İmren*, main square, mouth-watering display of lokum, helva and baklava, drinks served upstairs in café accompanied by soothing trickle of water in a little fountain.

Shopping

Safranbolu is well-known for its *lokum* (turkish delight) which can be bought in assorted boxes from Imren or any of the shops near Köprülü Camii. Also available is *yaprak helvası*, thin sheets of nougat separated by crushed walnuts. Locally produced saffron can be found in the shops near the Köprülü Camii. A tiny 1 gram packets will set you back about US$6, the high price reflecting its scarcity and the labour intensive harvesting techniques. The larger sachets contain much cheaper Iranian saffron.

Transport
The Ankara-Zonguldak railway passes through Karabük, but this is much slower than the bus

Dolmuş and belediye buses depart for Kıranköy and Karabük from the main square. The buses detailed below leave from the bus company offices around Sabri Artunç Caddesi, 100m west of the main roundabout, in Kıranköy. Ask for the 'otobüs yazıhane'. Ankara, 6 buses daily, 0500-1745, 4 hrs, US$6. **Bartın (Amasra)**, every 30 mins, 2 hrs, US$3.50. **Istanbul**, 4 daily, 7 hrs, US$10. **Kastamonu**, 4 daily, US$3.50, 2 hrs. **Trabzon**, 1 evening bus, 12 hrs, US$18.

Directory

Banks There is a small *İşbankası* with ATM at the bottom end of the arasta. There are lots more banks in Kıranköy. **Baths** See sights, Cinci Hamamı. **Post office** The small PTT is near the Cinci Hanı. **Tourist information** The tourist information office, T7123863, is in the arasta. Open everyday except Sun, 0900-1200, 1330-1700. The *Safranbolu Turizm Derneği* (Safranbolu Tourism Association), T7121047, also has an office on the corner of the main square.

The Hittite sites around Boğazkale

Around the modern-day village of Boğazkale lie the most impressive remains of the ancient Hittite empire which ruled much of Anatolia about 4,000 years ago. This barren area of brooding mountains scattered with outlying and fairly impoverished farming communities was once the core of the advanced Hittite civilisation which has left us with the extensive ruins of their capital Hattuşaş and the open-air temple of Yazılıkaya discovered nearby. Also in the area is Alacahöyük, another Hittite site of great significance.

*Phone code: 0364
Colour map 2, grid B3
Over 200 km to
the E of Ankara*

Ins and outs

By public transport access to the village of Boğazkale presents no real problems as it sits 21 km off the busy Ankara-Samsun highway, near the town of Sungurlu. Hourly direct buses depart from Ankara for Sungurlu (3 hrs, US$5) throughout the day; while you can make your escape on the regular Ankara-bound buses from Samsun or Amasya passing through the town. Dolmuş run between the bus-station in Sungurlu and Boğazkale regularly from 0715 to 1715, however, on Sundays this service is unreliable. From Yozgat there is no public transport to Boğazkale, although taxis make the 37 km journey for about US$18.

Getting there
A few travel agencies in Ankara may be willing to organize a tour to the area. Try Midas Tourism, Bestekar Sokak No 74/2, Kavaklıdere, 142/5943/44

Hattuşaş is spread over a large hillside to the south of Boğazkale, with the site entrance reached by passing up the villages main street and over a small bridge. A metalled road conveniently loops around the whole site taking-in all the main features. Without a car it is possible to walk around the area in about 3 hrs, although this involves some steep gradients. If you are feeling lazy you could accept a lift from one of the local farmers who hang around the entrance.

Getting around

Yazılıkaya is 3 km east of the village on the road towards Yozgat. Having looked around Hattuşaş, turning right outside the entrance brings you across a wooded valley to this road. Even at a very leisurely pace it's possible to see both sites on foot in a single day, possibly breaking for lunch in the village between.

Hattuşaş

Archaeological evidence has shown that the site was occupied a long time before the Hittites arrived in Anatolia by a shadowy race known as the Hatti. Assyrian traders established a commercial colony in the Hatti city around 1900 BC, however, within 200 years both this *kavrum* and the city were destroyed by a Hittite army. From the rubble rose the city of Hattuşaş, the new capital of the expanding Hittite Empire. During this period Hattuşaş was graced with public buildings, temples, palaces and artificial lakes, all surrounded by a 6 km long perimeter wall.

After a long period of hegemony in Anatolia, the Hittite Empire went into decline finally collapsing around 1200 BC. The site of Hattuşaş lay abandoned, to be partly reoccupied by the Phrygians some 300 years later. After this it slipped into obscurity, only to be rediscovered in 1834, becoming something of an enigma as archaeologists struggled to deduce its origins. The mystery was only solved with evidence from newly deciphered Assyrian cuneiform and Egyptian hieroglyphic texts, which referred to a people who lived in the 'Land of the Hatti'. Subsequent excavations at Hattuşaş by German archaeologists from 1910, unearthed over 10,000 cuneiform tablets, which when translated revealed details about all aspects of Hittite life.

The site

At the entrance local men will try and sell Hittite-style stone carvings to you or to offer their services as a guide. Many claim to have worked on the continuing archaeological excavations at the site & can be quite persistent

The first thing which strikes you about Hattuşaş, particularly if you're about to set-off on foot around the site, is its enormous size. Looking up at the huge expanse of tree-less hillside scattered with rocks, it is hard to create a mental image of this once-great city. The passage of 3,000 years has left little but stone foundations, however, there are several surviving features to give you an idea of its former scale and grandeur.

Once through the entrance the first remains are the foundations a large house, one of many which covered the slope above. Opposite are the huge limestone blocks which formed the base of the **Büyük Mabet**, (Great Temple) dedicated to the worship of the storm god Teshub and the sun goddess Hebut. It is easy to imagine how this massive structure took over 150 years to construct, finally reaching completion some time in the 13th century BC.

You pass into the structure through the remains of a ceremonial gateway as the Hittite King and Queen would have done, at the head of a large procession during religious festivals. At the heart of the temple was the sanctuary containing statues of the god and goddess surrounded by a large hall. Around the central hall were over 80 rooms, with the outer ones probably serving as archives and storerooms. Archaeologists deduced this from the large number of *pithoi*, large earthenware jars used for keeping produce, and cuneiform tablets found in these sections of the building.

From the Büyük Mabet the climb begins in earnest reaching a fork in the road after 350 m. Take the right-hand road which ascends steeply up to the crest of the ridge and the **Aslanlı Kapı**, (Lion Gate) one of eight gates which originally pierced the 6 km long city wall. Originally flanked by two large towers, the gate is guarded by a pair of stone lions to ward-off evil spirits and uninvited guests. The original carvings can be seen in the Museum of Anatolian Civilisation in Ankara.

Stretching southeast from the Aslanlı Kapı is a section of the city's outer defences. Taking advantage of the natural ridge-line, the wall was constructed on top of a 10-m high embankment and guarded by numerous towers.

Tablets tell the story

Clay tablets unearthed at Hattuşaş at the beginning of the last century, and then painstakingly deciphered by experts, have shed considerable light on the race who dominated Anatolia for nearly a thousand years and it now seems that the huge territorial extent of the Hittite empire was matched by its cultural sophistication.

As the realms of the Hittite Kings spread south and east across Anatolia, they instituted a feudal system to control their newly-won territory. At the top of the feudal pyramid was the Hittite priest-king who enjoyed absolute spiritual and temporal power and was worshipped as a deity. Poor communications and difficult terrain meant that a network of vassal rulers was established to govern in the king's name, though revolts and uprisings seem to have been common place. Also beneath the king sat an assembly known as the panku which also appeared to have wielded considerable power. A large bureaucratic class looked after the day-to-day administration of the empire.

Hittite society was further divided broadly between free citizens and slaves with both groups granted the right to own property and marry. Slaves, however, could be bought and sold, with many of the 200 statutes of the Hittite law code also distinguishing between the two groups.

They were governed by an extensive and, for its time, remarkably progressive body of civil and criminal law, many relating to marriage and agricultural matters. One law stated that the owner of a pig accidentally killed by a neighbour must be paid the cost of a replacement animal. Victims of crime were generally compensated through a system of fines levied against the criminal, with a 20 shekel fine for breaking a freeman's arm – though a similar offence against a slave only cost 10 shekels. The most serious criminal offences of bestiality, rape and treason carried the death penalty, though interestingly murderers were also fined.

In addition to their king the Hittites worshipped a confounding array of deities, many of them assimilated from other Anatolian peoples, though the pantheon's principal gods were the storm god Teshuba and the sun goddess Hebut. The gods were honoured through elaborate festivals, such as a Hittite new year held on the spring equinox, and animal sacrifices.

The road follows these defences to the **Yerkapı Kapı** (Earth Gate) also known as the Sphinx Gate after the two stone sphinxes that stood guard over it until they were carted off to museums in Istanbul and Berlin. This is the highest point of the defensive wall, a huge embankment faced with large rough cobble stones. Beneath it runs a 70 m tunnel constructed using a technique which predates the invention of the arch, known as the corbel arch. It is generally agreed that this entrance played some kind of ceremonial function and was not a means for soldiers to surreptitiously slip out of the city in the event of a siege. On the embankment above the tunnel and reached via a ceremonial staircase are the remains of the **Sphinx Gate**. This provides an excellent vantage point from which to survey the foundations of twenty-one **temple buildings** exposed by excavations on an artificially created flat area below. These all conformed to a similar plan, with the flat roofed chambers built around a central courtyard.

It is all downhill from here to the **Kral Kapı** (Kings Gate), another gap in the defensive wall, once guarded by representations of the god Teshub either side of the inner portal. The remaining sprightly-looking figure is a copy, to see the original you'll have to visit the Museum of Anatolian History in Ankara.

Further down the **Nişantepe** is an outcrop of rock into which a long Hittite inscription, believed to be a memorial to King Suppiluliuma II, is carved. On the other side of the road a path leads to the remains of the **Güney Kale** (South Fort) which was built by the Phrygians in the seventh century BC.

The path leads beyond the fort to a **cult chamber** containing a well-preserved relief of a warrior armed with a spear and sword, a bow slung over his shoulder. The right-hand wall is covered in equally well-preserved hieroglyphics. Mostly concerned with the contemporary achievements of the day, some parts of the final passage have led archaeologists to the conclusion that this was a symbolic entrance to the underworld.

From the Nişantepe you can look down on the **Büyük Kale** (Great Fortress), the fortified palace of the Hittite royalty. A flight of steps leads up to the summit of the naturally defendable outcrop from the road. Access to the palace was through a gate in this southwest corner, which gave onto a series of courtyards. The lower courtyards were occupied by servants and members of the royal household, while the imperial quarters were contained in the upper-most part of the citadel. ■ *0800-1730 daily. Joint ticket for Yazılıkaya and Hattuşaş US$1.50.*

Yazılıkaya

From 1500 BC Yazılıkaya, which translates as 'the Rock with Writing', served as an important religious complex at the centre of which is the largest known Hittite rock-sanctuary. This sanctuary consisted of two open-air chambers in a natural outcrop of rock, the walls of which are decorated with some of the most remarkable examples of Hittite carving ever found. Inscriptions at the site have added credence to the theory that it was the focus for celebrations marking the Hittite's principle religious festival at New Year, which fell on the spring solstice.

The site Arriving at the small car park in front of the site there may be a crowd of salesmen waiting to pounce on arriving coach parties. Having made your way through the mêlée proceed up the track past the rocky foundations of several temple buildings screened by a row of conifers on your left. There is a spring in the shade of some oak trees behind the ticket booth where you can refresh yourself and fill up your water bottle.

Follow the path into the larger (left-hand) chamber, the walls of which are decorated with long processions of figures marching towards the back of the cleft. The column on the left wall is made up predominantly of male gods, with the exception being three female deities hiding in the line, and that on the right is of goddesses. The gods are wearing conical headgear and shoes with curling toes which presumably were characteristic of the time, with the females sporting cloaks and flowing gowns. The rank of each male deity is denoted by the number of horns sprouting from its helmet, with the huge antler-like horns of the storm god Teshub showing his place as the principle Hittite god. Each figure is also identified by a hieroglyphic symbol carved above their outstretched arm. The two processions meet on the back wall where there are depictions of the storm god Teshub, standing atop the holy mountains Nanni and Hazzi, and his wife Hebut who is standing on a pair of panthers. Beside her is their son, Sharruma. Facing the back wall on a protrusion of rock is the well-preserved figure of King Tudhaliyas IV (1250-1220 BC) during whose reign the carvings were made. In his right hand he is holding above his head a winged sun-disc, a symbol of divine authority.

To the right of the large chamber a fissure leads into a second, smaller chamber, which was originally entered at its opposite end via a monumental gateway, now blocked by rockfall. Particularly well-preserved is a row of 12 gods armed with swords and wearing conical headgear marching in single-file. Opposite is the relief of a strange composite figure with a sword for its lower-body, two lions as its handle and topped by the head and shoulders of a man. Dubbed the 'Sword god', it is thought to be a representation of the Hittite god of the underworld, Neargal. Next to it is a depiction of King Tudhaliyas IV, the smaller of the two figures, being held tightly around the neck by the god Sharruma. ■ *0800-1730 daily. Joint ticket for Yazılıkaya and Hattuşaş US$1.50.*

D *Aşıkoğlu Hotel and Restaurant*, T4522004, F4522171, on the main road before the village. A favourite with tour groups so it can be crowded, most comfortable rooms in the village with en suite, also more simple doubles for US$20, a little over priced, the self-service restaurant has a utilitarian feel but serves tasty, reasonably priced food. **E** *Başkent Motel and Camping*, T4522189, F4522567, on the road up to Yazılıkaya. Similar rooms to the Aşıkoğlu and a good restaurant, camping and tent rental. Recommended. **E** *Kale Turistik Tesisleri*, T4522189, also overlooking the village on the road up to Yazılıkaya. Simple rooms with en suite, camping pitches. **G** *Hattuşaş Motel*, T4522013, on the main street before the village square. Plain rooms opening onto sitting area, some have balcony, cheaper waterless rooms, restaurant and carpet shop downstairs. Recommended budget option.

Sleeping
The hotels in Boğazkale are often booked-up with groups in the season, however, at other times of the year it is very quiet and you can probably get a good bargain

Amasya

Standing in a broad canyon beside the lazy waters of the Yeşilırmak River, Amasya is one of the most agreeable and interesting towns in all of Central Anatolia. It also has a considerable history with the grand rock-cut mausoleums staring-out over the town standing testament to its role as the capital of the Pontic Kingdom which rose to challenge Rome in the first century BC. From its time as an important Ottoman provincial centre and training ground for young princes, Amasya boasts a rich legacy of Islamic architecture. While on the river's northern bank survive the remnants of the town's historic civil architecture: a much-photographed line of wood-beamed houses enclosing a quiet district where a village-like atmosphere prevails. These attractions add-up to make Amasya far more than simply a place to break your journey to or from the Black Sea coast, with the town deserving a day or two of even the most rushed program.

*Phone code: 0358
Colour map 2, grid B4
Altitude: 392 m*

Getting there Close to the highway between Ankara and the Black Sea port of Samsun, Amasya is well-served by buses. There are also daily train services to Sivas and Samsun, although their progress is rather leisurely in comparison to the bus. **Getting around** The *otogar* is several kilometres northeast of the centre with regular dolmuş and belediye buses passing-by on the opposite side of the road, US$0.25, on their way in. A taxi costs US$3.50 into the centre. Once in the centre all the sights are within easy walking distance.

Ins & outs
See page 539 for further details

Amaseia, as it was originally known, first rose to prominence as the capital of the self-declared Pontic Kingdom set-up by the son of a Persian nobleman named Mithridates. It was a name that became widely known in the following three centuries, as the dynasty he established spread its control over much of Anatolia and his descendent Mithridates VI Eupator waged a series of bloody wars against the Romans. In 183 BC Amaseia lost its role as the seat of the Pontic kings to the newly captured port of Sinope, and with the subsequent Pontic defeat the town became part of the Roman province of Galatia-Cappadocia.

During Byzantine times, the town fell briefly to Arab invaders, becoming part of the Selçuk Empire after 1071. The medieval town was then ruled over by the Danışmendid, the Selçuks, the Mongols and the Eretnids, before falling to the Ottoman Sultan Beyazıt in 1391. As an Ottoman provincial capital, Amasya was the training ground for several sultans-to-be, subsequently

History

Central Anatolia

enjoying the benefits of generous imperial patronage. The results are still visible today in the rich architectural legacy that survives in the town. Something that you will certainly appreciate when the *ezan* (call to prayer) rings out from each of the mosques in the town, bouncing off the valley sides in a deafening cacophony.

Sights

Atatürk Meydanı with its large equestrian statue of Atatürk gazing out across the passing traffic to the river is found at the centre of town. This statue commemorates a famous speech made in Amasya by the nationalist leader and first president in the turbulent months leading up to the beginning of the War of Independence.

West of Atatürk Meydanı

The Sultan Beyazıt II Camii is 1 of the most beautiful mosques in Amasya

Flanking Atatürk Meydanı is the **Gümüşlü Camii**, a cream-coloured mosque built in 1326 of cut stone and much restored since. Walking west along Atatürk Caddesi about 100 m from the square is an old stone **bedesten**, the lofty interior of the four-domed structure still containing some shops. Across the road behind the Kileri Süleyman Ağa Camii, the **Taş Hanı** (1698), an Ottoman caravanserai, is home to small workshops despite its decrepit, crumbling state. From here the interesting spiral-fluted minarets of the **Burmalı Minare Camii** (The Spiral Fluted Mosque), a Selçuk structure built in 1242, are visible nearby.

Further west on Atatürk Caddesi, is the town's largest mosque, the **Sultan Beyazıt II Camii**. Set in well-tended gardens and flanked by a medrese and library containing over 20,000 volumes this mosque was built by Prince Ahmet in 1486. Have a look at the faded landscape painted onto the inside dome of the *şadırvan* (fountain) and the patterned faience and paintwork enlivening the multi-domed porch. Continue walking along Atatürk Caddesi to the archaeology museum (see below).

Amasya

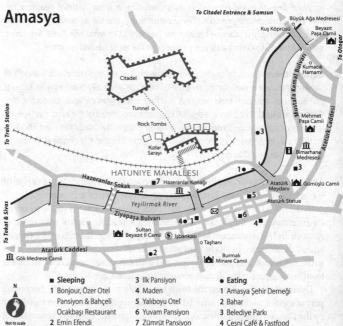

	Sleeping	3	İlk Pansiyon		**Eating**
1	Bonjour, Özer Otel	4	Maden	1	Amasya Şehir Derneği
	Pansiyon & Bahçeli	5	Yalıboyu Otel	2	Bahar
	Ocakbaşı Restaurant	6	Yuvam Pansiyon	3	Belediye Parkı
2	Emin Efendi	7	Zümrüt Pansiyon	4	Çeşni Café & Fastfood

Amasya is probably best known for the **Ottoman houses** which stand photogenically shoulder to shoulder along the north bank of the Yeşilırmak. Squeezed between these and the rocky acropolis, the narrow streets of **Hatuniye Mahallesi** are lined with many more 19th-century timber framed buildings. Saved from a fire which devastated the rest of the town in 1915, these buildings have only recently received the official protection that they deserve, with a handful being bought-up and restored as second-homes or pensions. The **Hazeranlar Konağı**, across the bridge from the post office, is one of the more handsome mansions. Built in 1872 by Hasan Talat Efendi, who served as minister of finance in the Ottoman government, the *konak* is now preserved as an ethnographical museum and art gallery. ■ *0900-1200, 1330-1730, US$1.25.*

Walking north from Atatürk Meydanı along Mustafa Kemal Bulvarı there is a row of interesting historical buildings. First up is the **Bimarhane Medresesi**, a treatment centre built in 1308 by the Mongol Sultan Ölceytu and recently restored. Used for the confinement of mental patients, the building was also a center of medical teaching and research. The intricately carved entrance portal is the most impressive feature of the building, demonstrating a strong continuity of style from Selçuk architecture. Instead of mental patients the medrese now hosts art exhibitions in its new role as Amasya's **Fine Art Gallery** (Güzel Sanatlar Galerisi). **North of Atatürk Meydanı**

Continuing north for about 200 m brings you to the **Kuş Köprüsu** (Bird Bridge), and the **Beyazıt Paşa Camii**, a solid looking early Ottoman mosque with the polychromatic marble arches of its domed porch supported by six thick square pillars. Opposite the bridge is the **Kumacık Hamamı**, a bath complex built in 1436, with what looks like glass jars protruding from the domed roof to allow light to penetrate into the steam room below.

Crossing the bridge, on the right is the eye-catching **Büyük Ağa Medresesi**, an octagonal building topped with pointed chimneys that was commissioned by the Chief Black Eunuch Hüseyin Ağa in 1438. It still functions as a Koranic school but you may be able to have a quick look inside.

The **Gök Medrese Camii** (Sky Seminary Mosque), named after the turquoise tilework on the octagonal topped tomb adjoining it, was built at the orders of the Selçuk governor in 1267. Now it houses the town's excellent museum, with interesting artefacts on display from the Bronze Age down through the Hittite, Urartian, Phrygian, Greek and Byzantine eras. These are complemented by various Selçuk and Ottoman exhibits including antique carpets and doors rescued from some of the Amasya's old houses. In the garden the Selçuk *kümbet* – or tomb – built for Sultan Mesut now contains some mummified bodies that were found during excavations at the Burmalı Camii in town. ■ *0830-1200, 1330-1730 daily except Mon. US$1.25. Getting there: A short distance beyond the Sultan Beyazıt Camii on the opposite side of Atatürk Caddesi.* **Archaeological & Ethnography Museum**

Staring out across the town from the cliffs of the acropolis mount, the rock-cut tombs of the early Pontic kings make a fascinating backdrop to the town, particularly when they're nocturnally flood-lit to very good effect. The sepulchres, of which there are fourteen in all, were hacked from the cliff wall and stand from three to over 10 m in height. One has been identified by an inscription as the last resting-place of Pharnacles I. **The Royal Tombs**

In front of the tombs stood the Kızlar Sarayı, or Palace of the Maidens, where the Pontic royalty are thought to have lived, however, little remains except the terrace wall and an Ottoman baths complex uncovered by recent excavations. A path to the left and tunnel, the rock worn smooth by feet over the centuries, gives access to two of the tombs, the furthest of which was used as a church in Byzantine times. Although visually more satisfying from a distance, proximity gives you the chance to appreciate the workmanship involved in cutting these structures from the cliff-side using only simple handtools.

Baring right from the top of the entrance stairway you'll find a café, toilets and a second group of smaller tombs. One of several tunnels is thought to descend to the river from here, giving access to water during times of siege. Peering inside many of the tombs you can see the evidence of grave robbers, who took hammer and chisel to the rockwalls in hope of finding treasure.

If you are feeling energetic and have a good head for heights, paths lead up the two prominent gullies from behind the Kızlar Sarayı, giving access to the castle above. Proper footwear should be worn for the ascent and care should be taken at several steep, rocky sections. Approximately halfway up the steep left-hand gully is another tunnel which bores down into the mountain. It is assumed that this also reached as far as the river, although now you can only carefully descend the weathered stairs about 30 m. It has also been suggested that these may have been blind tunnels used for the worship of deities of the underworld. ■ *0600-2000 daily. US$1. Cross the bridge opposite the post office into Hatuniye Mahallesi, follow signs under the railway line and up a set of stairs.*

The Citadel Crowning the double summit of the rocky acropolis, the citadel's origins pre-date the rise of the Pontic Kingdom. However, most of the extant ruins, parts of which have been rather unsympathetically reconstructed with new stone, date from much later. There are several chambers to explore and another tunnel which descends 150 steps into the bed-rock, but the main reason to make the climb is to enjoy the excellent view. From here you can follow the snaking course of the Yeşilırmak, while appreciating the strategic placement of the town in its tight valley, the steep sides of which now confine the growth of the modern town. ■ *Getting there: The Citadel is generally reached via a 2 km road which winds upwards from Zübeyde Hanım Caddesi about 500 m beyond the Büyük Ağa Medresesi. You cannot rely on there being a signpost, however, the left turn is 50 m before a flour factory with a large blue roof. For mountain-goats the steep paths up the gullies above the Kızlar Sarayı give much faster access, although it is probably then best to descend by the road.*

Essentials

Sleeping Amasya has a reasonable choice of accommodation including 2 very nice guest-houses in restored 19th-century mansions, both offering comfortable, idiosyncratically furnished rooms. There are several very cheap but much less atmospheric hotels on Ziya Paşa Caddesi in a small square facing the river.

B *Büyük Amasya Oteli*, T2184054, F2184056. Ugly concrete building on west bank of river, aspiring to luxury but the rooms are pretty average, all have en suite balcony, TV and telephone, on-site restaurant. **D-E** *İlk Pansiyon*, Hitit Sokak No 1, T2181689, opposite the tourist information kiosk. Armenian mansion lovingly restored by local architect Ali Yalçın, very atmospheric, all rooms are furnished and priced differently, some sleep up to 5, many original features preserved, meals served in leafy courtyard with very pleasant atmosphere, breakfast US$3, evening meal US$8. Booking ahead is recommended as it's a very popular. **D** *Emin Efendi*, Hazeranlar Sokak No 73, T2120852, F2121895. Recently restored 200 year-old Ottoman house overlooking the river, quiet location and loads of atmosphere, some rooms have river view, breakfast (US$3) and evening meals eaten in small courtyard. Recommended. **E** *Yalıboyu Oteli*, Ziyapaşa Bulvarı No 19/D, T2187029. Bright but fairly spartan rooms with TV, telephone, some have a view of the river and tombs but you can do better for the money. **E** *Hotel Maden*, Mustafa Kemal Paşa Caddesi No 5. This 2-star place is nothing exciting, but has bright, clean rooms though on the small side, en suite, TV, telephone, on-site restaurant. **E** *Yuvam Pension*, Atatürk Caddesi No 24/1. Guestrooms in an apartment block on the main street which is owned by a local chemist, clean, simple, use of kitchen and roof terrace, shared bathroom, rooms on top are quieter and have view. Recommended. Also **E** *Yuvam Pension 2*. Larger, quieter rooms in a residential house with garden for which you pay a little extra, very homely sitting area and kitchen, shared bathroom, large balcony, camping in the garden, tents available, contact *Yuvam Pension* on Atatürk Caddesi and someone will take you to this place. Recommended. **F** *Zümrüt Pansiyon*, Hazeranlar Sokak No 28, T2123554. Conspicuously modern block in the old quarter, functional rooms with and without shower closet, use of kitchen, roof terrace with unobstructed view of tombs. **G** *Özer Otel Pansiyon*, Ziya Bulvarı, Rüzgarlı Sokak No 1, T2181108. Has a slight edge over the other cheapies, nonetheless very bare rooms with shared bathroom. **G** *Hotel Bonjour*, Ziya Bulvarı No 35, T2184503. Basic waterless rooms, shared toilet is not the cleanest.

Midrange *Büyük Amasya Hotel Restaurant*, you could try this for a reasonably priced meal overlooking the river, *meze*, meat dishes and kebabs are on the menu, alcohol served. *Amasya Şehir Derneği*, situated in the 'Öğretmen Evi' (Teachers' Guesthouse), an ugly concrete building in a wonderful position across the river from the main square, selection of meze, ready-prepared dishes and grills, very reasonably priced and alcohol is served. **Cheap** *Adana Ocakbaşı*, Mustafa Kemal Paşa Caddesi, tiny place doing very cheap and tasty şiş and Adana kebabs. *Bahar Restaurant*, in alley next to Tokat Seyahat Office on Mustafa Kemal Paşa Caddesi, excellent selection of dishes including grilled meat, lahmacun and pide, also serves draught Efes, unaccompanied women travellers may not feel very comfortable here. *Bahçeli Ocakbaşı*, Ziya Bulvarı, in a small plaza facing the river, grilled meat, kebabs and steam-tray food, tables outside. *Belediye Parkı*, a riverside tea-garden reached across the bridge from the main square. *Çeşni Cafe and Fastfood*, Ziya Bulvarı, also in the small plaza, a modern place popular with students, pizza, köfte, also vegetarian dishes such as lentil and bean salads, also has outside tables in the summer. *Yayla Pizza*, İğneci Baba Sokak, in the road behind the Yalıboyu Hotel, pizza along with a huge variety of different pide and kebabs.

Eating
There is a row of ice-cream & cake shops on Ziya Paşa Caddesi near the Yalıboyu Hotel

Art galleries *Hazeranlar Konağı*, Hazeranlar Sokak, restored Ottoman *konak* beside the river, exhibits of local artists work.

Entertainment

Bus There are bus company offices on Atatürk Caddesi. **Ankara**, nearly every hr, 5½ hrs, US$7. **Istanbul**, evening buses, 10 hrs, US$15. **Kayseri**, several daily, 8 hrs, US$12. **Nevşehir**, 1100, 8 hrs, US$14. **Samsun**, at least every hr, 2 hrs, US$3.50. **Sivas**, 4 daily, 4 hrs, US$8. **Tokat**, 0900-1700, every 2 hrs, 2 hrs, US$3.50. **Trabzon**, 4 daily, 8 hrs, US$12.

Transport

Banks Banks with ATMs can be found on Atatürk Caddesi. **Baths** *Kumacık Hamamı*, built in 1436, relax in historic surroundings, opposite Kuş Köprüsü, Men: Sat-Sun, 1100-2400, Weekdays: 1700-2400, Women: Mon-Fri, 1100-1700. US$3 entry and assisted wash. **Communications Post office**:The PTT office is on Ziya Paşa Caddesi. **Internet**: There is no internet café at present in the town, but this is bound to change very soon. Try asking one of the town's many students. **Tourist information** On Mehmet Paşa Caddesi, near the main square. Open, summer, Mon-Fri, 1000-1200, 1400-1800, weekends, 1300-1800.

Directory

Central Anatolia

Tokat

Phone code: 0356
Colour map 2, grid B4
Altitude: 623 m

Sitting beneath a rocky castle-topped crag, Tokat is another central Anatolian town that history has left with a rich heritage of Islamic architecture. For the historically inclined this is also where Julius Caesar spoke the immortal words 'Veni, vidi, vici' (I came, I saw, I conquered) after a famous victory nearby, although disappointingly any tangible evidence of the man or his times is now deeply buried beneath the accumulated silt washed down from the eroded mountains. Present-day Tokat is a fairly unassuming and largely modern provincial centre, although some atmospheric, tumble-down neighbourhoods do still exist. Roughly equidistant between Sivas and Amasya, the town is a good place to break your journey, possibly staying overnight if your interest in mosques, medrese, tombs and caravanserais, has not yet been sated.

Ins & outs

See page 542 for further details

Getting there There are regular buses to Amasya, Sivas and other more distant destinations from the small *otogar*. **Getting around** It's a 15-min walk into the centre of town from the *otogar*; turn left out of the bus station and walk up to the roundabout, where a left turn onto Gaziosmanpaşa Bulvarı will lead you into town. A taxi is about US$2. Once in the centre all the sights and services are within walking distance.

History

Tokat enters history as an important stronghold of the Pontic Kingdom, with its citadel keeping watch over the approaches to the religious complex of Comana Pontica, 8 km to the north. Many battles of the Mithridates Wars were fought in the vicinity, and it was here that the legions of Julius Caesar finally extinguished any hope of an independent Pontic Kingdom by defeating Pharnaces I in 47 BC. Byzantine times were equally turbulent for the town, which was frequently attacked by marauding Arabs. Under Danişmendid rule a modicum of peace returned, only to be shattered again by the Mongol wave which swept across Asia Minor in the 12th century. The town was admitted into the Ottoman Empire by Sultan Beyazıt in 1392, although it had to endure conquest by the forces of Tamerlane before peace and stability could finally prevail.

Once Ottoman rule was established the town prospered, benefiting from its position on the east-west trade routes and its productive agricultural hinterland. The large Armenian population was particularly active in the mercantile and commercial life of the town up until the pogroms of the early 20th century.

Sights

The historic buildings are currently undergoing an extensive restoration programme sponsored by the Ministry of Culture. By the time you arrive they should be in better shape than in the past

Coming into town on Gaziosmanpaşa Bulvarı on the right is the **Sümbül Baba Türbesi**. Built in the 13th century it's now a rather weird sight with a house of much later vintage incongruously built on top of it. A short distance beyond a sidestreet on the left leads down to the **Burgaç Hatun Türbesi**, which is a state of advanced decrepitude at present but should improve with the on-going restoration work.

Walking onwards into the centre of town you pass the museum housed in the Selçuk Gök Medresesi (see below) and a large Ottoman caravanserai, the **Taşhanı**, just beyond. Built in 1631 this impressive stone caravanserai continues to fulfil a commercial role in the town with two floors of small workshops, still busy with artisans and traders, surrounding the pleasant courtyard. The **bazaar area** of narrow streets behind the caravanserai is also interesting to explore, with the tiny shopfronts displaying rows of shiny copper pots and pans and many other goods besides.

Just before reaching Cumhuriyet Alanı, opposite the Ali Paşa Hamamı, unmistakable with its domed roof covered in glass bulbs to let light into the steam-filled interior, the **tomb of Vezir Ali Paşa** is located in a small stone building with a glass dome in its roof. This dome allowed sunlight to shine onto the walls of the türbe, acting as a solar clock by which to tell the time for prayer.

Turning up the road which runs past the Ali Paşa Camii brings you along **Sulu Sokak** into what was the main bazaar area during Ottoman times. The streets are peppered with historical relics in the form of fountains, tombs, medrese and hans. Also in the backstreets, many characterful but crumbling timber-framed houses have survived in the shadow of the castle.

Several hundred metres beyond Cumhuriyet Alanı stands the **Latifoğlu Konağı**, a carefully restored 19th-century mansion which is open to the public. The interior recreates the style and atmosphere of a wealthy household of the times, with lavish decoration and exquisite furnishings. ■ *0900-1200, 1330-1700 daily except Mon. US$0.75.*

Tokat museum

The museum occupies one of the town's most famous historical buildings, the **Gök Medresesi** (Sky Seminary), named after its vivid turquoise tiles. Only a few of these now remain on the walls of the inner courtyard and approaching the building you may be forgiven for thinking that the seminary has sunk, with the entrance now well below the level of the street. In fact, the reverse is true as erosion of the surrounding hillsides has caused a gradual accumulation of material washed down over the centuries.

The medrese was constructed in the late 13th century by the Selçuk Emir Pervane Süleyman, who used the title Pervane (Butterfly) to denote his role as the Sultan's chief advisor. There is a türbe in one corner of the seminary, which contains 20 graves, one of which probably belongs to Pervane. Later during Ottoman times the medrese functioned as a hospital, before assuming its latest role as home for a well-stocked ethnographic and archaeological collection. Some of the highlights of the collection are displays explaining the local craft of making *yazmalar*, patterned cloth created by hand using wood-block prints. Also on show are antique clothing, weaponry and various unusual artefacts rescued from the churches of the area. ■ *0830-1230, 1300-1730 daily. US$1.25. The museum is on Gazi Osmanpaşa next to the Taşhan.*

Sleeping

B *Büyük Tokat Oteli*, T2281663, Demirköprü Mevkii, reached by crossing the river at the roundabout near the bus station and turning left, 1 km. A comfortable 4-star hotel, facilities include swimming pool. Recommended despite inconvenient position. **B** *Yeni Çınar Otel*, Gaziosmanpaşa Bulvarı No 2, T2140066. Newly opened, clean, modern rooms with en suite, TV, telephone and minibar, large family rooms available, most comfortable rooms in town. Recommended. **E** *Hotel Gündüz*, Gaziosmanpaşa Bulvarı No 200, 12141278, about 500 m from the centre. Nondescript place but comfortable looking beds, rooms have en suite shower, TV and telephone. Recommended. **E** *Hotel Taç*, Gaziosmanpaşa Bulvarı, T2141331, opposite Taşhanı. Very average rooms with TV, telephone, small shower. **E** *Hotel Çamlıca*, Gaziosmanpaşa Bulvarı No 86, T2141269, F2122899. Plain rooms with TV, telephone, old fittings in the bathroom. **F** *Çağrı Hotel*, Gaziosmanpaşa Bulvarı No 200, T2141278. New hotel with decent rooms with shower. Recommended. **F** *Belediye Oteli*, Gaziosmanpaşa Bulvarı No 153, T2128983. Next to the Taşhanı which is run by the municipality, a bit worn but passable budget option, waterless rooms also available for US$12, but may be noisy as they are at the front the street, discounts available.

Eating

The local speciality is Tokat kebabı, a slight variation on a well-known theme, which consists of chunks of lamb oven-roasted with peppers, tomatoes, garlic & spices

Murat Restaurant, next to Burgaç Hatun Türbesi, large smart dining room which is very popular at lunch, simple choice of ready-prepared dishes and grilled meat. *Zehra Ana Restaurant*, Cumhuriyet Alanı, next to belediye building, excellent place for a snack with very reasonably priced *gözleme* – pancakes filled with potato or cheese – and fresh, creamy *ayran* served at low tables. *Otel Yeni Çınar Restaurant*, Gaziosmanpaşa Bulvarı, a smart newly-opened place beneath the hotel of the same name, serves grilled meats and *kebabs* including the local speciality. *Şanlıoğlu*, Gaziosmanpaşa Bulvarı, a locally recommended pide and kebabs restaurant across from *Otel Yeni Çınar*.

Shopping Tokat is well-known for its copperware and for the production of *yazma*, colourful scarves printed with wooden stamps. The traditional centre of *yazma* production has recently moved from the venerable Yazmacılar Hanı in the old bazaar to a site on the Amasya road near the edge of town and reached by 'Sanayi' dolmuş from Osmanpaşa Bulvarı. Ask for the *yazmacılar*.

Transport **Bus** Amasya, 6 daily, 1½ hrs, US$3.50. Istanbul, several daily, 12 hrs, US$17. Samsun, 7 daily, 0900-2200, 4 hrs, US$8. Sivas, every hr from 0730, 1½ hrs, US$3.50. Trabzon, 3 daily, 10 hrs, US$16.

Directory **Banks** *İşbankası* and other major banks are on Gaziosmanpaşa Bulvarı near the centre. **Baths** You can't miss the large *Alipaşa Hamamı*, Cumhuriyet Alanı, built in 1572, separate male and female baths, US$3. **Post office** The PTT is on the west side of Cumhuriyet Alanı. **Tourist information** The tourist office is run by helpful Mr Erdoğan Horasan, who can organize local tours of any description and arrange for visitors to stay with local families. Find him in the kiosk next to the Taşhanı, or in his tiny office on the 2nd floor of the Taşhanı. No set opening hours.

Sivas

Phone code: 0346
Colour map 2, grid B5
Altitude: 1285 m

Stranded on the high Anatolian plateau, Sivas is a modern, rapidly growing city with a conservative god-fearing population of the central Anatolian mould. Winters are severe while after the brief green burst of spring the city seems marooned in a dun-coloured sea of desolate mountains. However, in the heart of the city is a surprisingly vibrant shopping district and a cluster of fine Islamic buildings raised when Sivas was an important trading centre and Selçuk town. These impressive monuments certainly justify a visit by anyone with a particular interest in Selçuk architecture. In the more recent past, the town hosted the Sivas Congress which was one of the defining events in the difficult birth of the Turkish Republic.

Ins & outs
See page 545 for further details

Getting there Sivas sits on important east-west lines of communication with buses and trains calling-in on their way to and from eastern Anatolia. **Getting around** The bus terminal is on the Ankara-Erzurum highway with dolmuş passing behind the building on the road near the 5-a-side football pitch into the centre. From the station catch any bus from outside on İnönü Caddesi, US$0.25. A taxi from the bus station into the centre costs about US$3. Once in the centre sights, hotels and restaurants are within walking distance.

History Despite its Hittite origins, it's not until Roman times that we know anything about Sivas. Sebasteia, as the city was then called, gained importance as a staging post on the caravan routes which crossed the empire. However the town really flourished with the arrival of the Selçuks in 1071 enjoying generous royal patronage as seen by the many fine public buildings which grace the place to this day. In common with other cities of the region, the Middle Ages were a time of reoccurring upheaval as wave after wave of foreign invaders crashed over the town. The final blow came in 1402 when the forces of Tamerlane overwhelmed the city's defences, razing it to the ground and massacring all its people. After this cataclysm, Sivas recovered slowly, becoming a fairly inconsequential provincial backwater in the Ottoman Empire.

However, as the site of the Sivas Congress held by Atatürk in 1919, the city has an important place in the history of the founding of the Turkish Republic. This was the first meeting of nationalist delegates from across the country, who under the leadership of Atatürk set-up a *de facto* government to rule over Anatolia. Since independence Sivas has become an increasingly industrial town, benefiting from its position on the national road and railway network. Also a conservative town, a gruesome incident occurred in 1993, when a group of radical muslims attacked a hotel in which the left-wing journalist Aziz Nesin and others attending a cultural festival in the city were staying. The crowd, enraged by the publication of Salman Rushdie's *'Satanic Verses'* and anti-religious comments made by Nesin, set fire to the hotel killing 37 people. It was an isolated outburst of religious violence and something the towns inhabitants try to forget.

Sights

The city's rich legacy of Selçuk architecture is conveniently clustered in and around a small municipal park beside Konak Meydanı which is filled with strolling families at the weekends. Nearest the junction is the **Bürüciye Medresesi** which dates from the period when the Mongol Ilkhanid dynasty ruled over the remains of the Selçuk Empire. Today, the theological school houses a rather sparse collection of archaeological artefacts, though the pleasant courtyard café and local carpet sellers are a much more interesting proposition.

Also within the park is the **Şifaiye Medresesi**, built as a medical centre by the Selçuk Sultan Keykâvus I in 1217 and used as a hospital up until 1916. Documents have revealed that medical practices used in the hospital in Selçuk times were remarkably progressive and included music therapy and hypnotism. Today, the doctors and patients have been replaced by stalls selling handicrafts such as leather goods and carpets, along with another café. The founder of the institution is buried in the small *türbe* to the right of the entranceway which is partially covered in beautiful faience work.

Just to the west of the Şifaiye Medresesi is the **Çifte Minare Medresesi** built in 1271 by an Ilkanid *vizier*. Only the typically impressive entrance portal embellished with ornate carving and the twin minarets – constructed of brick and picked-out with small blue tiles – which give the building its name, 'Seminary of the Twin Minarets', have stood the test of time. The rest of the structure lies in ruin.

Sivas

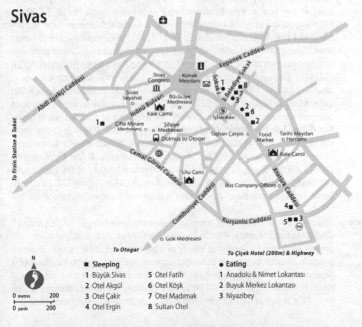

N

0 metres 200
0 yards 200

■ Sleeping		● Eating
1 Büyük Sivas	5 Otel Fatih	1 Anadolu & Nimet Lokantası
2 Otel Akgül	6 Otel Köşk	2 Buyuk Merkez Lokantası
3 Otel Çakir	7 Otel Madımak	3 Niyazibey
4 Otel Ergin	8 Sultan Otel	

South of the park on Cemal Gürsel Caddesi stands the city's oldest mosque the **Ulu Cami**, or Great Mosque. This plain building began life in 1197 with the recently added corrugated iron roof punctuated by numerous chimneys adding nothing to its charm. Inside, the rectangular hall is exceptional only for the rows of pillars supporting the low ceiling.

Beyond the Ulu Cami a right turn on Cumhuriyet Caddesi brings you after about 200 m to the **Gök Medresesi** (1271), a two-storey seminary built by Sahip Ata Fahrettin Ali, a benevolent Selçuk grand vizier whose other commissions grace Konya and Kayseri. The building is an outstanding specimen of Selçuk architecture with a dizzying mass of ornate carving – complex geometric and flowing floral patterns – around its imposing entrance portal. Rich decorative tilework in a variety of colours abounds, though the dominant shades are blue and turquoise giving the seminary its name, Gök meaning 'sky' in Turkish.

Sivas Congress & Ethnography Museum The museum is divided between an engaging collection of antique *kilims*, embroidery and various other bits-and-pieces on the ground-floor and the historic meeting hall above. Formerly an Ottoman-era secondary school, the hall that was commandeered for the Sivas Congress is furnished with wooden desks on which are displayed vintage snap-shots of the delegates who took part. Atatürk's bedroom and the vital telegraph cableroom, his link to the nascent independence movement, are also preserved as they were over 75 years ago. ■ *0830-1200, 1330-1730 daily except Mon. No fee. Located on İnönü Bulvarı across from the Kale Camii. The entrance is at the rear of the building.*

Essentials

Sleeping **B** *Büyük Sivas Hotel*, İnönü Bulvarı, T2254762, F2252323. Plushest place in town, comfortable rooms with en suite, TV and telephone, also a restaurant and bar – a rare species in this conservative town. **D** *Otel Madımak*, Eski Belediye Sokağı No 2, T2218027, reasonable with comfortable rooms equipped with small en suite, TV and telephone, the posted prices are a bit stiff so you try bargaining. **D** *Otel Köşk*, Atatürk Caddesi No 7, T2211150. Reasonable rooms with small en suite, TV and telephone, noisy in the front rooms. **E** *Sultan Otel*, Eski Belediye Sokak No 18, T2212986, F2219346. Much better value place with pleasant rooms with clean en suite. Recommended. **F** *Otel Akgül*, Atatürk Caddesi No 17, T2211254. Centrally located so expect some noise in the front rooms which are simply furnished with TV and television, waterless doubles for US$14, singles for US$8. **F** *Otel Fatih*, Kurşunlu Caddesi No 22, T2234313. Once you get past the hideous plastic flowers in reception the rooms, clean with en suite, TV and telephone, aren't bad, no breakfast. Recommended. **F** *Otel Çakır*, Kurşunlu Caddesi No 20, T2224526, F2218940. Passable rooms with en suite but more old-fashioned than the *Otel Fatih*, TV, telephone as standard but no breakfast. **G** *Yeni Belediye Terminal Oteli*, Yeni *Otogar* Yanı, T2261909. Next to the *otogar* this modern multi-story place has very characterless rooms with en suite shower, convenient for catching an early bus though, breakfast extra **G** *Otel Çiçek*, Atatürk Caddesi, Kepçeli Mevkii, T2215667, out at the far end of Atatürk Caddesi, basic rooms with old furniture, no breakfast. **G** *Otel Ergin*, Atatürk Caddesi No 80, T2212301. Seen better days but this is the cheapest place in town with basic waterless rooms.

Eating
You won't go hungry in Sivas but the options are limited to kebabs, pide & other standard fare

Niyazibey, Eski Belediye Sokak, soups and kebabs including yogurt-topped *iskender*. *Büyük Merkez Lokantası*, Atatürk Caddesi, near *Hotel Köşk*, bustling place with prompt service and a very good variety of ready-prepared dishes, soup, lahmacun and pide, all eaten beneath a sparkling chandelier. You could also try the *Hotel Köşk Restaurant* for something marginally more upmarket. There are a number of very cheap restaurants behind the PTT on Sokak 1: *Anadolu* and *Nimet Lokantası* are the best of the bunch at the moment serving up ready prepared dished and kebabs.

The protective pooch

The kangal köpeği *is a celebrated breed of working dog raised in the mountainous rangeland around the small town of Kangal. Bred to protect the flocks from roving packs of wolves or bears, these powerfully built dogs stand about waist high against an average sized man and weigh up to 60 kg. They typically have a short, sandy coloured coat with a black muzzle and ears, and a dusting of white fur on their chest. Naturally intelligent and good-natured animals, their instinct to protect is strong, as anyone who's had the misfortune of coming between a kangal and his flock will vouch for. With ears docked close to their heads and sporting leather collars with huge metal spikes* *they're an intimidating sight indeed.*

A distant cousin of the snow-white Kuvasz sheep-dogs of Hungary, kangals came to the attention of international breeders about 30 years ago. They've also recently made an appearance – minus the spiked collars – in the cities of western Turkey as family pets and popular fashion accessories. However, the kangal's status as Turkey's 'national breed' was confirmed by its appearance on a postage stamp issued by the PTT. Although no official kennel club exists, the government has established several breeding stations around the town of Kangal and the export of kangals now requires a license.

Sivas Seyahat, Istasyon Caddesi No 50, Yıl Sitesi 7-8, off İnönü Bulvarı. Local *Turkish Airline agents*. **Tour agencies**

Bus The *otogar* is well served by buses calling in en-route for destinations further east and west, including: **Amasya**, 4 daily, 4 hrs, US$7. **Ankara**, hourly, 6 hrs, US$10. **Divriği**, several daily, 3½ hrs, US$5. **Diyarbakır**, several daily, 9 hrs, US$12. **Kayseri**, hourly, 3½ hrs, US$5. **Erzurum**, several daily, 9 hrs, US$13. **Tokat**, every 2 hrs, 2 hrs, US$3.50. **Train** *Doğu Ekspresi*, passes through en-route for Erzurum and Kars everyday at 0545, 14 hrs; returning en-route for Istanbul via Kayseri and Ankara at 2345, 22 hrs. *Van Gölü Ekspresi*, passes through en-route for Malatya and Elazığ at 1915 on Mon, Wed and Sat, 9 hrs; returning at 0015, Tue, Thu and Sat en-route for Istanbul via Kayseri and Ankara, 23 hrs. *Güney Ekspresi*, passes through en-route for Diyarbakır at 1915 on Tue, Thu, Fri and Sun, 12 hrs; returning en-route for Istanbul via Ankara at 0015 on Mon, Wed, Fri and Sun, 23 hrs. **Transport**

Airline offices See tour agencies. **Banks** Banks with ATMs are on Atatürk Caddesi. **Baths** *Tarihi Meydan Hamamı*, Dikilitaş Caddesi No 39, just off Atatürk Caddesi in market area, newly restored Selçuk baths, US$3 for complete wash. **Post office** The PTT is on Konak Meydanı. **Internet** *Speed Internet Café*, on street behind the şifaiye Medresesi, US$1.50 per hr. **Tourist information** In the *Vilayet* building on Konak Meydanı. 0900-1700 daily except Mon. **Directory**

Surrounded by dry rolling hills, 90 km south of Sivas, Kangal is a small market town which is famed for its celebrated breed of sheep dog the *kangal köpeği* (see box). Nearby is the **Balıklı Kaplıca**, a most unusual hot-springs complex which has become the focus of a pilgrimage for suffers of the distressing skin disease psoriasis. Those afflicted by the disease immerse themselves in pools where several types of small resident fish nibble away at the dead and diseased skin. A cure involves wallowing in the water, which also contains beneficial minerals, eight hours a day for a period of three weeks. The centre, T4691151, F4573037, has several types of accommodation from simple chalets to reasonable hotel rooms, all of which are in great demand. ■ *Getting there: Dolmuş run every 30 mins from the main roundabout in Kangal to the springs.* **Kangal**

Divriği Lost in the rugged mountains to the southeast of Sivas, a trickle of visitors arrive in the small market town of Divriği each year to inspect a pair of buildings which have been designated as a World Heritage Site by UNESCO. The **Ulu Cami** and the adjacent **Darüşşifa** were built at the orders of the local potentate Ahmet Şah in 1228, and have both recently been carefully restored. The Ulu Cami was constructed as a place of worship in an enthusiastic Selçuk-style, with the geometric patterning carved into the limestone of its portal unrivalled in its richness and intricacy. The Darüşşifa next-door functioned as a hospital and its interior, reached via another elaborately decorated entranceway, abounds with idiosyncratic details such as the spiral-shaped drain for the central pool. ■ *Both buildings are on the hillside above the town centre and open from 0800-1700.*

Once you have had a look around the complex, there remains precious little else to do in town except wander the cobbled streets, looking out for the surviving Ottoman houses and several old mosques with curious wooden minarets. If you still have some time on your hands you could hike up to the scant ruins of the fortress on a rocky bluff overlooking the town.

Essentials There are several simple eateries on the main street and of the 3 hotels in town the **G** *Belediye Oteli*, T4181825, with simple doubles, en suite, balcony, is by far the best. It's under 1 km from the bottom end of town, about half-way to the railway station. A taxi from the *otogar* or station should cost under US$2. Regular dolmuş shuttle between Kangal and Divriği weekdays, 1½ hrs, US$3, and there are also 1 or 2 daily buses from Sivas. The *Doğu Ekspresi* train also stops at the station 2 km from town. If you are heading east the train is the best bet – unless you want to back track to Sivas – with an exciting and very scenic journey up the upper Euphrates valley in store for you.

The Black Sea Region

11

The Black Sea Region

550 Amasra

553 Sinop

556 Samsun

559 Ordu

559 Giresun

562 Trabzon

568 Sumela Monastry

571 Rize

573 Artvin

575 The Kaçkar Dağları

578 Ayder

579 Trekking from Ayder

579 The Upper Fırtına Valley

581 Yusufeli

Mostly ignored by foreign visitors, the Black Sea coastal region is distinct from any other part of Turkey, it's landscape more typical of northern Europe. Moisture laden winds blow off the sea causing sheets of rain to fall throughout the year. Woods and orchards cover the near-continuous mountain range backing the coast, pastures are grazed by dairy cows and tea plantations are dotted throughout the hills adding to the mix a feeling of being in a Himalayan hill station. The mountains have acted as an effective barrier to human movement, isolating the region from the Anatolian plateau to the south and so helping to shape a distinctive culture.

The western coast boasts long stretches of remote coastline, undeveloped except for the seaside centres of Amasra and Sinop. Boasting the ruins to prove their long historic pasts, they're now low-key resorts and fishing towns, refreshingly uncommercialized.

East from the grim industrial city of Samsun, the lushness of the terrain is hardly complemented by a string of drab concrete towns. A few reasonable beaches cater predominantly for a local crowd, though the narrow coastal strip is encroached on by a new multi-lane highway. A noteworthy exception is the port town of Trabzon with a fine architectural legacy from its days as the capital of the Byzantine Comneni empire. While perched spectacularly in the mountains nearby the Sumela Monastery ranks as the most visited attraction on the entire Black Sea coast.

Between Trabzon and the Georgian border the coastal range grows becoming the dramatic Pontic Alps, known in Turkish as the Kaçkar. Slashed by deep forested valleys and covered on their coastal slopes by tea plantations, this area is home to two of the country's most colourful and distinctive ethnic groups, the extrovert Laz and their neighbours the Hemşin. The mountainous country inland with peaks rising up to the summit of 3937 m Mount Kaçkar is a deserving destination for trekkers and climbers.

Amasra

Phone code: 0378
Colour map 2, grid A1
Population: 7,000

Amasra is a sleepy fishing town nestled on a rocky peninsula protruding from the rugged cliffed coastline. Snaking down a final set of tight switchbacks the town comes into view below, clustered on a narrow isthmus between two natural harbours. These are locally known as Küçük Liman (small harbour), to the west, and Büyük Liman (large harbour), site of the modern day port, to the east. With little of specific interest to occupy your time, after an initial investigation of its historic legacy or a visit to the nearby beaches, it's time to retire to one of the waterside fish restaurants for which the town is deservedly famed.

Ins & outs
See page 551 for further details

Getting there No direct buses to Amasra with travellers deposited in Bartın, 16 km away, from where regular dolmuş (US$1.25) climb over the coastal mountains. **Getting around** Once in the town everything is within walking distance.

History Well-endowed as a port and defensible position, a settlement was established by the Miletian Greeks in the sixth century BC, although references in The Iliad suggest a much earlier origin. Renamed by the Pontic Queen Amastris after herself, the peninsula was enclosed within thick defensive walls and a citadel built on its crown. With the demise of the Pontic Kingdom in the first century BC, Amastris came under Roman and then Byzantine control, with the Genoese holding a brief tenure before it was taken peacefully by the Ottomans in 1460.

Sights Extensive parts of the historic **fortifications**, mostly dating from the Byzantine era, remain visible around the shoreline of Küçük Liman and on the island of Boztepe, linked to the promontory by a robust Roman bridge. Once over the span, continue up quiet Nöbetçi Caddesi to the scant ruins of a Byzantine watchtower overlooking the sea. The view from the crest of the bluff is far more satisfying than the masonry remains themselves, and in summer you can enjoy a drink at a make-shift café while you savour the fresh salty air and watch the returning trawlers heading for the harbour.

Back in town, a path leads up from behind the Amasra Oteli to a narrow gateway in the walls of the citadel, several Genoese coats-of-arms visible in the stonework above the breach. Within the walls a quiet residential area hides two ruined **Byzantine churches,** converted after the Ottoman occupation for use as mosques.

Boat tours Boat tours are advertised along the wharf of Büyük Liman, but these consist merely of a short hour-long circuit around Boztepe to Küçük Liman- a timid after-lunch activity for Turkish landlovers. Perhaps, however, you can negotiate a more satisfying fishing trip on one of the small trawlers tied-up at the wharf. **Swimming** is possible in both the Küçük and Büyük Liman, although the water is not the cleanest. Better to head along the coast eastwards on a Cide or Kurucaşile-bound dolmuş to Bozköy or Çakraz, both of which have decent beaches.

Sleeping
Accommodation in Amasra is limited to small guesthouses, some in family houses, & a few fairly plain hotels although this will undoubtably change in the future

E *Otel Timur*, Çekilciler Caddesi No 57, Büyük Liman T3152589, on the main square. Plain rooms with ensuite, TV and telephone. **F** *Amasra Oteli*, General Mithat Ceylan Caddesi No 49, Büyük Liman, T3151722, also on the main square. Simpler rooms with shared toilet. **F** *Paşakaptan Oteli*, Çamlık Sokak No 1, Küçük Liman, T3151011. Set-back from waterfront, simple but homely rooms in rambling building, some have balconies, nice singles opening onto roof terrace for US$9. Recommended. **F** *Nur Turistik Pansiyon*, Çamlık Sokak No 3, Küçük Liman waterfront, T3151015. Pretty basic rooms, some with ensuite and seaview. **F** *Kale Pansiyon*, Kaleiçi, T3151251. Overlooking Büyük

Liman from the fortress, 5 rooms below family house, kitchen and shared toilet, shady terrace. Recommended for its quiet and scenic position. **F Otel Belvü Palas**, Küçük Liman Caddesi No 20, T3151237. On the waterfront, stark white rooms with concrete floors, balconies overlooking harbour, plans for renovation so the prices are set to rise.

Midrange Amasra is well-known for its fish restaurants with **Çınar Restorant**, serving up a range of reasonably priced seafood, meze and grilled meat on its waterside terrace overlooking Küçük Liman. Smarter and with a slightly wider selection of fish, but similar prices, is **Canlıbalık Restaurant**, also on Küçük Liman Caddesi. **Liman Restaurant**, beside Büyük Liman harbour, flashest place in town, smart interior, roof terrace, selection of meze, fish and meat dishes, slightly more expensive, attentive service. **Cheap** During the holiday season there's a row of wooden stalls beside the Büyük Liman harbour selling *midye tava* (fried mussels), *gözleme* (pancakes filled with cheese), toasted sandwiches and other snacks. **Şafak Pide ve Yemek Salonu**, Gazi Mithat Ceylan Caddesi, 1 road in from the Büyük Liman waterfront, serves decent pide, lahmacun, ready-prepared stews, excellent döner kebaps, although soup is a bit tasteless. **Balkaya Pastanesi**, across from Şafak Pide Salonu, cakes and biscuits.

Eating

Road Bus: All long distance buses arrive and depart from **Bartın**, which is linked by dolmuş leaving from near the PTT on Cumhuriyet Caddesi, every ½-hr (20 mins), US$1.25. **Özemniyet** have an office on Cumhuriyet Caddesi, Küçük Liman, where you can book tickets to **Ankara**, 5 hrs and **İstanbul**, 7 buses daily, 6 hrs, **İzmir**, 11 hrs and **Antalya**, 13 hrs, 1 daily bus. **Safranbolu**, 2 hrs, every hr, US$4. **Zonguldak**, every hr during day, 1½ hrs, US$3.50. **Dolmuş**: Along the coast to **Kurucaşile** and **Cide** 10 daily, 2/3 hrs, US$1.75/2.50, depart from Bartın before passing through Amasra.

Transport

Bank *İşbankası* is on Küçük Liman Caddesi. **Post office** The PTT is on Cumhuriyet Bulvarı, which runs roughly at equal distance to Büyük and Küçük Liman.

Directory

This section of the Black Sea coast, known in antiquity as Paphlagonia and frequently referred to in *The Illiad*, is ignored by all but a handful of visitors and remains one of the least developed stretches of the entire Turkish littoral. Green, forested mountains rise up from the sea, making communication with the rest of the country difficult and ensuring that tourist facilities have been very slow to develop. One narrow coastal road winds its way torturously along the coast and public transport is limited to dolmuş serving the various villages.

East from Amasra the narrow coastal road snakes its way past **Bozköy**, it's decent beach making it a popular day trip from Amasra, to sleepy **Çakraz**, where there are a few simple guesthouses. Next is **Kurucaşile**, a town with a tradition of boatbuilding and several small hotels. Once past **Gideros**, a pretty harbourside village watched over by a medieval fortress, the next sizeable place is **Cide**, known in ancient times as Aigialos and mentioned in the story of the Argonauts. The town centre, with a PTT and bank on the main street, is inland from the harbour and has a long 8 km stretch of pebbly beach. The **F** *Yalı Otel*, is on the seafront, reasonable rooms with ensuite, more comfortable rooms with TV, fridge are US$27.

Inebolu, 96 winding kilometres east, is a well-sited and sizable coastal town with several basic hotels and restaurants. **G** *Otel Özlü* and *Otel Altınöz*, both on Cumhuriyet Caddesi, have dull, basic rooms with bathroom. If you've had enough of the coastal road by this point there are dolmuş inland to Kastamonu every 30 minutes. If not, then it's 158 km east to Sinop, through quiet backwaters such as **Abana**, **Çatalzeytin** and **Helali**, and past several long stretches of beach.

Amasra to Sinop
If you are seeking to get off the beaten track, and particularly if you have your own transport, be it 2 or 4-wheeled, some time spent exploring the coast can be very rewarding

The Black Sea Region

● ●

Troubled waters

A kidney-shaped body of water roughly 1,000 by 500 km, the fertility of the Black Sea has long been celebrated by the people living around it. Paradoxically, however, more than 90% of the sea is infact dead: charged with lethal hydrogen sulphide and devoid of oxygen below a depth of about 180 m. This is the result of the natural process of decomposition in which bacteria consumed the huge quantities of nutrients washed into the sea by its rivers, using up all the oxygen and producing hydrogen sulphide. Although innocent in this case, the rich diversity of life which survives in the sea's thin surface layer is now threatened by human activity.

Pollution is a particularly grave problem because of the enclosed nature of the sea, with hundreds of tonnes of industrial pollution, including heavy metals and CFCs, washed in each year. Added to this is the waste water produced by 160 million people living in the area drained by Black Sea rivers, along with pesticides and inorganic fertilizers from farming.

Turkish fishermen have played an important role in the catastrophic depletion of Black Sea fish stocks, epitomized by the fate of the Black Sea anchovy. Locally known as hamsi, this staple of the Black Sea diet once swam in

immense shoals around the basin in an annual migration, arriving off the Turkish coast in November. In the main fishing grounds near Trabzon the schools of hamsi were traditionally met by fishermen who would reap a bountiful harvest. In the last 30 years, however, the shoals of hamsi have been dessimated by a veritable armada of trawlers using huge nets and sophisticated sonar equipment.

To add to the threat from overfishing, in the mid-1980s a jelly fish native to coastal waters off the eastern United States was accidentally introduced to the Black Sea from the ballast of a ship. Mnemiopsis leidyi thrived in its new home, multiplying rapidly and turning into an ecological nightmare as it fed on fish larvae. Thankfully in recent years scientist have reported a slow-down in the growth of the jelly fish population.

In the face of all these threats the six countries surrounding the Black Sea have realized the need to develop a coherent conservation policy for the basin, however, practical conservation efforts have been hampered by economic difficulties and conflict. Another major obstacle is making the other eleven countries in the Black Sea basin, as far away as Germany, responsible for what they dump into the sea via rivers such as the Danube.

● ●

Kastamonu
Phone code: 0366

There are many fine buildings built in Ottoman provincial style in the backstreets above town centre

Lost in a province of largely forested mountains, isolated Kastamonu has a rich Islamic architectural heritage of mosques, tombs, fountains, medrese and hamams, along with some fine traditional houses and a ruinous Byzantine castle on the slopes above the town centre. These, however, are probably insufficient reason to tempt most travellers to make a special journey, although you may well pass through on your way to or from Sinop.

The town is split by the Gökırmak river, with one-way Cumhuriyet Caddesi running down one bank (opposite side to the bus station), and Plevne Caddesi on the other side. From the *otogar* walk down Plevne Caddesi into town crossing the the old stone bridge, Nasrullah Köprüsü. Ahead the main square is flanked by **Nasrullah Kadı Camii**, with the recently restored Cemaleddin Firkenşah hamamı (1262), now housing a restaurant, opposite. The **Aşırefendi Han**, west of the square, is still busy by day with shoppers and traders, although the nearby **Kurşunlu Han** is empty except for after the spring and summer harvests when it hosts a bustling wheat market. Down the side street next to the Aşırefendi Han is **Yılanlı Camii**, a diminutive mosque built in 1271 with Ottoman gravestones in its well-kept courtyard, accessed through an engraved archway overhung by an old house.

Sleeping **D** *Otel Mütevelli*, Cumhuriyet Caddesi No 10, T2122018. Just past old bridge, a new hotel with comfortable but quite cramped rooms, TV, telephone, restaurant, bar. **E** *Rugancı Otel*, Cumhuriyet Caddesi No 27, T2149500, F2124343. Unexceptional rooms with bath, also newly renovated rooms for US$50 which are recommended. **F** *Otel İdrisoğlu*, Cumhuriyet Caddesi No 25, T2141757, 500 m from the *otogar*. Dated reception and similar rooms with basic bathroom, TV and telephone. **F** *Otel Selvi*, Banka Sokak No 10, T2141763, just east of the main square. A functional place with clean rooms, ensuite, telephone, singles available with/without bathrooms - US$6/$8. Recommended.

Eating *Kardelen Kebap*, Plevne Caddesi, across from *Otel İdrisoğlu*. New, smart, range of kebaps. *Plevne İşkembe Salonu*, also on Plevne Caddesi. Soups. *Uludağ Pide ve Kebap Salonu*, Cumhuriyet Caddesi, next to *Otel İdrisoğlu*. Recommended locally and always busy. *Frenkşalı Sultan Sofrası*, on the main square in restored hamamı. Pide and kebap, nicely decorated with interesting bits-and-bobs.

Transport **Bus**: Ankara, regular buses during the day, 4½ hrs, US$12. **Cide**, 3 daily, 3 hrs, US$6. **Inebolu**, every 30 mins, 1½ hrs, US$3. **Safranbolu**, 4 daily, 2 hrs, US$3.50. **Samsun**, 3 daily, 5 hrs, US$10. **Sinop**, 4 daily, 3 hrs, US$3.50.

Sinop

Set on the neck of a naturally defensible protrusion from the coast, Sinop enjoyed a grand past as capital and principal harbour of the Pontic Kingdom. Today, however, the initial impression of the town is a mixed one, with its superb position and the fragmentary, but still impressive, remains of the old city walls marred by the all-too-familiar tale of unsightly concrete and unchecked urban development. Still, once down in the pleasant harbour area with its waterside cafés and fish restaurants you'll probably be won over. There are some reasonable beaches in the area too, although compared to the Aegean or Meditteranean resorts Sinop remains uncommercialized and generally ignored by foreign visitors.

Phone code: 0368
Colour map 2, grid A3
Population: 26,000

Getting there Sinop is served by buses from Samsun (168 km), Kastamonu (235 km) and Ankara (440 km) and there is a small regional airport to the southwest of town. The TML ferry no longer calls in at the docks on its weekly journey up and down the coast. **Getting around** From the *otogar* it is a short 5-min walk past the prison and right down Tuzcular Caddesi to the harbour area where most of the accommodation and restaurants are found. Continuing along the main street, Sakarya Caddesi, brings you to the Alaeddin Camii and, 300 m beyond, the museum. Dolmuş pass the *otogar* on their way to the local beaches of Karakum, on the peninsula to the northeast of town, and Kumsal in the opposite direction.

Ins & outs
See page for further details

Legend attributes the towns name to the beautiful nymph Sinope who, coveted by the ill-intentioned Zeus, was granted anything that she desired. She chose eternal virginity and having skillfully thwarted Zeus' lustful advances, settled on the Inceburun Peninsula to live out her days, alone but happy.

Sinope became a free-city of the Roman empire prospering as a centre for maritime trade, exporting olives, olive oil and the amphorae used for their storage, continued for Sinope. The Byzantine era, however, saw a decline in the city's fortunes, as it was harrassed by Persian and Arab raiders before being taken by the Selçuks in 1214. The city changed hands often in the following centuries, first swamped by the Mongol invasions, then fought over by the Genoese and a local Turkic dynasty, the Isfendiyaroğlu. The city become part

History

of the Ottoman empire in 1458, the next notable date in local history being the Russian navy bombardment of the town in 1853, which destroyed much of the Ottoman fleet and sparked the Crimean war. Later, in the 20th-century Cold War stand-off between NATO and the Soviet Union, Sinop became the site of an important listening post, its electronic ears trained across the Black Sea.

Sights

Arriving at the *otogar* you have your first glimpse of the solid **defensive walls** which once ringed the isthmus, enclosing the city within about 3 km of battlements. Originally constructed by the early Greek inhabitants and much added-to subsequently, most of what you see today is from the Byzantine era. The walls remain the most interesting feature of the town, with an intact section near the harbour, called **Kale Burç**, offering a good view over the fishing trawlers lined-up along the wharf below.

The **Alâeddin Camii**, 500 m northeast along Sakarya Caddesi from the *otogar*, is a Selçuk mosque built after their conquest of the city in 1214. Behind it is the **Pervane Medresesi**, also built in the 13th century at the behest of Muinettin Süleyman, a Selçuk vizier whose power grew to eclipse that of the sultan, whom he unceremoniously dispatched. Within the medrese is the tomb Gazi Çelebi, an Isfendiyaroğulları Emir who ruled Sinop and was celebrated for his brave underwater exploits. When faced by a combined attack from Genoese and Comneni warships, he swam under the attacking vessels undetected and bored holes in the wooden craft, sinking the ships and winning the day.

Sinop Museum The museum's exhibits include Bronze Age artefacts with later Hellenistic, Roman, Byzantine, Selçuk and Ottoman pieces. Unusual, and well-worth a look, is the collection of icons rescued from Greek Orthodox churches in the local area. In the garden are what remains of a **Temple of Serapis** excavated in 1951, along with a memorial to the Turkish soldiers who died in the Russian

Sinop

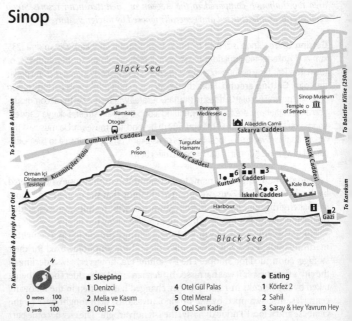

■ Sleeping
1 Denizci
2 Melia ve Kasım
3 Otel 57
4 Otel Gül Palas
5 Otel Meral
6 Otel Sarı Kadir

● Eating
1 Körfez 2
2 Sahil
3 Saray & Hey Yavrum Hey

The Black Sea Region

bombardment of 1853 which preceeded the Crimean War. ■ *Tue-Fri: 0800-1730, Sat-Sun: 0830-1700, Closed Mon. US$1.25. Getting there: Just northwest of junction of Sakarya Caddesi and Atatürk Caddesi.*

From the museum continue up Kemalettin Sami Paşa Caddesi for 250 m to **Balatlar Kilise,** part of the remains of an extensive Byzantine palace that once existed, later serving as a church.

Karakum beach is 2 km northeast of town, accessible on foot or by dolmuş from **Beaches** outside the *otogar*. A short stretch of dark sand overlooked by the bungalows, hotel and restaurant of the **Karakum Tatil Köyü,** a holiday camp development, it is hardly worth the bother. Better stretches of lighter-coloured sand are found to the southeast by taking a left fork 200 m after the *otogar* as you head out of town. First is the **Orman İçi Dinlenme Yeri**, run by the forestry department, which has shady picnic tables, camping facilities and a short stretch of sandy beach. Some 750 m beyond and reached on '*DSI*' dolmuş passing the *otogar* are stretches of beach accessible through the *Öztürkler Aile kampı* and *Kumsal Turistik Tesisleri* (see sleeping), while a short distance beyond is probably the best beach, backed by a summer house development, restaurant and the **D** *Beyaz Ev Motel*, Mobil Mevkii, T2612866. Homely, which has well-equipped rooms right on beach. Much more extensive is **Akliman,** a wide sandy beach several kilometres to the west of town past the airport. It attracts fewer people due to its more exposed northern aspect and reports of unpredictable currents. Dolmuş run from outside the *otogar* in the summer season.

Essentials

C *Hotel Melia ve Kasım,* Gazi Caddesi No 2, T2614210. Aspiring to be a quality hotel, falls well-short though, badly finished and ill-kept rooms, noisy, discounts available. **D** *Ayışığı Apart Otel,* Kiremitçiler Yolu No 21, T2613832. East of the town and *otogar*, reached along the road past the *Orman İçi Dinlenme Yeri*, well-designed split-level apartments set in lovely gardens overlooking sea, equipped with kitchenette, bathroom and telephone, family apartments available, restaurant. Well recommended. **F** *Otel Sarı Kadir* Derinboğazağzı No 22, T2601544, plain but clean rooms, well-equipped with TV, refrigerator, en-suite shower, some have harbour view. Recommended. **F** *Kumsal Turistik Tesisleri,* Kiremitçiler Yolu No 41, T2618777, 2 km from town by 'DSI' dolmuş, ugly concrete rooms facing sea, restaurant, good beach. **F** *Hotel Denizci,* Kurtuluş Caddesi, T2610904, simple rooms with high ceilings, some have ensuite, equipped with alarm clocks! **G** *Otel Meral,* Kurtuluş Caddesi No 19, T2613100. Clean, basic rooms with shared bathroom, no breakfast. Recommended. **G** *Otel Gül Palas,* Cumhuriyet Caddesi No 13, T2615286, just past the prison. 1/2/3/4 bed rooms, very basic but friendly owner.

Sleeping
A good selection of cheap pensions & hotels, filled in summer with Turkish holiday-makers, however, there is a lack of places at the more comfortable end of the market

Camping *Orman İçi Dinlenme Tesisleri,* Kiremitçiler Caddesi, coming in to town turn right after the *Orman Bölge Müdürlüğü,* about 200 m before the bus station. Conveniently close to town but quiet, pine-shaded pitches for tents and caravans, beach, crowded at weekends and in summer, rest of time you'll probably have it to yourself, tent (up to 4 people) or caravan US$4. *Öztürkler Aile kampı,* Kiremitçiler Yolu No 33, T2616060, about 1 km from town, pitches beside beach but limited shade, tent US$4, tiny rooms also available, equipped with kitchen and bathroom for US$11. There are also several camping sites at the far end of Akliman beach.

The Black Sea Region

Eating

There are plenty of restaurants serving up the fresh local catch in the harbour area

Midrange *Saray Restaurant*, Iskele Caddesi, waterside restaurant which is well thought-of locally, serves fish and seafood. Flanking the Saray restaurant are the slightly cheaper *Sahil* and *Hey Yavrum Hey*, both serving selection of fish, and also with pontoon dining areas. **Cheap** For good value fish try the *mezgit*, fried whitebait, at *Sahil restaurant*, which with a salad and drink costs about US$5. *Körfez 2*, facing harbour on Iskele Caddesi. Simple but popular place, pide, kebaps and ready-prepared soups and stews. *Ocakbaşı*, Kurtuluş Caddesi, opposite *Ziraat Bankası*. Tiny place where you cook your own şiş or Adana kebap at long grill. *Yalı Kahvesi*, Iskele Caddesi, café with nice shady tables beside the harbour.

Shopping

Ayhan Boat Shop, Iskele Caddesi, huge collection of hand-made model boats, from tiny ships in bottles to huge painted wooden steamliners.

Transport

Air *Turkish Airlines*, 1 weekly flight to Ankara on Mon. **Bus Ankara,** 3 daily, 6 hrs, US$14. **Ayancık,** every hr 0730-1945, 1 hr, US$3. **Istanbul,** 3 evening buses, 11 hrs, US$18. **Kastamonu,** 1000, 1400, 3 hrs, US$7. **Samsun,** 4 daily, 3 hrs, US$6. **Trabzon,** 2 daily, 6 hrs, US$12.

Directory

Banks Most major banks are found along Sakarya Caddesi. **Baths** *Turgutlar Hamamı*, Tuzcular Caddesi, US$4 entry and kese, women Tue 1200-1700. **Post office** On Atatürk Caddesi. **Internet** *FV1 Dreamshop*, Sakarya Caddesi, Büyükcamii Yokuşu 1/E, just off main street opposite Alaeddin Camii, US$2 per hr. **Tourist information** The office is near the *Hotel Melia ve Kasım*, 0800-1200, 1300-1800 in season.

Samsun

Phone code: 0362
Colour map 2, grid A4
Population: 310,000

A gritty port and industrial centre, Samsun sprawls around a large bay flanked by the agriculturally productive deltas of the Kızılırmak and Yeşilırmak rivers, which are renowned for their tobacco cultivation. The city has had a long history, although very little evidence survives above the concrete. In more recent times the city played a small but celebrated role in the formative days of the struggle for independence, as it was here that Atatürk disembarked from a ship having fled from British occupied Istanbul. However, despite looming large in the national psychy and Turkish history books, Samsun is a modern, working city which can be a bit grim, particularly if you arrive in the rain.

Ins & outs

See page 558 for further details

Getting there Samsun has good transport links with the rest of the country, and is served by buses, trains, daily flights to Istanbul and Ankara and the TML ferry service. **Getting around** The *otogar* is on the coastal highway several kilometres east of the centre. Pick-up a dolmuş (US$0.25) from across the road from the terminal, or a taxi (about US$3.50) into town. The train station is between the *otogar* and the centre and dolmuş passby outside. There are service buses between the *Turkish Airlines* office on Kazım Paşa Caddesi and the airport. Town the central landmark is Cumhuriyet Meydanı, a large expanse of concrete surrounded by ugly office and retail buildings. All the hotels, restaurants and services are found within walking distance. Cumhuriyet Caddesi runs west from the Cumhuriyet Meydanı. **Tourist information** The office is on the seaward side of Atatürk Bulvarı at the junction with Cumhuriyet Meydanı.

Background

The city of Amisus was founded as a trading colony just north of present-day Samsun by Ionian Greeks in the sixth century BC. Although not naturally as well-endowed as other harbours along the southern coast of the Black Sea, the city benefited from good links with the Pontic hinterland. It continued to flourish as part of the Pontic Kingdom, until the city was taken and burned by the Romans in 71 BC. Promptly rebuilt, the ports turbulent history continued thereafter, changing hands regularly down through the years. A long list of masters includes the Byzantines, the Comneni of Trebizond, the Selçuks, the Mongols and finally the Genoese, who set the city ablaze, once again, as they fled from the Ottomans in 1425.

Humbled by this last blow, Samsun remained a small inconsequential farming community up until the end of the 19th century when the railway came to town. Linked via Ankara to the rest of the country, locally grown tobacco could find its way to market and the economy boomed. Today, Samsun has fully regained its importance, becoming the largest port and industrial centre on the Black Sea coast.

Samsun also enjoys a significant place in the development of the Turkish Republic, as it was here on the 19 May 1919, that Atatürk landed having slipped out of British-controlled Istanbul by ship. He promptly began the task of organizing a nationalist movement and the date of his arrival in Samsun, celebrated as a national holiday, marks the beginning of the War of Independence.

Sights

Samsun's turbulent past and the rapid urban development of the modern era have left the city almost totally devoid of historical buildings. There are, however, three museums to keep you busy for a while, starting with the **Archaeology museum**, which has on display artefacts found at Karasamsun, ancient Amisus, which juts out into the sea to the northwest of the city centre and is off limits to the public within the perimeter of a military base. ■ *0830-1200 daily, 1330-1730. US$1.50. Off Atatürk Bulvarı near the harbour.* The **Atatürk Museum**, next door, has an extensive but fairly forgettable collection of Atatürk memorabilia ■ *Opening hours and price same as archaeology museum.* The **Gazi Museum**, another shrine to the great man housed in the former hotel where Atatürk stayed, is more interesting. ■ *0800-1200, 1300-1700 daily except Mon. Free. In the corner of Cumhuriyet Meydanı, right across from the* Vidinli Hotel.

Sleeping

B *Otel Yafeya*, Cumhuriyet Meydanı, T2444733, F2523559. Comfortably furnished and well-sized rooms, some suffer from traffic noise though, TV and telephone as standard, restaurant, carpark. Recommended. **C** *Otel Vidinli*, Cumhuriyet Meydanı, T4316050, F4312136, corner of square. Quieter than *Otel Yafeya*, single US$35, comfortable but slightly dated rooms with pine fittings, ensuite, TV, telephone and minibar, good restaurant. Recommended. **D** *Anakent Sosyal Tesisleri*. Set in gardens opposite the *otogar*, T2281470, access via foot-bridge from *otogar*, single US$20, plain but decent rooms with ensuite, TV and balcony, part of a complex including tennis courts and restaurant, set menu US$7, advantage of being away from hustle and bustle. Recommended. **E** *Şahin Otel*, Cumhuriyet Caddesi No 54, T4352001. Single US$16, reasonable rooms in new hotel, bit cramped but well-equipped with fan, telephone and cable TV as standard. Recommended. **E** *Otel Güllü*, Pazar Camii Sokak No 4, T4311717. Modern hotel with large rooms, TV, telephone, shower, dingy breakfast room, right opposite mosque so front rooms are blasted by call to prayer. **F** *Otel Gold*, Orhaniye Geçidi No 4, T4311959, off Cumhuriyet Caddesi near the Meydanı. Clean bright rooms with TV, telephone and a small shower, small singles US$11. Recommended. **G** *Hotel Bank*, Saathane Meydanı, Eski Telgrafhane Sokak No.10, T4311568. Row of flags visible from coastal road behind a carpark, 750 m west of central junction, compact rooms with wooden floors and ensuite shower, excellent value, some rooms have balcony, alcohol served in bar downstairs Recommended.

Eating

Midrange The *Hotel Vidinli restaurant*, T4316050, has a good international menu and pleasant surroundings. *Itimat Balık Lokantası*, T4200524, Cumhuriyet Bulvarı No 64, smart fish and seafood restaurant. **Cheap** Cumhuriyet Caddesi is lined with

The Black Sea Region

kebap restaurants and cheap lokantas, including the *Sila*, serving iskender, döner and other kebaps. *Başak Restorant*, Saat Kulesi Meydanı, serves good pide and lahmacun.

Transport **Air** *Turkish Airlines*, Kazım Paşa Caddesi No 11, T4315065, has 3 daily return flights from Istanbul and 5 per week from Ankara. There are free service buses to the airport. **Bus** **Amasya**, every 2 hrs, US$3.50, 2 hrs. **Ankara**, 6 daily, US$16, 6½ hrs. *Ulusoy* have buses at 0900, 1330, 2400. **Istanbul**, 3 daily, US$22, 11 hrs. **İzmir**, 1 evening bus, US$24, 15 hrs. **Sinop**, 0700, 1300, 1630, 1730, US$5.50, 3 hrs. **Trabzon**, every hr during day, US$8, 6 hrs. **Giresun** and **Ordu** buses leave every 30 mins from front of *otogar*.

Directory **Banks** There are lots of banks with ATM's around the centre. **Baths** *Büyük Şifa Hamamı*, just west of Saat Kulesi Meydanı, US$2.50. **Post office** The PTT is on Kazım Paşa Caddesi. **Tour agencies** *Kar Tur*, Kazım Paşa Caddesi No 5, T4312003, F4313060, airline reservations.

East of Samsun Once out of Samsun, the coastal highway proceeds across the fertile plain of the Yeşilırmak River, where locals say anything put in the ground will grow and stories abound of huge 3 kg aubergines. What you will definitely see are fields of broad-leaf virginia tobacco, used in the strong domestic brand of cigarettes, Samsun, growing beside fields of maize and corn. This verdant stretch of countryside was reputed to be the home of the Amazons, a tribe of fierce female warriors who worshipped Ares, the god of war. According to Strabo, out of necessity they coupled briefly with men from a neighbouring male tribe, the Gagarians, and when the offspring were born the females would be kept, while the male babies were raised by their fathers. To enable them to draw back a bow the Amazons' right breast was seared-off at birth.

Ünye
Phone code: 0452

About 25 km after rejoining the coast to the east of the Yeşilırmak Delta, numerous roadside pensions and campsites announce your imminent arrival in the small town of Ünye. A bustling but unexceptional market centre, there's little to see in the town itself apart from a few ramshackled buildings of Ottoman pedigree, however, on the western approaches are some of the nicest stretches of beach on the entire coast this side of Samsun. This white sand is the focus for a string of hotels, campsites and beachside restaurants catering for Turkish holidaymakers in the short summer season.

Some 7 km inland on the road towards Niksar stands the medieval castle of **Çaleoğlu**, associated with various legends and used up until the 18th century by a local *derebey* (landlord) as his keep.

Sleeping and eating To reach the seaside hotels head out of town on a green and white municipal minibus which stop across the coastal highway from Cumhuriyet Meydanı. A couple of kilometres west of town is the **F** *Belediye Çamlık Moteli and Camping*, T3231333, which has plain rooms and a restaurant set in woodland by the beach. Further-on are a series of more temporary camping places, most with basic restaurants and toilet facilities. About 4 km out the **D** *Hotel Talıp*, T3232238, is a 2-star place with comfortable rooms, a roof-bar and beach access. 500 m beyond the Talıp are a couple more basic places such as **G** *Şal Pansiyon*, T3120022, rooms with bathroom and a simple restaurant. There are also two decent hotels in town both just west of the small main square, Cumhuriyet Meydanı. **F** *Otel Burak*, Belediye Caddesi No 4, T3120186, homely rooms with tiny bathroom, TV and balcony. Recommended. **F** *Güney Otel*, Belediye Caddesi No 14, T3238406, Otel Burak just has the edge, but still good value rooms, some are a little cramped, US$11 with shared bathroom. *Adana Mutfağı*, next-door to the *Otel Burak* has a good choice of dishes including *çöp şiş* and lahmacun.

Directory Banks There is an İşbankası with ATM on Cumhuriyet Meydanı. **Post office** On Hükümet Caddesi, inland from football pitch. **Tourist information** The tourist information office is next to the football pitch on the main highway. Open irregularly during season.

Ordu

A well-to-do town in the middle of Turkey's hazelnut growing region. Although Ordu doesn't warrant any special attention, it is a possible place to break your journey. The town centre displays a degree of civic pride and investment unusual in Turkey with the pedestrianized main street, Sırrıpaşa Caddesi, lit by fancy street lamps and the public gardens along the seaside promenade well-tended. Despite this, the only thing of interest to the tourist is a **museum** housed in the 19th-century Paşaoğlu Konağı, a fine mansion typical of the period. The first floor is elegantly furnished in period style giving you an illuminating insights into provincial life in the late-1800s. To get to it follow the signposts up Hükümet Caddesi and past the PTT from the square. A Greek Orthodox church, easily recognizable just above the coastal highway heading west from the centre, has undergone careful restoration and is now being used as a mosque.

Phone code: 0452
Colour map ?, grid ??

E *Turist Otel*, Atatürk Bulvarı No 134, T2149115, F2141950, on the main road 200 m east of the centre, a well-appointed 2-star hotel, the large rooms have a ensuite bathroom, TV and telephone, some have a balcony with sea-view, on the downside they're also affected by traffic noise. **F** *Hotel Kervansaray*, Kazım Karabekir Caddesi No.1, T2141330, a large concrete building just east of central roundabout, unappealing concrete structure, the functional rooms have ensuite, no breakfast. **G** *Bacın Otel*, Sırrıpaşa Caddesi No 10, above Sağra confectioners, basic boarding house with shared toilet.

Sleeping

Aktaşlar Pide ve Lahmacun, inland from central roundabout, new place, lots of mirrors, good pide. *Deniz Restorant*, Süleyman Felek Caddesi, past the domed white fountain, modern place, serving kebaps, pide and pizza, garden. *Midi Restaurant*, on the pier in the middle of town, serves selection of fish, grilled meat and alcohol, similar experience to being at sea.

Eating

Road The *otogar* is on the coastal highway, 2 km east of the centre, and linked to it by taxi-dolmuş no 2. All the bus companies have offices in the centre. **Ünye** and **Samsun** dolmuş depart regularly all day from the seaward side of Atatürk Caddesi, just west of the main roundabout, 1½/2½ hrs, US$3/4.50. **Giresun**, dolmuş wait in front of the Belediye building on Atatürk Caddesi, US$1.50, 1 hr. There are also Ordu and Giresun Belediye buses leaving every 30 mins from the bus stand behind the Belediye building. **Sea** The **TML** pier is a 1 km west of the town centre (see page 47 for timetable).

Transport

Airline offices *Turkish Airlines*, Atatürk Caddesi, next to the main roundabout. **Banks** *İşbankası* is next to the *Kervansaray Hotel*. **Post office** The PTT is on Hükümet Caddesi. **Tourist information** On Atatürk Caddesi just to east of main roundabout. Open 0830-1730, weekdays.

Directory

Giresun

A pleasant and obviously prosperous town of mostly new apartment blocks, despite 3,000 years of history there's very little to detain you here. A steep climb leads up to the town's ruinous castle perched on a wooded promontory overlooking the town. Then there's the church of St Nicholas, now a rather

Phone code: 0454
Colour map 2, grid B6
46 km E of Ordu

The Black Sea Region

empty museum. Having inspected these two attractions you'll probably be ready to head onwards, though Giresun's varied choice of accommodation suggests it as a good place to overnight.

Ins & outs
See page 561 for further details

Getting there Long distance buses plying the coastal highway pass through the town stopping at the *otogar*, 3 km west of the centre. If you are arriving from the east ask to be let off at Atapark, the main square beside the highway, saving yourself the journey back in by dolmuş. Regular local bus and dolmuş services head east and west towards Ordu and Trabzon from east of Atapark. Giresun is also a port of call for the *Turkish Maritime Lines* ferry service. **Getting around** Possible to see the town's limited attractions on foot though it's a stiff climb to the castle. **Tourist information** There is a tourist information booth in the middle of Atapark. 0830-1900 daily in summer, 0900-1700 Mon-Fri in winter.

History
One of the best defensive positions on the entire Black Sea coast, an outpost was established on the outcrop in the eighth century BC by colonists from Sinope. The acropolis was known as Cerasous for most of its history, a name used by the local Greek population right up until their expulsion in 1923. The citadel of Cerasous was held by the Grand Comneni until 1461, when the conquest of Trebizond by the Ottomans heralded the demise of their empire.

Legend has it that it was from Cerasous that the first cherry tree was taken back to Italy by the Romans, giving the fruit its name, *is cerrasus*, in Latin. Today cherries are still grown in the coastal mountains, although hazelnuts are king in this part of the world.

Sights
The main sight of interest in Giresun is the **castle**, the fragmentary remains of which sit on top of a mountain jutting out from the coastline. There isn't much left of the Byzantine fortress or its Hellenistic foundations, but the extant masonry is set in a leafy park with several cafés. The greenery and views over Giresun and along the coast more than justifying the climb, also attracting crowds of picnicers and strollers at the weekend. ■ *Getting there: By car or on foot follow the 'Kale' signposts, which start 200 m up Gazi Caddesi from Atapark, on the left. Continue along the road as it winds around the seaward-side of the promontory for about 700 m.*

At the base of the castle mount, on the eastern side, stands what used to be the Greek Orthodox church of **St Nicholas**, which now houses a rather forgettable ethnographic museum. ■ *0800-1700 daily. US$1.50.*

It is also possible to take a small ferry from Ali Rıza Park jetty, east of the castle, to **Giresun Adası** visible several kilometres off-shore. The only island of any significant size on the entire Black Sea coast, it was known as the Isle of Ares (the god of war) in antiquity and legend has it that Jason and the Argonauts were attacked by vicious birds when trying to land on it. A black rock on the islet served as an Amazon shrine and to this day it's the focus of an endearing ceremony which is part of the annual **Giresun Aksu Festival** held on the 20 May. A celebration of spring which hails from pagan times, participants circle around the stone hand-in-hand, before throwing pebbles representing their worldly troubles into the sea. This is followed by a lively festival back on the mainland.

Sleeping
The town's hotels are found in the streets in the vicinity of Atapark

C *Otel Kit Tur*, Arif Bey Caddesi No 27, T2120245, F2123034, up Gazi Caddesi from Atapark on the left. Despite 3-star rating its a bit worn, much better value found elsewhere, pine fitted rooms with ensuite, TV and telephone, bar, sauna. **E** *Otel Çarıkçı*, Osmanağa Caddesi No 6, T2161026, F2164578. East of the fountain and Atapark, 85 year-old building although you wouldn't know it, quite small twins and doubles with shower, TV and telephone. **E** *Er-tur Oteli*, Çapulacılar Sokak No 8, T2161757, F2167762, walk east from Atapark and the fountain along Osmanağa Caddesi, turn right, clean newly fitted rooms in well-managed small hotel, excellent value, singles available, shower, TV, telephone. Recommended. **E** *Otel Serenti*, Arif Bey Caddesi No 12, T2129434, F2129555. Right after Vakıf Bank, newly-opened 2-star place, small comfortable rooms with ensuite shower, TV, telephone, slightly cramped, singles US$13. **F** *Bulut Otel*, Fatih Caddesi No 22, T2164115. From fountain take first right off Gazi Caddesi, 75 m down on right, bright and clean apart from the grimy carpets, single US$6, shared bathroom, no breakfast, rooms available with TV. Recommended budget option. **F** *Beyoğlu Oteli*, Fatih Caddesi No 7, T2161491. First right off Gazi Caddesi, 1/2/3 bed rooms in very basic boarding house, no breakfast.

Eating

Up narrow Köprülühan Sokak from the fountain, roughly parallel to Gazi Caddesi, are 2 good places which have tables out on the street in good weather. *Halil Usta Lokantası*, serves all types of kebap, as well as köfte, soups and stews, for vegetarians try the thick *mercimek çorbası* with tasty *bulgur pilav*. Next door is ***Kahramanmaraş Pide ve Kebap***, an excellent pide and lahmacun restaurant. Near the *Ulusoy* office facing Atapark is the spartan but popular ***Deniz Pide***, while up Gazi Caddesi heading inland from the fountain are lots of snack and fast food places. For something sweet try ***Balkaya***, 150 m up Gazi Caddesi on left, cakes, biscuits and 30 flavours of ice-cream. There are several all male places, including ***Sato Fıçı***, serving beer on tap east along Osmanağa Caddesi from the fountain.

Transport

Bus **Ordu,** Belediye buses leave every 30 mins from the minibus stand at the eastern (far) end of Osmanağa Caddesi, US$1.50, 1¼ hrs. **Samsun,** from Eray office around corner from İşbankası on main road, 5 times daily, US$4.50, 3½ hrs. **Trabzon,** dolmuş depart when full from the main road, around the corner from İşbankası, 0700-1900, US$3, 2 hrs. *Ulusoy* and several other companies have daily buses to other destinations including **Ankara**, **İstanbul**, **İzmir** and **Bursa**. Their offices are at the east end of Atapark from where service buses take you to the *otogar*. **Sea** The TML ferry calls in at the harbour, T2161620, F4451604, just north of Atapark (see page 47 for timetable).

Directory

Airline offices *Turkish Airlines*, T2124680, 750 m west of Atapark on coastal road. **Banks** *İşbankası* and other banks with ATM's are at the eastern end of Atapark and up Gazi Caddesi. **Post office** The PTT is on Gazi Caddesi. **Internet** *2005 Internet*, 3 kat, İşhanı, Gazi Caddesi, on 3rd floor of building next to *Otel Kit Tur*, US$1.50 per hour.

Tirebolu
38 km E of Giresun

The small town of Tirebolu, with its picturesque 14th-century sea-girt Genoese castle and its harbour, has managed to retain something of its former character. A few ramshackled Ottoman buildings have survived amidst the clutter of concrete buildings which climb the hill from the busy coastal road. There's also a tea-garden within the restored walls of the castle of St John, or you could stroll around the small harbour crowded with colourful fishing boats. Many of the menfolk are employed in the town's tea processing factory; while at Friday lunchtime the main street is blocked with worshippers praying on pieces of cardboard and prayer mats.

There are some reasonable beaches in the vicinity, the best of which is pebbly **Küçük Çay** set in a small bay several kilometres west of the centre. The **Belediye Plajı**, on the edge of town, is sandy but gets very crowded at weekends.

A short distance beyond Tirebolu the coastal highway crosses the **Harşit River**, a point of historical interest if nothing else, as this was the furthest west the imperial Russian army penetrated during its advance into Ottoman territory in 1916.

The Black Sea Region

Sleeping and eating Should you need a bed for the night try the **G** *Otel Huzur*, Gazipaşa Caddesi No 15, T4114093, climb up the main street, Gazipaşa Caddesi, 500 m from the overpass, very simple rooms, shared toilet, terrace with nice view over the town. There are several small *lokantas* on Gazipaşa Caddesi, while back across the bridge and past the Belediye building is the popular *Tirebolu Lahmacun and Kebap Restaurant*.

To Trabzon At **Akçakale** the ivy-covered remains of a well-preserved Byzantine keep, second only to Trebizond in the medieval empire of Comneni, are visible beside the road. **Akçaabat**, just 17 km short of Trabzon, has an area of old wood-beamed houses hidden up on the hill behind ranks of shoddily built concrete structures. The town, accessible by Belediye bus or dolmuş from Trabzon, also has a large and colourful weekly bazaar specializing mainly in food and clothing.

Trabzon

Phone code: 0462
Colour map 3, grid B2
Population: 151,000

Trabzon doesn't greet visitors with its best face: a seedy waterfront area with dreary buildings stretching along the busy coastal road and dock cranes punctuating the sky-line. But hiding above this unappetizing littoral up narrow cobbled streets, is a remarkably progressive town. A historic entrepot for trade at the western end of the Silk Route, Trebizond, as the city was formerly known, enjoyed its glorious apogee as the capital of the Byzantine Comneni empire; later becoming a significant provincial town where Ottoman princes learnt their statecraft. The loss of its Greek population in 1923 and changing patterns of trade left the town in what looked like a terminal decline. However, more recently it's been reinvigorated by its proximity to the emerging states of the former Soviet Union and the establishment of a Free Trade Zone. Container ships crowd the harbour and commercial agencies and brokerages line many of the streets. The narrow main thoroughfare is crowded with modern shops and clothing outlets; its restaurants choked with shoppers at the weekend. Heir to such a long and colourful history, the town quite naturally boasts a scattering of sites such as the fresco enlivened church of Aya Sofya and the bazaar district. It also makes a good base for a foray south into the cloud-shrouded mountains to visit the Sumela Monastery.

Ins & outs

Getting there
See page 568 for further details

Regular buses ply east and west along the winding 010 highway, linking Trabzon with other cities on the Black Sea coast. The airport, squeezed onto a narrow strip of land flanked on 1 side by the cliffed coastline, is 5 km east of the centre and served daily by *Turkish Airlines* scheduled flights. There are also cross-border ferry and bus links to Georgia, Russia and Azerbaijan.

Getting around
Dolmuş are available for private hire, although a price should be negotiated beforehand

The town has an abundant, and at times a street-clogging, supply of taxi dolmuş which ply set routes radiating from the main square, Atatürk Alanı. The airport, bus station and other principal sights are served by these dolmuş with fares set at US$0.45. Abundant public transport around town means it's best to abandon your car if you have one. **Tourist information** The tourist office is behind the İskenderpaşa Camii on Meydan Parkı Köşesi, T3214659.

Sights

The best way to see Trabzon is on foot with a walking tour of the attractions below taking, at a leisurely pace stopping for a drink or something to eat along the way, the best part of a day. To shorten the itinerary head directly westwards from Atatürk Alanı, missing out on the Avrasya Pazarı and St Maria. You can also break-off at the Gülbahar Hatun Camii and catch a dolmuş up to the Atatürk Köşkü (see below).

Your wanderings begin in the vicinity of **Atatürk Alanı**, the hub of the modern **A walking tour** town, where several lanes of slow moving traffic besiege a pleasant tree-shaded square where locals sit outside cafés drinking tea.

Down the hill to the east and housed in a long shed-like building stretched along the highway is the **Avrasya Pazarı**, which was formerly an emphorium of Soviet-era junk brought across the Caucasus by traders known as the Russian bazaar. Today it's considerably less fascinating, and after paying a small entrance fee you can browse the stalls, trawling through heaps of fairly mundane Turkish manufactured goods for something interesting to buy. There are several stalls selling handicrafts which are worth searching out.

The area surrounding the contemporary docks was historically the Genoese and Venetian quarter, with parts of a ruined Genoese fort standing as the only reminder of those times. Occupied by the army the castle is out-of-bounds to visitors, with the busy coastal highway burrowing beneath it a curving tunnel.

Heading back up to Atatürk Alanı, in the backstreets to the north of the square and reached down an alleyway beside the Güloğlu Restaurant, is the church of **Santa Maria**. A relic of the days when there was a sizeable Catholic community in Trabzon, the church was established in 1869 by the Capuchin order. It's still the centre of the town's small Catholic community. The hostel within the church compound offers the best budget accommodation in town (see below).

Uzun Sokak, a narrow cobbled street thronged with shoppers and choked with traffic, heads west from the corner of Atatürk Alanı. About 300 m along a left turn up Kasım Sokak brings you out in front of the **Kostaki Konağı**, a fine example of the late 19th-century mansions which once graced the streets of Trebizond.

Continuing along Uzun Sokak for 100 m, a road on the right just before the Tabakhane Camii leads passed a row of small silver workshops to the **Küçük Ayvasıl Kilise**, a ninth-century Byzantine church dedicated to St Anne. Currently being restored by the Ministry of Culture, only traces of the frescoes which once covered the walls are now visible.

Back on Uzun Sokak a left turn after the Tabakhane Camii, followed by a right before the Fatih Hamamı, leads you up to the **Yeni Cuma Camii** (New Friday mosque) in about 10 minutes. This was formerly a church dedicated to the patron Saint of Trebizond, St Eugenios, whose skull used to occupy pride of place in the building. This relic is reputed to have saved the city in 1223 from the Selçuk Turks besieging it. With the forces of Mehmet II camped outside the walls in 1461, the odds stacked against the city seem to have been too great though, and shortly after David II capitulated the church was coverted into a mosque.

Back down the hill the **Tabakhane Bridge** leads across a ravine, now crowded with houses and gardens, into the **Ortahisar** or Middle City. Superbly located on a narrow spur of land, this Byzantine fortified city was overlooked by a citadel and the palace of the Comneni Dynasty, the fragmentary ruins of which can be reached up Kale Caddesi. In the time of the Grand Comneni, the fortifications were extended across the western canyon and down to the harbour, enclosing an area known as the 'Lower city'. An extensive section of these later battlements remain intact between the **Zağnos Tower** and the **Kale Kapısı**, flanking Reşadiye Caddesi.

Across the Zağnos bridge is the **Gülbahar Hatun Camii** which was raised in 1514 after the death of Ayşe Hatun, the benevolent Greek wife of Sultan Beyazıt and mother of Sultan Selim I, who was known to her admirers as Gülbahar (Spring Rose). Beside the multi-domed mosque stands her tomb, along with a traditional timber farm building raised above the ground on mushroom-shaped stilts which was brought from the mountains of Rize province.

Walking down beside the walls of the 'Lower city', a right turn through the **Kale Kapısı** brings you onto Kahramanmaraş Caddesi. Continue up the hill to the Müftü Ismail Efendi Camii and the heart of the **bazaar area** just to the north. In the narrow streets of this lively district crowded with shoppers and traders, stands the baroque **Çarşı Camii**, a large late-19th-century mosque used by the local shopkeepers. To the south-east of the mosque is a crumbling **bedesten** originally constructed by the Genoese in the 14th century and still home to a cluster of shops and worshops.

Trabzon

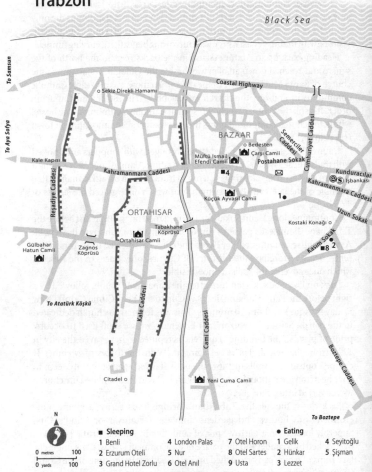

Black Sea

To Samsun

To Aya Sofya

o Sekiz Direkli Hamamı

Coastal Highway

BAZAAR

o Bedesten

Çarşı Camii

Müftü Ismail Efendi Camii

Postahane Sokak

Semerciler Caddesi

Cumhuriyet Caddesi

Kale Kapısı

Kahramanmaraş Caddesi

■4

Kunduracılar

@$ İşbankası

Kahramanmaraş Caddesi

Reşadiye Caddesi

Küçük Ayvasıl Camii

1 ●

Uzun Sokak

ORTAHISAR

Tabakhane Köprüsü

Ortahisar Camii

Kostaki Konağı o

Kasım Sokak

■8 2 ●

Gülbahar Hatun Camii

Zağnos Köprüsü

To Atatürk Köşkü

Kale Caddesi

Cami Caddesi

Boztepe Caddesi

Citadel o

Yeni Cuma Camii

To Boztepe

N

0 metres 100
0 yards 100

■ **Sleeping**
1 Benli	4 London Palas	7 Otel Horon
2 Erzurum Oteli	5 Nur	8 Otel Sartes
3 Grand Hotel Zorlu	6 Otel Anıl	9 Usta

● **Eating**
1 Gelik	4 Seyitoğlu
2 Hünkar	5 Şişman
3 Lezzet	

The Black Sea Region

Surrounded by gardens the church of Haghia Sofia commands a superb position on a hill overlooking the coast, 3 km to the west of the town centre. It originally formed part of a monastic complex established in the 13th century though the building was reconsecrated as a mosque in 1461. Unusually it incorporates Selçuk, Georgian and Armenian architectural features, however, it's mainly for the superb Byzantine frescoes decorating its interior that the church is known today. Painstakingly restored by a team of experts over six years from 1957, the surviving portions vividly illustrate scenes from the New Testament including the Miracles of Christ in the narthex and the Ascension on the vault of the central apse. All the paintings are clearly labelled in English and Turkish. Next to the ticket office is a typical old Black Sea house with its interior, carefully recreated in authentic style, open to the public as a museum. ■ *0830-1800 daily (closes at 1700 and on Mon during the winter). US$2.50 (museum an extra US$1.25). Getting there: Can be reached easily on the dolmuş marked 'Aya Sofya' which passes down Kahramanmaraş Caddesi from Atatürk Alanı.*

Aya Sofya

Don't miss the scenes from Genesis carved above the south porch & sealed with the Comneni imperial emblem, a single-headed eagle

Originally the home of a wealthy Greek banking family, the Karayannidhis, who were forced to abandon it in the exodus of 1923, this grand villa was built between 1890 and 1903. It was later presented as a gift to Atatürk by the city of Trabzon, however, he only stayed briefly in the house on three occasions before his death in 1938, when it was inherited by the nation. Now open to visitors, the house contains a museum taken-up mainly with photographs of the great man. Of more interest is the building itself which represents an architectural style common in the Black Sea region at the turn of the century. Set in well-tended gardens the villa also has a very pleasant outdoor café. ■ *0830-1900 daily, 1730 in winter. US$0.75. Getting there: over 6 km from the town centre it can be reached on dolmuş marked 'Köşk' from Atatürk Alanı. Buses also make the journey from Atatürk Alanı, passing via Gülbahar Camii (US$0.50).*

Atatürk Köşkü

A flat-topped hill to the southeast of the town centre, Boztepe has been attributed with religious significance since ancient Greek times when it was called Mount Minthrion. The site of early temples dedicated to the Persian Sun God Mithra and Apollo, later during the Christian era its slopes were peppered with churches and monasteries. Today, a café and picnic

Boztepe

The Black Sea Region

area overlooking Trabzon are the focus of a more temporal pilgrimage at weekends and on summer evenings, when locals arrive to barbeque and drink tea from silver *samovars*. It's a lovely spot with sweeping views across the city and the coast beyond. ■ *Getting there: Hop on a dolmuş marked 'Boztepe' from near the Halk Bankası on Atatürk Alanı, US$0.50.*

Kaymaklı About 3 km beyond the picnic area are the remains of a 15th-century Armenian monastery with some fairly well-preserved frescoes surviving on its internal walls. Called Kaymaklı, the monastic buildings are on a small farm with the *katholikon* (chapel) – which contains the best frescoes – now used as a barn. The resident Kantekin family are quite accustomed to showing visitors around, however, so far the local government hasn't granted any funds for the buildings preservation. ■ *Getting there: Buses and dolmuş for Çukurayır pass near the site. Ask the driver to let you off at the Misirli Camii from where you need to continue for 100 m, turning left down a rough track. At present there's no sign-post and the track may not be passable after heavy rain. Continue down for nearly 1 km, choosing a right-hand fork and then a right turn at a junction.*

Essentials

Sleeping The accommodation situation in Trabzon is surprisingly dire, particularly at the budget end of the spectrum. The problem is not that there is a lack of places, just that the majority of these play host to 'Natashas' – prostitutes from the states of the former Soviet Union. Although the red-light district is centred in the area from Iskele Caddesi down towards the docks, many of the establishments further west towards Atatürk Alanı, and even on the square itself, have turned to prostitution in the face of a slump in more conventional business. It goes to say that such hotels are not recommended, particularly for women travelling alone, and actually most do not accept tourists anyway. Such establishments are not included in the list below, however, for an up-to-date rundown of the situation talk to the tourist office.

AL *Grand Hotel Zorlu*, Maraş Caddesi No 9, T3268400, F3268458, 50 m down from Atatürk Alanı, the height of luxury in Trabzon with amenities such a gym, pool, Turkish bath, bar and restaurant. **B** *Hotel Usta*, Iskenderpaşa Mahallesi No 3, T3265700, F3223793, between Atatürk Alanı and Iskele Caddesi. Modern, well-fitted rooms, TV, minibar, a/c, restaurant, bar. Recommended. **C** *Otel Horon*, Sıramağazalar No 125, T3266455, F3216628, otelhoron@otelhoron.com.tr, on backstreet just to north of Atatürk Alanı. Recently refitted with comfortable rooms above modern lobby, TV, telephone and minibar, rooftop restaurant and bar. Recommended. **D** *Hotel Özgür*, Atatürk Alanı No 29, T3264703, F3213952, on the south side of Atatürk Alanı. Under renovation at time of visit so expect prices to rise. **E** *Otel Sartes*, Kazım Sokak No 23, T3216655, F3230928, off Uzun Sokak and past Kostaki Konağı. Formerly the Villa Pension, converted house with small garden, quiet and well away from red-light district, reasonable rooms with TV, telephone, shower, decent single rooms. Recommended. **E** *Hotel London Palas*, Maraş Caddesi No 71, T3265426, F3225861. Past PTT on left, 2 and 3 bed rooms with ensuite shower, TV, telephone, back ones have no window. **E** *Otel Anıl*, Güzelhisar Caddesi No.10, T3267282, down the road at the top of Iskele Caddesi on the right. Despite being in the red-light district this is a reputable place favoured by visiting businessmen, reasonably priced rooms with shower, recommended but some rooms suffer from traffic noise. **E** *Hotel Nur*, Camii Sokak No 15, T3230445, F3230447, next to the tourist information. Small bright rooms in quiet backstreet hotel, well-equipped with TV, telephone and refrigerator. Recommended. **F** *Erzurum Oteli*, Güzelhisar Caddesi No 15, T3225427, past the *Otel Anıl* in the red-light district. Deteriorated recently, dingy rooms with shower and telephone. **F** *Otel Kalfa*, Atatürk Alanı,

T3216748, F3212690, opposite the Belediye building. Tatty place in need of redecoration, bad plumbing, prostitute-free at present. **G** *Hotel Benli*, Iskenderpaşa Mahallesi, T3211022. Large old-fashioned boarding house, small rooms with washbasin, shared toilets, a bit musty but recommended in the absence of anything better.

The Catholic church of Santa Maria, Sümer Sokak No 26, Iskenderpaşa Mahallesi, T3212192, offers simple accommodation for travellers within its compound. To find it follow the street that starts beside the *Güloğlu Restaurant* on the north side of Atatürk Alanı. Quiet, clean double rooms with shared bathroom are available regardless of denomination for a voluntary donation. Particularly recommended for women travellers.

Midrange *Şişman Restaurant*, roof-top place at the Atatürk Alanı end of Maraş   **Eating**
Caddesi, a good selection of meze and grilled meat, predominantly male clientel,
alcohol served. The *Zorlu Hotel* has a good restaurant with an à la carte menu and
excellent buffets. **Cheap** *Lezzet Restaurant*, in the northwest corner of Atatürk Alanı,
bare, unassuming place recommended locally for *tandır kebap* (roast lamb) and
stews. *Gelik*, Uzun Sokak, 300 m down from Atatürk Alanı on the right, bustling modern place with a confounding array of ready-prepared dishes, soups also döner, delicious rice puddings and other deserts. *Çardak*, Uzun Sokak, down alley on right 5 m
from Atatürk Alanı, another local favourite, this time for pide served with an artery
clogging dollop of melted butter and an egg on top (ask for *tereyağsız* - without butter
- if you're watching your waist-line), tables outside beneath vine in summer.
Seyitoğlu, Uzun Sokak, at the Atatürk Alanı end on left, large lahmacun served on
plastic platters, cramped seating area upstairs. *Hünkar*, Kazım Sokak, off Uzun Sokak,
just past Kostaki Konağı, smart place serving delicious lahmacun and kebaps.
Kebabistan, Maraş Caddesi, across from *Hotel Zorlu*, all types of kebap, very busy at
lunchtime, delicious baklava. If you have a sweet-tooth try *Beton Helva*, Uzun Sokak,
Atatürk Alanı end on the left. Huge blocks of helva displayed in the window, also
ice-cream. Look out for *pestil* in the confectionary shops nearby. A locally produced
mixture of honey, milk, mulberries and hazelnuts, it takes on a leathery texture when
dried in thin sheets. Excellent food for the mountains.

There are cafés along the sea-front where you can enjoy a drink and the bracing sea   **Cafés**
air, accompanied by the background roar of traffic on the coastal highway. *Ganite*
Çay Bahçesi has tables on ivy covered terraces next to the Genoese castle, reached
down Güzellhisar Caddesi and across footbridge spanning coastal highway, it's
deservingly the most popular, particularly with local students. Popular with local families, especially at the weekends when it can be hard to find a free table, is the café at
Boztepe (see sights).

Şişman Restaurant serves alcohol accompanied by meze if you so desire. For a more   **Bars**
raucous, male-dominated affair try the *gazinos* (drinking clubs) and bars along Iskele   *The more-expensive*
Caddesi, however, these aren't recommended for unaccompanied women.   *hotels around Atatürk*
Alanı have bars

Sports Trabzon is home to the only successful non-Istanbul team in Turkish football   **Entertainment**
and its citizens are fanatical, even by Turkish standards, supporters of *Trabzonspor*.
Home matches are played at Hüseyin Avni Aker Stadyumu, reached by Aya Sofia
dolmuş from Atatürk Alanı

Kıyıtour, Iskele Caddesi No 50/B, T3215596, F2441118, airline tickets, ferry reserva-   **Tour agencies**
tions, car rental. *Afacan*, Iskele Caddesi No 40, T3215804, F3217001, air and ferry tickets, tours to Sumela.

The Black Sea Region

Transport **Air** *Turkish Airlines*, office on corner of Atatürk Alanı and Uzun Sokak, T3211680/3446, daily services to **Istanbul** and **Ankara**. Reservations must be made well in advance during the summer. There are no service buses to the airport, however, '*Havaalanı*' taxi dolmuş depart 24 hrs a day from just north of Atatürk Alanı, near the Hotel Horon, on Sıramağazalar Caddesi. **Bus** The bus companies have offices around the south-eastern corner of Atatürk Alanı and up the hill on Erzurum Caddesi from where you can buy tickets. *Ulusoy* departures for **Istanbul** and **Ankara** leave from their compound on Erzurum Caddesi. **Ankara,** 3 daily, US$20, 12 hrs. **Antalya,** 1030, US$30, 22 hrs. **Artvin,** regular buses, US$7, 5 hrs. There are also daily buses to **Batumi,** 1800, US$50, 15 hrs. **Bursa,** several daily, US$25, 18 hrs. **Erzurum,** 3 daily, US$10, 5 hrs. **Istanbul,** 1100, 1300, 1530, 1700, US$25, 18 hrs. Buses for other destinations leave from the *otogar*. **Samsun,** regular buses, US$10, 6 hrs. **Yusufeli,** 3 direct daily, US$10, 7 hrs. **Car rental**: *Avis*, Gaziosmanpaşa Caddesi No 20/B, T3223740, F3263520, also has an office at the airport T3255582. *Budget*, airport arrivals terminal, T3259774, F3259776. A recommended local firm, *Yıldız*, can be found on Maraş Sokak next to the *Zorlu Hotel*. **Ferry** *Turkish Maritime Lines*, Taksim Parkı Üstü, T3217096, F3221004, departs from the *Truva* docks in Trabzon, check timetable on page 47. *Karden Line Ferries* depart Tue and Fri for **Sochi**, Russia, cabins from US$60, seats US$50, tickets available from *Sarı Tur*, Iskele Caddesi, T3215596.

Directory **Banks** All the major banks are found along Maraş Caddesi. The main Işbankası 250 m down from Atatürk Alanı changes TCs. There are also private money changers around the centre. **Baths** *Sekiz Direkli Hamamı*, Pazarkapı 8, Direkli Hamamı Sokak, open 0600-2330, US$2.50, women only on Thu. **Communications Post office**: On Maraş Caddesi, 600 m west of Atatürk Alanı. **Internet**: *Internet cafe*, Maraş Caddesi, 2nd floor of building next to Işbankası, US$2 per hr. **Places of Worship** *Santa Maria*, Catholic church but all welcome (see sights and sleeping sections). **Useful addresses** Georgian Consulate, Gazipaşa Caddesi No 20, T3262226/2296, next to *Avis Office*, 100 m down from Atatürk Meydanı, transit (US$10) and 15/30 day tourist visas (US$30/$40) available. Russian Consulate, T3262600, Ortahisar, just uphill from the Ortahisar Camii, doesn't issue visas at present.

Sumela Monastery

The Greek Orthodox monastery of Sumela perched over 300 m up on the vertical side of the Altındere Valley is one of those recurring images of Turkey used on countless Tourism Ministry posters and brochures. Despite this exposure and the inevitable crowds which follow, Sumela can't help but leave a lasting impression. In the days of the Byzantine Comneni it grew powerful, enjoying the favour of the emperors in Trebizond and its role as an integral part of the imperial defence system guarding the narrow passes over the mountains. Abandoned since 1923, it has a forlorn and melancholy air, particularly when enveloped in the perennial mists and cloud that swirl up the forested valley. A visit to Sumela should be made as early in the day as possible when you have the most chance of a clear sky. It's worth considering that it's usually crowded with day-trippers at weekends during the summer.

History Legend has it that an icon of the Virgin Mary painted by St Luke took flight from the sinful city of Athens, flying over the Aegean and along the Black Sea coast, finally coming to rest on a small ledge on the precipitous side of Black Mountain. Two monks, Barnabus and Sophronicus, set out to search for the missing icon and helped by a vision, they finally tracked it down to the narrow valley of Altındere in the Pontic Alps. However, instead of taking it back to Athens they built a shrine around the picture, calling it Panayia tou Melas, 'Virgin of the Black Rock'.

Unfortunately there is no evidence to support this enchanting story, although there does seem to have been a monastery at the site since the 10th century at least. It was several centuries later, however, during the time of the Grand Comneni, that Sumela rose to prominence thanks to generous imperial patronage. Alexis III had the monastery rebuilt in 1360 and imperial edicts exempted it from taxation. The monastery was also granted extensive estates; while being charged along with several other strategically placed monasteries, with the task of guarding the Maçka valley and warning the imperial capital of approaching danger.

During Ottoman times Sumela maintained its privileged position, receiving several imperial visits and generous endowments. Its isolated position made it a popular place of exile for orthodox criminals who would live out their lives watched over by the monks. The monastery also attracted a steady flow of visitors, both to pay their respects and out of curiosity.

Sumela survived as a functioning monastery until 1923 when the last monks were evacuated as part of the Greek and Turkish population exchanges. Since then years of neglect and deliberate damage have left the monastery in a ruinous state, though, an on-going restoration programme is slowly putting this to rights.

The site

From the valley floor a steep path climbs up the valleyside in a series of switchbacks to a terrace where you'll find the ticket office and a café. The monastery itself is reached up a flight of stairs, at the top of which you pass through the gatekeepers quarters. In days gone by visitors would be offered a glass of rakı accompanied by cheese and olives while they signed the visitors book. This book with its last entry dated 24 June 1921 still survives in Greece.

A staircase descends from the gate to the main courtyard passing the guest and living quarters on the right. Against the back wall are the library and a cave church which is richly decorated with frescoes dating back to the 14th century, but much added to since. Unfortunately, these beautiful works of art have been badly scarred by vandals and thieves, although higher up on the ceiling they remain more or less intact.

Restoration work, which actually amounts to a virtual rebuilding of the structure, is severely behind schedule and it looks like it will be several more years before it's completed. Until then, you'll just have to ignore the piles of bricks and the workmen as you try to visualize what the monastery was like in its heydey.

On the way back down, 25 m below the terrace, a path on the right leads through the forest to a small ruined chapel and an excellent vantage point from which to view the monastery. A path descends from here through the forest to a track at the bottom which leads back down the valley to the main carpark. You can also ascend to the monastery on this less-busy path if you prefer.

■ *0900-1200, 1300-1800. US$1.25, car US$2.50. Keep you ticket for inspection before entering the monastery. Getting there: At an altitude of over 1200 m, 54 km inland from Trabzon and 23 km above Maçka. Most people visit Sumela on a day trip from Trabzon either by taxi dolmuş (US$12 each person, depart when full from the south side of Atatürk Alanı) or an organized tour, such as the one run by Ulutur from the Ulusoy office (US$4 return per person, not including the entrance fee, with minibuses leaving at 1000 and 1100, and returning mid-afternoon). On the way back the minibus normally stops at one of several inexpensive trout restaurants on the approach to Sumela, which also serve-up traditional Black Sea dishes such as muhlama, a heavy mixture of butter, eggs, flour and cheese.*

Essentials

If you're under your own steam you may also think about staying at the pleasant **F** *Çosandere Pansiyon*, T04625311190, 2 km above Maçka it has cozy rooms in a wooden house, clean shared bathrooms, restaurant serving up regional specialities. There's also a riverside campsite nearby. At the car park there's a small restaurant, a

The Black Sea Region

post office and a row of Forestry Department **cabins** which are available for rent. Ring T2302179, or contact the tourist office in Trabzon to make a reservation.

Trabzon to Rize East of Trabzon the mountains, cloaked in a mass of vegetation, march progressively closer to the coast, eventually leaving just enough room for the new multi-lane highway, and indeed in places even this has had to be laid on reclaimed land. If you are desperate for a swim there are some reasonable beaches near **Araklı** and **Sürmene** both accessible on a day trip from Trabzon. Just past Sürmene look out for the **Yakupoğlu Konağı**, one of the finest surviving Ottoman mansions on the coast. The wood and stucco mansion was home to the local feudal lords of the Yakupoğlu clan up until the 1970's, however, since they vacated it the building has been neglected and is slowly crumbling. Some 14 km east the road passes the Solaklı Çayı river and the ugly, concrete town of **Of**, unremarkable except as the centre of a Greek Muslim community who converted to Islam during Ottoman times.

Uzun Göl If the Sumela monastery is the most photographed sight on the Black Sea coast, then the calm lake of Uzun Göl, fringed by pastures and pine-forested mountains comes a very close second. Nestled at over 1,000 m in the mountainous hinterland above the coastal town of Of, Uzun Göl is a popular weekend get-away for the area's urbanites, who come by the car and van-load in summer to barbeque, picnic and maybe take a stroll. Needless to say, if you'd prefer to experience Uzun Göl minus the hullabaloo visit mid-week when things are considerably quieter.

The lower part of the village with its waterside mosque is a clutter of fairly uninspiring, newish buildings, however on the slope above, the old quarter harbours some more attractive wooden houses. There are quite a number of places to stay around the lake with **F-G** *Özkan Hotel*, T6566197, a large building on the lakeside near the mosque, offering simple 2/3/4 bed rooms with ensuite, breakfast and buffet dinner option available, closed in winter. Far nicer is the homely **E** *Huzur Pansiyon* half-way down the valley on the hillside above the road, which has clean rooms in a traditional house with lovely views from the balcony, also use of kitchen. Recommended. About 1 km beyond the village the friendly *Inan Kardeşler Motel*, T6566021, has clean wooden chalets sleeping two to 10 people, all of which are equipped with a bathroom and heating. Half and full-board options available with fresh trout from the adjacent fish farm featuring on the menu. Recommended. If you're only after a meal both the *Inan Kardeşler* and *Özkan* do very reasonably priced trout and salad, as well as local specialities such as *muhlama*.

Beyond the fresh air and scenic surroundings, Uzungöl suggests itself as a base for excursions into the wild and beautiful mountains ringing the village. There are a number of possibilities for day-hikes or longer treks to points such as the Soğanlı Pass (2330 m) or the Ziyaret Dağları (3,111m). Özkan, proprietor of the *Özkan Hotel*, is a useful source of information and can also act as a guide.

■ *Getting there: Uzungöl is reached up the Solaklı Çayı valley from a junction on the coastal highway to the west of Of. After passing through the town of Çaykara, 25 km from the coast, a left-hand turn takes you up a rougher 16 km road to the lake. There are mini-buses direct to Uzun Gol from Trabzon 3 times a day in the summer. They depart from the Çömlekci dolmuş stand next to the Avrasya Pazarı. Alternatively, get-off a dolmuş travelling along the coastal highway at the turn-off for Çaykara and wait for a dolmuş inland or hitch.* Afacan Tur *in Trabzon (see directory above) and* Ritur *in Rize (see directory below) organize daytrips to Uzungöl in summer.*

Rize

A modern town of apartment blocks squeezed onto the narrow coastal plain, Rize doesn't have much to detain the traveller. Its main claim to fame is as the centre of Turkey's tea growing region with fields of neatly clipped bushes marching up the surrounding mountainsides. The **tea research institute**, set in well-kept grounds on a hill-top overlooking the town, has a lovely garden where you can sip tea and enjoy the view. Follow signs for the 'Çay Araştırma Enstitüsü' up the hill for about 700 m from Atatürk Meydanı, easily recognized by the statue of Atatürk holding a flame at its centre. Continuing straight ahead from Atatürk Meydanı for about a kilometre will bring you to the ruins of Rize's diminutive castle where you'll find another café for refreshments. Back down in the town, inland from the roundabout on the coastal road, the main streets of Atatürk Caddesi and Cumhuriyet Caddesi run parallel to each other and the highway. Squeezed between the two is yet another large tea-garden which forms the focus for the town's civic life.

Phone code: 0464
Colour map 3, grid B2
Population: 54,000

Sleeping

A *Otel Kaptanlar*, Menderes Bulvarı No 172, T2130874, F2130883. Modern, on the coastal road 300 m west of the centre, comfortable rooms with TV, telephone and ensuite bathroom, breakfast extra, price seems excessive. **D** *Otel Kaçkar*, Cumhuriyet Caddesi No 101, T2131490, west of the main square. Newish building with small rooms, equipped with ensuite, telephone and TV. **F** *Hotel Evin*, Atatürk Caddesi No 420, T2131767. Simple rooms with shower closet in the corner, each bed also comes with a handy prayer mat. **F** *Otel Efes*, Atatürk Caddesi, T2141111, 100 m east of main square. Clean homely rooms with shower, TV and balcony. Recommended. **G** *Yüksel Otel*, Şehitler Caddesi No 18, on the front to the west of the roundabout. Basic is the only way to describe it. **G** *Otel Kent*, Maraşal Fevzi Çakmak Caddesi No 3, T2179854, west corner of the main square. Another very basic place but this one has suspect looking women hanging around in the reception.

Eating

Lale Restaurant, on the east side of main square, is a modern a/c place with excellent kebaps, the *kuru fasulye* (bean stew) is locally renowned but unsuitable for vegetarians due to the large chunks of meat in it, delicious *sütlaç* (rice pudding) with heaps of roasted hazelnuts on top. *Alaçoğlu Balık Lokantası*, Menderes Bulvarı, on the coastal road to the west of the roundabout and Belediye bus stand, fish restaurant above a shop selling the catch-of-the-day, very good selection and reasonable prices. For sweets and puddings try *Ismailoğlu* on the north side of the square, specialities include Laz Böreği, a creamy pudding wrapped with pastry.

Tour agencies

Ritur, Cumhuriyet Caddesi No 93, T2171484, F2171486, local agents for *Turkish Airlines* and *Turkish Maritime Lines* ferries, also have sightseeing and jeep tours to Uzungöl, Ayder and other places in the Kaçkar.

Transport

Road Bus: The *otogar* is just under a kilometre west of the centre. *Ulusoy* and *Show Turizm* have their offices on Cumhuriyet Bulvarı to the west of the main square and provide free service buses to the *otogar*. **Artvin**, every hr, 5 hrs, US$6. **Batumi**, 1 daily, 4 hrs, US$10. **Erzurum**, 2 daily, 6 hrs, US$7. **Hopa**, every hr, 1½ hrs, US$3.50. **Tbilisi**, 1 daily, 10 hrs, US$25. **Trabzon**, every 1½ hrs, 1¼ hrs, US$3. **Dolmuş** leave from the seaward side of the main roundabout on the coastal highway for Trabzon and Hopa. There is also a service in the summer to **Çamlıhemşin** and **Ayder** at 0900, 1100 and 1400. At other times get a *Hopa* dolmuş to Pazar and then change onto a dolmuş to Çamlıhemşin or Ayder.

The Black Sea Region

●●●

☞ *The Laz*

The Laz are an ethnic group who live along the eastern Black Sea coast between Pazar and Hopa. Numbering about 200,000, they are Caucasian people who speak Lazuri, a language closely related to modern Georgian. This has lead some researchers to speculate that they may infact be the legendary Colchians, guardians of the Golden Fleece. Far more certain is that the Laz migrated south from the Caucasus over a thousand years ago, adopting Christianity after their arrival in what is now northeast Turkey. A fiercely independent people, they maintained some degree of autonomy until the 16th-century Ottoman conquest, when they were converted to Islam. Even to this day, however, the Laz are not known for piety, instead gaining a reputation for their relaxed interpretations of Koranic law.

Typically tall and thin with blondy red hair, Laz are usually fairly easy to spot in a crowd. Their aquiline features and supposed slow-wittedness make them the butt of countless Turk-inspired jokes, though they also have a legendary
penchant for wise-cracking themselves.

Despite their distinctiveness, the Laz have always been keen participants in Turkish society and many now live far beyond the borders of Lazland. Well-known as seafarers and shrewd business men, the Laz play an important role in the Turkish shipping industry, as well as being inseparably associated with hamsi, the Black Sea anchovies caught off the coast.

Laz assimilation into Turkish society has inevitably led to an erosion of their own culture and traditions. In a controversial effort to halt this process a German academic, Wolfgang Feuerstein, created an alphabet of Latin and Georgian letters for the previously unwritten Lazuri language. Using this alphabet Feuerstein, working with a group of expatriot Laz, has compiled a Lazuri dictionary and created a written Laz history for the first time. Ever sensitive to the dangers of nationalism amongst its ethnic minorities the Turkish government has viewed these developments with great unease.

●●●

Directory **Airline offices** See tour agencies. **Banks** *İşbankası* is just inland of the main roundabout on the coastal highway. **Post office** The PTT is on Atatürk Meydanı, west of the main square. **Internet** *Internet Planet*, Atatürk Meydanı, top floor of building at the west end of Atatürk Caddesi. **Tourist information** There are small tourist information booths in the corner of the main square and on Atatürk Meydanı.

Pazar Pazar is about as unattractive as the other towns along this stretch of coast, however, it is an important departure point for dolmuş up to the high valleys and yayla of the Kaçkar mountains. Dolmuş generally depart early in the morning for the yayla (see page 575), returning in the evening or the next day. There are regular minibuses up to Çamlıhemşin and Ayder throughout the day. Should you need it there is a passable hotel on the main road west of the centre: **E** *Otel Martı*, T6122181. There is also an *İşbankası* on the main road.

To Hopa East of Pazar, the coastal road winds along between the green mountains and the grey brooding sea. This is the traditional homeland of the Laz people (see box), one of Turkey's most celebrated ethnic minorities. Unfortunately, the towns along this stretch of coast do little to complement the natural beauty of the landscape and are in fact distinguished, even by eastern Black Sea standards, by their ugliness and disorganization.

Hopa After 51 km the mountains retreat from the coast and you reach Hopa, the last
Phone code: 0464 Turkish town before the Georgian border, 22 km beyond. It's another fairly unappealing place in the typical Black Sea mould: a strip of high-rise blocks

with several lanes of traffic and plenty of concrete separating it from the waves. Adding to its attraction are the extensive docks from where copper mined nearby is loaded on to waiting ships. Arriving at the bus station the centre of town and hotels are several hundred metres to the east, and reached across a busy bridge spanning the Sundurna Çayı.

Sleeping The opening of the Turkish-Georgian border after the collapse of the Soviet Union has reinvigorated the local hotel trade, however, many of the places double as brothels. The hotels below were 'Natasha'-free when visited. **E** *Turistik Otel Cihan*, Ortahopa Caddesi No 5, T3512333, next to the Turk Petrol station 300 m east of the centre. Fairly standard 2-star hotel, rooms overlooking sea and coastal highway, ensuite, TV, telephone, balcony as standard. **F** *Otel Köşk*, Ortahopa Caddesi No 21, T3515024, one street back from the front just to the east of the Türk Petrol station, unassuming place with clean rooms with shower, TV, telephone, single US$13, breakfast extra. Recommended. **F** *Otel Huzur*, Cumhuriyet Caddesi No 25, T3514095, on the front west of the centre. Clean but unexciting rooms with shower. Recommended.

Eating *Cennet Lokantası, Pide & Kebap Salonu*, Ortahopa Caddesi, just to east of centre, as the name suggests this place has a wide selection of food, including breakfast and cakes. *Meydan Pide & Işkembe Salonu*, Cumhuriyet Meydanı, cheap place right in the centre with soups, pide and lahmacun. The *Belediye Çay Bahçesi*, east of the centre, is a good place for a glass of tea outside in the gardens.

Transport **Artvin**, every 30 mins, 1½ hrs, US$3. **Baku**, evening bus, 40 hrs, US$60. **Batumi**, evening bus, 1 hr, US$15. **Tiblis**, evening bus, 20 hrs, US$25. **Trabzon**, every 30 mins, 3 hrs, US$4. **Kemalpaşa/Sarp**, leave when full from next to the Türk Petrol station, 300 m east of the centre, US$1/1.50.

Directory Banks There is an *İşbankası* in the centre on Cumhuriyet Meydanı. **Post office** The PTT is also on Cumhuriyet Meydanı.

To the Georgian Border

Some 10 km east of Hopa is the town of **Kemalpaşa**, set back from a long pebbly beach with a tea-factory sited half-way along its length. This could be a possible outing if you are waiting for an evening bus into Georgia, although there are no facilities at present on the shade-less beach.

Less than 10 km beyond Kemalpaşa the small village of **Sarp** sits on the Georgian border. Dolmuş shuttle between Hopa and Sarp via Kemalpaşa regularly throughout the day. If you are crossing into Georgia you will need a visa obtained from the consulates in Ankara, Istanbul or Trabzon (see page 568). Evening buses leave from Hopa for Tiblis and Batumi, however, they arrive inconveniently in the middle of the night. You may prefer to take a dolmuş to the border and catch a taxi or minibus from the Georgian side into Batumi, US$15.

Artvin

The provincial town of Artvin has a wonderful position overlooking the deep Çoruh valley. Unfortunately, the uninspiring approach, past grim concrete blocks housing various arms of the local administration, sets the tone for what is a very disappointing town, devoid of any interest or charm. The only conceivable reason to visit is for the Kafkasör festival held on the last weekend in June in the mountains above town. This is a colourful three day event including poetry recitals, folk dancing, wrestling and culminating on the final day with the famous bull-fighting tournament. Crowds of up to 75,000 come from the surrounding region, and even from across the Georgian border, to camp in

Phone code: 0466
Colour map 3, grid A3
Altitude: 500 m
70 km inland from Hopa

The Black Sea Region

the meadows and indulge in around-the-clock merry-making. Outside this weekend tranquility reigns in the meadows and woods of Kafkasör, making it an excellent place to camp. Along with several restaurants, the local belediye has comfortable bungalows which are a pleasant alternative to staying in town (see sleeping). Dolmuş leave for Kafkasör from outside the Emniyet Müdürlüğü (Police headquarters) on İnönü Caddesi at 0700 and 1830, returning 30 minutes later.

With the limited prospects for employment in the local area, Artvinli have traditionally migrated west for up to 10 months of the year to work in Istanbul and the cities of western Turkey. Many hope that the mammoth Çoruh River project, consisting of a series of eight dams, the first of which is currently under construction to the southeast of town, will not just provide short-term employment, but may also help the local economy to diversify beyond forestry and farming.

Sleeping

There are lots of cheap hotels though most are given over to prostitution so don't expect an undisturbed nights sleep

C *Otel Karahan*, İnönü Caddesi No 16, T2122270, F2122420, reached through an arcade on İnönü Caddesi. The best place in town and natasha-free, reasonable rooms with ensuite but pretty over-priced, single rooms US$40. **E** *Çağdaş Otel*, İnönü Caddesi No 27/2, T2123333, F2124851. Newly opened hotel with small but clean wood-panelled rooms, each has ensuite, TV and telephone, also a suite with jacuzzi. Recommended. **F** *Kaçkar Hotel*, İnönü Caddesi, T2123399. Tall concrete building to th left of İnönü Caddesi, ill-fitting carpets and grimy walls but it's not a brothel, plain rooms with ensuite and sweeping views across the valley to make up for the mediocrity of the place. There are also lots of places to **camp** up at Kafkasör.

Eating

Midrange *Hanedan*, İnönü Caddesi, meze and grilled meat, a couple of tables have a great view, alcohol served. *Nazar*, at the bottom of İnönü Caddesi, has a similar menu and wonderful views over the Çoruh valley from its terrace, breakfast also served. **Cheap** *Saklıca*, down a set of stairs next to the *Divan Hotel* on İnönü Caddesi, don't be put-off by the plain interior, excellent soups and stews, unfortunately not suitable for vegetarians. *Kibar Aile Lokantası*, up steps beside the Emniyet Müdürlüğü on İnönü Caddesi, small non-descript place serving hearty pide and lahmacun. For breakfast and desserts try the *Köşk Pastanesi*, towards the top of İnönü Caddesi which has a good choice of pastries, cakes and biscuits.

Transport

Bus The bus station is on a terrace 500 m below the town centre, but all companies have free minibuses to and from their offices on İnönü Caddesi. **Dolmuş** also stop around the corner from the grim concrete government building on İnönü Caddesi. **Ankara**, 1600, 18 hrs, US$25. **Ardahan**, 2 buses daily, 3 hrs, US$7. **Erzurum**, 4 daily, 4 hrs, US$8. **Hopa**, every hr, 1½ hrs, US$2.50. **Istanbul**, 1300, 22 hrs, US$30. **Trabzon**, 5 daily, 5 hrs, US$9. **Yusufeli**, 4 daily, 1½ hrs, US$2.

Directory Airline offices The local agent for *Turkish Airlines* is the *Otel Karahan*, İnönü Caddesi. **Banks** All the major banks with ATMs are along İnönü Caddesi. **Post office** The PTT is on İnönü Caddesi. **Internet** *Televole*, above the Köşk Pastanesi at top end of İnönü Caddesi, US$1.50 per hr. **Tourist information** The tourist information office, with helpful English speaking staff, can be found on the second floor of the government building behind the Merkez Camii. To find it turn right at the huge concrete Vilayet building on İnönü Caddesi and then right again. Weekdays 0800-1200, 1330-1730.

The Kaçkar Dağları

The Kaçkar Dağları are the lofty eastern continuation of the Pontic mountains which run like a backbone along the entire Black Sea coast. To the southeast of Rize these peaks take on a grander scale, with the main ridge-line reaching beyond 3,500 m in a series of rocky summits. Reminiscent of parts of the Alps, the mountains are dotted with numerous icy tarns and cloaked on their northern haunches by huge swathes of undisturbed forest. The Kaçkar also have considerable human interest in the form of the mountain peoples who live in rustic villages of timber houses. These attributes attract a small but growing stream of foreign and domestic tourists who come to hike and climb in these magnificent mountains.

In recent years road builders have made great inroads into the Kaçkar mountains, linking most of the villages and *yayla* (high settlements traditionally occupied only during the summer) with the lower valleys. This policy, driven by the desire of local people who enjoy considerable political patronage, has been at a terrible cost to the environment. Tracks with obsurdly steep gradients have been bulldozed across forested mountainsides and beyond into the fragile alpine zone, initiating erosion and opening the way for illegal logging. In terms of trekking, these tracks, and the dolmuş that bounce up them, have made access to the *yayla* at the heart of the range very easy, at the expense of shortening the trekking routes, sacrificing the lower sections below the tree-line. Of course the enthusiast can still walk.

Access from the Black Sea coast is up the Fırtına Valley from Pazar. At Çamlıhemşin a side valley leads to Ayder, above which are the *yayla* of Avusor, Çaymakçur and Yukarı Kavron. Continuing up the Fırtına Valley gives access to the *yayla* in the southwest parts of the range including: Çat, Pokut, Palovit, Apıvanak and Orta Yayla. Dolmuş leave Pazar in the summer on a daily basis for many of the *yayla*, departing from 0700. From the south, a road above Yusufeli leads to Barhal, giving access to the Altıparmak range, and Olgunlar on the fringes of the central massif. There are daily dolmuş to both Barhal and Olgunlar from Yusufeli.

A wall of granite mountains, culminating in the country's third highest peak, 3972-m Mount Kaçkar, the range has a considerable effect on the regional climate, blocking the moisture laden air blown off the Black Sea and preventing it from reaching the Anatolian plateau. Conditions on the seaward side of the range are typically wet, with the mountains enveloped in mist and low cloud which rise-up during the morning on most days during the summer. On this side the mountains are cloaked in rich deciduous forest, giving way to mixed forests of pine and rhododendrum higher-up. The southeastern flank, facing the Anatolian interior, is drier and more sparsely vegetated, except around the villages where irrigation supports verdant orchards and cropland.

The seaward valleys are occupied predominantly by the Hemşin people (see box). The continental side of the range was home to Georgians and Armenians who have left the valleys dotted with churches and the local nomenclature scattered with names derived from their languages. These mountain folk traditionally migrated up from villages in the spring to graze their flocks on the lush grasses of the high pastures, or *yayla*, descending again at the end of summer. Although this pastoral existence is now almost extinct, killed-off by the huge exodus to find work in the cities of western Turkey, the *yayla* are not empty. Instead in summer they're occupied by locals returning to enjoy an extended holiday in the clean air and spectacular surroundings of their homeland.

Ins & outs

The area

The Back Sea Region

Trekking

The peculiarities of the local weather are the main factors to consider when planning the timing of a visit

Thick mists boil-up on the seaward side of the range most days until the end of August. September is generally a bit more settled, although by the end of the month most of the *yayla* are empty and the higher dolmuş services on the north-west side of the range have ceased. Earlier in the season (from late June onwards) trekking is of course possible, with the greater probability of wet, cloudy weather partially compensated by the wildflowers which carpet the alpine meadows.

Whatever the month, it's important to start early to take advantage of what are generally better conditions in the mornings. This is particularly true when negotiating high-passes from the north. As with any excursion into high mountains it's necessary to be adequately equipped with tent, stove, food, comfortable walking boots, and warm and water-proof clothing before setting-off. A compass is also handy for when you get caught in a pea-soup fog, but its usefulness will be limited by the lack of any detailed large scale maps of the area. As you might expect there aren't any problems finding water in the Kaçkar, although you may want to carry some water purification tablets. There are shops with a reasonable selection of supplies in Çamlıhemşin, Ayder, Yusufeli and Barhal, although specialist items should be brought with you. Ayder and some of the *yayla* also have small shops and even the odd bakery.

Guides Mehmet Demirci of *Türkü Tourizm* (see page 577) has excellent local knowledge and limited English. Guides can also be arranged through a number of the hotels in Ayder, such as the *Pirikoğlu* and *Klup Kaçkar*. In Yusufeli, contact the *Kayak Raft Dağcılık Ihtisas Derneği* (see page 581) who can organize guides and horses.

Trekking agencies *Anatolian Adventures*, T0207-8741107, psunshine@hotmail.com, a London-based company arranges trekking trips in the Kaçkar mountains. *Türkü Turizm* organizes walks, treks and sightseeing trips into the mountains.

Books & maps **Books** 'The Mountains of Turkey', **Karl Smith**, Cicerone Guide. Most comprehensive climbing and trekking guide to the range, though some trekking sections lack detail.
Maps There aren't any commercially produced maps of the Kaçkar available, although photocopies of military maps circulate amongst the pension owners and guides.

Kaçkar Dağları treks

Hemşin culture

The Hemşinli are an ethnic group who live more discreetly alongside their notorious neighbours the Laz, in the valleys which drain the northern flanks of the Kaçkar mountains. Originally of Armenian extraction, with the predominance of fair complexions to prove it, the Hemşinli converted to Islam sometime in the last century, thereby avoiding the fate which befell their Christian brethren.

Accustomed to living under difficult conditions, the Hemşinli are both resourceful and adventurous, with a tendency to travel widely in search of employment. Many sought their fortune in Czarist Russia until the revolution closed-off such avenues of opportunity, while in more modern times Europe has become the favoured destination. Of the 25,000 or-so Hemşinli, less than half currently reside on their home turf, something that is obvious in summer when every other car seems to have European plates.

It may have been while in Russia during the last century that the Hemşinli learnt the art of sweet-making, a skill at which they excel. Most of the best pastaneler in the country are either owned or run by Hemşinli, with the cake business being the foundation of many a local fortune.

Despite being part of such a far-flung diaspora, the Hemşinli strongly uphold their distinctive cultural identity part of which involves returning to their mountainous homeland each summer. Once in the Hemşin valleys the women don their colourful head-scarfs which are imported all the way from India. A part of the summer visit is spent in a yayla, a seasonal settlement high on the alpine pastures above the tree-line, enjoying the clean air and recharging their Hemşin-ness. The yayla, which can vary from a small cluster of low stone huts to village-like communities of wooden chalets, were traditionally occupied during the summer months as part of a transhumant lifestyle typical of mountain people. Each summer the Hemşin would move up with their flocks of sheep and cows to take advantage of the rich alpine pastures, descending again in autumn. Today, however, the herds grazing the high meadows are a fraction of what they used to be and most of the yayla's occupants are simply on holiday, with the month of August marked by lively festivities and get-togethers.

Çamlıhemşin
Phone code: 0464

The 22 km drive up the Fırtına Valley to Çamlıhemşin takes you into the forested foothills of the Kaçkar Mountains past steep tea plantations and several picturesque humpbacked bridges. After this approach and with all the expectation of arriving at the centre of the Hemşin valleys, the row of concrete buildings, squeezed between the foaming waters of the Fırtına Çayı and the precipitous valleyside, that greets you is more than a little disappointing. In fact there's very little to the one-street town at all with most of its population living in small communities scattered across the surrounding area. Crane your neck and high on the forested slopes above you'll catch a glimpse of magnificent wooden houses, surrounded by tea bushes and corn and connected to the valley by winch-driven cable cars. Indeed, except for some shops where you can stock-up on supplies and a couple of cheap cateries there is nothing to detain you in Çamlıhemşin.

A left turn at the upper edge of town leads across the Fırtına river and up to Ayder, straight ahead the road rapidly deteriorates into a track heading up the Upper Fırtına valley to Çat and numerous yayla above it. Dolmuş shuttle back and forth between Çamlıhemşin and Pazar during the day, though much less frequently on Sundays, US$1.25.

Directory Bank: There is a bank with ATM although don't rely on this working. They won't change TCs. **Travel agencies**: *Türkü Tourism*, İnönü Caddesi No 47, T6517230, run by Mehmet Demirci who can organize treks, yayla tours and jeep safaris, as well as horses and guides.

The Back Sea Region

Ayder

Phone code: 0464

Deep in the mountains 17 km above Çamlıhemşin, not-so-long ago Ayder was a small village of rustic log cabins with a nearby hot-spring. The ribbon of tarmac connecting it to the coast however has allowed Ayder to develop rapidly into a tourist centre. Promoting its fresh mountain air and beautiful scenery there are over a dozen hotels, several of them built illegally, and a huge new bath complex.

All this additional concrete has rather detracted from the natural beauty of the village's surroundings in a narrow forested valley cut by a ragging torrent. But, particularly during the month of August, the village gives visitors an unrivalled opportunity to experience the local culture. At this time Hemşinli converge on the village from all across Turkey and Europe for their annual holiday which takes on the form of a boisterous reunion. The focus of much of these festivities is the large meadow in the centre of the village where the *horon* is danced, accompanied by the discordant whine of an indigenous bagpipe-like instrument, the *tulum*. Empty rooms are few and far between during this period.

The *Ayder kaplıcaları* is the other reason to visit, with its piping-hot mineral waters, emerging from the ground at over 55ºC, said to be beneficial for various ailments. A wallow in the separate male and female pools, or the private baths, is certainly the best place to soak away those aches and pains after trekking. ■ *0700-2000 daily, US$2.* The original baths, much more modest in comparison, are below the new complex. ■ *0900-1700 for women; 1700-1900 for men, US$2.*

Sleeping & eating

There are several restaurants such as the Nazlı Çicek next to the bridge which serve trout, local dishes and alcohol. Most of the pensions in the village will also prepare evening meals on request

E *Ahşap Pansiyon*, Yukarı Ambarlık Mevkii, T6572162, up past the hot-baths and the meadow, visible above the road on the left, path begins beside a spring, newly built but traditional design, wooden house, small cozy rooms with ensuite, 2 apartments with kitchenette and sitting room US$35. Recommended. **F** *Ayder Hilton*, T6572024, near the hot-springs. Do not be fooled by the name. An ugly concrete structure, plain rooms with shared bathroom, breakfast extra. **F** *Clup Kaçkar*, T6572108, F6572109. Family-run pension in a wooden house down near the river at the lower end of village, quiet position, trekking information available. Recommended. **F** *Doğa Harikası Pansiyon*, T6572134, on the road above the hot-baths. Small simple rooms with shared bathroom, a good option for women travellers. **F** *Fora Pension*, T/F6517230. Small traditional-style house high above the road as you enter the village, reached by a path on left after *Pirikoğlu Otel*, peaceful position, homely atmosphere, simple rooms, shared bathroom, home-cooked meals, Mehmet who runs the pension also runs a local travel agency and can provide information. Recommended. **F** *Saray Hotel*, 6572001. Wooden building overlooking the bridge, becomes a busy Hemşin boarding house in Jul and Aug, when it's very crowded and lacks privacy, not to mention possible fire-risk. **F** *Yeşil Vadi Oteli*, T6572050, before the bridge on the right. Spartan twin-bedded rooms, shared bathroom, have more comfortable wood-panelled rooms with ensuite for US$16, kitchen on each floor. **G** *Çalayan Otel*, T6572073, just beyond hot-baths. Long wooden boarding house which is one of the village's original lodgings, no bathrooms due to proximity to hot-springs, simple traditional food prepared, manager Kadir Sarı is an experienced local guide. The Yüksel family, T6572095, have a very clean and comfortable **self-contained apartment** for rent below their house. Sleeps 4-5. Above hot-baths and meadow, new wooden house with red roof visible to the right of the road, no sign, US$35 per night, reserve well ahead in summer.

Transport

During the summer there are hourly **dolmuş** from Pazar to **Ayder**, 0900-1800, US$1.75. There are also 3 daily dolmuş to and from **Rize**. A **taxi** from Çamlıhemşin to Ayder costs US$15.

Trekking from Ayder

This two day route passes the enchanting lakes of Büyük Deniz and Karadeniz **Ayder**
Gölü, both set in spectacular surroundings, before crossing over the main **Çaymakçur**
ridge-line via the relatively easy Çaymakçur pass (3351 m) to the Düpedüz val- **Pass-Olgunlar**
ley. It is possible to extend this route from Olgunlar up the Büyük Çay to Mount
Kaçkar, returning via Deniz Gölü and the Kavron Pass to the northwest side of
the range (see Trans-Kaçkar), thereby encircling the entire central range.

1 Dolmuş leave Pazar for Yukarı Kavron Yaylası everyday during the summer
at 0700, passing through Ayder about one hour later.

2 Yukarı Kavron is a large *yayla* of over 300 houses with a small shop,
tea-house and a bakery that does delicious sesame rolls. It's also the starting
point for ascents of the glacier-hung north face of Mount Kaçkar via Öküz
Yatağı Gölü. From the *yayla* the path to Deniz Gölü zig-zags up the steep
valleyside to the east starting from near the bridge. Once you reach the lip, continue up easy-angled meadows on the right bank of the stream to a steep rocky
section where paths on either bank become visible (two hours). Once you have
ascended this section, break left away from the stream and climb-up several
hundred metres of steep scree to a plateau above and the placid waters of
Büyük Deniz Gölü. This makes an excellent campsite particularly if you have
been enveloped by the afternoon mists; with a spectacular view of Mezovit
(3760 m) and Mount Kaçkar to the south if you haven't.

3 From the small ridge just to the northeast of Büyük Deniz Gölü a steep path
descends to Karadeniz Gölü nestling like a piece of jade amongst the scree.
Before you drop down notice the path climbing the scree slopes beneath the
rocky pyramid of peak 3405 m to the southeast. Descend to the stream which
empties into Karadeniz Gölü and pick-up a well-marked trail climbing-up on
the other side. This track, marked regularly by cairns, zig-zags its way up to the
col in about 90 minutes.

4 The path drops steeply from the small col before passing along the
left-hand side of a sharp moraine. For the next 30 minutes the descent is in a
southeasterly direction over large slopes of broken rock, with the river and the
flat pastures of the Düpedüz Valley finally coming into view below you. A path
traverses left along the valley side above the meadows losing height slowly.

5 The Düpedüz Valley, its meadows carpeted with flowers early in the season
and its head guarded by an impressive crenellated ridge, makes a lovely place
to camp, but you may prefer to press on down the valley to Olgunlar. This
descent takes about 90 minutes, passing through the small *yayla* of Döbe as the
valley swings around to the right (southeast).

The Upper Fırtına Valley

Soon after leaving Çamlıhemşin the tarmac runs out and a pot-holed track
twists and turns its way up the Fırtına Valley, past magnificent wooden houses
perched high on the forested mountain sides. The beauty of this stretch of the
valley, if you can see out of the steamed-up windows of the dolmuş, is outstanding. Unfortunately, there is trouble in paradise as the government and a
consortium of foreign companies are hoping to harness the energy of the river
with a series of dams. The project has been repeatedly stalled in the courts by

The Black Sea Region

legal action, however, it seems to be progressing inexorably forward particularly in the face of only minor local resistance.

Some 12 km above Çamlıhemşin, the prominent tower of **Zil Kale** is an unmistakable landmark, standing forlornly on a bluff above the river. Built in the 12th or 13th century, it functioned primarily as a garrison to guard the upper valley, although it has also been suggested that it stood on what was an alternative route to the coast for the overland Silk caravans when the pass at Zigana was closed.

After another twelve bone-rattling kilometres, arriving at the small yayla of **Çat** is a relief. Spread-out on either side of the river, it's a tranquil spot except for the occasional car or dolmuş crawling up to the *yayla* above. The centre of things is the **F** *Otel Cancık*, T6544120, a warm friendly hotel, cum restaurant cum general store, with simple rooms. If the *Cancık* is full, which it probably will be in August, try the *Çat Tesisleri* at the bottom end of the village which has similar rooms with shared bathroom above a café/restaurant. A dolmuş leaves for Çat everyday at 0800 from Pazar, passing via Çamlıhemşin and returning in the afternoon. You could also get on a morning dolmuş from Pazar to Palovit or Başyayla which also pass through Çat.

Above Çat the track divides with the right-hand option leading up to Ortayayla and Çiçekliyayla, the jumping-off points for exploration of the southern-most section of the Kaçkar, the Verçenik range.

The left-hand track passes through the substantial *yayla* of **Elevit**, before dolmuş bump and grind their way up to **Tirevit**. From here the track claws its way up the valleyside in a series of ludicrously tight switch-backs, with dolmuş having to reverse to get around several of the tight corners. This ascent and the equally steep descent to **Palovit** are definitely not for the faint-hearted.

For a pleasant excursion returning to Çat or Elevit, catch a Palovit-bound dolmuş from Pazar, Çamlıhemşin or Çat and get-off at the small yayla of Karıç above Elevit. Cross the bridge and pick-up a well-defined path which traverses across the opposite side of the valley through pine forest. This path culminates at a grassy promontory above Elevit which boasts a superb view and lots of delicious wild strawberries at the end of August. The foundations of an Armenian church are just visible beneath the vegetation, while the sound of a spring filling a large water trough completes the mezmorizing peacefulness of the site.

To descend to Elevit you can either retrace you steps to the road or descend directly down the steep meadows to the valley below, where paths lead back to the *yayla*.

There is a guesthouse in Elevit which provides accommodation and serves-up local staples such as *muhlama* and soup. If you are still feeling energetic it's a 7-km walk down the forested valley to Çat.

Another possible day-trip starting from Elevit is to the lake of Yıldız Gölü, situated about three hours walk up the valley to the south of the yayla.

Palovit to Şenyuva or Ayder

This is an easy two-day route (actually possible in one long day if you are short of time) which takes you through some of the most beautiful Hemşin yayla and unspoilt forested scenery without the need for a tent or other heavy equipment. The setting-off point is the yayla of Palovit, reachable by dolmuş from Pazar via Çamlıhemşin on Thursday, Saturday, Monday, US$7. It's a bumpy three-hour ride which exacts a heavy price on the vehicles suspension, not to mention the passengers.

1 After arriving in Palovit continue down the valley for 45 minutes to the charming *yayla* of Amlakit, set on either side of the Palovit stream just above the tree-line. The dolmuş sometimes drives this section, but you'll probably have had enough of bouncing around inside it. At present this is where the jeep track ends, however, there are plans to drive it on to Pokut through the pristine forests of the lower Palovit valley.

2 Having crossed the river, the path descends from Amlakit on the right side of the valley through stands of pine, their trunks and branches cloaked in beard-like white moss. Some 20 minutes below the yayla is a bridge across a side-stream, after which the path climbs for an hour to the yayla of Hazindak.

3 Here you have the choice of descending directly to Ayder or continuing onwards to the yayla of Pokut. Each route takes about two hours. People in the yayla will be happy to point you in the right direction for either. The path down to Pokut passes through some of the most beautiful scenery on the entire route, perched high on a spur above the Palovit valley. The views on a clear day of the forested flanks of the Kaçkar are stunning. There is flat space to pitch a tent at the far end of the yayla, but if you fancy a bed for the night, there is also the homely (if slightly over-priced) **Pokut Demircioğlu Pansiyon**, offering simple rooms with wholesome breakfast and dinner for US$20 per head.

4 A path traverses through pines towards the neighboring yayla of Sal, visible on the same ridge less than a kilometre away. At a grassy col before the yayla, a path veers off right past a water-trough and begins its descent through broad-leaved forests into the Fırtına valley. A jeep track is presently being bull-dozed up from the valley and by the time you arrive this will almost certainly have reached both Sal and Pokut. Unfortunately, it has obliterated large sections of the old footpath down, while the surviving parts will soon be reclaimed by the forest if they are not used. At the moment it's a two hour descent through thick forest to reach the bottom of the Fırtına valley near the village of Şenyuva. There you'll have to wait for a passing lift down to Çamlıhemşin, 8 km away, not too much of a problem.

Yusufeli

Phone code: 0466

An administrative and market town serving the southern Kaçkar valleys, Yusufeli has lost much of its charm to the march of concrete. Its redeeming feature, however, is its setting in a rocky valley on the banks of the swift-running Barhal river, just above its confluence with the Çoruh. This position makes it a popular base for rafting and canoeing, with the Çoruh rated among the best descents in the world (see below). Unfortunately, the days of rafting on the Çoruh are numbered, with a huge staircase of dams, the first one under construction near Artvin, planned for the valley. The waters held-back by one of these barrages will also submerge Yusufeli itself, something that is generally accepted with quiet resignation by local people.

Trekkers and climbers heading for the southern side of the Kaçkar pass through Yusufeli, with access by dolmuş to Barhal, Yaylalar and Olgunlar from the town. Many people also use the town as a base from which to visit the nearby Georgian churches of Dörtkilise and İşhan (see below).

Rafting

The Çoruh is fed primarily by snowmelt from the Kaçkar Mountains with the river reaching its peak flow during May and early June, and dropping steadily thereafter. The main raftable stretch of the river is 135 km long and increases in severity to Grade 5 early in the season, Grade 4 after June.

A reputable Turkish company offering trips on the Çoruh is *Alternatif Turizm*, based in Marmaris, T02524135994,www.alternatifraft.com, who do four and eight day packages, for US$450 and US$700 respectively, which includes food, transfer from Erzurum and all camping equipment. A New Zealand based company *Adrift*, also offer a similar four day package for US$655, or US$825 including flights from London. UK office: T01488684509, www.adrift.co.nz. You can also get in contact with *Kayak Raft Dağcılık Ihtisas Derneği* (see useful addresses) who also organize rafting trips on the river.

Sleeping **G** *Çoruh Otel*, T8112155, 150 m up from bus station turn left and it's next to the footbridge. Basic rooms with shared bathroom, some rooms overlook river. **G** *Hotel Barhal*, T8113151, also next to the river opposite the *Çoruh Otel*. Basic rooms with ensuite. **G** *Çiçek Palas*, T8112102, Halitpaşa Caddesi. Very spartan place on main street 200 m from bus station. *Greenpeace Camping*, T8112271. Nice spot beside the river 750 m above the town. To get there cross the suspension foot-bridge in the centre of town, turn right and right again, camping pitches, rudimentary huts on stilts and tents provided, howerever, no bedding, US$2.50 per person, hot-water, pleasant waterside restaurant. Recommended. *Akın Camping*, 100 m before Greenpeace. Basic restaurant, plots are not very shady.

Eating **Cheap** *Arzet Lokantası*, opposite the bus station, local favourite serving thick soups, döner roasted horizontally over coals, saç kavurma (spicy lamb fried in a wok) and *alabalık* (trout). *Çınar Restaurant*, next to the suspension bridge, nice position beside the river, serves grilled meat as well as trout. *Yılmaz Pide Salonu*, left along alley before footbridge, tiny place serving pide and lahmacun. At *Greenpeace Camping* you can eat trout beside the river (see above).

Transport **Bus** **Artvin**, 3 morning buses, 1¼ hrs, US$3.50 **Erzurum**, 2 morning buses, 2½ hrs, US$4. **Trabzon**, Artvin buses continue on to Trabzon. For destinations further afield buses depart from Artvin. Buy you ticket in Yusufeli in advance. **Dolmuş** descend from **Barhal**, **Yaylalar** and **Olgunlar** in the morning, returning again sometime during the afternoon. Enquire early in the day around the bus station and try to secure a seat in advance. These services are year-round as all 3 settlements are permanently inhabited.

Directory **Banks** There is an *Işbankası* with ATM next to the mosque, 150 m up from the bus station on the right. **Travel agencies** *Kaçkar Outdoor Sports*, T8112393, F8113393, local company organizing treks and tours of the Georgian churches. Also organize rafting, however, they were closed for a time in 1999 for operating without a license. **Useful addresses** *Kayak Raft Dağcılık Ihtisas Derneği*, T8113151, at the back of the bus station, non-profit organization which can help organize guides for trekking and rafting, Sirali Aydin speaks some English and can give advice on routes in the Kaçkar, rafting equipment available for hire.

Georgian churches & monasteries **Dörtkilise** is a large 10th-century Georgian church set amidst orchards 13 km to the southwest of Yusufeli near the village of Tekkale. Without your own transport get on a dolmuş to Tekkale (Kılıçkaya and Köprügören dolmuş also pass through the village) from where a rough track, driveable with care, starts next to a campsite called the *Dört Kilise Resting Camp*, T8112908. This track reaches the church, obscured by vegetation on the left side of the valley, after 6 km. Finding a dolmuş back to Yusufeli in the afternoon is a problem and you will probably have to hitch or stay in the campsite. A taxi to the church and back from Yusufeli is about US$15.

At **Işhan**, a village of traditional houses high above the Oltu Çayı to the east of Yusufeli, you'll find another Georgian church built between the eighth and 11th centuries. Although the building is structurally intact, there are only fragmentary remains of the frescoes which once adorned the interior. There is no public transport to Işhan which is 6 km up a steep side road from the road heading towards Olur. Taxi drivers in Yusufeli charge US$20 return for the 30 minute journey.

Heading towards Erzurum the road follows the bottom of a towering rocky gorge, skirting the edge of the turquoise lake Tortum Gölü after about 20 km. Beyond the lake is a sign-posted turn-off for Çamlıyamaç village and the church of **Öşk Vank**, 7 km from the main road. In fact part of a 10th-century Georgian monastery, the large stone building is in reasonable repair with fragments of fresco suriving on the interior walls, although sections of the roof have collapsed. There's a café and simple shop beside the church.

About 15 km south of the Öşk Vank turn is another rough side-road leading to the village of **Bağbaşı**, set in a fertile valley 7 km off the road. Formerly the Georgian village of Haho, there's a 10th-century Georgian church half a kilometre above the settlement which, like Öşk Vank, was built by David the Great. There are several carved reliefs inside, such as a depiction of Jonah and the whale, and frescoes adorn some of the walls. The building is still in use as the local mosque so ask for the key in the village (*Kilise anahtarı, lütfen*).

Above Yusufeli a rough road follows the Barhal River as it cuts its way through the dry, rocky mountains past several ruinous Georgian fortresses and the irrigated fields surrounding numerous small farming communities. Sitting in a narrow valley at the junction of two rushing torrents, 30 km above Yusufeli, is Barhal, officially known as Altıparmak, which at first glance seems to consists of little more than several general stores, a bakery and a tea-shop. A village of 2,500 people, most of the wooden houses are hidden on the valley-sides upstream, cloaked in vegetation. Also tucked away in the greenery is a remarkably well-preserved 10th-century **Georgian church** which stands serenely beside the village school. Since the Georgians and Armenians fled this valley at the beginning of the century, it has been used as the local mosque and is often locked. Ask at the café in town for the key, although frankly the bare interior is hardly worth the bother. To find the church walk up the right-hand track (the left one leads to Yaylalar) for 10 minutes, looking out for a concrete aquaduct on the right. About 50 m beyond this is a path which initially climbs up beside a stream. Turn right at the top of the path and the church is a short distance ahead. From the church it's possible to walk up the valley following an aqueduct which clings to the steep hillside, passing through an idyllic landscape of meadows and orchards, outlying wooden houses and old timber hay lofts. This path emerges near the upper *mahalle* of the village, from where the rocky ridge of the Altıparmak Range is visible at the head of the valley. It takes about 10 minutes to return down the road to the village centre.

Barhal (Altıparmak)
phone code: 0466

Sleeping F *Karahan Pansiyon*, T2121800. Simple rooms in 1 of 2 traditional wooden houses sitting amongst the greenery above the church, in summer guests can sleep on the large covered balcony, the price includes breakfast and dinner. Recommended. **G** *Marsis Village House*, T8262002, 50 m before the bridge on the right. The most comfortable rooms in the village but the modern building is not the most inspiring, shared bathroom and sitting area, meals available. **G** *Barhal Pansiyon*. A wooden house beside the road as you enter the village, simple rooms with shared bathroom, balcony and seating area upstairs, reasonable meals on offer. **G** *Seher Köybaşı Pansiyonu*, T8262041, 25 m up from bridge, above shop. Rooms in friendly old lady's house, a bit musty but you can expect a very warm welcome. There is a lovely **camping** spot in a meadow beside the torrent several hundred metres along the road to Yaylalar.

Transport A dolmuş leaves at around 0800 for Yusufeli, with another coming past from Yaylalar a bit later.

Barhal to Karagöl & beyond A popular excursion from Barhal is up to the beautiful lake of Karagöl set at the head of the valley beneath the peaks of the Altıparmak range. This walk is possible as a day hike from Barhal, although, as it involves at least five hours of climbing, it wouldn't leave you much time at the lake before having to turn around again. Therefore consider camping at Karagöl, which also makes an excellent base for exploration of the surrounding mountains.

From Karagöl a steep path leads over the ridge to the southwest, dropping more-or-less straight down track-less slopes into the Önbolat Valley. There you'll pick up longitudinal paths leading up to the yayla of Pişenkaya and beyond to a campsite at Libler Gölü, at the base of the difficult Kırmışı Pass. Once over this, for the next day it is all downhill to Ayder passing through the yayla of Avusor, Dobaya and Taşlık.

Yaylalar (Hevek) & Olgunlar Despite its name, Yaylalar is a large permanently inhabited village ranged along the south side of the Büyük Çay river at 2100 m. This used to be the trail-head for trekking routes west along the valley, however, now the road continues another couple of kilometres to the village of Olgunlar. There is a **G** guesthouse with pleasant rooms above the village bakery and general store if you want somewhere to stay.

Olgunlar is a smaller settlement with some rustic old wooden houses and hay barns. Altogether twenty-five families live in the village, with all but two of the villagers descending to lower elevations during the winter. The first building you come to on the road, and rather out of keeping with the other houses, is the **G** *Olgunlar Pansiyon*, T8322044, run by Ismail Bayram, a school teacher from Sarıgöl. It has basic rooms with shared bathroom. Meals are prepared and there are basic supplies available. ■ *Getting there: A dolmuş arrives from Yaylalar at 0700, then turns around and descends all the way to Yusufeli, passing through Barhal about 1½ hrs later. It returns in the afternoon from Yusufeli.*

Trans-Kaçkar: Olgunlar to Palovit This route traverses from the relatively dry Büyük Çay Valley on the southeast side of the range, past the high mountains of the central massif, before descending down to the Hemşin yayla of Palovit. It is possible to do the route in three days, with an additional day necessary for the day hike to the summit of Mount Kaçkar. This ascent, although requiring no technical climbing, should only be undertaken by those who feel comfortable scrambling over rocky and sometimes exposed ground. From Palovit, a natural continuation of the route passes through several other Hemşin *yayla* and unspoilt tracts of forest to emerge in the Fırtına Valley (see page 580). This adds another day to the trek, but allows you to experience the full environmental diversity of the Kaçkar range. This trek can also be combined with the Ayder-Çaymakçur Pass-Olgunlar route (see page 579) to make a week long trek around the central Kaçkar.

1 Cross the bridge in Olgunlar and follow a good path along the left bank of Büyük Çay for 1½ hours to the yayla of Nazaf.

2 Continue up the main valley beyond Nazaf to an excellent camping spot at Dilber Düzü, reached about 3½ hours after leaving Olgunlar. The rocky flanks of Mount Kaçkar, ominously called Şeytan Kayaları (The Devil's Rocks), are visible on the opposite side of the valley.

3 Follow the valley nearly to its head before breaking right (northwest) and climbing towards Mount Kaçkar and Deniz Gölü, tucked in a deep cwm to the south of the peak. The ascent to the lake takes about two hours. It is a spectacular spot but there is only just enough room for two or three tents, and the pitch is rather rocky. If you are climbing to the summit on the following day you may prefer to camp at Dilber Düzü. Alternatively, if you are heading for the Kavron Pass you could make the short, steep ascent of the rocky pass due south of the lake and descend easily to Isimsiz Göl (Nameless Lake) where there is much more space to pitch camp. This takes about 30 minutes.

4 The route to the summit skirts around the right (north) shore of the lake before climbing up a shallow valley, grassy at first, to a saddle from where the whole south face of Mount Kaçkar is visible (30 minutes).

5 Descend the loose unconsolidated scree and walk along a grey rocky ridge to the right of a small glacier almost completely covered in debris. This ridge leads up to the base of a large dome-shaped rock.

6 A path, marked by cairns, zig-zags up the dome on ledges, however, you may to prefer to skirt around the right of it on easy-angled slabs.

7 From behind the dome a path is visible traversing right over a scree slope towards the obvious band of cliffs that guard the lower face (1½ hours from Deniz Gölü). Passing diagonally right above the first tier, the path then climbs up a long scree slope towards the ridge on the left. Before reaching the ridge the route again traverses right towards the summit, where a fine view over the entire range, weather permitting, and the summit book await you. Allow three hours for the ascent from Deniz Gölü, five hours from Dilber Düzü. Dropping back down to the lake takes about 1½ hours.

8 The initial part of the route onwards to the Kavron Pass is detailed in no 3. From the Isimsiz Göl head due west towards the obvious pass in the ridge ahead, which can be reached in about 30 minutes. From the top of this col the path drops down a steep rock and scree slope to where it levels-off. Bare left and continue losing altitude so that you pass around the bottom of a second ridge blocking your west-north-westerly path. Once around this ridge, traverse towards the flat meadows at the base of the Kavron pass (approx. north-west). There are several good camping spots below the pass which is reached in 60 minutes by following a well-trodden path.

9 From the Kavron pass (3270m) an old muleteers path with some intact sections of paving contours around the right side of the valley without losing altitude. There are excellent views down over the Palovit valley to the northwest, with the road climbing over the sharp rocky ridge to Tirevit in the valley beyond clearly visible. After 30 minutes the path brings you out onto the crest of the ridge separating the heads of the Kavron and Palovit valleys. At a tor-like outcrop of rock, a path drops very steeply down on the right to Derebaşı and Yukarı Kavron (two hours), from where there are several daily dolmuş down to Ayder. Bearing left down into the Palovit valley in a diagonal north-westerly direction, brings you to the yayla of Apıvanak in an hour, where there is plenty of scope for camping near one of the two old stone bridges (4½ hours from Isimsiz Göl, 6½ hours from Dilber Düzü).

10 Passing the small collection of sod-roooved stone huts hugging the ground, it is an easy hours walk down a jeep track to the lower, more substantial, yayla of Palovit. There are dolmuş down to Çamlıhemşin and Pazar from Palovit on Tuesday, Friday, Sunday at 0730, three hours, US$7. See page580, for the continuation of this route.

Northeast Anatolia

12

Northeast Anatolia

590 Erzurum

596 Kars

600 Ani

604 Doğubeyazıt

606 Around Doğubeyazıt

The country's northeast is a barren land of high mountain ranges, empty plateaus and deeply incised river valleys. At an average altitude of well over 1,500 m, the climate is severe with short summers and long icy winters. Communications with the rest of the country have always been difficult and despite the introduction of better roads and domestic air services, the region retains a feeling of isolation and backwardness. A stronghold of Islamic conservatism, the northeast, like the southeast, lags behind the rest of the country in developmental terms as the economy struggles to grow beyond its agricultural base. Most families still make a living from the land, cultivating potatoes, cereals and sugar where climate and topography allow or raising herds of goats, sheep and cattle. Poverty is widespread, though the people, after some initial reticence, are just as hospitable and friendly as in the rest of the country.

As well as being its largest centre, Erzurum is most people's introduction to the region. A predominantly modern city it has some impressive Islamic monuments and a certain rough sophistication imbued by its forbidding surroundings and isolation. Nearby, Palandöken is the better of two ski resorts in the region, the second being Sarıkamış near Kars. In the shadow of Mount Ararat, Doğubeyazıt is a chaotic frontier town, a stepping stone for those crossing into Iran, and a base for exploring some interesting and varied local sights. To the north the regular street plan and Russian architecture of Kars come as a surprise after the austerity of the surrounding steppe. It's no place to linger, though, with most people staying just long enough to visit the haunting medieval ruins of Ani tucked against the Armenian border.

Background Northeast Anatolia has never attracted many foreign visitors, however, the damage done to the region's nascent tourist industry by the Iranian Revolution and the 1991 Gulf War has been compounded by 17 years of Kurdish separatism. In fairness, apart from a few hot-spots along its Kurdish-populated southern fringe, the region has avoided the violence of the southeast, though its proximity to the fighting has certainly discouraged would-be visitors. Improvements in the security situation to the south, if they continue, will no doubt reverse this situation, while recent developments in Iran have also seen more 'overlanders' travelling through en-route for the frontier. Inspite of this the region remains woefully neglected by foreign visitors, which is a pity because it has some interesting sights.

As a result there are comparatively few facilities for tourists, with hotels typically catering for travelling businessmen and traders. Prices for accommodation and food are generally lower than in the rest of the country, reflecting the lower standard of living, however, paradoxically you may find yourself spending considerably more on transport. This is because there are insufficient tourists to support regular dolmuş or bus services to many sights, leaving the expensive alternative of hiring a taxi or taking a private tour as the only option.

If you're driving remember that the condition of some of the roads is very bad with rough or loose surfaces and potholes demanding constant attention from the driver. Added to these dangers is the possibility of snow and bad weather during much of the year. Petrol stations are also few and far between, so fill up your tank when you get the chance and never let it run down too low.

Erzincan to Erzurum Imprudently sited near the North Anatolian fault, Erzincan has frequently been levelled by earthquakes during its long history. The last major quake struck in 1933 when about 33,000 people were killed, although smaller tremors occur on a fairly regular basis. If that hasn't put you off a visit, it should be noted that all this seismic activity has robbed Erzincan of its architectural heritage, leaving a drab modern town in its wake. If you should need to stay try the **E** *Hotel Burcu*, T04462238360, F04462235081, Fevzipaşa Caddesi. One of several places on the main street within walking distance of the *otogar*. Continuing east towards Erzurum, **Tercan** is about equidistant between the two towns and a possible place to break the journey if you're driving. There are a few simple eateries on the main street, and the **Mama Hatun Türbesi**, an unusual 13th-century tomb on the hill above the highway, is a possible distraction. From the same period is the adjacent **caravanserai** which may or may not be unlocked.

Erzurum

Phone code: 0442
Colour map 3, grid B3
Altitude: 1853 m

The undisputed capital of Turkey's northeast, Erzurum sits in a wide treeless basin lost by winter in the snowy vastness of the east Anatolian mountains. Despite being isolated by such great expanses of rugged terrain it's an island of relative civilisation where you can find modern shops, wide tree-lined boulevards and a large university. By the standards of the western Turkey, however, Erzurum remains a poor and conservative backwater where women shuffle through the dusty streets cloaked in coarse brown robes or the black chador, and where you'll be hard pressed to find an alcoholic drink unless you know where to look. Earthquakes and conquest have left Erzurum uniformly modern in character, except, that is, for the few monumental structures surviving from its turbulent past. These now form the town's principle attraction, although there's also some of Turkey's best skiing on the exposed slopes of Palandöken Dağı, looming up 8 km to the southwest.

Northeast Anatolia

As an important regional transit point Erzurum's busy *otogar* is well-served by buses from destinations across the country. Daily trains link the city with İstanbul, Ankara and Kars to the east and there are also daily *Turkish Airlines* flights from Ankara. The main *otogar* is several kilometres to the west of the centre. Your bus company will probably provide a *servis* into town, but if not city bus no 2 passes by outside on its way into the centre. A taxi costs US$2-3. Buses from Artvin, Yusufeli and other towns to the northeast call at a smaller bus station, known as **Gölbaş Semt Garajı**, 1 km to the northeast of the centre, before sometimes continuing on to the main *otogar*. *Turkish Airlines* run a service bus from the airport, 10 km northwest of town, which drops passengers in the centre. The train station is 1 km north of the centre, and considerably closer to the hotels and restaurants at the top of Istasyon Caddesi. The old core of the city, centred on the junction of Menderes and Cumhuriyet Caddesi, is fairly compact and can easily be negotiated on foot.

Ins & outs
*See page 594 for
further details*

Sights

Most of Erzurum's sights are conveniently strung out along the main street, Cumhuriyet Caddesi, and can easily be visited on foot within three or four hours depending on your level of interest. Cumhuriyet Caddesi is also the main shopping street with modernish arcades and commercial centres dotted along its length.

Starting your tour just to the west of the busy crossroads where Cumhuriyet and Menderes Caddesi meet, set in a small park is the early 14th-century Yakutiye seminary, named after an Ilkanid Mongol emir, Kwaca Yakut, who administered Erzurum and the neighbouring town of Bayburt to the northwest. Its most distinctive feature is a thick minaret revetted with turquoise tiles which adds a welcome splash of colour to what can be a rather dour, monotone urban landscape. The upper section of the minaret, which was originally one of a pair, has been lost, though this does little to mar its pleasing ascetics. Around the front of the building an ornately carved portal gives onto a domed central hall, decorated with stalactite carvings around the ceiling and surrounded by cells where the theology students would have lived and studied.

**Yakutiye
Medresesi**

Since 1994 the interior has become a excellent venue for the town's **Museum of Turkish and Islamic Arts** with diplays including local costumes, handicrafts and jewellery made from the *oltu taşı* (black amber) for which the town is famous. Also on show are some vintage photographs of the city, so you can marvel at how much it's changed. ■ *Closed Mon, Wed and Sun at present, 0930-1730. US$0.75.*

Next to the *medrese* and usually guarded by a line of *boyacı* (shoe-shiners) sitting on the pavement beside their highly polished brass boxes, is the **Lale Mustafa Paşa Camii**. Dedicated by the gifted Ottoman *grand vizier*, Lale Mustafa Paşa, who held office during the 16th century, the mosque is built in classical Ottoman style and is said to have been designed by the imperial architect Mimar Sinan himself.

Walking east along Cumhuriyet Caddesi you come to the city's 'Great Mosque', or Ulu Cami, a large and very solid looking stone building standing on the opposite side of the road. Built in 1179 by an emir of the Saltuklu Turks, a branch of the Selçuk dynasty, the building has all the characteristics of the early Selçuk period with its simple internal space dominated by a forest of columns and lit by a small skylight above a stalactite dome.

Ulu Cami

Northeast Anatolia

Çifte Minareli Medrese Beside the Ulu Cami stands Erzurum's most famous building, the Çifte Minareli Medrese (Twin Minaret Seminary). It's considerably more interesting in design and detail that its neighbour, with the eponymous 30-m high minarets resembling a pair of pre-industrial chimneys. Access to the central courtyard is through a suitably impressive limestone portal decorated with beautifully worked patterns and designs. This wonderful stonework continues inside with intricately carved geometric designs and fanciful reliefs covering many of the interior surfaces.

Founded some time in the 13th century by Hüdavend Hatun, daughter of the Selçuk Sultan Keykubad II, the seminary was one of the largest in Anatolia with several hundred students lodged in the rooms on the second level. At the far end of the courtyard, which plays host to a café in summer and a huge drift of icy snow in the winter, is a large domed tomb thought to be the last resting place of the philanthropic foundress of the *medrese*. ■ *0830-1800 daily, US$0.50.*

Erzurum Kalesi When Emperor Theodosius fortified the town in the fifth century, he had a citadel constructed on the hill to the north of the Çifte Minareli Medrese. Rebuilt on several occasions since, the walls encompass on area of wasteland whose only feature is a small *mescit* (prayer hall) and a towering minaret originally built by the Saltuk Turks. Later converted into a clocktower, the structure remains one of the most conspicuous landmarks of the town's skyline, a Turkish flag fluttering in the wind from the top. A dark spiral staircase leads up inside the tower to a wooden platform which commands a superb view of the city with the mountains of the Palandöken range as a dramatic backdrop. ■ *0800-1200, 1330-1930 daily. US$0.75. Getting there: Walk up the narrow street opposite the Çifte Minareli Medrese, past several carpet shops.*

Erzurum

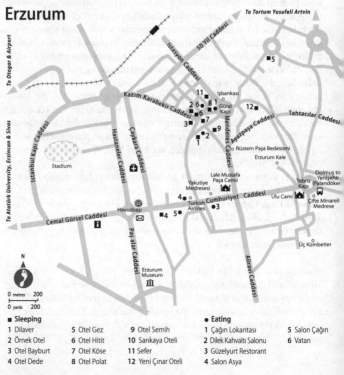

■ **Sleeping**

1 Dilaver	5 Otel Gez	9 Otel Semih
2 Örnek Otel	6 Otel Hitit	10 Sarıkaya Oteli
3 Otel Bayburt	7 Otel Köse	11 Sefer
4 Otel Dede	8 Otel Polat	12 Yeni Çınar Oteli

● **Eating**

1 Çağın Lokantası	5 Salon Çağın
2 Dilek Kahvaltı Salonu	6 Vatan
3 Güzelyurt Restorant	
4 Salon Asya	

Reached up the sidestreet that slips between the Çifte Minareli Medrese and **Other sights**
the Ulu Cami is a group of free-standing tombs known as the **Üç Kümbetler**
(Three Tombs). The largest of these is reported to be that of Emir Saltuk the
father of the dynastic offshoot from the Selçuk line that governed the area during the 12th and 13th centuries. The octagonal *türbe* is capped by a conical roof
and revetted with carved stone panels. There are also two other, less interesting, tombs in the small fenced enclosure which were constructed at a later date.

Back near the centre of town, the **Rüstem Paşa Bedesteni** is reached by
walking down Menderes Caddesi from Cumhuriyet Caddesi. You'll notice the
rows of peaked chimneys on the bedesten's roof on the right after about 250 m.
Commissioned by the gifted *grand vizier* of Süleyman the Magnificent,
Rüstem Paşa, the stone building harbours a pleasant courtyard which is the
focus of the town's jewellery and *oltu taşı* trade. A black volcanic stone similar
to obsidian, *oltu taşı* is sourced in the nearby town of Oltu, before being fashioned into highly polished beads traditionally used to make the*tespih* (prayer
beads) that Turkish men compulsively fiddle with. The stones are also set into
rings and earrings.

Branching off Menderes Caddesi down Ayazpaşa Caddesi brings you into
the **bazaar district** where the narrow sidestreets leading down the hill are lined
with shops selling shiny brass pots and pans, locally manufactured tin stoves,
shoes, blankets and all manner of other bits and bobs.

The museum's unexceptional collection is confined to artefacts uncovered at **Erzurum**
various archaeological sites in the surrounding area. These include examples **Museum**
of Urartian pottery, Hellenistic glassware and jewellery, Roman funerary
offerings and other assorted Selçuk pieces. There's also a grim display of evidence removed from mass graves where Turkish and Kurdish victims of
Armenian atrocities during the First World War were buried. It's obviously
mainly for local consumption because the labelling is in Turkish only.
■ *0800-1200, 1300-1700 daily except Mon. Entrance US$1. The museum is
inconveniently situated 500 m up Paşalar Caddesi, about 15 mins on foot from
the centre of town. You can also catch buses heading up the hill from Havuzbaşı,
although it's hardly worth it.*

Essentials

Erzurum has a reasonable selection of hotels, many of which are to be found around **Sleeping**
Gürcü Kapı, conveniently close to the railway station and only a 5-min walk from the
centre of things. Some of the cheapest boarding houses charge for using the shower,
so you may want to consider getting something a little more expensive with an
ensuite bathroom.

B *Hotel Dilaver*, Aşağı Mumcu Caddesi, Pelit Meydanı, T2350068, F2181148. Modern
3-star which is the best Erzurum has to offer, fairly uninspiring rooms but
well-equipped with A/C, TV, fridge, telephone and a hairdryer in the bathroom,
roof-top restaurant which serves alcohol and carpark. **D** *Otel Dede*, Cumhuriyet
Caddesi No 8, T2182591, F2345075. Modern, smallish rooms with tiled floors, ensuite
shower room. **E** *Hotel Sefer*, İstasyon Caddesi, T2186714, F2123775, convenient for
the station. Reasonable option, the rooms on the side of the building are larger and
less affected by traffic noise. **E** *Otel Polat*, Kazım Karabekir Caddesi No 4, T2181623,
F2344598. Newly renovated 2-star hotel, the clean rooms are newly furnished and
have sparkling bathrooms attached. Recommended. **F** *Örnek Otel*, Kazım Karabekir
Caddesi, T2181203. Guests are greeted by Hittite figures and a 50-year old switchboard in reception, basic rooms are adequate though a bit disappointing, no

breakfast. **F** *Otel Hitit*, Kazım Karabekir Caddesi No 27, T2187412, next door to the Örnek. Less appealing place where old fashioned rooms come with or without a shower. **F** *Otel Bayburt*, Kazım Karabekir Caddesi No 62, T2188140. Another cheap option across the road from the *Örnek Otel*, small rooms with basin, shared bathrooms on each floor. **F** *Otel Gez*, Kongre Caddesi No 88, T2182189. Newly converted office building 5 min-walk from Aşağı Mumcu Meydanı, slightly off patch, however, rooms are clean and good value, cheaper rooms without ensuite, triple rooms are cramped. Recommended. **F** *Yeni Çınar Oteli*, Ayazpaşa Caddesi No 18, T2121050, F2338963, in sidestreet opposite Gürpinar Cinema. Clean comfortable rooms with ensuite, TV and telephone make this the best value place in town. Recommended. **G** *Otel Semih*, Pelit Meydanı No 18, T2181618. Centrally located but rooms are basic, available with or without bathroom, smelly plumbing. **G** *Otel Köse*, Aşağı Mumcu Caddesi, No 40, T2339729. Once past the dingy reception the basic but clean rooms are not bad, shared bathroom, shower extra, best of the rock bottom cheapies.

Eating

Erzurum has a fairly good selection of excellent value kebap & pide restaurants, although as with most other Anatolian towns there isn't much beyond the standard fare

Midrange *Güzelyurt Restorant*, Cumhuriyet Caddesi, across from the Yakutiye Medresesi, good reputation as Erzurum's best and longest running (since 1928) restaurant, white table cloth place serving *meze* followed by varied, generally meat-based, menu, popular with wealthy *Erzurumlu* who enjoy a glass of beer or *rakı* with their meal, about US$10-15 per head with alcohol. You could also try the rooftop restaurant at the *Dilaver Hotel* which is also licensed, although the food isn't up to the standard of the Güzelyurt. **Cheap** *Salon Asya*, Cumhuriyet Caddesi, west of Yakutiye Medresesi on the north side of the street, large brightly lit restaurant with chandeliers hanging from the ceiling, excellent choice of food with every imaginable type of kebap including *iskender*, also pide and lahmacun. *Salon Çağın*, Cumhuriyet Caddesi, opposite the Salon Asya, another good value place with a similar menu, also sometimes has trout in the summer.

In **Gürcü Kapı** try *Vatan Restaurant*, opposite the *Polat Hotel* on Kazım Karabekir Caddesi, good selection of ready-prepared dishes and soup. *Çağın Lokantası*, across from the *Vatan Restaurant*, small cheery place serving kebaps, grilled meats and trout (US$1.50 each). For pastries and *baklava* there are several *pastane* on Cumhuriyet Caddesi to the west of the Yakutiye Medresesi including *Patisserie Zirve*. The cozy, old-fashioned *Dilek Kahvaltı Salonu*, just to the east of the *Hotel Dilaver*, is an excellent place for a breakfast of pastries or bread and honey with hot milk, tea or nest (sic) café.

Transport

Air *Turkish Airlines*, Caferiye Mahallesi, Cumhuriyet Caddesi, Eren Iş Merkezi No 88/3, T2181904, F2188530, has daily direct flights to **Ankara** and twice weekly services to İstanbul. *İstanbul Airlines* also has three weekly return flights to Erzurum. **Bus** Most bus companies have an office in the centre of town, usually along Cumhuriyet Caddesi, and operate free service buses to the *otogar*. **Ankara**, several, 12 hrs, US$18. **Artvin**, 6 buses daily, 4.5 hrs, US$7. **Diyarbakır**, 5 buses daily, 8 hrs, US$12. **Doğubeyazıt (via Ağrı)**, hrly buses during day, 4 hrs, US$6. **Erzincan**, every 30-60 mins, 3 hrs, US$5. **İstanbul**, several daily buses, 18 hrs, US$25. **Kars**, every hr, 3 hrs, US$4. **Sivas**, several buses, 6 hrs, US$10. **Tortum**, frequent dolmuş, 1 hr, US$2. **Van**, every 2-3 hrs, 6 hrs, US$10. **Yusufeli**, 4 buses daily, 3 hrs, US$4.

Directory

Banks There are plenty of banks with ATMs around Gürcü Kapı and on Cumhuriyet Caddesi, where you'll find Işbankası across from the Yakutiye Medresesi. **Baths** *Erzurum Hamamı*, Istasyon Caddesi, Gürcü Kapı, 0700-1030, men only. *Hanım*, in narrow street that winds between the Kale and Rüştem Paşa Bedesten, same hrs, female only. **Post office** The PTT is on the south side of Cumhuriyet Caddesi near Havuzbaşı. **Internet** *Internet Cafe*, Cumhuriyet Iş Merkezi, first floor, Cumhuriyet Caddesi opposite the PTT, very good set-up, US$1.50 per hr. **Hospitals** *Devlet Hastanesi*, Hastaneler Caddesi, north of Havuzbaşı. **Tourist information** The Tourist Information Office, T2185697, is at Cemal Gürsel Caddesi No 9, 200 m west of Havuzbaşı. Friendly, helpful staff. **Useful addresses** *Iranian Consulate*, T2183876, out of town along Aliravi Caddesi, across from

Eğitim Fakültesi, visa applications must be accompanied by a non-refundable fee of US$50, applications take up to 1 month to process and may be rejected.

As well as a dramatic backdrop to the town, the Palandöken Mountains, 6 km to the south of Erzurum, are home to one of Turkey's better ski centres. A system of five lifts give skiers access to about 30 km of runs on the northern slopes of Palandöken Dağı (3125 m). It's about 900 m from top to bottom and most of the runs, except for a couple of more challenging ones from the summit itself, are rated beginners or intermediate. The dry climate ensures light powdery snow, although it can get very cold on the exposed treeless mountain, particularly in January when conditions are at their best. Equipment can be hired at the *Dedeman Hotel* (see below) and there are also qualified instructors available for tuition. Although the resort is only in its infancy, looking out across the pristine mountains surrounding the resort the potential for future development at Palnadöken is enormous. **Palandöken**

At present Palandöken has two hotels: **AL** *Palandöken Dedeman*, T3162414, F3163607, at the base of the nursery slopes, reached by chairlift or a rough track from the bottom of the mountain, well-established 4-star hotel with comfortable rooms and cosy wooden beamed restaurant and bar. **A** *Tourinn Palan Otel*, T3170707, T3170700, palan.in.com.tr, newly opened, huge ugly building at base of the mountain, short walk from the lowest lift.

It is also quite feasible to stay in a hotel in Erzurum and take a day trip up to the ski resort. A taxi should cost about US$7 to the bottom of the mountain. There is no public transport to Palandöken although dolmuş leave from Tekir Kapı at the eastern end of Cumhuriyet Caddesi for Yenişehir. Tell the driver you're going to Palandöken and he'll drop you at the approach road from where you can walk or hitch the final 3 km.

East towards Kars

Once clear of Erzurum's sprawling army bases the E-80 highway sweeps across a dun coloured plain of rough pastureland and irrigated fields, with only the odd concrete pill box or crumbling fortification to break the monotony.

After 38 km Pasinler is a possible spot to stop for a breather. Guarded by the extensive remains of a hill top castle constructed by the Armenian Bagratids and later the base of one Uzun Hasan, the emir of the Türkoman Akkoyunlu tribe. The castle now stands partially ruined, although its formidable defensive wall are still worth a look if you fancy stretching your legs. **Pasinler**

Apart from the extra long loaves of bread that are churned out by the local bakeries the town is renowned for its hot springs. The *kaplıcalar* (bathhouses) are found on the south side of the highway beyond the railway and a small bridge. Admission to the separate male and female baths is US$1.50 and they're open 1030 to 1900. For those that wish an extended bathing session there are utilitarian rooms with ensuite available at the nearby **F** *Hotel Ter Tur*, T0442-6613538. The hotel also has private baths and a licensed restaurant. ■ *Getting there: Buses leave Erzurum every hr during the day for Pasinler, US$0.50.*

From Pasinler the highway follows the meandering Aras, the ancient River Araxes, which having left Turkey flows east acting as the frontier between Armenia and Iran before emptying into the Caspian sea in Azerbaijan. A landmark to look out for on the left is the 220-m long **Çobandede Köprüsü**, a graceful stone bridge built in the 16th century by Mimar Sinan, which spans the Aras in six well-proportioned arches 18 km beyond Pasinler. **Route**

Northeast Anatolia

At **Horasan** traffic heading for Ağrı, Doğubeyazıt and the Iranian border peels off to the right, while the E-40 and railway line continue winding along the Aras valley. After 45 km the vista flashing past the window changes dramatically as road and railway climb into stunning pine covered mountains reminiscent of the uplands along the Black sea coast.

Sarıkamış   Huddled amongst the conifers to the north of the highway, Sarıkamış is synonymous with one of the worst military disasters in recent Turkish history when, during the winter of 1914-15, commander-in-chief Enver Paşa ordered the Ottoman Third Army to attack Russian positions to the east. In the frigid arctic conditions 75,000 of the ill-equipped Turkish troops perished, mostly from hunger and exposure, leaving Erzurum open to a Russian counter-attack the following spring.

There's still a large military presence in the town today, with Turkish conscripts garrisoned, rather ironically, in the old Russian barrack houses. Logging is an important activity but the town fathers are clearly hoping that the small ski centre, 4 km away, will boost the local economy. Several new hotels have opened in the last few years and there are two operational chairlifts, with plans for a third on the drawing board. Even so, it's still a tiny resort and at the moment the pleasant pine forested terrain suggests itself more for cross-country skiing or snowshoeing.

Sleeping Simple accommodation is available in town at the **F** *Turistik Hotel Sarıkamış*, Halk Caddesi No 64, T0474-4134176, which is pleasantly decorated in Alpine-style. At the ski centre (*Kayak Merkezi*) try the **A** *Dedeman Oberj*, T0474-4136312, F0474-4136449, or the more simple *Çamlıkar Hotel*, T0474-4135259.

Transport There are regular buses to Kars, 30 mins, US$0.75. Erzurum-Kars buses also normally call-in to pick-up passengers.

Kars

Phone code: 0474
Colour map 3, grid B4
Population: 80,000
Altitude: 1768 m

Approaching Kars across a vast, empty land of swaying grass stretching as far as the eye can see, you have the feeling that you've arrived at the end of the world. The first impressions of the town with its drab concrete buildings and muddy pot-holed streets are hardly enticing either. However, once you've penetrated the shabby outskirts, the centre of town with its pedestrianized main street and tree-lined walkways dotted with the odd fountain is a significant improvement. Another nice surprise is the scattering of Belle Epoch buildings, left incongruously by the Russians during their last occupation and still elegant in spite of the peeling paintwork. Kars' sleepy, parochial atmosphere is also endearing, although the realities of living in such an isolated region, battered by some of the most severe weather in the country, are harsh. During the long winter temperatures rarely rise above -10°C, frequently dropping alot further, and the short summer months often see rain pelting down for hours from a brooding, leaden sky. The ruins of the Armenian city of Ani are what entice most people to make the long journey to Kars, although the town itself also has some things to keep you busy for an hour or two.

Ins and outs

Getting there
See page 600 for further details
Despite its isolation Kars is well linked into the national transport network with long distance buses from large western cities as well as smaller towns in the region. It's also served by daily flights from Ankara along with what is the longest train service

in the country departing İstanbul everyday at 0835 and arriving 38 hrs later, if you're lucky. Coming from Van or Doğubeyazıt will demand changing buses in Horasan or Iğdır respectively.

Getting around

Another legacy of the Russian occupation, a grid iron street plan, makes finding your way around the centre of town easy, with most things within strolling distance of each other. One notable exception is the provincial museum which is stranded out on the eastern edge of town, a 10-15 mins walk away or a short cab ride. Regular dolmuş shuttle into the centre from the train station, near the museum, and the *otogar*, several kilometres outside town to the east.

History

Kars first emerged from obscurity in the 10th century when it became the capital of the Armenian Bagratid dynasty. Although the capital was subsequently moved to nearby Ani, Kars remained an important Armenian garrison town until it fell to the Selçuks in the mid-11th century. The next millenium was characterized by turbulence and destruction as army after army swept through the city enroute for western Anatolia.

The Ottoman conquest brought a modicum of peace, though this was shattered in the 19th century as Czarist expansion in the Caucasus saw the area contested by its new belligerent neighbour. Known as 'the Caucasus Gate', the strategic town was subject to a prolonged siege by the Russians in 1828 and then again during the Crimean War in 1855, when an Anglo-Turkish force held out in the citadel for five months. The tenacious defenders were eventually overwhelmed but Kars was given back to the Ottomans as part of a wide ranging treaty signed by the two empires. Peace didn't reign for long though, as on the 24 April 1877 Russia declared war again, advancing on Kars. The town was taken after a bloody battle, beginning a period of Russian rule which

Kars

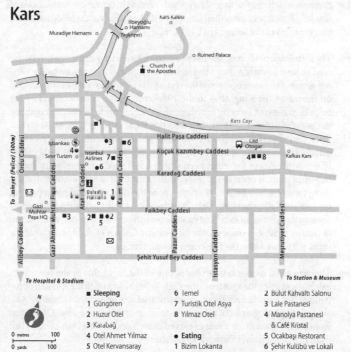

Sleeping
1 Güngören
2 Huzur Otel
3 Karabağ
4 Otel Ahmet Yılmaz
5 Otel Kervansaray
6 Temel
7 Turistik Otel Asya
8 Yilmaz Otel

Eating
1 Bizim Lokanta
2 Bulut Kahvaltı Salonu
3 Lale Pastanesi
4 Manolya Pastanesi & Café Kristal
5 Ocakbaşı Restorant
6 Şehir Kulübü ve Lokali

lasted over 40 years. During their tenure the Russians constructed a new town on the opposite side of the river to the castle, lining the streets with graceful buildings a few of which survive to the present-day. Kars was regained by a Turkish nationalist army commanded by Kazım Karabekir in 1920. It remains an important garrison town for the modern Turkish army and shaven headed conscripts are very conspicuous about town on Sundays when they are allowed off base.

Sights

The best place to look for the surviving domestic architecture of the Russian period is along Gazi Ahmet Muhtar Caddesi and Atatürk Caddesi. One particularly fine example, the **Gazi Muhtar Paşa Headquarters**, stands at the southern end of the former street and has been preserved for its role as Ottoman HQ during the war with Russia in 1877. The town's other buildings of historical interest are clustered to the north of the Kars Çayı river, where the old town crouched at the base of the fortress hill.

Church of the Apostles (Kümbet Camii) At the north end of Kazım Bey Caddesi stands what was formerly known as the Church of the Apostles. Constructed in the 10th century by King Abas of the Bagratid dynasty, it functioned as the town's cathedral right up until Ottoman times when it was converted into a mosque. Inside simple reliefs of the Twelve Apostles adorn the blind arches of the dome, however, unfortunately the building is generally kept locked these days.

Nearby, the **Taşköprü** is a 500-year old Ottoman bridge, rebuilt from basalt in the 18th century after being destroyed in an earthquake, spanning the murky brown waters of the Kars Çayı. Flanking the bridge are two historic hamams which despite their decrepitude are still in operation, with clouds of smoke billowing out from their chimneys. In the vicinity of the bridge there are also the ruins of the Selçuk era Ulu Cami.

Kars Kalesi The fortifications topping the hill above town have enjoyed a long and chequered history, being razed and then rebuilt on numerous occasions by the various armies that have conquered the region. The Armenian citadel constructed on the site by the King Abas in the 10th century, and later occupied by the Selçuks, was swept away by the Mongols in 1152, only to be restored again by the *grand vizier* of Murat III, Lale Mustafa Paşa, in 1579. Renovated several times during the Ottoman era it was destroyed during fighting between Turkish and Russian forces in 1855, only to be reconstructed yet again. Today, most of the castle, except the inner keep which is still used by the military and so out-of-bounds, is open to the public during daylight hours, although frankly there's not much to see. Local people make the climb to pay their respects at the tomb of Kahraman Celal Baba, a 14th-century spiritual leader, but the battlements also make an excellent vantage point from which to survey the town. ■ *Getting there: Continue up the hill past the Church of the Apostles and the ruins of a palace known as Beylerbeyi Sarayı. Free.*

Kars Museum The provincial museum is probably one of the highlights of the town with exhibits spanning the ages from the Early Bronze right up to the Russian occupation. Not surprisingly there are many artefacts unearthed at nearby Ani, along with photographs of other Armenian churches in the area. Of interest from the Russian era are a pair of carved church doors and a 19th-century bell from one of the town's Orthodox churches.

Upstairs the ethnographic section has beautiful examples of the distinctive Kars carpets and *kilims*, as well as other local handicrafts and traditional costumes. More grisly is a display containing documentary evidence of the attrocities carried out by Armenian partisans against the local Kurdish and Turkish populations. Before you leave have a look at the railway carriage behind the building which was the venue for talks between Russian Bolshevik and Turkish nationalist representatives that lead to the return of Kars to Turkey in 1920. ■ *0830-1730 daily except Mon. US$1.25. The museum is a 15-min walk from the centre of town.*

Essentials

Although the hotel situation in Kars is slowly getting better it still has quite some way to go. The cheapest places along Faikbey Caddesi are universally pretty dismal while those higher up the price ladder are certainly nothing to write home about, offering mediocre rooms at fairly inflated prices.

Sleeping

B *Hotel Karabağ*, Faikbey Caddesi No 142, T2123480, F2233089. Smallish rooms with TV, telephone, a/c and decent ensuite, comfortable but over-priced so try and bargain. **E** *Hotel Temel*, Kazım Paşa Caddesi No 4/Λ, T2121376. Old package hotel, very 1970s décor including dizzying floral wallpaper, simple rooms with shower are not a bad option. **E** *Hotel Güngören*, Halit Paşa Caddesi, Millet Sokak No 4. One of the better places in town, reasonable 1/2/3 bed rooms with bathroom, popular with visiting businessmen, restaurant and hamam next-door. Recommended. **E** *Yılmaz Otel*, Küçük Kazımbey Caddesi No 146, T2125174, F2125176, the Yılmaz and the **F** *Otel Ahmet Yılmaz*, T2124215, next-door used to be one and the same, however, the death of the owner saw the place divided between squabbling family factions. There is little to choose between the rooms which are pretty basic but equipped with TV, telephone and small ensuite, although the Ahmet Yılmaz charges considerably less. Lone women may not feel comfortable in either. **F** *Turistik Otel Asya*, Küçük Kazımbey Caddesi No 52, T2232299. Simple rooms with shower which are in need of redecoration. **F** *Huzur Otel*, Faikbey Caddesi No 171, T2234200. Reasonable size rooms with and without ensuite, shared squat toilets are dirty. **G** *Otel Kervansaray*, Faikbey Caddesi No 184, T2231990. Basic rooms with basin, some have simple ensuite, bareable rock-bottom cheapy.

The local speciality is *kaşar peyniri* (hard, medium fat cheese) and golden *bal* (honey) which are both sold in shops along Halit Paşa Caddesi. Combined with freshly baked bread, butter and tea, coffee or hot milk they make a delicious breakfast which is available in most of the town's *pastanesi*. Try *Bulut Kahvaltı Salonu*, on Faikbey Caddesi next to the Hotel Kervansaray, *Manolya Pastanesi* on Atatürk Caddesi or *Lale Pastanesi* on Halit Paşa Caddesi.

Eating
Thankfully for hungry travellers the restaurant situation in Kars is considerably better than the accommodation scene

Mldrange The restaurant in the *Hotel Karabağ* is a bit better than average, serves *meze*, kebaps and meat dishes with alcohol. In the *Şehir Kulübü ve Lokalı* on Karadağ Caddesi you can enjoy an alcoholic drink with a *meze* and kebap meal. **Cheap** *Cafe Kristal*, Atatürk Caddesi, cheery place which has good reputation locally, tasty soup, ready-prepared dishes and deserts, 3 courses and a drink will come to under US$4. *Bizim Lokanta*, Kazım Paşa Caddesi, Faikbey Caddesi end, bustling place serving ready-prepared dishes. *Ocakbaşı Restorant*, Atatürk Caddesi No 276, surprisingly chic interior, white table cloths and reasonable service make this meat restaurant stand out from the crowd, don't arrive too late in the evening though or your choice will be very limited, less than US$5 per head.

Northeast Anatolia

Tour agencies *Sınır Turizm*, T2123838, F2123841, Atatürk Caddesi No 80, *Turkish Airlines* agent, Ani tours, reservations.

Transport **Air** *Turkish Airlines* have 1 daily flight to Ankara. *İstanbul Airlines*, Atatürk Caddesi No 110, T2237539, F2125267, have 2 weekly flights to İstanbul.

Road **Buses** and **dolmuş** to the following destinations leave from the old bus station (*eski otogar*) at the eastern end of Küçük Kazım Bey Caddesi. **Ardahan**, every hr, 2½ hrs, US\$6. **Artvin**, several morning buses, 5 hrs, US\$8. Heading for **Doğubeyazıt** take a dolmuş to Iğdır (supposedly every hr, 0900-1500, 2½ hrs, US\$4.50) where you'll need to wait for another dolmuş onwards to Doğubeyazıt (hrly, 0500-1900, 45 mins US\$1.50). You should set-out in plenty of time to avoid getting stranded in Iğdır. **Long distance** and **Erzurum** services depart from the new terminal to the east of town, but bus companies provide free transport from their offices near the old bus station. Try *Kafkas Kars*, next to petrol station across from old *otogar*. **Ankara**, 3 daily buses, 15 hrs, US\$18. **Erzurum**, every hr, 3 hrs, US\$4. If there's no direct bus to **Van**, get on an Erzurum bus and ask to be let off at Horasan from where you can catch a bus east via Ağrı. However, don't leave too late in the day as the last bus from Erzurum passes mid-afternoon.

Train *Doğu Ekspresi*, departs İstanbul everyday at 0835, returns from Kars at 0710, 35 hrs. The *Doğu Ekspresi* and the local *Karma* service can be used to get to Erzurum although this takes a leisurely 5-6 hrs compared with 3 on the bus. Couchette reservations need to be made in advance as there is some demand for them.

Directory **Banks** *İşbankası* on Atatürk Caddesi is your best bet for changing TCs though even they may be reluctant. **Baths** Kars is well supplied with Turkish baths. The *Muradiye Hamamı* next to the Taş Köprü is pretty historic, and decrepid, women only. *Güngören Hamamı*, Millet Sokak, next to hotel of the same name, 0730-2300. *Belediye Hamamı*, Faik Bey Caddesi, 0730-2300, across from *Hotel Kervansaray*. **Communications** **Internet:** There's a café on the corner of Atatürk and Halit Paşa Caddesi, 1st floor. **Post office:** The PTT is on Ordu Caddesi. **Hospital** *Devlet Hastanesi*, off Ali Bey (Ordu) Caddesi in the south of town. **Tourist information** The tourist office, T2126817, Atatürk Caddesi, on 1st floor of government building next to the fountain. Weekdays 0830-1730.

Ani

45 km E of Kars
Colour map 3, grid B5

The reason most people come to Kars is to pay a visit to the desolate ruins of the Bagratid capital of Ani, squeezed up against the Armenian frontier. A large city of perhaps 100,000 people in its heyday, the ravages of time and tectonic activity have left us only fragmentary reminders of its former greatness in the form of a still impressive defensive wall; a handful of ruinous churches and various other scattered buildings. Although in themselves these remains may not measure up to much, particularly when compared with the marble greatness of Ephesus or the exquisite religious art of Cappadocia, their solitary setting on the grassy steppe, silhouetted against an immense cloud dotted sky and buffeted by the relentless wind is extremely evocative, more than justifying the trip.

Ins and outs

Getting there Ani lies between the village of Ocaklı and a deep gorge incised into the surrounding plateau land by the swift flowing Arpa Çayı, a tributary of the River Aras which empties into the Caspian sea, 600 km to the east. This gorge forms the uneasy frontier between the Republics of Turkey and Armenia, so any visit to Ani requires official permission from the authorities in Kars (see below). Getting to Ani without your own transport has always been difficult. Everyday a village dolmuş trundles out to Ocaklı, adjacent to the site, but unfortunately it's of little use because it doesn't return until the next morning and there's no accommodation in the village. The tourist office used to organize trips by taxi-dolmuş but because of the scarcity of tourists you may end up having to pay the entire US$30 fee yourself. A local entrepreneur with good knowledge of the site and some English, Celil Ersözoğlu, T2236323, mobile 05322263966, also takes groups out to the ruins for slightly cheaper. He sweeps the town's hotels every evening looking for interested parties so you may be able to split the cost with others. He's also available for longer tours of the region and takes care of the necessary documentation.

The procedure for getting permission is now fairly straight forward, although it does involve a certain amount of toing and froing. Complete a form issued by the Tourist Information Office in **Kars** and take it to the Emniyet Müdürlüğü (Police headquarters) on Faik Bey Caddesi, a 5-min walk west of the centre. With the stamped and approved paper in hand hike across town to the Kars museum where you can buy an entry ticket for the site (US$2). Tickets are not sold at the site. The whole process should take less than an hour and will give you a gentle insight into the elaborate and often highly frustrating procedures that govern any kind of official business in Turkey.

Getting permission

Don't be tempted to head out to the site without the correct documentation as you'll be turned back at the first checkpoint

History

Although there had probably been a settlement at the naturally defensible site since antiquity, Ani came to prominence in the 10th century as the capital of the Bagratids, an Armenian dynasty who carved themselves a kingdom from the mountains of eastern Anatolia. The city's rise was assured by King Ashot III's (952-977 AD) decision to move the Bagratid capital from Kars in 961 AD, and Ani blossomed into a strong fortress-city, endowed with many fine buildings and enriched by the caravan traffic passing through. Ani continued to prosper under Ashot III's successors, Smbat II and Gagik, however, the city went into a rapid decline early in the 11th century as Byzantine encroachment culminated in Gagik II ceding the kingdom to Constantinople in 1045.

This Byzantine interlude lasted less than two decades with the Emperor Romanus Diogenes' trouncing by the Selçuk Turkish army at Manzikert signalling the collapse of Byzantine power in Anatolia. The Selçuks controlled Ani until challenged by the Georgian King David IV, who succeeded in liberating the area from Muslim control, establishing a semi-autonomous kingdom. Ani and the surrounding region were governed by the feudal Zakhariad clan until a double catastrophe in the form of the Mongol invasions and a huge earthquake devastated the city. A shift in the east-west caravan routes

Ani

To Ocaklı Village of Kars

Car Park
Aslan Kapısı (Lion Gate)

Arpa Çayı

Arpa Çayı

ARMENIA

N

0 metres 300
0 yards 300

1 Church of the Holy Redeemer
2 Church of St Gregory (Tigran Honents)
3 Convent of the Virgins
4 Cathedral
5 Menüçehir Camii
6 İç Kale
7 Kız Kilisesi (Maiden's Church)
8 Church of St Gregory (Abighamrets)
9 Church of the Holy Apostles
10 Church of St Gregory (Abighamrets)
11 Selçuk Palace

Northeast Anatolia

sealed Ani's fate, consigning the once great city to oblivion. The city was 'rediscovered' by the outside world in the 19th century, attracting a steady stream of curious travellers ever since. During the Soviet era access to the ruins was severely restricted as the site fell within no-man's land between Turkey and the Soviet Republic of Armenia.

The site

The narrow pot holed road to Ani crosses an open landscape of cereal fields and lush meadows grazed by herds of cattle and horses, and dotted with beehives from which comes the regions famous honey. There are sweeping views across the Aras Valley and on a clear day the bulky cone of Mount Ararat is sometimes visible in the distance. You'll need to have your documentation and passport ready for inspection at several army checkpoints along the way.

Arriving in Ocaklı, a small collection of low stone houses, the outer wall of Ani looms over the flat sod roofs and television aerials. The impressive double wall, guarded by large watch towers, stretches along the north side of the triangular site, with the gorges of the Arpa Çayı and its tributary the Alaca Çay forming the city's other boundaries. The 10th-century fortifications are pierced by four portals with entry to the site through the **Aslan Kapısı** (Lion Gate), named after the relief of a lion carved onto the inner wall.

At the entrance your tickets will be checked and your passport taken into safe keeping by one of the soldiers guarding the site. Due to its proximity to the sensitive border with Armenia there are certain rules you must obey while touring the site, such as not taking photographs in the direction of the frontier, and these will also be explained to you.

Once the mini-briefing is over you're free to walk through the double gate for your first glimpse of the site: a rough plateau carpeted with grass and punctuated by the odd pile of masonry where rows of houses once stood. Today the area is peaceful except for the wind and it's hard to imagine that this was once a bustling city which contemporary sources likened to the splendid Byzantine capital of Constantinople. Jutting skywards above the pastureland like poignant memorials are the remnants of a number of the city's principal buildings, linked together by a network of paths which often correspond to the old street plan.

Church of the Holy Redeemer Bearing left brings you, after about 600 m, to the Church of the Holy Redeemer which having stubbornly stood its ground for nearly 1,000 years was partially destroyed by lightning in 1954. The remaining half of the structure bares an inscription recording a visit by Smbat III to Constantinople, where he received a fragment from the True Cross, an event that was celebrated on his return by the dedication of the church. The inside walls were decorated with frescoes of which a few faded examples can still be seen.

Church of St Gregory (Tigran Honents) A short distance to the east overlooking the Arpa Çayı is a small church dedicated to St Gregory the Illuminator. It is one of the best preserved of Ani's buildings and takes its Turkish

Church ruins, Ani

name, Resimli Kilise (Church with Pictures) from the lively frescoes that adorn its interior. Despite have suffered at the hands of vandals and religious zealots over the years you can still make out biblical scenes as well as depictions of important ecclesiastical events such as the trial and subsequent torture of St Gregory. A dedicatory inscription identifies the church's benefactor as one Tigrana Honents, a wealthy local nobleman.

From the Tigran Honents a path skirts the top of the escarpment above the Arpa Çayı before descending to a terrace overlooking the river. Surrounded by a perimeter wall the convent consists of two small chapels which were built at the beginning of the 13th century. Visible nearby is the truncated span of a medieval bridge which once spanned the rushing river and on the opposite, Armenian bank the watch towers - usually unmanned these days. **Convent of the Virgins**

Having clambered back up onto the plateau continue following the path west to the city's cathedral. Begun during the reign of Smbat II in 989 AD, the building wasn't completed until after his death under the patronage of Gagik I's wife, Queen Katramide. The unexceptional rectangular structure was the work of Trdat Mendet, an Armenian architect who had applied his expertise to repairing Haghia Sofia in Constantinople after the earthquake of 989 AD. In keeping with Armenian concepts of ecclesiastical architectural design he accentuated the height of the building which reaches up like a Gothic church spire towards the heavens. The central dome was supported on four thick columns, that is before it caved in. **The cathedral**

Beyond the cathedral, to the west, the Menüçehir Camii is easily recognized by its stripped red and black stonework and a truncated octagonal minaret which protrudes skywards. Fragmentary inscriptions found on the building's stonework suggest that it may have been a palace in the days before the Selçuk conquest, later being renovated and converted into a mosque. The vaulted interior of the building and the remnants of a ceiling mosaic certainly support this assumption, although local wisdom has it that the Menüçehir Camii, named after the first Muslim ruler of the city, is a contender for the title of oldest mosque in Anatolia having been built in 1072. Whatever its origins, the building is an interesting fusion of Armenian and Selçuk architecture. For those after a view, and an adrenaline rush, the tottering minaret can be scaled to its truncated top via a staircase inside. **Menüçehir Camii**

Ani's fortress occupies a mound at the south end of the site, though today it's often out-of-bounds to visitors. This is the oldest part of the city, pre-dating the Bagratid remains, and contains the ruins of several churches. Beyond, perched fantastically on a pinnacle of rock above the swirling waters of the Arpa Çayı, is a chapel known locally as the **Kız Kilisesi** (the Maiden's Church). **İç Kale (Inner Castle)**

Making your way back towards the site entrance you pass the ruins of another church dedicated to St Gregory (Abighamrets) which was raised during the 11th century by the architect responsible for the church of Tigran Honents. **Other remains**

Off the path on the right-hand side is the **Church of the Holy Apostles**, which was built in 1031 and converted later by the Selçuks into a caravanserai for accommodating visiting merchants. The entrance portal is the most notable feature, decorated with beautifully carved Armenian inscriptions.

There's little more than the foundations and some column bases left of yet another **Church of St Gregory (Abighamrets)** to the northwest of the caravanserai. Built by King Gargik at the beginning of the 11th century, even from these scant remains it's possible to see it was once an impressively large structure, though not very cleverly designed because the large central dome collapsed soon after its completion.

To complete your tour you may want to have a look at the **Selçuk Palace** built into the city's defensive walls overlooking the Alaca Çay.

Ağrı There's nothing to hold your interest in the dull provincial town of Ağrı and your visit will almost certainly be limited to a short stop in the small bus station, enroute for somewhere else. Even the eponymous mountain, Ağrı Dağı (Mount Ararat), is out of sight beyond the horizon 100 km to the east. If you're unlucky enough to be stranded overnight taxis and dolmuş passing outside the *otogar* take you into the centre where there are a couple of hotels and the usual choice of kebap and pide restaurants.

Doğubeyazıt

Phone code: 0472
Colour map 3, grid B5
Altitude: 1950 m

Just over 35 km west of the Iranian frontier, Doğubeyazıt sits on an extensive ova, or plain, encompassed by lofty mountains. On the northern edge of this large tectonic basin rears up the impressive 5137-m cone of Mount Ararat, which besides its biblical associations is also the highest peak in Turkey. Historically, the town has been a stopping point for caravans travelling along the Silk Route, and indeed it still functions as an important transit centre for goods and people crossing the border to the east. Doğubeyazıt once enjoyed a modest tourist industry up until the Iranian Revolution in 1979 interrupted the steady stream of 'overlanders' passing through. Then in the mid-1980s, the Kurdish troubles ensured the town was rubbed completely off the tourist map as PKK activity effectively put Mount Ararat, a popular destination for foreign and domestic trekkers, and other local sights out of bounds. Despite the spectre of Kurdish terrorism having been lifted from the area Iranian traders and businessmen still far outnumber tourists in the town's hotels, and probably will do for some time. This is a pity because there are enough interesting things to see in the area, such as the fanciful Ishak Paşa Sarayı; the hot-springs at Diyadin; a giant meteor crater and the what some believe to be the last resting place of Noah's Ark, to justify at least an overnight stay possibly two.

Ins & outs
See page 606 for further details

Getting there Doğubeyazıt is accessible by bus services via Ağrı as well as several morning dolmuş from Van. There are also regular dolmuş throughout the day to and from the Iranian border. **Getting around** The town itself is small and has a regular street plan, which makes finding your way around on foot pretty easy. The new *otogar* is on the east side of town, a 5-min stroll from the town's accommodation.

Sights The town itself is a rather chaotic, dusty grid of nondescript, semi-finished concrete buildings. Although there's nothing specifically to do the busy street activity, particularly along Ağrı Caddesi, can be interesting to watch. You may also like to trawl the bazaar area for interesting goods which have come across the border from Iran, though infact most of the shops stock the cheap manufactured goods sought after by Iranian buyers.

Excursions
See page 606 for further details

Despite the dearth of things to do in town there are several interesting places to visit in the area. Most of these sights can be reached independently unless there's been a drastic worsening of the security situation since the time of writing. However, if time is short you may prefer to enrol on a **tour** organized by *Mefser Tur* (see directory), although these do seem somewhat overpriced. Half-day tours include a visit to the Iranian border, Noah's Ark, the meteor crater and Ishak Paşa Sarayı or the hot springs at Diyadin and a Kurdish village in the area. Each of these options is about US$25 per person for a group of at least six people. A full day itinerary takes in all of the above sights for about US$35 per person in a similar sized group.

Doğubeyazıt has quite a good selection of hotels for such a small town, although these are frequented by traders and businessmen rather than tourists and consequently women travellers may feel uncomfortable in some. **Sleeping**

A *Hotel Nuh*, Büyük Ağrı Caddesi No 65, T3127232, F3126910. Newish hotel with car park, restaurant and bar, some of comfortable rooms have a view of Mount Ararat, posted rates are expensive but you'll probably be able to negotiate a discount. **B** *Hotel Ararat*, Belediye Caddesi, T3124987, F3127355, near the bus station. Supposedly 4-star, large concrete structure with restaurant and pool, though don't rely on it being full, small and, for the money, simple rooms with ensuite, TV and telephone.

D *Hotel Grand Derya*, Emniyet Caddesi, T3127531, F3127833. Very good value if prices don't change, comfortable rooms equipped with TV, telephone and ensuite shower, lounge with satellite-TV. Recommended. **D** *Hotel Ortadoğu*, Ağrı Caddesi No 105, T3124225, F3113681. Decent rooms which at the front have view of Ararat and busy Ağrı Caddesi from balconies, ensuite, TV, telephone and fridge as standard, internet access. Recommended. **D** *Hotel İsfahan*, İsa Geçit Caddesi No 26, T3125289, F3124470. Formerly a popular venue for tour groups, similarly equipped to the Ortadoğu but everything is a bit worn. **E** *Hotel Tahran*, Büyük Ağrı Caddesi No 124, T3112223, F3112460. Reasonable rooms with bathroom and telephone, a bit grubby but represents good value, friendly staff. Recommended. **E** *Hotel Urartu*, Belediye Caddesi, PTT Karşısı, T3127295, F3112450, opposite the PTT. Centrally located, small, simple rooms with telephone, TV and ensuite. **F** *Hotel İshakpaşa*, Büyük Ağrı Caddesi No 10, T3127036, F3127644, on the corner of Emniyet Caddesi opposite the police station. Simple 21 room place with ensuite shower and small balcony. **G** *Hotel Erzurum*, Belediye Caddesi No 22, T3125080. Basic guesthouse with small dirty lounge, tiny guestrooms with bathroom on each floor. **G** *Hotel Saruhan*, Emniyet Caddesi, T3113097, next to *Hotel Erzurum*. Larger and more salubrious rooms than next-door, some of partition walls are very narrow, shared bathroom. If you fancy something a bit different try the *İshak Paşa Restaurant*, overlooking the palace, where thin mattresses on the floor will set you back about US$2 each. Don't necessarily expect peace and quiet though as you may be entertained by an impromptu folk music session.

Camping *Murat Camping*, below İshak Paşa Sarayı on the left of the approach road, occasionally plays host to overland tours, simple meals prepared, US$1.25 per pitch.

Doğubeyazıt

To the Meteor Crater & the Iranian Frontier

■ **Sleeping**

1	Ararat	6	Nuh
2	Erzurum	7	Ortadoğu
3	Grand Derya	8	Saruhan
4	İsfahan	9	Tahran
5	İshak Paşa	10	Urartu

Not to scale

Northeast Anatolia

Eating There are several simple eateries along Belediye and Emniyet Caddesis which are perfectly adequate for a bite to eat. The imaginatively named *Lokanta*, opposite the *Hotel Saruhan*, is more welcoming than most, offering ready-prepared stews, kebaps and pide. For something a little more fancy try one of the hotel restaurants such as the *Ararat* or the *Grand Derya*.

Transport **Bus** Ağrı, every hr, 0700-1400, 90 mins, US$3. Every Ağrı-bound bus except the 1400 continues to **Erzurum**, 4 hrs, US$7. For **Artvin** and **Trabzon** change at Erzurum. **Van**, direct dolmuş leave across from where Belediye Caddesi meets Ağrı Caddesi at 0730, 0900, 1200 and 1400, 2-3 hrs, US$7. Alternatively, if you miss the dolmuş you can get a bus to Ağrı from where there are hrly services to Van. Total travelling time is about 6 hrs. Heading for **Kars** take a dolmuş to Iğdır (hourly, 0500-1900, 45 mins US$1.50) from opposite the *Hotel Ortadoğu* and then change onto a dolmuş to Kars (supposedly every hr, 0900-1500, 2½ hrs, US$4.50). You should set-out in plenty of time to avoid getting stranded in Iğdır, where you may have to wait for some time.

There are also daily departures from the bus station to more distant destinations such as Ankara

Into Iran Travellers crossing the Iranian frontier, 34 km southeast of Doğubeyazıt at Gürbulak, need to be in possession of a valid visa issued by an Iranian Consulate in Turkey or elsewhere. You may also be asked to present a bus or airline ticket for your return journey. Dolmuş for Gürbulak leave from near the petrol station on Ağrı Caddesi regularly, US$1.50. There's a restaurant, change facilities and several shops at the border post. Once you've completed the formalities catch an Iranian taxi to the town of Maku from where there are onward buses to Tabriz.

Directory **Banks** İşbankası on Belediye Caddesi sometimes changes TCs, but don't rely on it. In an emergency some of the town's hotels or jewellery merchants will change foreign currency but usually at pretty uncompetitive rates. **Post office** The PTT is on Belediye Caddesi. **Internet** At present there's no internet café in town although this may have changed by the time you get there. You could try the *Hotel Ortadoğu* on Ağrı Caddesi. **Hospitals** There's a fairly rudimentary healthcentre (*sağlıkocağı*) at the west end of Belediye Caddesi near the PTT, but for anything serious it's wise to head for Van, Ağrı or, even better, Erzurum. **Tour agencies** *Mefser Tur*, Belediye Caddesi No 6, T3126772, F3127776, *Turkish Airlines* agent, local tours.

Around Doğubeyazıt

İshak Paşa Sarayı
The palace is like something from a fairy tale

Set on a dramatic terrace looking out across the *ova* of Doğubeyazıt and backed by jagged, rocky peaks, you will almost certainly have seen a picture of the İshak Paşa Sarayı sometime during your visit to Turkey. The impressive setting is matched by the 366 room palace which was constructed by the Çıldıroğlu, a feudal dynasty who ruled over much of eastern Anatolia during the 18th century. Completed in 1784 by the Çıldıroğlu Lord İshak Paşa, the building is a weird and wonderful blend of Armenian, Georgian, Ottoman, Persian and Selçuk architectural styles. With its magnificent entry portal; whimsical striped minaret and Persian-style dome the building is aesthetically very pleasing. Delicate carving liberally decorates many of the stone surfaces within the palace, with particularly beautiful examples found on the tomb of İshak Paşa and his father, Abdi Paşa, in the main courtyard. No expense was spared with the more mundane practicalities of the building and it was fitted with both a heating and sewerage system. Unfortunately, recent restoration work has been carried out rather enthusiastically making parts of the palace look like they were built yesterday. İshak Paşa built up huge wealth and influence and in 1789 he assumed the highest post in the Ottoman administration, that of *grand vizier*.

Northeast Anatolia

In search of the Ark

One of the most celebrated biblical stories is that of Noah's Ark, recounted in The Book of Genesis, Chapter 6. In the Old Testament story God commands Noah to construct a wooden boat and to load on-board his family along with a pair of each living creature on the earth. He then lets loose the floodgates, inundating the world and cleansing it of all sin. After 40 days the floodwaters subside, the Ark comes to rest and its passengers disembark to repopulate the earth, this much is clear. Unfortunately, the Scriptures are less precise about where Noah actually landed, with the text vaguely defining the spot as 'hary urartu', or 'upon the mountains of Urartu'.

Urartu is the Assyrian name for 5,117-m high Mount Ararat, also lending its name to an ancient civilisation which flourished in the region between the ninth and seventh centuries BC. From this biblical scholars came to the conclusion that the mythical ship, if it really existed, must have landed somewhere on the huge volcanic cone.

This theory was supported by an Armenian tradition that a piece of the Ark was built into a sanctuary on the mountain called Jacob's Well. Though this shrine has long since disappeared, unsubstantiated sitings of the vessel have cropped up from time to time.

In 1955 there was great excitement when a party discovered a piece of ancient looking timber near the summit. Much to everybody's disappointment tests suggested that infact it was part of a 19th-century Russian theodolite, a surveying instrument for measuring horizontal and vertical angles with a rotating telescope. Ark-hunters were again aroused by aerial photographs taken by a Turkish mapping team which showed a mysterious boat shaped form on Ararat's flanks. These were later discounted as landslides, however, they encourage a flurry of expeditions, many of them funded by the American Evangelical movement. Hopes of finding the Ark were dashed in 1988 when scientists using sub-surface radar declared that there were no remains under the mountains ice cap. Shortly afterwards the mountain was effectively closed to would-be searchers by the guerilla war ranging between the PKK and the Turkish military.

At about this time an American named David Fusold claimed to have discovered the Ark on a mountainside near the village of Uzengili, 17 km southeast of Doğubeyazıt. Fusold's 'Ark' is a rocky boat-like shape, roughly corresponding to the dimensions of the vessel described in Genesis, which has been dismissed by sceptics as a geological formation. This seems to matter little to the Turkish authorities who, in an effort to promote local tourism, have dubbed the site 'Nuhun Gemisi' (Noah's Ark) and employed a custodian to show visitors around.

With the improving security situation the prospect of future expeditions scouring Mount Ararat for the Ark looks certain. However, a fresh interpretation of the biblical text suggests that these Ark-hunters may be barking up the wrong tree, with the ambiguous reference to 'the mountains of Urartu' infact referring to another peak entirely.

On the opposite side of a rocky defile are the ruins of a mosque constructed for Selim the Grim after his military success at Çaldıran (see page 652) in 1514, along with the remains of what is believed to have originally been an Urartian citadel, though much built on since. ■ *Getting there: The palace is 5 km east of town past the bus station and a large army base. It's easy enough to hitch on summer evenings or at weekends when locals go up to picnic in the hills, but at other times you may have to walk. Another option is to rent or borrow a bicycle from one of the shops or hotels in town, though the last section is pretty steep. A taxi should be about US$5 for the return journey, plus waiting time.*

Northeast Anatolia

Ağrı Dağı
(Mount Ararat)

Mount Ararat, Ağrı Dağı to the Turks, is a 5137 m volcanic cone which rises in spectacular fashion between Doğubeyazıt and the Armenian border. Frequently shrouded in ominous afternoon cloud, the top of the peak is capped by a permanent layer of snow and ice below which lie vast slopes of basalt and scree fields. The volcano last erupted in 1840, however a more immediate danger, that of PKK insurgency, has closed it to would-be summiteers for some time now.

It has been rumoured that with the general improvements in the security situation the military will soon be granting permission for foreign groups to tackle the peak again. As in the past though, any such expedition will first have to negotiate Ankara's Byzantine bureaucratic machine, with official requirements including the hiring of a Turkish Mountaineering Federation guide to accompany each group.

Mount Ararat is well-known to most as the supposed resting place of Noah's Ark, however, despite reported sightings as long ago as 70 AD no evidence of its existence has so far come to light. Not for want of trying it must be added (see box, page 607). ■ *Getting there: You'll need to get a taxi to the site which is signposted off the road to the Iranian frontier, about 18 km from town.*

Meteor crater

On a much smaller scale, but infinitely more accessible than Mount Ararat, is the crater left by a meteor which plummeted to earth in 1920 about 30 km east of Doğubeyazıt. Approximately 65 m long by 35 m wide the crater can be reached down a 3-km track, signposted the 'Meteor Çukuru', off the road to the Iranian frontier. ■ *Getting there: Catch an 'Iran Kapısı' dolmuş (every hr, US$2.50) from Ağrı Caddesi in Doğubeyazıt and ask to be let off at the Meteor Çukuru.*

Diyadin Kaplıca

About 40 km west of Doğubeyazıt near the village of Diyadin are a series of small geyser-like springs which spurt hot mineral rich water out of a rocky hillside. Over thousands of years the minerals deposited by these springs have built up into travertines, cascading downslope like a mini Pamukkale, enclosing a fast flowing river in a short tunnel. The hot mineral water is channelled into several simple concrete pools where local people come to bathe and relax. In the single sex communal pools the atmosphere is friendly, though the water, which is a milky white colour like *rakı*, may not immediately look that enticing. It's wonderfully hot though and according to local wisdom has curative powers for a variety of ailments. ■ *0730-1900, US$0.40. There's also a private pool which can be hired for about US$4.*

The thermal springs are also in the process of being tapped to provide the nearby community of Diyadin with hot water - a very progressive project in an area where some families struggle to afford to heat water for washing and cleaning. ■ *Getting there: A dolmuş ($2) for Diyadin leaves from Doğubeyazıt's Ağrı Caddesi opposite the Orta Doğu Hotel at about 0830 everyday. The journey takes you along the road to Ağrı through an open mountain landscape of rolling pastures and distant snow flecked mountains. The village is 6 km off the main road with the dolmuş dropping people at the springs 7 km beyond. The dolmuş returns at about 1200 for Doğubeyazıt, though unfortunately from the village, so you have to hitch a lift or walk pretty quickly back after a soak. If the driver knows you are returning to Doğubeyazıt he'll generally wait, but if you do miss it then hitch down to the main road and wait for a bus from Ağrı to pass.*

Southeast Anatolia

13

Southeast Anatolia

613 Karamanmaraş

615 Gaziantep

621 Nemrut Dağı

625 Around Nemrut Dağı

625 Malatya

627 Şanlıurfa

633 Harran

635 Diyarbahır

640 Mardin

643 Around Van Gölü

643 Tatvan

645 Tatvan to Van

647 Van

Sharing a border with Syria, Iraq and Iran, southeast Anatolia has a distinctly Middle Eastern, as opposed to Anatolian, flavour. Populated by ethnic Kurds and a substantial Arab population, Turks are a minority in this part of the country. Poor and underdeveloped, the southeast has also had a bloody separatist war between Kurdish guerrillas and the Turkish military to add to its woes. Some hope, however, is provided by the massive GAP project, which through its dams, irrigation projects and government investment is radically changing the character of the region, for better and for worse.

Because of the perceived dangers of travelling in southeast Anatolia most foreign visitors give it a wide berth, with only a trickle of intrepid travellers discovering its many and varied attractions. A trio of cities sit on the sweltering plains with bustling Gaziantep, ancient Şanlıurfa and chaotic Diyarbakır each offering its fair share of interesting, though rarely visited, sights, including crumbling citadels, venerable shrines and vibrant bazaars. On a hilltop overlooking the baked Syrian plain, Mardin has a few compelling Arab-style buildings; though the main draw is a Nestorian monastery nearby, still operational after 1,500 years. East towards the Tigris, the rocky tableland of Tür Abdin has several more isolated Syrian Orthodox monasteries; while the Islamic ruins of Hasankeyf are threatened with inundation by a new dam. In the barren mountainous north of the region the mystical stone statues of Nemrut Dağı are the area's principal tourist attraction, perched on a remote mountain peak with the stunning lake of Van to the east largely neglected by foreign and domestic tourists alike.

Southeast Anatolia

☛ ## The Kurds and the PKK

Kurds make up Turkey's largest ethnic minority with reliable estimates putting their number at 10 to 12 million. Historically a nomadic, pastoral people, their homeland consists of the rugged mountains and valleys of southeast Anatolia as well as parts of northern Syria, Iraq and the Iranian Zagros. Far from a homogeneous ethnic group, the Kurdish people are divided along linguistic lines, speaking four mutually unintelligible dialects, two of them in different parts of Turkey's southeast. They are further split by religious affiliation with various Sunni, Shiite and heterodox groups. In Kurdish society loyalty has traditionally been to the clan with the various tribes frequently coming to blows with each other and their Ottoman and Persian neighbours. There has never been a unified Kurdish state, although Kurdish nationalists came close to securing Great Power approval for such an entity after the First World War. Instead Kurds assimilated into Ottoman and then Turkish society, migrating to other parts of the country, principally large cities such as İstanbul where an estimated one million Kurds live today, and taking up positions in all walks of life.

However, many Kurds admit that their assimilation into Turkish society has come at the cost of abandoning, at least outwardly, their Kurdish identity. Any Kurd unwilling to do so finds themselves at the sharp end of state repression and violence. Add to this the grinding poverty and lack of opportunities in the southeast and you can easily explain the rise of the Kurdistan Worker's Party (PKK), a previously unknown Marxist organisation whose stated aim was to carve an independent Kurdish state from Turkish territory.

The PKK was established in 1978 by Abdullah Öcalan, a student of political science at Ankara University. In the aftermath of the 1980 military coup, Öcalan fled to Syria where he received support from the government in building a small guerrilla army. Trained in camps hidden away in Lebanon's Bekaa Valley, by 1984 the PKK was confident enough to launch attacks against isolated police and army positions inside Turkey. Over the next few years the tempo of violence increased, as teachers, doctors, landlords as well as civilians marked as "collaborators" became the target of PKK violence.

The government's response was to establish martial law over most of the

Ins and outs

Avoid travelling at night & remember that some roads, such as the highways between Diyarbakır and Bitlis, Van & Doğubeyazıt are under dusk to dawn curfew

Travelling in the southeast is undeniably more challenging than in other parts of the country. The tourist infrastructure is barely developed and people are far less used to dealing with foreigners than in the west of Turkey. Comparatively large distances between towns and cities makes for long tiring journeys and the summer heat, which peaks above 40°C on plains, can be debilitating. Having said that, exploring the southeast rewards you with a fascinating new angle on Turkey, offering a compelling insight into a world far from the resorts and urban centres most often seen by visitors.

The security situation has improved dramatically in recent years but it is still advisable to take certain precautions. Before you leave check-up on the latest advisories issued by your government. At present it's suggested that you send a fax to your consulate in Ankara (see page 24) telling them your intention to travel to the region and a rough outline of your itinerary, plus passport details. This may no longer be deemed necessary by the time you're going, but ask your consulate anyway. Be prepared to stop at military check-points and have your passport with you at all times. It's also not advisable to stray off unaccompanied into isolated rural areas either on foot or in a vehicle. In fact, these points are as much to do with avoiding unwanted trouble from the authorities, who may view foreigners travelling in the area with some suspicion, as because of the PKK threat.

Southeast Anatolia

region, with the army using massive force to try and crush its foe. As so often happens, innocent villagers became the main victims of the conflict: coerced into providing support for the insurgents on the one hand and punished by the army for such co-operation on the other. An estimated 3,000 villages were razed by the military to rob the PKK of it's support base, sending a flood of refugees towards the towns and cities, and resulting in widespread criticism from Human Rights organisations amd foreign governments. Public opinion, however, was firmly behind the generals, steeled by the images of young Turkish conscripts being buried on the nightly news. In such a political climate any moves towards a non-military settlement became impossible with government crackdowns against moderate Kurdish groups also receiving widespread popular support. On the international stage, however, the PKK enjoyed considerable sympathy despite it's known links to major drug trafficking and extortion operations.

By the late-1990s the military's strong arm tactics appeared, finally, to be making headway as massive cross-border incursions into northern Iraq destroyed rebel bases and security forces mounted increasingly successful anti-terrorist operations. The PKK's brutal tactics also alienated it from many of its supporters with the number of fighters dwindling from a peak of perhaps 10,000 in the early 1990s, to a hard-core of less than 1,000. The capture and subsequent trial of PKK leader Abdullah Öcalan in 1999 seems to have further weakened the organisation, although sporadic clashes continue despite his call for a general cease-fire.

Unfortunately, after 16 years of fighting, and the loss of an estimated 30,000 lives, there has been no progress on the fundamental issues which caused the conflict in the first place. Flushed by it's apparent success Ankara is maintaining its commitment to a military solution to the problem, while ignoring the modest demands of more moderate Kurds for cultural freedoms, such as the right to broadcast and educate their children in Kurdish. The ambitious GAP project is going someway to addressing the problems of underdevelopment and poverty in the region, however, without some concessions on the part of the government there seems little hope of a lasting solution.

Karamanmaraş

Set on the edge of a wide agricultural valley Karamanmaraş is a busy market town famous for its thick glutinous ice-cream and the locally produced *acı biber* (ground red chilly) which finds its way onto restaurant tables across the country. Formerly known simply as Maraş, in 1973 the town was belatedly awarded its cumbersome new epithet "Karaman" (Heroic) in recognition of its peoples dogged resistance to a brief period of French rule after the Ottoman capitulation of 1918. Despite its grand new name and a lengthy history, the ravages of war and numerous earthquakes have depleted the town's intrinsic interest.

Phone code: 0344
Colour map 5, grid B5
Altitude: 568 m

Unless you fancy breaking the journey between Kayseri & Gazlantep there's comparatively little to justify a special visit

The city had a significant Armenian population up until the pogroms of the early 20th century. The most infamous episode of recent local history occurred in the turbulent days leading up to the 1980 military coup, when right-wing activists, known as the Grey Wolves, targeted Alevis, members of a Shia sect, across the east because of their perceived left-wing sympathies. In Maraş the local authorities stood by as right-wing cadres rampaged through the town attacking Alevi homes and businesses. Order was finally restored by the military, but not before 31 people had been killed and hundreds injured in the violence.

History

Southeast Anatolia

Sights

Kıbrıs Meydanı is home to hotels, restaurants & the town's other sights are in easy strolling distance

Starting from **Kıbrıs Meydanı**, a roundabout decorated with fountains, walk up Atatürk Caddesi, which is thronged by day with shoppers and pedestrian traffic. On the left-hand side of the road is the Syrian-style **Ulu Cami** constructed at the beginning of the 16th century by a local Turcoman emir.

Across the road, the city's lively **bazaar area** runs parallel to Atatürk Caddesi and in summer the narrow covered streets provide a welcome respite from the intense sun. Along with stalls selling all manner of goods, the bazaar harbours workshops where coppersmiths bang away, shaping metal jugs and trays.

Continuing up Atatürk Caddesi you'll come upon the 14th-century **Taş Cami** and its various foundations, which is easily identified by the distinctive Syrian-style minaret projecting skywards. Behind the mosque the streets of Kurtuluş Mahallesi contain some pretty dilapidated 19th century Ottoman buildings that have escaped destruction by earthquake and modern developers.

Overlooking the Taş Cami is Maraş's strategic **citadel** whose much-repaired walls today encompass a pleasant café. The castle's walls also provide an excellent vantage point from which to gaze out over the urban sprawl which has exploded outwards from the historical core of the city.

Sleeping

Being a provincial capital & important market town, Maraş has several quite reasonable hotels

C *Otel Kazancı*, Kıbrıs Meydanı, T2234462, F2126942. Large concrete building up the hill from the fountain, centrally located yet quiet, comfortable, decently furnished rooms with a/c, refrigerator, telephone, TV and ensuite, restaurant. **C** *Hotel Belli*, Trabzon Caddesi No 2, T2234900/1, F2148282, 50 m from the fountain on busy Trabzon Caddesi. Popular with visiting businessmen, large, well-equipped rooms with everything that the *Otel Kazancı* has to offer at a slightly cheaper rate. Recommended. **C** *Otel Büyük Maraş*, Milli Egemenlik Caddesi No 7, T2233500/1, F2128894, left off Trabzon Caddesi by Akbank. Similarly equipped rooms to the *Otel Kazancı*. **D** *Hotel Çavuşoğlu*, Şeyhadil Caddesi No 50, T2253524, F2142303. Slightly simpler rooms which are clean with mod-cons such as telephone, TV and ensuite. **G** *Otel Çeltik Palas*, Şeyhadil Caddesi No 63, T2141638, opposite the *Hotel Çavuşoğlu*. Run-down boarding house with spartan but clean rooms, shared bathrooms with squat toilets, no breakfast.

Eating

Osman Usta, Trabzon Caddesi, on the same side as the *Hotel Belli*, a busy kebap place which is crowded with families and workers at meal times, serves soups, ready-prepared stews, lahmacun and kebaps, as well as regional specialities like *içli köfte* and *çiğ köfte*. For desert try the *Yaşar Pastanesi*, a fancy cake and ice-cream shop next to the *Hotel Belli* visited by political figures such as Tansu Çiller and Süleyman Demirel when they're in town. Alternatively, the less sophisticated *Ünal Pastanesi* on Atatürk Caddesi near the Ulu Cami also has the locally made *dövme dondurma* (beaten ice cream) served theatrically from metal drums with a long metal spoon. Thickened to a doughy consistency using *salep*, an extract gathered from orchids growing in the nearby mountains, it's a very different taste and texture sensation to western ice-cream.

Transport

Bus Local The *otogar* is just off the main highway, about 1.5 km west of the town's centre, Kıbrıs Meydanı. Dolmuş (US$0.30) ply regularly along Azerbaycan Bulvarı between the *otogar* and Kıbrıs Meydanı. Maraş's train station, 2 km from Kıbrıs Meydanı beside the main highway, is also connected to the centre by regular dolmuş. **Long distance** Adana, regular buses, 3½ hrs, US$5. **Adıyaman**, 5 daily, 0730-1930, 3 hrs, US$5. **Antakya**, regular buses, 4 hrs, US$6. **Kayseri**, 6 buses daily, 5 hrs, US$6. **Malatya**, several morning buses, 4½ hrs, US$5. There are also several daily departures for Ankara, İstanbul and İzmir. *Karamanmaraş Koop* run minibuses every 15 mins, US$2, to **Gaziantep**.

Banks *İşbankası* and several other banks have branches around Kıbrıs Meydanı. **Post office** The PTT is on Azerbaycan Caddesi between the museum and Kıbrıs Meydanı. **Tourist information** The provincial tourist office, T2126590, F2230355, is on the 3rd floor of Özgür Apartments, Dedezade Sokak No 6, walking down Trabzon Caddesi from Kıbrıs Meydanı it's the 3rd road on the right.

Gaziantep

An ancient city spread out across on a wide plain drained by a tributary of the mighty Euphrates, Gaziantep has metamorphosed in the last 30 years into a vibrant, modern city. Benefiting from huge state investment in the GAP project and the flight of capital and skilled labour from areas affected by Kurdish insurgency, the city is now the undisputed industrial and commercial hub of the southeast with sprawling industrial estates; newly-built concrete suburbs and chaotic shanty towns surrounding the centre. This economic transformation has inevitably affected the character of the city with much of Gaziantep's architectural and historical heritage submerged beneath concrete and steel. A handful of interesting sights have survived the onslaught though, including the ruinous citadel flanked by fascinating bazaar streets teeming with colourful mercantile activity and abounding with possible souvenirs.

Phone code: 0342
Colour map 5, grid B5
Altitude: 843 m
Population: 700,000

Ins and outs

Being an important regional centre, Gaziantep is well tied into the national transport network with regular long distance bus services to destinations across the country. The city is also linked to İstanbul by rail with frequent air connections to both İstanbul and Ankara daily. Approaching by road from the Mediterranean coast an excellent toll highway substantially reduces journey times.

Getting there
See page 619 for further details

The centre of town is a square flanked by a busy intersection known as Hükümet Konağı. Dolmuş (US$0.30) marked 'Devlet Hastanesi' leave regularly for the centre of town, passing near the railway station before reaching their terminus on Hürrıyet Caddesi, 500 m south of Hükümet Konağı. A taxi from the bus station costs less than US$3. From the airport there is a shuttle-bus to the Turkish Airlines office on Atatürk Bulvarı, just west of Hükümet Konağı.

Getting around
Most of the city's hotels & restaurants are within walking distance of Hükümet Konağı, as are the main sights

The Tourist Information Office, T2309960, F2340603, is housed in a pink and cream stripped building situated at the western end of the municipal gardens, behind the new Gaziantep Valiliği. Open weekdays 0830-1200, 1300-1730.

Tourist information

Sights

The city's citadel, crowning a hill to the northeast of the centre, is thought to date back to Roman times, although recent research has shown that the acropolis mound itself was built-up as a result of thousands of years of human occupation. The ramparts were repaired many times over the centuries with much of what you see today dating from the Selçuk and early Ottoman periods. Encircled by a dry moat, you enter the castle across a wooden bridge reached up a ramp opposite a small mosque. Partly as a result of the pounding it took during the War of Independence, the structure is in a bit of a sorry state these days, with only 12 of the 36 towers mentioned by the Ottoman chronicler Evliya Çelebi still standing. Renovation work does seem to be in progress though and the keep affords an excellent view across the roof tops of the city.

Gaziantep Kale

The lanes at the base of the Kale are lined with metalworkers shops and the air is filled with the sound of craftsmen taping away at brass kettles, carved silver trays and shiny pots. Continuing round the street at the base of the citadel a right-hand turn takes you past the Tahtanı Camii to a decrepit, crumbling *han* on the right which is home to yet more bustling workshops. A short distance down Uzun Çarşı a left-hand fork leads to the Alaüddevle Camii, a striking 14th-century mosque constructed with alternating coarses of black and white stone. This is a colourful bazaar district where the mouthwatering scent of mint, cumin and grilling meat hangs in the air at meal times. Less enticing is the *Et Halı* (meat market) which occupies the gloomy interior of an Ottoman bedesten.

Back in the centre of town a short stroll up Kayacık Sokak brings you to the 14th-century Syrian-style **Eyüboğlu Camii** and a signpost for the **Hasan Süzer Etnoğrafya Müzesi** (see below).

The 'old' town Before or after a visit to the museum it's worth having a wander around the narrow alleyways of the surrounding residential quarter which manages to retain its traditional atmosphere, along with a few old buildings. You'll notice that the windows of many houses are covered by traditional wooden screens, known as *kaffes*, or are placed high on the walls away from prying eyes. During the heat of the day the warren of narrow streets are almost completely deserted, although the sounds of family life filter out from behind net curtains and through partly open doors. During your exploration you'll probably stumble on the **Kurtuluş Camii**, a black and white stripped building which was built in 1892 as a church for the local Armenian community, but now serves as a mosque. Less than 300 m away on Hürriyet Caddesi you return to 21st-century Gaziantep where office workers and smartly dressed locals crowd the pavements and streetside kebap restaurants.

Archaeological Museum Gaziantep's museum is certainly one of the best in Eastern Anatolia with a well-displayed selection of artefacts spanning the millenia from the Paleolithic era down to the early 20th century. Some of the oldest pieces on show are stone hand-axes, pottery shards and clay figureens uncovered at sites in the region, with an interesting reconstruction of a Bronze Age tomb excavated by archaeologists before it was submerged beneath the reservoir formed by the Birecik Dam on the Euphrates. A considerably less ancient exhibit is a rusting 1915 steam-powered motorbike which was brought from a nearby community where the village elders insist that it once belonged to none other than TE Lawrence, better known in the west as Lawrence of Arabia. ■ *0900-1200, 1330-1700 daily except Mon. US$1.50. The museum is about 750 m north of Hükümet Konağı, past the city's stadium on Istasyon Caddesi. Dolmuş heading to and from the otogar pass outside.*

Hasan Süzer Etnoğrafya Müzesi The city's ethnography museum is housed in a beautifully restored Ottoman mansion which was donated to the municipality by the philanthropist businessman Hasan Süzer. Built around a shady central courtyard decorated with black and white pebbles, steps lead up to the Selamlık, or guest-quarters, on the first floor and the Haremlık, reserved for household members, on the storey above. Several of the rooms are decorated with traditional furniture and contain the predictable collection of plastic dummies possed unnaturally in local garb. There is also an exhibit of photographs, documents and other memorabilia dating from the War of Independence. Below street-level the cool depths of the residence's cellars, carved from the underlying bed rock, were used for storing food supplies and wine. ■ *0800-1200, 1330-1730 daily except Mon. US$0.75. Follow the sign-post up the alleyway opposite the Eyüboğlu Camii.*

Essentials

AL *Hotel Tilmen*, İnönü Caddesi No 168, T2202081, F2202091, a short walk south of **Sleeping**
Hükümet Konağı. Modern hotel with well-furnished, comfortable rooms equipped
with a/c, telephone and TV, good value 3 bed rooms for US$135, restaurant, car park
and dry-cleaning service. **A** *Otel Belkıs*, Karagöz Mahallesi, Çamurcu Sokak No 4,
T2202020/1, F2342675. Newly opened 2-star hotel, smart bedrooms but not overly
spatious, a/c, minibar, telephone and TV as standard, a little over-priced. **C** *Hotel
Kaleli*, Hürriyet Caddesi, T2309690, F2301597. Excellent value rooms which are bright
and spacious, if a little dated in appearance, a/c, telephone, TV and ensuite with bath-
tub, decent roof-top restaurant, ask for quieter room at the rear. Recommended.
D *Hotel Veliç*, Atatürk Bulvarı No 23, T2212212, F2212210. A newly redecorated
37-room hotel with reasonble rooms with a/c, telephone and TV as standard, bathrooms with shower are a bit on the small side. **D** *Hotel Çatuk*, Hürriyet Caddesi No 27,
12319480/1, F2330043. Pretty mediocre place offering fairly small bedrooms with
shower, a/c and telephone, breakfast extra. **E** *Hotel Katan*, İstasyon Caddesi No 58,
T2208450/1, F2208454. Overlooking the main road opposite the city's stadium, modern hotel with decent enough rooms equipped with ensuite, TV and minibar, to be
avoided on match nights. **E** *Hotel Güllüoğlu*, Suburcu Caddesi No 1/B, T2324363/4,
F2208689. Run by the local baklava mafia, small rooms with ensuite, telephone and

Gaziantep

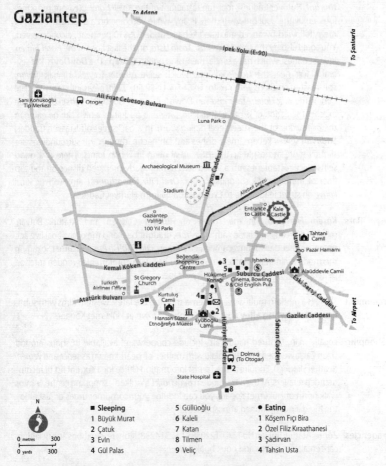

■ Sleeping		● Eating
1 Büyük Murat	5 Güllüoğlu	1 Köşem Fıçı Bira
2 Çatuk	6 Kaleli	2 Özel Filiz Kıraathanesi
3 Evln	7 Katan	3 Şadırvan
4 Gül Palas	8 Tilmen	4 Tahsin Usta
	9 Veliç	

0 metres 300
0 yards 300

TV, extra US$1.25 for breakfast. **E** *Hotel Büyük Murat*, Suburcu Caddesi No 16 Şahinbey, T2318449, F2311658. A short distance further down Suburcu Caddesi from the *Hotel Güllüoğlu*, this place represents better value with larger rooms equipped with telephone and TV above the tacky wood panelled reception. Recommended. **E-F** *Hotel Konfor*, Karagöz Caddesi, Kamber Sokak 2, T2312223, just off Karagöz Caddesi behind the Işbankası. Being redecorated when we visited so this may be a good one to check-out. **F** *Hotel Gül Palas*, Kayacık Sokak No 6, T2325213. Despite the name this certainly isn't a palace, pretty worn rooms with basin, newly fitted but dirty shared toilets, no breakfast, adequate budget option. **F-G** *Hotel Evin*, Kayacık Sokak No 11, T2313492. A short distance beyond the Gül Palas, nothing fancy but cleaner and more salubrious than its neighbour, shared bathrooms with shower, no breakfast. Good rock-bottom option.

Eating

The are many possibilities for budget dining around Hükümet Konağı & particularly along Suburcu Caddesi

Even by Turkish standards *Gaziantepli* have a seriously sweet-tooth and you can't take more than two steps in the centre of town without running into a shop with a tempting display of *baklava*, *kadayıf* (a desert made with shredded wheat, nuts and honey) and other super-sweet puddings in the window. Many of these brightly-lit outlets are run by members of the Güllüoğlu family who form a virtual caste of local sweet-makers. If you really want to push the boat out have clotted cream (*kaymaklı*) or a dollop of ice-cream (*dondurma*) on top of your pudding. **Midrange** *Kaleli Restaurant*, Hürriyet Caddesi, roof-top restaurant of the *Kaleli Hotel*, pleasant surroundings, enjoy the cool breeze, if there is any, while you dine on a decent selection of *meze*, followed by grilled meat and kebaps, under US$10 per head, alcohol served. You could also try the smart *ocak başı*, *Tasın Usta*, on the first floor of the *Hotel Tilmen*, İnönü Caddesi, which has a similar menu and prices. **Cheap** The *Doy Doy* is 1 of several places near the *Hotel Güllüoğlu* which serve quarter (*çeyrek*) or half (*yarım*) spit-roasted chickens with rice for US$1.50/ US$2.50. *Ekin*, pleasant courtyard café behind the *Veliç Hotel*, Atatürk Bulvarı. Down Suburcu Caddesi, the *Tahsin Usta* has an excellent selection of kebaps, lahmacun, pide and puddings which can be eaten in the *aile salonu* or the street-level dining room. In a backstreet off Istasyon Caddesi *Şadırvan* serves kebaps, meat dishes and lahmacun, though the surroundings are slightly more atmospheric than the usual neon-lit kebap joints. There is a good self-service restaurant with a varied selection of ready-prepared dishes on the top floor of the Beğendik shopping centre. *Özel Filiz Kıraathanesi*, atmospheric local *kahve* on street leading up to Eyüboğlu Camii from Hürriyet Caddesi.

Bars

Köşem Fıçı Bira, on the corner of Hürriyet Caddesi and Atatürk Bulvarı, rough-and-ready *meyhane* with *meze*, *rakı*, draught beer and the occasional live act, not recommended for unaccompanied women. *Old English Pub*, Hükümet Sokağı, in the modern cinema complex, trendy hang-out with comfortable wooden interior, perfect place if you need a temporary escape.

Entertainment

There is a modern multi-screen **cinema** showing the latest western films with subtitles and a **bowling alley** right in the centre of town at Hükümet Konağı.

Shopping

Locally manufactured handicrafts include copperware, available in shops around Uzun Çarşı; wooden furniture inlaid with mother-of-pearl, known as *sedef*, and *yemeni* (leather slippers). Enquire at the Tourist Information Office for a current list of recommended retailers. At the ultra-modern *Beğendik* ("We liked") shopping centre, 5-mins walk north of Hükümet Konağı, you can indulge your consumer urges or just enjoy the frigid air-conditioned atmosphere.

Tour agencies

Zöhre, Atatürk Bulvarı No 13/D, T2205857, F2314238, flight reservations and ticketing, car-rental, excursions and hotel booking.

Air *Turkish Airlines*, Atatürk Bulvarı No 30/B, T2301565, F2301567, operate several daily return flights to **İstanbul** and **Ankara** from the city's Oğzueli airport, 20 km to the southeast of the city. A shuttle-bus, US$2, departs from the *Turkish Airlines* office on Atatürk Bulvarı 90 mins before their scheduled departures. **Road Bus**: **Adana**, regular buses, 3½ hrs, US$4. **Adıyaman**, 4 daily buses, 4 hrs, US$5. **Ankara**, regular buses, 11 hrs, US$14. **Antakya**, regular buses, 4 hrs, US$5. **Diyarbakır**, regular buses, 5 hrs, US$7. **Malatya**, several buses daily, 4½ hrs, US$6. **Mardin**, 5½ hrs, several buses a day, US$8. **Şanlıurfa**, buses at least every hr, 2½ hrs, US$3. The premium company *Varan* operates over-night services to **İstanbul** (15 hrs) and **Ankara**, (9 hrs) for US$23 and US$16 respectively. **Car rental**: *Avis*, Ordu Caddesi No 15/A, *Şahinbey*, T3361194, F3363058. *Budget*, Fevzi Çakmak Bulvarı No 11/B, T3351230, F3351232. Local travel agents such as *Zöhre* (see above, tour agencies) can arrange car hire at competitive rates. **Train** *Toros Ekspresi*, departs İstanbul Tue, Thu and Sun at 0855, returning from Gaziantep on Tue, Thu and Sat at 1430, 27 hrs, calling at **Afyon**, **Konya**, **Karaman** and **Adana**. From **Ankara** you could catch the daily overnight *Çukurova Mavi Treni* to **Adana** and then transfer onto a bus for the final leg of the journey.

Airline offices *İstanbul Airlines*, Atatürk Bulvarı No 60, T2300048, F2307866. **Banks** *İşbankası* and several other banks with ATM machines can be found on Suburcu Caddesi. **Baths** *Pazar Hamamı*, Uzun Çarşı, near the Tahtani Camii. **Communications Post office**: The central PTT is on Hürriyet Caddesi. **Internet** *Well Net Cafe*, behind the cinema and bowling centre at Hükümet Konağı, in 1st floor of building opposite Vakıf Bank, US$1 per hr. **Hospitals** The state hospital is on Hürriyet Caddesi 600 m south of Hükümet Konağı. The *Sanı Konukoğlu Tıp Merkezi* is a modern, private health centre on Ali Fuat Cebesoy Bulvarı near the *otogar*. **Laundry** *Milano Kuru Temizleme*, dry-cleaning service, turn off Hürriyet Caddesi at the *Hotel Kaleli* and take the 1st right and it's 50 m down on the right.

Stranded in the brown, parched mountains of southeastern Anatolia, Adıyaman has to rank among the country's least pleasant provincial towns. its economy has traditionally been based on animal husbandry and the rain-fed cultivation of wheat and tobacco, fields of which you'll notice on either side of the road as you approach town. Though undoubtedly good for the impoverished local economy, the discovery of oil and the GAP project have done little to enhance Adıyaman aesthetically, helping transform it from a dusty one horse town into a rapidly expanding concrete mess. The only reason most people pass through is en route for Nemrut Dağı and with the town of Kahta, 32 km to the east, making a more convenient base for the day trip up to the mountain, there is little reason to linger.

Sleeping and eating D *Hotel Antiochos*, Atatürk Bulvarı No 141, T2163377, F2138456. Newish place inconveniently situated about 1 km east of the centre, decent rooms with a/c, telephone, TV and refrigerator, restaurant and swimming pool in the garden. **D** *Hotel Serdaroğlu*, Turgut Reis Caddesi No 20, T2164841, F2161554. Centrally located near the bus station, perfectly adequate for an overnight stay, slightly cheaper than the *Antiochos*, however, no pool, rooms do have a/c, telephone and TV. **F** *Beyaz Saray Pansiyon*, Atatürk Bulvarı No 136, T2162100, F2161580. Simple rooms with or without bathrooms, garden, restaurant and swimming pool make this a good budget option. There is a cluster of simple **eateries** around the bus station, though if you're staying you're probably best off eating in your hotel.

Transport Air *Turkish Airlines* operate a return flight from **Ankara** every Mon, Wed and Sat. *Inandı Turizm*, Atatürk Bulvarı Emniyet Yanı No 1, T2161436/7, F2161440, are the local sales agent, as well as organizing car rental and Nemrut Dağı tours. **Bus** **Malatya**, every 2 hrs, 3 hrs, US$3. For **Gaziantep** (4 hrs, US$5) and **Urfa** (90 mins, US$1.25) dolmuş depart regularly from outside the *Hotel Serdaroğlu*. There are also daily departures to destinations further afield such as **Ankara**, **İstanbul** and **İzmir**.

The GAP project

The Güneydoğu Anadolu Projesi (Southeast Anatolia Project), commonly known by the acronym GAP, is a massive project aimed at helping to develop Turkey's poorest region. The plan consists of a staircase of 22 dams on the Tigris and Euphrates Rivers, the centre-piece of which is the massive Atatürk Barajı, the fourth largest dam of its type in the world. Government planners forecast that when completed, sometime in 2005, the project's 19 hydro-electric plants will generate up to 26 billion kilowatt hours of electricity also providing water to irrigate three million hectares of farmland.

Thousands of miles of aquaducts have already been laid, with two massive tunnels channeling life-giving water from the reservoir impounded by the Atatürk Barajı to the parched plains near Şanlıurfa. Although only about 10% of the schemes have so far come on-line, the landscape around villages such as Harran has already been fundamentally changed. Where farmers previously struggled to produce one annual harvest of wheat from the dusty soil, now they can raise valuable crops of tomatoes, peppers, melons and, most importantly, cotton. Rural standards of living have already begun to rise, though Olcay Unver, the project's director, optimistically forecasts an eventual trebling of the region's average income.

The project's impact was not supposed to end there, with the combination of keenly priced hydro-electric power, cheap labour, raw materials and some very enticing tax breaks offered by Ankara attracting industries to set up in the area. Indeed this has been successful, notably around the now thriving city Gaziantep, though potential investors have generally been put off by the region's insecurity. Its detractors also complain that the GAP project is entrenching the region's highly unequal system of land distribution as large landlords reap most of the benefits, while poor farmers, unable to shoulder the high costs and risks involved in the new methods of farming, are forced off the land.

Inevitably such a gigantic project also has severe ecological implications with the shift to irrigated farming over such a large area causing a rise in water-borne infectious diseases, as well as the arrival of new ones such as malaria. The flooding of vast areas in a region dubbed "the cradle of civilisation" has also meant the loss of priceless archaeological treasures as dozens of ancient sites have disappeared underwater (see box, page 630).

The GAP project has also placed considerable strain on Turkey's relations with the downstream states of Syria and Iraq who rely on water from the Tigris and Euphrates. Both complain that Turkey is using far more than its share of the water with the Syrians formerly attempting to use their clandestine support for the PKK as a bargaining chip in negotiations with Ankara over water rights.

Kahta From the same uninspiring mould as Adıyaman, the small backwater town of Kahta has enjoyed a recent oil powered boom with over a hundred oil wells and a large refinery in the vicinity. Its proximity to Nemrut Dağı also puts it firmly on the tourist map as a favourite launching point for excursions up the mountain. Unless you visit during the *International Kahta Kommagene Festival* at the end of June, there's little to hold your interest.

Discounts can generally be negotiated during slack periods

Sleeping The in-flow of foreign visitors has frequently been interupted by instability in the region, most disastrously in 1999 when the PKK issued direct threats against the Turkish tourist industry. Competition is therefore stiff between the hoteliers. Several have deals with bus and dolmuş drivers to drop arriving travellers directly in front of their door. This can be very convenient, but if you don't like where you're being deposited continue to the minibus station. **C** *New Merhaba Otel*, Çarşı Caddesi, T7258055, F7257111. Reasonable rooms with telephone and TV in newish place, owned by amiable former actor, 15% student discount given. **F** *Hotel Mezopotamya*, Mustafa Kemal Caddesi No 20, T7255112, F7256229. Newly opened hotel on the right as you enter town, small rooms but decent for the price, some have a/c, swimming pool and restaurant. **F-G** *Hotel Kommagene*, Yeni Diyarbakır Yolu Üzeri, T7151092, F7257614. Plain but perfectly adaquate rooms with or without a shower, shady courtyard restaurant, like many of the other places in town can be a bit noisy, good budget option though. **G** *Anatolia Pension*, Adliye Karşı, T7256483. Basic rooms above crowded courtyard café, small terrace for guests use. **Camping** *Zeus Camping*, T7255695, Mustafa Kemal Caddesi, well-kept site, caravan US$6.50, tent US$4. They are currently building a hotel.

Eating There are several simple eateries on Mustafa Kemal Caddesi including *Şafak Lokantası*, which serves decent enough ready-prepared dishes, soup and kebaps, and the *Yudum* opposite. At the *Altın Şiş* on same road as the Anatolia Pension you'll find şiş kebaps and some other grilled meat. The best that Kahta has to offer is 5 km east of town where several restaurants overlook the vivid turquoise waters of the reservoir formed by the Atatürk Dam. Locals prefer the *Akropolian*, T7255132, which serves very reasonably priced *meze*, trout and meat on its terrace. Alcohol is also available, so try a glass of *rakı* accompanied by *şalgam*, a dark red juice made from turnips. Without transport it's easy to hitch a lift or alternatively hire a dolmuş for the ride.

Transport Many buses from Adıyaman actually start in Kahta, so there is plenty on offer, including daily departures to **İstanbul** (21 hrs), **Adana** (6 hrs), **Ankara** (12 hrs), **İzmir** (22 hrs) and **Kayseri** (8 hrs). There are also regular dolmuş to **Urfa** (2 hrs) and **Adıyaman** (25 mins) throughout the day. Several daily buses take the direct road via a dilapidated ferry across the reservoir formed by the Atatürk Dam to Siverek (1½ hrs), then connecting with buses to **Diyarbakır** (1½ hrs).

Directory Airline offices *Nemrut Turs*, T7256881, next to the *Nemrut Tur Otel*, ticketing agent for Turkish Airlines. **Banks** The town's *İşbankası* has an ATM and reportedly changes TCs too. **Post office** The PTT, which stays open until 2300, is off Atatürk Caddesi. **Tourist information** The Tourist Information Office, T7255007, is on Mustafa Kemal Caddesi opposite the *Hotel Bardakçı*. Call-in for local advice and current prices for Nemrut tours. 0830-1200, 1300-1700 weekdays.

Nemrut Dağı

Staring out across a barren, rocky landscape from their 2150-m eyrie, the stone heads of Nemrut Dağı have become the most recognizable face of Eastern Turkey. Only rediscovered by the outside world in the 19th century, today their collective gaze exerts an almost magnetic pull over visitors, drawing them eastwards and upwards to hold vigil on the summit, waiting for the golden light of the dawn or dusk sun to colour the ancient faces. It is a pleasant enough ritual and a fascinating spot, which you should be prepared to share with a small crowd of camera toting souls bused up for the experience.

Colour map 6, grid B1

Getting there Nemrut Dağı is situated between the towns of Malatya and Adıyaman in the mountains of the Anti-Taurus Range. A steep and, for the final section at least, rough road climbs up to within a 20-minute walk of the summit from the south side, with **Kahta** or **Adıyaman** most commonly used as bases for the trip. The well-signposted ascent is perfectly possible in your own vehicle but make sure you set off with a full tank of petrol. Allow about an hour for the ascent, although on the way you may decide to take the old road via Karakuş, Cendere and Arsameia. Conversely, you could visit these interesting sights on the way down. See page 624 for organised tours.

Ins & outs
Not to be confused with the extinct volcano on the shore of Lake Van

Southeast Anatolia

Climate Being at over 2,000 m snow lies on the peak for much of the year, so it's best to visit between the end of May and the beginning of Oct when the roads up to the summit are generally free of snow and passable. Even in mid-summer it can still be pretty cold at the top, particularly if you've arrived to watch the sunrise, so make sure you're dressed warmly. Good shoes are also advisable because the final ascent is across several hundred metres of loose scree.

History Stumbled upon in 1881 by a German engineer, Karl Puchstein, who was surveying the area for the Ottoman authorities, a preliminary investigation of the mountain top site was conducted some years later by the archaeologist Karl Humann, vilified in Turkey for having 'stolen' the altar of Zeus from Pergamum. It was to be 70 years, however, until a thorough study of Nemrut Dağı was conducted by a team from the American School of Oriental Research. Their research revealed that the mountain had been used as a temple complex and burial place by the Commagene Dynasty, who ruled over the surrounding area during the first and second centuries BC.

At that time the region, thickly forested and rich in resources, was a border province of the Seleucid empire. In 162 BC the governor broke away from the empire, setting himself up as the self-styled ruler of the Kingdom of Commagene. He was succeeded by his son Samos II (130-96 BC) who shrewdly managed to normalize relations with Seleucids, although the subsequent break-up of that empire during the reign of his successor, Mithridates I Callinicus (96-70 AD), saw Commagene allegiances switch to the new power in Asia Minor, the Romans. Benefiting from good relations with Rome and the Parthians to the east, it was under Antiochus I Epiphanes (64-38 BC) that the kingdom reached its zenith.

Antiochus I traced his lineage back to the Persian emperor Darius the Great and Seleucus I Nicator, founder of the Seleucid dynasty. But his shameless self aggrandizement didn't stop there as he believed himself to be a divine ruler who after death take his place alongside the other Gods in heaven. His vanity was the driving force behind the construction of the temple complex and tumulus on Nemrut Dağı, although soon after its completion he was brought crashing down to earth by the Roman Emperor Anthony, who deposed him for supporting the Parthians.

The summit Approaching from the south side of the mountain the end of the line as far as cars and minibuses are concerned is a carpark, flanked by a café serving hot and cold drinks as well as some simple snacks, which is several hundred metres beneath the top. Having paid the US$2.50 entrance fee, it's a 500-m walk up a rocky path to the summit of the peak itself, crowned by a 50-m high tumulus of crushed rock, laboriously heaped into a cone by ancient workers and thought by some to conceal the tyrant Antiochus' tomb. Terraces surround the mound on three sides, with the eastern one forming the temple's **main sanctuary**. This large flat area, occasionally used today as a helipad by visiting dignitaries, has a sacrificial altar near its edge and is overlooked by the much admired row of stone statues. Seated side by side they represent what Antiochus haughtily referred to as "the heroic company of my ancestors", a line of syncretic deities drawn from Greek and Persian mythology. First up on the left is Apollo, the Sun God; then comes Fortuna, Goddess of Fortune, although some suggest this may in fact be a personification of Commagene, a local goddess of fertility and abundance; Zeus-Ahurmazda, the largest figure is seated in the centre; followed by the deified Antiochus himself with Hercules-Ares beside him on the end. Each of the enthroned figures is several metres in height, though the heads have long since toppled off and now lie on the terrace in front. For most visitors these well-preserved heads, with their conical hats and long beards, are undoubtedly the big draw, complimented by the spectacularly lofty site commanding sweeping views across the surrounding mountains. The truncated figures are guarded by pairs of stone eagles and lions, with Greek inscriptions on the back of the statues explaining the procedure for ceremonial sacrifices carried-out on important days, such as the monthly celebration of Antiochus' birthday.

On the opposite side of the mountain and reached by a path around its base is the **western terrace**, overlooked by the same line-up of seated gods, their bodies badly worn by time. Surprisingly though, the heads scattered across the terrace below are in better shape than on the east side. There's also a row of interesting **reliefs** showing Antiochus greeting Apollo, Zeus and Hercules, with another carved panel depicting a lion, almost certainly meant to represent the Commagene state. Also worked into this panel are a constellation of 19 stars and planets, several of which are identified by inscriptions as Jupiter, Mars and Mercury, and modern historians have concluded this planetary alignment occurred on 7 July 62 BC, the year Antiochus received the support of Emperor Pompey in Rome.

Sleeping

There are several places to stay on the way up the mountain in and around the village of Karadüt, 12 km below the summit. There's no dolmuş to the village, though, so without your own transport you'll need to catch a lift in a passing minibus, of which there are plenty in season. **G** *Karadut Pansiyon*, T3727169. Basic rooms with shared bathroom in friendly family-run place on the upper edge of the village. **C** *Hotel Euphrat*, T7372175, F7372179. Several kilometres above the village on the left, basic rooms in unattractive barrack-like buildings, breakfast, lunch and dinner included in price. A short distance beyond is the far more appealling **F** *Kervansaray Turistik*

Stone faces,
Nemrut Dağı

Tesisleri, T7372190/1, F7372085. Cozy doubles with bathroom in a peaceful location, swimming pool (sometimes full in summer). If you have your own sleeping bag you can also stay in some very rudimentary concrete huts at the top of the mountain for about US$5 per person. Enquire in the café at the site entrance. A second road ascends from Malatya, passing through the village of Tepehan before reaching the end of the line at the **D** *Güneş Hotel*, a 3 km walk from the summit. A simple place charging US$20 per person for half-board accommodation, but it often fills up with tour groups from Malatya.

Tours

Without your own transport it's advisable to visit Nemrut Dağı on an organized tour departing from Adıyaman, Kahta, Malatya, as well as Şanlıurfa & even Cappadocia

Kahta The most popular base from which to make a visit because of its proximity to the mountain. Excursions are organized by the town's hotel owners who have generally abandoned the errant ways that gained them a bad reputation in the past, sticking instead to prices and itineraries fixed by the local tourist office. Visits are usually timed to coincide with either sunrise or sunset at the summit, although day time visits are also offered too. To witness the dawn means leaving before the cock crows at about 0300, though you'll be back down by 1130 for a nap. If you can't face getting up at such an ungodly hour, sunset is equally impressive, and means departing at a more civilized time during the afternoon, to return by 2100 for a late dinner. At the moment the going rate per minibus is US$35 for a "short tour", directly to the summit and back, or US$45 for the "long tour" which includes visits to the Karakuş tumulus, Cendere bridge and the Commagene capital of Arsameia. It's well worth signing up for the longer of the two as it would be a shame to miss these interesting sites.

Adıyaman If there's a group of you hoteliers or *İnandı Turizm* (see page 619) in Adıyaman can organize similar day trips up the mountain described above, although expect to pay a bit more because of the extra distance. The bus company *Ünal*, which has an office at the *otogar*, also lays-on reasonably priced trips for a minimum of 3 people, although you'd be wise to confirm the itinerary before handing over any money.

Malatya *Depet Tour* (see page 626) organizes overnight excursions to Nemrut Dağı for US$30 per person including transport, breakfast and dinner plus accommodation at the simple *Guneş Otel* near the summit. Park entrance fees and lunch are not included so you may want to pack yourself a picnic. Presuming there are enough people tours depart at midday from Malatya arriving in plenty of time for you to enjoy the sunset. They return at about 0700 the next day, giving you the chance to see sunrise as well if you wish, reaching Malatya by 1100. You could also enquire about a transportation only option, overnighting in the primitive huts at the carpark on the Kahta side of the summit, though you'll need a warm sleeping bag.

Şanlıurfa *Harran and Nemrut Tours* (see page 632) is the only company to offer excursions to Nemrut Dağı with an optional visit to the Atatürk Dam en-route. The 420-km roundtrip is possible in a very long day with the minibus leaving at 0700 and not returning until about midnight. A minimum of 4 people are required, which can be a problem if you're not with a group, and the price is US$30 per person. Alternatively, a more leisurely option is an overnight tour which costs US$40 each.

Cappadocia Numerous companies offer 2-3 day tours to Nemrut Dağı from here. Trips cost US$100-150 per person and typically include visits to Karatay *han* near Kayseri, Karamanmaraş and the other ancient sights on the mountain. If time is short such tours are a convenient way of seeing the mountain and getting a quick taste of Eastern Anatolia, although they do involve extended periods on the road. It is best to opt for a longer, 3-day excursion which gives you more time to appreciate things along the way.

Around Nemrut Dağı

There are a number of other sights, mostly of Commagene origin, on the southern flanks of Nemrut Dağı which can be visited by making a short diversion along what was the main route up the mountain before a new black-top was constructed between Karakuş and Narince. Minibus tours, such as the longer option from Kahta, usually include brief stops at these places on the way up or down from the summit.

Across a dry landscape punctuated by nodding donkeys and oil pipelines, the Karakuş tumulus rears up beside the road. Constructed by the Commagene King Mithridates II for his mother and several other female relatives, the royal tomb was located beneath the mound in the 1960s, however, much to the archaeologists' disappointment it was empty having been looted by ancient raiders. Around the perimeter of the tumulus stand a series of columns, one of which is topped by the headless statue of an eagle that gives the tumulus its name, meaning "Black bird".

Karakuş tumulus
9 km N of Kahta

A further 9 km from Kahta the Cendere Bridge spans a river issuing forth from a deep canyon onto a wide alluvial plain enclosed by mountains. The setting is dramatic and the single-arched Roman bridge, built during the reign of Emperor Septimius Severus (194-211 AD), is in excellent condition after recent renovation work, and is flanked at either end by commemorative columns. There's a small café on the road nearby if you're in need of refreshment.

Cendere Bridge & Eski Kahta

About 5 km beyond the bridge is a sign for the small farming community of Eski Kahta, which prior to the construction of the road up Nemrut Dağı was the trail-head from where you'd have to start walking. A river below the village is crossed by a Selçuk bridge and the remains of a 14th-century Mameluke castle which once guarded the crossing are visible on a bluff above.

The most interesting of the subsidiary Commagene sites in the Nemrut Dağı area is reached up a 2 km side road about 1 km or so beyond the Eski Kahta bridge. The capital of the Commagene Kingdom, Arsameia is situated on a rocky plateau overlooking the valley. From the small car park a path strikes off across the hillside passing what was formerly a funerary sanctuary, marked by a tall *stele* engraved with a depiction of the god Mithras. Further on, near a tunnel which descends to an ancient cistern, are more reliefs showing the Commagene kings Mithridates I and Antiochus I. Continuing along the path brings you to a wonderfully preserved relief set amongst the trees of Mithridates I greeting the god Heracles. Nearby is the mouth of a tunnel carved down into the bed rock, but despite local stories of it being a secret escape route to the valley below, German excavations in 1950s revealed that in fact it stops 158 m beneath the surface. Beside the tunnel a lengthy inscription identifies it as part of a funerary sanctuary dedicated to King Mithridates I Callinicus. ■ *US$1.25.*

Arsameia

Malatya

Malatya is a modern and, by eastern standards anyway, prosperous town. Set in a wide, fertile basin it has profited from a rich agricultural hinterland dedicated to arable farming and orchards. Mention Malatya to any Turk and the first thing that will spring to their mind is apricots. The town is the undisputed apricot capital of the country, producing thousands of tonnes of the fresh and dried fruit each year. Malatya's relative affluence, along with a sizeable student

Phone code: 0422
Colour map 5, grid B5
Population: 300,000
Altitude: 964 m

population, help it escape the dourness of many of the region's provincial capitals, and though there's nothing much to do in the town itself beyond a visit to the museum and a jaunt around the lively bazaar, its pleasant atmosphere and good transport links recommend it as an alternative base for the trip up Nemrut Dağı, or simply as a place to break your journey.

The origin settlement of Malatya, refered to as **Eski (Old) Malatya**, is located roughly 12 km north of the modern town. Established by the Roman Emperor Titus in the first century AD, it was occupied throughout Byzantine times, undergoing major restoration when the Selçuks ruled the area in the 12th century. The remains of the city walls, which at one time were guarded by 95 towers, are still visible, though other evidence of the city has been submerged beneath the modern settlement of Battalgazi. From the main square where buses from Malatya drop passengers, it's a short walk southwest past a restored 17th-century caravansarai to the Selçuk **Ulu Cami**, built in 1224, and the ruins of another Ottoman *han* beside it. ■ *Getting there: Reached on a city bus marked 'Battalgazi' (US$0.30) that stops on the opposite side of Buhara Bulvarı, reached by walking north through the bazaar district.*

Sleeping **A** *Altın Kayısı*, Istasyon Caddesi, T2383232, F2380083, appealingly called 'the golden apricot', inconveniently situated out near the station, most comfortable place in town, spacious and brightly decorated bedrooms, a/c, fridge, telephone, TV. **C** *Hotel Yeni Kent*, PTT Caddesi No 33, T3211053, F3249243. Comfortable 2-star hotel with a/c, telephone, TV and minibar in rooms, back rooms suffer from traffic noise. **E** *Malatya Büyük Otel*, Yeni Camii Karşısı, T3211400, F3215367. Behind the Yeni Cami, very good value rooms with a/c, telephone and TV as standard, small ensuite. Recommended. **F** *Otel Huzur*, Nasuhi Caddesi No 6. Helpful staff and decent rooms make this a good bet, shared bathroom. Recommended. **F-G** *Otel Kantar*, Atatürk Caddesi No 81, T3211510. Simply furnished 1/2/3/4 bed rooms, cheaper waterless rooms available, 10% discount in the kebap restaurant next-door. **G** *Park Otel*, Atatürk Caddesi No 17, T3211691, opposite the Belediye building. Reasonable rooms for the price, small ensuite. Recommended budget option if you don't mind noise from outside. **G** *Otel Tahran*, PTT Caddesi No 20, T3243615. Quieter location but basic rooms are a bit grubby, shared toilet, shower extra US$1.25.

Eating

Malatya doesn't have anything approaching haute cuisine, but there is a decent selection of well-priced restaurants & simple eateries. Unless it's stated otherwise assume that restaurants don't serve alcohol

The rooftop *Melita Restaurant*, T3224300, serves *meze*, grilled meat and kebaps at tables outside on its terrace; wine, beer and *rakı* are also available and there's live music in the evenings. Entrance is opposite *Depet Tour* in sideroad off Atatürk Caddesi. *Boğaziçi Lokanta*, locally recommended self-service restaurant near the *Otel Huzur*, good choice of soups, stews and salads, about US$3-5 per head. *Beyaz Saray*, Atatürk Caddesi near the *Park Otel*, busy kebap restaurant which also serves ready-prepared dishes and soup. *Öz Sinan Et Lokantası*, a short walk to the north of Atatürk Caddesi, is worth seeking out for its *kağıt kebabı*, a local dish of lamb baked in paper to keep it moist, also has other kebaps, lahmacun and pide with oven-baked rice pudding for desert. *Hürriyet Mangal*, Atatürk Caddesi, across from the Kent Otel, small place where you grill your own adana kebaps on hot coals, accompanied by salad and *ayran*, very cheap at US$1 per skewer. Around the corner on Sinema Caddesi, the *Mangal 2* is a larger version of the same idea. There's are plenty of cake shops on Atatürk Caddesi including the *Sevinç Pastanesi*.

Tour agencies *Depet Tour*, Atatürk Caddesi No 29, T3257576, F3264007, on 1st floor above Beydağı Turizm, sales agent for *Turkish Airlines*, car-rental and organizes overnight excursions to Nemrut Dağı (see page 624).

Air *Turkish Airlines* have one daily flight to both Ankara and İstanbul. A service bus **Transport** departs from outside the *Turkish Airlines* office 1½ hrs before departure. **Bus** The bus company *Zafer* have offices opposite the PTT so there's no need to trudge out to the *otogar* to buy your ticket. The otoger station is 5 km west of the city centre. Bus companies usually have a shuttle service into the city centre – if not cross the busy highway outside the station and flag down a dolmuş (US$0.30) heading for the centre. **Adana**, 5 daily buses, 8 hrs, US$9. **Adıyaman**, 5 daily, 3 hrs, US$5. These buses continue on to **Şanlıurfa. Ankara**, several daily, 10 hrs, US$14. **Elazığ**, every hr, 1½ hrs, US$2. **Gaziantep**, every 3 hrs during day, 4 hrs, US$7. **İstanbul**, several daily buses, 18 hrs, US$20. **Kayseri**, hourly during day, 6 hrs, US$9. Sivas, regular buses, 5 hrs, US$6. **Van**, 3 daily buses, 10 hrs, US$11. **Train** Malatya's station is situated several kilometres west of the city centre and is served by dolmuş departing from the minibus station in the bazaar area from the station get in a dolmuş marked 'vilayet' into the centre. **4 Eylül Mavi Tren**, departs Ankara everyday at 1940, returning via Malatya at 1455, 17 hrs. **Van Gölü Ekspresi**, departs İstanbul Mon, Wed and Sat at 2005, returning via Malatya on Tue, Thu, Sat at 1810, 17 hrs. **Güney Ekspresi**, departs İstanbul Tue, Thu, Fri, Sun at 2005, returning via Malatya on the same days at 1810, 17 hrs.

Airline offices *Turkish Airlines*, Kanalboyu Caddesi No 10, Orduevi Karşısı, T3211922, F3216489. **Directory** **Banks** There are several banks with ATM machines including *İşbankası* on İnönü Caddesi. **Baths** *Belediye Hamamı*, across from the *Malatya Büyük Otel*. Open 0730-2300, US$2.50 for entry and *kese*. **Post office** On PTT Caddesi near the junction with İnönü Caddesi. **Internet** *Çağrıut Internet Evi*, Sinema Caddesi, several hundred metres down, US$1.25 per hr. **Hospitals** Malatya's state hospital is a kilometre east of the centre on Hastane Caddesi, reached by walking along Atatürk Caddesi. **Tourist information** *The Tourist Information Office* is on the ground floor of the *Vilayet* building on İnönü Caddesi. 0830-1200, 1300-1730 weekdays.

The busy E-90 highway strikes eastwards from Gaziantep across an irrigated **Gaziantep** landscape of olive orchards and arable land towards the River Euphrates. At the **to Şanlıurfa** dusty town of **Birecik**, with its 11th-century crusader castle, the road crosses the mighty Euphrates, tamed now by the Atatürk and Birecik dams upstream, built as part of the ambitious GAP project (see box, page 620). The town gained notoriety as the former home of the bald ibis (*Geronticus eremita*) an ill-fated migratory bird, similar to a stork, which used to nest in large numbers on the cliffs above the settlement. Unfortunately, widespread use of chemical pesticides by local farmers and disturbance sent the population into a cataclysmic nosedive and despite a misconceived captive breeding progamme attempted by the WWF, the bald ibis seems to have been forced into extinction. A spring festival is still held in the town to celebrate the time when the bald ibis traditionally returned from over-wintering in the Ethiopian Highlands, although the guests of honour are now conspicuous in their absence.

Şanlıurfa

Historic Şanlıurfa, commonly refered to as Urfa, swelters away on the plains that Phone code: 0414 *extend southwards to the Syrian frontier. Revered as the birthplace of Abraham,* Colour map 6, grid B1 *the city is an important centre of pilgrimage for pious Muslims with a cluster of* Altitude: 547 m *well-kept mosques, a cave shrine and several pools filled with sacred carp forming the focus of the city's religious life. A medieval fortress and a colourful bazaar district are also worth exploring. Adding to the city's intrinsic interest is its very Middle Eastern flavour, with a vibrant composite population of Arabs, Kurds and Turks. Strolling through the streets you'll brush shoulders with ruddy-faced Arab villagers their heads wrapped in distinctive checked turbans, Kurds sporting*

Southeast Anatolia

baggy trousers hanging down to their knees and women cloaked in the all-encompassing black chador. As the water and investment made available by the GAP project transform the surrounding countryside, Urfa is experiencing an unprecedented building boom as shiny office blocks and hotels join the ancient mosques and tawny stone houses. The teeming shanty towns ringing the city have also exploded outwards as wave after wave of villagers head towards the bright lights in search of work and security. Urfa certainly has much to offer but since the Kurdish troubles its tourist sector has shrivelled with many of the town's hoteliers professing that it's been weeks since they've seen a foreign face.

Ins and outs

Getting there Şanlıurfa sits on the E-90 highway 137 km east of Gaziantep and 180 km southwest of
See page 632 for Diyarbakır. The city is not connected into the national rail network, so if you want to travel
further details by train Gaziantep is the closest station. It is well served by buses from destinations coun-
trywide, though many of these are coming from elsewhere in the region so may already
be full. The city's airport is served by daily domestic flights from Ankara and İstanbul.

Getting around The town's *otogar* is 1.5 km west of the centre beside the E-90 highway. Buses and
dolmuş ($0.30) to the town centre pass along the highway outside the bus station
before turning down Atatürk Caddesi. Alternatively, by taxi or on foot you can take a
more direct route with the former costing about US$1.50. The new Tourist Informa-
tion Office is just up a cobbled lane at the east end of the Göl Caddesi tunnel. Weekdays 0830-1200, 1300-1700.

Sights

Eski (Old) Urfa At the southern end of Sarayönü Caddesi, the city's busy main street widens into
& the bazaar Kara Meydanı, before narrowing again and continuing south into the bazaar
district district. Kara Meydanı is dominated by the unremarkable late 19th-century
Hüseyin Paşa Camii, though nearby the Ulu Cami is considerably older, having
been built in the 12th century when the city was under the control of the Zengi
dynasty, and more interesting. Reached through a narrow alleyway the courtyard is a peaceful haven, except at prayer time when it fills up with local traders.
Constructed in Syrian-style its flanked by an Ottoman graveyard and a tall
octagonal minaret which was originally the belfry of a Byzantine church, but
which now serves as a clock-tower, as well as a useful landmark.

Continuing down Divan Yolu Caddesi brings you to the **Gümrük Hanı**, a
solid 16th-century caravanserai which is occupied by petty traders and has a
pleasant central courtyard with several shady cafés, perfect for a glass of çay
before exploring the fascinating market district around it. The **Kapalı Çarşı**
(Covered market) is raucous and crowded – everything you'd expect from a
Middle Eastern bazaar – and seems to have changed little over the centuries.
Picking your way through the log-jam of itinerant traders, shopkeepers and
browsers you're treated to a sensory bombardment. The air is heavy with the
smell of aromatic spices, sun-ripped fruit and freshly oiled leather, and your ears
are filled with the hubbub of traders vocally hawking their wares in the three local
languages or striking a hard bargain. During your wanderings you're bound to
come across several more *hans* where the camel caravans of old would unload
their goods and trade having crossed the desert from Aleppo or Baghdad.

Dergah Legend has it that **Abraham** was born in this small cave in the cliff beneath the
city castle. Revered as a prophet by Muslims this grotto, known as the **Hazreti
Ibrahim Halilullah Dergahı** *(0800-1730)*, is an important pilgrimage site

attracting religious tourists from across Turkey as well as a few who've come from abroad. The cave is approached across carefully tended rose gardens, dotted with several mosques built at various times to accommodate visiting worshippers. Pilgrims file into the coolness of the cave through separate doors for each of the sexes and inside stand with hands upturned, their lips moving in silent prayer. Feel free to enter the cave or any of the attending mosques but remember that they are places of religious significance and worship and so you should dress and behave appropriately. A nearby cave holds a hair said to be from the Prophet Mohammed's beard which is equally popular with visiting devotees who take away plastic containers filled with water from a sacred spring outside.

Gölbaşı

Just to the west, Gölbaşı has more mosques, shrines and a shady waterside tea garden which is a world away from the ordered chaos of the city outside. It's a

Şanlıurfa

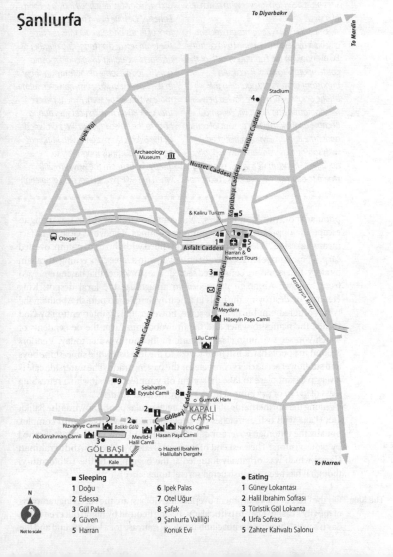

Southeast Anatolia

■ Sleeping		● Eating
1 Doğu	6 İpek Palas	1 Güney Lokantası
2 Edessa	7 Otel Uğur	2 Halil İbrahim Sofrası
3 Gül Palas	8 Şafak	3 Türistik Göl Lokanta
4 Güven	9 Şanlıurfa Valiliği	4 Urfa Sofrası
5 Harran	Konuk Evi	5 Zahter Kahvaltı Salonu

N

Not to scale

Disappearing beneath the waves

In a region so richly endowed with important ancient sites the GAP project and its associated dams and reservoirs have become what some archaeologists are describing as a national disaster. Hasankeyf in Batman province (see page 642), where the ruins of a medieval Islamic town are set to disappear beneath the waters impounded by the Ilısu Dam on the Tigris, has gained some notoriety due to the involvement of a British firm in the construction, however, many more sites have been lost forever with much less of a stir.

One such site is Zeugma, an ancient city built by Seleucus I in the third century BC overlooking the Euphrates north of the contemporary town of Birecik. An important fortress city guarding the bridge across which trade flowed between Mesopotamia and Anatolia, Zeugma became a fabulously rich provincial centre under the Romans, who embellished it with sumptuous villas and lavish public buildings. Unfortunately when choosing where to build his city Seleucus I could not have forseen that a huge concrete dam, the Birecik Barajı, was going to be constructed just 500 m downstream over 2,000 year later, flooding the site under metres of water.

When plans for the dam were unveiled local archaeologists from Gaziantep Museum, helped by a small team of foreign experts, began a frantic effort to save as much as they could before its completion. Ironically, this work revealed the wealth and size of the site, leading one archaeologist to described it as 'a second Ephesus'. Despite being hampered by a lack of funds and bureaucratic red tape, the team rescued a staggering number of artefacts including 15 splendid mosaic panels. Today, some of these are on show in the Gaziantep Museum, however, many more will never be seen. Experts believe that over 80 archeaological sites dating back to the Paleolithic era were drowned by the Birecik Dam alone, with hundreds, perhaps thousands more likely to disappear beneath the waves by 2005 when the GAP project reaches completion.

popular spot with local families, who come to stroll or drink tea, trying to escape the oppressive heat on summer evenings. The word Gölbaşı in fact means 'lakeside', referring to three ponds filled with shoals of plump, overfed carp. These pampered fish have been woven into a fable concerning Abraham by story-tellers and are considered sacred. The story goes that having emerged from his cave Abraham proceeded to antagonize the local despot, King Nemrut, by destroying the idols in a nearby temple. To punish Abraham the tyrant ordered him burnt at the stake, however, timely intervention by God turned the flames to water and the firewood into carp, the descendents of which you see swimming lazily around in the murky water today. Vendors around the pools hawk fish food to toss to the idle fish while shoe-shine boys and sunflower seed sellers compete for the passing trade. The waterside café is a very pleasant place to take the weight off your feet and sit with a refreshing glass of *ayran* or *çay* poured from a shiny metal *samovar*.

Along the northern side of the larger, rectangular pool, known as the Balıklı Göl (Lake with fish), stretches the triple-domed **Rizvaniye Camii** complex built by the Ottoman governor of Urfa in 1716 and now much photographed by pious visitors. The west end of the pool is enclosed by the **Abdürrahman Camii** which was originally founded at the beginning of the 13th century, though it has been reconstructed several times since.

The Kale   On the crest of the escarpment overlooking Gölbaşı are the surviving ramparts of the city's castle. They're particularly striking flood-lit by night, but even in the day it's worth braving the hot climb up a long staircase for a look around and the view. The contemporary remains date mostly from the 12th century when Urfa was the capital of the County of Edessa, although there was certainly a citadel on the spot long before that. Look out for a pair of 17-m high ancient columns at the top of the fortress hill. Called the **Throne of Nemrut** by locals after the biblical ruler of Urfa, a Syriac inscription on one of the columns reveals their origins are considerably less ancient, having been erected in the 10th century. ■ *US$0.75 when a warden is present.*

Halil Rahman Mosque

North of the town centre, Urfa's engaging archaeological collection is certainly worth a visit. The garden is filled with stone sculptures, ornately carved tombs and several mosaics; while inside there are artefacts dating from Neolithic to Ottoman times discovered at sites around the region. Upstairs, the enthnographic section has relics from the departed local Christian population as well as wooden furniture and shutters rescued from some of the city's old houses. There are also displays of antique carpets and embroidery. ■ *0830-1700 daily except Mon. US$0.75. The museum is on S Nusret Caddesi, several hundred metres west of the Vilayet building on Atatürk Caddesi.*

Archaeology Museum

Essentials

Urfa has a surfeit of cheap and grotty hotels which are adequate if you're only staying the night or are on a really tight budget. Most of these are used by visiting workers rather than foreign travellers. Moving up-market there are comparatively few choices in the middle price bands, so it's advisable to book ahead, particularly if you want to stay at the popular Şanlıurfa Valiliği Konuk Evi.

Sleeping

AL *Hotel Edessa*, Balıklıgöl Mevkii, T2164460, F2155589. Without a doubt the most comfortable hotel in town, conveniently situated 5-mins walk from Gölbaşı, well-appointed rooms some of which look out onto pools and castle, a/c, telephone, cable-TV, decent bathrooms, restaurant. Recommended. **B** *Hotel Harran*, Atatürk Bulvarı, T3132860, F3134918. Despite the old-fashioned exterior the rooms are well up to 4-star rating, equipped with a/c, telephone, minibar and ensuite with bath, large swimming pool at rear, restaurant. Recommended. **D** *Şanlıurfa Valiliği Konuk Evi*, Vali Fuat Bey Caddesi, Selahattin Eyyübi Camii Karşısı, T2159377, F3123368. Large Ottoman era residence transformed into Urfa's most interesting hotel, common areas are well-furnished, however, rooms are a let down, modern, bland furniture, a/c, telephone and TV as standard, nice courtyard café and restaurant. Recommended despite disappointing rooms, advance booking advisable. **E** *Hotel İpek Palas*, Köprübaşı, Şanmed Hastanesi Arkası No 4, T2151546, F2151290, in back street off Atatürk Caddesi. Plain, fairly ordinary rooms with shower cabinets in the corner, inflated price is supposed to be justified by the addition of a/c, TV and a telephone, still not very good value, singles are small. **F** *Hotel Güven*, Sarayönü Caddesi No 133, T2151700, F2151941. Newly renovated place which represents good value for money, clinical feel at present though, rooms are equipped with a/c, telephone and TV as standard, restaurant and bar on the top floor, laundry service. Recommended. **G** *Hotel Gül Palas*, Sarayönü Caddesi, Beyaz Sokak No 13/16, T2157701. A rambling old building with basic high ceiling rooms, probably the best of the rock-bottom cheapies. **G** *Otel*

Southeast Anatolia

Doğu, Sarayönü Caddesi No 131, T2151228. Bedrooms are disappointing after the bright, new reception, basic 1/2/3 bed rooms some with shower and toilet, very limited washing facilities for other rooms, shared squat toilets, not recommended for women alone. **G** *Şafak Oteli*, Göl Caddesi. Passable cheapy which at least is close to Gölbaşı, not the cleanest of shared bathrooms. **G** *Otel Uğur*, Köprübaşı Caddesi Belediye Karşısı No 3, T3131340. Fairly unsalubrious workers boarding house, though management have tried to perk things up with some plastic plants, once again not recommended for female travellers.

Eating

Urfalı do not really dine out all that much, so the choice of decent restaurants is pretty limited

Urfa is the home of southeastern culinary specialities such as *içli köfte* (deep-fried parcels filled with minced mutton and herbs) and *çiğ köfte* (raw lamb mince mixed with bulgur wheat and hot chilly). You may also fancy trying an *Urfa Kebabı*, the local variant on the kebap theme, which takes the form of minced lamb grilled on a skewer and served with peppers, tomatoes and onions. Most places don't serve alcohol, however the exceptions have been noted below. You can buy beer, wine and *rakı* in the small shop opposite the *Hotel Ipek Palas*. It's important to take extra care of what you eat in Urfa because the hot climate vastly reduces the time that food can be left around safely. Don't order ready-prepared dishes such as stews and soups unless they look fresh and you may also want to steer clear of *çiğ köfte,*unless you have fully acclimatized to the local diet.

Midrange *Hotel Edessa* has the most refined restaurant in town, with a varied menu to match the pleasant surroundings, some tables outside, from US$8 per head, alcohol served. *Urfa Sofrası*, Atatürk Caddesi, across from the stadium, new, modern branch of long running local favourite, selection of kebaps and grilled meat, pide, lahmacun and *içli köfte*, jump on a *otogar*-bound dolmuş if you don't want to walk from the centre. The restaurant of the *Şanlıurfa Valiliği Konuk Evi* (see sleeping) has a simple menu, but the surroundings on the terrace of this restored 19th-century mansion are perfect for a relaxed evening meal. **Cheap** *Güney Lokantası*, Köprübaşı Caddesi No 3/D, best of the cheap eateries around Sarayönü, conveniently placed for guests of the nearby hotels, serves soups, kebaps and ready-prepared dishes such as *kuru fasulye* (beans) and *bulgur pilavı* (couscous). There are several places to get breakfast nearby including *Zahter Kahvaltı Salonu*. *Halil Ibrahim Sofrası*, Göl Caddesi, part of the new development above the road tunnel, modern, reasonably priced meat-based menu. *Türistik Göl Lokanta*, Balıklı Göl, Gölbaşı, the nicest surroundings for a cheap bite to eat, *lahmacun*, *köfte* and other snacks brought to shady tables beside the fish pool. *Türistik Göl Çay Bahçesi*, a café next to the Balıklı Göl in Gölbaşı.

Tour agencies *Kaliru Turizm*, Köprübaşı Caddesi No 74/A, T2153344, F2163245, agents for *Turkish Airlines*, rent-a-car. *Harran and Nemrut Tours*, Özel Şanmed Hastanesi arkası, T2151575, F2151156, in the alley behind the Özel Şanmed Medical centre, run by local school teacher Özcan Aslan, tours organized to Harran, Nemrut and other sights in the region, call-in for a chat.

Transport **Air** *Turkish Airlines* have daily flights to **Ankara** and **İstanbul**. A service bus leaves for the airport about 90 mins before departure from the *Kaliru Turizm* office on Köprübaşı Caddesi. **Road Bus: Adana**, several buses daily, 6 hrs, US$8. **Adıyaman/Kahta**, regular minibuses, 2½ hrs, US$5. **Diyarbakır**, every 2 hrs, 0800-1800, 3 hrs, US$5. **Gaziantep**, hourly, 2 hrs, US$3.50. **Mardin**, regular buses, 3 hrs, US$5. **Van**, several daily buses, 9 hrs, US$12. There are also daily buses to more **long distance** destinations such as **İstanbul, Ankara, Antalya** and **İzmir**. **Car rental**: *Avis*, Ipekyolu Caddesi, Başbuğ Apt. No 121/A. T/F3122253. See also tour agencies.

Directory **Airline offices** (see tour agencies). **Banks** There are several banks with ATMs and *döviz* on Sarayönü Caddesi. **Post office** The PTT is on Sarayönü Caddesi just north of Kara Meydan 2.

Internet There's a very cheap internet service in the post office but you may have to wait a while for a terminal to become available. **Hospitals** *Özel Şanmed Hastanesi*, Köprübaşı Caddesi, private medical centre conveniently situated in the centre of town.

Harran

The village of Harran, near the town of Akçakale and the Syrian frontier, is thought to be one of the longest continually occupied settlements on the planet with a history dating back at least 5,000 years. Straddling a corridor of movement between southeast Anatolia and Mesopotamia, the settlement was a strategic watering hole and trading post in ancient times. The community is referred to in the Old Testament, most notably in reference to Abraham who is said to have lived there for a time:

Colour map 6, grid B1
45 km S of Urfa

And Terah took Abram his son, and Lot the son of Haran, his son's son, and Sarai his daughter-in-law, his son Abram's wife; and they went forth with them from Ur of the Chaldees, to go into the land of Canaan; and they came unto Harran and dwelt there. Genesis 11:31

This biblical association, along with the village's very unusual bee-hive shaped houses, attracts a trickle of inquisitive visitors. However the reality which greets you can be a little disappointing as much of ancient Harran lies buried underground while the distinctive conical houses have been vacated for more conventional buildings, occupants now tend to be their domestic animals. Even so, if you lower your expectations a trip to Harran can be interesting and worthwhile, also providing an insight into rural life in this rapidly changing region.

Long before the birth of Christianity Harran had developed as the principal religious centre for the worship of Sin, the god of the moon. This cult persisted through Classical and Roman times but despite the patronage of early Byzantine emperors, the great temple of Sin was demolished following Theodosius I's prohibition of pagan worship in 392 AD. However, the Byzantines found it impossible to stamp-out locally held beliefs in this peripheral region, and the Sabians, as the followers of Sin had become known, enjoyed a revival after the seventh-century Arab invasion. Under Arab tenure a university was established in Harran and the town flourished as a centre of learning and commerce until everything was levelled by the Mongols in 1260. Following this blow the town never regained its former significance, reduced to a small village of beehive-shaped dwellings clustered amongst the ruins.

Background

The design for these **beehive houses**, thought to date back several thousand years, was partly motivated by the harsh local climate with the thick mudbrick walls and high rooves helping to keep the interior cool during the scorching summer months. It was also probably a response to the scarcity of timber in the area with similar houses found in certain arid areas south of the Syrian border.

Harran's 6,000 or so inhabitants are predominantly Arab, the descendants of semi-nomadic pastoralists and farmers who traditionally inhabited this parched extension of the Syrian plain. In the past the arable land surrounding the village only supported one annual crop of wheat, so villagers supplemented their meagre incomes by smuggling across the Syrian frontier and working seasonally in the cotton harvest on the Çukurova Plain around Adana. Today, the cotton revolution has reached Harran thanks to irrigation water from the GAP project and if you arrive during the day things are likely to be quiet, with everyone bar a few children working in the fields. One of these youngsters will attach themselves to

The village

Southeast Anatolia

you and provide their services as an unofficial, but often well informed, guide. You'll be expected to pay for the service but this is a better way of making a small contribution to the community than giving in to the insistent demands for money, pens or cigarettes from other little kids you meet along the way.

The most conspicuous remnant of old Harran is the **Kale**, a ruinous fortress built during the 11th century on the foundations of what is believed to be the temple of Sin. The surviving arched chambers provide a welcome escape from the sun, though there's little to see inside except for scattered reliefs, the most interesting of which, depicting shackled dogs, is carved into the east gateway. A local man runs a café beside the castle, where you can enjoy a drink and have a look at his selection of souvenirs. The castle also provides an excellent lookout from which to survey the village with clusters of beehive houses sprouting like large fungi from between the modern buildings. You'll also be able to spot the square minaret of the nearby **Ulu Cami** which was founded in the eighth century by the Umayyad caliph, Marwan II. Formerly known by the evocative title *Cami al-Firdaus*, the 'Mosque of Paradise', it was reconstructed on several occasions, most recently in 1171. Around the mosque are the ruins of ancient Harran including its university, though avid enthusiasts apart there's little to get excited about.

For a closer look at one of the famous beehive dwellings the **Harran House** in the village is run by the municipality as a mini living-museum and gift shop. One of the dark, blissfully cool, chambers is furnished in traditional style and was formerly used as a guesthouse. If you want to stay overnight in the village enquire with the staff.

Tours Excursions arranged by *Harran and Nemrut Tours* in Urfa (see page 632) cost US$10 per person and leave daily at 0900 and 1600, giving you plenty of time to look around before returning to Urfa about 4 hrs later. The only snag is that a minimum of 4 people are required, unless you want to hire a van and driver yourself, and if you're on your own it's generally hard to muster that number of fellow tourists. Excursions to Harran are also offered by *Harran and Nemrut Tours* as part of a full-day itinerary also taking in the nearby sites of Han el Ba'rur, Şuayb and Soğmatar (see below) which are difficult to get to without your own transport. Again at least 4 people are needed which costs US$20 each including lunch with a local family.

Transport Under your own steam you'll need to drive south of Urfa following signs for Akçakale and a concrete irrigation canal which channels the life-giving waters from the Atatürk Dam on to cotton fields stretching towards the horizon. It's an almost dead-straight 20 km to a sign-posted turn-off on the left, from where it's another 10 km to Harran, known officially as Altınbaşak. There's no public transport along this final stretch but buses to Akçakale can drop you at the intersection where you'll have to wait for a lift. You're unlikely to have to wait long, although it's a baking, shadeless spot in summer; so come prepared with a hat and some water. Drivers offering you a lift may expect a contribution towards the petrol.

Around Harran

You'll need your own transport., dolmuş are non-existant. Take food & water as there are no facilities

To the northeast of Harran several rough blacktops cross huge swathes of cotton cultivation, before winding through a range of low hills, baked dry by the blistering summer sun. Just over 20 km beyond Harran is the **Han el Ba'rur Caravanserai**, a crumbling Selçuk *han* built at the beginning of the 12th century to accommodate passing camel trains. Another 23 km on are the **remains of Şuayb**, a large settlement inhabited from Roman times up until the Mongol invasion. As well as the remnants of buildings on the surface, there are a series of subterranean caverns that you'll need a torch to explore properly.

The main reason to venture out this way however is to visit the isolated village of **Soğmatar** (also called Sumatar), 15 km to the north of Şuayb. This ancient watering hole became an important centre for the Sabians, a community who integrated the practices of the cult of Sin into their own polytheistic religion, also worshipping Helios, god of the sun, and a whole pantheon of other celestial deities. The Sabian settlement at Soğmatar, built around the second century AD, was obviously an important ceremonial complex with eight groups of ruins, most with cave-temples, standing in an arc around a central mound. Each of these subterranean temples is thought to have been dedicated to a different god and there are carved inscriptions and figures on the walls of several. One of the contemporary villagers will almost certainly guide your around the various parts of the sites, for which they'll deserve a tip. The Sabians were looked upon with disdain by the other religious communities because of their beliefs and practices – said to include human sacrifices – and it is remarkable that they managed to survive as long as they did. Finally, however, in the 11th century they were forcibly converted by the local Muslim rulers, although some Sabian superstitions and beliefs are said to have persisted well into the Ottoman era.

Diyarbakır

Overlooking a bend in the Tigris River, Diyarbakır is a historic city with a troubled recent past. As a predominantly Kurdish centre and the capital of the southeast emergency rule region, during the late 1980s and early 1990s it became synonymous with the PKK and Kurdish insurgency. Things are considerably quieter these days, though the city's blistering summer heat and poverty combine to create what still feels at times like a very volatile atmosphere. At its heart the labyrinthine confines of the old city, embraced by black basalt walls, are crowded, dusty and hot; a sensory bombardment for the uninitiated, though for the seasoned traveller exploring the chaotic street can be an exciting and rewarding experience. The city makes a possible base for the trip south to Mardin, or a convenient place to break your journey between Şanlıurfa and Van.

*Phone code: 0412
Colour map 6, grid R2
Altitude: 650 m*

Getting there Being a major regional centre, Diyarbakır is served by buses from across the country. The city is also connected to İstanbul and Ankara by rail and regular air connections. **Getting around** The *otogar* is 3 km northwest of Dağı Kapısı on Elazığ Caddesi. Most bus companies provide a free shuttle service into Dağı Kapısı (where most of the accommodation is), but if not, dolmuş (US$0.35) regularly pass outside the front of the terminal. The train station is 1.5 km west of the centre at the end of Istasyon Caddesi. Dolmuş into the centre can be caught on the opposite side of the main road. A taxi is about US$3. A service bus links the airport, 3 km southwest, with the city.

Ins & outs
*See sights, page 636 &
transport, page 640, for
further details*

The city's strategic position in a volatile region is affirmed by the sprawling, barbed-wire encircled military installations around its edge. Another result of the PKK insurgency are the shanty towns ringing the city, occupied by villagers trying to escape the grinding poverty and insecurity of rural areas. These refugees have put a huge additional strain on the underdeveloped local economy, based largely on agriculture and processing industries, and the unemployment rate is thought to top 35%.

Background

With the army's recent success at combating the PKK, terrorist attacks in the city have almost completely died out. Anti-state feeling among the Kurdish population, however, still runs high and during your visit conversations will inevitably veer towards the "troubles". Needless to say, it is best to avoid becoming embroiled in overtly political discussions with strangers.

Despite all the hardship there is growing optimism that if the current stability continues badly needed investment can be attracted to the area, helping to encourage economic growth and raising standards of living. Until that happens though, the irresistible pull towards the west of the country, where better job prospects and greater opportunities await, will continue to encourage people to leave Diyarbakır and the southeast in droves.

Sights

Most of Diyarbakır's sights are conveniently located either inside or within a short walk of the city walls. The old city, however, retains much of its ancient street plan, so finding them if they're not on one of the principle thoroughfares running between the main gates is a different matter. With a good sense of direction and a bit of luck you'll stumble across some of them during your wanderings in the warren of backstreets; though to find others you'll definitely need to enlist the help of a local. This shouldn't be too much trouble as you'll almost certainly be approached by someone wanting to practice their hard-earned linguistic skills, who'll be glad to show you around in return for some conversational practice, or sometimes a small fee. Needless to say women travellers should be very careful about striking-up such relationships. To engage the services of a more formal guide enquire at the Tourist Information Office.

The City Walls

The old city is encompassed by a ring of solid, black basalt walls, guarded by 72 towers & pierced by four main gateways, as well as a number of smaller portals. The stone for the walls was taken from the nearby Karacadağ mountains

Originally dating back to Roman times, the contemporary ramparts were rebuilt at the orders of Sultan Melik Shah after the Selçuk capture of the city in 1088. Measuring 5.5 km in length and up to 12 m high, they've survived the depravations of time remarkably well and, except for two short sections removed in the modern era, remain virtually intact.

It's possible to walk along the top of the defences for much of their distance, though this shouldn't be attempted alone. You're first glimpse of the defences will probably be at **Dağı Kapısı** (the Mountain Gate), also known as Harput Kapısı, the northern-most breach in the walls which is guarded by a formidable looking pair of towers. Inscriptions carved onto the portal in Greek, Latin and Arabic identify famous historical personages, including the Byzantine Emperor Valens (364-375 AD), who graced the city with their presence.

Walking down Izzet Paşa Caddesi from Gazi Caddesi brings you to the **İç Kale**, or inner bastion of the city, built on a small hill overlooking the Tigris. Unfortunately most of the citadel is now occupied by a military establishment, so there's no chance of visiting either of the medieval churches inside. On the river side of the bastion, the **Oğrun Kapısı** leads out to an area of slum housing clinging to the side of the valley, from where you can get a glimpse of the sluggish, brown and, for much of the year, disappointingly small Tigris weaving across its floodplain below.

From the İç Kale the ramparts head south along the crest of the escarpment cut by the river to the **Yeni Kapısı** (New Gate) and then round to the **Mardin Kapısı**, straddling the road south to Mardin. The most rewarding section of the wall to walk is from the Mardin Kapısı west to Urfa Kapısı, a distance of about 1.5 km, and onwards if you so desire, though you'll have to cross Istasyon Caddesi at street level before climbing back up. This section is mostly pretty wide and in a good state of repair, providing an excellent vantage point from which to inspect the old city below. Along the way are two large bastions, **Yedi Kardeş Burcu** (Tower of the Seven Brothers) and **Melikşah Burcu**, both of which bare Selçuk inscriptions and motifs.

The Old City

Hopelessly crowded by day; an anarchic, noisy mass of people, handcarts & vehicles

South from Dağ Kapısı runs one of Diyarbakır's principal streets, Gazi Caddesi. Traders in baggy trousers and cloth caps loudly hawk fruit from barrows and çay boys skillfully negotiate the slow moving procession of shoppers, their silver trays stacked with glasses of tea. Shiny chrome stalls sell the region's speciality drink *şalgam,* a deep purple juice made from turnips (US$0.40), and mobile cassette salesmen assault your ear drums with loud *arabesque* blasted from flimsy speakers.

On your right near the Dağı Kapısı, the **Nebi Camii** (Mosque of the Prophet) is easily recognisable with its striking horizontal strips of black and white stonework, a common feature of Diyarbakır's religious buildings which utilizes the light-coloured sandstone and black basalt quarried nearby to great decorative effect. The mosque itself was endowed by the Turcoman Akkoyunlu dynasty in the early 16th century.

Continuing down Gazi Caddesi brings you into the city's buzzing bazaar area focused on the 16th-century **Hasan Paşa Hanı**, built by the grand vizier of the Ottoman Sultan Murat III. This is an interesting district to explore with narrow, twisting alleys lined with clothes shops, jewellery merchants and carpet outlets.

On the opposite side of the road you come to the city's most famous monument, the venerable **Ulu Cami**, partially hidden behind the unsightly entranceways to an underground shopping arcade. The building stands as the first major Selçuk mosque in Anatolia, constructed in 1091-92 during the reign of Melik Shah and strongly influenced by the Umayyad mosque in Damascus. It is typically Arab in form with a large, rectangular courtyard giving on to the low, flat roofed prayer hall. In the middle of the courtyard are two şadırvans and an ancient sun-dial, while the arcades surrounding it on two sides are supported by marble columns obviously pillaged from earlier Roman or Byzantine buildings.

To the northeast of the courtyard is the **Mesudiye Medresesi** constructed in 1198 by the Artukid Emir Qutb-al-Din Sökmen II and believed to be the oldest university in Anatolia. It still fulfils its original function as a Koranic school for local students.

Diyarbakır

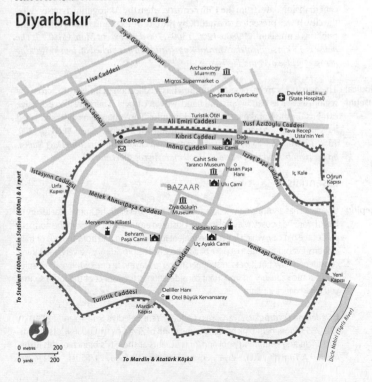

North of the Ulu Cami and reached along Ziya Gökalp Sokak you'll find the **Cahit Sıtkı Tarancı Museum** where a collection of vintage photographs, letters and poems is displayed in the beautifully restored house of Cahit Sıtkı Tarancı, a celebrated local poet. Despite the fairly forgettable nature of the exhibits, the building itself justifies a visit with its traditional furnishings and authentic decor. ■ *0800-1700 daily except Mon. US$1.*

Back on Gazi Caddesi a left turn down Yenikapı Caddesi brings you to the 16th-century **Dört Ayaklı Camii**, also called the Kasım Padışah Camii. Built by the Akkoyunlu Emir Kasım it has an unusual square minaret standing on four slender legs. To the left of the minaret a narrow street leads to one of Diyarbakır's churches, the **Kaldanı Kilisesi** (Chaldaean Church) which lurks unseen on the right behind a courtyard. The gate is kept locked and the caretaker isn't very keen on showing visitors around. You might have more luck at the **Meryemana Kilisesi** (Church of the Virgin Mary) buried in the backstreets of the old city's southwest quadrant. Built around a stone flagged courtyard, the church is still the centre of Diyarbakır's much shrunken Syrian Orthodox community, many of whom have fled abroad to escape persecution. Nearby the **Behram Paşa Camii** is the largest mosque in the city, dedicated by the Ottoman governor Behram Paşa in 1572.

At the southern end of Gazi Caddesi near the Mardin Kapısı a 16th-century Ottoman caravanserai called the **Deliler Hanı** has been converted into one of the most atmospheric hotels in town, complete with a swimming pool that's open to non-residents for a fee and a bar.

Atatürk Köşkü One of the best surviving examples of a traditional Diyarbakır house, the Atatürk Köşkü is found on the eastern bank of the Tigris to the south of town. Solidly built out of alternating courses of white and black stone, the magnificent mansion dates from the 15th century, when the Akkoyunlu dynasty ruled the city. It was presented to Atatürk by the city in 1937 and is now open to the public as a museum. ■ *0800-1200, 1300-1700 daily except Mon. US$0.75. The house is 2.5 km south of the Mardin Kapısı and can be reached on foot by walking across a bridge over the Tigris.*

Archaeological The province's archaeological museum has a collection of finds from across the
Museum region, as well as handicrafts and hand-woven carpets. There are also extensive exhibits on the Karakoyunlu and Akkoyunlu, Turcoman dynasties who ruled large tracts of Persian and Anatolia during the Middle Ages. ■ *0830-1200, 1330-1700 daily. US$1. A short walk along Ziya Gökalp Bulvarı from Dağı Kapısı, on the right behind the Dedeman Hotel and Migros supermarket.*

Essentials

Sleeping Diyarbakır has a surprisingly good selection of hotels, everything from 5-star luxury to basic boarding houses. Many places are clustered around Dağı Kapısı, in the northern part of the old city, which is very convenient for getting to and from the bus or train stations. Even in the cheaper price bands most hotels provide a/c – a very good thing considering how hot it gets in summer. If you're staying in one of the real cheapies without such a luxury an important consideration is the aspect of the room so that you avoid direct sunlight.

L *Dedeman Diyarbakır*, Ziya Gökalp Caddesi, Yeni Belediye Sarayı Yanı, T2288130, F2247353. Prominent pink building to the north of Ziya Gökalp Caddesi, lots of comforts including swimming pool and 2 restaurants at the city's branch of this luxury chain. **A** *Turistik Otel*, Ziya Gökalp Bulvarı No7, T2247550/1, F2244274, turistik@kaynet.com.tr Nearly 50 years old, looking good after recent refurbishment, pleasant public rooms, genteel atmosphere, comfortable bedrooms with a/c, telephone, TV, fridge, pool at the rear and restaurant. Recommended. **C** *Grand Güler Hotel*, Kıbrıs Caddesi No 13, Dağkapı, T2292221, F2244509. Newly opened, flashy reception all mirrors and marble, well-fitted rooms with small shower, TV, telephone, good value. **C** *Otel Büyük Kervansaray*, Gazi Caddesi, Mardinkapı, T2289606/7, F2239522. Housed in the Deliller Hanı, a restored Ottoman caravanserai, rooms don't really live-up to atmospheric surroundings, perfectly adequate but fairly average in terms of decor, equipped with a/c as standard, restaurant and large pool at the rear, courtyard nightclub which may keep you awake at night if you're a light sleeper. **C-D** *Büyük Otel*, ánönü Caddesi No 4, T2281295, F2212444. Rooms are bright and clean, well maintained, a/c and cable TV standard, roof-top restaurant. Recommended. **D** *Hotel Güler*, Kıbrıs Caddesi, Yoğurtçu Sokak No 7, T2240294, F2240294. Run by management of *Grand Güler Hotel*, decent rooms with bathroom, however, not as good value as it used to be. **D** *Demir Otel*, ázzetpaşa Caddesi No 8, T2288800, F2288809. Formerly popular with tour group, now starting to look very dated, rooms are perfectly comfortable and a/c. **D** *Balkar Otel*, Kıbrıs Caddesi No 38, T2281233, F2246936. Good value place, newish, pleasant rooms with small ensuite, a/c, telephone, TV and fridge come as standard, interesting photographs of the city in the 1950s hung in the lobby. Recommended. **D** *Hotel Kristal*, Kıbrıs Caddesi, Yoğurtçu Sokak No 10, T2293800/1, F224018/, opposite the Güler. Neat rooms with a/c, TV and telephone. **E** *Hotel Aslan*, Kıbrıs Caddesi No 23, T2247096, F2241179. Not a bad choice, quite spacious rooms with ensuite, telephone and TV, better value at the *Aslan Palas Oteli* next door. **F** *Otel Kervansaray 2*, ánönü Caddesi No 13 Dağkapı, T2216466, F2291837. Falls short of the standards set by its sister hotel, fairly plain rooms with a/c, TV and smal ensuite. **F** *Dicle Otel*, Kıbrıs Caddesi No 3, Dağkapı, T2235326, on the corner near Dağkapı. Good value rooms some with balcony, all have shower and telephone, may be hot in the summer. **F** *Hotel Kenan*, ázzetpaşa Caddesi No 20/B, T2216614. Clean rooms with ensuite and a/c, tiled floors give it a clinical feel, but represents good value for money. Recommended. **F** *Aslan Palas Oteli*, Kıbrıs Caddesi No 21, T2211227. Decent rooms with a/c, TV and small ensuite, some have balconies, another decent cheapy. **G** *Hotel Uçak*, Kıbrıs Caddesi No 31 Dağkapı, T2211076, simple place which is perfectly adequate if you're on a really tight budget, 1/2/3/4 bed rooms with squat toilet and shower, some have no external window. **G** *Otel Surkent*, İzzetpaşa Caddesi Sur Belediyesi Karşısı No 19 Dağkapı, T2216616. Basic rooms which aren't bad for such a low price, small ensuite, rooms on front may be hot.

Midrange For a refined meal try one of the town's better hotels where you'll also be able to enjoy a drink with your meal: *Turistik Otel Diyarbakır* has a good menu which features *meze*, fish and meat dishes, attentive service, pleasant poolside tables. *The Dedeman Diyarbakır* also has 2 upmarket restaurants frequented mainly by businessmen. **Cheap** Kıbrıs Caddesi has several decent restaurants where you can eat your fill for under US$5. The *Ünlü Kebabistanı*, next to the *Aslan Hotel*, has a selection of ready-prepared dishes, a thick and tasty *mercimek çorbası* (lentil soup) as well as kebaps. The *Sarmaşık Sofra Salonu* at Kıbrıs Caddesi No 32/A is another good place conveniently close to the Dağı Kapısı hotels. *Sarmaşık Ocakbaşı*, at No 17, specializes in *şiş*, *adana* and *urfa* kebaps grilled in front of you by the chef. *Tavacı Recep Usta'nın Yeri*, Yusuf Azizoğlu Caddesi, outside the city walls a short stroll from Dağı Kapı, modern place with tables outside, serves lahmacun, kebaps and *sac kavurma* (tasty chunks of lamb wok-fried with vegetables). Opposite the PTT on Kıbrıs Caddesi are a line of tea gardens, crowded with card-playing men in the evening. There are several döner stalls and places to get *çiğ köfte*, the regional specialty made from highly spiced, uncooked lamb mince, for US$1 per portion.

Eating
There isn't much action after dark in Diyarbakır, so your best bet is 1 of the more expensive hotels

Southeast Anatolia

Shopping With the collapse of the local tourist industry Diyarbakır could be a good place to pick up a carpet, however, don't expect to get any wild bargains. Try *Mesopotamia Carpet*, Gazi Caddesi, Celal Güzelses Yeraltı Çarşısı No 39, in the underground shopping mall in front of the Ulu Cami.

Tour agencies *Bianca*, İnönü Caddesi No 42, Dağı Kapı, local information and tours, plus ticketing.

Transport **Air** *Turkish Airlines*, İnönü Caddesi No 8, T2288401, F2288403, have several daily flight to **Ankara** and **İstanbul**. Service buses to the airport depart every 2 hrs from the THY office. **Bus** Most bus companies provide a free shuttle bus to the *otogar* from their offices around Dağı Kapı. **Adana**, every hr, 8 hrs, US$11. **Ankara**, hourly buses, 13 hrs, US$17. **Kahta**, several daily buses via Siverek, 3 hrs, US$6. **Malatya**, regular buses, 3½ hrs, US$6. **Şanlıurfa**, regular buses, 3 hrs, US$6. **Van**, 4 buses daily, 7 hrs, US$8. **Car rental** *Avis*, İnönü Caddesi No 6, Dağıkapı, T2290275, F2290276. **Train** Güney Ekspresi, departs **İstanbul** Tue, Thu, Fri, Sun at 2005, returning via Diyarbakır on Mon, Wed, Fri, Sun at 1136, 23 hrs.

Directory **Banks** There are several banks with ATMs on İnönü Caddesi and Gazi Caddesi. **Post office** The main PTT is on Kıbrıs Caddesi near Hindibaba Kapısı. **Tourist information** The Tourist Information Office is actually inside the Dağı Kapısı. Open weekdays 0830-1200, 1300-1730.

Mardin

Phone code: 0482
Colour map 6, grid B3
Population: 65,000
Altitude: 1083 m
100 km from Diyarbakır

Spilling down a flat top mountain crowned with military radar installations and antenna, Mardin stares out across a checkerboard plain of wheat fields towards the Syrian frontier, less than 20 km to the south. An ancient, strategic town of steep streets dotted with handsome Arab-style stone houses, its proximity to the border has ensured a turbulent recent history of ethnic violence and terrorist attacks. Though PKK activity in the area has cooled off under intense military pressure, Mardin sees few foreign visitors, with only a trickle of tourists passing through en route for the ancient Syrian Orthodox monastery of Deyrül Zafaran, a focus for the remnants of the area's once sizeable Christian population.

Sights

It's possible to pay a visit to the monastery & explore the old town as a day-trip, although there are several places to stay should you want to prolong your visit or continue E to Midyat & Hasankeyf

Arriving from the main highway Mardin's main street, the one-way Birinci Caddesi, climbs up through the new town of concrete apartments to the old city on the southern side of the mountain. At the western end of Birinci Caddesi is the Belediye Garajı where buses arrive and from where it's a short walk or dolmuş ride east to the main square, Cumhuriyet Meydanı. In the square itself the small collection of statuary and artefacts from the local Christian community on display in the **Mardin Müzesi** won't detain you very long. ■ *0800-1200, 1300-1700 daily except Mon. US$0.50.*

Downhill from the square is the town's interesting **bazaar district** where you'll also find the 11th-century **Ulu Cami**. Distinguished by its fluted minaret the building was badly damaged during the Kurdish rebellion of 1832 and has since lost much of its original character to heavy-handed restoration work.

Continuing east you'll pass a well preserved example of Mardin's vernacular stone architecture before reaching a staircase which leads up to the **Sultan Isa Medresesi**. Overlooking the town and the Syrian plain beyond, the 14th-century seminary built by an Artukid Emir has a magnificent carved portal, though the gate is usually locked so you may not be able to inspect beyond.

Above the Sultan Isa Medresesi the **citadel** affords an even better view of the town and Mesopotamian plain disappearing into the haze to the south. Originally constructed as a stronghold guarding an important trade route between

Anatolia and Mesopotamia, the castle was strengthened by the Byzantines before being occupied by the Arabs and the Selçuk Turks. As the capital of the Artukid emirate the fortress survived an eight month siege by the Mongols, only to fall later to a second attack. Within the outer walls, the subsequent rulers of Mardin, the Akkoyunlu, constructed a palace and mosque, both now in ruin and out-of-bounds as they fall within the perimeter of a military installation.

Lying on a rocky hillside is the monastery of Dar-ez-Zaferan, the so-called 'Saffron Monastery' in Arabic because it's said that petals from saffron crocuses were mixed into the mortar during its construction. Established at the end of the fifth century, it became the Patriarchate of the Syrian Orthodox Church in 1160, a role it filled until 1920 when the seat was moved to Damascus. Today, there's still a priest and several monks living in the monastery, although Mardin's Syriac population have mostly departed for less troubled lands. Until comparatively recently the monastery ran its own orphanage, however, pressure from the authorities, ever sensitive about proselytising, seems to have put a stop to such benevolent activities.

Dar-ez-Zaferan (Deyrül Zafran)
6 km SE of Mardin

The approach to the solid rectangular building is across fields and orchards carefully tended by members of the monastic staff. Although it may have lost its flock, it's obvious that the monastery is still well looked after, benefiting from donations by the widely spread Syrian Orthodox Diaspora. Once admitted by the warden, you climb a set of stone stairs to a peaceful courtyard filled with bird-song. The warden or one of the other members of staff will then conduct you around the building, showing you first an **underground chamber** which is thought to have been a sanctuary used by worshippers of the moon-god Sin prior to the monastery's construction. Next stop is a **mausoleum**, entered through an exquisite pair of 300-year old walnut doors, where the earthly remains of seven patriarchs and metropolitans (bishops) are interned in stone tombs. According to tradition the church-fathers are buried in full ceremonial gear seated at wooden thrones.

You'll then be shown the **chapel** where daily services are still held in Aramaic, the language spoken by Christ. Inside the cool interior the walls are decorated with simple paintings and a carved stone altar stands beside the patriarch's throne, carved onto the side of which are the names of all the patriarchs since 792 AD when the church was refounded. Next door are the wooden litters used to carry church officials in days gone-by.

On the first floor there are basic **guest-rooms** used by visiting theological students, as well as the patriarch's simple living-quarters. Paintings and photographs of the church patriarchs, including the present incumbent meeting the Pope in Damascus, stare down from the walls of a narrow room used for church meetings. Having completed the tour it's customary to make a small donation before taking your leave. ■ *0830-1130, 1330-1530 daily. As there's no public transport most people hire a taxi for the 10-min journey from Mardin. The trip costs about US$6 with the driver waiting to return you to town afterwards. You could also walk in about 90 mins, turning off the road southeast to Nusaydin at the yellow and black sign-post for Deyrülzafran.*

D *Otel Bilen*, Yenişehir, T2130315/6, F2122575, in the new part of town near the highway. 3-star, reasonable rooms with a/c, telephone, TV, fridge and small ensuite. **F** *Hotel Bayraktar*, Birinci Caddesi, Cumhuriyet Meydanı, T2121338. Very the worse for wear, tatty rooms, old furnishings, small ensuite, redeeming feature is excellent view from back windows. *Ünsal Yemek Salonu*, Birinci Caddesi, a restaurant east of Cumhuriyet Meydanı, ready-prepared dishes. There are several tea gardens at the east end of Birinci Caddesi near the PTT which are particularly nice in the evening.

Sleeping & eating
Don't leave dinner too late in the day as most of the town's simple eateries seem to close by 2100

Transport **Dolmuş** Diyarbakır, every hr, 90 mins, US$1.50. **Urfa**, several daily, 3 hrs, US$6.

Directory **Airline offices** The *Otel Bilen* (see sleeping) is the town's *Turkish Airlines* agent. **Banks** There are several banks on Birinci Caddesi near Cumhuriyet Meydanı. **Post office** The PTT, housed in a lovely old building, is at the east end of Birinci Caddesi. **Tourist information** The Tourist Information Office, T2125845, F2121852, is on Cumhuriyet Meydanı.

Midyat & the Tür Abdin

The main reason you might decide to stay in Midyat is as a base for exploration of the remote Tür Abdin plateau

Midyat is a small double town 60 km east of Mardin. The new part, know as Estel, is inhabited mainly by Kurdish families and doesn't warrant any special attention, though the Christian section of the settlement, just to the east, is far more atmospheric. Narrow, dusty alleyways squeeze between large old houses, the pale tan-coloured stone decorated with delicately carving. Originally home to a Syrian Orthodox community several thousand strong, many of the local Christians have fled in the last decade due to harassment by the PKK. There are a number of churches in the backstreets, though to gain access to their locked courtyards you'll need to find the often elusive caretaker. There's a simple guest-house **F** *Yuvam Otel*, T0482 4622531, near the dolmuş stop should you want to stay, but enquire about the local security situation as a dusk to dawn curfew has been imposed by the military in the past. ■ *Getting there: Dolmuş from Mardin run during daylight hours, dropping passengers at the main roundabout in Estel.*

The **Tür Abdin** is an area of parched limestone hills rolling eastwards to the River Tigris. Known as the 'Mountain of the Servant of God' the area developed an important monastic society in early Byzantine times with Syrian Orthodox monasteries and churches dotting the countryside.

Despite the troubled times several monasteries remain in operation serving as a focus for the beleaguered Christian population. About 20 km east of Midyat, Mar Gabriel was founded by Mar (Saint) Simeon in the fifth century, growing to become the largest and most important monastery in the area. Still home to the metropolitan of Tür Abdin, the monastery remains a working community with a small staff of monks who, in addition to their pious duties, cultivated the surrounding fields and orchards. If you turn up during the day you may be invited on a tour of the monastery, highlights of which include several mosaic decorated funerary chambers. However, before making the journey out there it's best to enquire at the Mardin Tourist Information Office. ■ *Getting there: Without your transport a taxi from Midyat with an hours waiting time at the monastery costs about US$25. You could be to hire a driver in Mardin for a day's excursion to Deyr-az-Zaferan, Midyat and Mar Gabriel which, depending on your bargaining skills, could be anything up to US$100.*

Hasankeyf

Set near the site of a ruined medieval city, the straggly modern village of Hasankeyf has been catapulted into the international media spot-light by the controversial Ilisu Dam being constructed downstream as part of the GAP project. When completed the barrage, second only in size to the Atatürk Dam on the Euphrates, will impound the River Tigris drowning scores of villages, as well as many of Hasankeyf's historic remains. In the face of strong international pressure the government has agreed to try and move certain buildings, although experts concede that even with the political will and adequate funding this will be a very difficult task.

Most of the extensive archaeological site is located to the southwest of the town on a terrace overlooking the Tigris gorge and reached down a road near the modern bridge. Originally established by the Romans as an isolated garrison guarding the strategically important valley, the town, known as Cephe, became a bishopric seat in Byzantine times. Overwhelmed by Arab invaders in the seventh century the town was renamed Hisn Kayfa, becoming the capital of the Turcoman Artukid dynasty in the 11th century. It's from this period that most of Hasankeyf's remains date, including a palace, a mosque, tombs and lots of ruined houses. The most photogenic, and hence best known, of the remains, however, stands alone on the opposite side of the river: the **Zeyn El-Abdin Türbesi**, a dome-topped masonry tomb sheathed in turquoise tiles. Unfortunately, the tomb, along with the remains of a medieval stone bridge, will be the first underwater when the flood gates close, so if you want to see them you'd better get there soon. ■ *Getting there: There are regular dolmuş from the grim provincial town of Batman, at the heart of the country's oil producing region, to Hasankeyf, or with your own transport you could also approach from Midyat to the south. Either way it would be wise to check locally on current security conditions in the area before proceeding.*

On the road between Diyarbakır and Tatvan, Bitlis is a small historic town squeezed into the narrow canyon of the Bitlis Çayı, a tributary of the Tigris. Founded in Byzantine times, from the 16th century it was the centre of a semi-autonomous Kurdish fiefdom. Guarded by a sinister looking citadel constructed from black basalt, the town has a picturesque humpback bridge and a fine 12th-century Selçuklu mosque, called the Ulu Cami, none of which really justify breaking your journey, unless you need a break from driving. ■ *Getting there: Dolmuş leave every hour for Tatvan, 20 mins, US$1. In the other direction frequent buses pass through town en-route for Diyarbakır, however, these may already be full.* | **Bitlis**

Around Van Gölü

There are a number of interesting sights scattered around the lakeshore with those at the southeast end – the Armenian church of Akdamar and the beaches at Edremit – within easy day trip range of Van town. Without your own transport though, it's necessary to have an overnight stay in Tatvan to explore the extinct volcano of Nemrut Dağı and the graveyard at Ahlat, possibly taking in the northern shoreline afterwards. Public transport between Van and Tatvan (144 km) is good, however from Tatvan you'll need to rely on dolmuş running between Ahlat, Adilcevaz and Erciş, often with waits in between.

Tatvan

Set against a backdrop of barren mountains on the southwestern shores of Lake Van, Tatvan is essentially a one street town strung out for several kilometres along the main road. Formerly the terminus for the *Vangölü Ekspresi* passengers would transfer here onto a ferry for the last leg of the journey across the lake to Van. Unfortunately for Tatvan and travellers alike, due to security problems along the final stretch the train now finishes its eastwards run in Elazığ and the TML ferries operate an, at best, sporadic service designed primarily for carrying freight. Tatvan still makes a convenient overnight base for trips up the nearby volcano of Nemrut Dağı, or for exploring the western shores of Lake Van. | *Phone code: 0432*
Colour map 6, grid A4

C *Hotel Tatvan Kardelen*, Belediye Yanı, T/F8279500, up street opposite the post office. Surprisingly modern 3-star hotel which is a popular venue for local weddings and functions, clean rooms equipped with telephone, TV, also a bar and restaurant on the premises. **E** *Hotel Altılar*, Cumhuriyet Caddesi No 164, T8274096/7, F8274098. Across from the post office, reasonably comfortable 1/2/3/4 bed rooms with TV, back rooms may be quieter, breakfast is extra. **G** *Hotel Üstün*, Hal Caddesi No 23, T8279014/5, F8279017. Best budget option, in backstreets near the lake, very quiet | **Sleeping & eating**
The town's hotels are all clustered within walking distance of the post office

Southeast Anatolia

Van Gölü

Up to 100 m deep; 130 km from shore to shore and 3,764 sq km in total area, it's no wonder that the ancient inhabitants of the region around Van Gölü (Lake Van) referred to it as the 'inland sea'. Ringed by lofty and, for much of the year, snow-capped mountains, the turquoise waters of Turkey's largest lake are a breathtaking sight. At an altitude of about 1,700 m above sea-level, the lake was formed millions of years ago by an eruption of the volcano Nemrut Dağı, at the western end of the lake, which formed a natural dam. The resulting body of water has no natural outlet with its level regulated by the balance between the amount of water washed in by rivers and the annual losses to evaporation. Concentrations of mineral salts have therefore built-up gradually in the water making the lake highly alkaline. For bathers this means that any cuts, scratches or sunburn sting severely though the alkalinity is a boon for local housewives, as there's no need to use soap for washing clothes. If you decide to test out the water yourself it's best to avoid swimming in the vicinity of Van, where pollution is a problem, though there are stretches of deserted beach all around the shoreline.

As with other large bodies of water Van Gölü is not without its tales of mysterious monsters in the Loch Ness mould. Called the Van Gölü Canavar (Lake Van Monster), or simply the Canavar, there have been a number of sightings by boatmen and villagers over the years, although rather tellingly the descriptions have often been wildly at odds. You're much more likely to see one of the lake's other endemic, and less fantastic, aquatic species, known locally as the inci kefal (thin mullet), on a plate in one of the lakeside restaurants.

position, simple but clean rooms with shared bathroom. **G** *Akgün Otel*, Hal Caddesi No 51, T8172374, in street parallel to Cumhuriyet Caddesi. Popular with visiting traders, basic rooms with handbasin. **G** *Otel Trabzon*, Ofis Caddesi No 18. Rudimentary place, shared bathrooms. There are a handful of small eateries sufficient for a simple meal along Cumhuriyet Caddesi. Otherwise try the *Hotel Tatvan Kardelen*.

Transport **Dolmuş** to **Bitlis** and **Ahlat** leave from outside the post office regularly during the day. The *otogar* is 2 km west of the centre on the main road, but buses heading for **Van**, 2 hrs, US$4, also stop in the town centre if they have empty seats.

Directory **Banks** There is an *Işbankası* on Cumhuriyet Caddesi. **Post office** The PTT is also on Cumhuriyet Caddesi. **Tourist information** There is an office of sorts next to the *Hotel Tatvan Kardelen*, T8276301, F8276300, little useful information. **Useful addresses** *Mehmet Sahli*, T4232203, local driver with some English who can arrange trips up Nemrut Dağı and to other sights in the area, overnight visits to villages in the vicinity, normally be found around the Tourist Information Office.

Nemrut Dağı Towering above the western shore of Van Gölü is the 2935-m high extinct volcano Nemrut Dağı. Not to be confused with its more famous, statue-topped namesake near Adıyaman (see page 621), this Nemrut Dağı created Lake Van when its eruptions blocked local drainage lines causing the mountain-girt basin to the east to fill up with water. This volcanic activity also left a deep crater which now contains a pair of lakes: one icy blue and swimmable only for the very brave; the other an evocative emerald green, warmed by hot springs around its edge. Nearby there is also a rather anti-climactic steam vent, but of more interest is the obsidian, a rare naturally occurring glass, scattered over the mountainsides. Varying in colour from a shiny black to opaque red and green, obsidian was prized in Neolithic times as a material for making razor sharp cutting tools and the deposits on Nemrut Dağı were at the centre of an ancient trading network which fanned out across the Near East.

The authorities generally discouraged visits to the volcano up until fairly recently due to supposed PKK activity in the area. However, with improvements in the security situation locals from Tatvan are again venturing up to bathe in the crater springs and picnic, though not in sufficient numbers to support a regular dolmuş service up the mountain. Therefore without your own transport it's a matter of finding a driver willing to make the rough 26 km climb up the mountain. Mehmet Sahli (see Tatvan, useful addresses) undertakes such trips for about US$40, though if you can't find him a taxi driver will probably want more. If you're driving up then the road, which soon deteriorates into a dusty track, starts near a Türk Petrol station on the western edge of Tatvan.

Tatvan to Van

East from Tatvan the main road passes through a bucolic landscape of small cereal fields, meadows and rushing streams. It's an idyllic looking land, though the harsh realities of rural life in such an underdeveloped region are brought home by the sight of villagers conducting the late-summer harvest with hand scythes. Indeed most agricultural activity in the area is unmechanized, subsistence farming with the men of the villages spending much of the year in the west of the country earning enough money to supplement their families' meagre incomes. There are several fortified checkpoints along the road where coaches and trucks are periodically stopped and searched so keep your passport handy. After winding up and over the 2234-m Kuskunkıran pass the highway regains the coast of Lake Van, where the island of Akdamar is visible offshore.

Perched on a small island 3 km from the shore is Akdamar Kilisesi, alternatively known as the **Church of the Holy Cross**. Used during medieval times as a place of refuge by the local Armenian population, in 921 AD King Gagik built himself a palace and stronghold on the island. There are few extant remains of these buildings, though the Armenian place of worship he also endowed is still standing. The reliefs within the church depict well-known biblical stories such as Adam and Eve, who are shown flanking the Tree of Life, about to make their fateful misdeed, on the middle part of the north wall (facing away from the shore). On the south wall is a lively frieze of David slaying Goliath, along with scenes from the story of Jonah and the whale. Other scenes that you may be able to identify are Abraham preparing to sacrifice his son, Isaac. Further up

Akdamar
A modest sandstone building, it's the unusually beautiful reliefs carved on to the exterior which are the church's most outstanding feature

Around Van Gölü

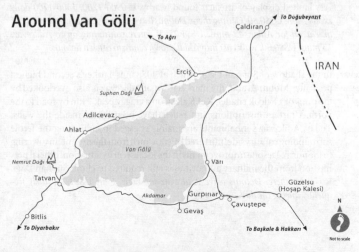

Southeast Anatolia

on the outside are exquisite bands of high relief depicting a veritable Noah's arc full of animated wild animals entwined within a long grape vine.

The rest of the small island is covered with almond orchards and rough meadows that make an excellent venue for a picnic. On a clear, still day the view across the lake to the snowy slopes of Süphan Dağı, reflected in the mirror-like surface is breathtaking. You may also be able to pick out the rarely visited island of Çarpanak, off the coast to the west of Van, which is also crowned by an 11th-century Armenian church.

■ *Getting there: Ferrymen wait at a small jetty beside the main road at Akdamar Iskelesi to take visitors across to the island. The 15-min crossing costs about US$20 per boatload. Approaching from Tatvan, Van-bound buses will let you off at the ferry departure point. From Van Akdamar dolmuş depart from a stop to the west of the bazaar area and the Ipek Otel, US$1. Alternatively, drivers on the route to Gevaş, 8 km east of Akdamar, may agree to take you the extra distance for about US$2-3. A taxi to Akdamar from Van costs in the region of US$25 which includes 90 mins waiting time, or you could combine it with a visit to Çavuştepe (see page 650) for a total of US$35-40.*

Gevaş & Edremit If you're fanatical about Islamic tombs and tombstones a visit to Gevaş, 42 km southwest of Van, may be in order for its **Halime Hatun Türbesi**, a Karakoyunlu mausoleum built for an important member of the clan in the the 14th century. It's surrounded by a cemetery of historic tombstones spanning from the 14th to the 17th centuries. At Gevaş and Edremit there are long stretches of beach with some rudimentary camping and restaurant facilities that are crowded with families from Van on summer weekends. See above for transport.

Ahlat On the northern shore of Van Gölü, 42 km from Tatvan, the small town of Ahlat is renowned for its extensive Selçuk cemetery. It was during the Selçuk era that the skilled local stonemasons crafted the various mausolea, tombs and headstones which form one of Anatolia's most extensive Islamic necropoli. On the western outskirts of town are a series of *kümbet*, two storey cylindrical tombs typical of the Selçuk period. The graveyard itself is a veritable forest of tall, thin tombstones decorated with delicate calligraphy and floral designs. Many are tipped at crazy angles having given up the vertical long ago and there's a certain romantic poignancy about the scene. A small **museum** next to the road has a very limited display of artefacts found nearby. ■ *0900-1200, 1300-1700 daily except Mon. US$0.30. Getting there: Dolmuş leave regularly from outside the PTT in Tatvan for Ahlat, 45 mins, US$1.25. If you're continuing on to Adilcevaz, 15 mins, US$0.50, walk east into Ahlat's town centre to catch a dolmuş.*

Adilcevaz In the shadow of Süphan Dağı, which at 4058 m is Turkey's second highest peak after Mount Ararat, the market town of Adilcevaz is also overlooked by the ruins of a Selçuk citadel, **Kef Kalesi**, on a craggy peak 7 km by road to the north. Urartian inscriptions and reliefs have been found inside the walls. Today, Adilcevaz's inhabitants are mainly engaged in cultivating the fertile surrounding countryside, nurtured by snowmelt from the mountain towering to the north. Despite improvements in the local security situation, official permission from the military authorities is still required to climb Süphan Dağı. ■ *Getting there: Dolmuş leave Adilcevaz for Erciş, 1 hr, US$1.25, fairly frequently during the day.*

Van

Van is the largest town in the mountains of southeast Anatolia. Its setting on a gently sloping plain beside the vast inland sea, Van Gölü, ringed by desolate expanses of tree-less mountains not dissimilar to parts of Central Asia, will appeal to those who appreciate open, rugged landscapes. In summer the temperature is moderated by the altitude, quite a relief if you've just arrived from the blistering heat of Diyarbakır or Urfa. Winter is less clement though with icy blasts of frigid wind driving temperatures down as low as -30°C.

Phone code: 0432
Colour map 6, grid A5
Altitude: 1727 m
1644 km E of İstanbul,
100 km as the crow flies
from the Iranian frontier

The town is a modern incarnation: a provincial centre with the government buildings, apartments blocks and busy shopping streets that go with it. The destruction of the First World War left scant evidence of the town's considerable historical legacy, confined now to Van castle and what's on display in the excellent provincial museum. Nonetheless the town makes an excellent base for excursions to other interesting sights such as Çavuştepe, Hoşap, Akdamar and the lake itself; and Van's hoteliers are hoping that a return to stability will help the area re-realize its obvious touristic potential.

Getting there Despite its relative isolation Van is served by regular long-distance buses from destinations all over the country. A faster way to reach the town is to fly, with several daily non-stop connections from İstanbul and Ankara. The *Vangölü Ekspresi* now terminates in Elazığ, still 8-9 hrs away by bus. **Getting around** With its regular street plan Van is fairly easy to negotiate. All of the accommodation and restaurants, plus the museum and tourist information are close to the main north-south thoroughfare, Cumhuriyet Caddesi. The *otogar* is several kilometres northwest of the centre just off the main highway. Most companies provide a free service bus, but these fill-up quickly and depart so don't miss it. Dolmuş, US$0.30, also pass by outside heading in to Beş Yol at the north end of Cumhuriyet Caddesi.

Ins & outs
*See page 650 for
further details*

Van's history begins in the ninth century BC when King Sarduri I succeeded in unifying the various Vannic tribes living in Eastern Anatolia around Lake Van. Discoveries of exquisite jewellery and armour demonstrate that the Urartians, as they came to be known, were both wealthy and gifted as craftsmen. They also gained a reputation as skilled engineers constructing elaborate fortresses and ambitious civil works such as a 65 km long canal which supplied Tuşpa with water. The Urartian domain was subsequently settled by the Armenians but over the following centuries the area rarely enjoyed its own independence, finding itself split into numerous cantons which came under the yoke of a succession of neighbouring empires. At the beginning of the 11th century Van was ceded to the Byzantines, although within 50 years the Battle of Manzikert heralded the beginning of Selçuk rule and the area's incorporation into the Sultanate of Rum. Waning Selçuk power saw Van controlled by various Turcoman emirs before it was annexed by the Ottomans in the 15th century. Under the Ottomans the city became an important garrison town and stop on the overland caravan routes.

History

In the closing years of the 19th century Van was not excluded from the anti-Armenian violence that broke-out across Anatolia. The city was, however, to witness far worse during the First World War when Russian forces aided by Armenian partisans occupied the city between 1915 and 1917. By the time the Ottoman army retook the city it had been reduced to rubble with the contemporary settlement constructed 4 km to the southeast following Turkey's independence.

Today, Van is the administrative and commercial hub of a large mountainous region peopled predominantly by Kurds. It has seen sporadic outbreaks of

South East Anatolia

terrorism in the last decade, although PKK activity has mostly been confined to more remote areas of the province. In addition to Kurds and Turks, the town's population also has a significant Iranian component, members of an estimated 400,000 strong exile community nationwide.

Sights

Van's turbulent recent history has not left much of interest in the town itself. However, a visit to its only surviving historical sight, the castle, and a look around the excellent provincial museum can easily occupy an afternoon. The frenetic **bazaar district** southwest of Beş Yol is also interesting.

Van Müzesi   Situated in a quiet backstreet to the east of Cumhuriyet Caddesi, Van's provincial museum has an interesting and well-displayed collection of artefacts found in the surrounding region. As you might expect Urartian exhibits feature strongly with an amazing horde of beautifully worked gold and silver jewellery, armour, pottery and seals. Upstairs, along with the usual antique carpets and local handicrafts are the macabre skeletal remains of Kurds and Turks massacred by Armenians during the First World War. Nothing is mentioned of the local Armenian population who also suffered similar atrocities. ■ *0800-1200, 1300-1700 daily except Mon. US$1.25.*

Van

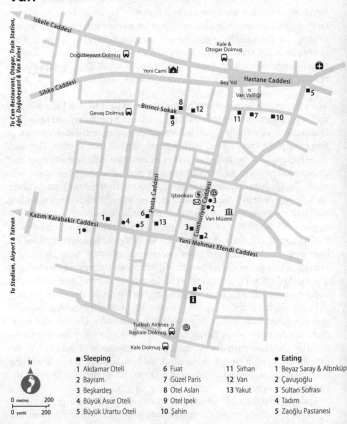

■ Sleeping			
1 Akdamar Oteli	6 Fuat	11 Sirhan	
2 Bayram	7 Güzel Paris	12 Van	
3 Beşkardeş	8 Otel Aslan	13 Yakut	
4 Büyük Asur Oteli	9 Otel İpek		
5 Büyük Urartu Oteli	10 Şahin		

● Eating
1 Beyaz Saray & Altınküp
2 Çavuşoğlu
3 Sultan Sofrası
4 Tadım
5 Zaoğlu Pastanesi

Near the lakeside to the southwest of the modern town a long, narrow spine of **Van Kalesi** rock juts vertically out from the flat alluvial plain. Known as the 'Rock of Van' this was the city's acropolis from ancient times as well as the focus of the old, pre-First World War, settlement.

The citadel is secured by two sets of defensive walls built by the Selçuks and later repaired during the Ottoman era. Nothing remains of the Urartian structure which was most probably constructed of mud bricks which decay quickly compared to stone.

One part of the Urartian complex that has survived is the **Sardur Burçu** (Sardur Tower), at the western end of the rock, which is thought to have been a fortified pier jutting into the lake. An Assyrian inscription on the tower identifies it with the Urartian monarch Sarduris I.

From the tower an ancient staircase hewn from the living rock leads up to a walkway which passes around to several **rockcut tombs** on the precipitous south face of the acropolis. A long cuneiform inscription on the cliff face proclaims the heroic deeds of King Argistis I (786-764 BC) who occupied one of the nearby sepulchres, with the others built for the Urartian monarchs Sarduris I and Menuas. Inaccessible further out on the cliff face is an inscription in Persian, Elamite and Babylonian left by the Persian king Xerxes sometime in the fifth century BC.

The crest of the ridge is a popular local picnic spot and is particularly nice in the late afternoon when the sun dips towards lake and you're reminded of the ancient Assyrian name for Van Gölü, 'The Sea Beyond the Sunset'. At the top is the **minaret** of the Süleyman Khan Camii which looks in danger of following the 16th-century Ottoman mosque which it once adjoined into oblivion.

Here you are rewarded with excellent views of the surrounding countryside, the lake & the town

A poignant and moving sight are the remains of **Old Van** to the south of the Rock which the First World War succeeded in removing from the map. Where the town formerly stood there's an expansive flyblown plain, pock marked with craters and scattered with rubble. Several of the old town's mosques have been restored and they now stand forlorn and lonely, accentuating the devastation around them. ■ *0900-1800 daily. US$0.50. Getting there. From Beş Yol at the north end of Cumhuriyet 'Kale' dolmuş, US$0.40, depart regularly for the castle.*

Essentials

A *Büyük Urartu Oteli*, Hastane Caddesi No 60, T2120660, F2121610. Across from state hospital, most luxurious place in town, spacious and comfortable rooms with ensuite bathroom, facilities include restaurant, bar, games room, sauna and swimming pool, prices open to discreet negotiation. **B** *Akdamar Oteli*, Kazım Karabekir Caddesi, T2149923, F2120868. 75-room modern hotel frequented by visiting businessmen, comfortable rooms with ensuite, telephone, TV and minibar, also has restaurant and bar. **B** *Hotel Yakut*, Posta Caddesi No 8, T2142832, F2166351. Similar clientel as the *Akdamar*, leather couches and TV in lobby, fairly small guestrooms but equipped with telephone, TV, fridge and a decent ensuite, smart restaurant with live music in the evenings. **D** *Hotel Fuat*, Posta Caddesi No 7, T2140780, F2166504, opposite *Hotel Yakut*. Large, well-furnished rooms with TV, television and minibar are good value, doubles have ensuite with bath, singles showers. Recommended. **F** *Büyük Asur Oteli*, Cumhuriyet Caddesi Turizm Sokak No 5, T2168792, F2169461. Plain, decent rooms with ensuite shower, relaxed sitting area overlooking the street, friendly and helpful staff, English-speaking, Saz-playing manager Remzi can give you lots of information on the area, sightseeing and camping tours also organized. Recommended. **E** *Otel Sirhan*, Hükümet Konağı Yanı, T2143463, F2162867. In the side street next to the provisional government building (Hükümet Konağı), unexceptional rooms with shower, roof-top

Sleeping

Southeast Anatolia

restaurant pumps-out very loud music late into the night. **E** *Hotel Beşkardeş*, Cumhuriyet Caddesi No 16, T2161116, F2166466. Couldn't get much more central than this one, small rooms with shower are pretty average though. **E** *Hotel Güzel Paris*, İrfan Baştuğ Caddesi, Hükümet Konağı Yanı, T2163739, F2167897, beyond the *Otel Sirhan*. The rooms are nothing special, but they are clean and good for the money, bathroom attached, helpful reception staff. Recommended. **E** *Otel Şahin*, İrfan Baştuğ Caddesi No 30, T2163062, F2163064. If the *Güzel Paris* is full you could try this one a short distance beyond, similar rooms and prices. **F** *Hotel Bayram*, Cumhuriyet Caddesi No 1/A, T2161136, F2147120. Centrally located, clean and, in some cases, spacious rooms with shower attached, prices have risen since redecoration. **G** *Otel Aslan*, Özel İdare Karşısı, T2162469. Very simple but adequate place in the bazaar district, clean rooms with tiled floors, small ensuite. **G** *Otel İpek*, Cumhuriyet Caddesi, Birinci Sokak No 3, T2163033. Basic boarding house used by bazaar traders, shared bathrooms. **G** *Hotel Van*, Cumhuriyet Caddesi Birinci Sokak, T2161733. Has the distinction of being the cheapest place in town, 2/3 person rooms with or without a shower, basic but perfectly adequate if you're counting every Turkish Lira.

Eating A local delicacy that you should try is *otlu peynir*, white cheese containing several fragrant local herbs, which is widely available at many of the delicatessens on Cumhuriyet Caddesi and makes perfect picnic fare. Van's restaurant scene offers nothing out of the ordinary, though there is a good choice of decent eateries offering fairly standard menus. Two good choices are: **Sultan Sofrası**, large glass-fronted place opposite the PTT, open 24 hrs for spit roasted chicken, rice and salad, US$1.25, *iskender kebabı* and other grilled meat dishes, comfortable chairs. *Tadım*, Kazım Karabekir Caddesi, busy place at lunch time, ready-prepared soups, stews and kebaps, *mercimek çorbası* (lentil soup), *bulgur pilavı* and salad for vegetarians. *Çem Restaurant*, Iskele Caddesi, about 1 km down Beş Yol towards the highway, locally recommended, serve yourself from an extensive buffet of *meze* followed by grilled meat dishes and kebaps, very reasonably priced. For alcohol with your meal head for one of the hotel restaurants such as *Büyük Urartu Oteli* or **Hotel Yakut**. Then there's also the roof-top **Beyaz Saray** (White House), where the *meze* and meat dishes are secondary to drinking and watching the show. *Çavuşoğlu*, Cumhuriyet Caddesi, slightly up-market patisserie, hot and cold drinks plus lots of goodies for those with a sweet-tooth.

Bars *Altınküp*, Kazım Karabekir Caddesi No 53, male dominated, smoky *meyhane*, not recommended for unaccompanied women. *Beyaz Saray*, Kazım Karabekir Caddesi, rooftop *gazino* where local starlettes put on a nightly cabaret show, Turkish-style, food served, if you sit outside you'll be expected to tip the performer when she sings at your table.

Shopping Several carpet dealers have manged to survive the lean times with the one beneath the *Büyük Asur Oteli* offering a good selection of local kilims and imports from Iran.

Tour agencies *Urartu Turizm Seyahat Acentası*, Cumhuriyet Caddesi, Büyük Asur Oteli Altı, T2142020, F2147262, airline ticketing and reservations. For local tours call-in for a chat with Remzi, the manager of the *Büyük Asur Oteli*.

Transport **Air** *Turkish Airlines*, Cumhuriyet Caddesi No 196, T2161241, F2161768, operate 2 daily return flights **Ankara** and 1 to **İstanbul**. A service bus leaves from outside their offices approximately 90 mins before scheduled departures. **Bus** Large local companies such as *Van Seyahat*, *Van Tur* and *Van Gölü* all have daily buses to distant destinations such as **Ankara** (20 hrs, US$22), **Antalya** (24 hrs, US$30) and **İstanbul** (up to 23 hrs, US$30). These companies provide a free shuttle service to the *otogar* for their passengers. There are also the following regional services: **Ağrı**, frequent buses, 4 hrs, US$5. **Diyarbakır**, 4 buses daily, 7 hrs, US$9. **Erzurum**, several buses, mostly morning,

6 hrs, US$11. **Hakkarı**, a couple of morning buses, 4 hrs, US$5. **Urfa**, 3 daily, 9 hrs, US$12. **Tatvan**, regular buses passing through, 2 hrs, US$4. The fastest and most convenient way to get to **Doğubeyazıt** is on the dolmuş departing every morning at 0700, 0900 and sometimes 1100 from Iskele Caddesi. These dolmuş fill up quickly so it's best to arrive well in advance and buy a ticket. The journey takes 2-3 hrs, US$7. If you miss the dolmuş you can get a bus to Ağrı from where there are services every 2 hrs to Doğubeyazıt. Total travelling time is about 6 hrs. There are no direct buses to **Kars** so you'll have to catch an Erzurum-bound bus and get off at the junction in Horasan, 5 hrs. Cross the road and wait for 1 of the regular Erzurum-Kars buses. **Train and ferry** With no passenger trains serving **Tatvan** anymore the ferry service across the lake runs very seldomly. If services should resume the quay can be reached by getting on an 'Iskele' dolmuş from Beş Yol.

Banks There are banks with ATMs and private change places on Cumhuriyet Caddesi. **Post office** The PTT is on Cumhuriyet Caddesi. **Internet** *Galaxy Cafe*, Cumhuriyet Caddesi, 1st floor of building across from the PTT, US$1.25 per hr. There is another internet café in the shopping arcade across from the *Turkish Airlines* Office. **Hospitals** *Devlet Hastanesi*, the state hospital is on Hastanesi Caddesi, east of Beş Yol. **Tourist information** The fairly useless Tourist Information Office, T2162018, F2163675, is at Cumhuriyet Caddesi No 127, just south of the *Büyük Asur Oteli*.

Directory

Along the crest of a long ridge stands the ancient Urartian fortified city of Sardurihinili. Established by King Sarduris II in the eighth century BC, the city, reached up a short track from the Van-Başkale road, was extensively excavated between 1961 and 1987, revealing many Urartian artefacts that now grace the provincial museum and the Museum of Anatolian Civilisation in Ankara. Çavuştepe was particularly valuable for archaeologists because it hadn't been built over by subsequent civilisations and so remains a purely Urartian site.

Çavuştepe
25 km SE of Van

Climbing up to the parking area from the road you'll notice the limestone foundations of the perimeter defences, originally topped with mud brick fortifications. The city stood, as it does today, at a strategic position guarding the approaches to Van, surrounded by the irrigated farmland of the Hoşap Çayı Valley. At either end of the ridge were temple complexes dedicated to Haldi, the god of war, and Irmushini, the god of fertility, two of the principle deities of the 72 strong Urartian pantheon. The knowledgeable site guardian, Mehmet Kuşman, gives visitors an illuminating tour of the area so it's worth turning up during working hours when he's on duty. During his 34 years at the site he's learnt to read Urartian cuneiform script and he deciphers fluently an inscription carved into a polished basalt gateway, which describes the foundation of the city and warns of retribution by the God Haldi against those who attack it.

Excavations at the site also revealed textile workshops used for the manufacture of woollen cloth; rows of *pithoi* (clay vessels) used for storing wine and foodstuff, water cisterns and what Mehmet claims is the oldest toilet in the world, a small hole opening onto a 4 m deep septic tank.

■ *Getting there: Başkale dolmuş, US$3, depart hourly from next to the Turkish Airlines office in Van passing both Çavuştepe and Hoşap Kalesi (see below). In a small group it is far more convenient to hire a taxi in Van for around US$35 for a return journey to the 2 sites. For an additional US$15 you could make a full day of it by also visiting Akdamar (see page 645).*

From Çavuştepe the Başkale road winds along the dry valley of the Hoşap Çayı, past a reservoir formed by the Zernek Dam. Situated at a strategic narrowing of the valley is Güzelsu, a scrappy collection of roadside restaurants and workshops serving trucks coming to and from Hakkarı and the Iranian border, backed by low mudbrick houses. Perched on a precipitous outcrop of rock

Hoşap Kalesi
33 km SE of Van

Southeast Anatolia

overlooking the village is the impressive citadel of Hoşap Kalesi which dates originally from Urartian times. Most of what is visible today, however, was constructed in 1643 by a local Kurdish warlord of the Mahmudiye tribe who controlled what is the only trade route between Van and the mountainous region of Hakkarı to the south.

The entrance to the castle is on the far side of the promontory, reached by crossing a small bridge. *US$1.* The site guardian lets visitors in through a small gateway in one of the keeps round defensive towers which gives access to a polished stone stairway carved into the bed rock. Scrambling around the outer citadel you pass the remains of a water cistern and *mescit* (prayer hall), before climbing to the upper fortress which commands a superb view across the desiccated mountains and the village below. The mudbrick defences have been remarkably well preserved in the arid climate, but take care when clambering around as it's a long drop. Protruding from the crest of a rocky ridge nearby is another jagged, sinister looking section of crenellated mudbrick wall.

Hakkarı
Altitute: 1748 m

An isolated mountainous province in the extreme southeast of the country, Hakkarı is very rarely visited by foreigners these days. Its rugged topography and long international frontiers have made it a particularly 'hot-spot' in the Kurdish conflict, with PKK guerrillas slipping regularly across from bases in Iran and Iraq to clash with the Turkish security forces massed in the area. The Turkish army have frequently returned the favour by making major sorties across the frontiers to seek and destroy terrorist camps, as well as depopulating rural areas inside Hakkarı to deny the PKK of any support.

Once a popular area for trekking and climbing in the stunning Cilo-Sat range, excursions into the mountains are not surprisingly impossible with the current security situation. With no interesting sights there's also very little reason to visit the provincial centre of Hakkarı, a depressing concrete town whose population has been swelled by refugees and military personnel. ■ *Getting there: 2 morning dolmuş from Van, 4 hrs.*

**Yüksekova &
the Iranian
frontier**

At the time of writing the Iranian border crossing 41km to the northeast of Yüsekova is open to foreign travellers with the necessary documentation (Iranian entry visa), though it would be wise to check at an Iranian Consulate about the current situation before making the journey. ■ *Getting there: A morning dolmuş leaves Van daily on the 4 hr journey to Yüksekova, from where you'll have to share a taxi or hitch to the frontier at Esendere.*

**Van to
Doğubeyazıt**
*Remember that the road
is closed after 1700*

On the three hour journey from Van to Doğubeyazıt the road skirts Van Gölü before forking off northeastwards across dramatic, inhospitable mountain terrain scarred by immense flows of solidified lava. Be prepared to stop at several army checkpoints along the way where passengers routinely have their baggage searched.

About 20 km after leaving the lake you reach the pretty waterfalls at **Muradiye** with surrounding moorland strangely reminiscent of the Scottish highlands. They are worth a pause if you're under your own steam.

At Çaldıran there's a large army base and a memorial to the victory that Selim the Grim secured over the forces of Shah Ismail of Persia here in 1514. The Sultan followed up this great military success by expanding the Ottoman realm across Syria, Palestine and parts of western Persia. The contemporary village is pretty bleak with its proximity to the Iranian frontier making smuggling an important activity for its menfolk. Beyond, the road passes within a few kilometres of the border, a fact which accounts for the curfew and the numerous checkpoints, before descending towards Doğubeyazıt (see page 604).

Background

14

654

Background

655 History

685 Economy

688 Modern Turkey

689 Culture

689 People

690 Ethnic make-up

692 Religion

696 Art

698 Architecture

700 Language

700 Literature

703 Cinema

704 Land and environment

704 Geography

706 Climate

707 Flora

708 Fauna

History

Anatolia, the land mass covered approximately by the Turkish Republic, has been inhabited by human beings since the earliest times, with evidence from recently discovered caves and rock-shelters, such as those at Karain near Antalya, suggesting settlement by early hunter-gathers as long ago as 8000 BC. Such people were distinguished from their ancestors by their use of simple tools made from flint and other natural materials. The ochre-coloured shapes daubed on to cavern walls with iron-oxide rich soil constitute the origins of artistic expression.

The **Neolithic Age** (7250-5250 BC) was an important milestone in the history of man as a general improvement in the climate was one of the triggers for the development of agriculture. Small communities, like the one discovered at Çatal Höyük near present-day Konya, began to farm the land and raise livestock. These early farmers cut their crops with scythes made from antler and ground the cereals in stone pestles. At Çatal Höyük they lived in sizeable villages of rectangular houses, built tightly up against each other and entered through a hole in the roof. Inside the plastered walls were decorated with simple paintings and the family shrines included simple clay representations of the revered fertility goddess.

Seashells found at Çatal Höyük demonstrate that there was limited inter-regional contact at the time and this developed during the **Chalcolithic Period** (5200-3000 BC) into the earliest trade networks. Such interaction with civilizations to the east, particularly in Mesopotamia, had a significant effect on indigenous people in south and eastern Anatolia. Technologies such as the potters wheel and primitive metallurgy were diffused westward along these early trade routes, paving the way for the emergence of more sophisticated civilizations, like the one discovered at Hacılar near Burdur.

The **Early Bronze Age** (3000-2000 BC) in Anatolia saw improvements in technology, foremost of which was the smelting and working of metals, which caused the development of new trade routes. Wealth amassed through mercantile activities and agricultural surplus fuelled the rise of local dynasties and the increasing complexity of indigenous societies. An indigenous written language had still not developed by this time, so we owe our present knowledge to Mesopotamian cuneiform inscriptions and careful archaeological detective work. On the Aegean coast, at an advantageous junction of east and westward trading routes, the walled settlement of Troy prospered. Coastal trade became more important and this aided the diffusion of technical knowledge, with the potter's wheel finally arriving in western Anatolia during this period. The spinning and weaving of cloth was now practised widely and jewellery-making, in common with the other arts, had reached new levels of sophistication and aesthetic beauty.

Little is known about the Hatti, a people who dominated much of central Anatolia during the **Middle** and **Late Bronze Age**, however, under their patronage, a network of trading colonies developed from the beginning of the second millennium BC. These *karum* were established between Konya in the west and Malatya in the east, the principle colony found at Kanesh, near modern-day Kayseri. Thanks to the meticulous record-keeping of the Assyrians, who documented many aspects of their commercial and social lives, we know that there was a highly organized trading system in operation between Anatolia and Mesopotamia at that time. Tin, textiles and perfumes were brought west from the Assyrian capital with the donkey caravans returning laden with Anatolian gold, silver and copper. Despite their sudden departure around 1700 BC, the Assyrians had a major influence on the development of the area, having imported not just the first writing system, but also having caused the hybridization of indigenous Anatolian, Syrian and Mesopotamian cultures.

The Hittites   It was on these foundations that the Hittites, an Indo-European people who migrated across the Caucasus some time in the third millennium, began to build what was to become the first truly great empire in Anatolia. This process was started by the King of Nesha who began conquering many small kingdoms, adopting indigenous Hatti deities and adapting the cuneiform alphabet and the literary conventions of Mesopotamian culture. Around 1600 BC, King Labarnaş I moved the capital to Hattuşaş and established the so-called 'Old Kingdom.' Hattuşaş grew into a magnificent capital graced with temples, palaces and public buildings of unprecedented scale and grandeur, surrounded by a mighty fortification 6 km in length.

After a brief period of internal instability which marked the end of the 'Old Kingdom', the territorial limits of the empire were pushed outwards again by warfare and diplomacy to eventually include a vast area of central Anatolia and Northern Syria. These military and territorial gains were matched by cultural developments which saw the Hittite civilization flower. They inevitably came into contact with the other great civilizations of the time, and like the Hatti before them, the Hittites were influenced by both Mesopotamian and Egyptian culture.

The zenith of Hittite power and cultural advancement came in the late 14th century BC, with Hittite forces engaging and beating the Egyptian army of Ramses II. Syria was partitioned between the two empires and the Egyptian Pharaoh later married a Hittite princess to seal the relationship. Considering its greatness, the rapidity with which the Hittite Empire collapsed has been a subject of much speculation. Around 1200 BC, Hattuşaş was conquered and burned by the Phrygians, former vassals of the Hittites, an event almost certainly made possible by decay within the empire itself. Some have attributed the downfall of the Hittites to the rise of an aggressive state in Assyria. Others see the hand of the mysterious 'Sea People', whose appearance in Anatolia coincided with widespread destruction and was the precursor to 300 years of turmoil, often referred to as the region's 'Dark Age'. The destruction of the Hittite Empire occurred at the same time as Troy was captured and burned by the Greeks, marking this period as one of widespread change.

Urartu & the   Urartu is a name first introduced to history by Assyrian inscriptions of the ninth
Phrygians   century. Initially a loose alliance of peoples scattered around Lake Van, it was the threat from the Assyrians to the south which encouraged the development of a unified state. Within a hundred years the Urartians had risen to prominence, seizing large tracts of territory and subduing, at least temporarily, their aggressive Assyrian neighbours. They strengthened their capital at Tushpa (Van), embellishing it with palaces and temples, and expanded their empire to include much of east and central Anatolia. The sophistication of the Urartian civilization is exemplified by the beautiful jewellery and handcrafted artefacts, particularly bronzeware, which was widely traded in the ancient world.

At the same time as the Urartians, the Phrygians, descendants of those who had burnt Hittite Hattuşaş several hundred years before, established a kingdom centred on the city of Gordion, west of present-day Ankara. They built a state which reached its peak in the eighth century BC. Despite controlling most of west and central Anatolia, the Phrygian capital was destroyed by marauding Cimmerian horsemen, a blow from which the kingdom never recovered. The huge burial mounds at Gordion, raised to heights of over 70 m, illustrate the wealth and power attained by the Phrygians before this catastrophe.

The Lydians   Under the reign of King Croesus, who ruled over much of western Anatolia for 150 years up until 546 BC, metal **coins** were first introduced, an innovation which helped the Lydians take full advantage of their position on important trade routes including the so-called King's Road that stretched east to Baghdad. The Lydians subdued all the states along the Aegean coast, also spreading their control inland, bringing them into competition with the Persians and leading to their ultimate defeat by the army of King Cyrus.

The Lycians (see box, page 344) were a people who lived along the coast of southwestern Anatolia, roughly between the contemporary towns of Fethiye and Antalya. Despite some Hittite references to a people called the 'Lukka', who may have migrated across the Mediterranean from Crete, the exact origin of the Lycians is a matter for speculation. What is certain, is that they formed a thriving **confederation** of city-states which attained a high level of cultural development. Although the Lycians were gradually affected by Hellenistic influences, they maintained their distinctive customs. They also struggled valiantly and with considerable success to maintain their freedom, and despite coming nominally under the Persian, Greek and Roman yoke, they managed to retain a great deal of autonomy.

The Lycians

The Greeks originally migrated in several waves across the Aegean, fleeing what is thought to have been an invasion of mainland Greece by the Dorians. First came the **Aeolians** in around 1000 BC, settling in small and initially very primitive settlements along the northern parts of the Aegean coast, followed later by the **Ionians** who established their communities further south. With time these communities grew, forming loose political confederations, such as the Ionic league.

The Greeks & Persians

From the eighth century onwards the Greek city status prospered, reaching impressive levels of cultural development and wealth. During this **Ionian renaissance**, a wave of adventurers, lead by the Milesians, set out to establish colonies around the Mediterranean and Black Sea, while at home some of the greatest ancient minds were pushing back the boundaries of knowledge in fields such as astronomy, physics and philosophy (see box, page 283).

The imperial Lydian overlords in Sardis were largely benign, collecting their annual tribute and themselves benefiting hugely from the developments of trade and commerce in the region. Even so, the Lydian defeat by Cyrus was widely celebrated and the **Persians** welcomed as liberators. Needless to say it didn't take long for attitudes towards the Persians to harden as a series of oppressive tyrants imposed their will. This antagonism finally crystallized in the **Ionian revolt** of 499 BC during which the Greeks rebelled, calling in vain on their kinsmen across the Aegean for support. Without this aid the rebellion was doomed to fail although it was five years before the Persians under King Darius finally stamped out resistance.

In fact, it was to take 150 years for the Greeks to be freed from the Persian yoke, when in 334 BC a young Macedonian king, later to be known as **Alexander the Great**, crossed the Hellespont with a modest army and defeated the Persians at Granicus. This was the beginning of a lightning campaign which within a year had rolled back Persian rule in Anatolia, and ensured its inspirational leader a place in history. By 323 BC when he died, Alexander the Great ruled over a huge swath of territory stretching eastwards as far as the Indus valley. However, this immense empire didn't last long, being contested by several of Alexander's generals after his death.

Of these, Seleucus Nicator eventually gained the upper hand establishing Seleucid dynastic control over much of west and south Anatolia. The following period was marked by the Hellenization of the region and the rise of powerful and sophisticated Hellenistic dynasties such as the Attalids. They benefited from the huge wealth generated by increased trade with their capital at **Pergamum** also becoming one of the foremost cultural centres in the ancient world (see box, page 239). However, it was Attalus III, last of the Attalid line, who issued in a new era by bequeathing his extensive kingdom to the Romans in 133 BC.

Under Roman rule, Anatolia became the **Province of Asia**, administered by a proconsul from its capital, Ephesus. Despite numerous challenges, the most serious

The Romans

of which came from the self-proclaimed King of Pontus, **Mithridates**, most of Asia Minor had come under Roman control by the middle of the first century AD. The main exception was the kingdom of Armenia which was maintained as a buffer-state between the Romans and the heirs to the Persian Empire, the Parthians. Most of Anatolia thrived under the Romans with commerce and trading activity particularly benefiting coastal ports such as **Ephesus**. A rich architectural legacy, visible today at archaeological sites across Anatolia, was left by the Romans as a testament to the richness and complexity of their civilization. However, tensions were building between the Latin and Greek-speaking portions of the empire. In an attempt to alleviate these problems, Emperor **Diocletian** split the imperial administration in half, granting the eastern section autonomy under its own ruler. This was only a partial solution which did little to relieve the underlying problems and soon after the empire descended into civil war.

Constantine emerged victorious and in 324 AD he established Byzantium, strategically placed on the shores of the Bosphorus, as the new Roman capital. New 'Rome', a symbol of the eastward shift of power within the empire, was embellished with the public buildings worthy of an imperial capital, and was renamed **Constantinople** in honour of its founder. Before his death, Constantine converted to Christianity, opening the way for its adoption as the state religion later that century. Theodosius the Great, his successor, went even further by banning pagan worship. He also goes down in the annals as the last emperor of the united Roman Empire, for shortly after his departure from the worldly stage the burdensome Latinate realms were cleaved from the Greek portions of the empire and left to fend for themselves.

The Byzantine Empire

The Byzantine Empire with its capital at Constantinople was essentially Greek in nature, although its ethnically diverse subjects were infact governed until the time of **Emperor Justinian** (527-565 AD) by institutions and laws left over from Romans times. This was corrected by an ambitious process of **internal reform** initiated by the emperor and his formidable wife, Theodora, which saw the development of a new and fundamentally Byzantine code of law. The energies of the state were also concentrated on **empire building** with military action pushing the imperial boundaries outwards to their maximum extent, incorporating such far-flung territories as Syria, Palestine, Italy, southern Spain and Egypt.

This period was a golden age, although the lustre quickly faded in the next two centuries as huge swaths of the empire were lost to the barbarian Goths and Lombards in the west and Arab and Syrian aggressors from the east. The resources of the state were also sapped by **religious conflict** within the supposedly ecumenical empire, and subjects in outlying regions, such as Palestine and Armenia, were mercilessly persecuted for their Monophysite beliefs. By the beginning of the eighth century the Byzantine Empire had contracted to include only the Anatolian heartland along with parts of Greece, southern Italy and the Balkans.

From this withered and battered state, the Byzantines managed to regain some semblance of their earlier greatness under the competent rule of **Basil I** (867-886 AD) and his successor Basil the Bulgar-Slayer (976-1025 AD). The Balkan territories were ruthlessly reclaimed and the empire's eastern borders were also pushed back. With the rest of Europe thrust into the barbarity of the Dark Ages, Constantinople became a haven of culture and enlightenment, while its economy enjoyed a trade-led boom.

However, such rosy times were to be short-lived. The simmering conflict between the empire's bureaucratic elite in Constantinople and the feudal lords who administered the provinces manifested itself at the very heart of Byzantine political life, creating a court that was characterized by **factionalism** and endless intrigue. Not only did this channel energy and resources away from dealing with external threats of the time, but it also meant that the very source of imperial power, the emperor himself, was often just a pawn installed by one faction or another, and so totally unqualified for the difficult job at hand. In addition to the threat from marauding invaders, the aggressive trade policies of the Venetians and Genoese ate into government revenues at a time when the Byzantines were becoming increasingly dependent on foreign mercenaries for their defence.

The Turks first crop up in history in Chinese references of the sixth century AD concerning a people known as the Tu-Kiu who established a kingdom in what is today Outer Mongolia. However, considerably earlier Turkic tribes had begun migrating from their homeland on the Central Asian steppes, driven westwards with their flocks by a combination of climatic, military and political factors. Shamanistic and nomadic groups, collectively described as Turcoman, they came into increasing contact with the settled civilizations of the Middle East, resulting much later in their conversion to Islam and adoption of more sedentary ways.

The early Turks

The most significant of these Turkic tribes were the **Selçuk Turks**. Enlisted by the Abbasid rulers of Baghdad for their military skills, the Selçuks usurped the sultanate and established a dynasty of their own, taking up orthodox Islamic practices and, ironically enough, becoming a conservative force increasingly at odds with the other, unruly, Turcoman tribes. This problem was solved by encouraging the Turcoman westwards into Anatolia, where the marauding bands found rich pickings in the remnants of the Byzantine Empire. They met only ineffective resistance from the divided Christian forces, who were woefully ill-prepared for fighting such a mobile and motivated enemy. Under the banner of a *jihad,* or holy war, the tribes pillaged the main towns, but they also found converts to their heterodox Islamic beliefs amongst the people, alienated by the rapaciousness and intolerance of late Byzantine rule.

In 1065 Alp Arslan led the regular Selçuk army into eastern Anatolia as much to subdue the wayward Turcoman tribes as to attack the Byzantines, who he actually wanted to form an alliance with. The two armies did eventually meet at **Manzikert** (Malazgırt), in the vicinity of Lake Van, and the Byzantines were routed. This engagement, although largely unplanned, was of huge significance because it left Anatolia at the mercy of the Turcoman raiding parties, who rapidly penetrated west to the Sea of Marmara and the Aegean.

The following years were characterized by almost constant conflict, with the Byzantines pitted against the Muslim hordes, but also frequently against each other. Selçuk military commanders and adventurers joined the Turcoman, encouraged by the glory of becoming a *gazi* or 'warrior of the faith', but also motivated by the huge fortunes to be made from the spoils of war. Some Selçuk and Turcoman leaders created their own principalities in captured territory, shunning direct control from Baghdad and establishing their own local dynasties.

It was from one such state in south-central Anatolia that the Selçuk **Sultanate of Rum** grew. At its peak at the beginning of the 12th century, the sultanate controlled most of Anatolia from its capital at Konya, reaching a state of peaceful coexistence with its Byzantine neighbours. In spite of their orthodox Sunni pedigree, the Selçuks were remarkably progressive and enlightened in outlook. Scholars and religious figures, including Mevlâna, the founder of the Mevlevi dervish order, were attracted from across the Muslim world by the generous patronage and freedoms accorded by the Selçuk court. Artistic expression also flourished, with the period particularly renowned for its exquisite tilework and delicate carving, a common feature of the public buildings commissioned at the time. These included numerous *caravanserai* (see box, page 487), built at regular intervals along trade routes as part of the Selçuk's policy of encouraging trade.

The flowering of the Selçuk state was cut short by the Mongol wave which broke over the Middle East, flattening all in its path. The Selçuk army was beaten in 1243 at the Battle of Köse Dağ, after which the Sultanate of Rum became a province of the massive Mongol Empire. This mighty entity disintegrated in its turn and was

Background

From beylik to empire

In the years following the establishment of the Ottoman Dynasty the area under their control grew rapidly. Osman Gazi's tiny frontier beylik, or principality, quickly evolved into a state and then an empire covering large areas on two continents, and made up of an ethnically and religiously diverse population. This rapid development required the Ottomans to develop institutions to organize and govern the new realms under their control.

Initially living by the sword, the Ottoman bey (leader) led his followers from the saddle with no capital and no administration above the traditional tribal organizations which had persisted from the earliest times. Each warrior's allegiance lay with his clan chief, who would submit to Ottoman authority only as long as there was the opportunity of finding wealth – which usually meant plunder – and grazing in their service. Tribal matters were still the preserve of each individual leader, while decisions on common policy were taken by a council in which the Ottoman bey enjoyed minimal superiority.

Such a tribal confederacy was fine for governing a small, quickly expanding emirate; however, as the territory under Ottoman control grew, so did the need for new institutions. The Ottoman leaders adopted the title 'sultan', adding legitimacy and authority to their rule. They also began to distance themselves from their subjects with the gradual development of elaborate court ceremonies particularly from the time Mehmet the Conqueror.

The growing complexity of state affairs made it necessary to delegate duties to ministers, called viziers, who would meet in the Imperial Council, or divan, to discuss matters of state and make decisions. The divan was initially headed by the sultan, although as time went on they gradually removed themselves from the day-to-day running of the empire, and were represented at these meetings by the so-called 'grand vizier', who became the acting head of state. This was a position

replaced in Anatolia by a dynamic patchwork of mutually antagonistic Turcoman principalities and Mongol emirates, opening a period known as the **Beylik Era**.

The Byzantines meanwhile had been ousted from their capital by the ill-disciplined rabble which constituted the **fourth crusade**, and were destined to spend half a century in exile in Nicaea before finally recapturing Constantinople in 1261. Despite a brief cultural resurgence started during the reign of Michael VIII Paleologus (1258-1282), Byzantine society was once more overtaken by internal conflict which finally degenerated into civil war.

Against this turbulent and fragmentary backdrop a young emir by the name of **Osman** began building on the lands granted to his father by the Selçuk Sultan Alâeddin. This small beylik around Söğut, near modern-day Eskişehir, was the begining of an empire which would last for over 600 years and which would at its zenith occupy huge territories spread across three continents. It was to become known as the Osmanlı or Ottoman empire, after Osman I who established the dynasty which was to rule over it for twenty-one generations.

Having declared his independence, Osman I embarked on a rapid period of expansion which was continued by his son, **Orhan**, who succeeded in occupying the Byzantine towns of Iznik and Bursa. It was to the latter of these, beneath the slopes of mount Uludağ, that the capital was moved in 1326. During its early history the development of the Ottoman state was primarily at the expense of the Byzantines, and Orhan avoided causing trouble with his more powerful Muslim neighbours to the east. **Turcoman** leaders and their gazi, united by the desire for glory and wealth, rallied behind the Ottoman banner in a jihad against the infidel

Background

of great power that would occasionally eclipse the sultanate; however, the post also carried enormous responsibility, with many a grand vizier paying the ultimate penalty for the sultan's displeasure.

As the Ottoman state became more established it could no longer rely solely on its traditional military forces, the tribal Turcoman, a disorderly and at times threatening rabble who would serve the sultan only if their interests coincided with those of the court. Gazi Orhan began to create a salaried army of Muslim and Christian soldiers, known as the Janissaries, in their place. The Turcoman were pushed to the frontier regions where they could cause the least disruption while continuing to harass the enemy.

Under Murat I the devşirme, literally translated as the "collecting," was started. This was a periodic tribute of young boys gathered from the Christian lands under Ottoman control, who were converted to Islam and trained, before entering the service of the sultan. Most became Janissaries, although some of the more gifted young pupils filled positions in the administration or palace, where they often rose to the very highest positions including that of grand vizier. The prolific 16th-century court architect Mimar Sinan (see page 102) was collected as part of the devşirme, serving as a janissary before becoming a military engineer.

Across the newly conquered realms the feudal administration and tax systems inherited by the Ottomans were left largely intact. Land grants were rewarded to military commanders for their service and in return they were expected to collect taxes, maintain security and supply soldiers to the imperial army when required. The empire was divided up into administrative units the largest being provinces governed by a beylerbeyi (governor-general). Aside from land granted to such Ottoman notables, religious foundations, known as vakıflar, were established to construct mosques, seminaries, public baths and fountains using funds raised by local taxation and donation.

Christians. They moved towards the Sea of Marmara securing its southern shores before crossing the Dardanelles into Thrace. Their increasingly powerful position allowed them to influence the affairs of court in Constantinople, with Orhan playing king-maker and aiding the accession of co-emperor Cantacuzene to the throne. He was rewarded with the hand of a Byzantine princess and a fort from which to launch such expeditions in the future.

From this foothold the Ottoman scourge raided deeper into Thrace, occupying strategic forts and consolidating their territorial gains by 'turkifying' the areas under their control with tribal nomads. In 1360 Orhan died and the Ottoman mantle was assumed by his second son. As leader, **Murat** rapidly built on the conquests of his father, capturing the town of Edirne before moving on to conquer Macedonia, Bulgaria and finally Serbia, after the defeat of a Serb coalition at the **Battle of Kosovo** in 1389. Murat continued the 'Turkification' of the Balkans, securing control over newly acquired territory by resettling Muslims from Anatolia, a policy that profoundly affected the ethnic make-up of the region and has had repercussions right up to the modern era. On the other hand, no concerted effort was made to convert Christians in the new realms mainly because the head tax levied on non-Muslims was an important source of revenue for the Ottoman treasury.

By this point the Ottoman had encircled Constantinople, cutting off land communications with Europe and reducing the Byzantines to little more than a vassal state. This caused considerable disquiet in the courts of Christendom; however, despite an **ill-fated crusade** by Frankish knights and their Hungarian allies which was annihilated by the Ottomans at the Battle of Varna, no concerted response ever materialized to relieve the once-great city.

Background

The rise and fall of the Janissary corps

The origins of the Janissary corps lie in the reign of Murat I, when a force of Christian soldiers and converts was created to serve the sultan. Christian boys were also collected as a periodic tribute from the Christian realms of the empire, a practice known as the devşirme. *These youths were converted to Islam before undergoing training which prepared them for service as Janissaries, or in the Ottoman palace and bureaucracy. The Janissaries became an elite force, their discipline and courage earning them the respect of their enemies. Their raison d'être was to serve the sultan, but they also had strong religious beliefs and were closely linked to the Bektaşi sect of dervishes.*

The Janissary corps was organized into regiments called ortas, *with each unit living a tightly knit communal existence, receiving daily rations from the sultan which were cooked in huge cauldrons. This practice had symbolic importance, representing the Janissaries acceptance of the sultan's authority. In times of revolt these kettles would be upturned, signifying the corps' displeasure with the palace and acting as the prelude to violence.*

Janissaries under Mehmet II played an important role in storming the defences of Constantinople; some years before, however, they had rioted in the capital Edirne, forcing Mehmet, then a young crown-prince, to grant them higher wages, an act of appeasement which was to set a dangerous precedent. At the time the corps numbered 12,000, although by the 16th century it had almost doubled in size due to the military demands of Ottoman expansionism. The Janissaries still represented an effective fighting force, although their political power had grown to a point where they threatened their master, the sultan. The 17th century saw numerous revolts by the Janissaries, with several sultans and grand viziers killed by the mutinous troops. Furthermore, during the reign of Mehmet IV (1648-1687) the state actually came under the control of a group of Janissary leaders.

Following Murat I's assassination by a Serb infiltrator in 1389, Beyazıt I was girded with the sword of Osman. Also known as *Yıldırım* (Lightning) on account of his rapid millitary deployments, he set about strengthening Ottoman control of the Balkans before turning his attention to the troublesome Turcoman principalities in Anatolia. Using Christian levies along with cannon and muskets for the first time, he succceded in overwhelming the smaller emirates, also coming to terms with the more powerful Karaman dynasty. This brought western and central Anatolia under his control although it also precipitated the worst crisis in early Ottoman history; one which the growing empire was lucky to survive.

In the east during this time the Mongol leader Tamerlane had built a huge Islamic empire stretching across Central Asia and Persia to the eastern margins of Anatolia. Ottoman actions seem to have antagonized him, and his formidable forces swept across the region. The Ottoman army was overwhelmed near Ankara in 1402 and Beyazıt I suffered the ignomy of confinement in a cage, dragged behind Tamerlaine's caravan until his death. However, the Mongol leader seems to have had no designs on his new territorial acquisition, and having reinstated the local Turkic leaders, did little to consolidate Mongol rule before his death in 1405.

Despite the dissipation of the Mongol threat, Ottoman empire building had been set back at least 50 years. A battle for succession raged between Beyazıt's four sons and the future of the House of Osman was far from secure . After 10 years of civil war Mehmet I finally emerged victorious, to begin reconstructing the Ottoman Empire.

The reigns of **Mehmet I** (1413) and his successor **Murat II** (1421-1451) were marked by almost continuous warfare at the end of which Ottoman authority had been returned to large areas of Anatolia and the Balkans. Despite the decrepitude of the Byzantine state, which at that time occupied little more than Constantinople itself,

Political power was accompanied by corruption in the corps. The law of celibacy was surreptitiously abandoned and admission into the corps was widened to include relatives and eventually any Ottoman citizen. Janissaries also grew to dominate certain aspects of commercial life in the main cities of the empire. No longer constrained by the devşirme, the force expanded rapidly, reaching well over 100,000 men by the early 19th century. This didn't mean the sultan had that many fighting men at his disposal, as the ranks were swelled by widespread and systematic fraud. Salaries were claimed for dead soldiers and paybooks were increasingly bought and sold as a valuable commodity. Needless to say, the Janissaries also became less inclined to fight, particularly when faced with the superior weaponry and techniques used by European armies, and would often turn a deaf ear to the call to arms.

By the end of the 17th century the corps had become a reactionary element blocking reform, not only within their own ranks but also to the Ottoman state. Aligned with the clergy, they frowned upon contact with Europe and the adoption of Western-style institutions, condemning them as un-Islamic. They also refused to use new military tactics or weapons developed in Europe resulting in a series of humiliating defeats for the sultan's army.

By the time Selim III came to the throne the need for radical change had been recognized but Janissary intractability frustrated reform and the sultan was deposed in 1807. His successor, Mahmut, decided upon a more radical solution. His opportunity came in 1829, when an uprising by the corps in Istanbul was brutally put down by loyalist forces. In what became known as the 'Auspicious Event': the disgraced Janissaries were herded into Et Meydanı, the square at the heart of their district and massacred to a man; a similar fate befell garrisons across the empire.

---

the 'Queen of Cities' had continued to elude the Ottomans in spite of several attempts to breach its formidable defensive walls. The taking of Constantinople was to become the first priority for the ambitious young man who became sultan in 1451.

In 1452 Mehmet II began preparations for his assault on Constantinople, ordering the construction of the fortress of Rumeli Hisar, opposite the existing keep of Anadolu Hisar on the Asian shore. The fortress was completed in under a year and in conjuction with a naval blockade effectively cut the city off from seaborne aid. Western experts were also engaged to construct artillery pieces, including the largest cannon ever built. A huge army was mustered and in the spring 1453, with his preparations completed, the Ottoman army lay siege to the city.

The conquest of Constantinople

Despite being massively out numbered, the defenders fought valiantly, holding out for 54 days. Eventually, however, worn down by repeated assaults and an almost constant artillery barrage, the defences were breached and the Ottoman horde poured into the city. The defenders fought to the last man with the Byzantine emperor himself dying unnoticed in the mêlée. As a customary reward for their services, the Ottoman host were allowed to ravage the city for three days, after which the sultan, from then on known as Fatih Mehmet (Mehmet the Conqueror), entered the city to reestablish order and begin reconstructing what would become the Ottoman imperial capital.

The capture of Constantinople sent shock-waves through Christendom and confirmed the Turks as a force to be reckoned with. Although there were some belated rumblings of a Crusade, these came to nothing. For the Ottomans this was also a hugely significant victory, giving them a new capital with an imperial pedigree and an excellent strategic position. On the other side of the coin, the

Background

The Ottoman Sultans

Osman Gazi *(1280-1324): a tribal emir who founded the Ottoman dynasty.*
Orhan Gazi *(1324-59): captured Bursa – then called Prusa- and adopted the title of sultan.*
Murat I *(1360-89): moved the capital from Bursa to Edirne giving the Ottomans a base for expansion into the Balkans.*
Beyaz2t I *(1389-1402): called "Y2ld2r2m" – the Thunderbolt- on account of the speed of his military campaigns. Unfortunately, his swiftness couldn't save him from Tamelane, who defeated the Ottomans and precipitated an eleven year war of succession between Beyaz2t's sons.*
Mehmet II *(1451-81): the much celebrated conqueror of Constantinople known to the Turks simply as Fatih (the Conqueror).*
Selim I *(1512-20): conquered large parts of the Middle East, claiming the title of caliph after annexing Arabia and Egypt. Known as Selim the Grim in the west because of his cruelty.*
Süleyman I *(1520-66): Süleyman the Magnificent presided over the empire during its golden age as territorial expansion in Europe brought the Ottoman horde to the gates of Vienna while in Istanbul the poets, artists and architects were hard at work.*
Selim II *(1566-74): referred to as Selim the Sot because of his preference for*
drinking and cavorting with his concubines over dealing with affairs of state, which were left to his wife Nurbanu and the grand vizier.
Mehmet III *(1595-1603): the period known as the "Sultanate of Women" continued under Mehmet III as the valide sultan, Safiye, became the power behind the throne.*
Mustafa I *(1617-18, 1622-3): the first of several mentally unstable sultans, Mustafa was deposed after just ninety-six days, only to be reinstated and overthrown again the following year.*
Osman II *(1618-1622): luckless Osman was brought to the throne to replace his insane uncle, Mustafa I, however, his unpopularity caused a rebellion and he was executed in the keep of Yedikule.*
Murat IV *(1623-40): Murat became an increasingly cruel and tyrannical leader, eventually dying of cirrhosis of the liver brought about by excessive drinking.*
Ibrahim I *(1640-48): Ibrahim the Mad emerged after 22 years of captivity insane and totally unfit to rule. Power was wielded instead by his mother Kösem and the grand vizier, while he frolicked in the harem.*
Mehmet IV *(1648-87): the youngest sultan, Mehmet IV ascended the throne when he was only six years old, however, he subsequently spent most of his time hunting rather than governing.*

storming of Constantinople finally extinguished the shrivelled remains of the Byzantine Empire which had been in existence for over 1,000 years.

Having captured Istanbul, Mehmet the Conqueror didn't rest, but began an aggressive campaign of conquest. Greece, Albania, the Crimea and the Black Sea Kingdom of Trebizon all fell under his rule, while in the existing Ottoman territories industries were established and trading rights granted to the Venetians and Genoese. These policies were continued after his death by Beyazıt II and then Selim I, who is remembered for his brutal treatment of Anatolia Shiites and his capture of vast tracts of the Middle East including the holy cities of Mecca and Medina. However, it was during the reign of Süleyman the Magnificent (1520-1566) that the Ottoman Empire reached its heady apogee of wealth and splendor.

Süleyman the Magnificent Sultan Süleyman came to power without a struggle as all potential rivals had been murdered by his father to assure his ascendency. The 26-year old embarked on a series of campaigns which brought huge new realms under Ottoman control. During his illustrious 44-year reign, the longest of any Ottoman sultan, Mesopotamia was occupied and the capture of Cyprus and Rhodes gave the

Süleyman II (1687-91): having spent 39 years imprisoned in the Cage, Süleyman II proved totally incompetent to rule.

Ahmet II (1691-95): another long-term resident of the Cage, Ahmet II died soon after becoming sultan.

Mustafa II (1695-1703): far more active than his predecessors, Mustafa II went on several campaigns before suffering a humiliating defeat at the hands of the Hapsburgs.

Ahmet III (1703-30): the reign of Ahmet III, known as the Tulip Period, was marked by elaborate court ceremonies and blatant consumption. There was also a modest cultural renaissance as the empire was opened-up to western influences.

Osman III (1754-57): a repressive sultan who made outings in disguise from the Topkap2 palace to ensure that his subjects were abiding by his many laws.

Abdül Hamit I (1774-89): an unremarkable sultan who was preoccupied with the pleasures of the harem.

Selim III (1789-1807): a westward looking moderniser and gifted musician who was deposed by the Janissaries for trying to introduce reforms.

Abdül Mecit I (1839-61). Abdül Mecit did away with many of the out-dated Ottoman court traditions, moving the imperial household to a European-style palace at Dolmabahçe and supporting the Tanzimat reforms begun by his father.

Abdül Aziz (1861-76): a keen amateur wrestler, Abdül Aziz developed extravagant tastes- including a huge harem of concubines – which emptied the much depleted Ottoman treasury.

Murat V (1876): a gifted and intelligent young man, Murat lasted just three months on the throne having descended into madness.

Abdül Hamit II (1876-1909): an increasingly authoritarian, and some say paranoid, ruler, Abdül Hamit II dissolved parliament and established a repressive police state which was finally toppled by the Young Turks.

Mehmet VI (1918-22): under the control of the British forces occupying Istanbul, Mehmet VI signed the humiliating Treaty of Sevres. He also found time to fall in love and marry a Greek girl forty years his junior before being spirited out of the city on a British warship.

Abdul Mecit II (1922-24): following the nationalists abolition of the sultanate, Abdül Mecit II remained as the nominal head of the Islamic faith until the Grand National Assembly dissolved the caliphate too, sending the last member of the House of Osman into exile. He spent his last days in Paris dying in 1944 as allied forces liberated the city from the Nazis.

strengthened Ottoman fleet, under the celebrated Admiral Barbarossa, bases from which to harass Christian shipping across the Aegean and eastern Mediterranean. In the Balkans, Süleyman took Belgrade and in 1529 led an army against Vienna. After a long siege, the sultan was forced to admit defeat, returning to Istanbul for the winter. There was rejoicing across Christiandom at this stemming of the Ottoman tide which some had feared would sweep across the whole of Europe.

At home, Süleyman the Magnificent's tenure saw a golden age for Ottoman culture. Poetry and the arts flourished, while the sultan's second grand vizier – the first was visited by the imperial strangler – produced an extensive document setting out the Ottoman legal and financial code, an achievement for which Süleyman gains his Turkish epithet, Kanuni (the law-giver). The inspirational architect Sinan (see box, page 102) was also busy gracing towns and cities across the empire with his fine public buildings one of the most splendid of which, the Süleymaniye mosque complex, was built in Istanbul to honour the sultan. All this came at a time when increasing contact with the West brought ambassadors and other visitors to witness the opulent grandeur of the Ottoman court.

Background

Life within Süleyman's harem was dominated by the sultan's wife Haseki Hürrem, known to the west as Roxelana. A slave girl of Polish or Ukrainian origin, Roxelana's influence went far beyond the confines of the Topkapı, and she was the first of several powerful women to exert control over Ottoman government.

Ottoman Süleyman the Magnificent's death while on campaign in Hungary triggered a
decline bloody struggle for succession from which Selim emerged victorious. During the reign of **Selim II** (1566-1574) earlier tensions began to resurface within the very fabric of the empire which would limit its ability to adapt to change and ultimately bring about its decline. The first of these was the power wielded by the reactionary Janissary corps and the influence of the conservative Islamic clergy, which stifled progressive forces and led to stagnation within the empire. Debilitating court intrigue was also encouraged by a series of weak men at the helm. Demonstrating a greater interest in the joys of the *harem,* Selim II, known in Europe as Selim the Sot on account of his penchant for high living, relinquished control over state affairs to his ambitious wife and grand vizier in what became known as the Sultanate of Women. The practice of fratricide, in which a newly appointed sultan would have his male relatives murdered thus removing any threat to his position, was also abolished. In its place heir-apparents were confined to the Cage within the Topkapı Palace, from which they would emerge after prolonged periods of isolation ill-equipped to rule the empire and open to manipulation.

Not surprisingly the 17th century saw a series of largely ineffectual sultans come to the throne, their reigns characterized, if nothing else, by their brevity. An exception was **Osman II** (1618-1622) who recognized the need for sweeping reform within the ruling class but whose efforts were frustrated by a Janissary uprising in which he and his grand vizier were killed. The tenure of **Mehmet IV** (1648-1687) is more symbolic of the period: just six years old at his ascendency, power was dominated by various elements within the palace and ruling class until a revolt by the Jannisary corps deposed him.

Another fundamental problem threatening the Ottoman state was the nature of its institutions, which were geared up to govern an ever-expanding empire. By the end of the 16th century the Ottomans had run up against strong and technically superior neighbouring states. In the Balkans, barriers to further expansion westward growth precipitated prolonged hostilities with the Hapsburg Empire. The second unsuccessful siege of Vienna in 1683 marked the high point of the Ottoman Empire, after which the Ottoman army went into retreat, suffering several humiliating defeats followed by the **Treaty of Karlowitz** (1699), which confirmed the conclusion of Turkish aspirations in Europe. With the possibilities of earning wealth and glory as a *gazi*, it was increasingly difficult to motivate the Janissaries and provincial levies to take up arms. At the same time economic problems meant the Ottoman treasury was less able to train and equip a professional army to stand in their place.

In the face of slow but inexorable imperial decline, the reign of Sultan Ahmet III (1703-1730) was surprisingly a time of cultural enlightenment in the empire. Known as the **Tulip Period** after the flowers which were imported from Holland and Persia to grace the gardens of the rich, European influences increased markedly. Ambassadors were sent to Europe and particularly France to observe and return with new ideas, while Western experts were imported to advise on the modernization of the military. The first printing press was established in Istanbul, a hugely significant development because of its near-heretical status in the eyes of the religious establishment. However, little progress was made in tackling the causes of Ottoman stagnation and decline in the face of strong opposition from elements within the state and clergy; if anything corruption and factionalism grew worse. A disastrous engagement with the Russian navy off Chios, which virtually wiped out the Turkish fleet, and the Russian invasion of the Crimea, forced the Ottomans to sign the Peace of Jassy in 1792, confirming their territorial losses, but more significantly giving Russia the power to protect Orthodox Christians living within the Ottoman realms.

By now the Ottoman Empire had become, to use the words of Tsar Nicholas I, "the sick man of Europe", and during the next hundred years it lurched from one crisis to the next, relegated to little more than a pawn in the European power struggle.

The desire for reform lived on in **Selim III** (1789-1807), but his efforts eventually came to nothing, except antagonizing the Janissaries to the point of revolt. His successor **Mahmut II** (1808-1839) had more success, reasserting nominal Ottoman authority over the provinces and clearing the way for the modernization of the armed forces by ridding himself of the reactionary Janissary Corps (see box, page 662). Despite these achievements, the sultan was faced with many problems, perhaps the most serious of which was the **Greek War of Independence** which broke out in 1821. Unable to subdue the Greek rebellion, the Porte was forced to enlist the help of their vassal Mehmet Ali, the ruler of Egypt. His modern army had more success, until reports of the bloody atrocities suffered by the Greek population (passionately articulated by Lord Byron), galvanized Britain, France and Russia into action. An Anglo-French fleet trounced the Ottoman navy in the **Battle of Navarino** (1827), while the Russian army advanced as far as Edirne before a truce was called. The Sublime Porte was forced to recognize Greek Independence in the subsequent treaty signed by the warring parties.

While the Ottomans were trying to reconcile this humiliation, Mehmet Ali, unrewarded for his loyalty and service during the Greek campaign, invaded Syria before pursuing the battered Ottoman army across Anatolia. With Istanbul threatened by his wayward vassal, Mahmut desperately sought help from the Russians who checked the Egyptian advance near Kütahya. However, such support came at a price with the Ottomans having to bow to Russian demands for a closure of the Straits. War broke out again in 1838 when the restive Mehmet Ali rejected Ottoman suzereinty; British support this time helped the Ottomans, although they were forced to accept a total loss of authority in Egypt.

Just when the Ottoman Empire seemed to be on the verge of total collapse, much-needed internal reforms were initiated during the reign of Abdülmecit I (1839-1861). This period became known as the **Tanzimat**, Turkish for reform, as attempts were made to revitalize the empire and reform its moribund institutions. A key reformer was Mustafa Reşit Paşa who had spent time as Ottoman ambassador in both London and Paris and was familliar with western politics. **The Gülhane Proclamation** of 1939 set out an ambitious agenda for change, promising the modernization of many aspects of the civil and military administration. Power was increasingly clawed back from the provinces, tax collection and local security were improved and the military reorganized along Western lines. However, the European powers became even more involved in domestic politics and the economy, with the colonial-style exploitation of agricultural resources. The first railways were built by Western business interests to help export raw materials to Europe, while the first banks and a postal services were established using foreign expertise.

In 1853 a relatively insignificant religious dispute between the French, Russian and Ottoman governments blew up into full-scale war, with France and Britain entering on the side on the Turks. The **Crimean War** was concluded after much loss of life three years later with a Russian surrender.

In spite of its positive outcome, the war had strained the empire and slowed the pace of internal change, encouraging the emergence of a younger generation of reformers, called the **Young Ottomans**. A group of well-educated men, many with first-hand experience of the Tanzimat bureaucracy, they also believed in the importance of economic development, modern education and new technology, but advocated such reform within a more traditional Islamic and imperial context. Many

Ottoman Reform

prominent Young Ottomans, such as the writer Nazik Kemal, were driven into exile by a government crackdown, only to continue their work from abroad.

The health of the empire continued to deteriorate during the 1860s and 70s as nationalist uprisings in the Balkans were accompanied by worsening economic distress. Sultan Abdülaziz was finally deposed in 1876 by a group of bureaucrats led by Mithat Paşa and supported by the armed forces. He was succeeded by Murat V, who promptly suffered a nervous breakdown and was deposed. **Abdülhamit II** then assumed the throne, granting popular demands for the formulation of a **constitution**. Mithat Paşa was appointed grand vizier and headed the body setup to draft the document, a process which was completed by the end of the year with the promulgation of the first written constitution in Ottoman history.

Abdülhamid and the Young Turks

The new constitution was very Western in character, granting power to new institutions such as a council of ministers and an elected chamber of deputies. It provided for an independent judiciary and a bill of rights which stressed the equality of all Ottoman subjects, irrespective of race or religion, thereby ridding the empire of the traditional *millet* system. The sultan was confirmed in his position as *caliph* and also retained significant powers for approving legislation and dismissing the chamber of deputies. Abdülhamid also had a clause added giving him the power to exile any subject on the grounds of national security, an ominous forewarning of events to come.

As an attempt at holding together the crumbling empire and possibly even reviving its fortunes, the constitution was never able to prove itself. To strengthen his position verses the constitutionalists' the sultan dismissed Mithat Paşa and sent him into exile. Abdülhamit then moved against the fledgling parliament, dissolving the council of deputies which didn't reconvene for 30 years. Abdülhamit's rule became increasingly autocratic and, suspicious of the bureaucracy's loyalty, he assumed personal control of the government from his palace, Yıldız Saray. Dissent in the press was silenced by strict censorship and he developed a large secret police force and a huge network of informers in all state institutions and walks of life, evidence of what many believe to be his mental instability and paranoia.

While this was going on Russia had attacked simultaneously in the Balkans and in eastern Anatolia under the pretext of protecting its Slavic brethren. The Turks were forced into signing a treaty which recognized the independence of Romania, Serbia and Montenegro, and left districts of the east in Russian hands. This *status quo* was revised at the **Berlin Conference** a year later at the insistence of Britain and the other European powers, with a moderately better outcome for the Turks.

All this activity had aroused the nationalistic aspirations of other Ottoman minorities and rebellions broke out across the empire. In eastern Anatolia elements within the large **Armenian population**, who felt oppressed by the state and harassed by their Kurdish neighbours, began agitating for an independent state. Separatist groups confronted the authorities in an attempt to provoke a violent reaction which they believed would bring the European powers into the fray on their side. Unfortunately, this dangerous gamble went tragically wrong as the authorities brutally put down the insurrection. This was followed by horrific massacres of innocent Armenians across the country by the army, but also with the collusion of Turkish and Kurdish civilians. Despite widespread indignation and disgust in the West, nothing more than a flurry of official protests reached Istanbul.

As the health of the empire continued to worsen, opposition to Abdülhamid's reign increased. State repression was intense so, to avoid persecution, opponents fled abroad or joined clandestine organizations. The secret Committee of Union and Progress (CUP), also known as the **Young Turks**, was set up in 1889 by a group of disaffected young military officers who were in favour of modernization along Western lines, but hated European meddling in Ottoman affairs and the authoritarian nature of Abdülhamit's rule. The CUP established a network of **underground cells** and enjoyed particular strength in the provinces where state control was weaker. Salonika, home to the Ottoman Third Army, was an important base of support and in June 1908 CUP members staged a rebellion. With units of the Third Army behind them, the CUP leaders sent a telegraph message to the sultan demanding the restoration of the 1876 Constitution. Fearing for his own survival, Abdülhamit relented to the CUP demands.

The **restoration of the constitution** was greeted with significant popular support and in Istanbul crowds took to the streets in celebration. Restrictions on the press were lifted and political exiles returned from abroad. General elections in 1909 consolidated the CUP's hold on power and later that year the newly elected government deposed the sultan and sent him into internal exile.

With his successor Mehmet V on the throne, the powers of the sultanate were severely curtailed, while the influence of the CUP grew steadily despite a proliferation of political parties and groups within the parliament. CUP domination of politics and its increasingly anti-democratic tendencies dramatically escalated after the 1913 coup led by Enver Paşa. The government was transformed into a military dictatorship with power concentrated in the hands of three ministers: Enver Paşa, Minister of War; Talât Paşa, Minister of the Interior and Ahmet Cemal, Minister of the Navy.

This slide back to authoritarian rule was accompanied by disastrous defeats on the battlefield. Ottoman rule in the Balkans was effectively extinguished in the **First Balkan War** by a Greek, Serbian and Bulgarian alliance, with Turkish forces only managing to claw back Edirne when the allies began fighting amongst themselves the following year. Meanwhile expansionist Italy had invaded the province of Tripoli (Libya) and occupied the Dodecanese Islands.

As the dark clouds of war gathered over Europe in 1914, the government was split over the role Turkey should play in the impending conflict. Enver Paşa was sympathetic to the German cause, playing on traditional fears of Russia (which had joined with Britain and France) in order to win over those of the cabinet who favoured neutrality. A secret pact was signed on 2 August 1914 and with stalemate on the western front in Europe, Berlin pressured their secret ally to enter the war. Enver Paşa finally yielded in November ordering the Ottoman fleet – commanded by a German admiral – to bombard Russian Black Sea ports. Within months of **declaring war** Ottoman forces, already weakened after years of bloody conflict in the Balkan, were fighting simultaneously on multiple fronts in the Balkans, Anatolia and the Middle East. This stretched resources and manpower to the very limit and despite the dogged determination and courage displayed by Turkish soldiers, their position became untenable.

Destined to fight a largely defensive war, one of the few major Turkish offensives was launched by Enver Paşa in the winter of 1914-15. Aimed at dislodging the Russians from eastern Anatolia this ill conceived attack was an unmitigated disaster as the poorly equipped Turkish ranks were decimated by the cold, followed by a Russian counter attack the following spring. Armenian partisans also aided the Russians, giving Enver Paşa the pretext to order the deportation of all **Armenians** from Anatolia, citing them as a threat to national security. What followed was one of the darkest episodes of 20th-century history, with about one million Armenians perishing due to hunger, exposure and brutality during the forced march to camps in Syria. Despite overwhelming documentary evidence, the charges of genocide levelled at the CUP regime have been flatly denied by Turkish governments ever since and the issue remains highly emotive and politically charged to the present day.

In the spring of 1915 the Allies launched a major landing on the **Gallipoli Peninsula** which was intended to secure the straits and allow a naval force to bombard Istanbul, a blow that was supposed to knock Turkey out of the war for

The First World War

Background

good. What was meant to be a lightning assault degenerated into an infamous debacle which only ended after enormous loss of life when the Allied expeditionary force was finally evacuated in January, 1916. This was a very important victory strategically, but also psychologically, for the battered Ottoman forces. It was also during the fearsome battles to defend Gallipoli that a young colonel,**Mustafa Kemal**, distinguished himself, displaying the bravery under fire and sound leadership which would later bring military success to the Turkish nationalists.

Ottoman forces also successfully defended Baghdad from British attack in 1915, although they were eventually driven from Mesopotamia two years later. There was more trouble in Arabia where an Arab revolt aided by the British and later immortalized by the story of T E Lawrence, gathered momentum from 1916. By the end of 1917 Arab and British forces were advancing inexorably through Palestine and Syria, finally capturing Damascus after intense fighting. In the face of this onslaught Mustafa Kemal, who had assumed control of the Syrian front, began to pull back what was left of his exhausted army in expectation of the **armistice**, signed on 30 October 1918.

Under the terms of the armistice the Ottoman humiliation was complete. Allied warships anchored in the Golden Horn, and the Ottoman army was rapidly demobilized. In addition to the ignominy of losing all its imperial territories, large chunks of the Turkish heartland were also occupied by foreign troops. French forces advanced into southern Anatolia; the Italians took land along the south west coast and worst of all, the Greeks, who most Turks viewed as subjects, invaded the Aegean region around Izmir. Predictably, defeat also precipitated the collapse of the CUP government, with the three strong men, Enver, Talât and Cemal, spirited out of Istanbul on a German warship.

In April 1920 the Allies gathered in San Remo, Italy to set out their intentions for dividing up the Ottoman Empire and Anatolia along lines largely agreed in secret during the war. The **Treaty of Sèvres** was the resulting document signed by representatives from the warring parties including Sultan Mehmet VI. The treaty confirmed the partition of Anatolia and also granted the Armenians an independent homeland in eastern Anatolia, although it fell short of realizing Kurdish aspirations for a state. However, the terms of the treaty never became reality due to the emergence of a vigourous nationalist movement led by Mustafa Kemal which challenged the authority of the sultan's government and began fighting to eject the occupying armies.

The War of Independence The birth of the nationalist movement can be traced back to Mustafa Kemal's departure from Istanbul in 1919, ostensibly to take up a position as inspector-general of the army in eastern Anatolia. In fact, his intentions were to form a nationalist army which could resist the dismemberment of the Turkish homeland. On 19 May he landed in the Black Sea port of **Samsun**, an event held to be the beginning of the **struggle for Independence** and celebrated as a national holiday. A month later the nationalists set out their aims at a congress in Erzurum, where representatives drafted the **National Pact**. This document defined in uncompromising terms the objectives of the movement, including the establishment of an independent nation, free from outside intervention, in what was considered to be the Turkish homeland at the core of the Ottoman Empire. Territorial claims outside this boundary were relinquished, although, the protocol saw the requisite inclusion of Istanbul and the Straits in the future state. The National Pact was ratified at a second, better attended, congress in Sivas some months later, at which the Representative Committee under the chairmanship of Mustafa Kemal began operating as a *de facto* government. To avoid alienating the public opinion, the authority of the sultan was once again affirmed, although the nationalists justified their actions by stating that he was currently under Allied control.

An election called in January 1920 returned a large nationalist majority, but before convening the representatives gathered in **Ankara**, a small provincial town which was to serve as the nationalist headquarters and future capital. Even more alarming for the Allies was the approval of the National Pact in the Istanbul parliament, which caused the British to impose martial law in the city and exile numerous deputies. In a bold response the nationalists created the **Grand National Assembly** in Ankara on 23 April which duly elected Mustafa Kemal as its president.

Any authority retained by the sultan's administration in Istanbul was eroded by the signing of the humiliating Treaty of Sèvres. The nationalists refused to recognize the treaty, declaring that the sultan no longer represented the will of the nation and therefore had no right to sign such a document. A constitutional law drafted in January 1921 by the Grand National Assembly strengthened this position by stating that sovereignty belonged to the nation, with the nation represented solely by the new parliament in Ankara. The rift between the palace and the nationalists had now become irreconcilable.

While these political developments were occuring, the **military situation** facing the nationalists had become critical. Upon landing in Samsun, Mustafa Kemal had secured the loyalty of the Turkish army in eastern Anatolia commanded by his old friend General Kâzim Karabekir. This force was to form the backbone of the nationalist army, which was swelled over the following months by irregular partisans and unruly guerrilla bands. With great skill Mustafa Kemal created a cohesive force from these disparate units, while also devoting huge energy to finding the equipment and supplies needed to support them. Diplomatically isolated, the nationalists had to rely on their own resources, although some aid was received from the communist regime in Moscow. Nationalist resistance to the French in the south was particularly fierce, helping to dull both French and Italian enthusiasm for continuing the occupation. Both nations, increasingly impressed by the viability of the nationalist government in Ankara, were also uneasy about the **Greek occupation** of Izmir which had developed with British encouragement into a full-scale invasion of western Turkey. During 1920-21 the Greeks pushed east from the coast, driven by ambitions of reclaiming territory lost by their forefathers, the Byzantines. Several brave stands by the nationalist army at the small town of Inönü, to the west of Eskişehir, failed to check the Greek advance and in desperation Mustafa Kemal ordered a strategic retreat, buying himself time to prepare a last ditch defence at the Sakarya River, within a 100 km of Ankara.

Despite considerable opposition from deputies in the Assembly, Mustafa Kemal was given personal command of the nationalist army, and on 13 August the Greeks attacked. The **Battle of Sakarya** raged fiercely for three weeks before the Greek Expeditionary Force finally disengaged in the face of dogged opposition and retreated to new positions. Apart from the immediate success of having saved Ankara, for which the ecstatic National Assembly bestowed the title of *gazi*, warrior of the faith, on Mustafa Kemal, the nationalist victory also persuaded the French to withdraw from southern Anatolia. This released extra troops which were massed along the front for a decisive counter-offensive launched at **Dumlupınar** in August 1922. The Greek lines rapidly faultered under the determined attack, with the Turkish troops immediatly pressing their advantage. Within hours the occupying forces were on the retreat westwards, leaving a trail of destruction in their wake. The remains of the Greek army and thousands of civilians were hastily evacuated from **Smyrna**, present-day Izmir, ahead of the nationalists' triumphant arrival in the city on 9 September. In the mopping up operations which followed, alleged atrocities carried out against the remaining Greeks by Turkish soldiers and civilians culminated in a catastrophic fire that destroyed much of the city.

Although a great victory, celebrations were premature as the nationalists squared up against a large Greek army in Thrace and the British forces still guarding the Straits. This was a dangerous situation with the explosive potential for dragging Turkey back into conflict with the European powers. Thankfully a truce proposed by the British was accepted and in compliance with its conditions the Greeks pulled out of eastern Thrace. It was agreed that the British would remain in place until a permanent settlement could be worked out, a process which began in Lausanne, Switzerland. Invitations to the conference were issued to both the Istanbul and the Ankara government, however, Mustafa Kemal was determined that the nationalists should be the sole Turkish representatives. This forced his controversial move to abolish the sultanate, while maintaining the sultan's role as Muslim leader or *caliph*. There was considerable opposition to this from conservative deputies and members of the clergy, but they were eventually won over by Mustafa Kemal's forceful argument. In November 1922 the Grand National Assembly passed a motion separating the caliphate from the sultanate, dissolving the latter and effectively ending over 600 years of Ottoman rule. Some time later Mehmet VI unceremoniously slipped on to a British warship which transported him into exile on the island of Malta, while his cousin, Abdülmecid was appointed caliph.

The members of the nationalist delegation, led by the celebrated military commander and close friend of Mustafa Kemal's, Ismet Paşa, were now the sole Turkish representatives at the Lausanne conference table. With the principles of the National Pact forming the basis of their negotiating position, Turkish intransigence over many issues, but particularly the right to absolute sovereignty, caused the talks to drag on for months. Finally, however, the Treaty of Lausanne was signed on 24 July 1923 in what was a huge diplomatic victory for Ismet Paşa and the nationalist movement. The treaty acknowledged complete Turkish sovereignty within the country's present borders and ended the capitulations. Turkish claims to Mosul and the Hatay were rejected, although plans for Armenian and Kurdish homelands to be carved out from eastern Anatolia were both scrapped. Greek territorial claims were also abandoned, with Turkey and Greece agreeing to exchange most of their respective minority populations. Turkish sovereignty over the Straits was also recognized, although management of the strategic seaway, which was to become a demilitarized zone, was handed over to an international commission. The contrast with the humiliating settlement signed at Sèvres just three years earlier could not have been more complete and on 29 October 1923 the Grand National Assembly proclaimed the Republic of Turkey, naming Mustafa Kemal as its first president.

The Republican era

The establishment of the Turkish Republic was a hugely significant moment, but it was actually only the first step of a process in which its ambitious new leader, Mustafa Kemal, sought to rework the country into a modern, Western-style democracy. Over the next 15 years the pace of change was dramatic, as reform after reform swept away old institutions and eroded traditions, leaving no part of Turkish society untouched. Such a progressive agenda was not without its precedent, important periods of change had taken place during Ottoman times, but without the constraints of the empire innovation was much easier. The existence of an experienced bureaucracy and a functioning system of local administration was also a great boon for the young republic. Of course this is not to belittle the achievements of the era, or its remarkable leader whose energy and determination reshaped the country.

Mustafa Kemal had grown to view religion as a block to progress and his energies were initially focused on **secularization**. To begin the process of separating the mosque from government, and to consolidate his own and the Republic's position, he decided that the **caliphate** must be removed. He enlisted the help of the press and influential reformers to begin a campaign against the caliphate, spreading the message that such a religious institution would hinder the country's development. On the 3 March 1924, the Grand National Assembly passed a motion removing the caliphate and sending Abdülmecit, the last of the House of

Osman, into exile. This legislation was accompanied by a series of other laws which eroded the importance of religious institutions. The Islamic courts were abolished, as were the seminaries where students received religious instruction, while the administration of pious foundations was placed under the control of the prime minister. The post of *Şeyh-ül-islam*, head of the country's religious hiearchy and a possible source of competition, was also dissolved. These important steps were reinforced in the new **constitution of 1924** which set out the secular nature of the Republic, with Islam as its official religion, but sovereignty lying firmly in the hands of the nation, to be exercised by the Assembly in the new capital, Ankara.

A year earlier Mustafa Kemal had established the **Republican People's Party** as a broad church in which to gather the diverse elements of the nationalist movement. As the country's president as well as the leader of the only political party, Mustafa Kemal now enjoyed unrivalled power. This anti-democratic trend worried some politicians, including several of Kemal's staunchest allies from the early days of the struggle for independence. Two of these men, Kâzım Karabekir and Ali Fuad, resigned from the Republican People's Party and, in a move against one-man rule, created a rival political organization called the **Progressive People's Party**. This new party advocated true multi-party democracy along with civil rights and was viewed with great distrust by the government. The excuse to clamp down came in 1925, when a **Kurdish rebellion** broke out in eastern Anatolia. The military quickly controlled the situation but some elements within the Republican People's Party pressed for a strengthening of the government's already considerable powers and the draconian **Law for the Maintainance of Order** was passed. Under this new legislation dervish orders in the east of the country were closed down and 'Special Courts', set up to deal with the rebels, sentenced 46 of the leaders to death in Diyarbakır. Meanwhile, in Istanbul, several newspapers critical of the regime were closed down and the Progressive People's Party was banned, ending any effective opposition to the government.

Atatürk also used these new powers to push through other important reforms, the best known of which was the **Hat Law** banning the traditional red felt hat, called the fez. First introduced to replace the turban by the reforming sultan Mahmut II, the fez became a symbol of Ottoman society, embodying all the traditional and 'backward' characteristics detested by reformers such as Mustafa Kemal. The campaign against the fez was initiated by the President himself who, having made vague references about more 'civilized' headgear, appeared in public sporting a Panama hat. This seemingly innocuous action had a huge effect, scandalizing the more conservative elements of society who viewed such hats as Western, but more importantly, as un-Islamic. Following the example of their leader, members of the bureaucracy began to don the offending headgear and some enterprising merchants made a quick fortune importing hats from Europe. In November 1925, the fez was officially proscribed sparking riots in the east; the rioters were severely dealt with by the 'Special Courts'. Unlike the fez, the veil was considered too sensitive an issue for legislation, although Atatürk made his opinions on its use quite clear.

The government also moved against the **dervish orders** whose heterodox teachings enjoyed widespread popular support, therefore making them a possible threat to the process of reform. The tombs of sufi prophets, such as Mevlâna and Hacı Bektaş, as well as dervish lodges across the country were closed, driving the organizations underground.

The brisk pace of change continued in 1926 with the introduced of the **Gregorian calender** to replace the Islamic lunar calender previously used. Also of major significance was a complete overhaul of the **Turkish law system** undertaken that year. Ottoman penal and commercial law, already modified during the Tanzimat and Young Turk periods, were replaced by systems modelled on the Italian and German codes, while the civil law code, essentially Islamic in nature, was

Background

swept away in favour of the Swiss model. Polygamy was now illegal, although in conservative areas the practice would remain widespread for many years, and divorce could now be demanded by either party. Women and minority groups, such as the remaining Jews, Greeks and Armenians, also enjoyed complete equality in the eyes of the law for the first time. This was an important step in the **emancipation of Turkish women**, a process which some would say has yet to culminate. Woman began playing a greater economic role, taking jobs in new industries as well as the bureaucracy. In recognition of this social change women were allowed to participate for the first time in the 1930 elections, and just five years later 17 women were elected to the assembly as deputies.

Both Mustafa Kemal's style of leadership and the reforms he introduced met with considerable opposition, and in 1926 a **plot to assassinate the president** during a visit to Izmir was uncovered. The chief conspirator was a disgruntled former deputy who disagreed with certain government policies and held a personal grievance against Kemal. The 'Special Courts' swung into action, condemning the deputy and 15 co-conspirators to death, though several leaders of the People's Progressive Party were acquitted of involvement. Opposition had again been crushed and the reform process was free to continue unhindered, although the dizzying pace of change seen in the first years of the republic slowed markedly. In 1927 Mustafa Kemal delivered a monumental speech to the Assembly in which he charted the history of the nationalist movement and summed up its achievements to date, a task which took six days.

The first systematic **census** was carried out with the help of Belgian experts on 28 October 1927. According to the results, the republic had a population of approximately 13.5 million, a vast majority of whom lived in rural areas and were employed in the agricultural sector. The government clearly had a long way to go with its plans for economic development, while the census also highlighted the deficiencies in the education system with only one in ten Turks able to read. These findings gave new vigour to the government's efforts to improve literacy and education, and encourage industrialization.

During 1927-28 the government began preparations to abandon the Arabic script in favour of the **Latin alphabet**. Such a radical change was encouraged by the success of language reform in the Soviet states of Central Asia, where a similar switch had been sucessfully made. Not only would romanization bring Turkey into line with the other 'civilized' countries of Europe, but the new script would be much easier to learn, so helping to boost literacy levels.

The Latin alphabet was modified by a special commission to create a phonetic 'Turkish' alphabet of 29 characters, specifically designed for the special sounds used in the Turkish language. On 9 August the language reform was announced by Mustafa Kemal in Istanbul. With typical energy and enthusiasm he then set off across the country teaching the new alphabet in schools and town halls. Adults were forced back into the classroom alongside children, and by November the Assembly passed legislation banning the use of Arabic script in the public domain. Such strong tactics were quickly justified as jumps in literacy were accompanied by increases in the number and readership of newspapers, books and other printed material. However, such practical benefits were accompanied by strong nationalistic motivations for the switch. The new alphabet pushed the country westwards, creating a national identity which was tied less closely to its Ottoman past and the Islamic world. The alphabet reform was accompanied by moves to simplify and purify the Turkish language (see page 700) by purging Arabic and Persian syntax and grammatical forms. There was also a major drive to improve education through the creation of *Halkevleri* (People's Houses) from 1932 to serve as community centres hosting classes, lectures, workshops and films. The *halkevleri* also filled a political role acting as the lowest organ of the Republican People's Party bureaucracy.

Name hunting

Up until 1934 most Turks had made do without a surname. Only a few people of noble descent had family names, with the vast majority using their christian name in conjunction with the name of their father, their birthplace or even a personal characteristic. Names such as Kayserili Mehmet (Mehmet from Kayseri) or Kör Ahmet (Blind Ahmet) were perfectly adequate in a traditional society where people didn't move around very much. However, in a modern and increasingly mobile society the possibilities for confusion were huge, not least in the government tax and census records.

The official announcement in 1934 that everybody must adopt a surname was followed by a nationwide hunt for suitable names. In tribute to his achievements the president was granted the honorific appellation 'Atatürk' - Father of the Turks - by the National Assembly. His deputy Ismet chose Inönü after the town where he won a great victory in the War of Independence.

Some people chose a name which reflected a character trait, such as Ali Elibol (Ali Generous) or Mehmet Mutlu (Mehmet Happy); or an aspect of their physical appearance like Cafer Güler (Cafer Smiler) or Volkan Uzun (Volkan Tall). Other names were far less flattering such as or Cengiz Topal (Cengiz Cripple) or Onur Şişko (Onur Fatty).

Occupations were naturally quite common such as Emre Kasap (Emre Butcher) or Kaya Demircioğlu (Kaya Ironsmith's Son); names from nature were also popular like Hüseyin Şimşek (Hüseyin Lightning) or Fuat Toprak (Fuat Soil). Then there were the plain bizarre ones such as Refik Adıvar (Refik Has-a-Name) or Sevim Yılanlı (Sevim With-a-Snake).

Along with requiring everyone to adopt a surname, the government abolished the traditional titles which had preceded names: Bey (Mister), Efendi (Sir) and Hanım (Lady) were replaced by Bay (Mr) and Bayan (Mrs/Miss); however, the old honorific terms are still in popular usage today. So, you're just as likely to be addressed as Jack Bey, as Bay Smith.

The government's efforts to encourage the development of a strong national identity also came through the creation of official histories concerning the origin of the Turkish people and language. A particularly inane example was the **'sun-language theory'** which suggested that the root of all languages could be traced back to the sound uttered by the first man — quite naturally a Turk – when he looked at the sun. More plausible, but equally fallacious, stories gave the Turks a primary role in the evolution of civilization, tracing their ancestry back to the Hittites, among others.

The reform processes continued during the 1930s, albeit at a slower rate, with the resulting social and cultural changes stirring up popular resentment against what amounted to one-party rule. To address this, an official opposition party was formed in 1930. However, this experiment in democratization was quickly reversed as the new party became a rallying point for strong anti-government feeling.

In contrast to these domestic problems, Turkey conducted itself with great success in the **international arena**. Icy relations with its long-standing enemy Greece had thawed with the signing of a treaty in 1930, while the rapport between Moscow and Ankara grew steadily during the 1920s. The rise of fascist, expansionist regimes in Europe and particularly worries about Italian territorial aspirations after Mussolini's invasion of Ethiopia, encouraged Ankara to seek agreements with its Balkan and eastern neighbours. Security concerns also led Ankara to successfully petition the League of Nations for an end to the demilitarized status of the Straits. All this progress was aided by the non-revisionist nature of state policy towards its international frontiers, a principle enshrined in the constitution. One exception was the Hatay, where a large Turkish population lived under French administration in the mandate of Syria. In the run up to Syrian independence, Atatürk secured concessions from the French granting the area significant autonomy, while recognizing Turkish as one of its official languages. Later, under intense pressure from Ankara and in the face of growing disorder, the French agreed to allow a plebiscite in the region. The result of the 1938 election, open to considerable Turkish manipulation, was the short-lived **Republic of Hatay** whose parliament voted for a union with Turkey less than a year later.

After a period of decline **Atatürk died in 1938** from cirrhosis of the liver caused by heavy drinking, leaving the nation in mourning for a leader who had achieved so much in such a short time, shaking off the shackles of the Ottoman Empire and shaping the destiny of modern Turkey through his ambitious reform program. In just 16 years great progress had been made towards his goals of modernization and secularization, while the institutions to continue such change were firmly rooted. The reins of power were smoothly taken up by **Ismet Inönü**, Atatürk's deputy and close friend, who was confirmed as president in a unanimous vote on 11 November 1938.

The Second World War and Post-War change

Ankara's foreign policy aim in the run-up to the Second World War was to foster closer relations with France and Britain in the face of German and Italian aggression. Memories of the disastrous Great War, however, hardened the political will to remain neutral and the Nazi occupation of Greece in 1941 precipitated the signing of a non-aggression pact with Germany. Ankara's cautious attitude prevailed in spite of pressure from both sides, and it was only in 1945 that Turkey finally declared war on Germany in order to secure itself a seat at the post-war conference table. Despite taking no active part in the hostilities, the war had a huge effect on the country, disrupting trade and undermining the economy at a time when military expenditure was stretching the government's purse. Inflation and shortages drastically reduced standards of living and encouraged black marketeering. One of the official responses was an ill-conceived punitive tax imposed on wealthy merchants and landowners, most of whom came from the non-Muslim minorities left in Istanbul and Izmir. Deeply unconstitutional the 'Wealth Tax' displayed a further shift towards authoritarianism by the party and succeeded in alienating the remaining Greeks, Armenians and Jews.

The end of the war in Europe brought little improvement for Turkish security, as the country was now faced with a grave threat from her traditional enemy to the north. Russian designs had been revealed by captured communiqués, and with the Soviet occupation of Bulgaria and Moscow's renouncement of non-aggression, things did not bode well. Russian belligerency in the Caucasus, coupled with demands for a reappraisal of the Strait's status heightened anxiety and brought Britain and, more importantly, North America in on Turkey's side. Under the **'Truman Doctrine'**, economic and military aid began pouring into the country from 1947, as Turkey became an important partner in US-led attempts to contain the Soviet Union and prevent the spread of communism.

The conclusion of the war also saw the beginnings of significant **political changes** which were the result of growing dissatisfaction in the arbitrary and repressive nature of RPP rule. Repeated calls for democratic reform from inside the party led to the dismissal of several influential deputies, including businessman Celâl Bayar and Adnan Menderes, a wealthy landlord, who established the **Democratic Party** (DP). Campaigning for the 1947 general election on a platform of improving democracy and instituting the rule of law, the DP won a significant minority in parliament, going on to secure a landslide victory three years later, ending over a quarter of a century of RPP rule.

The first years of Democratic rule, with Adnan Menderes assuming the presidency, were characterized by general prosperity thanks to a series of bumper harvests and US economic and military aid. The Soviet Union was perceived to be the greatest threat to the status quo, so Turkey naturally gravitated towards the Western allies, also later signing a mutual defence agreement with Iraq, Iran and Pakistan. In 1950, Ankara sent a brigade to fight in the Korean War and two years later Turkey's position in the Western Alliance was confirmed by an invitation to join **NATO**. Due to its geopolitical importance, the country benefited from massive US support under the Marshal Plan, and along with military aid came loans to shore up the economy, and also equipment and expertise to help in the developmental process.

Relations with the **Arab world** were not so cosy due to Ankara's recognition of Israel, while Turkish-Greek relations deteriorated as a result of the worsening situation in **Cyprus**, where there had been an upsurge of Greek terrorism against British rule. Concerned for the safety of the Turkish-Cypriot minority after independence, Turkey advocated partitioning Cyprus; the tense atmosphere between Athens and Ankara was further poisoned by the anti-Greek riots which rocked Istanbul in 1955.

In the **domestic arena** the decade of Democratic rule had done nothing to improve democracy, rather the opposite. Having previously opposed anti-democratic legislation, once in power the DP leaders grew to resent criticism. Laws governing the press were tightened and the RPP found itself the victim of government oppression as party assets were seized and local headquarters shut down. A landslide victory at the polls endorsed such actions in the eyes of the leader, who became more confident and autocratic.

Nevertheless, opposition to the government was brewing within the DP and more importantly, in the armed forces which had been badly affected by the worsening economic problems. The 1957 election was indicative of the political climate: the DP lost a little ground but the official figures were never released by the government. Menderes resorted to increasingly populist policies while also stepping up state repression of opponents. Tensions mounted to new and dangerous levels during 1959 and elements within the army led by General Gürsel prepared to seize power. In 1960 violent student demonstrations gave the army the excuse it needed to step in, imposing martial law and arresting members of the government, including Adnan Menderes and Celâl Bayar, while the bloodless *coup* was celebrated by rapturous crowds on the streets Istanbul and Ankara.

The **Committee of National Unity** (CNU), made up of military officers and headed by General Gürsel, took over control having ousted the DP government and dissolved parliament. This was generally seen by the army as an interim measure to allow time for the drafting of a new constitution which would then be subject to a referendum. The new constitution confirmed many of the secular foundations layed down in the Republican era, but also went on to introduce a variety of new measures, including a senate and a constitutional court in order to prevent a return to authoritarian rule.

On 9 July 1961, the nation went to the polls with 62% of voters in favour of the new constitution. Despite achieving a majority, the military junta was shaken by the size of the 'No' vote, which was rightly interpreted as a vote of support for Menderes and the deposed regime. In response, the CNU ratified harsh sentences handed down to over 400 former DP members; Menderes and two other Democrat leaders were hanged. Instead of bringing the DP story to a conclusion, the hangings caused great bad feeling, particularly in the rural areas where Menderes was raised to the status of a martyr.

The elections of 1961 returned Turkey to **civilian rule** but the new constitution had changed the face of Turkish politics. General Gürsel resigned his commission to become the Republic's third president, a position which was now meant to be

1950s: Democratic Party rule

The 1960s: from military rule to democracy & back

above party politics. The RPP had failed to win a majority in either the senate or the assembly, only scoring a narrow victory over the second-place Justice Party, which was made up largely of former Democrats. This not only disappointed the military, but also led to four years of unstable coalition rule, with the army continually in the background prodding the various parties into cooperation.

The problem of **Cyprus** once more reared its ugly head in 1963 when Greek attempts to alter the constitution caused an eruption of inter-communal violence which threatened to drag Greece and Turkey into the conflict. A flurry of diplomatic activity averted military intervention and a United Nations peacekeeping force was given the unenviable task of controlling the violence. Meanwhile, tense relations between Athens and Ankara were aggravated by the expulsion of the remaining Greeks from Istanbul.

In the run up to the 1965 elections, the RPP-dominated coalition was toppled by an alliance led by the Justice Party, under its new leader **Süleyman Demirel**. Formerly a state water engineer with some business experience, Demirel demonstrated his popular appeal at the polling booths where the Justice Party secured an overall majority. This resounding victory has also been attributed to the 'Menderes factor' which saw grass-roots support for the Democratic Party fall squarely behind its new incarnation as the Justice Party.

Stability prevailed under the new administration as Demirel adhered to responsible policies. Despite unresolved problems the economy improved steadily as industrialization continued. Land reform and rural development were largely neglected, but conditions in the countryside improved due to large-scale migration to the cities and abroad. **Emigration** to Germany and other European countries had begun in earnest, with Turkish 'guest workers' repatriating valuable foreign exchange, as well as Western goods and ideas.

In the general atmosphere of freedom and **improved civil rights** the growing industrial workforce became increasingly politicized, while in university students formed associations to encourage political debate. In response to the growth of left-wing groups, such as the Turkish Workers' Party, the right also began to mobilize itself, causing a gradual polarization of Turkish society. Of particular consequence was the ultra-nationalist **MHP** (National Action Party), led by an ex-army officer, Alparslan Türkeş, which became involved in violent confrontations with left-wing activists based in the universities. Unrest was encouraged by rapidly changing social conditions and frustration at the economy; in addition, events on the world stage, such as the student uprising in Paris, and the Russian invasion of Czechoslovakia, also encouraged the disorder.

The Demirel government, its position weakened by internal disagreement and defections, was unable to control the dangerous situation, so on the 12 March 1971 the armed forces took over the country's administration in what became known as the '**coup by memorandum**'.

1970-83:
Political
violence and
another military
coup

The military tried to restore order by closing left-wing organizations, including the Turkish Worker's Party, and bringing their leaders to trial. State repression was intensified in the face of an upsurge of leftist terrorism, with the indiscriminate arrest and widespread torture of thousands of students, academics, intellectuals and trade union members. At the same time right-wing vigilante groups, often with the connivance of soldiers or police, targeted suspected left-wing sympathizers.

Against this backdrop of political violence and fear, a **government of national unity** was established drawing its members from all the main political parties. Military involvement in the administration was gradually reduced, until in 1973 the National Assembly rejected the armed forces' candidate for president, instead choosing Fahri Korutürk. The **parliamentary elections** of the same year brought victory for the RPP and its new leader Bülent Ecevit. However, the highly fragmented political scene – the

The Turkish military: guardian or threat?

Turkey has a large standing army of about 800,000 men, making it the second largest, after the United States, in NATO. Indeed, wherever you travel in the country those khaki uniforms are a common sight. However, quite apart from its pervasive presence, the army has also always played a central role in Turkish society.

Conscription brings the military into every home, as all able-bodied 18 year-old men, with the exception of university students who can defer, serve up to 18 months national service. Few look forward to the call-up, although, on the whole, the rigours, the boredom and, if you're posted to the southeast, the very real dangers of serving your askerlik are suffered stoically, forming a source of great pride once it's all over.

Since independence, and despite Atatürk's wishes to the contrary, the army has often been heavily involved in Turkish politics. This will hardly come as a surprise when you learn that six of the republic's ten presidents, including the first two, Atatürk and İnönü, were military men. Indeed, in the eyes of many Turks the military actually embodies the state, with the army standing as the protector of the nation. In turn, the generals see themselves as the guardians of the Kemalist principles of a secular, Westernizing state laid down by Atatürk.

In this role as national saviour the army has seized control on three separate occasions during the last 40 years when it felt these principles were at stake. Since the last coup in 1980, though, it has exercised its influence through the National Security Council, a committee made up of the top brass: president, prime minister and three key ministers. It was through this body that it achieved what's been called a 'post-modern coup', forcing the Islamist government of Necmettin Erbakan to stand down in 1997, while also pushing for a series of anti-Islamic reforms.

In spite of all this meddling in the name of democracy, and its convoluted economic interests, the army remains Turkey's most trusted institution, viewed by most Turks as a cut above the corrupt and self-serving politicians who supposedly run the country.

assembly was divided between five parties – meant a return to unstable coalition rule with small parties such as the fascist MHP enjoying their first taste of political power. Bolstered by their official position the MHP's paramilitary youth wing, known as the **Grey Wolves**, stepped up their campaign of intimidation and violence, attacking political opponents as well as members of the minority Alevi and Kurdish communities. **Attacks on the Alevi community**, targetted for their supposed left-wing sympathies, reached a climax in December 1978 when Grey Wolves went on a bloody rampage in the provincial town of Karamanmaraş. The local authorities did nothing to intervene and the violence claimed 31 lives before eventually being brought under control by the army.

The turbulent political situation was accompanied by severe economic difficulties brought on in part by the oil price rise of 1973. International relations were no less fraught as a coup backed by Athens toppled the government of Archbishop Makarios III in **Cyprus**. In response to the threat of annexation by the Greeks, Bülent Ecevit sanctioned an invasion and on 20 July 30,000 Turkish troops landed on the island's northeast coast and advanced rapidly towards the capital, Nicosia. A UN-brokered ceasefire only halted the fighting briefly and within two months the Turkish army controlled approximately 40% of the island, effectively partitioning it between the two communities. And so it has remained to the present-day despite considerable effort on the part of the international community to broker a deal between the two sides.

Background

On the international stage Cyprus was at least partly to blame for a cooling in US-Turkish relations, as an irritating lack of support for the Turkish cause from Washington was impounded by an arms embargo imposed by Congress. The Turkish government also played lip service to mounting domestic opposition to the US military and economic presence in the country, renouncing a bilateral defence agreement and taking over several American military installations. Things improved considerably in 1978 with a relaxation of the embargo; however, it was the dramatic **Islamic Revolution** which swept the Shah from power in neighbouring Iran the following year that put things back on their old footing. Turkey's strategic importance to NATO and the West was reaffirmed, particularly as the Soviet invasion of Afghanistan, also in 1979, meant a new escalation of the Cold War.

Back at home, the late 1970s saw an increase of **terrorism and violence** as right-wing death squads roamed with impunity and radical leftist groups launched frequent attacks against the state. The police force was itself deeply divided, some factions in open collusion with groups such as the Grey Wolves, and a succession of weak coalition governments was unable to halt the bloodshed. People increasingly looked towards the military, the only institution with the strength to restore order. Finally, on 12 September 1980, the armed forces under the command of their Chief of Staff General Evren took contol in a **bloodless *coup d'état***, the third military take over in two decades.

After seizing power the generals wiped the slate clean, dissolving all political parties and banning their deputies from re-entering politics. The labour unions were abolished and the universities brought under strict control, while efforts were also made to depoliticize the bureaucracy, which generally meant ridding its institutions of left-wing sympathizers. Under strict **martial law** terrorist organizations were ruthlessly hunted down, but other more benign groups also fell foul of indiscriminate military repression. Politicians, union members, intellectuals, students, teachers, and even members of the Peace Association, a group campaigning for nuclear disarmament, were imprisoned. An EEC committee estimated that 30,000 people were in custody at the height of the crack-down, and despite vociferous international condemnation, the use of torture was widespread.

Having energetically flattened the political landscape, the military took a small step towards re-establishing democratic institutions in 1981 by setting up a civilian cabinet led by Bülent Ulusu, a retired admiral and one of the masterminds of the military take over. This **nominally civilian government** was made up of bureaucrats, retired military officers and professors, but real power still resided with the four-member National Security Council (NSC) headed by General Evren. Unobstructed by partisan politics, Turgut Özal, who the junta had kept on as minister of finance, continued implementing a rigorous stabilization program for the debt-crippled Turkish economy. Foreign policy also maintained an even keel with relations between Turkey and its Western allies as a central concern. Later in 1981, civilian rule came another step closer with the creation of a consultative assembly, hand-picked by the military, to draft a new constitution which would be presented for endorsement in a referendum. In sharp contrast to its predecessor which espoused civil liberties and freedom, the **new constitution's** main aim was to ensure law and order. The presidential form of government was maintained with the head of state's position strengthened by a clause prohibiting any legal action against his orders. Also disturbing were controls on the press and the unions, which had their right to strike severely curtailed. Widespread criticism was checked by a ban on all negative comments about the document or General Evren but, realizing the potentially embarrassing situation if the constitution was rejected, the junta went on a major offensive to win over the electorate. Evren toured the country giving daily television and radio broadcasts, while his earlier warnings about not relinquishing control until the conditions were right left little doubt about the outcome of a 'No' vote.

However, the results of the **plebiscite** stunned even the generals themselves as 91% of the electorate voted in favour of the constitution. This was widely interpreted as a victory for the NSC and an endorsement of General Evren's harsh rule. Indeed for a majority of Turks the end – a return to stability and some kind of democracy – seems to have justified the means.

In April 1983 the ban on party politics was lifted with 15 groupings formed practically overnight. By October when the **election campaign** officially began, most of these had self-destructed or been outlawed by the NSC on the grounds that they were linked to formerd political organizations. Of the three remaining parties which fought the election, Turgut Özal's **Motherland Party** (ANAP), a broad church containing various political viewpoints, achieved victory. A former bureaucrat with extensive foreign connections, **Özal** was to play a prominent role in politics for the next decade. He was also to dominate the Motherland Party – referred to by some as the 'Turgut Özal fan club' – appointing friends and relatives to key positions and maintaining loyalty through generous patronage. It was this patronage, dispensed through a huge system of funds directly controlled by the prime minister, which bought support for the Motherland Party but also institutionalized corruption.

1983-93: the Özal years

After local election success in 1984, the Motherland Party's position became even more secure, allowing the government to continue unhindered with its ambitious economic programme. In contrast, the process of democratization was largely neglected and made little progress. Martial law remained in force across much of the country and a scathing report by Amnesty International highlighted continuing press censorship and the use of systematic torture by the security services, as well as the **denial of civil rights** for the country's Kurdish population.

Following the relaxation of the ban on pre-1980 politicians, the elections in 1987 saw several new parties led by old faces, including Süleyman Demirel making a come back as leader of the True Path Party (DYP). Local administrative control had also been clawed back from the military with civilian rule now extending across most of the country. However, despite these modest gains no attempt had been made to alter the body of repressive laws contained in the constitution. Indeed Özal's words,"Economy first, then democracy", left little question about where his priorities lay.

Despite support for the government being steadily eroded by high inflation and endemic corruption Özal announced his intention to replace Evren as president when his term expired. Ignoring a humiliating local election defeat for his party, he achieved this in October 1989 aided by an opposition boycott of the presidential vote.

Not surprisingly the opposition parties were openly hostile towards the **new president**, questioning both his integrity and his moral authority to lead the country. Özal's departure had also left the Motherland Party government weak and divided, unable to deal with a catalogue of problems facing the country. Among the most pressing of these was Kurdish insurgency which had been escalating in the south east of the country since 1984 (see page 612).

The **Iraqi Invasion of Kuwait** in 1990 therefore came as a welcome distraction from the tales of domestic woe and helped raise flagging support for the embattled president. Özal took personal charge of diplomacy offering the Western allies his country's active support. This pledge manifested itself in the closure of the Turkish pipeline used to export Iraqi oil. Allied aircraft also used Turkish airfields and troops were cleared for participation in the conflict. However, there was considerable domestic opposition to involvement in the war with regular anti-war protests and terrorist attacks on US targets. Özal clearly hoped to be rewarded for his country's enthusiastic support of the allied cause, perhaps through a reinvigoration of Turkey's EU application. In the event the country did less well, earning a package of aid from the Arab states.

More importantly the Gulf War gave Turkey a chance to reaffirm its importance as a stable, Western ally in the region. This came at a time when **the disintergration of the USSR** had altered the strategic concerns shaping Turkey's relationship with the West. A state visit by Bush in 1991 helped to underline the country's continuing importance, particularly in view of emerging concerns about the threat posed by Islamic fundamentalism.

The break up of the Soviet Union also left Turkey to develop its influence in the newly independent republics of the **Caucasus** and **Central Asia**. The policy of encouraging political, economic and cultural ties with their Turkic cousins – not without its precedent – was actively pursued by Özal and the new prime minister Demirel, who both toured the region in the early 1990s signing bilateral agreements and dispensing paternal advice. But Ankara's high aspirations were ultimately frustrated by its weak economic position and the emergence of Russia as the dominant influence in the region. Nevertheless, Turkey has developed strong diplomatic and trade links with several countries in the region, including **Azerbaijan**, and now looks poised to benefit from a pipeline for exporting Caspian Sea oil which is to be built across its territory.

The fall of the communist regimes in Europe presented Turkish foreign policy with additional challenges. Relations with the new democratic government in **Bulgaria** improved dramatically as human rights' abuses against the Bulgarian-Turkish minority, 300,000 of whom had been forced to flee across the border into Turkey during 1989, ceased. Things were less straight forward as **the former Yugoslavia** descended into bloodshed. Public opinion was aroused by the plight of the Bosnian Muslims and Ankara became frustrated at the lack of firm action taken by the international community against the Serbs. It was therefore with considerable ardour that the Turkish government backed NATO's air campaign against Serbia in 1999, aimed at halting the atrocities being carried out by Serb forces in Kosovo.

On the domestic front the moderately right-wing **True Path Party** (DYP) emerged victorious in the 1991 elections. Having failed to achieve the necessary parliamentary majority, Süleyman Demirel, whose fortunes had come full circle since his political exile following the military take over, was forced to seek a coalition with the left of centre Social Democratic Party (SHP). Despite disappointment at the return to coalition rule, this union was greeted optimistically and some steps were taken to address the Kurdish problem as President Özal abolished the law prohibiting the use of Kurdish in music and speech. However, efforts towards granting greater Kurdish cultural rights were frustrated by opposition within the government and **the death of Turgut Özal** from a heart attack in 1993.

Turgut Özal remains a controversial figure who has the power to evoke violently contrasting emotions in Turkish people. To his supporters he was an energetic Westernized leader with a strong vision of where Turkey should be both economically and in the world order. In pursuit of his economic aims he instituted radical change, which although painful in the short-term, was necessary for the future prosperity of the nation. Meanwhile, on the world stage his assertive diplomacy certainly raised Turkey's profile. To his detractors, on the other hand, he promoted all the worst aspects of capitalism, encouraging the development of a profit-driven, corrupt society in which a small minority with the right political connections made a fortune at the expense of the rest. There is undoubtedly some truth in both these views, but few could contest the fundamental effect, for better or worse, that Özal had on the country.

Towards the Millennium Shortly after Özal's untimely death, Süleyman Demirel announced his intention to become president, a move which forced his resignation from the DYP and the government. In his place the party elected **Tansu Çiller**, the first woman to lead a Turkish political party or to head a government. The news was greeted as a victory for

A veiled threat?

One of the most controversial elements of the government crack-down on Islamic radicals who supposedly threaten the state, was its ban on the wearing of headscarves by civil servants and students. A seemingly innocuous piece of patterned cloth used by millions of Turkish women to cover their heads for reasons of practicality as well as Islamic modesty, in the eyes of staunch secularists the headscarf had become an overtly political symbol of revivalist Islam.

Universities expelled thousands of teachers and students who refused to comply with the ban and there were ugly scenes on campuses across the country as some of those excluded protested at what they saw as an infringement of their personal freedom. Headscarf wearers rubbished claims that the veil was a political message, insisting that they covered their heads simply because of their religious beliefs. This assertion was supported by the findings of a student survey conducted by a human rights association, with the questionnaire also showing that few girls were forced to cover up by their families - another secularist allegation.

The headscarf cause was championed by Merve Kavakçı, an Islamist deputy who arrived at the opening session of parliament with her head covered. This infringement of the parliamentary dress code landed her in predictably deep hot water, as she lost her seat and her citizenship on charges of "seeking to incite hatred based on religious difference".

Despite continued resentment at the ban, the government has stuck to its guns, no doubt steeled by the rumblings of the secularist generals. Many commentators, however, insist that such authoritarian tactics play into the hands of the radical Islamists, handing them support on a platter.

women's rights and an important milestone in the process of social reform started by Atatürk. A westernised academic educated in the US, Çiller's appointment also met with approval from foreign governments and financial institutions. But these hopes quickly evaporated as she displayed her total inability to deal effectively with the bloody conflict continuing in southeast Anatolia. Her mismanagement of the economy also caused deepening distress for the man on the street as inflation topped 100% per annum in 1994. Added to her obvious incompetence were accusations of gross corruption which began to surface regularly in the press.

Fuelled by public disenchantment at the secular parties and growing economic hardship, the early 1990s saw the meteoric rise of the **Islamic Welfare Party** (Refah Partisi). Founded a decade before by seasoned politician Necmettin Erbakan, the Welfare Party had profited from a modest Islamic revival under Turgut Özal. Özal held that religion was an important part of the Turkish identity and that its suppression since Atatürk's secular reforms had been both unsuccessful and damaging. The Welfare Party became the mouthpiece for a generation educated in the *Imam-Hatip* (Religious Schools) which had proliferated during the 1980s, and its calls for a return to traditional Islamic values also found widespread appeal in the poorer urban neighbourhoods and conservative east.

Welfare achieved success in the 1989 and 1990 elections, but it was the municipal elections of 1994, when its candidates snatched control of towns and cities across the country, that signalled its arrival as a true political force. Most shocking of all for avowed secularists and the military establishment were its victories in Ankara and Istanbul, considered two of the most secular and progressive cities in the country. Once in power, the Islamists impressed many people with their efficient management of municipal government, while Çiller's sleaze-splattered administration limped from one scandal to the next. The success of the Welfare Party continued in the 1995 general election when it became the largest party in

Background

the assembly, although without a significant majority it was kept out of government by an unholy marriage between Çiller and the uninspiring Motherland boss Mesut Yılmaz. This coalition soon foundered but to save herself from criminal investigation on corruption charges, Çiller shamelessly formed a new government with her avowed enemies in the Welfare Party. This abrupt U-turn angered even her staunchest supporters and to the horror of Turkish secularists, including the military top brass, it opened the way for Erbakan to become the first Islamist prime minister. Once in government, however, the Welfare Party's Islamic agenda was watered down, though not enough for the generals, whose veiled threats of intervention were enough to cause the coalition's collapse in 1997.

In the endless merry-go-round of Turkish politics, it was left to the dour Mesut Yılmaz to form a coalition with the left-wing DSP, signalling Bülent Ecevit's return from the political wilderness. The coalition made reasonable progress in key areas such as the economy and Yılmaz also bent to pressure from the military to crack down on the Islamic movement, purging Welfare supporters from universities, schools and the civil service (see box, page 683) and bringing charges against the party itself in the Constitutional Courts. These proceedings eventually led to the closure of the Welfare Party in 1998 and a lifetime political ban on its leader, although other Islamist deputies promptly rallied behind a new banner, the Virtue Party. Encouraged by the generals, the government went on to attack the *Imam-hatip* religious schools which were seen as promoting the spread of radical Islam. This was achieved by extending the length of compulsory state education from five to eight years, thereby restricting the schools' intake to students over fourteen – by which time children would be less vulnerable to Islamic 'brainwashing'.

The claims of sleaze finally caught up with the prime minister in November 1998, when he was censured by the assembly for his role in the crooked sell-off of a state-owned bank for US$600 million. That left Ecevit, still untainted by charges of corruption, to act as caretaker prime minister until the elections scheduled for early 1999. Buoyed by his clean and nationalistic credentials, being the man who ordered Turkish troops into Cyprus in 1976, Ecevit's campaign also benefited from the capture of the PKK leader, **Abdullah Öcalan**. Considered to be public enemy number one by most Turks, Öcalan had been on the run since being forced from Syria by intense diplomatic and military pressure. Some weeks later he resurfaced in Italy, where authorities refused to extradite him to face what many in Europe believed would be an unfair trial and a possible death sentence. Angry protests by both Turks and Kurds across Europe proved that Öcalan had become a political hot potato and after floating the idea of sending him to Germany to face terrorism charges there, he was freed. Back on the run, he was finally captured in Kenya by Turkish special forces. His return was greeted with huge celebrations across Turkey, while European capitals witnessed a wave of counter-demonstrations by PKK supporters. A high-security courthouse was rapidly prepared on an island in the Sea of Marmara and the Turkish public gleefully watched as the sensational trial unfolded. From his bullet-proof glass stand, the PKK leader struck a conciliatory tone, calling his fighters down from the mountains and urging the resolution of the Kurdish issue through political means. But this was dismissed by many Turks as a ploy to save his own neck. During the lengthy trial, televised live to an enthralled nation, he revealed the inner workings of the PKK, including confirmation of the long-suspected link with Athens. The trial concluded with Öcalan condemned to death, a sentence ratified by the Supreme Court later in 1999. Only a parliamentary vote now stands between the PKK chief and the gallows, but despite popular opinion being strongly behind the execution, pressure from abroad and particularly the EU, which finally agreed on a timetable for Turkey's entry into Europe, could sway the final decision.

Riding high on the publicity created by the Öcalan affair, Ecevit's DSP was catapulted to victory in the April elections. More surprising was the success of the nationalist MHP which, having cleaned up an image tainted by the political violence of the 1970s and other illegal activities, also benefited from the wave of nationalistic sentiment sweeping the country to come second in the polls. So it was left to the 73-year-old political survivor, Bülent Ecevit, to form a government with the nationalist MHP, an unlikely marriage even by Turkish standards.

The new government was faced not only with the still-smouldering conflict in the southeast and continuing economic distress, but also a natural disaster of immense proportions. In the early hours of August a huge earthquake measuring 7.3 on the Richter scale struck northwest Turkey (see box, page 173). Centred between the towns of Izmit and Adapazarı, the quake caused widespread devastation, though the true scale of the disaster only became apparent in the following days; reliable sources now put the death toll at over 40,000. However, one positive thing to emerged from the disaster was a thaw in Turkish-Greek relations, as the generosity and depth of feeling shown by the Greek nation in the aftermath surprised its neighbours.

Economy

At independence in 1923 the republican government inherited a backrupted country ruined by years of war. The economy was overwhelmingly agricultural and Ottoman industry had failed to develop in the face of foreign competition and the Capitulations – advantageous commercial agreements secured by the Great Powers. The loss of Ottoman territory at the end of the war had also cut Turkey off from its traditional markets, while the Armenian pogroms and Greek emigration had robbed it of its entrepreneurial class, as well as valuable capital and expertise.

Despite these dire beginnings the Turkish economy achieved some success in the 1920s as low tariffs – a requirement of the Treaty of Lausanne – encouraged trade, and limited investment was secured by public and private concerns. However, impatience at the slow pace of progress led the state to assume a more active part in organizing and running the economy, a policy which became known as **étatism**. Launched by the government in 1931, this strategy drew on the example of State Planning in the Soviet Union, but was also motivated by a strong desire to maintain Turkey's economic independence. The primary concern was rapid industrialization and under the first Five-Year Plan, from 1934 high tariffs were imposed and domestic production stimulated by a state-led 'buy Turkish' campaign. The government also began establishing State Economic Enterprises (SEEs) in key areas of the economy such as manufacturing, mining and infrastructure.

Despite the agricultural sector constituting by far the most important part of the economy and employing most of the workforce it was generally neglected. Nevertheless it achieved a remarkable recovery, although the collapse of world prices brought on by the Great Depression led to widespread stagnation and a drop in national prosperity.

Etatism achieved some success and, as the world's economic climate improved in the mid-1930s, Turkey's economy grew by up to 6% per annum. The 1940s, however, brought stagnation as government investment was channeled into defence, and foreign trade all but ceased.

The post-war Turkish economy benefited handsomely from its strategic alliance with the anti-Communist West. Under the Marshall Plan investment and aid poured into the country helping to stimulate growth in the industrial and agriculture sectors. Thousands of tractors were imported under a US credit scheme and the area under cultivation expanded rapidly, particularly on the central plateau where vast new areas were brought under the plough. Output grew impressively, though

The early years of the Republic

1945-1979

Background

much of the new land proved to be marginal at best, resulting in low yields and a disastrous increase in soil erosion which by 1970 affected 50% of all farmland.

Even so, the commercialization of the agricultural economy brought about by mechanization and improved transportation resulted in a rise in rural incomes. This stimulated demand for consumer goods which contributed to the rapid development of Turkish industry during the period. Annual growth rates of up to 8.6% were achieved in the sector, which between 1950 and 1979 doubled its share of GDP to 25%.

The head-long dash for industrialization also created major problems in the Turkish economy, some of which are still only partially resolved today. Protected by subsidies and tariff barriers, the industrial sector, though particularly the SSEs, were woefully inefficient. Under the policy of import-substitution Turkish companies remained safe from the very international competition which would have forced the much-needed increases in productivity. Ironically, such autarkic policy also required ever-larger imports of plant machinery and components which in turn negatively affected the country's balance of trade. The real crunch, however, came with the oil price rises of the 1970s as the economy's dependence on imported petroleum was cruelly exposed. Inflation spiralled and unemployment reached about 30%, stoking the flames of an already volatile political scene. With the contraction of the country's export market, the trade deficit ballooned to $4 billion and state bankruptcy loomed as foreign creditors refused to grant further loans. Emergency measures, including a 10% devaluation of the Turkish Lira, were brought in by the government of Süleyman Demirel narrowly averting disaster. However, by December 1977 things had continued to worsen and the new prime minister, Bülent Ecevit, was forced to implement an IMF-approved stability program, paving the way for a rescheduling of Turkey's debt and a much-needed international loan.

Unfortunately, the austerity programme failed to improve matters as industrial output and exports continued to decline and the country had to be bailed out again by international financial institutions. Another change of government in November 1979 brought another stabilization scheme, this time to be implemented by a Western-educated economist named Turgut Özal. He'd barely started the job, though, when the worsening political instability and violence precipitated a military coup.

The Özal years: 1980-1993 Following the 1980 coup the military junta made Turgut Özal minister for economic affairs and unhindered by party politics he began implementing a wide-reaching reform programme. His policies aimed to liberalize the Turkish economy with specific measures to reduce the state's involvement in the economy; decrease subsidies and price controls; establish a realistic exchange rate and foster exports and foreign investment. The liberalization program essentially involved a radical reorientation from import substitution to an outward-looking, export-driven economy. Attempts were made to increase efficiency in the SSEs by freeing prices, which until that time had been set by government, and managers were granted more autonomy. Özal also mooted scrapping the monopolies held by many SSEs.

By 1983 when Özal became prime minister, the reforms were starting to have some success at boosting trade and improving the country's balance of payments. Helped by a devalued currency the manufacturing and agricultural sectors became more competitive and exports rose accordingly. Despite sharp cutbacks in public expenditure, by 1981 the economy had also returned to positive growth, registering a 3% annual rise in GNP between 1981 and 1985. Foreign investment began to trickle cautiously into the economy and joint ventures were set up with international firms. This progress helped Turkey regain its creditworthiness, allowing it to borrow on the international capital markets.

Unemployment and inflation were more stubborn problems which challenged the Özal team throughout the decade. In 1984 the official proportion of the

Background

workforce without a job was 13%, although the true figure was undoubtedly much higher; by 1987 inflation was running at 70% per annum and was seriously affecting the government's popularity.

The 1991 Gulf War hit the economy hard as UN sanctions put an end to lucrative Turkish-Iraqi trade. Two pipelines which transported Iraqi oil across the country to the Mediterranean coast were also closed, robbing the country of an estimated US$300-US$500 million per year in revenues, in addition to part of its domestic oil supply. However with the help of a compensation package the economy bounced back.

Turgut Özal's death in 1993 brough to a close a period of immense economic change. The Özal years had seen a fundamental shift in government policy with steps taken towards the creation of a free-market economy. The industrial sector had benefited from a more liberalized trade regime and a vigorous private sector had emerged. A cornerstone of Özal's reform program had been export-led growth and between 1979 and 1988 exports quadrupled. Foreign investment had also increased significantly, although the external debt had grown to over $65 billion putting strain on the country's balance of payments. Despite good intentions there had also been very limited progress at reducing the bloated state sector with loss-making SSEs continuing to burden the public finances. As previously stated, unemployment and inflation remained high and the government's policies were also widely blamed for widening the gap between rich and poor.

The period from 1993 to 2000 proved a turbulent one for the Turkish economy, in part reflecting the inconsistencies and mismanagement of a string of weak coalition governments. Despite her credentials as a Western-educated economist, the government of Tansu Çiller plunged the country into **crisis** by failing to restrain government expenditure with generous pay awards for civil servants and investment in state-run industry. These measures stoked inflation which reached 73% in mid-1993, while the overvalued lira slowed exports and built up a hefty trade deficit. The government borrowed heavily to cover its budgetary shortfalls and the country's external debt mushroomed to US$65 billion by the end of the year. At home growing concern over the handling of the economy led to a steady 'dollarization' of the economy as people changed their savings into hard currency. However, it was the downgrading of the country's hard-earned credit rating which confirmed these worries, causing **a collapse of the exchange rate** as capital fled the market. Despite efforts to stop its precipitous slide, the lira lost over 75% of its value against the dollar in just a few months and the country went into recession. Somewhat belatedly an austerity program was introduced, securing a standby loan from the IMF on the face of government pledges to reduce expenditure, raise tax revenue and speed up the sell-off of SSEs.

The financial crisis resulted in a drop in GNP for 1994, though the economy returned to positive growth by the following year. A more immediate problem for Turkish people, however, was **continuing high inflation** which gravely affected those on fixed salaries, such as teachers, doctors and civil servants. With consumer price inflation topping 99% in 1997, this group saw their incomes steadily eroded as biannual pay increases failed to keep pace with the rising cost of living. Growing hardship and poverty in general helped the Islamist Refah Party achieve a victory at the polls.

Turkey's continuing political instability proved a disincentive to badly needed foreign investment, as did the continuing frustration of its attempts to join the EU. On a more positive note a customs union with the EU began to produce benefits as it contributed to a steady increase in trade.

Unfortunately, growing optimism about the country's prospects was dealt a severe blow by the 1998 **Asian financial crisis** which halved the value of the

Economic progress: 1993-2000

Background

Istanbul Stock Exchange overnight and battered investor confidence in developing markets. The subsequent meltdown of the Russian economy – Turkey's second largest export market after Germany – also hit the economy hard. However, worse was to come as the **1999 earthquake** levelled a heavily industrialized area which accounted for a third of the country's gross domestic product. The disaster stretched public finances to the limit with huge state spending on the clear-up demanding the introduction of emergency taxes such as one on mobile telephones. It also forced the government to agree to yet another IMF-sponsored reform program, freeing loans of US$4 billion over three years.

Modern Turkey

Despite such an inauspicious start to the new millennium, with the country still reeling after its worst natural disaster in modern times, Turkey has made huge progress since the foundation of the republic 77 years ago. This period has witnessed the country's transformation from a traditional agrarian society into a modern industrial one. Over half the population now lives in cities, with this proportion set to rise rapidly as country-folk continue to drift towards the cities in search of work and a better standard of living. The last two decades, in particular, have witnessed economic liberalization which has encouraged growth and the emergence of a dynamic private sector competing successfully on the world stage.

As in other developing countries, however, economic development has not been without its costs. Detractors point to growing disparities between rich and poor, and to the fact that the benefits of economic growth have bypassed a large segment of the population who continue to live in poverty. Glaring inequalities have also emerged between the regions with the underdeveloped east of the country lagging far behind the more industrialized west. Widespread unemployment is also a persistent problem with the growth of a large black economy of petty traders and manual workers, many of whom barely eke-out an existence. The government has also shown itself willing to ignore environmental concerns and the destruction of its historical heritage in the search for economic growth.

The future performance of the economy depends largely on the government sticking to a comprehensive three-year reform plan worked out with the IMF. Two years into this programme the signs look promising with the government continuing to meet its monthly inflation targets and privatization. However, tough choices lie ahead, such as the need to trim the bloated bureaucracy and end support for inefficient, loss-making state industries – dubbed 'black-holes' on account of their insatiable appetite for government funds.

The present administration has already shown some willingness to curb endemic corruption, though not enough for the new crusading president, Ahmet Sezer, who precipitated a crisis in February 2001 by accusing the Ecevit government of dragging its feet in the fight against sleaze. A heated argument between Ecevit and Sezer sent a tidal wave through the Turkish economy as foreign investors withdrew from the Turkish economy in droves, siphoning off an estimated US$8 billion from the Central Bank reserves and sending the Istanbul Stock Exchange crashing 18% – its biggest ever single-day loss. The banking system was thrown into temporary chaos and the IMF – sponsored reform programme appeared to be in jeopardy. However, as political tempers have calmed, the battered economy looks like stabilizing, while the average Turk has been left with even less faith in the politicians who run the country.

On the Kurdish front, initial optimism that the capture of Öcalan might lead the conflict into a new, more positive phase has been disappointed. Although the tempo of violence has decreased markedly since a ceasefire in 1999, sporadic clashes still occur between the security services and the PKK. Meanwhile, no headway has been made towards finding a political solution to the underlying causes of the conflict. Instead the only Kurdish political party, HADEP, which the authorities insist has 'organic links' to the PKK, finds itself subjected to state harassment and repression. Revelations have also recently surfaced about support from elements of the establishment for Hizbullah, an armed Islamic group which liquidated hundreds of suspected PKK sympathizers during the 1980s and 1990s. Looking on the bright side, the government's massive investment in the South East Anatolia Project (GAP) is improving standards of living in the Kurdish heartland, while many Kurds are privately pinning their hopes on Turkey's eventual entry into the EU, when they'll be guaranteed their cultural rights and freedom of expression.

So how far off is Turkey's entry into the European Union? Having lodged its formal application over 14 years ago, the country was only accepted as a candidate in 1999, with prime minister Bülent Ecevit optimistically setting 2004 as the date for integration. In reality Turkey may have to wait considerably longer as it struggles to meet the strict criteria for membership. Despite rapid economic growth income levels are still just a third of the EU average, while inflation remains in double figures. Progress will also have to be made on the country's terrible human-rights record and the generals will need to keep their noses out of government. Then, of course, there's the long line of other candidates from Eastern Europe and the Baltic who are also queuing up to join. All in all integration seems quite a long way off yet, although the country is certainly moving in the right direction.

Culture

People

At the time of the Turkish Republic's first official census in 1927 the country's population was 13.6 million. Today, that figure has more than quadrupled to about 65 million people. What's more, it's estimated that at current growth rates the population will top 100 million by the year 2030.

In common with other developing countries this rapid expansion has been due to improvements in health care and sanitation which have helped people live longer, healthier lives. At the same time many Turks are still encouraged by poverty and tradition to have lots of babies. For nearly 40 years after the establishment of the republic in 1923, the government also encouraged population growth seeing people as a valuable resource. Contraceptives were banned and the state even provided financial incentives to promote larger families.

All this began to change in the 1950s as officials started to see the country's rapidly growing population as a threat to economic development. The government began disseminating information on family planning and in 1967 abortion was decriminalized. Voluntary organizations worked alongside officials and even some members of the Sunni clergy became involved, assuring their flocks that it wasn't un-Islamic to adopt birth control. These efforts had some success in reducing the birth rate, although in rural and eastern Turkey large families continued to be the norm.

As you'll quickly notice when you're walking round provincial town or villages, or in the poorer districts of larger cities, Turkey has a very youthful population with roughly a quarter of all people under the age of fourteen. This creates huge challenges for the state not least of which is providing classrooms for 12 million children and paying the salaries of 523,000 teachers.

Considering its size, about that of the UK and France combined, Turkey's present population of over 65 million doesn't seem excessively large. Indeed the feeling of emptiness and space as you're travelling across the Anatolian plateau or the

Population distribution

Background

mountains of the east supports this idea. And so do the population density figures, at first glance: 79 people per sq km, less than half the average for Britain or Germany. However, a closer look at the distribution of people across the country reveals that nearly half the population live on less than 25% of the land – a narrow coastal belt which stretches from Zonguldak to Istanbul, around the Sea of Marmara and south to Izmir. Within this area things are considerably more crowded and it will hardly come as a surprise to learn that Istanbul is the most densely populated province in the country with over 1,300 people squeezed into every sq km. Parts of the Black Sea coast and Mediterranean are also fairly crowded, though at the opposite extreme, central and eastern Anatolia have very low population densities.

Urbanization In common with other developing countries Turkey has experienced an unprecedented movement of people from the countryside to the cities. In 1950 about 80% of the population lived in villages; however, in just 50 years, this situation has been reversed with over two thirds of Turkish people now living in towns and cities. If you've visited an isolated Anatolian village reached along a rutted track, several hours journey from the nearest hospital and where farming is the sole economic activity, it's easy to appreciate the pull of the cities. Villagers are lured by the opportunities for better employment, healthcare and education for their children, and the larger the city the greater the pull. Istanbul with its concentration of industry and commerce attracts a lion's share of rural migration, although the other big cities like Ankara, Izmir and Bursa have also experienced a rapid influx.

Such rapid urbanization has inevitably led to problems such as congestion, urban unemployment and an acute shortage of housing with many of the new arrivals living in squatter settlements that ring the large cities. Known as *gecekondu*, which translates as 'founded in the night', these areas of shacks and shoddy concrete buildings are generally constructed on state-owned land by migrants taking advantage of an unrepealed Ottoman law protecting houses built during the hours of darkness. By 1980 researchers reckoned that over half the residents of the largest cities lived either in *gecekondu* or squatter settlements that had been incorporated into the city.

Ethnic make-up

Turks About 85% of modern Turkey's population are ethnic Turks, an Altaic people related to the Mongols, Manchus, the Bulgars and possibly the Huns, with the rest of the people belonging to one of several other distinct ethnic groups. The majority of these non-Turkish minorities were inherited from the Ottoman Empire at independence. However, despite their widespread assimilation into modern Turkish society, the government remains very sensitive to the perceived threat such groups pose to national unity. Since 1965 ethnic differences have not been recognized in the national census and the use of non-Turkish languages in the education system is outlawed.

Kurds The best-known and most troubled of Turkey's minorities are the Kurds (see box, page 612), an ancient race who are mentioned by Xenophon in the fifth century BC. They occupy a homeland which stretches across the mountains of southeast Turkey, as well as parts of Syria, Iraq and Iran. In Turkey they speak two dialects: Zaza, around Tunceli, Erzincan, Erzurum and Bingöl, and Kermanji, across the rest of the region. Their numbers are estimated at around 11 million, although this figure is hotly disputed by the government.

Arabs The second largest ethnic group, thought to be about a million strong, are the Arabs who live mainly in the Hatay, a province in south Turkey that until 1939 was part of the French Protectorate of Syria. Speaking a local dialect of Arabic, they maintain strong social and economic ties with their brethren in Syria, also migrating in large numbers to work in other countries of the Middle East.

Several much smaller ethnic groups live along the Black Sea coast with the most celebrated being the Laz, a people who originated in the Caucasus and are thought to have descended from the Colchians, the guardians of the mythical golden fleece. The Laz converse in a language, known as Lazi, which is closely related to no other and which until the recent efforts of a German academic was unwritten (see box, page 572). They number about 200,000 and inhabit the area between the towns of Pazar and Hopa. Laz are easily recognized by their distinctive fair complexions and red hair, features which, along with their supposed slow-wittedness, have become a popular raw material for Turkish humour. Then there are the Hemşinli (see box, page 577), an even smaller group numbering perhaps 15,000, who speak a dialect of Armenian and live in the lush northern valleys of the Kaçkar mountains. Industrious and entrepreneurial, despite having spread themselves across the country and indeed the world in search of commercial opportunity, they remain a remarkably cohesive group, returning each summer to their native villages for boisterous reunions. Finally, there is also a significant Georgian-speaking minority along the mountainous Turkish-Georgian frontier.

Laz & Hemşinli

Greeks formerly made up a large proportion of Anatolia's population, living mainly along the Aegean and western Mediterranean coast; as well as parts of central Anatolia and the Black Sea coast. In the towns and cities they were predominantly engaged in trade and commerce or they worked as craftsmen. Following the Turkish War of Independence, two million Anatolian Greeks were forcibly resettled in Greece under the provisions of the 1923 Treaty of Lausanne. About 200,000 Greeks, mostly in Istanbul and on the Aegean islands of Gökçeada and Bozcaada were permitted to stay however, this number has slowly declined in the face of official persecution and periodic outbreaks of violence against the community. There are estimated to be about 20,000 Greeks living in Turkey today.

Greeks

Another formerly significant minority, whose recent history is even more tragic than that of the Greeks, are the Armenians. A race of Caucasian origin whose homeland is in the mountains of eastern Anatolia, Iran and the Republic of Armenia, during the Byzantine and Ottoman periods they spread widely across the empire and most cities of the region include a large Armenian quarter. Like the Greeks they often worked as merchants or craftsmen and were governed by their own leaders as part of the Ottoman *millet* system.

Armenians

Having lived more or less peacefully with their neighbours until the end of the 19th century, communal tensions were fanned by growing Armenian nationalism. Isolated protests and terrorist incidents by Armenian revolutionaries provoked a government crack-down. The resulting atrocities, perpetrated by Ottoman soldiers as well as Kurdish and Turkish civilians, left thousands dead and caused an exodus of about 100,000 Armenians. And worse was to come: the Russian army, aided by Armenian partisans, pushed into eastern Anatolia at the beginning of the First World War; in response, the Ottoman government ordered the mass deportation of Armenians to internment camps in Syria. In the forced marches that followed hundreds of thousands lost their lives as a result of starvation and violence. This appalling episode, which Armenians insist was a state-directed policy of genocide, remains a highly contentious issue with the Turkish government flatly refusing to acknowledge any wrongdoing on the part of the Ottoman government.

Not surprisingly, in view of past events, the country's remaining Armenian community – now estimated at about 40,000 people concentrated in Istanbul – keeps a fairly low profile. Generally a pretty wealthy group involved in commerce and banking, they have extensive contact with members of the Armenian diaspora spread across the world. The community also supports its own newspapers and churches.

Jews Jews have a long history in Anatolia with large, wealthy communities existing in several cities, such as Sardis, in early Roman times. In common with other minorities they were afforded religious and administrative freedom by the Ottomans and in 1492 Shepardic Jews expelled by the Spanish Inquisition were invited to settle in the empire by Beyazıt II. Most of present-day Turkey's 20,000 Jews descend from these exiles and they still use a version of old Spanish called Ladino as their mother tongue. The Sephardic community, along with two smaller and mutually quite distinctive Jewish groups – the Karaites who use Greek as their native language, and the Ashkenazic who descend from Yiddish-speaking European immigrants – live mainly in Istanbul and have traditionally been heavily involved in the commercial and financial sectors.

A third, rather obscure Jewish group are known as the **Dönme** – a Turkish word meaning 'convert', also used to describe transvestites, which has strong negative connotations. Followers of the 17th-century false messiah, Sabbatai Sebi, who was forcibly converted to Islam, the Dönme follow a curious faith which incorporates aspects of Judaism and Islam. Scorned by both communities they were subject to periodic persecution. Today, however, they are a wealthy group who count many successful businessmen among their number.

An estimated 30,000 Jews from all three groups left Turkey in 1948 for the newly established state of Israel. Emigration continued to whittle away the community during the following two decades with up to 1,000 people leaving each year, however, since 1970 the group's population has stabilized.

Religion

Turkey's population is 99% Muslim but the proportion of strict adherents is much lower. Most Turkish Muslims belong to the orthodox Sunni sect, although there is also a significant Shia minority. The largest Shia group are known as Alevi and constitute anything up to 30% of the population; however, without census information the exact size of the community is unclear.

At independence in 1923, the Turkish Republic was declared a secular state with the separation of religion and government achieved over the following years by Atatürk's reforms. Despite this, as a traveller in Turkey the outward signs of Islam – the mosques, the minarets and the exotic sounding call to prayer – abound. But, although strongholds of religious conservatism do exist in the country, in the main Turks are fairly relaxed about religion. Having said that, Islam has had a widespread popular revival in recent years with a minority openly supporting the imposition of *sharia* (Islamic) law (see page 683). Needless to say, the fiercely secular state institutions, along with much of the population, are virulently opposed to such plans.

Despite its important role in the early development and subsequent history of Christianity, only a small Christian community - mostly Syrian Orthodox, but also Armenian and Greek Orthodox as well as Roman Catholic - now remains in Anatolia. There is also a small Jewish community (see above) mostly living in Istanbul and other large cities in the west of the country.

Islam Islam, which translates as 'submission to God', is a monotheistic religion whose followers believe that Allah (God) transmitted divine messages to the Prophet Mohammed (570-632 AD), a citizen of Mecca. Allah's revelations to the Prophet were set down in the Koran, a book of beautifully composed rhyming verse which is the ultimate authority on Islamic teachings and faith: a spiritual guide for mankind.

The Koran sets out five principal tenets, often described as the 'five pillars' of the religion. According to the first pillar, "There is no God but God and Mohammed is the Prophet", a verse repeated by Muslims during prayer.

The second pillar is prayer (*namaz*), which Muslims should perform at five proscribed times every day having completed a ritual ablution. Prayer is directed towards Mecca and consists of a series of ritual movements, bowing, kneeling and then prostrating with the forehead touching to the ground, symbolizing submission to Allah. Muslims can pray anywhere by unrolling a rug on the ground; however, they are expected to pray in a mosque as often as possible, and particularly on the Muslim holy day of Friday. Women are also expected to pray but they can do so in private; if they choose to attend a mosque they must use the specially designated area, usually screened off from the rest of the hall.

Almsgiving (*zekat*) is the third pillar whereby devoted Muslims are expected to distribute a part of their wealth to the needy.

The fourth pillar is an annual fast (*oruç*) during the month of Ramazan when no food must pass the lips of the faithful between dawn and dusk. The purpose of fasting is to renew the spirit and concentrate the mind. The night between the 27th and 28th days of Ramazan carries particular significance as the time that Mohammed is said to have received the revelations from God. Known as *Kadir Gecesi* it's marked by a night of prayer in mosques across the country.

The final pillar is the *hac*, a pilgrimage to Mecca in the twelfth month of the Islamic year during the festival of *Kurban bayramı* (Sacrifice Holiday), which every able-bodied Muslim must make if possible during his or her lifetime.

In addition to these central tenets the Koran and the *hadis*, an authenticated collection of Muhammed's sayings, set out an ethical code, essentially the same as that prescribed in the Bible, which Muslims should live by. Included are a prohibition on eating pork and drinking alcohol, as well as the belief that all men should be treated equal regardless of race or creed. Indeed, the Koran recognizes the prophets of the Jewish and Christian faiths, including Christ, although it doesn't accept his divine nature. As in the Christian faith the reward for following the precepts laid down in the Koran is the attainment of heaven after death.

Muslim sects   After Mohammed's death his followers disagreed over who should succeed him as caliph – an intermediary between Allah and mankind and the spiritual leader of all Muslims. The divisions were along political and ethnic, as well as theological, grounds with one group claiming Ali Ibn Abu Talib, the Prophet's cousin and son-in-law, as legitimate successor. The opposing group, held that the caliph should be appointed and that the leader of the Umayyad clan, Muawiya, was in fact the rightful successor. In the subsequent fighting Ali was murdered and the caliphate assumed by the Umayyad. This was not the end of the matter though, as the supporters of Ali rallied behind his son, Hussein, fighting at Kerbela and losing to the Umayyad in 680 AD. This defeat led to an unreconciled rift between the two camps, with the followers of Ali evolving into the entirely separate **Shia sect**; meanwhile, the Umayyad dynasty controlled the caliphate from Damascus and became the hereditary leaders of the **Sunni faith**. That is until the institution was taken by the the Abbasids, who ruled from Baghdad until 1258, when the city fell to the Mongols and the caliph was executed.

The position then remained unfilled for more than two and a half centuries, until Selim the Grim defeated the Egyptian Mameluks and brought a large part of the Middle East, including the Holy cities of Mecca, Medina and Jerusalem, under Ottoman control. Carting the sacred Holy relics back to Istanbul, Sultan Selim revived the title of caliph in 1517, declaring himself 'Commander of the Faithful' and the earthly leader of all Muslims. The Ottoman sultan's enjoyed this highly symbolic title for over 400 years, until the caliphate was abolished in 1924 by the newly formed Turkish Grand National Assembly.

All dressed up for the chop

Across the country the beginning of the summer holidays in June sees thousands of young boys prepared for their sünnet – circumcision. Rather than being snipped at birth, in Turkey the simple operation – performed for inextricably entangled reasons of faith and hygiene – is left until the boy is between five and 10 years old. Naturally anticipated with some trepidation by the subjects, it's a major event for families and, like a batmitzfah in the Jewish culture, marks the symbolic transition to manhood.

In typically Turkish style, ostentation is the order of the day with the proud, but nervous, victim dressed in a shiny white suite and fur-lined cape, a crown perched on his head and a sceptre in his hand. Looking every bit the little prince, boys were traditionally mounted on a horse to tour the neighbourhood and be admired. Today, however, an open-top vintage Cadillac is more the norm, leading a snaking convoy of cars, vans and trucks loaded with family and friends. This procession is serenaded by a cacophony of horn blowing and the frantic, discordant sound of the zurna (reed flute) and the incessant beating of the davul (drum).

Performed under local anaesthetic by a professional sünnetçi, the circumcision is preceded by a prayer from a hoca (holy man) presiding over the affair. The young patient is then sat on a soft cushion decorated with ribbons to recover as a stream of family and friends file past to congratulate him and wish him 'Geçmiş Olsun' – May it be in the past. It's customary for these well-wishers to leave gifts of money and gold – a welcome distraction from the obvious discomfort – before the festivities begin in earnest.

Along with the division between Sunnis and Shias, each sect was further split. Eminent Sunni theologians interpreted the Islamic texts in different ways creating four recognized schools of Islamic law. In present-day Turkey most Muslims belong to the Hanafi and Shafii schools, named after their leaders. Shia Muslims were also divided over the spiritual leadership of the sect, with the Twelve Imam Shias, who held that Ali and his eleven descendants were the rightful successors to the Prophet, becoming the dominant school. However, the majority of Turkish Shias belong to a heterodox sect established in the ninth century by Muhammad ibn Nusayr and known in Turkish as the Alevi.

The **Alevi sect** – who make up about 70% of Turkish Shias – claims adherents from the Arab, Kurdish and Turkish communities and has traditionally been associated with the southeast of the country. Having suffered centuries of persecution by the Sunni majority, they are an introverted group who generally keep themselves, and their religious beliefs and rituals, to themselves. This veil of secrecy led Sunnis and Twelfth Imam Shias to conclude that the sect engaged in heretical practices. In truth, Alevi doctrine does depart from established Islamic orthodoxy on many subjects, for example encouraging a more liberal view towards women, but the Alevi do not, as often claimed, worship Christian saints or conduct strange rituals.

In the modern era the Alevi community became known for its left-wing sympathies, an association which made it the target for right-wing vigilantes and police harassment; while there are occasional flare-ups of intercommunal violence between Alevi and radical Sunni elements.

In addition to the Alevi, other **heterodox Shia** sects were imported into Anatolia by Turkic tribes from the 12th century on. Such Sufi groups followed the mystical teachings of a respected master, or şeyh, and organized themselves into brotherhoods. Incorporating elements of Shia mysticism with folk-religion and even Christian beliefs, these tarikatlar proved enormously popular, attracting those that had trouble identifying with the rigidity and austerity of orthodox Islam. Perhaps the most famous dervish brotherhood are the Mevlevi, followers of the teachings of Mevlana who practise a spinning dance to achieve spiritual union with God. However, there were a number of other, larger orders including the Bektaşi, who were closely associated to the janissaries. These brotherhoods grew to exercise significant political influence in Ottoman times and it was to curb their power that Atatürk outlawed all such groups in the 1920s. But this action did little to diminish the popularity of the *tarikatlar* and they survive in modern Turkey as an important religious and even political force.

Anatolia is steeped in Christian history. Within the boundaries of modern Turkey are numerous places mentioned in the **Old Testament** such as Harran where Abraham lived for a time with his family; while the so-far fruitless search for Noah's Ark (see page 607) has focused on the slopes of Mount Ararat near the Turkish frontier with Iran. It was in Antioch, present-day Hatay, around 40 AD that the term 'Christian' was first coined to describe the followers of Christ with the city becoming a important base from which the religion spread across the region. **Paul** set out with Barnabas on the first of three missionary journeys from Antioch, visiting in the course of the next decade towns and cities across western Anatolia, as well as further afield. Among the centres he visited during his far-reaching travels were Iconium (Konya), Attalia (Antalya), Myra, Patara, Alexandra Troas, Assos, Miletus and Ephesus, where he lived for over two years before being forced to flee following the riot of the silversmiths.

Christianity

Christianity found fertile ground amongst the Jewish and Gentile communities in Anatolia but as the number of converts increased so did **persecution by the Roman authorities**. In a famous episode in 156 AD the bishop of Smyrna Polycarp was burnt at the stake along with some of his followers while an assembled crowd bayed: "This is the teacher of Asia; this is the destroyer of our gods; this is the father of the Christians."

One hundred years later as Roman rule in Anatolia wavered under assaults by the Goths and Persians, the community became a convenient scapegoat. Widespread persecution continued under his successor, Diocletian. However after **Constantine's victory** in the Roman civil war conditions improved significantly and in 324 AD Christians were granted equality of rights and idolatry was officially proscribed. Although not baptized until on his death bed, Emperor Constantine is reputed to have become sympathetic to Christian beliefs having had a vision of a burning cross before entering battle.

The **Nicene Creed**, issued after an ecclesiastical council in Nicaea, established the relationship between state and church, with Constantine confirmed as both temporal and spiritual leader of the empire. Meanwhile the church was organized into five metropolitans – Rome, Constantinople, Alexandria, Antioch and Jerusalem.

The Christianization of Anatolia continued under Theodosius I and paganism was banned in 392 AD. Many temples were destroyed by Christian zealots, though in more remote areas the old beliefs would linger for centuries to come. In the following century the church was split by yet more doctrinal disputes with the bishop of Constantinople, Nestorius, promulgating his belief that Christ and the Virgin Mary were of a human, rather than divine nature. This caused a mighty stir with the Council of Ephesus in 431 AD denouncing him as a heretic and deporting him to Egypt. Despite this harsh response his doctrine continued to attract adherents in southeast Anatolia where it gave rise to the Nestorian Church.

Controversy over the nature of Christ was to rumble on for centuries with the Monophysites – who contrary to orthodox opinion believed that Christ had only a divine nature – maintaining a position on the margins of the empire far from the centre of church power in Constantinople. The Monophysite creed was to become the basis of the Syrian Orthodox or Jacobean Church, named after the sixth-century bishop of Edessa, Jacobus Baradeus, who was an active proponent.

Background

As well as hosting the ecclesiastical councils which shaped the doctrines of the early church, Anatolia was home to many of the great Christian leaders. Among these was **Basil the Great**, the Bishop of Caesarea (present-day Kayseri), who lay down the foundations of a monastic society which thrived in the caves and rock-cut retreats of the region.

The sixth and seventh centuries were a time of insecurity for Christians in Anatolia as the Arab invasions swept through the region. But having finally suppressed this danger from the east, the empire was engulfed in a disruptive internal conflict over the representation of Christ and other religious figures. In contrast to Judaism and the newly emerged Islamic faith which prohibited such images, icons and statues had become a focus of veneration for Christians. In the face of considerable opposition, moves were made by successive emperors to purge the church of such heretical practices. The iconoclastic controversy which raged from 726 to 843 AD provided a useful excuse for the state to reassert its control, closing the powerful monastic orders and confiscating their assets. Iconoclasm was publicly condemned by the Pope in Rome, just one of the doctrinal disputes which eventually led to the schism between the Orthodox and Roman Catholic churches in 1054.

The arrival of the **Selçuk Turks** in Anatolia in the 10th century brought with it a certain amount of brutality towards the Christian population. Some were massacred, forced to convert, or enslaved; other Christian peasants chose to adopt the religion of the conquerors. Conversion was hastened by the confiscation of church property and the taxation of non-Muslims in the 12th century.

Later under the **Ottomans** the remaining Christians in Anatolia, predominantly Greeks and Armenians, were guaranteed religious freedom and given autonomy to administer their own affairs under the *millet* **system**. This gave authority over each community – *millet* meaning nation – to its own religious leaders, although the Orthodox and Armenian patriarchs as well as the Jewish grand rabbi were ultimately appointed by the sultan. Such tolerance towards religious minorities was in keeping with Islam's positive attitude towards 'peoples of the book', though Christians suffered some disadvantages for their faith. A head tax was payable by all non-Muslims and no Christian could enter the Ottoman administration or army unless he'd converted.

From the introduction of the *millet* system in the 16th century, Christians co-existed remarkably peacefully with the Muslim majority for about four centuries. However, the awakening of nationalistic aspirations in the various Christian minorities during the 19th century saw an end to such tolerance, as the Greek and Armenian communities were increasingly perceived as a threat to national integrity.

The Christian minorities were severely depleted by the Armenian pogroms and the Turkish-Greek population exchanges of 1923, and although religious freedom has been guaranteed to all under the **Turkish Republic**, periods of harassment and official discrimination have encouraged many more to leave. By 1995 the number of Christians had been reduced to about 140,000 found mostly in the western cities and in southeast Anatolia, where a once-sizeable **Syrian Orthodox** community lives around Mardin and Midyat. Formerly numbering about 500,000, since the mid-1980s these Jacobites have found themselves caught between government forces and the PKK, with many fleeing to Istanbul or abroad.

Art

Turkey has a rich and varied artistic heritage dating mainly, but not exclusively, from the Islamic period. The Islamic prohibition on the representation of living things – though not always strictly adhered to – was a significant influence on the development of artistic expression. Instead of representational work, Selçuk and Ottoman artists generally concentrated on decorative artforms such as tile making, paper marbling and calligraphy.

One of the most important Ottoman artforms was calligraphy, an ornate and highly stylized form of writing used by the ruling class. Each sultan had his own elaborate calligraphic monogram, known as a *tuğra*, and several rulers became respected masters of the art themselves. Calligraphy was used to decorate the Koran and other religious texts; it was also used by the Ottoman court and bureaucracy for correspondence, edicts and deeds. The demise of the empire and the introduction of a Latin-based script saw its virtual extinction.

Calligraphy

The art of tile making was introduced into Anatolia by the Selçuk Turks, although an earlier tradition of ceramic and mosaic production existed during Byzantine and Roman times. Glazed tiles, particularly in white, turquoise and cobalt blue, are a common characteristic of Selçuk architecture used to decorate both the inside and outside of palaces, mosques, tombs and medrese. The Selçuks also produced tiles decorated with lively plant motifs, as well as people and animals in spite of the religious ban.

Tile making

This tradition was continued through the *beylik* period into Ottoman times, when it was refined with the introduction of new techniques. More complex and detailed designs were made possible using the *cuerda seca* technique with borders outlined by a mixture of beeswax and manganese to stop the various coloured glazes running together. Benefiting from imperial patronage, tile making reached its zenith in the beautiful geometric and floral patterned ceramics produced in Iznik (see box, page 175) during the 16th century, although it continues to this day in Kütahya (see box, page 441).

Known in Turkish as *ebru*, paper marbling was developed in the Ottoman Empire during the 15th century. A unique pattern created by laying a sheet of paper onto the surface of water which has been sprinkled with dye, *ebru* was used for the borders surrounding Ottoman miniatures and on the inside covers of books. Handmade *ebru* have now been replaced by manufactured marble paper, although the craft persists on a small-scale as an art form in its own right.

Paper marbling

Members of the Ottoman elite were particularly fond of painted miniatures which often contradicted Islamic law by depicting historical scenes, battles and famous personages. In a similar vein to Persian miniatures they were painted with great attention to detail using strong, vivid colours.

Painted miniatures

Embroidery was widely used in Selçuk and Ottoman times to decorate military banners, tents and pavilions. Religious items such as Koran covers and hangings, as well as everyday things like blankets, headscarves and towels, were also delicately embroidered with geometric and floral patterns. Embroidery and lace-making are still widely practised in villages across the country today. Another traditional folk art, thriving due to commercial demand, is **carpet weaving** (see box, page 60).

Embroidery

It wasn't until the 19th century that Western-style painting began to emerge in Turkey with the establishment of the Academy of Fine Art by the accomplished artist Osman Hamdi Bey. Turkish artists were sent to Europe to learn new techniques and skills, while foreign artists were invited to Istanbul. This process was encouraged by the new republican government and Turkish artists were influenced by European artistic movements. Today, the country has a diverse art scene with a growing number of galleries in the major cities exhibiting the work of domestic artists.

Western-style painting

Background

Architecture

Turkey is an architectural treasure trove having witnessed over 8,000 years of building by a long and distinguished list of civilisations. Indeed, it's a fact that the country has more ancient Greek ruins than Greece and more ruined Roman cities than Italy. Sites such as Ephesus have benefited from extensive restoration with monumental buildings, such as the Library of Celsus, standing much as they would have done 2,000 years ago. Invariably the most impressive feature of these ancient cities are their amphitheatres, the banks of seating cleverly propped against a hill or mountainside or supported by huge arching vaults. Pergamon's 10,000 seat theatre, carved out from a steep mountainside, is one of the narrowest and steepest in Anatolia; while Aspendos' Roman theatre with its multi-storey backstage building and semi-circular cavea - a characteristic feature of the period- remains amazingly intact.

Under the Byzantines the building boom continued with the imperial architects lavishing much of their attention on the capital, Constantinople. The huge dome of Haghia Sophia, designed in the fifth century by the mathematicians Anthemeus of Tralles and Isidorus of Miletus for the emperor Justinian, pushed back the limits of contemporary building know-how, becoming an architectural benchmark for the next thousand years. Superlatives aside later Byzantine architects left a rich endowment of smaller, more decorative buildings like Istanbul's Church of the Pantocrator, with its multi-domes and alternating courses of stone and red brick. Inside the decorators were equally busy enlivening the walls with rich mosaics and frescoes such as those adorning Trabzon's Haghia Sophia or the church of St Saviour in Chora, near the city walls in Istanbul. These Theodosian ramparts are a feat of civil engineering in themselves: raised in a hurry the double walls were guarded by close to 200 towers. However, finally they were overcome by the Ottomans, ushering in a new era for Anatolian architecture.

Infact new architectural styles had already made an appearance in Anatolia, brought from the east by Turkic invaders from the 11th century. The most influential of these were the Selçuks whose fusion of Turkic, Persian and Arab traditions is characterised by the solid stone seminaries and caravanserais which dot the Anatolian heartland. These typically have richly embellished portals covered with lavish geometric carving and brick minarets picked-out with pieces of coloured tiles, echoes of the extensive tilework often found inside. Although externally rather nondescript, some of the finest mosques from this, and the subsequent *beylik*, period are the so-called "forest mosques" whose interiors are divided by rows of wooden columns, often topped by carved capitals.

Early Ottoman architecture as seen in the first capital, Bursa, shows great continuity with earlier Selçuk design, although by the 15th century a more refined and distinctly Ottoman-style was emerging. This was to be perfected over the next century reaching its pinnacle of excellence with the work of the inspirational court architect Mimar Sinan (see box, page 102). Synonymous with the great imperial mosque complexes of the Süleymaniye in Istanbul and the Selimiye in Edirne, with these buildings Sinan finally surpassed the technical achievements of the builders of Haghia Sophia, creating huge central domes supported on a series of half-domes and just four massive piers. Uncluttered and airy on the inside, from the outside the arching central domes surrounded by cascading clusters of semi-domes framed by pencil thin minarets also provide a breathtaking profile on the skyline. These large complexes aside, the industrious Mimar Sinan built a vast number of smaller mosques, baths, medrese, tombs and assorted other buildings: an immense body of work which defined what has become known as the Classical Ottoman-style.

Post-Sinan Ottoman architects struggled to attain the ascetic or technical brilliance of their predecessor, gradually succumbing to European influences from the mid-17th century. The resulting 'Turkish Baroque' as seen in the palace of

Football crazy

Turks are fanatical about football. The whole nation settles down in front of the television for a big game and the major cities fall eerily silent only to erupt into chaos when a positive result comes in. Boisterous fans pile into cars and vans to tour the streets waving flags and blaring their horns. It's also not uncommon for jubilant supporters to fire guns into the air, a celebratory practice which sometimes leads to tragedy. Top players are afforded superstar status and rub shoulders with the glitterati at the hottest night-spots and parties, while a host of tabloid TV-shows and newspapers follow their every move.

The Turkish league championship is dominated by three Istanbul teams, Galatasaray, Beºiktaº and Fenerbahçe, who monopolise not just the talent and advertising revenue, but also the adulation of the nation. Matched, or rather mismatched, against these three giants are the poorly funded provincial

teams, who invariably lose. Trabzonspor, from the Black Sea port city, are the only team to have threatened Istanbul's hegemony of the league, although they've lagged behind in recent years.

Lately, Turkish teams have had some success in European competitions, although the country also gained notoriety for off the pitch violence in 2000 when two British supporters were stabbed to death in Istanbul during the UEFA cup tie between Galatasaray and Leeds. This incident provoked ugly pitched battles between Turkish and British fans in Copenhagen when Arsenal and Galatasaray squared-up later that year.

If you fancy watching a match, don't be dissuaded as Turkish fans are noisy, excitable but far less inclined to violence than their European counterparts. Your best bet for quality of play on the field and atmosphere in the terraces is an Istanbul derby. See page 163 for where to get tickets.

Dolmabahçe or the Nuruosmaniye Camii in Istanbul, has been far less well received, and is often scorned for its over-exuberant decoration and confused style.

European economic involvement in the Ottoman empire during the 19th century witnessed an increasing number of foreign architects working in the capital. Among these was Sir Charles Barry, designer of the Houses of Parliament in London, who was responsible for the neo-renaissance British embassy building constructed off Istiklal Caddesi in 1845. The Swiss Fossati brothers were also very active in Istanbul during this period; while an Italian, Raimondo d'Aronco, served as the imperial architect at the turn of the century, building art nouveau structures such as the Egyptian embassy in the Bosphorus suburb of Bebek.

The founding of the republic saw a reversal of this westernising trend as an indigenous architectural movement, named the First National Movement, was pioneered by Vedat Tek and Kemalettin Bey. Drawing heavily on their Ottoman architectural heritage, these architects used modern materials to create buildings such as the Hotel Merit Antique in Istanbul's Laleli district, which was originally constructed for families left homeless by a huge fire during the First World War.

The economic dislocation of the 1930s saw the First National Movement largely replaced by stark internationally inspired modernism with most activity concentrated in the republic's new capital Ankara. However, shortages of modern construction materials and a desire to remain independent during the Second World War witnessed a Second Nationalist Movement spearheaded by the prolific architect, Sedad Hakk2 Eldem. This movement was short-lived and post-war Turkish architecture has been dominated by the need to provide for a rapidly growing and urbanising population. Consequently, the traditional character and skyline of towns and cities across the country has been transformed by a rash of utilitarian concrete apartment blocks and cheap housing. Meanwhile many historic buildings have fallen into disrepair or been ripped down with only the most significant enjoying any kind of imperfect state protection. Sadly much of Turkey's architectural heritage has already been lost in this way, though in some areas the importance of conserving old buildings for future generations-and as an attraction for domestic and international tourists- has been belatedly recognised.

Language

Turkey's official language is Turkish, although a significant minority of the population speaks Kurdish, Arabic or another language as their mother tongue (see page 690). These non-Turkish languages aren't officially recognized and are not taught in school; indeed until the 1980s, even speaking Kurdish, for example, in public meant risking arrest.

Modern Turkish includes many words of Persian and Arabic origin, although since 1923 efforts have been made by the government to 'Turkify' the language by ridding it of these foreign borrowings. As part of this process the country switched to a Latin-based script of 29 letters in 1928. Today, the process of 'Turkification' is continuing, albeit at a much slower pace, under the aegis of an academic body known as the Turkish Linguistic Association who are charged with creating new words using old Turkic roots. Indeed a measure of their progress is the fact that a modern Turk cannot read the original version of Atatürk's mammoth six-day speech without a glossary. However, many Arabic words are still in common usage including *teşekkür* (thanks). Modern Turkish is also littered with Western borrowings, though only a very few words – such as *yoğurt* – have been passed in the opposite direction.

Despite the common misbelief that their language is the most difficult to learn in the world, Turkish has a very logical and systematic grammar which is almost completely devoid of the irregularities that make English so impenetrable to new learners. Its strictly phonetic pronunciation is also a boon once you've learnt the basic sounds. Having said that, a different sentence structure and its alien agglutinated form, whereby suffixes are added to the root of a word to change its meaning, are at first confounding to speakers of Latin-based languages.

Literature

The roots of Turkish literature can be traced back to the oral traditions of the Turkic tribes who roamed the Central Asian steep over a thousand years ago. These early stories were past down from generation to generation, although several epics of the sixth and seventh centuries have also been preserved in stone as monumental inscriptions. As the Turks migrated westwards they came into contact with Islam and the well-developed literary traditions of Persia and the Middle East. These influences along with the gradual adoption of a more sedentary lifestyle caused the emergence of the first written works of Turkish literature. It also resulted in the emergence of two distinct types of literary expression from the 10th century onwards.

Divan The first of these was *divan*, a classical literary form that drew heavily on Persian and Arabic grammatical structures and style, and which was eventually hybridized as the court language of the Ottomans. *Divan* poets concerned themselves primarily with creating beautifully crafted passages which adhered to strict principles of structure and form. This literary style reached its apogee in the 16th century under the generous patronage of Süleyman the Magnificent. Among the more familiar *divan* poets are Fuzuli, Baki and Nedim, while one of the best-known works of Ottoman prose is the *Seyahatname*, an exhaustive description of the experiences of the much-travelled Ottoman court official Evliya Çelebi.

The Turkish Bath

The hamam or Turkish bath holds a special place in traditional Turkish society. Conceived long before the advent of domestic plumbing, the hamam was where grimy Turks from all walks of life would turn-up for a scrub. With the importance attached to physical, as well as spiritual, cleanliness in the Islamic faith, those who could afford to visited the baths regularly. In Ottoman towns each neighbourhood had a hamam and baths were a feature of most pious foundations with well over 2,000 existing in Istanbul alone a hundred years ago.

However, they were far more than simply a place for a good wash. As Irfan Orga remembers in Portrait of a Turkish Family, in Ottoman Istanbul they "...were hot beds of gossip and scandal-mongering... the excuse for every woman in the district to have a day out." In the steamy, sexually segregated world of the local baths men would talk business, while women chatted, sang and eyed potential suitors for their eligible sons. For such extended bathing sessions ladies often brought with them baskets of goodies and sweet serbets to sip.

A ceremonial scrub was also the prelude to marriage – the Ottoman equivalent of a hen night – and babies were traditionally brought for a wash 40 days after their birth. The hamam was also the venue for a person's final bath, a ritual ablution performed on the corpse before it was buried.

In the modern era the proliferation of showers and baths in private homes has been at the expense of hamams and many have been forced to close. Others remain open largely for tour groups and offer a modified, though still enjoyable, experience including mixed sex bathing, alcoholic beverages and hot oil massages.

The grandest historic baths, such as **Cağaloğlu** and **Çemberlitaş**, are in Istanbul, although Bursa's **Eski Kaplıca** also has an impressive Ottoman pedigree; lots of white marble and the bonus of naturally-heated spring water. Travelling around the country you'll also come across lots of smaller, less opulent hamams still used by local people and which offer excellent value for money as well as a truly relaxing, skin-tingling experience.

A session begins in the camekan, a reception area where you disrobe in private cubicles and swap your clothes for a piece of checked cloth to wrapped around your waist. Modesty demands men keep this peştemal on at all times, though in some women's baths greater nudity is acceptable. You'll also often be issued with a pair of wooden clogs, known as takunya, which make shuffling across wet marble floors a difficult and potentially dangerous proposition. Suitably attired it's time to progress through the soğukluk – a cool area equipped with toilets and showers – to where the action is in the hararet. Usually a marble-decked hall lit by small holes pierced in the domed ceiling, the atmosphere is hot and steamy with the hararet traditionally centred on the göbektaşı or "navel stone," a large slab of marble surrounded by small basins at which you wash with piping hot water. It's quite acceptable to wash yourself using your own soap and shampoo, though people who want to get really clean plumb for a kese – an assisted wash. Performed by the resident keseci, this consists of being doused in hot water, soaped and then rubbed all over with a rough cloth traditionally made from camel hair and not unlike a brillo pad. You emerge, minus several layers of skin and lots of ingrained dirt, positively gleaming. For many, however, a hamam visit isn't complete without a massage, generally a fairly rough but invigorating pummeling conducted on the göbektaşı. Following this you can relax in the hararet for as long as you like, emerging into the soğukluk to be swaddled in towels by the attendant. Refreshments are usually on offer in the camekan to help you rehydrate and it's customary to relax on one of the chairs or beds, summoning up the energy to get dressed and depart feeling like a new person.

Folk literature Using the Persian-influenced language of court, *divan* literature was inaccessible to the great mass of ordinary people in Anatolia. This led to the development of a parallel body of folk literature based on Central Asian traditions but similarly adapted by Islamic influences, in this case the mystical philosophies of *sufi* teachers such as Yunus Emre. The poems of this genre were typically recited to the accompaniment of a *saz* by tourbadours who wandered between Anatolian towns and villages. Knows as *aşıklar* – or lovers – because of their preoccupation with tragic, unrequited love, these itinerant minstrels also worked issues affecting the common people into their poetic songs. The last aşıklar disappeared during the 20th century, their way of life and heterodox beliefs viewed with increasing suspicion by the establishment. Unfortunately, many of their poems have been lost with them, though some have entered popular consciousness or been written down.

Another form of folk poetry known as Tekke poetry – a tekke being a dervish lodge – was concerned primarily with the mystical interpretations of Islam followed by the various sufi orders. While in the realms of prose, folk stories such as the anonymous 14th-century 'Tales of Dede Korkut' remain extremely popular to this day.

Western styles During the 19th century the over-elaborate *divan* style was slowly replaced by more concise and accessible Western styles. The translation of Western novels and plays helped this process, encouraging a flurry of original work heavily influenced by these new forms. The **Tanzimat period** also saw the emergence of a whole new school of writers, many of whom were concerned with defining a new Ottoman identity in the face of the empire's inexorable decline. Authors such as Namık Kemâl and Ziya Paşa imbued their work with strong Ottoman patriotism, with a play by the former entitled *Vatan* (Home Country) causing passionate street demonstrations in Istanbul after its opening in 1878. Also keen supporters of the constitution and democracy, many of these intellectuals fled to European countries during the repressive years of Abdülhamit's reign, from where their works criticizing the government were smuggled back into the country.

The work of Young Ottoman writers such as Namık Kemâl was an inspiration for a group of nationalistic journalists and playwrights who formed part of the National Literature Movement which developed between 1911 and 1923. Writers such a Ziya Gökalp, a prominent journalist, developed the idea of a distinctly Turkish, as opposed to Ottoman, identity in their work. The National Literature Movement itself was a broad church which included novelists, poets and playwrights whose defining feature was their use of concise, clear language and their preference for issues affecting the country and its people as subject matter. Poets of this period, such as Kemâlettin Kamu and Orhan Orhon also concentrated on producing work in the poetic forms and syllabic metre of traditional Anatolian folk poetry, while using the lives of ordinary people as their material.

This 'Turkification' of literature was reinforced by the government's introduction of the Latin script in place of Arabic in 1928. Deemed necessary by Atatürk on nationalistic as well as practical grounds, this meant that within a generation the Turkish people had effectively been cut off from their Ottoman literary heritage. A committee of scholars was also charged with the task of inventing new words based of old Turkic roots to replace the Persian and Arabic vocabulary that had entered the Turkish language over the preceeding 1,000 years.

Another important break with tradition came in 1941 when Orhan Veli published a collection of poems entitled 'Garip' (Strange). In this work the poet had completely disregarded the formal rules of rhyme and analogy which had hitherto governed Turkish poetry, instead preferring to express feelings in the straightforward terms of free verse. This revolutionary development was quickly taken up by a growing number of writers, spawning a minor poetic movement known as the Garipler.

I kiss you!

Mahir Cagir is a very 21st-century phenomenon. A journalist from Izmir, in November 1999 Mahir decided to join the growing number of people with a personal presence on the world wide web. A friend constructed him a simple website which included a clumsily worded physical description, a list of his hobbies and a few flattering poses of the moustachioed man himself. With typical Turkish hospitality, he also extended an open invitation, clearly aimed at members of the fairer sex: "Who is want to can come to Turkey I can invite. She can stay my home (sic)."

Following its cyber debue at ikissyou.org, Mahir's site was promptly hijacked by some internet funsters who replaced the original photographs with something a little more raunchy. Dismayed at this attack on his personal domain, Mahir approached the authorities, who were at a loss about how to deal with such cyber crimes. However, much to his surprise ikissyou.org was attracting a lot of attention. Whether because of its catchy name or naively comical and mildly pornographic content, the site received hundreds, then thousands of hits per day. Mahir was inundated with emails and telephone calls accepting his offer of hospitality and praising his site. A few less charitable individuals also mocked his terrible English.

Topping 500,000 visits per day, it wasn't long before the financial possibilities of achieving cyber cult-status dawned on Mahir. Magazine interviews and lucrative advertising contracts followed, while his admirable hit-rate earned him a place in the Guinness Book of Records. A signing with EMI was the next step with the unlikely star's debue single - "I kiss you!"- due out in 2001. Meanwhile, Mahir has become a self-styled cultural ambassador and philanthropist raising money for the victims of the 1999 earthquake and the war in Chechnya. However, despite all the attention Mahir remains disarmingly down-to-earth about his meteoric rise to stardom: "Somethings in life are beyond your control just like having an accident, winning a prize or having something fall on your head."

Cinema

The first film was shown in Turkey in 1896 at a performance by the Lumière brothers in the Yıldız Palace, Istanbul. Immediately popular with the European and Christian residents of the city, public shows were put on in the Beyoğlu and Şehzadebaşı districts in the following years. However, it wasn't long before the government cottoned on to the possibilities of propagandizing through the new medium with a series of documentaries produced by the newly formed Central Cinema Directorate.

Independence in 1922 opened a new chapter in Turkish film-making as actor Muhsin Ertuğrul established the country's first private studio. Over the next seventeen years he directed 29 films establishing himself as the father of Turkish film-making. Ertuğrul was influenced heavily by the Turkish theatre, but he also produced officially sanctioned docudramas dealing with matters such as the First World War.

The 1940s saw several more studios open with output heavily weighted towards patriotic films and documentaries inspired by the war. A lack of funds also encouraged the making of cheap melodramas based around very simplistic storylines – a genre which remains popular with a large segment of the population today.

The post-war years witnessed a huge expansion of the film industry, although, strict government censorship introduced in 1932 continued to stifle creativity. By the mid-1960s there were over 50 directors producing films in the country, a few of which, such as Metin Erksan's 1964 film, *Susuz Yaz* (Dry Summer), won international acclaim. At about this time cinema courses were introduced at several universities and the Union of Turkish Film Producers was established. These developments, coupled with a spectacular increase in the number of cinemas across the country, led to what's been called 'cinematic inflation' – the proliferation of low-budget, poor-quality films – with over 300 films produced in 1972. The vast majority were frivolous comedies and corny melodramas which are still popular fare on local television stations and the occasional long-distance bus journey.

However, a small number of film-makers were also making higher-quality films which addressed social and economic issues affecting the country. The influential director Lütfi Akad started this trend in 1952 with *Kanun Namına* (In the name of the Law), a true-to-life drama set in an Anatolian village. Other younger directors, like Zeki Ökten and Yavuz Özkan, also dealt with subjects such as feudal landlordism and changing social structures in their films. In the 1970s Ömer Kavur directed the first Turkish film about prostitution; while the actor-director Yılmaz Güney made a series of celebrated films dealing with prison life, urban poverty and social injustice. Imprisoned himself for attempting to kill a judge, Güney made several films from behind bars with the collaboration of other directors, later escaping to France where he directed several highly acclaimed films including *Yol* (The Road), about the trials and tribulations of a group of prisoners on temporary release.

During the 1970s and 80s the Turkish film industry went into decline caused by growing competition from television and video; as well as rising production costs. Domestic films also had trouble competing with the impressive effects and racy storylines of Hollywood blockbusters. The number of Turkish-made feature films plummeted during this period, though looking on the bright side, the quality of the two dozen or so movies now produced each year is much higher. Recent home-produced hits include *Eşkiya* (The Bandit) starring Şener Şen, which broke box office records when it was released in 1996.

Land and environment

Geography

Turkey is a large rectangular country stretching about 1,500 km east to west and 550 km from north to south, making it roughly the same size as the UK and France combined. Of this land, 97% is on the continent of Asia and the remaining portion, to the northwest of the Sea of Marmara, is classed as continental Europe. Surrounded on three sides by the Aegean, the Black Sea and the Mediterranean it has over 8,000 km of coastline, also sharing almost 3,000 km of land frontier with Syria, Iraq, Iran, Armenia, Azerbaijan, Georgia, Greece and Bulgaria.

The country has a population of about 64 million people, 15 million of whom live in and around Istanbul (by far the largest city). About 50% of the population live along the coasts with large areas of sparsely inhabited countryside in the central and eastern parts of the country.

The Turkish landscape is dominated by a high central plateau bordered by mountains formed when the southward moving Eurasian plate collided with the continent of Gondwanaland. Stretching along the southern edge of the plateau, parallel to the Mediterranean coast, are the Taurus mountains; while along the northern margin the Pontic range run the length of the Black Sea coast from near Istanbul to the Georgian border. In the eastern part of the country these two ranges meet the Zagros mountains to form an extensive knot of high altitude terrain.

Thrace & Marmara On the European side of the Sea of Marmara, Thrace is an area of gently sloping hills and wide valleys that drain into the River Meriç, which forms the Greek-Turkish frontier. A range of comparatively high hills extend along the coast continuing southwest to form the Gallipoli Peninsula. This part of the country is divided from Asiatic Turkey by two narrow straits, the Dardanelles and the Bosphorus, which were formed by the movement of underlying plates. The same tectonic forces which created these two channels and the Sea of Marmara between are still at work, with the North Anatolian fault zone, responsible for the cataclysmic 1999 earthquake, continuing in an east-west line from Sakarya and Izmit beneath the sea.

The southern Marmara coast is characterized by a series of narrow bays inland of which are a number of small, relatively shallow lakes, such as Iznik Gölü, and discontinuous mountains ranges like the 2543-m high Uludağ massif near Bursa. All this means that travelling is relatively time consuming with a combination of road and ferry services necessary to get between points more quickly.

As you'll soon discover if you're travelling along the coastal road, the Aegean shoreline is a highly indented and convoluted one with numerous deep bays, such as the Gulf of Edremit and Izmir Bay, which the north-south highway has to make long diversions around. Sizeable peninsulars and rocky headlands also project out from the coast towards a string of off-shore islands – Lesbos, Chios, Samos, Kos and Rhodes – which are under Greek sovereignty. Backing the sea are mountains of 1,000-1,800 m divided by several wide, agriculturally important irrigated valleys such as the Gediz and the Menderes. The rivers that formed these valleys generally rise on the eastern margins of the central plateau, snaking gently towards the sea in a lazy series of meanders. Indeed it is from the classical River Meander, known today as the Menderes, that the word "meander" entered the English language. These rivers carry large quantities of sediment which, by the standards of geological time, are rapidly extending the coastline in certain areas. The region produces a diverse range of crops from olives to vegetables, cotton to tobacco.

The Aegean coast

Turkey's Mediterranean coast is backed along its entire length by the Taurus Mountains, which are predominantly formed from karstic limestone. In the west the range arches southwards forming the Lycian Peninsula between Fethiye and Antalya. The loftiest local massifs are the Akdağlar and Beydağları which reach just over 3,000 m and are divided by the high Elmalı basin.

East of Antalya a wide alluvial plain bordered by long sandy beaches – the focus for large scale touristic development – extend 10 to 15 km south from the mountains. Known in ancient times as Pamphylia, this coastal strip is watered by a number of rivers, such as the Köprülü Çay, which cut steeply down through the Taurus. Behind the mountains a series of karstic basins have filled with water forming the lakes and marshlands of the Lake District.

The Taurus bulge south again between Alanya and Mersin and the mountains descend straight into the sea. With no coastal plain to speak of along most of this stretch, settlement and tourist development have been restricted, except, that is, at Anamur and Silifke where rivers have extended the coastline sufficiently to allow areas of cultivation.

The eastern part of the coast is dominated by the Çukurova, a flat and extremely fertile alluvial plain laid down by the Seyhan and Ceyhan Rivers. Cultivated since the Neolithic Revolution 10,000 years ago, today it's the country's main cotton producing area, also hosting a large textile industry. Along the seaward margins of the delta large freshwater lakes and marshland rich in wildlife are enclosed by long dune-backed beaches.

The Mediterranean

Usually talked about as a single, uniform region, the central plateau is quite a diverse area made up of various undulating plateaus divided by hills and mountain ranges. It is an important agricultural area producing about a third of the country's wheat, as well as other crops such as potatoes, sugar beet and opium. Major

The Central Plateau

landforms include the monotonous rolling grass and arable land of the Konya Ovası, known as Turkey's bread-basket, and the Tuz Gölü, a shallow salt lake at the centre of a large basin to the south of Ankara. Further east large parts of Niğde, Nevşehir and Kayseri provinces are covered with layers of volcanics such as the soft tufa responsible for the highly eroded landscape around Göreme. These were laid down by the now-extinct volcanoes of Hasan Dağı (3258 m), to the south of Aksaray, and Erciyes Dağı which towers over Kayseri. The country's longest river, the 1,355 km long Kızılırmak, named the "Red River" after its sediment laden waters, curls its way from Sivas southeast to Cappadocia before bending back north again past Ankara to the Black Sea coast.

The Black Sea Similar to the Mediterranean, the Black Sea coast is dominated by mountains, although these increase remarkably in size and stature as one progresses eastwards, attaining the impressive 3,000 m plus heights of the Kaçkar range between Trabzon and the Georgian border. Apart from the deltas formed by the Kızılırmak near Bafra and the Yeşilırmak to the east of Samsun, both important centres of tobacco cultivation, there's very little coastal plain with the mountains deeply incised by swift-flowing rivers such as the Harşit, the Fırtına and the Çoruh. The last of these flows down the south side of the Kaçkar mountains from near Bayburt, before cutting itself an awe-inspiring gorge from Yusufeli to Artvin. The mountainous topography all along the coast makes agriculture difficult while also isolating the region from the rest of Anatolia and ensuring its relative underdevelopment.

Eastern Anatolia This is a large region of high desolate mountains between 3,000 and 5,137 m above sea-level, the latter being the height of the volcanic cone of Ağrı Dağı (Mount Ararat) near the Armenian border which clocks-in as Turkey's tallest peak. Another notable feature is Van Gölü by far, the country's largest inland water body. Mildly alkaline and fringed with decent beaches the lake would be a major tourist draw were it not for the region's history of instability. Between the extensive mountain ranges are deeply incised valleys and wide tectonic basins, such as those around Erzurum, Ağrı and Van, where the region's limited agricultural activity, largely subsistence rain-fed cultivation of grains and animal husbandry, is concentrated. The east is Turkey's poorest region with standards of living far below those found in the west of the country. The area's largest river is the Aras which forms part of the Armenian frontier before flowing eastwards to the Caspian sea, with the Euphrates and Tigris also rising in the mountains.

The Southeast The area between Gaziantep, Şanlıurfa and Mardin forms a northern extension of the Syrian plain which rises from an average altitude of 400 m at the frontier into hills and mountains like the 1900-m Karacadağ range southeast of Diyarbakır. Much of the region falls between the mighty Tigris and Euphrates rivers which are fed by snow-melt in their mountainous upper basins to the north, flowing south across Syria and Iraq to the Persian Gulf. These rivers are presently the focus of the ambitious GAP project of dams, irrigation schemes and hydroelectric project (see box, page 620), which is dramatically altering the region's landscape with the introduction of extensive areas of irrigated cropland. Despite such change it remains a poor and underdeveloped area.

Climate

Defying commonly-held stereotypes of an arid, desert-like country, Turkey has a diverse climate which varies enormously over its surface area due to the interplay of altitude, physical relief and regional weather patterns. Generally speaking, however, the country can be divided into six climatic zones.

This part of the country experiences pleasantly warm summers, with average temperatures of 25°C, and mild winters, with the January mean across most of the region at 2°C. Winter depressions result in most of the area's 600-900 mm of annual rainfall, with the occasional dump of snow and sub-zero temperatures due to southward incursions of cold air from the Balkans. Precipitation in summer usually comes in short, sharp downpours followed by long dry spells.

Marmara & Thrace

A Mediterranean-type climate characterized by mild winters and hot summers, with an average temperature range of 25-30°C, predominates in this region. Most rain falls in heavy, and often prolonged, downpours during the winter and early spring, though the summer is dry except for the odd thunderstorm. Temperatures and humidity increase as you progress southwards, with Antalya becoming uncomfortably hot and sticky in August. It is cooler and generally also wetter in the mountains with snow covering the higher peaks of the Taurus for two to six months each year.

Aegean & Mediterranean

The central region has a continental climate with large temperature variations between summer and winter; day and night. Dominated by a zone of high pressure for much of the winter, the weather is cold but pretty dry; with any precipitation usually falling as snow. Spring is the wettest season with a long dry summer the norm. Temperatures are moderated by the altitude and usually drop significantly at night.

Central Anatolia

This is the wettest region with the dominant northwesterly winds, laden with moisture from the sea, dropping up to 2,400 mm of rain throughout the year. Winters are mild and summers cool, though high humidity when the sun does show its face makes it seem much warmer than it actually is. Precipitation increases and temperatures decrease as you climb into the mountains, however, beyond the main ridge line there's a dramatic "rain-shadow" effect with the southern flanks on the Pontic range receiving much less rainfall.

The Black Sea

A long distance from the moderating influences of the sea and at a high altitude, Eastern Anatolia has a continental climate with severe winters when thermometers in towns such as Erzurum and Kars frequently drop to -30°C. Snow lies on the ground for up to four months of the year. Summer temperatures are much cooler than the rest of the country and It's generally dry.

Eastern Anatolia

The southeast is the country's hottest region with sizzling summer highs of up to 48°C, though 40-45°C is more usual. There is also a pronounced summer drought with most of the area's 400-550 mm of rain falling during the mild winter months.

The Southeast

Flora

Due to the diversity of its climate and terrain, Turkey supports a wide variety of plant life. The country also finds itself at the junction of three botanical regions with plant species typical of the Irano-Turanian, Euro-Siberian and Mediterranean areas all found within its borders. When combined these factors produce a remarkable biodiversity with over 10,000 plant species – an impressive 3,000 of which are endemic. In comparison, the whole of continental Europe has only about 11,500 species, 2,500 of which occur nowhere else.

However, In a comparatively short time man has wrought immense changes on Anatolia's natural vegetation. The rolling grassland of the central plateau was formerly covered in huge expanses of primeval forest with the ancient Greek historian, Herodotus, describing the peninsular as a 'sea of oak forests'. Clearance for agriculture and timber exploitation has put paid to much of this though. The pace of deforestation has been especially rapid in the last hundred years, a period that

Background

Bulbs and the beasts

To the alarm of conservationists evidence of a large illicit trade in wild Turkish bulbs was uncovered in the 1980s with tens of millions of specimens dug-up and exported each year to garden centres and bulb merchants in Europe. A serious threat to populations in the wild, the Turkish Society for the Protection of Nature (DHKD), funded by the WWF, has recently begun a scheme to encourage villagers to propagate bulbs for export. Sown by a group of families onto shady terraces around the village of Dumlugöze in the high Taurus, the bulbs of Galanthus elwesh, a delicate white snowdrop, were left to multiply. After three years the new bulbs were large enough to sell, providing a good income for the participants. Although still in its infancy, it's hoped that this Indigenous Propagation Project will spread to other villages, helping to take the pressure off wild bulbs and also boosting incomes in poor mountainous communities like Dumlugöze.

The Dumlugöze snowdrops are available in the UK by mail order from John Shipton Bulbs, T44(0)1994240125. In Turkey try contacting the DHKD, Büyük Postane Caddesi No 43-45, Kat 5-6, Sirkeci, Istanbul, T02125282030, www.dhkd.org

has witnesses the total area of forestland reduced from 20.2 million to 5.5 million ha. Some large areas of forest, mainly under Forestry Service management, do still exist today, with particular concentrations in the mountains of the Black Sea and Mediterranean regions.

The deciduous forests cloaking parts of the eastern end of the Pontic range are especially worthy of note, particularly when the autumn colour change sets whole mountainsides ablaze. Only relatively small areas of undisturbed forest remain with an estimated 86% degraded by tree felling. Higher up below the alpine meadows rhododendrons and azaleas grow in abundance.

In the mountains of the Mediterranean and Aegean pine forests are the norm, although the higher slopes of the Taurus mountains also harbour much-reduced stands of ancient cedar of Lebanon (*Cedrus libani*) and juniper. Large areas of these regions are also covered with *marquis*: a scrubby and usually fairly prickly mix of bushes and plants including holly oak and fragrant herbs like sage and thyme, cropped low to the ground by the ever-present roaming goat herds. In spring the *marquis*, as well as adjacent meadows and orchards, are filled with an abundance of wildflowers such as daisies and scabious Spring and autumn rains also unleash a wealth of wild flowering bulbs with many of the varieties favoured by European gardeners (see box), familiar names such as snowdrops, cyclamen and crocus, having originated in the mountains and meadows of Anatolia.

On the Anatolia plateau and in the east spring comes later, but is nonetheless accompanied by an impressive display of wild flowers. Many Aegean bee-keepers take advantage of the tardy spring bloom in the rolling countryside of the interior, loading their hives on to trucks and driving hundreds of kilometres when the flowers are parched and withered near the coast. In time the meadows and rough grazing land of the interior are also burnt by the sun, leaving lines of poplar and orchards of fruit trees around settlements as the only green in a virtual sea of brown.

Fauna

The country's animal life has experienced a similar man-induced decline as its plant species and it's clear from historical sources that Anatolian wildlife was far more abundant in the past. Habitat loss to agriculture and urbanization as well as widespread hunting and fishing are generally blamed for this reduction, however, a more insidious role has also been played by organophosphate poisoning from agricultural pesticides and pollution. Despite this the country still harbours a varied and interesting array of mammals, birds and reptiles; although your chances of seeing some of them is rather slim.

Large mammals

Particularly elusive are the large mammals. Villagers in the Taurus and the east still report the occasional sighting of a wolf or wild cat and trekkers in the forests of the Kaçkar Mountains may also spot a brown bear or deer. Ibex and chamois still roam in the higher more remote areas. Badgers, porcupines and foxes are a more common sight darting across the road in front of cars at night, or the unlucky ones squashed by the roadside. The most ubiquitous sizeable mammal, however, found in forest and scrubland across large swathes of the country, is the *yaban domuzu* or wild boar. Walking through woods or *marquis* you'll often come across areas of disturbed ground where boar have been digging for roots and bulbs; and while the Islamic proscription on eating pork doesn't stop locals hunting boar for sport or in tourist areas to sell to hotels and restaurants, the animal seems to be thriving.

Reptiles

Tramping around the numerous archaeological sites in the Aegean and Mediterranean regions you'll come across dozens of small lizards which scuttle off beneath a stone or into a crack as you approach. The camouflaged and slow-moving chameleons are more difficult to spot. You may also catch one of Turkey's vipers or grass snakes basking in the sun, although if you make plenty of noise as you approach they'll slither off before you get close. Tortoises are common in the Southern Aegean and Mediterranean, while terrapins also occupy freshwater bodies in the south of the country.

Birds

Located on migration routes between Eurasia, Africa and the Middle East, many different bird species stop-off in Anatolia each spring and autumn, with more northern species overwintering in the area. Seasonal visitors include waterfowl like the white-fronted goose, red-throated diver, white-headed duck, tufted duck, pygmy cormorant, red-breasted merganser, teal, dalmatian pelican and flamingo. There are also visiting birds of prey such as the osprey, marsh harrier or the extremely rare honey buzzard. Add to this the large number of indigenous species and it's easy to understand why Turkey is so popular with ornithologists.

Native raptors include species such as the Egyptian vulture, seen thermalling high over the central plateau and in the east, golden eagles, hawks and buzzards, along with rarities such as the white-tailed kite. There are also ten species of owl – the eagle owl, fishing owl and long-eared owl amongst them – living in Anatolia.

Turkey is particularly rich in wetland habitats with Birdlife International and the DHKD having identified 97 "important birds areas" (IBA) in the country of which over a third are marsh, lake or riverine ecosystems. Areas such as Sultansazlığı near Kayseri (see box, page 524) and Manyas Gölü, south of Bandırma, have been designated as *Kuş Cenneti* – "Bird Paradises" – and as national parks enjoy official protection; although many more are under threat from irrigation and land reclamation projects; agricultural and industrial pollution and hunting.

Other good places for bird-watching are the Meriç delta in Thrace; the Lake District; the Esmekaya Marshes north of Konya; Tuz Gölü north west of Aksaray; the Göksu delta near Silifke; the Çukurova delta south of Adana; the Aladağlar and the eastern Black Sea mountains. A useful publication about the 97 Turkish IBAs - entitled '*Important Bird Areas in Turkey*' –, which includes site descriptions, species lists and local threats, is available from the DHKD head office in Istanbul.

Marine life

Due to intensive fishing and pollution the health of Turkey's coastal waters has become a matter for some concern. Indiscriminate trawling using sophisticated equipment has caused an alarming drop in fish stocks with species such as the

Black Sea anchovy, or *hamsi*, being overfished to the point where even if fishing was stopped today it would take years for populations to regenerate. This has affected the livelihoods of coastal communities and small-scale operators in some areas have been forced out of business.

Further up the food chain large marine mammals like dolphins do still live in Turkish waters, although their continued survival is under threat from human activity. The two species of marine turtle which nest on Turkish beaches (see box, page 325) are threatened by tourist development and fishermen's nets, while the Mediterranean monk seal (see box, page 243) is on the brink of extinction.

Footnotes

15

Footnotes

713 Basic Turkish for travellers

718 Glossary

720 Food glossary

725 Index

728 Shorts

729 Map index

739 Colour maps

Basic Turkish for travellers

A-Z Pronunciation

Aa vowel similar to the 'u' in cut
Bb as in bet
Cc like j in jelly
Çç like ch in chess
Dd as in deaf
Ee as in let
Ff as in ferry
Gg as in get
Ğğ a silent letter which lengthens the preceeding vowel
Hh as in hell
Iı vowel similar to the e in label
İi like ea in tea
Jj like the s in treasure
Kk like the c in cut
Ll as in leisure
Mm as in met

Nn as in nest
Oo similar to the o in hot
Öö like the sound e in her
Pp as in pet
Rr as in ran
Ss as in set
Şş like sh in shell
Tt as in test
Uu like the u in full
Üü like the ew in dew
Vv as in vet
Yy as in yet
Zz as in zest
Xx only in foreign words, used as ' ks' in Turkish like Meksika-Mexico.
Ww only in foreign words

Numbers

0	sıfır	60	altmış
1	bir	70	yetmiş
2	iki	80	seksen
3	üç	90	doksan
4	dört	100	yüz
5	beş	200	Ikıyüz
6	altı	300	üçyüz
7	yedi	1,000	bin
8	sekiz	2,000	ikibin
9	dokuz	300,000	üçyüzbin
10	on	1,000,000	bir milyon
11	onbir		
12	oniki		The most important ordinal numbers
19	ondokuz		are:
20	yirmi	First	Birinci
30	otuz	Second	İkinci
40	kırk	Third	Üçüncü
50	elli	Fourth	Dördüncü

Days

Sunday Pazar
Monday Pazartesi
Tuesday Salı
Wednesday Çarşamba

Thursday Perşembe
Friday Cuma
Saturday Cumartesi

Months

January *Ocak*	July *Temmuz*
February *Şubat*	August *Ağustos*
March *Mart*	September *Eylül*
April *Nisan*	October *Ekim*
May *Mayıs*	November *Kasım*
June *Haziran*	December *Aralık*

Seasons

Spring *İlkbahar*	Autumn *Sonbahar*
Summer *Yaz*	Winter *Kış*

Greetings

Good morning *Günaydın*	Hi *Selam*
Good afternoon *İyi Günler*	Goodbye *Güle güle*
Good evening *İyi Akşamlar*	Welcome *Hoş geldin*
Good night *İyi Geceler*	See you later *Görü şürüz*
Hello *Merhaba*	Bon voyage *İyi yolculuklar*

Basics

Yes *Evet*	There is/are... ...*var*
No *Hayır*	There isn`t/aren`t ... ...*yok*
No there isn't any *Yok*	Right/Wrong *Doğru/Yanlış*
Please *Lütfen*	Enough/More *Yeter/Daha*
Thank you *Teşekkür ederim*	Good/Bad *İyi/Kötü*
Thank you very much *Çok teşekkür ederim*	New/Old *Yeni/Eski*
Thanks *Teşekkürler, Sağol, Mersi*	Open/Closed *Açık/Kapalı*
You're welcome *Bir şey Değil*	Big/Small *Büyük/Küçük*
Pardon Me/Excuse me *Affedersiniz*	Hot/Cold *Sıcak/Soğuk*
Sorry *Pardon, Özür dilerim*	Vacant/Occupied *Boş/Dolu*
Help yourself *Buyrun*	Cheap/Expensive *Ucuz/Pahalı*
OK *Tamam*	Fast/Slow *Hızlı/Yavaş*
Certainly *Tabii*	Quickly *Çabuk*
Maybe *Belki*	With/Without meat *etli/etsiz*
I don't know *Bilmiyorum*	Not... ...*değil*
I don't understand *Anlamıyorum, anlamadım*	And *Ve*
	Or *Veya*
I understand *Anladım*	Mr... ...*Bey*
Wait a minute *Bir dakika*	Mrs... ...*Hanım*
I want... ...*istiyorum*	Miss... *Bayan...(used only with forenames)*

Questions

What? *Ne?*	Which one? *Hangisi?*
Where is...? ...*nerede?*	How much? *Kaç para?*
Why? *Neden? Niçin?*	How many? *Kaç tane? Ne kadar?*
Who? *Kim?*	What does it mean? *Ne demek?*
How? *Nasıl?*	What is it called in Turkish? *Türkçesi nedir?*
When? *Ne zaman?*	
What's this? *Bu ne?*	

Small talk

How are you? *Nasılsın? Nasılsınız?*
I'm fine, thank you *İyiyim, teşekkürler*
Nice to meet you *Memnun oldum*
What's your name? *İsminiz ne?*
Do you speak English? *İngilizce biliyor musunuz?*

Where are you from? *Nerelisiniz?*
How old are you? *Kaç yaşındasınız?*
I'm ... years old *... yaşındayım*
I'm English/Scottish/Irish/Australian *İngilizim/İskoçyalıyım/İrlandalıyım/ Avustralyalıyım*
I'm sightseeing *Geziyorum*

Time

Now *Şimdi*
Later *Sonra*
Then *O zaman*
Always *Her zaman, Hep*
Never *Hiçbirzaman, Asla*
Sometimes *Bazen*
Early/Late *Erken/Geç*
Today/Tomorrow *Bugün/Yarın*
Yesterday *Dün*
...(two) days later *...(iki) gün sonra*
In the morning *Sabah*
In the afternoon *Öğleden sonra*

At noon *Öğlen*
In the evening *Akşam*
At night *Gece*
At what time? *Saat kaçta?*
At (four) *Saat (dörtte)*
Minute *Dakika*
Ten minutes *On dakika*
Hour (also watch or clock) *Saat*
Two/three hours *İki/üç saat*
What time is it? *Saat kaç?*
It is ...(four) o`clock *Saat...(dört)*

Weather

Weather *Hava*
How is the weather? *Hava nasıl?*
It`s sunny/cloudy/rainy/snowy/foggy/ windy *Güneşli/bulutlu/yağmurlu/ karlı/sisli/rüzgarlı*

Directions

Left/Right *Sol/Sağ*
Turn left/right *Sola/sağa dön*
Here/There *Burada/Orada*
Near/Far *Yakın/Uzak*
North/South *Kuzey/Güney*
East/West *Doğu/Batı*
Straight *Düz*
Toward *Doğru*
A bit further *Az daha uzakta*
Uphill/Downhill *Yokuş yukarı/ Yokuş aşağı*
Steep *Dik*
Wide/Narrow *Geniş/Dar*
From... *...dan*
Until... *...a kadar*

Before/After *Önce/Sonra*
Behind/In front of *Arkasında/Önünde*
Between *Arasında*
Across from *Karşısında*
At the end... *...sonunda*
Street *Cadde*
Road *Yol*
One-way street *Tek yön*
Dead-end *Çıkmaz sokak*
Crossroads *Dörtyol,Kavşak*
No entry *Araç giremez*
Road work *Yol çalışması*
Road closed *Yol kapalı*
Pedestrian crossing *Yaya geçidi*

Travelling

Bus *Otobüs*	Adult/child/student *Tam/çocuk/öğrenci*
Mini bus *Dolmuş*	A ticket to… *…a bir bilet*
Aeroplane *Uçak*	Can I make a reservation? *Rezervasyon*
Train *Tren*	*yaptırabilir miyim?*
Car *Araba*	Can I book a seat? *Yer ayırtabilir miyim?*
Ferry *Vapur, Feribot*	What time does it leave? *Kaçta kalkıyor?*
Ferry terminal *İskele*	How long does it take? *Ne kadar sürer?*
Bicycle *Bisiklet*	How far is it? *Ne kadar uzaklıkta?*
Taxi *Taksi*	How many kilometres is it? *Kaç*
Motorcycle *Motorsiklet*	*kilometre?*
Ship *Gemi*	When do we arrive? *Ne zaman varırız?*
Hitch-hiking *Otostop*	When is the next bus/train/ferry? *Bir*
On foot *Yaya*	*sonraki otobüs/tren/vapur ne zaman?*
Bus station *Otogar*	Where does it leave from? *Nereden*
Bus stop *Otobüs durağı*	*kalkıyor?*
Railway station *Tren istasyonu*	Which platform does it leave
Arrival/Departure *Varış/Kalkış*	from? *Hangi perondan kalkıyor?*
Seat *Koltuk*	Which bus goes to …? *Hangi otobüs…*
Cabin *Yataklı*	*a gider?*
Single/Double *Tek/Çift*	Do I have to change? *Aktarmalı mı?*
Price *Ücret*	Is there a delay? *Rötar var mı?*
Ticket *Bilet*	Can I get out here? *Burada inebilir miyim?*
Return *Gidiş-dönüş*	

Accommodation

Hotel *Otel*	Quilt *Yorgan*
Pension *Pansiyon*	Hot/Cold water shower *Sıcak/Soğuk*
Tent *Çadır*	*sulu duş*
Campsite *Kamping*	Light/Dark *Aydınlık/Karanlık*
Room *Oda*	Comfortable/Uncomfortable *Rahat/*
Single/Double/Triple room *Tek/Çift/Üç*	*Rahatsız*
kişilik oda	Clean/Dirty *Temiz/Pis*
With shower/Bathroom *Duşlu/Banyolu*	Noisy/Quiet *Gürültülü/Sakin*
With telephone *Telefonlu*	Mosquito *Sivrisinek*
Air-conditioned *Klimalı*	Is there a hotel nearby? *Yakınlarda bir*
Key *Anahtar*	*otel var mı?*
Suitcase *Bavul*	Do you have a double room for
Towel *Havlu*	one/two nights? *Bir/iki gecelik çift*
Toilet *Tuvalet*	*kişilik bir odanız var mı?*
Toilet paper *Tuvalet kağıdı*	Can I see the room? *Odayı görebilir*
Shampoo *Şampuan*	*miyim?*
Soap *Sabun*	Is breakfast included? *Kahvaltı dahil mi?*
Bed *Yatak*	Can we camp here? *Burada kamp*
Sheet *Çarşaf*	*yapabilir miyiz?*
Pillow *Yastık*	I want… *…istiyorum*
Blanket *Battaniye*	

Emergencies

Help! *İmdat!*
Stop! *Dur!*
Go away! *Git lütfen!* (stronger *Defol!*)
Stay away from me! *Bana yaklaşma!*
You are making me uncomfortable!
Beni rahatsız ediyorsunuz!

I need a doctor! *Doktora ihtiyacım var!*
Where is the hospital? *Hastane nerede?*
Can you call the police? *Polisi arar mısınız?*

Walking

Walking *Yürüyüş*
Mountain *Dağ*
Forest *Orman*
Valley *Vadi*
Plain, Plateau *Ova*
River *Nehir, Irmak*
Lake *Göl*
Sea *Deniz*
Shore *Kıyı*
Beach *Kumsal*
Bridge *Köprü*
Cave *Mağara*
Field *Tarla*
Village *Köy*
Hut *Kulübe*
House *Ev*
Peak, Summit *Zirve*

Ridge *Sırt*
Hill *Tepe*
Cliff *Uçurum*
Slope *Yamaç*
Ridge *Sırt*
Pass *Geçit*
Rock *Kaya*
Cemetery *Mezarlık*
Tower *Kule*
Mosque *Cami*
Church *Kilise*
Monastery *Manastır*
Ruins,remains *Harabe, yıkıntı*
Turkish bath *Hamam*
Mud *Çamur*
Camera *Fotoğraf Makinası*
Water bottle *Matara*

Civilities

Hoş geldin Welcome
Hoşbulduk used as a reply to welcome
Allahaısmarladık Goodbye (said by the person departing)
Güle güle Goodbye (said by the person staying)
Buyrun used to invite (people somewhere) or offer (food, drinks...), could also be used as 'help yourself'
Şerefe In your honour, to your health
Elinize Sağlık Traditional compliments to the person who cooks
Afiyet Olsun Phrase used as a reply to the above and also said to someone sitting down to a meal
Kolay Gelsin! May your work be easy
Geçmiş Olsun! May it be in your past (said to someone who is ill, stressed or has just overcome an accident, injury or difficulty)
Sıhhatler Olsun! May you have a good health (said to someone who has just had a bath or shower, a hair cut or shave
Hoşçakal Stay happy (used as an alternative to goodbye)
Başınız Sağolsun said to someone who has just experienced a death in the family or friends
Çok Yaşa! Bless you!
Sende gör! Phrase used as a reply to Bless you
Canın Sağolsun! May your soul be safe and harmless (said to someone who has just accidentally done something)

Glossary

acropolis high point in an ancient city which was the site of a fortress and temples

agora a market place

aile salonu part of a Turkish restaurant reserved for families or single women

altgeçit underpass

apse semi-circular or polygonal recess for the alter in a church

araba car

arasta shops which formed part of a religious foundation, rent would be used for the upkeep of the mosque

asker(i) soldier/military base

bakal grocery shop

banliyö suburban

bedesten vaulted stone hall with strong gates where valuable goods were traded

Belediye town hall/municipal administration

billet ticket

bouleuterion council hall or meeting place in Hellenistic city

cadde(si) road

cami(i) mosque

caravaserai a fortified inn for accommodating overland caravans

çarşı(sı) a market or bazaar

çay(ı) tea or a river

çeşme a spring, tap or fountain

çevreyolu ring road

dağ(ı) mountain

danışma information desk

deniz sea

deniz otobüsü hydrofoil

derviş member of a religious sect or brotherhood such as the Mevlevi

dinlenme yeri a rest or picnic area

dikkat caution/beware

dolmuş communal minibus or car running set route

dur stop

eczane chemist/pharmacy

emniyet mudurluğu police HQ

erkek man/men's toilet

eski old

ev(i) house

ezan the call to prayer

garson waiter

gazino nightclub

gece night

geçit mountain pass/col

geniş araç wide vehicle

hastane hospital

hamam(ı) Turkish bath

han(ı) an inn built for accommodating trade caravans

hararet hot part of a Turkish bath

harita map

hazır yemek ready-prepared dishes usually kept warm in steam trays

Hellenistic a period of strong Greek influence in Anatolian from death of Alexander the Great to the 1st century BC

hesap bill

heyelan landslide

heykel statue

hisar(ı) castle/fortress

hookah free-standing waterpipe

hükümet konağı provincial government building

hünkar mahfili the area of a mosque reserved for the sultan

içilmez unpotable

içme suyu drinking water

ilkokul primary school

imam Islamic clegymen

imaret(i) the soup kitchen attached to a mosque

indirimli discounted/reduced

iskele(si) a quay or wharf

jandarma a branch of the army who are responsible for law and order in the countryside

kale(si) castle, citadel

kapı(sı) gate or door

kapıcı caretaker

kaplıca hot-springs or thermal baths

karakol police station

karayolları roads/highways

kat storey

katlı otopark multi-storey car-park

kaynak spring

KDV *Katma Değer Vergisi* Value Added Tax

kilise(si) church

konak mansion

köprü(sü) bridge

köşk(ü) villa or pavilion

köy(ü) village

külliye(si) a mosque complex which usually includes a hospital, seminary, arasta and hospital

kümbet free-standing mausoleum

küsetli a train or ferry cabin with a couchette
lastik tyre
lastikçi tyre repairs
liman(ı) harbour
loge private box or enclosure in a theatre
medrese Islamic seminary
meydan(ı) main square
mihrab an ornamented niche found in all mosques which indicates the direction of Mecca
mimber preachers pulpit in a mosque, often highly ornamented
minare(si) tall tower or spire from which müezzin calls faithful to prayer
müezzin the man who calls the faithful to prayer
müze museum
narthex anti-chamber or porch area of a church
nave the central aisle of a church
necropolis cemetery
nymphaeum public fountain
oda(sı) room
okul school
okul taşıtı school bus
Osmanlı Ottoman
otobus durağı bus stop
otoyol(u) motorway
park yeri car park
patika footpath
pazar weekly market
pencere window
rakım altitude
şadırvan mosque fountain where Muslims wash before praying

samovar a metal teapot often with a charcoal burner beneath it
saray(ı) palace
sarcophagus a stone or rock-cut tomb with a lid
selamlık the part of an Ottoman residence reserved for men or entertaining visitors
şehir city
şehit(ler) martyr(s)
Seljuk Selçuk Turks
servis dahil service included
sokak (sokağı) street
su water
sürücü adayı learner driver
tam full fare
tatil köyü holiday village
tehlikeli madde dangerous load
Tekel the state tobacco and alcohol monopoly
Tekel Bayii Off-licence/liquor store
tekke(i) a dervish lodge or meeting hall
tuğra the Ottoman imperial monogram
türbe(si) mausoleum/tomb
Türk Hava Yolları (THY) Turkish Airlines
uzun araç long vehicle
valilik (valiliği) provincial government building
yalı waterside mansion
yasak bölge out-of-bounds, entry forbidden
yayla summer community, usually in the high mountains
yol(u) road
yol onarımı/yapımı road construction
zahlye dervish hostel
zil door bell

Food glossary

Kebaps and other meat dishes

Kebaps are typically served with salad, rice or chips, or wrapped in a wheat pancake

Adana kebabı spicy hot minced lamb grilled on a skewer

Beyti kebabı minced lamb or chicken grilled on a skewer

Biftek/Bonfile steak

Böbrek fried kidneys

Ciğer liver

Çöp şiş chunks of lamb grilled on small bamboo skewers

Döner kebabı wrapped in wheat pancake (*dürüm*) or in half a loaf of bread (*yarım ekmek*)

Dana/sığır eti beef

Inegöl köftesi finger sized meatballs originally from Inegöl near Bursa

Iskender kebabı slices of *döner* meat on a pide bread soaked in tomato sauce, yoghurt and melted butter, a speciality of Bursa

Kağıt kebabı lamb and vegetables baked in paper

Karışık ızgara mixed grill

Kiremitte köfte meat balls roasted on an earthware tile, also covered with melted cheese (*kaşarlı*)

Koç yumurtası/Billur ram's testicles

Köfte grilled meat balls often served with *piyaz* (white bean salad)

Kuzu eti lamb or mutton

Pastırma dried, spiced meat

Pirzola lamb chops

Saç kavurma spiced meat and vegetables brought sizzling to the table in a wok

Şinitzel wienerschnitzel

Şiş kebabı grilled skewers of lamb (*kuzu şiş*) or chicken (*tavuk şiş*)

Sucuk garlic sausage

Tandır kebabı oven roasted mutton

Tavuk/piliç chicken

Urfa kebabı minced lamb grilled on a skewer

Hazır Yemek (Ready-Prepared dishes)

Biber dolması peppers stuffed with rice and meat

Bulgur pilavı bulgar rice sometimes cooked with a meat stock

Et yemeği meat stew

Etli türlü meat stew with vegetables

Güveç meat and vegetable stew

Karnıyarık aubergines stuffed with mince meat

Kuru fasulye (v) white beans in a tomato sauce

Makarna (v) pasta

Mantı ravioli-like meat filled parcels covered in garlic yoghurt sauce

Menemen (v) fried eggs with tomatoes, onions, peppers and garlic

Musakka a lamb stew with aubergines

Patates yemeği potatoes cooked in a meat sauce with other vegetables

Pilav (v) rice

Sebzeli Türlü (v) vegetable stew

Tas kebabı mutton stew

Pideci

Pide long piece of dough, kneeded flat and topped with cheese (*peynirli/kaşarlı*), egg (*yumurtalı*), mince (*kıymalı*), chunks of meat (*kuşbaşı*) or chicken (*tavuklu*)

Lahmacun frequently called "Turkish pizza", a layer of spiced lamb smeared on to a thin dough base

Sade pide (v) round flat bread

Street food

Badem içi (v) fresh almonds, usually sold chilled by weight on mobile stalls

Çiğ köfte a spicy mix of raw lamb-mince and bulgar wrapped in a wheat pancake – a speciality of the southeast

Dürüm döner meat (chicken or beef) wrapped in a wheat pancake with salad

Gözleme (v) Turkish pancakes filled with cheese (*peynirli*), potatoes (*patatesli*) or mince (*keymalı*)

Kestane (v) roasted chesnuts sold by street vendors in the cities in winter

Koköreç grilled sheep's intestines flavoured with cumin and eaten as a sandwich

Midye mussels stuffed with peppery rice and pine-nuts

Simit/gevrek sesame covered bread rings

Söğüş brain and offal wrapped with tomatoes and onions in a wheat pancake

Tost toasted sandwich with cheese (*peynirli*) or salami (*karışık*)

Turşu (v) (*suyu*) pickles served as a drink

Soups

Balık çorbası fish soup

Domates çorbası (v) tomato soup

Düğün çorbası (v) so-called 'wedding soup' made from lemon and eggs

Ezo gelin çorbası tomato and lentil soup flavoured with mint, may contain meat stock

İşkembe çorbası tripe soup

Mercimek (v) lentil soup

Paça çorbası a soup made from various boney parts of a sheep boiled with garlic

Sebze çorbası (v) vegetable soup

Şehriye çorbası noodle soup

Tarhana çorbası (v) yoghurt and vegetable soup

Tavuk çorbası chicken soup

Yayla çorbası (v) yoghurt and barley soup

Tatlı (sweets)

Turks have a particularly sweet tooth, with lots of creamy puddings and what, to the western palate, are super sweet desserts

Aşure a delicious, sweet stew of pulses, nuts and fruit flavoured with cinamon

Ayva tatlısı a quince pudding normally eaten with cream

Baklava an oven-baked pastry made with layers of nuts and syrup

Dondurma ice-cream

Güllaç layers of fine pastry and walnuts baked with milk and rose water

Helva a semolina-based pudding with pinenuts

Kabak tatlısı very sweet pumkin pudding topped with walnuts

Kadayıf shredded wheat pudding with nuts and syrup

Kuymak clotted cream

Kazandibi a creamy pudding called 'the bottom of the pan' on account of its caramalized topping

Kemalpaşa tatlısı doughy balls soaked in super sweet syrup

Keşkül milk-based pudding sprinkled with nuts, often eaten with ice-cream (*dondurma*)

Komposto stewed fruit

Künefe shredded wheat with mild cheese and syrup, a speciality of the southeast

Kurabiye biscuits

Lokma fried dough balls in sugar syrup

Lokum Turkish delight

Muhallebi creamy pudding made with rice flour

Pasta cream cake

Supangle thick chocolate pudding, from corruption of the words 'Soup Anglais' (English soup)

Sütlaç rice pudding, typically baked in the oven (*fırında*)

Tahin helvası blocks of sesame *helva* with nuts or cocoa

Tavuk Köğsü creamy pudding made with shredded chicken

Yoğurt tatlısı a cake drenched in syrup and topped with walnuts

Zerde sweetened rice flavoured with saffron

Kahvaltı (Breakfast)

In all but a few hotels breakfast is included in the price of your room. Such hotel breakfasts are a fairly standard affair consisting of bread and cheese, tomatoes, cucumber, olives, honey or jam, and tea or coffee.

Bal honey
Börek an oven-baked pastry filled with cheese, vegetables or meat
Ekmek bread
Peynir cheese

Reçel jam
Tereyağı butter
Yumurta eggs
Zeytin olives

İçecekler (Non-alcoholic drinks)

Ayran a yoghurt drink usually drunk with meals
Boza a thick fermented millet drink
Buz ice
Çay tea
Kahve coffee
Kola coke
Meyve suyu fruit juice
Neskafe generic term for instant coffee
Portakal suyu orange juice

Salep a hot, sweet drink made with extract of *Orchis mascula*, a rare wild orchid
Şalgam turnip juice, a violent coloured speciality of the southeast which is often drunk with *rakı*
Şıra unfermented grape juice
Su water
Süt milk
Türk kahvesi Turkish coffee
Vişne suyu sour cherry juice

İçkiler (Alcoholic drinks)

İçkili alcohol served
İçkisiz no alcohol served
Bira beer
Cin gin
Fıçı bira draught beer
Kokteyl cocktail
Konyak cognac

Likör liqueur; *nane likörü* (sweet mint liqueur drunk with coffee at end of meal)
Rakı strong aniseed spirit
Şampanya champagne
Şarap wine; *beyaz şarap* (white); *kkırmızı şarap* (red); *roze şarap* (rose)
Viski whiskey
Votka vodka

Meyve (fruit)

Armut pear
Ayva quince
Çağla green almond
Çilek strawberry
Dut mulberry
Elma apple
Erik green plums usually eaten before they're ripe
Frambuaz raspberry
Greyfurt grapefruit
İncir fig
Karpuz watermelon

Kavun melon
Kayısı apricot
Kiraz cherry
Limon lemon
Mandalin mandarin, tangerine
Muz banana
Nar pomegranate
Portakal orange
Şeftali peach
Üzüm grape
Vişne sour cherry

Sebze (Vegetables)

Acı biber hot peppers
Bakla broad beans
Bamya okra
Barbunya red beans
Bezelye peas
Biber peppers
Domates tomato
Enginar artichoke
Fasulye beans
Havuç carrot
Ispanak spinach
Kabak courgette
Karnabahar cauliflower

Lahana cabbage
Mantar mushroom
Marul lettuce
Pancar beetroot
Patates potato
Patlıcan aubergine
Roka rocket
Salatalık cucumber
Sarmasak garlic
Soğan onion
Taze fasulye green bean
Taze soğan spring onion

Çerez (Nuts)

Antep fıstığı pistachio
Badem almond
Çekirdek sunflower seeds
Ceviz walnut
Fındık hazelnut

Fıstık peanut
Kabak çekirdeği dried pumpkin seeds
Kestane chestnut
Kuru yemiş dried fruit
Leblebi roasted chickpea

Peynir (cheese)

Beyaz peynir white cheese similar to *feta*
Çökelek mild, crumbly cheese used in börek and gözleme
Kaşar peyniri yellow cheese, varies from mild (*taze*) to mature (*eski*)

Keçi peyniri strong flavoured white cheese made from goats milk
Teneke peyniri tasty, white cheese cured in aluminium containers
Tulum peyniri dry, crumbly cheese made in a goat skin

Baharat ve otlar (Herbs and spices)

Dereotu dill
Fesleğen basil
Hardal mustard
Karabiber black pepper
Kekik thyme

Kimyon cumin
Maydanoz parsley
Nane mint
Pul biber crushed chilly
Tuz salt

Cooking terms

Acı spicy
Az pişmiş rare
Buğulama steamed
Ezme paste or purée
Fırında baked
Haşlama boiled
İyi pişmiş well done

Izgara grilled
Kızartma fried
Mangal barbeque
Sıcak hot
Soğuk cold
Yumurtalı with egg
Zeytin yağlı cooked with olive oil

Cutlery

Bardak glass
Bıçak knife
Çatal fork

Kaşık spoon
Peçete napkin
Tabak plate

General Vocabulary

Afiyet olsun Bon appetit
Bahşiş tip
Elinize sağlık "Health to your hands", traditional response to *Afiyet olsun*
Hesap bill (*Hesap, lüften!* the bill, please)

Şerefe cheers!
Vergi tax
Vergi dahil tax included
Kahvaltı breakfast
Öğle yemeği lunch
Akşam yemeği dinner

Index

A

Abana 551
accommodation 38
Acıgöl 511
Adana 422
Adilcevaz 646
Adrasan 367
adventure tourism 64
Adıyaman 619
Aegean Region 213
Ağaçlı 305
Ağlasun 451,452
Ağrı 604
Ağrı Dağı 608
Afyon 445
Ahlat 646
Aizanoi 444
Ak Vadi 496
Akbük 308
Akçaabat 562
Akçakale 562
Akçakıl 410
Akçay 230
Akdamar 645
Akkum 264,416
Aksaray 488
Akşehir 449
Akyaka 308
Akyarlar 305
Aladağlar 523
Alahan 416
Alanya 397
alcohol 57
Alexandria Troas 225
Alibey 232
Altınkum 284
Alıparmak 583
Amasra 550
Amasya 535
Anamur 406
Anazarbus 428
Andriake 363
Anıl 600
Ankara 466
Antakya 431
Antalya 376
Antioch ad Pisidiam 456
antiques 61
Aperlae 360
Aphrodisias 287
Apollonia 361
appearance 35
Araklı 570
army 683
Arsameia 625
art 700

Artvin 573
Arykanda 365
Aspendos 389
Assos 226
Atatürk airport 27,74
Atatürk, Mustafa Kemal
    470
Avanos 511
Aya Sofya 82
Ayaş 419
Ayder 578
Ayder Çaymakçur
    Pass-Olgunlar 579
Aydıncık 409
Ayvalı 508
Ayvalık 230

B

Babakale 226
Bademli 235
Bağla 305
balloon flights 499
Balıklova 261
Bandırma 192
Barhal 583
Barla 456
Barla Massif 460
Bayırköy 318
Bayramhacı
    Kaplıcaları 513
Behramkale 226
Belevi 275
Belisırma 490
Bergama 236
Beydağları Coastal
    National Park 368
Beyşehir 457
Bitez 305
Bitlis 643
Black Sea Region 547
boats 47
Bodrum 298
Boğazkale 531
Boğsak 410
books 68
Boz Dağı 248
Bozburun 319
Bozcaada 224
Bozköy 551
Boztepe 565
Bozyazı 409
Bülbül Dağı 269
Burdur 452
Bursa 178
bus 42

Butterfly Valley 339
Büyük Çaklı 352
Büyük Menderes
    Valley 279
Byzantine 662

C

Çakraz 551
camel wrestling 285
Çamlıhemşin 577
camping 41
Çanakkale 216
Çandarlı 235,241
Çandır 457
Cappadocia 492
car 43
caravanserai 487
carpet 60
Castle of St John 301
Çat 580
Çatalzetin 551
Çavdarhisar 444
Çavuşin 503
Çavuştepe 651
Çayağız 363
Çayağızı 349
Cehennem 417
Cennet 417
Central Anatolia 463
Çeşme 260
Ceyhan 427
children 34
christianity 699
Cide 551
Cimbar Canyon 524
Çıralı 368
Claros 264
climate 20
clothing 35
coffee 57
consulates 24
costs 26
credit cards 25
Çukurova 425
culture 693
Cumalıkızık 192
currency 25
customs 23,35
Cyaneae 356
cycling 45,64

D

Dalaman 331
Dalyan 324

Datça 319
Davraz Dağı 460
Dedegul 461
Demircili 414
Demre 361
Denizli 289
Derinkuyu 510
Didyma 284
Dikili 235
Dilek National Park 278
Dimçay Valley 399
disabled travellers 32
diving 66
Divriği 546
Diyarbakır 635
Doğubeyazıt 604
dolmuş 45
drink 57
drugs 36

E

earthquakes 173
**Eastern
    Mediterranean 403**
Ereahat 207
economy 689
Edirne 196
Edremit 230,646
Efes 269
Eğirdir 457
Ekincik 323
Elevit 580
Elmalı 366
embassies 24
emergency telephone
    numbers 33
Emli Valley 527
Ephesus 269
Erciyes Dağı 520
Erzurum 590
Esenboğa airport 466
Eskişehir 440
etiquette 35

F

fax 52
festivals 62
Fethiye 332
Fındıkköy 444
Finike 364
Fırtına Valley 579
First World War 673
flights 27
Foça 242

food 53
Frig Valley 444

G

Gallipoli Penisula 205
GAP 620
gay and lesbian
travellers 34
Gaziantep 615
Gazlıgöl 448
Gelibolu 206
Gemiler 342
Gevaş 646
Gideros 551
Giresun 559
Göcek 332
Gökçeada 212
Gökova 308
Göksu Delta 412
Gölköy 307
Gordion 478
Göreme 497
Greeks 661
Güllük 298
Güllük Dağı National
Park 386
Gülpınar 226
Gülşehir 514
Gümbet 305
Gümüldür 264
Gümüşlük 306
Gündoğan 307
Güvercinlik Vadisi 496
Güzelyurt 491

H

Hacıbektaş 514
haggling 58
Haghia Sophia 82
Hakkarı 652
hang gliding 65
hans 487
Harran 633
Hasandağı 491
Hasankeyf 642
Hatay 429
Hattuşaş 532
Havsa 203
health 66
heat and cold 68
Helali 551
Hemşin 577
Heracleia under
Latmos 294
Hevek 584
Heybelli 448
Hierapolis Castabala 429
Hisarönü 340
Hisarönü Peninsula 318
history 659
hitch-hiking 46
Hittite sites 531
Hittites 660
holidays 62

Hopa 572
Horasan 596
hotels 38
price codes 39
Hoşap Kalesi 651
Huzur Vadisi 332

I

İasos 297
İhlara Canyon 489
İhsaniye 448
İnebolu 551
İnli 444
İnsuyu Mağarası 452
international dialling
codes 51
internet 50
İpsala 204
İshak Paşa Sarayı 606
İskenderun 430
Islam 696
İsparta 450
İstanbul 71
İşhan 582
Işıkkale 415
itineraries 19
İzmir 249
İznik 173

J

Janissary corps 666

K

Kaçkar Dağları 575
Kadikalesi 306
Kadırga 230
Kale 359,361
Kaleköy 212
Kalkan 350
Kangal 545
kangal köpeği 545
Kanlıdivane 419
Kaputaş 352
Kapıkırı 294
Karaburun 262
Karaburun Peninsula 261
Karadedeli 415
Karagöl 584
Karahayıt 293
Karakabaklı 415
Karamanmaraş 613
Karatepe-Arslantaş
National Park 428
Kargı 305
Kars 596
Karşıyaka 253
Kastamonu 552
Kastellorizo 353
Kaş 351
Kaya Köyü 341
kayaking 65
Kaymaklı 510,566
Kaynarpınar 262

Kayseri 515
Kekova 357
Kekova Island 360
Kemalpaşa 573
Kemer 374
Kestanbolu Kaplıca 226
Keşan 204
kilims 60
Kilitbahir 207
Kıyıkışlacık 297
Kizkalesi 417
Kızılçukur 505
Knidos 320
Konya 480
Köprülü Kanyon
National Park 390
Kordon 252
Kovada Gölü
Milli Parkı 457
Köyceğiz 321
Kozak 235
Kuçukbahçe 262
Küçükkuyu 230
Kültepe 519
Kumbağ 204
Kurdistan Worker's
Party 612
Kurucaşile 551
Kuşadası 275
Kuşcenneti Milli
Parkı 192
Kütahya 440
Kuzu Limanı 212
Kyaneai 356

L

Lake Bafa 294
Lake District 449
language 25,704
Laodiceia 293
Laz 572
leather 60
Letoön 345
Liman Ağızı 352
Limyra 365
literature 704
Lycian Way 339
Lycians 661
Lydians 660

M

magazines 52
Malatya 625
Manavgat 396
Manisa 244
Mardin 640
**Marmara
Region 169**
Marmaris 314
Mazıköy 511
medicine 67
Meis 353
Mersin 420
Mevlâna Museum 483

Mevlâna, Celaleddin
Rumi 482
Mevlevi 482
meze 53
Midyat 642
Milas 296
Milet 281
Miletus 281
military 683
mining 240
money 25
Mordoğan 262
Mount Mycale 279
Mount Pion 269
Mount Siphylus 246
mountain biking 45,64
Muğla 309
Mustafapaşa 508
Mut 416
Myra 362

N

Narlıkuyu 416
Nazilli 286
Nemrut 644
Nemrut Dağı 621
Nevşehir 493
newspapers 52
Niğde 521
Noah's Ark 607
**Northeast
Anatolia 587**
Nysa 286

O

Ocaklı 600
Of 570
Olgunlar 584
Ölüdeniz 338
Olympos 368
Ömer 448
Önbolat Valley 584
Open Air Museum 498
opening hours 33
Ordu 559
Ören 230,307
Orhaniye 318
Ortaca 323
Ortahisar 504
Ottomans 664
Ovacık 340
Özdere 264
Özkonak 511,513

P

Palandöken 595
Palovit 580
Pamphylian Plain 387
Pamukkale 289
paragliding 65
Paşabağı 504
Pasinler 595
Patara 347

Pazar 572
pensions 38
Pergamum 236
Perge 387
Persians 661
Phaselis 373
Phrygians 660
Pınara 344
PKK 612
planning 19
police 38
population 693
post 51
poste restante 51
prehistoric 659
Priene 279

R

radio 52
rafting 65
reading 68
religion 696
Republican era 676
Reşasiye Peninsula 318
restaurants 54
Rize 571
rock-climbing 65
Romans 661

S

Sabuncupınar 444
safety 37
Safranbolu 528
Sagalassos 451,452
Sahilevleri 264
Şahinkaya 212
Saklıkent 343
Samsun 556
Şanlıurfa 627
Sarayiçi 199
Sardis 247
Şarköy 205
Sarıgerme 331
Sarıkamış 596
Sarımsaklı 233
Sarp 573
Sart 247
Sartmustafa 247
season 20
Second World War 680
Seferhisar 264
Selçuk 265
Selçuk Turks 663
Selge 391
Selime 490
Selimiye 318
Sema 483
shopping 59
Side 392
Sığarcık 264
Silifke 411
Sillyon 388
Simena 359

Simi 319
Sinop 553
Sipahili 409
Şirince 274
Sivas 542
Sivri Dağı 459
skiing 65
Soğanlı 509
Soğmatar 634
Söğüt 444
Söke 279
**Southeast
 Anatolia 609**
Spil Dağı 246
sport 64
student travellers 33
Sultanahmet 81
Sultanhanı 488
Sultaniye 323
Sultansazlığı 521
Sumela Monastery 568
Sürmene 570

T

Tahtalı Dağı 377
Tarsus 421
Taşucu 410
Tatvan 643
taxi 46
tea 57
Tekirdağ 204
telephone 51
television 52
Tenedos 224
Teos 264
Tercan 590
Termal 172
Termessos 386
Thrace Region 193
Thracian coast 204
time zone 33
tipping 36
Tirebolu 561
Tirevit 580
Tlos 342
tobacco 229
Tokat 540
Topkapı Palace 85
Torba 307
tour operators 21
tours 21
Trabzon 562
train 47
Trans-Aladağlar 526
transport
 to Turkey 27
 within Turkey 41
travellers' cheques 26
trekking 64
Troad 220
Troy 220
Truva 220
Turica Valley 199
Tür Abdin 642
Turgutreis 306
Turkish Airlines 41

Turkish Maritime Lines
 fares 31
 offices and agents 31
Turunç 317

U

Üçağız 358
Uçhisar 495
Uğurlu 212
Uludağ 190
Ünye 558
Urartu 660
Ürgüp 505
Urla 261
Uzun Göl 570
Uzuncaburç 414
Uzunköprü 204

V

vaccinations 23
Van 647
Van Gölü 643
vegetarians 54
Veli, Hacı Bektaş 517
visas 23
voltage 33
volunteering 35

W

walking 64
War of Independence
 674
water 57
websites 23
weights 33
Western Anatolia 437
**Western
 Mediterranean 311**
whirling dervishes 483
women travellers 33
working 34

X

Xanthos 346
Xanthos Valley 342

Y

Yakapınar 427
Yalıkavak 307
Yalova 172
Yaylalar 584
Yazılı Canyon 457
Yazılıkaya 334
Yenibahçe 415
Yeşilovacık 410
Yüksekova 652
Yumurtalık 427
yurt 332
Yusufeli 581

Z

Zelve 503
Zerk 391
Zeytinlik 212
Zindan Mağarası 457

Shorts

470	'Father of the Turks'	182	Phantom plays
451	A scent of roses	441	Potty about pottery
325	A turtle change	524	Sultansazlığı: bird paradise
687	A veiled threat?	533	Tablets tell the story
246	An affair of the eyes	173	The 1999 earthquake
55	An A-Z of meze	225	The discovery of Troy
60	Anatolian carpets	620	The GAP project
47	Black Sea ferry timetable	252	The Kordon
315	Blue Water Voyage	612	The Kurds and the PKK
59	Carpet talk	572	The Laz
240	Controversial mining	239	The library of Pergamum
285	Deve Güregi-Camel wrestling	344	The Lycians
51	Dialling out	217	The mythology of the strait
630	Disappearing beneath the waves	545	The protective pooch
		666	The rise and fall of the Janissary corps
54	Fish for a dish		
703	Football crazy	487	The Selçuk caravanserai
664	From beylik to empire	283	The thinkers of Miletus
517	Hacı Bektaş Veli and the Bektaşi order	705	The Turkish Bath
		683	The Turkish military: guardian or threat?
577	Hemşin culture		
607	In search of the Ark	273	The Virgin Mary (Meryemana)
175	Miles of tiles	58	Tips on haggling
679	Name hunting	494	To Cap it all
43	No rules of the road	52	Toll free numbers
200	Oiled wrestling	552	Troubled waters
243	On the brink: the Mediterranean monk seal	224	Troy: Fact or Fable
		644	Van Gölü

Map index

424	Adana	82	Haghia Sophia
446	Afyon	291	Hierapolis
525	Aladağlar treks	489	Ihlara Canyon
536	Amasya	75	İstanbul orientation
407	Anamur area	250	İzmir
601	Ani	176	İznik
468	Ankara centre	576	Kaçkar Dağları treks
432	Antakya	378	Kaleiçi
376	Antalya	597	Kars
227	Assos	353	Kaş
511	Avanos	472	Kavaklıdere
231	Ayvalık	516	Kayseri
461	Barla Massif trek	358	Kekova area
238	Bergama	321	Köyceğiz
300	Bodrum	277	Kuşadası
306	Bodrum Peninsula	442	Kütahya
180	Bursa	645	Lake Van area
183	Bursa centre	282	Miletus
218	Çanakkale	78	Old İstanbul
493	Cappadocia region	292	Pamukkale Village
261	Çeşme	374	Phaselis
100	Covered Bazaar	280	Priene
326	Dalyan	529	Safranbolu
460	Davraz Massif trek	629	Şanlıurfa
461	Dedegul & Kartal Tepe trek	266	Selçuk
637	Diyarbakir	394	Side
605	Doğubeyazıt	554	Sinop
454	Eğirdir	104	Sirkeci & Eminönü
270	Ephesus, Plan of	543	Sivas
592	Erzurum	94	Sultanahmet
334	Fethiye	86	Topkapi Palace
118	Galata & Taksim Square	564	Trabzon
205	Gallipoli Peninsula	222	Troy
617	Gaziantep	506	Ürgüp
114	Golden Horn, North of the	648	Van
498	Göreme	346	Xanthos

Footnotes

Sales & distribution

Footprint Handbooks
6 Riverside Court
Lower Bristol Road
Bath BA2 3DZ England
T 01225 469141
F 01225 469461
discover
@footprintbooks.com

Australia
Peribo Pty
58 Beaumont Road
Mt Kuring-Gai
NSW 2080
T 02 9457 0011
F 02 9457 0022

Austria
Freytag-Berndt Artaria
Kohlmarkt 9
A-1010 Wien
T 01533 2094
F 01533 8685

Freytag-Berndt
Sporgasse 29
A-8010 Graz
T 0316 818230
F 3016 818230-30

Belgium
Craenen BVBA
Mechelsesteenweg 633
B-3020 Herent
T 016 23 90 90
F 016 23 97 11

Waterstones
The English Bookshop
Blvd Adolphe Max 71-75
B-1000 Brussels
T 02 219 5034

Canada
Ulysses Travel Publications
4176 rue Saint-Denis
Montréal
Québec H2W 2M5
T 514 843 9882
F 514 843 9448

Europe
Bill Bailey
16 Devon Square
Newton Abbott
Devon TQ12 2HR. UK
T 01626 331079
F 01626 331080

Denmark
Nordisk Korthandel
Studiestraede 26-30 B
DK-1455 Copenhagen K
T 3338 2638
F 3338 2648

Scanvik Books
Esplanaden 8B
DK-1263 Copenhagen K
T 3312 7766
F 3391 2882

Finland
Akateeminen Kirjakauppa
Keskuskatu 1
FIN-00100 Helsinki
T 09 121 4151
F 09 121 4441

Suomalainen Kirjakauppa
Koivuvaarankuja 2
01640 Vantaa 64
F 09 852751

France
FNAC – major branches

L'Astrolabe
46 rue de Provence
F-75009 Paris 9e
T 01 42 85 42 95
F 01 45 75 92 51

VILO Diffusion
25 rue Ginoux
F-75015 Paris
T 01 45 77 08 05
F 01 45 79 97 15

Germany
GeoCenter ILH
Schockenriedstrasse 44
D-70565 Stuttgart
T 0711 781 94610
F 0711 781 94654

Brettschneider
Feldkirchnerstrasse 2
D-85551 Heimstetten
T 089 990 20330
F 089 990 20331

Geobuch
Rosental 6
D-80331 München
T 089 265030
F 089 263713

Gleumes
Hohenstaufenring 47-51
D-50674 Köln
T 0221 215650

Globetrotter Ausrustungen
Wiesendamm 1
D-22305 Hamburg
T040 679 66190
F 040 679 66183

Dr Götze
Bleichenbrücke 9
D-2000 Hamburg 1
T 040 3031 1009-0

Hugendubel Buchhandlung
Nymphenburgerstrasse 25
D-80335 München
T 089 238 9412
F 089 550 1853

Kiepert Buchhandlung
Hardenbergstrasse 4-5
D-10623 Berlin 12
T 030 311 880
F 030 311 88120

Greece
GC Eleftheroudakis
17 Panepistemiou
Athens 105 64
T 01 331 4180-83
F 01 323 9821

India
India Book Distributors
1007/1008 Arcadia
195 Nariman Point
Mumbai 400 021
T 91 22 282 5220
F 91 22 287 2531

Israel
Eco Trips
8 Tverya Street
Tel Aviv 63144
T 03 528 4113
F 03 528 8269

For a fuller list, see www.footprintbooks.com

Italy
Librimport
Via Biondelli 9
I-20141 Milano
T 02 8950 1422
F 02 8950 2811

Libreria del Viaggiatore
Via dell Pelegrino 78
I-00186 Roma
T/F 06 688 01048

Netherlands
Nilsson & Lamm bv
Postbus 195
Pampuslaan 212
N-1380 AD Weesp
T 0294 494949
F 0294 494455

Waterstones
Kalverstraat 152
1012 XE Amsterdam
T 020 638 3821

New Zealand
Auckland Map Centre
Dymocks

Norway
Schibsteds Forlag A/S
Akersgata 32 - 5th Floor
Postboks 1178 Sentrum
N-0107 Oslo
T 22 86 30 00
F 22 42 54 92

Tanum
Karl Johansgate 37-41
PO Box 1177 Sentrum
N-0107 Oslo 1
T 22 41 11 00
F 22 33 32 75

Olaf Norlis
Universitetsgt 24
N-1062 Oslo
T 22 00 43 00

Pakistan
Pak-American Commercial
Hamid Chambers
Zaib-un Nisa Street
Saddar, PO Box 7359
Karachi
T 21 566 0418
F 21 568 3611

South Africa
Faradawn CC
PO Box 1903
Saxonwold 2132
T 011 885 1787
F 011 885 1829

South America
Humphrys Roberts
Associates
Caixa Postal 801-0
Ag. Jardim da Gloria
06700-970 Cotia SP
Brazil
T 011 492 4496
F 011 492 6896

Southeast Asia
APA Publications
38 Joo Koon Road
Singapore 628990
T 865 1600
F 861 6438

In Hong Kong, Malaysia,
Singapore and Thailand:
MPH, Kinokuniya, Times

Spain
Altaïr
C/Balmes 69
08007 Barcelona
T 933 233062
F 934 512559

Altaïr
Gaztambide 31
28015 Madrid
T 0915 435300
F 0915 443498

Libros de Viaje
C/Serrano no 41
28001 Madrid
T 01 91 577 9899
F 01 91 577 5756

Il Corte Inglés – major
branches

Sweden
Hedengrens Bokhandel
PO Box 5509
S-11485 Stockholm
T 08 611 5132

Kart Centrum
Vasagatan 16
S-11120 Stockholm
T 08 411 1697

Kartforlaget
Skolgangen 10
S-80183 Gavle
T 026 633000
F 026 124204

Lantmateriet Kartbutiken
Kungsgatan 74
S-11122 Stockholm
T 08 202 303
F 08 202 711

Switzerland
Office du Livre OLF
ZI3, Corminboeuf
CH-1701 Fribourg
T 026 467 5111
F 026 467 5666

Schweizer Buchzentrum
Postfach
CH-4601 Olten
T 062 209 2525
F 062 209 2627

Travel Bookshop
Rindermarkt 20
Postfach 216
CH-8001 Zurich
T 01 252 3883
F 01 252 3832

Tanzania
A Novel Idea
The Slipway
PO Box 76513
Dar es Salaam
T/F 051 601088

USA
Publishers Group West
1700 Fourth Street
Berkeley
CA 94710
T 510 528 1444
F 510 528 9555

Barnes & Noble, Borders,
specialist travel bookstores

Will you help us?

We try as hard as we can to make each Footprint Handbook as up-to-date and accurate as possible but, of course, things always change. Many people write to us - with corrections, new information, or simply comments.

If you want to let us know about an experience or adventure - hair-raising or mundane, good or bad, exciting or boring - we would be delighted to hear from you. Please give us as precise information as possible, quoting the edition number (you'll find it on the front cover) and page number of the Handbook you are using.

Your help will be greatly appreciated, especially by other travellers. In return we will send you details about our special guidebook offer.

email Footprint at:
tur1_online@footprintbooks.com

or write to:
Elizabeth Taylor
Footprint Handbooks
6 Riverside Court
Lower Bristol Road
Bath BA2 3DZ
UK

Footprint travel list

Footprint publish travel guides to over 120 countries worldwide. Each guide is packed with practical, concise and colourful information for everybody from first-time travellers to travel aficionados . The list is growing fast and current titles are noted below. For further information check out the website **www.footprintbooks.com**

Andalucía Handbook
Argentina Handbook
Bali & the Eastern Isles Hbk
Bangkok & the Beaches Hbk
Bolivia Handbook
Brazil Handbook
Cambodia Handbook
Caribbean Islands Handbook
Chile Handbook
Colombia Handbook
Cuba Handbook
Dominican Republic Handbook
East Africa Handbook
Ecuador & Galápagos Handbook
Egypt Handbook Handbook
Goa Handbook
India Handbook
Indian Himalaya Handbook
Indonesia Handbook
Ireland Handbook
Israel Handbook
Jordan Handbook
Jordan, Syria & Lebanon Hbk
Laos Handbook
Libya Handbook
Malaysia Handbook
Myanmar Handbook
Mexico Handbook
Mexico & Central America Hbk
Morocco Handbook
Namibia Handbook
Nepal Handbook
Pakistan Handbook

Peru Handbook
Rio de Janeiro Handbook
Scotland Handbook
Singapore Handbook
South Africa Handbook
South American Handbook
South India Handbook
Sri Lanka Handbook
Sumatra Handbook
Thailand Handbook
Tibet Handbook
Tunisia Handbook
Venezuela Handbook
Vietnam Handbook

In the pipeline – London, Kenya, Rajasthan, Scotland Highlands & Islands, Syria & Lebanon

Also available from Footprint
Traveller's Handbook
Traveller's Healthbook

Available at all good bookshops

Turkey

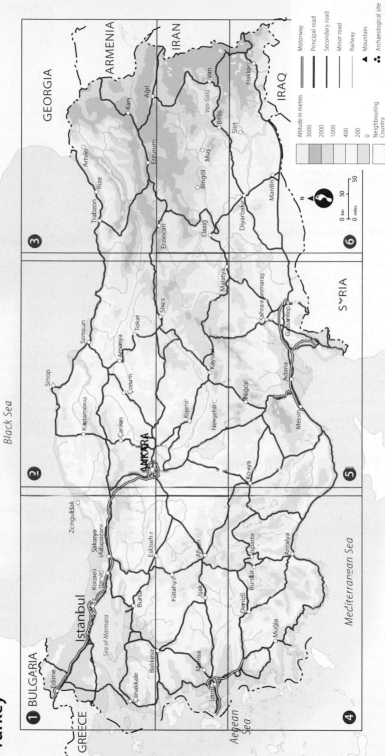

Legend:

- Motorway
- Principal road
- Secondary road
- Minor road
- Railway
- ▲ Mountain
- Archaeological site

Altitude in metres
- 3000
- 2000
- 1000
- 400
- 200
- 0
- Neighbouring Country

N

0 km 50
0 miles 50

Countries/Regions:
BULGARIA, GREECE, GEORGIA, ARMENIA, IRAN, IRAQ, SYRIA

Seas:
Black Sea, Sea of Marmara, Aegean Sea, Mediterranean Sea

Places:
Edirne, İstanbul, Zonguldak, Sakarya (Adapazarı), Kocaeli (İzmit), Çanakkale, Balıkesir, Bursa, Eskişehir, Kütahya, Uşak, Manisa, İzmir, Muğla, Denizli, Burdur, Isparta, Antalya, Afyon, Ankara, Çankırı, Kastamonu, Sinop, Samsun, Amasya, Çorum, Tokat, Kırşehir, Nevşehir, Niğde, Konya, Mersin, Adana, Kayseri, Gaziantep, Kahramanmaraş, Sivas, Malatya, Elazığ, Diyarbakır, Mardin, Siirt, Erzincan, Trabzon, Rize, Artvin, Kars, Ağrı, Erzurum, Bingöl, Muş, Bitlis, Van, Hakkari

Van Gölü

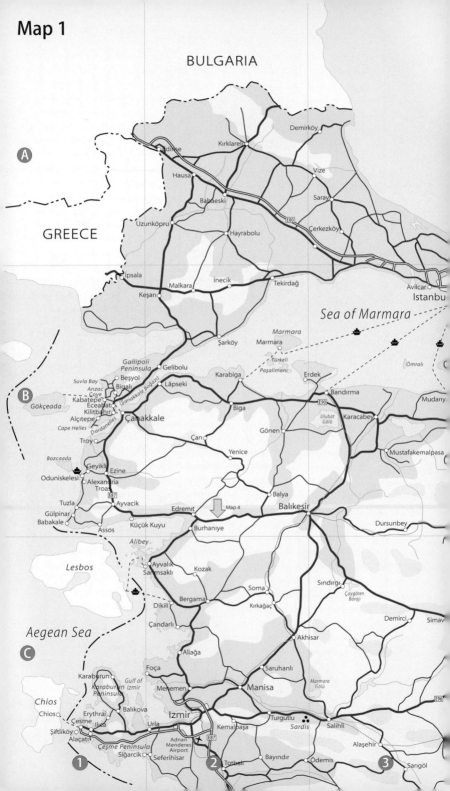

Map 1

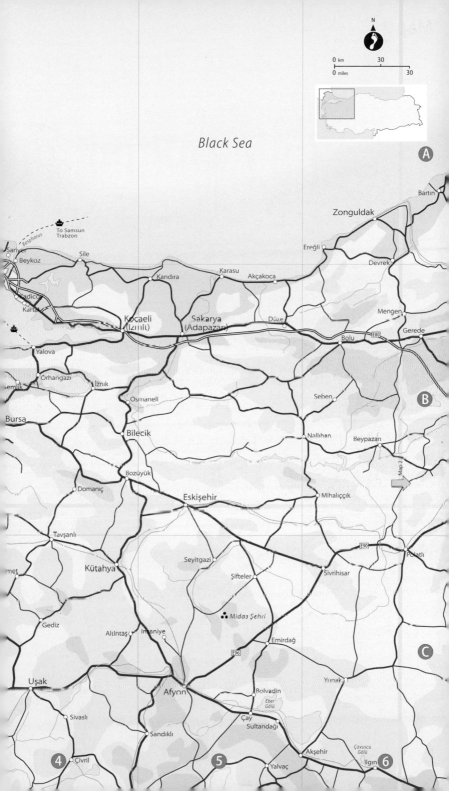

Map 2

Sinop

A
Amasra
Cide
Inebolu
Abana
Ayancık
Gerze

Bartın
Ulus
Küre

Safranbolu
Daday
Devrekani

Karabük
Kastamonu

Map1

Mengen
Tosya
Osmancık

Gerede
Kurşunlu
Ilgaz
E80

E80
Iskilip

B
Çankırı
Çorum

E89
Çubuk

Sungurlu
Yazılıkaya
Boğazkale
Hattuşaş

ANKARA
Elmadağ
Delice
Map 5
Yozgat

E88
Kırıkkale
Sorgun

Gordion
Yorköy

Polatlı
Sarıkay

Balâ

Haymana
Kaman
Boğazlıyan

Kulu
Kışehir

C
Mucur

Şereflikoçhisar
Hacıbektas

E90
Özkonak
Bayramhacılı

Ortaköy
Gülşehir
Avanos
Boğazköprü

Nevşehir
Uçhizar
Göreme
Ürgüp
Ince

Acıgöl
Mustafapaşa

Cihanbeyli
Kaymaklı
Avvali
Mazıköy

Derinkuyu
Güzelöz

Melendiz
River
Yukarı
Soğanlı
Yeşilhisar

Aksaray

1
2
3

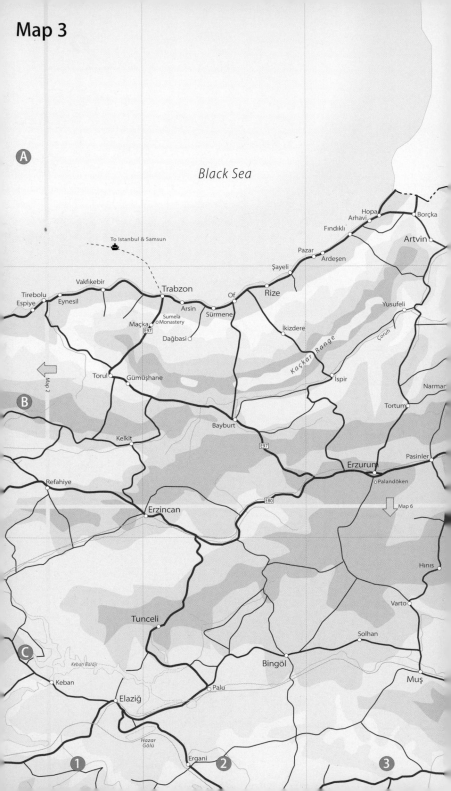

Map 3

Black Sea

To Istanbul & Samsun

Hopa
Arhavi
Borçka
Fındıklı
Artvin
Pazar
Ardeşen
Şayeli
Trabzon
Of
Rize
Tirebolu
Vakfıkebir
Espiye
Eynesil
Yusufeli
Arsin
Sürmene
Maçka
Sumela
Monastery
İkizdere
Dağbasi

Kaçkar Range

Çoruh

Torul
Gümüşhane
İspir
Narmar
Tortum
Bayburt
Kelkit
Pasinler
Refahiye
Erzurum
Palandöken
Erzincan

Hınıs

Varto

Tunceli

Solhan

Keban Barajı

Bingöl
Muş

Keban
Palu
Elazığ

Hazar Gölü

Ergani

1   2   3

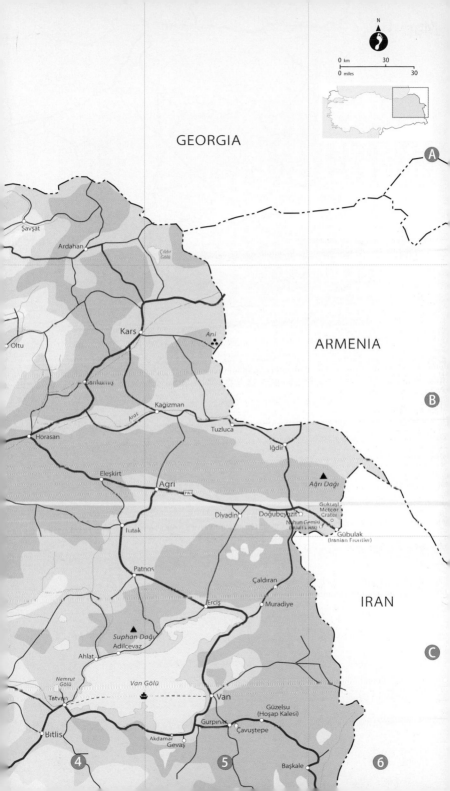

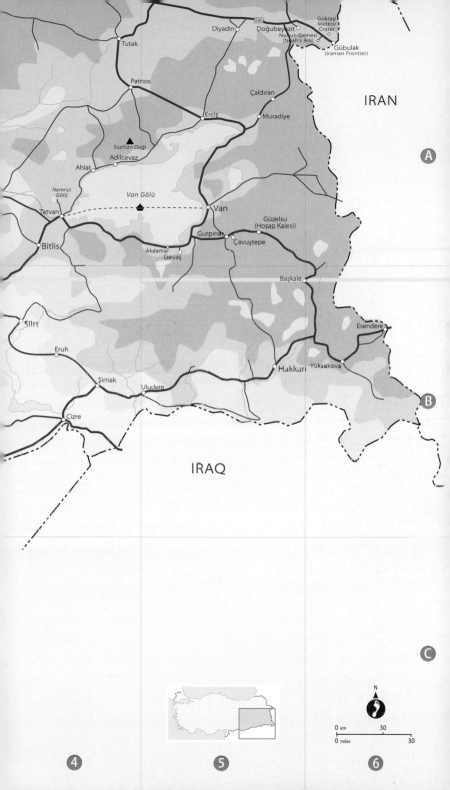

What the papers say

"The guides for intelligent, independently-minded souls of any age or budget."
Indie Traveller

"Footprint can be depended on for accurate travel information and for imparting a deep sense of respect for the lands and people they cover."
World News

"Footprint Handbooks, the best of the best."
Le Monde, Paris

"If 'the essence of real travel' is what you have been secretly yearning for all these years, then Footprint are the guides for you."
Under 26

"The titles in the Footprint Handbooks series are about as comprehensive as travel guides get."
Travel Reference Library

Mail order
Available worldwide in bookshops and on-line. Footprint travel guides can also be ordered directly from us in Bath, via our website **www.footprintbooks.com** or from the address on the imprint page of this book.

Acknowledgements

Thank you to Terry Richardson, a freelance writer and photographer living in Antalya, who contributed to the Lake District section and wrote the lakeland trekking piece, and to Süleyman Baştutan who proof read the Cappadocia section.

I'd also like to thank the following for their help and hospitality: Simla Akkoyun, Rupert Birch, Sue Brophy and Joao, Neslihan and Teoman Guimaraes in Istanbul; Ibrahim and Sabrina Baştutan in Cappadocia; Remzi Boybag and the staff of the *Büyük Asir Oteli* in Van; the Davidson clan in Trabzon and particularly Gary for his companionship and cooking in the mountains and for the low-down on Uzun Göl; Kate Clow in Antalya; Mehmet and Kader Demirci in Ayder; Yusuf Kamil in Demre; Huseyin Kurt at the Silifke Turizm Müdürlügü; Tim Goodman in Izmir; Ali and Yusuf Pehlivan in Üçagiz; Ali Yıldız and family in Çıralı; the staff at Anzac House in Çanakkale.

Thank you also to Liz and Dek Messecar for putting me up in London. And last, but not least, Pelin Güler for her endless patience and assistance.

Dominic Whiting

Dominic's first taste of Turkey was on a family skiing holiday in 1985. After a degree in geography and spells on the road in southeast Asia and India he set off across Europe in an old Dutch postal van. Arriving in Turkey he found work as a university English teacher and using the generous holidays to work as a guide he explored the country from corner to corner. He found ample opportunity to indulge his passions for trekking and climbing in the Turkish mountains and later established an adventure travel company. Back in London now, Dominic works as a freelance writer, photographer and occasional guide, returning frequently to Turkey for both work and pleasure.